Words of the Vietnam War

WORDS OF THE VIETNAM WAR

The Slang, Jargon, Abbreviations, Acronyms,
Nomenclature, Nicknames, Pseudonyms,
Slogans, Specs, Euphemisms, Double-talk,
Chants, and Names and Places of the Era
of United States Involvement in Vietnam

by Gregory R. Clark

McFarland & Company, Inc., Publishers
Jefferson, North Carolina, and London

British Library Cataloguing-in-Publication data are available

Library of Congress Cataloguing-in-Publication Data

Clark, Gregory R., 1948–
    Words of the Vietnam War : the slang, jargon, abbreviations, acronyms, nomenclature, nicknames, pseudonyms, slogans, specs, euphemisms, double-talk, chants, and names and places of the era of United States involvement in Vietnam / by Gregory R. Clark.
        p. cm.
    ISBN 0-89950-465-5 (lib. bdg. : 50# alk. paper) ∞
    1. Soldiers—United States—Language (New words, slang, etc.)—Dictionaries.   2. Vietnamese Conflict, 1961–1975—Language (New words, slang, etc.)—Dictionaries.   3. English language—United States—Slang—Dictionaries.   4. Americanisms—Dictionaries. 5. Military art and science—Dictionaries.   6. United States—History, Military—20th century—Dictionaries.   I. Title.
PE3727.S7C57   1990
959.704'3'03—dc20   89-43639
                                                                          CIP

Manufactured in the United States of America

McFarland & Company, Inc., Publishers
    Box 611, Jefferson, North Carolina 28640

To those who lost more in Vietnam
than just their sleep
and their innocence...

Acknowledgments

With special thanks to Major Daniel McDowell, U.S. Air Force Auxiliary, and Virginia Alvord, whose support helped make this book possible. And deep appreciation to my parents who did not throw out the baby with the bathwater. And to Sven Uff'Da, wherever you are, thanks.

Introduction

In this dictionary are about 10,000 entries (including *see* references), with more than 4,300 definitions. Two major sections of alphabetical (see page 1) and numerical (see page 572) listings contain the names of persons, places, events, terrain features; military installations, operations, units, equipment, specifications and weapons; euphemisms, slang, graffiti, acronyms, and abbreviations; and foreign words and phrases. Also included are words, slogans, and phrases from the antiwar, hippie, and civil rights movements of the late sixties. The entries range much further than just the foul mouthed slang of the grunts and the diplomatic double-talk of the United States' highest executives.

These are the words of an era, not just a war. A dictionary cannot answer the "how" or "why" questions about Vietnam, and the compiler has not tried to. Inevitably, however, a description of what the Vietnam War era was does come through the words of its soldiers, leaders, opponents, and victims. The words touch upon all the participants in the war from the GI in the field to the REMFs to the protesters on campus to the Chinese advisors to the ROK Marines to the politicians to the Muong tribes of the Central Highlands.

The primary focus of this dictionary is the period of direct American involvement in Southeast Asia, from 1961 when United States advisors occupied South Vietnam, to the fall of Saigon in 1975. There are some entries nevertheless that reflect the linguistic situation as far back as 1945 and as far forward as the late 1980s.

My aim has been to compile a comprehensive dictionary of value to libraries, schools, educators, linguists, history buffs, the three million Americans who served in Vietnam, and those interested in military history or the nature of language. My research has involved hundreds of books, manuals, military reports, and recorded media. Interviews and contacts with veterans, antiwar activists, and personal experience have added to the accuracy of this collection.

The format of each entry herein is the word, name, or phrase, followed by either the definition or where the definition is located within the book. Some definitions also include (in parentheses between the word and the definition) other words or acronyms which are synonymous with or related to the main word or phrase. Other entries related to the main word are listed as "See also" and are found at the end of the definition.

All references in this book are to American forces unless otherwise noted. Units are sometimes listed in the abbreviated format of "company (troop) / battalion (squadron) / brigade (regiment) / division."

Vietnamese names are listed in their traditional form, last name first, middle name, then first name, i.e., Nguyen Ngoc Loan. In addition some Vietnamese words are accompanied by a "GI" pronunciation which is enclosed in brackets [   ].

These abbreviations are frequently used in the definitions:

ARVN—Army, Republic of
  Vietnam
FWF—Free World Forces
GVN—Government of South
  Vietnam
NVA/VC—North Vietnamese/
  Viet Cong
NVN—North Vietnam

RVN—Republic of Vietnam
SEA—Southeast Asia
SFG—U.S. Special Forces Group
SVN—South Vietnam
US/ARVN—U.S./ARVN Forces
USSF—U.S. Special Forces
VC—Viet Cong

A

A & D (Admission and Dispositions Section) Admissions section of a field or evacuation hospital.

A Kit *see* **ACAV Kit**

A Shau Special Forces Camp The A Shau Special Forces Camp was located 95kms southwest of Da Nang, almost on the Laotian border, straddling the Ho Chi Minh Trail. The camp was defended by a battalion sized ARVN and CIDG force. In March '66 an NVA regiment attacked and surrounded the isolated camp. Poor weather in the area reduced air support to a minimum, and several days after the attack began the camp defenses began to collapse. Some of the ARVN and CIDG defenders deserted the camp and "chieu hoi'ed" to the NVA. The camp was abandoned and the USSF team and 172 CIDG troops were extracted by Marine helicopters. The NVA immediately took over and developed the area into a major infiltration route and logistics base area. *See also* **A Shau Valley.**

A Shau Valley (Shotgun Alley) Rugged dense jungle valley near the SVN/Laotian border, 75kms southeast of Khe Sanh and 40kms southwest of Hue in Thua Thien Province. Major NVA/VC base area and infiltration route into the I Corps. Operation Delaware, in April '68, was the first major allied assault into the valley. U.S. Army operations in the area encountered stiff enemy resistance and heavy AA fire used against U.S. helicopters. Most remembered for heavy U.S. losses by troopers of the 101st Abn, while taking Hamburger Hill (Hill 937) in May '69. Shortly after securing the hill, the U.S. high command ordered it abandoned. *See also* **Hamburger Hill, Operation Delaware, Operation Somerset Plain.**

A-1 (Skyraider, Sandy, AD-6, Spad,

A-1E, -1G, -1H) Single engine, prop driven fighter used for close air support of ground troops. The Skyraider was manufactured by Douglas Aircraft and was used by the U.S. Navy (AD-1 thru AD-6) as a fighter-bomber until replaced by the A-4 Skyhawk. The A-1 was armed with four 20mm cannons, had up to an 8,000-pound bomb payload and had a maximum speed of 322mph and a range of 1,800kms. The A-1E/G was the dual seat version. In June '65 while on RESCAP, Navy A-1's were attacked by NVAF MiG-17's. One of the A-1's outmaneuvered the jets and shot down one of the MiG's with his 20mm cannons. During the war two MiG's were downed by the prop-planes. The U.S. Air Force, Navy and VNAF used the A-1 for CAS and SAR missions.

A-26 *see* **B-26**

A-3 *see* **B-66**

A-4 (Scooter, Skyhawk, A-4E/F) Douglas Aircraft Co. single engine, single seat jet attack bomber. The bomber was used extensively by the Navy and Marines in the airwar over Vietnam. The ground or carrier based bomber had a bomb payload of up to 8,200 pounds (standard load of 3,000 pounds), with a max speed of 685mph and a range of 1,480kms. A-4C/D models were the standard versions used by the Navy and entered service in '62. The A-4E was a later version with an upgraded, more powerful engine. A-4F entered service after '67 and featured a more powerful engine and was equipped with advanced avionics systems and was often used in the SAM suppression role. A-4s flew more combat bombing missions than any other aircraft operated by the Navy in Vietnam. *See also* **TA-4F.**

A-5 (Vigilante, RA-5, Viggie) Carrier based Navy attack bomber (A-5) converted

1

for use as a photo reconnaissance aircraft (RA-5C) for use over Vietnam. The twin engine jet Vigilante ("Viggie") was manufactured by North American Rockwell and had a maximum speed of 1,385mph, a range of 4,800kms. In the bomber mode it could carry nuclear or conventional bomb loads. During the Vietnam War the Vigilante was operated by a two man crew and used exclusively for photo recon work.

A-6A (Intruder, KA-6 Tanker) All weather bomber used by the U.S. Navy and Marines. The Grumman A-6 Intruder entered service in '63 and featured twin jet engines with a max speed of 685mph, a max payload of 15,000 pounds and a range of 3,000kms. The two-seat bomber was used extensively in the tactical ground support role in South Vietnam and also in strategic bomb runs over North Vietnam. The Intruder was primarily carrier based and was equipped with advanced navigational systems allowing it to effectively attack targets at night and in bad weather. The EA-6A/B were the ECM versions of the A-6 and were used to attack and jam enemy SAM and radar gun sites. The KA-6 was the air tanker version of the A-6A. *See also* **Digital Integrated Attack Navigation Equipment, EA-6A.**

A-7 (Corsair II, A-7E) Navy single engine, all-weather, light attack aircraft. Manufactured by Ling-Temco-Vought, the A-7 could carry 20,000 pounds of ordnance, had a max speed of 679mph and a range of 4,500kms. The Corsair was equipped with advanced navigational, weapons and radar systems allowing it to attack targets at night and in bad weather. The carrier based bomber was also designed to sustain major damage from enemy guns and still remain airworthy. The A-7s first operated in Vietnam in '67. In '70 an upgraded version, the A-7E, was deployed to Vietnam. It featured a more powerful engine and the aircraft was armed with a 20mm cannon.

A-37 (Dragonfly, T-37) Manufactured by Cessna Corporation, the T-37 functioned as a jet trainer. The A-37 was an upgraded version of the trainer featuring more powerful engines and eight underwing hardpoints for mounting ordnance. The twin engine jet was in Vietnam in a ground support role. The two man crew sat side by side in the cockpit. The A-37 had a maximum speed of 507mph, a range of 1,600kms, a bomb load of 5,000 pounds and was armed with one 7.62mm minigun. The A/T-37 was used by the Air Force as a trainer and TAC bomber in Vietnam. The A-37 was one of the two tactical jet fighter aircraft in the VNAF inventory, replacing the older prop-driven A-1 Skyraider. *See also* **Combat Dragon Deployment.**

A-Gunner (Assistant Machine Gunner) Part of the machine gun team which consisted of a gunner and the assistant gunner. The A-Gunner helped feed ammunition to the machine gun and also spotted targets for the gunner. The A-Gunner carried extra ammunition for the machine gun and also collected extra belts of ammo carried by other members of the unit. In a typical infantry squad each member of the squad might carry one hundred-round belt of machine gun ammo. During a firefight it was the A-Gunner's responsibility to gather up the extra ammo belts and keep the machine gun supplied. In the event anything happened to the machine gun operator, the A-Gunner took over.

A-Shaped Ambush (U-Shaped Ambush) Ambush set up in the shape of the letter "A" or in a semicircular "U." The ambush was effective if a large number of troops were available to man the site. The enemy walked into the open end of the ambush and had to retreat to extricate himself from it. Attempting to move through the A-shaped ambush was difficult because much of the fire power and the heaviest guns were concentrated at the front of the "bush." If the force being ambushed was small, the elements at the open end of the ambush could move towards each other, completely encircling the kill zone. *See also* **Ambush, L-Shaped Ambush.**

A-Team Basic field operating unit of the U.S. Special Forces. A-Teams consisted of 10–12 men cross-trained and specialist in weapons, communications, medical, engineering, tactics and counterinsurgency operations. The field teams trained, organized and led the CIDG and Strike Forces in the defense of Vietnam's mountain villages. As the war expanded, the A-Teams and their CIDGs became more aggressive against the NVA/VC and started operations involving long range recon and ambush against the NVA lines of infiltration into South

Vietnam. Recon and ambush ops often and secretly crossed the border into Laos and Cambodia. The first A-Teams began operations in South Vietnam in '62, establishing Special Forces Camps throughout Vietnam, with the bulk of the camps being located along the Cambodian and Laotian borders. Four to five A-Teams were under the control of a B-Team, with three B-Teams controlled by a C-Team. The typical A-Team consisted of a commanding officer, executive officer, operations sergeant, heavy weapons leader, intelligence sergeant, light weapons leader, medical and assistant specialist, engineer sergeant, engineer and radio operator and supervisor. *See also* **B-Team, C-Team.**

AA *see* **Antiaircraft Guns**

AA Gunsites North Vietnamese AA and AAA gunsites were generally organized around a centrally located target acquisition radar/computer, around which 5–8 AA/AAA guns were located. The computer fed the guns with the firing information and commanded the fire. Many of the sites were mobile, moving every few days to avoid U.S. AA suppression attacks. The U.S. had a special operation called Commando Sabre that used jet aircraft to hunt for the gunsites. The gunsites were deployed around truck parks, fuel and supply transfer points and storage areas. *See also* **Commando Sabre Missions.**

AA-2 AAM *see* **Atoll Missile**

AAA *see* **Antiaircraft Artillery**

AAA-0 *see* **39th Infantry Regiment (Infantry)**

AAACV *see* **Australian Army Training Team, Vietnam**

AAAGV *see* **Australian Army Assistance Group, Vietnam**

Aachen II *see* **1st Infantry Division Fire Bases**

AAFES *see* **Post Exchange**

AAM (Air-to-Air Missile) Generic name for air-to-air missiles. Missiles fired from aircraft to other targeted aircraft. The aircraft could be planes, helicopters or other missiles. The AAMs used guidance systems based on heat detection (IR), radar, and radio control. *See also* **Atoll Missile, Sidewinder Missile.**

AAR *see* **After Action Report**

Aardvark *see* **F-111**

AATTV *see* **Australian Army Training Team, Vietnam**

AB Triple-C *see* **Airborne Battlefield Command and Control Center**

Abandoned Equipment, '75 (Captured Equipment '75) With the fall of South Vietnam in April '75, large quantities of U.S. equipment were abandoned by the ARVNs. Rough estimates on the equipment captured by the NVA from the routed ARVN were: .45cal pistols (90,000); M-16 rifles (791,000–1,600,000); M-67 RR (200); M-60 GPMG (15,000); M-79 (47,000); M-72 (63,000); mortars (14,900); M-14, M-1/2, sub-mg (857,580); artillery pieces (1,600); M-113 (1,380); M-41/48 tanks (550); ammunition (tons) (200,000+). Also: trucks/jeeps (several thousand); WPB patrol boats (26); swift boats (107); PBR (293); ASPB (84); monitors (64); ATC–LCM-6 (100); CCB (8); RPC (27); other craft (800). Also: A-1, F-5, A-37 aircraft (16 squadrons); UH-1 helicopters (17 sq.); CH-47 helicopters (4 sq.); C-7 Caribou (3 sq.); C-130 Hercules (2 sq.); other aircraft (13 sq). (These squadrons encompass in excess of 2,000 aircraft.) In addition, large quantities of ammunition, military and medical supplies, fuels, spare parts, communications equipment, building materials and facilities were surrendered to the North Vietnamese. *See also* **U.S. Aircraft Losses.**

Abandonment of the Central Highlands (Rout of the Central Highlands) In early March '75 three NVA divisions overran Ban Me Thuot, headquarters for 23d ARVN Division. South Vietnam's President Thieu ordered the withdrawal of ARVN troops from the northern provinces of the II Corps Central Highlands to the coast. The withdrawal quickly turned into a rout with ARVN forces running to the coast for safety. Panic among the ARVNs spread to the civilian population resulting in a mass exodus from the Highlands and eventually spread down the coast to Saigon. In the meantime, I Corps was cut off from the south and by the end of March Da Nang was in the hands of the NVA. *See also* **Ban Me Thuot.**

Abatis *see* **Porcupine Fence**

ABCCC *see* **Airborne Battlefield Command and Control Center**

ABD *see* **Acoustic Bullet Detector**

Abel Mabel *see* **Operation Abel Mabel**

Abilene *see* **Operation Abilene**

ABN *see* **Airborne**

Above the Rest *see* **101st Airborne Division (Airmobile)**

Abrams, General Creighton W. Abrams served as General Westmoreland's deputy commander of U.S. ground forces in Vietnam (MACV) until he assumed Command of MACV in July '68. Abrams directed U.S. ground forces in Vietnam until the last combat units were withdrawn in '72. Abrams changed the Army's ground war policy from the large scale operations favored by Westmoreland, to small scale operations designed to keep pressure on the NVA/VC while limiting American casualties. Abrams also initiated the Accelerated Pacification Program in an effort to put more of SVN under the control of US/GVN units. Abrams served as Army Chief of Staff from '72 until his death in '74. *See also* **Accelerated Pacification Program.**

Absent Without Leave (AWOL) A soldier absent from his unit or assigned post, without permission, is unaccounted for, and whose absence is not due to hostile action. AWOL was distinguished from "desertion" by the technical definition of desertion, which was the intent to remain permanently absent from the military. If an absent soldier retained one piece of his military equipment or uniform, he was not considered to have deserted, but would be charged with AWOL. *See also* **Deserters.**

Abzug, Bella (Patsy Mink) Two members of the U.S. House of Representatives, Bella Abzug and Patsy Mink, met with the head of the communist PRG, Nguyen Thi Binh, in Paris in April '72. Binh was in Paris as part of the ongoing peace talks between the U.S. and North Vietnam. House representatives Abzug and Mink later denounced the continued U.S. bombing of targets around Hanoi and Haiphong and "promised" Binh to step up their efforts, in the U.S. Congress, to stop the Nixon administration from continuing the war. Mink was the House Representative from Hawaii, and

Abzug was from New York. Abzug was also part of a congressional fact finding team that visited South Vietnam in early '75.

AC *see* **Aircraft Commander**

AC-1 *see* **C-7A**

AC-47 (Spooky, Gooney Bird, Dragon-ship, Puff-the-Magic Dragon) C-47 aircraft modified to perform as a gunship, beginning in November '65. The C-47 was redesignated the AC-47 and was fitted with three electrically operated 7.62mm Gatling guns (miniguns), each firing 6,000 rounds per minute from an altitude of 4,000 feet. The ship also carried a large supply of aerial flares. The gunship was frequently called out at night to provide support to friendly ground units. It was also used for interdiction missions along enemy supply lines in Laos and Cambodia. In '69 some USAF AC-47s were gradually transferred to VNAF and replaced by the AC-130 gunship. The gunships were operated by U.S. Air Force crews of the Air Commandos and Special Operations Squadrons. *See also* **AC-130, Pylon Turn, Project Big Eagle.**

AC-117 *see* **C-117**

AC-119G (Shadow, Gunship III, Combat Hornet Deployment) Fairchild C-119 cargo aircraft converted by the Air Force for use as a gunship and designated the AC-119G "Shadow." The Shadow was armed with four miniguns, NODs, flare launcher and a high intensity searchlight. The gunship was used in support of friendly ground forces and deployed to Vietnam in December '68 under the Combat Hornet Deployment. The guns on the Shadow were computer controlled to keep the ship from firing on friendly troops, based on their acknowledged position on the ground. AC-119s were eventually transferred to VNAF as the AC-130 fulfilled the fixed-wing gunship role in the U.S. Air Force. *See also* **C-119, AC-119K, AC-130, AC-47.**

AC-119K (Stinger) Fairchild C-119 cargo aircraft converted by the Air Force for use as a gunship and designated the AC-119K "Stinger." The Stinger was armed with four 7.62mm miniguns, two 20mm cannons and electric sensor monitoring equipment. The AC-119K was used to patrol the Ho Chi Minh Trail and was able to react to electronic sensor activations from implanted equipment along the trail. The Stinger was also equipped with two jet engines in addition to its twin propeller engines giving the modified C-119 extra power and burst speed to move out of range of NVA/VC ground fire. *See also* **C-119, AC-47, AC-130, AC-119G.**

AC-130 (Spectre, Gunship II) The U.S. Air Force AC-130 gunship was a modified C-130 transport equipped with weapons, NODs, and sensors to detect enemy troop concentrations and perform as a gunship. The AC-130 was armed with 2–4, 20mm cannons, four miniguns, a 105mm howitzer as well as flares and cameras. Some versions of the gunship also carried 40mm cannons. The weapons were mounted along the left side of the aircraft and were aimed by the pilot by adjusting the position of the aircraft. The AC-130 began to replace the AC-47 gunship in '69. As the AC-47 faded out, troops began to call the AC-130s by the old AC-47's nickname of "Spooky" and "Puff." *See also* **AC-47, AC-119G, AC-119K, C-130.**

ACAU *see* **Australian Civil Affairs Unit**

ACAV *see* **Armored Cavalry Assault Vehicle**

ACAV Kit (A Kit, B Kit) M-113 APCs used in Vietnam were modified to perform as armored cavalry assault vehicles. In order to modify the M-113 the Army devised two retrofit kits for it. Kit A was used by the 11th Cav before its deployment to Vietnam in '66. And Kit B was used to convert existing APCs in Vietnam to the ACAV. The A Kit included gun shields for the .50cal machine gun, three gun mounts and two shields to be used by the extra M-60 machine guns that were to be fitted on the vehicle. The B Kit consisted of only the .50cal gun shield and was used on the M-125 81mm mortar carrier. *See also* **Armored Cavalry Assault Vehicle.**

ACB *see* **Amphibious Construction Battalions**

ACC *see* **M-577 ACC**

Accelerated Pacification Campaign *see* **Accelerated Pacification Program**

Accelerated Pacification Program (APP, Accelerated Pacification Campaign, Le Loi) U.S. backed program initiated in November '68 by MACV Com-

mander, General Abrams, in an effort to increase the number of friendly villages under the control of the GVN and speed up the deployment of the SVN military to the point that they would be a confident, self-reliant force able to protect the country from the NVA/VC. The program was placed under the direction of William Colby. The Phoenix Program of VCI elimination was part of this program. The program had limited success and began to fall apart as U.S. troop levels began to decrease. The VCI were never completely eliminated and the GVN forces were not able to maintain control. The GVN's name for the program was "Le Loi." *See also* **Phoenix Program.**

Accelerated Turnover to Vietnam (ACTOV, Sequential Turnover Plan) Navy program established by Admiral Elmo Zumwalt in '68 to carry out Vietnamization of the war. The program trained the Vietnamese in the maintenance and operation of naval equipment that was transferred to them as U.S. participation in the war was reduced. The heart of the plan used an OJT system called "Sequential Turnover." Under the system, one VNN crewman was placed aboard a U.S. boat and trained to replace one of the American crewmen. When he was sufficiently trained the American crewman left the boat and another Viet sailor was brought onboard. This continued until the entire crew was Vietnamese. The Navy ACTOV program was one of the more successful Vietnamization programs. *See also* **Vietnamization.**

Acceptable Loss Level Phrase for what the military determined to be "acceptable" losses of men and equipment incurred during combat operations. Official military "acceptable loss levels" were not always acceptable to the U.S. public. Loss levels were based on such factors as the number of men or aircraft participating in the attack, enemy defenses, weather considerations, ordnance available and the condition of the attacking force. These factors were culminated into an estimate of losses and an acceptable loss level was established. Some observers, less impressed with the military method, believed the loss estimates were based on the "WAG" principle.

Accessory Packet Sealed foil packet that was found in a box of C-Rations. The waterproof brown packet contained a book of matches, two pieces of chewing gum (hard), a packet each of instant coffee (strong), sugar (caked), cream substitute and salt, a packet of folded toilet papers (never enough) and a box of four cigarettes (stale). One accessory packet was packed inside each box of Cs, and there were 12 C-Ration meals to a case. *See also* **C-Ration, SP Pack.**

Accommodations *see* **Live and Let Live**

Accompanied Tour (Unaccompanied Tour)   Military designation that indicated a tour of duty assignment allowed an individual soldier's dependents to accompany him to his new duty station. Dependents were not allowed in war or hazardous duty zones, such tours being designated "unaccompanied tours." Accompanied tours to Vietnam were allowed until '64 when all U.S. military dependents were evacuated from South Vietnam.

Accordion Wire *see* **Concertina Wire**

Ace (Air Ace)   American fighter pilots who shot down five or more aircraft were called "Aces." During the Vietnam War, two Navy pilots, one Air Force pilot and two Air Force Electronic Weapons Officers became the only American aces of the airwar in Vietnam. The aircraft kills had to be confirmed by other friendly aircraft to qualify.

Ace of Spades *see* **Calling Cards**

Acetylene Gas   One of the gases U.S. units sometimes pumped into Viet Cong tunnel systems. The gas served to displace the limited oxygen that was in the tunnels and when ignited it burned up the tunnel's remaining air supply. Because the tunnels were constructed with a series of breaks, trapdoors and several levels, the gas could not be distributed to all the branches within the tunnel system. *See also* **Tunnels of Cu Chi, Tunnel Rats.**

Acey-Deucy Club   NCO club located at the Naval Fuel facility on Vinh Loc Island. *See also* **Vinh Loc Island.**

ACG-35/68M *see* **Seismic Tunnel Detector**

ACH-47 *see* **Go-Go Bird**

Acheson, Dean   Dean Acheson served as Foreign Policy Advisor to both Presidents

Kennedy and Johnson. In '66 Acheson began voicing opposition to President Johnson on the way the war was going in Vietnam. Acheson was one of the members of the "Wise Old Men," an unofficial policy group that advised President Johnson on various matters. The group advised Johnson in '68 that they believed the war in Vietnam was unwinnable and that U.S. forces should be withdrawn.

Acid *see* **Lysergic Acid**

Acid Rock (Heavy Metal)   Rock music of the sixties characterized by high decibel chords from electric guitars. Most often identified with the hippie movement. Drug use was prevalent among many of the rock performers of the day. In the mid sixties, Acid (LSD) was often used by some rock groups to intensify their performance.

ACM *see* **Army Commendation Medal**

ACOU-SID *see* **Acoustic Sound Intrusion Device**

Acoustic Bullet Detector (ABD)   Experimental "bullet" detector for use on Army helicopters. The system consisted of an acoustically sensitive sensor located on the belly of the helicopter. When the enemy fired at the chopper the plate "heard" the rounds and sounded a warning in the cockpit. The system never went very far because most helicopter crews could tell they were taking rounds by the loud "rips" and "tings" the enemy bullets made as they tore at the aircraft's skin.

Acoustic Sound Intrusion Device (ACOU-SID)   Acoustic sensor monitoring enemy troop activity. The sensor was activated when the noise level exceeded the normal ambient noise level established by the device. When activated, the sensor would transmit a coded radio signal and 10 seconds of audible sound to a remote receiver. Activation could be accomplished by voices, artillery, vehicles or even screeching monkeys. The device could be dropped from aircraft to lodge in trees or could be carried to the target area and hidden in the trees. The ACOU-SID was about three feet long and four inches in diameter. A small drag chute was used when the sensor was deployed by air. *See also* **Electronic Sensors.**

ACR *see* **Air Cavalry Regiment, Armored Cavalry Regiment**

Across the Pond *see* Vietnam (GI Names)

ACS *see* Air Cavalry Squadron

ACSC *see* Air Command and Staff College

ACT *see* Air Cavalry Troop

Acting Jack (Acting Sergeant, Temporary Sergeant) Nickname for an enlisted man temporarily appointed to the rank of sergeant. In old Army terminology it referred to a corporal placed in command of a section. In Vietnam it referred to an E-4 temporarily appointed to the rank of sergeant. The acting sergeant was blessed with the authority, privileges, and responsibilities of the rank, but continued to be "paid" at the E-4 rank.

Acting Sergeant *see* Acting Jack

ACTIV *see* Army Concept Team in Vietnam

Active Light System *see* IR Scope, Starlight Scope

ACTOV *see* Accelerated Turnover to Vietnam

Acute Situation Reaction *see* Combat Fatigue

ACV *see* Army Air Cushioned Vehicles, PACV

ACY *see* Armed Combat Youth

AD *see* Aviation Detachment, Administrative Discharge

Ad Hoc Task Force on Vietnam Special group composed of President Johnson's advisors convened by the President to consider the February '68 request by General Westmoreland for 200,000 more U.S. troops, to be immediately deployed to Vietnam. The group decided against the 200,000 troop escalation and advised the President to deploy only an additional 20,000 troops to Vietnam. The ability of the NVA/VC to launch the widespread attacks of Tet '68, with 500,000 U.S. troops in Vietnam, cast grave doubt on the glowing reports by Westmoreland on the progress the U.S. military was making in Vietnam. Members of the Ad Hoc Task Force were Clark Clifford, Walt Rostow, Paul Nitze, Paul Warnke and Generals Maxwell Taylor and Earle Wheeler.

AD-6 *see* A-1

ADA *see* Air Defense Artillery

Adams, Sam (Adams-Westmoreland Controversy) In '65 CIA Intelligence Officer Sam Adams challenged MACV estimates of the number of NVA troops that were operating in, and infiltrating into, SVN. Adams used captured enemy documents and enemy interrogation reports to show that MACV estimates of enemy troop strength were deceptively low. When MACV Commander Westmoreland was confronted with the CIA information he refused to adjust the enemy totals, preferring to use the lower MACV estimates. In '82 a CBS News documentary charged Westmoreland with conspiracy to falsify enemy totals. Westmoreland sued CBS and the figures and sources used by Adams came to light. CBS and Westmoreland settled the suit out of court.

Adams-Westmoreland Controversy *see* Adams, Sam

ADC *see* Assistant Division Commander

Adjustable Ranging Telescope *see* M-14 Sniper Rifle

Adjutant General (AG, AGC, Adjutant General's Corps) Army administrative staff responsible for noncombat/non-logistical command functions such as statistical records, personnel records, Army publications and orders, postal services, awards, and general administrative functions. The AGC operated as an arm of the Army's Chief of Staff.

Adjutant General's Corps *see* Adjutant General

Adjutant's Office *see* S-1

Administrative Discharge (AD) A military administrative procedure for discharging an individual from military service. ADs included all discharges except those ordered as a result of a court-martial. Undesirable, General, Honorable, and Hardship Discharges were issued under administrative guidelines. The AD was particularly useful in issuing UDs for "substandard performance of duty, numerous minor discipline infractions, or diagnosed character behavior disorders." Soldiers with a record of drug abuse, sale or supply of drugs, or persistent disciplinary problems could easily be "booted" out of the service without going through the lengthy process of a court-martial. The AD became a prominent method of dealing with drug related problems and militant black soldiers in Vietnam after '69. *See also* Bad Paper, Discharges.

Administrative Leave Military leave granted to an individual but not charged to his normal yearly leave allowance. Administrative leave could be granted for religious functions, to attend civilian awards presentations, or any other function approved by the commanding officer.

Administrative Line 1939 *see* Brevie Line

Admiral (Vice Admiral, Rear Admiral) Highest ranking officer grades in the U.S. Navy. The admiral grades were equivalent to the "general" grades in the Army, Air Force, and Marines. The highest admiral rank was Admiral of the Fleet, followed by Admiral, Vice Admiral, Rear Admiral (upper) and Rear Admiral (lower), respectively equivalent to the Army ranks of General of the Army, General, Lieutenant General, Major General and Brigadier General. *See also* General Officers.

Admiral *see* Navy Sailors, Admiral

Admiral, The *see* Electronic Warfare Officer

Admission and Dispositions Section *see* A & D

Adrenaline Junkie (TIC, Tango India Charlie) Slang name for the person who has a need to be extremely active and busy, a sort of slave to the excitement caused by combat, the nearness of death and subsequent "high" it caused. This applied to grunts, pilots, aircrews and many of the nurses who served in Vietnam. The rush and pressures of working on critically wounded patients gave the nurses a sense of exhilaration and purpose in Vietnam that, for many, could not be matched when they returned to work in the States. Many of the nurses had a need to be under pressure to function, and without such pressure, their lives were incomplete or, seemingly, no longer fulfilling. Some pilots continually sought out missions of high stress to fill their need for excitement. For some pilots three of the sweetest

words to their ears were "troops in contact" (TIC, Tango India Charlie), which meant the pilots would be flying into hostile fire instead of routine bomb runs. For troops on the ground the rush of excitement was no less addicting. Many sought out the enemy with a passion.

ADSID *see* Air Delivered Seismic Intrusion Device

Advance *see* Pay Advance

Advance Leave During the Vietnam War many soldiers were granted "advance leave." Normal rules entitled a soldier to one 30-day leave per year. Eligibility for such leave was available after a year had been served in the military. Many soldiers being sent to Vietnam were granted their 30-day leave in advance because they often were shipped to Vietnam on completion of their advanced training, less than four months after entering the service. The advanced leave was generally granted if the unit commander believed there was a reasonable chance the soldier would repay the used leave in the time he had remaining in service. Lost leave records from 201 files allowed some soldiers to take more than their allotted leave. *See also* Pay Advance.

Advanced Individual Training *see* Advanced Infantry Training

Advanced Infantry Training (AIT, Advanced Individual Training, Second-Eight) Upon completion of Basic Infantry Training, U.S. Army soldiers were assigned to an advanced training program. Advanced Infantry Training was for those soldiers whose primary job would be in the infantry, artillery, or armor. Advanced Individual Training prepared soldiers for the other jobs that made up the Army, i.e., cooks, clerks, medics, logistics, transports, etc. Advanced Infantry Training typically lasted eight weeks, and many graduates of the training, after a 30-day leave, were Vietnam bound.

Advanced Research Project Agency (ARPA, Project Agile) U.S. Department of Defense agency whose primary purpose was the testing of new weapons, devices and techniques for counterinsurgency. The ARPA had field test teams operational in SVN throughout the war monitoring weapons trials, new equipment and jungle warfare techniques. In '61 ARPA operated under the code name of Project Agile. The ARPA's field test teams in Vietnam were designated the "Army Concept Team in Vietnam," ACTIV. *See also* **ACTIV, TIARA Project, DCPG, Tech Rep.**

Advanced Tactical Support Bases *see* **Ammi Barge**

Advanced Technology Training (ATT) An Army holding program for troops returned from Vietnam who could not be assigned to other overseas duties, but could not be released from the military. Soldiers in that category included those with more than five months to go in service, but less than ten months on their enlistment. Other troops in the holding program were those with less than five months to go in service who did not qualify for the early-out program. *See also* **Early-Out.**

Advisor *see* **Combat Assistance Team, MACV, Quan Su**

Advisory, Training and Operations Mission (ATOM; Training, Relations and Instruction Mission; TRIM) Combined American and French team organized to coordinate the transition from a French to an American advisory effort, established in '54. In '55 the team was reorganized and renamed the Training, Relations and Instruction Mission (TRIM). The American members of ATOM, and later TRIM were part of the MAAGV force. In '56 the French left Vietnam and the Americans assumed full training and advisory functions to the South Vietnamese. *See also* **TRIM Program.**

AEC *see* **Atoms for Peace**

Aerial Field Artillery (AFA) A rename of helicopter gunships previously called Aerial Rocket Artillery. The new name primarily applied to AH-1 cobra gunships assigned as aerial artillery gunships. *See also* **Aerial Rocket Artillery, AH-1G.**

Aerial Flares Parachute suspended flares dropped from aircraft, used for ground illumination. Aerial flares had an output of over one million candle power and were typically dropped from a flare ship at an altitude of 1,000 feet. *See also* **Smokey Bear, AC-47.**

Aerial Observer *see* **Airborne Observer**

Aerial Rocket Artillery (ARA, Air Artillery, Rocketeers) Heavily armed helicopter gunships, loosely known as "Rocketeers," used to provide fire support to ground units. Typically armed with rockets and miniguns. Various types of rocket systems were used on the gunships, but most often seen were the XM-158, 7-rocket pod and the XM-159 or XM-200, 19-rocket pod or the XM-3, 24-rocket pod. The pods were used in pairs, and sometimes mixed or mounted with other weapons systems such as miniguns, cannons and grenade launchers. *See also* **XM-158, XM-159, XM-3 Rocket Launcher, Aerial Field Artillery.**

Aerial Tankers *see* **KA-6, KB-50, KC-130, KC-135**

Aerial Weapons Company (AWC) Army helicopter company consisting of gunships. Initially gunship platoons in Vietnam consisted of UH-1B/C Huey Hogs, but later in the war AH-1G Cobras were used to fill out the weapons platoons. The AWC provided fire support to ground units and operated as armed, aerial reconnaissance teams. *See also* **Avn, LFT, HFT.**

Aerial-Denial Ordnance Strikes Air Force technique of surrounding a downed airman with a continuous ring of bombs, rockets and cannon fire in an effort to keep the enemy from capturing him before he was rescued. *See also* **Gravel Mine, U.S.**

Aero Rifle Platoon (ARP, Blue Team, Blues, All American Team) The infantry platoon of an air cavalry troop. The ARP or "Blue Team" as they were called, were transported by the Huey Slicks of the troop's "Lift Platoon." The lift platoon consisted of 8–9 UH-1D/H Hueys. The troop's scout platoon (Pink and White Teams) usually operated in two and three ship elements that sought out the enemy. When contact was made the "Blues" would be called in to pin the enemy while the gunships of the troop's "Red Platoon" provided fire support. An "All American Team" was field slang for a complete Red, White and Blue Team, combined for a mission. *See also* **Air Cavalry Troop.**

Aero Scout Platoon (ASP, White Platoon, Whites, White Teams) The scouting platoon of an air cavalry troop. The platoon consisted of several light observation helicopters that operated alone, in pairs or with gunships seeking out the NVA/VC.

The primary helicopter used by the "Whites" was the OH-6 Loach. The White Teams often worked with gunship teams from the troop's aero weapons platoon in 2–3 ship teams called "Pink Teams" or "Hunter-Killer Teams." The job of the scouts was to locate the enemy so the firepower of the gunships and artillery could be brought to bear and the infantry of the troop's aero rifle platoon could be brought in to close with and finish the enemy. *See also* **Air Cavalry Troop.**

Aero Weapons Platoon (AWP, Reds, Red Platoon, Guns) Helicopter weapons platoon of an air cavalry troop. The AWP was also called the "Red Platoon" or "Guns." The platoon usually operated in two ship elements providing close support for its rifle platoon that operated on the ground. The Guns also operated with the reconnaissance element of the troop in "Pink Teams" that sought out the NVA/VC. The Pink Team usually consisted of an observation chopper and one or two gunships. The gunship platoon operated AH-1G Cobras and Huey Hog gunships. *See also* **Air Cavalry Troop.**

Aeromed *see* **Aeromedical Evacuation Units**

Aeromedical Evacuation Units (Aeromed, 10th Aeromedical Evacuation Group, 10th Aeromed) U.S. Air Force Group responsible for flying the wounded out of Vietnam. The 10th Aeromed consisted of the 34th, 55th, 56th, and 57th Aeromed Squadrons and their associated detachments. *See also* **Air-Evacuation.**

Aeroscouts *see* **Helicopter Scouts**

Aerospace Rescue and Recovery Service (ARRS, Pararescuemen, PJs, That Others May Live) USAF rescue service specialists, known as PJs, were ranger trained medics, parachute and frogman qualified. PJs would often go down to wounded aircrewmen to give them first aid and get them into the rescue chopper. The ARRS worked from air bases in South Vietnam and Thailand using HH-3 and HH-53 Jolly Green Giant helicopters. ARRS crews deployed to SVN in April '62 and by the time they departed SVN in '73 they had rescued 3,883 downed aircrewmen at a cost of 71 ARRS personnel. Rescues in enemy territory required an armed task force to accompany the ARRS. The ARRS motto; "That Others May Live."

See also **Search and Rescue.**

AFA *see* **Aerial Field Artillery**

AFDL (Drydock) Small, towed, Navy floating drydock. AFDLs were originally designed to support amphibious operations providing smaller assault and cargo craft with drydock repair facilities. AFDLs were used in Vietnam by riverine and naval support forces. *See also* **Ammi Barge.**

AFH-1 Helmet *see* **APH-5 Helmet**

AFLC *see* **Air Force Logistics Command**

Afloat Base *see* **Mobile Riverine Base**

AFQT *see* **Moron Corps**

Afro (Afro Comb) The Afro was a hairstyle that became popular with many young blacks during the sixties and seventies. The Afro featured long hair, uniformly rounded about the head. In order to keep the hair fluffed out, a special comb, the Afro comb, was used. The comb had several long teeth and a handle. The Afro comb caused some problems in the military because it was too long to fit completely in a soldier's pocket, exposing the handle. This was a violation of the regulations regarding the military uniform which dictated that nothing was to stick out of the uniform's pockets. *See also* **Black Power, Clenched Fist, Klan; Same Mud, Same Blood.**

Afro Comb *see* **Afro**

AFRS *see* **American Forces Vietnam Network**

AFSC *see* **Armed Forces Staff College, Quaker Prosthetics Center**

AFSEA *see* **Air Force Special Elements Activity**

AFSP *see* **Air Police**

After Action Report (AAR) Army system requiring field officers to make written reports after an enemy action. The reports were later organized and analyzed by an Army strategies group in an effort to continually upgrade Army tactics and strategies, based on past actions. AARs were called in by radio from field units, while major operations were written up in detailed reports at the battalion and brigade level. *See also* **Friendly Initiated Incident.**

Afterburner (Dry Thrust, Wet Thrust, Burners) During normal jet engine operation, intake air is mixed with fuel, the burning fuel-air mixture produces superhot gases which are exhausted from the engine, generating the thrust (dry thrust) to move the aircraft forward. To increase the thrust, and the speed of the aircraft, raw fuel can be injected directly into the exhaust chamber where it burns with the gases, greatly increasing the thrust (wet thrust) produced. Afterburning greatly increases aircraft power, but also uses enormous amounts of fuel. Heavily loaded fighter-bombers in Vietnam used their afterburners during takeoffs. Going into "burners" was also used in aerial combat to give the aircraft speed advantages in pursuing targets, and for evasion and avoidance tactics.

AFV Lobby *see* **Iron Mike**

AFVN *see* **American Forces Vietnam Network**

AG *see* **Adjutant General**

AG-44 *see* **Saucer Cap**

AGC *see* **Adjutant General**

Agency, The *see* **Central Intelligence Agency**

Agent Blue Used as part of the defoliation program in South Vietnam, Agent Blue was a desiccant type herbicide used primarily to kill growing rice crops that were suspected of belonging to or destined for the enemy. The defoliants were codenamed after the identifying color bands on the herbicide containers. Agent Blue was a fast acting contact herbicide of cacodylic acid, and was very effective against rice crops and as a locally applied defoliant around base camps and along roads. Agent Blue caused the leaves of the plant to shrivel and drop off. *See also* **Defoliation**.

Agent Orange (2-4-5-T, 2-4-5-D) Chemical herbicide used to defoliate vegetated areas in Vietnam. The defoliants were codenamed after the identifying color bands on the herbicide shipping containers. The defoliant caused plants, shrubs and trees to grow at such a fantastic rate that the cells of the vegetation ruptured and died within 5–7 weeks. The effects lasted 7–12 months before reapplication was required. Agent Orange was composed of the defoliants

2-4-5-D and 2-4-5-T; the latter contained the contaminant Dioxin as a by-product, which at the time was the most powerful and toxic poison created by man. Dioxin was linked to birth defects and a myriad of other diseases and health problems. *See also* **Defoliation, Dioxin Poisoning, SS Vulcanus**.

Agent Pink *see* **Defoliation**

Agent Purple *see* **Defoliation**

Agent White Part of the American program of defoliation in South Vietnam. Agent White was sprayed around American bases in an effort to kill off growing brush and weeds, to clear fields of fire and deny the enemy cover. The defoliant was sprayed by helicopter, from truck mounted pressurized sprayers, and from man-carried backpack pump sprayers. The defoliants were codenamed after the identifying color bands on the herbicide containers. Agent White consisted of a mixture of picolinic acid and 2-4-D herbicide, and provided extended herbicide control for a longer period of time than that provided by Agent Blue. *See also* **Defoliation**.

Aggression from the North *see* **White Paper: Aggression from the North**

Aggressive Defense (Static Defense) When American combat Marines were first deployed to SVN in March '65, their mission was to defend the U.S. air base located at Da Nang. Their mission was labeled "static defense." After several weeks of holding the perimeter around Da Nang the Marines were ordered to begin offensive operations against the VC around Da Nang; their new mission was labeled "aggressive defense." The rationale was the Marines would search out and destroy the enemy before the enemy could attack the base. A major factor influencing the decision to put the Marines on the offensive was the swiftly eroding position of the ARVNs in their battle with the VC. *See also* **Search and Destroy**.

AGM (Air-to-Ground Missile) Generic name for air-to-ground guided missiles. Various types used different methods of guidance. The primary common feature was that they were fired from aircraft to ground targets. *See also* **AGM-12, AGM-45, AGM-78A, XM-22, Zuni, SS-11, TOW**.

AGM-12 (Bullpup) Air-to-ground missiles used by U.S. aircraft in Vietnam.

The 250-pound warhead missile was wire guided to the target, by the pilot, after the missile was dropped from the aircraft. The maximum range of the missile was 11kms, but effective targeting range was closer to 4kms, at a speed of 1,360mph. The Bullpup was one of the first "smart bombs" (guided bombs) used by U.S. aircraft against North Vietnamese targets. There were several versions of the Bullpup available to the Air Force and Navy featuring larger warheads and more powerful rocket engines. *See also* **Smart Bombs, AGM.**

AGM-45 (Shrike ARM) U.S. air-to-ground, antiradiation guided missile (ARM) fired from an aircraft. The missile used the enemy radar emitted by the SAM and AAA gun sites as a beacon and rode the signal to its source to destroy the site. The 10-foot long AGM-45 had a maximum effective range of 8kms (max range of 29–40kms) and packed a 145-pound HE warhead. The Shrike missile was first used by Wild Weasels in May '66 in missions against NVN to suppress SAM activity on bombing raids. The Shrike was later replaced by the AGM-78. Fan Song and Fire Can radar were used by NVN to aim their SAM missiles and higher calibre antiaircraft artillery guns. *See also* **Fan Song, Fire Cans, Wild Weasel, Iron Hand, AGM.**

AGM-62 *see* **Electro-Optical Guided Bomb**

AGM-78A (Standard ARM) U.S. surface-to-air missile that was adapted for use as an air-to-ground antiradiation missile. The missile was originally developed by General Dynamics for the Navy and was called the "Standard." The AGM Standard ARM was 15 feet long, had a launch weight of over 1,400 pounds, and featured greater range and a larger warhead than the AGM-45 ARM. The AGM-78 was used by the Navy and the Air Force in the SAM suppression role, and had a max speed of about 1,900mph. The Navy used the A-6 Intruder as its primary SAM suppressor aircraft, and the Air Force used the F-105 and F-4.

Agnew, Spiro T. Vice-President to Richard Nixon, Agnew was a highly outspoken critic of those members of Congress and the press that criticized the Nixon administration. Agnew was later accused of bribery and tax evasion. In October '73

Agnew pleaded no contest (nolo contendere) to tax evasion and resigned from the Vice-Presidency. He was replaced by Gerald R. Ford.

Agricultural Reform Tribunals (Ho's Land Reforms) Program established in North Vietnam by Ho Chi Minh in '55. The focus of the tribunals was the elimination of the "landlord class" that controlled the rural farmlands of North Vietnam. The program was based on Ho's strict adherence to Marxism. Ho formed cadres that installed themselves in rural villages across NVN, staging tribunals to determine who were "landlords." Selected "landlords" were executed or sent to labor camps. The cadre were given quotas of landlords to identify and they relied heavily on the input from the peasants who worked the land. Some of the peasant input was based on lies and old grudges. The Reform Program totally disrupted NVN's agricultural economy and the program was repudiated in mid-'56.

Agroville Program One of Premier Diem's government programs, adopted from the French, designed to improve the lifestyles of rural villagers and farmers. The '59 plan called for the resettlement of rural groups into government built villes and hamlets. The object was to protect the people from harassment by the VC and gain the support of the people. Most of the people were relocated from VC controlled areas, many forceably. Some of those relocated resented the government for uprooting them from their ancestral homeland and the new, "safe" relocation camps eventually came under the influence and attack of the VC. The program was later modified and called Strategic Hamlets in '61. *See also* **Strategic Hamlet Program, Restructuring.**

AH-16 *see* **Repose**

AH-17 *see* **Sanctuary**

AH-1G (Cobra, Snake, Red Bird, Huey Cobra) Bell Aircraft attack helicopter which deployed to SVN September '67. The production model was the AH-1G, which was armed with a combination of rockets, 40mm grenades, miniguns and later antitank missiles. The Cobra could carry over 1900 pounds of ordnance and was used extensively to provide fire support to ground troops and all types of air-to-ground attacks on enemy positions. The Bell Cobra became the Army's primary gunship, and in '69 began service with the Marines and later the Navy. The two man crew utilized tandem seating with the pilot seated behind and slightly higher than the gunner. *See also* **Gunship, AH-1J, Heavy Hog.**

AH-1J (Sea Cobra) Twin engine version of the Bell AH-1 Cobra helicopter developed for use by the U.S. Marine Corps. The AH-1J, designated the Sea Cobra, became available to the Marines for combat testing in Vietnam in '71. The Sea Cobra was slightly faster than the single engine Cobra but had a little less range. *See also* **AH-1G.**

AHC *see* **Assault Helicopter Company, Avn**

AID *see* **U.S. Agency for International Development**

Aid Bag *see* **Unit One**

AIM-7 (Sparrow, SAR, Semiactive Radar Guidance) U.S. air-to-air missile. Sparrow missiles used in Vietnam had a max speed of over 2,200mph and a range in excess of 16kms. The AIM-7 had a 66-pound warhead and a launch weight over 400 pounds. The missile used semiactive radar (SAR) guidance and was a Navy/Marine standard AAM. SAR guidance systems used the aircraft's radar to mark the target; when the missile was launched it would home in on the marker signal and chase down the target aircraft.

AIM-9 *see* **Sidewinder Missile**

Aiming Stakes Wooden sticks positioned around a gun pit (mortar or howitzer) used as reference points for quick aiming of the weapon.

Air Ace *see* **Ace**

Air America (Civil Air Transport Company, CIA Air Force, CAT) Cover name used by the CIA air force in Indo-China supporting their covert COIN activities in the region. The CIA Air Force in Southeast Asia previously fronted under the name of Civil Air Transport Company. Air America provided air support for clandestine CIA activities throughout Southeast Asia and also provided legitimate air cargo services throughout the same area. The aircraft of Air America were primarily transport and included both fixed and rotary wing craft.

Both marked and unmarked aircraft were used. Air America continued to operate in SVN until the country collapsed in April '75. *See also* **Spook Plane, Freedom Train.**

Air Artillery *see* **Aerial Rocket Artillery**

Air Blowers (Mighty Mite, Buffalo Turbine, Mars Generator, Resojet, Tunnel Flusher) During the Vietnam War the U.S. Army experimented with several different air blowers. The gasoline powered air blowers received the military designation of "Tunnel Flushers" and were used to pump gases and smoke into enemy tunnel systems. Of the four blowers used, the "Mighty Mite" was the most successful based on weight of the unit and fuel consumption. The Mighty Mite did not blow air at a rate as high as the other units, but it was more mechanically dependable and man-portable in the field. *See also* **Tunnel Warfare, Resojet Air Generator, Buffalo Turbine, Mighty Mite, Mars Air Generator.**

Air Cav *see* **Air Cavalry**

Air Cavalry (Air Cav) Infantry troops, organized as a unit, that transported and assaulted via helicopter. In the old west, cavalry soldiers were mounted on horseback; in Vietnam they were helicopter or APC mounted. The 1st Air Cav was the first division formed completely around the helicopter as the cavalry workhorse. *See also* **1st Air Cavalry.**

Air Cavalry Regiment (ACR) Light infantry regiment that used helicopters for maneuver and deployment. The regiment consisted of 3–4 troops and at least one organic artillery battalion. The regiment also included maintenance and support units, all designed to be mobile. In Vietnam, elements of the air cavalry regiment primarily operated as a reconnaissance and screening force, functioning as the eyes and ears (and sometimes the teeth) of the ACR's parent division.

Air Cavalry Squadron (ACS) Basic element of a cavalry regiment. In Vietnam the ACS operated as the reconnaissance arm of the division. The 1st Squadron/9th Cavalry acted as the eyes and ears of the 1st Cavalry Division. The 1st/9th Cavalry consisted of a Headquarters Troop, three Air Cavalry Troops, and a Ground Reconnaissance Troop. The air cavalry troop had a headquarters element, a scout platoon of LOHs, a gun platoon of helicopter gunships, and a rifle platoon equipped with its own lift helicopters. The ground recon troop consisted of jeep mounted and "leg" elements. *See also* **1st Squadron, 9th Cavalry (Aerial Recon), Air Cavalry Regiment.**

Air Cavalry Troop (ACT) Air elements of a cavalry or air cavalry squadron, the squadron consisting of 2–4 troops. The air cav troop typically consisted of a headquarters section and four platoons. The platoons were identified by name as well as color. The White Platoon consisted of 2–3 helicopter scout teams; Aero Scout Platoon (White Teams). The Red Platoon consisted of the troop's gunships; Aero Weapons Platoon, which also operated in teams. The Blue Team was the Aero Rifle Platoon and consisted of a platoon of infantry that was transported by an 8–9 ship platoon of UH-1D/H Huey Slicks. The scouts and gun teams often operated together forming Pink Teams. *See also* **Hunter-Killer Team, Aero Rifle Platoon, Aero Scout Platoon, Aero Weapons Platoon.**

Air Cofat (NSA Courier Service) Naval Support Activity Courier Service operated from the Navy offices in the Cofat Compound in Saigon. Air Cofat operated C-45, C-47 planes and CH-46 helicopters which made the circuit of Navy installations from Da Nang to An Thoi delivering dispatches, personnel and high priority cargo. Cofat aircraft was based at Tan Son Nhut and operated three days a week. NSAD also operated flights two days a week between Saigon and Da Nang. *See also* **NSAD, NSAS, Cofat Compound.**

Air Cofat–Sealords (Sealords) U.S. Navy utility lift helicopter detachment of the Naval Support Activity. The detachment operated under control of HAL-3 from a base in Saigon to provide transport, courier, lift and supply services for Navy units in and around the Delta. Air Cofat also provided limited lift capacity for Navy SEAL operations, with the Seawolves providing air cover and support. Lift operations were later expanded and a helicopter base was established at Binh Tuy. The Binh Tuy detachment was known as the "Sealords." *See also* **Seawolves, Air Cofat.**

Air Command and Staff College

(ACSC) Air Force institution of advanced learning which was attended by senior officers. Courses and seminars were held in a variety of managerial related fields such as communications, operations and personnel. The ACSC was located at Maxwell Air Force Base, Alabama. *See also* **Air War College.**

Air Commando Wing (Special Operations Wing, 14th Special Operations Wing, SOW) Air Force units that operated in Vietnam conducting counterinsurgency warfare. The wing included those specialized units that provided ground support and special missions against the NVA/VC. In mid-'68 the Air Commando Wing and its squadrons were redesignated the Special Operations Wing and Special Operations Squadron. The Air Commandos (14th SOW) operated the Air Force's A-37s, gunships (AC-47/119/130), PSYOPS and "Green Hornets" in Vietnam. *See also* **AC-47, -119, -130; UH-1F, Special Operations Squadron, NPK, Project Mule Train.**

Air Cushioned Vehicles *see* **Army Air Cushioned Vehicles, PACV**

Air Defense Artillery (ADA, 97th Artillery Group) Army designation for its air defense missile units during the Vietnam War. The Army deployed two Hawk surface-to-air missile batteries to Vietnam. The 6th/56th Artillery operated at Tan Son Nhut, Long Binh, and Chu Lai. The 6th/71st Artillery operated at Qui Nhon and Cam Ranh Bay. Both battalions were part of the 97th Artillery Group which was responsible for Army air defense. Group headquarters was at Tan Son Nhut. By '69 both battalions had departed Vietnam, the threat of a North Vietnamese air attack against U.S. installations considered highly unlikely. *See also* **Hawk Missile.**

Air Delivered Mines *see* **CBU Mines**

Air Delivered Seismic Intrusion Device (ADSID, Tropical Tree) Seismic sensor dropped from a plane or helicopter used to monitor enemy movement. When dropped, the sensor lodged itself in the ground and when activated sent a coded radio signal to a remote monitoring unit. The unit was activated by ground vibrations in the immediate vicinity of the sensor, the source of which could be the movement of enemy troops, impacting artillery or even a passing water buffalo. The battery powered ADSID weighed 25 pounds, was four inches in diameter and two feet long with a pointed end that lodged in the ground. The attached antenna was one inch in diameter, four feet long and shaped like the branch of a leafless tree. The NVA/VC called the ADSID the "Tropical Tree." *See also* **Electronic Sensors.**

Air Force Academy *see* **U.S. Air Force Academy**

Air Force Bases, Vietnam   The U.S. Air Force operated from 11 major air bases in South Vietnam from '61 until the end of '72. The air bases at Saigon, Bien Hoa, Pleiku, Nha Trang and Da Nang were operational prior to the introduction of American combat troops in '65. The bases at Binh Thuy, Vung Tau, Phan Rang, Cam Ranh Bay, Tuy Hoa and Phu Cat became operational in '65 or later.

Air Force Cross   Our nation's second highest award for bravery awarded to Air Force personnel by the President. Equivalent to the Navy Cross and the Army Distinguished Service Cross.

Air Force Engineers *see* **RED HORSE Engineers**

Air Force Logistics Command (AFLC) Air Force command responsible for insuring that Air Force units were equipped and kept supplied with necessary armament and munitions. The Navy Military Sealift Transport System provided cargo transports to move Air Force munitions from the U.S.A. to staging bases in the Philippines and the Pacific. From the staging bases the supplies were airlifted by elements of the Air Force's Military Airlift Command to staging points in South Vietnam. From these staging bases the Air Force Southeast Asia Airlift System (SEAIR) distributed the munitions to air bases within Vietnam and Thailand. Some munition runs were also made to smaller fields supporting air operations in Laos and Cambodia. *See also* **Southeast Asia Airlift System.**

Air Force Personnel *see* **Flyboys**

Air Force SP *see* **Air Police**

Air Force Special Elements Activity (AFSEA)   U.S. Air Force detail assigned to the American Embassy security group. The detail provided after-curfew security and escort service to Embassy VIPs who lived off the embassy grounds. The detail also performed other embassy related security functions in conjunction with the Army and Marine security elements.

Air Head   An area secured for use as a landing zone and collection point for troops and supplies. The area was secured by an advance party either parachuted or helicoptered into the area. Similar to a beachhead formed by amphibious troops.

Air Liaison Officer (ALO)   Air Force personnel assigned to coordinate the use of aircraft in support of ground combat units. The ALOs and Forward Air Controllers operated at various headquarter levels and in the skies over units in contact with the enemy. *See also* **Forward Air Controller.**

Air Mattress *see* **Rubber Bitch, 82d Airborne Division**

Air Medal (Air Mission Points) Awarded in the President's name for meritorious service or heroism during air related duties. An Air Medal with a "V" attachment denotes the award was for valor: Pilots and aircrews were eligible. The Air Medal ranks behind the Distinguished Flying Cross. Twenty-five helicopter combat assaults, and at least six months in-country were required to get the Army Air Medal in Vietnam. The Marines' requirement for an Air Medal was the accumulation of 20 points, one point for each air mission, two points if you took enemy ground fire or flew above or north of the DMZ.

Air Mission Points *see* **Air Medal**

Air Mobile, Light *see* **AML**

Air National Guard *see* **USS Pueblo**

Air Operations Center (AOC)   A joint U.S. Air Force and South Vietnamese Air Force command center established in late '62 to coordinate air operations throughout South Vietnam. *See also* **Tactical Air Control System, Control and Reporting Post.**

Air Panels (VS17, Identification Panels) Brightly colored plastic panels used by U.S. forces on the ground to identify themselves to friendly aircraft. The panels, sometimes called VS17s, were laid out in the open so friendly aircraft attacking enemy positions would be able to identify the friendly lines.

Air Pirates *see* **Yankee Air Pirates**

Air Police (AP, Security Police, AFSP, Air Force SP, Apes) The Air Force's military police force. Equivalent to the MPs (Military Police) in the Army, and the SPs (Shore Patrol) in the Navy. In addition to the APs (nicknamed Apes) a special Air Force security force, the Security Police (Air Force SPs), were deployed to Vietnam to provide security for U.S. air bases. The SPs used guard dogs and provided complete base perimeter security. A more aggressive Air Force security force was created in '67 called the Combat Security Police which assisted in providing security for Air Force installations in Vietnam and Thailand. *See also* **Combat Security Police.**

Air Strike *see* **Bring-Smoke**

Air Strike Technique (Pop-Up) The technique involved the attacking plane flying at extremely low altitude (contour flying). Just before reaching the target, the aircraft quickly climbed, "popped-up," to the correct bombing altitude and released its bomb load. After the attack, the plane dove back to contour altitude. This technique allowed the aircraft to avoid enemy radar for much of the inbound flight, but it did open the plane up to more AA/AAA ground fire. SAMs and radar controlled AAA guns were not as effective unless they could get a good fix on the attacking aircraft. *See also* **Nap-of-the-Earth.**

Air Studies Group *see* **SOG Groups**

Air Support Operations Center *see* **Direct Air Support Center**

Air Support Radar Team (ASRT) U.S. Marine mobile radar units initially stationed at Da Nang to provide radar support for air operations, prior to the full expansion of air facilities at the base.

Air Tankers *see* **KA-6, KB-50, KC-130, KC-135**

Air to Ground Missile *see* **AGM**

Air Traffic Control Company *see* **Air Traffic Control Detachment**

Air Traffic Control Detachment (ATC Detachment, ATC, Air Traffic Control Company) Army aviation element that provided air traffic control to its aviation units. *See also* **Avn.**

Air Vietnam The government-owned and operated airline of South Vietnam. The airline provided service to Vietnam's major cities and had several international routes.

Air War College (AWC) Advanced training facility attended by Air Force officers above the rank of captain. The AWC conducted classes related to interpersonal communications, management skills, personnel interaction, and command level air war tactics and procedures. The AWC was located at Maxwell Air Force Base, Alabama. *See also* **Air Command and Staff College.**

Air Wing *see* **Wing**

Air-Assault Technique of using helicopters to deploy troops for combat assault. Most basic tactic of Air Cav units. Sometimes referred to as "vertical assault" by the Marines. *See also* **Combat Assault.**

Air-Evac *see* **Air-Evacuation**

Air-Evacuation (Air-Evac) Evacuation of medical patients by aircraft, usually fixed-wing military transports. Air-evacs were used to transport the wounded to field hospitals in Vietnam. The more seriously injured were flown to Japan and or the United States. *See also* **Medevac.**

Air-to-Air Missile *see* **AAM**

Airboat (Aircat) Flat bottomed boat, driven from the rear by a large vertical propeller blade, used by U.S. riverine and Special Forces in the Delta. The small boats were noisy, but were excellent for crossing the swamps and flooded areas of the Delta. The boats could carry 7–8 troops at speeds of up to 40 knots and were sometimes called "aircats."

Airborne (Abn) Infantry Parachute Troops. *See also* **173d Airborne Brigade, 82d Airborne Division, 101st Airborne Division.**

Airborne Battlefield Command and Control Center (ABCCC, AB Triple-C, Airborne Computer Control Center) Air Force and Navy aircraft used as aerial command center. The aircraft were fitted with sophisticated radar and communications equipment and could remain airborne for long periods of time. Specially fitted C-130s were often used in the ABCCC role. ABCCC aircraft were instrumental in assisting in the evacuation of Saigon in April '75. "Blue Chip," "Red Crown," "College Eye," and "Crown" were the code names for some of the ABCCCs active over the skies of SEA throughout the airwar. *See also* Skyspot, EC-121, P-3, C-54, C-130.

Airborne Computer Control Center *see* **Airborne Battlefield Command and Control Center**

Airborne Helicopter Refueling *see* **High Drink**

Airborne Observer (AO, Aerial Observer) Airborne spotter in either a plane or helicopter. Aerial observers frequently accompanied FAC and LOH pilots on reconnaissance and surveillance missions throughout SEA.

Airborne Radio Relay Communications equipment mounted in some Army helicopters used for the relay of radio traffic. Radio relays were used to allow ground units to communicate with headquarters when operating beyond the normal range of the radio equipment they carried. Terrain features such as mountains and valleys also could interfere with radio transmissions. These obstacles could be temporarily overcome by spotting an airborne radio relay position between the ground elements that needed to maintain radio contact. Helicopters were typically used, but Army fixed-wing utility aircraft were also employed. *See also* Radio Relay.

Airborne Training (Jump School; Ft. Benning, Georgia; Ground-Tower-Jump Week) Army parachute training took place at Ft. Benning, Georgia. The rigorous course took three weeks to complete. The physical training involved was extensive. Jump trainees ran everywhere they went for the three weeks they were in the school. The training was broken down into three one-week sessions; ground week, tower week and jump week. Those who successfully completed the course were awarded a pair of prestigious jump wings, and allowed to walk again.

Airburst An artillery round that detonated in the air above the target, instead of on impact with the ground. Airburst could be achieved by mechanically timed fuses or variable timed fuses. The variable timed fuse used radar to determine detonation and exploded 20 meters above the target. Mechanical fuses could be set to explode the shell at a variety of heights above the target. *See also* **VT Round.**

Aircat *see* **Airboat**

Aircraft *see* **Birds**

Aircraft Carrier Forces During the Vietnam War the U.S. deployed aircraft carriers off the coast of North and South Vietnam for use in the air war against the NVA/VC. The carriers operated as part of Task Force 77 and 2–6 carriers were usually deployed in the coastal waters of Vietnam throughout the war. *See also* **USS America, Bon Homme Richard, Constellation, Coral Sea, Enterprise, Forrestal, Franklin D. Roosevelt, Hancock, Hornet, Independence, Intrepid, Kearsarge, Kitty Hawk, Midway, Oriskany, Ranger, Saratoga, Shangri-La, Ticonderoga, Yorktown, 7th Fleet, TF 77.**

Aircraft Commander (AC) Pilot in command of an aircraft.

Aircraft Rockets Rocket systems used on fixed-wing aircraft for attacking ground targets. In Vietnam the primary rocket used was the 2.75-inch folding fin rocket, mounted in pods attached under the wings or on the pylons of the aircraft. Some of the same rockets and pods used by fixed-wing aircraft were fitted for use by attack helicopters and gunships. The Navy used a larger, 5-inch rocket called the "Zuni." *See also* **XM-159C, Zuni, LAU-3.**

Airman First Class *see* **E-4**

Airman Second Class *see* **Private First Class**

Airman Third Class *see* **E-2**

Airmobile (Ambl, AM) Reference to infantry units that deployed using helicopters, the helicopters being an integral part of the unit. Also applied to Army helicopter companies that operated as troop transports. *See also* **Heliborne, 11th Air Assault Division, 1st Air Cav, Avn.**

Airstrike *see* **Strike**

AIT *see* **Advanced Infantry Training**

AK *see* AK47

AK Amp (At-the-Knee Amputation)
Abbreviated format, medical slang, for a
traumatic amputation that occurred at the
knee. In Vietnam, usually the result of a
land mine or damage from large calibre
machine guns.

AK Booby Trap (Spiked Rounds)
One of the tricks used by some USSF troops
was to booby trap enemy weapons. Cartridges used in the AK-47 and SKS rifles
would be carefully taken apart and a small
piece of C-4 explosive or Det Cord inserted
into the shell. The bullets were reassembled
and loaded into enemy weapons. The
weapons or spiked ammo was then dropped
along trails or near areas of enemy activity.
The NVA/VC would collect the weapons
and when they were fired the booby trapped
rounds would explode in the face of the
firer. The booby trap was effective, though
limited in its scope. It took the Viet Cong a
while to realize that the rounds were being
sabotaged. *See also* **Booby Trap.**

**AK47 (Kalashnikov 47, AK, Type 56,
Type 56-1, AKM, AKMS, Automat Kalashnikova'47)** Universal communist assault rifle, originally Soviet made. The PRC
manufactured versions were the Type 56
(AK47) and Type 56-1 (AKM). The 7.62mm
rifle could fire a single shot or full auto,
30-round magazine fed, gas operated and
extremely dependable and easy to use. The
AK featured a high muzzle velocity which
caused the bullet to spin resulting in extensive damage to the tissue impact area . A
loaded AK weighed about 11 pounds. The
AKMS had a folding metal stock, and the
AKM had a fixed wooden stock that could
accommodate a bayonet. The AMD-65 was
a Hungarian version of the AKMS. The
Type 56 had a fixed folding bayonet and
became the most common rifle used by the
NVA/VC. Also known as the AK-47 and
T-56. Nicknamed "Alpha Kilo."

AKA *see* **Attack Cargo Ship**

AKL Light cargo ship used by the Navy
as a "lighter" for harbor transfer of cargo.
Also used as a general resupply ship by the
Naval Support Activity. The NSA used the
small cargo ship to run regular resupply
shuttles along South Vietnam's coast, from
Da Nang to An Thoi. The AKL was armed

with 20mm guns and had a max speed of 12
knots. *See also* **Southern Shipping Company, YFR, Lighter.**

AKM *see* **AK47**

AKMS *see* **AK47**

Ala Moana *see* **Operation Ala
Moana**

Alamo Apartments Large apartment
complex located in downtown Da Nang.
Most of its occupants were American civilians working as contractors or Consulate
personnel.

Alamo Hilton "Alamo Hilton" was the
nickname for a large, deeply buried, under-
ground bunker at Khe Sanh Combat Base.
The bunker was constructed by Navy SEA-
BEES, and used to house "visitors" to KSCB.
See also **Khe Sanh.**

Albatross *see* **HU-16**

Albumin *see* **Serum Albumin**

Alcatraz *see* **Hanoi Hilton**

Alcoholics *see* **Juicers**

**Alerts (Alert: Red ... Yellow ...
White)** Most major Army bases in Vietnam operated under an "alert system."
Based on intelligence information, a subjec-
tive rating was given to the likelihood of an
enemy attack on the base. According to the
rating, an alert status was issued to base personnel. Alert status was described by color:
1) white = normal, low probability of enemy
attack; normal guard routine. 2) yellow =
cautious, possible attack; 50 percent of base
personnel on the line. 3) red = enemy attack
is imminent; 75–100 percent of base personnel on the line.

Ali, Muhammad (Cassius Clay)
Olympic Gold Medal winner in boxing and
three-time Heavyweight Boxing Champion
of the World. Ali applied for a conscientious
objector deferment based on his Black Muslim religious beliefs when he was classified as
1-A by his draft board in '66. His deferment
was denied and he was drafted. He refused
to serve and was tried and convicted of
violating the Selective Service Act in '67. His
conviction was later overturned by the
Supreme Court saving him from a $10,000
fine and five years in federal prison. Ali was
born Cassius Marcellus Clay in '42, but
changed his name in '64 in keeping with his

conversion to the Muslim religion. Ali refused to fight for the government, saying "No Viet Cong ever called me Nigger."

ALICE (All-Purpose Lightweight Individual Carrying Equipment, Ruck[sack]) U.S. Army field pack system used by the individual soldier to carry weapons, ammunition, tools and supplies and other equipment. The system consisted of a pack (lightweight rucksack) with an assortment of pockets, a tubular aluminum pack frame, various rings, straps, pouches and attachments to fit the required load. Two pack sizes were available in SVN, with max rated loads of 50 and 70 pounds. The actual average loads in the field were closer to 65 and 95 pounds. "If you couldn't get it in your ruck, you didn't need it." *See also* **NVA Rucksack, ARVN Rucksack, Jungle Rucksack.**

Alkies *see* **Juicers**

All American Division *see* **Almost Airborne**

All American Team *see* **Aero Rifle Platoon**

All the Communists Have to Do to Win... *see* **Pham Van Dong**

All the Way *see* **173d Airborne Brigade**

All Weather Air Delivery System (AWADS) Air Force system using a combination of computer control and radar guidance to direct the parachute delivery of supplies in any kind of weather. *See also* **Station Keeping Equipment.**

All-Afro *see* **82d Airborne Division**

All-Purpose Lightweight Individual Carrying Equipment *see* **ALICE**

All-Secure-Situation-Remains-the-Same *see* **Alpha-Sierra-Sierra-Romeo-Sierra**

Allotment (Living Allowance) Deduction made from a soldier's pay usually associated with support of his dependents. For a married soldier the government would send his wife a "living allowance," part of which came out of the soldier's regular pay. An Army private E-1 in '68 received approximately $98 gross pay, from which $50 was paid to his wife as part of her allotment; after taxes and insurance he was left with

roughly $35 a month. *See also* **Finance.**

ALMAR Orders *see* **Commandant**

Almost Airborne (All American Division) One of the nicknames for the 82d Airborne Division based on the unit's patch. In the center of the dark red square patch was a dark blue circle with two white "A's" side by side. Worn across the top of the patch was a crescent-shaped blue tab with "Airborne" embroidered in white. The division was also nicknamed the "All-Afro," the "Eighty-Deuce," and the "All American" Division. *See also* **82d Airborne Division.**

ALO *see* **Air Liaison Officer**

Aloui *see* **LZ Aloui**

Alpha Boat *see* **ASPB**

Alpha Bravo *see* **Ambush**

Alpha Kilo *see* **AK47**

Alpha Mike Radio *see* **AM/FM Radio**

Alpha Strikes Code name for naval air strikes against targets in North Vietnam. Alpha Strikes involved all carriers, available strike and support aircraft. Reconnaissance missions and small air strikes by Navy carrier craft were not considered Alpha Strikes unless most of the ship's complement of attack aircraft took part in the strike.

Alpha-Sierra-Sierra-Romeo-Sierra (All-Secure-Situation-Remains-the-Same) Marine radio jargon used by units in the field to report their current status to headquarters indicating their position was quiet, with no enemy contact or activity as was the previous status or situation report. *See also* **Situation Report.**

Alphabet (Military Alphabet, Phonetic Alphabet) U.S. military phonetic alphabet: A—alfa (alpha), B—bravo, C—charlie, D—delta, E—echo, F—foxtrot, G—golf, H—hotel, I—india, J—juliet, K—kilo, L—lima, M—mike, N—November, O—oscar, P—papa, Q—quebec, R—romeo, S—sierra, T—tango, U—uniform, V—victor, W—whiskey, X—xray, Y—yankee, Z—zulu. The South Vietnamese military also used a similar phonetic alphabet. *See also* **ARVN Phonetic Alphabet.**

ALQ-87 ECM Pod (ALQ-101 ECM Pod, ALQ-105 ECM Pod) Air Force, wing mounted, Electronic Counter Measures pod. The ALQ-87 was found to be effective at jamming some Fan Song radar signals. The ALQ-101 was another of the Air Force's ECM pods used by early Wild Weasel aircraft. The ALQ-105 was an updated version of the -101 and was fuselage mounted under blisters along the sides of the aircraft. Previous ECM equipment had been pod mounted on the wing pylons. *See also* **Electronic Counter Measures.**

ALQ-101 ECM Pod *see* **ALQ-87 ECM Pod**

ALQ-105 ECM Pod *see* **ALQ-87 ECM Pod**

ALR-31 LWR *see* **F-105F/G**

ALSG *see* **TG 76.4**

Alternative Service Some conscientious objectors (C.O.s) were given the option of performing "alternative" humanitarian service instead of serving in the military. The alternative service could be performed in the States or the C.O. could volunteer to serve overseas or in Vietnam as a member of one of the many civilian organizations that provided humanitarian aid to the rural population of South Vietnam. *See also* **USAID, IVS, CORDS, Conscientious Objector.**

Alvarez, Lieutenant Everett, Jr. (First American Airman Shot Down...) The first American airman to be shot down and captured by the North Vietnamese. He was held prisoner for 8½ years. Alvarez was shot down over North Vietnam on August 5, 1964, during Operation Pierce Arrow, the first U.S. air raid against North Vietnam. The raid was in retaliation for NVN gunboat attacks on U.S. Navy ships operating in the Gulf of Tonkin. Alvarez was piloting an A-4 Skyhawk from the USS *Constellation* when he was shot down. *See also* **Gulf of Tonkin Incident, Operation Pierce Arrow.**

Always Faithful *see* **Semper Fidelis**

AM *see* **Airmobile, Avn**

AM-2 Mats *see* **Short Airfield for Tactical Support**

AM/FM Radio (Alpha Mike, Foxtrot Mike) The two primary methods of radio communication used by military sets were AM (Amplitude Modulation–Alpha Mike) and FM (Frequency Modulation–Foxtrot Mike). The type of modulation referred to the manner in which the radio wave carrying information was transmitted. For AM the radio wave was changed according to the amplitude of the signal while the frequency of the signal remained constant. In FM radios the amplitude of the signal remained the same but the frequency of the wave was changed. AM radios typically operated in the 20–50,000 hertz range, while FM radios operated in the 100,000 + hertz range. FM transmissions had greater range and a better signal-to-noise ratio than AM. *See also* **Radio.**

Amatol Explosive compound used in the construction of some military ordnance. The compound was a mixture of ammonium nitrate and Trinitrotoluene (TNT). *See also* **TNT.**

Ambl *see* **Airmobile**

Ambulatory *see* **Walking Wounded**

Ambush (Bush[ed/ing], Alpha Bravo) Surprise attack on an enemy force by a well concealed attack force. A "good ambush," or "bush" as some GIs called it, was one in which all of the enemy in the kill zone were either killed or wounded. In a "perfected bush" the enemy never returned fire. Ambushes slowed down advancing enemy forces and caused the enemy to commit more forces to the ambush area to relieve ambushed units. The NVA/VC were experts at bushing. Ambushes utilizing small units were most effective. U.S. Recon, USSF, Ranger/LRRP and some specialized units were very effective at bushing the NVA/VC. "Alpha Bravo" was sometimes used to denote an ambush during radio communications. *See also* **L- , A-Shaped, Linear, Hasty or Prepared Ambush, Helicopter Ambush, Aquabush, Baited Ambush.**

Ambush Academy Nickname for the familiarization and in-country orientation courses conducted by the larger commands in Vietnam. The courses served to acclimate replacement troops and orient them to some of the dangers of the NVA/VC and Vietnam. Replacements spent a few days in the course before they were sent to the field to join their new units. *See also* **T M & B School, SERTS.**

Ambush Alley (Highway 19) GI nickname for the section of Vietnamese Highway 19 in the Central Highlands between Duc Co, near the Cambodian border and An Khe in II Corps. The NVA/VC made numerous attempts to close the highway which was a major overland route used to supply Pleiku, Kontum and Dak To. Highway 19 crossed the SVN/Cambodian border near the Ia Drang Valley and Duc Co, and continued east through Pleiku and An Khe to Highway 1 near Qui Nhon.

AMCAL *see* **American Division**

AMCRASH Nickname for a Marine LVTP-5 used at Chu Lai for a fire and rescue vehicle. The amtrac was fitted with fire equipment and floodlights and was used to reach crashed aircraft in the sandy areas off the runway. *See also* **LVTP-5**.

AMD-65 *see* **AK47**

Amer-Asian Vietnamese children, the product of GI fathers and Vietnamese mothers. During the final days of South Vietnam several Amer-Asian orphans were airlifted out of the country. After the fall of Vietnam a program was established by Congress to expedite the emigration of Amer-Asian children from Vietnam to the U.S. Estimates of the number of Amer-Asian children that remained in Vietnam after '75 vary between 7,000 to 12,000. *See also* **Operation Babylift, Orderly Departure Program.**

America's Puppet *see* **Ngo Dinh Diem**

America, Love It or Leave It *see* **One Country, One Flag; Love It or Leave It**

America, USS *see* **USS America**

Americal Division (23d Infantry Division [Americal], Metrecal Division, AMCAL, Amerikill) The division, created September '67 in Vietnam, consisted of the 11th, 196th and 198th Infantry Brigades, seven artillery battalions and miscellaneous other units including recon and aviation, serving in the three southern provinces of I Corps. The division, headquartered at Chu Lai, was closed and withdrawn November '71. Low morale in the division and troops poorly trained, equipped, and led, contributed to the Americal's poor reputation. Incidents such as My Lai and FSB Mary Ann added to the division's woes. Troopers of the division referred to it as "The Metrecal Div. sponsored by General Foods" and the "Amerikill Division." *See also* **My Lai, Americal Patch.**

Americal Patch Compared to some of the other American unit patches of the Vietnam War the Americal patch was plain and simple. The shield-shaped, dark blue patch was flat across the top forming a rounded point at the bottom of the patch. On the patch was one large, one small, and two medium-sized white stars. The largest of the stars was at the bottom of the patch and a medium star at the top. A medium star was located on the left side of the patch and the small star was located on the right. *See also* **Americal Division.**

AmeriCalley Division *see* **Americal Division**

American *see* **My**

American Advisor *see* **Co Van My**

American Country Teams *see* **Buon Enao**

American Defectors *see* **Garwood, PFC Robert (Bobby)**

American Forces Vietnam Network (AFVN, Armed Forces Radio Station [AFRS], Radio Vietnam) Recreational military radio and TV for U.S. troops in Vietnam. The radio station was on the air 24 hours a day, broadcasting various types of music, radio shows, news, and weather. The AFVN TV network broadcasted news and weather, and reruns of popular American TV programs. The reruns were mostly sitcoms, westerns, and adventure series. After the departure of U.S. combat units from Vietnam English-language broadcasts were carried by "American Service Radio." *See also* **Chickenman, American Service Radio, Bobbie.**

American Friends of Vietnam *see* **Iron Mike**

American Friends Service Committee *see* **Quaker Prosthetics Center**

American GI Film Ratings (Skin 1 . . . Fuzz 1 . . .) System used by GIs to rate the films they were shown at their bases. The ratings were Skin 1, Skin 2, Skin 3, Fuzz 1, Fuzz 2 and Fuzz 3. "Skin" referred to the amount of nude skin seen in the film, and "Fuzz" referred to the amount of pubic hair that was to be seen. The higher the number, the better the film. Skin 3, Fuzz 3 was the highest rating, which equated to lots of nudity, and plenty of fuzz.

American Gold Star Mothers Maternal organization in which all of the members had lost a son in the military. Prior to the Korean War, the government awarded the deceased military man's mother a Gold Star, in addition to any other posthumous awards the man had earned. The Gold Star Mother's headquarters was in Washington, D.C. The mothers shared annual meetings and were supportive of each other. The government ceased its award of the Gold Star with the Korean War. The organization continued to grow through the Korean War, and into the Vietnam War, even without the government-issued star.

American Grass A special strain of grass developed for the Army and used in Vietnam. The special grass was very coarse and fast growing, requiring very little water. As the grass dried out it was periodically burned. The grass was planted in some of the free-fire-zones located in III Corps and used to burn off vegetation which concealed enemy bunkers and tunnel entrances. The grass reduced erosion from cleared areas.

American Imperialist Air Raiders see Fonda, Jane

American Nazi Party see White Power

American Pilots see Yankee Air Pirates

American POWs Officially 591 American POWs were returned to American control as a result of the January '73 Paris Peace Accords. The POWs had been held in North Vietnam, Laos and China. Most were military personnel, but several were civilians and one was a CIA agent. During their captivity the Americans were subjected to torture, malnutrition, brutality, solitary confinement, and refused medical attention. The last of the POWs were released from communist control in March '73. The fate of 2,300+ Americans, still unaccounted for, is unknown. Rumors persist that some Americans are still being held by the North Vietnamese. Many alleged sightings of Americans held as prisoners have come from Vietnamese, Cambodian and Laotian refugees

and several private, and illegal, paramilitary missions have been attempted seeking to verify the reports of American POWs still held in Vietnam. As of January '90 the Socialist Republic of Vietnam (North Vietnam) insists it is not holding any U.S. prisoners, but of the more than 3,000 Americans declared missing during the Vietnam War, less than 25 percent have been accounted for or repatriated. *See also* **4th POW Wing, Prisoner of War, Torture, Operation Homecoming.**

American Red Cross (ARC, Programming) The ARC provided noncombatant personnel to serve in Vietnam. At many of the larger base camps and cities there were Red Cross centers that provided off-duty troops a nonmilitary environment. The ARC also sent workers out to the field to entertain the troops with games, conversation and a touch of home. The ARC called their efforts a "program," and tried to visit as many field units as security and the situation would allow. ARC personnel that visited troops in the field were usually women. *See also* **Donut Dollies.**

American Red Cross Women *see* **Donut Dollies**

American Service Radio (ASR) ASR took over English-language broadcasting in South Vietnam after the departure of Armed Forces Radio in March '73. The station broadcasted news, weather, music, and information. On April 29, 1975, the station played "I'm Dreaming of a White Christmas" several times. This song was the "secret" cue to U.S. Embassy personnel that it was time to evacuate Saigon and they were to get to the Embassy as soon as possible. *See also* **American Forces Vietnam Network.**

American Servicemen's Union (ASU) Antiwar group which consisted of civilian and military members. The aim of the group was to get military personnel to refuse orders to fight in, or go to Vietnam.

American Women *see* **Round Eyes**

American Women's Association of Saigon (AWAS) Women's group established in Saigon in the mid-sixties. Most of the members were the wives of U.S. Embassy and Foreign Service personnel. Some wives of local U.S. civilian contractors were also members. The group functioned as a social outlet for some American women in the combat zone who were restricted in their travels. The group also organized charity events on behalf of various Vietnamese organizations and volunteered their time to other groups.

Americans Do Not Like Long, Inconclusive... *see* **Pham Van Dong**

Americans Without Dollars (Russians) After the fall of Saigon to the communists in '75, a steady flow of Soviets and personnel from Eastern Bloc countries began to trickle into Vietnam. Many were technicians and advisors to the communist government of Vietnam, examining captured American equipment and expanding the Soviet naval presence at Cam Ranh Bay. The street vendors in Saigon (Ho Chi Minh City) called these Europeans "Americans without dollars," because they were similar in appearance to the Americans, but not generous in their spending habits as the Americans that preceded them had been.

Amerikill *see* **Americal Division**

AML (Air Mobile, Light) Army helicopter which transported and supported light infantry. *See also* **Light Infantry.**

Ammi Barge (Pontoon Barges, Advanced Tactical Support Bases, ATSB) Large pontoon barges that were linked together and used as small operating bases for riverine operations in South Vietnam. The barges were also used as mobile artillery and helicopter pads by riverine forces in the Delta. During Operation Slingshot, near the Parrot's Beak, the barges were used as bases for riverine operations against NVA/VC supply lines and called Advance Tactical Support Bases (ATSB). The Ammi pontoon barge was 90 × 25 × 5 feet and could also be linked together to form piers. The barge also found use with the Navy as a small, mobile dry-dock facility and general vehicle for a variety of storage and transfer needs. *See also* **Artillery Barge, Helicopter Barge, YFND, AFDL.**

Ammo Dump (Ammo Point) Area where ammunition was stored. The dump was usually located in a remote area of the base and bunkered and bermed to protect it from enemy fire. It was one of the main targets of enemy sappers during ground assaults on base camps. An ammo point was a scaled down version of the ammo dump. Small quantities of ammo points were strategically located at various points around a fire base to allow for ease of access. The main ammo dump was usually located at some distance from the center of the base to insure that an explosion didn't wipe out the base.

Ammo Point *see* **Ammo Dump**

Amnesty Box *see* **Shakedown**

Amnesty Program *see* **Carter, President Jimmy; Ford Clemency Review**

Amoebic Dysentery *see* **Ho Chi Minh's Revenge**

Amphetamines *see* **Speed, Dexamphetamines**

Amphibious Assault Ship *see* **USS Iwo Jima**

Amphibious Cargo Carrier *see* **M-76 Cargo Carrier**

Amphibious Cargo Ship *see* **Attack Cargo Ship**

Amphibious Construction Battalions (ACB) Large SEABEE units that deployed to Vietnam in '64–'66 to assist with construction of U.S. combat bases. The ACB's prime function was military and several battalions operated throughout I Corps. SEABEE Technical Assistance Teams continued to operate throughout the country primarily working on civic improvements and pacification projects while the ACBs concentrated on the military mission. *See also* **SEABEES, SEABEE Technical Assistance Teams.**

Amphibious Logistics Support Group *see* **TG 76.4**

Amphibious Ready Group/Special Landing Force (ARG/SLF) Special landing force of the U.S. Marine III Amphibious Force, 7th Fleet. The force conducted amphibious landings in the I Corps area until September '69. The landings were usually part of larger ground operations in the landing area, and included infantry and armored units, and sometimes included elements of the South Vietnamese Marines or ROK Marines. *See also* **Special Landing Force.**

Amphibious Tractor Operator *see* **Military Occupation Specialty, LVT**

Amphibious Training Center *see* **Coronado Island**

Amphibious Transport Dock (LPD) Navy amphibious assault ship used to transport Marines and their equipment. The LPD could carry 930 troops, their equipment and six UH-34 or UH-46 helicopters or four LCM landing craft. The LPD was also equipped with two LCM-6 or four LCPL landing craft stored on the boat deck and available for use by the amphibious landing force. The ship was operated by a crew of 490 men and could make 20 knots, and its internal docking well allowed troops to be quickly loaded into their landing craft. LPDs were designed as replacements for the Navy's older AKA transports. *See also* **Attack Cargo Ship.**

Amphibious Transport Ship *see* **Attack Transport Ship**

Amplitude Modulation Radio *see* **AM/FM Radio**

Amtrac(k) *see* **LVTP-5**

Amyl Nitrate *see* **Poppers**

An Giang Province IV Corps province where GVN pacification programs were relatively successful. The primary reason for the programs' success was that the entire province was a Hoa Hao (wa how) sect stronghold. The Hoa Hao were fiercely anticommunist. The province was centered 50kms from the Cambodian border and less than 50kms from the Gulf of Thailand. The Viet Cong were very active in most of the Delta provinces, but they were very careful to avoid An Giang. *See also* **Hoa Hao.**

An Hoa Village located 30kms southwest of Da Nang, in the An Hoa Valley. Home of the Marines and later the 1st Squadron/9th Cavalry at LZ Two Bits. An Hoa was located in the heart of the Que Son Valley, a highly active NVA/VC base area throughout the war. The valley was first patrolled by the Marines and later by elements of the Americal Division. *See also* **Arizona Territory, Que Son Valley.**

An Hoa Valley *see* **An Hoa**

An Khe *see* **Camp Radcliff**

An Loc (Battle of An Loc) The provincial capital of Binh Long Province, located 105kms north of Saigon, was the site of a major battle fought during the NVA '72 Easter Offensive. NVA armor and troops surrounded An Loc and pounded it with artillery and ground attacks in an attempt to overrun it. For three months the NVA were beaten back by An Loc's 5th ARVN Infantry Division defenders and American air power. The NVA were unable to take An Loc and withdrew to bases across the Cambodian border, 18kms away.

An Nhon Tay *see* **Ho Bo Woods**

An Thoi (USS Krishna) Village located on the southwestern tip of Phu Quoc Island. An Thoi served as a Vietnamese naval base and as the joint Coastal Surveillance Center of the Fourth Coastal Surveillance Zone. An Thoi also served as the anchorage for the USS *Krishna* during the monsoon season. The *Krishna* provided support to the cutters of Coast Guard Squadron One that operated as part of the coastal surveillance force of TF 115, operating in the Gulf of Thailand and along SVN's eastern coastline. Many Vietnamese considered An Thoi the "nuoc mam" capital of SVN, supposedly producing the best of the best. *See also* **WPB, Phu Quoc Island, Nuoc Mam.**

An/AAQ-5 *see* **FLIR**

AN/APQ-92 *see* **VAH-21**

AN/APS-94 *see* **SOTAS**

AN/ASC Radio Console The AN/ASC Radio Console was developed by the Army Signal Corps to provide infantry unit commanders with a system of radios that they could use to communicate with ground and air units while airborne in their "command and control" helicopters. The consoles featured a variety of scramblers, FM, UHF, VHF and radios. Model numbers of the AN/ASC installed during the course of the Vietnam War were the -6, -10, -11 and -15. The radios allowed the commander to maintain contact with his ground units and at the same time coordinate air with artillery support and other units in the vicinity. *See also* **U.S. Radios, Command and Control.**

AN/GUQ-10 (IOS Binoculars, Integrated Observation System) The AN/GUQ-10 Integrated Observation System consisted of long-range binoculars electronically merged with an image intensifier. The IOS system allowed enemy targets to be spotted at great distances and the range and target angle automatically calculated by the system. The IOS could be used day or night and was only affected by weather that reduced visibility, such as rain or fog. The AN/GUQ-10 was used as an artillery targeting tool.

AN/MPQ-4 Radar (MPQ-4)   Countermortar radar set used to detect the location of enemy mortar fire. The MPQ-4 was a trailer mounted, towed unit. *See also* **Counter-Mortar Radar.**

AN/PAS-8 *see* **SU-50 Electronic Binocular**

AN/PPS-4/5 *see* **Ground Radar**

AN/PRC-10 (PRC-10)   The PRC-10 was the standard Army field radio in the early sixties. It had a 170-channel capacity, weighed 26 pounds, and a maximum range of 5–8kms. The PRC-10 FM radio was replaced in U.S. units by the AN/PRC-25 which had a greater range, a 920-channel capacity and was lighter in weight. *See also* **AN/PRC-25, U.S. Radios.**

AN/PRC-25 (PRC-25, Prick-25) Standard field radio, man transported. Maximum, unobstructed range (on a very good day) was about 25kms. The actual average range was less than 8kms, depending on terrain and antenna used. The PRC-25 had 920 FM channels and weighed 23 pounds and replaced the AN/PRC-10 in most regular Army units in Vietnam after '67. The radio had a short "whip" antenna and a longer shock-cord jointed antenna. The PRC-25 was notoriously sensitive to the elements, and the RTOs that carried them took great care to keep them functional and supplied with batteries. The handsets, sensitive to moisture, were often operated wrapped in the waterproof plastic bags in which replacement batteries were packaged. *See also* **U.S. Radios.**

AN/PRC-41 (PRC-41)   U.S. UHF radio, often used by Air Force FACs. *See also* **U.S. Radios, Forward Air Controller.**

AN/PRC-64 (Key Radio, CW Radio) U.S. military radio first used in Vietnam in '64. The small, 10-pound portable, battery powered radio was used primarily for keyed (Morse Code) radio transmissions. The Radio was "voice-capable," but was unreliable in the voice mode. The PRC-64 found use at USSF camps as a CW (Continuous Wave) radio. *See also* **U.S. Radios.**

AN/PRC-74 (PRC-74)   Army radio

used by some Special Forces units for long-range AM radio communication by Morse Code (CW) or voice. The PRC-74 had a range in excess of 10kms and was normally used at the company and battalion level for long distance communications. *See also* **U.S. Radios.**

AN/PRC-77 (Monster, Krypto, PRC-77, Talk-Quick Radio, KY-38 Crypto Set) Field radio with a Cryptographic (KY-38) scrambler/descrambler attached. Used to make radio calls over a secure net. Only other KY-38 sets on the net could decipher the message, sometimes nicknamed the "Talk-Quick Radio" or "Krypto." The PRC-77 was an improved version of the PRC-25 radio. Attached to the PRC-77 was the KY-38 Crypto Set. It was also known as the Monster because of its bulk and excess weight that had to be carried by RTOs in the field. The KY-38 was connected to the PRC-77 by a cable. The cable and its connectors were a constant source of headaches for RTOs in the field. Sometimes the Monster was divided, the RTO carrying the PRC-77 and another man lugging the KY-38. *See also* **U.S. Radios.**

An/PRC-90 *see* **Survival Radios**

AN/PRR-9 (AN/PRT-4)   U.S. lightweight portable radios with a max range of about a mile. The PRR-9 was a helmet mounted receiver and weighed about one-half pound and could only receive. The PRT-4 was a handheld transmitter that weighed about 1.5 pounds and was only able to transmit. These radios were designed for use at the platoon and squad level, with the squad leader having both the PRR-9 and the PRT-4, while squad members had the PRR-9 receiver. Due to poor performance and limited range, the units were not widely used in the field. The receiver used the helmet as an antenna and many troops operating in the jungle did not wear their helmets. *See also* **U.S. Radios.**

AN/PRS-3 (Metal Detector, Mine Detector)   Handheld metal detector used by U.S. engineer units for minesweep operations. The detector's signal was broadcast through a set of earphones worn by the operator as he swept over the ground with the flat detector plate. *See also* **Land Mines.**

AN/PRT-4 *see* **AN/PRR-9**

AN/PVS-2 *see* **Starlight Scope**

AN/PVS-5 see SU-50 Electronic Binocular

AN/TPS-25 see Ground Radar

AN/TPS-33 see Ground Radar

AN/TRC-90 (TROPO Radio, TRC-90) U.S. radio system used in Vietnam that bounced its radio signals within the earth's troposphere. The troposphere is the lowest layer of the earth's five atmospheric levels. The TRC-90 TROPO radio had a maximum range of 240kms and transmitted 45 channels. The TRC-90 was used to transmit voice and teletype radio signals. See also U.S. Radios.

AN/TVS-2 NOD see Night Observation Devices

AN/TVS-4 NOD see Night Observation Devices

AN/URC-10 see Survival Radios

AN/URC-68 (URC-68) Long-range FM radio used by the U.S. Special Forces for some cross border operations. The radio was extremely heavy, but provided good communications over long distances. See also U.S. Radios.

AN/VSS-3 Searchlight see Xenon Light

ANACDUTRA see Annual Active Duty for Training

ANC see U.S. Army Nurse Corps

Ancestral Ghost see Ma Ruoc Hon

Andersen Air Force Base see Guam

Anderson, Admiral George see Chief of Naval Operations

ANG see USS Pueblo

Angel's Wing An area in Cambodia along the SVN/Cambodian border used by the NVA as a base for operations into SVN. The Angel's Wing was centered about 25kms south of Tay Ninh and northwest of Saigon in Tay Ninh Province, III Corps. On a topographical map the boundary between South Vietnam and Cambodia resembles an angel's wing.

Animal Farm see Holding Company

Animals of the Army see Long-Range Reconnaissance Patrol

Animated Crotch Rot see Venereal Diseases

Ann-Margret (Fire Base) Ann-Margret was the nickname of one of the 25th Infantry Division's forward observation posts located north of the division base camp at Cu Chi. The platoon sized base was located near the southern edge of the Fil Hol Rubber Plantation. The plantation, and its extensive underground tunnel complex, was used by the VC to launch rocket and mortar attacks against the division base camp. Ann-Margret was abandoned in '67 because better surveillance methods were available to the division. Ann-Margret was also one of many American entertainers that performed stage shows for U.S. troops in Vietnam. See also Hope, Bob.

Annam (Central Vietnam, Trung-Bo) The name given to the area ruled by the Chinese in the seventh century, Trung-Bo in Vietnamese. The area covered the southern part of NVN and the northern area of SVN. In the 1800s the French ruled the same area and it was known as Vietnam. The French partitioned the country into three districts or Protectorates: Annam (central), Tonkin (north) and Cochin (south). Annam encompassed the area between the 20th Parallel in the north, and roughly the 12th Parallel in the south. The people living in this area were known as Annamese or Annamites. The capital city of Annam was Hue. See also Cochin China, Tonkin, Annamese.

Annamese (Annamites, Mites) French description for those who inhabited the region of Annam in the central part of Indo-China. The French also referred to the Vietnamese in general as Annamese or Annamites. "Mites" was the derogatory name the French used during their colonial occupation in reference to the Vietnamese. See also Annam.

Annamese Cordillera see Annamite Cordillera Mountains

Annamite Cordillera Mountains (Annamese Cordillera, Chaine Annamitique) Mountain range running from the southern portion of North Vietnam and eastern Laos down to the northern provinces of II Corps in South Vietnam and the northeastern corner of Cambodia. The mountains peaked at 8,500 feet.

Annamites *see* Annamese

Annapolis *see* U.S. Naval Academy

Annex, The *see* Hanoi Hilton

Annual Active Duty for Training (ANACDUTRA, AT, Annual Training, Unit Training Assembly [UTA]) National Guard and Army Reserve units received annual training to upgrade their skills. For the period of their annual training, two or more weeks, they were considered active duty personnel with all rights and privileges. The weekly active duty training sessions were referred to as "Unit Training Assembly" (UTA).

Annual Training *see* Annual Active Duty for Training

Anti-Draft-Card-Burning-Bill *see* Bill 392

Anti-Intrusion Devices Devices used by U.S. troops to protect their base camps and perimeters. Several different types of devices were used experimentally and became a regular part of the perimeter defenses. Some of the devices used were radar sets that could detect enemy ground movement and identify the firing area of enemy mortars, various wire obstacles such as concertina and razor wire, night scopes, seismic sensors, trip flares, and tin cans with rocks inside hanging on the wire. The various devices made it increasingly difficult for the enemy to attack American base camps but the NVA/VC continued to probe and attack American bases until the end of the war.

Anti-Riot Law *see* H. Rap Brown Law

Antiaircraft Artillery (AAA, Flak, Triple-A's) Large calibre guns, 57mm or greater, used to shoot down aircraft. The NVA made widespread use of AAA weapons for defense in NVN, especially 57mm, 85mm, 100mm and 130mm guns. At times AAA gunners were "chained" to their guns to prevent them from retreating from U.S. aircraft flak suppression attacks. *See also* Antiaircraft Guns.

Antiaircraft Guns (AA) General reference to guns used to shoot down aircraft. The NVA used 23mm, 37mm and 57mm guns extensively in North and South Vietnam for air defense against U.S. helicopters

and aircraft. Various size machine guns were also used in the air defense role. Automatic weapons and assault rifles were also used. The NVA/VC were trained to fire their automatic weapons, en masse, straight up so that attacking American aircraft would fly through the fire, instead of trying to "lead" the aircraft and fire on it as it flew by. *See also* Antiaircraft Artillery, 23mm AA, 37mm AA, 57mm AA, Cotton Balls, AA Gun Sites.

Antiaircraft Radar *see* Fire Cans

Antimotion Triggers *see* M-5 Triggers

Antipersonnel Radar *see* Ground Radar

Antiradiation Missile (ARM) Air-to-ground guided missiles that used a ground/water based radar signal as guidance to the target. The source of the signal was usually enemy search radar; the ARM locked on to the enemy signal and followed it down to its source. During the VNW the U.S. made use of the ARMs to help suppress enemy SAM sites in NVN. SAM suppression missions were conducted as part of the Air Force's Iron Hand missions by the specially equipped F-100 and F-105 Wild Weasel aircraft. *See also* AGM-45, Wild Weasel, Operation Iron Hand, Surface-to-Air Missile.

Antiseptic (Field Expedient) *see* Honey

Antitank CBU *see* MK-20 CBU

Antitank Guided Missiles (ATGM) In '72 during the Eastertide Offensive the NVA/VC began using the Soviet Sagger ATGM-3 antitank guided missile. The ATGM-3 was a semiautomatic command line of sight guided missile used against US/ARVN armor. In response to the NVA's use of tanks in '72, the U.S. began using their M-151 TOW antitank guided missiles against NVA armor. Both missiles were wire guided. When the missile was launched it unreeled wire as it moved toward the target. The wire was connected to a joystick controller used by the gunner to guide the missile. *See also* M-151 TOW, ATGM-3, SS-11 AGM.

Antiwar Movement *see* Peace Movement

Anvil and Hammer U.S. tactic of

positioning a blocking force (Anvil) in place and having another force (Hammer) sweep toward the block, hopefully pinning an enemy force between the anvil and the hammer resulting in high enemy casualties. The tactic was only partially successful in Vietnam because the NVA/VC were often able to slip away before they could be trapped. The NVA/VC's strategy was to wait until they had fire superiority or the element of surprise in their favor before they engaged American units.

Any One Who Runs Is... "Any one who runs is a Viet Cong, any one who stands still is a 'well disciplined' Viet Cong." Rationale used by some GIs to fire at Vietnamese working in the fields. The reasoning was if you shoot at them and they run they "must" be Viet Cong. *See also* the Vietnam Solution.

Anything, Anywhere, Anytime, Bar Nothing *see* 39th Infantry Regiment (Infantry)

ANZAC *see* Australian–New Zealand Army Corps

Anzio *see* FSB Anzio

AO *see* Airborne Observer, Area of Operation

Ao Dais (Long Costume) Traditional Vietnamese dress. The long dress was split on both sides from the hem to the waist and worn over baggy silk trousers. Considered more of a formal type of dress, primarily worn by women, but some men wore them ceremonially. For the female the hem of the dress was around the ankles. For the males the hem stopped at the knees.

Ao Quan *see* Coffins, Viet Cong

AOC *see* Army Operations Center, Air Operations Center

AP *see* Air Police, Armor Piercing Round, Hamlet

Ap *see* Village

Ap Bac *see* Battle of Ap Bac

Ap Bia Mountain *see* Hamburger Hill

Ap Doi Moi *see* Really New Life Hamlets

AP Round *see* Armor Piercing Round

AP-2H *see* VAH-21

APA *see* Attack Transport Ship

Apache Force (Combat Recon Patrols) USSF and CIDG force which oriented U.S. combat units on operating in Vietnam. The Apache Force would accompany the U.S. unit and field OJT them to the "ins and outs" of combat with the NVA/VC in Vietnam. With the announcement of the withdrawal of U.S. combat forces, the Apache Force was renamed Combat Recon Patrols and assigned normal patrol duties.

Apache Snow *see* Operation Apache Snow

Apaches *see* 1st Squadron, 9th Cavalry (Aerial Recon)

APB (Barracks Ship, Self-Propelled) Modified U.S. Navy LST used as a floating barracks by elements of the Mobile Riverine Force. The APB along with other barracks barges and modified LSTs were used as bases by the Mobile Riverine Force. The armored ships were capable of speeds of 11 knots, were armed with 40mm cannons and could house up to 800 men (sardine style). Four APBs were part of the MRF: USS *Benewah*, *Colleton*, *Mercer* and *Nueces* (Nieces). *See also* APL, Mobile Riverine Force.

APC *see* M-113

APCs *see* Army Aspirins

Apes *see* Air Police

APH-1 Helmet *see* APH-5 Helmet

APH-5 Helmet (Helicopter Crew Helmet, APH-1, Brain Bucket, AFH-1) Helmets worn by Army aircraft crews. The helmet featured an attached boom mike and built-in ear pieces and a retractable visor. An upgraded version of the helmet, the APH-5 was made of ballistic-nylon and phenolic resin. The helmets were nicknamed the "brain bucket" and did not provide enough acoustic and crash protection to the wearer. A modified version of the aircraft helmet became standard issue in '65 and was designated the AFH-1 (Crash Ballistic Protective Flying Helmet, Nylon Outer Shell). The Army flight helmet was again upgraded to the SPH-4 in '69. *See also* SPH-3 Helmet.

APHE *see* HEAP Round

APL (Barracks Barge; Barracks Ship, Non–Self-Propelled) Modified U.S. Navy barge used as floating barracks ship by elements of the Mobile Riverine Force. Two versions of the floating barracks ship were used. The APL was not self-propelled and was towed into position and could provide cramped housing for up to 650 men. The ship was not armored and was armed only with machine guns. The APB was a modified LST used as a barracks ship and was self-propelled. *See also* **APB, APA.**

APO *see* **Army Post Office**

APP *see* **Accelerated Pacification Program**

Apple *see* **FSB Apple**

APR-26 Launch Warning Receiver *see* **WR-300**

Apricot Ears *see* **Mutilations**

April 30 Revolutionary (Late Revolutionaries) Nickname for Vietnamese who had previously been neutral in their support of the GVN or the NLF who suddenly threw their support to the NLF when it appeared, without a doubt, that the NLF would win in South Vietnam. Especially representative of those Vietnamese that joined the NLF cause on the day Saigon, and the GVN, fell April 30, 1975.

APU *see* **Auxiliary Power Unit**

Aquabush Nickname for ambushes conducted by elements of the 9th Infantry Division operating in the Delta of IV Corps. Small ambushes were set up along streams and canals to interdict Viet Cong movement at night. *See also* **Ambush.**

AR *see* **Armed Recce, Army Regulation**

AR-15 *see* **Article 15, M-16 Rifle**

ARA *see* **Aerial Rocket Artillery, Avn**

Arabic Method Interrogation technique used by the ARVN, supposedly learned from their CIA advisors. The technique involved blindfolding the subject and tying him naked to a straight-backed chair. After several hours of sitting in isolation the interrogation began. The subject became disoriented and his resistance quickly broke down. *See also* **Torture, ARVN.**

ARC *see* **American Red Cross**

Arc Light (B-52 Airstrikes, Heavy Arty, Operation Arc Light) Code name for B-52 bombing missions against targets in SEA started in '65. The B-52's guidance to the target and bomb release could be controlled by ground radar to improve bombing accuracy from very high altitudes and through cloud cover. The typical bomb loads were 108 (500 lbs) or 53 (750 lbs) bombs. Ground vibrations caused by Arc Light strikes could be felt up to 16kms away from the strike zone. Ear drums could be blown out up to 1km away. Craters created by the bombs were over 30 feet in diameter and 25 feet deep. Most of the damage was caused by the concussion wave released when the bomb detonated. The strikes were sometimes called "Heavy Arty." *See also* **Big Stuff.**

ARC/RT-10 *see* **Survival Radios**

ARCOM *see* **Army Commendation Medal**

Are You North Vietnamese? *see* **Noi Bac-Viet?**

Area Fire (Artillery) *see* **Mini-Arc Light Strikes**

Area of Operation (AO) Area where a unit or units conduct operations. American AOs in Vietnam were assigned to reduce the chance of friendly units firing on each other. A unit assigned to an AO worked that area, with all other friendly units keeping clear. If a friendly unit needed to operate in another AO the unit sought permission and clearance and coordinated its movement within the other unit's AO. AOs tended not to overlap, and the NVA/VC would use the seam created between AOs for unobstructed movement. An AO and a TAOR were virtually the same thing. *See also* **Tactical Area of Responsibility.**

Area Recon by Fire (Mad Minute, Mike-Mike) When all weapons around the perimeter of a U.S. base fired out in front of their positions, at a range of 200–600 meters, for about a minute. This minute of sustained, random directional fire was designed to kill any enemy infiltrators or snipers hidden beyond the perimeter. Routinely done at small patrol or fire bases in hostile territory. Also used at night when the enemy's presence was felt, but his location was unknown. The mad minute was also used at first light and tended to relieve some of the pressure on watchful, tense troops. Mad minutes were also referred to as Mike-Mikes for radio traffic.

Area Support and Coordination Committee (ASCC) Joint committee established within a province at the district level. The committee coordinated the efforts of US/ARVN units, civil authorities and intelligence groups conducting military and pacification efforts within the district. The ASCC was usually chaired by the district chief.

Area Warfare Term used to describe U.S. combat objectives in Vietnam. As stated by MACV, "U.S. Forces objective is to destroy enemy forces, not to seize and permanently hold any specific terrain, except on a temporary basis."

ARG *see* **Amphibious Ready Group**

ARG/SLF *see* **Amphibious Ready Group/Special Landing Force.**

Arizona Territory (Arizona Valley, An Hoa Valley) Valley area centered 30kms southwest of Da Nang. The valley was bordered on the east by the Que Son mountains and mountains of the Chaine Annamitque bordered on the west. The village of An Hoa was located on the valley floor, east of the Song Thu Bon river which wound through the valley. In the mountains surrounding the valley were NVA/VC base areas and most of the villagers in the valley were pro–NVA/VC. During the Marines' stay in Vietnam they operated constantly in the valley, suffering a great many casualties. Because of the heavy enemy activity the Marines nicknamed the An Hoa Valley the "Arizona" or the "Badlands." *See also* **An Hoa, Liberty Bridge, Operation Georgia.**

Arizona Valley *see* **Arizona Territory**

ARL (Landing Craft Repair Ship) Modified Navy LST used as a floating repair facility by craft of the Mobile Riverine Force. The ARL operated as part of the MRF Base and had docking facilities and repair barges to support riverine operations.

ARM *see* **Anti-Radiation Missile**

Armalite (M-16A2, Colt M-16) Original manufacturer of the AR-15 rifle which

later became the M-16 rifle. The AR-15 was first designed in the mid-fifties and licensed to Colt Industries for production in '59 and redesignated the M-16A1. Mass produced for the military, it was sometimes referred to as the Colt M-16. An improved version, the M-16A2, soon followed. Today the M-16 is the most widely used and recognized rifle in the world. The weapon's high muzzle velocity and stability allow for a heavy volume of fire, which was important in jungle combat at close ranges. The light weight of the 5.56mm bullets had less stopping power at longer ranges, but the tumbling of the bullet inflicted heavy body damage at the nearer ranges experienced in jungle warfare. *See also* **M-16A1.**

Armed Combat Youth (ACY) GVN program to train youth groups in the use and care of weapons. Similar to armed Boy Scouts. At its peak, the program boasted of having 30,000 youth members. The ACY was formed into small platoons that were established at the village and hamlet level and used to promote government policy and aid the locals of the village. The ACY actually functioned as a GVN police group that tried to force GVN policy and compliance on the villagers.

Armed Falcons of the 20th ARA *see* **20th Artillery (Aerial Rocket)**

Armed Forces Qualification Test *see* **Moron Corps**

Armed Forces Radio Station *see* **American Forces Vietnam Network**

Armed Forces Staff College (AFSC) Staff college that trained officers from all four branches of the military in joint operations and procedures. AFSC was located at Norfolk, Virginia.

Armed Recce (AR) Armed reconnaissance. In the case of fighter planes, Search and Destroy. Aircraft would search for enemy targets and then attack them when they were found. During a normal ground reconnaissance mission the object was to get into the area to be reconned, and get out without making enemy contact. In an armed recce, reconnaissance was the main mission, but the enemy was not avoided, and was sometimes sought. *See also* **Hunter-Killer Operations.**

Armed Struggle (Vietnamese) *see* **Dau Tranh**

Armor   Various types of armored vehicles were used by the U.S. and its allied forces. Some of which included M-24, M-41, M-48, M-113, M-50, V-100, M-551, M-88, M-56, M-42 and Centurions. The NVA did not make widespread use of armored vehicles until the Eastertide Offensive of '72, although several PT-76s did participate in the overrun of the Special Forces camp at Khe Sanh in '68. The main armored vehicles of the NVA were the PT-76, T-34, T-54 and the T-59. The NVA used massed armor formations in their Final Offensive in '75, outnumbering ARVN armor by a ratio more than 3–1.

Armor Ambush   *see*   **Hardspot**

Armor Piercing Round (AP)   An armor piercing tank round that penetrated the target and then exploded. Also used against vehicles and bunkers as well as the armored vehicles it was designed to destroy. The designation "AP" was used for several types of ammunition with armor piercing qualities.

Armor-Plated Shorts   *see*   **M-1955 Flak Jacket**

Armored Cars   Several different types of armored cars were used during the Vietnam War. The V-100 was used by American forces primarily for convoy escort and base security. The South Vietnamese initially used WWII vintage American M-8, Ford Lynx II, and British Dingo armored cars. *See also* **V-100, M-8, Dingo.**

Armored Cavalry Assault Vehicle (ACAV)   A modified M-113 served armored cavalry units as an assault vehicle. The modification primarily consisted of adding a gun shield to the .50cal machine gun to protect the gunner and the addition of two M-60 machine guns, with shields, mounted to the top sides of the APC. The added machine guns were used by the cavalry troops assigned to the vehicle. *See also* **ACAV Kit, M-113.**

Armored Cavalry Regiment (ACR)   The 11th Armored Cavalry Regiment was the largest American armor unit to operate in Vietnam. The regiment consisted of three armored cavalry squadrons, an air cavalry troop and related support companies (maintenance, medical, engineer, etc.). Each squadron consisted of three troops of Armored Personnel Carriers, one M-48 tank troop, and a 155mm Self-Propelled artillery battery. The M-551 light tank entered service with the regiment in '69 and functioned in the armored reconnaissance mode. *See also* **11th Armored Cavalry Regiment.**

Armored Cavalry Troop   *see*   **Cavalry Troop**

Armored Command Carrier   *see*   **M-577 ACC**

Armored Girdle   *see*   **M-1955 Flak Jacket**

Armored Personnel Carrier   *see*   **M-113**

Armored Rail Cars   *see*   **Wickums**

Armored Reconnaissance Vehicle   *see*   **M-551 ARV**

Armored Seats (Chest Protectors)   UH-1 Huey helicopters used in Vietnam featured armored seats for the pilot and copilot. The 175-pound highbacked armored seats provided the pilots with back and side protection from small arms fire. A special armored breastplate (chest protectors) fit across the front of the seat to add protection for the chest. The 1st Cav was the first large helicopter force to deploy to Vietnam in '65 and their Hueys were fitted with the armored seats, but there were initial shortages of the front breastplates. The side armor plates were movable and could be slid into position when necessary. *See also* **Body Armor.**

Armored Troop Carrier   *see*   **ATC, Armored Troop Carrier**

Armored Troop Carrier-Helicopter   *see*   **ATC, Armored Troop Carrier**

Armored Truck   *see*   **Hardened Convoy**

Armored Vehicle Launched Bridge   *see*   **M-60 AVLB**

Armpit of the World   *see*   **Vietnam (GI Names)**

Armpit Sauce   *see*   **Nuoc Mam**

Army ACV   *see*   **Army Air Cushioned Vehicles**

Army Air Cushioned Vehicles (Army ACV)   Army version of the PACV used by the Navy in Vietnam. The Army's 3d

Brigade/9th Infantry Division operated a platoon of the air cushioned vehicles in the Delta of IV Corps. The ACV was radar equipped and armed with .50cal machine guns and grenade launchers. *See also* **PACV.**

Army Air Force The Army "Air Force" consisted of its own fleet of small fixed-wing aircraft. These aircraft were originally designated to provide remote field resupply to Army units and also function as reconnaissance and surveillance aircraft. Later in the Vietnam War some of the aircraft were armed with machine guns, rockets and bombs and used for direct tactical support of ground units. Some of the Army's fixed-wing aircraft were O-1, CV-2, OV-1, U-6, U-1, U-10, U-8, U-21. Armed fixed-wing aircraft were assigned to FWT, SURV and RAC aviation companies. *See also* **Avn.**

Army Aircraft Carrier *see* **USNS Corpus Christie**

Army and Air Force Exchange System *see* **Post Exchange**

Army Aspirins (APCs) Standard military aspirin containing a compound of Aspirin, Phenacetin, and Caffeine. *See also* **Drug List.**

Army Authorization Document System (TAADS) Administrative system used within the Army to initiate, maintain, record, and document organization changes in the Army. Changes in unit specifications and TOE changes were processed through this system.

Army Bases *see* **Golden Ghettos**

Army Call Signs (2, 3, 4, 5, 6, 6 Actual) 2 = Intelligence officer (Bn or above); 3 = Operations officer (Bn or above); 4 = Command sgt or lead NCO; 5 = XO or second in command (sergeant at the platoon level); 6 = Unit commander (added to the call sign of the unit for platoon or larger). Example: "Foxfire-6 Actual" was the company commander, "Foxfire-6" was the commander's RTO. Messages often passed between commanders through their RTOs. Foxfire-1-6 would be the commander of the first platoon of the company, Foxfire-2-6 would be the second platoon, etc. Some GIs nicknamed God "Supreme-6." *See also* **Call Signs.**

Army Combat Engineers *see* **Com-**bat Engineer Team

Army Commendation Medal (ACM, ARCOM) Award given for service. Most enlisted men received an ACM for serving in Vietnam.

Army Concept Team in Vietnam (ACTIV) Army teams in SVN which evaluated new weapons and techniques for possible permanent incorporation into the Army TOE or SOP. The teams began operating in the early sixties and tested a wide variety of weapons systems throughout the war. ACTIV was first established in SVN in '62 and was under the direction of the Department of Defense's Advanced Research Projects Agency. *See also* **Advanced Research Projects Agency.**

Army Construction Engineers The Army deployed two types of engineer units to Vietnam. The combat engineers operated in the field constructing and fortifying combat bases, mine clearing, demolitions, and generally spent a great deal of time under fire. The Army construction engineers focused their efforts on structures, facilities and base camp improvements. The construction engineers also worked on local civic projects for the Vietnamese and trained ARVN engineers in construction techniques. *See also* **Combat Engineer Team, Engineers.**

Army GP *see* **General Medical Officer**

Army Green Uniform *see* **Class A's**

Army Hamburger *see* **Gaines**burgers

Army Helicopter Flight School *see* **Fort Rucker**

Army Infantry *see* **Queen of the Battles**

Army Instructor *see* **Lane Grader**

Army Mortuary (U.S. Army Mortuary, Oakland) The U.S. Army Mortuary located at Oakland Army Base, California, was the primary port of entry for the remains of U.S. servicemen returning from Asia.

Army Nurse Corps *see* **U.S. Army Nurse Corps**

Army Operations Center (AOC) United States Army, Vietnam (USARV) control center, originally located in Saigon and later relocated to Long Binh. USARV functioned as the administrative and logistical support command for U.S. Army forces in South Vietnam and was established in '65. *See also* **U.S. Army Vietnam.**

Army, Republic of Vietnam (SVA, Vietnamese National Army, VNA, ARVN) As part of the French Union Forces in '50, the Vietnamese National Army was formed to fight the Vietminh. After the defeat of the French in '54 the VNA remained intact, and under Diem became the Army of the Republic of Vietnam. The Army was equipped and advised by the U.S. under MAAG and finally MACV. The ARVN as a whole suffered from poor leadership and even poorer morale. Although some ARVN units distinguished themselves in combat against the NVA/VC, those units tended to be the exception rather than the rule. Many Americans in Vietnam saw the ARVNs as eager to avoid the enemy and extremely reluctant to take the initiative in combat. After the ARVN suffered several setbacks while fighting the VC the U.S. decided American troops would be required to fight the communists in Vietnam. Military service was mandatory in Vietnam, but often the wealthy could pay to keep their sons out of the Army or buy them commissions as officers. The ARVN Officer Corps suffered from corruption, infighting and a preoccupation with status and power. ARVN soldiers often had no strong convictions about the war and a general distrust of their own government, a self-serving government fraught with corruption, instability, greed and fear. During the final days of SVN the military had nearly a million men under arms, yet in an all-out offensive, NVN rolled the ARVN forces back in less than two months. During the course of the war it is estimated that South Vietnam's military forces suffered 235,000+ KIAs and 600,000 WIAs. The "ARVN" technically represented Army troops; the term was used loosely to represent any South Vietnamese military personnel. *See also* **ARVN, Corruption, South Vietnamese Armed Forces, Battle of Ar Bac.**

Army Peace Corps *see* **Sneaky Petes, Special Forces**

Army Personnel File *see* **201 File**

Army Post Office (APO, FPO, Fleet Post Office) All Army and Air Force troop mail bound for Vietnam was processed through the Army Post Office system. Vietnam-bound mail was dispatched from the APOs at Seattle, Washington and San Francisco, California. The Navy and Marine Corps used a separate postal system called the Fleet Post Office.

Army Recruit *see* **Twinks**

Army Regs *see* **Army Regulations**

Army Regulations (AR, Army Regs) Rules of conduct and action established by the U.S. Army which were applicable to all Army personnel.

Army Security Agency (ASA, USASA, Radio Research Unit, RRU, Radio Spooks) Highly classified Army group that intercepted enemy radio transmissions, and was responsible for maintaining the secrecy of Army signal and electronic intelligence gathering activities. The group was headquartered in Saigon with intercept stations located throughout SVN. The group originally deployed to Vietnam in '61, departing in March '73. Over that period the group was known as the following USASA Groups: 400th, 82d, 53d, 509th, and USASAGV (U.S. Army Security Agency Group, Vietnam). As part of their cover the ASA groups were frequently referred to as "Radio Research Units." The technicians that operated stations were nicknamed "Radio Spooks." *See also* **National Security Agency.**

Army Special Warfare Center (John F. Kennedy Center for Special Warfare) The Army's special warfare center was located at Fort Bragg, North Carolina, and trained Special Forces troops in counterinsurgency operations. The Center was renamed the "John F. Kennedy Center for Special Warfare" shortly after Kennedy began to support the concept of a specialized force to counter communist insurgents. *See also* **Special Forces.**

Army Tan Uniform (Tropical Worsted Uniform, TW Uniform) Army dress uniform. The tan uniform was similar in design to the Class A uniform which it preceded. The uniform was made of a lightweight wool worsted blend and polyester/gabardine mix. The TW was the primary uniform worn by officers and senior NCOs traveling to SVN. The TW was eventually replaced by the Class A, Army Green Uniform. *See also* Class A's.

Army Transport Corps (ATC) U.S. Army organization responsible for arranging in-country transportation required by the Army. The ATC coordinated the necessary air, land and sea transport required to meet the Army's needs. Under control of the ATC was a wide variety of transport equipment. The ATC managed LCMs, BARC and LARCs, small ships, and a small fleet of utility aircraft. ATC also managed Newport, the Army's port facility located in Saigon. *See also* **Newport Terminal Facility.**

Army Transportation Corps *see* **Army Transport Corps**

Army War College (AWC) The United States Army War College was established in the early 1900s to provide senior military officers a means to study, analyze and disseminate information relating to the art and the science of war. War college doctrine was used as an advisory tool to the government and as a tool for formulating military policy. The college was located at Carlisle Barracks, Pennsylvania.

Army's Aircraft Carrier *see* **USNS Corpus Christie**

Army's War (Nixon's War, Kennedy's War, Johnson's War) Perception by some Americans during various phases of the Vietnam War that the war was actually the personal war of the Army (the military), or one of the Presidents who happened to be in office at the time (Presidents Kennedy, Johnson or Nixon). Some critics argued Vietnam was the only war the military had and they were trying to make the best of it. Still others believed that all aspects of the war were somehow personally orchestrated by the President.

ARP *see* **Aero Rifle Platoon**

ARPA *see* **Advanced Research Project Agency**

ARRS *see* **Aerospace Rescue and Recovery Service**

ART Scope *see* **M-14 Sniper Rifle**

Article 15 (AR-15) U.S. Army disciplinary action against a soldier usually resulted in some, or all of the following: loss of pay, extra duties, restriction to base or

barracks, and loss of rank. Nonjudicial in nature.

Article 118 U.S. Army Uniform Code of Military Justice's code for murder committed against a civilian population. The charge was brought against 1/Lt. William Calley, Jr., in September '69, for his actions in the village of My Lai in '68. *See also* **Calley, My Lai.**

Artillery Barge (Fire Support Barge, Forward Fire Support Base, Mobile Fire Support Base) Flat topped barges used for artillery platforms by units of the Mobile Riverine Force in the Delta. Each barge could support two 105mm or 155mm howitzers, the gun crews and ammunition. The barges were usually attached to LCM-8 landing craft and moved into support position. The LCM provided space for the gun's command post and functioned as a Fire Direction Center. The LCM-8 also provided some security with its .50cal machine guns. The barges were used as forward fire support bases and effectively allowed artillery support to be available wherever riverine operations might pursue the enemy. *See also* **Barge, LCM-8.**

Artillery Barrage *see* **Bring-Smoke**

Artillery CBU *see* **ICM Round, Firecracker, CBU**

Artillery Kill Zone *see* **Kill Zone**

Artillery Safety Margin (Danger Close) Artillery term used by an artillery spotter in the field requesting artillery support. The term indicated to the firing artillery battery that the coordinates and adjustments of the requested artillery rounds would be falling very close to friendly troops (most likely the unit requesting the support). How close the rounds were called on to friendly troops was the responsibility of the command requesting the fire. Allowances had to be made for the type of artillery being fired, atmospherics, and who was doing the firing (U.S. or ARVN). The safety margin for most units was 200–600 meters depending on the tactical situation. If ARVN artillery was firing in support of U.S. units the safety margin was often extended. *See also* **Danger-Close Range.**

Artillery Umbrella Technique employed by most FWF units in Vietnam stressing that they operate in the field within the range of supporting artillery. Reconnaissance units operated in the field regardless of the artillery umbrella. With the use of helicopter borne aerial rocket artillery units could operate outside of the artillery umbrella, and still receive fire support. By only operating within the range of the artillery, U.S. units were somewhat restricted in their operations. In order to go deeper into enemy territory it was necessary to establish fire bases closer to those areas, and with the increase in fire bases a like increase in logistical support for those bases arose. See also **Fire Base Psychosis.**

Artillery, NVA   The NVA made use of Soviet and Chinese made artillery pieces and rockets. The Viet Cong typically used 60mm and 81/82mm mortars. The use of the larger calibre weapons was usually restricted to main force VC units and the NVA. Such weapons included 120mm mortars, 130mm and 152mm guns and various rockets. The larger calibre guns were primarily found along the border areas where they operated from relatively safe sanctuaries. The large guns were difficult to move and out of character for the highly mobile NVA/VC forces that operated in SVN. Rockets provided the bulk of long-range fire support for the enemy in-country. After '71 the use of larger weapons became more frequent.

Artillery, U.S. (Arty)   U.S. units in Vietnam made extensive use of artillery throughout the war. Artillery pieces were defined by type and size. The type of weapon was indicated by the trajectory path of the shell. Mortars (81mm, 4.2-inch, etc.) had a high arcing trajectory, lobbing their shells. Howitzers (105mm, 155mm, etc.) had a medium, rounded trajectory and guns (175mm, 16-inch) fired on a low arc or flat trajectory. The diameter of the weapons barrel was designated in millimeters or inches, i.e., 105mm, 175mm, 4.2-inch and 16-inch. The typical artillery pieces used by US/FWF units in Vietnam were 60mm, 81mm and 4.2-inch mortars; 105mm, 155mm howitzers; 175mm, 5-inch, 8-inch and 16-inch cannons. See also **Cannons.**

Artillerymen see **Redlegs**

Arty see **Artillery**

Arvin see **ARVN**

Arvin Telephone Exchange see

Tiger Phone Exchange

ARVN (Arvin, Marvin-the-Arvin, As-Really-Very-Nervous, Our Vietnamese, Luc Quan)   Generic name used in reference to any South Vietnamese soldier or member of the military; "Our Vietnamese." American GIs generally did not hold a very high opinion of most of the ARVN they encountered, although there were some outstanding ARVN units in Vietnam. ARVNs were seen to avoid the enemy and were at times easily routed by the NVA/VC. A GI field description of "ARVN" was: "As-Really-Very-Nervous." "Army" in Vietnamese was "Luc Quan." The rural Vietnamese referred to ARVN troops as "Republican troops." See also **Search and Avoid; Army, Republic of Vietnam; The Vietnamese, Luc Luong Dac Biet.**

ARVN 1st Inf Div Recon Company see **Hac Bao**

ARVN Airborne (Division Airborne) The ARVN Airborne Division was first organized in '68 from previously organized airborne battalions and brigades and was one of the best fighting units in the South Vietnamese military. The ARVN Airborne operated in all four Corps Zones during the division's existence and was generally held in reserve for critical situations. The ARVN Airborne participated in the Laos Incursion, Lam Son 719, and suffered heavy casualties during its withdrawal from Laos. See also **Lam Son 719.**

ARVN Deserters see **Rattlesnakes**

ARVN Long Rats (Indigenous Rations) Vietnamese dehydrated rations. Unlike the American dehydrated rations that consisted of several different meals, the Vietnamese rations consisted only of rice and a small packet of flavoring. The flavoring packet consisted of small amounts of dried fish, lamb, beef or vegetables and dried peppers. The rice could be eaten straight from the bag or re-hydrated with water. The dehydrated rice was available on a limited basis to LLDB and CIDG forces that operated for long periods of time in the field. The rations were packaged in plastic and included several pieces of peanut candy, wrapped in edible rice paper. USSF/LRRP units sometimes used the ARVN long rats to supplement their diet. See also **LRRP Rations.**

ARVN Marines *see* **Republic of Vietnam Marine Corps**

ARVN Phonetic Alphabet South Vietnamese military phonetic alphabet: A—anh-dung, B—bac-binh, C—cai-cach, D—dong-da, E—e-de, F—foxtrot, G—gay-go, H—hong-ha, I—im-lang, J—juliet, K—kinh-ky, L—le-loi, M—manh-me, N—non-nuoc, O—oanh-liet, P—phu-quoc, Q—quang-trung, R—rach-gia, S—son-tay, T—tu-tuong, U—ung-ho, V—ve-vang, W—wit-ki, X—xung-phong, Y—yen-bai, Z—zulu. *See also* **Alphabet.**

ARVN Queers (Queers, Gook Faggots) It was a social practice among some Vietnamese males to hold hands in public. For the Vietnamese it was considered normal and acceptable for friends to walk down the street hand-in-hand. American GIs who saw the practice immediately judged such behavior to be homosexually related and began categorizing Vietnamese men as "queers" or "gook faggots." To try to short-circuit the aspersions, Vietnamese hand-holding in public declined. The practice began to return in late '71 as the number of U.S. troops in Vietnam dwindled, reducing the chances of misconceptions by Vietnam's allies.

ARVN Rangers *see* **Biet-Dong-Quan**

ARVN Rucksack (Ranger Pack, Indigenous Rucksack) U.S. developed rucksack for use by the South Vietnamese Army. The pack was made of nonwaterproof cotton duck material and was mounted on spring-steel "X" shaped frames. The pack featured a large compartment and two external pockets as well as attaching hooks and straps for other equipment. The pack was produced outside of Vietnam and general distribution to ARVN troops began in '64. A similar version of the pack was produced for the Thai Army and a version of the ARVN Rucksack became available to American troops in '68. *See also* **Jungle Rucksack, ALICE, NVA Rucksack.**

ARVN SEALs *see* **Lin Dei Nugel Nghai**

ARVN Special Forces *see* **Luc Luong Dac Biet**

ARVNSF *see* **Luc Luong Dac Biet**

As-Really-Very-Nervous *see* **ARVN**

ASA *see* **Army Security Agency**

ASAS *see* **Australian Special Air Services**

ASCC *see* **Area Support and Coordination Committee**

ASEAN *see* **Association of Southeast Asian Nations**

ASG *see* **SOG Groups**

ASH *see* **Assault Support Helicopter Company, Avn**

Asian Deer *see* **Barking Deer**

Asian Elephant *see* **Elephants**

Asian-American Special Forces *see* **Peregrine Group**

Asiatic Cobra Up to seven feet long, the cobra was usually found living among the roots of trees or in small, dark holes. The cobra possessed a highly toxic nerve venom that could be fatal in 2–24 hours. It could either strike or spit its venom. The venom could cause blindness on contact with the eyes. *See also* **Snakes.**

ASOC *see* **Direct Air Support Center**

ASP *see* **Aero Scout Platoon**

ASPB (Assault Support Patrol Boat, Alpha Boat) American MRF patrol boat. The 50-foot ASPB could do 16 knots and was operated by a crew of five. The armor-plated boat was armed with two 20mm cannon/.50cal machine gun turrets, and an 81mm mortar and 40mm grenade launcher. The ASPB was used for patrols, scouting, mine-sweeping and providing fire support for ATCs and assault troops during river operations. The ASPB, or "Alpha Boat," was specially designed for river warfare and featured an underwater engine exhaust system that significantly quieted the boat's normal engine noises. ASPBs operated with TF 116 and TF 117 before being transferred to the VNN. *See also* **TF 117, TF 116.**

Aspirant (Chuan-Uy, Sinh-Vien Sy-Qu, Student Officer) Vietnamese officer rank below second lieutenant. Below Chuan-Uy the lowest officer rank was the Student Officer, Sinh-Vien Sy-Qu.

ASR *see* **American Service Radio**

ASRT *see* **Air Support Radar Team**

Ass-and-Trash Runs (Routine Missions)
Pilot slang for routine helicopter missions, such as ferrying supplies, passengers, equipment or courier runs. This was opposed to missions involving combat assault, medevac, extractions or "hot" LZ logistic resupply runs. *See also* **Log Bird.**

Ass-in-the-Grass-Test A form of military "field audit" to roughly evaluate the number of soldiers a unit had patrolling in the field compared to the actual number of troops available to the unit. In Vietnam, during the height of the war, on any given day less than 15 percent of the American manpower in Vietnam was actually assigned to combat duty. The remaining 85 percent provided support, operated clubs, were on R & R, were suffering from malaria, heat exhaustion or battle wounds, were new personnel just arriving in-country, or troops DEROS-ing. *See also* **Tooth-to-Tail-Ratio.**

Ass-Kicker Anything that was hard, difficult, exhausting, a big problem or bad news... a real bitch.

Assassination Bureau *see* **Phoenix Program**

Assault Engineers *see* **Combat Engineer Team**

Assault Helicopter Company (AHC)
The assault helicopter company consisted of slicks and gunship helicopters working together to provide infantry troops the ability to assault an area by helicopter, and to provide them with direct aerial gunship support. *See also* **Avn.**

Assault Hospital Ship *see* **LPH**

Assault Support Helicopter Company (ASHC) Army medium helicopter company that provided troop lift and support. During the Vietnam War the CH-47 was the Army's medium lift helicopter. A single CH-47 could move an infantry platoon or a 105mm howitzer section, its ammunition and crew. A typical ASHC operated with 16 helicopters. *See also* **Avn, CH-47.**

Assault Support Patrol Boat *see* **ASPB**

Assembly of Unrepresented People
1960s peace group whose focus was ending war in general. They used acts of civil disobedience to further their goals.

Asshole of the World *see* **Vietnam**

(GI Names)

Assistant Division Commander (ADC)
Some American infantry divisions operated with two ADCs. Assistant Division Commander-A was generally responsible for tactical field operations of the division. ADC-B coordinated the remainder of the division's functions such as administration and logistic support. In smaller U.S. divisions one ADC performed both roles.

Assistant Machine Gunner *see* **A-Gunner**

Associated States of Indo-China *see* **Indo-China**

Association of Southeast Asian Nations (ASEAN) Association founded in '65 to promote growth and cooperation between its member nations. The members were the Philippines, Thailand, Singapore, Malaysia and Indonesia. The association was non-military oriented.

ASU *see* **American Servicemen's Union**

AT *see* **Annual Active Duty for Training**

At-the-Knee Amputation *see* **AK Amp**

ATC *see* **Army Transport Corps**

ATC Detachment *see* **Air Traffic Control Detachment, Avn**

ATC, Armored Troop Carrier (Armored Troop Carrier, Armored Troop Carrier-Helicopter, ATC-H, Tango Boat)
Armored LCM-6 landing craft used by the American MRF for tactical transport of troops. The ATC had the standard bow ramp and was fitted with standoff armor for protection against enemy RPGs. The boats were armed with a 20mm cannon, two .50cal machine guns and sometimes a 40mm grenade launcher. A hard top was also located over the holding area to reduce the effectiveness of enemy mortars. The ATC-H was fitted with a landing platform that could accommodate one helicopter. One ATC-H in a group was assigned as the Battalion Aid Station on operations. The helipad allowed troops, fuel, supplies and medevac operations to take place on the water. The ATC, known as a Tango Boat, could carry a 40-man platoon of troops.

ATC-H *see* **ATC, Armored Troop Carrier**

ATF *see* **Australian Task Force**

ATGM *see* **Antitank Guided Missiles**

ATGM-3 (Sagger, AT-3 ATGM) Soviet made antitank guided missile, first used against FWF by the NVA during their '72 Eastertide Offensive. The 25-pound missile was wire guided, max speed of 120mph with a minimum range of 500 meters and a maximum of 3,000 meters; armor penetration was 400mm. The man pack unit came in a cluster of four missiles that were fired independently. The missile needed to be guided by the operator to the target. If the operator could be made to lose sight of the target, due to suppressive fire, or the target using evasive maneuvers, then the target stood a good chance of avoiding the missile. *See also* **Antitank Guided Missiles.**

Atlanta *see* **Operation Atlanta**

Atlas Wedge *see* **Operation Atlas Wedge**

Atoll Missile (AA-2 AAM) Soviet air-to-air missile (AAM) carried by North Vietnamese Air Force MiG-21s. The AA-2 Atoll was a copy of the U.S. Sidewinder missile, and was available in infrared and radar homing versions. The missile carried a 13.2-pound warhead, had a range of 6,000kms, was a little over 9 feet long, and had a launch weight of 154 pounds. Two Atoll missiles were deployed on the NVAF MiG-21s for aerial combat with American aircraft over North Vietnam. *See also* **MiG-21, Sidewinder Missile.**

ATOM *see* **Advisory, Training and Operations Mission**

Atomic Energy Commission *see* **Atoms for Peace**

Atoms for Peace (Nuclear Reactor) In the mid-sixties the U.S. built a small, nuclear power plant near the city of Dalat, 230kms northeast of Saigon. The plant was built as part of the U.S. Atoms for Peace program under the guidelines of the U.S. Atomic Energy Commission. Critical components (radioactive fuel rods) and reactor documentation were evacuated or destroyed in early April '75 before they could fall into the hands of the NVA.

Atrocical *see* **Americal Division**

ATSB *see* **Ammi Barge**

ATT *see* **Advanced Technology Training**

Attack Cargo Ship (AKA, Amphibious Cargo Ship, LKA) Armed Navy cargo ship usually assigned to an amphibious force for resupply operations of an amphibious force. The AKA could transport 300 troops, their equipment and supplies, and 18 LCM landing craft. The ship could make a maximum speed of 20 knots and was operated by a crew of 330 men. The AKA was redesignated the LKA (Amphibious Cargo Ship) in '69. *See also* **AKA, LPD.**

Attack Carrier *see* **CVA**

Attack Helicopter Squadron *see* **HMA**

Attack Transport Ship (APA) Armed troop transport ship. Navy APAs had a troop capacity of 1,500 and were initially used in WWII to transport troops for amphibious assaults. APAs were used as barracks ships during the Vietnam War and typically housed 900–1,000 men over extended periods of time. The APA was used by riverine forces and by U.S. personnel operating the harbor facilities at Da Nang. The AKA was redesignated the LPA (Amphibious Transport Ship) in '69. The ship had a maximum speed of 17 knots. The LPA was eventually replaced by the LPD which assumed the duties of transport and support of amphibious troop landings with the Navy. *See also* **APL, LPD.**

Attleboro *see* **Operation Attleboro**

Aussie Hats *see* **Digger Hats**

Aussies *see* **Australia**

Austin II *see* **Operation Austin II**

Australia (Aussies) Australia first deployed advisors to Vietnam in July '62 as the Australian Army Training Team, Vietnam. In '65 Australian combat troops of the Royal Australian Regiment began deploying to SVN as the 1st Australian Task Force. Additional units deployed over the years including more advisors, RAAF bombers and helicopters, medical, engineering, artillery, armor units, destroyers, helicopter crews and frogmen from the Australian Navy (RAN). The Australians primarily operated in Phuoc

Tuy Province, III Corps, and did extensive training with the ARVN and RF/PF forces. Of the 50,001 Aussies that served, 496 died and 2,398 were wounded. *See also* RAR, AATTV, Australian SAS, HMAS Hobart, AAACV, ATF, ANZAC.

Australian Army Assistance Command, Vietnam *see* **Australian Army Training Team, Vietnam**

Australian Army Assistance Group, Vietnam (AAAGV, AAACV; Australian Army Assistance Command, Vietnam) The AAAGV, sometimes referred to as the AAACV (Australian Army Assistance Command, Vietnam), was first organized in March '72 to provide advisory assistance and training to the ARVN. The group was headquartered in Saigon until their departure from Vietnam in January '73. *See also* Australian Army Training Team, Vietnam.

Australian Army Training Team, Vietnam (AATTV; Australian Army Assistance Command, Vietnam [AAACV]; The Team) In August '62 Australia deployed a training team to Vietnam to assist the ARVN forces. Throughout the war the AATTV advised and trained ARVN and CIDG troops in patrol and recon techniques. Many of the advisors were members of the Australian SAS, who specialized in patrolling and reconnaissance work. The AATTV paralleled the work of the USSF's in operating CIDG strike units. In December '72 the last of the AATTVs departed Vietnam. Australian advisory and assistance duties were taken up by the Australian Army Assistance Command, Vietnam (AAACV) until their departure in January '73. *See also* Australia.

Australian Civil Affairs Unit (ACAU) Australian version of civic action programs conducted by the American military in Vietnam. The ACAU helped the Vietnamese civilian population in their area with projects such as the construction of schools, irrigation and road improvements, and general help to the local population. The ACAU also conducted medical screening and limited intelligence gathering in the villages. *See also* Combined Action Platoon.

Australian Communist Party *see* **Vietnam Action Committee**

Australian GI *see* **Digger**

Australian SAS *see* **Australian Special Air Services**

Australian Special Air Services (SAS, Australian SAS [ASAS]) Special Air Services troops were specialists in patrolling, reconnaissance and jungle warfare. The first Australian SAS troops deployed to SVN as advisors to train ARVN Rangers and CIDG troops. When Australian combat troops entered the war the SAS expanded its presence assuming a role parallel to the USSF's. The SAS organized and led CIDG and ARVN Rangers through operations in and around Phuoc Tuy Province, III Corps. From '66–'71 at least one SAS squadron was serving in Vietnam. Like other Australian units, the SAS rotated whole squadrons. *See also* Australia.

Australian Task Force (Nui Dat, ATF, 1st Australian Task Force) Australian Task Force that operated in Phuoc Tuy Province, III Corps. The ATF was headquartered at Nui Dat, 60kms southeast of Saigon. The task force consisted of several Royal Australian Regiments (RAR), SAS, armor, engineer, artillery, signal and logistics support units. Australian units deployed as a complete force with most of the members of the unit rotating out of Vietnam at the same time, and a new unit rotating in to take its place. The ATF primarily operated in the Province of Phuoc Tuy. The last "Aussie" combat units departed Vietnam in early '72. *See also* Australia, FSB Coral.

Australian–New Zealand Army Corps (ANZAC) Australian Army advisors deployed to Vietnam in '62, followed by Australian combat troops in '65, designated the Australian Task Force. Also in '64, New Zealand deployed a small group of advisors to Vietnam, followed by a battery of the Royal New Zealand Artillery and later SAS, engineers and infantry. A combined force of the New Zealanders and Australians formed the Australian–New Zealand Army Corps; ANZAC. Both countries increased their commitment to the South Vietnamese over the course of the war. During the war 469 Australian and New Zealand soldiers died in Vietnam. *See also* New Zealand, Australia.

Authorized Strength *see* **Fat Unit**

Automatic Ambush *see* **Booby Trap**

Automat Kalashnikova '47 *see* AK47

Automatic 8th *see* **8th Artillery Regiment**

Automatic Weapons (AW) Individual small arms weapons with a high rate of fire. Automatic weapons included assault rifles (M-14, M-16, AK47) and machine guns. AW generally referred to modern individual weapons which automatically loaded a new round into the firing chamber after ejecting the previously fired round. This was in comparison to older rifles that required the firer to manually operate the bolt of the weapon to eject the fired round and load a new round.

Autonomous Cities There were 11 autonomous cities in South Vietnam. They shared the same administration privileges and local control as that of a Province. The cities were Vung Tau, Saigon, Hue, Da Lat, Da Nang, Qui Nhon, Nha Trang, My Tho, Can Tho, Rach Gia and Cam Ranh.

Autorotation (Forced Landing, Controlled Crash, Counter-Rotation) Landing maneuver performed by a helicopter when it lost rotor power. The procedure involved neutralizing the pitch of the rotor blades. The rotors would continue to turn from centrifugal force providing limited lift allowing the craft to go into a fast glide. The speed of the glide was reduced just prior to impact with the ground by changing the tilt of the rotor mast causing the nose of the ship to flare up. Changing the pitch of the blades at this time would allow the aircraft to settle roughly to the ground. Sometimes described as a "controlled crash" by U.S. helicopter pilots. Called "counter-rotation" by Australian pilots. *See also* **Hammerhead Stall.**

AUTOVON Military telephone system interconnecting military installations. The AUTOVON network had access to civilian phone systems, but was a totally separate system allowing military facilities to communicate over land lines even if the civilian phone system was down.

Auxiliary Minesweeper *see* **YMS**

Auxiliary Power Unit (APU) External power unit used to start turbine aircraft engines. The unit consisted of a very small, portable, turbine generator. Hot exhaust air from the APU was pumped into the aircraft's jet engine, causing the aircraft's turbine to turn. When the turbine reached the proper speed, fuel from the aircraft could be injected into the hot exhaust, and the subsequent ignition of the fuel would start the aircraft's engine. The APU connection could then be removed. The APU also provided the electrical power to the aircraft during the start-up process.

Auxiliary Tug, Small *see* **YTL Tug**

Average Age of the U.S. Soldier... *see* **19**

Avgas (Av-gas) *see* **Jet Fuel**

Aviation Battalion *see* **Combat Aviation Battalion**

Aviation Company *see* **Avn**

Aviation Detachment (AD) Units separated from their parent unit and detailed (detached) to operate with another unit. Such detachments usually performed special functions or missions needed by the unit to which they were attached. In Vietnam aviation units often operated with attached units to augment their forces. In the 1st Cavalry Division ADs consisted of attached aerial artillery, maintenance sections and cavalry squadrons.

AVLB *see* **M-60 AVLB**

Avn (Aviation Company) Military abbreviation of aviation. Prior to '63 Army helicopter units were designated Transportation Companies, with their prime function being the transport of troops and equipment. With the advent of the UH-1, the role of the helicopter was expanded to include fire support and air assault. In '63 Army aircraft companies were redesignated Aviation Companies and classified according to their primary mission. The main classifications were AHC (Assault Helicopter Company), AM (Air Mobile), AML (Air Mobile Light), ARA (Aerial Rocket Artillery), ASH (Assault Support Helicopter), ATC (Air Traffic Control), AWC (Aerial Weapons Company), CAC (Corps Aviation Company), Escort (Armed Helicopter Escort), FWT (Fixed-Wing Transport), FWU (Fixed-Wing Utility), GS (General Support), HH (Heavy Helicopter), MH

(Medium Helicopter), RAC (Reconnaissance Airplane Company), SAC (Surveillance Aircraft Company) and SURV L (Surveillance Aircraft, Light). A typical assault or airmobile helicopter aviation company in Vietnam consisted of two platoons of transports (slicks), a platoon of gunships (guns). *See also* **Combat Aviation Group, Combat Aviation Battalion.**

AW *see* **Automatic Weapons**

AWADS *see* **All Weather Air Delivery System**

Award Packet *see* **Package A/B Awards**

Awards *see* **Gongs**

AWAS *see* **American Women's Association of Saigon**

AWC *see* **Air War College, Aerial**

Weapons Company, Avn

AWOL *see* **Absent Without Leave**

AWOL Bag   Black leather/Naugahyde luggage bag popular with troops in the military. The bag looked like a large version of the open topped doctor's bag. The AWOL bag was zipper-closed across the top, with two top positioned carrying handles. The bag was about 20 × 12 × 12 inches high, and when zippered closed, it had a rounded top. *See also* **Valpac.**

AWP *see* **Aero Weapons Platoon**

AWSP *see* **M-42 Duster**

Azimuth (Shoot An Azimuth)   A directional bearing taken from Magnetic North in reference to a map and compass. To "shoot an azimuth" was to take a directional reading.

B

B & S Ration *see* **Beer and Soda Ration**

B Kit *see* **ACAV Kit**

B-1 Kit *see* **Unit One**

B-1 Unit (B-2, B-3)   Army C-Ration boxes were identified by the contents of the main entrée and a designation of the type of dessert included in the box; a B-1, B-2 or B-3 unit. The units consisted of a small can of crackers. Also included in the can would be candy or a tin of jam, jelly, or cheese spread, or cocoa powder. C-Rations were available from different manufacturers, and the contents of the boxes varied accordingly. Sometimes the peanut butter, cheese spread or jams were loosely packed in the box, or they were found sealed in the "B" unit can. *See also* **C-Rations, B-2 Unit.**

B-2 Unit (Water Biscuits, Cheese, Marmalade, Crackers, Peanut Butter)   Can from a box of C-Rations containing four round crackers and a tin of peanut butter, jelly, cheese, marmalade, candy or cocoa powder. *See also* **Peanut Butter, C-Rations, B-1 Unit.**

B-3 *see* **Military Regions, NVA/VC**

B-3 Unit *see* **B-1 Unit**

B-4 Bag (Valpak)   Air Force issue soft-sided, folding suitcase. The B-4 was original issue to Air Force flight crews. The suitcase was made of canvas or rubberized canvas, and when opened, folded flat. Uniforms were laid inside and secured by a strap across the center of the bag. When the bag was closed it folded in half, and was secured by a zipper around the edge. A strap and clasp arrangement, located on the opposite ends of the closed bag, kept it from accidentally opening if the zipper failed. A handle was attached to the center line of the closed bag. There were two large, flat pockets on the outside of the bag for miscellaneous storage. The bag was colored OD or sage green. The Valpak (Valpac) was a similar type bag which featured a hook on one end allowing the bag to be hung. On the B-4, the bag was folded in half and then zippered closed; on the Valpak the zipper was on the inside of the bag and zippered shut, then the bag was folded in half and secured by straps. *See also* **AWOL Bag.**

B-5 Front   Communist headquarters responsible for NVA/VC operations in the two northernmost provinces of South Vietnam (Quang Tri and Thua Thien). During the course of the war several divisions and independent regiments and battalions were controlled by the B-5 Front. During the NVA's Final Offensive in '75 the Front controlled the 304th, 312th, 320b and 325th NVA Divisions and over 16 separate regiments and battalions.

B10/11 RCL (B11 RCL, Type 65 RCL) Soviet made recoilless rifle used by the NVA/VC. The 82mm, B10 RCL weighed 125 pounds and was mounted on a two-wheel cart to enable the weapon to be more easily moved. The B10 fired an eight-pound HEAT round to a maximum effective range of 900 meters. The PRC version of the B10 was the Type 65 RCL. The B11 RCL was a heavy recoilless rifle weighing over 600 pounds. The B11 was cart mounted and could direct fire 20 or 30 rounds to 1,200 meters, or indirect fire HE rounds out to 6,500 meters. The NVA/VC made wide use of recoilless rifles against FWF armored vehicles and combat base defensive positions. *See also* **Recoilless Rifle.**

B-10/11 Recoilless Rifles *see* **PRC RCL**

B11 RCL *see* **B10/11 RCL**

B-12 (Vitamin B)   One of the more dependable hangover remedies available to some U.S. troops. When available, vitamin B-12 was injected by sympathetic medics at base camp and battalion aid stations.

B-26 Bomber (RB-26, Invader, A-26) WWII vintage bomber used by the VNAF as a tactical bomber. U.S. B-26 bombers were first given to the French in early '54, and again provided to VNAF in '62. The aircraft was manufactured by Douglas and called the "Invader." The RB-26 was fitted with cameras and used for photo reconnaissance work. The twin engine, propeller driven B-26 had a max speed of 355mph, a range of 2,880kms, was armed with 10–18 .50cal machine guns and a bomb load of 4,000 pounds. The U.S. Air Force version of the bomber first operated in Vietnam in '64 was called the A-26. Stocks of the aircraft were turned over to the Vietnamese when Air Force jet aircraft began combat missions in SVN.

B-29 Bomber   American bomber that was tentatively scheduled to provide air support to the French in '54 at the siege of Dien Bien Phu. The U.S. Government formulated a plan in early '54 to use the B-29 in support of French forces, but President Eisenhower never authorized the plan to be executed. *See also* **Operation Vulture.**

B40   *see*   **Rocket-Propelled Grenade**

B41   *see*   **Rocket-Propelled Grenade**

B50   *see*   **Rocket-Propelled Grenade**

B-52 Airstrikes   *see*   **Arc Light**

B-52 Bomber (BUFFs, Beast, Big Ugly Fat Fellows [Fuckers], Stratofortress, Steel Cows)   Strategic bombers used to bomb targets in North and South Vietnam and enemy sanctuaries and supply routes along the SVN/Cambodian and SVN/Laotian borders. The planes acquired many nicknames because of their huge size and their less than graceful appearance. Nicknames such as BUFF, Beast, and Big Ugly Fat Fuckers. The NVA/VC called them "Steel Cows." The safety margin to protect friendly troops on the ground from B-52 strikes was initially 3,000 meters, but as the bombing accuracy of the B-52 increased the bomb line was eventually lowered to 1,000 meters. The B-52 had a maximum ceiling of 55,000 feet and a speed of 660mph and a range of 13,600kms. The Boeing manufactured aircraft could carry up to 66,000 pounds in bombs with typical bomb loads of 84 500-pounders and 24 750-pound bombs. Bombs were carried internally and mounted on wing pylons. B-52 strikes against NVN were limited to the area below the 20th Parallel, but in '72, B-52s hit Hanoi for the first time in the war. During the war B-52s operated from bases on Guam, Okinawa and Thailand. *See also* **Combat Skyspot, Big Belly B-52s, Operation Linebacker, Flying Artillery, Kadena.**

B-52D   *see*   **Big Belly B-52s**

B-57 Bomber (Canberra, RB-57, EB-57)   Air Force twin engine jet bomber deployed to SVN in '64, first used in retaliation for VC attacks against American installations and later saw an expanded role as a night bomber. The RB-57 was fitted with cameras and used for photo reconnaissance. The EB-57 was equipped with electronic sensors and used as a night bomber against the Ho Chi Minh Trail. The B-57 was a U.S. production of the British Canberra bomber. The B-57 had a maximum speed of 582mph, a range of 3,600kms, was armed with eight .50cal machine guns and could carry 6,000 pounds in bombs. At the start of the VNW the B-57s were pulled out of retirement for use in Vietnam for recon and ground support. Some B-57s were eventually transferred to VNAF. See also **Project Patricia Lynn, B-57G.**

B-57G (Tropic Moon III) Specially equipped Air Force B-57 detachment which deployed to SEA in September '70. The B-57G Canberra bomber was equipped with special radar devices, NODs, LLTV, and a laser sight, and was used at night against the Ho Chi Minh Trail. The special bomb group operated under the code name of Tropic Moon III from the Air Force base at Ubon in Thailand. The B-57G electronic equipment allowed accurate bombing at night or in poor weather. The Tropic Moon detachment was withdrawn from Thailand in April '72. See also **B-57 Bomber.**

B-66 (Skywarrior, EA-3, KA-3, RA-3, A-3, Whale, Destroyer) McDonnell Douglas twin engine jet bomber, called the "Destroyer." The bomber was used in various configurations by both the Navy and the Air Force. The EA-3 and EKA-3 were Navy ECM aircraft used for jamming enemy radar and aircraft tracking. The KA-3 was the Navy's carrier-based aerial tanker (nicknamed the "whale"). The RA-3 was equipped with infrared sensors and was used for surveillance and detection missions along the Ho Chi Minh Trail. The A-3 was the Navy version of the bomber and was the largest aircraft used aboard Navy carriers. The B-66 had a maximum speed of 594mph and a range of 3,200kms. See also **EB-66, EKA-3.**

B-B-B see **Burn-Bash-Bury**

B-Detachment see **B-Team**

B-Team (B-Detachment) U.S. Special Forces group that supported four to five A-Teams in the field, providing them with supplies, munitions and other support as required. The B-Team consisted of 20–25 men commanded by a major. Three to four B-Teams were under the command of a C-Team. The B-Team consisted of six officers and 18 NCOs. The team members were all Special Forces qualified, with additional specialties in logistics, intelligence and medicine. See also **A-Team, C-Team, Special Forces.**

B-TOC see **Brigade Tactical Operations Center**

Ba (Woman, Father) Vietnamese word with many meanings such as woman, father, 3, wave, count, lady, father's eldest brother/sister, sow, 100, and spread. For the GI it meant woman, and the number 3. GIs called most older Vietnamese men "papasan."

Ba Gia (Battle of Ba Gia) Village located approximately 12kms west of Quang Ngai in I Corps. In '65 the 1st and 2d VC Regiments attacked three ARVN battalions in the area. The ARVNs were quickly routed leaving behind their weapons. The ARVN general in command of troops in the area refused to send his troops into Ba Gia to drive out the VC; instead he requested that U.S. Marines based at nearby Chu Lai be used to counterattack the enemy. U.S. Marines supported by U.S. aircraft eventually drove out the VC. The ARVN's inability to hold Ba Gia or counterattack indicated to U.S. policy makers the ARVN's inability to hold out alone against the NVA backed Vietcong without U.S. troop support. See also **Ap Bac, Dong Xoai, Binh Gia.**

Ba-Me-Ba Beer see **Vietnamese Beer, Ba-Mi-Ba**

Ba-Mi-Ba One of the better Vietnamese beers. See also **Vietnamese Beer.**

Baby Boomers Reference to the generation of Americans born between '45 and '55. The birth rate jumped during that period as U.S. soldiers returned home from WWII and started families in a prosperous and growing America. The "baby boomers" made up the largest portion of the U.S. troops that went to Vietnam. The average age of the soldier in-country during the period of the war '65–'73, was "19." See also **19.**

Baby Doctor see **Spock, Dr. Benjamin**

Baby Killers Shoot Yourself, Not the Vietnamese Antiwar phrase sometimes hurled by protesters and antiwar activists at GIs recently returned home from Vietnam.

Baby-San (Virgin Soldier, Cherries) GI slang for a young Vietnamese child, baby or young girl. Vietnamese prostitutes called a young GI, who was a sexual virgin, a baby-san. GIs also referred to other GIs who were sexual virgins as "baby-sans" and "cherries." *See also* **New Troop.**

Babylift *see* **Operation Babylift**

Bac *see* **Chinese**

Bac Bac VC *see* **Ban**

Bac Bo *see* **Democratic Republic of Vietnam**

Bac Ho *see* **Ho Chi Minh**

Bac-Bo *see* **Tonkin**

Bac-Ky *see* **Tonkin**

Bac-Si (Quan-Y-Si, Doctor) Vietnamese for "doctor." The rural Vietnamese referred to doctors and medics as "Bac-Si." "Quan-Y-Si" was Vietnamese for a military doctor.

Bac-Viet *see* **Democratic Republic of Vietnam**

Bach Mai Hospital During the intensive bombing of Hanoi in December '72 the Bach Mai Hospital was severely damaged. Early reports by Eastern Bloc reporters and American antiwar activists claimed the hospital had been totally destroyed. Less than 500 meters from the hospital grounds was a small airfield that was the actual target of the attack. The NVN reportedly made a habit of placing SAM missile sites and AAA gun positions throughout populated areas without regard to the possible consequences to the civilian population. A reported 1,700 civilians died in the 11 days of intensified bombing. *See also* **Christmas Bombing, Surgical Bombing.**

Bachelor Officer Quarters (BOQ) On-base living quarters for military officers. Living facilities at the BOQ were for the officers only, not their families or dependents. Most U.S. military officers stationed in Saigon lived in one of several BOQs scattered around the city. In the early days of the U.S. advisory effort the MACV Compound located near Tan Son Nhut was used for administrative purposes and for the billeting of personnel. Some of the names of the BOQs were Five Oceans BOQ located in a hotel in Cholon, Brinks BOQ located in a hotel behind the Continental Palace Hotel, Metropole on Tran Hung Dao Street, Hong Kong on Ngo Quyen Street, Rex on Le Loi Street and Hialeah on Nguyen Van Street. There were more than thirty BOQs in the Saigon area during the war.

Back Bird (De-Log Ship) As part of a resupply mission, platoon or company size, the excess items, trash, unused items, etc. were taken out by the back bird. It was the last ship in the resupply operation, sometimes called a "de-log" ship. *See also* **Log Bird.**

Back Scratching Tank technique of one tank firing its machine gun on enemy soldiers that have climbed aboard another nearby tank while the tank's occupants stay buttoned up inside.

Backblast *see* **Signature**

Backblaster *see* **Recoilless Rifle**

Backload Term for a maneuver by assault troops returning to their initial assault point for extraction. For U.S. troops, helicopters and riverine craft were the most commonly used troop assault vehicles.

Backseater *see* **Weapons Systems Operator**

Bad Bush *see* **Boonies**

Bad Conduct Discharge (BCD) Discharged from military service based on bad conduct while in the service. The BCD was not as damning as the Dishonorable Discharge, but for employment purposes a BCD still made it difficult to get a decent job. *See also* **Bad Paper.**

Bad Country *see* **Indian Country**

Bad Luck *see* **Hard-Luck**

Bad Paper Nickname for the less-than-honorable (LTH) types of discharges which were available from the military. Bad paper discharges were Bad Conduct, Undesirable, and Dishonorable. Soldiers receiving such discharges were not eligible for VA benefits or medical coverage for service connected disabilities. Holding bad paper made it virtually impossible to obtain a federal job or be seriously considered by most private sector employers. Bad Conduct and Dishonorable Discharges were issued as a result of a court-martial, and a soldier could accept an Undesirable Discharge instead of facing a court-martial trial. An estimated 34,000 Dishonorable and Bad Discharges were issued to Vietnam Era Veterans. *See also* **Discharges, Undesirable Discharge.**

Bad Scene *see* **Bummer**

Bad Situation *see* **Bummer**

Bad Time *see* **Good Time**

Bad Trip *see* **Get High**

Bad-Ass Territory *see* **Boonies**

Badlands Marine name for the Arizona, an area southwest of Da Nang that was part of a major NVA/VC base area and was heavily booby trapped. Badlands was also used in a general sense to describe a particularly hostile enemy area. *See also* **Arizona Territory, Boonies.**

Baez, Joan American folk singer who joined the antiwar movement in the sixties. In '73, as Jane Fonda had done in '72, she visited Hanoi and claimed American air raids had caused widespread damage to the city.

Bagged *see* **Drunk**

Bahnar *see* **Montagnards**

Baie de Tourane *see* **Da Nang**

Bail Out *see* **Punch-Out**

Bailey Bridge A military bridge used to span short distances. The bridge was made of prefabricated steel girders and panels welded in place by the engineers. The bridge sections could be trucked in and rapidly assembled to cross small riverbeds, streams and gullies. The original Bailey Bridge was designed by a British engineer for use by Allied forces in WWII. The Bailey Bridge design soon became a standard engineering item of the U.S. military. The bridges were used in Vietnam to span rivers and streams along the main roads in places where the original bridges had been destroyed by the Viet Minh or the Viet Cong. *See also* **M-60 AVLB, Balf Bridge.**

Baited Ambush Tactic of ambushing and pinning a small force in order to cause a larger force to come to its aid. As the larger force approached, a preplanned ambush was sprung on the larger force. A common tactic

of the NVA/VC. *See also* **Cong Don Da Vien, Lame Duck Ambush.**

Baker *see* **Operation Baker**

Balancing Pole *see* **Chogi Stick**

Balf Bridge A folding, scissors bridge deployed across obstacles to enable armor and vehicles to pass. The bridge was carried and deployed from a modified M-113 APC. *See also* **M-60 AVLB, Bailey Bridge.**

Ball-Buster *see* **Hump(ing)**

Ballad of the Green Berets *see* **Sadler, Sergeant Barry**

Ballad of the Yellow Beret (Bob Seger, Beach Bums) A tongue-in-cheek ballad about America's yellow quail, the American draft dodger. The song was sung by Bob Seger and the Beach Bums, and it satirized the draft dodger and resister as cowards for their refusal to serve their country. According to the song, only the "best" at convincing the draft board not to induct them were awarded the "yellow beret." The song was available in the late sixties as a 45-RPM single, and was a takeoff on the "Ballad of the Green Berets," by Sergeant Barry Sadler. *See also* **Sergeant Barry Sadler.**

Ballistic Firing Phrase used to describe the firing of guided missiles, normally radar controlled, without those controls engaged. During Operation Line Backer II North Vietnamese SAM sites fired ballistically hoping to hit the waves of U.S. B-52s that were striking the Hanoi-Haiphong area. The NVN turned off their radar guidance because with them on they were easy targets for U.S. Wild Weasel suppression missions. The unguided SAMs were ineffective at hitting the bombers. The SA-2 contained a proximity fuse that caused the missile to detonate in the vicinity of a target it was homing in on. The missiles automatically detonated at a preset altitude if the missile missed its assigned target. *See also* **Wild Weasel, SA-2.**

Balmoral *see* **FSB Balmoral**

Bam Me Lam *see* **Dirty Thirty**

Bamboo Bangalore *see* **Bangalore Torpedo**

Bamboo Cuts *see* **Bamboo Poisoning**

Bamboo Litter (Poncho Litter) Stretcher made of cut bamboo poles, used as a litter for carrying casualties. Between two bamboo poles fatigue shirts or ponchos were used to complete the litter. Ponchos or poncho liners alone, without the poles, were often used in the field to move casualties.

Bamboo Mine (Bamboo Pipe Bomb) Viet Cong mine that was actually a bamboo pipe bomb. A length of bamboo was filled with rocks, nails, glass and explosive. A friction fuse was attached for detonation. *See also* **Booby Trap.**

Bamboo Pipe Bomb *see* **Bamboo Mine**

Bamboo Poisoning (Bamboo Cuts) GI name for the pus filled sores that could cover the arms and faces of grunts who operated in thick jungle and bamboo thickets. The sores were a result of the skin being cut and scraped on leaves and branches as troops moved through dense jungle. In the hot, wet, tropical climate the wounds quickly became infected and were slow to heal. *See also* **Gook Sores.**

Bamboo Viper (Step-and-a-Half Snake) Extremely poisonous greenish/yellow snake that called Vietnam home. The venom contained a powerful nerve toxin. Called a step-and-a-half by U.S. troops because that's about how far you got after being bitten before your terribly painful, agonized death began. *See also* **Snakes.**

Ban (Shoot, Bac Bac VC) "Ban" in Vietnamese meant to shoot or fire. It was bastardized to "bac bac" by GIs attempting to communicate with Vietnamese peasants in the field. "Bac Bac VC" meant to shoot the NVA/VC. *See also* **Sat Cong, Kill.**

Ban Chong Dau Co Moc (Barbed Spike Plate Booby Trap) VC booby trap. Three-four wooden, barbed spikes mounted on a small board and concealed in the vegetation, spike side up. These were usually placed along trails or in areas where enemy troops would be likely to fall on them. They were often used around an ambush zone. When the ambush was sprung the enemy troops would seek cover in the bushes and vegetation along the trail and impale themselves on the spikes. Punji stakes were used in a similar way. *See also* **Punji Pit/Stakes, Booby Trap.**

Ban Kara Eboo *see* **Camp Cobra**

Ban Me Thuot (Battle of Ban Me Thuot, Daughter of Thuot) Capital of Darlac Province, Central Highlands, II Corps. Headquarters for the ARVN 23d Infantry Division. Also headquarters for a brigade of the U.S. 4th Infantry Division. Ban Me Thuot was located 255kms northeast of Saigon, in the center of South Vietnam. In early March '75 NVA troops overran the city in the opening moves of North Vietnam's Final Offensive to take over South Vietnam. Three NVA divisions attacked a two regiment sized defensive force of the 23d ARVN Division overwhelming them in two days' time. Ban Me Thuot meant "Daughter of Thuot" to the Montagnard tribes that populated the area. *See also* **Abandonment of the Central Highlands.**

Banana *see* **Chuoi, Souvenir Me**

Banana Clip Ammunition magazine used in carbines and rifles. The magazine featured a slight curve and held more cartridges than the straight or standard magazine. The M-16 banana clip held 30 rounds compared to the normal 20-round magazine. The AK47 rifle and the M-2 Carbine also used banana clips.

Banana Grove *see* **Chuoi**

Band-Aid *see* **Combat Medic**

Bandit Hill *see* **1st Infantry Division Fire Bases**

Bandits of the 118th Avn *see* **118th Aviation Company**

Bandolier Cloth slings used to carry ammunition. The bandoliers contained pockets for holding rifle magazines, grenade rounds or boxes of ammunition. The slings could then be carried over the shoulder or draped as necessary. Cotton M-16 bandoliers came packed with the ammunition, boxed in cardboard. The ammunition had to be transferred from the boxes to the magazines. Once the magazines were loaded with the rifle rounds they could be carried in the bandolier. Bandoliers also came with a large safety pin attached, which was used for adjusting the sling of the bandolier. Belts of M-60 machine gun rounds were often worn in the field draped across the shoulders and over the chest, similar to the old banditos of the West.

Bangalore Torpedo (Bamboo Bangalore) Explosive devices used to breach holes in barbed wire defenses and obstacles. The "torpedo" consisted of tubes of explosives connected together, then slid under the wire and exploded. The Bamboo Bangalore was the Viet Cong version of the torpedo, which was made out of bamboo stalks packed with explosives.

Bangkok (Venice of the East) Because of its beauty and many waterways, Bangkok was often compared romantically to Venice, Italy. Bangkok was one of the official R & R centers used by U.S. troops during the VNW. *See also* **R & R.**

Banh Chung Vietnamese ceremonial cake prepared to celebrate the Tet Holiday. The cake consisted of rice, soybeans and pork wrapped in banana leaves and steamed for several hours.

Banh Da (Rice Cookies) Vietnamese cookies made from rice paste and sesame seeds, cooked or dried until crisp.

Banh Duc A Vietnamese jelled rice dish consisting of rice, flour, limestone powder and water.

Banh Giay (Ben-Gay) Vietnamese rice cake usually served on ceremonial occasions. GIs bastardized the name to "Ben-Gay."

Bank Shot (Skip Shot) Tanker term for firing a delayed fuse tank shell in such a way that it ricochets around a corner into the desired target, usually a bunker or gun implacement. The delayed fuse allowed the shell to be skipped off the ground or a wall without immediately detonating. The technique limited the tank's exposure to enemy RPG fire and was used with some success against NVA/VC bunkers in Vietnam.

Banner Sun *see* **Project Banner Sun**

Banquet *see* **Bua Chen**

Banyan Trees (Fig Trees) East Indian fig tree that populated much of Vietnam.

Bao Dai (Playboy of Paris) Last Emperor of Vietnam (1925–46 and 1949–55). Bao Dai ruled Vietnam before it was partitioned into North and South Vietnam. During the French and Japanese occupations of Vietnam, Bao Dai was the figurehead ruler of Vietnam. In '55 he was dethroned by Diem, who established the Republic of South Vietnam with himself as its first president. Bao Dai was known as the "Playboy of Paris" because of his long and frequent visits

to the "pleasure centers" of Paris. Bao Dai remained in Paris to live in exile.

Bao Loc Provincial capital of Lam Dong Province, located 143kms northeast of Saigon in the southern portion of II Corps Central Highlands. *See also* **Provincial Capitals.**

Bao Tri *see* **Khiem Cuong**

Baptism of Fire *see* **Bust-Your-Cherry**

BAR *see* **Browning Automatic Rifle**

Bar Armor *see* **Standoff Armor**

Barbed Spike Plate Booby Trap *see* **Ban Chong Dau Co Moc**

Barbed Wire *see* **Tanglefoot**

Barbershop *see* **Whorehouse**

Barboa *see* **LZ Barboa**

BARC *see* **LARC**

Bareback *see* **Ride Bareback**

Barefoot Boots *see* **Special Boots**

Barge *see* **Ammi Barge, Artillery Barge/Helicopter Barge**

Barge, Amphibious Resupply Craft/Cargo *see* **LARC**

Baria *see* **Phuoc Le**

Barking Deer (Asian Deer) Small Asian deer. The 40-pound deer was about the size of a small dog, and got its nickname, the "barking deer," from the small barking sounds it made to sound warnings and signal other deer in the area.

Barn Door *see* **Tactical Air Control System**

Barracks Bag *see* **Laundry Bag**

Barracks Barge *see* **APL**

Barracks Ship, Non–Self–Propelled *see* **APL**

Barracks Ship, Self-Propelled *see* **APB**

Barrage *see* **Artillery Barrage**

Barrel Meltdown *see* **Fire Discipline**

Barrel Roll *see* **Operation Barrel Roll**

Barrier Island Narrow strip of land located along the coast in Quang Tin

Province, I Corps. The strip was called Barrier Island and was bordered by the South China Sea to the east and separated from the rest of the province by a series of interconnected rivers and streams. The island was 49kms long and 6kms at its widest point and several hundred meters wide at its narrowest point. The island ran roughly northwest to southeast with the northern tip 5kms east of Tam Ky and the southern tip 11kms northwest of Chu Lai.

Barrier Patrols *see* **TF 115, Delta Barrier Operations**

Barrier Reef *see* **Operation Barrier Reef**

BAS *see* **Battalion Aid Station**

Base Area (Base Area 353) An area used for logistics, defense or any other physical structures utilized by a force, with the force operating out of the base. Units operating in their base area were usually more difficult to deal with because they knew the terrain and had time to set up defenses, escape routes and ambush sites. The U.S. referred to areas of SVN and adjacent Cambodia and Laos that were under NVA/VC control as enemy base areas. The major enemy base areas were assigned numbers for recognition purposes. Base Area 353 was located north of Tay Ninh, along the SVN/Cambodian border. Base areas that were targets during Operation Menu also had code names as well as base area numbers. *See also* **Operation Menu.**

Base Area 353 *see* **Base Area**

Base Area 604 *see* **Tchepone**

Base Area Targets—Operation Menu *see* **Operation Menu Targets**

Base Camp (Static Defensive Position) A semipermanent home or base used by U.S. tactical units operating in the field. Size of the camps varied, but a company base camp was usually the smallest and division size the largest. Base camps usually had at least one artillery battery present. In the case of the company base camp it might be supported by its own 4.2″ mortars, or one or more artillery batteries. The larger base camps, brigade and division, tended to be permanent facilities, while company and battalion size camps were usually temporary. *See also* **NVA/VC Base Camps.**

Base Camp Commandos *see* **Rear-Echelon-Mother-Fuckers**

Base Exchange *see* **Post Exchange**

Base-Camp-Desk-Jockey *see* **Rear-Echelon-Mother-Fuckers**

Baseball Cap (Beanies, Pinhead Caps, Utility Cap, Soft Cover) The Army Utility Cap became standard issue in '62. The cap was an OD green polyester baseball cap. Versions of the cap were worn by all branches of the service, worldwide. The caps were not popular with field troops in Vietnam. The polyester fabric was hot to wear and stained easily. The cap became available in a variety of colors. The ARVN also produced their own version of the baseball cap. It featured a higher peak than the U.S. version. A U.S. commercial version of the cap was also available. It featured a shorter bill and a lower peak, reducing the "pinhead" effect. The Marines called their utility hats "soft covers."

Baseball Grenade *see* **M33/M59 Fragmentation Grenade**

Basic Combat Training (BCT, Basic, Basic Training, Cruits) Initial combat training given to new Army recruits. During the Vietnam War Army Basic Training ran eight weeks, Marine Basic Training lasted 13 weeks. During the initial orientation "career" testing took place to determine IQ scores and into what field an individual should be placed to best meet the needs of the service. New recruits in the Army were almost universally referred to as "cruits" or other less endearing or complimentary names. *See also* **Basic Training Camps, Infantry Training Regiment, Twinks, New Troop.**

Basic Load *see* **Field Load**

Basic Training *see* **Basic Combat Training**

Basic Training Camps, U.S. Army During the Vietnam War U.S. Army basic training took place at the following bases: Ft Benning, GA; Ft Bragg, NC; Ft Lewis, WA; Ft McClellan, AL; Ft Campbell, KY; Ft Jackson, SC; Ft Gordon, GA; Ft Ord, CA; Ft Dix, NJ; Ft Polk, LA. Basic training lasted six–eight weeks.

Basic Training Camps, U.S. Marines *see* **Marine Corps Recruit Depot**

Basketball Ship *see* Firefly

Bassac River (Sampan Road, Sampan Alley, Sampan Valley, Song Hau Giang) French name for the southern arm of the Mekong River called the Song Hau Giang. The Bassac River paralleled the Mekong River from Phenom Penh in Cambodia to its junction with the Mekong and Hau Giang rivers near Cho Moi in South Vietnam's Delta. The Bassac was used as a major infiltration route by the NVA/VC, and was known as "Sampan Alley," "Sampan Road," and "Sampan Valley" by troops that tried to close the route down.

Bassac RPG *see* **Game Warden River Groups**

Bastard Unit (Composite Unit) A unit consisting of smaller units of different purpose, mixed together to perform a variety of assignments. Officially known as a "composite unit," but more appropriately known as a "bastard unit." Composite groups would be assembled to perform specific details or special operations. When the mission was completed the units were returned to their parent organization. A "bastard unit" could also refer to a unit of uncertain purpose or whose parent unit was not immediately known. During the heat of battle, in which many units were involved, a unit could get separated from its parent unit and temporarily be assigned to operate under a different higher headquarters.

Bastogne *see* **Operation Bastogne, FSB Bastogne**

Bastogne Bulldogs *see* **327th Infantry (Airborne) Regiment**

Bata Boots (Jungle Tennis Shoes) High top, olive drab tennis shoe worn by CIDG troops. Most ARVN troops wore black combat boots, but some did wear the tennis shoe or open sandals. The Bata Boots were similar to the jungle shoes worn by the NVA. Bata Boots were manufactured in Vietnam. *See also* **NVA Boots.**

Batangan Peninsula Peninsula centered 28kms southeast of Chu Lai along the coast of Quang Ngai Province, I Corps. The area was a longtime Viet Cong base area from which the VC were voluntarily supported by the farmers and the peasants in the region. The Batangan Peninsula and the Phuoc Thuan Peninsula were host to several

U.S. ground operations aimed at decreasing VC influence in the area. Villages in the area were very hostile to U.S. troops and several "incidents" took place between uncooperative villagers and U.S. troops sweeping for the Viet Cong. *See also* **Operation Piranha, My Lai, Song Tra.**

Batcats *see* **Electronic Intelligence Aircraft**

Batship (RIIS, Remote Image Intensifier System) Early experimental image intensifier system used for target acquisition. The RIIS system was mounted aboard Huey gunships. The system consisted of a nose mounted camera that electronically enhanced ambient moonlight and displayed the picture on a CRT monitor in the aircraft. The Hueys were nicknamed "Batships." The system proved ineffective and further testing of the system under combat conditions was halted. *See also* **INFANT, FLIR.**

Battalion (Bn) Basic U.S. Army maneuver and combat element, usually commanded by a lieutenant colonel. Battalion sizes varied, but generally consisted of two or more companies, with a projected field strength of up to 920 men. During Vietnam U.S. Infantry Battalions had a strength of approximately 800 men, on paper, but actually fielded closer to 400–500 men in four companies. A field artillery battalion consisted of 18 guns in three batteries. ARVN unit organization was patterned after U.S. units with actual field troop levels closer to the projected field strength. Battalions were combined to form regiments and brigades. *See also* **Battalion, NVA/VC; Regiment.**

Battalion Aid Station (BAS, Regimental Aid Station, Brigade Aid Station) Small medical aid station located in the field at the battalion level. The BAS provided general first aid for the unit, sick call and initial treatment for casualties at the battalion headquarters. In Vietnam helicopters allowed casualties to bypass BAS and go directly to hospital facilities, C & C company for the Marines and evacuation hospitals for the Army. BAS also provided limited care to the local civilian population. In the Marines a similar sized aid station was located at the regiment level. In the Army an aid station was also located at brigade. For the MRF the BAS was located aboard ATC-Hs, which could use their deck pads for medevac. *See also* C & C Company, Dispensary.

Battalion Days in the Field Report (BDF Report) Army administrative report tracking the number of days a battalion spent on field operations. The report was used to monitor the battalion's activity and efficiency.

Battalion Landing Team *see* **Regimental Landing Team**

Battalion Reconnaissance Element *see* **Hawks**

Battalion RIF Reconnaissance in force operations were carried out by units varying in size from platoon to division. The Battalion RIF entailed Bn HQ establishing a fire base equipped with artillery support. The battalion's companies would patrol out from the base, within range of the arty guns. When enemy contact was made the arty and air support were called in to pound the target. The Bn commander typically climbed in his C & C and directed the infantry follow-up from the air. He was sometimes known in the field as a "Flying-Squad-Leader." *See also* **Search and Destroy, Reconnaissance in Force, Flying-Squad-Leader.**

Battalion, NVA/VC A typical main force Viet Cong battalion, at full strength, consisted of about 700 men organized into three infantry companies and a support element armed with light mortars, heavy machine guns and recoilless rifles. The NVA/VC battalion strengths were estimated at 300–700 men. The NVA/VC operated organic (belonging to a specific regiment or division) as well as independent battalions throughout South Vietnam. *See also* **Battalion, Organic.**

Battery Basic artillery unit. U.S. artillery batteries in Vietnam were usually commanded by a captain and fielded 70–100 men. A battery generally consisted of six artillery tubes (howitzers) or guns. Other types of batteries were also available including searchlight, machine gun, countermortar and targeting batteries. Battery designations applied to towed and self-propelled artillery units and not to the mortars (81mm and 4.2 inch) operated at the company level of an infantry unit. A 105/155mm battery in Vietnam consisted of about 100 men, six guns

(in three platoons/six sections), and headquarters, communications, ammunition and vehicle transport sections.

Battery C/4th/77th (ARA) 101st ABN *see* **Death on Call**

Battery Chief *see* **Exec Post**

Battery Registration (Gun Registration, Registration Fire) Firing artillery at predetermined points to establish the necessary corrections to be made to the weapon to achieve accurate fire. Guns were registered everytime they were relocated. The procedure involved firing at a known map coordinate and having a spotter adjust the fire to impact the spot. The range and deflection settings required to hit the registration target could then be calculated and used later for accurate firing on any target within range of the battery. Registration fire was one of the first tasks of the gun crew once the weapon was set up and ready to fire.

Battle *see* **Campaign**

Battle Fatigue *see* **Combat Fatigue**

Battle for Hue During the NVA/VC Tet '68 Offensive three NVA regiments and numerous VC units attacked and held parts of Hue. The 6th NVA Regiment and several VC units made their final stand in the walled portion of the city called the Citadel. It required house to house fighting along with artillery and airstrikes to finally clear the enemy out of Hue. In the process over 65 percent of the structures within the city were destroyed, over 3,000–5,000 civilians died and over 500 American and ARVN soldiers were killed. There were 3,000–8,000 estimated NVA/VC losses. The NVA/VC held the Citadel for 24 days before they were eliminated. *See also* **Citadel, Hue.**

Battle Neurosis *see* **Combat Fatigue**

Battle of An Loc *see* **An Loc**

Battle of Ap Bac (Ap Bac) In January '63 elements of the ARVN 7th Division attacked VC units near the village of Ap Bac, less than 20kms south of Saigon in the Delta. ARVN APCs swept in while infantry forces were air assaulted into the area making contact with a reinforced VC battalion. The 2,000+ ARVN troops were pinned down and suffered heavy casualties before the 400 VC holding Ap Bac withdrew from the area. Thirteen Army helicopters were destroyed or damaged and three American advisors were killed on the ground. The Battle of Ap Bac in '63 was one of the most public and humiliating defeats for the ARVNs and the U.S. program that was trying to form them into an effective force. *See also* **Dong Xoai, Ba Gia, Binh Gia, Vung Ro Incident.**

Battle of Ba Gia *see* **Ba Gia**

Battle of Ban Me Thuot *see* **Ban Me Thuot**

Battle of Binh Gia (Binh Gia) In December '64 elements of the 9th VC Division attacked the village of Binh Gia in Phuoc Tuy Province, III Corps. The village was located 35kms northeast of Vung Tau and 60kms east of Saigon. During the course of the battle the 33d ARVN Ranger and 4th SVN Marine battalions were destroyed. ARVN reinforcements eventually caused the VC to withdraw. The VC later claimed that the guerrilla phase of their war on the GVN was over and they were now ready for all-out operations against ARVN and U.S. forces. The VC division had been newly formed from the 272d and 273d VC regiments and was commanded by an NVA general from the north. *See also* **Battle of Ap Bac.**

Battle of Dak To November '67 battle between elements of the U.S. 173d Airborne/1st Cav, the 4th Inf Div and NVA regulars in the Central Highlands around the Special Forces camp at Dak To. Dak To, located just 20kms from the Laos/Cambodian border, was the site of heavy fighting between American and NVA units. American casualties (347 dead) were very high compared to the confirmed enemy casualty figures (1,200+ dead). Most of the U.S. casualties occurred during the capture of Hill 875. Elements of the 174th NVA Regiment held the hill until the end of November when elements of the U.S. 503d and 12th Infantry took the hill. *See also* **Operation Mac Arthur, Hill 875, Dak To.**

Battle of Dong Xoai *see* **Dong Xoai**

Battle of Hamburger Hill *see* **Hamburger Hill**

Battle of Ia Drang (Ia Drang) October '65, first full-scale NVA offensive in SVN. The 32d, 33d and 66th NVA regiments attacked the Plei Me Special Forces Camp in a drive to the east to cut SVN in two. The Ia Drang Valley, located southwest of Pleiku, was the first major combat assault by the 1st Air Cav, with elements of the 1st Brigade engaging the three NVA regiments. After a month of search and destroy, units of the 5th, 7th and 9th Cavalry had inflicted heavy casualties on the NVA units causing them to withdraw to sanctuaries across the nearby Cambodian border to regroup and refit. The kill ratio for 1st Cav troops was almost 6:1 (enemy KIA to U.S. KIA). *See also* **Ia Drang Valley, Task Force Ingram, Operation Silver Bayonet, Chu Pong Massif, Turkey Farm.**

Battle of Khe Sanh *see* **Siege of Khe Sanh**

Battle of Loc Ninh In October '67 elements of the 9th Viet Cong Division attacked the U.S. Special Forces Camp at Loc Ninh, 115kms north of Saigon and less than 15kms from the Cambodian border. Six U.S. infantry and artillery battalions from the U.S. 1st Inf. Div. and ARVN units were moved into the area to reinforce the camp. The VC were thrown back and forced to retreat to their sanctuaries across the Cambodian border. *See also* **Loc Ninh.**

Battle of Long Tan *see* **Long Tan**

Battle of Tam Quan (Tam Quan) In December '67 recon elements of the 1st Bde, 1st Cav made contact with NVA/VC units near the town of Tam Quan, 92kms north of Qui Nhon, on the coast in Binh Dinh Province, II Corps. The 1st Cavalry Division was operating in the area as a part of Operation Pershing. Army and ARVN units poured into the area inflicting heavy casualties on the enemy force. As a result of Operation Pershing enemy activity in the area was greatly reduced and Binh Dinh Province was one of the quietest provinces during the communist '68 Tet Offensive. *See also* **Operation Pershing.**

Battle of Tan Hiep *see* **Tan Hiep**

Battle of Vinh Thanh *see* **Operation Crazy Horse**

Battle-Sight Zeroing Technique of adjusting a weapon's sight for accuracy at a set distance. Done on all direct fire weapons, i.e., rifles, machine guns and cannons.

Battlefield Religion The revelation that some GIs had that during combat they would not be able to kill as required because of a sudden resurrection of moral conviction against taking a human life. They often brought their moral dilemma to the unit chaplain in hopes that he could pull them out of combat or perhaps get them C.O. status. Many of these GIs had not followed religion regularly in the States, but turned to it in the Nam, hoping that it might somehow help them. Most chaplains were sympathetic, but rarely interfered. *See also* **Foxhole Convert.**

Bay Bang Vien Dan (Cartridge Trap) VC booby trap using an unfired cartridge. A small hole was dug in the ground six–ten inches deep and large enough to accommodate a booted foot. A short nail or pin was driven through a small board and a hollow bamboo tube was centered over the pin and attached to the board. The board was placed in the hole and an unused cartridge placed in the hollow tube, resting on the nail. The hole was then camouflaged. When someone stepped through the hidden hole they forced the cartridge down against the nail, firing the bullet through the victim's foot. Various size rifle and machine gun rounds were used. *See also* **Booby Trap.**

Bay Ten Sat (Steel Arrow Trap) VC booby trap. The trap consisted of a steel arrow mounted on a board and powered by a rubber band made from a tire inner tube. The trap was buried at an angle just below ground and camouflaged. When the trip wire was pulled the arrow was released and shot up out of the ground, spearing anyone in its flight path. *See also* **Booby Trap.**

Bayonet *see* **M-1905 Bayonet, K-Bar**

Bazooka *see* **M-20 Rocket Launcher**

BB-62 *see* **USS New Jersey**

BC *see* **Body Count**

BCD *see* **Bad Conduct Discharge**

BCT *see* **Basic Combat Training**

BDA *see* **Bomb Damage Assessment**

Bde *see* **Brigade**

BDF Report *see* **Battalion Days in the Field Report**

BDQs *see* **Biet-Dong-Quan**

Beach Bums *see* **Ballad of the Yellow Beret**

Beachmaster U.S. Navy personnel that directed communication, traffic and salvage operations during amphibious landings.

Beacon Drops *see* **RABFAC**

Beagle *see* **IL-28**

Beanie Weenies *see* **Beanies-and-Weenies**

Beanies *see* **Baseball Cap**

Beanies-and-Weenies (Beans and Franks, Beanie Weenies) One of the popular C-Ration delights. The weenies were tasty even if the lardy beans were too stiff to eat.

Beans and Franks *see* **Beanies-and-Weenies**

Beans-and-Motherfuckers (Ham and Lima Beans, Ham-and-Mothers) One of the less appetizing C-Ration entrées. The ham was tough and the beans had the consistency of lard. Traditionally one of the meals you tried to leave behind in the C-Ration case. Rated "Numba 10,000" on the GI menu, officially, ham and lima beans, but more popularly known as "ham-and-mothers" or "beans-and-motherfuckers." *See also* **C-Rations.**

Bear Cat (Long Thanh) Name of a division size base camp located at Long Thanh, 28kms east of Saigon and 55kms north of Vung Tau, Bien Hoa Province, III Corps. From '66–'71 Bear Cat served as the base camp for units of the U.S. 9th Infantry Division, Queen's Cobras and the Royal Thai Army Force.

Bear Trap Viet Cong booby trap that was made of two boards, each about 18 inches square, with wooden or steel stakes attached to the board. The boards were placed side by side with the stakes pointed up in a shallow hole. The boards pivoted independently on bamboo rods and the trap was covered and camouflaged. When a soldier stepped into the hole his foot plunged down between the two boards which pivoted the stakes into his leg above the tops of his boots. The stakes were typically covered with human waste or a poison called "Elephant's Trunk" to increase the chance of infection. *See also* **Booby Trap, Punji Stakes.**

Bearcat *see* **F-8F**

Beast *see* **B-52, Caucasian**

Beast Barracks   Nickname for the facility used to indoctrinate cadets on the finer points of West Point etiquette. New cadets attending West Point Military Academy were put through a quick course on the way things were done at "The Point." New cadets were referred to as "beasts."

Beat-Feet   *see*   **Book, Sky**

Beat-Off   *see*   **Masturbate**

Beatnik   Beatniks entered upon the American scene in the early fifties. As a group, beatniks tended to shun traditional American values through their distinctive art, poetry and music. Many of them were intellectuals, artists or social dropouts. They lived and moved in a world apart from the rest of society and were the first socially recognized group to flaunt their use of illicit drugs.

Beau Charger   *see*   **Operation Beau Charger**

Beaucoup (Boo Coo, Boo Koo)   Much or many. Used by the GIs and the Vietnamese to communicate quantity. Derived from the French and universally known.

Beautiful   *see*   **Dep**

Beautiful Spring   *see*   **Madame Nhu**

Beaver   *see*   **U-6**

Bedbug People Detector   *see*   **People Detector**

Bedcheck   Nighttime check by an NCOIC to verify that the troops under his charge were in their authorized area, i.e., not missing from the company area. Bedchecks were performed by some U.S. units in Vietnam at the larger bases and in the cities. The purpose of the checks in Vietnam was to verify the soldiers were not living off the base, shacked-up someplace in Saigon, Da Nang or any of the larger cities. It was against Army regulations for enlisted men to live off the base without authorization. Such authorization was seldom granted in Vietnam because of the hostile situation. The regulation was not enforced by all units in Vietnam, and many soldiers in rear areas lived off the base with their Vietnamese girlfriends, wives, and even a few "boyfriends." *See also* **Shack Up.**

Beech Craft Model 18   *see*   **Volpar**

Beef and Potatoes   *see*   **Beef and Rocks**

Beef and Rocks (Beef and Potatoes)   One of the main C-ration entrées available was a 5.5 ounce can of sliced beef and potatoes. It was more appropriately described as "beef and rocks," due in part, to the potatoes' texture, weight and less than appealing taste. *See also* **C-Rations.**

Beehive Round   *see*   **M-546, Flechette, Shotgun Flechette**

Beep Codes, Sensors   *see*   **Portable Seismic Intrusion Device**

Beeper   An emergency signal transmitted from an air crewman's survival radio when he bailed out of his plane. The audible radio frequency was used by rescue aircraft to pinpoint his location. The radio was attached to the parachute and was automatically turned on when the parachute was deployed. *See also* **Survival Radios.**

Beer and Soda Ration (B & S Ration)   Army and Marine units operating in the field, without access to a PX or EM Club, were granted a ration of beer and or soda for each soldier in the unit. The beer and soda were provided by the Army/Marines. In some units the ration was based on the number of days a man spent in the field. Accordingly, he received one can of beer or one can of soda (or two of each). Some commands allowed a can of each, and for some other units the ration was two cans of beer, with a load of soda being thrown in unrationed. Other commands limited the ration to two cans of beer a month. The field troops usually received their B & S ration on stand-down when they were periodically rotated off the line.

Beer Can Grenade (Coke Bomb)   Viet Cong homemade hand grenade consisting of a small can packed with explosive, placed inside a beer can (or softdrink can). The space between the two cans was filled with gravel, nails, metal or broken glass. The fuses used on the grenade were from dud–American grenades or nonfunctioning old French hand grenades. The crude grenades were more powerful than the standard U.S. hand grenade, but the dud rate was much higher with the VC grenade. The cans used for the grenade were often taken from American trash dumps, collected by pro-Viet Cong peasants that rummaged through American landfills. Trash carelessly discarded by GIs was often turned against them by the VC. *See also* **C-Rat Grenade, Burn-Bash-Bury.**

Beer Can Insignia (Distinctive Insignia, DI)   Distinctive insignia (DI), identifying the various military organizations and functions. Most of the specialized insignia worn in Vietnam were not authorized or official, but were generally allowed. The insignia consisted of locally made embroidered patches, flashes, tabs and badges. Many of the larger ARVN and Army units designed their own insignia and had them locally produced. The metal insignia were hand stamped from brass (usually beer cans) and hand painted and were referred to as "beer can insignia." The unauthorized insignia were tolerated by many American units in Vietnam, but were not allowed to be worn in the States. *See also* **Shoulder Tabs.**

Beer, Vietnamese *see* **Vietnamese Beer**

Beetle Stompers *see* **Infantry Soldier, The**

Believer (Dead Enemy Soldier)   GI slang for a dead enemy soldier; a "believer" in the power of the unit that killed him.

Bell Jet Ranger *see* **OH-58**

Below the Knee Amputation *see* **BK Amputation**

Belt, The   Viet Cong name for a series of tunnels, interconnected bunkers and fighting positions strategically located around the U.S. 25th Infantry Division base camp located at Cu Chi, in III Corps. From these positions the Viet Cong were able to ambush and harass American units in the area. The "belt" was connected to the massive tunnel system beneath the Cu Chi district area.

Belts, Machine Gun (Pocket Belt, Disintegrating Belt)   Modern belt-fed machine guns primarily used either a pocket belt or a disintegrating belt. The pocket belt was made of fabric and the individual rounds fit in small pockets in the belt. The disintegrating belt featured individual rounds interconnected by means of metal links that were slipped onto the cartridges.

BEM *see* **Business Executives Move for Peace**

Ben Hai River (Song Ben Hai)   Geographical boundary between North and South Vietnam. The '54 Geneva Accords called for the temporary partitioning of Vietnam at the 17th Parallel. The Ben Hai River was used as the physical line of demarcation to indicate the demilitarized buffer zone between North and South Vietnam. *See also* **Demilitarized Zone.**

Ben Hai River *see* **Demilitarized Zone**

Ben Nghe River (Saigon River, Song Sai Gon River)   Large river that runs through Saigon and empties into the South China Sea between Go Cong and Vung Tau. The river allowed Saigon to become a major port city through the 72km river passage to the open sea. The river had its origins in the mountainous area northeast of Tay Ninh, III Corps. The Song Sai Gon merged with the Song Dong Nai just east of Saigon, turning into the Song Nha Be. *See also* **Saigon, Song Dong Nai.**

Ben Suc   A fortified VC village in the Iron Triangle, 25kms from Saigon. The village remained under VC control until '67 when units of the 26th Infantry/1st Infantry Division, under command of Lt. Col. Alexander Haig, removed the villagers and their possessions, relocating them to the GVN resettlement camp at Phy Loi. The area in and around the village was honeycombed with VC tunnels. Ben Suc was leveled and some of the tunnels destroyed. The U.S. operation to clear and destroy Ben Suc and its tunnel complex was part of Operation Cedar Falls. Shortly after U.S. troops left the area the VC returned and began resurrection of their tunnel system. *See also* **Operation Cedar Falls, Colonel Alexander Haig.**

Ben Tre (We Had to Destroy the Town..., Truc Giang)   Provincial capital of Kien Hoa, destroyed by U.S. air strikes during the Tet '68 Offensive. The town had been occupied by well entrenched enemy forces of the 516th and 550th VC battalions. Massive air and artillery strikes were required to dislodge the enemy. It's rumored that this is where the phrase "we had to destroy the town in order to save it" was coined by a U.S. Army officer involved in the clearing of Ben Tre. This is comparable to General Custer's statement, before the Little Big Horn, about the Indians; "we'll bring peace to this land if we have to kill them all." Ben Tre was also known as Truc Giang and was located 11kms south of My Tho and 43kms east of Vinh Long, IV Corps.

Ben-Gay *see* **Banh Giay**

Bends-and-Motherfuckers (Squat-Thrust Exercises) Slang for military training squat-thrust exercises. From a standing position you squat to the ground, placing your hands on the ground in front of you, between your legs. You then support your weight on your hands and thrust your legs out behind you as in the push-up position. The feet and legs are then brought back up to the squat position, and the move is ended by returning to the standing position, at attention. The exercise was done in four counts.

Benoctol *see* **BTs**

Berchtesgaden *see* **FSB Berchtesgaden**

Beret Flash (Flash) Shield shaped unit insignia worn on the military beret. The flash was similar in design to the pocket emblem and shoulder patch normally worn on the uniform. The U.S. Special Forces was the first American Army unit authorized to wear the beret as part of their uniform. The flash was worn on the side of the beret and identified the wearer's unit. There was a different flash design for each of the Special Forces Groups (1st, 5th, and 7th). Berets became fashionable for other units in Vietnam; they also had distinctive unit flashes.

Berm (Berm Line) A raised mound of dirt or an embankment erected around a fortification to increase its defensive capabilities. Sometimes rice paddy dikes were referred to as berms. The Viet Cong frequently constructed bunkers in the berm lines around villages. From the berms they could ambush troops crossing the open area facing the berm line. *See also* **Defilade.**

Berrigan, Father Daniel *see* **Catonsville Nine**

Berrigan, Father Philip (Father Philip Berrigan) Catholic priest and antiwar activist. In October '67 Father Berrigan, along with a group of antidraft protesters entered the Selective Service Board at the Baltimore Customs House and poured duck blood on draft classification files. Berrigan was tried and convicted, becoming the first Catholic priest in the U.S. to be convicted of a political crime. While awaiting sentencing in May '68, Berrigan, his priest brother Daniel, and seven other protesters entered the Catonsville SSB and burned several hundred draft classification records. He was eventually sentenced to six years in prison. In '73 he performed his own marriage to Catholic nun Elizabeth McAlister, and in '74 they had a baby girl. *See also* **Catonsville Nine.**

Bertrand Russell War Crimes Tribunal (War Crimes Tribunal [WCT]) Stockholm based organization founded under the name of British pacifist Bertrand Russell. The WCT collected evidence based on accusations by the North Vietnamese that the U.S. bombing of NVN was criminal and genocidal. Various international teams visited NVN during the war collecting evidence for the tribunal. Visits to NVN were strictly controlled and orchestrated by the North Vietnamese and included bringing in bomb victims from outside areas to display to visiting dignitaries. At various times American antiwar activists accompanied the teams to NVN, reporting back to their factions in the U.S.

The Best Go West Phrase referencing the fact that during the U.S. advisory effort between '61–'65 American troops that served in Vietnam were for the most part volunteers and professional soldiers. Between '65 and '67 most American combat troops were regular Army troops deploying to Vietnam as whole units. After '67 large numbers of draftees were used to fill the ranks of the Army in Vietnam. For Army officers prior to '65, Vietnam was the "place to go to enhance your career," and after '65 it became a place where they "had to go for their career." *See also* **Ticket-Punching.**

Betel Nut (Black Gums) Tree-grown Vietnamese nut chewed by the locals (men and women), that possessed opium-like qualities and stained the teeth and gums dark reddish black. The nut and leaves of the Indian palm tree were mixed with lime and tobacco. The mixture, simply known as betel nut, when chewed numbed the tongue and gums. Like chewing tobacco, the juice was not swallowed and the chewer was required to spit often.

BGM-71 *see* **M-151 TOW**

Bicycle *see* **Xe Tho, Bicycle Bomb, Pedicab**

Bicycle Bomb (Min Xe Dap) Viet Cong booby trap device used for terrorist attacks. The bomb was a bicycle with explosives stuffed down the tubing supports and under the seat. A detonator was hidden inside the support tubing and connected to a watch timer and battery hidden in the bike's headlight. The bike could be ridden to the location that was to be bombed and left. The booby-trapped bike looked like any other bike that might be on the street. Several pounds of TNT could be packed into the bicycle's tubing. *See also* **Booby Trap.**

Bien Hoa Capital of Bien Hoa Province, III Corps. Headquarters for the ARVN III Corps Command, Headquarters for the U.S. II Field Force and a major U.S. air base and logistics center. Bien Hoa was 20kms from Saigon, the national capital. Bien Hoa was one of the three largest U.S. Air Force bases in Vietnam.

Bien Hoa Commute (General's Commute) Senior U.S. officers of the II Field Force commuted from the II FFV headquarters at Long Binh to their quarters, located in old French villas in the nearby city of Bien Hoa. The generals commuted by helicopter to the war in the morning and returned to their villas at the end of the day. The headquarters' complex was located on the outskirts of Bien Hoa in a suburb of Long Binh. The practice was halted in early '67 by the new II FFV commander, General Bruce Palmer, Jr. The practice had begun with the buildup of U.S. combat forces and the establishment of the Field Force headquarters in '66. *See also* **II FFV.**

Bien Hoa Heliport *see* **Spartan**

Biet-Dong-Quan (ARVN Rangers, BDQs, South Vietnamese Rangers, Vietnamese Rangers) South Vietnamese Rangers (Special Mobile Corps) trained by U.S. Rangers and Special Forces. The ARVN Rangers were some of the best troops in the South Vietnamese Army. They were officially referred to as the Luc Luong Dac Biet, or Vietnamese Special Forces. The ARVN Ranger units were often used to fortify weakened regular ARVN units in critical battles, deploying company or battalion size units. The ARVN Rangers were primarily used as a quick reaction force and rarely functioned in the recon mode. U.S. Rangers also served directly with the BDQ as field advisors. There were three ARVN Ranger training centers in Vietnam: Trung Lap, Tet Son and Duc My. *See also* **Luc Luong Dac Biet.**

Big Belly B-52s (B-52D) Nickname for B-52Ds that operated with a structural modification to the aircraft that enabled them to carry 60,000 pounds of bombs in their internal bomb bay and wing mounted pylons. Unmodified B-52s normally carried a maximum bomb load of 27,000 pounds. A flight of six B-52Ds could saturate a target area 1km wide and 2kms long from a typical altitude of 30–35,000 feet. The modified B-52s were nicknamed "big bellies." Bombing accuracy of the B-52 was enhanced by radar controlled systems (Combat Skyspot) which allowed the bombers to provide direct support to ground troops. *See also* **B-52, Combat Skyspot, Flying Artillery.**

Big Bird *see* **Freedom Bird**

Big Dead One *see* **1st Infantry Division**

Big E *see* **USS Enterprise**

Big Eagle *see* **Project Big Eagle**

Big Eye *see* **EC-121**

Big Gunny in the Sky *see* **God**

Big H, The *see* **Heroin**

Big Iron Birds *see* **Freedom Bird**

Big Look *see* **EC-121**

Big Minh *see* **Duong Van Minh**

Big Mothers *see* **SH-3**

Big O's (Marijuana Cigarettes) *see* **OJs (Marijuana Cigarettes)**

Big Patch *see* **Operation Big Patch**

Big Px, The *see* **U.S.A.**

Big Red One *see* **1st Infantry Division**

Big Red One Patch The patch of the 1st Infantry Division was one of the simplest of all American units that served in Vietnam. The five sided patch was brown or dark green, straight across the top and pointed at the bottom. In the center of the patch was a large red number "one." *See also* **1st Infantry Division.**

Big Shotgun *see* **M-40A1 RCL**

Big Stuff (Heavy Stuff) GI slang for artillery fire or air strikes, especially heavy artillery such as eight-inch, 175mm Army guns, the 16-inch guns of the USS *New Jersey* and B-52 Arc Light strikes. *See also* USS New Jersey, Arc Light.

Big Ugly Fat Fellows *see* B-52

Big Ugly Fat Fuckers *see* B-52

Big Wheels *see* Command

Big-Mothers *see* SH-3, CH-3

Bill 392 (Anti-Draft-Card-Burning-Bill) On August 30, 1965, Bill 392 was signed into law by President Johnson. The new law made it a crime to knowingly destroy, mutilate or deface a draft card. If convicted, the law provided for a $10,000 fine and five years in prison. The law was in response to the growing disrespect for the Selective Service System by some factions of the antiwar movement and their disregard for those serving in the armed forces. *See also* Burn Yourselves, Not Your Draft Cards; Catholic Workers Movement.

Billings *see* Operation Billings

Bin Thuy *see* Binh Thuy

Bin Tin, Colonel *see* Colonel Bin Tin

Bingo Point in a flight at which a pilot needed to return to base because of low fuel. When he reached his Bingo point he had just enough fuel (including his reserve) remaining to get him back to base. Pilots on roving patrol, or flying cover, had to constantly monitor their fuel situation. In the heat of battle and during dogfights with enemy MiGs, fuel considerations were critical.

Binh Gia *see* Battle of Binh Gia

Binh Nhat *see* E-2

Binh Tay *see* Operation Binh Tay

Binh Thuy (Bin Thuy, Binh Tuy) Town along the Bassac (Mekong) River 120kms southwest of Saigon and 10kms northwest of Can Tho in Phong Dinh Province, IV Corps. Binh Thuy was the site of the only major U.S. Air Force base in IV Corps. The Air Force base at Binh Thuy was turned over to VNAF in '70.

Binh Tram (Road Repair Crews) NVA units that worked along the Ho Chi Minh Trail, primarily doing maintenance to keep the trail open. Over the years crews consisted of tens of thousands of soldiers and civilians that maintained the roads and trail networks, and the various logistics facilities located along the system. The North Vietnamese claimed that "loyal" volunteers made up the Binh Tram, but many of those who worked on the trail system were actually conscripts. The conscripts were from Lao, Cambodian and Montagnard villages in the vicinity of the trail.

Binh Tuy *see* Binh Thuy

Binh Xuyen An organized Vietnamese gang that operated out of Cholon in Saigon and the Rung Sat and maintained its own small army. The gang consisted of a small group of followers that controlled prostitution, drug and gambling interests in the Saigon-Cholon area. The group's leader, Le Van Vien, controlled the police and security forces in the area until '55. The Binh Xuyen fought the French until the Viet Minh pushed the Binh Xuyen out of the Rung Sat in '47. They then joined the French to fight the communists. When the French left Vietnam the Binh Xuyen rebelled against the Diem regime and were destroyed by the South Vietnamese military in '55. Those members that survived joined the Viet Cong. *See also* Hall of Mirrors.

Binh-Tri-Thien (Ho Chi Minh Sandals, Ho Chi Minh Slippers, Gook Shoes) Vietnamese for the black rubber soled sandals worn by the VC and the NVA. The sandal's soles were made from discarded tire treads and the straps were made from strips of inner tubes. *See also* NVA Boots.

Bino(s) *see* Binoculars

Binoculars (Bino[s]) Field binoculars.

Bipod An assembly consisting of two legs that attached to the front end of a weapon. The legs were used to support the weapon during firing. M-60 machine guns carried in the field had folding bipods attached to the weapon. The M-14 rifle and BAR also had bipods for support. Several of the automatic weapons used by the NVA/VC also featured bipods. *See also* Light Machine Guns.

Bird *see* LZ Bird, Penis, Helicopter

Bird Air Small charter air service that operated throughout South Vietnam. During the collapse of SVN (during the NVA Final Offensive in March '75), Bird Air was under charter to the U.S. to evacuate Vietnamese refugees from various cities throughout South Vietnam.

Bird Colonel *see* **Colonel**

Bird Dog *see* **L-19**

Bird Watcher Missions Missions conducted by elements of the U.S. Marines' Force Recon. The missions involved the recon units operating deep in enemy territory in Laos and NVN, collecting intelligence and targeting information. *See also* **Force Recon.**

Bird, The (The Finger) Universal derogatory gesture made by forming a loose fist with the hand and then extending the middle finger upward. In general it meant "fuck-you" or "get screwed." American GIs used it on each other and the Vietnamese, and they in turn, especially the children, used it on the GIs. Sometimes called "flipping" someone the bird or the finger.

Bird-Dogging *see* **Column Cover**

Birds (Aircraft, Ships) Generic military slang for any type of aircraft. Helicopter crews sometimes referred to their aircraft as "ships."

Birmingham *see* **FSB Birmingham**

Biscuits *see* **John Wayne Crackers**

Bitch Box (Radio Amplifier) Radio speaker assembly used to amplify incoming radio traffic. "Bitch Boxes" were frequently used at the company level and above so the commander could more easily monitor the activity of his platoons in the field, leaving his hands free to use his map or another radio handset to call in support.

BK Amputation (Below the Knee Amputation) Amputation of the leg, below the knee.

Black American Soldier (Black GI) During the early days of the war the black soldier shouldered an unusually heavy share of the burden. Prior to '66 blacks represented 8 percent of the military, 10 percent of the force in Vietnam, and nearly 25 percent of the combat troops on line. Blacks represented 11 percent of the American population yet they accounted for nearly 24 percent of the military's KIAs. After '66 the

military made efforts to reduce the number of black troops in front line units to more accurately reflect blacks' proportion of the American population. Between '66–'70 blacks represented over 12 percent of the KIAs in Vietnam, and nearly 16 percent of the combat troops in-country. By the end of '71 blacks made up 12.3 percent of the EMs in Vietnam, and 2.7 percent of the officers. The Army was the most liberal of the military departments, with blacks representing 14.3 percent of the enlisted ranks, and 3.6 percent of the officers. The Navy was the most racially conservative, with blacks representing 5 percent of the enlisted men, and fewer than 1 percent of the Navy's officers. *See also* **Project 100,000.**

Black Beret In February '69 U.S. Rangers of the newly organized 75th Rangers were authorized to wear Black Berets. Black berets were also worn by some U.S. advisors assigned to Vietnamese units, reflecting the beret worn by their counterparts in the unit. The Vietnamese National Police, Armor Corps and MAT Teams wore the black beret as part of their uniform. The black beret was also worn by U.S. Navy SEALs and river patrol forces. *See also* **SEAL, TF 117, TF 116, Seawolves, Long-Range Reconnaissance Patrol.**

Black Bird *see* **SR-71**

Black Cats of the 282d Avn *see* **282d Aviation Company**

Black Crow Sensor System One of several electronic sensor systems used aboard Air Force surveillance aircraft. The Black Crow system was able to detect the static emissions from a truck engine from altitudes in excess of 7,000 feet. The system was mounted onboard AC-130 Spectre and AP-2H aircraft and used extensively over the Ho Chi Minh Trail from '68 to the end of U.S. involvement in the Vietnam War. *See also* **Electronic Sensors, TRIM Program.**

Black Ditch Monument *see* **Vietnam War Memorial**

Black Flights (Secret Evacuations, High-Risk Vietnamese) Secret evacuation of "high-risk" Vietnamese from South Vietnam during the country's collapse in '75. The CIA made arrangements to have former Vietnamese intelligence officers, GVN officials, military leaders and spies quietly flown out of Vietnam before the communist victory. During the course of the evacuation these individuals were referred to as "priority," "endangered," "sensitive," or "politically sensitive" Vietnamese. In most instances the families of such Vietnamese were also evacuated. *See also* **Final Evacuation of Saigon.**

Black Gash of Shame   *see*   **Vietnam War Memorial**

Black GI   *see*   **Black American Soldier**

Black Gums   *see*   **Betel Nut**

Black Handicap Message   Test message used to check the communications channels along the chain of command at major U.S. installations in Vietnam. The message consisted of a string of numbers. The message would be initiated at a defensive bunker on the base perimeter and called into successively higher levels of command, until it reached the top of the chain. The end message was compared to the initiated message for accuracy and the amount of time required for the message to be passed from bunker to the top of command. The exercises were carried out in Vietnam occasionally to test the chain of command at the larger bases, which seldom saw any serious action.

Black Hats (Pathfinders)   Special Army teams inserted into an LZ to manage the direction, clearing and air traffic control of a major size LZ. Using a combination of radios and navigational aids the teams directed air operations at the LZ. Pathfinders were primarily used for large operations when increased air traffic was expected at an LZ. This would include large helicopter assaults, captured enemy cache extractions or evacuations of large groups of civilians. Nicknamed "Black Hats" because the team members wore black baseball caps instead of the regulation OD green cap. The Black Hats performed a similar function as the Air Force's Combat Controllers. *See also* **Combat Controller.**

Black Hawk Missions   Quick reaction force which consisted of a Mobile Strike Force company commanded by a USSFs team. The "Black Hawk" mission consisted of an MSF company on-call to react to reconnaissance by recon units of the 7th Squadron/1st Air Cavalry Regiment. Elements of the 7th/1st Cavalry Division would conduct recon missions along the Cambodian border in the Plain of Reeds. When they located the enemy a Black Hawk mission would be initiated and an MSF company air assaulted into the area. Black Hawk operations were similar to "Eagle Flights." *See also* **Eagle Flights, Mobile Camp Operations.**

Black Knights   *see*   **5th Cavalry**

Black Leech   *see*   **Leeches**

Black Lions   *see*   **28th Infantry Regiment**

Black Magic   *see*   **M-16 Rifle**

Black Man   *see*   **Soul Brother**

Black Market (Le Loi Street, The Black) All manner of goods could be acquired through the black market. Military supplies, weapons, food and medicines, most of which were stolen or traded for, found their way to the market. In Saigon, Le Loi Street was the heart of the market. Americans traded items for money or for other items and the VC traded in the same markets. Since many corrupt GVN officials profited from the market activity, there never was any real effort by the GVN to close it down. On "the Black" in '69, a two dollar case of coke, bought in a U.S. PX, could be sold for five dollars.

Black Pajamas (Black PJs)   The primary uniform of the local VC consisted of a loose fitting black cotton shirt and black pants with a drawstring waistband. The "black pajamas," as they were called, were not limited to the Viet Cong. Many farmers and villagers also wore black "pj's," or a combination of colors. The black pajama was also worn by members of the GVN's Rural Development Cadre. The local populace tended to shy away from wearing the black pj's because of the increased possibility of being mistaken for a VC by FWF and American troops.

Black Panther Division (Royal Thai Army Volunteer Force, RTAVF, Royal Thai Expeditionary Division)   The Thailand Black Panther Division began deployment to South Vietnam in July '68, replacing the Queen's Cobra Regimental Combat Team. The division operated throughout Bien Hoa Province and was based at Bear Cat. In '70, the division was renamed the Royal Thai Army Volunteer

Force, and remained in Vietnam until March '73, when the last troops left. The division was at times referred to as the Royal Thai Expeditionary Division. *See also* **Thailand.**

Black Panthers Black militant group formed in '66. The primary founders were Huey P. Newton and Bobby Seale. The Panthers advocated black involvement in all aspects of American society, and urged the white power structure to work towards full employment and housing for blacks. The Panthers also urged blacks to take control of their own destiny by seizing control of the black community. The head of the FBI, J. Edgar Hoover, proclaimed the Panthers to be subversive and dangerous "cop killers," and proceeded to destroy them. Several Panthers were killed by police in one-sided gun battles. *See also* **SNCC, Black Power.**

Black Panthers (ARVN) *see* **Hac Bao**

Black PJs *see* **Black Pajamas**

Black Ponies *see* **Light Attack Squadron 4**

Black Power (Black Power Bracelet) During the black struggle for equality in America in the sixties, certain factions of the various civil rights movements came to believe the only way to change the current system in America was through the aggressive use of power by the people. For the black community this translated to "Black Power." Not only the power of the vote, but economic and educational power. For some militant black groups Black Power meant armed struggle and violence in order to win the rights they sought. The symbol used for Black Power was the raised "Clenched Fist." Blacks in the military, sympathetic to, or part of the Black Power Movement, began to wear "bracelets," woven from the bootlaces of their friends killed in combat. *See also* **Clenched Fist; Afro; Dap; Klan; Same Mud, Same Blood; Brown, H. Rap; SNCC.**

Black Power Bracelet *see* **Black Power**

Black Psyche CIA term for disruptive (and hopefully untraceable) rumors and propaganda spread throughout a population with the aim of causing fear, discontent, dissension and mistrust against the subject of the attack. CIA teams used Black

Psyche and sabotage to attempt to weaken the new communist government that took control of North Vietnam in '54. The teams printed up counterfeit money in an effort to destabilize NVN's monetary base and they also contaminated crops which were vital to the economy. The CIA's goal was to weaken the Ho Chi Minh government while at the same time trying to strengthen the SVN regime. *See also* **White Psyche; Lansdale, Edward.**

Black Rifle *see* **M-16 Rifle**

Black Scarves *see* **2d Infantry Regiment**

Black Spot (NC-123K) Code name for an Air Force program that modified two C-123s to be used against North Vietnamese traffic on the Ho Chi Minh Trail. The two C-123s were equipped with forward looking radar, low level television equipment and laser illumination/detection devices. The C-123s were also armed with CBU dispensers allowing them to "bomb" any targets that they found. The modified aircraft were designated the NC-123K and operated against the trail from November '68 to June '70. *See also* **Operation Commando Hunt.**

Black Syph *see* **Syphilis**

Black Virgin Mountain *see* **Nui Ba Dinh**

Black Woman *see* **Sister**

Black, The *see* **Black Market**

Blackbird *see* **LZ Blackbird**

Blackhorse Base Camp *see* **Xuan Loc**

Blackhorse Patch The unit patch of the 11th Armored Cavalry Regiment was nicknamed the "scared horse." The shield shaped patch was bordered in black, flat across the top and pointed at the bottom. The patch was diagonally split down the center with the upper portion in red and the lower portion in white. Centered in the patch was the silhouette of a large black horse, reared on its hind legs. *See also* **11th Armored Cavalry Regiment.**

Blackhorse Regiment *see* **11th Armored Cavalry Regiment**

Blackjack Operations (Operation Blackjack, MGF, Mobile Guerrilla Force, MGC) Series of operations conducted by

CIDG and USSF units operating as part of the MACV/SOG program, which included Projects Delta, Omega, Gamma and Sigma. The operations included crossing into Laos and Cambodia to harass and disrupt enemy activities in their base areas. The Blackjack forces were officially known as the Mobile Guerrilla Force and operated at the same level as the VC. The MGF was active from October '66 to July '67 after which they became part of the larger Mobile Strike Forces. An MGF typically consisted of a USSF A-Team, 150-man CIDG mobile guerrilla company (MGC) and a 30–34 man combat reconnaissance platoon (CRIP). *See also* **Projects: Delta, Omega, Gamma, Sigma.**

Blacklist   List kept by South Vietnamese intelligence of known and suspected Viet Cong. The list was maintained by the National Police and augmented by information from U.S. and South Vietnamese military intelligence sources. The Viet Cong had a "blacklist" of their own containing the names of GVN officials (administrators, police, teachers, etc.) and those that showed any favoritism or support for the GVN or worked for the Americans. Several thousand Vietnamese on the VC's blacklist were executed during the '68 Tet Offensive during the VC's attempt to eliminate the GVN support structure and "rally" the population to their side. The rally they sought never took place and large numbers of the VC died in the attempt.

Blackspot   *see*   **C-123K**

Blackwater Fever   *see*   **Malaria**

Bladder Bird (Cow, Flying Cow, Fuel Bladder)   Nickname for a C-123 or C-130 transport fitted with 4,500-gallon fuel bladders in the cargo bay for the air transport of various fuels. Bladders were available in various sizes, from 2,000–50,000 gallons, and were transported by truck and by sling beneath helicopters. The bladders were rubberized and collapsible. *See also* **Blivet.**

Blade Time (Helicopter Allocation) Routine helicopter use was allocated on a daily basis depending on the functionally available aircraft and previous commitments. The time allotted to units for routine resupply, command and control and noncombat related transport missions was referred to as "blade time" and did not apply to medevac or combat support operations.

Blanket Division   Nickname for the 1st Cavalry Division because of the large size of the unit's patch. The 1st Cav patch was the largest American unit patch of the Vietnam War. The gold colored patch was in the shape of a shield, edged in black. A wide black bar bisected the shield diagonally. On the upper portion of the bisected shield was the black silhouette of a horse's head. The bright yellow and black patch was not worn on field uniforms in Vietnam; instead a subdued version in black and green was available. *See also* **1st Cavalry Division.**

Blanket Party   Retaliatory "party" held in honor of an erring recruit. One of the Army and Marine training tactics was to punish an entire platoon or company for the mistakes of one man. If the same man continued to "screw up," the platoon continued to suffer for his mistakes. In an effort to bring the man in line, platoon members would hold a blanket party for the man after lights-out. The usual tactic was to creep up on the target and throw a blanket over him, pinning him to the bed, then the rest of the platoon would commence to "beat the hell" out of him. Fist or bars of soap wrapped in bath towels were the usual weapons. After such a party the man usually got the message and cleaned up his act. *See also* **GI Shower.**

Blast Out   *see*   **Operation Blast Out**

Blasting Caps (Caps, M-6)   Used with Det Cord to detonate C-4 explosives. The cap was crimped to the end of the det cord or fuse, and then inserted into the C-4. The M-6 was the blasting cap most often used with C-4 explosive and in the M-18 Claymore Mine. Blasting caps came in two varieties: electrical, and nonelectrical detonation. There was an art to crimping the ends of the blasting cap. A crimp in the wrong place, or with too much force would cause the cap to detonate in your hand. The blasting cap was powerful enough to take off several fingers when detonated. Some GIs used their teeth to crimp the caps. *See also* **M-18 Claymore Mine, Detonator Cord, Sympathetic Detonations.**

Blastout I   *see*   **Cam Ne**

Blinker (Quads, Quadriplegic)   Callous GI hospital slang for a quadriplegic. Quads were paralyzed from the neck down and the most movement they were capable of was to blink their eyes.

Blister (Bumps) Electronic, navigational or communications equipment partially mounted on the exterior of an aircraft were usually sealed in a "blister." The blisters provided aerodynamic cover for the equipment and were usually not part of the original design of the aircraft. Blisters were sometimes referred to as "bumps."

Blivet (Pod, Seal Bin, Lug-a-Lug) A 500-gallon rubberized bladder, sometimes called a "pod" or "seal bin," used to transport water and fuels to units in the field. The bladder could be slung under a resupply helicopter and moved wherever necessary. A three- and five-gallon man-carried version of the blivet, nicknamed a "lug-a-lug" was also used in the field to carry water; it was easier to manage than multiple canteens. *See also* **Bladder Bird.**

Blockade As early as '65 the U.S. Joint Chiefs of Staff proposed the blockade of North Vietnamese ports to cut off the war supplies received from Russia, China and Soviet-Bloc countries. The mining of North Vietnam's harbors did not happen until May '72. Once North Vietnam's three major and four minor ports were mined and blockaded by U.S. Navy ships the seaborne flow of supplies was quickly cut off. The NVN ports of Haiphong, Hon Gai, Cam Pha, Thanh Hoa, Vinh, Quang Khe and Dong Hoi were closed as part of Operation Linebacker. *See also* **Haiphong, Operation Linebacker, River Mines.**

Blocking Force *see* **Hammer-and-Anvil**

Blocs (Tank Treads) Individual tank tread sections, linked together to form the tank tracks.

Blood Bath *see* **Political Purification**

Blood Expander *see* **Serum Albumin**

Blood Money *see* **Solatium**

Blood Trail Trail of blood left by the wounded. After a firefight, ambush, airstrike or enemy contact a search was made of the contact area to count the enemy dead and retrieve their weapons and documents. During such searches blood trails were usually found indicating the enemy dragged off their dead and wounded. Some of the wounded were able to move away under their own power, leaving a trail of blood behind. Troops following up on these blood trails would run upon wounded enemy soldiers, or the trail would just disappear, or a dead body would be found, or the trail could end in an ambush for the troops tracking it. *See also* **Body Hooks.**

Blood Weapon (Captured Weapon) Field term for a weapon taken from a dead enemy soldier, especially if the soldier capturing the weapon was responsible for killing the enemy soldier in combat.

Blood Wings *see* **Jump Wings**

Blood(s) *see* **Soul Brother**

Bloody One *see* **1st Infantry Division**

Bloody-Assholes *see* **9th Infantry Division**

Blooker *see* **M-79**

Bloop Tube *see* **M-79 Grenade Launcher**

Blooper Gun *see* **M-79 Grenade Launcher**

Blossoming Lotus General Van Tien Dung's name for the NVA tactic of attacking a target. The tactic involved a large force quickly thrusting to the center of the objective; units then attacked out or "blossomed" outward to attack enemy units in all directions from the center of the objective. The tactic had the potential to take enemy units by surprise, since they normally expected the assault to come from outside their perimeter. The tactic could also prove disastrous for the NVA attackers if the defender was able to coordinate his supporting fires, concentrating them on the center of the NVA thrust.

Blouse (Unblouse) U.S. military terminology for having your uniform pants bottoms tucked into your boot tops. Unbloused pants were worn loose around the top of the boots; not tucked into the boot tops. Army troops were required to wear their fatigue pants bloused when worn with combat boots. Requirements varied in the combat zone, but bloused fatigues reduced the number of bugs and leeches that could enter a man's pants leg as he moved through the jungle and infested streams. The Australian and New Zealand troops referred to their uniform or fatigue shirts as "blouses."

Blow Away *see* **Kill**

Blowjob *see* **Fellatio**

Blowtorch *see* **Komer, Robert**

BLT *see* **Regimental Landing Team**

BLU-82/B *see* **Daisy Cutter (Instant LZ)**

Blue Beach *see* **Operation Tailwind**

Blue Chip *see* **Airborne Battlefield Command and Control Center**

Blue Dragons *see* **Republic of Korea Marine Corps**

Blue Feature Referred to rivers, streams, aqueducts, ponds, lakes, and canals, and in general any water feature as pictured on topographical military maps. Tactical radio conversations mentioned "blue features" by coordinates or reference without announcing over an unsecure net exactly what the feature was. The theory was that if the enemy was monitoring the radio traffic he would be unable to pinpoint the location or know the unit's intentions. The theory was good but the NVA/VC were experts at tracking and surveillance, and generally knew the locations of large U.S. units as they operated in the jungle.

Blue Hueys *see* **Seawolves**

Blue Light *see* **Operation Blue Light**

Blue Marlin *see* **Operation Blue Marlin**

Blue Max of the 20th ARA *see* **20th Artillery (Aerial Rocket)**

Blue Spaders *see* **26th Infantry Regiment**

Blue Stars *see* **48th Aviation Company**

Blue Team *see* **Aero Rifle Platoon**

Bluejackets *see* **Navy Sailors**

Bluelegs *see* **Infantry Soldier, The**

Blues *see* **Aero Rifle Platoon**

Bluper *see* **M-79 Grenade Launcher**

BM14/21 (140mm Rocket) Soviet made multiple rocket launchers. The BM14 was 140mm, 16-tube, fin and spin stabilized, with a 6km range. The BM21 was 122mm, 40-tube, fin stabilized, with a range of 11–20kms depending on rocket used. Both launchers were vehicle mounted. A single tube version of the BM21 was available to the NVA/VC for guerrilla use. It was lighter and could be broken down and man carried. *See also* **DKZ-B**.

Bn *see* **Battalion**

Bo Doi (Soldier) Vietnamese for "soldier," especially those of the People's Army of North Vietnam; NVA.

Bo-Chi-Huy *see* **Headquarters**

Boat People Vietnamese refugees fleeing South Vietnam by boat after the communist takeover in 1975. Estimates range as high as 1,300,000 for the number of Vietnamese that fled by boat from the communist regime in South Vietnam after '75. The refugees used anything that would float and paid dearly to escape from Vietnam. Of the 1.3 million people that attempted to get away by boat it is believed that 20 percent of them died at sea due to exposure, drowning, dehydration and pirates.

Boat Support Unit *see* **SEAL Team Assault Boat**

Boatswain Mate (Warrant Officer) Navy rank equivalent to the grade of Warrant Officer. In Vietnam some river patrol craft were commanded by boatswain mates as well as lower ranking Petty Officers. *See also* **Warrant Officer**.

Bobbie (Bobbie-the-Bubbling-Bundle-of-Barometric-Brilliance) Bobbie-the-Bubbling-Bundle-of-Barometric-Brilliance was the TV weather girl who did the in-country weather reports for Armed Forces Radio Service, Vietnam. The weather report was the most current, official, uncensored news allowed out on the airwaves to U.S. troops in SVN. *See also* **AFVN**.

Bobbie-the-Bubbling-Bundle *see* **Bobbie**

Bobcats *see* **5th Infantry Regiment (Mechanized)**

Bobcats of the 20th ARA *see* **20th Artillery (Aerial Rocket)**

Bodes *see* **Cambods**

Body Armor (Chicken Plate, Bullet Proof Vest) Armored ceramic breastplate that was worn by some helicopter door gunners. Nicknamed the "chicken plate," the wrap-around vest weighed 25 pounds and provided the chest and back areas protection from small arms fire. Because of its weight, it was only worn by those soldiers who "rode" everywhere they went . Door gunners often carried extra chicken plates to sit on, adding a little bit of extra security for those "private areas" so dear to their hearts. *See also* **M-1955 Flak Jacket, Flak Jacket, Leg Armor, Special Flak Suit, Armored Seats.**

Body Bag (Rubber Bag) The bodies of U.S. soldiers killed in action were put into green or black body bags to be removed to morgue facilities and from there, to be returned home. The bag had a full length zipper down its center, and was less than airtight. Reinforced plastic handles were attached to the ends of the bag to facilitate carrying. When body bags were not available, bodies were wrapped or slung in a poncho or poncho liner to enable the remains to be moved. *See also* **Graves Registration.**

Body Cooler (Temporary Morgue) Refrigerated building used at military medical evacuation hospitals as a temporary holding facility for the dead. The bodies were later removed by Graves Registration personnel to the military morgue for processing. Each evacuation hospital had its own temporary morgue facility. At some of the field units refrigerated conexes were used as temporary morgues. *See also* **Reefers, Zipper Room.**

Body Count (Statistical Indicators of Military Success, BC) In RVN, because of a lack of terrain objectives, the U.S. military needed some other method to measure the progress of the war. The method used was a running tally of the enemy dead. MACV issued guidelines as to how the body count was to be collected. The individual units determined how high-kill ratios were to be rewarded. The more enemy dead, it was reasoned, the better the war was going. The pressure to achieve higher body counts to raise the statistics eventually led to abuses of the system and a loss of accuracy. As the system deteriorated and the body counts inflated the philosophy of the body count became "if it's dead and Vietnamese, it's VC." Officially body counts were called "Statisti-

cal Indicators of Military Success." *See also* **Confirms, Partial Body Count, Kill Ratio; Victory Medals, Viet Cong.**

Body Count (Viet Cong) *see* **Victory Medals, Viet Cong**

Body Hooks Locally manufactured grapnel hooks used by the NVA/VC to recover their dead and wounded. Standing NVA/VC tactics dictated that the bodies of the dead and wounded were to be recovered whenever possible to keep the enemy (US/ARVN) from knowing the exact extent of NVA/VC casualties. The hooks were thrown out from the cover of jungle or grass, hooking the bodies, which were then pulled in. *See also* **Blood Trails.**

Bofors Guns *see* **M-42 Duster**

Bogus In GI slang; bad, defective, poorly (or un-) planned or false. *See also* **Fucked-Up.**

Bohlen, Charles *see* **Wise Old Men**

Boi Loi Woods Heavily wooded area located along Highway 14, 18kms north of Cu Chi, just west of the village of Ben Suc in Binh Duong Province, III Corps. The woods and the surrounding environs were a longtime VC base area.

Bold Dragon I *see* **Operation Bold Dragon I**

Bolling *see* **Operation Bolling**

Bolo *see* **Operation Bolo**

Bomb Damage Assessment (BDA) Assessment of the effectiveness of a bomb strike. The assessments were made by aircraft, following the strike, or by ground units going into the target area. BDA for targets in NVN were usually done by aerial reconnaissance flights. BDA along the Ho Chi Minh trail and for targets just north of the DMZ were conducted by air or by Special Forces teams infiltrating the area. *See also* **Drones.**

Bomb Haiphong... "Bomb Haiphong...
...Better yet, get bombed
.....Only Lifers get bombed
......Then bomb Haiphong with Lifers." GI graffiti expounding the virtues of bombing Haiphong. *See also* **Boozers.**

Bomb Line Imaginary line in front of

friendly troops, beyond which aircraft can attack without getting clearance from the friendly ground unit. The bomb line was used to reduce the chance of friendly aircraft accidentally bombing their own troops. The bomb line usually reflected the safety margin allowed and varied from several hundred meters for jet fighter-bombers to several kilometers for B-52 strikes. The slower an aircraft could operate, the closer he could deliver his ordnance in support of ground troops. Helicopters were able to provide the closest support.

Bomb Release Switch *see* **Pickling**

Bomb Vietnam Back Into the Stone Age *see* **LeMay, General Curtis**

Bomber Cell (Wave) Air Force bomber cells consisted of three aircraft each. A group of cells attacking the same target was called a "wave."

Bombing Beacon Electronic navigational device used to direct aircraft to a target. Equipment in the aircraft utilized the signal given from the beacon as a reference point. From the beacon's reference point the target was given as an azimuth (direction) and range. Targets could be attacked with great accuracy. Beacons had to be emplaced by ground teams. This was usually done by USSF or LRRP teams. *See also* **Radio Beacon, Combat Skyspot.**

Bombing Halt *see* **Bombing Pause**

Bombing of Cambodia *see* **Secret Bombing of Cambodia**

Bombing Pause (Bombing Halt) During the U.S. airwar against NVN, '65–'69, there were 16 bombing pauses during which U.S. aircraft did not attack targets in NVN. Most of the pauses were used by the Johnson administration as peace overtures to Hanoi and followed U.S. peace initiatives. Temporary pauses took place at Christmastime. NVN used the periodic bombing halts to rebuild their facilities, enhance their defenses and increase their infiltration of troops and supplies to SVN. U.S. peace attempts were denounced by Hanoi. Ho Chi Minh refused to talk peace until the U.S. withdrew all its forces from Vietnam and recognized his regime as the one true representative of all Vietnam. *See also* **Operation Proud Deep, Christmas Bombing.**

Bombing the Dikes *see* **Red River Delta**

Bon Homme Richard *see* **USS Bon Homme Richard**

Bong *see* **Montagnards, Pipe**

Bong Son (Hoai Nhon, the Plains, Bong Son Plain) Village located about 77kms north of Qui Nhon, Binh Dinh Province, II Corps. The village was one of many on the coastal Bong Son Plain. It was located 75kms north of Qui Nhon and 10kms from the coast. The plains, the surrounding hills and valleys, were a longtime VC base area until U.S. combat troops began operations in the area. Bong Son became the home of elements of the 173d Airborne Brigade, '69–'71, who referred to the area as the "Plains." *See also* **Operation Masher-White Wing, 506 Valley.**

Bong Son Campaign *see* **Operation Masher-White Wing**

Bong-Sung-Song *see* **Buong-Sung-Xuong**

Bonnie Dick *see* **USS Bon Homme Richard**

Bonze *see* **Thich Quang Duc**

Boo Coo *see* **Beaucoup**

Boo Coo Dep *see* **Dep**

Boo Koo *see* **Beaucoup**

Booby Trap (Widow Maker, Automatic Ambush) Wide range of devices used to inflict casualties on an enemy. Sometimes called "Widow Makers" or an "Automatic Ambush." The NVA/VC were very resourceful in the use of booby traps. Discarded U.S. equipment, dud ammo and even trash were used against GIs with disastrous effectiveness. The booby traps slowed American troop movement and created a psychological pressure that was almost as debilitating as the injuries inflicted by the trap. The VC were experts at camouflaging their traps, which varied in size from a fountain pen to a pit large enough to trap an armored personnel carrier. It is estimated that booby traps caused over 17 percent of U.S. casualties and 11 percent of the U.S. KIAs. *See also* **Punji Stakes, Bouncing Betty, Steel Arrow Trap, Cartridge Trap, Coconut Mine, Bridge Trap, Punji Pit, Barbed Spike Plate,**

Bamboo Mine, Malayan Gates, Malay Log, Scorpion Trap, Shoebox Mine, Bicycle Bomb, Land Mines, Ban Chong Dau Co Moc, Parker-51, Mud Ball, Hand Grenade Traps, Bear Trap, Bubonic Plague, Tiger Trap, Sorry 'Bout That Trap, Toe-Poppers, AK Booby Trap, Time Pencil, Min Mine, PMD-6/7 Antipersonnel Mine, PMN Antipersonnel Mine, PRC-4 Mine; Gravel Mine, U.S.; TM-41 Antitank Mine, VC Claymore, Cast Iron Mine, MDH-7 Antipersonnel Mine, Mechanical Ambush.

Book (Beat-Feet, Haul-Ass, Hotel Alpha, Most Ricky-Tick[y], Make-a-Hat) To leave, get out, move, or vacate the area. Originally credited as being an old Navy/ Marine term. Before going on liberty, from ship or shore, personnel were required to sign out in the Duty Officer's or NCO's Log Book. To book out or book became synonymous with leaving in a hurry. To add emphasis or indicate an accelerated departure "haul-ass" or its phonetic translation, Hotel Alpha, was used. Another Marine variant was "most ricky-tick(y)," filtered down from Japan via WWII and Okinawa, and "make-a-hat." *See also* **Di Di, Sky, Un-Ass.**

Boom-Boom (Sex, Hump, Honeymoon, Get Laid, A-Piece-of-Tail, Pom-Pom, Short-Time, Nooky) Lowest common denominator, except for the word "fuck," between the Vietnamese language and the English language for GIs and the Vietnamese to communicate their desire for sex with each other; "di lai" and "viec giao cau" in Vietnamese. Most of the GI/Vietnamese encounters only lasted a few minutes and were referred to as a "short-time" or "quickies." Because of the high incidence of venereal diseases the military medical powers strongly suggested that GIs use condoms. A GI that had his sex without the use of a condom was known as "going in" or "riding" bareback. On Okinawa GIs used the word "honeymoon" to communicate their desires to the local women. *See also* **Ride Bareback, Whorehouse, Water-Point.**

Boomers Air Force nickname for refueling boom operators. On the KC-135 the refueling boom was a telescoping rigid tube fitted with two short wings which help stabilize the boom during refueling operations. *See also* **KC-135.**

Boondocker Shoes *see* **Brogans**

Boondocks *see* **Boonies**

Boondoggle *see* **Cluster Fuck**

Boonie Hat *see* **Jungle Hat**

Boonie Rat *see* **Infantry Soldier, The**

Boonie Time *see* **Bush Time**

Boonies (The Bush, Boondocks, The Field, Up-Country, The Sticks, Indian Country) Infantry term for any place the infantry operated outside of base camps, fire bases, villes and towns. Generally speaking any place lacking civilization; hostile areas away from the relative security of the base camps and cities. "Indian Country" and the "Badlands" were Marine names for those areas of the boonies where the enemy roamed and owned the countryside and if there was contact it would be heavy. The worst of the boonies was known as the "bad bush," "bad-ass territory," "Indian Territory," and "the Badlands." *See also* **The Shit, FEBA, Sitdown, Tiger Country, Arizona, Indian Country.**

Boot *see* **New Troop, Second Lieutenant**

Boot Brown Bar *see* **Second Lieutenant**

Boot Zippers (Lace-In Zippers) Laced in boot zippers that allowed combat and jungle boots to be opened and closed using a tongue zipper instead of the regular boot-laces. Gen. Abrams, MACV Commander, didn't approve of troops wearing the boot zippers and regulated against them after he took command in '68. MACV regulations dictated that only personnel working in or around port facilities or troops operating in water covered areas could wear boot zippers. Regulations notwithstanding, many GIs continued to wear the zippers. The zippers were mostly a luxury of rear area troops. Grunts in the field tended to stick with laced boots which didn't jam or break apart as the zippers were prone to do.

Bootleg Whiskey A Vietnamese concoction of black market American beer diluted with Coca Cola. The Vietnamese, who didn't drink this mix themselves, sold it to the Americans who frequented the small bars and whorehouses near the larger American base camps.

Boots   Various types of boot wear were used in Vietnam. *See also* **Jungle Boots, Special Boots, Bata Boots, NVA Boots.**

Boozers *see* **Juicers**

BOQ *see* **Bachelor Officer Quarters**

Border Battles   Late '67 series of battles by U.S. and ARVN units against large NVA units along the western border of South Vietnam. *See also* **Operation Mac Arthur, Operation Shenandoah II, Battle of Dak To.**

Border Rangers   South Vietnamese troops manning border outposts, many of which had previously been occupied by U.S. Special Forces and CIDGs. With the start of the withdrawal of U.S. troops many of the USSF CIDG camps were converted to border outposts. The former CIDG troops had been absorbed into the ARVN as "Border Rangers" and were under the command of ARVN rangers (red berets) at the camps. Under command of the ARVNs the former CIDGs were much less aggressive and gradually fell into a "bunker mentality." *See also* **Bunker Mentality.**

Border Surveillance Missions (BS Missions)   Missions usually carried out by reconnaissance units monitoring enemy activity along the border. MACV-SOG, Ranger and LRRP units were primarily responsible for border and cross border operations. *See also* **LRRP, Greek Operations.**

Border Surveillance Program (Trail Watcher Program)   USSF program that used specially trained CIDGs to monitor enemy trail and infiltration route activity along South Vietnam's western border. The Border Surveillance Program, started in '63, was an extension of the Special Forces' earlier Trail Watcher Program, which had carried out the same function. The surveillance teams gradually worked their way into Laos and Cambodia to observe enemy activity.

Bore Brush   Small metal bristled brush usually attached to a rod, used to clean the barrel of a rifle or pistol.

Boston Whaler (Skimmer)   16/18 foot, shallow draft boat used by U.S. forces throughout the Delta. The Boston Whalers, powered by a 50 or 75hp outboard engine, were often used to insert or extract SEAL teams and for harbor patrol duties by the Navy's Harbor Patrol Force. The small open boat, nicknamed the "Skimmer," could make 20 knots and transport 4–6 troops. Some of the boats were fitted with pedestal mounts for an M-60 machine gun, but most boats were unarmed except for the weapons carried by the crew and passengers. The Boston Whalers were also used by some Army units patrolling along river areas in I Corps. *See also* **SEAL Team Assault Boat.**

Bought-the-Farm *see* **Kill**

Bouncing Betty (M-2 Bounding Mine, OZM-3 Antipersonnel Mine)   Cone shaped mine buried in the ground. When triggered, it bounced about three feet into the air, about groin level, then exploded, causing extensive shrapnel damage to the lower part of the human body. The more popular VC version used a 60mm mortar round. The U.S. version of the bouncing betty was the M-2 Bounding Mine. The OZM-3 Antipersonnel Mine was a Soviet version of the bouncing betty used by the NVA/VC. The OZM-3 was cylinder shaped, 3 inches in diameter, 4.7 inches high and 9.9 pounds in weight. *See also* **Booby Trap.**

Bounties   During the course of the Vietnam War some Americans were singled out by the Viet Cong as being especially dangerous. These individuals or groups had a "bounty" placed on their heads by the Viet Cong. The VC offered to pay, in cash, anywhere from ten to several hundred thousand piastres for Americans with a bounty on their heads. Americans singled out for bounties had been effective at hurting the Viet Cong militarily or had won the support of local peasants and farmers. American Special Forces, snipers, LRRPs, CAP members and CIA agents and American Officers were usual targets of the VC bounty offers. *See also* **Hathcock, Gunnery Sergeant Carlos; Special Forces.**

Bowls (Pipes)   Nickname for pipes used to smoke marijuana, hash or opium. *See also* **Marijuana.**

Box *see* **Vagina**

Boxcars of the 178th Avn *see* **178th Aviation Company**

Boxer *see* **USS Boxer**

Boxing the Target *see* **Bracket**

Boys-in-Saigon (Newsmen in Vietnam)   The corporate news media often referred to their news crews reporting from Vietnam as the "boys-in-Saigon." Initially the views held on America's progress in the war, by the boys-in-Saigon, were far less optimistic than the views held by their bosses within the corporate structure. As the war dragged on and public support for it dwindled, media coverage in Vietnam shifted from an optimistic conclusion to the war to a negotiated settlement and stalemate with the communists. *See also* **Kam Nhe.**

BQM-34L Drone *see* **Drones**

Bra Chute *see* **T-10 Chute Malfunctions**

Bracket (Bracketing, Boxing the Target) Firing several rounds of artillery and adjusting until one round falls just short of the target and the next round falls slightly beyond the target. When this had been achieved the target was said to be bracketed. When the target was so bracketed its range was pinpointed allowing any subsequent rounds to be fired without further adjustments. Sometimes called back-to-front "boxing of the target." *See also* **Straddle.**

Brain Bucket *see* **APH-5 Helmet**

Braniff Airlines *see* **Commercial Carriers**

Brass *see* **Command**

Brasso (Spit Shine) Generic name for brass and copper cleaner used in the military as a metal polish, most notably on the standard issue brass belt buckle and insignia of rank. Brassoed belt buckles and spit shined boots were the epitome of "stateside" or garrison duty. *See also* **Mickey Mouse.**

Bravo *see* **Combat Medic, Medic, Operation Bravo**

Break Squelch Keying the transmitter on a radio to stop the normal static received when the radio is idle (no incoming traffic). Used for signaling to another radio set when the transmitting set, the one breaking squelch, is unable to use voice transmission because of the proximity of enemy troops. The technique was standard procedure on night LPs and recon missions.

Breakbone Fever *see* **Dengue Fever**

Breakfast, BA 353 *see* **Operation Menu Targets**

Breaking Tape (Taping Up) LRRP

term used to describe part of the preparation procedures before a long-range reconnaissance mission. All loose equipment carried on the patrol was tied down or taped to eliminate excess noise and rattles. The success of the LRRP mission depended on their ability to move undetected through enemy territory. A flapping uniform or bouncing piece of equipment could easily give their position away, and a six man team in the middle of an enemy company or battalion area did its utmost to go undetected. *See also* **Noise Discipline.**

Breechcloth (Loincloth) Traditional tribal dress worn by members of the various Montagnard tribes. It was a long wraparound dress, ankle length with an overlapping split. The top of the breechcloth tied at the waist. For hunting, gathering and other active duties the Montagnards usually wore loincloths. Montagnards that were part of the CIDG or the village defense force wore a mixture of ARVN type fatigues and traditional shirts.

Brevie Line (Administrative Line 1939) Geographical and administrative line that extended into the Gulf of Thailand and separated South Vietnamese territory from Cambodian territory. The line extended from Cambodian/South Vietnamese border above Ha Tien, southwest 47kms to a point just off the coast of Phu Quoc Island. From there the line traced north around the coast of the island to a point 15kms south of Duong Dong and 3kms from the western coast of the island. From that point the line continued southwest, into the gulf, along the original axis of the line from the main coast. All territorial waters north of the Brevie Line were Cambodian, those to the south were Vietnamese.

Briarpatch *see* **Hanoi Hilton**

Bridge Trap *see* **Cau Bay**

Briefs *see* **Skivvies**

Brig An area of confinement aboard a ship; a jail. Marine and Navy personnel referred to any jail, ship or land based, as a brig. *See also* **Long Binh Jail.**

Brigade (Bde) Unit commanded by a colonel or brigadier general; generally three or more assigned battalions and necessary support units (admin, logistics, medical, artillery, etc.). A U.S. Army division was composed of three to four brigades; 15,000–20,000 troops. Prior to '61 the division consisted of 2–3 regiments of battalions. After '61 the term "regiment" was replaced with "brigade." Infantry units still refer to themselves in the historical context of the regiment (12th Infantry Regiment, 27th Infantry Regiment, 4th Artillery Regiment, etc.), but under the ROAD system infantry, artillery and nonarmored cavalry units were officially designated by their branch (12th Infantry, 7th Cavalry, 1st Aviation, etc.). *See also* **Regiment, ROAD.**

Brigade Aid Station *see* **Battalion Aid Station**

Brigade Tactical Operations Center (B-TOC, BTOC) Brigade level tactical operations center used to control the combat elements assigned to the brigade. Abbreviated "B-TOC" or "BTOC." *See also* **Tactical Operations Center.**

Brigadier General A one-star general officer in the U.S. Army, Marines and Air Force. The equivalent rank in the Navy was Rear Admiral (Lower). *See also* **General Officers.**

Brigham Control Ground based radar installation that provided air control functions for U.S. aircraft over North Vietnam. Brigham Control was located in Thailand at Nakhon Phanom RTAFB. *See also* **NKP.**

Bright Light Missions Code name for MACV-SOG ground operations conducted in enemy held territory to rescue downed U.S. aircrews.

Bring-Heat *see* **Fire (shoot)**

Bring-Smoke (Air Strike, Artillery Barrage, Fire for Effect) GI slang for calling in artillery or an air strike on a target. Normal procedure involved firing one to several rounds to precisely place the impacting artillery on the target, and then issuing the command "fire for effect" to commence the barrage by all guns in the battery. Also used in a general sense to refer to any type of fire against a target. *See also* **Fire (Shoot).**

Bring-the-Max *see* **Kill**

Brinks BOQ *see* **Brinks Hotel**

Brinks Hotel BOQ (Brinks BOQ) Served as a BOQ for some U.S. military officers. The Brinks, located in downtown Saigon behind the Continental Palace Hotel, was bombed on Christmas Eve '64, by Viet Cong sappers. Two Americans were killed and more than 70 Vietnamese and Americans were wounded. *See also* **Bachelor Officer Quarters.**

BRJ *see* **RMK-BRJ**

Bro *see* **Soul Brother**

Brogans (Combat Boots, Boondocker Shoes) General reference to combat boots, especially those of the larger sizes, that tend to use up a lot of space. GIs in the field wore the leather and nylon jungle boots, while aircrews usually wore the all leather combat boots. Some rear area personnel in the larger cities, and some Air Force ground personnel, also wore the standard issue low quarter shoes. The leather combat boots were worn by aircrews because they provided more protection from fire in the event of a crash. The nylon of the jungle boot easily caught fire and literally melted the foot it surrounded. *See also* **Jungle Boots.**

Bronco *see* **OV-10A**

Bronze Star (Officers Award) Traditionally awarded for meritorious or heroic service in a military operation against an armed enemy, not associated with aerial flight or combat. A "V" on the award indicated valor. In Vietnam many officers, of all rank, received Bronze Stars just for having been in-country. This reduced the worth of the award in the infantryman's eyes and clouded the real meaning behind the award. For many the Bronze Star was known as an "officers award." *See also* **Gongs.**

Brothel *see* **Whorehouse**

Brother *see* **Soul Brother**

Brother Black *see* **Soul Brother**

Brown *see* **FSB Brown**

Brown, General George *see* **Chief of Staff**

Brown, H. Rap Former leader of Student National Coordinating Committee, renamed from the Student Nonviolent Coordinating Committee in '67, after Brown took over the group's leadership from Stokely Carmichael. Brown was radically militant and supported the use of armed revolt to accomplish racial equality in America, and he was a strong advocate of the Black Power Movement which advocated the use of violence to accomplish racial change in America. Brown, known to his parents as "Hubert," was charged in absentia with conspiracy to incite a riot during black riots in Cincinnati, Ohio. In '70 he made the FBI's "10 Most Wanted List," and during a holdup in '71, was captured in New York City after a shootout with police. *See also* H. Rap Brown Law, SNCC.

Brown Bar *see* Second Lieutenant, New Troop

Brown Krait Snake *see* Cham Quap, Snakes

Brown Leech *see* Leeches

Brown-Root-Jones Construction *see* RMK-BRJ

Brown Shoes (Navy Aircrews) Navy pilots and aircrewmen were nicknamed "brown shoes " because they wore brown shoes, while the rest of the Navy wore black shoes, jungle boots or white shoes.

Brown Water Navy *see* TF 116

Browning 9mm Pistol (GP35, 9mm Pistol) 9mm pistol popular with U.S. reconnaissance forces. The Browning GP39 was similar in design to the Army M1911 .45cal pistol and carried 13 rounds, compared to the seven-round magazine of the .45cal. The muzzle velocity of the GP35 was 1110 feet per second. The GP35 was not standard Army issue but several thousand models of the pistol were available in SVN throughout the war. Some had been brought in from source countries such as Canada and Belgium, others entered via NVA/VC officers that carried the weapon, which had been supplied by the Red Chinese who had captured the pistol from the Nationalist Chinese. *See also* Type 59 Pistol.

Browning Automatic Rifle (BAR, M-1918A2) Vintage WWII light machine gun (.30cal automatic rifle) that was given to French troops in Vietnam in the early fifties and later used by RF/PF units and some ARVN units. The BAR was later replaced with .30cal and M-60 machine guns, but captured BARs were used by the VC. The BAR weighed 16 pounds, unloaded, and was fed from a 20-round magazine. The heavy BAR was usually operated with a bipod for support and used as a squad weapon. Because of its heavy weight the BAR was not a favorite with the ARVN and they replaced it as soon as .30cal and M-60 machine guns became available to them.

Browning Heavy Machine Gun *see* M-2 HMG

Browning Medium Machine Gun *see* M-1919A6 MG

Bru *see* Montagnards

Brush-Fire War *see* Guerrilla War

BS *see* Bullshit

BS Missions *see* Border Surveillance Missions

BSU *see* SEAL Team Assault Boat

BTs (Benoctol) French drug available in Vietnam without a prescription. Benoctol, nicknamed the BTs, was taken in pill form, and induced an excited state of violent aggression in the consumer. The BTs were mixed with other illicit drugs used by some American GIs in Vietnam. *See also* Illicit Drugs.

Bua Chen (Banquet, Tiec Lon) Vietnamese banquet or party.

Bubble *see* OH-13

Bubbleless SCUBA System *see* CCR-1000

Bubonic Plague U.S. troops en route to Vietnam were required to take plague shots before they were allowed to enter the country. Bubonic plague was active throughout most of Southeast Asia. In March '67 a routine U.S. patrol near Cu Chi found dead rats tethered in a VC tunnel along with a syringe and a vial containing a yellow liquid. A U.S. medical intelligence team found that one of the rats had bubonic plague. Some Tunnel Rats believed the VC were purposely using the plagued rats as part of their tunnel defenses. *See also* Shot Card, Tunnels of Cu Chi.

Buck Sergeant (Sergeant E-5, Trung-Si, Specialist-5) Lowest ranking NCO, Grade E-5, equivalent to a Staff Sergeant in the Air Force or Petty Officer Second Class in the Navy. In the Army and Marine Corps, Sergeant E-5s were originally authorized to direct a squad, but due to shortages of NCOs and officers after '68 some were put in charge of platoons. Specialist-5 (Spec-5) was also an E-5 rank in the Army, and a non-infantry leadership position. Trung-Si [trung c] was Vietnamese for "sergeant." *See also* **Specialist 5th Class.**

Buck-Rogers Secret Decoder *see* **CIRCLE Wheel**

Buckeye Nickname for the shanty town located just outside of the U.S. 25th Infantry Division base camp at Cu Chi. *See also* **Dogpatch.**

Buckle *see* **Throwin' Hands**

Buckshot Round, M-79 *see* **M-576**

Buckskin *see* **Operation Buckskin**

Buddha Head Slang for persons of Japanese or Chinese ancestry, especially the Japanese. *See also* **Chinks.**

Buddha Grass *see* **Marijuana**

Buddha's Birthday *see* **Tet**

Buddha, The *see* **Rusk, David Dean**

Buddhism Religious and philosophical system founded by Gautama Siddhartha in the sixth century B.C. Buddhism emphasizes the seeking of perfect morality, compassion and wisdom leading to a transformation and enlightenment. Buddhism belief is that life moves in ever repeating cycles of reincarnation. Hinayana Buddhism is the ancient religion of Vietnam. It came into contention with Confucianism that was introduced to Vietnam in 1009. Vietnam's Emperors adopted Confucianism and modeled their government around it, effectively squeezing out the influence of Buddhism, which was Vietnam's major religion representing 95 percent of the people. Vietnam's upper classes followed Confucianism. *See also* **Confucius.**

Buddhist Barbecues *see* **Thich Quang Duc**

Buddhist Revolt During '65 SVN's government was ruled by a military junta headed by Nguyen Cao Ky. Buddhists across SVN began protesting against the military rule in favor of a civilian government. The Buddhist protest became increasingly disruptive and Ky sent his personal forces to Hue to crush the revolt.

Buddy System Field term used in the early days of Vietnamization when ARVN units were paired with U.S. units for operational training. It also referred to pairing a new GI to the field (FNG) with an experienced field troop, allowing the new man a chance to learn the ropes. *See also* **Double Force, Vietnamization.**

BUFFs *see* **B-52**

Buffalo *see* **Operation Buffalo**

Buffalo Boy *see* **Water Buffalo**

Buffalo Hunter *see* **Drones**

Buffalo Soldiers *see* **1st Squadron / 9th Cavalry (Aerial Recon)**

Buffalo Turbine Large air blower used experimentally by the Army in Vietnam for tunnel warfare. The 800-pound unit could blow a considerable volume of air through an enemy tunnel complex, but the unit was so large and awkward to use that the Army deemed it inadequate for field use. The unit was usually air transported to the field by helicopter and moved to the tunnel entrance by jeep or APC. Four men were then required to position the Buffalo for use. *See also* **Tunnel Warfare, Air Blowers.**

Buffalo-DHC-5 *see* **C-8A**

Buffs *see* **Water Buffalo**

Bug Juice (Insect Repellent) The military-issued insect repellent was nicknamed "bug juice." It was marginally effective against mosquitoes, but when poured directly on imbedded leeches caused them to stop feeding. Bug juice mixed with the peanut butter from C-Ration meals made an excellent fuel which could be used in the C-Rat stove. *See also* **Peanut Butter, Insect Repellent.**

Bugville *see* **Soc Trang**

Bui Phat Shanty town located across the Saigon River from the French settlement in Saigon. The shanty town, named Bui Phat, was mostly inhabited by former North Vietnamese Catholics who had fled the North in '54 after the Geneva Accords had partitioned North and South Vietnam. Bui Phat's inhabitants were staunch supporters of Ngo Dinh Diem.

Buick Flight *see* **Takhli Royal Thai Air Base**

Buis, Major Dale *see* **First American to Die...**

Bull Session *see* **Hangar-Flying**

Bull Simons *see* **Simons, Colonel Arthur "Bull," Son Tay Raid**

Bulldozer *see* **Caterpillar D7E Tractor**

Bullet Blotter *see* **Infantry Soldier**

Bulletproof Vest *see* **Body Armor**

Bullet Shot I-V Deployments (Operation Freedom Porch Bravo) Code name for a series of Air Force emergency deployments of B-52s to Andersen Air Force Base in Guam in response to the April '72 NVA Eastertide Offensive. Immediately after deploying to Guam the B-52s began bomb strikes against NVA targets north of the DMZ that were providing support for the offensive against SVN. The B-52 strikes were part of Operation Freedom Porch Bravo which focused on the invasion force's lines of communication. *See also* **Constant Guard I–IV, Eastertide Offensive.**

Bullet Stabber (Tank Loader) Usual starting position for a new man joining a tank crew. Least desirable of the tank crew positions. The loader sat in a cramped corner of the turret to load the shells fired by the tank's main gun.

Bullpup *see* **AGM-12**

Bullshit (BS, Bullshit Net) To lie, to con, to be unbelievable and or to exaggerate beyond belief. During quiet periods of no enemy action RTOs sometimes passed on small bits of information and rumors between platoons on the same radio net; unofficially the "bullshit net." RTOs were also a source of information and rumors passed within the unit. From their position as platoon or company RTO they could monitor the traffic of other units in the area and listen to command decisions passed between headquarters. *See also* **Stateside Bullshit, Command Net.**

Bullshit Bombers Air Force slang for aircraft used for psychological warfare operations. The aircraft were primarily used to drop leaflets and make loudspeaker broadcasts to enemy soldiers and civilians. C-130s were often used to drop leaflets because their large cargo capacity allowed the planes to "bomb" several villages in one flight, reducing the aircraft's exposure to enemy fire. *See also* **Psychological Operations, Controlled Littering.**

Bullshit Net *see* **Bullshit**

Bummer (Pisser, Sucks, Bad Scene) Bad news situation, no good, downer, an adverse condition, an unfortunate occurrence but not as bad as "the shits" or a "fucked situation." Bad situations and some individuals "suck." *See also* **Fucked-Up.**

Bumps *see* **Blister**

Bundy, McGeorge National security advisor to President Kennedy and later a senior advisor to President Johnson. Bundy was one of the President's "Wise Old Men" advisory group. In earlier years Bundy had been a strong advocate of fighting communism in Vietnam. By '68 his attitude had changed and he backed the group's proposal to the President that the war should be ended as quickly as possible through negotiation instead of military force. Bundy's brother, William, was also an advisor to both Kennedy and Johnson. *See also* **Wise Old Men; Bundy, William.**

Bundy, William State Department Foreign Affairs advisor to both Presidents Kennedy and Johnson. Bundy helped draft the original Gulf of Tonkin Resolution and was instrumental in the development of the U.S. bombing policy of North Vietnam, Operation Rolling Thunder. Bundy's brother, McGeorge, was also an advisor to Presidents Kennedy and Johnson. *See also* **Bundy, McGeorge.**

Bung (NLF Guerrillas) South Vietnamese guerrillas' (Viet Cong) nickname for themselves. "Bung" in Vietnamese meant a marshland or swamp area used for cover and concealment. An area used by resistance forces. *See also* **Viet Cong, National Liberation Front.**

Bunji Cord *see* **Bunji Strap**

Bunji Strap (Bunji Cord, Monkey Strap, Safety Strap) Flexible cord attached to the machine guns used by some helicopter door gunners. This cord, or strap, greatly increased his field of fire. With the usual fixed mounted machine gun the gunner could fire down, to the front and sides, but the bunji increased his field of fire allowing him to fire behind and under the helicopter. The gunner could lean out of the chopper and fire behind it, something he couldn't do with the fixed gun mount. The gunner was tethered in the ship by a safety strap (nicknamed a "monkey strap"). This increased flexibility with the gun also increased the gunner's exposure to enemy fire. *See also* **Door Gunner.**

Bunker A defensive position of fortified walls and ceilings, fitted with a firing window or slot used to provide fire and bomb protection for its occupants. A bunker was the typical location for a machine gun position. In Vietnam, American bunkers varied in their construction and size. For the average troops, bunkers of sandbags and PSP were the standard; for larger or command bunkers concrete was often used. The NVA/VC used bunkers in their base areas and around villes. There construction usually consisted of mounded dirt with log reinforced walls and roofs, extremely well camouflaged and highly resistant to direct fire and aerial attack. *See also* **Bunkerline, Bunker Mentality, Family Bunkers.**

Bunker Bunnies Women's softball team of nurses from the 12th Evacuation Hospital located at Cu Chi, III Corps. The off-duty nurses played softball with GIs in the area. The only special rules that applied were, men were not allowed to catch the Bunnie's fly balls, and left handed GIs had to bat right handed and vice versa. *See also* **12th Evacuation Hospital (Semi-Mobile), GWINK.**

Bunker City Nickname for a large enemy bunker complex captured by elements of the 1st Cavalry Division during the May '70 U.S. incursion into Cambodia. The bunker complex served as an NVA/VC supply depot and communications center. *See also* **Cambodian Incursion, The City.**

Bunker Mentality The "bunker mentality" referred to the tendency of combat units to confine operations to the immediate vicinity of their bases and not to conduct large scale operations to seek out the enemy in his own base areas. Prior to '69 U.S. forces actively took the war to enemy base areas. After Tet '68 U.S. units increasingly took a more defensive approach in combating the enemy. The French in Vietnam were guilty

of this, concentrating most of their forces in base camps and reacting to enemy attacks, instead of taking the battle to the enemy. The South Vietnamese forces also tended to avoid large scale operations that would take them deep into enemy contested zones. *See also* **Enclave Policy, Fire Base Psychosis.**

Bunker, Ellsworth America's ambassador to South Vietnam from '67 to '73. Bunker supported the Thieu Government of South Vietnam until '71 when evidence came to light that during Vietnam's national elections Thieu had forced Nguyen Cao Ky and Duong Van Minh, his only opponents, out of the election.

Bunkerline (Lines, Stand Lines) Defense bunkers placed around the outer perimeter of a base camp. The bunkers were usually arranged to provide mutual supporting, interlocking fields of fire. At the larger U.S. permanent base camps, the bunkers "on the line" were usually tied into the base command center by telephone land lines. At the smaller base camps communication was by word of mouth and runners carrying messages. The bunkers provided overhead cover and were the first line of defense after the rows of concertina, tanglefoot and trip flares. Troops that manned the bunkerline at night referred to the duty as having to do "lines," or "standing lines." *See also* **Bunker.**

Buon Enao (American Country Team) Rhade Montagnard village, located near Ban Me Thuot in the Central Highlands that was the prototype for the Strategic Hamlet program in South Vietnam. The plan called for the GVN to help the villagers to provide their own security from the VC and at the same time improve their social and economic condition. Civic improvements were provided by various Vietnamese agencies under the direction of the USAID. Local villagers were taught by the USSF how to fortify and defend their village. Buon Enao, as an experiment, was successful. The program later failed when applied to the rest of Vietnam. *See also* **Strategic Hamlet Program.**

Buong-Sung-Xuong (Bong-Sung-Song) Vietnamese phrase meaning "throw down your weapons." The American version sounded like "bong-sung-song." The phrase was used by Americans attempting to capture armed NVA/VC encountered in the field. There was some question as to how many of the enemy actually were able to understand the American pronunciation.

Burke, Admiral Arleigh *see* **Chief of Naval Operations**

Burn Call *see* **Police Call**

Burn Hanoi, Not Our Flag One of the pro–Johnson administration slogans used by demonstrators supporting America's war effort in Vietnam. In some cases demonstrators against antiwar groups were less concerned with administration policy, and were more concerned with the antiwar groups' lack of respect for tradition; the government and hard work. It was primarily a conflict between young and old. The old going by their previous ways, and the young wanting change.

Burn Yourselves, Not Your Draft Cards (Roger La Porte, Norman Morrison) One of the chants by anti-antiwar hecklers. Each antiwar or antidraft demonstration had its counter, or pro-government demonstrators. This particular chant was related to the Morrison incident in which 32-year-old Norman Morrison poured gasoline over himself and set himself on fire. Morrison staged his antiwar protest on the steps of the Pentagon. The event took place during a protest, November 2, 1965. A second self-immolation took place outside the United Nations Building, November 9, 1965, by Roger La Porte. *See also* **Bill 392.**

Burn-Bash-Bury (B-B-B) Aussie policy of trash disposal. Trash was burned, cans were crushed and buried. The object of the policy was to keep the trash out of the hands of the Viet Cong who could skillfully turn it into deadly booby traps or utilize the trash for their own needs. Australian troops rigidly followed the policy. U.S. troops were also aware of the enemy's ability to fabricate weapons from their discarded trash, but many GIs were less conscientious with their trash and its correlation to weapons and booby traps. *See also* **Beer Can Grenade, C-Rat Grenade.**

Burners *see* **Afterburner**

Burning Shit *see* **Shit Burner**

Burp Gun *see* **M-3A1 SMG**

Burt *see* **FSB Burt**

Bush Beetles *see* **Infantry Soldier, The**

Bush Cover *see* **Jungle Hat**

Bush Hat *see* **Jungle Hat**

Bush Knife *see* **Machete**

Bush Rag *see* **Bush Towel**

Bush Shave *see* **Dry Shave**

Bush Time (Hump Time, Boonie Time, Trigger Time, Combat Time) Amount of time a grunt spent out in the field and the bush; combat time. Also referred to as boonie time, hump time, and trigger time. *See also* **The Shit, Boonies.**

Bush Towel (Bush Rag) Standard Army/Marine issue, OD green bath towel, worn around the neck by grunts in the field, who used it to wipe the sweat from their hands and face as they humped in the boonies. The towel was also worn under the shoulder straps of the rucksack to reduce sores and abrasions caused by the straps and ruck cutting into the skin. The towels were sometimes cut and worn as crude shirts by field troops who were overdue for uniform exchange. The terry cloth towel measured 29 × 45 inches and was one of the standard issue items for Vietnam.

Bush(ed/ing) *see* **Ambush**

Bush, The *see* **Boonies**

Business Executives Move for Peace (BEM) An organized group of business executives that opposed the war in Vietnam. BEM opposition to the war was primarily based on economics. The war in Vietnam was very expensive to run. Besides the up-front cost of munitions, supplies, transport, etc., there were many hidden costs such as veteran insurances, claims, benefits, V.A. facilities, etc. Some estimates put the cost of the war in excess of a million dollars a day. Other costly side effects of the war were rising inflation and interest rates.

Bust(in') Caps *see* **Fire (Shoot)**

Bust-Your-Cherry (Baptism of Fire) A cherry was a new man to the field, no combat experience, no field experience and a danger to the seasoned troops around him. A cherry's baptism of fire came with his first firefight, and his initiation to combat. When the new man busted his cherry, surviving his first combat, he became less of a threat to his fellow soldiers. *See also* Cbt.

Busted (Reduction in Grade)   GI slang for a soldier being reduced in rank; i.e., sergeant reduced to corporal or corporal reduced to private, etc. Such reductions were associated with a disciplinary action against the soldier and usually carried other punishment such as restriction to post, extra duty and reduction in pay. *See also* Article 15.

Bustin' Bush   *see*   Cut(ting) Trail

Bustle Rack   Exposed pipe frame assembly attached to the rear area of a tank turret, used for the carrying and storage of additional supplies.

Butcher Brigade   *see*   11th Infantry Brigade (Light)

Butcher of Vinh   One of President Johnson's many nicknames bestowed on him during antiwar demonstrations in '66, this particular one was in reference to Navy bombing raids on the NVN city of Vinh. Antiwar activists falsely claimed that the Navy had bombed Vinh out of existence. The POL facility at Vinh was one of the first NVN sites bombed by U.S. aircraft in retaliation for NVN gunboat attacks against U.S. destroyers operating in the Gulf of Tonkin in '64. The name "Butcher of Vinh" was a parallel to the "Butcher of Budapest," the nickname Soviet Premier Khrushchev had acquired due to his actions against Hungary in '56. *See also* Vinh.

Butt Pack (M-56 Harness, M-1956/1961 Combat Field Pack)   Small military field pack that was attached to the pistol belt and supported by the M-1956 harness and suspenders. The M-1956 harness featured padded shoulder straps that were attached by hooks to the combat web belt. The harness allowed field packs, pack boards, radios and various other equipment to be carried. The M-1956 version of the pack was made of cotton duck. Later versions were designated the M-1961 Combat Field Pack, and were made

of nylon. The butt pack had less than half the capacity of the lightweight rucksack. *See also* **M-1956/1967 Individual Load Carrying Equipment, Web Gear.**

Butt Stroke   *see*   **Vertical Butt Stroke**

Butter Bar   *see*   **Second Lieutenant**

Butterfly Mine   *see*   **Cluster Bomb Units**

Butterfly Trigger   The push-button trigger on the Browning .50cal heavy machine gun. The trigger mechanism was shaped like the wings of a butterfly, and had to be depressed, using both thumbs, to fire the weapon.

Button Hook Bush (Double Back Ambush)   Ambush technique used by U.S. troops operating in dense jungle. The NVA/VC often had small observation/recon units follow larger U.S. units as they patrolled the jungle. A small force from the main U.S. column would be detached, and move off the trail. The force would move parallel to the trail and away from the main column, doubling back the way the column originally came. The detachment would then reenter the trail and come up behind the NVA/VC tracking force ambushing them from the rear. This tactic was sometimes successful, but not popular because the ambush detachment was separated from the main body and had to cut its way through the dense jungle to get around the enemy force, whose exact size was usually undetermined. *See also* **Stay-Behind Ambush.**

Button Up   To button up in a tank or armored vehicle, the crew got completely inside the vehicle, closed all the hatches, and viewed the war through periscopes and hatch portals. The button up maneuver was not very popular in the heat and humidity of Vietnam.

Buzz   *see*   **Get High**

BX   *see*   **Post Exchange**

Byrd   *see*   **Operation Byrd**

C

C & C *see* **Command and Control**

C & C Company (Collection and Clearing Company, Medical Clearing Station) C & C Company was part of the Navy medical battalion that provided medical services to the Marine Corps. The battalion consisted of a headquarters company and four C & C companies. Each C & C company was composed of a headquarters, two clearing and one collecting platoon. The collection platoon assembled the casualties received from battalion aid stations or directly from the field and distributed them to the clearing platoons for immediate medical aid. Stabilized casualties requiring more extensive care were transferred to larger hospital facilities. The medical battalion headquarters maintained the unit's records, motor transport, preventive medicine section and the command element. *See also* **Battalion Aid Station.**

C and S *see* **Clear and Hold**

C Zone *see* **War Zone C**

Cs *see* **C-Rations**

C-1 Trader (E-1 Tracer, C-1A, EA-1) Navy carrier based transport. The C-1, twin engine, prop-driven transport could carry nine passengers or 3,500 pounds of cargo. The E-1 Tracer was a C-1 variant that was packed with radar and communications equipment and featured a wing mounted saucer shaped radome. The Grumman manufactured aircraft had a max speed of 265mph and a range of 2,300kms. The C-1/E-1 were used on a limited basis during the Vietnam War by carriers operating off the coast of Vietnam. The Marine Corps also used the C-1 for transportation of passengers and light cargo.

C-2A (Greyhound) Grumman twin engine, prop-driven aircraft. The Navy operated two versions of the Greyhound, both carrier operational. The C-2 was used as a carrier landable transport. The E-2 Hawkeye was used as a radar search aircraft providing early warning of approaching enemy craft. The C-2 had a max speed of 352mph, a range of 2,600kms and could transport 39 troops or 10,000 pounds of cargo. *See also* E-2 Hawkeye.

C-3 Explosive A plastique type explosive used in the early years of the Vietnam War. The C-3 explosive was very similar to the C-4 explosive that replaced it, except it was not as pliable and was less flexible in its uses. *See also* **Composition-4 Explosive, TNT.**

C-4 *see* **Composition-4 Explosive**

C-5A (Galaxy) Four engine Air Force jet transport manufactured by Lockheed Aircraft. The C-5 was the largest transport in the world with a lift capacity of 221,000 pounds or 345 passengers. The C-5 had a maximum speed of 571mph and a range of 6,000kms. It also featured a drop ramp for rear loading. The nose section swung up and out of the way to allow for front loading of the cargo bay. The C-5 was used extensively for transport services between Vietnam and the States.

C-7A (CV-2, Caribou, STOL, DHC-4A, AC-1) Medium transport, especially effective at using short or rough airstrips (STOL-Short Takeoff and Landings). Manufactured by the de Havilland Aircraft Corp of Canada, the Caribou could move 32 troops or three tons of cargo. The Caribou was originally part of the Army inventory and was designated the AC-1, and later redesignated the CV-2. The Air Force complained so loudly that the Army was usurping the Air Force's supply mission, that the Army's Caribous were turned over to the Air Force in '67 and redesignated the C-7A. The twin engine, prop driven Caribou had a cruising speed of 182mph and a range of 2,100kms. As part of the Vietnamization program the Caribous used in Vietnam were transferred to VNAF.

C-8A (Buffalo-DHC-5) STOL transport aircraft manufactured by de Havilland Aircraft of Canada and used by the Air Force to provide support to locations with short and or rough airstrips. The C-8 was similar to the C-7A Caribou, but featured twin turbo-prop engines with a max speed of 290mph, a range of 1,110kms and a passenger capacity of 41 troops or 18,000 pounds of cargo. The C-7 and C-8 looked much alike except the C-8 had a high horizontal tail stabilizer (the C-7 had a low horizontal tailplane) and a small, round button nose (the C-7 had a rounded nose). *See also* C-7A.

C-10 VC Sapper Battalion *see* U.S. Embassy, Tet '68

C-40 Claymore *see* VC Claymore

C-45 (Expediter) Beechcraft twin engine transport used by the Army / Air Force and the Navy shortly after WWII. The small transport had a max speed of 225mph, a range of 1,900kms and could transport 6–8 people or cargo. Several of the C-45s were given to VNAF and used for courier service and aerial reconnaissance.

C-46 (Curtis Commando) Vintage WWII cargo aircraft used on a limited basis in Vietnam. The C-46 and C-47 were the primary transports used by the CIA's airline, Air America, to support its covert operations in Laos, Cambodia and Vietnam. The twin engine C-46 had a maximum speed of 269mph, range of 1,903kms and could transport 50 passengers, or cargo. The C-46 had a little more speed, range and lift capacity than the C-47. The C-46 featured a large rounded tail with the cockpit windows blending into a smooth, round nose. *See also* Air America, C-47.

C-47 (SC-47, RC-47, Skytrain, DC-3) WWII vintage transport aircraft. The twin engine, propeller driven aircraft saw extensive use in Vietnam. VNAF used the C-47 for transport. The SC-47 was loaded with flares and used in night operations as a flare ship to light ground targets and ARVN outposts under attack. A photo recon version, the RC-47, was used by VNAF for aerial recon work. The U.S. Air Force used modified C-47s as gunships and redesignated them AC-47s. First manufactured in '41 by Douglas Aircraft for use in WWII. The DC-3 was the civilian designation for the C-47. The C-47 had a max speed of 230mph, a range of 2574kms and transport capacity of 28 troops. *See also* AC-47, R4D, Night Angel, C-117.

C-54 (Skymaster, SC-54, Rescuemaster) Vintage WWII transport that saw limited service in Vietnam with the Marine Corps. The C-54 was manufactured by Douglas Aircraft and was powered by four prop-engines with a max speed of 265mph and a range of 6,200kms. The C-54 Skymaster operated with a crew of six and could transport 30–50 passengers. During the early days of the war the C-54 transported passengers and priority cargo to Vietnam until replaced by the faster C-141 and C-5A. Some C-54s, designated SC-54 (Rescuemaster), were converted for temporary use as airborne command posts and used early in the war for SAR duties. The SC-54s were based out of Thailand and were eventually replaced by HC-130s. *See also* ABCCC, C-130s.

C-69 *see* C-121

C-117 (AC-117) Marine and Navy transport that was an improved version of the C-47. The C-117 featured slightly more powerful engines and was primarily used for courier and transport duties. It was not carrier qualified. In Vietnam some C-117s were used as flare ships, airborne radio relay stations, aerial control centers and for general transport duties. A few C-117s were temporarily outfitted as gunships and used by the Marines for close support. *See also* C-47, AC-47.

C-118 (Liftmaster) Military version of the DC-6 commercial airliner manufactured by Douglas Aircraft. The four engine, prop-driven transport was used by both the Air Force and Navy for the movement of cargo and personnel. The C-118 had a maximum speed of 360mph, a range of 6,100kms and could move 27,000 pounds of cargo or 74 troops. The C-118 saw limited service in Vietnam.

C-119 (Flying Boxcar) Twin engine transport manufactured by Fairchild and operated by the Air Force. The C-119 was called the "Flying Boxcar" and had a maximum speed of 243mph and a range of 2,800kms. The C-119 was a medium transport which could carry 62 troops or 30,000 pounds of cargo. Several C-119s were in the VNAF inventory. Some surplus Air Force C-119s in Vietnam were converted to gunships and designated the AC-119G/K. The Air Force C-119s were replaced by C-123 and C-130 aircraft. *See also* AC-119G/K.

C-121 (C-69, Constellation, Connies) The Lockheed Constellation first entered service in '44 as the C-69, a military transport that was an adaptation of a civilian designed airliner. After WWII the C-69 was designated the C-121 and used for commercial aviation and as a transport by the Air Force and Navy. The C-121 had a max speed of 330mph, a range of 3,800kms and could transport cargo or 60 passengers. As newer, more powerful transports entered service the C-121 was eased out of the transport role and was packed with sophisticated radar, navigational and communications equipment and used for monitoring of enemy radar and radio communications and as an airborne air controller. *See also* EC-121.

C-123 (Provider)   Twin engine propeller driven transport used by the Air Force in Vietnam. The aircraft featured good short-strip takeoff/landing capabilities and was sometimes fitted with auxiliary jet power boosters for quick climbing from "hot" or extremely short landing strips. The aircraft was manufactured by Fairchild and had a maximum speed of 205mph, a range of 2,300kms and a payload of about 23,600 pounds or 61 passengers (70 Vietnamese troops). C-123s were first deployed to SVN in '61 to provide transport for ARVN troops and were the primary aircraft used for the aerial spraying of defoliants during the war. *See also* **Operation Ranch Hand, Mule Train, Black Spot, Candlestick.**

C-123 Lightship   C-123 transport used as a high altitude battlefield illuminator. The C-123 was fitted with banks of high intensity arc lamps mounted on the underbelly of the aircraft. The bank of lights was fixed in position and from an altitude of 5,000–12,000 feet could illuminate a 670–1,600 meter diameter area on the ground. At such altitudes the aircraft was out of danger of small arms fire as it provided a constant light source over the target area. The lightship was used to provide support to units in open areas under attack. The lights and flares were less effective over jungle areas because of the shadows produced and the dense overhead jungle cover that limited light penetration. *See also* **Firefly, Nighthawks.**

C-123K (Blackspot)   C-123 transport fitted with special night optics equipment, and with a special bomblet dispenser fitted into the belly. The bomblets were released over suspected enemy areas pinpointed by the night optics system.

C-124 (Globemaster)   Four engine, propeller driven aircraft used by the Air Force as a long-range strategic transport. The big plane could transport 200 troops or 68,500 pounds of cargo. The C-124 had a maximum speed of 304mph and a range of 6,400kms. During the early days of the war in Vietnam the Globemaster was used to transport priority cargo and personnel to Vietnam. The C-124 was later replaced by the faster C-141 and C-5A transports.

C-130 (Hercules, Herc, RC-130, HC-130)   Four engine, turbo-prop medium cargo transport manufactured by Lockheed Aircraft. The C-130 had a cruising speed of 340mph, a range of 6,100kms and a payload of 35,000 pounds or 92 passengers. The Hercules was the primary transport aircraft used by U.S. forces in Vietnam. The aircraft was reliable and was used extensively for airlift and resupply operations. Some C-130s were later converted for use as gunships (AC-130) and replaced the aging AC-47 gunship. The RC-130 was equipped with cameras and used for photo reconnaissance missions. The HC-130 was a command and control ship that was used to monitor enemy air activity, U.S. air operations over NVN and SAR missions. *See also* **AC-130, ABCCC, KC-130.**

C-133 (Cargomaster)   Large four engine, propeller driven, long-range strategic transport operated by the Air Force. The Cargomaster, manufactured by Douglas, had large rear doors that allowed large cargos to be airlifted. The C-133 could transport 200 troops or 110,000 pounds of cargo. The plane's maximum speed was 359mph and a range of 6,400kms. The C-133 was the largest operational transport in the Air Force inventory in '65 when U.S. combat troops began deploying to Vietnam. The C-133 was later replaced by the C-141 and C-5A.

C-135 (Stratolifter, EC-135, KC-135, WC-135, RC-135)   Military version of Boeing's commercial airliner, the Boeing 707. The C-135 functioned as an Air Force personnel and cargo transport. The four engine jet had a max speed of 600mph and a range of 1,800kms. The C-135 operated with a crew of six and could transport 87,000 pounds of cargo or 126 troops. The KC-135 was the aerial tanker version. The EC-135 operated as airborne command post for the Strategic Air Command. Several RC-135s were used for reconnaissance and aerial mapping missions. The WC-135 was a radar and weather, electronic reconnaissance version. *See also* **KC-135, EC-135.**

C-140 (Jetstar)   Air Force twin engine, utility jet transport. The Lockheed manufactured jet was operated by a two man crew and could transport 10–16 passengers. The jet had a maximum speed of 573mph and a range of 3,400kms. During the Vietnam War the small jet was used for VIP transport and by the Air Force Communications Service to verify the accuracy of worldwide military navigational aids and sites.

C-141 (Starlifter)   Air Force four engine, turbo-jet, long-range transport, manufactured by Lockheed Aircraft. The C-141 had a lift capacity of 70,800 pounds or 154 passengers, a cruising speed of 570mph and a range of 6,445kms. The C-141 first entered service in SEA in '65 and became the backbone of the Air Force's lift command. The Starlifter was used to transport personnel, supplies and equipment with some aircraft being outfitted to serve as airborne ambulances to transport the wounded to hospitals in Japan and the States.

C-Biscuits   *see*   **John Wayne Crackers**

C-Detachment   *see*   **C-Team**

C-Rat Grenade (VC Hand Grenade) Homemade Viet Cong hand grenade. The grenade used an empty C-ration can packed with explosive, small rocks, metal, ground glass or nails. The can was attached to a hollow bamboo handle six–eight inches long. Inside the tube was a crude friction fuse attached to a piece of string with a loop of bamboo or wooden knob. As the grenade was thrown, the thrower held on to the bamboo loop. When the grenade flew out of his hand the friction fuse was activated and the grenade was armed. The grenade had a very short range, but was very powerful. The homemade grenade was also used as a stationary booby trap. The Viet Cong were very effective at using the trash thrown away by U.S. soldiers. *See also* **Hand Grenades, Beer Can Grenade, Burn-Bash-Bury.**

C-Rat Stove (Marine Stove)   Small field utility stove, used by GIs to heat their C-rations and boil water for coffee or hot chocolate. The stove was made of an empty C-ration can, the top removed, and holes punched into the sides of the can around its bottom. A small piece of C-4 or Comp-8 explosive was placed in the bottom of the can and then ignited. The explosive burned with an intense flame, sufficient to quickly warm a can of food or heat a canteen cup of water. Many a claymore mine sacrificed its contents to serve as fuel for hungry grunts in the field. Sometimes called a Marine stove. *See also* **Fuel, Compressed, Trioxane.**

C-Ration Cookies   *see*   **John Wayne Cookies, C-Rations**

C-Ration Crackers   *see*   **John Wayne Crackers, C-Rations**

C-Rations (Cs, C-Rats, Combat Rations, Charlie-Rats)   Combat rations. Individual meals issued to troops where no hot food or kitchen facilities were available. The boxed meal consisted of a canned main entrée (beef, pork, poultry), canned fruit and canned dessert; bread; pound, fruit or pecan cake, and a can of crackers or biscuits. Also included in the box was an accessory packet containing salt, sugar (caked), spoon, cigarettes (stale), matches, toilet paper (never enough), candy coated gum (hard) and a packet of cream substitute and instant coffee (extremely strong). Some of the cans were dated from the 40s. Typical weight of one boxed meal was two pounds and the meals were designed by nutritionists to provide 3,000 calories per day. The list of canned C-ration delicacies included jam spreads (grape, apricot, pineapple, peach, blueberry), peanut butter & crackers, ham & lima beans, peaches, ham with water added, chicken & noodles, beef & potatoes, pound cake, fruit cocktail, marmalade, water biscuits, beans & meatballs in tomato sauce, cheddar cheese spread, beans & franks in tomato sauce, chopped ham & eggs, pecan or orange nutroll, spaghetti & meatballs, beef with spice sauce, applesauce, turkey loaf, pork stew, pears, apricots, fudge brick, date pudding, beef stew, beef with noodles, fruit cake, bread, boned chicken, beefsteaks with juices, tuna, pork slices with juices. *See also* **LRRP Rations, Accessory Packet, SP Pack, John Wayne Cookies or Crackers, Tobasco Sauce.**

C-Team   **(C-Detachment, Special**

Forces Company)   The U.S. Special Forces C-Team commanded three to four B-Teams in the field. A typical C-Team consisted of 20 men under the command of a lieutenant colonel. The C-Team was the organizational equivalent of a regular Army company and was referred to as a Special Forces Company. The B-Teams were equivalent to a platoon and the A-Teams were equivalent to squads. *See also* B-Team, A-Team, Special Forces.

C. Turner Joy   *see*   **Tonkin Gulf Incident**

C.M. Hoo   *see*   **Ho Chi Minh**

C.O.   *see*   **Conscientious Objector**

CA   *see*   **Combat Assault**

Ca Lu   *see*   **LZ Stud**

Ca Mau Peninsula (Quan Long)   Extreme southern tip of South Vietnam where the Gulf of Thailand on the western coast meets the South China Sea on the east coast. The provinces that made up the peninsula were An Xuyen, Bac Lieu, Kien Giang and Chuong Thien. This area was heavily infested with the Viet Cong throughout the war. Ca Mau (Quan Long), the provincial capital of An Xuyen, was located 115kms southwest of Can Tho in the middle of the peninsula.

CA-73   *see*   **USS Saint Paul**

CAB   *see*   **Combat Aviation Battalion**

Cables (Loose Threads)   GI slang for loose threads on the uniform.

CAC   *see*   **Combined Action Company, Corps Aviation Company, Avn**

Cache   Hidden supplies. In Vietnam the NVA/VC made wise use of caches to store such items as weapons, ammunition, explosives, medical supplies, and food stocks. One of the more routine functions of Free World Forces in Vietnam was the continuous search for enemy caches. When caches were discovered their contents were usually transported back to rear base areas for inspection and display. Foodstuffs were usually transported to the rear and redistributed to local area peasants. If a cache could not be moved because of its size or lack of transport it was destroyed in place.

CACO   *see*   **Casualty Assistance Call Officer**

Cacodylic Acid   *see*   **Agent Blue**

Cacti   *see*   **35th Infantry Regiment**

Cade River   *see*   **Song Cu De River**

Cadillac   *see*   **Medic**

Cadre (Can-bo, VC Song and Dance Teams, Political Officer)   Members of the central leadership group of a unit or organization. The NVA/VC cadre formed the nucleus around which the combat forces operated. The cadre operated the political propaganda machine at the hamlet and village level, interfacing with the people on a personal level. NVA/VC troops conducted combat and retaliatory operations while the cadre proselytized the peasantry. The GVN used their own Revolutionary Development Cadre program in an attempt to win over the rural population. The RD cadre used some of the same techniques as the NVA/VC cadre, but the program was started too late in the war and lacked sufficient support to be successful. *See also* **RD Cadre, Viet Cong Infrastructure.**

CAG   *see*   **Combat Aviation Group, Combined Action Groups**

Cai Be   *see*   **Operation Quyet Chien**

Cai Tang (Reburial)   Vietnamese custom of reburying the dead. If a family could not afford the proper ancestral burial, the body would be buried in a temporary grave. When the proper burial could take place the bones of the corpse were dug up, washed and reburied in the proper manner. This was especially the case with refugees who had been displaced from their ancestral lands. They believed that the spirits of the dead could not be calmed until the remains were buried in the proper location.

Cairn (Trail Marker)   Methods used by the NVA/VC to mark trails and locations, indicating such things as booby traps, caches or other important locations. NVA/VC markers of stones or branches were left in a coded pattern to mark special locations. They also used markings on trees. These markings served as warning signals for other NVA/VC moving through the area. Through experience, some American scouts and pointmen became familiar with some of the trail marks used, allowing them and the units they led to avoid ambushes and booby traps. *See also* **Kit Carson Scout.**

Calcutta (Solitary Confinement Cell) American POWs' nickname for a solitary confinement cell that measured 6 × 2 feet with one 6 × 2 inch window. *See also* **Torture, NVA Methods.**

Call Signs Coded identification names used by the military. The coded names identified units, individual commanders, aircraft, special teams, and basically any unit, individual, vehicle, aircraft or installation that had a name. Some call signs were permanent fixtures of a unit while other call signs lasted only as long as the mission to which they were associated. Code name selection could be computer generated, or selected to meet a specific need or occasion. Proper radio procedure dictated that call signs were to be used to prevent the enemy from identifying the speaker or his position. *See also* **Army Call Signs.**

Calley, Lt. William, Jr. (Rusty Calley) Court-martialed and convicted for the murder of Vietnamese civilians in the village of My Lai, March '68. Calley was a platoon leader in Co C/1st Bn/11th Bde/20th Inf/ Americal Division. Lt. Calley's defense was that he valued the lives of his men above those of the Vietnamese. He believed the villagers had been supporting the VC in the area, the same VC that had booby-trapped and mined the area in which his men had been mauled and the same VC that sniped at them as they moved through the area. Calley was sentenced to life imprisonment; he served three years under house arrest before being paroled. *See also* **My Lai, Koster.**

Calling Cards (Death Cards, Ace of Spades) Some U.S. combat units operating in the field had printed cards identifying their unit and usually including their nickname, date, unit symbol or other identifying logo. Also included would be the unit's motto or perhaps a short message to the enemy. These "calling cards" were left on the bodies of enemy soldiers the unit killed or were attached to enemy prisoners on their way to a hospital or interrogation. The cards served as a notice to the enemy that their unit was operating in the area, and were there to "kick ass." Various types of calling cards were also used by some Special Forces

and LRRP units. *See also* **Gunfighters, Mutilations.**

Calls *see* **Jody Calls**

Caltex *see* **Shell Oil Company**

Cam Lo Marine base camp located along Highway 9, 14kms west of Dong Ha in Quang Tri Province, I Corps. The Marine base was located 14kms south of the DMZ and was the southwestern anchor for "Leatherneck Square." *See also* **Leatherneck Square.**

Cam Lo River *see* **Song Cau Viet River**

Cam Ne (Operation Blastout I) During operations near Duong Son, I Corps, elements of the 3d Marines and ARVN units were operating near the village of Cam Ne as part of Operation Blastout I. The Marines took fire from the village and, after evacuating the inhabitants, burned the village to the ground. The scene of U.S. Marines torching the grass hooches was caught on film by a CBS news crew led by Morley Safer. The burning was broadcast nationwide in America with commentary by Morley Safer. The White House was not pleased with the selective broadcast, claiming it was incomplete and showed the Marines in a less than favorable light.

Cam On (Lam On) Vietnamese equivalent to "thank you" (cam on), and "please" (lam on).

Cam Pha *see* **Turkestan, Haiphong**

Cam Ranh Bay (CRB, World's Biggest Sand Trap) Large seaport in SVN, located in Khanh Hoa Province, II Corps. It was converted into one of the largest U.S. logistics centers in SVN. It was the home of the 22d Replacement Battalion, responsible for Army replacements throughout I and II Corps. CRB was one of the Air Force's major air bases in Vietnam. Bob Hope called the base the "world's biggest sand trap" because of the fine grain sand that got into everything. CRB was occupied by the Soviet Navy after the collapse of SVN in '75. CRB is currently their largest base on the Pacific Rim. During the war Cam Ranh Bay was considered the safest location in all of South Vietnam. In '69 Viet Cong sappers raided the facility destroying or damaging several structures and killing two GIs.

Cambodia (Kampuchea, Phnom Penh, Khmer Republic) Officially the Khmer Republic was located between SVN and Thailand, with its capital of Phnom Penh located along the Mekong River. During much of the VNW it was politically neutral. NVN used the border area in Cambodia as a pipeline to infiltrate supplies, equipment and men into SVN. In '70, after a change of government, Cambodia moved away from its neutral stance and became pro–West. U.S. and ARVN forces crossed the border into Cambodia in an effort to break up the NVN supply activities; an effort only partially successful. On April 20, 1975, the anticommunist government of Cambodia fell to the communist Khmer Rouge, who renamed the country Kampuchea. *See also* Year Zero, Operation Eagle Pull.

Cambodian Black *see* Marijuana

Cambodian Bombing *see* Secret Bombing of Cambodia

Cambodian Campaign *see* Cambodian Incursion

Cambodian Incursion (Cambodian Invasion, Toan Thang 43–45, Cambodian Campaign) In April '70 US/ARVN ground units crossed the SVN/Cambodian border in an effort to destroy NVA sanctuaries in Cambodia. The NVA/VC had been operating out of the sanctuaries in neutral Cambodia for years. Because of this neutrality no large scale assaults had ever been launched by US/ARVN forces. It was believed that COSVN Headquarters was somewhere in the area, but it was never found. Large quantities of NVA arms and ammunition were removed or destroyed. Enough supplies and weapons were uncovered to outfit ten enemy divisions. With the ground attack the airwar against the sanctuaries was also increased. An estimated 10,000 enemy soldiers were killed and material losses set the NVA/VC back at least 10–18 months. U.S. units involved in the incursion began to withdraw into SVN at the end of June. ARVN units remained in Cambodia a while longer. The operation was a success, but incomplete because U.S. ground units were only allowed to penetrate 30kms into Cambodia and couldn't press the attack on the retreating NVA/VC. The ARVN advance was limited to 60kms and without the

Americans they were not aggressive in their pursuit of the enemy. The invasion into Cambodia caused the NVA/VC to move deeper into Cambodia, somewhat weakening Lon Nol's ability to deal with the Khmer Rouge. The invasion led to massive antiwar demonstrations in the U.S. *See also* Operation Rock Crusher; Operation Binh Tay; Operation Tran Huong Dao XI; City, The; Kent State.

Cambodian Invasion *see* Cambodian Incursion

Cambodian Liberation Army *see* Khmer Rouge

Cambodian Red *see* Marijuana

Cambodians *see* Cambods

Cambods (Cambodians, Bodes) GI nicknames for the Cambodian people; "Bodes" or "Cambods."

Cammies *see* Jungle Camouflage Uniform

Camo Cover *see* Camouflage Cover

Camo Grease *see* Camouflage Paint

Camo Paint *see* Camouflage Paint

Camouflage Cover (Camo Cover, Helmet Cover) Fabric cover used on U.S. helmets. The cover fit over the helmet and was tucked in between the outer helmet and helmet liner. The cover was then secured by an elastic or rubber band around the outside. The cover had slits that were used for holding twigs and leaves to break up the outline of the helmet for camouflage purposes. The outer rubber band was often used by GIs to secure such things as matches, cigarettes, insect repellent, toilet paper, etc. on the outside of the helmet. The cover also served as billboard for GI graffiti or short-timer calendars. The cover came in OD green and camouflage patterns. *See also* GI Helmet.

Camouflage Fatigues *see* Jungle Camouflage Uniform, Tiger Fatigues

Camouflage Paint (Camo Paint, Camo Grease, Grease Paint, Camouflage Sticks) Black and green grease used to camouflage the hands and face during night operations and recon missions. The paint came in tubes, one inch in diameter and three inches long, two colors per tube; green paint on one end, black on the other. The flat, no gloss paints were used to break up the natural lines of the face and hands, and conceal exposed skin.

Camouflage Sticks *see* **Camouflage Paint**

Camouflaged Concentration Camps Viet Cong propaganda name for the Strategic Hamlets established by the Diem regime. The hamlets were fortified villages that were supposed to protect the people from the VC, but the program was extremely faulty and died shortly after Diem's assassination in '63. The Viet Cong claimed the villagers were forced into the camps and held against their will, yet in '75 after the communist victory in Vietnam, NVN/PRG opened scores of "reeducation camps" where South Vietnamese who had been pro–GVN, pro–American or were not active supporters of the NVA/VC were imprisoned and suffered far less freedom than those who had been relocated to the GVN camps in the early sixties. *See also* **Reeducation Camps, Strategic Hamlet Program.**

Camp Blackhorse *see* **Xuan Loc**

Camp Carroll Marine fire base located along Highway 9, 22kms west of Quang Tri, I Corps. Later in the war Army self-propelled 175mm artillery guns were based at Camp Carroll to provide support to Army and Marine units operating within range of its guns. The fire base was occupied by the Army after the Marines departed Vietnam.

Camp Cobra (Ban Kara Eboo) U.S. Army jungle training center located near Korat, Thailand. The center was located about 210kms northeast of Bangkok and established in the early sixties. The training camp and its mock Vietnamese villages were the Army's attempt to train and acclimatize some of their troops for combat in Vietnam. The training stressed large scale operations against enemy guerrilla forces, but did not adequately address the true nature of the Viet Cong and their interaction with Vietnam's rural populace. Training at the facility gradually ended as U.S. combat troops began deploying to South Vietnam. Ban Kara Eboo was the name of the center's mock village. *See also* **SAWTOC.**

Camp Davis American compound located at Tan Son Nhut Airport in Saigon. After the withdrawal of U.S. forces from

Vietnam the compound became the home of the North Vietnamese and PRG (NLF) delegates to the Four Part Joint Military Team. *See also* **Four Part Joint Military Team.**

Camp Davis (Duc Hoa) *see* **Davis, SP4 James T.**

Camp Eagle (Phu Bai) Large Army base camp established as the headquarters of the 101st Airborne Division in early '68. The base camp was located along Highway 1, 3kms south of Phu Bai, Thua Thien Province, I Corps. The base camp was previously occupied by Marine units. Phu Bai was 8kms south of Hue. *See also* **Screaming Eagle Replacement Training School.**

Camp Enari Headquarters of the 4th Infantry Division, which was located at Pleiku, in the Central Highlands of II Corps. *See also* **4th Infantry Division, Pleiku.**

Camp Evans Headquarters of the 3rd Brigade/101st Airborne Division, located 22kms northwest of Hue, I Corps. The camp was previously occupied by elements of the 3d Marine Division. *See also* **101st Airborne Division.**

Camp Faith *see* **Hanoi Hilton**

Camp Friendship U.S. Army base located at Korat, Thailand.

Camp Goodman Special Forces team compound for USSF advisors in the Saigon area.

Camp Haskins (32d Naval Construction Regiment, 32d SEABEES) Headquarters of the 32d Naval Construction Regiment. The camp was located on Red Beach just north of Da Nang on the harbor crescent. In March '70 Camp Haskins became the headquarters for the III Marine Amphibious Force which moved from Camp Horn when XXIV Corps H.Q. took control of I Corps. *See also* **Camp Horn.**

Camp Holloway (Christmas Tree Heliport) U.S. Special Forces advisory compound located 6kms from Pleiku in the Central Highlands of II Corps. Pleiku served as II Corps headquarters. In February '65 the Viet Cong attacked the camp and the Air Force base located at Pleiku in one of the early enemy attacks against U.S. personnel. The camp was named after CWO Charles Holloway, the first member of the 52d

Aviation Battalion to be killed in Vietnam, July '62. The camp was used as a forward helicopter base by the 1st Cav. and was nicknamed "Christmas Tree Heliport" because of the distinctive design of the taxiways and main landing strip. *See also* **Pleiku, Turkey Farm.**

Camp Hoover   One of the base camps of the 9th Marine Amphibious Brigade established in '65 at Da Nang. The camp was located at the base of Hill 268 and Hill 327, between the hills and the air base at Da Nang.

Camp Hope   *see*   **Son Tay Raid**

Camp Horn (III MAF Headquarters) Until March '70, command post for the III Marine Amphibious Force. Camp Horn was located on the Tien Sha Peninsula, directly across from Da Nang, sharing the peninsula with Monkey Mountain. III MAF moved to Camp Haskins on Red Beach west of Da Nang. Camp Horn later became the headquarters for the XXIV Corps.

Camp Long Binh   *see*   **Long Binh**

Camp Radcliff (The Golf Course, An Khe)   1st Cavalry Division base camp established at An Khe in August '65, 408kms northeast of Saigon. The base camp was one huge helicopter pad that supported more than 500 aircraft and the 20,000 troops of the division. Camp Radcliff was named after the first 1st Cav pilot to be killed in Vietnam, Major Don G. Radcliff. The camp covered six square kilometers on a grassy mountain plain and was nicknamed the "Golf Course" because the rolling plain resembled a golf course, fully equipped with holes furnished by early enemy mortar and rocket attacks. *See also* **1st Cavalry Division (Airmobile).**

Camp Site   *see*   **Harbour Site, Night Defensive Position**

Camp Strike Force (CSF)   Locally organized CIDG (Civilian Irregular Defense Group) that operated out of and provided security for the Special Forces camp. The CIDG camps were located along the border and their mission was surveillance of enemy infiltration routes. Their mission was later expanded to include interdiction and harassment of the enemy. During the peak of the U.S. Special Forces effort in SVN a typical camp force consisted of a battalion of CIDGs

(400–600 troops), a combat recon platoon, a Nung security team and the Special Forces A-Team. *See also* **Special Forces, Civilian Irregular Defense Group, CRP Platoon.**

Camp Tien Sha   Headquarters compound for the Naval Support Activity, Da Nang. The camp was located on the Tien Sha peninsula on the harbor side of Da Nang Harbor. The camp was in the shadow of Monkey Mountain which was located on the northwestern edge of the camp. The NSA camp was established in July '65 and previously belonged to elements of the 2d ARVN Division. NSA, Da Nang, coordinated logistical support for Navy and Marine units throughout the I Corps area. *See also* **Naval Support Activity, Da Nang.**

Camp Unity   *see*   **Hanoi Hilton**

Camp Woodson (334th Avn)   Army compound for the crews and support personnel of the 334th Aviation Company. The company operated out of Bien Hoa and consisted of slicks and gunships. The company operated in Vietnam from '66–'72, under the call signs "Dragons" and "Peacemakers."

Camp Zinn   *see*   **2d Battalion/503d Infantry Regiment**

Camp Zuma, U.S. Army Evacuation Hospital (Zuma)   The main U.S. military hospital located in Japan during the Vietnam War. Severely wounded GIs, evacuated from Vietnam, were treated at Zuma or at one of the other U.S. Army hospitals near Tokyo.

Campaign (Battle, Large-Scale Operation)   Officially large-scale American operations in SVN were termed "campaigns." Large military battles were also referred to as campaigns. The political mood of the American government at the time dictated that in an undeclared war, such as the Vietnam War, it would not be in the public interest to refer to operations in Vietnam that resulted in high body counts, as "battles." "Campaign" had a less ominous sound, and could cover a broad spectrum of military activities and results.

Campaign 275   *see*   **Final Offensive**

Campaign Hat (Smokey-Bear Hat, Ranger Hat)   Distinctive head gear worn by U.S. Army and Marine Corps drill instructors. The wide, flat brimmed campaign hats were similar to those worn by U.S. Park Rangers, and more famously, by "Smokey-the-Bear," of forest fire prevention fame.

Can Cuoc *see* **Good Guy Card**

Can Lao (Secret Police) Name of the SVN Secret Police, organized and commanded by Ngo Dinh Nhu, the brother of then–President Ngo Dinh Diem. The Can Lao operated as Nhu's personal police force and was notorious for its terror tactics against non–Diem factions in Saigon. The secret police force operated as the "strong-arm" of the Can Lao Nhan Vi Cach Mang Dang, Nhu's revolutionary movement. *See also* **Can Lao Nhan Vi Cach Mang Dang.**

Can Lao Nhan Vi Cach Mang Dang (Revolutionary Personalist Labor Party, Can Lao) Political party created in '54 by Ngo Dinh Nhu, brother of SVN's President Diem. Nhu organized the party to provide political support for his brother and a base of pro–Diem officials that could be used to fill political and administrative positions within the regime. Most of the members of the party were Northerners who had escaped from NVN after the '54 partition of the country. Nhu financed the party efforts through a network of government corruption, racketeering and vice schemes. The Can Lao was effective until the death of the Ngos in the '63 coup, after which the party members became frequent assassination targets of the Viet Cong. Also known as the National Revolutionary Movement or Can Lao. *See also* **Can Lao.**

Can Opener *see* **P-38**

Can Opener Tank *see* **Dozer Tank**

Can Tho ARVN IV Corps Headquarters and provincial capital of Phong Dinh Province. Can Tho was located on the Song Hau Giang (Mekong) River 120kms southwest of Saigon.

Can-Bo *see* **Cadre**

Canada The prime country of exile chosen by American males escaping military service. Between 30,000 and 80,000 draft age men fled to Canada to escape induction into the military. Some of the "exiles" were deserters from the military. Canada also participated in the control commissions established to monitor the '73 Paris Peace Accords. Throughout the war the U.S. was one of Canada's major customers, purchasing large quantities of war munitions and supplies. *See also* **ICC, ICCS.**

Canberra *see* **B-57 Bomber, Royal Australian Air Force**

Candlestick Nickname for a C-123 transport aircraft fitted with flares for flying illumination missions over friendly trouble spots at night. *See also* **C-123.**

Candy-Ass (Wimp, Pussy) Nickname for someone who is emotionally and or physically weak, lacking strength or stamina. Such individuals were also referred to as "wimps" or "pussies."

Canh-Sat Quoc-Gia *see* **National Police Force**

Canister Round *see* **Flechette, M-546 Beehive Round**

Cannabis *see* **Marijuana, Hashish**

Cannibalization *see* **Strategic Reappropriation**

Cannon General classification of large caliber weapons (20mm or greater), typically referred to as artillery. Cannons were further subdivided into three categories: mortars, howitzers, and guns. Mortars were low velocity, high trajectory, short barrel, short range, muzzle loaded artillery pieces (60mm, 81mm, etc.). Howitzers were medium velocity, low-high trajectory, medium barrel, medium range, breech loaded artillery (105mm, 155mm). Guns were flat trajectory, high velocity, long barrel, long range, breech loaded artillery (175mm, 8-inch, etc.). The terms gun, howitzer, and cannon were often used interchangeably. Gun also was used in reference to 20mm and 30mm automatic cannons mounted on aircraft or ships. *See also* **Redlegs, Mortar.**

Cannon Cockers *see* **Redlegs**

Canopy (Double Canopy, Triple Canopy) Thick, overhead jungle foliage which could completely conceal the jungle floor from aerial view. The canopy could consist of two and three (double and triple canopy) layers of tree cover which blocked the sun from reaching the jungle floor. Enemy trails, camps, bunkers and storage areas under the canopy usually went undiscovered until ground units stumbled upon them during operations, or recon teams came upon them.

Cantigny *see* **1st Infantry Division Fire Bases**

Canton   A district or subdivision of a province in Vietnam. Equivalent to a county in the United States.

Cantonment (Compound)   Military term for a camp or base, usually consisting of temporary structures used by troops. The cantonment, or "compound," was usually self-contained providing its own perimeter security and facilities to support its troops. U.S. and Free World Force units built compounds all over SVN. Some U.S. compounds were established on existing South Vietnamese bases, creating compounds within compounds.

Cao Dai (Dai Dao Tam Ky Pho Do Sect)   Vietnamese religious order centered in the Province of Tay Ninh. During the mid-fifties the Cao Dai, officially known as the Dai Dao Tam Ky Pho Do Sect, had their own private army, which was supported by the French, and fought against the Viet Minh. When the French departed Vietnam the Cao Dai integrated some of its forces into the Vietnamese Army under pressure from Premier Diem. Later the USSF organized some of the order into a CIDG to fight the communists in the mountains of Tay Ninh Province. The Cao Dai as a religion was a combination of the teachings of Confucianism, Buddhism, Christianity and Islam mixed with Vietnamese nationalism.

Cao Lanh   Provincial capital of Kien Phong, located on the southwestern edge of the Plain of Reeds in IV Corps. Cao Lanh was 113kms southwest of Saigon near the Song Tien Giang (Mekong) River.

CAP *see* **Combined Action Platoon, Fire (Shoot)**

Cap St. Jacques *see* **Vung Tau**

Capital Division, ROK *see* **Capital Republic of Korea Infantry Division**

Capital Military District (Capital Special Zone, CMD, CSZ)   The city of Saigon and the immediate surrounding area. Saigon, as the capital of the Republic of Vietnam, was designated as a separate military district and garrisoned accordingly. The CMD was also part of the Capital Special Zone which included Gia Dinh Province, which provided the river links from Saigon to the South China Sea. *See also* **Saigon.**

Capital Republic of Korea Infantry Division (CRID, Tiger Division, Capital Division)   The ROK Capital Division deployed to SVN in '65, and operated in the Qui Nhon area of II Corps. The division consisted of cavalry and infantry regiments and several artillery battalions. The ROK units operated effectively against NVA/VC units until their withdrawal from SVN in March '73. The ROK soldiers were particularly effective at killing the VC, generating kill ratios of 10–100 VC for every ROK soldier killed. The ROKs were not prone to taking prisoners and were hard-hearted when it came to waging war. They were also extremely vindictive, seeking out enemy units that ambushed or booby-trapped them. ROK areas of control tended to be relatively quiet because of their heavy-handed, but effective methods. *See also* **Republic of Korea.**

Capital Special Zone *see* **Capital Military District**

Capping *see* **Fire (Shoot)**

Caps *see* **Blasting Caps**

Capt *see* **Captain**

Captain (Capt, Railroad Tracks, Company Commander, Dai-Uy)   Highest ranking of the company grade officers. Insignia of rank represented by two parallel gold bars, nicknamed "railroad tracks." A captain in the field usually commanded a company. Like lieutenants, company commanders (captains) only spent six months in the field before they were rotated to staff positions at the battalion or brigade level. Field grade officers in Vietnam were plagued by a casualty rate greater than 90 percent. "Dai-Uy" was the Vietnamese equivalent rank. *See also* **Company Grade Officers.**

Captain's Mast (Request Mast)   U.S. Navy disciplinary proceeding performed by the commanding officer for infractions by enlisted personnel. The commanding officer heard the complaint and assigned the punishment. The Mast was held for nonserious breaches of discipline. The Captain's Mast could also be convened for the presentation of awards and commendations. The Mast procedure applied to Navy and Marine Corps personnel. Any individual could also "request mast" to speak with the commanding officer to air a grievance or make a formal request.

Captured Equipment '75 *see* **Abandoned Equipment, '75**

Captured Radios *see* **NVA/VC Radios**

Captured Weapon *see* **Blood Weapon**

Captured, Unaccounted For *see* **Discrepancy Case**

CAR *see* **Combat Action Ribbon**

Car Wash *see* **Whorehouse, Water-Point**

CAR-15 (XM-177E2, Commando Rifle, Shortie, Colt Commando) The CAR-15, Commando Rifle, was a modified M-16A1 Carbine. The CAR-15 featured a shorter barrel and a short, expandable metal stock. The handgrip surrounding the barrel was round instead of the triangular plastic of the M-16. The CAR-15 also had a special flash suppressor to reduce noise and conceal some of the muzzle flash. The XM-177 was the experimental version of the CAR-15 used by the Air Force. The XM-177E1 was the Army's experimental version and featured the "forward assist" (cartridge lock) missing on the XM-177. The XM-177E2 was the final experimental version. The carbine was widely used by USSF/LRRPs and was originally issued with 30-round "banana" clips (magazines). Testing of the weapon was conducted by ACTIV. Test weapons were issued to several U.S. units for evaluation in '66. Army airborne, Special Forces, air cavalry and armored cavalry used the test weapons under combat conditions. The shorter version of the M-16 proved effective and well liked by the troops that used them. The XM-177 had some problems with erratic rates of fire and clogging of the fire suppressor. Modifications to correct those problems were not approved and production of the weapon was halted in '70. Since U.S. troops were getting out of the combat business it was decided to discontinue the program. The weapon remained in use primarily with USSF/LRRP troops that maintained the CAR-15 until the end of the war in Vietnam.

Caravell Petition A petition circulated and signed by some of South Vietnam's leading political figures in '60. The petition was presented to President Diem requesting that he institute a system of political reform throughout South Vietnam. Diem ignored the petition and his brother Nhu took steps to harass those who had backed the petition drive. *See also* **Can Lao.**

Caravelle *see* **Hotel Caravelle**

Carbine *see* **M-1 Carbine**

Card *see* **MSTS Card**

CARE (Cooperative for American Relief Everywhere) A nonprofit, nonsectarian relief agency, fully approved by the U.S. government. CARE provided humanitarian aid on a worldwide basis. In Vietnam CARE teams distributed food, clothing, medical aid, and building products to help Vietnam's refugee population. Goods distributed by CARE often found their way to the Viet Cong, through the peasant population CARE was attempting to help. CARE teams also helped the Vietnamese farmer with agricultural projects and enhancements.

Cargo Pod *see* **Universal Military Pod**

Cargomaster *see* **C-133**

Caribou *see* **C-7A**

Carl Gustav *see* **L14 RCL**

Carmichael, Stokely *see* **Student Nonviolent Coordinating Committee**

Carolina Moon (Project Carolina Moon, Mass-Focus Weapon, Operation Carolina Moon) USAF project in May '66 to float large, flat, 5,000-pound mines down the Song Ma River in NVN, in an effort to explode the magnetically detonated mines under the Thanh Hoa Bridge. The "mass-focus" mine was designed to concentrate its explosive force from the outer edge inward. The bridge was a major transport artery moving supplies south for the NVA war effort. The Air Force had been unable, up to this point, to destroy the bridge with conventional bombing. Two attempts were made using the mines; neither destroyed or significantly damaged the bridge. The mine was so large, eight feet in diameter and over two feet thick, that it required a C-130 transport for delivery. *See also* **Thanh Hoa Bridge.**

Carpet Bombing (Saturation Bombing)
Deliberate widespread area bombing. Civilian casualties and property destruction resulted from the widespread bomb dispersal pattern, which covered a much greater area than the original military target. Hanoi falsely accused the U.S. of carpet bombing during the bombing of North Vietnam in '72. Had carpet bombing been employed by Air Force B-52s, there would have been little left standing in Hanoi. Carpet bombing techniques were used to bomb several free-fire-zones, especially those in the Cu Chi and Iron Triangle areas of III Corps. Such massive bombing was very effective for collapsing enemy tunnel systems in the area. *See also* **Christmas Bombing, B-52.**

Carrier Pigeons   In the very early sixties U.S. Army advisors experimented with "carrier pigeons," using them to carry messages within South Vietnam. SVN had no nationwide communications system that would allow GVN officials at the district and village levels to communicate with the provincial capitals. Military advisors experimented with various means to enhance communications within the GVN and its remote offices. Carrier pigeons proved unworkable. Pigeons raised in New Jersey for carrier work were no match for the tropics and the many diseases of Vietnam. The carrier pigeon experiment was very short-lived.

CARS   *see*   **Combat Arms Regimental System**

Carter, President Jimmy (Pardon, Amnesty Program)   Thirty-ninth President of the United States, Democrat from the state of Georgia. Shortly after taking office in '77 Carter announced an unconditional pardon for all Vietnam Era draft evaders. The pardon applied to all those men who had left the country, or were in hiding within the United States. The pardon did not apply to military deserters, but a special discharge review program was established. The program reviewed the cases of individual deserters who applied to the board for a pardon or an upgrade of an Undesirable Discharge. The review process did not apply to those who had deserted while stationed in Vietnam, or those convicted by court-martial. *See also* **Deserters, Discharges.**

Cartridge Belt   *see*   **Clutch Belt**

Cartridge Trap   *see*   **Bay Bang Vien Dan**

CAS   *see*   **Close Air Support, Central Intelligence Agency**

Case Officer   *see*   **Spook**

Case-of-the-Ass   *see*   **Pissed**

Casevac   *see*   **Medevac**

Cash Sales   One of the Marine nicknames for troops new to the field in Vietnam. On Marine posts in the U.S. "Cash Sales" was a military store where soldiers could buy new uniforms. The store had a distinctive smell of musk and chemically treated cotton poplin. Replacement troops arriving in Vietnam, in their newly issued jungle fatigues, brought that characteristic smell of Cash Sales with them. *See also* **New Troop.**

Cast Iron Mine   NVA/VC cast iron mine. Egg shaped, 10 inches long, 5 inches in diameter with serrated sides. The mine was most reliable when command detonated, but it could be rigged to detonate with a trip wire. *See also* **Booby Trap.**

Castillo, Manolito   *see*   **First American Woman to Die...**

Castle   Call sign for the control tower located at the Long Binh Heliport.

Castle   *see*   **FSB Castle**

Casuals   Military personnel in transit, either waiting for transportation to or from a duty station, or waiting to receive orders to a duty station. Some larger units had a Casual or Holding Company, where troops were held until they could be shipped out of the base or assigned to a regular unit. *See also* **Holding Company.**

Casualties   *see*   **Pushes, Vietnam War Casualties**

Casualty Assistance Call Officer (CACO)   Marine Corps officer assigned to notify a fellow Marine's next-of-kin of the Marine's casualty condition, and assist them with funeral or hospital arrangements. *See also* **Survival Assistance Officer.**

Casualty Classifications   Army casualty classifications used for reporting purposes were identified as heavy, moderate, and light. The wound or injury a soldier might suffer was classified as light, moderate, severe, or critical. For medical evacuation the Marines classified their casualties as emergency, priority, routine, and nonevac. See also **Medevac Priorities, Medic.**

Casualty Codenames see **KIA/WIA Code Names**

Casualty Collection Point Designated point, usually well to the rear of a combat action, where casualties were brought and given temporary medical treatment until they could be evacuated from the area. In Vietnam combat casualties were usually extracted by helicopter. The collection point was usually located far enough to the rear of the action to allow choppers to get in without harassing enemy fire. At times the collection point came under enemy fire, making the medevac of the wounded and dead difficult, and on some occasions impossible until a later time. Chopper pilots often ignored enemy fire if they believed they could get into a hot LZ to extract the wounded. See also **Medevac.**

Casualty Priorities Casualty admission to U.S. combat hospitals was handled on a priority basis. The highest priority was an American and the lowest was a Vietnamese civilian. The full order was: Any U.S. personnel, a dog from a U.S. scout dog team, an NVA prisoner, a Viet Cong prisoner, any ARVN soldier, and finally, Vietnamese civilians. Many field hospitals had regulations against treating any Vietnamese civilians except in the most extreme life threatening situations, but even those were sometimes referred to civilian Vietnamese hospital facilities, of which there were few. See also **Triage.**

Cat see **Caterpillar D7E Tractor**

CAT see **Combat Assistance Team, Air America**

Cat Fever (Catarrhal Gastroenteritis) Common inflammation of the mucous lining of the stomach and intestines, nicknamed "Cat Fever" by the medics and doctors in Vietnam. Cat fever caused diarrhea and cramping, and if left untreated could lead to ulceration of the walls of the stomach or intestines.

Cat Hole Single use, individual field latrine. Troops in the field not privy to the luxury of a formal latrine would carve out a small hole in the ground for their excre-ment, covering it with dirt when they were finished. The cat hole was the only latrine available for troops in the field that had to remain in the same area for any length of time. If troops were moving through an area the cat hole was dispensed with. See also **Latrine.**

Cat Lo Village located 7kms northeast of Vung Tau, on the bay (west) side of the peninsula. Cat Lo was used as a Navy base by the South Vietnamese and was the main base used by U.S. Navy units of TF 116 operating in the Rung Sat Special Zone. See also **TF 116, Southern Shipping Company.**

Catarrhal Gastroenteritis see **Cat Fever**

CATC see **Combat Controller**

Catch Some Zs see **Zs**

Catcher's Mitt 1st Infantry Division nickname for the heavy jungled area located 20kms northeast of Phu Loi and 20kms east of Lai Khe. The Catcher's Mitt was used as a base area by various NVA/VC units operating in Binh Duong, Phuoc Long and Bien Hoa provinces. On the Army maps the area vaguely resembled a baseball glove. See also **1st Infantry Division.**

Caterpillar (Convoy) GI slang for a convoy operating on a secure section of road. Such convoys usually moved with minimal or no armed escort. Most convoys operated in Vietnam with several security vehicles. In some cases the security vehicles were augmented by overhead helicopter or FAC surveillance. Aircraft would scout ahead of the convoy looking for possible enemy ambush sites. If the convoy did come under fire the aircraft would provide additional support. Ground security vehicles which were sometimes used for convoy duty included APCs, tanks, gun jeeps, V-100 armored cars, and specially equipped gun trucks. See also **Column Cover.**

Caterpillar D7E Tractor (D7E [Cat] Tractor, Cat, Dozer, Bulldozer, D5E Bulldozer, T6 Bulldozer) Full tracked bulldozer tractor manufactured by Caterpillar Corp. and used extensively by Army engineers in Vietnam. Cats were used for road and fortification construction as well as land clearing operations and enemy village demolition. The driver operated from an open cab and was vulnerable to sniper fire. The Rome Plow was fitted to the D7E and used for forest clearing. The D5E bulldozer was widely used by Army engineers for the building of remote fire bases. The D5E could be heli-lifted into place by the CH-54 helicopter. The T6 dozer was primarily used by Navy SEABEES and was also air transportable. *See also* **Rome Plow, Dozer-Infantry.**

Cates *see* **LZ Cates**

Catheter Bottles *see* **Foley Bag**

Catholic Refugee Program *see* **Passage to Freedom Program**

Catholic Relief Services (CRS) In Vietnam the Catholic Relief Services assisted the Vietnamese refugee population, providing food, clothing, shelter and community programs.

Catholic Worker Movement (David Miller) 1960s antiwar group located in New York. One of the group's members, David Miller, 22 years old, burned his draft card outside the Whitehall Street Army Induction Center in Manhattan, New York. Miller burned his draft card during a protest, October '65, and the scene was picked up and broadcasted on nationwide television. Miller, the first card burner to be prosecuted, was convicted and served over 2½ years in jail. *See also* **Bill 392.**

Catonsville Nine (Father Daniel Berrigan) Nine antiwar protesters entered the Catonsville, Maryland, Selective Service Board in May '68 and removed a large number of draft classification records to the Board's parking lot and burned them. Fathers Daniel and Philip Berrigan, priests of the Roman Catholic Church, were two of the nine. The Berrigans were subsequently convicted of conspiracy and the destruction of government property and sentenced to three years in prison. They refused to surrender to serve their time and stayed on the run until '70 when they were captured by the FBI. *See also* **Berrigan, Father Philip.**

CATS *see* **Civic Action Teams**

Cattle Truck A military semitruck with trailer used to transport troops. The trailer was about thirty feet long, opened top, with low, wooden side panels. Inside the trailer were long rows of narrow wooden seats for the troops to sit on. Cattle trucks were commonly used at Army training bases in the States.

Cau *see* **Montagnards**

Cau Bay (Bridge Trap) Booby trap used by the VC on some of the small, narrow bridges which crossed dikes and small streams or gullies. The selected bridge was cut in the center, and braced underneath with slivers of bamboo and the cut camouflaged with dirt. Beneath the bridge, punji stakes were placed. The bridge was usually braced enough to allow one small man to cross without it collapsing. Enemy troops attempting to cross the bridge in numbers or with their field gear on would be sufficient in weight to cause the bridge to collapse at its center, dropping them on to the hidden spikes below. *See also* **Booby Trap.**

Cau Viet River *see* **Song Cau Viet River**

Caucasian (Chuck, Ofay, Cracker, Southern Cracker, Grays, Whitey, Redneck, Honky) Slang references by blacks to Caucasians. Southerners were usually referred to as Crackers, Southern Cracker, Redneck or Peckerwood and usually singled themselves out by their southern drawl or bigoted attitudes. Militant blacks referred to the white man as the Beast or White-Beast. Some other names for whites: Rabbits, the Man and Mister Charlie.

Caught-His-Lunch *see* **Kill**

Caution Crossing Armor term for the method used to cross a damaged or unstable bridge. Only one tank at a time was allowed on the bridge and the crossing was made at a constant speed between five and ten miles per hour. The tank making the crossing would not change gears, pivot or stop.

Cav *see* **Cavalry**

Cav of the Cav *see* **1st Squadron/ 9th Cavalry (Aerial Recon)**

Cavalry (Cav) In Vietnam cavalry consisted of the Air Cav and the Armored Cav. Air Cav was infantry, mounted in helicopters with their own helicopter gunship support. Armored Cav was infantry, mounted in APCs with tanks for support. *See also* **1st Cavalry Division, 11th Armored Cavalry Regiment.**

Cavalry Troop (Trp, Air Cavalry Troop, Armored Cavalry Troop) A company size unit of armor or light infantry operating as a cavalry force. A troop usually consisted of three to four platoons, labeled A–D. Two or more "troops" made up a Cavalry Squadron. An Air Cavalry troop consisted of four platoons and the troop headquarters element. The four platoons of the troop were aero scout, lift (slicks), weapons (gunships) and an aero rifle platoon (infantrymen). An armored cavalry troop would also have had a headquarters element and four platoons which were scout, weapons and two cavalry platoons. The weapons platoon usually consisted of tanks and the scout platoon consisted of APCs and or M-551 light tanks. *See also* **Air Cavalry Troop.**

Cay The Vietnamese word for "tree."

Cay Champedak *see* **Jackfruit**

Cay Chuong *see* **Punji Pit**

Cay Dua *see* **Palm Trees**

Cay Dua Nuoc *see* **Palm Trees**

Cay Giep Mountains *see* **Crescent, The**

Cay May *see* **Palm Trees**

Cay Mit *see* **Jackfruit**

Cay Thien Tue Cycad tree sometimes mistaken for a fern or a palm tree in Vietnam. The tree grew to a height of about twenty feet along coastal areas and lowland forests. The leaves, buds, fruit, and stems of the tree were highly poisonous and could be lethal if eaten. The seeds and young leaves of the tree could be eaten if they were prepared correctly and extensively cooked. Troops moving through areas where the trees were densely packed experienced trouble breathing because the cycad pollen irritated the lungs and throat. *See also* **Palm Trees.**

Cayuse *see* **OH-6**

CBMU *see* **Construction Battalion Maintenance Unit**

CBS Evening News *see* **Cronkite, Walter; Kam Nhe**

CBSS *see* **Combustible Case Ammunition**

Cbt (Combat, The Elephant) Military abbreviation for the word "combat," used in reports and documentation. "The Elephant" was an old Army term for combat. When a soldier had seen "The Elephant," he had experienced armed combat; baptism of fire.

See also **Bust-Your-Cherry.**

CBU Mines (Gravel, Dog Shit Mines, Air Delivered Mines) Small antipersonnel mines delivered by aircraft. The 3-inch diameter mines were encased in cluster bomb units that dispersed the mines over the target area. Once the mine hit the ground a series of attached wires sprang out from it. These wires served as the triggering mechanism that detonated the mine. The small mines were less powerful than a hand grenade, but deadly enough to blow off a hand, arm or foot. Exploding mines also released shrapnel. A variant of the air delivered mine featured camouflaged mines in the shape of dog feces. The Air Force code name for the CBU was "Gravel," and downed pilots awaiting rescue were often surrounded by a field of mines for protection. *See also* **MK-20; Gravel Mine, U.S.**

CBUs *see* **Cluster Bomb Units**

CBU-24 (CBU-46) Antipersonnel cluster bomb unit used by the Air Force. When the bomb was released over the target the casing would open releasing 460–600 smaller bombs (bomblets). The smaller bombs were dispersed over a wide area. The bomblets were about 2 inches in diameter, each containing 250–300 steel pellets that exploded on contact with the ground or just above ground level. The CBU-46 was a similar type of cluster bomb; each bomblet was fitted with small fins to allow for a wider pattern of bomblet dispersal. *See also* **Cluster Bomb Unit.**

CBU-35 *see* **M-35 CBU**

CBU-46 *see* **CBU-24**

CBU-55 (Ethylene Oxide Bomb, Earthquake Bomb) The CBU-55 was a cluster bomb that used a variant of Fuel-Air Munitions technology. The 300-pound CBU consisted of three individual canisters that separated from the main bomb. On impact the canisters ruptured, releasing a cloud of ethylene oxide. After a delay to allow the three clouds to spread, a detonator ignited the cloud. The exploding gas cloud created a tremendous blast creating downward and outward pressures of over 300 psi. The blast covered an area of more than 30 meters in diameter and was capable of collapsing bunkers, blowing down trees and crushing anyone under the cloud. Sometimes called the "earthquake bomb." *See also* Fuel-Air CBU, Cluster Bomb Units.

CC *see* Command and Control, Company Commander

CCB (Command and Communications Boat, Command and Control Boat) A modified Monitor used as a command and communications boat by American riverine forces in Vietnam. The CCB was armed the same as a Monitor except the 81mm mortar was removed, and the mortar compartment used for extra radio and communication equipment. *See also* Monitor.

CCC *see* MACV-SOG Command and Control

CCK Air Base *see* Nationalist China

CCN *see* MACV-SOG Command and Control

CCR-1000 (Closed-Circuit SCUBA System, Bubbleless SCUBA System) Military SCUBA diving system that recycled the air exhaled by the diver into breathable air. The recycling of the breathed air kept exhaled air bubbles from rising to the surface. The system was used on missions requiring total secrecy and to avoid detection by the enemy.

CCS *see* MACV-SOG Command and Control

CCT *see* Combat Controller

CDEC *see* Combined Documents Exploitation Center

CDS *see* Container Delivery System

Cease Fire *see* Paris Accords, Check Fire

Cedar Falls *see* Operation Cedar Falls

Celebrities *see* Watch List

Celer, Silens et Mortalis *see* Swift, Silent and Deadly

Census Grievance Program US/SVN program to take the census of South Vietnam's population and at the same time listen and make note of the problems voiced by the people. The focus was on the rural population of SVN. The theory was that the GVN would use the information to help the people and thus win their trust and support.

Many of the rural Vietnamese refused to cooperate in the census. Some were afraid that if they cooperated with the GVN there would be reprisals against them by the Viet Cong. Still others believed if they complained about the government that GVN would retaliate against them. This latter belief was based on propaganda that had been circulated by the Viet Cong.

Centerline Tank *see* Drop Tanks

Central Highlands (Plateau du Darlac, Highlands) Highlands area of II Corps covering 14,000 square kilometers of mountains and plateau. Pleiku, Kontum, Ban Me Thuot and Dak To were some of the more familiar names of the mountain region. The mountain areas were mostly inhabited by Montagnard tribes. The coastal areas were inhabited by the South Vietnamese. The Highlands were strategic. If the NVA could have taken and held them, they would have cut SVN in half from the Cambodian border, east to the sea. The Highlands served as a major NVA/VC base area and supply and infiltration route, and was the scene of many battles between American and enemy forces. During the '75 Final Offensive the NVA took the Highlands which led to the collapse of SVN.

Central Intelligence Agency (CIA, The Agency, The Company, CAS) Many of the early counterinsurgency programs in South Vietnam were directly CIA sponsored. The CIA had a network of spies and informants stationed throughout SEA. As the U.S. military began to take a more active interest in Vietnam the CIA gradually lost control of the war it was waging against the communists. Throughout the war conflict existed between the CIA's and the military's analysis of the war. The CIA office in Saigon was referred to as "CAS." *See also* Spook, Air America.

Central Office South Vietnam (COSVN, Mimot Rubber Plantation) Headquarters for all communist forces operating in SVN, formed in '62, and responsible for coordination of the VC political and military effort in South Vietnam. COSVN directly controlled VC units, and indirectly controlled NVA units. For some time it was believed the COSVN HQ was located in Cambodia near the border with SVN in the III/IV Corps junction area, and was one of the objectives of the American incursion into Cambodia in '70. COSVN was actually located on the Mimot Rubber Plantation on the border north of Tay Ninh. The HQ was never captured because its exact location was never determined by American forces, although during the secret bombings of Cambodia in '69, it was hit, but not destroyed, by B-52s. *See also* **Tri-Thien Front.**

Central Vietnam *see* **Annam**

Centurion (Mark 5) British made heavy tank used by Australian armor forces in Vietnam. The Centurion was armed with an 83mm cannon, one .50cal and two .30cal machine guns, and weighed over 50 tons.

CEP *see* **Combat Engineer Team**

Cercle Sportif Old French sporting club located on Hong Tap Tu Street, near the Presidential Palace in Saigon. The club was a social gathering place for the remaining French nationals that lived in Vietnam, and soon became a hangout for upper echelon American diplomats, Embassy personnel and notables. The club had tennis courts, a swimming pool and a large bar.

Certain Victory *see* **Operation Quyet Thang**

CES Request (Combat Essential Supply Request, Emergency Resupply Request) Military jargon for an "emergency resupply request." For combat units in the field such requests were necessary when the normal resupply procedures would not be adequate to fill the units' needs. CES was often requested for units in contact with the enemy when supplies of ammunition or fuel were running low. Normal logistics channels would attempt to keep up with a unit's needs, but special events such as heavy enemy contact or destruction of a POL or ammo dump could easily raise the urgency level associated with resupply.

Cessna 0-2 *see* **0-2**

Cessna 170 *see* **L-19**

CET *see* **Combat Engineer Team**

CEV *see* **M-728 CEV**

CG *see* **Civil Guards, Commanding General**

CG College *see* **Fort Leavenworth**

CG-11 *see* **USS Chicago**

CGC Point Welcome (Point Welcome, U.S. Coast Guard Cutter) In August '66 the U.S. Coast Guard cutter *Point Welcome* was attacked by U.S. Navy aircraft off the coast of South Vietnam near the DMZ. The *Welcome* was performing routine night patrol duties as part of TF 115 when the ship was mistaken for an enemy trawler. The cutter was repeatedly attacked and unable to identify herself to the attacking planes. The *Welcome* was eventually beached near the DMZ. When the attack was over two crewmen were dead and three wounded. The *Point Welcome* was eventually repaired and returned to service. *See also* **Friendly Fires.**

CH-3 (Jolly Green Giant, HH-3, Pelican, Big-Mothers) Sikorsky S-61R helicopter used by the Air Force and the Coast Guard as a rescue and transport helicopter. The Air Force version was called the CH-3E and nicknamed the "Jolly Green Giant"; the Coast Guard version was the HH-3F, called the "Pelican." Several of the Air Force CH-3Es were modified for SAR work which included helicopter armor, aerial refueling capacity and extra fuel tanks. These modified CH-3s were designated HH-3Es and used for SAR missions in Vietnam. Coast Guard versions of the CH-3 were similar to the HH-3E, without the armor. The Pelican also had additional navigation equipment. The CH-3 could transport up to 26 troops, with a max speed of 164mph at a range of 800kms. *See also* **SH-3.**

CH-19 *see* **H-19**

CH-21 (Shawnee, H-21, Flying Banana) The Boeing-Vertol (Piasecki) H-21 Shawnee was the first major U.S. helicopter to be used in Vietnam. The "Flying Banana" was primarily used to transport ARVN troops and cargo. The chopper had a single engine located in the rear which drove two rotors atop the front and back of the ship. The CH-21 had a max speed of 130mph and a range of 450kms and was armed with door mounted light machine guns or rifles. The underpowered chopper was rated for up to 20 troops, but typically only transported 10–12 ARVNs. In '61 the CH-21 was the first Army helicopter used in Vietnam for combat transport, operated by U.S. crews of the 8th, 57th and 93d Transport companies based at Bien Hoa, Saigon and Soc Trang, joined later by the 33d and 81st.

CH-34 (H-34, Choctaw, UH-34, H-35, Seabat, Seahorse, S-58, HUS, SH-34) Single engine utility helicopter used by the Army, Marines and the Navy throughout the late '60s. The Sikorski S-58 had a max speed of 123mph and could transport 12–18 troops or over 2,900 pounds of cargo and was unarmed. The Navy version was called the Seabat or (SH-34) H-35. The Army version was called the CH-34 or Choctaw. The Marine version was called the Seahorse, H-34 (HUS), and was the Marine workhorse helicopter until the CH-46 Sea Knight came on the scene. Field Marines nicknamed the Seahorse the "Shudder-and-Shitboxes." Marine helicopters first arrived in Vietnam in April '62 providing lift support to the ARVNs. When American troops arrived in '65, the Seahorses supported Marine operations.

CH-37 (Mojave, H-37, S-56) Sikorsky, twin engine, S-56 heavy lift helicopter was used by the Army, Navy and the Marine Corps. The Army version, CH-37 or H-37, was called the Mojave and was the first U.S. heavy lift helicopter deployed to Vietnam. The CH-37 could transport cargo or 23–36 troops, and had a top speed of 130mph and a range of 230kms. In '68, because of the Mojave's limited range and slow speed, it was replaced in Army units by the CH-47 Chinook. The Marines and the Navy replaced their version of the CH-37 with the CH-46 Sea Knight and the CH-53 Sea Stallion. *See also* **CH-46, CH-53.**

CH-46 (Sea Knight, H-46, The Frog, UH-46) Twin engine medium lift transport helicopter used by the Navy and Marines. The Boeing-Vertol manufactured CH-46A was unofficially called the "frog" by field Marines and had a maximum speed of 166mph, a range of 380kms and room to transport 25 combat troops or 4,500 pounds of cargo. The chopper featured a rear cargo/entry ramp and began replacing the older H-34 helicopters in '66. The CH-46 operated with a three man crew and was unarmed except for a window mounted machine gun manned by the crew chief. The Navy model was officially designated the UH-46. The CH-46D was an upgraded model with more powerful engines and better reliability; it entered service in Vietnam in late '67.

CH-47 (Chinook, Shit-Hook, Hooks, Pipesmoke) Medium transport helicopter, manufactured by Boeing-Vertol. The Chinook functioned as the Army's prime cargo helicopter. It was able to move 3–4 tons of cargo or up to 33 troops. Cargo or artillery pieces such as the 105mm howitzers could be sling loaded and transported to almost any place in Vietnam. The CH-47 had a cruising speed of 150mph and a range of 390kms. The Chinook was primarily used unarmed, but some aircraft were fitted with window mounted machine guns in the forward section of the cargo bay. The Go-Go Bird was an experimental program to use the CH-47 as a gunship, but after testing, the program was dropped. *See also* **Go-Go Bird.**

CH-53 (HH-53, Sea Stallion, S-65A, Super Jolly Green Giant) Heavy lift helicopter used by the Air Force, Marines and the Navy. Manufactured by Sikorsky, the S-65A was designated the CH-53A "Sea Stallion" by the Marines and the Navy. The HH-53B was the Air Force version, and was nicknamed the "Super Jolly Green Giant." The CH-53 functioned as an unarmed transport capable of a max speed of 195mph and a range of 415kms. The twin engine Sea Stallion could carry up to 37 combat troops or 24 litters and its internal cargo compartment could accommodate jeeps or field artillery pieces. The CH-53E, Super Stallion, was an enhanced version of the helicopter, featuring three engines, a range of 500kms and the capacity to transport up to 55 troops. *See also* **CH-53E, Pedro, Super Jolly Green Giant.**

CH-53E (Super Sea Stallion) Improved and enhanced version of the Sikorsky S-65A helicopter which featured three engines, a seven blade rotor, a three man crew, and a lift capacity of 55 troops. The Super Sea Stallion entered limited service with the Navy and the Marines, but was not used as an assault troop transport in Vietnam. *See also* **CH-53, Pedro.**

CH-54 (Sky Crane, Tarhe, CH-54A, CH-54B) Sikorsky Aircraft Company, heavy lift helicopter. The twin turbine helicopter had no passenger or cargo compartment. The heavy transport helicopter could move containerized cargos of troops or supplies, and with its 20,000 pound payload capacity could transport boats, dozers, artillery, damaged aircraft and any other item that could be slung beneath its belly. Up to 80 troops could be transported in the Tarhe's troop pod. The CH-54A had a lift capacity of 20,000 pounds; the CH-54B had a capacity of nearly 40,000 pounds. The maximum speed of the Tarhe was 127mph, with a range of 404kms. *See also* **Universal Military Pod.**

Cha Gio Traditional Vietnamese dish of vegetables, noodles, crab and small pieces of pork, wrapped in rice paper and deep fried.

Cha Tom Vietnamese dish; sugar cane sticks soaked in shrimp paste and then grilled.

Chaff Small strips of metal (tin foil) dropped from aircraft in an effort to confuse and interfere with enemy ground radar. By the time the U.S. launched its new air offensive against NVN in '72, chaff equipped planes were regularly assigned to accompany attack aircraft en route to their targets. Chaff caused considerable confusion and false readings for NVN radar units.

Chaffee *see* **M-24 Light Tank**

Chaine Annamitique *see* **Annamite Cordillera Mountains**

Chalk Number Number assigned to a parachutist prior to his loading and jumping from the aircraft. The number was traditionally "chalked" on his helmet for easy identification. The chalk number was supposed to match the flight manifest maintained by the loadmaster responsible for loading the troops onto the aircraft. The jumpmaster verified that troops jumped in the proper order and that all got out of the aircraft over the drop zone. *See also* **Shoe Tags.**

Cham Quap (Brown Krait Snake) Highly poisonous ground snake found in the jungles of South Vietnam. This small brown krait blended well into the surrounding jungle and took a heavy toll on the NVA/VC. U.S. units operating in the field tended to make a lot of noise which scared the snakes away. U.S. infantrymen were also very conscious of snakes and the high number of lethal snakes in SEA. The NVA/VC occupied many underground and sublevel complexes which were frequently explored by the snake. Another reason for the higher loss of NVA/VC troops to poisonous snakes was the reduced availability of antidotes for the snake venom. *See also* **Snakes.**

Chamberlain *see* **FSB Chamberlain**

Champa *see* **Chams**

Champedak *see* **Jackfruit**

Chams (Champa) The ancient, Indian-like coastal inhabitants of the area along the Vietnam coast from the Red River Delta to the Mekong Delta; to them the area was known as Champa. The Champa kingdom later came to be called Annam by the Vietnamese. The ethnic Vietnamese began the displacement of the Chams from the area in A.D. 900 and took over the entire area by 1471. The Chams survived by fishing and high seas/coastal piracy, but gradually faded from dominance under Vietnamese pressure. Some Champa descendants existed as part of Vietnam's minority population, and were not supportive of the Vietnamese in any form (GVN, VC, or NVA). *See also* **Annam, FULRO, Nguoi Thuong.**

Chancroid *see* **Venereal Diseases**

Changeover Day *see* **MPC Changeover**

Chanh Long *see* **Dog Leg**

Chao Ba (Chao Ong) Traditional greeting to a Vietnamese woman, used to say "hello" or "good morning," "good afternoon" or "good evening." Chao Ong [chow ung] was used to greet a man.

Chao Oi *see* **Choi Oi**

Chao Ong *see* **Chao Ba**

Chaos *see* **Operation Chaos**

Chaplain Corps *see* **God Squad**

Chapman, General Leonard *see* **Commandant**

Charge of Quarters *see* **CQ**

Charge of Quarters Runner *see* **CQ Runner**

Chairman Joint Chiefs of Staff *see* **Joint Chiefs of Staff**

Charles *see* **Enemy, The**

Charlie *see* **Enemy, The**

Charlie Charlie *see* **Command and Control**

Charlie Med Company C of an Army medical battalion. Component companies of a battalion used alphabetic designations for the company name. The designations started with "A" and used sequential letters of the alphabet until all the companies were assigned. In the field the medical companies were simply referred to by the phonetic name—Bravo Med, Charlie Med, etc.

Charlie One *see* **FSB Charlie One**

Charlie Ridge Marine nickname for a small ridge located 13kms southwest of Da Nang and 6kms west of Hill 55 in Quang Nam Province, I Corps. The ridge overlooked the An Hoa Valley and formed the northern rim of Happy Valley. The ridge acquired its nickname because of the high level of Viet Cong activity that greeted the Marines when they began offensive operations in the area in '65; the ridge belonged to Charlie.

Charlie-4 *see* **Composition-4 Explosive**

Charlie-Rats *see* **C-Rations**

Chas. *see* **Number One; Enemy, The**

Chase Ship A backup helicopter that flew to the rear and at a higher altitude behind another helicopter(s) for the purpose of extracting the crew and occupants should the lead ship crash. This technique was most often used for VIP helicopters or Medevacs going into hot LZs. Medevacs going into LZs to pick up wounded were frequent targets of the NVA/VC. Some Medevac flights consisted of two helicopters; should the first helicopter be unable to get out once it got into the LZ, then the chase ship would attempt to go in and get the wounded out.

Chau Phu Provincial capital of Chau Doc Province, IV Corps, located 100kms northwest of Can Tho and about 3kms east of the Cambodian border. Chau Phu was located on the southern bank of the Bassac River.

Che Vietnamese dessert; a pudding made of beans, noodles and coconut.

Cheap Charlie Anyone, especially a GI, who was tight or stingy with his money. A common cry in the Saigon bars if a GI didn't buy a bargirl a Saigon Tea. *See also* **Saigon Tea.**

Cheap Heart *see* **Purple Heart**

Check Fire Command issued to immediately stop the firing of weapons. The term was primarily used to stop the firing of artillery weapons when such fires were believed to be firing on friendly forces or on the wrong target. "Check fire" heard on a radio net brought instant response from firing artillery and was distinctly different from "cease fire" orders which were issued at the end of a normal firing mission. When a check fire order was received all firing guns were checked to insure they were correctly set and the target coordinates were rechecked for accuracy.

Check Point (CP, Checkmate) Defensive strong points along a road, responsible for the security of a given section of road. A convoy's progress along a road could be monitored by the check points through which it successfully passed. Sometimes referred to as a "checkmate." The North Vietnamese also had a series of check points located at intervals along the Ho Chi Minh Trail, feeding NVA troops into the South. For most NVA troops, prior to '75, the passage south along the trail was a one-way trip. High ranking NVA officers, political figures and some seriously wounded soldiers were allowed to pass through the trail's checkpoints, headed north.

Checkerboard U.S. patrol tactic of placing small units in a checkerboard search pattern in order to locate enemy defensive positions. The typical search pattern involved a half-full platoon patrol searching a one square kilometer area (100 × 100 meters). When the area had been searched, the patrol moved on to the next square, 3–5km area directly diagonal to the one just searched. This pattern continued until contact was made or the operation was called off. These small search units were sometimes called "Recondos." The small size of the patrol force made it an appetizing target for larger NVA/VC units in the area. The American patrols considered themselves, and none too happily, bait trying to draw out the enemy. *See also* **Recondos, Infantry Search Patterns.**

Checkmate *see* **Check Point**

Cheese *see* **B-2 Unit**

Chemical Warfare The deployment of nonexplosive, chemical agents designed to kill, harass, or incapacitate enemy forces. This also included the use of chemical agents to destroy enemy materials or to contaminate areas vital to the enemy. The U.S. was accused of using chemical warfare against the NVA/VC. The U.S. did use chemical defoliants to denude areas used by the NVA/VC for bases and ambushes. Herbicides were used to kill food crops believed to be used by the enemy, and CS gas was used to flush the enemy out of bunkers and tunnel complexes. CS crystals were also used to contaminate old U.S. fire bases, and as part of the perimeter defense around some U.S. bases. *See also* **Defoliation, Operation Ranch Hand, CS Gas, Chemical Weapons.**

Chemical Weapons (Chem) Various types of chemical (chem) weapons were used in Vietnam. The primary chemical weapons used by the U.S. were CS (Riot) gas, and chemical defoliants. The NVA, on occasion, used CS gas, most of which had been captured from US/ARVN units. *See also* **Defoliants, CS Gas, Hobart.**

Chennault, Anna (Dragon Lady) Chinese born widow of Army Air Force General Claire Chennault, of the Flying Tigers of WWII. She chaired the "Republican Women for Richard Nixon" Committee during the '68 presidential campaign. Anna Chennault, who was nicknamed the "Dragon Lady," was sent to Saigon in '68, prior to the U.S. presidential election, to talk with South Vietnam's President Thieu. She was dispatched by then-"presidential candidate" Richard Nixon to encourage Thieu not to agree to the recently convened Paris peace talks between the U.S. and North Vietnam. She urged Thieu to hold out until after the November '68 elections because he would be offered a better "deal" from the Nixon administration. After Anna Chennault's visit to South Vietnam, Thieu promptly stated he would not participate in the peace talks that were taking place in Paris. President Johnson announced that peace talks with NVN would begin in May '68, and encouraged the South Vietnamese regime to cooperate. During presidential campaigning, Nixon repeatedly pledged not to interfere with the Johnson administration's peace efforts, yet he violated his pledge by sending Anna Chennault to Saigon to secretly sabotage those efforts. President Thieu was not eager for peace talks between the U.S. and NVN to begin because NVN insisted that Thieu be removed

from power before a cease-fire could take place. Thieu embraced the Nixon overture and backed away from the Johnson peace initiative.

Cheo Reo (Hau Bon) Provincial capital of Phu Bon Province, II Corps, located in the Central Highlands 97kms west/northwest of Tuy Hoa. Cheo Reo was strategically located near the intersection of Highways 7 and 14, and served as a major U.S. base camp. Cheo Reo was also referred to as Hau Bon.

Cherry *see* **New Troop, Baby-San**

Cherry Hill 3d Battalion/16th Artillery Regiment base camp located just outside of Chu Lai in Quang Tin Province, I Corps. The 3d/16th Arty was originally part of TF Oregon and later was attached to the Americal Division. The base camp was named "Cherry Hill" because the hill had not been attacked by the NVA/VC during the '68 Tet Offensive. The 3d/16th Arty operated 155mm howitzers.

Cherrypicker *see* **M-578 VTR**

Chest Protectors *see* **Armored Seats**

Chi-Huy *see* **Headquarters, Commanding Officer**

Chicago *see* **USS Chicago**

Chicago 7 (Bobby Seale) Eight antiwar activists were charged with inciting to riot and conspiracy at the '68 Democratic convention. Judge Hoffman, the presiding judge, declared a mistrial for the defendant, Bobby Seale, separating him from the other defendants. Overnight the "Chicago 8" became the "Chicago 7." Seale was charged with 16 counts of contempt of court, and sentenced to four years in prison. *See also* **Chicago 8.**

Chicago 8 (Chicago Conspiracy Trial) Trial of 8 antiwar activists charged with conspiracy to cause a riot during the Democratic national convention in Chicago, August '68. The '69 trial resulted in heated arguments between the presiding judge, Julius Hoffman, and the eight defendants and their lawyers. During the course of the trial, all the defendants, and their lawyers, were charged with several counts of contempt. The eight defendants were Bobby Seale, David Dellinger, Tom Hayden, Abbie Hoffman, Rennard Davis, Lee Weiner, Jerry Rubin and John Froines. The defendants were acquitted of conspiracy charges, but Hayden, Dellinger, Davis, Hoffman and Rubin were found guilty of rioting. The convictions were later overturned on appeal. *See also* Chicago 7.

Chicago Conspiracy Trial *see* **Chicago 8**

Chickasaw *see* **H-19**

Chicken Bus (Military Bus) Nickname for military buses used in Vietnam to transport troops. The windows of the bus were covered with wire grate screening to keep out hand grenades that could be thrown into the vehicle as it passed through crowded city streets. The buses were used in the larger cities, and U.S. bases.

Chicken Colonel *see* **Colonel**

Chicken Coop *see* **Quiz Room**

Chicken Plate *see* **Body Armor**

Chicken Shit Colonel *see* **Colonel**

Chickenman (Wonderful White Winged Weekend Warrior, Winged Warrior, Fantastic Fowl) Through '69 and early '70, American Forces Radio, AFVN, broadcasted a radio serial called "Chickenman, the most fantastic crime fighter the world has ever known... (Chickenman ... he's everywhere ... he's everywhere)." The Fearless Feathered Fighter fought crime and or evil on the weekends in Midland City, USA. The show aired five days a week, five times a day, a different episode each day lasting about two minutes. The tongue-in-cheek comedy brought a smile to the lips of many a grunt, who was fortunate enough to hear Chickenman on the radio.

Chickenshit Details *see* **Scut Duty**

Chicom (Chinese Communist) Common reference to military equipment made in Communist China. The NVA/VC were supplied with both Soviet and Chinese weapons.

Chicom Hand Grenade *see* **Type 59 Grenade**

Chief Master Sergeant *see* **E-9**

Chief of Naval Operations (CNO) Highest ranking officer in the U.S. Navy, responsible for all naval operations. During the Vietnam War the admirals that held the post were Arleigh Burke, George Anderson, David McDonald, Thomas Moorer, Elmo Zumwalt and James Holloway.

Chief of Operations (CHOPS) Title for a controlling officer.

Chief of Smoke *see* **Exec Post**

Chief of Staff The senior officer of the U.S. Army, and the Air Force, occupy the position of Chief of Staff. The Chief of Staff is the highest ranking officer for his branch of the service and is responsible for all operations of his service. During the Vietnam War, the Chiefs of Staff for the Army were Generals Maxwell Taylor, Lyman Lemnitzer, George Decker, Earle Wheeler, Harold Johnson, William Westmoreland, Creighton Abrams and Fred Weyand. Air Force Chiefs of Staff were Generals Thomas White, Curtis LeMay, John McConnell, John Ryan, George Brown and David Jones.

Chief Petty Officer *see* **E-7**

Chief Warrant Officer *see* **Warrant Officer**

Chieu Hoi Program (Open Arms Program) Means "Open Arms," a GVN program granting amnesty to any NVA/VC soldier who chose to defect from the communist side and give support to the GVN. Those who chose to "rally" to the GVN were called Hoi Chanhs or ralliers. Some went to work for the military and became scouts for U.S. units; they were known as Kit Carson Scouts. After a time of being under GVN control, some of the Hoi Chanhs would slip away and rejoin their old communist outfits. Some of the VC changed sides several times during the course of the war. The program ended in '73. In America's haste to evacuate Saigon in '75 records containing the names of Hoi Chanhs and many of the CIA's Vietnamese spies and operatives were not destroyed, and fell into the hands of the NVA/VC victors. *See also* **Hoi Chanhs, Kit Carson Scouts, Early Word**.

Chiggers *see* **Vets**

Chil *see* **Montagnards**

Chin Turret *see* **XM-28, TAT 101**

China *see* **People's Republic of China**

China Beach   U.S. Marine in-country R & R center located on the east coast of the Tien Sha Peninsula about 7kms north of Marble Mountain and east of Da Nang.

China Card (Chinese Intervention) Prior to the commitment of U.S. combat troops to Vietnam in '65 there was much discussion in government circles as to what Communist China's reaction would be if U.S. troops entered the war in Southeast Asia. The administration knew China was supplying NVN with weapons and there was much concern that U.S. intervention in Vietnam would bring China into the war on the side of the North Vietnamese. The "question mark" was what China would do; this was called the "China Card," and no one was sure how China would play it. Thoughts of the Chinese intervention on behalf of the North Koreans during the Korean War heavily influenced the Johnson administration's policy during its initial U.S. strategy in Southeast Asia. Because of the administration's fears of China entering the war in SEA, many restrictions were placed on the air war the U.S. waged against North Vietnam. Administration advisors seemed to totally ignore the true relationship between North Vietnam and China. The two countries had long been enemies, with China occupying, and at war with Vietnam many times over the past centuries. There was also some doubt that due to political turmoil taking place in Red China in the mid-sixties, and Sino-Soviet tensions, that China was in any position to provide NVN with anything more than materiel support.

China Marines   see   **4th Marine Regiment**

Chinese (Chinks, Bac, Trung Cong) During the Vietnam War, a large portion of Vietnam's population consisted of ethnic Chinese. They lived throughout Vietnam with a large concentration located in the Chinese section of Saigon, called Cholon. The ethnic Chinese were called "Chinks" by some GIs and occupied nonagrarian positions such as craftsmen, vendors, bankers and foreign traders. Based on years of friction between the Chinese and the Vietnamese, Vietnam's ethnic Chinese population was mistrusted and resented by the ethnic Vietnamese. "Bac" was Vietnamese for "northern" and used in general to refer to the Chinese. "Trung Cong" meant "Communist Chinese" in Vietnamese. See also **China Card.**

Chinese Advisors (Chinese Regulars) On several occasions U.S. reconnaissance and raiding teams encountered Chinese soldiers in the border areas along South Vietnam's borders. Military intelligence speculated that the Chinese soldiers were assisting the North Vietnamese in an advisory role. Large numbers of Chinese troops were not encountered by American forces during combat operations in Vietnam.

Chinese Checkers   see   **Elephant Chess**

Chinese Communist   see   **Chicom**

Chinese Hand Grenade   see   **Type 59 Grenade**

Chinese Intervention   see   **China Card**

Chinese MiGs   see   **Shenyang J-6**

Chinese New Year   see   **Tet**

Chinese Push-Ups   see   **Push-Ups**

Chinese Regulars   see   **Chinese Advisors**

Chinese-Fire-Drill   see   **Cluster Fuck**

Ching Chuan Kang (CCK)   see   **Nationalist China**

Chinh Huan (Indoctrination Sessions) North Vietnamese indoctrination sessions that were mandatory for all North Vietnamese Communist Party members.

Chinks   see   **Chinese**

Chinook   see   **CH-47**

Chinook Gunship   see   **Go-Go Bird**

Chipped Beef on Toast   see   **Shit-on-a-Shingle**

Chit Book   At most EM and NCO clubs in Vietnam drinks and snacks could only be purchased using "chits." A 2 x 4-inch book of 20–40 tear-out chits was sold at the club and all subsequent purchases of beer, alcohol, and snacks were paid for with the chits. In many of the on-base clubs local Vietnamese civilians were hired to work as waitresses and in the kitchen. To keep American MPC out of the hands of the Vietnamese, chits were used. The chits were useless outside of the club where they were sold, and they allowed the Americans that operated the club to better control the flow of money. See also **EM Club.**

Chloracne Painful acne condition that seemed to have a high incidence rate among Vietnam veterans who had been exposed to Agent Orange. The acne was most evident around the neck and shoulders. *See also* **Dioxin Poisoning, Agent Orange.**

Chloroquine (Horse Pill, Monday Pill) Orange colored antimalaria pill taken weekly to prevent contracting malaria. The large pill was a mix of chloroquine and primaquine, and all U.S. personnel were supposed to take the pill for the duration of their tour in Vietnam. Called a horse pill because of its large size. Sometimes called a Monday pill because some units tried to issue them always on Monday, for consistency. Widespread side effects of the pill were diarrhea and yellowing of the skin. Dapsone was a second antimalaria pill that was taken on a daily basis, along with the weekly "horse pill." *See also* **Dapsone, Primaquine.**

Cho (Marketplace) Vietnamese for "marketplace." The Vietnamese marketplace served as a central gathering place where farmers and craftsmen could sell their wares. A marketplace was typically located near a village or town crossroads and was an essential part of the rural Vietnamese economy. *See also* **Tax Collecting.**

Cho Long *see* **Cholon**

Chocks (Wheel Blocks) Portable blocks or wedges placed in front of, and to the rear of, aircraft tires to keep the plane immobile while it was parked, or just prior to takeoff.

Choctaw *see* **CH-34**

Chogi Stick (Balancing Pole) Wooden pole four to six feet long used by the Vietnamese to carry various goods. The pole was balanced over the shoulders with two loads or baskets equally distributed at either end of the pole. Men and women used this method of transport at the village and farm level. Loads in excess of 200 pounds could be easily moved by a single individual.

Choi Oi (Chao Oi) Vietnamese exclamation meaning "alas," "oh!" "Heavens!" or stretched to "My God!" In Vietnamese it was actually "chao oi," [chow oi] but it was Americanized to "choi oi."

Cholon (Cho Long) Section of Saigon predominantly occupied by Vietnamese of ethnic Chinese origin. Cholon was a small city within a city. During the NVA/VC Tet Offensive of '68, Cholon was used as a base and staging area for attacks throughout Saigon. During the fighting to clear Cholon of the NVA/VC, many parts of the city were destroyed. Cholon was located in the southern area of Saigon, west of the Saigon River along the Kinh Doi Canal.

Chop Slang for transport by helicopter. "At 0700 we chop to LZ Stud, and patrol from there northeast along the road."

Chop-Chop (Food) Vietnamese Pidgin English for "food." Frequently used by Vietnamese children begging food from GIs. When U.S. combat troops first deployed to Vietnam, some of them would throw C-Ration cans of food at the Vietnamese as they drove through the villages and towns. As encounters between Vietnamese children and GIs became more deadly, the friendly attitude of the GIs began to fade and was displaced by suspicion, apprehension and caution. The VC used some children to attack U.S. soldiers by booby-trapping them or having them leave bombs or grenades in areas frequented by the GIs. A group of children seeing GIs approach would run up to them begging for food (chop-chop), cigarettes or whatever they could get. *See also* **Fellatio.**

Chopper *see* **Operation Chopper, Helicopter**

Choppers *see* **UH-1**

Choppers of the 118th Avn *see* **118th Aviation Company**

CHOPS *see* **Chief of Operations**

Chrau *see* **Montagnards**

Christian Missionary Alliance (CMA) One of several religious organizations providing help to the various factions of the South Vietnamese population.

Christmas Bombing (Operation Linebacker II) Operation Linebacker II was an intensified bombing campaign aimed at pressuring NVN to negotiate, in good faith, for peace in Vietnam. The "Christmas Bombing," as it came to be called, started in December '72 and lasted 11 days, striking POL and dock facilities, airfields, supply depots, radar and SAM sites, transportation links and power plants. Many targets previously restricted were hit, and for the first time B-52s were used against targets in Hanoi and Haiphong. Several B-52s were downed by SAMS, but by the end of December, the massive and highly accurate bombing campaign against Hanoi and Haiphong encouraged NVN to resume meaningful negotiations in Paris. *See also* **Operation Linebacker I, Bach Mai Hospital.**

Christmas Tree Heliport *see* **Camp Holloway**

Christmas Tree ID Nickname for an identification system used by ground units of the 1st Infantry Division in III Corps. The system was devised in order for airborne generals to identify units on the ground and track their progress during operations. The system called for infantry squads to "pop" a specific color of smoke as they were deployed into the landing zone. Each subsequent landing of troops would use a different color. As the ground units advanced and popped smoke to identify their location the commanders, overhead in their C & C ships, could monitor the progress of the operation. Various states of confusion arose overhead as the ground smoke mixed in the rotor wash generating new, undefinable colors. *See also* **Flying-Squad-Leader, Pop Smoke.**

Christmas Truce Every Christmas and Chinese New Year (Tet) that U.S. troops were in Vietnam, a unilateral truce was declared by the Free World Forces. The truce period varied from 36–72 hours and called upon the NVA/VC to temporarily cease fighting to observe Christmas. U.S. offensive operations were placed on hold, and U.S. troops, and bases, attempted to celebrate the holiday. Every year the truce was announced, and every year the NVA/VC violated the truce by conducting mortar and rocket attacks on U.S. bases, ambushes or terrorist attacks in the larger towns. Usually within hours of the start of the declared truce the NVA/VC would begin harassing attacks, or attempting to overrun a remote base or two. *See also* **Tet Offensive, Ho Chi Minh Truce.**

Chru *see* **Montagnards**

Chu Lai Major U.S. base constructed on the coast of SVN in Quang Tin Province, I Corps, home of the Marine Air Station. Chu Lai was located 75kms southeast of Da Nang. The Marine airstrip, located at Chu Lai, was one of the first SATS strips to be laid and consisted of interlocking AM-2 aluminum mats. Chu Lai provided the Marines in the southern part of I Corps with air and helicopter support. The base was constructed on an empty strip of beach between Tam Ky and Quang Ngai in May '65. In September '65 the Marines deployed a Hawk SAM battery to protect the base from enemy aircraft. *See also* **Short Airfield for Tactical Support.**

Chu Loc *see* **Main Force VC**

Chu Pao Pass (Rock Pile) Mountain pass on Highway 14 between Kontum to the north and Pleiku in the south. After the NVA/VC Eastertide Offensive in '72, the area around the pass was held by the NVA/VC. As long as they held the pass Kontum was cut off except for resupply by air. U.S. advisors called it the "Rock Pile."

Chu Pong Massif (Chu Pong Mountains) Southwestern part of the Annamitique mountain range. The 6,880-foot high Chu Pong Massif was located near the border junction of Laos, Cambodia and South Vietnam, west of Pleiku in II Corps. The valley below the Chu Pong was the Ia Drang, site of several large battles between U.S. and NVA/VC forces. *See also* **Ia Drang Valley, Battle of Ia Drang.**

Chu Pong Mountains *see* **Chu Pong Massif**

Chuan-Tuong *see* **General Officers**

Chuan-Uy *see* **Aspirant**

Chuck *see* **Caucasian, Enemy**

Chumming Technique used by aircraft to draw enemy fire, exposing the enemy position to retaliation from accompanying aircraft. Navy Black Ponies, flying in pairs, used the tactic at night. One would fly low and slow over an enemy area; the second plane flew high above with his lights off. When the plane flying low drew enemy fire, the upper plane attacked the source of the fire, lighting it up for the other plane to join the attack. Army "Pink Teams" performed similar missions using a light observation helicopter to fly low and slow, attempting to draw enemy fire. When the enemy fired, Cobra gunships would attack. *See also* **Skunk Hunt, Hunter Killer Teams.**

Chunker *see* M-79, M-5 Grenade Launcher

Chuoi Vietnamese for "banana," Vuon Chuoi, a "banana grove." *See also* Souvenir Me.

Chuong Duong *see* Operation Platypus

Chuong Thien, Province (Vi Thanh) South central province in the Delta region of IV Corps which was used by the NVA/VC as an infiltration route through the Delta, from the Gulf of Thailand to the east coast of Vietnam, the provinces of Vinh Binh, Vinh Long, Kien Hoa and Go Cong. The capital of Chuong Thien was Duc Long, also known as Vi Thanh.

Chup Rubber Plantation During the ARVN incursion into Laos in February '71, a parallel push was made by ARVN elements into the Cambodian Chup Rubber Plantation area located 85kms northwest of Tay Ninh City. The area was used as a major base by the NVA/VC who were attempting to reestablish bases to compensate for losses suffered during the US/ARVN Cambodian Incursion in '70. The operation to clear out the Chup area collapsed when the ARVN commander, General Do Cao Tri, was killed in a helicopter crash. The attacking ARVN forces folded back into SVN and NVA/VC forces at Chup continued to grow and refit. *See also* Lam Son 719, Cambodian Incursion.

Chupata Bread Vietnamese bread.

Church, Senator Frank *see* Cooper-Church Amendment

Churchill of Asia *see* Ngo Dinh Diem

CIA *see* Central Intelligence Agency

CIA Air Force *see* Air America

CIB *see* Combat Infantryman's Badge

CIC *see* Combat Information Center

CID *see* Criminal Investigations Division

CIDG *see* Civilian Irregular Defense Group

CIDG Training Center *see* Phu Quoc Island

CIDG Ville *see* Dependent Village

Cigarette Roll *see* T-10 Chute Malfunctions

CINCPAC *see* Commander-in-Chief, Pacific Command

CINCPACAF *see* Commander-in-Chief, Pacific Air Force

CINCPACFLT *see* Commander-in-Chief, Pacific Command

Cinderella Liberty *see* Liberty Call

CIP *see* Counterinsurgency Plan

Circle Pines *see* Operation Circle Pines

CIRCLE Wheel (Buck-Rogers Secret Decoder) U.S. Army coding device introduced for use in Vietnam in '70. The CIRCLE encryption wheel was the Army's attempt to standardize its encoding techniques used for secure communications on the battlefield. Sometimes called the "Buck-Rogers Secret Decoder" by GIs not overly impressed with the workings of the code wheel.

CIT *see* Counterintelligence Team

Citadel (Imperial City, Walled City) The walled, enclosed portion of the city of Hue, I Corps. The walls were 30 feet high and 20–90 feet thick, and were surrounded by a water filled moat. Sight of heavy fighting during the January '68 Tet Offensive. Prior to Tet '68 there had been little fighting or terrorist activity in the city. After the battle for Hue it was discovered that more than 3,000 GVN leaders and employees and their families had been killed by NVA/VC death squads while the NVA held the city. The Citadel was finally cleared by the U.S. Marines in house-to-house fighting at the end of February '68. Hue was captured by the NVA in March '75 during their Final Offensive. *See also* Hue, Battle for Hue, Hue Massacre.

Citizen Soldiers *see* Reserves

City, The (Rock Island East, Bunker City) Name given to a large NVA complex discovered during the US/ARVN incursion into Cambodia in '70. The complex was a major storage depot and terminus on the Ho Chi Minh Trail. The 10km square complex was located in the "Fish Hook" area, north-west of Loc Ninh, in Cambodia. The complex was nicknamed "The City" and sometimes referred to as "Rock Island East." Thousands of tons of equipment were captured including ammunition, communications equipment, crew served weapons, medical supplies, POLs and over 400 trucks. Military officials estimate enemy troop losses at 11,000 KIA while U.S. losses for the operation were 1,800 killed or wounded. *See also* **Toan Thang 40–45, Bunker City, Fish Hook.**

Civic Action Teams (CATS, Village Action Teams, VATS) Navy teams that operated in hamlets in the Da Nang area. The Navy CAT program operated similar to the Marine Combined Action Program, providing the villages with support for civic improvements. CAT members lived in the hamlets they supported and operated health and hygiene clinics as well as civic construction projects. A similar Navy program called "VATS," Village Action Teams, operated at the village level. The programs operated under the Naval Support Activity and ended with the withdrawal of Navy logistical support forces in '70. *See also* **Combined Action Program; NSA, Da Nang.**

Civil Air Transport Company *see* **Air America**

Civil Guard *see* **Regional Forces**

Civil Operations and Revolutionary Development (Civil Operations and Rural Development Support, CORDS) A U.S. program activated in '67 under control of MACV. CORDS operations were centered on pacification efforts to help the GVN gain the control and the allegiance of the rural population. CORDS was supported by the U.S. military, CIA, and various State Department agencies. The Phoenix Program, part of CORDS, was designed to identify and eliminate the VC infrastructure and its effect on the people. The CORDS program was ineffective and plagued by corrupt Vietnamese officials and the U.S. military's desire to put more emphasis on combat rather than on nation building. When U.S. combat troops withdrew from Vietnam in March '73, CORDS was renamed RRO. *See also* **Office of Civil Operations, Pacification, USOM, OSAFO, Phoenix Program.**

Civil Operations and Rural Develop-

ment Support *see* **Civil Operations and Revolutionary Development**

Civil Rights Act '64 *see* **Johnson, President Lyndon Baines**

Civil Support for Revolutionary Development *see* **Pacification**

Civil War *see* **Vietnamese Civil War**

A Civil War ... A Losing War ... "A civil war ... a losing war ... a self-defeating war ... a dangerous war ... an undeclared war ... an immoral war: what kind of America is it whose response to poverty and oppression in South Vietnam is napalm and defoliation, whose response to poverty and oppression in Mississippi is ... silence?"—Copy from a March '65 SDS ad for an antiwar rally.

Civilian Clothes *see* **Civvies**

Civilian Construction Workers *see* **Tiger Ladies**

Civilian Irregular Defense Group (CIDG, Sidge, Irregulars, Indigenous Troops, Digs) Local defense forces, organized, trained and directed by U.S. Special Forces A-Teams. The "Sidge," as they were called by their Green Beret leaders, were company and battalion size forces drawn from the Montagnard tribes inhabiting the mountains and border areas of SVN. The CIDG was originally established by the CIA to provide local security for Montagnard villages against the NVA/VC. The CIDG was later expanded to include recon and raiding missions into enemy controlled areas. The program was taken over by USSF in '63. CIDGs were extremely loyal to their American advisors and as mercenary soldiers were not part of the regular South Vietnamese Army. Because of a long-standing hatred between the Montagnard tribes and the Vietnamese people, the CIDGs were controlled entirely by the U.S. Special Forces. By '71 all CIDG operations were put under command of the South Vietnamese Special Forces as the USSF personnel were withdrawn to the United States as part of the Vietnamization program. The effectiveness of the CIDG quickly deteriorated under the command of the Vietnamese. *See also* **Special Forces, Mobile Strike Force, Montagnards.**

Civilian War Casualties (CWC) The number of Vietnamese civilians killed during the Vietnam War, CWC (Civilian War Casualties) ranged between 250,000 to over 1,000,000. Few official tallies were kept on civilian deaths, and most of those that were kept were lost when Saigon fell to communist forces in '75. Postwar accounting of the dead has been further hampered by the closed society of the Social Republic of Vietnam (North Vietnam) and the U.S. lack of recognition for the communist victors in South Vietnam. See also **Vietnam War Casualties, SVN.**

Civilianization Program to utilize South Vietnamese civilians in some jobs previously performed by U.S. military personnel. The civilians were hired to work at some of the less sensitive logistics centers, performing support functions, allowing more U.S. military personnel to perform other war related duties.

Civvies (Civilian Clothes) Slang for normal, civilian clothes. In general any form of attire, excluding military uniforms, worn by a serviceman.

CJCS see **Joint Chiefs of Staff**

Clacker (Clacquer, M-57, Klacker) Hand held firing mechanism used to detonate the U.S. M-18A1 claymore mine. There were two types of hand detonators used, a manual and an electric version. The M-57 hand held clacker generated a 3-volt electric pulse when the handle of the device was squeezed or struck on a hard surface. A later version of the M-57 contained two flashlight batteries to generate the pulse which detonated the electric blasting cap that in turn detonated the claymore. See also **M-18A1.**

Clacquer see **Clacker**

Clap see **Nonspecific Urethritis, Venereal Diseases**

Clark Air Force Base see **Philippines**

Class A's (Army Green Uniform) The Class A green uniform became the Army Standard lightweight uniform in '64, replacing the Army Tan uniform. The Class A uniform was worn by enlisted and officer personnel and became the standard dress and travel uniform of the Army. Troops in transit to and from Vietnam usually wore fatigues or khakis. The Class A featured a four pocket coat with matching pants. The

uniform was worn with low quarter shoes, except by airborne troops, who were allowed to wear jump boots. See also **Army Tan Uniform.**

Class I Provisions (Perishable Food, Frozen Food, Refrigerated Food, Class II Provisions) Military name for frozen, dry and refrigerated perishable food items. Other food items were classified as Class II Provisions.

Class II Provisions see **Class I Provisions**

Class Six Store Military liquor store which restricted the sale of packaged liquor items to NCOs and officers. Regulations dictated that enlisted men could only purchase hard liquor in the EM Club. As with most of the Army's rules this one was usually ignored and GIs at base camps managed to obtain their share of bottled spirits "outside" the boundaries of the EM Club. See also **EM Club, Chit Book.**

Clausewitz see **Principles of War**

Clay, Cassius see **Ali, Muhammad**

Claymore see **M-18, VC Claymore**

Claymore Bag (M-18A1 Antipersonnel Mine Carrier) The cloth bag used to carry the M-18 claymore mine was often used by U.S. troops to carry extra ammunition, rifle magazines and grenades. The bag featured two separate compartments and a shoulder strap.

Claymore Mine see **M-18 Claymore Mine**

CLCV see **Clergy and Laity Concerned About Vietnam**

Clear a Weapon Clearing a weapon involved firing several rounds from the weapon, clearing the chamber, to insure it was functioning properly. In the case of helicopter door gunners, this clearing usually took place while airborne over supposedly uninhabited terrain. A number of water buffalo fell victim to the weapon clearing tactics of some door gunners. Troops preparing to load helicopters for an assault or on entering a base camp were directed to "clear their weapons." The troops would remove the magazine from their weapon and eject the shell in the chamber. Clearing the weapon this way greatly decreased the chance of an accidental discharge in the chopper or inside the perimeter of the base camp. *See also* **Lock-n'-Load.**

Clear and Hold (C and S, Clear and Secure, Cordon and Search, Mopping Up Actions) Encircling an area, then conducting a search, often used in conjunction with the pacification program. U.S. Army units would cordon off an area, search and clear it of the enemy; then ARVN/RF/PF forces would be used to hold the area and provide security for the CORDS pacification teams working with the villagers in the area. In I Corps, the Marines conducted C & S operations, then a CAP would perform the pacification and long-term security. The French equivalent was called "Mopping Up Actions." The Army operations were usually successful at clearing the area, but SVN forces typically were unable to keep the NVA/VC from returning to the cleared area causing the operation to be repeated ... many times.

Clear and Secure *see* **Clear and Hold**

Clearance In many areas of Vietnam it was necessary for U.S. units to get permission before a target could be fired on. For artillery and airstrike targets near populated areas, clearance to fire had to be granted by the US/ARVN headquarters in the area, and the controlling Province Chief or his designate. Seeking clearance usually created delays that reduced the effectiveness of the requested fire. No clearance was required to fire in free-fire-zones. In known enemy controlled or hostile populated areas fire could be returned without clearance if the enemy initiated contact. In open, uninhabited areas no clearance for fire was required. *See also* **Free-Fire-Zone.**

Clearing Company Forward medical unit serving as a collection point for casualties. It provided emergency aid and arranged evacuation to rear area hospitals for those cases requiring more extensive treatment. *See also* **Battalion Aid Station.**

Clearing Station *see* **C & C Company**

Clenched Fist Sixties hand salute signifying racial identity (and Black Power) among black Americans. Black "brothers" would greet each other in Vietnam with a raised, clenched fist. The Army outlawed these salutes, Afro hairstyles, and the "dap" handshake. The Army's contention was that the blacks' use of the salutes and handshakes was not in keeping with proper military form and was causing derision within the ranks. White units flying the Confederate flag were ignored by the military command structure. In '71 after several protests by black GIs, and violent confrontations, the Army rescinded its ban on Afros, daps, etc., and attempted to reduce its discriminatory policies. *See also* **Black Power; The Klan; Afro; Dap; Same Mud, Same Blood; Ju-Ju.**

Clergy and Laity Concerned About Vietnam (CLCV) A coalition of religious groups established in '65 to oppose the war in Vietnam. The CLCV's leaders included Dr. Martin Luther King, Father Daniel Berrigan, and Rabbi Abraham Heschel. The CLCV was nonviolent and advocated a negotiated settlement to end the war in Vietnam, the total withdrawal of all U.S. military forces, and an end to continued support for the South Vietnamese government.

Clerical Collar *see* **Dog Collar**

Clerks and Jerks *see* **Rear-Echelon-Mother-Fuckers**

Click *see* **Kilometers**

Clifford, Clark M. Served as an advisor to Presidents Kennedy and Johnson on matters of foreign affairs and Vietnam. Clifford was appointed Secretary of Defense in '68 after Robert McNamara resigned the same position. Clifford supported the Administration's war policy until early '68 when he advised President Johnson of the high drain in funds and manpower the war had created. Clifford advised Johnson to establish limits to the U.S. war effort and seek a negotiated settlement with North Vietnam. *See also* **Ad Hoc Task Force on Vietnam, Secretary of Defense.**

Clipping-Off *see* **Cooking-Off**

Close Military terminology meaning to move into close proximity to combat an enemy force. Example: Units of the 2d Battalion were unable to close with the enemy because of intervening terrain ... yet elements of the 3d Battalion closed with the enemy company, inflicting heavy casualties before the enemy withdrew. *See also* **Contact.**

Close Air Support (CAS) System of using combat aircraft to give fire support to ground units in contact with the enemy. Tactical fighters, fighter-bombers and fixed-wing gunships provided the support, usually directed by a ground Forward Observer or a Forward Air Controller, overhead, in a small observation plane. The effectiveness of the support was dependent on the accuracy of the information on enemy strength, disposition, proximity to friendly units and the accuracy of the delivered ordnance. Most strikes were directed parallel to friendly lines. Strikes that approached from the front or rear of friendly lines had to be extremely accurate because the slightest error could drop the ordnance in on the friendly troops. *See also* **FAC**.

Close Embrace Tactics *see* **Hugging**

Close-Order Drill (Marching) Military marching. The marching drills were designed to instill discipline and coordination, and enhance the teamwork principles of the military. The most concentrated period of marching was during basic training when the soldiers' attitudes and skills were being formed. During basic training the soldiers would literally drill for hours to achieve perfection and precision on the parade ground. *See also* **Grinder**.

Closed Breech Scavenging System *see* **Combustible Case Ammunition**

Closed-Circuit SCUBA System *see* **CCR-1000**

Closing the Back Door (Rear Guard) Air Force slang for aircraft providing rear security for strike missions to insure that the strike aircraft were not attacked by enemy fighters as they departed the strike zone. *See also* **Tail-End Charlie**.

Cloud Pass *see* **Hai Van Pass**

Cloud Seeding Operations (Weather Micro-Modification Projects, Silver Iodide Crystals During the U.S. offensive against North Vietnam in '70, U.S. aircraft seeded the monsoon clouds above Hanoi with silver iodide crystals in an effort to increase seasonal flooding in parts of NVN's Red River Delta. The secret seeding operations were later judged to have had extremely minimal impact in disrupting ground activity in NVN, but may have caused higher than normal flooding to the valley area around the POW camp at Son Tay, resulting in the camp's evacuation. Other experimental cloud seeding projects were also tested in an effort to hamper NVN supply activities, but, again, results of artificial rainmaking attempts proved ineffective. The seeding efforts were officially referred to as "Weather Micro-Modification Projects." *See also* **Son Tay Raid**.

Cloverleaf U.S. Army circular patrol pattern. Patrol units were sent out in three directions from a central base to try to make contact with enemy units. From the central base, patrols would make a circular sweep out from the base, completing the circle near the base. The resulting circular sweeps looked like a large cloverleaf. Using this method three patrols could cover a 270-degree arc from the base. The base provided fire support for the patrols, and a secure location for their return. If no enemy contact was made, the base advanced and the search pattern began again. *See also* **Infantry Search Patterns**.

Club Cammies (Profile Suits) Nickname for the camouflaged fatigues typically worn by U.S. recon and Special Forces troops in Vietnam. The club cammies were worn off-duty by troops around the larger base camps and clubs. The fitted tiger suits were clean, pressed and decorated with the various patches, tabs and insignia of the man's unit. The uniforms were not officially sanctioned by the Army but, for the most part, tolerated in Vietnam, in deference to the highly skilled nature of long-range reconnaissance work. When such troops operated in the field, camouflaged fatigues were worn, minus the patches and insignia. *See also* **Jungle Camouflage Uniform, Tiger Fatigues**.

Cluster Bomb Units (CBUs) A single bomb that broke apart over the target dispersing hundreds of small antipersonnel bomblets over a wide area. Several types of CBUs were air delivered, and late in the war an artillery fired shell, called the Firecracker, was introduced to accomplish the same function. CBUs were effective antipersonnel weapons, but were not discriminate in their detonation. If a farmer or buffalo-boy entered a CBU mined area they could be killed as easily as an NVA soldier. Each bomblet had the destructive power of a small hand grenade. Each bomb carried 250–450 bomblets. *See also* Firecracker, Fuel-Air CBU, MK-20, CBU-24, CBU-46, WAAPM-CBU, CBU Mines, SUU-30, M-35 CBU, CBU-55, COFRAM, Parcel Bomb.

Cluster Fuck (Chinese-Fire-Drill, Boondoggle, Ratfuck Operation) Disorganization, mass confusion, or a situation where nobody seems to know what is going on; where nothing is being accomplished, or whatever is being done is being done completely wrong. Botched or poorly planned military operations were often called "boondoggles," "cluster fucks," or "ratfuck operations." *See also* SNAFU.

Clutch Belt (Cartridge Belt) Cartridge belt carrying ammo, worn by U.S. Marines. *See also* 782 Gear, Web Gear.

CMA *see* Christian Missionary Alliance

CMB *see* Combat Medical Badge

CMD *see* Capital Military District

CMEC *see* Combat Materiel Exploitation Center

CMH *see* Congressional Medal of Honor

CMIC *see* Combined Military Interrogation Center

CMPSF *see* Composite Military Police Strike Force

CNAG *see* Naval Advisory Group

CNO *see* Chief of Naval Operations

Co (Co Cong, Female Viet Cong) Vietnamese for young girl or unmarried woman. GIs sometimes referred to the female Viet Cong as "Co Cong." *See also* The Enemy.

CO *see* Commanding Officer

Co A/7th Battalion *see* 5th Infantry Division (Mechanized)

CO Call (Commanding Officer Call) "Visit" paid to a unit by its commanding officers. CO calls were usually made by battalion level commanders to individual company or battery base camps. The commander would pass on orders for operations and brief his subordinate commanders. The CO call allowed the commander to visit several of his units in the course of a day, allowing the subordinate unit commanders to remain in the field with their units. In Vietnam artillery batteries were frequently split up between two or three fire support bases making assembly of all the commanders in one place a time-consuming task. The CO call allowed all units to be kept informed with a minimum of disruption.

Co Chien RPG *see* Game Warden River Groups

Co Cong *see* Co

Co N/75th Infantry (Rangers) *see* Delta Teams

Co Tuong *see* Elephant Chess

Co Van My (American Advisor) Vietnamese name for an "American advisor."

Co-Ax *see* Coaxial Machine Gun

Co. *see* Company

Coast Guard Cutter *see* WPB

Coast Guard Squadron One *see* TF 115, WPB

Coast Guard Squadron Three *see* TF 115, WPB

Coastal Blocking Group *see* TF 194 Groups

Coastal Force *see* Junk Force

Coastal Raiding Group *see* TF 194 Groups

Coastal Surveillance Center *see* Coastal Surveillance Zones

Coastal Surveillance Force *see* TF 115

Coastal Surveillance Zones (Coastal Surveillance Center, Contiguous Zones) The coast of SVN was divided into four coastal zones for patrolling by ships and aircraft of the U.S. Navy's TF 115, Operation Market Time, and the Vietnamese Navy. Zone 1 extended from the DMZ to Duc Pho, with Da Nang as the zone's Coastal Surveillance Center (CSC). Zone 2 extended from Duc Pho to Phan Thiet, with Qui Nhon and Nha Trang as CSCs. Zone 3 extended from Phan Thiet to Vinh Loi, with Vung Tau the CSC. Zone 4 covered the remaining coast and the island of Phu Quoc, with the CSC located at An Thoi on Phu Quoc Island. The CSCs coordinated search and surveillance missions carried out in their respective zones. The zones were nebulously referred to as the "Contiguous Zones." *See also* **TF 115.**

Coaxial Machine Gun (Co-Ax) A machine gun mounted on a tank turret, parallel with the tank's main cannon, allowing the same sighting to be used for either weapon. The M-48 used a 7.62mm machine gun as its co-ax.

Cobra *see* **AH-1G, UH-1B, Asiatic Cobra, LZ Cobra**

Cobra Training School *see* **USARV Cobra Transition School**

COC (Command of Camp) Administrative headquarters for a large U.S. base camp. The COC was responsible for the camp's operation, but was not the tactical control headquarters for combat operations in the area. The COC was responsible for such things as billeting of troops, garbage and waste disposal, defensive structures, mess hall facilities, traffic control, recreation facilities, etc. COCs were only found on very large base camps typically at the division and brigade level. *See also* **Tactical Operations Center.**

Coc Dau (Kill) Vietnamese, literally meaning to "bump one's head." For the GIs and Vietnamese, "coc dau" [cock-a-dow] was bastardized, meaning "to kill." When Vietnamese children would get frustrated or angry with a GI they would sometimes say, "VC coc dau you." The GI might respond with, "Me coc dau beaucoup VC" or "You VC, I coc dau you." *See also* **Kill.**

Cocaine Cocaine was one of the many illegal drugs in use within the U.S. The hippie movement made extensive use of cocaine throughout the sixties and seventies. Cocaine use in Vietnam was relatively minor compared to use of other illicit drugs such as heroin, marijuana, morphine, methamphetamines, etc. *See also* **Speed, Illicit Drugs, Drug List.**

Cochin China (Southern Vietnam, Nam-Bo) Prior to French colonization of Vietnam, the country was divided into the three smaller countries of Tonkin, Annam and Cochin China. Cochin China was the southernmost country, and in ancient times

it had been controlled by Annam, China and Cambodia. Cochin China covered the area of Vietnam south of the 12th Parallel and west of Longitude 108, or from the foot of the Central Highlands, south to the China Sea and the Gulf of Thailand. The Delta area of Cochin China (Nam-Bo) was prime agricultural land. Saigon was the capital and largest city in the country. In '49, Cochin China became part of the country of Vietnam. *See also* **Tonkin, Annam.**

Cochise Green *see* **Operation Cochise Green**

Cock *see* **Penis**

Cock-Rot (Drippy-Dick) Nicknames for a wide variety of sexually transmitted venereal diseases that were prevalent in Vietnam. *See also* **Venereal Diseases.**

Cockroach Races One of the pastimes practiced by some GIs at base camps was cockroach racing. The cockroaches in Vietnam were very large and some of them were quite fast. To relieve some of their boredom GIs would capture several roaches and race them for money.

Cocoa Beach *see* **Vinh Loc Island**

Coconut Mine Viet Cong booby trap that consisted of a hollowed out coconut filled with explosive. The coconut was buried in a shallow hole with several rocks stacked on top of it. A trip wire activated a friction fuse that detonated the explosive, throwing the rocks. *See also* **Booby Trap.**

Code of Conduct (Executive Order 10631, Military Code of Conduct, MCC) The Code of Conduct states the standards to which all members of the United States Armed Forces are to adhere in the event they are involved in combat with, or captured by the enemy. The Executive Order was signed by Dwight D. Eisenhower, President of the United States, and Commander-in-Chief of the armed forces, at the White House, August 17, 1955. All members of the armed forces were to be familiar with the code and expected to live up to its high moral standard. Code of Conduct for Members of the United States Armed Forces: I) I am an American fighting man. I serve in the forces which guard my country and our way of life. I am prepared to give my life in their defense. II) I will never surrender of my own free will. If in command I will never surrender my men while they still have the means to resist. III) If I am captured I will continue to resist by all means available. I will make every effort to escape and aid others to escape. I will accept neither parole nor special favors from the enemy. IV) If I become a prisoner of war, I will keep faith with my fellow prisoners. I will give no information or take part in any action which might be harmful to my comrades. If I am senior, I will take command. If not, I will obey the lawful orders of those appointed over me and will back them up in every way. V) When questioned, should I become a prisoner of war, I am required to give my name, rank, service number, and date of birth. I will evade answering further questions to the utmost of my ability. I will make no oral or written statements disloyal to my country and its allies or harmful to their cause. VI) I will never forget that I am an American fighting man, responsible for my actions, and dedicated to the principles which made my country free. I trust in God and the United States of America.

Cofat Compound The Cofat Compound was located in Cholon, in Saigon and was named after the French cigarette company that built it. In '63 U.S. Navy headquarters personnel began to occupy offices in the compound. From the compound the Navy coordinated dispatch deliveries to field units by way of Air Cofat, the Navy courier service which operated out of Tan Son Nhut. *See also* **Air Cofat.**

Coffins, Viet Cong (Ao Quan) Before large scale attacks by the Viet Cong, the VCI would have each Vietnamese village and hamlet in the area of the attack make several wooden coffins. The coffins (ao quan, in Vietnamese) would not be openly displayed but would be kept out of sight behind hootches and walls. The wooden coffins were for the Viet Cong who were going to die in the attack. The Viet Cong would supposedly fight more fiercely and with more conviction in the attack if they believed that should they be killed they would receive a ritualistic burial.

COFRAM Round (Controlled Fragmentation Munition) U.S. antipersonnel weapon. The weapon was similar to a cluster bomb except that it was fired from a 155mm howitzer. The COFRAM round had a time fuse that exploded the shell casing over the target, releasing 60 small bombs (submunitions) that exploded on impact with the ground. Each of the small bombs was equivalent to a small fragmentation hand grenade. The scattering of the submunitions could be controlled by varying the time fuse that exploded the shell casing. The maximum range of the COFRAM round was 18,000 meters. *See also* **Cluster Bomb Units, Submunitions.**

COIN *see* **Counterinsurgency**

COIN Operations *see* **Pacification**

Coke Bomb *see* **Beer Can Grenade**

Col *see* **Colonel**

Colby, William Was CIA Station Chief in Saigon in '59, where he organized the start of the CIDG and the Strategic Hamlet Programs. In '68 Colby took over direction of CORDS operations under MACV command and was also responsible for the Phoenix Program of VCI elimination. In '73 Colby was appointed director of the CIA. *See also* **Phoenix Program, CORDS.**

Colco Island *see* **Vinh Loc Island**

Cold LZ *see* **Hot LZ**

Cold Tunnels *see* **Hot/Cold Tunnels**

Collapsible Canteen (2-Quart Canteen, LP Bladder) Plastic canteen used by U.S. troops in Vietnam. The canteen entered service in '69 and featured soft plastic sides that allowed the air to be squeezed out of the canteen as the water was removed. With the air removed the remaining water in the canteen didn't "slosh about" and make noise. The thin plastic canteen was carried in a nylon carrier. The prototype, the Limited Production Bladder, was called the LP bladder by the troops who field tested it. Other versions of the collapsible canteen were tried but were unsuccessful. *See also* **5-Quart Bladder.**

Collateral Civilian Damage Official military terminology used to describe damage or destruction to civilian property as a result of friendly units attempting to destroy the enemy or deny him the use of structures, locations or terrain features; damage to civilian property caused by a military attack. *See also* **Military Phraseology, Surgical Bombing.**

Collection and Clearing Company *see* **C & C Company**

Collectivization (Land Reform) Shortly after the defeat of the French by the Viet Minh the new government of North Vietnam, under Ho Chi Minh's communist control, began a program of collectivization throughout many of the provinces of North Vietnam. The program centered around land reform and the redistribution of the farmland. Although most of the farms were small, they were still subject to the collective process. The program angered small farm owners, many who revolted against the communist program. The revolts were typically crushed with military force, resulting in thousands of deaths and imprisonments. Ho later repudiated the program, blaming its failure on Communist Party leader Truong Chinh. Ho replaced Chinh with Le Duan. *See also* **Lao Dong.**

College Eye *see* **Airborne Battlefield Command and Control Center**

Collins, General Joseph L. (Lightning Joe) General Collins commanded the U.S. 25th Infantry Division on Guadalcanal during WWII. His troops named him "Lightning Joe." The 25th Infantry was known as the "Tropic Lightning Division." Lightning Joe was sent to Saigon in '54 as a Special U.S. Representative with the job of evaluating the political situation in SVN and organizing the GVN. General Collins recommended that the U.S. not back Prime Minister Diem because of his harsh policies and weak national appeal. Collins' recommendations were not followed and the U.S. proceeded to back the Diem regime.

Collins 32S-3 (32S-3 Radio) One of the long-range radios used by U.S. Special Forces throughout Vietnam to maintain communications with remote USSFs camps. *See also* **U.S. Radios.**

Colonel (COL., Full Bird, Full Bull, Bird Colonel, Chicken Colonel, Dai-Ta) Highest ranking field grade officer below the rank of general. Insignia of rank was a Silver Eagle with spread wings, known by a variety of nicknames in the field. Colonels in field commands typically commanded a brigade or regiment. Dai-Ta was the Vietnamese equivalent rank.

Colonel Bin Tin Highest ranking NVA officer in Saigon. On April 30, 1975, he accepted the formal surrender of the South Vietnamese government, headed by General "Big" Minh.

Colonel Computer *see* **Combat Martin Operations**

Colons (French Colonialist) French nickname for the French nationals who lived in France's foreign colonies, including Vietnam.

Colorado *see* **Operation Colorado**

Colt Commando *see* **CAR 15**

Colt M-16 *see* **Armalite**

Colt .45 *see* **M-1911A1**

Column Cover (Bird-Dogging) Aircraft assigned to fly above a ground convoy or formation. Light observation helicopters were typically used, but sometimes gunships flew the cover if the area through which the convoy was moving presented a high probability of enemy ambush. The choppers frequently buzzed suspected areas attempting to draw fire or prematurely trigger an ambush. Sometimes referred to as "bird-dogging." *See also* **Caterpillar.**

Combat *see* **Cbt**

Combat Action Ribbon (CAR) Badge awarded to U.S. Marine infantrymen who served in combat against a hostile force. Service and support personnel were not eligible for this award. It was equivalent to the Army's CIB. *See also* **Combat Infantryman's Badge.**

Combat Air Traffic Controller *see* **Combat Controller**

Combat Arms Regimental System (CARS) Official Army policy established in '57 to recognize and continue the tradition of the Army regiment. Regimental lineage, established by units since the Army was founded, was passed on to subsequent units under the regimental name. The regiments retained their names and histories, but were reorganized into brigades under the Army's ROAD system. Traditionally, regiments operated together, but during Vietnam some regiments were split up with their battalions serving in different parts of the world. A further reorganization of the Army in the early '80s has attempted to regroup separated battalions with their parent regiment for assignment to the same brigade force. *See also* ROAD.

Combat Assault (CA, Heliborne Combat Assault, Vertical Assault, Vertical Envelopment) Armed air assault of an area. Generally understood in Vietnam to mean a helicopter assault by infantry troops. Infantry troops were transported by helicopter and inserted into an "LZ"; once on the ground the troops continued to press the assault on the target. The Marines referred to such helicopter-borne insertions as "Vertical Assaults" and "Vertical Envelopments." An Army helicopter assault battalion typically consisted of 64 Slicks for transport of about 500 troops. During the Vietnam War the 1st Cavalry Division was organized as airmobile cavalry. The Marines had no specific air cavalry units, but utilized the helicopter in the combat assault role. *See also* Air-Assault.

Combat Assistance Team (CAT) In mid '68 the title of U.S. military advisor teams that operated with the ARVN at the battalion level and above was changed to "Combat Assistance Teams." The change was made as part of the Vietnamization process. Pentagon policymakers wanted the Vietnamese command structure to see that the U.S. wanted to "assist" the Vietnamese in their struggle against the NVA/VC rather than take the position of telling the ARVN what to do and how to fight the war. *See also* Military Assistance Command, Vietnam.

Combat Aviation Battalion (CAB, Aviation Battalion) One of the basic elements of an Army aviation group. An aviation group consisted of several aviation battalions that provided helicopter support to other Army units. An aviation battalion consisted of several different types of aviation companies. The companies performed such functions as troop lift, medium and heavy helicopter support, fixed-wing reconnaissance, gunships, fixed-wing transport, and various other duties. *See also* Combat Aviation Group, Avn.

Combat Aviation Group (CAG) Army aviation group that provided helicopter and fixed-wing support to Army units. Several aviation groups were active during the Vietnam War. A group consisted of 2–6 aviation battalions that provided troop and equipment helicopter support, and several

separate companies and platoons that performed special functions such as fixed-wing reconnaissance, heavy helicopter lift, general support, aerial weapons, maintenance, and utility. The aviation groups active during the Vietnam War were 11th, 12th, 16th, 17th, 101st, 160th, 164th, and the 165th. *See also* Combat Aviation Battalion.

Combat Boots *see* **Brogans**

Combat Clerks *see* **Rear-Echelon-Mother-Fuckers**

Combat Controller (CCT, Combat Air Traffic Controller, CATC) Air Force ground teams that coordinated certain Air Force missions from the ground were sometimes referred to as "Combat Air Traffic Controllers" or "CCTs." Missions included large aerial delivery of supplies, parachute drops or special targeting. CCT teams often operated with long-range reconnaissance units to direct air strikes and bombing missions. CCTs worked closely with USSF units operating in the field. The members of the teams received intensive weapons and counterinsurgency training. The Army had their own version of the CCT called Pathfinders or Black Hats. *See also* Black Hats.

Combat Crazy *see* **Flip Out**

Combat Dragon Deployment Air Force code name for the first deployment of A-37 aircraft to Vietnam for combat. Twenty-five aircraft of the 604th Air Commando Squadron deployed to Bien Hoa in July '67 as part of the 3d TFW. Many of the A-37s operated in Vietnam were eventually transferred to VNAF as part of the Vietnamization program. *See also* A-37.

Combat Emplacement Evacuator *see* **Entrenching Tool**

Combat Engineer Party *see* **Combat Engineer Team**

Combat Engineer Team (Assault Engineers, Combat Engineer Party, CET, CEP) Engineer team inserted into an LZ to enlarge it or to create a fire support, patrol or temporary base. Teams consisted of 6–10 men, using tools brought in by helicopter. Using demolitions, chain saws and heavy equipment, a defensive perimeter could be established in just a few hours. The U.S. Army deployed two types of engineer units to Vietnam: Combat and Construction Engineers. The Navy SEABEES performed the engineering task for the Marines and Navy in I Corps. The NVA also used combat engineers; they were called the Dac Cong. *See also* Dac Cong, SEABEES, Army Construction Engineers, Engineers.

Combat Engineering Vehicle *see* M-728 CEV

Combat Essential Supply Request *see* CES Request

Combat Exhaustion *see* Combat Fatigue

Combat Fatigue (Shell Shock, Battle Fatigue, Battle Neurosis, Operational Exhaustion) Extreme case of fatigue, stress, and mental illness caused by prolonged and or intense exposure to the rigors of combat. In many instances the man was unable to function as a soldier. His mental condition would sometimes leave him detached from the reality of the war around him, making him a danger to himself and those surrounding him. The condition has had several names; in WWI it was "shell shock," in WWII it was "battle fatigue," and "combat exhaustion," in Korea it was called "battle neurosis" or "operational exhaustion," in Vietnam it was called "combat fatigue" and "acute situation reaction." It has also been labeled as "delayed stress" and "situational trauma." In Vietnam the symptoms varied, but the general indications were the soldier's inability to function under the stress of combat. For U.S. combat forces operating in the field, the combination of heat, disease and exhaustion took a heavy toll. The usual treatment was to pull the man out of the field for a few days and rest him at a base camp. After the rest he was usually returned to his unit. Severe cases required prolonged rest or reassignment. In an effort to relieve some of the stress related to combat, units were periodically rotated out of the field to stand downs at base camps. But due to the vagaries of war, it could be several weeks between stand downs for combat units in the field. Because the total number of American forces available for combat was so small, line units saw an inordinate amount of combat. *See also* Post-Traumatic Stress Syndrome, Flip Out, Combat Psychiatrist.

Combat Fatigues *see* Fatigues

Combat Field Pack *see* Butt Pack

Combat Hornet Deployment *see* AC-119G

Combat Infantryman *see* Infantry Soldier, The

Combat Infantryman's Badge (CIB) Army badge awarded to infantrymen for having been under enemy fire in a combat zone. Generally speaking, service and support troops were ineligible for this award. The CIB signified that the wearer served as an infantryman under hostile fire. Equivalent to the Marines' Combat Action Ribbon. *See also* Combat Action Ribbon.

Combat Information Center (CIC, NOC, Naval Operations Center) Artillery targeting information was received at the center and evaluated. Gunnery information was then calculated and passed on to the gun-control equipment for setup and firing by the artillery battery. Each Navy combat ship had a CIC that coordinated battle actions and was equivalent to the Army TOC or the Marine COC. For shore based Navy units, such as the coastal and riverine task forces, the CIC was called the "Naval Operations Center" or NOC. *See also* Tactical Operations Center.

Combat Lancer Deployment Air Force code name for the first deployment of the F-111 for combat in Vietnam. The F-111 was one of the Air Force's newest bombers, capable of delivering over 30,000 pounds of ordnance, in any weather, using NOE and low level contour flying. The first detachment of six F-111As were deployed to Takhli RTAFB in March '68. Due to structural failure and combat half of the detachment crashed in less than a month. The remaining planes returned to the States for modifications and corrections. The F-111 did not return to combat until mid '72, a much improved and dependable aircraft. *See also* F-111.

Combat Martin Operations (Colonel Computer, Electronic Backseater) Air Force missions designed to jam the communications channels between North Vietnamese MiGs and the ground control radar units that directed them. The Combat Martin missions were flown with F-105F aircraft that had the rear seat in the cockpit removed. The rear cockpit area was stuffed with electronic jamming equipment. The electronic "backseater" was nicknamed

"Colonel Computer" by Air Force crews. *See also* **F-105F/G.**

Combat Materiel Exploitation Center (CMEC)   U.S. government agency charged with the responsibility for monitoring enemy weapons usage. The CMEC attempted to secure new enemy weapons which appeared, test and evaluate those weapons, and issue reports to the military regarding the weapons' characteristics and abilities.

Combat Medic (Bravo, Band-Aid, Doc, Bac-Si, 91 Bravo)   Medic that accompanied Army units in the field. The first line of first aid given to wounded soldiers was provided by the medic. Though they were normally unarmed and noncombatant many medics in Vietnam carried a pistol for self-protection. The NVA/VC made medics, officers, and RTOs their prime targets. They would purposely wound a GI so there would be a call for a medic to come up. The enemy would then try to kill the medic. Different units called their medics by different names in an attempt to avoid letting the enemy know a medic was required for a down soldier. A Navy medic operating with the Marines was called a "corpsman." The Vietnamese referred to medics as "Bac-Si." *See* **Corpsmen, Unit One, Medic.**

Combat Medical Badge (CMB)   U.S. Army badge awarded to combat medics who perform their duties with a unit under hostile fire. The job of the combat medic was one of the most difficult, and perhaps one of the most rewarding during the Vietnam War.

Combat MOS   *see*   **11 Bravo**

Combat Nurses   *see*   **U.S. Army Nurse Corps**

Combat Operations Center   *see* **Tactical Operations Center**

Combat Pay   *see*   **Hazardous Duty Pay**

Combat Psychiatrist (Shrinks)   Psychiatrists were assigned to the larger Army hospitals in Vietnam to treat some of the mental problems caused by the stress of combat. Combat "shrinks" typically worked on three basic principles: immediacy, proximity and expectancy. Immediacy: Quickly addressing the problem, not allowing it to linger or go unattended. Proximity: Treatment to begin as close to the action as possible; this meant in the combat zone itself. Expectancy: An attitude that the patient would recover and be returned to duty. The patient needed to understand this if the treatment was to be successful. Troops with problems were returned to combat as soon as possible in an attempt to keep their problems from becoming chronic, or buried under other symptoms.

Combat Rations   *see*   **C-Rations**

Combat Recon Patrols   *see*   **Apache Force**

Combat Reconnaissance Platoon   *see* **CRP Platoon**

Combat Refusal (Mutiny, Field Refusal)   In Vietnam incidents of field troops refusing to follow combat orders increased significantly after '69. The Army used the term "combat refusal" and "field refusal" to disguise the actual mutiny that took place; such a refusal under combat conditions was "officially" a capital offense. There were many reasons for the refusals; most common were the field troops' lack of trust in the officers leading them. Many times officers with no combat experience were attempting to lead troops who had spent many months in combat, and who had more combat experience and better knowledge of the situation. Another reason for some soldiers' reluctance to fight was their belief that the war effort was doing no good and men were dying and being maimed for no valid reason. They argued that the ARVN didn't even fight for their own country, so why should they. By '69 most of the original soldiers which had come to Vietnam with their units were gone and were replaced with increasing numbers of draftees, many who didn't want to be in the Army or Vietnam in the first place. As U.S. offensive combat operations were reduced, troops experienced more idle time and lack of purpose. Many troops had difficulty coping with the increasing unpopularity of the war. This coupled with the easy, cheap access to abusive drugs, greatly increased problems throughout the services. The Army was hardest hit because it provided the largest source of manpower in Vietnam, much of it filled through the draft. Combat refusal was not the norm in the Army, but the instances of it increased until American combat troops were finally withdrawn from Vietnam. Few wanted to be the last to die while following seemingly senseless orders for a nation and its people who would not fight for themselves. *See also* Frag(ging).

Combat Security Police (CSP, 1041st Security Police Squadron, Operation Safeside) Special Air Force security police of the 1041st Security Police Squadron. CSP squadrons were established under Operation Safeside in '67 to assist regular Air Force Security Police with the defense of U.S. air bases. The CSPs were trained at the Army Ranger school and were organized into heavily armed sections that operated inside the base wire and around the outer perimeter of the base, using dogs, and Ranger ambush and surveillance techniques. Squadrons operated worldwide, with at least one squadron constantly in Vietnam between April '68 and February '71. *See also* **Air Police.**

Combat Skyspot (Skyspot) Name for an Air Force technique used to guide B-52s to their target. The system used ground based, computer controlled radar that directed the bombers over the target and signaled when the bombs should be released. The system was introduced in '66. It greatly increased the bombers' accuracy, and went a long way toward removing the weather as a significant factor in high altitude bombing. Skyspot was used extensively for the secret B-52 bombings against NVA/VC sanctuaries located along the Cambodian border. Skyspot was similar to a Marine system called TPQ-10 which was more portable, but had a shorter directional range. *See also* **TPQ-10, Operation Menu, Ground Control Approaches, SKE, TPQ Missions.**

Combat Strength *see* **Paddy Strength**

Combat Support Aviation Battalion (CSAB) 1st Cavalry Division's aviation battalion that provided the division with medium helicopter support. The battalion was equipped with up to 48 CH-47 Chinook helicopters, in three companies. The CH-47s provided artillery and troop lift support, as well as logistic resupply. The CH-47 could move a 105mm howitzer, its crew and ammunition in one sortie. Heavy lift support was provided by the CH-54s which could move the division's 155mm howitzers and other heavy assets. *See also* **Assault Support Helicopter Company.**

Combat Time *see* **Bush Time**

Combat Tracker Team *see* **Dog Team**

Combat Veteranitis A phrase used by author Philip Caputo to describe a condition many Vietnam combat veterans faced after their departure from the combat zone and return to the United States. The veterans' symptoms included, but were not limited to: "an inability to concentrate, a childlike fear of the darkness, a tendency to tire easily, chronic nightmares, an intolerance of loud noises . . . alternating moods of depression and rage" instigated for no apparent reason. *See also* **PTS.**

Combination Tool *see* **Entrenching Tool**

Combined Action Company (CAC) Combined U.S. Marine and Popular Force unit formed in '65 to provide security and civic action programs at the hamlet level. The CAC consisted of several squads, each squad containing several Marines and PF troops. The squad lived in the PF's local hamlet and provided security for the villagers in the hamlet as well as medical assistance and help with civic projects such as digging wells, communal buildings, road repair, etc. The program allowed the PF soldiers to gain valuable experience in defending their villages, and also raised the villagers' awareness to the positive effects of keeping the VC out of their villages. In '67 the program was reorganized into the CAP. *See also* **Combined Action Platoon.**

Combined Action Groups (CAG) NVA/VC cadre teams organized to perform as pacification teams in rural areas. The teams in a particular area operated out of one base camp, visiting several hamlets during the course of their travels. The enemy program was similar to the U.S. Marine CAP program. The enemy CAG base camps provided logistics support, security, training and command control. *See also* **Combined Action Platoon.**

Combined Action Platoon (Combined Action Program, CAP) U.S. Marine pacification program operated in rural I Corps hamlets. Each CAP platoon consisted of a Marine rifle squad (12–14 men + corps-man) and a PF platoon (30–35 men). The CAP organized the hamlet defense and lived in the hamlet on a 24-hour basis. Besides hamlet security, CAP teams provided the villagers medical care and assistance with hygiene and disease related problems. CAP teams also built simple structures and roads and conducted a variety of other civic projects aimed at helping the people. The Marine pacification program was successful in screening the people from the VC and in large part insulating them from some of the corruption and abuses of the GVN. CAP teams were a reorganization of the '65 Marine Combined Action Company. The CAP program started in '67 after the CAC proved pacification efforts could work. Because the CAPs were so successful at screening the VC from the people they were often the targets of VC attacks and attempts to overrun the hamlets. In '70 the Marine CAP program was expanded to include a Marine rifle company working with an RF/PF battalion, and renamed the Combined Action Group. The program ended with the withdrawal of the Marines in '71. After the departure of the Marines the GVN was unable to adequately support the villages or provide them with security, allowing the VC to return. *See also* **Combined Action Company, Combined Action Groups.**

Combined Action Program *see* **Combined Action Platoon**

Combined Documents Exploitation Center (CDEC) Army intelligence center that deciphered and analyzed captured enemy documents. The center was located in Saigon.

Combined Military Interrogation Center (CMIC) Manned by U.S. and Vietnamese intelligence groups specializing in the interrogation of captured and suspected NVA/VC.

Combined Reconnaissance and Intelligence Platoon (CRIP Platoon) Mixed unit of U.S. and SVN personnel whose mission was to combine their efforts in gathering intelligence on the enemy. The SVN personnel included ARVN soldiers, Kit Carson Scouts, and some PRUs. CRIPs operated independently and pretty much ran their own show. Some U.S. units had their own CRIP or CRP platoons which provided intel-ligence on enemy activities in the vicinity of the base camps from which they operated. CRIP platoons also ran ambush missions and sought targets for artillery and air strikes. *See also* **CRP Platoon, Hunter-Killer Operations, Hawk Team.**

Combined Studies Group (CSG) U.S. Embassy level office in Saigon used as a front by the CIA in the early '60s. The front was similar to the Programs Evaluations Office used in Laos. *See also* **Programs Evaluations Office.**

Combustible Case Ammunition (CBSS) Special round developed for the M-551 ARV. The M-551 was equipped with a 152mm main gun capable of firing an anti-tank guided missile or HEAT round. The HEAT round (XM409) consisted of a projectile (warhead) and a combustible case that contained the propellant which launched the HEAT round. In theory the case was consumed when the round was fired. This eliminated the need for brass shells to hold the projectile. The theory did not work well in Vietnam. The combustible case was not always consumed, which left the gun tube "trashed." M-551s in Vietnam were eventually modified with a "closed breech scavenging system" (CBSS) which cleaned the tube with a blast of compressed air after each firing. *See also* **M-551 ARV.**

COMCINCPACFLT *see* **Commander-in-Chief, Pacific Command**

Come Quickly *see* **Lai Day**

Comics *see* **Topographical Maps**

Command (Big Wheels, Gears, Wheels, Brass) Soldier's slang for generals and their command staffs, those who made the decisions that affected the military man's life.

Command and Communications Boat *see* **CCB**

Command Control (C & C, CC, Charlie Charlie) Headquarters controlling a given unit, action or operation. From the battalion level up, each field commander usually had a personal helicopter assigned to him that he used for C & C over his units in the field. From the C & C, the commander could monitor the combat situation on the ground and coordinate air and artillery support. Division level C & C helicopters were usually equipped with several different types of radios that allowed the general and his command group to simultaneously maintain radio contact with several ground, artillery and air support units. *See also* **AN/ASC Radio Console, Flying-Squad-Leader.**

Command and Control Boat *see* **CCB**

Command and General Staff College *see* **Fort Leavenworth**

Command Detonated Mine Mines detonated from a distance by an individual in sight of the mine location. The mine was usually detonated electrically, but some of the cruder VC mines used string or even vines attached to the triggering device. Many discarded American flashlight and radio batteries got a second lease on life as part of the electrical circuit used to command detonate Viet Cong mines. The batteries were collected along trails where they had been discarded by troops moving through an area. SVN civilian workers at U.S. Army trash dumps would secretly collect the used batteries during the day and pass them on to the VC at night. *See also* **Booby Traps.**

Command Junks Junks were used as part of South Vietnam's coastal patrol, the Junk Force. The command junk was motorized, about 55 feet long, armed with .30 and .50cal machine guns and used to provide overall command for an operating junk group. A junk group consisted of from one to three command junks and six to sixteen various other patrol junks. *See also* **Junks, Junk Force.**

Command Mess Mess facilities reserved for command generals and selected colonels. Their mess hall was located at the large, rear area division base camps and cities. The facilities were luxurious, featuring cloth table coverings and napkins, silverware and crystal. These senior officers had the best of food prepared by an Army "chef," and were served by Vietnamese waitresses with U.S. enlisted men as DROs and busboys. A far cry from the C's the grunts ate, or the mess hall food at a fire base. *See also* **General's Mess.**

Command Net Radio net established

for communications between Company CPs and higher headquarters. At the company level, at least one radio was used exclusively for communications between the Company CP and its platoons, as well as one radio on the command frequency connecting the Company CP with Battalion HQ. *See also* **Bullshit Net.**

Command of Camp *see* **COC**

Command of Quarters *see* **CQ**

Command Post (CP) Headquarters section and command center for a unit(s). Generally, units of platoon size and larger established a CP. The CP was usually located near the center of a moving formation or camped unit.

Commandant (Generals; Pate, Shoup, Greene, Chapman, Cushman, ALMAR Orders) Most senior officer, and commander, of the U.S. Marine Corps. The generals who commanded the Marines during the Vietnam War were Randolph Pate, David Shoup, Wallace Greene, Leonard Chapman, and Robert Cushman. ALMAR Orders were directives issued by the commandant and applicable to all U.S. Marines.

Commandement Command boat, usually heavily armed and armored, that provided command control during riverine operations. Used by the French and South Vietnamese river forces. The usual commandement was a modified LCM with the front ramp replaced with a curved bow, and the boat armed with 20mm cannons and machine guns. The commandement had a crew of ten and was equipped with radar and additional radios allowing it to perform as a control and fire support boat.

Commander of the U.S. Military Assistance Command (COMUSMACV) The Commander of the Military Assistance Command, Vietnam, had overall responsibility for controlling U.S. forces in SVN, and implementing the policies and strategies generated in Washington and at CINC-PAC. The commander was also responsible for the advisory efforts to the South Vietnamese government and military. From '62 to '73 the MACV Commanders in Vietnam were Generals Harkins ('62–'64), Westmoreland ('64–'68), Abrams ('68–'72) and Weyand ('72–'73). *See also* **Military Assistance Command, Vietnam.**

Commander U.S. Naval Forces, Vietnam (COMNAVFORV, NAVFORV; Naval Forces, Vietnam) The overall command of all Navy forces in Vietnam, with responsibility for all Navy construction, logistical support of Navy and Marine personnel and command of the Navy Advisory Group. The command was created in April '66. The Marines in Vietnam were under the command of CINCPACFLT and operationally controlled by MACV, yet their logistic support was under the control of COMNAVFORV. COMNAVFORV (Navy forces in Vietnam) was under the operational command of CINCPACFLT (7th Fleet) while being under the operational control of MACV. *See also* Operational Command.

Commander-in-Chief, Pacific Air Force (CINCPACAF) Command center for all U.S. air operations in the Pacific Command Area, reported to CINCPAC. *See also* Commander-in-Chief, Pacific Command.

Commander-in-Chief, Pacific Command (CINCPAC, COMCINCPACFLT) Command center governing all U.S. military operations in the Pacific Command Area. One admiral had command/control of the Pacific Theater. CINCPAC was also known as CINCPACFLT, Commander-in-Chief, Pacific Fleet. During the Vietnam War the Navy CINCPAC commanders (COMCINCPACFLT) were admirals Harry Felt; U.S. Grant Sharp; John McCain and Noel Gayler. The CINCPAC Commander reported directly to the Secretary of Defense. The MACV Commander in Vietnam reported directly to CINCPAC. Although the MACV Commander had overall authority for forces in Vietnam CINCPAC was responsible for all forces in the Pacific.

Commanding General (CG) Officer grades 7 through 11, commanding a unit or army. *See also* General Officers.

Commanding Officer (CO, The Old Man, Chi-Huy) Officer in charge, with ultimate responsibility for the unit he commands. The CO of a unit, company size or larger, was often referred to by the troops as "The Old Man," especially if the men under his command respected and or trusted him. "Chi-huy" was Vietnamese for commander.

Commanding Officer Call *see* CO Call

Commando *see* V-100

Commando Bolt Code name for U.S. air strikes along the Ho Chi Minh Trail near the area where the trail entered Laos. The strikes were part of Operation Steel Tiger; both Navy and Air Force aircraft participated. *See also* Operation Steel Tiger, Ho Chi Minh Trail.

Commando Hunt *see* Operation Commando Hunt

Commando Rifle *see* CAR-15

Commando Sabre Missions (Misty FACs, Deliverers of the White Death) Special Air Force strikes against NVN targets north of the DMZ, code named Commando Sabre. The strikes were directed by F-100 aircraft being used as FACs. The F-100 used its speed as partial protection from the high concentration of enemy AA positions in the area. The F-100s would mark targets such as truck parks, fuel depots, convoys and AA gun positions for immediate strikes by other aircraft. The call sign used by the F-100 FACs was "Misty." The two seat recon version of the aircraft was armed with smoke rockets for target marking, and 20mm cannons. The F-100s trolled the low level skies over southern NVN drawing fire to identify targets. The Misty crews were reportedly called the "Deliverers of the White Death" by NVN AA gunners.

Commando Vault *see* Daisy Cutter (Instant LZ)

Commercial Carriers (Sea-Tac) The U.S. government contracted with commercial air carriers to transport American troops to and from Vietnam. Various carriers were chartered to make the flights, most of them leaving from either Travis Air Force Base, California, or Seattle-Tacoma (Sea-Tac) Airport, near Fort Lewis, Washington. Flying time to Vietnam was 20–24 hours with several stops along the way for fuel and aircraft crew changes. In-flight meals provided to the troops were usually box lunches. Officers and female personnel sat in the front of the aircraft, with the EM filling out the rest of the 200+ seats. Some of the commercial carriers used were Continental, Pan American, TIA, Braniff, World Airways and Flying Tiger Lines.

Committee for Nonviolent Action

1960s antiwar group, located in New York City.

Commo (Communications) Military slang for communications and any related signal equipment or personnel. *See also* U.S. Radios.

Commo Check (Radio Check) Radio transmission quality check between two or more radio sets. "Lima Charlie," "five-by-five," or "loud and clear" were the typical responses to the radio check, if the quality or reception was good. Hopefully the station you were conducting the radio check with also was receiving you "loud and clear." *See also* Lima Charlie.

Commo Track *see* M-577 ACC

Commo Wire (WD-1 Communication Wire, Day Dien) Multipurpose electrical wire used in a variety of ways. It was used for field phones, detonator wire, bootlegged lighting systems, field radio antennas and many other uses, including as bindings for prisoners. "Day Dien" [day den] was Vietnamese for electrical wire/commo wire.

Communication Tunnel Viet Cong tunnels used to interconnect chambers, rooms and other tunnels. The communication tunnels, many of which were several kilometers long, connected hamlets and villages within the tunnel system. *See also* Tunnels of Cu Chi.

Communications *see* Commo

Communist China *see* People's Republic of China

Communist Daily Newspaper *see* Nanh Dan

Communist Party *see* Lao Dong

Communist Party of Australia *see* Vietnam Action Committee

COMNAVFORV *see* Commander U.S. Naval Forces, Vietnam

Comp-B *see* Composition-4 Explosive

Company (Co) Basic element of a battalion, consisting of two or more platoons. Independent companies had numerical names (3d Transport Co, 542d Medical Co, 74th Aviation Co). Companies that were a permanent part of a battalion had alphabet names (Company B or Bravo Co; Company

D or Delta Co, etc.). Company size varied with the purpose of the unit, but a line infantry company generally consisted of 3–4 platoons and a headquarters element (approx. 140–160 men). In artillery battalions, a "Battery" was equivalent to a company, and in cavalry squadrons, a "Troop" was equivalent to a company. A tank company consisted of 17 tanks, in three platoons. *See also* Company, NVA/VC.

Company(–) (Co[+]) Graphic representation of a company minus one of its platoons. Used for maps, reports and briefings. The Battalion(–) or Bn(–) represented a battalion minus one of its companies. Platoons or companies were sometimes detached from their parent company or battalion and temporarily assigned to the control of another headquarters, Bn (+).

Company, NVA/VC A main force Viet Cong company, at full strength, consisted of about 180 men. An NVA company varied in size depending on the type of company it was. Sapper and artillery companies were generally smaller than line infantry companies. An NVA line company was 150–200 men strong.

Company, The *see* Central Intelligence Agency

Company C/D, 52d Infantry Two separate companies from the 52d Infantry Regiment were deployed to SVN as Rifle Security units. Company C deployed December '68, and departed August '72, and operated as guards in the Saigon area under command of the 716th MP Battalion and later the 18th MP Brigade. Company D served two separate tours in Vietnam. The first tour, as security, was with the 95th MP Battalion at Long Binh, in November '66 to November '69. Their second tour as security, June '71 to November '72, was at Qui Nhon with the U.S. Army Support Command.

Company Clerk *see* Morning Report

Company Commander (CC) Army and Marine combat companies were generally commanded by a captain. In Vietnam when there was a shortage of captains, a company would be commanded by a 1st lieutenant. *See also* Company, Captain.

Company E/14th Infantry *see* 14th Infantry Regiment

Company E/F, 52d Infantry Companies E and F were separate companies of the 52d Infantry Regiment operating in Vietnam as Long-Range Reconnaissance Patrols. Both companies deployed December '67 and were withdrawn February '69. Company E served the 1st Cav operating in the An Khe area of II Corps. Company F served with the 1st Infantry Division operating in the Lai Khe area of III Corps. The two companies were redesignated Companies H and I of the 75th Infantry, Rangers. *See also* **Rangers.**

Company Grade Officer Officer grades, O-1 through O-3; 2d lieutenant, 1st lieutenant and captain. During the Vietnam War the casualty rate of company grade officers was greater than 90 percent. Company grade officers typically only spent six months in the field before being rotated to staff positions at the battalion/brigade or division level.

Compassionate Leave (Emergency Leave) Leave granted allowing a soldier to return home because of a death or serious illness in the family. GIs in Vietnam normally remained in-country unless they were dead, wounded or on R & R. Exceptions to the rule: a 30-day U.S. leave was allowed if the soldier extended his tour in Vietnam, or was allowed to the U.S. on compassionate leave. Examples of situations that qualified a soldier for the leave were the death of a parent and the necessity to make arrangements to take care of the surviving parent; or if a man's wife had severe medical complications, or if there were other traumatic family oriented disasters. Requests for compassionate leave were usually presented to the man's CO and coordinated through the chaplain and the Red Cross.

Compassionate Loan Army phrase for the temporary assignment of a soldier to another unit. The assignment usually involved two members of the same immediate family, one in the hospital and the other assigned nearby. Compassionate loan was granted on several occasions in Vietnam when two brothers or a father/son were serving in-country at the same time and one of them was seriously wounded. Army regulations could not force family members to serve in the same war zone simultaneously; it had to be on a voluntary basis. *See also* Sole Survivor Rule.

Compensation Payment *see* **Grievance Payment**

Composite Battery (Mixed Artillery, MXD) U.S. artillery battery that was composed of more than one type of artillery weapon. In Vietnam a composite battery of three 175mm and 8-inch guns was a standard configuration, and 105mm/155mm mixed artillery batteries (MXD) were also common. *See also* **Artillery, U.S.**

Composite Military Police Strike Force (MP SWAT Team, CMPSF) Military version of the SWAT Team, Special Weapons and Tactics, used by civilian police forces in the States. The MP Strike Force was used in sensitive situations where an armed soldier refused to surrender for arrest. The CMPSF was used more frequently after '69 as the number of drug related shoot-outs and violence increased. *See also* **Military Police.**

Composite Unit *see* **Bastard Unit**

Composition B *see* **Composition-4 Explosive**

Composition-4 Explosive (C-4, Charlie-4, Composition B, Comp-B) Soft, gritty plastic explosive used by the military. White, grainy textured, packaged in two sticks requiring a blasting cap to detonate. Extremely stable explosive which could be shaped, dropped, burned or struck without exploding. C-4 burned with a very intense flame. GIs used small chunks of C-4 to heat C-Rations and water in the field. Damp or wet conditions didn't affect the properties of the explosive and C-4 was readily available. C-4 had toxic qualities if taken internally. It was the explosive portion of the M-18 Claymore Mine. Composition B was a variant of C-4. *See also* **C-Rat Stove, C-3 Explosive, TNT.**

Compound *see* **Cantonment**

Compromised Codes *see* **Shackle Cards**

COMUSMACV *see* **Commander of the U.S. Military Assistance Command**

Con Son Correctional Center *see* **Poulo Condore**

Con Son Island *see* **Poulo Condore**

Con Son Province *see* **Province, Con Son Island**

Con Thien (Hill of the Angels) Vietnamese translation for "Hill of the Angels." Series of low hills located 27kms NW of Quang Tri and less than 3kms from the DMZ. Con Thien was one of the northernmost Marine outposts in I Corps. In September '67 the NVA attacked Marine hill positions with infantry supported by long-range artillery and rockets from across the DMZ. For nine days the Marines were bombarded and assaulted by elements of the 324B, NVA Division. The Marines held and forced the attacking NVA to retreat across the DMZ. In support of the Marines, the Air Force mounted special bombardment missions to silence the enemy guns located along the DMZ. *See also* **Operation Neutralize, SLAM.**

CONARC *see* **Continental Army Command**

Conceived in Doubt . . . Operation Lam Son 719, the South Vietnamese Invasion of Laos: "The operation, conceived in doubt and assailed by skepticism, proceeded in confusion." A view, attributed to Henry Kissinger, of the South Vietnamese incursion into Laos in '71. *See also* **Operation Lam Son 719.**

Concentrated Fire Combining a force's available firepower on one target. The firepower could be from direct or indirect fire, weapons or aircraft. *See also* **Fireballing.**

Concentration Camps *see* **Reeducation Camps**

Concertina Wire (Accordion Wire) Coiled barbed wire used in defensive positions. The wire could be permanently staked down and intertwined with regular barbed wire fortifications. Concertina was carried by some armor units and used as part of the defensive perimeter setup around the vehicle. When the unit was ready to move out the wire was recoiled and stored onboard the vehicle. Sometimes called "accordion wire." *See also* **German Wire, Tanglefoot.**

Concordia *see* **Operation Concordia**

Concussion Grenade *see* **MK-3A2 Offensive Hand Grenade**

Conex Large corregated metal shipping container used for the storage and transport of supplies and equipment. Approximately 8 × 8 × 8 feet. Some of the conex containers were insulated and fitted with small refrigeration units. These refrigerated conexes, or "reefers," were used to store perishables and as temporary morgues at some base camps. The containers were used for storage, bunkers, command post and a variety of other unauthorized uses. The term "conex" was derived from the official name of the metal boxes and their intended use, "Continental Exchange" shipping containers. The containers could be packed and easily transported worldwide. *See also* **Reefers, Ro-Ro Containers.**

Coney Island Nickname for the Marine combat base at Khe Sanh in '67–'68. The Green Berets located at the Lang Vei Special Forces called the Marine base "Coney Island," because they had so many lights visible at night. *See also* **Khe Sanh.**

Confidential (v) *see* **Kin**

Confirmed *see* **Confirms**

Confirmed VC *see* **Viet Cong Suspect**

Confirms (Confirmed) Military slang for a "confirmed kill" or body count. That translated to a dead body or a piece of an enemy body (death caused by combat, air strike, artillery, etc.). In theory enemy body counts required confirmation before they would be accepted into the official record; in practice, the confirmation process was sometimes very loosely executed and subject to exaggeration and falsification. *See also* **Body Count, Partial Body Count.**

Confucianism *see* **Confucius**

Confucius (Confucianism) Philosophy founded by Confucius in the fifth century B.C. emphasizing man's moral duty to man, the worship of the family, one's ancestors, and the development of fearlessness, sincerity, compassion and wisdom. Emphasis was placed on man accepting life as it is and working within the framework of society; "not rocking the boat." Confucianism, once the state religion of China, was brought to Vietnam and accepted by Vietnam's emperor in 1009. After this most civil servants and higher authorities were Confucians. In order to find favor with the emperor it was necessary to be a Confucian. The Buddhists resented this new form of religion; Confucianism came to be Vietnam's moral philosophy while Buddhism struggled on as its religion. *See also* **Buddhism.**

Cong Don Da Vien   NVA/VC name for the tactic of attacking an isolated GVN or RF/PF outpost, causing it to call for help and reinforcements. The NVA/VC then set up a massive ambush to attack the relief force attempting to reach the besieged outpost. The tactic was used successfully against the French and later the South Vietnamese. It was also used against American troops but was not always as effective because U.S. units had the benefit of increased mobility by way of the helicopter. U.S. units also had an abundance of firepower available.

Cong, The   *see* **Enemy, The**

Congress of Racial Equality (CORE) 1960s civil rights group active in the South, its membership consisting of young blacks and liberal whites, trying to eliminate the system of segregation in the South. CORE actively participated in the black voter registration drive in the South. CORE was also very active in "freedom rides" conducted throughout Alabama and Mississippi. Southern rules dictated that blacks riding public buses must ride in the rear of the bus and not be allowed to sit down unless all the whites on the bus had a seat. Freedom riders ignored the rules and integrated the buses in a show of contempt for the Southern rules of segregation.

Congressional Medal of Honor (Medal of Honor, CMH, MH)   Highest U.S. award for outstanding acts of bravery against an armed enemy. The first Medal of Honor recipients of the Vietnam War were Captain Roger H.C. Donlon (Army), CM3 Marvin G. Shields (Navy), Captain Donald G. Cook (Marines) and Major Bernard F. Fisher (Air Force). *See also* **Captain Roger Donlon, Dong Xoai, Major Bernard Fisher, Captain Donald Cook.**

Congressionals   A letter of inquiry presented to a military headquarters or command from a congressional source. The letters were initiated via the Legislative Liaison Office of the Congress and generally dealt with a question, complaint or issue raised by one or more of a congressman's (senator's) constituents. The inquiry was usually addressed by the commander of the unit, or his designate. Parents sometimes complained to their legislators about the conditions their sons were in, the food, lack of letters, etc. Sometimes the complaints to the legislators came straight from the troops themselves. Such inquiries were referred to as "Congressionals" within the military, and although not well received, required a response.

Conical Hat   *see*   **Non**

Connie   *see*   **USS   Constellation, C-121**

Connies   *see*   **EC-121**

Conscientious Objector (C.O.)   American Army C.O.s occasionally found themselves in Vietnam. Because they refused to fight or carry a weapon they were usually not sent to the field or to bases where hostile action was likely. Instead they worked as clerks and in other rear area duties in places such as Saigon or Cam Ranh Bay. Some C.O.s did go to the field as medics. Other C.O.s were allowed to avoid the military by performing "alternative" humanitarian services with civilian organizations. C.O. status was granted to practicing members of the Quakers, Jehovah's Witnesses, Mennonites, and other selected religious orders that opposed participating in war based on their religion. C.O. status could also be granted to an individual who opposed war based on strong moral or philosophical grounds. The individual had to argue his case before his Selective Service Board. More than 170,000 C.O. classifications (1-O and 1-AO) were granted during the Vietnam War. *See also* **Alternative Service, Draft Classification.**

Conscripts   *see*   **Draftee, National Servicemen**

Constant Guard I–IV Deployments Code name for a series of Air Force deployments of air combat units from bases in the U.S. to bases in Thailand and South Vietnam in response to the NVA Eastertide Offensive in April '72. Over a dozen combat and support squadrons deployed to SEA in less than 30 days. Prior to the NVA attack three Air Force F-4 squadrons, a squadron of A-37s and a detachment of AC-119Ks were in SVN. With the help of massive air support the South Vietnamese were able to stop and turn the NVA invasion. *See also* **Eastertide Offensive, Bullet Shot I–V Deployments.**

Constellation   *see* **USS Constellation, C-121**

Constipation *see* **Ho Chi Minh's Revenge, Peanut Butter**

Construction Battalion Maintenance Unit (CBMU) Navy SEABEE battalion that operated out of Da Nang, under the Naval Support Activity. The CBMU functioned as a maintenance unit supporting the Navy's logistical operations in I Corps. The battalion maintained and repaired equipment and facilities directly related to the NSA's support role. *See also* **NSA, Da Nang; SEABEES.**

Contact (Engage) Engaging the enemy with direct fire or being fired on by the enemy. Maintaining close proximity and or contact with the enemy. *See also* **Close, Troops in Contact.**

Contact Fire Mission *see* **Fire Mission**

Container Delivery System (CDS) U.S. Air Force cargo delivery system that used containerized cargo to allow more accurate resupply of units in the field. Normal supply loads were dropped from about 1000 feet, but containerized loads could be dropped from 600 feet, allowing the load to fall faster, with less drift away from the drop zone, and still remain intact. Standard supply loads required more altitude, allowing more time for the parachute to slow the load's fall, reducing impact speed, but this increased the potential for load drift away from the drop zone. *See also* **Low Altitude Parachute Extraction System.**

Containerized Cargo *see* **Ro-Ro Containers**

Containment U.S. theory and policy that surfaced after WWII on how to deal with the spread of communism throughout the world. The main strategy was to keep communism from spreading outside of the Soviet Union and Mainland China. As communism did begin to spread to other countries the focus of containment was on keeping it within the borders of the newly affected country. The strategy was not to go on the offensive by taking the war to the communist country supporting the insurgency, but to play a defensive role and try to limit the enemy expansion within the borders of the affected country, slowly snuffing it out with democracy and U.S. Foreign Aid.

Contested Area *see* **Indian Country**

Contiguous Zone, The *see* **Coastal Surveillance Zones**

Continental Airlines *see* **Commercial Carriers**

Continental Army Command (CONARC) Headquarters command for U.S. Army units in the continental United States.

Continental Hotel *see* **Continental Palace**

Continental Palace (Continental Hotel) International hotel in Saigon that served as a press camp during the American war years in South Vietnam. The hotel was located on Tu Do Street almost next door to the Hotel Caravelle. *See also* **Caravelle.**

Continental United States (CONUS) Military reference to the United States. *See also* **The World.**

Contour Flying *see* **Nap-of-the-Earth**

Control and Reporting Center *see* **Control and Reporting Post**

Control and Reporting Post (CRP, 507th Tactical Control Group, CRC, Control and Reporting Center) Mobile Air Force radar installation used to monitor aircraft. A CRP was deployed to South Vietnam in September '61 to monitor the airspace over Saigon and provide radar training for technicians of South Vietnam's Air Force. The CRP was originally manned by members of the 507th Tactical Control Group. Other CRPs followed and were deployed at Da Nang and Pleiku. Information from the radar post was transmitted to the Control and Reporting Center located at the Air Operations Center at Tan Son Nhut. *See also* **Tactical Air Control System.**

Control Questions Series of questions used to interrogate a prisoner/agent (spy). The answers to the questions were already known by the interrogator and were used to verify the trustworthiness and accuracy of the prisoner's responses.

Controlled Cannibalization *see* **Strategic Reappropriation**

Controlled Crash *see* **Autorotation**

Controlled Fragmentation Munition *see* **COFRAM Round**

Controlled Littering (Leaflet Missions, White Envelope Missions) A phrase sometimes used to describe U.S. PSYWAR leaflet missions. One of the more successful leaflet operations was the "White Envelope" missions. Leaflets encouraging the Viet Cong to surrender were dropped over enemy areas. Included in the envelope was a letter which granted amnesty to the bearer as authorized by the GVN, and a "safe conduct pass" that was to be presented to any GVN official or military unit. The letters, which were dropped over free-fire-zones and enemy sympathetic areas, also applied to Viet Cong family members. *See also* **Psychological Operations, Bullshit Bombers.**

CONUS *see* **Continental United States**

Conventional Bombs *see* **Iron Bombs**

Conventional Warfare *see* **Set-Piece Battle**

Converged Sheaf *see* **Sheafs of Fire**

Converts *see* **Foxhole Converts**

Convoy *see* **Caterpillar**

Convoy of Tears When the NVA launched their final offensive in April '75 the ARVNs began abandoning positions en masse. The ARVNs abandoned the Central Highlands, headed southeast along Highway 7, and along with thousands of refugees from the Highlands, jammed the highway, the main route to the coast. There was great loss of life in the panicked crowds that swept south attempting to outrun the advancing NVA Army. The NVA shelled the retreating column with artillery further increasing the panic and confusion. The same scene was later repeated along Highway 1 as refugees and soldiers retreated along the coast toward Saigon. *See also* **Final Offensive.**

Coogee *see* **FSB Coogee**

Cook *see* **Stew Burner, REMF**

Cook, Captain Donald G. The Marine Corps' first Medal of Honor winner. Cook received the award for heroism after being taken prisoner by the Viet Cong in December '64. While operating as an advisor to the South Vietnamese Marines, Cook and the ARVN Marines were ambushed in Phuoc Tuy Province, III Corps. During the ambush Cook was wounded and

deserted by the ARVNs. During his captivity he was constantly moved from camp to camp, and continually beaten and abused by his guards as he continued to resist. Cook died a POW in December '67 as a result of a near-starvation diet, and malaria. Cook was buried by other POWs who shared his captivity.

Cooking-Fire Recon *see* **Red Haze**

Cooking-Off (Clipping-Off) Ammunition exploding and discharging because of heat from a fire. A common occurrence when a vehicle carrying ammunition began to burn. It also happened when a hootch was burned and hidden ammunition and explosives began to discharge and explode. Also called "clipping-off."

Cooper, Senator John *see* **Cooper-Church Amendment**

Cooper-Church Amendment June '70 congressional amendment that restricted the use of U.S. ground troops in Cambodia or Laos without express congressional approval. The amendment was cosponsored by Senators Frank Church (D-Idaho) and John Cooper (R-Kentucky) and was voted down in the House of Representatives but passed in the Senate. A modified version of the amendment passed both houses of Congress in late '71; it restricted the use of U.S. ground troops in Laos and Thailand. Congressional efforts to restrict the use of U.S. troops served notice to President Nixon that he did not have "carte blanche" with U.S. forces in an increasingly unpopular war in SEA. As a result of the amendment U.S. troops did not accompany ARVN forces into Laos in '71. *See also* **Cambodian Incursion, War Powers Act, Hatfield-McGovern Amendment.**

Cooperation Plan *see* **Hop Tac Plan**

Cooperative for American Relief Everywhere *see* **CARE**

Copperheads *see* **162d Aviation Company**

Coral *see* **FSB Coral**

Coral Sea *see* **USS Coral Sea**

Cordon and Search *see* **Clear and Hold**

CORDS *see* **Civil Operations and Revolutionary Development**

CORE *see* Congress of Racial Equality

Coronado *see* Operation Coronado

Coronado Island (Navy Special Warfare Operations Training Center, Amphibious Training Center) Coronado Island, located just off the coast of San Diego, California, was the site of the U.S. Navy's amphibious and special warfare training centers. The base was the initial stateside training facility for Navy SEAL personnel and riverboat crews destined to operate in Vietnam with TF 116 or TF 117. *See also* **SEAL, TF 116, TF 117.**

Corporal *see* **E-4, Private First Class**

Corps Corps had five meanings in Vietnam. 1) Vietnam was divided into four tactical areas for military operations called the Corps Tactical Zones, identified as I, II, III and IV Corps. 2) U.S. Marine Corps operated in Vietnam; "The Corps" to Marines. 3) Corps referred to specialized groups within the military performing a given function such as the Medical Corps, Transportation or Signal Corps. 4) There were four U.S. Corps headquarters controlling combat activities in Vietnam; I & II Field Force, III MAF and XXIV Corps. 5) NVA Army Corps brought about the collapse of SVN in '75. *See also* **Corps Tactical Zones, I or II Field Force, III MAF, XXIV Corps.**

Corps Aviation Company (CAC) Army Corps level aviation company that provided the command headquarters element with helicopter transport and support. In Vietnam, CACs were assigned to the various U.S. divisions and separate brigades.

Corps Tactical Operations Center (CTOC) Operational control center responsible for military units within a Corps Tactical Zone. Each of the four Corps (I–IV) in Vietnam had its own tactical operations center that coordinated military operations. *See also* **Tactical Operations Center.**

Corps Tactical Zones (CTZ) Prior to July '70 SVN was divided into four zones for administration of the war effort. The zones were Corps I, II, III and IV. After July '70 the Corps Zones were redesignated Military Regions I–IV.

Corps, The *see* **Crotch, The**

Corpseman *see* **Corpsmen**

Corpsmen (Medical Corpsmen, Navy Hospital Corpsmen, HM, Quack, Doc, Corpseman, Squid) Navy medics attached to the Marine Corps to provide all of the Marines' medical care. Also referred to Army medical personnel working in the hospitals and aid stations as opposed to the medics that operated in the field with combat troops. Medics had a variety of nicknames such as Doc, Quack and Squid. "Squid" was the general nickname given to Navy personnel by the Marines. The Vietnamese referred to medics as "Bac-Si." "Corpseman" was a nickname jokingly given to the Navy medics. *See also* **Combat Medic, Unit One, Medic.**

Corpus Christi *see* **USNS Corpus Christi**

Corruption Corruption was as much a part of the South Vietnamese way of life as death was a part of war. Corruption could be found at all levels of government and within the military. Part of the system of corruption was the Black Market, and its associated activities. Americans, as well as other Free World Forces, dabbled in the market with the Vietnamese. The bribing of government officials was the norm, and in many cases for any progress to be made bribes and "favors" had to continuously flow from the Americans. As American forces withdrew from Vietnam the effects of corruption within the military and the government became much more evident. In some cases ARVN medevac flights to RF/PF outposts were held up until an arrangement for "payment" could be made between the requesting unit and the commander of the medevac unit. More and more U.S. equipment turned up on the Black Market for sale to "anyone" able to pay the price. In Phuoc Binh (Song Be) the ARVN infantry commander had to pay the artillery commander in order to receive fire support. After '70 the incidence of high level ARVN officers selling arms and equipment to the NVA/VC greatly increased, especially in the III Corps area. High level staff officers of the ARVN 5th and 18th divisions sold equipment, claymore mines, and ammunition to the Viet Cong. In '74 the commander of the 25th ARVN Division was arrested for selling government rice supplies to the Viet Cong. Corruption was at the heart of the South Vietnamese system, and it was never adequately addressed by the

U.S. government or the successive American military commands that directed the war. *See also* **Black Market, Phuoc Binh, 25th ARVN Division, Grievance Payment.**

Corsair II *see* **A-7**

Cosmoline (Gun Grease) Protective grease used on firearms to prevent rust. The grease was applied to firearms at the factory of manufacture to protect the weapons during shipment and storage. Excess grease was removed and the weapon thoroughly cleaned before it was used.

Cost of the War *see* **Guns and Butter Financing**

COSVN *see* **Central Office South Vietnam**

Cotter Pin *see* **Spoon**

Cotton Balls (Flak Burst) Pilot slang for enemy antiaircraft flak. For U.S. pilots flying missions against North Vietnam, the flak explosions came in three distinctive colors; white, blue, black. 37mm flak bursts were white puffs that looked like "cotton balls" in the sky. 57mm flak bursts were bluish-gray; some pilots said the 57mm rounds coming up at them "looked like fiery red golf balls." The larger AAA flak bursts were large black clouds with exploding orange centers. *See also* **Antiaircraft Guns.**

Cougar *see* **F-9**

Cougars *see* **214th Aviation Battalion, 57th Avn**

Cough Syrup *see* **GI Gin**

Counter Culture *see* **Hippie**

Counter Recoil Operated Weapon Launcher *see* **CROW Grenade Launcher**

Counter-Mortar Fires (Counter-Rocket Fires) Mortar or artillery fire missions used for the purpose of attempting to silence enemy mortar or rocket fire. At larger base camps radar units were used to spot enemy mortar and rocket sites. Sometimes direct observation of the enemy firing position was used to fire the missions. The NVA/VC usually only fired a few rounds, not a sustained barrage, moving their mortars to a new position and firing a few more rounds. This method made it extremely difficult to accurately fix the enemy's firing location or guess where the next rounds would come from. *See also* **Counter-Mortar Radar.**

Counter-Mortar Radar Long-range radar unit designed to detect the location of enemy mortars and rockets as they fired. Radar could be used to detect the rounds as they left the tubes, but were of limited effectiveness against short attacks because by the time the radar could lock on to the location the enemy had ceased fire. When the NVA/VC used mortars for harassment they generally only fired several rounds, instead of a sustained barrage, or after firing a few rounds they would move the mortar to another location and fire a few more rounds. Once the sites were identified, artillery units would fire counter-mortar (counter-rocket) missions to silence the enemy attack. *See also* **AN/MPQ-4 Radar.**

Counter-Rocket Fires *see* **Counter-Mortar Fires**

Counter-Rotation *see* **Autorotation**

Counter-Sniper Using a sniper to seek, locate and eliminate an enemy sniper.

Counterinsurgency (COIN) Military strategy of neutralizing an enemy insurgent force conducting guerrilla warfare. Revolutionary guerrilla warfare sought to overthrow the existing government by means of political subversion and military force. To counter this attack the government must be willing to meet the guerrilla at his own level on the battlefield, and at the same time keep the political climate in the country open to maintain the trust and respect of the people. An effective means of fighting guerrilla warfare was to use some of the same tactics employed by the guerrillas. The Viet Cong proved that military might alone was not enough to stop insurgent forces. *See also* **Guerrilla War, Pacification.**

Counterinsurgency Plan (CIP) Kennedy Administration plan formulated in '61 to increase U.S. military aid to South Vietnam. The increased aid was to finance increases in the strength of South Vietnam's regular army by 20,000 troops and expand the Civil Guard by an additional 32,000 men. The increases were to counter Viet Cong activities aimed at the destruction of the Diem regime in South Vietnam.

Counterinsurgency Support Office (CSO) U.S. Army logistics command that supported U.S. Special Forces operations in SEA. The CSO was based at Okinawa and provided direct logistics support to USSF units and their associates (CIDG and MACV/SOG) in SEA.

Counterintelligence Detachment *see* CID

Counterintelligence Team (CIT) U.S. Marine counterintelligence teams worked closely with ITTs (Interrogator/Translator Teams) to gather information on enemy activities. This information was used by Marine commanders for strategy and tactics, and eventually became the basis for several large scale Marine operations.

Counterpart Formal name used by U.S. military advisors to refer to the South Vietnamese military officers they advised. In some ARVN units the commanders were turned over so often that higher American advisory headquarters simply referred to a particular advisor's "counterpart" in briefings rather than trying to keep track of the new commander's name.

Countries Aiding South Vietnam *see* Turtle Monument

Country Joe and the Fish *see* I-Feel-Like-I'm-Fixin'-to-Die Rag

Country Teams Diplomatic jargon for foreign military advisory or support teams working with the forces of the host government. The members of the teams were officially part of the embassy staff, and not an independent military force. The U.S. had such teams throughout Asia. Most of the team members were in the field with government forces, providing them training and advice.

Country, The *see* Vietnam (GI Names)

County Fair *see* Operation County Fair, County-Fair Operations

County-Fair Operations (Minipacification Operations) Marine slang for a cordon and search operation. A village would be surrounded and the people in the village were offered food and clothing and a MEDCAP was conducted; a minipacification program. National Police or ARVN accompanying the Marines performed a search for

weapons and contraband and made a check of the villagers' ID cards. Those without cards or with forged cards were arrested as VCS and taken away. As part of the operation limited civil action improvements were carried out, such as road/bridge repair, hootch roof repairs, well expansion, irrigation projects, etc. GVN teams also held propaganda sessions aimed at winning the confidence of the people. The operation lasted 3–5 days. *See also* **Hamlet Festival.**

Coup Troops (Voting Machines) Nickname given to ARVN Armor units because of their political effect on the ruling parties in the early days of the GVN. No coup could be successful without the backing of the armor unit and its commander. Before any coup could be attempted the group preparing to stage the coup had to win the trust and support of the ARVN armor commander. Because of the importance of armor in withstanding coups, Diem kept the ARVN armor units close to Saigon. In '63 Diem lost the support of the ARVN armor commander, and a successful coup toppled his regime and resulted in his execution. The tanks of the ARVN armor were nicknamed "voting machines."

Course Instructor *see* **Lane Grader**

Cover (Soft Cover, Jungle Cover) Military terminology for headgear, hat or helmet. "Soft cover" was the Marine utility hat. "Jungle cover" was the soft, broad brimmed jungle hat. *See also* **Jungle Hat.**

Cover Down Cover Down was an order issued to troops standing in formation, ordering them to form up their lines with the ranks and files of the formation aligned in a "military manner."

Cover-Your-Ass *see* **CYA**

Cow *see* **Bladder Bird**

Cowboy, The *see* **Nguyen Cao Ky**

Cowboy Hat *see* **Jungle Hat**

Cowboy Scouts (Vietnamese Interpreters) Nickname used by some GIs for the Vietnamese interpreters that accompanied American units operating in the field. Sometimes these interpreters were just regular ARVN soldiers that could speak both Vietnamese, and enough English to get by. Some of the Vietnamese working with American units were actual scouts, performing the dual role of scout and interpreter. *See also* **Kit Carson Scout.**

Cowboys (Honda-Girls, Cowgirls) Young South Vietnamese hoodlum element that roamed the streets of Saigon (and the larger urban areas) on motorcycles and motorscooters, many of them draft dodgers from the Army. Many were from wealthy families and heavily involved in the black market trade. Cowboys typically operated in pairs and were known for their quick, snatching thievery and quick getaways. Some were involved in prostitution, pimping for their girlfriends. The cowboy's girlfriend or sister (called a Honda-Girl) would ride on the back of the motorcycle in areas frequented by GIs. The GI would flag one down and look at the girl and haggle price. The fee ran from $6 to $20 and was divided between the girl and the cowboy. *See also* **Prostitute.**

Cowboys of the 335th Avn *see* **335th Aviation Company**

Cowgirls *see* **Cowboys**

Coxswain Flat Location aboard a boat or ship where the coxswain stands to steer the vessel.

CP *see* **Command Post, Check Point**

Cpl *see* **E-4**

CQ (Charge of Quarters, Command of Quarters) Noncommissioned officer in charge of a unit headquarters at night, outside of normal duty hours. The CQ was in administrative command of the unit and responsible for maintaining the chain of command between the unit's higher headquarters and subordinate units or troops under the CQ's command. The company level CQ was responsible for maintaining order within the company area, messaging, bed checks, special wake-up calls and other functions as required. Field units in Vietnam did not run CQs, but the larger base camps and facilities ran CQ nightly. The CQ was sometimes referred to as Command of Quarters and was assisted in his duties by one or more CQ Runners. *See also* **Officer of the Day.**

CQ Runner (Charge of Quarters Runner) The CQ was the NCO in charge of a headquarters during the night hours. He had at his disposal enlisted men who functioned as runners. These runners typically handled such duties as carrying messages, passing on orders, wake-up calls for the cooks and KPs and any other miscellaneous duties the CQ came up with. *See also* **CQ.**

Crabs *see* **M-29C, Venereal Diseases**

Crachin Field term for seasonal climatic conditions in the mountains of I and II Corps featuring very low cloud ceilings mixed with drizzling rain and sometimes, heavy fog. The low clouds socked in the valleys between the mountain peaks and ridges making supply and combat support difficult for American units operating in the area. *See also* **Monsoons.**

Crack Up *see* **Flip Out**

Cracker *see* **Caucasian**

Crackers *see* **B-2 Unit**

Crash *see* **Zs**

Crash Ballistic Protective Flying Helmet *see* **APH-5**

Crater Charge Explosive charges placed in an enemy tunnel. When the charges detonated the tunnel was supposed to collapse. The placing of such charges was normally done by the engineers, but it was sometimes done by regular grunts, when no engineer teams were available. *See also* **Tunnel Rats, Engineers.**

Crazy (Flaky, Dinky Dau, Wrapped-Too-Tight, Dingy, Head-Case) GIs had many terms for calling each other crazy or out of balance with the world around them. Some of the phrases included flaky, wrapped too tight, not playing with a full deck, fucked-up, Section 8 (Section 212 material), dinky dau, head-case. Craziness manifested itself in a multitude of ways in Vietnam; the one common thread among all of Vietnam's "crazies" was that "crazy people were totally unpredictable!" *See also* **Dinky Dau.**

Crazy Horse *see* **Operation Crazy Horse**

CRB *see* **Cam Ranh Bay**

CRC *see* **Control and Reporting Post**

Creamed Beef on Toast *see* **Shit-on-a-Shingle**

Creative Federalism *see* **Great Society, The**

Credibility Gap Sixties buzzword used to define the differences between what the nation's policymakers were telling the public and what those policy leaders were actually doing. The government's credibility to the public steadily crumbled as the truth of U.S. policy of war mismanagement leaked out. The public's access to the news media, Tet '68, Watergate and the Pentagon Papers fiasco, all contributed to the increasing distrust of the American public for its government and its stated policies.

Crescent Plain *see* **Crescent, The**

Crescent, The (Phu My, Cay Giep Mountains, Crescent Plain) GI nickname for the Cay Giep Mountains. The 3,199-foot high, coastal mountain range located between Phu My and Vinh Thanh, in Binh Dinh Province, II Corps. The peak of the range was located 27kms northeast of An Khe, and 27kms northwest of Phu Cat. Phu My was located along Highway 1, 24kms north of Phu Cat, in the coastal lowlands nicknamed the "Crescent Plain." Like much of Binh Dinh Province the Crescent area was infested with the Viet Cong, who enjoyed considerable support from the local populace.

Crest (Hill) *see* **Military Crest**

Crew Served Weapons Scope *see* **Starlight Scope**

Cricket *see* **Operation Cricket**

CRID *see* **Capital Republic of Korea Infantry Division**

Criminal Investigations Division (CID) Military organization that investigated criminal activities within the military. During the Vietnam War the CID focused many of its investigations on the sale, use, and trafficking of drugs within the military. They also investigated smuggling, Black Market activities and other criminal activities conducted by U.S. servicemen. The CID frequently used undercover agents, placed in field and base camp units, to gather evidence. The CID was generally disliked by most GIs, worldwide. *See also* **OSI.**

Crimp *see* **Operation Crimp**

Crimson Tide *see* **Operation Crimson Tide**

CRIP Platoon *see* **Combined Re-**connaissance and Intelligence Platoon

Crispy-Critters (Napalm Victims) Slang nickname for the burned bodies of a napalm or flamethrower attack. *See also* **Naphthenic-Palmitic Acid.**

Crocodiles *see* **119th Aviation Company**

Cronkite, Walter (CBS Evening News) Popular television newsman who anchored the CBS Evening News throughout the Vietnam War. Cronkite was generally supportive of administration efforts in Vietnam until Tet '68, when he withdrew his support of the Johnson Administration and publicly questioned America's ability to win in South Vietnam. Cronkite was trusted and respected by the American public and his change in attitude toward the war signaled a growing change in the nation's perception and support of the war.

Crook *see* **FSB Crook**

Crop Denial US/SVN program with the objective of destroying crops suspected of belonging to, or destined for use by the NVA/VC. The destruction or denial methods used on the crops included: chemical poisoning, burning, and destruction by artillery or air strikes. Crops already harvested were either destroyed or removed from the VC area and later distributed to GVN facilities. The term "Crop Denial Program" sounded less hostile and heavy-handed than "enemy food supply poisoning" or "food supply destruction." The basic premise of the crop denial program was, destroy the rice and there won't be any for the enemy; a starving enemy would have to give up the fight. *See also* **Ranch Hand, Resource Management, Defoliation, Big Patch, Rice Denial.**

Cross Border Patrols (Out-of-Country Patrols) Reconnaissance and raid missions conducted by USSF units across South Vietnam's border into Laos, Cambodia and North Vietnam. The main purpose of the patrols was to gather information on enemy sanctuaries and infiltration routes along the border. Cross border patrols were the primary source of information about the sanctuaries since no major US/ARVN ground operations took place into the area until '70. Cross border operations also included raids and ambush attacks in the enemy's rear areas. Out-of-country patrols were occasionally performed by U.S. LRRP teams, but such missions were usually part of USSF and MACV-SOG operations. *See also* **Roadrunner Teams, Greek Operations.**

Cross Burning *see* **Klan**

Crossbows *see* **173d Aviation Company**

Crossovers *see* **Garwood, PFC Robert (Bobby)**

Crotch Rot *see* **Jungle Rot**

Crotch, The (U.S. Marine Corps, Mother Green) "Mother Green" was a nickname for the Marine Corps used by career soldiers. Marines in general referred to the "Corps" as the "Crotch."

Crow *see* **LZ Crow**

CROW Grenade Launcher (Counter Recoil Operated Weapon Launcher) Experimental multiple-shot grenade launcher developed by Colt Firearms. The CROW used the high velocity M-383 40mm grenade, which, when fired, utilized the increased recoil from the high velocity round to operate the automatic loading mechanism of the launcher, chambering the next round to be fired. *See also* **Grenade Launcher.**

Crow's Foot (Eagle's Claw) Valley area near the Bong Son Valley of Binh Dinh Province where the mountains fan out into ridges and small valleys that, on the map, look like a bird's foot. The area, about 73kms northwest of Qui Nhon, was nicknamed by members of the 1st Cavalry Division that operated in the area in '66. Sometimes referred to as the "Eagle's Claw." *See also* **Bong Son.**

Crow's Nest Area along the SVN/Cambodian border, in Cambodia, used as a sanctuary and base by the NVA for launching attacks into SVN. On military maps the roughly "nest shaped" area was located 85kms west of Saigon and 70kms north of Vinh Long in the Delta. The Crow's Nest dipped into South Vietnam in Kien Tuong Province, IV Corps. *See also* **Parrot's Beak, Dog's Head, Angel's Wing, Fish Hook.**

Crown *see* **Airborne Battlefield Command and Control Center**

Crows *see* **Electronic Warfare Officer**

CRP *see* **Control and Reporting Post**

CRP Platoon (Combat Reconnaissance Platoon) "Eyes and ears" of the Special Forces CIDG Camp. The CRP platoon conducted reconnaissance and small raids in support of the CIDG camp from which they worked. The CRP platoon was part of the camp's "Camp Strike Force." The platoon consisted of 30–36 CIDGs who were typically better equipped, trained and disciplined than the regular CIDG soldier. The CRP platoon was usually commanded by a member of the USSF, and operated in the general area of the camp. *See also* **Combined Reconnaissance and Intelligence Platoon.**

CRS *see* **Catholic Relief Services**

Cruits *see* **New Troop, Twinks, Basic Combat Training**

Crunchies *see* **Infantry Soldier, The**

Crusader *see* **F-8**

CRV *see* **M-114 CRV**

Cry Baby Grenades *see* **Grenades, Gas**

CS Gas (Tear Gas, E8 CS Gas Dispenser) Chemical irritant used for riot control; tear gas. The U.S. military sometimes made use of CS gas in an effort to "smoke" out the enemy from entrenched bunkers and tunnel systems. The CS could be delivered by hand grenade or artillery. The E8 CS Gas Dispenser was also used by troops in the field. On occasion the enemy used captured CS gas grenades or mortar rounds against U.S. positions. CS was available in "persistent" (crystals) and "nonpersistent" (gas) forms. Nonpersistent CS was the smoke form commonly used in riot control. In Vietnam it was typically dispersed by hand grenade or artillery. *See also* **Grenades, Gas; Persistent CS, E8 CS Gas Dispenser, M-17 Protective Mask.**

CS Grenades *see* **Grenades, Gas**

CS-1 *see* **Persistent CS**

CSAB *see* **Combat Support Aviation Battalion**

CSF *see* **TF 115, Camp Strike Force**

CSG *see* **Combined Studies Group**

CSO *see* **Counterinsurgency Support Office**

CSP *see* Combat Security Police

CSWS *see* Starlight Scope

CSZ *see* Capital Military District

CTF-77 *see* TF-77

CTOC *see* Corps Tactical Operations Center

CTT *see* Dog Team

CTZ *see* Corps Tactical Zones

Cu Chi (Dong Zu) Home of the U.S. 25th Infantry Division in Vietnam. The division's base camp was located just off Highway 1, 24kms northwest of Saigon and 3kms north of Cu Chi Town in Hau Nghia Province, III Corps, on a large open field, known as Dong Zu, previously used by the South Vietnamese for parachute training. Just north of the base camp was a maze of underground tunnels that laced the area. The Viet Cong tunnel system consisted of hospitals, rest centers, ammunition and weapons storage, fighting positions, headquarters, kitchens, weapons factories and more, all underground with expertly camouflaged entrances and breathing holes. The VC called the Cu Chi District "Iron Land." *See also* **Tunnel Rats.**

Cu Chi Computer Center (NCR 500, UNIVAC 1005) The NCR 500 and the UNIVAC 1005 computers were used by the U.S. Army intelligence section to analyze enemy "patterns of activity" in the northern and western areas of III Corps. The computers were maintained in air conditioned trailers located at Cu Chi, the 25th Infantry Division base camp. The center was also part of a network of computers that provided data used by the HES, Hamlet Evaluation System. *See also* **Hamlet Evaluation System, Pattern Activity Analysis.**

Cu Chi Express GI nickname for the road convoys that traveled between the 25th Infantry Division base camp at Cu Chi and the U.S. logistics center located at Long Binh. Supply convoys were plagued throughout the war by Viet Cong mines and ambushes. Eventually a series of fire bases was established along Highway 1, between Cu Chi and Saigon, which reduced enemy activity along the road. *See also* **Cu Chi, Long Binh.**

Cu Chi Music Ensemble (Viet Cong USO) Group of Viet Cong entertainers that performed in the Cu Chi area during the Vietnam War. The group performed short propaganda plays for VC troops and selected peasants of the area in the underground tunnel complexes near Cu Chi. The group performed plays and song and dance routines, and conducted patriotic sing-alongs. The ensemble, and other similar NVA/VC groups, performed throughout Vietnam providing troops with entertainment while reinforcing the communist political agenda. Such groups were the Viet Cong's version of the American "USO Show." *See also* **Hope, Bob.**

Cu Chi National Guard *see* **25th Infantry Division**

Cu Loc Prison *see* **Zoo, The**

Cua Viet Village located at the mouth of the Song Cua Viet River in Quang Tri Province, I Corps. The river connected Quang Tri City and the Marine logistics center at Dong Ha with the South China Sea. A small naval base was established at Cua Viet to support river patrol and supply operations. Larger ships, unable to negotiate the river, off-loaded their cargoes to smaller craft operating on the river. The river served as the lifeline for Dong Ha with Navy and Marine units in constant contention with the NVA/VC to keep the river open. Cua Viet served as the support base for PBRs of TF Clearwater. *See also* **Song Cua Viet, TF Clearwater.**

Cunningham *see* **Dewey Canyon Fire Bases**

Cunt Cap (Garrison Cap, Side Cap, Piss-Cutter, Soft Cap) Soft, foldable hat with variants worn by all branches of the service. The cap was spread open to be worn on the head and folded flat when not in use. The Army nicknames for their garrison hat were "cunt cap" or "side cap." The Air Force called theirs "cunt caps." And the Marines and Navy called theirs "piss-cutters."

Curfew The curfew was a constant part of the Vietnam War. It affected both the Vietnamese and the Free World Forces. The curfew hours varied depending on the locale and the situation. Generally in the larger cities no one except security personnel were to be on the streets between midnight and 6 A.M. In the rural areas the curfew for the

Vietnamese was sunset to sunup; any Vietnamese civilians encountered after those hours could be considered Viet Cong. In hostile areas no lights were allowed in hootches after sunset. In March '75 as the military situation deteriorated in SVN the curfew was progressively extended and the start hour changed to 10 P.M., 8 P.M., and on the last day before Saigon's collapse a 24-hour curfew was declared, and mostly ignored by the populace.

Curtis Commando *see* C-46

Cushman, General Robert *see* Commandant

Cut(ting) Trail (Bustin' Bush, Trail Blazing) To move through jungle or dense vegetation, hacking out a trail as you went instead of following an already defined trail or track. Lead elements cut a path that became more defined as each man in the group moved through. Machetes were used to cut the path. If noise was a consideration the group moved through the jungle without cutting; this was a very slow and difficult process. Avoiding already established trails in enemy territory greatly reduced the chances of tripping enemy booby traps and getting caught in an ambush. In especially dense terrain the point man cutting the trail was rotated often. Cutting through jungle vines and brush was extremely hard work in the humid jungle heat, a task made more difficult with a 60–70-pound rucksack and weapons. *See also* **Machete.**

Cut-Down (I.V.) Medical term used to describe the procedure used to locate an artery/vein in order to insert a needle or I.V. to administer medication. The procedure involved cutting a deep slit on the inside of the arm, where it bends at the elbow, and searching for the artery, then raising it for I.V. insertion. The cut-down was performed when the artery could not be located near the surface due to its collapse from injury, blockage or dehydration. Cut-downs were sometimes performed in the field by medics when medical evacuation was delayed.

Cut ... a Hus *see* **Lighten-Up**

Cut ... Some Slack *see* **Lighten-Up**

Cuts *see* **Recycle**

Cuu Long 44-02 A January '71 ARVN operation into Cambodia to open Route 4,

the road between Kampong Song and Phnom Penh. The road had been closed by communist rebels, the Khmer Rouge, who were fighting the Cambodian government. The ARVN's successful operation to open the road was at the Cambodian government's request.

Cuu Nuoc & Thong Nhat (National Salvation) Two newsletters circulated in various areas of South Vietnam. The papers were written and distributed by members of the VCI and the NLF. Cuu Nuoc meant "national salvation" and Thong Nhat meant "unification."

CV-2 *see* **C-7A**

CVA (CVAN, CVS, CVN) Navy designation for its attack aircraft carriers. CVAN was the designation for the Navy's nuclear powered aircraft carrier, the USS *Enterprise,* CVAN-65. The *Enterprise* was the world's first nuclear powered carrier to see combat duty. CVS were aircraft carriers fitted for antisubmarine warfare. All three types of carriers saw action in the waters off Vietnam, providing air support to troops in South Vietnam, and conducting air operations against North Vietnam, Laos, and Cambodia. *See also* **Aircraft Carrier Force, USS Yorktown.**

CVA-14 *see* **USS Ticonderoga**

CVA-19 *see* **USS Hancock**

CVA-31 *see* **USS Bon Homme Richard**

CVA-34 *see* **USS Oriskany**

CVA-41 *see* **USS Midway**

CVA-42 *see* **USS Franklin D. Roosevelt**

CVA-43 *see* **USS Coral Sea**

CVA-59 *see* **USS Forrestal**

CVA-60 *see* **USS Saratoga**

CVA-61 *see* **USS Ranger**

CVA-62 *see* **USS Independence**

CVA-63 *see* **USS Kitty Hawk**

CVA-64 *see* **USS Constellation**

CVA-66 *see* **USS America**

CVAN *see* **CVA**

CVAN-65 *see* **USS Enterprise**

CVC Helmet Fiberglass helmet worn

by U.S. armor crewmen. The helmet was large with an internal headset and boom microphone. The CVC helmet was shaped like a modified football helmet.

CVN-65 *see* **USS Enterprise**

CVS *see* **CVA**

CVS-10 *see* **USS Yorktown**

CVS-11 *see* **USS Intrepid**

CVS-12 *see* **USS Hornet**

CVS-33 *see* **USS Kearsarge**

CVS-38 *see* **USS Shangri-La**

CW Radio *see* **AN/PRC-64**

CWC *see* **Civilian War Casualties**

CWO *see* **Warrant Officer**

CYA (Cover-Your-Ass) The old philosophy of self-protection.

Cycad Tree *see* **Cay Thien Tue**

Cyclic Rate of Fire The maximum rate of fire of a weapon in a fixed period. The rate was usually measured in the number of rounds per minute the weapon could fire if it had an unlimited supply of ammunition available. Some examples of cyclic rates of fire: AK47, 600rds; M-60, 550rds; M-16, 800rds; M-3, 450rds.

Cyclo *see* **Pedicab**

D

D5E Bulldozer *see* **Caterpillar D7E Tractor**

D7E (Cat) Tractor *see* **Caterpillar D7E Tractor**

D Zone *see* **War Zone D**

D-D *see* **Di Di**

D-Ring *see* **Stabo Rig**

DA 483 *see* **Dream Sheet**

DA 2635 *see* **Dream Sheet**

DA Form 1 *see* **Morning Report**

Da Lat Provincial capital and resort located in the Central Highlands of Tuyen Duc Province, II Corps. Da Lat was connected by rail to Phan Rang, southeast near the coast, and was 78kms west of Cam Ranh Bay. Da Lat was prized as a resort by the "upper class" Vietnamese and was the site of South Vietnam's Military Academy for its officer staff. *See also* **Lang Bian.**

Da Nang (Tourane, Baie de Tourane, DNG) Port city in Quang Nam Province, I Corps, located on the mouth of the Ca De Song River. Headquarters for U.S. Marines, Army XXIV Corps and SVN military forces in I Corps. Da Nang, RVN's second largest city, was a major logistic base and airfield, and its name became synonymous with the

U.S. Marine Corps in Vietnam. The French called Da Nang, Baie de Tourane. Da Nang was a major Buddhist stronghold during their revolt in '66. The air base outside the city suffered several attacks, but it was never overrun until the NVA offensive in '75. During the U.S. airwar against NVN, Da Nang supported air operations of the Marines, Navy and Air Force. *See also* **Half Moon Bay.**

Da Nang Harbor *see* **Half Moon Bay**

Dac Cong (DACON Companies, NVA Combat Engineers, NVA B-52, Viet Cong Special Forces) North Vietnamese Army (Viet Cong) combat engineers, sometimes called Sappers; also referred to as the Viet Cong's Special Forces. The Dac Cong (DACON) used bangalore torpedoes, satchel charges and other combined explosives to open up holes in the defensive wireworks surrounding allied base camps and fortifications. They used an assortment of bamboo ladders and mats to cover defensive wire to allow NVA assault troops to enter the enemy's defensive perimeter. Once inside the perimeter the sappers would use satchel charges on enemy strong-points, command bunkers and ammo dumps. Ho Chi Minh called them NVN's answer to the American

B-52. *See also* Combat Engineer Team, Sappers, F-100 Battalion.

DACON Companies *see* **Dac Cong**

Dai Dao Tam Ky Pho Do Sect *see* **Cao Dai**

Dai Kim Do (Great Golden World) Large dance hall located in the Cholon area of Saigon, on the same property as the famous whorehouse, the Hall of Mirrors. The Hall of Mirrors was closed down in '55 by Diem during his crackdown on the Binh Xuyen, but the dance hall remained open for dancing until '62 when Madame Nhu banned public and private dancing throughout South Vietnam. After the fall of the Diem regime in '63, dancing in Saigon re-emerged. *See also* **Hall of Mirrors, Dance Ban**.

Dai Uy Vietnamese for chief, leader, someone in charge, or the honcho. Vietnamese military rank equivalent to a U.S. Army captain. *See also* **Captain**.

Dai Viet (Nationalist Party of Vietnam) Vietnamese nationalist party founded in '39 in Hanoi. The party, the Dai Viet Quoc Dan Dang (known as the Dai Viet), was extremely nationalistic, anti–French and anticommunist. The Dai Viet was formed by the followers of Phan Boi Chau, a staunch nationalist who attempted to gain Vietnamese independence by revolting against the French in the early 1900s. After the communist takeover of NVN, the Dai Viet was outlawed and its remaining members fled to South Vietnam, settling in upper I Corps. Various factions of the Dai Viet surfaced, but they could never consolidate into a political force capable of affecting Vietnamese politics.

Dai-Ta *see* **Colonel**

Dai-Tuong *see* **General Officers**

Dai-Uy *see* **Captain**

Daily-Daily *see* **Dapsone**

Daisy Cutter (Homemade) Nickname for any number of "homemade," or "field utility" bombs custom-made by GIs in the field. Some examples of field utility daisy cutters were a stick of C-4 explosive wrapped with part of an M-60 machine gun ammo belt; several concussion and WP grenades wrapped around a stick of C-4; a can of engine oil with a thermite grenade attached to it; a can of gasoline or napalm with a WP grenade attached; a stick of C-4 with rocks imbedded into it. These and other examples were used by GIs against the enemy. Sometimes helicopter aircrews carried one or two variants of the daisy cutter which they could drop on the enemy if the opportunity presented itself.

Daisy Cutter (Instant LZ) (Commando Vault, BLU-82/B) 10,000/15,000-pound bombs used to clear an instant LZ in thick jungle. The 10,000-pound BLU-82/B was dropped by helicopter (CH-54), and could create a 100-meter diameter hole in the jungle. The bomb was fitted with a special extended fuse that allowed the bomb to detonate several feet above the ground, creating a smaller crater and increasing the area of vegetation destruction. Some of the bombs were delivered by C-130s, with the bombs being slid off the rear cargo ramp; a drag chute attached to the tail of the bomb slowed its fall. During the final days of the war, in '75, VNAF dropped some of the bombs on NVA troop concentrations. The Air Force version was called the Commando Vault and weighed 15,000 pounds.

Daisy Cutters (GP Bombs) Nickname for 250- and 500-pound general purpose bombs that exploded slightly above ground level. Attached to the fuse end of the bomb was a metal shaft, 4–5 feet long. The shaft caused the bomb to detonate 3–4 feet above the surface of the ground, greatly increasing the effectiveness of the bomb blast and shrapnel. Bombs that detonated at ground level were not as effective against enemy personnel concentrations on the ground, but were better used against entrenched enemy bunkers and fortified positions. *See also* **Airburst**.

Dak Pek Hamlet which became the sight of a U.S. Special Forces camp, located on Highway 14, 120kms north of Pleiku, 12kms east of the Laotian border.

Dak Seang Village located in the Central Highlands of Kontum Province, 15kms northwest of Dak To. Dak Seang was also the site of a U.S. Special Forces CIDG camp located astride a major NVA/VC infiltration route. In April '70 elements of 3–4 NVA regiments attempted to overrun the small outpost. The camp was defended by less than 350 CIDG troops and its USSF complement. The camp was supported by air and artillery and eventually relieved by two Mike Force battalions that fought their way to the camp.

Dak To Vietnamese town located on Highway 14 in the Central Highlands of Kontum Province, II Corps. Dak To was located less than 20kms from the Laos/Cambodian border near a main NVA/VC infiltration route into SVN. In '65 the USSF established a camp near Dak To to monitor enemy activity. In '67 U.S. and NVA units battled for the hills around Dak To. The U.S. successfully moved the NVA off the hills, but NVA infiltration through the area continued throughout the war. *See also* Battle of Dak To.

Dallas *see* **Dewey Canyon Fire Bases**

Dan Cong Civilian laborers working for the NVA/VC, farming, fishing, repairing weapons, doing road/trail work and other tasks as required. By using civilians to do jobs that would have otherwise required troops, the NVA was able to assign more of its forces to combat duties. Not all of the laborers were "volunteers" and over the years of the war thousands of civilians were coerced, intimidated or simply drafted into service of the NVA/VC. *See also* **Tinh Nguyen, Tooth-to-Tail Ratio**

Dan Quan *see* **People's Self-Defense Force**

Dan Sinh Vietnamese phrase meaning "popular livelihood." VC propaganda slogan used to point out the shortcomings of the GVN while claiming how much better things would be in the future when the war was over and the communists had triumphed. Based on the number of South Vietnamese that have escaped Vietnam since the communist victory in '75, it appears the communists should have qualified their "dan sinh" slogan to indicate just "who" would actually benefit from their victory.

Dan Ve (Village Militia) Village militia organized under the Diem regime as a local self-defense force to protect rural villages from the Viet Cong. The Dan Ve were poorly armed, barely trained, and ineffectively led. Many of the militia were part of Diem's corrupt system and used the Dan Ve for their own benefit. Some members of the militia were actually VC and used the Dan

Ve as a source of equipment to outfit VC units in the field. The Dan Ve served as the forerunner of the Regional and Popular defense forces (RF/PFs). *See also* **Popular Forces, Regional Forces.**

Dance Ban (Prohibition Against Dancing, Morality Law) In '62 Madame Nhu, sister-in-law of South Vietnam's President Diem, announced a ban on all dancing, public or private, in South Vietnam. According to Madame Nhu, the ban, or "Morality Law," was imposed to "protect the purity and honor of Vietnamese womanhood." The ban remained in effect until November '63 when the Diem regime was overthrown in a military coup, after which dancing returned to Vietnam. *See also* **Madame Nhu, Dai Kim Do, Taxi Dancer.**

Dandy Fever *see* **Dengue Fever**

Danger *see* **FSB Danger**

Danger Close *see* **Artillery Safety Margin**

Danger-Close Range Marine field term for close range artillery or air strikes called on to enemy positions. "Danger-Close" range allowed 50 meters of safety clearance between the strike area and the friendly unit calling in the strike. The 50-meter proximity to friendly units was considered critical and was used to break up enemy concentrations closely engaged with friendly units. *See also* **Hug, Artillery Safety Margin.**

Daniel Boone *see* **Operation Daniel Boone**

DAO *see* **Defense Attache Office**

Dao Phu Quoc *see* **Phu Quoc Island**

Dap *see* **Soul Handshake**

Dapsone (DDS, Daily-Daily, White Pill) Antimalaria pill taken by American troops to reduce the risk of contracting malaria. The small white pill was taken daily and was usually called the "daily-daily" or the "white pill." *See also* **Chloroquine, Primaquine.**

DARMA *see* **Defensive Contact Artillery Fire**

DARMA Fires (Defense Against Rocket and Mortar Attack) Artillery technique designed to suppress enemy rocket or mortar attack. The procedure concentrated artillery fires at preplotted target locations that had been selected as possible enemy 107/122mm rocket launcher or mortar sites. DARMA was a variant DEFCON fires. *See also* **Defensive Contact Artillery Fire.**

DART *see* **Deployable Automatic Relay Terminal**

Darvons Commonly prescribed pain medication issue in the Army. Darvon was the name of a compound of aspirin and a synthetic narcotic called propoxyphene. Darvons were available in capsule form and usually prescribed for the relief of mild pain. Like many other narcotic drugs, Darvon was sometimes abused and addictive. Overuse of the drug could lead to severe constipation and urine retention. *See also* **Drug List.**

DASC *see* **Direct Air Support Center**

Dash-Twelve (12 Logbook, Helicopter Log Book) The -12 was a page from the helicopter logbook; an updated logbook was kept with each aircraft. The logbook was updated each time the craft was operated or serviced. The "dash-twelve" page of the logbook was turned in to the operations section of the helicopters unit which tracked the hours flown by the crews and hours of operation of the aircraft.

DAT *see* **District Advisory Team**

Date Eligible to Return from Overseas Service (DEROS, Tour of Duty) The scheduled date a tour of duty was over in Vietnam. The date to DEROS was memorized and counted down on special calendars, called Short-Time-Calendars. These calendars were conspicuously posted on walls and lockers; some troops even kept a copy etched on their helmet covers. DEROS was probably the most anticipated day in a soldier's tour. DEROS was officially defined as Date of Expected Return from Overseas. The Army tour lasted 12 months, the Marine tour was 13 months and Navy SEABEES rotated, as a unit after eight months. *See also* **Tour of Duty Phases, Rotate, Short-Timer Calendar, One Year Tour.**

Date of Expected Return from Overseas *see* **Date Eligible to Return from Overseas Service**

Dau Dam (Funeral Procession) For-mal Vietnamese funeral procession featuring an altar, horse drawn hearse, and marchers carrying wreaths, banners and flags. Formal funerals were usually only available to the rich and those in high government positions.

Dau Tieng (Tri Tam) Vietnamese town located along Highway 14, 25kms east of Tay Ninh City, 60kms northwest of Saigon in Binh Duong Province, III Corps. Dau Tieng was also known as Tri Tam, and was located near the southwest edge of the Michelin Rubber Plantation. The entire area around Dau Tieng was a longtime Viet Cong base area and NVA infiltration route. The U.S. Army established a large fire base at Da Tieng which was manned by elements of the 1st Infantry Division and later by units of the 25th Infantry Division. *See also* **Michelin Rubber Plantation, Iron Triangle.**

Dau Tranh (Dau Tranh Vu Trang, Dau Tranh Chinh Tri) Vietnamese phrase for struggle, the basis for communist strategy in Vietnam. The North Vietnamese struggle was in two parts; Dau Tranh Vu Trang was the armed or violent struggle against the GVN and its allies, and Dau Tranh Chinh Tri the political struggle. The political struggle was used early in the war and when it became ineffective the armed struggle began.

Dau Tranh Chinh Tri *see* **Dau Tranh**

Dau Tranh Vu Trang *see* **Dau Tranh**

Daughter of Thuot *see* **Ban Me Thuot**

Davis, Rennard *see* **Chicago 8**

Davis, SP4 James T. (Camp Davis) U.S. Army Specialist-4, James T. Davis was killed in a VC ambush just outside the village of Duc Hoa, west of Saigon, December 22, 1961. Davis was an Army communications specialist working with the ARVN, monitoring Viet Cong radio transmissions in the area. He was officially the first American to be killed (in combat) in Vietnam. In his honor the American MACV Compound located at Duc Hoa was named Camp Davis. Camp Davis later became headquarters for the MACV advisory group that was attached to the ARVN 25th Inf. Div. *See also* **First American to Die...**

Day *see* **Dung Lai**

Day Dien see Commo Wire

Day Thep Gai see Tanglefoot

Day-Glo Paintings and posters using "Day-Glo" paints were popular during the sixties. The Vietnam version of the paintings were usually done on black velvet or velvetine material by Vietnamese artists, and were popular among some of the base camp GIs. The Day-Glo paints used were fluorescent in color and glowed under "Black Lights." Day-Glo paintings and posters were also popular amongst the hippie and antiwar sects back in the States.

DC-3 see C-47

DCC see Komer, Robert

DCPG see Defense Communications Planning Group

DCS see Strategic Communications Command

DD (Destroyer, Destroyer Escort [DE]) U.S. Navy classifications for its destroyers (DD) and destroyer escort (DE) ships. Both were used for coastal surveillance and interdiction duties off the coast of South Vietnam. The destroyers were capable of making 35 knots and were armed with a combination of 3-inch, 5-inch, and 40mm guns, as well as torpedo launchers and ASROCs (Antisubmarine Rockets). The DEs were a little larger than the DDs, similarly equipped, with maximum speeds in the range of 27 knots. See also TF 115, DER.

DD-731 see USS Maddox, Tonkin Gulf Incident

DD-951 see Tonkin Gulf Incident

DDS see Dapsone

DE see DD

De Soto Patrol Code name for regular U.S. Navy intelligence and surveillance patrols carried out along the coast of NVN. It was during one of these patrols that NVN patrol boats fired on the USS *Maddox* in '64, eventually resulting in the Gulf of Tonkin Resolution and escalation of U.S. involvement in Vietnam. Similar patrols had been carried out along the coast of North Korea, China and the USSR and were designed to monitor and record enemy radar and radio transmissions for further analysis. See also Tonkin Gulf Incident, Ferret Operations, OPLAN-34A.

De-escalation see Escalation

De-Log Ship see Back Bird

Dead see Kill

Dead Enemy Soldier see Believer

Dead Space An area within the range of a weapon or observer that cannot be brought under fire by the weapon or seen by the observer because it is hidden or screened by the terrain. This pertained primarily to direct fire weapons such as rifles, machine guns and rockets. See also Field of Fire.

Deadlined Military term for a vehicle that is out of service awaiting parts and or repairs.

Deadly 2d Lieutenants see Second Lieutenant

Dealers of Death see Gunfighters

Deans, The see 120th Aviation Company

Dear John Letter A letter received by a soldier, from his wife or girlfriend, informing him that she was going to divorce him, separate from him, or break up with him. In short, she wanted the soldier out of her life. The letters used a variety of excuses and sometimes went into great painful detail as to why the breakup was taking place. Frequently the woman was leaving the soldier for another man (Jody), or was just fed up with military life, was tired of waiting, found a new love, or just couldn't stomach the soldier any longer. Dear Johns received overseas were particularly devastating because of the distances involved, the emotional isolation, and difficulty in addressing problems until the man's tour ended. See also FREE, Jody Call.

Death Before Dishonor One of the mottoes of the U.S. Marine Corps. Also the motto for the 1st Squadron/9th Cavalry. The motto was painted on the 1st/9th Cav's helicopters with their emblem, "crossed cavalry swords."

Death Cards see Calling Cards

Death on Call (Battery C/4/77 [ARA] 101st ABN; Love by Nature, Live by...) Nickname of Battery C/4th Battalion/77th Artillery (Aerial Rocket) was "Death on Call." The gunships of the 77th began deploying to Vietnam October '68 and operated with the 101st Airborne, providing aerial rocket artillery support. Their "calling card" featured an eagle holding the crest of the 101st ABN, and a thunderbolt, with the inscription, "Love by nature, Live by luck, Kill by profession." *See also* **Calling Cards, 77th Artillery Regiment.**

DEB *see* **Division Engineer Battalion**

Debridement *see* **Delayed Primary Closure**

DECCA British-developed, night and low visibility, navigational aid initially used by the U.S. in South Vietnam. The system used low level radio signals which proved to be ineffective for the terrain and atmospheric conditions of Southeast Asia. The system was eventually phased out of use.

Decent Interval Reference to a lull in the North Vietnamese Final Offensive, April 20–25, 1975. The NVA had effectively surrounded Saigon and had paused in its final push to crush the GVN. Some historians speculate that the lull was orchestrated by North Vietnam in an effort to allow the remaining U.S. personnel in Vietnam a "decent interval" to depart the country, before the final attacks on Saigon by the NVA. Hanoi further directed the commander of its offensive force in SVN (Gen. Van Tien Dung) not to interfere with the U.S. evacuation that was taking place in Saigon. The NVA did not fire directly on evacuation aircraft; but on April 29 artillery and air strikes did render the airstrip at Tan Son Nhut unusable. *See also* **Fall of Saigon.**

Decker, General George *see* **Chief of Staff**

Deckhouse IV *see* **Operation Deckhouse IV**

Decks *see* **Party-Pack**

Declaration of Honolulu *see* **Honolulu Conference**

Declaration of War The United States never officially declared war on North Vietnam. Many political and military leaders believed the lack of declaration doomed American involvement in SEA to failure because the nation's full military resources were not mobilized and the public was fed the war on a piecemeal basis. North Vietnam used the lack of a declaration of war against U.S. POWs, claiming such prisoners

were not subject to the rules and protections of the Geneva Convention and were in fact criminals who had committed crimes against the Vietnamese people. Since NVN was not a signatory of the '49 Geneva Convention, it is doubtful that U.S. POW treatment would have been any better. *See also* **Geneva Convention, War Powers Act.**

Dee-Dee *see* **Di Di**

Deep Serious *see* **Fucked-Up**

Deep Shit *see* **World of Hurt**

Deep-Sixed *see* **Kill**

Deer Gun Single-shot pistol developed for use by CIA operatives in SEA. The small handgun was less than five inches long and weighed less than a pound. The 9mm bullet was loaded by removing the barrel, and setting the hammer was done by a small, pulled cocking lever at the rear of the gun. Several rounds of ammunition could be carried in the small hollow butt of the weapon. The range of the Deer Gun was limited and its single shot capacity dictated that it would have to be used at extremely close range to be effective. The weapon was to have been air-dropped to indigenous agents, but the operational use of the weapon was never approved and most of the several thousand manufactured guns were destroyed.

Deer Teams Code name for U.S., OSS teams that trained and equipped the Viet Minh to harass the Japanese during their occupation of Indo-China during WWII. The first Deer Team parachuted into Japanese occupied Tonkin in early '45 and in addition to training and equipping the Viet Minh, were to identify Japanese targets for the Air Force and pass on intelligence information to the American command. The Deer Teams eventually supplied a small force of Viet Minh soldiers with small arms, several mortars and machine guns. *See also* **Office of Strategic Services; Dewey, Major Peter; Patti, Archimedes L.A.**

DEFCON *see* **Defensive Contact Artillery Fire**

Defeat in Detail (Divide and Conquer) Military strategy of dividing a large enemy force into smaller forces and defeating the reduced forces one at a time until the enemy is defeated. A rephrase of "divide and conquer."

Defense Against Rocket and Mortar Attack *see* **DARMA Fires**

Defense Attache Office (DAO) Under direction of the U.S. Ambassador to SVN, the DAO coordinated U.S. military assistance to SVN. The DAO took over the task of coordinating U.S. military assistance to South Vietnam as MACV and U.S. troops completed their withdrawal in '73. The offices of the DAO were located at the old MACV complex located near Tan Son Nhut Airport in the northwestern corner of Saigon.

Defense Communications Planning Group (Jason Group, DCPG) Secret U.S. intelligence think tank formed in the early '60s charged with the responsibility of inventing and generating new ideas on new electronic warfare devices and techniques to be used in Vietnam. The name of the group was formally changed from the Jason Group to the DCPG in '67. The group had many ideas that were put into practice with varying results. Some examples were the McNamara Line, Igloo White and the Turd SID. *See also* **Advanced Research Projects Agency, Tech Rep, Igloo White, Electronic Sensors.**

Defense Communications System *see* **Strategic Communications Command**

Defense Intelligence Agency (DIA) U.S. agency operated by the Pentagon, established in '61 to coordinate the collection, digestion and dissemination of military intelligence. The agency was a joint services organization.

Defense Concentration *see* **Defensive Contact Artillery Fire**

Defensive Contact Artillery Fire (DEFCON, Ringing-the-Perimeter, Defensive Concentration) U.S. practice of preplotting artillery fires for use around a base or Night Defensive Position. The artillery was plotted to encircle the position and the coordinates were registered with the artillery unit that would be called to provide the fires. Should the position be attacked during the night, the fire could quickly be called in on the prearranged coordinates, "ringing the perimeter with steel." DEFCONs, defensive concentrations, were routinely plotted as Standard Operating Procedure by U.S. units in Vietnam and were one of the first tasks accomplished when a unit stopped for the night. *See also* **Defensive Targets, DARMA Fires, Shooting the Donut.**

Defensive Line *see* **Main Line of Resistance**

Defensive Targets (DTs, Delta Tangos) Targets preestablished with an artillery battery. The target coordinates were called in to the battery prior to their use and given a number. In the event of enemy activity, the preplotted targets could simply be called by number, instead of the time-consuming and error prone request by coordinates that normally took place during the heat of battle. Defense targets were plotted by the unit commander or forward artillery observer attached to the unit. He usually selected the most likely avenues of approach the enemy might use, or areas the enemy could use as an ambush site. DTs were also routinely plotted to circle an entire position with artillery fire. *See also* **Defensive Contact Artillery Fire.**

Defiant Stand *see* **Operation Defiant Stand**

Defilade (Hull Down) To position your forces behind an obstacle to give them protection from enemy fire coming from another elevation. The obstacle could be natural as in the bank of a stream, or the edge of a hill, or a ground depression; or the obstacle could be a man-made mound of dirt, piled logs, or a sandbagged position. A tank or armored vehicle in defilade is said to be "hull down." *See also* **Berm.**

Defoliation (Agents: Orange, Blue, White, Pink, Purple, Herbicides) Military method of destroying vegetation used by the enemy for cover and concealment. Powerful herbicides were sprayed on various areas of SVN to clear areas of vegetation that were used by the enemy. The program started in '61 and was discontinued in '70 when the toxic and long-lasting effects of the agents became publicized. The defoliants were sprayed by air, by boat along riverbanks, and by hand sprayers around military installations. Over 19,000 defoliation sorties were carried out between '61–'70, deploying 12.8 million gallons of herbicides. *See also* **Ranch Hand; Resource Control; Agents: Orange, White, Blue, Pink, Purple; Operation Pink Rose.**

Degtyarova Pakhotnyi LMG   *see*   DP LMG

Degtyaryov Shpagin 38 HMG   *see* Type 54 HMG

Delaware   *see*   Operation Delaware

Delayed Primary Closure (DPC, Debridement)   For shrapnel and fragmentation wounds the usual procedure was to remove the metal from the wound, and the dead tissue surrounding it (debridement), clean the area and leave the wound open (Delayed Primary Closure). The open wounds were regularly cleaned out for several days, and then sutured closed.

Delayed Stress Syndrome   *see*   Post-Traumatic Stress Disorder

Delaying Action (Delay)   A retrograde movement by the main body of a force moving away from an enemy force. A small element of the retrograde force remained behind to attack the advancing enemy in an effort to slow him down. The delay force attempted to inflict as much damage as possible on the enemy and disrupt the enemy advance long enough to allow his parent force the time to move away. The NVA/VC made excellent use of delay tactics. Often an enemy squad could hold up an entire American company or larger force, providing the necessary minutes for their comrades to escape. Such small delaying forces sacrificed their lives as U.S. artillery and air strikes were brought to bear. *See also* Retrograde Movement, Retreat, Retire, Roll-Up Force.

Delinquency Report   *see*   DR

Deliverers of the White Death   *see* Commando Saber Missions

Dellinger, David   *see*   Chicago 8

Delta   *see*   Project Delta, LZ Delta

Delta Air Force   *see*   Navy's Delta Air Force

Delta Barrier Operations   Series of operations conducted by TF 194, codenamed SEALORDS, throughout the western and northwestern provinces of South Vietnam. The four operations, Barrier Reef, Giant Slingshot, Foul Deck (Tran Hung Dao) and Search Turn, specifically targeted NVA/VC infiltration routes along the Cambodian border. The operations were effec-tive in reducing NVA/VC activity in areas they had previously controlled, virtually uncontested. The operations started in late '68 with U.S. forces from TF 115, 116 and 117, and continued into late '71 with the use of ARVN troops and U.S. advisors. *See also* TF 194, Operations: Barrier Reef, Giant Slingshot, Foul Deck, Search Turn.

Delta Butcher, The (Ewell, Gen. Julian J.)   U.S. 9th Infantry Division soldiers' nickname for their beloved division commander in Vietnam. *See also* 9th Infantry Division.

Delta Dagger   *see*   F-102

Delta Deltas   *see*   Donut Dollies

Delta Footwear Program   Army program in Vietnam established to test and evaluate experimental footwear to be worn by U.S. soldiers in wet tropical zones. Various types of socks and boot designs were tried in an attempt to reduce the problems of the foot soldier with his feet and his footwear. *See also* Delta Sox.

Delta Regional Aviation Command (DRAC)   Unified command established to coordinate and control U.S. air assets in the Delta of IV Corps providing support to ARVN units. As U.S. ground units withdrew from the Delta, U.S. helicopter support for the ARVNs remained. The aviation command coordinated its activities with the Delta Regional Assistance Command which had overall responsibility for U.S. units assisting the ARVN in IV Corps.

Delta Sox   Nylon socks that became standard Army issue to Vietnam troops in '70. The socks were lightweight and designed to survive continued wet usage. The socks worked well in the wet climate, but were not flame resistant and melted at a low temperature. Because of this, the nylon socks and the nylon sided jungle boots were not usually worn by aircraft crews. Prior to '70, wool socks were standard issue to Army troops, even those en route to Vietnam. The decision to use nylon socks in Vietnam was, in part, based on an Army study done during the mid sixties which experimented with different types of socks and boots for use in wet tropical zones. *See also* Delta Footwear Program.

Delta Tangos   *see*   Defensive Targets

Delta Teams (Co N/75th Infantry

[Rangers], 74th Infantry LRRP) Name for long-range reconnaissance teams of the 173d Airborne Brigade that operated in Vietnam. The teams were redesignated as the 74th Infantry Detachment (LRP) in December '67. In February '69 the detachment was redesignated Company N, 75th Infantry (Rangers). The small teams performed long-range reconnaissance for the brigade until August '71.

Delta, The *see* **Mekong Delta**

Demilitarized Zone (DMZ, The Z, Song Ben Hai River) Demarcation line separating opposing countries from each other generally located along border lines. The zone was an area on either side of the line that was to remain clear of all military forces and installations. The DMZ in Vietnam was five miles wide, and positioned at the 17th Parallel. The actual demarcation line was the Song Ben Hai River that ran roughly west–east below the 17th Parallel. *See also* **Geneva Accords.**

Democratic Republic of Vietnam (DRV, NVN, North Vietnam, Bac Bo, Bac-Viet) Official name of North Vietnam. Ho Chi Minh, and the Viet Minh, formally founded the DRV in '50, naming himself as President. The name was changed to the Socialist Republic of Vietnam (SRV) in '76 after the fall of Saigon, and the reunification of North and South Vietnam into one country. The communist government of Ho Chi Minh was first recognized by China and the Soviet Union in January '50. *See also* **Socialist Republic of Vietnam.**

Dengue Fever (Breakbone Fever, Dandy Fever) One of several different fevers prevalent in Vietnam, also called Breakbone or Dandy Fever. The viral disease was characterized by painful swelling of the joints, sore muscles, high fever, and skin rash. The virus was transmitted through the bite of a mosquito, and treatment consisted of rest, and consumption of plenty of fluids. Dengue fever was usually not fatal, unless the disease was coupled with other complications.

Denounce the Communist Campaign *see* **To Cong Campaign**

Denton, Commander Jeremiah U.S. Navy pilot shot down near Hanoi in June '65. During a televised interview, orchestrated by the North Vietnamese, Commander Denton used his eyes to blink out the word "torture." He survived the Hanoi Hilton and was released in the prisoner exchange per the Paris Peace Accords in '73. *See also* **Prisoner of War.**

Denver *see* **USS Denver**

Dep (Pretty, Beautiful, Boo Coo Dep) Vietnamese for "pretty." The GI version was "boo-coo dep"; very pretty.

Department of Defense *see* **Secretary of Defense**

Department of Information (VDGI) Vietnamese government information department that functioned in a fashion similar to the U.S. Public Information Office. Media personnel who wanted to accompany Vietnamese operations, or ride as observers on Vietnamese aircraft needed government approval through the DGI. After '65 the large numbers of U.S. operations in Vietnam made it easier for correspondents to move around in the war with U.S. troops, and requests to accompany Vietnamese units declined.

Department of State *see* **Secretary of State**

Dependent Village (CIDG Ville) Village where the families of CIDG troops lived. The dependents of the CIDG troops were not allowed to live within the perimeter of the camp's compound. In some cases the families occupied bunkers and hootches around the periphery of the camp creating a camp within a camp. In other cases a small, independent village was constructed for the dependents adjacent to the CIDG camp.

Deploy *see* **Set-In**

Deployable Automatic Relay Terminal (DART) Ground based radio relay station that was used to intercept radioed readings from electronic sensors placed along the Ho Chi Minh Trail, and forward the data to the ISC at NKP for evaluation and targeting. Several relay sites were situated along the Cambodian and Laotian border to augment data collection duties performed by Air Force surveillance aircraft. DART was used in conjunction with Commando Hunt operations conducted against enemy trail activity. *See also* **Electronic Sensors, Commando Hunt, EC-121, Pave Eagle, NKP, Infiltration Surveillance Center.**

Deputy Civilian Commander of MACV see **Komer, Robert**

DePuy Foxhole Systematic spacing and locating of defensive positions to ensure their interlocking fire, named after General William DePuy, commander, 1st Infantry Division in Vietnam in '66. *See also* **Interlocking Fire.**

DER (Radar Picket) U.S. Navy destroyer escort class ships used for "radar" picket duty along the coast of South Vietnam, part of TF 115; Operation Market Time. The ships were DE Class destroyers with their torpedo launchers removed, and additional long-range radar equipment installed. The pickets normally operated around the perimeter of the fleet, conducting surveillance against enemy aircraft. In Vietnam the DERs were used to monitor Vietnam's coastal activities in an effort to reduce North Vietnam's waterborne infiltration of supplies and equipment into SVN. *See also* **TF 115, Market Time, DD.**

DEROS *see* **Date Eligible to Return from Overseas Service**

Deserters (RITA, FRITA, FUFA, Fed-Up-with-the-Fucking-Army) As U.S. involvement in Vietnam increased and antiwar sentiment in America grew, more and more members of the Armed Forces became resistant to service in Vietnam. The AWOL and desertion rates were greatest in the Army. Many underground organizations were created to help soldiers avoid fighting in Vietnam and were active in many countries worldwide. Countries such as England, Sweden, Canada, Spain, Switzerland, Ireland, and others would help deserting soldiers hide or escape to other anti–Vietnam War countries. The reasons for desertion varied but most were related to a fear of dying or killing, or objections to the war on moral grounds. An estimated 93,000 U.S. soldiers deserted the military during the Vietnam War. Nearly 22 percent of those who deserted did so after having served a normal tour of duty in Vietnam. Antiwar groups and deserter support groups sometimes referred to deserters or antiwar soldiers as RITAs, FRITAs or FUFAs. RITA was a war resister-in-the-army and a FRITA was the friend of a resister. FUFAs were those soldiers who were fed-up-with-the-fucking-

army, and were willing to do almost anything to avoid further military duty or any service in Vietnam. Government estimates for the number of deserters for the period '65–'73 exceed 550,000; most of these were short-term AWOLs. 100,000 hardcore deserters were actually discharged from the military. Officially there were 5,000 cases of desertion in-country and 32,000 cases of failure to report or return to Vietnam. *See also* **Amnesty Program, French Leave.**

Desertion During the war in Vietnam desertion among the combatants was highest within the South Vietnamese military. The average rate of desertion for the SVN military was about 20 percent per year from '61 to '75, with the rate greatly increased prior to '65 and after '72. ARVN deserters tended to return to their home villages and often found themselves "recruited" by the VC. The NVA/VC defected to the GVN under the Chieu Hoi program which granted them amnesty for their fighting against the government. American deserters from the war were small in number, but increased as the war continued. *See also* **Chieu Hoi Program, Deserters, French Leave, Bad Paper.**

Designer Fatigues *see* **Pegged Fatigues**

Desk Jockey *see* **Rear-Echelon-Mother-Fuckers**

Dessert, BA 350 *see* **Operation Menu Targets**

Destroyer *see* **DD, B-66**

Destroyer Escort *see* **DD**

Det Cord *see* **Detonator Cord**

Detachable Cargo Pod *see* **Universal Military Pod**

Detachment Alpha (Alfa) *see* **Mine Division 112/113**

Detachment B-36 *see* **Project Rapid Fire**

Detachment B-50 *see* **Project Omega**

Detachment B-51 U.S. Special Forces detachment that trained the Vietnamese Special Forces (LLDB) at the training center in Dong Ba Thin.

Detachment B-52 *see* **Project Delta**

Detachment B-55 U.S. Special Forces detachment that controlled the operations of the CIDG Mobile Strike Forces in SVN. *See also* **Mobile Strike Force.**

Detachment B-56 *see* **Project Sigma**

Detachment B-57 *see* **Project Gamma**

Detonator Cord (Det Cord, Prima Cord) Cord used to detonate explosives or booby traps. When detonated, a length of cord exploded along its entire length so fast it appeared that the entire length of cord was exploded simultaneously. In fact, the exploding charge was swiftly moving down the length of the cord. A length of det cord could be wrapped around a small tree; when detonated the tree would be blown down. In the field, det cord and blasting caps were separately carried by different men to reduce the chance of the blasting caps accidentally detonating the det cord. Also known as "prima cord." *See also* **Blasting Caps.**

Detox (Detoxification Centers, Johnson Island, Drug Testing) In an effort to reduce the number of drug addicted soldiers who returned to the U.S. from Vietnam the military established 11 drug rehabilitation and detoxification centers in-country. By '70 soldiers returning to the U.S. through unit withdrawal or DEROS were required not only to be tested for venereal diseases but also for drugs (urine testing for drugs started in '71). Those who did not pass were not allowed to leave Vietnam until their detoxification was complete or their VD cured. One of the more persistent rumors which floated around at DEROS time was that all the men that caught incurable cases of VD were sent to Johnson Island in the Pacific until cured or dead.

Detoxification Centers *see* **Detox**

Deuce-and-a-Half *see* **M-35 Truck**

Developing Community Spirit *see* **WHAM**

Devil Flight (632d Security Police Section) Name of the Air Force security reaction force for the U.S. Air Base at Binh Tuy. The force consisted of about 160 men and officers from the U.S. Air Force 632d Security Police Section and Vietnamese Air Force

Security. Binh Tuy was the Air Force's major air base located in the central Delta of IV Corps.

Devil's Asshole American riverine unit's nickname for a particularly hostile area of the Delta. The enemy infested area was a maze of narrow canals and river channels located in dense jungle south of Sa Dec near the center of IV Corps.

Dew *see* **Marijuana**

Dewey Canyon *see* **Operation Dewey Canyon**

Dewey Canyon Fire Bases (Riley, Razor, Dallas, Erskine, Cunningham, Turnage) During January–March '69 the 9th Marines plus two 1st ARVN Division battalions conducted operations in the A Shau Valley as part of Operation Dewey Canyon. During the operation they established six fire bases from which they operated and provided fire support. The fire bases were named Riley, Razor, Dallas, Erskine, Cunningham, and Turnage. At the end of the operation the Marines and ARVNs were withdrawn, and the bases abandoned. *See also* **Operation Dewey Canyon.**

Dewey, Major Peter (Operation Embankment) First American killed in Vietnam, September '45. Dewey was an Army OSS officer and part of Operation Embankment. He was in command of a team assigned to help repatriate Allied prisoners of war, seek out war criminals, and observe the actions of the French in Vietnam. Major Dewey was killed in a Viet Minh ambush near the team's quarters in Saigon; his body was never recovered, and at the time he was officially declared MIA. Dewey's MIA status made him the first American MIA in Vietnam, and he is considered to be the first American soldier to have died in Vietnam after the end of WWII. *See also* **First American to Die. . . , Deer Teams.**

Dexamphetamines (Uppers, Special Forces Popcorn, Dextro Amphetamine, Greenie, Green Bomb) Amphetamines used by some Special Forces and some LRRPs to temporarily overcome exhaustion and sleep deprivation in order to maintain alertness and stamina. The pills also depressed the appetite allowing for less food to be taken on long-range patrols. The uppers were supposed to be used on a limited basis, but some SF troops went for long periods of time, continually "popping" the pills. Several different types of "uppers" were available, in varying strengths. "Greenies" or "green bombs" were green encapsulated amphetamines that were generally available to combat pilots and USSF/LRRP units. *See also* **Illicit Drugs, Drug List, Speed.**

Dextran *see* **Serum Albumin**

Dextro Amphetamine *see* **Dexamphetamines**

DFs (Disposition Forms) Just about every action in the Army paperwork chain had to be preceded by, accompanied by and followed by a DA-Disposition Form. The Department of the Army DF was the civilian equivalent of the corporate "memo" or cover letter.

DFC *see* **Distinguished Flying Cross**

DH-5/DH-10 Claymores *see* **VC Claymore**

DHC-4A *see* **C-7A, STAS**

DHC-5 *see* **C-8A**

DI *see* **Drill Instructor, Beer Can Insignia**

Di An *see* **Four Corners**

Di Di (Dee-Dee, Dee-Dee-Mau, Di Di Mow, Didi, D-D, Di Di Mau) "Di di mau" [dee dee maow] was a Vietnamese colloquial phrase meaning to get away or to hurry. "Di" was Vietnamese for leave, change position, to go or move away. "Mau" meant quick, rapid or fast. The GI version was less pronounced and Americanized and sounded more like "d d mao" or similar variants. *See also* **Book, Sky.**

Di Di Mau *see* **Di Di**

Di Di Mow *see* **Di Di**

Di Lai *see* **Boom-Boom**

DIA *see* **Defense Intelligence Agency**

Diamond Division *see* **5th Infantry Division (Mechanized)**

DIANE *see* **Digital Integrated Attack Navigation Equipment**

Diarrhea *see* **Ho Chi Minh's Revenge**

Dick *see* **Penis**

Dicks *see* **Enemy, The**

Diddy-Bop Originally a black term associated with a free and easy style of walking. Diddy-bopping in Vietnam was used to describe anyone walking in a careless, unattentive, indifferent, reckless or unconcerned manner. Diddy-bopping in the field could prove most hazardous, and was usually reserved for base camps and rear areas.

Didi *see* **Di Di**

Died of Wounds *see* **DOW**

Diehard Tunnel Rats (Rat-6, Non Gratum Anus Rodentum) Code name for the tunnel rat team of the 1st Engineer Battalion/1st Infantry Division. In '67 Army engineers of the 1st Infantry Division took over primary responsibility for tunnel warfare in their AO. A Diehard Tunnel Rat team consisted of an officer (call sign name Rat-6), an NCO, 2–3 enlisted men, a medic, RTO and two Kit Carson Scouts. The team was based at Lai Khe and was helicoptered to the field for tunnel exploration. The team's motto was "Non Gratum Anus Rodentum" — "not worth a rat's ass." *See also* **Tunnel Warfare, Tunnel Rats.**

Diehards *see* **Fink Release Program, Hardliners**

Diem *see* **Ngo Dinh Diem**

Diem My *see* **My Dinh Diem, Ngo Dinh Diem**

Diem's Angels (Presidential Bodyguard) The presidential bodyguard force for President Diem was nicknamed "Diem's Angels." The elite guard was barracked a short distance from the Presidential Palace. During the military revolt and overthrow of the Diem government in '63, the bodyguard was surrounded by rebel military forces and took heavy casualties before they surrendered.

Diem-ocracy Slang reference to the government of President Ngo Dinh Diem's form of democracy in South Vietnam; part dictatorship, part monarchy. *See also* **Ngo Dinh Diem.**

Dien Bien Phu (Navarre Plan) French outpost, located in an isolated valley on the border between Laos and North Vietnam. In May '54 Viet Minh forces defeated the

French there in a decisive battle that ended the French Indo-China War. 7,420 of the 11,000 French defenders at Dien Bien Phu were killed or wounded and most of the rest were taken prisoner, many of them dying enroute to Viet Minh prison camps. The Navarre Plan used the French troops as bait, hoping the Viet Minh would make a conventional attack and be decimated by the French Forces. The U.S. Marine position at Khe Sanh in '68 was often compared to the French position at Dien Bien Phu; but during the siege of Khe Sanh, the NVA were unable to overrun the U.S. forces. *See also* **Operation Vulture.**

Dien Bien Phu Kitchen (Smokeless Kitchen)   Viet Cong underground "smokeless kitchen," named after small subterranean field kitchens first constructed in trenches used by the Viet Minh. The VC version of the kitchen was located further underground. Smoke from the cooking fires was channeled through a series of ducts that was mixed with outside air to dilute the smoke. The diluted smoke was vented through several different exit holes making the smoke practically undetectable by aerial reconnaissance. In areas patrolled by the enemy (FWFs) the stove fires were started after dark and extinguished before first light. The stoves were very inefficient, often causing the smoke to back up into the tunnels. Above ground cooking was the preferred method, when possible. *See also* **Tunnels of Cu Chi.**

Dien Bien Phu Survivors   *see*   **Dong Hoi**

Dien Cai Dau   *see*   **Dinky Dau**

Diet Cong   *see*   **Sat Cong**

Digger (Australian GI)   Australian nickname for their infantry soldiers; Australian GI. *See also* **Infantry Soldier, The.**

Digger Hats (Aussie Hats)   Soft widebrim hats popularized by Australian troops in WWII. The Digger hats survived WWII and many of them found their way to Vietnam to be worn by some French troops in the early fifties and later by Australian troops in the sixties.

Digital Integrated Attack Navigation Equipment (DIANE)   Sophisticated navigational and weapons system used aboard Navy A-6 Intruders that started

carrier deployment to SVN in July '65. The system allowed the aircraft to fly and maneuver at extremely low altitudes for prolonged periods of time, greatly increasing the aircraft's ability to reach and strike its target. *See also* **A-6A.**

Digs   *see*   **Civilian Irregular Defense Group**

Dikes   *see*   **Red River Delta**

Dime-Nickel   *see*   **M-101A1 Howitzer**

Dimes   *see*   **Number-10s**

Dinassauts (Naval Assault Division, French)   Combined French Navy and Army force used to conduct riverine operations. The size of the dinassaut varied depending on the mission, but the basic force consisted of two patrol boats, two fire support boats and six to eight transport craft, usually LCMs. The Navy operated the boats, and Army units were transported and used for assault operations. The French dinassaut structure was passed on to the Vietnamese who formed their first dinassaut in April '53. As U.S. advisors took over, the scope of the river assault force was expanded and the name changed to River Assault Groups. *See also* **River Assault Group.**

Ding   *see*   **Kill**

Dingo   British made, four wheel, armored scout car. A limited number were available to the ARVNs who used them for base camp security and convoy escort duty during the mid-sixties. *See also* **Armored Cars.**

Dingy   *see*   **Crazy**

Dinh Hills   *see*   **Nui Thi Mountain**

Dining Room Orderly (DRO, KP, Kitchen Police)   In a military mess hall the setting of the tables, cleaning, arrangement of food, serving and most other noncooking duties are performed by the DRO. Also known as KPs or Kitchen Police. The KPs prepared foods under the direction of the cooks, and when the cooking was finished the KPs took on the job of DRO. In Vietnam most large bases that had mess halls were staffed by Vietnamese civilians to do the KP and DRO work under guidance of the military cooks. Most U.S. troops avoided KP duty whenever possible, although some troops preferred KP to combat duty in places like the Ia Drang, A Shau or the DMZ. *See also* Hots.

Dink Vietnamese nickname used to describe U.S. soldiers. It was supposedly a derogatory word that meant "hairy men from the jungle." The word was quickly adopted by GIs in Vietnam to refer to all Vietnamese, friend and foe alike. *See also* Enemy, The.

Dinky Dau (Dinky Dow, Dien Cai Dau) Bastardized Vietnamese for crazy or ridiculous. A belief held by many South Vietnamese on the mental state of the Americans in Vietnam. In Vietnamese "dien" meant to be crazy or mad and was combined in the phrase "dien cai dau" [dinky daow], which became Americanized as "dinky dau." *See also* Crazy, Tight.

Dinky Dow *see* **Dinky Dau**

Dinky-Dau Smoke *see* **Marijuana**

Dinner *see* **Operation Menu Targets**

Dinner, BA 352 *see* **Operation Menu Targets**

DIOCC (District Intelligence and Operations Coordination Center, PIOCC) Vietnamese intelligence center located at the district (DIOCC) and the province (PIOCC) levels. Intelligence information gathered by ARVN and NPFF units was collected at the centers. The information was further coordinated with U.S. intelligence data. The centers took on more of the intelligence gathering efforts after '69 as U.S. troop strength declined. DIOCCs were established in those districts where the GVN controlled the district capital. Each province had a PIOCC (Province Intelligence and Operations Coordination Center) even though its effectiveness was questionable.

Dioxin Poisoning In '69 a research study revealed that Dioxin, a toxic by-product in Agent Orange, caused tissue damage and birth defects in test animals. Dioxin is a long-lasting poison able to remain toxic in excess of thirty years. Vietnam veterans exposed to Agent Orange in the field began complaining of a higher incidence of soft tissue cancers, skin and liver disorders, chloracne, nervous system problems and various other unexplained ailments. Many of these problems were not statistically normal for these veterans when compared to men in their age group who had not been to Vietnam or exposed to Agent Orange. *See also* Agent Orange.

Direct Air Support Center (DASC, ASOC, Air Support Operations Center) Part of the Tactical Air Command system for the allocation, control and direction of Close Air Support activities. Each Corps Tactical Zone in Vietnam had a DASC that coordinated requests for tactical air support and the allocation of assets. Air support activity in the CTZs was originally coordinated by the Air Support Operations Center (ASOC), but as U.S. air involvement increased in SVN the role of the ASOC was greatly expanded and the centers redesignated DASCs. The center was manned by Vietnamese and U.S. Air Force crews that allocated aircraft within the CTZ. If the Corps could not respond the ASOC/DASC sought help from the Joint Operations Center. *See also* Air Support Operations Center, Joint Operations Center.

Direct Exchange (DX) In military jargon "DX" meant direct exchange. Goods and items within the military were often required to be exchanged on a one for one basis. Such exchanges were simply referred to as DXed. Combat troops in the field made direct exchanges of their uniforms as the uniforms became dirty or worn out. Uniforms that were in reusable condition were laundered and returned to the unit's reserve clothing stockpiles to be redistributed to other troops in the field as required. DX also became GI slang meaning "to kill." To "DX a gook" was to kill a Vietnamese (many GIs equated any dead Vietnamese with the NVA/VC). *See also* Kill.

Direct Supply Unit *see* **DSU**

Dirty Bird *see* **Hanoi Hilton**

Dirty Thirty (Bam Me Lam) Nickname given to the group of 30 American pilots temporarily assigned to fly VNAF C-47 aircraft. The American pilots were part of Operation Farmgate, the U.S. Air Force advisory effort to VNAF. The April '62 assignment allowed the release of some VNAF C-47 pilots to man T-28 fighter aircraft providing combat support to ARVN ground units. The Dirty Thirty were withdrawn to the U.S. in December '63. The motto of the group was "Bam Me Lam," a colloquial

Vietnamese phrase which supposedly professed the sexual prowess of the goat. *See also* Operation Farmgate.

Dirty War, The *see* Indo-China War

Discharge Review Board *see* General Discharge

Discharges Administrative discharges: Honorable Discharge—full VA benefits; General Discharge—VA benefits and less-than-honorable (LTH); Hardship Discharge —under honorable or less-than-honorable conditions; Undesirable Discharge—no VA, LTH; Clemency Discharge—no VA, LTH. Court-Martial designated discharges: Bad Conduct Discharge—no VA, LTH; Dishonorable Discharge—no VA, LTH.

Discrepancy Case (Captured, Unaccounted For) Classification used to identify a specific type of American MIA in Southeast Asia, also referred to as "Captured, Unaccounted For." The classification applied to Americans known to have been taken prisoner during the Vietnam War, yet they were not part of the POWs repatriated in '73 nor were their remains returned to American control. Verification of the POW's capture was by means of photographs released by the NVA/VC or by sightings and or communication with other POWs in the various NVA/VC prison camps. *See also* Missing in Action.

Disembark *see* Un-Ass

Dishonorable Discharge *see* Bad Paper

Disintegrating Belt *see* Belts, Machine Gun

Dismemberment *see* Traumatic Amputation

Disneyland East *see* Vietnam (GI Names)

Dispensary Military aid stations located at the smaller bases and fire bases. The aid stations provided basic first aid treatment and were manned by field medics. Seriously ill or wounded patients were medevaced to battalion aid stations or evacuation hospitals. *See also* Battalion Aid Station, Evacuation Hospital.

Displaced Person *see* Refugee

Disposition Form *see* DFs

Distinctive Insignia *see* Beer Can Insignia

Distinguished Flying Cross (DFC) Awarded for individual heroic or distinguished action during flight related circumstances. The award was available to all branches of service.

Distinguished Service Cross (DSC) America's second highest award for bravery, awarded by the U.S. Army. Equivalent to the Air Force Cross and the Navy Cross.

District *see* Province

District Advisory Team (DAT, District Senior Advisor, DSA) U.S. advisory efforts at the district headquarters level were conducted by 8 to 10 man advisory teams, headed by the District Senior Advisor who was the counterpart to the GVN's District Chief. The DAT worked in conjunction with the pacification effort, advising at the district level regarding security, RF/PF training, refugee assistance, medical and civic projects, economic issues, the Phoenix Program; the total operations of the district and its inhabitants. The typical DAT consisted of the DSA and his deputy, intelligence officer and NCO, medic, two RTOs and sometimes an attached specialist (engineer, demolitions, etc.), all members of the U.S. military. *See also* Province Senior Advisor.

District Intelligence and Operations Center *see* DIOCC

District Senior Advisor *see* District Advisory Team

Div *see* Division

Divide and Conquer *see* Defeat in Detail

Division (Div) A combined group of tactical units forming an organization capable of sustained combat. The group consisted primarily of infantry or armor, artillery, engineers, transport and other support groups as necessary. U.S. Army Division size varied, but typically consisted of several brigades (regiments) of 12,000 to 20,000 troops. The Air Force division consisted of two or more combat wings. The Navy division consisted of similar type ships grouped under one command. The Marine division consisted of several regiments.

Division 55 *see* River Division 55

Division Airborne *see* **ARVN Airborne**

Division Aviation Assets *see* **Organic Aviation Unit**

Division Civil Affairs *see* **G-5**

Division Engineer Battalion (Force Engineer Battalion, DEB, FEB) The Marines operated two types of engineer units. The Division Force Battalion was primarily a combat engineering arm that supported a Marine division. The DEB handled fortification construction, improvements, mine clearing and demolitions. The Force Engineer Battalion supported larger Marine operations and units providing construction of billets, landing facilities, airstrips, etc. When necessary, Marine engineers were augmented by Navy SEABEES. *See also* **Engineers.**

Division Intelligence *see* **G-2**

Division Operations *see* **G-3**

Division Personnel Staff *see* **G-1**

Division Senior Advisor (DSA) U.S. senior military advisor to an ARVN Division Commander. The DSA was usually a colonel and interfaced directly with the ARVN general that commanded the division. The DSA was colocated with the division headquarters and was responsible for the American advisory staff that assisted the other ARVN units that composed the division. The DSA and the advisory staff under him were part of MACV. *See also* **Military Assistance Command Vietnam.**

Division Supply *see* **G-4**

Divisional Aviation Assets *see* **Organic Aviation Unit**

Divisional Tactical Operations Center (DTOC) All tactical operations carried out by the division, or units attached to it, were coordinated and supported through the Division TOC. Similar TOCs were operational at the brigade and battalion levels.

Dixie Cup (Navy Hat, Nurse Hat) Traditional white hat, with upturned sides, worn by Navy enlisted personnel. Sometimes the white "winged" hats worn by nurses were also referred to as a "Dixie Cup." Redcross Workers were also called "Dixie Cups." *See also* **Donut Dollies.**

Dixie Station U.S. Navy staging area in the South China Sea used by American carriers during air operations in South Vietnam, first established in '65. Dixie Station was off the coast of SVN due east of Saigon, about 160kms southwest of Cam Ranh Bay at 11 degrees north, 110 degrees east. The station also served as a "primer area" for carriers on their way to operate off Yankee Station. Strikes launched from Dixie Station struck at targets in SVN where the threat of enemy AA/AAA fire was not as great, and no SAMs, MiGs or large AAA guns would be encountered. Dixie Station allowed pilots a chance to "warm up" to the combat zone. *See also* **Yankee Station.**

DKZ-B (122mm Rocket, Katushas) Soviet made rocket launcher used by the NVA in Vietnam. The 122mm Katusha rocket was tripod mounted, six feet long, fin and spin stabilized, weighed 100+ pounds and had a range of 11kms. An attached extra motor extended the rocket's range to 17kms. The DKZ-B carried HE, smoke or chemicals, but the NVA primarily used the HE version. The single tube rocket and launcher could be broken down and man carried to its launch site making it an ideal weapon for guerrilla and foot infantry forces. During the NVA siege of Khe Sanh more than 5,000 of the rockets were fired into the base. *See also* **BM14/21, Rockets.**

DMS Boot *see* **Jungle Boot**

DMZ *see* **Demilitarized Zone**

DNG *see* **Da Nang**

Do Ma (Mother-Fucker, Du Ma, Mo-Fo) Colloquial Vietnamese phrase loosely translated as "mother-fucker" (Mo-Fo); figurative translation, fuck-mother. GIs were quick to pick up on the phrase.

Do Unto the VC . . . "Do unto the VC as they have done to the GVN," unofficial theme of the Phoenix Program of '68–'72. *See also* **Phoenix Program.**

Do-28 (Dornier Skyservant, Skyservant) German made twin engine, prop-driven STOL transport. The Do-28 had a cruising speed of 178mph and a range of 1,800kms. Several of the Skyservants found their way into the Air America inventory in SEA and were used for COIN operations throughout the region. The plane manufactured by Dornier Aircraft, in Germany, had an unusual design; the engine nacelles were mounted on the fuselage, on the sides of the cockpit. Most aircraft with multiple engines had them mounted on the wings. *See also* **Air America.**

Do/Did *see* **Kill**

Doan-10 Viet Cong sapper group that operated in the Rung Sat Special Zone with the Song Long Tau River as their prime target. The Doan-10 operated several elements along the river using water mines, mortar, rocket and RPG attacks to ambush Allied ships. The Doan-10 operated from bases located in the extreme northern portion of the RSSZ and in the Nhon Trach district. Nhon Trach was centered about 20kms east of Saigon in Bien Hoa Province, III Corps. The Doan-10 operated successfully against Allied shipping until June '69 when a series of operations was conducted to clear out enemy base areas, in the Nhon Trach. *See also* **Rung Sat, Nhon Trach.**

Doc *see* **Combat Medic, Corpsmen**

Doc Lap Dong Minh Hoi *see* **Viet Minh**

Doc Lap Palace *see* **Gia Long Palace**

Doctor *see* **Bac-Si**

DOD *see* **Secretary of Defense**

Dodge City Marine nickname for a small valley between Charlie Ridge and Hill 55, where frequent firefights occurred with the NVA. The area was the operational home of the 2d NVA Division and 90th Regiment of the NVA. Dodge City was also one of the nicknames for Hanoi used by some Air Force crews; and was also the name of one of the BEQs on Benning Avenue at the MACV compound located near Tan Son Nhut Airport.

Dog *see* **LZ Dog, Village Deer**

Dog Collar (Clerical Collar, Roman Collar) Slang nickname for the clerical collar worn by ministers and priests. Catholic priests (military chaplains) wore a rabbit, which was a combined Roman collar and a white dickey. *See also* **God Squad.**

Dog Leg (Chanh Long) GI nickname for the town of Chanh Long, located north of Saigon in Binh Duong Province, III Corps.

Dog Meat *see* **Village Deer**

Dog Patch *see* **Dogpatch**

Dog Shift Slang for the work shift from 1800 (6 P.M.) to 0600 (6 A.M.) hours.

Dog Shit Mines *see* **CBU Mines**

Dog Tags Military identification tags worn by U.S. troops bearing name, birthdate, serial number, religion, and blood type. The ID was worn on two oval shaped metal plates. In theory, when a soldier was killed in the field, one tag was removed and given to the unit commander for next-of-kin notification, the other tag remained with the body for identification. The commander used the tag to begin the notification and paperwork process.

Dog Team (Combat Tracker Team, CTT) U.S. dog teams operated in SVN, used to detect the enemy. The dogs were teamed with a handler and a tracker and used for base security and on patrols in the bush. Some dog teams trained at the 25th Infantry's Tunnels, Mines and Booby Trap School located at Cu Chi. Because of the possibility of foreign diseases returning to the States with the dogs, and possible control problems, the dogs were not returned to the U.S. with their handlers as U.S. troops were withdrawn to the States; instead many of the dogs were destroyed. A five man tracker team was composed of a team leader, RTO, dog handler, cover man and visual tracker.

Dog's Head An area along the South Vietnam/Cambodian border used by the NVA as a base for operations into SVN. On a topographical map the boundary between South Vietnam and Cambodia in this area resembles a dog's head, facing west. The Dog's Head was located in Tay Ninh Province, III Corps, 40kms northwest of Tay Ninh and east of Phnom Penh, Cambodia.

Doggie Straps The wide pack straps used on ALICE field packs were in high demand by Marines who nicknamed them. They were in such demand because they were more comfortable to wear. The wide straps gave better distribution to the pack weight than the narrow straps on the Marine field packs. *See also* **ALICE.**

Doggies *see* **Infantry Soldier, The**

Doghouse Helicopter pilot slang for the box shaped housing on top of the helicopter's fuselage which housed part of the transmission, rotor shaft and linkages. OH-6A Loaches used for scouting and reconnaissance in Vietnam were difficult to see from above when they scouted at low altitude. In order to make them more visible by other helicopters and aircraft that might be operating above them, a white (or other high visibility color) stripe was often painted on the top of the tail boom and the "doghouse." The "doghouse" was also the nickname for the housing found on the rear deck of the LVTP amtrac. The housing covered the vehicle's exhaust and intake air system. *See also* **OH-6, LVT.**

Dogpatch   GI nickname for the Vietnamese shanty towns that sprung up outside the gates of many U.S. base camps. The shacks were made of scavenged cardboard, wood, and tin, and featured small open air shops selling a variety of items and souvenirs. A restaurant, barbershop, and coke stand were dogpatch regulars. Dogpatches usually featured a makeshift whorehouse, or two, and illicit drugs were readily available and cheaply priced. Sometimes the whorehouses were disguised as massage parlors or jeep/truck washes, or were found at the rear of the barbershop. *See also* **Water Point, Four Corners, Buckeye, Johnsonvilles.**

Dollar Ninety-Worst   *see*   **197th Infantry Brigade**

Dolphins   *see*   **Killer Dolphins**

Dom   *see*   **STP**

Domino   Principle   *see*   **Domino Theory**

Domino Theory (Domino Principle, Red Menace)   American theory that if South Vietnam was taken over by the communists, the rest of Southeast Asia, India, the Middle East and possibly even Europe could fall under the "Red Menace," communist domination. The "dominoes" referred to at the time were South Vietnam, Laos, Cambodia, Burma and Thailand. The '54 theory, developed by the National Security Council, and championed first by President Eisenhower, was often used as one of the justifications for an American presence in SEA. To date only Thailand and Burma of the original dominoes, remain free, noncommunist nations.

Don Muang Royal Thai Air Base (631st Combat Support Group)   Thailand air base that was used by the U.S. Air Force to conduct missions throughout SEA. Don Muang was home for the 631st Combat Group and was located about 20kms northeast of Bangkok.

Don't Mean Nothin' (Don't-Give-a-Shit; Fuck-It, Just Doin' My Time, Keep on Steppin')   Frequently used GI comment on a bad situation, bad luck, a buddy's death, a change in the hump direction or any number of other negative circumstances. It meant whatever was happening wasn't going to get to them, bring them down, make them give in or acknowledge that the situation really hurt or bothered them; a "don't-give-a-shit" attitude, no regrets. In the field it was more often heard as "Fuck-it, don't mean nothin'." A similar saying was "just doin' my time," which reflected the grunt's lack of interest in everything around him except his immediate survival through the next day in his tour.

Don't Sweat the Small Stuff   One of the many GI philosophical ideas on how to survive the war in Vietnam.

Don't-Give-a-Shit   *see*   **Don't Mean Nothin'**

Donc   *see*   **Rock Apes**

Done-Beens   *see*   **Vinh Binh Cigarettes**

Dong   *see*   **Penis, Piasters**

Dong Ap Bia Mountain   *see*   **Hamburger Hill**

Dong Ba Thin   Village located just north of Cam Ranh Bay on Highway 1. A U.S. Army base located there was the home of several aviation companies throughout the Vietnam War.

Dong Den   3,300-foot mountain overlooking Elephant Valley in I Corps. One-time home of elements of the 3d Marine Regiment. Approximately 25kms northwest of Da Nang. *See also* **Elephant Valley.**

Dong Ha   Town in Quang Tri Province, I Corps, located 15kms northwest of Quang Tri and less than 20kms from the DMZ. Dong Ha served as a major logistics and combat base for Marine and Army units operating in the province. Dong Ha was located near the Song Cam Lo River near the junction of Highways 1 and 9. Highway 9 ran west to Khe Sanh and into Laos. During the Tet '68 Offensive the 320th NVA Division attacked from across the DMZ in an attempt to overrun the Marine base. Marines and ARVN troops held the base causing the NVA division to retreat back into NVN. At the time of the '73 cease-fire Dong Ha was in the hands of the NVA, and remained so until the end of the war.

Dong Ha River Security Group *see* **TF Clearwater**

Dong Hoi (Dien Bien Phu Survivors) City on the coast of North Vietnam, 150kms northwest of Hue. After the fall of Dien Bien Phu in '54 the Viet Minh marched the captured French survivors over 600kms to Dong Hoi where they were repatriated to the French military. The survivors suffered from malnutrition, disease and infection. Only a few hundred of the original 8,000 survivors of the French garrison at Dien Bien Phu survived the march to the coast. In May '72 the small port facilities at Dong Hoi were mined by the U.S. Navy as part of Operation Linebacker. The mines and naval blockade closed the port to foreign shipping, restricting war materials destined for NVN. *See also* **Dien Bien Phu.**

Dong Nai Regiment Main force Viet Cong regiment operating in the central III Corps area throughout much of the war.

Dong Nai River *see* **Song Dong Nai River**

Dong Tam (United Hearts and Minds) Brigade base camp of the 9th Infantry Division which operated as part of the Mobile Riverine Force. The 600-acre base was located on the Mekong River 7kms west of My Tho in Dinh Tuong Province, IV Corps. The base was constructed on silt and sand dredged from the Mekong, and was named by General Westmoreland after the Vietnamese phrase "dong tam" meaning "united hearts and minds."

Dong Thap Regiment *see* **1st Viet Cong Regiment**

Dong Tien Vietnamese for "progress together." The Vietnamese used the term to describe the U.S. program of pairing an ARVN unit with a U.S. unit in order to train and advise the ARVN unit while working toward the U.S. goal of Vietnamization. *See also* **Vietnamization.**

Dong Tre Special Forces Camp (SF Team A-222) U.S. Special Forces camp located 33kms northwest of Tuy Hoa, Phu Yen Province, II Corps.

Dong Xoai (Battle of Dong Xoai) District capital in Phuc Long Province, III Corps, 85kms north of Saigon. Dong Xoai Special Forces camp was attacked and overrun by elements of the 9th VC Division in June '65. The CIDGs and their families at the camp suffered over 200 killed and 20 of the 24 Americans at the camp were killed or wounded. It was for his actions in defense of the camp at Dong Xoai that CW3 Marvin G. Shields became the Navy's first Medal of Honor winner of the Vietnam War. ARVN Rangers were later inserted into the area to search for the enemy units that had attacked the camp. During the search, the Viet Cong ambushed the Rangers, creating such a panic among them that the ARVNs threw away their weapons and fled into the jungle, an early indication of ARVN battle readiness. *See also* Ap Bac, Ba Gia, Binh Gia.

Dong Zu *see* **Cu Chi**

Donkey Sight (Iron Idiot, Range-Gunnery Computer) A gunsight used for manually aiming the main gun of a tank. The target was centered in the sight and the tank's gunner made the necessary cannon adjustments for the approximate range of the target. The donkey sight reduced the tank's accuracy, but increased its reaction speed. The gunnery system of the tank was designed for the targeting of enemy armor and "hard" targets, but in Vietnam the lack of enemy armor greatly reduced the need for the gun computer for most close-range targets. Armor doctrine dictated that when a target was spotted its range and speed were calculated on the range-gunnery computer (nicknamed the "iron idiot") and the cannon appropriately aimed. In Vietnam the iron idiot was used to calculate gun information when the tank fired long-range support missions.

Donkey-Dick GI nickname for the flexible tin spout which could be attached to the opening on the Jerry Can. The foot-long spout made it easier to fill the fuel tanks on military vehicles. The Jerry Can had an angled opening, but no spout for pouring. "Donkey-dick" was also the nickname for the large round cable connector used to interconnect the electrical systems of military vehicles and or trailers. *See also* **Jerry Can.**

Donlon, Captain Roger (First Vietnam Medal of Honor Recipient) In July '64 the U.S. Special Forces Camp at Nam Dong in the northwestern corner of South Vietnam was attacked by at least a battalion of VC. The camp was defended by two reinforced companies of local Civil Guards and a 12-man American A-Team. During the attack the enemy managed to enter the camp and attempted to overrun the inner compound. Although wounded three times, Captain Donlon rallied and directed the camp's defenders and kept the VC from taking the camp. *See also* **Congressional Medal of Honor.**

Donut Dollies (American Red Cross Women, Dixie Cups, Delta Deltas) American Red Cross women who comforted and assisted wounded U.S. soldiers in the major hospitals and provided other services to the troops in Vietnam. The workers would read to the wounded, help them with letters, talk with them and do what little they could to ease some of their pain, fear, suffering and loneliness. In the field the workers provided games and conversation. The Donut Dollies (Delta Deltas) also manned stopover points offering donuts and coffee to the troops in transit to and from the war zone. *See also* **American Red Cross, SRAO, Donut Six, Dixie Cup.**

Donut Six (6) Nickname for the chief of the Red Cross women, the "Donut Dollies." In the Army the number "six" was attached to the call sign of a unit commander for radio communications. The chief of the ARC women was awarded the same distinction. *See also* **Army Call Signs, Donut Dollies.**

Doobie *see* **Marijuana**

Door Gunner (Shotgunner) Assault and transport helicopters in Vietnam were usually armed with M-60 or .30cal machine guns; these were manned by the door gunner and aircraft crew chief. Door gunner positions were usually filled by volunteers because their job was so hazardous, but there was a waiting list of grunts trying to become door gunners. For a grunt to get out of the field to become a gunner, he usually had to extend his tour in Vietnam. On gun-

ships, the gunner/crew chief monitored the performance of the weapons and was available to clear jams or hung rockets in-flight. Door gunners were sometimes called "shotgunners." *See also* **Bunji Strap, Hell Hole, Hang Fire.**

Dope *see* **Illicit Drugs**

Doper (Junkie, Pothead, Freak, Head) References to consistent users of illicit drugs such as marijuana, heroin, opium, hashish, barbiturates and LSD. After '68 the unauthorized use of such drugs increased steadily throughout the U.S. military in Vietnam. *See also* **Heads.**

Dork *see* **Penis**

Dornier Skyservant *see* **Do-28**

Double Back Ambush *see* **Button Hook Bush**

Double Canopy *see* **Canopy**

Double Eagle *see* **Task Force Delta**

Double Force Catchword used to describe operations in '67 around Saigon, involving the U.S. 199th Light Infantry Brigade and ARVN 5th Ranger Group. The object was for the units to operate together on a one-for-one basis, in an effort to train the ARVN in equipment use and tactics. This was an early attempt at Vietnamization. *See also* **Vietnamization, Buddy System.**

Double Point When two point elements were used to move at the head of a formation. The double point increased the chances of detecting an ambush, but it also put more troops out away from the main body, making the points more vulnerable to enemy fire and isolation. *See also* **Walking Point.**

Double Veteran (Rapist-Killer) GI term for a soldier who raped a woman before he killed her.

Doubtfuls GI term for those Vietnamese they could neither confirm to be friendly or enemy. Often used to refer to Vietnamese spotted from a distance, with no weapons visible and no positive indication of their status. The "doubtfuls'" status was further confused if they did not run when approached by U.S. units. In Vietnam if a Vietnamese ran away from a GI he was generally considered to be Viet Cong or at the very least a Viet Cong suspect. *See also* **Viet Cong Suspect.**

Doughnut *see* Shooting the Donut, Donut Dollies

Dove Unit *see* Korean Military Assistance Group, Vietnam

Doves and Hawks *see* Hawks and Doves

DOW (Died of Wounds) Category of U.S. casualties in Vietnam. Soldiers who died as a result of their wounds were sometimes classified separately if they died en route to, or at the hospital. This separate category sometimes led to inaccuracies in casualty reporting because only those soldiers who died on the field were counted as KIA even though more soldiers actually died as a result of combat operations or enemy attacks. *See also* Wounded.

Dow Chemical Company *see* Dow Shalt Not Kill

Dow Shalt Not Kill (Dow Chemical Company) 1967 slogan used by antiwar activists protesting the use of napalm in Vietnam. Dow Chemical Company was the primary manufacturer of napalm used by the U.S. *See also* Napthenic-Palmitic Acid.

Down (Shoot Down, Splash) 1) To shoot down an aircraft. 2) To be depressed or of a depressing nature or bad situation, as in "downer." 3) To remove a device from active service. To "down" a tank because of transmission trouble or to "down" a helicopter because of a hardware malfunction. *See also* U.S. Aircraft Losses, Mission Ready.

Down with the American Imperialists... "Down with the American imperialists and their Saigon puppets," one of the frequently sounded communist propaganda slogans heard in Vietnam.

Dozens, The Verbal shootout, usually between two "brothers." "Playing the dozens" or "throwing the dozens" involved the two participants taking turns insulting each other, one always trying to outdo the other's insult. No topic was sacred, be it personal, family, or parentage. The audience which witnessed the exchange determined the winner, based on how "low" or "cold" the insults were. The thrower of the lowest, coldest insult was the winner.

Dozer *see* Caterpillar D7E Tractor

Dozer Tank (M-8A1 Dozer Blade, Can Opener Tank) M-48 Army tank fitted with the M-8A1 bulldozer blade. The "dozer tank" was used to destroy enemy bunkers and earthworks. The blade weighed over 8,000 pounds and provided the tank with a limited mine clearing ability. Nicknamed a "can opener tank." *See also* Dozer-Infantry.

Dozer-Infantry Team of bulldozers, dozer tanks, Rome Plows and infantry in combined operations in heavy jungle. The heavy equipment was used to flatten jungle areas during infantry sweeps and "jungle busting" operations. *See also* Jungle Busting, Dozer Tank, Rome Plow.

DP *see* Refugee

DP LMG (DPM, Degtyarova Pakhotnyi LMG) Soviet made 7.62mm light machine gun. The DP was gas operated, drum fed with a loaded weight of over 23 pounds. The gun was the Soviet Army's main light machine gun until the fifties when it was distributed to communist block countries. The DP found its way into the hands of the Viet Minh and later the NVA/VC. The DP was fed by a 47-round drum that was mounted on the top of the gun. The DPM was an upgraded version of the DP and featured a pistol grip and improved bipod. In Russian units the DP was eventually replaced by the RPD series of machine guns. *See also* RPD LMG.

DPC *see* Delayed Primary Closure

DPM *see* DP LMG

DR (Delinquency Report) Military citation issued by the MPs for misdemeanor infractions of Military Regulations or standing orders. DRs could be issued directly to a soldier for offenses such as traffic violations, missing equipment, uniform violations, etc. The DR was forwarded to the soldier's immediate headquarters for disciplinary action.

Dr. Pepper Nickname given by U.S. Air Force pilots to one of the SAM firing patterns used by the North Vietnamese. Three missiles would be fired at an aircraft, so the missiles approached the plane from the ten, two and four o'clock positions, simultaneously. "Ten, Two and Four" was the slogan for the Dr. Pepper soft drink. *See also* Surface-to-Air Missiles, SA-2.

DRAC *see* Delta Region Aviation Command

Draft, U.S. The draft increased from 17,000 men a month to over 35,000 men in July '65. The increase was necessary to support America's growing war effort in South Vietnam. During the war an estimated two million young men between the ages of 18–26 were drafted, out of 27 million draft age men. The number of draftees required by the government began to decrease after mid-'69 as plans were made to reduce the U.S. presence in Vietnam. President Nixon officially ended the draft in December '72, and President Ford terminated draft registration in '75. In '77 President Carter pardoned all those who had been convicted of violations of the Selective Service Act, and in '79 he reinstituted mandatory draft registration. *See also* **Hobson's Choice.**

Draft, Viet Cong *see* **VC Draft**

Draft, Vietnamese For South Vietnamese males the draft age was 20 years old, compared to 18 years old for Americans. The Viet Cong drafted males between 16–18 years of age. The Viet Cong used propaganda and nationalism in their quest for more recruits; when the "call to the cause" failed the VC used force, coercion and terror to gain their recruits. Desertion rates among GVN forces was very high. In most years ('61–'75) the rate of desertion exceeded the number of volunteers. GVN draftees were most often taken from the rural villages. The more affluent Vietnamese residing in the major cities bribed local draft board officials to overlook their sons. The ARVN had continual problems in trying to draw willing recruits into the military.

Draft Classification (1-A, 2-S, 4-F, 1-Y, 1-O, 1-AO) Some of the draft classifications available to America's male youth in the sixties and the seventies: 1-A—highest classification, meant (according to the draft board) that you were physically and mentally eligible for military service; 1-AO—C.O. eligible for military service as a noncombatant (medic, etc.); 1-O—Conscientious Objector (C.O.), must perform alternative service; 1-Y—unfit for service for psychiatric or medical reasons, or unable to pass the IQ qualification test; 2-S—military deferment while attending college; 4-F—unqualified for military service (physical reasons).

Draft Counseling Efforts established by various antiwar groups to counsel prospective draftees on ways to avoid the draft. The counseling advised on ways to leave the country and had a refined list of methods that were successful at helping the prospective draftee fail the preinduction physical. Some of the methods included starvation, to beat the weight minimum (obesity, to exceed the limit), drug addiction, convincing homosexuality, mental instability and the taking of various drugs that would throw blood tests off. There were also references to other doctors, psychiatrists and dentists who could write up papers or install appliances that could keep the draftee out of the military. *See also* **Draft Dodging.**

Draft Dodging Draft dodging was raised to an art form during the Vietnam War as thousands of young, able-bodied American males between the ages of 19 and 26 went to great lengths to avoid military service to their country. Most of the dodges required the dodger to falsify his physical, mental, or emotional condition to be successful. The vast majority of draft dodgers were from America's middle and upper classes, which resulted in the burden of the draft falling upon the shoulders of the less educated, and economically depressed low–middle, and lower class. Some of the dodges were attending divinity school, teaching school or becoming a professional educator, attending college and continuing on to graduate school (effective until '68), marriage (effective until '66), excessive weight loss/gain which would put the individual outside of the accepted weight brackets, "needle tracks" on the body, (habitual IV drug addicts were shunned by the military), proof of prolonged illicit drug use, proof of having been convicted of a felony (convicted murderers couldn't go to Vietnam to kill), deferments based on occupation, wearing of braces accompanied by a doctor's excuse stating they had to be worn for a prescribed period of time (some dentists would put braces on, for a price), a doctor's statement indicating specific mental treatment or psychiatric care in progress, taking various drugs just before the physical exam (the drugs would cause one to fail the exam), amputation of a limb (self-inflicted amputation of the trigger finger, or toes, worked for several dodgers), homosexuality (real or imagined, the performance had to be convincing to the board's doctors), some skin diseases (especially those which were contagious or required special treatment), ingesting large quantities of foods which would throw off blood tests, having a close family member dependent on you for their care (alcoholic or drug dependent wife; also worked if the wife was seeing a psychiatrist), acting crazy or retarded, breaking a bone and not having it set correctly (permanent self-inflicted crippling), etc. *See also* **Draft Counseling**.

Draft Lottery (Selective Service Youth Advisory Committee (SSYAC) In '69 the Selective Service began using a lottery system to select draftees. The system was based on date of birth. Capsules with numbers 1–366 were selected by the Selective Service Youth Advisory Committee. The capsules were randomly drawn with the number in the capsule corresponding to a birthday date. The first day was 1-Jan: Whatever the first number drawn, it was assigned to 1-Jan. The second number drawn was assigned to 2-Jan. This continued until all the days of the year were assigned a drawn number. The numbers, 1–366, then corresponded to the order that the draft for the year would proceed. In addition to the numbers drawn, the 26 letters of the alphabet were randomly drawn. The letters indicated the order in which the names of the draftees, for the selected dates, would be called up. All draft eligible men whose birthday corresponded to the lottery number one were to be drafted first. The lower the lottery number the more likely an individual was to be called for the draft. The lottery system was devised to eliminate many of the previous draft exemptions and arbitrary actions by local boards. Previous exemptions from the draft favored the wealthy and the educated, and burdened low and middle class Americans with fulfilling draft quotas to support the war in Vietnam. The draft ended in December '72. *See also* **Selective Service, Draft Exemptions**.

Draft-Card-Burning As part of the antiwar movement in '65, some protesters burned their draft cards as a symbolic gesture against the war. In retaliation, Congress passed a tough law against such burnings. The law didn't stop the burnings, and several protesters were arrested and convicted. *See also* **Bill 392; Catholic Workers Movement; Burn Yourselves, Not Your Draft Cards**.

Draftee (Conscripts) An individual selected for compulsory military service in the armed forces. During the VNW most draftees were inducted into the Army, but there were instances when the Marine Corps used personnel from the draft register. In Australia individuals drafted into the military were called conscripts, and the draft process was called conscription. Although Australia drafted several thousand men into the service during the Vietnam War, service in Vietnam for Australian troops was on a volunteer basis. Australian forces served in Vietnam as a unit, the entire unit rotating back home after a year's service. *See also* **Selective Service, Hobson's Choice, National Servicemen, Australia**.

Drag Slang for administrative, political or social power, clout, or influence. Sometimes called being "well connected," having the right connections with influential people or those in control. Having drag in Vietnam was very important for specialized units that required special supplies or support. *See also* **Tail-End Charlie**.

Drag Bombs *see* **Retarded Bombs**

Dragon Eye Regiment *see* **Republic of Korea Marine Corps**

Dragon Fruit (Eyes of the Dragon, Litchi Fruit) Sweet fruit from the Chinese litchi (lychee or lichee) tree, planted and harvested in Vietnam. The small, round, one-inch diameter fruit grew in clusters and was eaten raw, cooked or dried. When the fruit was dried it was called "litchi nuts." The meat of the fruit was whitish-pink and surrounded a large, brown seed. The Vietnamese called the fruit "the eyes of the dragon"; "dragon fruit."

Dragon Lady *see* **Madame Nhu, Anna Chennault**

Dragon Ship *see* **Helicopter Gunships**

Dragon's Jaw *see* **Thanh Hoa Bridge**

Dragonfly *see* **A-37**

Dragons of the 334th Avn *see* **334th Aviation Company, Camp Woodson**

Dragonship see AC-47

Dragoons see 7th Squadron, 1st Cavalry Regiment (Dragoons)

Dragunov Rifle see SVD Rifle

Dream Sheet (DA 483, DA 2635) Slang for the official Army Station Assignment Request form. The form was used for specialized branches of the Army and higher level officers. The form was filled out by the members of graduating classes such as nursing and physician classes. Candidates noted where they wanted (dreamed) to serve, and the Army determined where they would serve. The form was designated DA Form 483, for officers, and DA Form 2635, for enlisted men.

Drill Instructor (DI)   Basic Training instructor who shepherded new troops through their first few weeks of military life. Perhaps the first person the new recruit quickly learned to fear and hate when he entered the service. Drill instructors in the Army and Marines wore wide, flat brimmed campaign hats, like those worn by U.S. Park Rangers and Smokey-the-Bear. The DI "mothered" recruits through Basic Training, and was responsible for their bodies 24 hours a day. The only time the DI got a break from his charges was when he turned them over to the control of a course instructor for an hour or two. See also Lane Grader.

Drill Sergeant see Drill Instructor

Drippy-Dick see Venereal Diseases, Cock-Rot

DRO see Dining Room Orderly

Drones (Buffalo Hunter, BQM-34L) Throughout the war, the Air Force used unmanned drone aircraft to fly photo reconnaissance missions over North Vietnam. The BQM-34L was one of the drones launched by Air Force C-130 aircraft under the code name "Buffalo Hunter."

Drop Tanks (Centerline Tank)   Auxiliary fuel tanks primarily used on fighter and fighter-bomber aircraft. The extra tanks allowed the aircraft more range and or loiter time. When the tanks ran empty they could be jettisoned. Fighters usually dropped their tanks before they engaged in dogfights with enemy aircraft. The additional weight and drag of the tanks adversely affected the performance of the aircraft during high speed dogfight maneuvers. 300- or 450-gallon drop tanks were mounted on the wing pylons or a single 600-gallon "centerline tank" could be attached to the aircraft's belly.

Drop Your Cocks and... "Drop your cocks and grab your socks...." Familiar morning serenade used by Drill Instructors as they moved through the barracks rolling recruits out of the rack.

Drop Zone (DZ, DZ Charlie)   Designated area used for the landing of paratroops or parachute delivered supplies. During the Vietnam War the only combat parachute drop by a large U.S. force was conducted in February '67 by the 2d Battalion/ 503d Infantry/173d Airborne Brigade. The drop zone was named "Charlie" and was located deep in War Zone C near the Cambodian border, Tay Ninh Province, III Corps. The troops and their artillery support were dropped in enemy territory without incident. The drop was part of Operation Junction City. See also Operation Junction City, 2d Battalion, 503d Infantry.

Drop Zone Charlie see Drop Zone

Drug High see Get High

Drug List   Partial list of some of the familiar medical drugs used in Vietnam: Dexamphetamines—uppers; Methamphetamines—uppers; Ritalin—downer in kids, upper in adults; Amyl Nitrate (poppers)—used for angina attacks—upper; Amytal—tranquilizer; Quaaludes—sedative; Meprobamate—tranquilizer; Epinephrine—heart stimulant; Lidocaine—injectable local and topical anesthetic; Lomotil—antidiarrhea pill; APC—military aspirin (aspirin/phenacetin/caffeine). See also Illicit Drugs.

Drug Testing see Detox

Drugs see Illicit Drugs, Drug List

Drumming-Out   Practice of automatically (and sometimes arbitrarily) kicking a Marine out of the Corps if he was found guilty of a court-martial offense. When General David Shoup assumed command of the U.S. Marine Corps in '59 he outlawed the practice.

Drung see Montagnards

Drunk (Sauced, Tanked, Get Blind, Shit-Faced, Ripped, Polluted, Bagged)

Slang for alcohol intoxication. Sometimes "stoned" was used to refer to drunkenness, but it was more often used to refer to being high on drugs. *See also* **Get High.**

DRUT *see* **F3D-2**

DRV *see* **Democratic Republic of Vietnam**

Dry Hole (Wild Goose Chase) Intelligence slang for a "wild goose chase." Intelligence information used to coordinate combat operations was not always accurate. Sometimes combat units would be inserted into an area expecting to find an enemy force or cache, but came up empty-handed. The information used was based on interviews with informants or captured enemy soldiers, reconnaissance missions and accumulated data on a given area.

Dry Monsoons (Dry Season) The weather cycle in SEA followed a pattern of predictable rains. The dry part of the year was sometimes referred to as the "dry monsoon season" and was a time when most large scale military offensives took place. During the rainy monsoon season movement was difficult and little significant military action took place. The dry season generally ran from April to October in I and II Corps, and November to April in III and IV Corps. *See also* **Monsoons.**

Dry Season *see* **Dry Monsoons**

Dry Shave (Bush Shave) Shaving with a safety razor without the benefit of water or shaving lather. Trainees in Basic Training who did not shave sufficiently to satisfy their drill sergeants were sometimes forced to dry shave. The resulting shave was usually painful and marked by nicks and cuts. GIs in the field in Vietnam sometimes dry shaved using a safety razor or just the double-edged razor blade. Such field shaves in arid areas were called "bush shaves" and were usually ordered after some high ranking officer visited troops in the field and commented on the "unmilitary appearance" of the men. The result would be an order from subordinate commanders that the men shave in the field, dry or otherwise.

Dry Thrust *see* **Afterburner**

Drydock *see* **AFDL**

DSA *see* **District Advisory Team, Division Senior Advisor**

DSC *see* **Distinguished Service Cross**

DShK HMG *see* **Type 54 HMG**

DShK38/46 HMG *see* **Type 54 HMG**

DSS *see* **Post-Traumatic Stress Disorder**

DSU (Direct Supply Unit) Army logistics unit providing supply items to units operating in the field. DSUs made deliveries to combat bases and outposts. Supply items were then redistributed to line units in the field.

DTs *see* **Defensive Targets**

DT-1 VC Regiment *see* **1st Viet Cong Regiment**

DTOC *see* **Divisional Tactical Operations Center**

Du Ma *see* **Do Ma**

Dua La *see* **Nipa Palms**

Dua Nuoc *see* **Nipa Palms**

Dua Tree *see* **Palm Trees**

Duan *see* **Montagnards**

Duc Hotel One of the fortified residential hotels used by the CIA to house its personnel. The hotel complex was located several blocks from the U.S. Embassy in downtown Saigon.

Duc Lap (Duc Lap Special Forces Camp) Village located 50kms southwest of Ban Me Thot and just 10kms from the Cambodian border. Duc Lap was also the site of a Special Forces Camp that the 1st NVA Division attempted to overrun in August '68.

Duc Long (Vi Thanh) Capital of the Delta province of Chuong Thien, located 43kms southwest of Can Tho. Duc Long was also known as Vi Thanh.

Duc My Town located 34kms northwest of Nha Trang and 20kms from the coast in Khanh Hoa Province, II Corps. Duc My was located along Highway 21 and was the location of one of the ARVN Ranger Training Centers. *See also* **Biet-Dong-Quan.**

Duc Pho U.S. base located at the southern tip of I Corps. Duc Pho was located along Highway 1, 38kms south of Quang Ngai, and less than 2kms from the coast.

The base was located near a small 480-foot hill nicknamed Montezuma Mountain by Marines that first occupied the base. When the elements of the 1st Cavalry Division took control of the base they renamed it LZ Montezuma. The base was finally occupied by elements of the 3d Bde/4th Infantry Division. *See also* **LZ Montezuma.**

Duck, The *see* **V-100**

Duck Suit Nickname for the spotted brown camouflage suits worn by some Special Forces and CIDG troops. The pattern consisted of various, irregular sized spots in three shades of brown over a tan background. The pattern and color was the same as that used by "duck hunters" in the U.S. The color pattern was not very popular with U.S. Special Forces, and was worn for a limited time by some ARVN Special Forces.

Duckbill Shotgun Shotgun that fired its buckshot in a horizontal spray pattern instead of the customary circular pattern. Used for close combat by scout and recon units to cover a wider area. *See also* **Shotgun.**

Ducky *see* **Le Duc Tho**

Dud *see* **Explosive Ordinance Disposal**

Dufflebag Operational code name for American effort to train and advise the 25th ARVN Division in the use of unattended ground sensor equipment. As the U.S. began to withdraw from Vietnam existing sensor strings and new implants became the responsibility of the ARVNs. ARVN implant and monitoring operations were restricted to enemy active areas near ARVN base camps. The U.S. continued to monitor sensor strings placed along the Ho Chi Minh Trail. Data was collected by specially equipped aircraft which flew over the trail system. Collected data was transmitted to the ISC at NKP for analysis and targeting. *See also* **Electronic Sensors, ISC.**

Dufflebag (Seabag) Army standard issue storage bag. The bag was OD green, 21 inches wide and 36 inches long when fully packed. A carrying handle was attached to the side of the bag, as well as a strap that secured the top of the bag. The top-loading dufflebag was available in cotton duck or nylon, and could be padlocked for security. The strap used to secure the top of the

bag doubled as a carrying strap for slinging the bag over the shoulder. The Seabag was used by the Navy and the Marines, and was similar in design.

Dulles, John Foster Served as the U.S. Secretary of State in '53 in the Eisenhower Administration. Dulles was a staunch anticommunist and believed the Viet Minh to be an instrument of the Soviets. Dulles advised President Eisenhower to intervene militarily to aid the French in Indo-China, and specifically advocated the execution of Operation Vulture, the U.S. plan to bomb the Viet Minh. *See also* **Operation Vulture.**

Dummy Load The condition of a radar unit being on, but not actually scanning or emitting radar search signals. When in this state the radar station, part of a SAM site, could not be detected by enemy aircraft. Radar emissions, when the unit was in the search mode, could be used by enemy aircraft to locate and destroy the SAM site before it could launch its missiles. *See also* **ECM, Wild Weasel.**

Dump Truck *see* **Igloo White**

Dung Lai (Halt) Vietnamese order to stop or halt. One of the first Vietnamese phrases learned by GIs who had to deal with Vietnamese civilians. Dung lai [dung lie].

Duong Mon Ho Chi Minh *see* **Ho Chi Minh Trail**

Duong Tu Do *see* **Tu Do Street**

Duong Van Minh (Big Minh, General Minh) One of the coup leaders who took control of the GVN after the assassination of President Diem, November '63. He was ousted January '64 in a bloodless military coup. He again took control of the GVN after the resignation of President Thieu in April '75. Two days later he formally surrendered Saigon and South Vietnam to Colonel Bin Tin of the NVA.

Dust *see* **Kill**

Dust Devils Small swirling tornadoes that sucked dust and dirt from cleared, barren areas around firebases and helicopter landing pads, depositing the contents into the machinery, weapons and clothing of the nearby inhabitants.

Dust Eater The last vehicle in a convoy. All the dust raised by vehicles traveling along dirt roads tended to hang in the air, and the last vehicle in the convoy usually caught most of it. The dust eaters in Vietnam were the rear security elements of the convoy. *See also* **Tail-End Charlie.**

Duster *see* **M-42 Duster**

Dustoff *see* **Medevac**

Dutch Mill *see* **Infiltration Surveillance Center**

DX *see* **Kill, Direct Exchange**

Dylan, Bob Popular folk-rock singer of the sixties. Through his songs Dylan spoke of injustices, women and the new drug culture. He is usually identified with the antiwar movement because some of his songs dealt with current issues. None of his songs were about Vietnam but they did focus on some of the ills of society. Dylan's real name was Robert Zimmerman; born in Duluth, Minnesota, in '41.

Dynamic Defense (Mobile Defense) U.S. Army term to describe field operations of U.S. combat units after '71, providing defensive security for U.S. bases and strategic locations in Vietnam. These operations consisted of U.S. ground combat units patrolling the area around cities and installations to keep the NVA/VC from launching rocket attacks, while the ARVN pursued Vietnamization, and hopefully the NVA/VC in the outer areas of the country. The U.S. operations were a modification of the old Enclave Policy, which originally sought to provide defensive security for U.S. combat units. *See also* **One War Plan, Economy of Force.**

Dysentery *see* **Ho Chi Minh's Revenge**

DZ *see* **Drop Zone**

DZ Charlie *see* **Drop Zone**

E

E-1 Lowest grade in the U.S. military. In the Army, Marines and Air Force it was designated the rank of recruit or private. In the Navy it was called seaman recruit.

E-1 Amtrac *see* **LVTE**

E-1 Tracer *see* **C-1 Trader**

E-2 (Private, Airman Third Class, Seaman Apprentice) The grade of E-2 in the U.S. military was equivalent in rank to private in the Army and Marines, airman third class in the Air Force and seaman apprentice in the Navy. In the Vietnamese army the equivalent rank was binh nhat (private first class), their lowest ranking soldier.

E-2 Hawkeye (Hawkeye) The Hawkeye was a twin engine propeller driven aircraft used by the Navy for airborne navigational control of its aircraft and to provide aerial surveillance and early detection of enemy aircraft. The Grumman manufactured aircraft was equipped with a huge radar dish mounted on a pedestal

above the wings and could operate from aircraft carriers or land bases. *See also* **C-2A.**

E-3 *see* **Private First Class**

E-4 (Corporal [Cpl], Specialist-4, Airman First Class, Ha-Si-Nhat) U.S. military grade. In the Army an E-4 was equivalent to the rank of corporal or specialist-4 (Spec-4). In the Air Force the rank was equivalent to an airman first class. For the Marines the equivalent rank was corporal. For the Navy the rank was petty officer third class. Ha-si-nhat was the Vietnamese equivalent rank for corporal first class.

E-5 *see* **Buck Sergeant**

E-6 *see* **Staff Sergeant**

E-7 (Gunnery Sergeant, SFC, Platoon Sergeant, Spec 7, SP/7) U.S. military NCO rank of E-7 was called a sergeant first class, platoon sergeant or specialist 7th class in the Army. Gunnery sergeant was the equivalent Marine rank. In the Air Force an E-7 was a master sergeant, and in the Navy an E-7 was a chief petty officer. Trung-si-nhat was the equivalent ARVN rank.

E-8 (First Sergeant, Master Sergeant, Spec 8, SP/8)   U.S. military NCO rank of E-8, which in the Army included specialist 8th class, master sergeant and first sergeant. In the Marines the rank was equivalent to a master sergeant. For the Air Force the rank of E-8 was a senior master sergeant, and in the Navy the rank was a senior petty officer. Thuong-si was the equivalent Vietnamese rank.

E-8 CS Gas Dispenser   Multiple tube CS gas dispenser. The portable unit was equipped with 16 35mm tubes that fired CS gas rounds. The dispenser weighed 35 pounds, and was used for base defense by some Army units. After the 16 cannisters were fired the launcher was discarded; it was not reloadable. *See also* **CS Gas.**

E-9 (Sergeant Major, E-Nine, Chief Master Sergeant, Master Chief Petty Officer)   Grade E-9, the highest ranking noncommissioned officer. The senior NCO, in the Army, was called a sergeant major or specialist 9th class; in the Marines he was called a master gunnery sergeant or a sergeant major; in the Air Force he was called a chief master sergeant; and in the Navy he was called a master chief petty officer. The master gunnery sergeants of the Marines and the sergeant majors of the Army usually refer to positions within the command structure of combat units. The specialist 9th class (Spec 9) and Marine master gunnery sergeant usually refer to leadership in the technical area. Thuong-si-nhat was the Vietnamese equivalent rank.

E-Eight   *see*   **E-8**

E-Nine   *see*   **E-9**

E-Tool   *see*   **Entrenching Tool**

EA-1   *see*   **C-1 Trader**

EA-3   *see*   **B-66**

EA-6A (Prowler, EA-6B)   Electronic warfare aircraft used by the Navy and Marines to jam NVN radar during American air strikes. The planes accompanied strike aircraft on the mission allowing for more effective jamming of enemy radar controlled weapons. The EA-6A and the EA-6B (Prowler) were specially modified versions of the Navy's A-6A all-weather bomber. They not only jammed enemy radar but also attacked SAM and radar controlled AAA gun

sites. EA-6s used by the Navy were carrier based while most of the aircraft used by the Marines were land based at Da Nang. *See also* **A-6A, SAM Suppression.**

EAD   *see*   **Extended Active Duty**

Eagle   *see*   **LZ Eagle, Camp Eagle**

Eagle Flight   Special helicopter assault force used to close with the enemy, or as a reaction/reinforcement force for engaged friendly units. The typical Eagle Flight consisted of one command ship (C & C), 7–10 troop transports (Slicks), 5 gunships (Hogs) and one Slick used as a Medevac. The Flight fielded a platoon or reinforced platoon and sometimes several Eagle Flights were combined. Because the troops and ships were dedicated to the assault task, they could be quickly placed into action without the usual planning required for an infantry assault by helicopter. Eagle Flights were first used by USSFs in '63 and consisted of 5–6 Americans and 30–40 CIDGs. Later other airmobile units used the technique. *See also* **Pacifier, Blue Team, Black Hawk Missions, Insertion of Opportunity.**

Eagle Flight   *see*   **Eagle Flight, Insertion of Opportunity**

Eagle Pull   *see*   **Operation Eagle Pull**

Eagle's Claw   *see*   **Crow's Foot**

Eagle's Nest   *see*   **FSB Eagle's Nest**

Ear Mutilations   *see*   **Mutilations**

Early Evening Nautical Twilight   *see* **EENT**

Early Word   Psychological warfare method first used by the 1st Infantry Division operating in III Corps. An enemy soldier who rallied (Chieu Hoi) to the side of the GVN was immediately coaxed to call upon his comrades to surrender. A helicopter equipped with a loud speaker system and radio relay unit flew over the area occupied by the rallier's unit. From nearby the rallier spoke to his former comrades over the radio; his voice was relayed to the broadcast system on board the chopper. His voice was then directly broadcast to the enemy troops in the area. Prior to the "early word" technique the method used by other Psywar teams involved the rallier making a taped message on field portable recording equipment. The taped plea for surrender was then rebroadcast over the area where the rallier had

Chieu Hoi'ed. The older system meant there was a considerable time delay between the time the man Chieu Hoi'ed, recorded the plea, and then returned to the field for broadcast. By the time the tape was brought out to the field the rallier's comrades had usually left the area. The "early word" system allowed such broadcasts to be made as soon as the enemy soldier rallied. *See also* **Chieu Hoi Program.**

Early-Out (150-Day Early-Out) U.S. Army program to grant a soldier an early release from the service. If a soldier returned from Vietnam with less than 90 days before his ETS he was eligible for the early-out. The program also allowed an early-out with 150 days remaining if the soldier had pre-enrolled to attend college or trade school. This kept soldiers from missing the start of school because their enlistment ended in mid-semester. Some soldiers extended their Vietnam tours in order to qualify. Soldiers with a two year enlistment could be out of the Army in 19 months if they survived a 14 month tour of duty in Vietnam, instead of the normal 12 month tour.

Earthquake Bomb *see* **CBU-55**

Earthworks Defensive fortifications made of mounds of dirt, usually with trenches or holes for additional cover. The NVA/VC made extensive use of earthworks in the construction of their bunker systems and base camp defenses. *See also* **Berm.**

Easter Offensive *see* **Eastertide Offensive**

Eastertide Offensive (Spring Offensive, Easter Offensive, Nguyen Hue Offensive) April '72 NVA invasion of SVN, an unsuccessful attempt to overrun the ARVN and take over SVN. The NVA made wide scale use of armor for the first time in ground assaults. Several NVA divisions attacked Quang Tri, Binh Long, Kontum and Binh Dinh provinces. The offensive was turned back through the efforts of ARVN forces and U.S. air power. Most U.S. ground combat forces had already been withdrawn from Vietnam, and limited American air power from bases in Vietnam and Thailand was immediately available. As the offensive continued more U.S. air units were redeployed to SEA for support. Estimates of NVA KIA ranged as high as 100,000. *See also* **Constant Guard, Bullet Shot.**

Eat the Apple, Fuck the Corps... Field Marine's catchall phrase which described his attitude toward the vagaries of Command. A capricious Command which had him take a hill from the NVA one day, only to abandon the hill within a few days. The same Command which had him return a few weeks later to again take it from the NVA. *See also* **FTA.**

EB-57 *see* **B-57**

EB-66 Air Force ECM aircraft used to jam and monitor enemy radar. The EB-66 was a modified B-66 bomber which operated with a crew of four EWOs (Crows) and two pilots. EB-66 aircraft frequently led Air Force strikes into North Vietnam. The information gathered by the EB-66 was used to adjust attack patterns of the strike aircraft. *See also* **B-66.**

EC-121 (MiG Watch, Big Look, Rivet Top, Connies) Airborne radar and communications center. Air Force and Navy EC-121s were used over the Gulf of Tonkin during the U.S. airwar against North Vietnam to monitor air traffic. The "Connies" monitored enemy MiG activity (MiG Watch/Rivet Top), providing early warning to American strike aircraft, as well as navigational monitoring of American aircraft over North Vietnam. EC-121s were also used to monitor electronic sensors placed along the Ho Chi Minh Trail as part of Commando Hunt operations. Information gathered from the sensors was relayed to the ISC at NPK for evaluation and targeting. *See also* **C-121, Electronic Sensors, ISC.**

EC-135 Air Force C-135 aircraft modified for ECM duties. The EC-135 was loaded with electronic countermeasure and operated by Air Force technicians. The EC-135 was first used in Vietnam during Operation Linebacker. The C-135 was the military version of the commercial Boeing-707 airliner. The RC-135 was a reconnaissance version of the C-135 fitted with radio and radar monitoring equipment. *See also* **C-135, ECM.**

ECM *see* **Electronic Counter Measures**

Economic Aid to North Vietnam (American) *see* **Reconstruction Aid**

Economy of Force (Strategic Defense) Military term to explain the post-Tet '68 strategy of reducing U.S. offensive operations in SVN and moving towards a more defensive posture, concentrating on city and base defense and Vietnamization. U.S. military policy centered on defense instead of a heavy reliance on offensive operations against the enemy. In Vietnam this also meant no ground attacks into NVN. According to Army policy Economy of Force was the prudent use of available resources to accomplish the military mission with a minimum expenditure of those resources. The strategy was also known by phrases such as "Dynamic Defense" and "Mobile Defense." *See also* **Strategic Offensive, Dynamic Defense, One War Plan.**

EE-8 Field Telephone (Field Telephone, Land Lines) WWII vintage military field telephone used by the Army and Marines. The phones were interconnected by commo wire. Each phone set had its own ring generator that had to be cranked to ring another station on the line.

EENT (Early Evening Nautical Twilight) Twilight as seen from aircraft. EENT was a little later in time than ground level viewed twilight due to the difference in the observation altitudes.

EF-10B *see* **F3D-2**

EF-105F/G *see* **F-105F/G**

Eggbeater *see* **HH-43**

Egress *see* **Ingress**

Eight-Inchers *see* **M-110 8-Inch SPA, M-55 8-Inch SPA**

Eight-Klick Ville (Fire Base Mongoose) Area worked by elements of the 501st Infantry/101st Airborne. The area consisted of a string of hamlets about 8kms long along the coast of SVN, southeast of Hue. The 501st established a small fire base called Mongoose at the northern end of the area. The entire area was used as a base of operations by the VC, with the villagers in the area very sympathetic and supportive of them.

Eighty-Deuce *see* **82d Airborne Division**

Eisenhower, President Dwight D. 34th President of the United States and Commander in Chief of Allied forces in Europe during WWII. Eisenhower provided equipment and supplies to aid the French in their war effort in Indo-China, but he never authorized the use of U.S. combat forces in the area. Eisenhower sought support from the British in the form of a joint force to assist the French in Indo-China, but the British were not interested. The Eisenhower Administration backed the Diem regime after the collapse of the French and gradually increased American advisors in Vietnam while continuing to provide economic and military aid to the GVN. *See also* **Operation Vulture.**

Eject *see* **Punch-Out**

EK-3B *see* **EKA-3**

EKA-3 (Tacos, EK-3B) Navy A-3 aircraft that functioned as a radar jammer and air tanker. The EKA-3 Tacos was a modified version of the A-3 Skywarrior used for standoff-jamming to confuse enemy radar controlled weapons. Standoff-jamming was less effective than the electronic jamming aircraft which accompanied strike aircraft to their targets. *See also* **B-66, EB-66.**

El Paso I & II *see* **Operation El Paso**

Electro-Optical Guided Bomb (EOGB, Walleye, AGM-62) Aircraft delivered bombs that were aimed through a TV camera mounted in the nose of the bomb. The EWO or WSO electronics officer in the attack aircraft would lock in the target using the bomb's nose TV camera. When the bomb was released it was remotely guided to the target. The 1,000–3,000 pound Walleyes were some of the most commonly used "smart bombs" deployed during the VNW. The Walleye made its Navy debut in March '67. Subsequent versions of the EOGB introduced during the '72 bombing campaign proved even more accurate and effective than the first Walleyes. *See also* **Smart Bombs, Laser Guided Bomb.**

Electric Fence *see* **McNamara's Wall**

Electric Strawberry Nickname for the 25th Infantry Division. The division patch was shaped like a leaf. The border of the bright red leaf was yellow and in the center was a yellow thunderbolt. The division was also nicknamed the "Cu Chi National Guard" because during the division's four years in Vietnam it was continually headquartered at Cu Chi. The official name of the 25th Infantry Division was the "Tropic

Lightning." *See also* 25th Infantry Division.

Electronic Backseater *see* **Combat Martin Operations**

Electronic Countermeasures (ECM, Ferrets) System of electronic devices used to jam, confuse or otherwise reduce the effectiveness of enemy radar and tracking systems. ECMs were part of overall electronic warfare. During the U.S. airwar against North Vietnam several different types of ECM specific aircraft were used, as well as onboard ECM systems on individual attack and reconnaissance aircraft. Aircraft that specialized in ECM were nicknamed "ferrets" and were mainly used by U.S. Navy and Air Force attack aircraft against NVN. *See also* **Wild Weasel, EB-66, Chaff, ALQ-87, EA-3, EC-121, EWO.**

Electronic Intelligence Aircraft (ELINT, Batcats) Air Force and Navy aircraft used as airborne control centers to monitor enemy ground activity. ELINT aircraft were primarily used along the border areas of SVN where difficult terrain limited the U.S. ground war against enemy sanctuaries. The aircraft monitored sensor equipment, relaying the information to the Air Force Infiltration Surveillance Center located at Nakhon Phanom in Thailand. "Batcats" was one of the code names used for C-130s that regularly flew the relay missions. *See also* **Electronic Sensors, ISC.**

Electronic Sensors Electronic equipment used by the U.S. to monitor enemy activity on the battlefield. The U.S. made widespread use of such equipment as small personnel detecting radar sets, low light intensifier scopes, infrared spotlights, and a variety of electronic sensing equipment. Remote sensing equipment in enemy areas radioed back information about enemy movement and deployments. The unattended sensors allowed enemy areas to be monitored with a minimum of exposure by U.S. troops. *See also* **Ground Radar, Starlight Scopes, ADSID, G-SID, P-SID, MAGNA-SID, SID, ACOU-SID, Dufflebag, Igloo White, ISC, Unattended Ground Sensors, Sensor String, OP-2E, F-4, TRIM, EC-121, Pave Eagle, DART, MicroGravel Mines, Black Crow Sensor System, Seismic Intrusion Devices.**

Electronic Warfare Officer (EWO, Crows, The Admiral) Officer onboard an aircraft who was responsible for the operation of the electronic sensing and evasion equipment as well as offensive targeting and tracking. On Air Force aircraft the EWOs were sometimes nicknamed "Crows" and the senior EWO was nicknamed the "Admiral." *See also* **ECM.**

Elephant, The *see* **Cbt**

Elephant Chess (Co Tuong, Chinese Checkers) Oriental version of checkers; Chinese Checkers, called "Elephant Chess" by the Vietnamese. The game was widely played by Vietnamese males and the ability to play well was a form of "status symbol." The game was highly visible within the Vietnamese social structure.

Elephant Grass (Knife Grass, Tranh Grass, Razor Grass) Razor sharp grass common to Vietnam. The tall clumps of grass grew to heights of 12 feet or more, blocking vision and cutting the skin and clothing of those who moved through it. In addition to the cutting qualities of the grass, troops moving through it, during the dry season, would cause the fine pollen of the plant to go airborne, making breathing difficult. The Nung mercenaries called it knife grass.

Elephant Intestines (Rice Rolls, Rice Tubes, Rice Belts, Tube Socks) NVA/VC nickname for the cotton tubes or rolls they used to carry their ration of rice in the field. The tube was filled with rice and was carried slung over the back and shoulders. A filled tube could carry about 16 pounds of rice. U.S. soldiers used a similar method to carry C-Rations. Field troops conducting extended missions often packed extra cans of C-Rations inside their wool socks. A pair of socks could carry 12–14 cans of Cs. The ends of the "tube socks" would be tied off and carried draped across the soldier's rucksack or around his neck.

Elephant Valley Small valley located approximately 25kms northwest of Da Nang near Dong Den, part of an NVA/VC base area. During a night in June '65 elements of the 3d Marine Regiment made contact with a VC convoy in the valley. The Marines requested offshore artillery fire. When the smoke had cleared several elephants and numerous VC were found killed by the barrage. The VC were using the elephants to transport supplies and small artillery pieces.

From that point on the valley was nick-named Elephant Valley by the Marines. *See also* **2d Battalion/3d Marine Regiment, Elephants.**

Elephant's Foot Nickname for the lowland marsh area located in the Plain of Reeds, in Kien Tuong Province, IV Corps. The area was situated north of Muc Hoa, along the Cambodian border, and was used by the NVA/VC to infiltrate equipment and supplies eastward toward Saigon.

Elephant's Trunk *see* **Punji Pit**

Elephants Small numbers of wild elephants roamed the remote reaches of the Central Highlands and the jungle border areas of Cambodia and Laos. The Viet Minh, and later the NVA, made limited use of domesticated elephants to transport supplies and heavy weapons along border infiltration routes. The small Indian elephants were soon written out of the NVA TO&E because of the many difficulties they caused. The elephants were difficult to hide from American aerial reconnaissance and the trails they left were like highways through the jungle. Another important factor was the expense in time and manpower required to keep the elephants fed.

The Elephants Have Moved Out in Front... "The elephants have moved out in front and everybody else is stumbling through their shit." A colorful description of the mass evacuation of ARVN forces from the Central Highlands areas of Kontum and Pleiku in the face of the NVA offensive in early '75. ARVN armor, trucks, and troops moved southeast from Pleiku along a little-used unpaved road called Route 7B. The rain soaked road was turned into mud and mush by the ARVN's heavy vehicles, making movement difficult. Intermingled with and following the ARVN units were thousands of civilians on foot, bicycles and vehicles also trying to outrun the advancing NVA, all mired in the mud on 7B. The description was attributed to Thomas Polgar, Saigon CIA Station Chief.

Eleven Bravo *see* **11 Bravo**

ELINT *see* **Electronic Intelligence Aircraft**

Elixir of Terpin Hydrate *see* **GI Gin**

Elliot *see* **Red Devil Road**

Ellsberg, Daniel Released the Pentagon Papers to the press in '71. The Papers were a secret study, commissioned by Secretary of Defense Robert McNamara in '67 on the U.S. involvement in Vietnam and the war's winability. The Pentagon Papers showed how the government had purposely misled the American public as to the extent and necessity of U.S. involvement in Vietnam. This led to a large gap in the government's credibility with the public. Ellsberg was indicted for the theft of classified information in June '71. In the middle of his trial the charges were dismissed, based on misconduct by the government, due to illegal activities against Ellsberg's psychiatrist and attempts by Nixon to influence the trial judge. *See also* **Pentagon Papers.**

Elope Term used by some Americans for their civilian Vietnamese patients who left the hospital before their treatment was complete. The hospitals were sponsored and supported by various humanitarian organizations attempting to provide rural Vietnamese civilians with medical care. Patients would sometimes disappear before their treatment was complete, returning to their home villages, because they believed they no longer required treatment, didn't believe the treatment was working, or had simply had enough of hospital life.

Elysee Agreement A 1949, formal agreement between Vietnam's Emperor Bao Dai and the French government which detailed the terms of Vietnamese independence, as recognized by the French. This agreement was supposed to allow Vietnam, under Bao Dai's leadership, to unify Vietnam and control its own affairs. This was just one of many "formal" recognitions by the French government that had little meaning in actual practice. *See also* **We have granted Vietnam "full independence...."**

EM *see* **Enlisted Man**

EM Club On-base serviceman's club for enlisted personnel below the rank of E6. At least one club was located on the larger bases and at most base camps. On larger bases NCOs had a club of their own; on the smaller bases NCOs used the EM's club. The NCO clubs were for NCOs, grades E-5 to E-9, and were generally only found on very large military installations with an NCO population to support the club. *See also* Chit Book, Class Six Store.

Embankment *see* **Dewey, Major Peter**

Emergency Channel *see* **Guard Channel**

Emergency Evac *see* **Medevac Priorities**

Emergency Evacuation LZ *see* **Purple-Out-Zone**

Emergency Leave *see* **Compassionate Leave**

Emergency Radio *see* **Survival Radios**

Emergency Resupply Request *see* **CES Request**

Emergency Room *see* **ER/OR**

Emus *see* **135th Aviation Company**

Encircle *see* **Vertical Envelopment**

Enclave Policy (Ink Blot Policy) Early policy adhered to by U.S. combat troops in SVN. The policy was designed to limit the use of troops to the protection of established enclaves or holding areas, providing protection for air bases and port facilities. U.S. troops were to clear an area on the coast and keep it clear of the enemy, allowing a base of support for ARVN units operating outside the enclaves. The policy was never fully enacted. Shortly after the deployment of U.S. troops for defensive security, they went on the offensive and sought contact with the enemy. This "ink blot" approach was supported by the Marines, while the Army wanted more extensive contact with the enemy through search and destroy operations. *See also* Bunker Mentality, One War Plan, Dynamic Defense.

Endangered Vietnamese *see* **Black Flights**

Endotracheal Tube *see* **Tracheotomy**

Endsweep *see* **Operation Endsweep**

Enemy, The GIs had many names for their Vietnamese enemy. The names applied to the NVA regulars (NVR) and the communist guerrillas. Sometimes the names applied to the Vietnamese people and the ARVN in general. Some of the names were Viet Cong, Victor Charlie, VC, Charlie,

Charles, Chuck, Chas., Ghost, the Cong, Little People, Zips, Zipperheads, Dinks, Gooks, Gooners, the Opposition, Luke the Gook, Hos-tiles, Slopes, Little Guys, Dicks, Nguyen, Regulars, Gomers, Nguyen Charlie, Yellow People, November Victor Alpha, the Night or Shadow Government of Vietnam and the NVA. *See also* Vietnamese, The; Viet Cong; North Vietnamese Army; Dink; Noggies.

Enemy Territory *see* **Boonies, Tiger Country**

Enfilade A head-on firing or sighting position that allowed for fire to be directed down the length of a troop formation, or the length of a trench or stream bed. *See also* Grazing Fire.

Engage *see* **Contact**

Engineer Research and Development Laboratory *see* **ERDL**

Engineers During the Vietnam War the U.S. military deployed several different types of engineer units. Each branch of service had a dedicated engineer force. The Army operated Combat and Construction Engineer Battalions. The Marines deployed the Division and Force Engineer Battalions. The Navy had the SEABEES and the Air Force had the RED HORSE Engineers. In addition to military engineers several commercial engineering companies contracted with the military to work on construction projects throughout SVN. The largest U.S. civilian contract company doing military construction in SVN was RMK-BRJ. *See also* RMK-BRJ, Tiger Ladies.

English *see* **LZ English**

English North *see* **LZ English North**

Enhance Plus *see* **Operation Enhance Plus**

Enlisted Man (EM) Soldiers with the grade E1-E9, nonofficer personnel. The largest body of personnel in the military.

Enlisted Reserve *see* **U.S. (Serial Number)**

ENSURE (Expedite Nonstandard Urgent Requirements for Equipment) Army program that expedited the delivery of essential equipment and supplies. The program bypassed the normal logistics channels acquiring the necessary items as quickly as possible and transporting them by the fastest means available. The ENSURE program was used often in Vietnam to provide troops specialized equipment until sufficient quantities of the equipment became available and could be supported through the normal logistics procedures. The program also involved the securing of non-military, commercial items for use by the military if the need for such nonstandard equipment could be justified.

Ensure 202 Mine Detector   Land mine detonator. The device consisted of a set of heavy roller wheels that were attached to the front on the M-48 tank. As the tank moved forward along the road, the pressure from the roller wheels detonated undetected land mines. The system was only marginally effective. Much time was lost repairing and replacing the mangled wheel sections as mine damage took its toll on the device.

Enterprise *see* **Operation Enterprise, USS Enterprise**

Entrenching Tool (ET, Personal Engineering Implement, E-Tool, Combination Tool)   Small folding shovel/pick combination carried by field troops. Used for filling sandbags and the individualized rearrangement of the terrain (digging foxholes). Two versions of the E-Tool were used by U.S. troops in Vietnam. The Combination Tool had an adjustable pick and blade attached to a wooden handle. The lightweight E-Tool was a three section, all metal folding shovel with a tubular triangular handle. The shovel blade could be positioned at a right angle to the handle to allow the tool to be used as a pick/ax or scraper. The E-Tool was also euphemistically known as a "Combat Emplacement Evacuator" or "Personal Engineering Implement."

EOC *see* **Human Relations Committee**

EOD *see* **Explosive Ordinance Disposal**

EOGB *see* **Electro-Optical Guided Bomb**

EP-3C *see* **P-3**

Epinephrine   Adrenal gland extract that was administered to the wounded to increase blood pressure. The hormone extract was injected into the body and caused the blood vessels to constrict and stimulate the pumping action of the heart. In Vietnam epinephrine was administered to fight blood loss and shock in attempts to stabilize the patient's blood pressure.

Equal Opportunity Committee *see* **Human Relations Committee**

Equation of Advantages   Term coined in '68 by the chairman of the senate's Foreign Relations Committee, Senator J. William Fulbright. At the time he believed it would be difficult for America to enter into peace negotiations with NVN, because militarily he believed them to have the advantage. And unless their advantage could be reduced there was no incentive for them to negotiate for peace when there was a chance they could win on the battlefield. The "equation of advantages" needed to be evened out to produce a better atmosphere for negotiations. For America this meant an escalation of the bombing, and troop increases in Vietnam. Fulbright's comment: "It is extremely difficult for a party to a negotiation to achieve by diplomacy objectives which it conspicuously failed to win by warfare.... The hard fact of the matter is that our bargaining position is at present a weak one; and until the equation of advantages between the two sides has been substantially altered in our favor, there can be little prospect of a negotiated settlement which would secure the independence of a non–Communist South Vietnam."

ER *see* **U.S. (Serial Number)**

ER/OR   Standard abbreviations for "emergency room" and "operating room."

ERDL (U.S. Army Engineering Research and Development Laboratory)   Army laboratory that developed and tested various items used by the military. They developed the standard "leaf pattern" camouflage design that was adopted by the Army for its standard camouflage uniform. The ERDL pattern consisted of four colors: yellow/green (48 percent), dark green (28 percent), brown (16 percent) and black (8 percent) in irregular shapes. *See also* **Jungle Camouflage Uniform.**

Errand Boy *see* **Pony Express**

Erskine see Dewey Canyon Fire Bases

Escalated Response see Graduated Response

Escalation (De-escalation, Gradualism, Measured Response) The words escalation and de-escalation often made front page headlines during the Vietnam War. U.S. and North Vietnamese forces continued to increase (escalate), while the American White House called for the cooperation of the North Vietnamese in reducing (de-escalation) its infiltration of troops in support of the Viet Cong in South Vietnam. The terms "gradualism" and "measured response" were also used to describe the Johnson Administration's policy of escalating force in Southeast Asia. See also Ratcheting.

Escort Ship see Gunship, Avn

Eskimo Boats see Skilak

Esprit de Corps see Semper Fidelis

Essential Load see Field Load

Essex Class Aircraft Carrier see USS Yorktown

Esso see Shell Oil Company

ET see Entrenching Tool

Ethylene Oxide Bomb see CBU-55

ETS see Expiration Term of Service

Evacs see Evacuation Hospital (Semimobile)

Evacuation Hospital (Semimobile) (Semimobile Evacuation Hospital, Meat Factories, Evacs) Army hospitals that used permanent and semipermanent structures to house their medical facilities. Evac hospitals generally had a 200+ bed capacity allowing them to serve a wide range of illnesses and injuries. The primary function of the Evac hospital was the stabilization of patients for their transfer to other, larger medical facilities, in and out of Vietnam. Evac hospitals were not as mobile or transportable as the MASH and MUST units, and tended to be long-term facilities. Nicknamed "meat factories" by the hospital's nurses. See also Evacuation Hospitals: 12th, 24th, 85th, 91st, 95th; MUST; MASH.

Evacuation of Saigon see Final Evacuation of Saigon

Evan see FSB Evan

Every Day in the World... "Every day in the world a hundred thousand people die. A human life means nothing." This quote, attributed to General Giap commander of the NVA, reflected the overall Vietnamese philosophy of life and death. This in part explained North Vietnam's commitment to the war in Vietnam, even though their casualties numbered in the hundreds of thousands. The individual life meant nothing in comparison to the goal of a unified Vietnam under North Vietnamese Communist rule. See also Giap, General Nguyen Vo, You Can Kill Ten of My Men...

Ewell, Gen. Julian J. see Delta Butcher, The

EWO see Electronic Warfare Officer

Exec Post (Chief of Smoke, Battery Chief) Position in an artillery battery occupied by the executive officer, charged with the responsibility of firing the battery. From the Exec Post, orders and firing data from the Fire Direction Center were relayed to the gun crews. The "Chief of Smoke" (Battery Chief) assisted the XO, and honchoed the battery in the absence of the executive officer.

Executive Officer (XO) An officer, second in command, of a unit (company, battalion or brigade), also equivalent to the chief of staff of a large unit (task force or division).

Executive Order 10631 see Code of Conduct

Exfiltrate see Sky

Exit Visa see Laissez-Passer

Expectants see Triage

Expedite Nonstandard Urgent Requirements... see ENSURE

Expediter see C-45

Expend Shells Not Men Military reasoning for the massive use of air strikes and artillery against the NVA/VC. In theory U.S. units would seek out the enemy and when contact was made they would back off far enough to allow air and artillery strikes to hit the target. The NVA/VC understood this tactic and attempted to engage U.S. units as closely as possible and pin them down so they could not disengage and call in added firepower. The NVA/VC seldom allowed themselves to be trapped in large numbers by U.S. forces or engage in a set-piece battle unless they believed they had the advantage. These factors made it difficult for the U.S. to bring their fire superiority to bear against the enemy. *See also* **Hug, Set-Piece Battle.**

Experimental Military Unit *see* **135th Aviation Company**

Experimental Model *see* **XM**

Expiration Term of Service (ETS) The date when a soldier's active duty enlistment was over and he was eligible to get out of the Army, probably the most important date in a draftee's career. During the Vietnam Era, draftees served a two year enlistment in the service. After their release they were required to spend another four years in the Reserves. For those soldiers who had served in Vietnam, the requirement that they serve in the Active Reserve was waived. Non-Vietnam veterans were required to attend the monthly reserve meetings and two weeks of active duty during the summer. At the end of the Reserve period the soldier would receive a certificate discharging him of his military obligation.

Explosive Ordnance Disposal (EOD, Dud) Military teams that disarmed and disposed of unexploded ordnance (duds), mines, booby traps and any munitions that threatened friendly troops or the civilian population. The NVA/VC used dud ammunition and ordnance in the construction of booby traps and mines against FWF units. Because of the large quantities of ordnance used in Vietnam and a shortage of EOD teams, much of the EOD effort fell upon regular infantry troops that patrolled in the field.

Extend *see* **Extended Active Duty**

Extended Active Duty (EAD, Extend, Extension) Extending one's active duty commitment to the military in order to gain a promotion in rank or to attend a specific service school. In order for a draftee, with a two year active duty commitment, to apply for Helicopter Flight School, he had to extend his service time to three years. Extending in Vietnam was often done by GIs to avoid finishing their enlistment at an Army post in the States. In some units an extension of 6 months brought with it an additional R & R. Some grunts extended their tours in Vietnam to get out of the field and into safer jobs at the base camps. The typical Army extension in Vietnam was 2–5 months. *See also* **Door Gunner.**

Exterminate Communist *see* **Sat Cong**

Extraction *see* **Insert(ion)**

Eye Corps *see* **I Corps**

Eyes of the 26th Marines *see* **3d Marine Division Reconnaissance Company**

Eyes of the Dragon *see* **Dragon Fruit**

F

F and M *see* **Fire and Maneuver**

F1 Frag (F1 Frag NK) Soviet made fragmentation grenade used by the NVA/VC. The grenade was 3.75 inches long and 2.5 inches in diameter, weighed one pound and had a serrated outer shell similar to the U.S. MK2 grenade. The pineapple or egg shaped grenade had an effective blast range of about 22 meters. The North Korean version of the grenade was called the F1 Frag NK; it was 3 inches in diameter and 4 inches long. The one-pound grenade had a smooth surface and a blast range of 18 meters. The North Korean grenade was also widely used by the NVA/VC. *See also* **Hand Grenades.**

F1 Frag NK *see* **F1 Frag**

F3D-2 (EF-10B, Skyknight, DRUT) Twin engine jet fighter manufactured by

Douglas Aircraft. The twin seat fighter was one of the Marine Corps' primary aircraft during the fifties and saw limited service during the Vietnam War. The fighter was equipped with electronic jamming and detection equipment and was used as an ECM aircraft by the Marines for night operations over NVN. The F3D-2 Skyknight was redesignated the EF-10 and operated until '69 when it was replaced by the EA-6A Intruder. The F3D had a max speed of 600mph, a range of 1,930kms and was armed with four 20mm cannons. The Marines nicknamed the EF-10 the "DRUT," which was "turd" backwards. *See also* EA-6A.

F-4 (Phantom II, Phantom, Fast Mover, Flying Brick) McDonald-Douglas Phantom II, twin engine, all weather tactical fighter-bomber. Various versions of the F-4 saw combat in Vietnam generally with a max speed greater than 1,500mph, 16,000-pound bomb load (standard load of 5,000–7,000 pounds) and a range of 800kms. The model J had a range of 1,400kms and the model E was equipped with an internal, nose mounted 20mm cannon. The RF-4 was the photo reconnaissance version. The aircraft was operated by the Marines, Navy, and Air Force and was land and carrier based. During the course of the war, F-4s downed 146 enemy MiGs, while losing 528 aircraft to ground fire, SAMs, MiGs and mechanical problems. The F-4C was the twin seat version and was used as a Wild Weasel. The F-4 was also used in early '68 to implant electronic sensors along the Ho Chi Minh Trail. F-4s carried 16 sensors (ADSID or ACOUSID) in each SUU-42 pod and dropped them along the trail. The F-4 allowed high speed drops to be made at tree top level with minimum aircraft exposure to hostile fire. *See also* RF-4, Wild Weasel, F-4 Weasels, Electronic Sensors.

F-4 Weasels The F-4C Phantom was used to augment the F-105 Wild Weasel force that flew SAM suppression missions against North Vietnam. The Weasel Phantom entered service in '69 but did not operate against SAM sites until the bombing of NVN was resumed in late '72. F-4Cs carried ECM gear, Shrike missiles, bombs and CBUs, but was not able to carry the Standard ARM. The F-4C was later replaced by the F-4G which was a dedicated Wild Weasel

mission aircraft featuring extensive ECM equipment and new ARM ordnance. *See also* Wild Weasel, Iron Hand, F-105, F-100.

F-5 Tiger (Freedom Fighter, F-5E, Skoshi Tiger) Small twin engine jet fighter manufactured by Northrop Corp. In '65 the U.S. Air Force deployed F-5s to Vietnam for evaluation under the code name Skoshi Tiger. The aircraft proved suitable for use by VNAF and training was begun. In '66 VNAF began using the F-5 operationally. The jet could cruise at 1,064mph and had a maximum bomb load of 4,000 pounds; it was also armed with two 20mm cannons and two Sidewinder missiles. The Freedom Fighter, as it was known, was highly maneuverable and easy to maintain. An upgraded version, the F-5E, Tiger II, became available in '72. Several were given to VNAF before U.S. support for Vietnam ended. The F-5E had a 7,000-pound payload and more powerful engines.

F-5E *see* **F-5 Tiger**

F-8 (Crusader, RF-8) Single engine, single seat, all weather jet interceptor/ fighter-bomber. The F-8 was gradually replaced by F-4Js, most phased out of service by May '68. The F-8 was the only Marine aircraft to be both land and carrier based during the VNW. The Crusader was manufactured by LTV Aerospace and had a maximum speed of 1,120mph, a range of 1,770kms and was armed with four 20mm cannons, two AAMs and 32 rockets. The F-8 was used by both the Navy and the Marines to provide ground support in South Vietnam. The RF-8 was the photo reconnaissance version of the aircraft and remained in limited service with the Marines/Navy throughout the war.

F-8F (Bearcat) U.S. single engine, prop-driven fighter given to the French in '50 during their war against the Viet Minh. The F-8F was manufactured by Grumman Aircraft. Surplus stocks of the aircraft were used by Navy and Marine Reserve squadrons. The F-8F had a maximum speed of 421mph, a range of 1,700kms and was armed with four 20mm cannons, and could also deliver several hundred pounds of bombs in the close support role. Those few Bearcats that survived the First Indochina war were absorbed into the VNAF after the French departed Vietnam. The F-8Fs in the

VNAF inventory were eventually replaced with U.S. A-1 Skyraiders. *See also* **A-1**.

F-9 (Cougar, Panther)   Grumman Aircraft single engine jet fighter used by the Navy and Marines, manufactured in two models. The "Panther" had straight wings, the Cougar was swept winged. The aircraft represented one of the Navy's first jet fighters, entering service in the mid-fifties. The two seat version of the Cougar saw service in Vietnam as a tactical support fighter early in the war. The Marines later used the Cougar as a tactical air coordinator aircraft directing air strikes and performing reconnaissance. The F-9 was phased out in '67 and replaced by the TA-4F. The F-9 Cougar had a max speed of 690mph, a range of 1,600kms and was armed with 20mm cannons and a 4,000-pound bomb load capacity. *See also* **TA-4F, Tactical Air Coordinator.**

F-14 (Tomcat)   Advanced Navy fighter that began deploying to Navy aircraft carriers in the early '70s. The F-14 was not used in combat in Vietnam, but was available on carriers of the 7th Fleet that participated in the evacuation of Americans and South Vietnamese from Saigon in April '75. The F-14 had a speed in excess of Mach 2 and carried air-to-air missiles.

F-80   *see*   **T-33**

F-100 (Supersabre, Hun, RF-100)   Air Force single engine jet fighter bomber used extensively in the air war in Vietnam. Manufactured by North American Aviation, nicknamed the Hun by Air Force crews. The RF-100 was the photo reconnaissance version of the F-100. The twin seat version, the F-100F, was used by the Wild Weasels during Iron Hand missions to suppress enemy SAM missile sites in NVN. The F-100 had a maximum speed of 864mph, a range of 2,400kms, four 20mm cannons and could carry external fuel tanks and 7,500 pounds of bombs. *See also* **Iron Hand, Wild Weasel, SA-2.**

F-100 Battalion   Specially formed unit of Viet Cong commandos that performed terrorist bombings and assassinations in Saigon and the surrounding area. The F-100 battalion consisted of small groups of saboteurs that operated from underground bases located near Cu Chi. The unit was just one of the Viet Cong's "Dac Cong" type units

that operated throughout South Vietnam. The F-100 group was rendered ineffective by '72 due to the effects of the Phoenix Program and the destruction of many of the unit's tunnel bases in the Cu Chi area. *See also* **Sapper, Dac Cong.**

F-101   *see*   **RF-101**

F-102 (Delta Dagger)   The first Air Force jet aircraft used in SVN for intercept missions. Prior to the use of F-102 aircraft, the only jets used over Vietnam were RF-101 reconnaissance aircraft. The single engine, single seat F-102s deployed to Tan Son Nhut in March '62 and also operated from Da Nang. Later they were replaced by Navy aircraft operating from carriers off the coast of SVN. The F-102 was manufactured by Convair/General Dynamics, had a max speed of 825mph, a range of 2,170kms and was normally armed with air-to-air missiles.

F-104 (Starfighter)   Single engine, single seat jet fighter manufactured by Lockheed Aircraft. The Air Force fighter was used in a limited role in Vietnam. The F-104 had a max speed of 1,530mph, range of 930kms, a bomb load of 4,000 pounds and was armed with a single 20mm cannon. F-104s operated in Vietnam from '65 to '67 as MiG interceptors, after which they were gradually phased out of service and replaced by the F-4 Phantom.

F-105 (THUD, Lead Sled, Ultra Hog, Squash Bomber, Thunderchief)   Single engine fighter-bomber made by Republic Aviation, originally designed as a nuclear fighter-bomber. The Air Force began using the F-105D Thunderchief in Vietnam in '64 and it saw extensive use throughout the war. During the late sixties it was the heaviest single seat fighter plane in the world. Its high speed and low level ordnance delivery made it effective against both tactical and strategic targets. The F-105 had many nicknames and had a max speed of 1,390mph, range of 1,840kms, a bomb load of 14,000 pounds and was armed with a 20mm cannon. The F/G models also saw service in Vietnam. F-105s downed 27 MiGs in the eight years they operated in SEA with a loss of 334 aircraft from enemy SAM and ground fire. *See also* **Wild Weasel.**

F-105F/G (EF-105F/G, ALR-31, LWR)   Twin seat version of the Republic F-105 fighter-bomber used in Vietnam by the U.S. Air Force. The EF-105F was the designation for the twin seat F-105s used for SAM suppression by the Wild Weasels. The F-105G was a later version "Weasel" with an upgraded Launch Warning Receiver (ALR-31) and ECM equipment that was mounted in a blister on the aircraft's fuselage. ECMs were previously carried in a pod mounted on a wing pylon. The 105G also had the ability to carry the larger AGM-78A ARM. The "G" model began operations against North Vietnam in early '68. See also **Wild Weasel, F-105, ARM.**

F-111 (Aardvark) Twin engine, all weather, jet fighter-bomber designed by General Dynamics. The F-111, named the Aardvark, was equipped with computerized radar and bombing systems; its wings could be pivoted to different positions to improve the aircraft's performance. F-111s were initially deployed to SEA in March '68 and were plagued with many problems but later modifications greatly improved their performance and dependability. Based out of Thailand in '72 the F-111 flew combat missions against NVA infiltration routes and SAM sites. The F-111 had a max speed of 1,450mph, range of 4,707kms, bomb load of 31,500 pounds and was armed with a 20mm cannon and had a two man crew. See also **Combat Lancer Deployment.**

F-227 Fairchild-Hiller twin engine aircraft used by the Marines as a light transport. The F-227 had an 11,600-pound payload, or it could transport 20–48 troops depending on the aircraft's configuration. The aircraft operated with a two man crew, had a max speed of 290mph, and an extended range of 4,300kms.

F.I.C. see **Indochina**

FA-CBU see **Fuel-Air CBU**

FAC see **Forward Air Controller**

FADAC see **Field Artillery Digital Automatic Computer**

FAE see **Fuel-Air CBU**

Fagot see **MiG, MiG-15, ARVN Queers**

Fairfax see **Operation Fairfax**

FAL-FAR see **Royal Laotian Army**

Falana, Lola see **Hope, Bob**

Falciparum see **Malaria**

Falcons of the 335th Avn see **335th Aviation Company**

Fall of Cambodia see **Operation Eagle Pull**

Fall of Phnom Penh see **Operation Eagle Pull**

Fall of Saigon In March '75 the NVA/VC began their spring offensive. So successful were their initial attacks against South Vietnamese positions that they launched an all-out assault. Within a matter of several weeks they had completely overrun all of South Vietnam's defenses. South Vietnam surrendered to communist forces April 30, 1975. An estimated 52,000 South Vietnamese were evacuated by American military aircraft, another 10,000 escaped on commercial aircraft, and several thousand more Viets evacuated Vietnam in small boats, making their way to U.S. ships stationed off the coast. See also **Final Offensive, Operation Frequent Wind, Decent Interval; Abandoned Equipment, '75.**

Falsies (Silicone Injections) Because of a distinctive lack of pronounced breasts in Vietnamese women, "stuffed" brassieres were a social must among urban working women. A wide variety of materials were used to enhance the figures of Vietnamese women who worked around American men or catered to the GI quest for "breast" on their women. Many of the GIs did not appreciate the diminutive Vietnamese figure; in an effort to attract more GI business to bars, bargirls and whores attempted to Americanize their bodies by stuffing their bras. Other Vietnamese women turned to silicone injections to inflate their way into the hearts and hands of the American GI.

Family Bunkers In most of the rural villages and hamlets of Vietnam the people had constructed underground bunkers where they could go at night or when the war raged near their ville. The bunkers were large enough to provide a family with extremely cramped protection from small arms fire, but many of the bunkers could not survive a direct hit by bombs or artillery. In some areas of high enemy tunnel activity, the bunkers were interconnected by a series of narrow tunnels. Through the tunnel passages the enemy could easily move beneath the village, and between fighting positions, harassing American units and then disappearing from sight. The only way to be sure a bunker was clear was to frag it and then conduct a search.

Family Syndrome   Phrase used to identify one of the problems that plagued ARVN units during the war and especially during the NVA's Final Offensive in early '75. Most ARVN soldiers moved their families near to the area where they were stationed. The NVA began their final push throughout SVN and GVN forces retreated; many of the ARVN troops were more concerned with the evacuation of their families than fighting a delaying action against the NVA. ARVN troops left their defensive positions to tend to their families, crippling the units' ability to slow the NVA thrust with an organized "fighting withdrawal." ARVN Marine and Navy units were much less affected by the family syndrome because many of their families were located in the relative safety of Saigon.

Famous Fourth   *see*   **4th Infantry Division**

Fan Song   U.S. code name for the North Vietnamese ground radar detection system used to track and target attacking aircraft. The radar equipment was mobile, mounted in a wheeled van, and provided targeting information for the SA-2 SAM missile. *See also* **Surface-to-Air Missile, SA-2, Fire Cans, Ground Control Intercept.**

FANK   *see*   **Forces Armees Nationale Khmer**

Fantail MiG   *see*   **MiG-15**

Fantastic Feathered Fowl   *see*   **Chickenman**

Fantastic Fowl   *see*   **Chickenman**

FAO   *see*   **Forward Observer**

Farmer   *see*   **Shenyang J-6**

Farmgate   *see*   **Operation Farmgate**

Fast Mover   *see*   **F-4**

Fat Bombs   During early American air involvement in Vietnam there was a shortage of advanced technology aircraft ordnance. Much of the ordnance on hand in late '65 and '66 was Korean War vintage bombs. These bombs had a large diameter which caused a high drag ratio when mounted on the newer, high speed jets. The old bombs were called "Fat Bombs." As bomb production increased in the U.S., stocks of newer design, low drag coefficient ordnance made their way to aircraft used in Vietnam.

Fat Rat Jobs   *see*   **Skatin'**

Fat Rats (Water Bladder)   Nickname for the Army issue five-quart, collapsible water bladder. The plastic bladder was contained inside an OD green, ripstop nylon carrier. The instructions on the cover of the "Fat Rat" said the bladder could be "inflated" with air and used as a flotation device, supposedly able to support up to 10 pounds of equipment. The bladder and its nylon cover were 10 x 12 inches. GIs speculated that the only thing the air inflated bladder could support was a wet rat.

Fat Unit (Authorized Strength)   Slang for a unit operating at or above full strength. U.S. units in Vietnam, due to casualties, illness, R & Rs and rotations, were seldom operated at their full authorized strength. A typical Army infantry platoon had an authorized strength of 44 men, but the actual combat strength (paddy strength) was 24–32 men. When the first American combat troops deployed to Vietnam they arrived as "fat units," up to strength. *See also* **Paddy Strength.**

Father   *see*   **Ba**

Father Hoang Quynh   *see*   **Luc Luong Dai Doan Ket**

Fatigues (Fats, Stateside Fatigues, Combat Fatigues, Utility Fatigues, Utilities)   Military work uniform. During the Vietnam War there were "Stateside Fatigues" (Utilities) and "Jungle Fatigues" (Tropical Combat Uniform). The stateside (utility) fatigues were OD cotton; the shirt, with two breast pockets, was worn tucked into the pants. The four pocket, belt looped pants were worn bloused with boots by Army and Marine troops or unbloused with regular shoes. Both utility and jungle fatigues were worn by U.S. forces. Most ARVN forces wore American style utility fatigues. *See also* **Jungle Utilities, Jungle Camouflage Uniform, Pegged Fatigues.**

Fats   *see*   **Fatigues**

FAWS   *see*   **Fixed Axial Weapons**

FDC   *see*   **Fire Direction Center**

FDO   *see*   **Fire Direction Officer**

Fearless Feathered Fighter *see* **Chickenman**

FEB *see* **Division Engineer Battalion**

FEBA *see* **Forward Edge of the Battle Area**

FEC *see* **French Expeditionary Corps**

Fed-Up-with-the-Fucking-Army *see* **Deserters**

Feet Dry/Feet Wet Aircraft pilot's reference to the part of a flight that operated over water (feet wet). When the flight crossed land, that part of the flight was referred to as feet dry.

Fellatio (Blowjob, Suckie-Suckie, Chop-Chop) Oral sex. The Vietnamese-American nicknames for this were "suckie-suckie" or "chop-chop." It was easy for both the Americans and the Vietnamese to say and understand. Oral sex was not one of the more popular practices of Vietnamese prostitutes, especially the Buddhists among them and it often required extra payment and a lot of long-winded convincing by GIs. Oral sex was generally easier to obtain in the larger cities where larger groups of non–Buddhist prostitutes tended to gather. Since over 90 percent of Vietnam's population was Buddhist the chances of "chop-chop" in the rural villages and towns were greatly reduced. *See also* **Chop-Chop.**

Fellowship of Reconciliation (FOR) Worldwide Christian organization founded in Great Britain in '14 that advocated peace and nonviolent social reform. During the VNW the American FOR chapter opposed the war in Vietnam, the draft, and they supported the civil rights movement in the States. Many of FOR's small membership were religious leaders that provided support for other antiwar and civil rights groups such as the American Civil Liberties Union, War Resisters League, Congress of Racial Equality, Clergy and Laity Concerned About Vietnam, and others.

Felt, Admiral Harry *see* **Commander-in-Chief, Pacific Command**

Female Viet Cong *see* **Co**

Fence, The (Mekong River) U.S. aircrews that flew attacks against North Vietnam out of Thailand nicknamed the Mekong River the "Fence." The Mekong River formed much of the border between Thailand and Laos. Once returning aircraft saw the broad and winding Mekong pass under their wings they knew they were home free. *See also* **Mekong River.**

Fenuge *see* **New Troop**

Ferret Operations Secret military intelligence gathering operations designed to test an enemy's defenses. The operations were designed to provoke the enemy into using his defense systems. The enemy's reactions could then be monitored and later evaluated. During '64 the USS *Maddox* was on such a ferreting mission monitoring North Vietnam radar and radio transmissions when it was attacked by NVN gunboats in the Gulf of Tonkin. *See also* **Tonkin Gulf Incident, De Soto Patrol.**

Ferrets *see* **Electronic Counter Measures**

Fetch *see* **SH-3**

Fever-of-Undetermined-Origin (FUO Fever) Patients admitted to field hospitals with a high fever, and no other specific symptoms, were classified as FUOs, their fever not being immediately identifiable as one of the big three fever producers: malaria, dysentery or dengue fever. Many GIs who came down with FUO fever accused the antimalaria pills that they took of actually masking symptoms of malaria instead of preventing it. They claimed the unknown fever was actually a mild case of malaria. Medical authorities argued that the antimalarial drugs were effective, but they were never able to adequately identify what the FUO fever was, or its source. *See also* **Malaria, Dengue Fever.**

FF *see* **Field Force**

FFAR *see* **XM-159C Rocket**

FFF *see* **Find, Fix and Finish**

FFZ *see* **Free-Fire-Zone**

Fiddler's Green *see* **FSB Fiddler's Green**

Field, The *see* **Boonies**

Field Artillery *see* **Tube Artillery**

Field Artillery Digital Automatic Computer (FADAC) Artillery computer used to manipulate target data for the generation of gun data used to fire on a target. The electronic gun data computer was first used in the U.S. Army in Vietnam in '68. Prior to that time gun data was calculated by hand. The gun computer calculated range, deflection and powder charge required to impact the target and also kept a record of all the firing data and calculations for future reference. Computer calculated gun data was double-checked by hand by members of the FDC. *See also* **Fire Direction Center.**

Field Commission *see* **Mustang**

Field Force (FF) U.S. Corps level headquarters used for the tactical control of military operations within the Corps Area of Operation. Field Force Headquarters also coordinated logistic, pacification programs and use of advisory forces. Three field force headquarters were established in Vietnam: I FFV, II FFV and XXIV Corps.

Field Force Reserve Combat units that were designated as an emergency reserve force. In Vietnam Field Force Reserve units functioned as normal combat elements, but were generally committed in such a fashion that they could be withdrawn from their current operation and activated as an emergency reserve. Such a reserve force could quickly be moved to trouble spots within the Field Force's AO. Airmobile cavalry units were usually selected as the Field Force Reserve because of their organic helicopter support.

Field Goal *see* **Operation Field Goal**

Field Grade Officers Officers holding the rank of colonel, lieutenant colonel or major.

Field Jacket *see* **M-1951 Field Coat**

Field Load (Basic Load, Essential Load) Weapons and ammunition loads taken to the field for combat. Vietnam era infantry companies' standard weapons included M-16 rifles, M-79 grenade launcher, M-60 machine gun, LAWs, 81mm mortar, .45cal pistol, and sometimes shotguns. The term "field load" was often used interchangeably with the term "basic load," the basic load of ammunition a man or unit carried to the field on normal operations. The load varied from unit to unit, but one such load was 10–14 loaded M-16 magazines, 2–4 grenades, and 400–800 rounds of machine gun ammo. Additionally, M-79 grenade, smoke, C-4

plastique and LAW rounds were included in the load mix. In addition to weapons and ammunition, the typical field load included a poncho, rations, E-Tool, bayonet, poncho liner, extra canteens and first aid kit. Part of the load could also include a bush-towel, extra socks, and an abbreviated shaving kit (razor, soap, toothbrush, toothpaste, toilet paper). Other optional items included an extra bolt for the M-16 rifle, rope, det cord, extra grenades, a claymore mine, air mattress, extra grenades and ammo, LAW, and various other items. For some missions an "essential load" was required. This load mostly consisted of weapons, ammunition, first aid packet, and water. The soldier carried a minimum of equipment essential to combat. Such missions were, by design, very brief and specific in their purpose. After the mission the man would retrieve his regular equipment load. *See also* **782 Gear, Light(s).**

Field Manual (FM, ST, TM) All official Army procedures, recommendations and doctrine were assembled in a series of manuals designated FM—Field Manual, ST—Special Text, TM—Technical Manual. The manuals were identified by a publication number and descriptive title. TMs covered technical issues such as weapons, communications devices, munitions, etc. STs were specially printed manuals dealing with a specific subject not covered by an FM, or new information not yet included in a current FM. FMs dealt with operations, doctrine, usage and all other aspects of the military.

Field of Fire (FOF) The area that a weapon or group of weapons could fire on effectively from their current position, without obstruction from terrain or the limits of dead space. *See also* **Dead Space, Principal Direction of Fire.**

Field Phone *see* **EE-8 Field Telephone**

Field Radio (Horn, Hook, RT, Radio Telephone) Various types of radios were used in Vietnam. U.S. field radios were man carried, most common of which were the AN/PRC-25 and AN/PRC-77. The former was known as the Prick-25, and the latter was known as the monster or Krypto because of its heavy weight. The handset used on these sets was sometimes referred to as a hook, and the radio itself as the horn. A limited number of Soviet built radios were used by the NVA/VC. U.S. radios were regularly used down to the squad level, while NVA/VC units made very limited use of radios below battalion and company. *See also* **Radio Telephone Operator, U.S. Radios, NVA/VC Radios.**

Field Rations *see* **C-Rations, LRRP Rations**

Field Reappropriation *see* **Midnight Requisition**

Field Refusal *see* **Combat Refusal**

Field Telephone *see* **EE-8 Field Telephone**

Field Training Exercise *see* **FTX**

Field Utility Nonmilitary issue item. Reference to any piece of equipment or device that was locally fabricated or homemade, and used in the field. Troops often designed items and devices to enhance their operations or survivability. Such field utility items were usually nonstandard, varying from unit to unit.

Field-Day (GI Party) Marine slang for cleaning; as in sweeping, mopping, washing, dusting and general housekeeping and custodial duties. In the Army it was referred to as "GI"; as in, "GI the latrine," or a "GI party."

Field-Transport Pack *see* **782 Gear**

Fierce Tiger II *see* **Operation Fierce Tiger II**

Fifty-Cal *see* **M-2 HMG**

Fig Trees *see* **Banyan Trees**

Fight (Fist) *see* **Throwin' Hands**

Fighter Jocks *see* **Flyboys**

Fighter Pilots *see* **Flyboys**

Fighting for Peace Is Like Fucking for Virginity An expression by an unknown author about the counterproductivity of war.

Fighting Hole *see* **Fox Hole**

Fighting I *see* **USS Intrepid**

Fil Hol Rubber Plantation Viet Cong base area that was located in the abandoned French rubber plantation less than 10kms north of Cu Chi. The area was laced with interconnecting tunnels that extended throughout the district of Cu Chi. *See also* **Cu Chi.**

Film Rating System *see* **American GI Film Ratings**

Final Evacuation of Saigon In mid–April '75 when it appeared the ARVN could not, or would not, be able to hold back the NVA Final Offensive, the U.S. began the evacuation of American personnel and their dependents. On April 29 the last of the Americans and their dependents were ordered evacuated; these included embassy staff, civilian workers, and the military security force. In addition, Vietnamese nationals who would be at risk, because of their association with the Americans, were also evacuated. Evacuees departed by airplane until Tan Son Nhut was closed; evacuation was continued by helicopter from the embassy roof until April 30. An estimated 65,000 people were evacuated from Vietnam; nearly 55,000 of those were Vietnamese. *See also* **Operation Frequent Wind.**

Final Offensive (Ho Chi Minh Campaign, Campaign 275, Great Spring Victory) The NVA started a major offensive in early March '75, which resulted in the country-wide collapse and rout of SVN military units. The NVA/VC began their push in late '74, and were so successful with their initial advances that they made their final push for the entire country in March '75. The NVA continued their push through SVN until Saigon and SVN fell to the communists on April 30, 1975. The NVA/VC motto for the offensive was "marvelous speed, boldness, surprise and certain victory." The campaign, under the command of General Van Tien Dung, was known as "Campaign 275" or "Great Spring Victory," and was also called the "Ho Chi Minh Campaign" in honor of Uncle Ho.

Finance (Pay Voucher, Money Order) Administrative section (department) of a headquarters unit that handled the troop's pay records. During Vietnam enlisted men were typically paid in cash according to a "pay voucher" that indicated the soldier's rate of pay and extra allowances for flight or combat duty. The voucher also indicated any special allotments (withholdings for dependents), savings or deductions for disciplinary actions. The soldier signed the voucher indicating he had received the cash payment. In Vietnam many soldiers turned over portions of their pay to the Payroll Officer who, in turn, purchased money orders for the troops so they could send some of their wages home. *See also* **Pay Advance, Allotment.**

Find 'Em, Finger 'Em... *see* **R & R**

Find, Fix and Finish (FFF) Traditional military doctrine for dealing with an enemy force. "Find" the enemy and "Fix" him in position using superior firepower, and then "Finish" him off with ground troops. The doctrine was not always effective in Vietnam because the enemy was so difficult to pin down to one location. U.S. troops were constantly searching for the NVA/VC, and usually only found them when the enemy was ready to be found. GIs called the FFF doctrine "Find, Fix and Fuck 'em over if you can."

Finger, The *see* **Bird, The**

Fini Hut Bastardized combination of French and Vietnamese which meant that something was over, the end, destroyed, gone, or no more. "Fini" from the French, meaning to end, or over. And "het" (Americanized to "hut") from the Vietnamese which meant to end or finish. The phrase was used by both Americans and Vietnamese in their dealings with each other.

Fink Release Program (Diehards, Finks) American POWs who cooperated with the North Vietnamese were said to be participating in the "Fink Release Program." The prisoners who continued to resist the North Vietnamese were considered "diehards" or "hardliners" and labeled those who cooperated with the North Vietnamese, "Finks." The Finks were kept separated from the other prisoners and in exchange for information, confessions and public appearances, were granted special treatment such as more and better food, exercise and better living conditions. *See also* **Prisoner of War; Hardliners; Garwood, PFC Robert (Bobby).**

Finks *see* **Fink Release Program, Hardliners**

Fire (Shoot) (Bust[in'] Caps, Lit-Up, Lite-Up, Fire-Up, Bring-Heat, Scunnions, Hose-Up) To shoot or fire your weapon or be shot at.... To saturate an area with automatic and small arms fire. GI slang

meaning to bring massive amounts of firepower to bear on a target, in hopes of "blowing it away," causing severe damage or at least cause it to stop shooting back at you. The term "bustin' caps" or "capping" was originally credited to the Marines who claimed the firing of the M-16 rifle sounded like a "cap pistol." The term was later absorbed by all branches of the service and came to mean the firing of any weapon. *See also* **Bring-Smoke, Kill.**

Fire and Maneuver (F and M) Basic infantry strategy of moving in to close with the enemy and using maximum firepower to destroy him. U.S. infantry doctrine called for elements of the force to advance on a target using fire and maneuver. The elements would alternate, one element laying down a base of covering fire while the other element advanced. The elements would alternate movement and fire until the objective was taken.

Fire Base Small U.S. base camps used as patrol bases in South Vietnam. The bases usually did not have their own artillery but sometimes did have 81mm or 4.2-inch mortars. The base was usually manned by a company or platoon sized force. Fire bases were often constructed around an LZ and the terms were often used interchangeably. A fire base with artillery pieces was upgraded to a "fire support base" and usually featured a few more creature comforts. A fire base usually consisted of several bunkers surrounded by rolls of concertina wire, tangle foot and claymores. Fire bases were established to provide security for a particular area or a base from which patrol units operated. *See also* **Patrol Base, Fire Support Base, Landing Zone.**

Fire Base Ann Margret *see* **Ann Margret**

Fire Base Nancy *see* **FSB Nancy**

Fire Base Oasis *see* **FSB Oasis**

Fire Base Psychosis A grunt-generated term describing a soldier's fear of operating very far from an artillery fire support base. As the VNW started to wind down in '70 some Army infantry units were hesitant to operate outside the range of the fire support base from which they patrolled. Patrolling within range of the FSB guns afforded patrols some protection in the event they came under fire from the enemy, this surrendered the area beyond artillery range to the enemy. *See also* **Artillery Umbrella, Bunker Mentality.**

Fire Base Thunder (Thunder I–III) During operations of the 1st Infantry Division in its Area of Operation north of Saigon, a series of small, temporary fire bases were established. The bases were built along Highway 13 and were called Thunder I, II and III. The bases were established to control Highway 13, the road link between Saigon and the northern III Corps provinces, and especially the towns of Loc Ninh and An Loc.

Fire Cans (Antiaircraft Radar) Nickname for the radar sets used by the North Vietnamese to direct their radar controlled antiaircraft guns. *See* **Fan Song, Ground Control Intercept.**

Fire Direction Center (FDC) Controlled an artillery battery's indirect fire support activities. The FDC interfaced with units in the field requesting artillery support, calculated the necessary gun information and provided the data to the guns for firing. Gun firing data was calculated by hand until '68 when the FADAC electronic gun computer entered service with the Army. The gun computer calculated range, deflection and powder increments to be used to fire the shell to the designated target. *See also* **Field Artillery Digital Automatic Computer.**

Fire Direction Officer (FDO) Artillery officer responsible for the fires of a battery.

Fire Discipline (Barrel Meltdown) Controlling a unit's firepower in an effort to control ammunition consumption. For patrols engaged in a firefight, it was essential that they use well-placed fire in short bursts since they did not carry an unlimited supply of ammo. Resupply was dependent on the unit's accessibility in the jungle, weather, and the volume of enemy fire. Continuous firing of the M-60 machine gun caused the barrel to heat up, prematurely detonating the cartridges, causing jams and barrel meltdowns. Fire discipline also referred to not using machine gun fire to respond to enemy probes of the perimeter, since such a response would reveal the gun's position. Hand grenades were used to discourage such probes.

Fire for Effect *see* **Bring-Smoke**

Fire Guard (Fire Watch) Soldier assigned to patrol the troops' sleeping area on watch for fire. The fire guard's duty was to sound the alarm in the event of a fire. Fire guard only took place during basic training. Generally one man per hour stood fire watch during the normal sleep hours, with the watch rotating through the entire training platoon. The watch began with lights out and continued until the first wake up call about 0500 or 0600 hours. Trainees stood the watch until they graduated basic and left the training company.

Fire Mission (Contact Fire Mission) A barrage fired by an artillery battery, or a request by a field unit for indirect fire support. A "Contact Fire Mission" was requested by troops in the field that were in immediate contact with enemy forces. In Vietnam all fire missions not plotted for free-fire-zones required clearance to fire from the battery's headquarters and the Vietnamese district chief. For various reasons clearances could be very difficult to obtain. *See also* **H and I.**

Fire Superiority The ability to deliver a greater concentration of accurate fire onto a target than the fire that could be returned by the enemy. In Vietnam the FWFs had fire superiority over the NVA/VC, but were unable to use it effectively because the enemy usually avoided contact with FWFs unless he had distinct advantage over them or believed he could defeat them in a battle.

Fire Support Barge *see* **Artillery Barge**

Fire Support Base (FSB, Howard Johnsons) Forward artillery or infantry patrol bases created to provide fire support to units operating in the field. The bases were generally remotely located, temporary, self-contained, secured by infantry and supplied by air. Sometimes an abandoned base would be reopened when ground operations shifted back into the area. Infantry troops called the FSBs "Howard Johnsons" because they represented a degree of civilization and some comfort compared to the terrible conditions associated with field operations. "Fire bases" were temporary, but generally remained in operation longer than a patrol base. "Fire support bases" generally remained open for longer periods of time, and had a few more refinements than the patrol or fire base. The FSB might feature some rough structures and better defenses for the gun crews, or it might be a semipermanent installation with many of the features of a larger base, only on a much smaller scale, such as underground bunkers, electric generators, buildings, EM Club, etc. The name "fire support base" was sometimes used interchangeably with the name "LZ," and "fire base." *See also* **Patrol Base, Fire Base, FSSB, Landing Zone.**

Fire Support Coordination Center (FSCC)   A fire support center used to control the fires of artillery and the planning for strategic air strikes. The center digested target information and coordinated the use of available indirect fire assets, offshore guns, when available, and air strikes.

Fire Support Surveillance Base (FSSB) Fire support base merged with surveillance and target acquisition equipment employed by elements of the 173d Airborne Brigade above 506 Valley in Binh Dinh Province, II Corps. Surveillance equipment used by the base included ground based radars, electronic sensors and night scopes. The FSSB was located near the heavily traveled enemy route and base area in the valley. Once the surveillance equipment identified targets, the organic artillery at the base could open fire, and fires from other bases and air strikes could be brought to bear. The FSSB program was first initiated in early '70. *See also* **Fire Support Base, Ground Radar.**

Fire Team (FT)   Tactical U.S. Marine infantry unit consisting of 3–5 men. A squad was made up of two or three fire teams. The Army infantry squad consisted of two fire teams, each containing 4–5 men.

Fire Watch   *see*   **Fire Guard**

Fire-for-Effect   Command given to an artillery battery to fire continuously and rapidly on a given target until a cease-fire order was received.

Fire-in-the-Hole   Warning yelled out when a planned detonation was about to take place. Anyone near the area when the warning went out was aware that some type of friendly placed demolition charge or grenade was about to explode.

Fire-Up   *see*   **Fire (shoot)**

Fireballing (Concentrated Fires) Slang for large amounts of concentrated artillery fire applied to a target. *See also* **SLAM.**

Firecracker   Code name for an American artillery shell that was similar to an aircraft delivered Cluster Bomb Unit. The Firecracker did not detonate on impact; instead the shell casing burst open and scattered hundreds of golfball-sized bomblets over a wide area. Within a few seconds the dispersed bomblets exploded simultaneously. The Firecracker was first used by the Marines during the Siege of Khe Sanh in Jan '68. *See also* **Cluster Bomb Unit.**

Firefight   Brief, violent exchange of fire between two opposing forces, sometimes extending into lengthy drawn out battles.

Firefly (Foxtrot Foxtrot)   Night helicopter missions consisting of two gunships, and one helicopter fitted with searchlights, arc lamps or large aircraft landing lights. Sometimes the helicopter with the searchlight (Basketball Ship) also was equipped with a starlight or infrared scope. The lightship would seek out the enemy in the darkness and illuminate the area if a target was found; the gunships would then attack the target. The VC initially fired on the lightships when the missions first started, but the gunships brought them such grief that they learned from the experience, and avoided contact and disclosure of their position. The fireflys (Foxtrot Foxtrot) were also called Lightning Bugs, Basketball Ships and Lightships. *See also* **C-123 Lightship, Nighthawks, Night Hunter Operations.**

Firing-from-the-Hip   Tanker term describing the ability of a tank to fire at point-blank range into a bunker or fortification.

First Aid Kit   *see*   **Unit One**

First American Airman Shot Down... *see*   **Alvarez, Lieutenant Everett, Jr.**

First American to Die...   The American soldier identified as the first to die in SVN is dependent on the period of U.S. involvement studied. SP/4 James T. Davis is officially listed as the first American to die in combat in Vietnam in December '61. Two MAAG advisors, Master Sergeant Chester Ovnand and Major Dale Buis, were killed during a VC attack on their advisor's compound near Bien Hoa in July '59, and Major

Peter Dewey, an OSS liaison officer, was killed September '45 in a Vietminh ambush near Saigon. Buis and Ovnand's names are the first names on the wall of the Vietnam War Memorial. *See also* **Dewey, Davis.**

First American Woman to Die... (Barbara Robbins, Manolito Castillo) On March 30, 1965, an automobile packed with explosives was parked outside the U.S. Embassy in Saigon; the car exploded, killing or wounding over 200 Americans and Vietnamese. Manolito Castillo and Barbara Robbins were the only Americans to die in the blast. Castillo was in the Navy and Barbara Robbins, who was on the embassy's secretarial staff, became the first American woman to die in the Vietnam War.

First Aviation Brigade *see* **1st Aviation Brigade**

First Cavalry *see* **1st Cavalry Division (Airmobile)**

First Cavalry Division *see* **1st Cavalry Division (Airmobile)**

First Field Force Vietnam *see* **I Field Force**

First In and Last Out *see* **Wild Weasel**

First in the Nam, Second to None Unofficial field motto of the 173d Airborne Brigade in Vietnam.

First Indochina War *see* **Indochina War**

First Infantry Division *see* **1st Infantry Division**

First John *see* **First Lieutenant**

First Lieutenant (1lt., 1st Lieut., First John, L.T., Trung-Uy) Ranked above a second lieutenant, Army and Marine first lieutenants normally commanded a platoon size unit. In Vietnam due to a shortage of captains, first lieutenants were sometimes placed in command of company size units in the field. Promotion was to the rank of captain. Combat infantrymen often called their platoon leader L.T., for Lieutenant. Trung-Uy was the Vietnamese equivalent rank. *See also* **Company Grade Officers.**

First Logistical Command *see* **1st Logistical Command**

First Marine Air Wing *see* **1st**

Marine Air Wing

First Marine Division *see* **1st Marine Division**

First Shirt *see* **Gunnery Sergeant**

First Signal Brigade *see* **1st Signal Brigade**

First Special Forces Group *see* **1st Special Forces Group**

First Team *see* **1st Cavalry Division (Airmobile)**

First U.S. Air Force Aircraft... The first official loss of a U.S. Air Force aircraft and its crew occurred in February '62. During a Ranch Hand defoliation mission a C-123 Provider crashed and its crew of three were killed.

First Vietnam Medal of Honor Recipient *see* **Donlon, Captain Roger**

First-Light Recon (Last-Light Recon) Air reconnaissance performed by light observation helicopters at dawn and at dusk. The recon involved the helicopter making a pass over suspected enemy areas of activity such as hamlets and villages. The Viet Cong often moved in to support villes at dusk when US/ARVN troops had secured for the night. The same VC would leave the villes just before dawn to avoid US/ARVN units that might sweep through the area during the day. The dawn and dusk recon flights were attempts to gather intelligence information that could be used for future operations against suspected enemy villes.

First-Light-Readiness *see* **Stand-To**

Fish Hook An NVA/VC base area in Cambodia along the SVN/Cambodian border, believed to be the location of the communist headquarters for South Vietnam, COSVN. The Fish Hook area was located 33kms north of the boundary of South Vietnam and Cambodia, where Tay Ninh and Binh Long Provinces met the Vietnam/Cambodian border in III Corps; 25kms northwest of Loc Ninh. On a map the boundary between SVN and Cambodia in this area resembled an upside down fish hook. During the US/ARVN incursion into Cambodia in '70, a large enemy complex containing large quantities of enemy weapons and supplies was discovered in the Fish Hook west of Loc Ninh. *See also* **Rock Island East; City, The.**

Fish Sauce *see* **Nuoc Mam**

Fishbed *see* **MiG, MiG-21**

Fisher, Major Bernard F. The Air Force's first Medal of Honor winner during the Vietnam War. Fisher received the award for bravery for combat actions in March '66. Fisher and five other A-1 Skyraiders were providing air support to the A Shau Special Forces camp when one of the A-1s, piloted by Lt. Col. Dafford Meyers, was hit by enemy fire and made an emergency landing at the camp's chewed-up airstrip. While under fire, Fisher landed his plane on the pockmarked airstrip to rescue the downed pilot. Fisher's plane took several hits from enemy gunners before he was able to squeeze Meyers into the single seat cockpit of the plane. Fisher managed to avoid obstacles on the strip and get airborne, safely returning to base.

Fishes-and-the-Sea Reference to the way some policymakers and diplomats viewed the Viet Cong. The Viet Cong represented the "fishes" in the "sea" of civilians throughout Vietnam. It was argued that the way to eliminate the VC was to deprive them of the sea that sheltered them and gave them life. From these views the U.S. developed policies to deprive the VC contact with the people, much as the British had done in Malaya. Thousands of villagers were removed from their ancestral homes to relocation camps under programs called "Strategic Hamlets" and "New Life Hamlets." Once removed, the areas previously inhabited were declared Free-Fire-Zones. *See also* **Strategic Hamlet Program, New Life Hamlet, Forced Urbanization.**

Fistfight *see* **Throwin' Hands**

Five Mountain Program *see* **Ngu Hanh Son Program**

Five O'Clock Follies (MACV Daily Press Briefings) The U.S. military command in Vietnam, MACV, held daily briefings for the news media to inform them on the progress of the war and political items within the country. The 5:00 P.M. briefings were conducted at the JUSPAO office in Saigon by the U.S. military, embassy personnel and on occasion members of the Vietnamese military. The news media, and later (unofficially) MACV, began to refer to the daily briefings as the "Five O'Clock Follies," a reflection of the validity, accuracy, and usefulness of some of the information being presented, and the inability or lack of interest of the news media to digest or seek to verify the information. *See also* **Joint U.S. Public Affairs Office.**

Five Oceans BOQ *see* **Bachelor Officer Quarters**

Five-by-Five *see* **Lima Charlie**

Five-O-Deuce *see* **502d Light Infantry Brigade**

Five-Ss *see* **POW Handling Practices**

Five-Square *see* **Lima Charlie**

Fixed Axial Weapons (FAWS) Military jargon for attached helicopter weapons systems that only fired straight ahead; axially. Weapons such as machine guns, cannons, rocket and gun pods were all fixed in position, firing straight, to the front of the helicopter. Door mounted machine and miniguns, chin mounted turret weapons, and flex guns were flexible in their field of fire and not restricted to axial fire. *See also* **XM-6 Machine Gun.**

Fixed-Wing Transport Company (FWT) Army aviation company that operated the fixed-wing, CV-2 Carribou. Through the CV-2 the Army was able to provide much of its own local field support by air. The CV-2 was an excellent short strip takeoff/landing aircraft. In '67 the Army had to give up its Carribous to the Air Force, who had complained to the JCS that the Army was usurping their mission of providing air transport and cargo support. When the Air Force took over the CV-2s in '67 they were redesignated the CV-7A and continued their STOL mission in SEA. *See also* **Avn, C-7A.**

Fixed-Wing Utility Company (FWU, Utility Airplane Company [UAC]) Army fixed-wing aircraft company that provided transport and support services. In Vietnam a variety of aircraft were assigned to the company, but most were of the U- series of light transports: U-1, U-6, U-7, etc. The fixed-wing transport company was also known as a "Utility Airplane Company," UAC. *See also* **Avn.**

Flagellated Protozoan *see* **Ho Chi Minh's Revenge**

Flags... VC—Red (top half), blue (bottom half), gold (yellow) star in center. NVA—Solid red with gold star in center. RVN—Solid yellow with three red horizontal stripes through its center. *See also* **When They're Not Red...**

Flak *see* **Antiaircraft Guns**

Flak Apron Protective apron worn by some U.S. soldiers in Vietnam operating in heavily booby-trapped areas. The flak apron was boot length and secured around the waist by a belt. It wrapped around the back of the legs providing them and the groin area some protection from shrapnel. The apron was heavy and awkward, reducing mobility, and was seldom worn by troops in the field. It was primarily used by bomb disposal teams attempting to defuse enemy mines or booby traps. *See also* **Flak Jacket.**

Flak Birds (Flak Suppression) Group of aircraft assigned the task of enemy ground flak suppression. The group accompanied a larger strike formation and was responsible for knocking out troublesome AA implacements around the assigned target.

Flak Burst *see* **Cotton Balls**

Flak Happy *see* **Flip Out**

Flak Jacket (Flak Vest, M-1952 Body Armor) Army sleeveless armored vest designed to stop shrapnel wounds to the chest, back and stomach. 8.5 pounds in weight, with a zippered or string tied front, the ballistic nylon vest was totally useless against rifle and machine gun rounds. A standard issue item in Vietnam, most field troops left them at their base camps because of their added weight and lack of bullet protection. Heavier armor vests were available but were seldom worn by field troops. The Marines had a heavier version of the flak jacket called the M-1955. *See also* **Body Armor, M-1955 Flak Jacket, Flak Apron.**

Flak Suppression *see* **Flak Birds**

Flak Vest *see* **Flak Jacket**

Flaky *see* **Crazy**

Flameout Engine failure of a jet aircraft; the failure of the normal mechanics of combustion. The reason for the failure could be from battle damage, running out of fuel, or during a high altitude climb when the air thins to the point that it no longer supports engine combustion (over 55,000 feet). Bat-tle damage could include fuel line blockages, blocked air intakes, electrical ignition failure, etc. Flameouts in Vietnam were usually fatal for the aircraft, but survivable by the pilot.

Flamethrower *see* **M-2A17, M-132, M-67A3**

Flaming Dart I & II *see* **Operation Flaming Dart**

Flank (Flanker, Flanking Element) Left and or right sides of a formation, fortification, or position, with the front of the body facing the enemy. Flankers were men or elements of a unit assigned to the left and or right sides of the main body. The elements on the flank provided security for the main body, engaging an enemy force attempting to move around and attack the main body from the sides or the rear. A "flanking element" could also be used in an attack, attempting to move around the main enemy body, or front, to attack from the sides and or the rear.

Flank Speed Nautical term meaning "full" speed.

FLAR *see* **SLAR**

Flare Launcher *see* **LAU-74A Flare Launcher**

Flare Ship *see* **Flares**

Flares (Flare Ship, Moonshine, Smokey-the-Bear) Magnesium based pyrotechnic devices used for illumination and signaling. Illumination flares were artillery or air delivered, suspended in air with a small parachute. Early in the war the Army experimented with helicopters as flare ships, but because of their limited loiter time they were not used; instead the fixed-wing SC-47 became the standard. Air Force AC-47, AC-119 and AC-130 gunships later replaced the SC-47 flare ship and were able to remain airborne over trouble spots dropping million-candle power flares and firing on enemy positions. A flare ship was sometimes nicknamed "moonshine" or "Smokey-the-Bear." *See also* **Trip Flare, Aerial Flares, Hand Flares, AC-47, AC-130, Night Angel, Illumination Rounds; Grenades, LAU-7, Illumination, Magnesium Flares.**

Flaring *see* **Rotor Wash**

Flash *see* **Beret Flash**

Flechette (Canister Round, Beehive

Round, Fletchettes) Tank, rocket, or artillery round filled with finned, steel darts, fired point-blank into enemy concentrations. A highly effective antipersonnel round at close range. Flechette is French for dart. Depending on the caliber of the round, each shell contained 1,300–90,000 of the 1–3 inch long darts. The shells were sometimes loaded with 1,200–1,500 buckshot instead of the darts. Flechette rounds were also available for the 12-gauge shotgun, M-79 grenade launcher and the 2.75-inch rocket. *See also* **2.75-inch Flechette Rocket, M-546 Beehive Round, Shotgun Flechette, M-576 Canister Round, M-551 ARV.**

Flechette Rocket *see* **2.75-inch Flechette Rocket**

Flechette Round, M-79 *see* **M-576**

Flechette, Shotgun *see* **Shotgun Flechette**

Fleet Marine Force, Pacific (FMFPAC) Command element for all U.S. Marine units operating in the Pacific region. The commander of FMFPAC reported to CINCPAC. *See also* **CINCPAC.**

Fleet Post Office *see* **Army Post Office**

Fletchettes *see* **Flechette**

Flex Guns *see* **XM-6 Machine Gun**

Flight U.S. Air Force designation for a 3–5 aircraft group with a similar mission or function. Generally four flights to a squadron. *See also* **Wing, Tactical Fighter Squadron.**

Flight Line Air base parking area reserved for flight ready aircraft.

Flight Pay Additional pay received by U.S. pilots and flight crews on active flight status. A minimum number of flight hours were required each month for an individual to maintain his flight status, and the associated extra pay.

Flip Flops *see* **Rubber Thongs**

Flip Out (Crack Up, Flak Happy, Combat Crazy) Slang for mental instability. For some Americans the stress of combat in Vietnam was too much to bear. When a soldier could no longer maintain his mental or emotional balance he broke down. Each individual handled the breakdown differently. Some became withdrawn, unreachable empty shells; others would throw all caution to the wind, acting recklessly; still others would just fall to pieces and be no use in combat or at anything else. The GIs had various names for it, but officially, in Vietnam, it was called combat fatigue. *See also* **Combat Fatigue.**

FLIR (Forward Looking Infrared Sensor) Aircraft mounted, forward looking infrared sensing systems that create a video image based on a target's thermal qualities. The FLIR was used on some Army helicopters and Navy/Air Force surveillance/reconnaissance aircraft in conjunction with other systems used to detect enemy movement at night. The system used by the Army in its INFANT helicopter system was designated the AN/AAQ-5; it weighed more than 200 pounds, and was attached to the helicopter's nose. Air Force and Navy systems were used extensively for night truck-busting missions along the Ho Chi Minh Trail. *See also* **Infrared, SLAR, NOD, Black Spot, INFANT.**

Floating Mines *see* **Limpet Mine**

Floating Rice Variety of rice that was grown on the open flood plains of IV Corps. Normally rice was grown in a paddy surrounded by low dikes, the water used to grow the rice kept at a uniform level. Floating rice was able to adapt to any water level and was commonly grown in the flat flood regions of the Delta where the water levels fluctuated with the tides, seasons and the rains.

Flop Hat *see* **Jungle Hat**

Flotation Bladder Assembly *see* **5-Quart Bladder**

Flower Child *see* **Hippie**

Flower Power Division *see* **9th Infantry Division**

Flower Power Patch Through the 9th Infantry Division's colorful patch the unit acquired several nicknames: Flower Power, Psychedelic Cookie, and Bloody Asshole. The patch was round with a dark green border and background. An eight-pointed (octofoil) leaf design filled the center of the patch. The upper half of the octofoil design was red and the lower half was dark blue.

In the center of the patch was a solid white circle. *See also* **9th Infantry Division.**

Floyd *see* **FSB Floyd**

FLR *see* **Stand-To**

Fly Catcher *see* **Project Flycatcher**

Flyboys (Zoomies, Air Force Personnel, Fighter Pilots, Fighter Jocks, Jet Jockeys) Grunt's reference to Air Force personnel, aircrews in particular. Jet aircraft pilots were also referred to as Zoomies, Wing Wipes, Flyboys, and Fighter Jock(ey)s.

Flying Artillery Nickname for the B-52s that bombed targets in conjunction with friendly ground operations. B-52 bombing accuracy was greatly increased in '65 with the introduction of computer/radar guided bomb runs as furnished by Combat Skyspot. The increased bombing accuracy allowed the B-52s to be used in direct support of ground troops. Several B-52s were kept on alert at their base on Guam to respond to tactical needs, as opposed to an assigned bombing mission. A flight of six B-52s could bomb a path 1km wide and 2kms long, from an altitude so high their approach couldn't be heard from the ground. Such a flight could deposit more than 360,000 pounds of bombs on a target area in one pass. *See also* **B-52, Combat Skyspot.**

Flying Banana *see* **CH-21**

Flying Boat *see* **P-5**

Flying Boxcar *see* **C-119**

Flying Brick *see* **F-4**

Flying Bubble *see* **OH-13**

Flying Butterknife Nickname for the 173d Airborne Brigade based on the unit's distinctive patch. The top and bottom of the patch was rounded and bordered in white. On a dark blue background a large white wing held a red bayonet. Attached at the top of the patch was a dark blue, crescent shaped tab; embroidered in white on the tab was the word "Airborne." *See also* **173d Airborne Brigade.**

Flying Cow *see* **Bladder Bird**

Flying Crane *see* **CH-54**

Flying Dragons *see* **52d Aviation Battalion**

Flying Egg *see* **OH-6**

Flying Helmets *see* **APH-5, SPH-3 Helmet**

Flying Horses *see* **Helicopter**

Flying Minimums *see* **Minimums**

Flying Nuns Nickname for nuns from the Catholic convent located near Vinh Long, who, on occasion, caught rides to and from Saigon aboard U.S. Army helicopters from the base at Vinh Long.

Flying Telephone Pole *see* **Surface-to-Air-Missile**

Flying Tiger Lines *see* **Commercial Carriers**

Flying-Squad-Leader (Squad-Leaders in the Sky) Grunt's reference to a commander who directed ground units while he was airborne in a C & C helicopter; particularly, battalion commanders who tried to direct individual squads on the ground, rather than using the normal chain of command. Airborne commanders had an overview of ground operations but could not always see what was actually happening to the troops on the ground. This sometimes led to the airborne commander overriding the ground commander's orders which further added to the confusion of the battle. In some instances "airborne commanders" were "stacked" above a battle; the battalion CO would be airborne, above him would be the brigade CO, and above him would be the division CO. *See also* **Command and Control, Christmas Tree ID, Battalion RIF.**

FM 31-18 LRRP Manual *see* **Ranger's Bible**

FM-Field Manual *see* **Field Manual**

FMFPAC *see* **Fleet Marine Force, Pacific**

FN FAL *see* **L1A1 SLR**

FN GP35 *see* **L9A1 Pistol**

FNG *see* **New Troop**

FO *see* **Forward Observer**

FOs *see* **Fragmented Orders, Forward Observer**

FOB 1-4 *see* **Forward Operating Base**

FOD *see* **Foreign Object Damage**

Fodding *see* **Foreign Object Damage**

FOF *see* Field of Fire

Fog Oil *see* XM-52 Smoker

Folding Fin Aerial Rockets *see* XM-159C Rocket

Foley Bag (Catheter Bottles) A foley bag was a plastic bag attached to a catheter tube used to collect fluids draining from the body. It was used to drain various body cavities but was most often used for cathetered urine drainage. American medical units in Vietnam used empty medical bottles for drainage because of severe shortages of the foley bags.

Fonda, Jane (Hanoi Jane, American Imperialist Air Raiders) American actress who became an anti–Vietnam War activist in the late sixties. She was originally remembered by many GIs for her nude scenes in the movie *Barbarella,* but in '72 the GIs remembered her for her pro–NVN propaganda trip to Hanoi. Journalists nicknamed her "Hanoi Jane" when she went to Hanoi and spoke to selected American POWs and toured buildings damaged by U.S. air strikes. She posed for pictures wearing an NVA helmet while seated on an NVA AA gun used to fire on U.S. aircraft, and reportedly urged the NVA gunners to shoot down "American imperialist air raiders." She later married antiwar activist Tom Hayden. Many Vietnam veterans remain bitter over her Hanoi visit and the propaganda boost it gave the North Vietnamese. *See also* Visits to Hanoi, Vietnam Veterans Against the War.

Foo Gas *see* Fou Gas

Food *see* Chop-Chop

Footprint of the American Chicken *see* Fuck-Peace Sign

Footprintless Boots *see* Special Boots

FOR *see* Fellowship of Reconciliation

For Nation, Forget Self Slogan used by the NVA to spur on their soldiers. NVN used nationalistic zeal as a driving force to push its soldiers, and people to victory. Under Ho Chi Minh, NVN was willing to fight as long as necessary, regardless of cost, to rid Vietnam of all foreigners and place a unified North and South Vietnam under the communist flag, and Hanoi's rule.

Force Engineer Battalion *see* Division Engineer Battalion

Force Recon (Marine Force Recon) U.S. Marine special reconnaissance force, equivalent to the Army's Special Forces/Rangers/LRRPs and the Navy SEALs. Force Recon operated in small groups conducting intelligence gathering and raiding missions in enemy territory. The Marine recon units operated throughout I Corps, sometimes crossing the border into Laos and North Vietnam. In addition to their recon duties Force Recon served as advisors with I Corps CIDGs, operated with MACV-SOG and conducted air strike targeting missions against the enemy. *See also* Bird Watcher Missions, Stingray Missions.

Forced Landing, Helicopter *see* Autorotation

Forced March Military method of infantry movement characterized by quick marching or movement with an almost total lack of rest stops, resulting in the troops arriving at their destination in an exhausted or nearly exhausted state. Not a popular formation among the troops. In Vietnam forced marches were used by U.S. units attempting to reach sister units that were trapped or pinned down by the enemy. For such relief missions the usual complaints heard from the troops were minimal. *See also* Hump(ing).

Forced Relocation *see* Restructuring

Forced Rural Resettlement *see* New Economic Zones

Forced Urbanization (Forced-Draft Urbanization) Description of the forced relocation programs in Vietnam. The Strategic Hamlet and New Life Hamlet programs were designed to relocate rural Vietnamese peasants to new fortified, government protected hamlets in an effort to remove them from the dangers of the VC. The programs often involved the forced relocation of the peasants to refugee camps, isolating them from their ancestral homes and the land they farmed and forcing them to find other means of livelihood in the "cardboard and tin" cities that were the refugee camps. The peasants were forced into a modern environment and the urban ills associated with it. *See also* Strategic Hamlet

Program, Fishes-and-the-Sea, Operation Sunrise.

Forced-Draft Urbanization *see* **Forced Urbanization**

Forces Armees Nationale Khmer (FANK, Vietnam Individual Training Group, VITG) Khmer National Armed Forces, Cambodian army troops of the Khmer Republic (Republique Khymer): fighting the communist guerrillas of the Khmer Rouge. FANK units were trained in counterguerrilla operations by a special unit of the U.S. 1st Special Forces Group. Some Khmer troops were trained in Vietnam by the USSF Vietnam Individual Training Group (VITG) which was organized in '70. The program was deactivated in December '72. FANK forces continued to be supplied and supported by the U.S. until NVA-backed communist Khmer Rouge troops seized Phnom Penh in early '75. *See also* **Khmer Rouge.**

Ford, President Gerald R. Vice-President Ford became the 38th President of the United States when Richard Nixon resigned the Presidency in August '74. In March '75 after the NVA began their Final Offensive in South Vietnam, Ford requested one billion dollars from Congress to aid the South Vietnamese in their fight against the NVA. The Democratically controlled Congress granted 300 million dollars to be used only for humanitarian aid and the evacuation of U.S. personnel from SVN. In May '75 Cambodian communist forces captured the U.S. merchant ship *Mayaguez*; Ford ordered the Marines to retake the vessel and rescue the crew, even though the Cambodians had agreed to voluntarily release the ship and its crew. *See also* **SS Mayaguez.**

Ford *see* **Medic**

Ford Clemency Review Board (Shamnesty Board) Review board established during the Ford Administration to grant a form of amnesty to Vietnam AWOLs who surrendered to the military. If an AWOL soldier turned himself in the board could waive arrest, and issue the man an Undesirable Discharge. If the man performed 24 months of alternative service, the UD could be upgraded to a Clemency Discharge (CD). Veterans groups considered the board a sham because it did not address the problem of the Vietnam veteran who had fought in

the war before going AWOL (deserted). The board's UDs and CDs were still less-than-honorable discharges; "bad paper" in the eyes of would-be employers. The board was nicknamed the "Shamnesty Board." After much public pressure the UDs of wounded and decorated veterans were upgraded to General or Honorable Discharges. The board was also empowered to review the cases of draft evaders, who left the country during the war, and could grant them a "full pardon." *See also* **Bad Paper, Discharges.**

Ford Lynx II Armored Car *see* **Armored Cars**

Foreign Aid to North Vietnam *see* **Reconstruction Aid**

Foreign Object Damage (Fodding, FOD) Damage to aircraft of a noncombat nature. Debris on the runway could be sucked into the engine, or kicked-up by the aircraft's wheels causing damage to the fuselage. Birds sucked into engine intakes were also considered FOD. In Vietnam there were instances of friendly aircraft being sabotaged by our own troops. Such incidents took place toward the end of the war, and were attributed to the overall decline of morale within some military units in Vietnam. The Air Force and Navy referred to such sabotage as "fodding."

Foreign Service Officers (FSO) U.S. civilian personnel that worked under the AID program in South Vietnam. FSOs operated in the larger towns in an attempt to aid the rural populace with a variety of agricultural, social and economic programs. *See also* **U.S. Agency for International Development, Pacification, Spooks.**

Foreign Service Reserve Officer *see* **Spook**

Forest of Assassins *see* **Rung Sat**

Forest of Darkness *see* **U Minh Forest**

Forest Penetrator *see* **Penetrator**

Forrestal *see* **USS Forrestal**

Fort Campbell One of the U.S. Army training facilities during the Vietnam War. Fort Campbell was located in Kentucky.

Fort De Russy Army's Hawaiian point of entry and departure for Vietnam assigned R & R troops. The base was located near the beach at Waikiki, on the island of Oahu, southeast of Honolulu, Hawaii.

Fort Jacks *see* **Fort Jackson**

Fort Jackson (Fort Jacks) One of the Army's Basic Training facilities during the Vietnam War. Fort Jackson was located in South Carolina.

Fort Leavenworth (Leavenworth, Command and General Staff College, CG College) Home of the Army's Command and General Staff College, located in Kansas, for the purpose of higher military education of general officers and their staff (colonels) relating to command administration and policy. Leavenworth also served as home of the Army/Air Force maximum security military prison, formally known as the "U.S. Disciplinary Barracks."

Fort Leonardwood *see* **Lost-in-the-Woods**

Fort Rucker (Army Helicopter Flight School, Fort Wolters) Army preliminary helicopter flight training took place at Fort Wolters, Texas. Advanced flight training was conducted at Fort Rucker, Alabama. Helicopter flight training was 32 weeks long, roughly four months at each flight school. Preliminary flight school was conducted in an atmosphere similar to basic training, i.e., harassment, inspections, regimentation, etc. *See also* **TH-55A Helicopter.**

Fort Sam *see* **Fort Sam Houston**

Fort Sam Houston (Fort Sam) Fort Sam Houston, San Antonio, Texas, one of the U.S. Army's primary training facilities. The Army's medic and nurse training courses were conducted at Fort Sam. During the Vietnam War, large numbers of newly graduated medics were routinely assigned to Vietnam to gain their experience on the battlefield. Nurses usually worked at other Army facilities for 3–12 months before volunteering for duty in Vietnam.

Fort Sill U.S. Army base located in Oklahoma, primary field artillery training facility during the Vietnam War.

Fort Wolters *see* **Fort Rucker**

Forty *see* **Grenade Launchers, 40mm**

Forward Air Controller (FAC) Airborne observer who controlled and coordinated aircraft and artillery attacks against ground targets. FACs would identify enemy targets and, if possible, mark them with smoke rockets, then direct strike aircraft. FACs also worked in conjunction with friendly ground units directing and adjusting artillery fires. Except for the smoke rockets FACs were unarmed, slow moving, light observation aircraft. Through most of the war FACs used single engine O-1, and twin engine OV-2 and OV-10 aircraft. In addition to target spotting, the FACs did after strike, BDAs. A FAC crew consisted of the pilot and a radio operator/observer, but often FAC pilots flew alone. *See also* **Tactical Air Coordinators, Commando Saber Missions.**

Forward Air Controller, Ground Marine Forward Air Controllers, assigned at the battalion and regimental headquarters level, who coordinated air strike activities from the ground. When necessary, the ground FACs would accompany combat units in the field, adjusting and directing air strikes in support of the units. Ground FACs sometimes used ground based radar beacons (RABFAC) to direct strike aircraft. The beacon fixed the FACs position and the air strike could easily be adjusted accordingly, allowing accurate strikes in bad weather or at night.

Forward Artillery Observer *see* **Forward Observer**

Forward Edge of the Battle Area (Front Line, FEBA) Military terminology for the front line, where most combat took place. In Vietnam there was no real "front line"; battles could erupt almost anywhere. The areas around the major bases were the most secure, making all the other areas possible combat zones. In Vietnam the only real distinction between the "rear" and the "front" was the difference in the attitudes of the various levels of command and the creature comforts available to the troops. *See also* **Boonies, Sitdown.**

Forward Fire Support Base *see* **Fire Support Base, Artillery Barge**

Forward Looking Airborne Radar *see* **SLAR**

Forward Looking Infrared Sensor *see* **FLIR**

Forward Observer (FO, Forward

Artillery Observer, FAO) Artillery liaison officer who accompanied infantry units in the field, directing and adjusting artillery fires in support of those units. In U.S. infantry units FOs were normally assigned at the company level, but often accompanied smaller units on special missions. With an FO present the unit commander was able to concentrate his efforts on the battle at hand. The unit commander assumed the FO duties if the observer was out of action.

Forward Operating Base (FOB) Small base set up forward of a larger base, used as a jump-off point for ground operations into an enemy area. Such bases were moved frequently in an effort to maintain contact with the enemy. FOBs were self-contained, providing support for units operating from the base and usually provided limited artillery support, similar to a fire base, but more mobile. MACV-SOG operations were carried out from forward bases located at Ban Me Thuot (FOB-1), Kontum (FOB-2), Khe Sanh (FOB-3) and Da Nang (FOB-4). In '67 the MACV-SOG FOBs were consolidated into three Command and Control Centers, which performed the same function. *See also* **MACV-SOG Command and Control, Fire Support Base.**

Forward Rearm and Refuel Point (REARF, FREARF) Fuel and ammunition supply points set up close to an operation or action. In Vietnam forward REARF points were used to increase the ability of helicopters to support ground operations. The FREARF points reduced the turnaround time required by helicopters. Normally helicopters involved in combat would return to their base when they ran low on fuel and ammo. The bases were typically located 30 minutes to an hour from the more remote areas where combat often flared. Establishing a FREARF point greatly reduced the helicopters' turnaround time allowing them to remain longer on-station. FREARF points were usually established at fire bases or LZs near the action, and were only temporary. *See also* **Hot–Turn Around, Loiter Time.**

Forward Support Area (FSA) Reference to the area supported by a forward operating base. The FOB was established to provide logistic and artillery support for friendly units operating in the immediate area of the base. *See also* **Fire Support Base,**

Forward Operating Base.

Fou Gas (Fou Gasse, Phougas, Foo Gas, Homemade Napalm, Fu-gas, Jellied-Gasoline) Fifty-five gallon drum filled with a mixture of gasoline, diesel fuel or aviation fuel, and a chemical thickener, dispersed by a stick of dynamite or C-4 explosive and ignited by a flare or themite grenade. Sometimes the "jellied-gasoline" mixture consisted of gas and laundry soap. When exploded, the contents of the drum were sprayed across a large area (80–100 meters), into attacking troops, similar to napalm dropped from an aircraft. A flare or grenade ignited the mixture. The homemade napalm was used as part of defensive fortifications around some U.S. base camps and was especially effective for hilltop defenses where gravity enhanced the spreading effect of the jellied-gasoline. *See also* **Napalm.**

Fou Gasse *see* **Fou Gas**

Foul Deck *see* **Operation Foul Deck**

Four Corners (Di An, Little Appalachia) Nickname given to the Vietnamese town of Di An by troops of the 1st Infantry Division. Di An served as 1st Infantry Division Headquarters and was located 12kms northeast of Saigon, about halfway between Saigon and Bien Hoa. Di An also served as the location of the U.S. Army's MAT school that trained the South Vietnamese who in turn trained RF/PF forces in the field. The term "Four Corners," like "Dogpatch," was used by many GIs in Vietnam to mean any shantytown near an American base. 1st Inf Div HQs was also nicknamed "Little Appalachia" because of the initial poor living conditions at the base camp. *See also* **Dogpatch.**

Four Fs *see* **R & R**

Four No's South Vietnam's President Thieu was adamantly opposed to any peace agreements that included the Viet Cong. He had a policy of four "no's" that expressed his view of the communist Viet Cong and dealings with North Vietnam: no political concessions, no territorial concessions, no commercial or trade exchanges, and no recognition of the communist party in SVN. Thieu was eventually pressured by the U.S. to conceed to a coalition style government with the Viet Cong and acceptance of territorial acquisitions made by the NVA in SVN prior to the '73 cease-fire. *See also* **Paris Accords.**

Four Party Joint Military Commission (FPJMC, JMC, Joint Military Commission)   Commission established by the Paris Peace Accords in January '73 to oversee the withdrawal of all foreign combat troops from SVN, monitor the cease-fire, oversee the exchange of prisoners, and resolve status of U.S. MIAs. After the withdrawal of U.S. combat troops in March '73 the commission was disbanded and replaced by the FPJMT. The four parties of the commission were the U.S., SVN, NVN and the Viet Cong. The commission flew an orange flag with the number 4 printed on it and members of the commission wore a similar orange armband. The FPJMC never resolved the question of U.S. MIAs and the cease-fire was ignored by the VC, NVN and SVN. *See also* **Four Part Joint Military Team, War of the Flags, Landgrab Campaign.**

Four Party Joint Military Team (FPJMT) Established March '73 as part of the Paris Peace Accords to resolve the status of American MIAs during the Vietnam War. The team had no real power to force the NVA/VC to cooperate and disbanded with the fall of Vietnam in April '75. *See also* **Four Party Joint Military Commission.**

Four Point Twos   *see*   **M-30 4.2-inch Mortar**

Four Ss (Shit, Shine, Shower & Shave) Basics of American military hygiene.

Four-Deuce   *see*   **M-30   4.2-inch Mortar, M-106 Four-Deuce**

Four-Holer   *see*   **Latrine**

Fourth Estate   Old nickname for journalist or journalism as a profession.

Fourth Infantry Division   *see*   **4th Infantry Division**

Fourth Marine Regiment   *see*   **4th Marine Regiment**

Foxhole (Individual Fighting Position, Titty-Deep, Fighting Hole)   Infantry defensive position consisting of a hole or depression dug in the ground. The foxhole might be big enough for one man or perhaps several. The military has extensive documentation on the proper way to dig such a hole. In Vietnam, GIs dug fresh foxholes at their NDPs, refilling the holes before they departed the area in an attempt to deny them

to the enemy. In the Central Highlands the ground was so hard that many times foxholes dug at an NDP were shallow, or "titty-deep." GIs humping in the boonies sometimes carried sandbags with them which were used to improve their night defensive positions. On other occasions sandbags were flown in by helicopter. *See also* **Spider Hole, DePuy Foxhole, Entrenching Tool, Sandbags.**

Foxhole Convert (Converts)   A GI who became devoutly religious as a result of his combat experiences. The fear-induced-converts would "promise" God all manner of sacrifice and repentance if He spared them. The new convert usually had an antireligious attitude and was highly skeptical about the workings of God as put forth by the Chaplain Corps. Foxhole conversions peaked during heavy enemy attacks, but many of the converts forgot their "promises" to God when the threat was over and returned to their old ways until the fear struck again. *See also* **God Squad, Battlefield Religion.**

Foxhole Strength   *see*   **Paddy Strength**

Foxtrot Foxtrot   *see*   **Firefly**

Foxtrot Mike Radio   *see*   **AM/FM Radio**

FPJMC   *see*   **Four Party Joint Military Commission**

FPJMT   *see*   **Four Party Joint Military Team**

FPO   *see*   **Army Post Office**

Fractured Cross   *see*   **Operation Fractured Cross Alpha**

Frag(ging)   Anonymous act of using a hand grenade or other explosive in an attempt to kill a fellow soldier. Officers and senior NCOs were the most common targets of fragging, but racially and drug motivated incidents against enlisted men also took place. The targeted officer/NCO was viewed by his attacker as either incompetent, cruel or overzealous in his leadership duties, or harassed the men below him. The grenade was typically thrown into the target's sleeping quarters while he slept. As a warning, a smoke grenade would sometimes be tossed or the safety pin from a hand grenade left in a conspicuous place. If the offending officer/

NCO didn't change his ways or get transferred out of the unit, his men would frag him. Fraggings became more frequent in the Army after '69 as the U.S. war effort tapered off. In addition to the fraggings, late in the war there were several highly suspicious incidents of an officer/NCO being the only casualty during a patrol in which no other members of the patrol were wounded, and no enemy body count or captured weapons were part of the incident. Investigations indicated the dead officer/NCO had not been regarded very highly by the members of the platoon, and on previous occasions had unnecessarily or recklessly endangered their lives. The Marines suffered fewer fragging incidents because of tighter control procedures. See also Operation Freeze, Lifers.

Fragged see **Frag(ging), Fragmented Orders**

Fragmentary Orders see **Fragmented Orders**

Fragmentation Suit see **Special Flak Suit**

Fragmented Orders (Fragged, Fragmentary Orders, FOs)   The short or abbreviated form of a standing order, typically associated with aircraft mission assignments. The standing or current order could involve a general mission, such as the interdiction of enemy supply lines. The "fragged" order would indicate the specific target or mission, for a specific attack group. Sometimes aircraft en route to one target in Vietnam were "fragged" to a more urgent target. Frag orders contained information regarding the number of aircraft assigned to the target, course data (speed, altitudes, routing), rescue and command and control information as well as the type of ordnance and what to expect in the way of enemy defenses around the target.

Frags see **Grenades, Fragmentation** or **U.S. Frags**

Frags, U.S. see **U.S. Frags**

Francis Marion see **Operation Francis Marion**

Francis, Connie see **Hope, Bob**

Franklin D. Roosevelt see **USS Franklin D. Roosevelt**

Freak see **Doper, Radio Frequency**

FREARF see **Forward Rearm and Refuel Point**

FREE (Sugar Reports, World News)   Soldiers mailing letters home from Vietnam were not required to use stamps on their outbound letters; instead they simply wrote "FREE" where the stamp would normally go. Mail from home was nicknamed "Sugar Reports" and the "World News." See also Dear John Letter.

Free Khmer see **Khmer Serei, Khmer Issarak**

Free Love see **Hippie**

Free Speech Movement (FSM)   A September '64 student movement led by Mario Savio to protest the University of California, Berkeley's banning of student political activity on campus, viewed as an infringement of their right of free speech. The confrontations between university authorities and the student body resulted in hundreds of arrests. Eventually the school acceded to students' demands for freedom of political expression, grudgingly acknowledging their rights. The movement demonstrated the power such groups could have on altering policy and public opinion, further strengthening the power of other antiwar and civil rights groups.

Free Time see **Ghost Time**

Free World Military Forces (FWF, FWMF, Free World Forces, Free World Military Assistance Forces, FWMAF)   Name for the group of countries which provided military aid and support to SVN during the war years '59 to '75. Forty-three countries participated in the economic, humanitarian and or military support of South Vietnam. The countries that provided combat forces to aid the SVN government were the U.S., Korea, Thailand, Australia, Philippines, New Zealand, Taiwan and Spain, in order of total combat personnel. Excluding the U.S., the South Koreans, Australians and Thais provided the largest number of combat forces. The FWF was also referred to as the Free World Military Assistance Forces (FWMAF). See also "Turtle Monument" for the complete list of countries that provided economic/military assistance to South Vietnam.

Free World Forces see **Free World Military Forces**

Free World Military Assistance Forces *see* **Free World Military Forces**

Free-Fire-Zone (No-Fire-Zone, War Zones, FFZ) Designated area in which no clearance was required to fire on any target in the area. Any buildings, cattle or civilians could be fired on without restriction. Anyone, other than friendly military personnel, in such a zone was suspected as enemy, and subject to attack. Attacks outside free-fire-zones normally required clearance from higher headquarters and approval by the Vietnamese before a target could be fired on. The use of free-fire-zones was viewed by some VNW critics as the indiscriminate use of American fire power against innocent civilians. The zones were created in areas of known enemy base camps and remote areas. Some villagers were relocated from their homes in VC controlled areas to relocation camps and the vacated area declared a free-fire-zone. The villagers often sought to return to their ancestral lands. The military believed it was necessary to cut the VC off from his source of food, manpower and support. Artillery would be randomly fired (H & I Fire) into free-fire-zones in an effort to keep the enemy off guard. No-fire-zones were all other areas that required clearance before they could be fired on: U.S. troops had to wait until the enemy fired on them before they could "request" permission to fire back. Free-fire-zones were sometimes referred to as "war zones." *See also* **Fish-and-the-Sea, Strategic Hamlet Program, Restructuring, Rules of Engagement.**

Free-the-Army *see* **Fuck-the-Army**

Free-Tubing *see* **M-19 60mm Mortar**

Freedom and Democracy *see* **Tu Do Dan Chu**

Freedom Bird (Big Bird, Big Iron Birds) Reference by U.S. troops to any aircraft that returned them home, to the States, at the end of their tour of duty in Vietnam. Aircraft, chartered commercial and military, were used to transport American troops to and from South Vietnam. *See also* **Commercial Carriers.**

Freedom Deal *see* **Operation Menu**

Freedom Fighter *see* **F-5 Tiger**

Freedom Now, Withdraw Now 1960s antiwar protest slogan.

Freedom Porch Bravo *see* **Bullet Shot I-V Deployments**

Freedom Train CIA nickname for the Air America flights that evacuated American and Vietnamese personnel from Da Nang in late March, just prior to the fall of Da Nang to the communists on March 30, 1975.

Freedom Train *see* **Operation Freedom Train**

Freeze *see* **Operation Freeze**

French Colonialist *see* **Colons**

French Expeditionary Corps (FEC) French military force that provided security for French colonies. The first expeditionary force arrived in Vietnam in 1880. After WWII a large French force was sent to Vietnam to reclaim the former French colony from the Japanese. It was this expeditionary force that Ho Chi Minh and the Viet Minh battled for independence in the early fifties. The FEC primarily consisted of French nationals and European volunteers. Southeast Asian indigenous troops (Cambodians, Laos, Vietnamese) and a variety of others composed the bulk of the French Union Forces. At their peak the FEC numbered 178,000 men and the French Union Forces (FUF) numbered 339,000 men. Between '46 and '54 an estimated 90,000 French troops died in Vietnam. *See also* **French Union Forces.**

French Indochina *see* **Indochina**

French Leave (Desertion) A kind phrase used to describe desertions by some South Vietnamese forces from outpost and bases just prior to an enemy attack. The soldiers taking "French leave" would disappear or "wander off" the night before an NVA/VC attack. The sudden disappearance of Vietnamese nationals also occurred at U.S. installations where Vietnamese civilians were employed. Often before a major enemy attack the civilian workers would leave their jobs early or just not show up for work. Usually within 24 hours of such a demonstration the facility was hit by a major enemy attack. *See also* **Desertion, Deserters.**

French Union Forces (FUF) French forces that fought in Indochina, '45 to '54. The force mostly consisted of native Vietnamese and some Cambodians and Laotians that fought the Viet Minh with French Expeditionary Corps in Indochina. The FUF fought the Viet Minh who were seeking independence from French colonial rule. The South Vietnamese units which fought with the French were not antiindependence, but did not want to fall under the domination of the communist-led Viet Minh; instead they sought a democratic form of independence from the French. *See also* **French Expeditionary Corps.**

Freq *see* **Radio Frequency**

Frequency Modulation Radio *see* **AM/FM Radio**

Frequent Wind *see* **Operation Frequent Wind**

Fresco *see* **MiG, MiG-17**

FRI *see* **Friendly Initiated Incident**

Friction Detonator *see* **Lucifer Match**

Friendly Fires (Incontinent Ordnance Delivery)   Any type of weapons fire received into a position from forces friendly to your own. Also referred to as "incontinent ordnance delivery." Such accidental fires into friendly positions were not uncommon in Vietnam. Mistakenly directed air strikes, artillery rounds that fell short, caused casualties. If a unit got lost or was in the wrong position it could be mistaken for the enemy and fired on by its own troops. Unit location and identification were critical factors in calling in artillery and air strikes. Safety margins for how close artillery and air strikes could be brought in to friendly positions were established to try to eliminate the effects of rounds falling short, or an air strike being slightly off target. Wounds or deaths suffered as a result of friendly fires were not included in the statistics for military casualties. Casualties from friendly fires were considered a result of nonhostile action, even though the fire could have resulted as part of a routine fire mission or as part of a defensive fire request. Fire accidents caused by ARVN artillery, troops or aircraft, inflicted on American troops were also considered "friendly fires." *See also* **Vietnam War Casualties, U.S.; KIA; WIA; Short Round; Shooting the Donut; Friendly Wounds; CGC Point Welcome.**

Friendly Initiated Incident (FRI, FRY,

Military Reporting)   Reporting procedures in the military were extensive. Officers were required to make radio and sometimes written reports on all incidents related to their unit, reports such as "After Action Report" following combat, plans for operations, casualty reports, intelligence reports, and a host of others. A system of phrases and terms littered the reports. Many reports simply amounted to a series of acronyms, times, coordinates and numbers. The FRI (pronounced FRY) indicated that the reported incident had been initiated by a friendly unit. *See also* **After Action Report.**

Friendly Wounds   Wounds received as a result of being fired on by forces friendly to your own; wounds not inflicted by enemy operated weapons. *See also* **Friendly Fires.**

Friendship *see* **Operation Platypus**

Frigging   Slang word, used in place of the word "fucking," during colorful conversations in the presence of "ladies," high ranking diplomats or military officers. "Frigging" was most often used by career NCOs in those situations where the vulgarities of military language would not be tolerated. "Frigging" and words like it were also used by those who had the need to express themselves with strong language, but avoided blatant profanity. *See also* **Fuck.**

FRITA *see* **Deserters**

Frog, The *see* **CH-46**

Froines, John *see* **Chicago 8**

Front Line *see* **Forward Edge of the Battle Area, Sitdown**

Front Unifie pour la Liberation (FULRO)   Officially the Front Unifie pour la Liberation des Races Opprimees; the Unified Front for the Liberation of Oppressed Peoples. FULRO was an anti–Vietnamese group, within SVN, with members from the Montagnard tribes, Chams and ethnic Khmers. In '65 Montagnard tribes and the GVN agreed to a temporary truce. In return, the tribes agreed to fight on the side of the GVN, under the direction of the U.S. Special Forces. The tribes fought the NVA until the fall of SVN in '75. Montagnard survivors in Vietnam are still strongly anti–Vietnamese and continue to oppose the new Vietnamese government of the SRV. *See also* **Chams.**

Front, The *see* Sitdown

Frontal Lobe *see* Give-a-Shit-Lobe

Frozen Food *see* Class I Provisions

Frozen Smile *see* Shit-Eatin'-Grin

Fruit-Salad *see* Trash

FRY *see* Friendly Initiated Incident

FSA *see* Forward Support Area

FSB *see* Fire Support Base

FSB 30 & 31   Fire support bases 30 and 31 were established during the ARVN Task Force which entered Laos during Operation Lam Son 719. The fire bases were established on small hills overlooking Highway 9. ARVN artillery pieces were deployed by helicopter to provide artillery support to the ARVN force attacking along Highway 9 from South Vietnam to Tchepone in Cambodia. Both fire bases were located in Laos about 25 and 35kms from Khe Sanh, north of Highway 9. *See also* **Operation Lam Son 719.**

FSB Anzio   One of the fire support bases of the XXIV Corps Artillery. The base was located near Phu Bai, south of Hue in I Corps. During '69, FSB Anzio was home of the 2d Battalion/138th Artillery and their 155mm self-propelled howitzers, one of the few National Guard units to serve in Vietnam. The 2d/138th Arty was from Kentucky.

FSB Apple   Apple was an Army fire support base located along Highway 1, between Xuan Loc and Long Binh, near the village of Trang Bom, Bien Hoa Province, III Corps.

FSB Balmoral   One of the Australian fire support bases located in Bien Hoa Province, III Corps. The base provided fire support for Australian operations in the area and mutual supporting fire for FSB Coral, the Aussie fire base located 5kms south of Balmoral.

FSB Bastogne   An Army fire support base used to support elements of the 101st Airborne Division during operations into the A Shau Valley. The fire base was located east of the valley in Thua Thien Province, I Corps.

FSB Berchtesgaden   Berchtesgaden was one of the temporary fire support bases

established in '68 to support Operation Somerset Plain. The operation involved elements of the 1st Cavalry, 101st Airborne, and 1st ARVN Division operating in the A Shau Valley.

FSB Birmingham (Hue Southwest)   101st Airborne fire support base located 10kms south of Hue and 20kms southwest of Phu Bai. The large FSB was also known as "Hue Southwest" and functioned as a forward supply and helicopter base for units operating in the A Shau Valley and along the Laotian border. *See also* **A Shau Valley.**

FSB Brown   Temporary fire support base established by elements of the 5th Battalion/7th Cavalry in Cambodia during the '70 Cambodian Incursion by US/ARVN forces.

FSB Burt   One of several temporary fire support bases used by the 3d Brigade/25th Infantry Division during operations in War Zone C. FSB Burt was nearly overrun during Operation Yellowstone by the 271st and 272d Viet Cong regiments. During the attack the base was defended by 2d & 3d Battalions/22d Infantry, who managed to throw back the Viet Cong attack. *See also* **Operation Yellowstone.**

FSB Castle (FSPB Castle)   Fire support and patrol base established in late '69 on May Tao Mountain, northeast of Vung Tau. The base was manned by elements of the 1st Australian Task Force which was conducting operations on the mountain. The mountain served as a major base camp for NVA/VC troops in the area. *See also* **May Tao Mountains.**

FSB Chamberlain   A temporary fire support base of the 25th Infantry Division. One of the units to man the 105mm howitzers at the base was the 2d Battalion/77th Artillery.

FSB Charlie One   Marine fire support base located 8kms north of Dong Ha, along Highway 1, in Quang Tri Province, I Corps.

FSB Coogee   Australian fire support base established in '68 about 25kms north of Bien Hoa and 5kms northeast of FSB Coral. The base was established by elements of the 1st ATF conducting operations in the area.

FSB Coral   Fire base of the 1st Australian Task Force. The base was located at

Khu Tru Mat on the Song Be River, 22kms north of Bien Hoa. A battery of 105mm howitzers provided fire support to Australian and ARVN troops in the area. *See also* **Australian Task Force.**

FSB Crook A temporary fire support base of the 25th Infantry Division located 14kms northwest of Tay Ninh City, III Corps. The base was established in '69 in a matter of hours and equipped with personnel-detecting radar and night vision scopes. Crook was purposely established on a known enemy infiltration route as bait. Elements of the 9th Viet Cong Division attacked the base which was defended by a company from the 3d Battalion/22d Infantry and two batteries of 105mm howitzers. Defenders at the base inflicted heavy casualties on the VC (more than 400 killed) while suffering only four American casualties. The NODs and radar enabled the base's guns to pinpoint the enemy and crush the attack.

FSB Cunningham *see* **Dewey Canyon Fire Bases**

FSB Dallas *see* **Dewey Canyon Fire Bases**

FSB Danger Fire support base located near Giao Duc in western Dinh Tuong Province, IV Corps. FSB Danger served as the battalion base camp for the 4th Battalion/39th Infantry, which operated as part of the 1st and 3d Brigades/9th Infantry Division. *See also* **39th Infantry Regiment, Hardcore Battalion.**

FSB Eagle's Nest Temporary fire support base established during Operation Delaware by elements of the 1st Cavalry Division in April '68. The FSB was re-occupied by elements of the 101st Airborne during Operation Somerset Plain in July '68 to support operations in the A Shau Valley. *See also* **Operation Somerset Plain, Operation Delaware.**

FSB Elliot *see* **Red Devil Road**

FSB Erskine *see* **Dewey Canyon Fire Bases**

FSB Evan One of the fire support bases established in Cambodia to provide fire support for the U.S. incursion in '70. The base was manned by elements of the 1st Battalion/12th Cavalry which was part of the 1st Cavalry Division. *See also* **Cambodian Incursion.**

FSB Fiddler's Green One of the fire support bases of the 2d Squadron/12th Cavalry. The base was located east of Saigon in the 2d/12th's area of operations.

FSB Floyd Fire support and surveillance base operated by elements of the 3d Battalion/503d Infantry/173d Airborne Brigade. The base was located at the northern end of the 506 Valley in Binh Dinh Province, II Corps. *See also* **506 Valley.**

FSB Fuller The northernmost American fire base in South Vietnam. Fuller was perched on top of a 1,800-foot mountain on the edge of the DMZ. Six 105mm howitzers were squeezed onto the narrow peak and were manned by the Army until the position was transferred to the ARVN in '72.

FSB Georgia Temporary fire support base established near the A Shau Valley to support operations by the 101st Airborne during Operation Somerset Plain in August '68. *See also* **Operation Somerset Plain.**

FSB Gold U.S. fire base located 88kms northwest of Saigon and northeast of Tay Ninh City in III Corps. The base was established in March '67 in War Zone C to support Operation Junction City. The base was manned by the 2d Battalion/77th Artillery/25th Infantry Division. Five battalions of the 272d VC Regiment attempted to overrun the base in a daylight attack. Enemy units entered the defensive perimeter, nearly overrunning the base. Defenders, using beehive rounds, supporting artillery, and air strikes managed to hold onto Gold until relief forces from the 22d Infantry and the 34th Armored were able to turn back the attack.

FSB Kelly *see* **LZ Kelly**

FSB Klaw II Fire support base established in Kien Hoa Province in '68 to provide fire support for operations of the 2d Brigade/9th Infantry Division. The base was manned by C Battery/3d Battalion/34th Artillery and directly supported the 3d Battalion/47th Infantry operations in the area. *See also* **Tiger's Lair.**

FSB Maureen One of the fire bases operated by the 101st Airborne Division near Hue, I Corps.

FSB Moore One of the 9th Infantry

Division's fire bases providing support for riverine operations in the Delta. The fire base was located just west of Dong Tam and east of Cai Be in Dinh Tuong Province, IV Corps.

FSB Myron   Temporary fire support base established during the '70 Cambodian Incursion providing support to US/ARVN units. Myron was manned by elements of the 2d Battalion/12th Cavalry/1st Cavalry Division.

FSB Nancy   Army fire base located near Phu Bai, south of Hue in I Corps. The fire base was the operational home of the 1st Battalion/39th Artillery. Their batteries consisted of self-propelled 175mm guns and 8-inch howitzers. The battalion was part of XXIV Corps Artillery, but it operated under control of the 101st Airborne Division in the I Corps area. *See also* **1st/39th Arty.**

FSB Nuts   A temporary fire support base of the 1st Battalion/327th Infantry/101st Airborne Division.

FSB Oasis   Army fire support base established in the Central Highlands, 25kms southwest of Pleiku. The base provided support to elements of the 1st Cavalry, and the 4th and 25th Infantry divisions operating along the border during Operation Paul Revere. *See also* **Operation Paul Revere, TF Walker.**

FSB Picardy   One of the 1st Infantry Division's fire support bases located north of Saigon. The base was manned by elements of the 28th Infantry Regiment.

FSB Razor   *see*   **Dewey Canyon Fire Bases**

FSB Rendezvous   Fire support base of the 101st Airborne Division located near Phu Bai in I Corps. The base supported operations of the 2d Battalion/327th Infantry that operated in the area in '71.

FSB Riley   *see*   **Dewey Canyon Fire Bases**

FSB Ripcord   Army fire support base located on the edge of the A Shau Valley. Ripcord was manned by elements of the 101st Airborne Division which suffered heavy casualties while defending the base. The NVA made a concerted effort to wipe Ripcord out, nearly overrunning the base in July '70. Under heavy pressure from the NVA, Ripcord was abandoned.

FSB Sheraton Rock Pile   *see*   **Rock Pile, The**

FSB Son   Temporary fire support base established in July '68 to support Operation Somerset Plain in Thua Thien Province. The fire base was located west of FSB Birmingham and was manned by elements of the 2d Battalion/320th Artillery which was part of the 101st Airborne Division. The fire base provided support for operations into the A Shau Valley. *See also* **Operation Somerset Plain.**

FSB Sophia   Fire support base established by elements of the ARVN Task Force during their '71 Laos Incursion, Operation Lam Son 719. FSB Sophia was located in Laos about 50kms west of Khe Sanh and south of Highway 9 overlooking the town of Tchepone, an NVA logistics center on the Ho Chi Minh Trail.

FSB Tempest   A temporary fire support base established in the hills near Duc Pho in '67. The base supported operations of the 1st Battalion/14th Infantry/4th Infantry Division.

FSB Terri Lynn   Temporary fire support base established by elements of the 1st Battalion/5th Cavalry during the '70 Cambodian Incursion. The fire base was located in the Fishhook area of Cambodia. *See also* **Cambodian Incursion.**

FSB Thunder One   U.S. fire support base located along Highway 13 (Thunder Road), between Loc Ninh and Saigon. Thunder One was one of several 1st Infantry Division fire bases established along Highway 13 to support the division's efforts to keep the road open.

FSB Turnage   *see*   **Dewey Canyon Fire Bases**

FSB Vanderdrift   U.S. fire base located along Highway 9 in Quang Tri Province, I Corps. The fire base was used by Marine and Army units operating in the northern area of I Corps.

FSB Veghel   Fire support base established by elements of the 101st Airborne Division on the outskirts of the A Shau Valley in I Corps. The base supported 101st Airborne and 1st Cavalry Division operations into the valley. *See also* **A Shau Valley.**

FSB Verna   One of the fire support bases of the 199th Light Infantry Brigade. The base was manned by elements of the 2d Battalion/40th Artillery, which operated 105mm howitzers.

FSB Victory   Originally a Marine fire support base located 19kms south of the DMZ. In '69 elements of the 101st Airborne Division took control of the base and began operations in the area. The base was also known as "FSB Victory 12."

FSB Xray   1st Cavalry Division fire support base established in Cambodia during the '70 US/ARVN incursion into Cambodia. *See also* **Cambodian Incursion.**

FSCC   *see*   **Fire Support Coordination Center**

FSM   *see*   **Free Speech Movement**

FSO   *see*   **Foreign Service Officers**

FSPB Castle   *see*   **FSB Castle**

FSSB   *see*   **Fire Support Surveillance Base**

FT   *see*   **Fire Team**

Ft Benning, Georgia   *see*   **Airborne Training**

FTA   *see*   **Fuck-the-Army**

FTX (Field Training Exercise)   Military abbreviation for "field training exercise." The exercises were designed to improve a soldier's proficiency in some selected aspect of field operations.

Fu-gas   *see*   **Fou Gas**

Fuck   In its many variants, probably the most commonly used word in the American GI's vocabulary. It expressed awe, sadness, disbelief, contempt, affection, admiration, fornication, and a wealth of other feelings that could be summed up in this one four-letter word. *See also* **Frigging.**

Fuck-It, Don't Mean Nothin'   *see* **Don't Mean Nothin'**

Fuck-Peace Sign (Footprint of the American Chicken, Peace Sign)   Opposite of the "two finger" peace sign, the extended index, middle and ring finger; the fuck-peace sign. Used by anti-antiwar activists during counter rallies and demonstrations during the Vietnam War. The "peace sign" was also called the "Footprint of the American Chicken" by some of America's "silent majority."

Fuck-the-Army (FTA, Free-the-Army)   A common sentiment towards the military as a career, expressed by many Army draftees. FTA could be found stenciled and written on many walls and helmet covers in Vietnam. Lifers resented the FTA attitude and tried to make life rough for soldiers that were too vocal on the subject. FTA also stood for "Free the Army," a Hayden/Fonda program aimed at U.S. soldiers. FTA attempted to show American soldiers the error of military ways and encouraged them to resist being a part of the military's role in Vietnam. Hayden and Fonda took their program to coffeehouses and GI gathering places located near Stateside military bases. *See also* **Teach-In, I'd Rather Throw Up . . . , Eat the Apple. . . .**

Fuck-Up (Screw-Up, Hose-Up, Mess-Up)   To make a mistake or grievous error; to do something really stupid. Hose or hose-up had a dual meaning; it could mean to screw up or mess up in some way, or it could refer to firing a weapon. Fuck-up also referred to a GI who was a chronic, habitual screw-up or to a troop with continual discipline problems. *See also* **Fire (Shoot), Goldbricking.**

Fuck-You Lizard (Gecko Lizard)   A gecko lizard common to Southeast Asia. At night when the weather was warm the lizards would croak out a staccato song that seemed to go on all night. GIs who heard the lizard's song swore it was screaming "fuck-you . . . fuck-you."

Fucked-Up (Screwed-Up, Fugazi, The Shits, Deep Serious)   —A really bad situation, a mess, screwed-up. The Marines also called this "fugazi." —To be wounded, dead, mentally or emotionally imbalanced, crazy or in pain. —To get high on drugs or alcohol. —A description of a badly wounded or mutilated individual, place or thing. *See also* **Bogus, Fuck-Up.**

Fuckin' A   Absolute, emphatic or positively yes, used to respond positively to a question or statement. "Fuckin' A" meant yes, with authority.

Fuckin' New Guy   *see*   **New Troop**

Fuckin' Off   *see*   **Goldbricking**

Fuel Bar   *see*   **Fuel, Compressed, Trioxane**

Fuel Bladder   *see*   Bladder Bird

Fuel Depot   *see*   Tank Farm

Fuel Tablets   *see*   Fuel, Compressed, Trioxane

Fuel Tanker   *see*   M-131

Fuel Tanker Trailer   *see*   M-123 Tractor

Fuel Trailer   *see*   M-131 Fuel Trailer

Fuel, Compressed, Trioxane (Fuel Bar, Heat Tabs, Fuel Tablets, Trioxane, Hexamine Fuel Tablets)   Compressed fuel tablets used in the field to heat canned rations. These white bars were approximately 3 × 1 × ½ inches thick, had the texture of mothballs and were packaged three to a box. The fuel bar was designed to be used with a small, foldup wing stove, but an empty ration can was often used. One bar was sufficient to warm one can of C-Rations, taking several minutes to accomplish this. The preferred method was still the C-Rat stove with a pinch of C-4. A much older version of the fuel bars was Hexamine fuel tablets which were about 1 inch in diameter and ¾ inch thick. *See also* **C-Rat Stove, C-4.**

Fuel-Air CBU (FA-CBU, Fuel-Air Munitions, FAE, Fuel-Air Explosive CBU)   The Fuel-Air CBU was first used in Vietnam in '75 in defense of Saigon during the NVA's Final Offensive. The FA-CBU consisted of a number of smaller bombs encased in a larger bomb. The larger bomb would split open over the target, releasing the bomblets. At an altitude of 1,000–1,500 feet each bomblet would release a liquid chemical in droplet form that, on contact with the air, formed a small explosive cloud. The smaller clouds linked together to form a large descending cloud which was detonated by timed fuses in the bomblets. The result was a massive downward explosion (pressures greater than 300 psi) and an instantaneous fire that consumed all the oxygen from the area beneath the cloud. *See also* **Cluster Bomb Unit, CBU-55, Ord.**

Fuel-Air Explosive CBU   *see*   Fuel-Air CBU

Fuel-Air Munitions   *see*   Fuel-Air CBU

FUF   *see*   French Union Forces

FUFA   *see*   Deserters

Fugazi   *see*   Fucked-Up

Fulbright, Senator J. William   During the Vietnam War, Senator Fulbright served as the chairman of the powerful Senate Foreign Relations Committee and helped President Johnson get the Gulf of Tonkin Resolution passed through Congress in '64. Fulbright's support of the President's Vietnam War policies began to falter in the mid-sixties. In '67/68 the Senate's Foreign Relations Committee held public hearings that provided national exposure for supporters and critics of the Vietnam War. Afterwards Fulbright began to urge for withdrawal of American forces from Vietnam.

Full Bird   *see*   Colonel

Full Bull   *see*   Colonel

Fuller   *see*   FSB Fuller

FULRO   *see*   Front Unifie pour la Liberation

Funeral Detail   Army assignment that involved the notification of a dead soldier's next-of-kin (NOK), providing the NOK with any assistance required to facilitate the dead man's burial. The detail consisted of an officer and at least one enlisted man. The size of the detail was increased if the dead soldier was to receive a military burial at a private cemetery or if the remains were to be interred at a military cemetery. Additions to the detail might include pallbearers, Honor Guard, and Color Guard. During the Vietnam War, enlisted men on the detail were mostly drawn from troops recently returned from Vietnam, soldiers awaiting their ETS: not enough time remaining in service for an overseas assignment, but too much time for an early-out.

Funeral Procession   *see*   Dau Dam

FUNK   *see*   Khmer Rouge

Funky Fourth   *see*   4th Infantry Division

Funky-Light Project   *see*   TIARA Project

Funny Money   *see*   Military Payment Certificates

Funny Papers   *see*   Topographical Maps

FUO Fever   *see*   Fever-of-Undetermined-Origin

Fusil Mitrailleur Modeles 1924/29 *see* Mle 24/29

FWF *see* Free World Military Forces

FWMAF *see* Free World Military Forces

FWMF *see* Free World Military Forces

FWT *see* Fixed-Wing Transport Company, Avn

FWU *see* Fixed-Wing Utility Company, Avn

G

G-1 (Division Personnel Staff, J-1) Division Level Headquarter's Personnel Staff. The J-1 was a similar position at a higher command level, part of a joint force such as the MACV J-1. *See also* **S-1.**

G-2 (Division Intelligence, Two-Shop, J-2) Military Intelligence Staff at the Division Headquarters level. The J-2 was a similar position at a higher level, part of a joint force such as the MACV J-2. *See also* **S-2.**

G-3 (Division Operations, J-3) Operations Staff personnel at the Division Headquarters level. The J-3 was a similar position at a higher level, part of a joint force such as the MACV J-3. *See also* **S-3.**

G-4 (Division Supply, J-4) Supply and Logistics Staff personnel at the Division Headquarters level. The J-4 was a similar position at a higher level, part of a joint force such as the MACV J-4. *See also* **S-4.**

G-5 (Division Civil Affairs, J-5) Division Headquarters Staff personnel responsible for the coordination of military affairs with civilian affairs and dealing with civilian problems that arose due to the division's military actions. The J-5 was a similar position at a higher level, part of a joint force such as the MACV J-5. In most U.S. units the G-5 also was responsible for psychological warfare operations. *See also* **S-5.**

G-SID *see* **Ground Seismic Intrusion Device**

G-Suit Pressurized aircraft flight suit used to reduce the effects of gravity (Gs) on pilots in flight. The zippered suit was worn over the outside of the flight uniform. Without the G-Suit a jet pilot making high speed maneuvers could easily pass out at the controls of his plane.

Gainesburgers™ (Army Hamburger) Nickname for Army hamburger patties. In Vietnam the ground beef patties came in cans and reportedly had the texture, consistency and taste of the commercial dog food "Gainesburgers." Some troops in Vietnam were fed water buffalo steaks, which were said to be worse than the Army's "Gainesburgers."

Galaxy *see* **C-5A**

Game Warden *see* **TF 116**

Game Warden River Groups (River Patrol Groups, River Patrol Flotilla 5, RIVPATFLOT 5) Task Force 116, Operation Game Warden consisted of five river patrol groups (RPG) that operated on the waterways of the Delta. The Upper Delta RPG (RIVRON 55) worked the enemy sanctuaries on the Cambodian border above Cho Moi. The Rung Sat RPG (RIVRON 59) worked the RSSZ out of Vung Tau. The My Tho RPG (RIVRON 53) worked the My Tho River south of Saigon. The Co Chien RPG (RIVRON 57) primarily worked the river between Vinh Long and the mouth of the Mekong near Phu Vinh. And the Bassac RPG (RIVRON 51) operated along the southern arm of the Mekong River between Chau Duc and the river's mouth. In September '68 the five RPGs were classified as River Patrol Flotilla 5. *See also* **TF 116.**

Gamma *see* **Project Gamma**

Gamma Globulin (GG Shot) Injections of gamma globulin was given to all American troops before going overseas as a hedge against contracting hepatitis. The GG shot was memorable for the pain encountered as the serum was injected into the buttocks.

Gamma Goat *see* **M-561 Cargo Carrier**

Garand Rifle *see* **M-1 Rifle**

Garbage *see* **Burn-Bash-Bury**

Garbage-Pickers *see* **Vietnamese, The**

Garfield *see* **Operation Garfield**

Garrison Cap *see* **Cunt Cap**

Garry Owen Regiment *see* **TF Garry Owen**

Garwood, PFC Robert (Bobby) (Crossovers) U.S. Marine private captured by the Viet Cong in August '65. Shortly afterwards he voluntarily joined the Viet Cong to fight against American troops. Garwood, fluent in Vietnamese, not only fought with the enemy but on occasion handled American POWs. Garwood was one of several American defectors, known as "crossovers," to the NVA/VC during the war.

Gas Mask *see* **M-17 Protective Mask**

Gates, Thomas, Jr. *see* **Secretary of Defense**

Gators *see* **119th Aviation Company**

GAU-2/A Minigun Pod *see* **SUU-11 and GAU-2/A Minigun Pods**

Gayler, Admiral Noel *see* **Commander-in-Chief, Pacific Command**

GCA *see* **Ground Controlled Approaches**

GCI *see* **Ground Control Intercept**

Gears *see* **Command**

Gecko Lizard *see* **Fuck-You Lizard**

Gelignite Nitroglycerin based explosive compound that was composed of ammonium, cellulose nitrate and wood pulp. Gelignite was widely used throughout the war for demolition duties.

Gen *see* **General**

General (Gen.) A four-star general officer in the U.S. Army, Marines and Air Force. The equivalent rank in the Navy was an Admiral. During the Vietnam War nearly twice as many generals were in Vietnam under the command of General Westmoreland as there were under General Omar Bradley during the Allied invasion of Europe in '44. In addition Gen. Bradley commanded more than four times the number of troops commanded by Gen. Westmoreland in Vietnam. During the Vietnam War there was a glut of Army officers, field grade and above, yet at the same time there was a shortage of company grade officers to lead troops in the field. *See also* **General Officers.**

General *see* **General, General Officers**

General Discharge Military discharge granted to some American soldiers who voluntarily sought drug treatment and rehabilitation for their drug dependency. Those who sought treatment were not prosecuted for their drug use, but were subject to other charges such as trafficking, and crimes related to drug use. Those men with a General Discharge were eligible for veterans' benefits and medical care. Undesirable Discharges could be upgraded to Generals through the DOD's Discharge Review Board or by the Ford Clemency Review Board for deserters. General Discharges were also granted for medical or psychiatric reasons. *See also* **Ford Clemency Review Board, Discharges, Bad Paper.**

General Edward Lansdale *see* **Lansdale, Edward**

General Giap *see* **Nguyen Vo Giap**

General Issue *see* **GI**

General Loan *see* **Nguyen Ngoc Loan**

General Maxwell Taylor *see* **Taylor, Maxwell**

General Medical Officer (GMOs, Army GP) Army medical officers providing nonspecialized general medical services, in comparison to surgical officers specializing in various fields. In Vietnam many of the GMOs were interns or residents with little combat medical or trauma experience. The GMO was the military equivalent of a civilian general practitioner.

General Minh *see* **Duong Van Minh**

General of the Army/Air Force *see* **General Officers**

General Officers (Senior Grade Officers, Vietnamese General Officers, Tuongs) Senior military officers above the rank of colonel. In the Army and Air Force a 5-star general is the General of the Army/Air Force. For the Army, Air Force and Marines the following apply: 4 gold stars, General; 3 stars, Lieutenant General; 2 stars, Major General; 1 star, Brigadier General. A Commanding General (CG) usually commanded a division size force or larger. In the South Vietnamese Army the general officers wore silver stars of the following rank: 5—General of the Army (Thong-Thong), 4—Lieutenant General (Dai-Tuong), 3—Major General (Trung-Tuong), 2—Brigadier General (Thieu-Tuong), 1—Sub Brigadier General (Chuan-Tuong). *See also* Admiral.

General Purpose (GP) Military name for any item without a specific purpose. *See also* Daisy Cutters (GP Bomb).

General Purpose Bomb *see* GP Bomb

General Purpose Machine Gun *see* M-60 MG

General Support Company (GSC) An Army aviation company that provided general support to the division headquarters. The company provided C & C ships used by the command general and his staff, general transport, dispatch duties and VIP passenger services for division headquarters.

General Uprising *see* Khoi Nghia

General Van Tien Dung *see* Van Tien Dung, General

General Vang Pao *see* Meo

General Waste-MORE-Land *see* Westmoreland, General William C.

General's Commute *see* Bien Hoa Commute

General's Mess Eating facilities used by the commanding general of a unit. In field units the general's mess consisted of a separate room, apart from the officer's mess, in which the general was served his meals, with admittance to other officers by the general's invitation. *See also* Command Mess.

Generals Awards *see* Package A/B Awards

Geneva Accords (Geneva Agreements, 1954, 17th Parallel) Vietnam peace agreement between the French and the Viet Minh, July '54, ending the First Indo-China War. The agreement called for the temporary partitioning of Vietnam at the 17th Parallel (the DMZ), requiring all French forces to move south of the partition, and Viet Minh forces to relocate north of the DMZ. South Vietnamese forces were aligned with the French and were required to do the same. Countrywide elections were to be held for the Vietnamese people to determine if the two Vietnams were to be united, and under what government. The agreement also called for the eventual withdrawal of all foreign troops from Vietnam, Laos and Cambodia. Civilians were to be allowed to freely move across the DMZ and settle without threat of reprisals or discrimination from the pro-democratic government of the South or the Communists of the North. Neither government was allowed to import military supplies or equipment, except as replacements for existing equipment. Foreign troop reinforcements were also banned, but existing troops could be replaced with fresh troops. The countries signing the final agreement were Cambodia, the Democratic Republic of Vietnam (North Vietnam), France, Laos, People's Republic of China, the Soviet Union, and the United Kingdom. The United States and the State of Vietnam (South Vietnam) refused to sign. SVN strongly and continually protested against the agreement and refused to honor much of it, contending that the agreement was between the French and NVN, and that SVN was a sovereign state and not part of France or subject to French obligations.

Geneva Agreement, 1954 *see* Geneva Accords

Geneva Agreement, 1962 (Laotian Accords) 1962 Geneva Agreement between warring civil factions in Laos that established Laotian neutrality and ordered the withdrawal of all foreign troops from the country. The agreement established a coalition government in Laos between the Neutralist, Pathet Lao, and the Rightist. The coalition government, headed by Prince Souvanna Phouma, took effect in July '62, and lasted until mid-'63 when the coalition broke down and factional fighting resumed. As part of the agreement NVA troops supporting the Pathet Lao, and U.S. advisors supporting the Royal Lao government (Rightist) were ordered to withdraw. U.S. advisors withdrew, but more than 10,000 NVA troops moved deep into the Laotian interior and continued fighting the RLA.

Geneva Convention (International Red Cross, IRC) International agreement adhered to by most members of the civilized world regarding the treatment of prisoners of war. Rules and protections of the '29 and '49 Geneva Convention were to be granted to the captured soldier provided he was in uniform, carried arms openly and obeyed the rules and customs of war. The rules regarding the treatment of prisoners and civilians in a war zone were under the supervision and administration of the International Red Cross (IRC) with individual countries responsible for the action and education of their soldiers. Countries were morally bound by the rules, but several countries (especially Asian communist), do not honor the terms and conditions of the Geneva Convention. During the Vietnam War the NVA/VC refused to acknowledge the terms of the Geneva Convention because legally no state of war existed between North Vietnam and the United States. The general terms of the convention called for a captured soldier to reveal only his name, rank and identification number. His captors were to provide him with adequate food, water and medical care. Captives were to be allowed correspondence with family members and to receive parcels. Prisoners attempting to escape were not to be punished and there was to be no torture, harassment or other abuse. The IRC or other neutral states were to have access to prison facilities for routine inspections. *See also* **Declaration of War.**

Geographical Bachelors Army nurse's slang for married doctors and other married men who socialized as if they were not married. Serving in Vietnam afforded some married men the option of acting the part of a "bachelor" during their tour of duty.

Georgia *see* **FSB Georgia, Operation Georgia**

German Tape *see* **German Wire**

German Wire (Razor Wire, German Tape) Coiled wire, similar to concertina wire, but instead of barbs there were inch-long razor sharp blades, double-edged, spaced ½ inch apart. Used as a defensive barrier, usually along the tops of fences, structures or in conjunction with barbed or concertina wire. Razor wire was more difficult to cut than regular barbed wire, and more difficult to handle. A 40-pound roll of "razor wire" could be stretched to 20 meters and the 30-inch-high rolls could be stacked and interlaced with tangle foot defenses to create perimeter barricades. *See also* **Tanglefoot, Concertina Wire.**

Geronimo Regiment *see* **501st Infantry Regiment (Airborne)**

Get Blind *see* **Drunk**

Get High (Tripping, Stoned, High, Drug High, Skulled-Out, Get-a-Buzz, Get Ripped) Slang for getting high on drugs. In the case of drugs, such as LSD, getting high resulted in the user taking a "head-trip" and hallucinating. Sometimes the "trip" was more like a nightmare and was called a "bad trip." For marijuana and hash, stoned or getting ripped were the operative words. *See also* **Drunk.**

Get Laid *see* **Boom-Boom**

Get Ripped *see* **Get High**

Get-a-Buzz *see* **Get High**

Get-Rid-of-Westmoreland-Now *see* **GROWN**

Get-Some... GI slang for killing the enemy, seeking revenge; payback. Soldiers in Vietnam said it to each other as an encouragement, similar to dancers telling one another to "break a leg." The phrase served to vocalize a sense of revenge or purpose. *See also* **Payback.**

Get-Tight To get tight with someone was to become friends with them, or identify with them. In some circles it also meant to get drunk or high on drugs.

Get-Your-Rocks-Off *see* **Masturbate**

Get-Your-Shit-Together (Squared Away) To compose or pull yourself together, organize and regroup, straighten up or put your head on straight; to be squared away. "Having-your-shit-together" was a vital necessity when operating in the field against the NVA/VC.

Getcha Vines *see* **Wait-a-Minute Vines**

Gettin' Over   Succeeding, winning at something or over someone. *See also* **Score, Skate.**

GG Shot *see* **Gamma Globulin**

Ghost *see* **Enemy, The**

Ghost Time (Free Time, Off Duty Hours, Slack Time)   GI slang for free time or off duty. Units in rear areas generally worked a 10–12 hour day and rotated extra duty, KP and guard duty; any remaining time was usually their own, and they were considered off duty. Troops in the field did not get off duty time until they were pulled out of the field for stand-down. Field troops sometimes had days, or portions of a day, when their field activity was light, such as when they were waiting for transport, resupply or "walks in the sun." These light periods were sometimes referred to as "slack time." *See also* **Stand-Down.**

Ghostin' *see* **Goldbricking**

GI (General Issue, Government Issue)   The universal name for the American soldier, popularized in WWII when GI originally meant Government Issue or General Issue; it came to apply to American soldiers in general. Many of America's WWII soldiers were not career soldiers, but general inductees. The Vietnamese tended to look upon all Americans in Vietnam as GIs. *See also* **Trooper, Digger, Bo Doi.**

GI (Clean-Up) *see* **Field-Day**

GI Film Rating System *see* **American GI Film Ratings**

GI Financier *see* **Shylocker**

GI Gin (Cough Syrup, Terpin Hydrate)   GI slang for government issue cough syrup; elixir of terpin hydrate.

GI Helmet (Steel Pot, M-1 Helmet, Piss-Pot)   U.S. military helmet, the M-1 weighed approximately 3.5 pounds and was worn by many armies worldwide. Commonly known as a "steel pot" by most soldiers. The WWII vintage helmet consisted of five basic parts: outer steel shell, laminated nylon liner, sweat band, chin strap and optional camouflaged helmet cover. The cover had slits to allow the insertion of branches and grass for more effective camouflaging. Ballistics tests with Chicom 82 and 120mm mortars proved the helmet to be just marginally effective in protecting the head from the shell fragments. *See also* **Camouflage Cover, Helmet Liners.**

GI Insurance ($10,000)   U.S. government–sponsored insurance plan for the military. Any American serviceman killed in the line of duty was covered by a $10,000 policy, the proceeds paid to his next-of-kin or selected beneficiary.

GI Joe *see* **Gungi Marine**

GI Party *see* **Field-Day**

GI Phrase Book   Halt (stop)—Dung Lai; Lay down your weapon—Buong sung xuong; Put up your hands—Dura tay len; Keep your hands on your head—Dura tay len dau; I will search you—Toi kham ong; Do not talk—Durng noi chuyen; Walk there—Lai dang kia; Turn right—Xay ben phai; Turn left—Xay ben trai; Come here—Lai day; Thank you—Cam on; Please—Lam on; Kill VC—Coc dau VC; American Advisor—Co van my; Come quickly—Lai mau; Are You North Vietnamese—Noi Bac-Viet; I don't understand—Toi khong hieu; I don't know—Khong biet.

GI Shower   One of the perils of basic training for a recruit who did not bathe often enough, thoroughly enough or did not have sufficient command of his body odor. Such a recruit would be thrown into the platoon's shower area and scrubbed down with scrub brushes and cleanser by offended members of the platoon. The shower left the recruit scratched, bruised and educated. These showers were the result of the recruit offending the noses of his fellow platoon members or somehow offending the drill instructor's sense of smell or field of vision. Such offenses usually led to the entire platoon being punished because of the excesses of one man. The GI shower was an attempt to make the offender toe-the-line. *See also* **Blanket Party.**

GI Tent *see* **Shelter Half**

GI Towel *see* **Lucky Towel**

GI Trots *see* **Ho Chi Minh's Revenge**

GI-rines *see* **U.S. Marines**

Gia Dinh   The capital of Gia Dinh

Province. The province also encompassed the national capital of Saigon. Gia Dinh was located on the outskirts of Saigon. *See also* Saigon.

Gia Hoi *see* **Strawberry Patch**

Gia Lam *see* **MiG Airfields**

Gia Long (Nguyen Dynasty, Nguyen Phuc Anh) Born Nguyen Phuc Anh in 1792, he was one of the ruling warlord of Cochin China. With the help of French mercenaries and a missionary, Nguyen Phuc Anh defeated the king of Tay Son, who had all but conquered Cochin China. The king of Tay Son was from the central region of Annam and with his brothers had conquered Tonkin and Cochin China. When Nugyen Phuc Anh defeated the king, he proclaimed himself Emperor Gia Long, establishing the Nguyen Dynasty. The dynasty survived until Bao Dai abdicated the throne in '55. Under Gia Long, Tonkin, Annam and Cochin China were united as Vietnam, with the capital located in Hue. For their help he granted France unrestricted trade and access to Cochin China.

Gia Long Palace (Presidential Palace, Doc Lap Palace, Independence Palace) Presidential mansion that served as the residence for South Vietnam's president. The palace was located in the heart of Saigon and was previously known as Duc Lap Palace or Independence Palace. In '62 the palace was bombed and strafed by two VNAF pilots disgruntled with President Diem. *See also* **Palace Air Strike.**

Gia Nghia Provincial capital of Quang Duc, II Corps. Gia Nghia was located in the Central Highlands 173kms northeast of Saigon, less than 40kms southeast of the Cambodian border.

Giai Phong Vietnamese for "Liberation and Independence," one of the VC's propaganda phrases.

Giant Slingshot *see* **Operation Giant Slingshot**

Giap *see* **Nguyen Vo Giap**

Gibbon *see* **Rock Apes**

Gibraltar *see* **Operation Gibraltar**

Gibs *see* **Weapons Systems Operator**

Gimlet *see* **21st Infantry Regiment (Light)**

Gin and Wink *see* **Gwink**

Ginsberg, Allen One of the fathers of the hippie movement. Ginsberg believed that LSD was the path to spiritual enlightenment and that everyone in America over the age of 14 should try LSD at least once. Ginsberg promoted love and peace, using drugs to accomplish his goal. *See also* **Leary, Timothy; Hippie Movement.**

Gio Linh Marine outpost located less than 4kms south of the DMZ, it represented the northeastern anchor of "Leatherneck Square." The village of Gio Linh at one time straddled Highway 1, but it was evacuated and the Marine outpost established. Gio Linh was 14kms north of Dong Ha and its close proximity to the DMZ left the camp's occupants under constant threat from the NVA. *See also* **Leatherneck Square.**

Girls Only Say Yes to Men Who Say No Campus antiwar slogan meaning college girls said yes to sex with men who said no to the war.

Gitcha Vines *see* **Wait-a-Minute Vines**

Give-a-Fuck (A-Rat's-Ass) To care about something or someone, to be concerned, or to be involved. Typically used in the sarcastic negative sense to express a lack of interest, as in, "Who gives-a-fuck...?" or, "I could give-a-fuck less if he jumps." The phrase was used interchangeably with "a-rat's-ass," as in "Who gives a-rat's-ass...?"

Give-a-Shit-Lobe (Frontal Lobe) Slang reference to the frontal lobe of the brain. If the frontal lobe was damaged the patient was in a condition in which he "didn't give-a-shit about anything." Because of the destructive nature of modern weapons, head wounds received in Vietnam were particularly dibilitating.

Gives-Me-the-Ass *see* **Pissed**

GKR (Government of the Khmer Republic) Lon Nol's anticommunist government of Cambodia during the early '70s. *See also* **Cambodia, Lon Nol.**

Gladiators *see* **57th Aviation Company**

Glide Bombs *see* **Smart Bombs**

Globemaster *see* **C-124**

GM100 *see* **Groupement Mobile 100**

GMOs *see* **General Medical Officer**

Go Cong Provincial capital of the Province of Go Cong in IV Corps. Go Cong was located 45kms south of Saigon and 12kms from the coast.

Go-fers *see* **Kite-Tails**

Go-Fors *see* **Liaison Section**

Go-Go Bird (Chinook Gunship, Guns-a-Go-Go, ACH-47) Nickname for CH-47 helicopter, armored and armed, tested in '66 as a gun platform or gunship, designated the ACH-47. The Chinook was armed with 20mm miniguns, 40mm grenade launchers, .50cal machine guns and rockets. The test helicopters were assigned to the 1st Air Cav and were used to support helimobile operations. The ACH-47 was tested for two years with three of the four test aircraft being destroyed. Though it possessed much firepower it was deemed too slow and too large a target for practical use. *See also* **CH-47.**

Go-to-Hell Rag *see* **Lucky Towel**

Go/No Go (Mechanized and Armor Combat Operations, Vietnam) Term used in an Army armor study conducted to evaluate the feasibility of using armor in a country such as South Vietnam. The study, "Mechanized and Armor Combat Operations, Vietnam," focused on the terrain, weather conditions, and the road network within the country. The terrain of South Vietnam was subdivided into Go/No Go areas. "Go" areas were able to support armor operations, "No Go" areas were not. The study concluded that 58 percent of SVN's terrain would support tank operations, and 65 percent of the terrain would support APCs. When Army troops initially deployed to Vietnam in '65 they left their armor elements behind. The Marines deployed their armor during their initial buildup in Vietnam and demonstrated that tanks could be used effectively.

God GI nicknames for God: Supreme-6, Sky Honcho, Big Gunny in the Sky. *See also* **Army Call Signs.**

God Squad (Chaplain Corps, Sky Pilot) Nickname for the military Chaplain Corps. Chaplains were sometimes nicknamed "Sky Pilots." *See also* **Dog Collar.**

GOER 4 × 4 *see* **M-553 Cargo Carrier**

Going Downdown Phrase used by U.S. pilots to describe air strike missions against Hanoi in North Vietnam.

Going-Low-Level *see* **Nap-of-the-Earth**

Gold *see* **FSB Gold**

Gold Room (The Tank, JCS Conference Room) The Joint Chiefs of Staff held their meetings in a windowless briefing room located in the bowels of the Pentagon. The room was called the "Gold Room" or the "Tank." *See also* **Joint Chiefs of Staff.**

Gold-Bar *see* **Second Lieutenant**

Goldberg, Joseph Served as the U.S. ambassador to the United Nations from '65 to '68. Goldberg believed the only solution for the U.S. in Vietnam was through a negotiated settlement, and participated in advising President Johnson in March '68 as one of the "Wise Old Men." Goldberg's stance against the war became increasingly vocal after he stepped down from his position at the U.N. *See also* **Wise Old Men.**

Goldbricking (Slacking, Ghostin', Sandbagging, Fuckin' Off, Lagging, Half-Stepping) Avoiding a work detail or the performance of duty. Using devious means to avoid work. Infantry considered anyone who goofed off in the field, or who did not respect the hostile surroundings to be half-stepping or slacking. Lack of attention could lead to members of the unit suffering because one man wasn't "taking care of business." Many grunts considered anyone who obtained a rear area job at the expense of another grunt to be untrustworthy, cowardly, lazy and in general a life form to avoid. For the grunt the role model for the typical "goldbrick" was an REMF. The Marines labeled their goldbricks "shitbirds." *See also* **Rear-Echelon-Mother-Fuckers, Malingering, Fuck-Up, Skatin', Sandbagging a Patrol/Ambush, Shit-Bird.**

Golddiggers All-girl dance troupe that sometimes accompanied Bob Hope on his entertainment tours for U.S. troops in Vietnam. The dancers "had legs up to their necks" and were very popular with the GIs. *See also* **Hope, Bob.**

Golden Dragons *see* **14th Infantry Regiment**

Golden Fleece *see* **Operation Golden Fleece**

Golden Ghettos (Army Bases) Marine slang name for the larger U.S. Army base camps in South Vietnam that were equipped to give Army troops in the camps the "feel of home." The camps had Vietnamese civilians to do the soldier's laundry, the cleaning of their living quarters, kitchen duties, food service and at some bases even sandbag filling and bunker construction. The Army troops also enjoyed USO clubs and hobby activities, EM clubs and various other amenities to make their stay in Vietnam as comfortable as possible. This was in contrast to the spartan comforts available to the Marines. In the later years of the war Marine bases in Danang became almost as luxurious as the Army's divisional base camps. *See also* **Ice Cream Soldiers.**

Goldfish Bowl *see* **OH-13**

Goldwater, Senator Barry Hawkish senator from the state of Arizona. He was unofficially credited with being the first public official to characterize the conflict in Vietnam as a "war," and was very vocal on ways it could be settled. During his '64 run for president, he commented on the use of tactical nuclear weapons against VC strongholds, and the possible bombing of NVA supply lines linked to Communist China. The hawk mentality dictated, "if you have to be in a war, then fight to win." Goldwater criticized the Johnson administration for not defining America's objective in Vietnam and he believed America should do whatever was necessary, short of using nuclear weapons, to support its soldiers in the field, or else get out of the war altogether.

Golf Course, The *see* **Camp Radcliff**

Gom Dan Derogatory Vietnamese term used by the VCI to describe GVN resettlement and refugee camps near the cities, literally meaning herding or gathering. The VCI used the term during their propaganda speeches to rural villagers in an attempt to turn the people against the GVN. The VCI told the villagers of the horrible conditions at the government camps and what they could expect if they chose to "voluntarily" relocate from their village. The VCI urged the people to fight along with the VC to stop the government's forced relocation program. *See also* **New Life Hamlet.**

Gomers *see* **Enemy, The**

Gongs Derogatory term used to describe American military awards and decorations distributed during the latter half of the Vietnam War. Because of a lowering of the standards required to receive such awards thousands were issued to people who didn't deserve them. The respect and true meanings of the awards were greatly diminished because of the ease with which they could be obtained. In '68 the ratio of combat deaths to awards was 28–1, yet, in '70 after a reduction in overall combat and drastic decreases in major American offenses, the ratio was 132–1. *See also* **Bronze Star, Package A/B Awards.**

Gonorrhea *see* **Venereal Diseases**

Good Bush *see* **Ambush**

Good Chute Air Force phrase describing the state of a pilot or crewman who has bailed out of his aircraft. A "good chute" indicated the stricken aircraft's pilot or crew was able to eject or jump clear of the plane before it disintegrated or crashed. The fact that a parachute deployed was a good sign that the pilot was at least well enough to get out of the aircraft.

Good Guy Card (South Vietnamese Identification Card, ID Cards, Can Cuoc) Nickname for the South Vietnamese government issued identification cards; can cuoc [can cook]. All Vietnamese civilians were supposed to have legitimate ID cards. The cards were to be presented to the authorities for inspection when they were requested. The lack of an ID, or a forged ID, was reason to arrest an individual as a suspected VC until he could produce his card or prove he was not the enemy. GIs nicknamed the cards "good guy cards" and in many cases it was the only means they had to judge whether the bearer of the card was friend or foe. The cards did not impact VC operations because forged cards were readily available to them, and they used the fake cards to pass through checkpoints and move about the country.

Good Time (Bad Time) Active duty time credited toward an individual's enlistment commitment. "Bad time" was time a soldier spent in confinement (jail) or while AWOL. Bad time was not credited toward the soldier's enlistment, and it had to be made up before his enlistment was considered complete. The time was repaid by adding the bad days to his enlistment, or he could accept a forfeiture of pay, equal to the number of bad days owed.

Gook Beer *see* **Tigerpiss**

Gook Booze *see* **Tigerpiss**

Gook Faggots *see* **ARVN Queers**

Gook Shoes *see* **Binh-Tri-Thien**

Gook Sores (Ringworm) Ulcerous sores common among GIs who spent extended periods of time operating in the boonies. The open sores typically covered the arms, neck and legs. The sores were caused by the unsanitary field conditions and the ease with which infection set up in the body. Lacerations from elephant grass and general cuts and scrapes quickly became oozing, puss filled sores. Such conditions only warranted local field treatment and troops remained in the field until rotated into base camp. Many other parasites were rampant; ringworm the most common. *See also* **Bamboo Poisoning.**

Gook Syndrome (The Only Good Gook Is a Dead Gook) An opinion held by some GIs that all Vietnamese were bad. Some considered the Vietnamese people, friend and foe, as less than human, therefore of little value as human beings, so that the loss of Vietnamese lives was not considered meaningful or important. The GI outlook was reinforced by the actions of the Vietnamese themselves. For many young Americans it was difficult to comprehend the extremely low standard of living experienced by the rural Vietnamese, as well as the Viet Cong's disregard for the lives of their fellow countrymen. For many, the Vietnamese as a people were regarded as "gooks," and "the only good gook was a dead gook." *See also* **Mere-Gook-Rule, Every Day in the World..., When They're Not Red....**

Gooks GI slang reference to anyone of Asian origin. The word originated during the Korean War and found its way to Vietnam by way of American Korean War veterans. The term was universally applied to Vietnamese civilians and the NVA/VC. *See also* **Enemy, The; Vietnamese, The.**

Gooners *see* **Enemy, The**

Gooney Bird *see* **AC-47**

Gophers *see* **Liaison Section**

Gorks (ICU Patients) Army medical slang for the patients in the Intensive Care Unit.

Got-the-Ass *see* **Pissed**

Government Issue *see* **GI**

Government of the Khmer Republic *see* **GKR**

Government of Vietnam (GVN) The noncommunist government of South Vietnam at war with the communist forces of the Viet Cong and North Vietnam. North Vietnam sought the reunification of North and South Vietnam and supported the communist Viet Cong forces within the country attempting to overthrow South Vietnam's government. The government was referred to by several names including GVN, Saigon Government, SVN Government. *See also* **Republic of Vietnam, L & M.**

GP *see* **General Purpose**

GP Bombs (General Purpose Bomb Mk-81, Mk-82, Mk-83, Mk-84) During the Vietnam War the U.S. made use of a variety of air delivered ordnance. The standard general purpose "iron bombs" delivered by the Air Force, Navy, and the Marines were Mk-81 (250 pounds), Mk-82 (500 & 750 pounds), Mk-83 (1,000 pounds), and the Mk-84 (2,000 pounds). Other special ordnance bombs were also used such as 3,000/10,000/15,000-pounders, laser guided bombs, CBUs, FAEs, drag bombs, and several others. *See also* **Retarded Bombs.**

GP35 9mm Pistol *see* **Browning 9mm Pistol**

GPES *see* **Ground Proximity Extraction System**

GPMG (General Purpose Machine Gun) *see* **M-60 MG**

GR Point *see* **Graves Registration Point**

Grab 'em by the Balls and... After Tet '68 there was a concerted effort by the military to gain the support of the Vietnamese peasantry through a program called Pacification. The theory was if you won the hearts of the people, their minds would follow, thus the program became widely known as Winning the Hearts and Minds. The more cynical elements of the U.S. military didn't have much faith in the program and came up with a slogan of their own: "Grab 'em by the balls and their hearts will follow." *See also* **Pacification, WHAM.**

GRADS *see* **Ground Radar Aerial Delivery System**

Gradualism *see* **Escalation**

Graduated Response (Escalated Response) The established strategy of the Johnson administration in dealing with communist aggression from North Vietnam. The strategy called for the gradual increase of military pressure on the North Vietnamese; the pressure to be in the form of direct bombing by American aircraft against targets in NVN. It was hoped that by starting softly and increasing the pressure, NVN would see the eventual outcome, and halt their aggression and support of the guerrillas in the South. The military didn't agree with the gradual response and wanted all-out heavy attacks in order to limit American losses. President Johnson decided to go with the "Gradual Response." *See also* **Escalation, Ratcheting.**

Grail *see* **Surface-to-Air-Missile**

Grass *see* **Marijuana**

Gravel *see* **CBU Mines**

Gravel Mine, U.S. (XM-27 Mine, MicroGravel Mines, Small Gravel Mines) Extremely small antipersonnel mines used by the U.S. in SEA. The mines were dropped from aircraft and were about two inches in diameter and shaped like a gray rock or piece of gravel. When compressed or stepped on, the mine would explode. The gravel mine had no metal parts and could not be detected with a mine detector. The first version of the mines was supposed to deteriorate after several weeks' exposure to the elements, known as "self-sterilizing." But in practice all the mines didn't deteriorate at the same rate and gravel mine fields continued to be lethal several weeks beyond their official sterilization cutoff. A second version of the mine more closely controlled the self-sterilization process. In addition to the new gravel mine that was produced, two other versions entered service. The Small Gravel Mine was a smaller version of the original gravel mine. Both mines were capable of blowing off a foot or a hand when detonated. The MicroGravel Mine was developed to function as a warning device and caused no bodily injury. When the MicroGravel was stepped on it exploded with a loud pop that could activate electronic sensors or sentries. Thousands of the gravel mines were dropped along the Ho Chi Minh Trail and in areas of heavy enemy activity. *See also* **CBU Mines, Aerial-Denial Ordnance Strikes.**

Gravel Mine, Viet Cong Locally manufactured antipersonnel mine used by the Viet Cong — a homemade claymore. The mine was a can or bag packed with gravel and an explosive charge. When the mine detonated the gravel became as deadly as the shrapnel from an artillery round. Sometimes the mine was also packed with nails or broken glass to increase its effectiveness. *See also* **M-18 Claymore Mine; Gravel Mine, U.S.**

Graves, Theresa *see* **Hope, Bob**

Graves Registration *see* **Graves Registration Point**

Graves Registration Point (GR Point, Graves Registration) Military terminology for the point on a base where the dead were collected from. From the smaller bases the bodies were transferred to larger facilities to be processed for return to the States. At the larger bases the GR Point included morgue facilities for refrigerated storage of the bodies. Identification and the initial embalming process of the body also took place at Graves Registration. *See also* **Green Ghouls.**

Graveyard, The Vietnamese whorehouse located at Soc Trang in the Delta of IV Corps. The house was primarily used by ARVN troops until '65 when they were displaced by the increasing numbers of American troops. The Americans had much more money to spend and, eventually, economically squeezed the ARVNs out. *See also* **Shrinking Bird Disease.**

Gray Propaganda *see* **House 7 Radio Group**

Gray Radio *see* **House 7 Radio Group**

Gray Tigers *see* **57th Aviation Company**

Grays *see* **Caucasian**

Grazing Fire   Fire directed toward a target in which the bullet's trajectory is roughly parallel to the ground, and is consistently at or below chest level. Grazing fire was particularly effective at slowing the charge of enemy troops, pinning them in position. Effective grazing fire was typically directed from firing elements positioned at a slightly higher elevation than the target area. *See also* Enfilade.

Grease   *see*   **Kill**

Grease Gun   *see*   **M-3A1 SMG**

Grease Paint   *see*   **Camouflage Paint**

Great General Offensive and People's Uprising   *see*   **Tet Offensive**

Great Golden World   *see*   **Dai Kim Do**

Great Neutralizer, The   Reference to the jungle, which at night favored neither side, provided the forces involved did not move, and remained vigilant. The advantage went to the army that learned how to use the jungle, without trying to conquer it.

Great Society, The (Creative Federalism)   When President Johnson took office in '64 he had a broad plan to eliminate poverty in America and institute domestic reform. He envisioned America and its society, through his leadership, becoming richer and more powerful; a great society. In order to accomplish Johnson's Great Society, changes in America's racial and economic lifestyle were necessary. Administration efforts early in Johnson's term yielded advances in overcoming some of the poverty and racial inequities that plagued America. Johnson's plan included massive improvements in the country's education system, full Social Security for the elderly, jobs for all those willing to work, and an all-out war to immediately reduce, and eventually eliminate poverty in America. The Great Society was an expensive effort, as was the ever-expanding war in Vietnam. The country was capable of financially supporting one or the other, but not both. In the end Johnson's Great Society paid the price, and the war went on. Johnson's plan for the country was originally called "Creative Federalism," before it was renamed the "Great Society." *See also* Johnson, President Lyndon Baines; War on Poverty.

Great Spring Victory   *see*   **Final Offensive**

Greater Unity Force   *see*   **Luc Luong Dai Doan Ket**

Greek Operations   Field name for a series of USSF/CIA reconnaissance and intelligence gathering operations conducted into the border areas of SVN. The individual projects came under the control of MACV-SOG in '67 and were generally referred to as the "Greek Projects." Under projects Delta, Sigma, Omega and Gamma, long-range reconnaissance missions were conducted into Cambodia, Laos and NVN. *See also* Project: Delta, Sigma, Omega, Gamma.

Greeley   *see*   **Operation Greeley**

Green Beret   Distinctive headgear worn by the U.S. Army's Special Forces. The green beret was made of wool with a leather binding around the edge. A braid was threaded through the binding and used to adjust the size of the beret. In '61 President Kennedy authorized the beret as part of the USSF's uniform. Initially the USSFs were the only Army unit authorized to wear a beret. *See also* Special Forces.

Green Berets   *see*   **Special Forces**

Green Bomb   *see*   **Dexamphetamines**

Green Cord Uniform (WAC Uniform)   Standard uniform of the Army Women's Corps. The uniform featured a short sleeved shirt/coat and skirt in a light shade of green. Duty nurses wore the traditional white nursing uniform. WAC and nurse personnel also wore fatigues and jungle fatigues in Vietnam.

Green Dragon   *see*   **M-113**

Green Ghouls   Marine nickname for GIs that worked Graves Registration. *See also* Graves Registration Point.

Green Giant   *see*   **CH-3**

Green Hornets   *see*   **UH-1F**

Green Leech   *see*   **Leeches**

Green Machine (Veterans Administration, VA)   Nickname for the Regular U.S. Army and the U.S. Marine Corps. During the VNW the Army consisted of career soldiers who had enlisted, and draftees who weren't making the Army a career. After the war the term was also used by Vietnam veterans to refer to the Veterans Administration.

Green Tracers *see* **Tracer Round**

Green Troop *see* **New Troop**

Green Wave *see* **Operation Green Wave**

Green-Up Switch setting indicator in the cockpit determining the ready state of the ordnance load. When the red indicator on the switch was showing, the weapons were not armed. Green-up indicated the weapon system was ready to be fired or released.

Greene, General Wallace *see* **Commandant**

Greenie *see* **Dexamphetamines**

Greenie Beanies *see* **Special Forces**

Greenseed *see* **New Troop**

Grenade *see* **Hand Grenades**

Grenade Launcher *see* **M-79 Grenade Launcher**

Grenade Launchers, 40mm The U.S. used several different types of grenade launchers in Vietnam. They all fired a 40mm grenade round, and were manually or electrically operated. Grenade launchers were generally nicknamed "Forties or Forty," except the M-79 Grenade Launcher which had several nicknames. *See also* **M-406 Grenade; M-576 Canister Round; Grenade Launchers: M-79, M-75, M-129, XM-174, XM-94, XM 13 Grenade Launcher; Grenade Launchers, Navy; CROW Grenade Launcher; XM-28 Turret.**

Grenade Launchers, Navy (Mk-10/18/ 19/20 Grenade Launchers) The U.S. Navy experimented with several different types of multiple-shot grenade launchers to support their riverine operations in the Delta of Vietnam. The Mk-10 and 18 were belt fed, hand cranked grenade launchers used on some riverine craft. These launchers used the standard 40mm grenades which were fed into the launcher on a fabric belt. The Mk-19 and 20 used the higher velocity M-383 grenade round that was used by aircraft grenade launchers; both launchers were self-reloading (automatic). *See also* **Grenade Launchers.**

Grenades, Fragmentation (Frags) An antipersonnel grenade that, when exploded, scattered jagged fragments of metal across a wide area. The grenades had either a serrated exterior that broke apart on detonation, or a smooth exterior with an internal coil of wire that broke into pieces when detonated. The egg shaped, serrated type was of WWII vintage and was commonly referred to as a pineapple grenade. The smooth grenades were of more recent vintage, lighter weight with a greater blast radius. Soviet, North Korean, Chinese and American frags were used in Vietnam. *See also* **NVA/VC Frags; U.S. Frags.**

Grenades, Gas (CS Grenades, Tear Gas Grenades, M-7 CS Hand Grenade, Cry Baby Grenades) Hand grenades containing tear gas designed for use in riots and crowd control. CS grenades were often used in Vietnam in an effort to dislodge the enemy from bunkers and tunnels. The M-7 grenades were cylinder shaped, 3 inches in diameter, 5.5 inches long and weighed a little over a pound. Burn time for the gas was 20–60 seconds over a radius of 35 meters with the CS gas causing upper respiratory difficulty, nausea, vomiting and extreme eye irritation. The grenades were sometimes called "Cry Baby" grenades. *See also* **CS Gas.**

Grenades, Illumination (M-79 Flare) Rifle grenade used for illumination. The 3–4 pound grenade was attached to the muzzle of the rifle and fired; on impact with the ground the illuminating material within the grenade ignited and burned for approximately 45 seconds. The intensity of the light was nearly 80,000 candlepower and in clear, flat terrain, illuminated a radius of 100 meters. An illumination round was also available for the M-79 Grenade Launcher. The small flare was fired from the M-79, ignited overhead and drifted to the ground under its attached parachute. *See also* **Flares.**

Grenades, Smoke (M-8 Smoke Grenade, M-18 Smoke Grenade, Smoke Canister Grenade) U.S. hand grenades used to generate smoke. The M-8 generated white smoke and the M-18 generated colored smoke (red, green, yellow, purple/ violet). The grenade was cylinder shaped, 3 inches in diameter, 5.5 inches long and weighed 20 ounces. The smoke was designed to cling to the ground and the grenade burn time was 90–120 seconds condensed over a radius of 35 meters for a total of about 250,000 cubic feet of smoke. Smoke grenades were used for signaling and to provide cover or screening for troops. Sometimes referred to as Smoke Canister Grenades.

Grenades, Thermite (Thermite Grenade) U.S. incendiary grenade composed of powdered aluminum and metal oxides. The grenade was cylinder shaped and contained thermite, which when ignited burned for approximately 30 seconds at 4,300 degrees Fahrenheit. This temperature was high enough to burn completely through a truck engine block. The incendiary grenade was used for the burning of enemy materiel and damp foodstuffs. *See also* **Incendiaries.**

Grenades, White Phosphorus (White Phosphorus Grenade, WP Grenade, Willie Peter Grenade, M-34) U.S. antipersonnel hand grenade. When detonated the grenade scattered small particles of white phosphorus that burned intensely when exposed to the air. The burning particles clung to clothes and the body and continued to burn until all air was removed or the particle consumed itself. WP even burned underwater. Particles embedded in the skin would continue to burn until the particle was dug out, burned through the tissue or burned up. As the particle burned it also burned the tissue adjacent to it. Each WP grenade weighed a little over 2 pounds. *See also* **White Phosphorus.**

Grenadier (Thump Gunner, Thumperman) Man assigned to carry and operate the M-79 Grenade Launcher. *See also* **M-79.**

Greyhound *see* **M-8 Armored Car, C-2A**

Grid Coordinates System used by the military to reference terrain and locations on a map. Military maps contained a superimposed grid system that allowed any point on the map to be referenced by a set of six or eight numbers. Maps of Vietnam used in the field were 1:50,000 scale, divided into 100 × 100km grids identified by a two character code, i.e., XS, WR, YR, etc. Added to this code would be six numbers that would pinpoint a spot on the map to within 100 meters. XS863914 was the 100-meter square area where the Saigon City Office and the Rex BEQ were located. "863" represented the horizontal and "914" the vertical coordinates.

Grievance Payment (Solatium, Compensation Payment, Go-Minh Money) U.S. military officials often made payments to Vietnamese civilians for accidental losses they suffered as a result of U.S. military operations. The payments ranged from several dollars to several hundred dollars and were paid as compensation for the loss of a "loved one" and the grief associated with that loss; solatium. Payments were also made for property damage to buildings, crops, farm animals and personal possessions. The Vietnamese had to file their claim directly with the U.S. military or through their district or province chief. GVN officials and landowners were well known for filing false and inflated claims, in attempts to fatten their pockets. Some GVN officials attempted to channel the peasants' claims in their area directly through their office. The officials would modify (exaggerate/inflate) the claims and present them to the Americans to be resolved. Collecting the money from the Americans, the officials would skim part of it into their pockets, distributing the paltry remainder to the peasants. In the peasants' eyes it appeared that the Americans were not making just restitution for the damages they caused, and to the Americans it appeared that the peasants were "crooks," taking unfair advantage of the program. When the Americans realized the corruption was at the GVN level they began requiring the peasants to make their claims only to the Americans, at which time they were paid directly. The payments were nicknamed "Go-Minh" money. Go-minh was Vietnamese for "extracting oneself from a predicament."

Grinder (Parade Ground) Marine slang for a Parade Ground. *See also* **Close-Order Drill.**

Ground Control Intercept (GCI) Technique using ground radar to locate attacking enemy aircraft, then vectoring fighters to intercept them. NVN used the technique to vector MiGs to intercept U.S. planes inbound to targets in NVN. GCI was also used in conjunction with NVA radar controlled aircraft guns and surface-to-air missiles. *See also* **SA-7, Fan Song, Fire Cans.**

Ground Controlled Approaches (GCA)
Aircraft attempting to land, using landing approach instructions received from the ground control tower. Because of weather or instrument failure a pilot might be unable to make a normal visual approach. GCA approaches were also used to direct some B-52 bomber raids along the Ho Chi Minh Trail and against NVA/VC base areas. Ground control approach equipment consisted of a control station and navigational radar. *See also* **RABFAC, Combat Skyspot.**

Ground Pounder *see* **Infantry Soldier, The**

Ground Proximity Extraction System (GPES, Hook and Cable Delivery System)
Air Force cargo delivery system designed to resupply combat units in the field when the cargo plane was unable to land due to hostile fire or lack of an adequate runway. The cargo to be delivered was pallet loaded and placed at the rear ramp of a C-130; a large arresting hook was attached to the load. A cable system was stretched across the runway and the C-130 would fly in low (5–10 feet) hooking the cable with the arresting hook. As the C-130 moved away from the cable the load would be jerked out of the plane. The system worked but was extremely dangerous. The GPES system was originally called the "Hook and Cable Delivery System." It was eventually replaced by the LAPES system. *See also* **LAPES, LOLEX.**

Ground Radar (AN/TPS-25, AN/TPS-33, AN/PPS-4/5, Antipersonnel Radar, GSR) Short-range, directional Ground Surveillance Radar sets first issued in '67 used by some U.S. units to detect enemy movement. Most of the radars used were relatively large sets that were positioned at base camps. The AN/PPS-4 was a small man-packed unit with a maximum range of 1,500 meters. Although the unit was man portable it was usually helicoptered into a company position for nighttime surveillance. When a moving target was detected identification tones would be heard through the unit's headset. The AN/PSS-5 was a larger unit with a range of 5,000 meters and was not man portable. The PSS-5 featured an audio indicator as well as a small scanning scope display. Other versions of ground radar included the AN/TPS-25 and the TPS-33. The TPS-33 had a maximum range

of about 1,800 meters and could be broken down into man portable loads. The radars could detect vehicle and personnel movement, and an experienced operator could tell the difference between male and female personnel, their speed and direction of movement. *See also* **FSSB.**

Ground Radar Aerial Delivery System (GRADS) System using ground radar to guide an aircraft over a drop zone. The supply drop was made from 6,000–9,000 feet above the target after the aircraft was positioned using the radar. *See also* **Ground Control Approaches, LAPES, LOLEX.**

Ground Seismic Intrusion Device (G-SID, Mini-SID) The G-Sid was a seismic sensitive sensor used by the U.S. The device consisted of a watertight metal box approximately 12 inches square. Inside the box were electronic circuits, a radio transmitter and batteries. Sandwiched between the circuit-boards of the device were several magnesium panels. Once the device was activated a tilt switch was enabled; if the device was tilted to an angle greater than 15 degrees the box would self-destruct, the magnesium plates igniting, destroying the electronic components in the box. Attached to the top of the box was an 18-inch antenna. The G-SID was deployed by digging a hole deep enough to conceal the box yet allowing 10–12 inches of antenna to be exposed. Several devices (called a string) would be planted along a trail. The seismic sensor within the G-SID was extremely sensitive to ground vibrations, which activated the unit causing it to transmit a two-digit numerical code. The code would be displayed on a special remote receiver. Based on where the string was implanted and the codes received an operator could determine the direction of enemy travel, size of force and even their speed. The Mini-SID was a smaller version of the G-SID. *See also* **Electronic Sensors, P-SID, TurdSID.**

Ground Studies Group *see* **SOG Groups**

Ground Surveillance Radar *see* **Ground Radar**

Ground Week *see* **Airborne Training**

Grounder Pounder *see* **Infantry Soldier, The**

Group   Military designation for several units under one command. For the Army a group represented several battalions, organized for a specific function, under one brigade command. In Vietnam groups were usually part of larger support commands such as Aviation, Military Police, Signal, Support, etc. The Air Force, Navy and Marines also deployed forces arranged in "groups."

Group 559/759   North Vietnamese logistic support groups whose sole function was to transmit supplies from North Vietnam to NVA/VC units in South Vietnam. Groups 559 and 759 began operations in the late fifties, down trails along the Laos and Cambodian border; later the trails came to be collectively known as the Ho Chi Minh Trail. *See also* **Ho Chi Minh Trail.**

Group Alpha, MRF (Group Bravo, MRF)   In September '68 the MRF was expanded from three to four River Assault Squadrons. These squadrons were divided into Group Alpha and Group Bravo. Alpha consisted of five River Assault Divisions, operating in the area of Kien Hoa Province. Group Bravo consisted of three River Assault Divisions, operating throughout the lower Delta area. *See also* **TF 117.**

Group Bravo, MRF *see* **Group Alpha, MRF**

Group Mobile 100 *see* **Groupement Mobile 100**

Groupement Mobile 100 (GM100, Group Mobile 100)   An elite French armored force that operated in the Central Highlands of Vietnam against the Viet Minh. The force consisted of over 3,000 men, armored vehicles and artillery. Within six months of the unit's deployment to the Highlands, the Viet Minh had all but eliminated the GM100 as a fighting force. The French armored unit suffered its worst defeat at the Mang Yang Pass when the group was ambushed. The pass was through the mountains along Highway 19 between Pleiku and An Khe. During American involvement, French defeats and tactics were frequently used in comparisons to American situations and results in Vietnam. *See also* **Mang Yang Pass.**

Grow-Your-Own (Promotion from Within)   Practice of filling a unit's NCO vacancy from within the unit's pool of enlisted men. The "promote from within" method maintained unit cohesion and usually brought better results than bringing in an NCO from outside the unit to fill the vacancy. Unit cohesion was especially important in small specialized units such as EOD, LRRP and recon teams.

Grown (Get-Rid-of-Westmoreland-Now)   A group of junior Pentagon officers formed a secret society advocating the replacement of General Westmoreland as the MACV Commander in Vietnam. The group was disgruntled over the backlash caused by the communist Tet '68 Offensive. Prior to the communist Tet Offensive Westmoreland had given the indication that the U.S. was winning the war in Vietnam.

Gruening, Senator Ernest *see* **Morse, Senator Wayne**

Grunt *see* **Infantry Soldier, The**

GSC *see* **General Support Company**

GSG *see* **SOG Groups**

GSR *see* **Ground Radar**

GSW (Gunshot Wound)   Military abbreviation for "gunshot wound," used for reporting and statistical purposes.

GTL *see* **Gun-Target-Line**

Guam (Tin City, Andersen Air Force Base, Rock, The)   U.S. protectorate located about 4,000kms from Vietnam and about 6,300kms from the States. During the Vietnam War B-52s based at Guam (nicknamed the "Rock" by aircrews), made regular attacks on targets in SEA. During the mass evacuation of Vietnamese in '75 Andersen Air Force Base on Guam was used as a rest stop for Vietnamese refugees en route to permanent homes. The refugees were temporarily housed in sheet metal barracks that came to be known as "Tin City." Additionally 25,000 Vietnamese were allowed to permanently settle on the island. *See also* **Wake Island, Bullet Shot I-V Deployments, B-52.**

Guam Conference   Guam was the site of a '67 high level conference between President Johnson and President Thieu of South Vietnam. The conference was convened by President Johnson to show U.S. support and resolve to the Vietnamese government and to introduce America's new ambassador to SVN and a new deputy who would work under General Westmoreland at MACV to Vietnam's President Thieu and premier Nguyen Cao Ky. Also in attendance at the meeting were Dean Rusk, Robert McNamara, Ellsworth Bunker, Robert Komer and generals Abrams and Westmoreland. *See also* **Honolulu Conference.**

Guard, The *see* **Reserves**

Guard Channel (Emergency Channel, Guard Frequency)   U.S. military radio channel (UHF-243/VHF-121.5mHz) used by aircrews as an emergency radio frequency. The "Guard Channel" was the radio frequency that aircraft in trouble switched to, enabling them to communicate with other friendly aircraft in their area. Emergency radio sets used by downed aircrews also had access to the Guard Channel and used it to notify rescue aircraft of their condition and coordinate rescue efforts. The North Vietnamese used captured U.S. emergency radios to try to lure rescue aircraft into an area in an attempt to shoot them down.

Guard Frequency *see* **Guard Channel**

Guardian *see* **13th Aviation Battalion (Combat)**

Guerre à Outrance (War to the End)   French for "war to the end." The North Vietnamese used the phrase to describe their outlook on the struggle for reunification of North and South Vietnam.

Guerrilla War (Insurgency, Unconventional Warfare)   The use of irregular forces to harass and demoralize a larger enemy army. The irregulars continued this tactic until a regular army force became available, or the enemy force capitulated. The forces conducting the guerrilla operations were largely made up of local or indigenous personnel, usually with some type of foreign support. Guerrilla warfare was difficult to fight using conventional methods of war. One of the prime considerations was eliminating the guerrilla from his sources of support, both in and outside of the subject country. Another important factor in fighting guerrillas was the ability to be able to identify them. Eliminating the

guerrilla's base of support and identifying him was not successfully done in SVN. Because of restrictions placed on the U.S. military the guerrilla support sources outside of SVN were not subject to direct ground attack. And making the distinction between the guerrillas and the people was nearly impossible because at times they were one and the same. Conventional forces and weapons were used to fight an unconventional war. Prior to Vietnam, using conventional forces to fight and contain guerrillas required from 10–15 soldiers per guerrilla, but with the introduction of the helicopter during the Vietnam War the ratio of regular army troops per guerrilla was reduced to 5–1. *See also* **Limited Conventional War.**

Guideline *see* **Surface-to-Air Missile, SA-2**

Gulf of Siam *see* **Gulf of Thailand**

Gulf of Thailand (Gulf of Siam)   Sea gulf shared by South Vietnam, Cambodia and Thailand. The gulf was located to the west of Vietnam and was previously known as the Gulf of Siam. Enemy supply and infiltration operations crossed the gulf to Cambodia forming a southern supply terminal and infiltration route to Vietnam. *See also* **Sihanouk Trail.**

Gulf of Tonkin Incident *see* **Tonkin Gulf Incident**

Gulf of Tonkin Resolution *see* **Southeast Asia Resolution**

Gun, The *see* **M-60 MG**

Gun Birds *see* **Gunship**

Gun Camera *see* **KA-60 Gun Camera**

Gun Crew *see* **Gun Section**

Gun Grease *see* **Cosmoline**

Gun Jeep (Jeep, M-151)   Standard U.S. quarter-ton jeep, armed with a pedestal mounted gun. In Vietnam gun jeeps were usually armed with an M-60 or .50cal machine gun. Later versions of the gun jeep appeared armed with a TOW, minigun, automatic grenade launcher or 106mm recoilless rifle. The gun jeep was used extensively by all branches of the service, in the security role. The unmodified jeep had a maximum speed of about 65mph and was used throughout Vietnam by the ARVNs and the Free World Forces. A jeep could accommodate 3–4 passengers and a driver. Jeeps in Vietnam used gasoline for fuel; some military cargo/utility vehicles could use different types of fuel. *See also* **Rat Patrols.**

Gun Pets *see* **Parapets**

Gun Registration *see* **Battery Registration**

Gun Run (Rolling Hot, Run) A strafing run made by a helicopter gunship. The "run" was against a specific target/area or was used to prep an LZ before a helicopter assault. Gunship pilots typically announced the beginning of such an attack as "Rolling Hot." This announcement was made in the clear so other aircraft in the area would be aware the gunship was making a run, and also to inform troops on the ground that ordnance was on the way. Gun runs also referred to fixed-wing aircraft that strafed targets with machine gun or cannon fire.

Gun Section (Gun Crew) The gun crew for a field artillery or self-propelled artillery piece. The 105mm howitzer had an authorized crew strength of 8 men and the 155mm was crewed by 11 men. The M-107, -108 and -110 SPA guns operated with a five man crew and the M-109 SPA operated with a six man crew. In Vietnam most towed artillery units operated 1–3 men short of the authorized strength. Normally a battery consisted of 6 guns or tubes. *See also* **Artillery, U.S.; NVA.**

Gun Truck *see* **Hardened Convoy**

Gun Tub Nickname for the forward, twin .50cal machine gun turret located in the bow of a Navy PBR. *See also* **PBR.**

Gun-Target-Line (GTL) An imaginary line between a firing artillery gun and its target. Any friendly units located along the line would have the shells from the gun traveling directly overhead, creating a possible problem should one or more of the gun's rounds fall short. *See also* **Short Round.**

Gundecking Falsification of operational reports. The South Vietnamese Junk Force was notorious for inflating the number of boats they claimed to have conducting routine patrols. By claiming high patrol numbers the various groups of the force could request more manpower, equipment and support, making life a little easier for the few boats that did go on patrol. The practice continued until the Junk Force was merged with the Vietnamese Navy in '65. The practice of gundecking was not limited to the Junk Force. Many ARVN units submitted false reports on operations, weapons lost, desertions, etc., throughout the war. American units were not above gundecking, some U.S. units were guilty of inflated enemy body counts, and President Nixon ordered the "alteration" of reports on the secret bombing of Cambodia.

Gunfighters (1st/6th/198th LIB, 366th Tactical Fighter Wing, 366th TFW) Nickname of Company A/1st Battalion/6th Infantry Regiment/198th Light Infantry Brigade. The motto used on their "death cards" was "Dealers of Death." The card was an ace of spades, with a skull and crossbones in the center of the card along with their name, unit and their motto. "Gunfighters" was also the unit name of the 366th Tactical Fighter Wing, Air Force F-4s operating out of Da Nang. *See also* **Calling Cards, 6th Infantry Regiment.**

Gung-Ho (Hard-Charger) In Chinese it meant to "pull together"; in the military it generally referred to any one who was overenthusiastic, overeager or overzealous about his military duties; a lifer or potential lifer (career soldier).

Gungi Marine (GI Joe, Sergeant Rock) Marine name for the kind of Marine most grunts would want in the field with them. The Gungi Marine was trustworthy, loyal to his fellow grunts, a natural leader, strong, bush smart, cunning, had a sense of humor, was aggressive yet careful, perhaps a little crazy at times; the man you wanted in your foxhole with you, on your fire team or as your squad leader. Marine version of "GI Joe" or "Sergeant Rock" of WWII comic book fame.

Gunner's Quadrant A leveling device used to measure the angle of a weapon's barrel in relation to a horizontal reference point. The quadrant measured the angle of elevation in degrees, with respect to the ground (horizontal reference).

Gunnery Sergeant (Gunny, Top, GySgt, First Shirt, 1st Sergeant, The Topper) First or senior NCO of a unit, generally a company size or larger. Platoon sergeants were also referred to as "Gunny."

"Gunny" was strictly a Marine term. The other names for the senior NCO of a unit applied to both the Army and the Marines. In the Marine Corps a gunnery sergeant held the grade of E-7. *See also* **E-7.**

Gunny *see* **Gunnery Sergeant**

Guns The Marine nickname for the weapons squad or weapons platoon. The name also was used in reference to the company or platoon's machine gun teams. "Guns" was also the nickname for the helicopter gunships of the Army's Aero Weapons Platoon. *See also* **Gunship, Aero Weapons Platoon.**

Guns and Butter Financing Term used during the Vietnam War referring to the difficulties in balancing the cost of the war in Vietnam ("guns") and financing the domestic reforms ("butter") of President Johnson's "Great Society." The Reforms proposed and legislated by the President were expensive, and each day the cost required to support the expanding war in Vietnam grew. With the inflation rate rising, Johnson had to decide whether to curtail defense spending or reduce the goals for his domestic programs. Not wanting to give up on Vietnam and his goal to stop communist aggression, Johnson was forced to cut back on his domestic reforms. Estimates for cost of the war years was in excess of $150 billion, with additional costs to be incurred as time goes on. *See also* **Great Society, The.**

Guns-a-Go-Go *see* **Go-Go Bird**

Gunship (Escort Ship, Guns, Gun Birds) Name applied to helicopters and some fixed-wing aircraft used exclusively in the ground support role. AH-1, UH-1B and UH-1C helicopters provided an accurate and heavy volume of fire on enemy targets. Air Force C-47, C-119, and C-130 transport aircraft were modified and armed with various weapons that allowed them to be used as airborne gun platforms delivering a heavy volume of fire to enemy positions. In the early days, armed U.S. helicopters in Vietnam were called "Escort" ships. Gunships were referred to as "Guns" by helicopter crews or "gun birds" by the Marines. *See also* **AC-47, AC-130, AC-119G, UH-1C, AH-1G, Go-Go Bird, Helicopter Gunship, UH-1F, UTTCO, FAWS.**

Gunship II *see* **AC-130**

Gunship III *see* **AC-119G**

Gunshot Wound *see* **GSW**

Gunslingers *see* **Those Who Kill for Pleasure...**

Guy in Backseat *see* **Weapons Systems Operator**

GVN *see* **Government of Vietnam**

GVN by Day, NLF by Night *see* **Xoi Dao**

GWINK (Gin and Wink) One of the popular drinks shared by members of the 12th Evac at Cu Chi. The drink consisted of gin and Wink. Wink was a commercial, carbonated grapefruit drink. *See also* **Bunker Bunnies.**

Gypsy Operations Military operations in which small combat or fire bases were established for short periods of time, and subsequently moved and reestablished in several different locations throughout the course of the operation.

Gyrenes *see* **U.S. Marines**

GySgt *see* **Gunnery Sergeant**

H

H & I *see* **H and I**

H & S Company (Headquarters and Supply Company) Battalion headquarters and supply (service) group of a Marine infantry battalion. A normal Marine infantry battalion consisted of four rifle companies, supply group and the battalion headquarters.

H and I (Harassing and Interdiction Fires, Targets of Intelligence, HI Fires,

Raking) Random artillery fires on pre-selected targets in an effort to disrupt unseen enemy activity, disturbing their sleep, weakening morale and restricting their movement. The enemy targets usually chosen were suspected assembly areas, trails, campsites or previously discovered positions. The name H and I was changed later in the war to Targets of Intelligence, by higher command, or referred to as I & I Fires (Intelligence and Interdiction). Army public relations people believed Targets of Intelligence had a less sinister sound in the press than Harassment and Interdiction Fire. "Raking-Over" was the French name for H & I Fires.

H I Fires *see* **H and I**

H-3 *see* **SH-3**

H-6 *see* **LVTH-6**

H-13 *see* **OH-13**

H-19 (Chickasaw, UH-19, CH-19, S-55) The Sikorsky S-55 (H-19) was the only helicopter available to the South Vietnamese until the first arrival of American helicopters in '61. The H-19s were leftovers from the French and were not well-suited to troop carrying operations. The H-19, or UH-19 "Chickasaw" as it was designated by the U.S. Army, was also used by the Navy, Air Force, and the Marines, as the CH-19. The UH-19 operated with a two man crew and could transport ten men, with a max speed of 112mph and a range of 570kms. The H-19 was quickly replaced by the CH-21, 34, and 37 as the prime helicopter used to transport the ARVNs prior to '65.

H-21 *see* **CH-21**

H-23 *see* **OH-23**

H-34 *see* **CH-34**

H-35 *see* **CH-34**

H-37 *see* **CH-37**

H-43 *see* **HH-43**

H-46 *see* **CH-46**

H-48 *see* **UH-1F**

H-Hour Military reference to the time a mission or operation was to begin.

H. Rap Brown Law (Anti-Riot Law) A law that was attached to the '68 Civil Rights Act, and was designed to give the police more legal power in controlling politically motivated riots and civil disorder. The law was in response to H. Rap Brown's incitement to crowds of black demonstrators to take up arms to force a change in black-white relations and achieve social reform. *See also* **Brown, H. Rap.**

Ha's *see* **Hawk Missile**

Ha-Si *see* **Private First Class**

Ha-Si-Nhat *see* **E-4**

Hac Bao (Black Panthers, ARVN 1st Inf Div Recon Company) One of the better ARVN units to fight in Vietnam, operated in I Corps throughout the war. The 1st ARVN Division was headquartered in Hue. *See also* **1st ARVN Infantry Division.**

Hades *see* **Operation Ranch Hand**

Hai Lang Small village located outside of Hue, scene of heavy fighting by elements of the 501st Infantry/101st Airborne, during Tet '68.

Hai Quan *see* **Republic of Vietnam Navy**

Hai Van Pass (Cloud Pass, Le Col des Nuages) Strategic pass on Highway 1, between Hue and Quang Tri in I Corps. Highway 1 was South Vietnam's major north/south road connecting the DMZ; Quang Tri and Hue, north of the pass, with Da Nang, Chu Lai and Quang Ngai, south of the pass. With no suitable ports available to Allied shipping north of the pass most supplies needed to be trucked or airlifted in. Possession of the pass was critical to the American and South Vietnamese war effort. The NVA made repeated attacks on US/ARVN units in the area, but were unable to close the pass. If the NVA had been able to close the pass, the extreme northern provinces of South Vietnam would have been isolated and denied overland supply. The Americans called the pass "Cloud Pass." *See also* **Hawk Missile, Iron Bridge Ridge.**

Haig, Lt. Col. Alexander Commanded the 1st Battalion/26th Infantry during the "restructuring" of the village of Ben Suc in the Iron Triangle, during Operation Cedar Falls, in January '67. Haig joined the Nixon administration as a National Security Council advisor in '68 and in less than 5 years was promoted, by President Nixon, from the rank of colonel to "4-star" general and appointed vice-chief of staff of the U.S. Army. Haig's promotion was above the heads of several senior officers on the promotion list. Haig continued to advise Nixon on national security matters. After Nixon's resignation, Haig remained Ford's national security advisor and in '80 became Ronald Reagan's short term secretary of state.

Haight-Ashbury (Hashbury)   District in San Francisco, California, that became the hippie capital of the world in the mid-sixties. "Hashbury," as it was known to its occupants, also attracted teenage runaways, winos, motorcycle gangs, professional and amateur drug dealers, con artists and miscellaneous psychos and "weirdos."

Haiphong (Haiphong Harbor)   North Vietnam's major port city, improved by the French, and connected to Hanoi by a 100km rail line. U.S. intelligence estimated that 85 percent of NVN's war materiels passed through the port. The harbor itself was not targeted for air strikes until '72, but the city was targeted several times. In May '72 U.S. naval forces mined the port in an effort to slow the NVA supply buildup. The mines were removed in July '73 as part of the '73 Paris Peace Accords. North Vietnam's major ports of Thanh Hoa, Cam Pha and Hon Gai were also mined. The port minings were part of Operation Linebacker I. *See also* Operation Linebacker I, Blockade, River Mines.

Hairhead   *see*   **Hippie**

HAL-3   *see*   **Seawolves**

Halang   *see*   **Montagnards**

Half Moon Bay (Da Nang Harbor)   The natural harbor at Da Nang was crescent shaped and was called "Half Moon Bay." The harbor was 8kms wide at its opening and about 15kms across at its widest point. *See also* Da Nang.

Half-Stepping   *see*   **Goldbricking**

Hall of a Thousand Mirrors   *see*   **Hall of Mirrors**

Hall of Mirrors (Le Van Vien, Hall of a Thousand Mirrors)   Reportedly the largest brothel in Southeast Asia prior to '55. The whorehouse was run by Le Van Vien, leader of the Binh Xuyen. The brothel was located in the Cholon area of Saigon. Le Van Vien controlled the national police in the Saigon

area and dominated all the major vice activities within the city. In '55 South Vietnam's Prime Minister Diem used the Army to shut down the operations of the Binh Xuyen. The survivors relocated to the Rung Sat Zone and joined the Viet Cong. Le Van Vien managed to escape to France with a considerable fortune. *See also* Binh Xuyen, Dai Kim Do, Dance Ban.

Hallucinogens (LSD, Mescaline, Psilocybin, STP)   Variety of drugs that induced hallucinations in the user. These drugs had varying effects on the individual user, such as altering his perception, consciousness, self-worth and perceived reality. The drugs also could induce hazards such as psychosis and genetic defects. *See also* LSD, STP.

HALO (High Altitude, Low Opening Parachute Jump)   Special type of parachute jump used to infiltrate enemy territory. The jump involved the transport aircraft traveling at an extremely high altitude so it would not be heard on the ground, and the parachute jumper making his free-fall to within several hundred feet of the ground before deploying his chute. This allowed him to enter an area presenting himself as the smallest possible target for the minimum amount of time.

Halt   *see*   **Dung Lai**

Ham and Lima Beans   *see*   **Beans-and-Motherfuckers**

Ham Chong   *see*   **Punji Pit**

Ham Rung Bridge   *see*   **Thanh Hoa Bridge**

Ham Tan   Capital of Binh Tuy Province, III Corps. Ham Tan was located 110kms east of Saigon and about 4kms west of the coast.

Ham-and-Mothers   *see*   **Beans-and-Motherfuckers**

Hamburger Hill (Battle of Hamburger Hill, Dong Ap Bia Mountain, Hill 937, Ap Bia Mountain)   During Operation Apache Snow, in the A Shau Valley of I Corps, elements of the 101st Airborne, 187th Infantry made contact with two battalions of the 29th NVA Regiment on Hill 937, May 11, 1969. Except for the NVA troops dug-in on the hill, 937 had no other tactical significance. The division commander (Zais) ordered the hill taken, and on May 20, after

11 assaults and 442 American WIA/KIAs the hill was taken. One week later, the hill was abandoned by U.S. troops, and the division commander quietly replaced. The sacrifice offered by 3d/187th Infantry far outweighed the marginal importance of "Hamburger Hill" at a time when the U.S. war effort was beginning to wind down. *See also* **Apache Snow; Zais, General Melvin; 187th Infantry Regiment.**

Hamlet (Ap) A small group or cluster of houses, huts or hootches, forming a unit. Several hamlets composed a village. GIs generally referred to a single hamlet as a ville or village, but officially a village consisted of several hamlets. Hamlets were often used by the VC to ambush U.S. troops. The VC could force unwilling villagers or enlist the aid of sympathetic villagers to help them construct defensive positions within the ville. Such positions were well camouflaged and highly resistant to U.S. air and artillery strikes. The VC used the Americans' reluctance to fire on villages as an offensive weapon, repeatedly ambushing U.S. troops from the safety of the villages. "Ap" was used to denote a hamlet on military maps (Ap Hung Tho, Ap Bac Lan, etc.). *See also* **Village.**

Hamlet Chief *see* **Province**

Hamlet Evaluation Survey   *see* **Hamlet Evaluation System**

Hamlet Evaluation System (HES Report, HES 70, Hamlet Evaluation Survey) A '67 computer rating system used by MACV to evaluate the loyalty of villages to the GVN. All inhabited areas of SVN were included in the report. The HES survey was used, in part, to determine the progress of the Accelerated Pacification Program. Ratings ran from A (loyal to Saigon) to E (a VC sympathetic location) or V (a VC controlled location). Input for the computer's decisions was based on the responses from representative hamlets in the field. The information was frequently falsified to make the report more favorable to the GVN. The flawed system was used by the American command to demonstrate the supposed effectiveness of the GVN to gather and hold popular support among its rural populace.

Hamlet Festival U.S. Army name for limited pacification operations carried out in

I and II Corps in late '65. The operations were patterned after Marine "County-Fair Operations" that involved U.S. and ARVN units surrounding a hamlet to seal it off. At first light units would sweep into the sealed village. The occupants would be questioned and their ID cards checked. The hamlet was thoroughly searched and the villagers given medical aid and food. The operation would last two–three days with the U.S. unit providing perimeter security, medical aid and food while the ARVNs did the questioning and searching. *See also* **County-Fair Operations, Pacification.**

Hamlet Militia *see* **People's Self-Defense Force**

Hammer-and-Anvil (Blocking Force, Leavenworth Plan) Military tactic that involved setting up a blocking force (anvil) of friendly units and using another friendly force to drive (hammer) the enemy into the blocking force, pinning the enemy between the two forces. U.S. forces used the tactic repeatedly in Vietnam. The helicopter allowed large numbers of troops to be moved quickly into blocking positions when the enemy was found. Sometimes artillery and air strikes were used to provide the blocking element, forcing the enemy to move through an exploding curtain of steel to avoid the driving force. When airborne or airmobile troops were deployed as the blocking force, and armor units conducted the sweep, the maneuver was referred to as the Leavenworth Plan. *See also* **Stopper.**

Hammerhead Stall Stall condition experienced when an aircraft is performing a high speed vertical climb following a dive. As the aircraft climbs it begins to lose power as it reaches its maximum climbing altitude. If the aircraft continues to climb it eventually stalls. The recovery procedure from such a stall involves sharply yawing the aircraft into a dive, picking up speed and hopefully restarting the engine. A similar condition occurs in helicopter flight if the chopper loses power at a high altitude. As the chopper falls, the blades are autorotated, at the proper speed the engine could be restarted. Hammerhead stalls were routine parts of flight training. In helicopters the stall was simulated by shutting off the engine while at a high altitude. *See also* **Autorotation.**

Hammersley *see* **Operation Hammersley**

Hammock (NVA Hammock) Four types of hammocks saw service with U.S. units in Vietnam. The WWII vintage canvas model was used at some base camps; weighing 15 pounds, it was not a field carried item. An improved, 4-pound version was available in the early sixties. In '68 the Army started using two models patterned after the NVA hammock. Both versions were made of nylon netting with supporting nylon ropes. One version (NVA copy) was 3 × 8 feet, the larger version was 5 × 9 feet and was used as a multipurpose net and hammock. Both versions weighed less than two pounds.

Hancock *see* **USS Hancock**

Hand Flare (M-127, White Star Flare, Slap Flare) Small hand launched aerial flare. The flare was fitted in a cardboard tube; holding the tube vertically and striking the bottom end fired the flare, which rocketed upward. At the peak of the rocket's climb the flare ignited and drifted to the ground by parachute. *See also* **Flares.**

Hand Grenade Booby Traps The VC made extensive use of hand grenades for booby traps. A grenade's handle would be wrapped with electrical tape and the safety pin removed; the grenade would be dropped in the gas tank of a vehicle. Some time later the gasoline would dissolve the glue on the tape, releasing the handle and blowing up the vehicle. Another simple method was to place a grenade in an empty can with the pin removed. When a tripwire attached to the grenade was pulled, the grenade would be pulled out of the can and detonate. The NVA/VC would booby-trap the dead bodies of their own troops, and when possible booby-trap the bodies of dead GIs. The use of grenades as booby traps by U.S. troops was limited in scope. Some U.S. patrols would booby-trap their trash, catching the scavenging VC by surprise. *See also* **Booby Trap.**

Hand Grenade Handle *see* **Spoon**

Hand Grenades (Grenade) Small antipersonnel bombs designed to be thrown by hand, detonating on contact or by internal timer. There were various types of hand grenades: fragmentation, smoke, illumination, incendiary, white phosphorus, gas and concussion. Both FWFs and NVA/VC forces made wide use of hand grenades in defensive, offensive operations and in booby traps. Most hand grenades operated with a fused timer that allowed a 4–7 second time delay before detonation. With the delay removed the grenade would detonate instantly when the handle (spoon) was released. *See also* **Grenades: Fragmentation, Illumination, Gas, Concussion, Smoke, White Phosphorus, Thermite; Grenade Launchers; Rifle Grenade; Spoon; C-Rat Grenade.**

Hang Fire (Misfire, Hung Rocket) Failure of a round to fire after having been struck by the firing pin, or the failure of the explosive charge to detonate. When a "hang fire" occurred with a mortar round, the mortar tube had to be carefully inverted to allow the round to slide out and be gingerly removed for disposal. The round was considered armed and subject to detonation at any time. A similar problem could occur with the 2.75-inch rockets used aboard helicopter gunships, if the triggered rocket failed to leave the tube in which it was loaded. The failure could be in the rocket motor, or the spring loaded tail fins could "hang-up," causing the armed rocket to be lodged in its launcher. It was the aircraft's crew chief/door gunner's responsibility to remove the misfire.

Hang Time *see* **Loiter Time**

Hangar-Flying (Bull Session) "Hangar-flying" referred to the animated conversations between combat pilots as they described some of their combat flights and experiences, mentally reflying the mission; similar to a "bull session."

Hanoi (Thanh Long) Capital of North Vietnam, and after the fall of South Vietnam in '75, the capital of all of Vietnam; the Socialist Republic of Vietnam. Hanoi is located on the Red River, in the Red River Delta, and served as the French capital of Indochina until their defeat in '54. In ancient times it served as the capital of Tonkin and was known as Thanh Long. Hanoi provided the guidance, support and later the manpower to carry on the NVA/VC war effort in the south. Rail and industrial centers were occasionally targets of U.S. bombing raids, but no major air strikes hit Hanoi until December '72, when the Christmas bombing took place. *See also* **Bach Mai Hospital, Christmas Bombing.**

Hanoi Hanna　GI nickname for North Vietnamese female broadcasters on Radio Hanoi, equivalent to Tokyo Rose (of WWII fame) or Peking Polly (Korean War). Hanna read communist slanted news and propaganda in English for the consumption of U.S. troops in SVN. Hanna knew the disposition of most regular U.S. units incountry and mentioned some units by name. During her broadcast she would deliver inflated casualty reports for U.S. units and target black troops for special consideration in an effort to get them to rebel against the military system. Hanoi Hanna was not just one woman; several North Vietnamese women did the broadcast, but the GIs lumped them all under the name of Hanoi Hanna. *See also* **Radio Hanoi.**

Hanoi Hilton (Hao Lo Prison, Hell-Hole Prison)　Central Hanoi Prison in NVN, used for holding U.S. POWs. The prison complex consisted of a number of smaller prison units, each given a name by the POWs. The main prison was used for extended interrogations, and housed various torture devices used to extract information or as harassment. Hao Lo roughly translated in Vietnamese meant "hell-hole." Conditions at the prisons were poor, medical attention was rarely available, the food was marginally edible and torture and isolation were the norm rather than the exception. Sanitation facilities were extremely poor, and the cells were infested with lice, insects and rats. Psychological torture was used extensively for punishment, harassment and subjugation of U.S. POWs. Hoa Lo was divided into several sections, nicknamed: Heartbreak Hotel, Little Vegas, Camp Unity and New Guy Village. Some of the nicknames of other POW prisons in and around Hanoi were The Zoo, Briarpatch, Son Tay, The Annex, Dirty Bird, Alcatraz, Camp Faith, The Plantation and The Powerplant. When it became evident to the NVA that the Paris Peace Accords would be signed the treatment of the prisoners greatly improved and the torture practices ended. *See also* **Torture, NVA Methods; Zoo, The; Tap Codes; Prisoners of War; Heartbreak Hotel.**

Hanoi Jane　*see*　**Fonda, Jane**

Hanoi-Haiphong Sanctuaries　During the initial U.S. bombing campaign against North Vietnam targets, the cities of Haiphong and Hanoi were excluded from the list of acceptable targets released by the White House. Also excluded from the original list were several airfields in North Vietnam where MiG fighters were based. In '67 the first strikes against MiG bases were authorized, and in '69 limited targets were authorized in the Hanoi and Haiphong areas. NVN made use of the bombing restrictions to greatly increase their war effort, storing supplies, munitions and weapons in the bomb safe zones. Massive bombing of the Hanoi-Haiphong Sanctuaries did not take place until the Christmas bombings of '72. *See also* **Operation Linebacker II.**

Hao Lo Prison　*see*　**Hanoi Hilton**

Happening on the Green　Courtyard located at Clark Air Base in the Philippines. During the evacuation of Saigon in late April '75 several thousand Vietnamese refugees took up temporary lodging in the courtyard. The refugees were eventually moved from Clark AB to permanent residences in communities throughout the U.S. *See also* **Philippines.**

Happy House　The tribal ritual center of a Montagnard village. The Happy House was usually constructed in the center of the village and housed the village's spirit. In the larger villages the Happy House was also the communal sleeping area for the unmarried men of the village. The house also served as a social gathering place for the men and was off limits to the village women. *See also* **Longhouse.**

Happy Smoke　*see*　**Marijuana**

Happy Valley　*see*　**Vinh Thanh Valley, Happy Valley (Marines)**

Happy Valley (Marines)　Viet Cong base area located 36kms southwest of Da Nang and 17kms northwest of An Hoa. The mouth of the east/west valley was located at the village of Ha Tan. The valley ended 28kms to the west of Ha Tan, in dense terrain which was just 30kms from the Laotian border. The western end of Charlie Ridge formed part of the northern rim of Happy Valley. The NVA/VC occupied the valley using it as a major infiltration route to the coast until Marines began patrolling on a regular basis. The valley was laced with mines, booby traps, and snipers; and sudden, vicious ambushes by the NVA/VC were always a threat. "Happy Valley" acquired its nickname from the Marines, who patrolled the area, and were always so "happy" to leave the valley.

Harassing and Interdiction Fires *see* **H and I**

Harbor Entrance Central Post *see* **SEASHARP**

Harbor Explosive Ordnance Disposal Teams *see* **SEASHARP**

Harbor Operations and Maintenance Support *see* **SEASHARP**

Harbor Patrol Force *see* **SEA-SHARP**

Harbor Site (Campsite)   Recon Marine phrase for a campsite or night defensive position; temporary patrol base. From the campsite the Recon Marines performed short reconnaissance missions in the area, returning to the harbor site for security and rest. The Australian infantry used the term "harbour site" to reference a night campsite or NDP. *See also* **Night Defensive Position, Patrol Base.**

Harbor Tug, Large *see* **YTB**

Harbor Utility Craft *see* **LCU**

Hard Points *see* **LAU-77/78/80**

Hard Stripes *see* **Specialist Class**

Hard Targets (Soft Targets)   Military targets were defined as either hard or soft. Soft targets were personnel, unarmored vehicles (cars, trucks, jeeps, etc.), thatch hooches, wooden boats, and basically any targets that could be easily penetrated by small arms and automatic weapons fire. Hard targets were all armored vehicles, fortifications, concrete-steel-brick structures, ships, and any other targets not easily penetrated by the smaller caliber weapons.

Hard-Case Lifers *see* **Lifers**

Hard-Charger *see* **Gung-Ho**

Hard-Luck (Bad Luck)   Slang reference to bad luck. Some men and units seemed to fall into bad situations, one after the other. They were known as hard-luck platoons or hard-luck companies, and their reputation usually preceded them.

Hardcore Battalion   The 4th/39th Infantry was nicknamed the "Hardcore Bat-

talion" because of the extreme methods they used to combat the Viet Cong in the Delta. The 4th/39th primarily operated in Dinh Tuong Province and functioned as a counterguerrilla force against the Viet Cong. The battalion's four companies' primary mode of operation was the night ambush. One company conducted ambushes around the fringe of the battalion's AO, a second company operated within 10kms of the battalion base camp. The other two companies operated as guerrilla companies throughout the AO. Techniques used by the highly disciplined and professional 4th/39th were extremely effective in western Tuong Province. *See also* **39th Infantry.**

Hardened Convoy (Armored Truck, Hardened Truck, Gun Truck)   U.S. cargo trucks used for convoy duty, specially fitted with armor plate and sandbags to protect the drivers and their loads from NVA/VC ambushes en route. Many of the "hardened trucks" were used for convoy escort duties as well as transports and were fitted with a variety of heavy weapons which included miniguns, quad .50cal machine guns and grenade launchers. The armored gun trucks were also used for base camp defense.

Hardened Truck *see* **Hardened Convoy**

Hardliners (Softliners)   Nickname for some American POWs based on their interpretation of the Military Code of Conduct that was to be followed by American servicemen. In the prisons of Hanoi the "hardliners" or "diehards" believed in following the MCC to the letter with no variance, and considered anyone who did not do so a collaborator or enemy. The "softliners" believed you should resist as long as possible, eventually yielding (as little as possible) without giving in completely: The object being survival. Navy pilots and some Air Force pilots tended to take the hardline, while the rest took the softline; a few completely cooperated with the NVA and were labeled "Finks," and worse.

Hardship Discharge   Administrative discharge from military service, granted to allow an individual to address a severe family problem, or hardship requiring his full attention. For instance a soldier could be released to care for a surviving invalid parent. A hardship discharge could also be granted to allow a soldier to care for his chronically ill wife or parent, or other extenuating circumstances. *See also* **Discharges.**

Hardspot (Armor Ambush)   GI slang for an ambush setup using armor. Armor ambushes were difficult to conceal in Vietnam; the vehicles made so much noise when they moved and were so easy to see that they were not effective as a mobile ambush force. But an effective use of armor in ambush was against NVA/VC infiltration routes at distances in excess of 600 meters. Night scopes and infrared searchlights mounted on the tanks allowed them to quietly engage targets at long distances.

Hardstand   Flat platform constructed of PSP steel plating, asphalt or concrete. Hardstands were used as helipads or parking areas in soft sand or muddy terrain. Hardstands were also used to support artillery pieces. Hardstands made of PSP steel plate could be quickly constructed and provided maximum support without the weight and construction time associated with concrete hardstands. *See also* **PSP.**

Hardwick's Sea Snake   *see*   **Hook-Nosed Sea Snake**

Harkins, General Paul D.   First commander of the U.S. Military Assistance Command, Vietnam. General Harkins commanded MACV from '62 until '64, when Gen. William Westmoreland took command. MACV was established in Saigon in '62, and assumed the advisory and training duties formerly controlled by MAAGV. *See also* **Military Assistance Advisory Group, Vietnam.**

Harriman, Averell   Served as ambassador-at-large in the Kennedy and Johnson administrations and as under secretary of state for political affairs. Harriman was one of Johnson's policy advisors and one of his "Wise Old Men." In '68 at the onset of peace negotiations with the North Vietnamese, Harriman served as the U.S.'s chief negotiator. Harriman advised Johnson to seek a negotiated settlement in Vietnam and bring the U.S. troops home. *See also* **Wise Old Men.**

Harvest Moon   *see*   **Operation Harvest Moon/Lien Ket 18**

Hash   *see*   **Hashish**

Hash Marks   Insignia worn on the lower sleeves of the military uniform. On Army uniforms the hash mark appeared as a diagonal, braided "slash" indicating the wearer had reenlisted in the Army. Subsequent reenlistments were marked by identical slashes, placed in parallel, on the sleeve.

Hashbury   *see*   **Haight-Ashbury**

Hashish (Hash)   One of several illicit drugs abused by some U.S. troops in Vietnam. Hash was also one of the many illegal drugs and substances in use in the States. The hippie movement made extensive use of such drugs throughout the sixties and seventies. Hashish was derived from the resin extracted from marijuana plant tops and sprouts; in its final form it was usually sold as a small black ball of sticky gum that was mixed with tobacco and smoked in a pipe. *See also* **Marijuana.**

Hastings   *see*   **Operation Hastings**

Hasty Ambush   Ambush quickly set up as a result of a surprise encounter with an enemy force. Hasty ambushes usually resulted when a small, undetected recon patrol came upon an enemy force. The recon force would quickly deploy into an ambush. Normally, ambushes were prepared in advance, with the ambushing force moving into position well in advance of any possible enemy contact. The hasty ambush was used when the enemy force encountered was small and the ambush force felt it could easily overwhelm them. Hasty ambushes were one of the main tactics of U.S. recon and hunter-killer teams. Such ambushes were nearly impossible for platoon or company size units because of their inability to move undetected through the jungle. *See also* **Ambush.**

Hasty Defenses (Hasty Perimeter) Perimeter defense hastily deployed usually while in contact with, and under fire from an enemy force. The hasty perimeter defense usually did not have the benefit of foxholes or improved defensive positions, but attempted to use the available terrain to defensive advantage. During routine sweeps U.S. troops were often thrown into hasty defenses when ambushed by the enemy.

Hasty Perimeter   *see*   **Hasty Defenses**

Hat Dich   Village located 33kms north

of Vung Tau and 14kms west of Binh Gia in Phuoc Tuy Province, III Corps. The village and the area surrounding it served as a base of operations for elements of the 5th Viet Cong Division.

Hatchet Force   Platoon size force composed of 4–5 USSF and 30 CIDG troops conducting Project Omega and Project Sigma missions in enemy controlled areas, many of which were in Laos, Cambodia and North Vietnam. The force operated deep in enemy territory conducting raids and ambushes from their MACV-SOG Command and Control bases in I and II Corps. The force also acted as a quick reaction element to provide backup and followup for Spike Recon Teams. The Hatchet Force was itself backed up by SLAM Companies. *See also* **MACV-SOG Command and Control; Projects: Omega, Sigma; Spike Recon Team; SLAM Company.**

Hatchet Teams   Long-range reconnaissance teams of the 2d Battalion/502d Infantry (Airborne). The small recon teams provided intelligence and special ambush patrols for the 2d Brigade/101st Airborne Division during operations in Vietnam. The teams were later reclassified as LRRP units and were eventually consolidated into Company L/75th Infantry (Rangers) in February '69.

Hatfield-McGovern Amendment   '70 congressional amendment sponsored by Senator Mark Hatfield, R–Oregon, and Senator George McGovern, D–South Dakota, that required that all U.S. troops in South Vietnam be withdrawn by the end of '71. The amendment failed to pass in the Senate, but gave a clear indication to the Nixon administration that America had grown weary of the war and the secret dealings at the White House. Hatfield opposed the war and frequently criticized the Nixon White House. *See also* **Cooper-Church Amendment, War Powers Act.**

Hathcock, Gunnery Sergeant Carlos (The White Feather, Long Tra'ng du K'ich)   U.S. Marine sniper Sgt. Carlos Hathcock. He was nicknamed White Feather because of the small, white, chicken feather he wore in his bush hat. During Hathcock's two tours in Vietnam he had 93 confirmed kills and many other probables. He operated in the Duc Pho area of I Corps

in '67, harassing the NVA/VC. So successful was he that the NVA/VC placed a $10,000 bounty on his head. In September '69, while on patrol, the amtrac he was riding hit a mine; he was seriously burned and returned to the States. He retired from the Marine Corps in April '79 as a gunnery sergeant. Long Tra'ng du K'ich is Vietnamese for White Feather Sniper. *See also* **Sniper; Waldron, Sergeant Adelbert F., III.**

Hau Bon   *see*   **Cheo Reo**

Hau Giang River   *see*   **Bassac River**

Haul-Ass   *see*   **Book**

Having Your Shit Together   *see* Strac, Get-Your-Shit-Together

HAW   *see*   **Heavy Antitank Weapons**

Hawk Hill   GI name for the fire support base located on a small hill 10kms northwest of Tam Ky and 50kms southeast of Da Nang. The fire base was located less than 4kms west of Highway 1 and served as a fire base for the Americal Division.

Hawk Missile (SAM, U.S.; 2d Light Antiaircraft Missile Battalion, LAAM)   The Marines deployed surface-to-air Hawk missile systems at Da Nang and Chu Lai air bases. Hawk missile (Ha's) antiaircraft batteries of the 1st LAAM were placed on Hill 55 south of Da Nang, Hill 327 west of Da Nang, Hai Van Pass north of Da Nang and on Monkey Mountain east of Da Nang. The 2d LAAM deployed its batteries around the air base at Chu Lai. "HAWK" (Homing All-the-Way Killer) missiles were manufactured by Raytheon Co. Three missiles were mounted on a towed launcher; each warhead weighed 100 pounds, traveled at a speed of 1,900mph to a max range of 30kms. The battery's organic radar illuminated enemy aircraft as targets for the missile. Marine Hawks in SVN never fired in combat. *See also* **Hill 55, Hill 327, Air Defense Artillery.**

Hawk Team   Long-range reconnaissance teams composed of volunteers from the 2d Bn/327th Infantry (Airborne). The recon teams provided their battalion and the 1st Brigade/101st Airborne Division with recon and intelligence information. The teams were later formalized into LRRP units that were redesignated Company L/75th Infantry (Rangers) in February '69. *See also* **Tigers.**

Hawk Team, 173d Airborne Nickname given to small teams of 6–8 men that were inserted into the jungle foothills around Phu My in Binh Dinh Province, II Corps. The teams operated in the hills for 3–5 day periods seeking out small enemy units. The Hawk team concept around Phu My was initiated by elements of the 173d Airborne operating in the area in early '70. The concept was similar to other methods such as the CRIP Platoon and Hunter-Killer operations. *See also* **CRIP, Hunter-Killer Operations.**

Hawkeye *see* **E-2 Hawkeye**

Hawkeyes Nickname for hunter-killer teams of the 4th Infantry Division. The Hawkeyes operated as LRRP teams that specialized in long-distance sniping. The teams consisted of 3–5 men that operated independently in the field for several days at a time.

Hawks Generic nickname for the reconnaissance element of some U.S. infantry battalions, more formally designated "Battalion Reconnaissance Elements."

Hawks and Doves In the early sixties two schools of thought existed on dealing with communism in Vietnam; the Hawks believed the best way to eliminate the communists' influence on the people was to kill the VC; the people would give their allegiance to whoever could protect and provide for them. Doves believed in gaining the confidence and trust of the people to eliminate the influence of the VC, demonstrating that the government was on their side and interested in their well-being. Other issues were part of the hawk/dove discussion, but basically the hawks wanted to kill the VC and cut them off from the population, while the doves wanted to squeeze the VC out with kindness and a minimum of violence.

Hawthorne I & II *see* **Operation Hawthorne I & II**

Hayden, Tom *see* **Chicago 8; Fonda, Jane**

Hazardous Duty Pay (Combat Pay) Vietnam was considered a combat or hostile fire zone, allowing all military individuals operating in the zone to be eligible for Hazardous Duty Pay. The pay was $65 per month in addition to the individual's normal pay. The $65 rate applied to all military personnel operating in Vietnam, including Navy and Air Force personnel operating in the skies and coastal waters of Vietnam. *See also* **Jump Pay.**

HC-1 *see* **Rowell's Rats**

HC-130 *see* **C-130**

HE (High Explosive) Standard artillery and mortar high explosive rounds. "Hotel Echo" was the military phonetic alphabet equivalent, used for radio communications.

He Who Enlightens *see* **Ho Chi Minh**

Head *see* **Doper**

Head Case *see* **Crazy**

Head Lice *see* **Lice**

Head Shed *see* **Headquarters**

Headache Bar Steel bars welded to the top of the operator compartment on Rome Plows and tree clearing bulldozers. The bars kept branches and trees from hitting the operator during jungle clearing operations. In Vietnam extensive jungle clearing operations were conducted by American Army Engineers and SEABEES. *See also* **Rome Plow.**

Headquarters (HQ, Head Shed, Bo-Chi-Huy) Command element of a unit or group of units. Chi-huy was Vietnamese for commander, bo-chi-huy referred to headquarters. *See also* **Commanding Officer, Headquarters Company, Headquarters and Headquarters Company.**

Headquarters and Headquarters Battery *see* **Headquarters and Headquarters Company**

Headquarters and Headquarters Company (HHC, HHB, HHT) HHC: Headquarters element of an infantry/armor battalion (Headquarters and Headquarters Company). HHB: Headquarters element of an artillery battalion (Headquarters and Headquarters Battery). HHT: Headquarters element of a cavalry squadron (Headquarters and Headquarters Troop). Each of the headquarters elements controlled their respective subordinate companies, batteries or cavalry troops.

Headquarters and Headquarters Troop *see* **Headquarters and Headquarters Company**

Headquarters and Service Company *see* **H & S Company**

Headquarters and Supply Company *see* **H & S Company**

Headquarters Battery *see* **Headquarters Company**

Headquarters Company (Headquarters Troop, Headquarters Battery) Command element of a company sized unit. The headquarters element in an Army infantry company usually consisted of the company commander, his executive officer, 1st sergeant, company clerk, supply sergeant, supply clerk, 1–3 RTOs and the company medic. There could also be an attached artillery forward observer and his RTO. For infantry units operating in the field in Vietnam the XO, supply sergeant, supply clerk and company clerk remained in the rear at the brigade or division base camp. The small rear component of the headquarters element was responsible for the company records, resupply, mail, etc. Headquarters Troop and Headquarters Battery were similar command elements of the cavalry troop and the artillery battery, respectively.

Headquarters Specialist *see* **Rear-Echelon-Mother-Fuckers**

Headquarters Troop *see* **Headquarters Company**

Heads (Pothead, Smokers) In Vietnam soldiers that "got high" in the field or in base camps were classified, by their peers, into one of two groups, either Heads or Juicers. Juicers got high on alcohol, and Heads used drugs, primarily marijuana, opium or hash (other drugs were also used). The Heads had a very pessimistic outlook on the military role in Vietnam and tended to be pro Peace Movement. A large percentage of Heads were draftees and occupied the lower enlisted ranks. As the U.S. war effort in SVN decreased they tended to grow in number and get more vocal in their discontent. *See also* **Juicers.**

Healy, General Mike U.S. Army Special Forces general who commanded American advisory units in II Corps during the withdrawal of American combat troops in '72–'73. Best known for the "third" dog tag he wore around his neck that stated, "If you are recovering my body, fuck you."

Healy, Kenneth World Airways pilot who evacuated 54 Vietnamese orphans from Saigon in late March '75 as the rest of Vietnam was falling to the communists. Healy piloted a DC-8 cargo plane and was denied clearance to remove the children from VN because the plane was unheated and did not have adequate safety seating. The U.S. Embassy refused to help and denied Healy's request for milk and food for the children. Healy departed Saigon without clearance and eventually flew the orphans to Oakland Airport, World Airways' base of operation. The children were housed at the Army's Presidio in San Francisco until permanent homes could be found for them.

HEAP Round (APHE) High explosive armor piercing round designed to penetrate an armored vehicle and explode inside. HEAP rounds were fired by tanks and antitank weapons. HEAP rockets were also available for use by aircraft. *See also* **HEAT Round.**

Heart *see* **Purple Heart**

Heartbreak Hotel American POWs' nickname for the interrogation area inside Hao Lo Prison. *See also* **Hanoi Hilton, Prisoner of War.**

Hearts and Minds *see* **WHAM**

HEAT *see* **HEAT Round**

Heat Casualty *see* **Heat Prostration**

Heat Prostration (Heat Casualty) The effects of heat prostration and heat stroke took a high toll on American GIs in combat. The typical equipment load of a field grunt weighed from 60 to 100 pounds. Maneuvering this weight load in a fire fight in the high heat and humidity of Vietnam created many casualties. Dehydration added to the problem because usually the only source of drinkable water available to field grunts was the 2–5 quarts of water they carried with them. Drinking untreated water from local streams or wells could prove very hazardous. *See also* **Water Purification Tablets.**

Heat Retentive/Moisture Resistant Sleeping Shirt *see* **Jungle Sweater**

HEAT Round (HEAT) High Explosive Anti-Tank round fired by tanks and tank killers (antitank guns). HEAT rounds were also available for aircraft ordnance, notably 2.75-inch HEAT rockets. The round was designed to detonate on impact. Against armored targets, the cone shaped, hollow charge burned during the large explosion caused by the detonation of the warhead. The burning gases emitted from the exploding charge burned through the armor. The explosive nature of the charge made the HEAT round especially effective against targets such as bunkers, fortifications and structures. *See also* **HEAP Round, Combustible Case Ammunition.**

Heat Tabs *see* **Fuel, Compressed, Trioxane**

Heavies *see* **Monitor**

Heavy *see* **HVY**

Heavy Antitank Weapons (HAW) Long-range, heavy antitank weapons; HEAT missiles. HAW missiles didn't enter service in Vietnam until '72. The U.S. TOW, M151, was used effectively against NVA armor in the '72 Eastertide Offensive. The NVA used the Soviet made Sagger, AT3, which was more difficult to use and required more practice to fire accurately than the U.S. TOW. *See also* **M151, AT3.**

Heavy Artillery *see* **M-114A1 155mm Howitzer**

Heavy Arty *see* **Arc Light**

Heavy Fire Team *see* **Heavy Helicopter Section**

Heavy Helicopter Company (HHC) Army Aviation company, composed of 12–16 CH-54 Flying Cranes. The HHC provided heavy lift support allowing the CH-54 to transport 155mm howitzers, medium bulldozers, or nearly 20,000 pounds of cargo. The CH-54s were also used for the recovery of downed helicopters. *See also* **CH-54.**

Heavy Helicopter Section (Heavy Fire Team, HFT, HHFT, Heavy Helo Fire Team) Army helicopter fire team that consisted of three gunships called "Heavy Helo Fire Teams." Navy three ship HHFTs operated on a limited basis, the two ship fire team (LHFT) being the standard configuration. Heavy fire teams were also referred to as "Red Teams." *See also* **Seawolves, Light Helicopter Section.**

Heavy Helicopter Squadron *see* **HMH**

Heavy Helo Fire Team *see* **Heavy Helicopter Section**

Heavy Hog Nickname for the AH-1 Cobra helicopter that operated with four XM-159 rocket pods. Each pod carried 19 2.75-inch folding fin rockets. The Cobra was also armed with a chin mounted minigun or combination minigun/grenade launcher. *See also* **AH-1, Huey Hog.**

Heavy Hunter-Killer Team A helicopter hunter-killer team that consisted of one OH-6 Loach, two AH-1 Cobra gunships, and one UH-1D/H as a chase ship. The Loach was the bait, the Cobras provided instant fire power if the enemy took the bait. The chase ship often carried a recon team that would be inserted into the area where the gunships fired on the enemy. Recon's job was to search the area and check the body count. Should the Loach or a Cobra get shot down, the Chase ship was there to extract the crew. *See also* **Hunter-Killer Team.**

Heavy Machine Gun (HMG) Large calibre machine guns, .50cal (12.7mm) or greater. The HMG was too large to be man carried in the field and was usually tripod or carriage mounted. The American heavy machine gun used in Vietnam was the M-2, .50cal. The NVA/VC made use of the DShk or Type 54, and the Japanese Type 92 heavy machine gun. *See also* **M-2, Type 53 HMG, Type 54 HMG, Type 57 HMG, KPV, Japanese Machine Guns.**

Heavy Metal *see* **Acid Rock**

Heavy Salvage Ship *see* **LHC**

Heavy Section Term used to describe three tanks or three helicopters (gunships) operating together as a unit.

Heavy Stuff *see* **Big Stuff**

HECP *see* **SEASHARP**

Heliborne Being airborne in a helicopter as opposed to fixed-wing aircraft. *See also* **Airmobile.**

Heliborne Combat Assault *see* **Combat Assault**

Helicopter (Chopper, Flying Horses, Helo, Bird, Ship) The helicopter changed the face of war by giving infantry troops and artillery unprecedented mobility. Four classes of U.S. Army helicopters (choppers) were used in Vietnam: OH—observation,

UH—utility, CH—cargo and AH—attack. The Air Force, Marines, and Navy also made widespread use of several different types of helicopters in Vietnam. The Air Cavalry referred to the helicopter as their "flying horses." Helicopters were referred to as "choppers," "birds," "helos," "copters," and "ships."

Helicopter Allocation *see* **Blade Time**

Helicopter Ambush (Rotor Bumpers) To combat the effectiveness of the American helicopter the NVA/VC developed several methods to ambush the aircraft. In open LZs long stakes were shoved into the ground. On top of the stake a small wooden propeller was attached, through a piece of string, to the safety pin on a hand grenade. The downdraft from approaching helicopters spun the propeller, taking up the slack in the string, pulling the pin from the grenade causing it to explode as the helicopter was landing. The VC laced LZs with punji stakes that impaled American troops as they disembarked from their helicopters. There were so few natural LZs in the jungles of the Central Highlands that the enemy was able to cover most of them with booby traps, mortars, machine gun teams or command detonated mines. Another of the NVA/VC tactics was the "rotor bumper." Posts, 12–15 feet long, were placed vertically in an LZ. Helicopters were unable to put down in the LZ because the tall post would hit the rotors, shearing the blades off. Unable to land, the troops would have to jump the 15+ feet to the ground, which was a long fall with a 70-pound pack on their shoulders. The NVA/VC also placed the DH-10 mine in trees, aimed to blast skyward. A simple friction fuse was attached to the tree tops. The downdraft from landing helicopters would detonate the mine, spraying shrapnel into the helicopters. *See also* **Ambush.**

Helicopter Assault *see* **Combat Assault**

Helicopter Attack (Light) Squadron 3 *see* **Seawolves**

Helicopter Barge Barges used by riverine forces for helicopter landing pads. U.S. riverine units used large pontoon barges as mobile helicopter bases during operations in the Delta. The barges could land 2–3 helicopters simultaneously and were fitted with bladders to provide a refueling capacity. The barges were usually towed into position by LCM-8 landing craft allowing remote riverine operations to be conducted with full helicopter support. *See also* **Barge.**

Helicopter Crew Helmet *see* **APH-5 Helmet**

Helicopter Detachment 1 *see* **Rowell's Rats**

Helicopter Flight School *see* **Fort Rucker**

Helicopter Gunship Fire Team *see* **Light Helicopter Section**

Helicopter Gunships (Dragon Ship) During America's initial involvement in Vietnam experiments with armed helicopters were carried out. It was not until the Hughes UH-1 helicopter became available that a helicopter was successfully equipped and operated as a gunship in South Vietnam. The first helicopter gunships were the UH-1Bs. As improvements were made to the helo's performance the UH-1C became the standard Huey Gunship. The Huey represented a transport helicopter modified to perform as a gunship. Later the Bell AH-1 Cobra entered service as the Army's first helicopter designed specifically as a gunship. *See also* **UH-1B, UH-1C, AH-1G, Go-Go Bird.**

Helicopter Landing Zone *see* **Landing Zone**

Helicopter Log Book *see* **Dash-Twelve**

Helicopter Scouts (Scoutships, Aeroscouts) Light observation helicopters employed by the Army to perform reconnaissance and surveillance missions. The primary choppers used by the Army for scout missions were the OH-6, OH-13, and OH-23, and OH-58. The OH-13 and -23 were old observation aircraft that were slow and vulnerable to enemy fire, and were replaced by the OH-6. The OH-6 was a faster, more maneuverable ship that could be armed with a fixed mounted minigun, as well as carry a door mounted machine gun and gunner. The OH-58 represented the last helicopter to enter service with the Army in Vietnam. It featured speed and maneuverability and was used extensively in the scouting role. *See also* **Air Cavalry Troop, Aero Scout Platoon.**

Helicopter Valley (Song Ngan Valley)
Nickname given to Song Ngan Valley near the DMZ during Operation Hastings by the 3/4 Marines in July '66. During the air assault two CH-46 helicopters collided and crashed on approach to the LZ. A third crashed nearby attempting to avoid hitting the first two choppers and a fourth CH-46 was brought down by sniper fire. Several Marines in the LZ were butchered as they tried to escape the disintegrating rotor blades of the crashed choppers. *See also* **Operation Hastings.**

Helio Courier *see* **U-10**

Hell Hole Nickname for the observation hole in the floor of a CH-53. The observation port was used to direct the pilot for accurate positioning of the helicopter over a cargo, or sling load during pickup or delivery. In a UH-1D/H helicopter the wells on either side of the engine and rotor shaft mechanism were also called "hell holes." The hell holes were occupied by the crew chief and the door gunner. The hole's occupants sat on an aluminum tube and canvas seat, facing out over the door mounted machine gun. The life expectancy of a helicopter door gunner entering a hot LZ was measured in seconds if the ship was on the ground for longer than a minute. The pilots sat in armored seats, but the door gunner's only protection was the armored vest he wore. *See also* **Door Gunner, Body Armor.**

Hell No, We Won't Go Chant frequently used by antidraft demonstrators. Many groups became antidraft, as well as antiwar. Organizations such as the SNCC and SDS supported those individuals who refused the draft. The SNCC's contention was that blacks, from the less affluent neighborhoods across America were being drafted at a higher rate than whites, and having to shoulder more of the responsibility for the ground war in Vietnam. Draft refusals first started showing up in mostly white antiwar groups, but later spread to black sponsored antiwar groups and individuals.

Hell's Angels (Protest Busters) On many occasions during an antiwar protest rally, there would be a counter rally staged by those supporting government policy regarding the Vietnam War. In October '65, near Berkeley, several members of the Hell's Angels motorcycle club took exception to the antiwar protesters and crashed their cycles into the crowd, wreaking havoc before police could wade in and separate the two groups. In November the leader of the Hell's Angels, Sonny Barger, met with Allen Ginsberg and arranged a truce between the Angels and the peace/antiwar groups. The truce was so effective that the Angels began to accept the peace movement, and on several occasions "rode shotgun" for demonstrations in the Berkeley area.

Hell-Hole Prison *see* **Hanoi Hilton**

Hello (Greeting) *see* **Chao Ba**

Helmet *see* **GI Helmet**

Helmet Cover *see* **Camouflage Cover**

Helmet Liners The nylon helmet liner worn inside the U.S. M-1 Helmet. The liner was often worn alone in situations where the steel helmet was not necessary. In the field combat troops that didn't wear their steel pots wore soft hats instead of the helmet liners. The liners were used at guard post, training bases, and for ceremonies, and were usually painted and decorated with unit identification labels and or badges. *See also* **GI Helmet.**

Helo *see* **Helicopter**

Helo Fire Team *see* **Light or Heavy Helicopter Section**

HEOD *see* **SEASHARP**

Hep Duc *see* **Hiep Duc Valley**

HEP Round (High Explosive Plastic)
Tank round used against fortifications and personnel. The round consisted of a large charge of high explosive plastique which detonated on impact. The round was effective against personnel, soft bunkers and vehicles, but couldn't penetrate armor or fortified bunkers.

Herbicides *see* **Defoliation**

Herc *see* **C-130**

Hercules *see* **C-130**

Herd, The *see* **173d Airborne Brigade**

Heroin (Scag, Smack, Skag, The Big H) Narcotic derivative of morphine. Highly addictive, heroin was one of many illicit drugs available to American personnel in Vietnam. Heroin could be "shot-up" intravenously, smoked (laced with the tobacco from a normal cigarette) or snorted. Heroin had no distinctive odor when smoked, and could easily be used without detection. Abuse of the drug increased greatly in the Army after '70, when it became available to U.S. troops on a widespread basis, supplied by countries such as Thailand and Laos, and marketed by the South Vietnamese. Heroin obtained in Vietnam was especially addicting because it was 95 percent pure. (Heroin sold on the street in the States was only 5–10 percent pure.) The "H" was so potent that prolonged contact with the skin could cause skin rashes and lesions. The Army estimated that 7 percent of the enlisted population in Vietnam in '71 were addicted to heroin. *See also* **Illicit Drugs.**

Herringbone   Defensive reaction taken by American armored vehicles while traveling in column formation. When attacked the vehicles pivoted to face the sides of the road. The vehicles alternated their facing so roughly half the column faced the left side of the road, while the other half faced the right side of the road. The alternate facing allowed the vehicles to cover each other's back and use maximum firepower without hitting other friendly vehicles in the formation.

HES 70   *see*   **Hamlet Evaluation System**

HES Report   *see*   **Hamlet Evaluation System**

Hexamine Fuel Tablets   *see*   **Fuel, Compressed, Trioxane**

Hey, Hey, LBJ...   "Hey, Hey, LBJ, How many babies did you kill today?" One of the chants shouted by Australian antiwar demonstrators at President Lyndon Johnson on his visit to Australia in October '66. The American version was most often heard as "Hey, Hey, LBJ, How many boys did you kill today?"

HFT   *see*   **Heavy Helicopter Section**

HH   *see*   **HVY, Avn**

HH-1H   *see*   **UH-1H**

HH-1K   (Huey Trainer)   UH-1 helicopter trainer used to familiarize and instruct new pilots on flight operations of the Huey. *See also* **UH-1.**

HH-1N   *see*   **UH-1N**

HH-3   *see*   **CH-3**

HH-43   (Huskie, Eggbeater, Husky, H-43, OH-43)   Kaman Corp. helicopter used by the Air Force for SAR and fire fighting duties. The Husky was well suited for crew recovery in terrain that would not allow the helicopter to land. By means of a winch and basket system casualties and survivors could be lifted from the water, or out of the jungle as the helicopter hovered overhead. The Navy designation for the HH-43 was the OH-43 and it was used for liaison and transport duties; it was land and carrier based. In the Marine Corps and the Navy the OH-43 was replaced by the UH-1E. The HH-43 had a max speed of 120mph, a range of 806kms and could transport cargo or up to five passengers.

HH-53   *see*   **CH-53**

HH-53B/C   *see*   **Super Jolly Green Giant**

HHB   *see*   **Headquarters and Headquarters Company**

HHC   *see*   **Heavy Helicopter Company, Headquarters and Headquarters Company**

HHFT   *see*   **Heavy Helicopter Section**

HHH   *see*   **Humphrey, Vice-President Hubert Horatio**

HHT   *see*   **Headquarters and Headquarters Company**

Hickory   *see*   **Operation Hickory** (Army) or (Marine)

Hiep Duc Valley (Hep Duc)   Valley located around the village of Hiep Duc, 40kms west of Tam Ky and 50kms south of Da Nang. The valley was located at the west end of the Que Son Valley in Quang Tin Province, I Corps. The entire area was an active NVA/VC infiltration route and was continually patrolled by U.S. units and was the site of several full-scale operations.

Hieu Giang River   *see*   **Song Cau Viet River**

High   *see*   **Get High**

High Altitude, Low Opening Parachute Jump   *see*   **HALO**

High Angle Hell (Mortar Fire)   GI slang for mortar fire. *See also* **Incoming.**

High Drag Bombs *see* **Retarded Bombs**

High Drink (Airborne Helicopter Refueling) Refueling system carried onboard some U.S. Navy destroyers which operated off the coast of NVN. The system, through a series of hoses and pumps, allowed SAR helicopters to refuel while hovering over the rear fantail of the ship. This allowed SAR helicopters to operate at greater distances from their "base" aircraft carrier. The system worked for several types of helicopters.

High Endurance Cutters *see* **WHEC**

High Explosive *see* **HE**

High Explosive Armor Piercing *see* **HEAP Round**

High Explosive Plastic *see* **HEP Round**

High Points CIA and MACV briefing terminology used to describe brief periods of intense enemy activity, usually centered around attacks on military installations or civilian centers.

High-Risk Vietnamese *see* **Black Flights**

Higher *see* **Honcho**

Higher-Higher *see* **Honcho**

Highland *see* **Operation Highland**

Highland Redlegs *see* **42d Artillery Regiment**

Highlands *see* **Central Highlands**

Hightop *see* **M-577 ACC**

Highway 1 (Street Without Joy, Purple Heart Trail) Vietnam's main highway running from the Chinese/North Vietnam border to Saigon in South Vietnam. Most of the highway wound along the coast. In NVN, just north of Thanh Hoa the road turned inland, passing through Hanoi, and passing into China at Dong Dang. In the South the highway turned west from the coast near Phan Thiet, heading inland to Saigon and onward to Phnom Penh, Cambodia. Labeled "The Street Without Joy" by the French writer Bernard Fall. Also known as "Purple Heart Trail." *See also* **Purple Heart Trail, Street Without Joy.**

Highway 2 Interprovincial highway that connected Vung Tau with Highway 1 at the road junction just south of Xuan Loc. Camp Blackhorse was located just off Highway 2; Phuoc Tuy and Long Khanh provinces, III Corps.

Highway 4 National highway that connected Saigon to the Delta. The highway ran southwest from Saigon to My Tho, through Vinh Long, Can Tho and Soc Trang to Ca Mau.

Highway 5A Interprovincial highway that connected Saigon with Go Cong; Go Cong and Long An provinces, III and IV Corps.

Highway 7A Interprovincial road that connected Vinh Long with Phu Vinh; Vinh Long and Vinh Binh, IV Corps.

Highway 7B Interprovincial road that junctioned with Highway 14 south of Pleiku, near My Thach, and continued southeast through Cheo Reo to junction at Highway 1 near Tuy Hoa; Pleiku, Phu Bon, and Phu Yen provinces, II Corps. *See also* **The Elephants Have Moved Out in Front...**

Highway 8A Interprovincial road that connected Ha Thien through Rach Gia with Long Xuyen; Kien Giang and An Giang provinces, IV Corps.

Highway 9 (Route 9) National highway that crossed the SVN/Cambodia border near Sa Tiac and Lang Vei, then proceeded eastward through Khe Sanh to junction at Highway 1 near Dong Ha in Quang Tri Province, I Corps. Also frequently referred to as Route 9. *See also* **Operation Lam Son 719.**

Highway 10 Interprovincial highway that connected Chau Duc with Long Xuyen; Chau Duc and An Giang provinces, IV Corps.

Highway 11 National highway connecting Da Lat with Phan Rang and Highway 1; Tuyen Duc and Ninh Thuan provinces, II Corps.

Highway 13 *see* **Thunder Road**

Highway 14 National highway connecting Phu Cuong (just north of Saigon) through Ban Me Thuot, Pleiku, Kontum and Dak To to Ha Tan, southwest of Da Nang. The highway negotiated the central part of South Vietnam between Bien Hoa in the south and nearly to Da Nang in the north.

Highway 15 National highway that connected Vung Tau, through the junction at Xa Phuoc Le with Bien Hoa. The U.S. base camp at Bear Cat was located just off the highway; Bien Hoa and Phuoc Tuy provinces, III Corps.

Highway 19 *see* **Ambush Alley**

Highway 20 National highway that connected Xuan Loc (Long Khanh Province, III Corps) with Da Lat (Tuyen Duc Province, II Corps).

Highway 21 National highway that connected Ban Me Thuot City with Highway 1 at Ninh Hoa; Darlac and Khanh Hoa provinces, II Corps.

Highway 21A Stretch of national highway located south of Da Lat that connected Highway 20 at Lien Khuong with Highway 11 near Lac Xuan, in Tuyen Duc Province, II Corps.

Highway 22 Section of national highway located primarily in Tay Ninh Province, III Corps, which junctioned with Highway 1 at Go Dau Ha, then proceeded north through Tay Ninh City to Thien Ngon, and across the border into Cambodia.

Highway 23 Interprovincial highway that connected Vung Tau, through the junction at Xa Phuoc Le to a junction with Highway 1, 25kms southwest of Phan Thiet; Phuoc Tuy and Binh Tuy provinces, III Corps.

Highway 24 Provincial road that connected Go Cong with My Tho; Dinh Tuong and Go Cong provinces, IV Corps.

Highway 26 Provincial road that connected My Tho, through Ben Tre to Ba Tri; Dinh Tuong and Kien Hoa provinces, IV Corps.

Highway 27 Interprovincial road that connected Long Xuyen with Can Tho; An Giang and Phong Dinh provinces, IV Corps.

Highway 31 Interprovincial highway that connected Can Tho with Vi Thanh; Phong Dinh and Chuong Thien provinces, IV Corps.

Highway 535 *see* **LZ Ross**

Highways (QL, LTL, TL) South Vietnam's primary road network consisted of national, interprovincial and provincial roads, loosely called "highways." The main national highways, designated "QL" (Quoc-Lo), were 1, 4, 9, 11, 14, 15, 20, 21, and 22. The interprovincial highways, designated "LTL" (Lien Tinh Lo), were 2, 5, 7, 8, 10, 23, 27, and 31. The main provincial roads, designated "TL" (Tinh Lo), were 24 and 26. Highway 1 was South Vietnam's longest, best paved highway. Many of Vietnam's "highways" were little more than graded dirt roads. *See also* **Individual Highways.**

Hill (Military Hill) In military terminology a "hill" was designated (named) by its elevation (measured in meters or feet, depending on map used) which was printed on military maps; i.e., Hill 937 or Hill 875. If two hills of equal height were located close together or separated by a low saddle or ridge, the hills were further identified by their relative position to each other; i.e., Hill 881 North, and Hill 881 South. The elevation printed on military maps represented the hill's highest point above sea level. In Vietnam the standard map used by FWFs was the 1:50,000 scale map prepared by the U.S. Army Topographic Command. Hill and terrain elevations were measured in meters. *See also* **Military Crest.**

Hill 55 Served as part of the Marines' perimeter defense around Da Nang Air Base and the city of Da Nang. The small hill was located about 13kms south of the air field and 16kms northeast of An Hoa, Quang Nam Province, I Corps. *See also* **Hawk Missile.**

Hill 64 *see* **Rock Quarry**

Hill 268 *see* **Hill 287**

Hill 287 (Hills 364, 268, 327) Four small hills west of Da Nang Air Base that were occupied by the U.S. Marines as part of the perimeter defense of the city of Da Nang and the air base. The hills were arranged in roughly a north-south line in the following order: 287, 364, 268, and 327. Hill 287 was the farthest north and about 8kms from the air base with Hill 327 the farthest south and about 4kms from the air field. *See also* **Hawk Missile.**

Hill 327 *see* **Hill 287**

Hill 364 *see* **Hill 287**

Hill 861 *see* **Hill Fights**

Hill 875, Dak To In October/November '67, during Operation MacArthur, elements of the 173d Airborne cleared the hills of enemy units around the base camp at Dak To. During the operation some of the heaviest fighting occurred on Hill 875 where two-thirds of the 2d Battalion/503d Infantry were killed or wounded taking the hill from the well-entrenched troops of the 174th Regiment/1st NVA Division. More than 300 GIs died in securing the hills around Dak To. During the final assaults on Hill 875 elements of the 1st Battalion/12th Infantry were deployed to assist in taking the hill. *See also* **Battle of Dak To, Operation MacArthur.**

Hill 881, North/South *see* **Hill Fights**

Hill 937 *see* **Hamburger Hill**

Hill Battles *see* **Hill Fights**

Hill Fights (Hill Battles) Battle by Marines in April '67 to take Hill 881 (North and South) and 861. The hills were held by the NVA, until taken by the Marines. The hills were about 7kms northwest of Khe Sanh Combat Base, and became part of the outer defenses of Khe Sanh during the NVA siege of the base in early '68. The Marines referred to the struggle to clear the hills of the NVA as the "Hill Battles." *See also* **Khe Sanh.**

Hill of the Angels *see* **Con Thien**

Hilsman-Forrestal Report Report presented to President Kennedy on the Vietnam fact-finding mission conducted by Roger Hilsman and Michael Forrestal. Hilsman was a State Department expert on the Far East and Forrestal was part of the White House National Security staff. The mission was initiated by Kennedy, and prompted by the different and often contradictory information the President was receiving from the military, his advisors and the news media. The report concluded that the Diem regime and the ARVNs were ineffective because of corruption and that Diem had lost touch with the people. The report also stated that some progress was being made, but U.S. involvement in Vietnam would be longer than originally projected.

Hippie (Hairhead, Flower Child, Longhairs, Counterculture) Hippies in the 60s were characterized as having evolved from the beatnik generation. Hippies tended to be antiwar, antiauthority and antiestablish-

ment. They rejected the established American way of life and believed in the power of free love, long hair, and spiritual happiness to overcome conflict. Their free flowing lifestyle was based on mysticism as they championed drugs as the answer to total harmony. To the casual observer the hippie movement and the peace movement seemed to blend into one. "Flower power" was the hippie slogan, the flower being their symbol of peace and tranquility. The hippie movement and counterculture spread nationwide, and were eventually felt around the world.

Hit Parade (Strike Damage) Early nickname for the official records kept in aviation units detailing the strike damage (number of hits) inflicted by enemy fire on American aircraft.

Hit Teams *see* **Provisional Reconnaissance Unit**

HLZ *see* **Landing Zone**

HM *see* **Corpsmen**

HMA (Attack Helicopter Squadron) Designation for a Marine attack helicopter squadron. In '69 Marine attack helicopter squadrons were outfitted with the AH-1G Cobra. Before '69 a limited number of UH-1 Hueys had been pressed into service as Marine gunships. *See also* **Gunship.**

HMAS Hobart (Royal Australian Navy [RAN], HMAS Perth) The HMAS *Perth* and *Hobart* were two Royal Australian Navy destroyers that operated with U.S. naval forces patrolling the coastal waters of South Vietnam. During the course of the war four Australian Navy destroyers operated off the coast of Vietnam providing fire support and interdiction duties. The RAN also provided advisor teams to the SVN Navy as part of the AATTV. RAN frogman teams instructed the Vietnamese on underwater demolitions and harbor security measures. RAN helicopter crews operated with the U.S. 135th Aviation Company providing support to the 1st Australian Task Force. *See also* **135th Aviation Company, Australian Task Force.**

HMAS Perth *see* **HMAS Hobart**

HMG *see* **Heavy Machine Gun**

HMH (Heavy Helicopter Squadron) Designation for a Marine heavy helicopter squadron. The Marines used the CH-37, later replaced by the CH-53, as their heavy lift helicopter. *See also* **CH-53, Marine Air Squadron Designations.**

HML (Light Helicopter Squadron) Designation for a Marine light lift helicopter squadron, typically outfitted with UH-1Es after '65. *See also* **UH-1E, Marine Air Squadron Designations.**

HMM (Medium Helicopter Squadron) Marine Corps' designation for their medium lift helicopter squadron. The squadrons initially operated the CH-34 helicopter; it was replaced by the CH-46 as their medium lift ship. Most large scale Marine operations used the CH-46 because of its increased transport capacity over the UH-1E. *See also* **CH-46, Marine Air Squadron Designations.**

HMM-163 *see* **Marine Medium Helicopter Squadron 362**

HMM-362 *see* **Marine Medium Helicopter Squadron 362**

Hmong *see* **Meo**

Ho *see* **Ho Chi Minh, Sister**

Ho Bo Woods Heavily wooded area along the Saigon River, north of Cu Chi in Hau Nghia and Binh Duong Province, III Corps. U.S. troops nicknamed the village areas of An Nhon Tay and Phu My Hung "Ho Bo Woods." The area beneath the woods was honeycombed with enemy tunnels that were tied into the massive tunnel complex just north of Cu Chi. During the war the village of Phu My Hung served as the VC's Saigon area command headquarters. *See also* **Tunnels of Cu Chi.**

Ho Chi Minh (Uncle Ho, Nguyen Tat Thanh, Nguyen O Phap, Nguyen Ai Quoc, Bac Ho) Believed born Nguyen Sinh Cung in central Vietnam in 1890, but known by many aliases in his life. Ho Chi Minh (he who enlightens) directed the Vietnamese campaign to oust the French from Indo-China and later led the drive to reunite North and South Vietnam. He ruled NVN from '54 until his death in '69. His goal was to unite all of Indo-China under his Communist Party. His Viet Minh forces defeated the French in '54 in the First Indo-China War. He helped organize and support southern communist efforts against the GVN. In the late fifties he sent elements of

his army south to complete his plan for unification of Vietnam, and the ejection of any foreign powers that stood in the way of that unification. In the early years Ho preached nationalism. This helped him gather the backing of small Vietnamese groups seeking independence. Ho declared independence from the French and founded the Democratic Republic of Vietnam in '50. Under the flag of nationalism, communist and noncommunist groups fought the French in Indo-China. Ho was always a hard-core communist, and used nationalism as a screen to gather support. In '60 the same screen was used to organize nationalists/communists to fight for unification of North and South Vietnam, which was opposed by the anticommunist Diem government. Ho died in '69. As Ho aged he was known as Bac Ho (Uncle Ho) to his people. After the fall of SVN in April '75, Saigon was renamed Ho Chi Minh City in his honor.

Ho Chi Minh Campaign *see* **Final Offensive**

Ho Chi Minh City After the fall of South Vietnam to the communists in April '75, Saigon was renamed Ho Chi Minh City in honor of the father of Communist North Vietnam, Ho Chi Minh. *See also* **Saigon.**

Ho Chi Minh Corner Nickname for the area about 30kms southeast of Saigon in the Rung Sat Special Zone patrolled by the River Patrol Force, TF 116. The area was infested by the VC who used the RSSZ as a base area throughout the war. Ho Chi Minh Corner was part of the main shipping channel to the port in Saigon. *See also* **TF 116.**

Ho Chi Minh Highway Just prior to the Eastertide Offensive in '72 the NVA started a massive construction project to improve the Ho Chi Minh Trail. With the signing of the '73 Paris Peace Accords the NVA was able to widen and improve the trail unmolested by U.S. aircraft. North Vietnam even extended fuel pipelines from North Vietnam to support armor operations that were part of their master plan for defeating the ARVN forces in South Vietnam. The Ho Chi Minh Trail became so wide and smooth it was nicknamed the "Ho Chi Minh Highway." *See also* **Ho Chi Minh Trail.**

Ho Chi Minh Sandals *see* **Binh-Tri-Thien**

Ho Chi Minh Slippers *see* Binh-Tri-Thien

Ho Chi Minh Trail (The Trail, Duong Mon Ho Chi Minh) A major infiltration route used by NVN to move men and materiel into SVN, called Duong Mon Ho Chi Minh by the Vietnamese. The trail ran south from Hanoi toward the DMZ and then south along the border of Laos and Cambodia into SVN. The trail was one major route with many side trails that led into the interior of SVN. U.S. bombing campaigns were never able to permanently cut the route. The trail was believed to be the major supply route used by the NVA/VC, but evidence indicates that a greater percentage of the supplies used in the south by the NVA/VC came by way of the Sihanouk Trail from the Gulf of Thailand east to SVN. *See also* Sihanouk Trail, Lam Son 719, Truong Son Corridor, Group 559/759, Commando Hunt, Ho Chi Minh Highway.

Ho Chi Minh Truce During the course of the Vietnam War the only temporary truce honored by the NVA/VC during U.S. involvement in Vietnam was a three day truce in September '69, called in honor of the death of Ho Chi Minh. *See also* Truce.

Ho Chi Minh's Revenge (GI Trots, Diarrhea, Runs, Flagellated Protozoan, The Shits, Squirts) Due to a wide variety of ailments and conditions, American troops in Vietnam suffered from frequent bouts of stomach cramps and diarrhea. GIs referred to the persistent or serious bouts of diarrhea as Ho Chi Minh's Revenge. The most common cause of the "runs" in Vietnam was amoebic dysentery (Flagellated Protozoan). For troops in the field the "squirts" could sometimes be temporarily relieved by eating C-ration peanut butter and crackers, and limiting the intake of water. This field expedient caused temporary constipation, reversing the trend. For many troops the antimalaria tablets issued were also a cause of diarrhea. Medics typically treated severe cases of the runs with Polymagma or Intromycin. *See also* Polymagma.

Ho, Ho, Ho, Ho Chi Minh... "Ho, Ho, Ho, Ho Chi Minh. The NLF Is Going to Win." One of the antiwar chants that surfaced in the early '70s.

Ho, Ho, Whattaya Know, White Folks Gotta Go One of the SNCC chants. The SNCC was very wary of whites who wanted to join the organization. The SNCC believed if there was to be equality between the races their organization would have to push for it, and if whites were allowed membership in the group, their presence and participation would ultimately hold back any progress that the SNCC might achieve. This view was completely opposite the views of the SCLC, who believed the only way to change the current system in American society was if blacks and whites worked together for progress and change. *See also* Student Nonviolent Coordinating Committee, SCLC.

Ho Thi Thien *see* Thich Quang Duc

Ho's Land Reforms *see* Agricultural Reform Tribunals

Hoa Binh Trong Nhut "Vietnamese for Peace, Independence and National Reunification," a VC propaganda slogan.

Hoa Hao (Huyuh Phu So) An independent Buddhist sect centered in the An Giang area of the Delta in South Vietnam, founded by Huyuh Phu So in 1919. They had their own private army similar to the Cao Dai in Tay Ninh. They were almost as anti–French as they were anti–Viet Minh, but the French did manage to recruit them to fight the Viet Minh during the First Indo-China War. In '55 after the French defeat the Hoa Hao began to rebel against the new South Vietnamese government of Premier Diem. The rebellion was put down by the SVN Army and the Hoa Hao's military power crushed. Later the Americans quietly hired some of the remaining Hoa Hao as mercenaries as part of USSF, CIDG forces in the Delta. *See also* An Giang.

Hoa Loc *see* MiG Airfields

Hoai Nhon *see* Bong Son

Hobo Woods *see* Ho Bo Woods

Hobson's Choice During the Vietnam War some individuals standing before criminal court judges were given "Hobson's Choice" — go to jail or join the military. The criminal court system across America was given a new tool to control some of America's wayward youths. Because the nation's reserves were not called up, there was a critical shortage of manpower in the military. To satisfy the needs of the service normal restrictions against military service eligibility were often waived. Because of Vietnam, minor crimes were overlooked by recruiters in their effort to fill manpower quotas. The ranks of both the Marines and the Army were increased by reckless American youth caught in the wheels of the justice system. *See also* **Draftee, Draft.**

Hoc Bao *see* **MACV-SOG Command and Control**

Hoffman, Abbie *see* **Chicago 8**

Hog *see* **UH-1C, UH-1B**

Hog Flight *see* **UH-1C**

Hogjaws *see* **Rome Plow**

Hognose *see* **M-75 Grenade Launcher Turret**

Hoi An Provincial capital of Quang Nam Province in I Corps. Hoi An was located near the coast, 21kms southeast of Da Nang along the Song Thu Bon River.

Hoi Chanh (Rallier, Quy Chanh, Returnee) A participant in the GVN Chieu Hoi program. The program rewarded NVA/VC soldiers who defected to the GVN. Under the program the "returnees" were debriefed on their participation with the NVA/VC. Some ralliers were then given the opportunity to work as scouts for American units. Most of the ralliers were relocated to government camps and hamlets located far from the area of their defection. "Quy Chanh" was Vietnamese for "defector." *See also* **Chieu Hoi Program, Kit Carson Scout.**

Holdin' (Possession) Slang reference to a person armed with a concealed weapon or being in personal possession of drugs or other controlled or restricted items.

Holding Barracks *see* **Holding Company**

Holding Company (Animal Farm) The holding company contained soldiers that were in transit between duty stations, not assigned to a regular unit, waiting for orders to go to a new unit or waiting for paperwork to process for their release. Individuals in the holding company were not part of a regular unit and didn't have scheduled duties; because of this they were assigned a variety of temporary duties such as KP, grounds cleaning, and the typical

"shit details" for which none of the regular units wanted to give up personnel. Ft Benning's holding company was nicknamed the Animal Farm. Soldiers assigned to the holding company took temporary quarters in the "holding barracks." *See also* **Casuals, Scut Duty.**

Holiday Inn *see* **1st Infantry Division Fire Bases**

Holiday Inns (Waikiki East) GI nickname for large U.S. base camps where troops from the field would stand down. Company and battalion stand-downs at the larger base camps allowed grunts an opportunity to take showers, eat hot meals and become human and civilized for a few days. During the stand-downs at the "holiday inns" the troops usually performed perimeter guard at night. "Waikiki East" was the name for one of the stand-down centers located at Cu Chi, 25th Infantry Division headquarters. *See also* **Stand-Down.**

Holloway, Admiral James *see* **Chief of Naval Operations**

Holloway, CWO Charles *see* **Camp Holloway**

Hollyhock *see* **Operation Hollyhock**

Hollywood Marines *see* **Marine Corps Recruit Depot**

Home Boy *see* **Soul Brother**

Homecoming *see* **Operation Homecoming**

Homeguard *see* **Popular Forces**

Homemade Napalm *see* **Fou Gasse**

Homestead *see* **Operation Homestead**

Homing All-the-Way Killer *see* **Hawk Missile**

HOMS *see* **SEASHARP**

Hon Co Island (Tiger Island) North Vietnamese island located 25kms off the coast of NVN, northeast of Mui Lay. The island was about 47kms north-northeast of Quang Tri and less than 30kms northeast of the DMZ. The island was occupied by NVA troops and several patrol boats. The island was nicknamed "Tiger Island" by American Navy sailors. U.S. ships that strayed too near the island were frequently fired on by enemy troops on the island. "Straying" of U.S. cargo ships was usually a result of bad weather or a breakdown in the ships' navigational gear.

Hon Dai *see* **Penis**

Hon Gai *see* **Haiphong**

Hon Tre (Special Forces School, In-Country) Island just off the coast of South Vietnam, 2kms across the bay from Nha Trang in II Corps. Hon Tre was the in-country training center of the U.S. Special Forces, MACV Recondo School. *See also* **MACV Recondo School.**

Honcho (Higher-Higher, Higher) Field term for the leader of a unit, not necessarily an officer, but the man who actually directed the unit; leader. The "honcho" was usually well respected and trusted by the men he led. "Higher-Higher" or simply "Higher" was Marine slang for stuffy or stuck-up officers. Such officers usually had a poor rapport with the men they commanded and seemed only interested in advancing to the next command step in their career.

Honda *see* **Motorcycles**

Honda-Girls *see* **Cowboys**

Honey (Antiseptic) Bee honey was used as an ancestral folk remedy by the Vietnamese. Applied to a wound, the drying honey acted as an antiseptic. In remote areas where medical antiseptics were not available, honey was used to aid the healing process of open or sutured wounds.

Honey Buckets (Shit Pots) In Vietnam, because of the terrain, slit trenches for latrines were seldom used; instead a 55-gallon drum was used as a holding container. A 55-gallon drum was cut into thirds; the top and bottom of the drum were then used as "shit pots" or "honey buckets." These buckets were placed in the latrines under the toilet seats. Once a day the buckets were removed and the contents burned using kerosene. The shit burning detail was avoided at all cost by U.S. troops, and aptly fit the description of the true "shit detail." At larger bases the Vietnamese were employed for bucket duty. *See also* **Shit Burner, Shit Details.**

Honeymoon *see* **Boom-Boom**

Hong Kong Hill Large hill located just north of Highway 19 forming part of the western border of the 1st Cavalry Division's base camp at An Khe in II Corps.

Hong Kong Special Very large fireworks display made in Hong Kong and used in Vietnamese celebrations during Tet, the Lunar New Year.

Honky *see* **Caucasian**

Honolulu Conference (Declaration of Honolulu) In '65 and '66 high level conferences were held in Honolulu, Hawaii, to determine the course of U.S. actions in Vietnam. The April '66 conference was attended by President Johnson, Robert McNamara, Maxwell Taylor and William Bundy resulting in 40,000 additional troops being deployed to SVN in support of the Thieu regime. The February '66 conference was attended by the President; McNamara; Taylor; Gen. Westmoreland; and Henry Cabot Lodge, Jr.; and South Vietnam's heads of government, Nguyen Van Thieu and Nguyen Cao Ky. After the conference the US/SVN governments pledged to address the issues of political/social reform, refugees, inflation, economic growth in SVN and the defeat of the Viet Cong. *See also* **Guam.**

Honorable Discharge Highest ranking discharge granted by the military. In general a soldier qualified for an Honorable Discharge if he completed his service commitment to the country, and kept out of serious trouble with the military authorities. The majority of discharges granted from the Vietnam era were honorable. Between '52 and '74 some Honorable Discharges carried an SPN code which detailed a particular negative circumstance associated with the discharge. An Honorable Discharge could also be granted for medical or psychiatric related reasons. *See also* **Discharges, SPN Number, Section 212.**

Honorable Peace *see* **Honorable Solution**

Honorable Solution (Honorable Peace) Phrase often used during the mid-sixties to describe the Johnson administration's search for a way to end the war in Vietnam. For the administration the solution meant NVN would compromise and cease the infiltration of troops and supplies into SVN, and work out peace terms with South Vietnam. For some politicians in Washington, the honorable solution meant the U.S. would compromise on its goals for Vietnam in an effort to end the war and stabilize the region. After his election in '68, President Richard Nixon began speaking of an end to the Vietnam War in terms of an "honorable peace." *See also* Peace with Honor.

Hooch (Hootch)   GI term for a rural Vietnamese hut or house, usually made of thatch and bamboo with a mud floor. A GI hooch was a bunker, or small building used to sleep and live in. Hooch also applied to makeshift shelters made of ponchos and tarps in the field, usually built over or around a fighting position or foxhole. *See also* Foxhole.

Hooch Ba (Hooch Maid, Hooch Girl, Housegirl)   Vietnamese woman who did the general cleaning of a GI's hooch at the larger base camps. On a daily basis, for a few dollars a month, a GI could get a Vietnamese woman or girl to come to the American base and sweep the floor, do his laundry, mend and even polish his boots. At the larger bases where several GIs occupied the same hooch, they would all chip in a few dollars to pay for the maid service. It was commonly believed that through these and other base civilian workers, military intelligence related to the camp found its way to the NVA/VC. The Australians did not hire civilians to do their cleaning chores; instead they went to great lengths to keep the Vietnamese out of their bases. The Aussies believed the Vietnamese civilians compromised the bases' security.

Hooch Girl   *see*   Hooch Ba

Hooch Maid   *see*   Hooch Ba

Hook   *see*   Field Radio

Hook and Cable Delivery System   *see* Ground Proximity Extraction System

Hook-Nosed Sea Snake (Hardwick's Sea Snake)   The hook-nosed sea snake and Hardwick's sea snake were both quite plentiful along the coastal waters and river mouths of Vietnam. The hook-nosed sea snake had a reputation as being the most vicious of all the water snakes in Vietnam and was about 5 feet long. The Hardwick sea snake was the most common of the two snakes and was about 3 feet long. Both snakes possessed a highly toxic venom that affected the muscles. *See also* Snakes.

Hooks   *see*   CH-47

Hoosier LRRPs (151st Infantry [LRP], Indiana National Guard)   Company D/151st Infantry (LRP) was an LRRP company of the Indiana National Guard. The company was formed in late '67 and trained in long-range reconnaissance and patrolling, and had the distinction of being the only National Guard LRRP unit to serve in Vietnam. In March '68 the "Hoosier LRRPs" were activated for regular duty, one of the few National Guard units to be activated during the Vietnam War. After additional training the company was deployed to Vietnam in December '68. The company operated under control of II Field Force with Company F/51st Infantry (LRP), both companies providing II FFV with recon and intelligence. Company D returned home in November '69. *See also* Reserves, LRRP.

Hootch   *see*   Hooch

Hop Tac Plan (Quadrillage, Cooperation Plan)   Pacification program established in '64 by General Westmoreland in the seven province areas around Saigon. ARVN troops were to clear and secure rural areas from the VC, allowing government pacification teams to enter the area to distribute U.S. supplies, winning the support of the people. The plan was discontinued in '65 due to the inability of the ARVN troops to clear or secure the areas for the teams; also because of government corruption, few of the supplies were distributed as planned. The French attempted a similar program called "Quadrillage," but they did not have the manpower to provide continuous protection to all the areas that required pacification. Hop Tac meant "cooperation" in Vietnamese. *See also* Strategic Hamlets GVN, Pacification.

Hope   *see*   LZ Hope

Hope, Bob   Bob Hope made several USO tours to Vietnam, beginning as early as Christmas '65. During his show tours he brought along an ample supply of talent in the form of dancers, singers, and comedians. Some of the stars which accompanied him on the tours were Raquel Welch, Connie Stevens, Martha Raye, Mary Tyler Moore, Theresa Graves, Ann-Margret, Connie

Francis, Jill St. John, Nancy Sinatra, Lola Falana. *See also* **Cu Chi Music Ensemble.**

Horn *see* **Field Radio**

Hornet *see* **USS Hornet**

Hornets of the 116th Avn *see* **116th Aviation Company**

Horny *see* **Randy**

Horse Collar (Survival Sling) Nickname for the large sling used to hoist personnel onboard a helicopter. The sling was attached to a cable and winch, and was used for rescue and recovery missions. *See also* **Penetrator.**

Horse Pill *see* **Chloroquine**

Horseshoe Nickname for one of the NVA artillery entrenchments that fired on Khe Sanh and its surrounding outposts, particularly Hill 881 South. The NVA mortar position was located about 2,500 meters from Hill 881 South and was repeatedly bombed by Air Force and Marine aircraft, but the tubes continued to fire until the end of the siege. *See also* **Khe Sanh.**

Horseshoe, The (Phuong Ho) Marine nickname for the area around the village of Phuong Ho, 16kms southeast of Da Nang along the coast. Many of the hamlets in the area were sympathetic to the Viet Cong and the area was heavily booby-trapped.

Hos-tile, A-gile and Mo-bile Motto of the 101st Airborne Division (Airmobile) in Vietnam, and U.S. airmobile operations in general. *See also* **1st Cavalry Division.**

Hos-tiles *see* **Enemy**

Hose *see* **Kill**

Hose-Up *see* **Fuck-Up, Fire (Shoot)**

Hospital Ships *see* **Repose, Sanctuary**

Hostile Intent *see* **U.S. Air Rules of Engagement, Lavelle**

Hot LZ (Cold LZ, Red Smoke, Red LZ) Landing Zone receiving enemy fire. In Vietnam, NVA/VC troops often attacked FWFs during helimobile operations. The attacks included direct fire, mortar and sometimes booby traps. Helicopters, as well as the troops they unloaded, were targeted by the enemy. Helicopters coming into a hot or "Red LZ" to drop off troops barely touched down, to minimize their time as a target. A Cold LZ was one in which no enemy units opposed the landing of friendly troops. Hot LZs were usually marked with red smoke so other aircraft approaching the LZ would know it was hot. *See also* **Landing Zone, Helicopter Ambush.**

Hot Pad Alert Fighter aircraft kept ready for immediate takeoff, with the aircraft crews standing by. Later in the Vietnam War helicopter gunships also stood hot pad alert. The gunships were armed and fueled, their crews in a shack or bunker within a few feet of the aircraft. Aircraft were kept on hot pad alert to enable quick reaction to tactical situations. Hot pad alert was usually rotated through all the crews in the unit. *See also* **Ramp Alert, Whiplash.**

Hot Pursuit The legitimate right, under International Law, for the forces of one country, under attack by irregular or guerrilla forces, to pursue the irregular attacking force into another country. In the case of Vietnam, NVA/VC forces would launch attacks against SVN, then retreat to sanctuaries in Cambodia to avoid U.S. retaliatory attacks. Cambodia did nothing to stop or discourage the NVA/VC from using Cambodia as a sanctuary. Under International Law the U.S. had the right to pursue the NVA/VC into Laos and Cambodia, but U.S. law forbid such hot pursuit because the U.S. was at peace with the Cambodian government and diplomatic ties existed. It wasn't until '70 that U.S. forces "officially" attacked NVA/VC forces in Cambodia. In '67 Prince Sihanouk, of Cambodia, did make overtures to the U.S. government to allow U.S. ground forces to pursue NVA/VC into Cambodia, based on "hot pursuit," but Sihanouk requested guarantees that Cambodians living along the border areas, where the NVA/VC had their sanctuaries, would not be harmed. President Johnson did not seek to expand the war into Cambodia and did not communicate further with Sihanouk on the matter. General Westmoreland's requests to pursue the NVA/VC into Cambodia were repeatedly denied. *See also* **Operation Menu, Operation Daniel Boone, Secret Bombing of Cambodia.**

Hot Shit Someone who excels at something, an expert, a professional; or one who "thinks" he is those things. *See also* **My Shit Don't Stink.**

Hot Shot *see* **My Shit Don't Stink**

Hot Spot *see* **Operation Big Patch**

Hot War *see* **Other War, The**

Hot-Stuff (Napalm) *see* **Naphthenic-Palmitic Acid**

Hot-Turn Around Technique used by some aircraft to decrease the time interval required to refuel and or rearm. When the aircraft landed at the Rearm and Refuel point the engine was not turned off and the crew didn't leave the aircraft, except to assist the ground crews. When the REARF was complete the aircraft departed to continue its fine support mission. *See also* **Forward Rearm and Refuel Point.**

Hot/Cold Tunnels "Hot tunnels" for Army tunnel rats involved direct enemy contact. The enemy was in the immediate tunnel system which was being searched. "Cold tunnels" involved no enemy contact, the enemy having withdrawn. *See also* **Tunnel Rats.**

Hotel *see* **LZ Hotel**

Hotel Alpha *see* **Book**

Hotel Caravelle (Caravelle) One of the favorite hotels used by journalists in Vietnam. The Caravelle was 10 stories tall with a continental dining room located atop the 10th floor. The hotel was located on Tu Do Street, across from Le Loi Square, not far from South Vietnam's presidential palace. *See also* **Continental Palace.**

Hotel Continental Palace *see* **Continental Palace**

Hotel Echo *see* **HE**

Hotel-Mike *see* **Corpsmen**

Hots (Mess Hall Food) GI slang for hot meals, usually served in a base camp mess hall. Troops operating in the field generally ate C-Rations. Some field units were able to get one hot meal a day if the meal could be flown in by helicopter. Conditions of weather, enemy contact, accessibility to an LZ and aircraft availability were factors which affected hot meals getting out to the field. Base camps of battalion size or larger usually had field kitchens. The larger Army base camps had mess halls where Vietnamese civilians did the KP duties under the direction of Army cooks. *See also* **Dining Room Orderly, Mermite Cans.**

Hourglass Spray System *see* **Operation Ranch Hand**

House 7 Radio Group (Gray Radio, Voice of Southern Nam Bo, Voice of the Sacred Sword) Secret CIA operated radio station established in March '73 to harass the NVA/VC. The station's broadcast studio was located at No. 7 Hong Tap Tu Street and the broadcast group was called "House 7." The station broadcasted anticommunist propaganda, news and music, in Vietnamese and Cambodian, into Cambodia, North and South Vietnam. The CIA station broadcasted under the names of the "Voice of Southern Nam Bo," "Voice of the Sacred Sword" and "Mother Vietnam." Because the broadcasts claimed no political or government affiliations they were called "gray radio" or "gray propaganda." The House 7 crew and their families were successfully evacuated from Vietnam in late April '75.

House Fighting, VC Style *see* **Xuyen Oc**

Housegirl *see* **Hooch Ba**

Hovercraft *see* **PACV**

How-Six *see* **LVTH-6**

Howard Johnsons *see* **Fire Support Base**

Howie *see* **Howitzer**

Howitzer (Howie) The 105mm, 155mm, and 8-inch howitzers were widely used by FWFs during the Vietnam War. The 105mm and the 155mm were available as towed or self-propelled weapons. The 8-inch howitzer was self-propelled. The howitzers were medium range (11,000–16,000 meters), low/high trajectory, were breech loaded, and fired a variety of medium velocity shells. The towed 105mm and 155mm howitzers were light enough to be air transported by helicopter. Howitzers were nicknamed tubes, howie, hows. *See also* **Cannon, M-101, M-108, M-114A1, M-110.**

Hows *see* **Howitzer**

HPE *see* **SEASHARP**

HQ *see* **Headquarters**

HRC *see* **Human Relations Committee**

Hre *see* Montagnards

Hroy *see* Montagnards

HT-1 Radio Small walkie-talkie radio set used by some Special Forces units in Vietnam. The small hand-held voice radio that operated on flashlight batteries was also used at the hamlet level. Early versions of the HT-1 featured a "self-destruct" mechanism that destroyed the radio's circuit board. The feature was incorporated in the radio to keep it out of the hands of the VC. *See also* U.S. Radios, TR-20.

HU-1A *see* UH-1

HU-16 (Albatross, SA-16, UF-1) Air Force/Navy seaplane, nicknamed the "Albatross," used for search and rescue duties. The twin engine, propeller aircraft was manufactured by Grumman Aircraft and had a maximum speed of 236mph, a range of 5,100kms, and operated with a five man crew. The Air Force designation for the HU-16 was the SA-16 and the Navy called them the UF-1. Some versions of the Navy UF-1 were outfitted as antisubmarine search aircraft, but most of the HU-16s that saw service in Vietnam were used by the Air Force as SAR aircraft. *See also* **SAR.**

Hue (Imperial City, Old City) Cultural and religious center of South Vietnam and the country's third largest city, located northwest of Da Nang in I Corps, it was once the Imperial Capital of Vietnam, and the capital of Annam. Situated on the Perfume River, 8kms from the coast, it was the provincial capital of Thua Thien and headquarters for the ARVN 1st Division and MACV Headquarters in I Corps. During the '68 Tet Offensive, the NVA/VC captured the Citadel within the city. Extensive damage was done to the old city, after 31 days of house-to-house fighting US/ARVN forces cleared the city. *See also* **Citadel, Annam, Hue Massacre, Open City.**

Hue Massacre During the communist Tet Offensive of '68 the NVA/VC captured the Citadel in old Hue City and held it for 31 days. When the city was finally retaken by U.S. and ARVN forces, they discovered the mass graves of over 3,000 people who had been systematically executed by the NVA/VC. Hundreds of other inhabitants were missing and presumed dead. The victims of the massacre consisted of those who

supported the GVN or gave aid to the general populace and included GVN personnel, teachers, local leaders, priests, foreign medical teams, students and others who were opposed to, or were neutral toward communist rule. *See also* **Political Purification, Khmer Rouge, Hue.**

Hue River *see* **Perfume River**

Hue River Security Group *see* **TF Clearwater**

Hue Southwest *see* **FSB Birmingham**

Huey *see* **UH-1**

Huey Cobra *see* **AH-1G**

Huey Cobra Gunship *see* **UH-1C**

Huey Gunship *see* **UH-1C, UH-1B**

Huey Hog *see* **UH-1C, UH-1B**

Huey Trainer *see* **HH-1K**

Hug(ging) (Close Embrace Tactics) Tactic (effectively used by the NVA/VC) of engaging enemy forces at extremely close range. Firefights at ranges of 20–30 meters were so close that it was difficult to call in fire support from air strikes or artillery without the possibility of hitting friendly troops. The NVA/VC tactic of using the "close embrace" was very effective because it greatly nullified the use of the U.S.'s superior firepower. When the enemy used hugging, the U.S. unit would attempt to break contact and withdraw far enough to allow air or artillery strikes to be called in on the enemy position. It was usually during the pullback of the U.S. units that the enemy would withdraw, leaving behind a small delaying force. *See also* **Danger-Close Range.**

Hull Down *see* **Defilade**

Human Relations Committee (HRC, Race Relations Board, RRB, Equal Opportunity Committee, EOC) Groups, committees, and councils established in the early 70s within the military to try to improve relations between the various races in the military. These groups attempted to reduce the tension and confrontations caused by the clash between ethnic values and attitudes and the military regulations and requirements. The efforts of the committees eventually brought about changes throughout the entire U.S. military structure, enabling minorities to maintain more of their social structure and a recognition of their particular needs by the military.

Human Relations Councils *see* **Human Relations Committee**

Human Wave Attacks Technique used by the NVA/VC to attack a defensive position. Successive waves of troops lined one behind each other at regular intervals. The first few waves in the attack group were armed; the waves behind those were unarmed. As the attack began the troops surged forward; as the first waves were cut down by U.S. fire, the waves of men behind them filled the gaps, picked up the dropped weapons and continued to press the attack. The NVA/VC randomly used human wave attacks on remote base camps and small NDPs. The same technique was used effectively by the Chinese in the Korean War. The massive amounts of firepower an American unit could bring to bear was usually sufficient to break up the NVA/VC human wave attacks. *See also* **Hug.**

Hump *see* **Humping,** **Boom-Boom, Operation Hump**

Hump Time *see* **Bush Time**

Hump(ing) (Ball-Buster) To move, march or patrol in the boonies, mountains, rice paddies or the jungles; to carry. Field gear, coupled with rough terrain and jungle heat, enemy booby traps and snipers, made movement a painful effort in Vietnam. "Ball-buster" humps were really difficult humps through extremely heavy jungle and undergrowth. Vines and tangles in thick jungle hampered movement to such an extent that it could take several hours just to move a couple hundred meters. *See also* **Boom-Boom, Forced March.**

Humphrey, Vice-President Hubert Horatio (HHH) Senator from Minnesota who served as Vice-President during the Johnson administration in '64. Humphrey was strongly in favor of using U.S. troops to stop communism in Vietnam: He spent a good deal of his time traveling within the U.S. and abroad defending the President's Vietnam policy. He was the Democratic candidate for president in '68, losing to Richard Nixon by less than 1 percent of the popular vote. Humphrey was reelected to the Senate in '70.

Hun *see* **F-100**

Hundred-Mission Crunch *see* **100 Missions**

Hung Dao Hotel Old hotel on Tu Do Street, in Saigon, that was one of the better known whorehouses frequented by Americans.

Hung Rocket *see* **Hang Fire**

Hungry *see* **ICCS**

Hunter-Killer Ambushes *see* **Hunter-Killer Operations**

Hunter-Killer Operations (Hunter-Killer Ambushes) Special ambush operations usually conducted by Lurp or Ranger teams. The ambush team consisted of 6–15 men. When contact was made with the enemy, the team attempted to follow and maintain contact with the retreating enemy. In a normal ambush after contact was made, the ambush team tried to break contact and get as far away from the ambush site as possible. The Hunter-Killer teams remained in the area attempting to expand the engagement, thereby pinpointing a larger enemy force. This larger force would then be engaged by American air and artillery, and a larger followup ground force to close with the enemy. *See also* **Hawk Team, CRIP Platoon.**

Hunter-Killer Operations, SEALS Operations conducted by U.S. Navy SEAL teams from their bases in the Delta. The operations included raids, ambushes, reconnaissance and surveillance of the NVA/VC. The SEAL Hunter-Killer team usually consisted of three to four men.

Hunter-Killer Team (Pink Team, Visual Reconnaissance Team [VR Team]) Air cavalry team of two Army helicopters working together to engage the enemy. The team consisted of an OH-6 Loach and an AH-1 Cobra gunship. The Loach would fly low and slow attempting to draw fire from the VC; if the VC fired on the Loach it would pull out of the way and the Cobra, which had been following out of sight at a higher altitude, would move in on the enemy and "lite-up" the area with minigun, grenade and rocket fire. Pink Teams operated as armed reconnaissance, frequently calling in "Blue Teams" (Aero Rifle Platoons) as a ground element to follow-up enemy contacts. Pink

Teams were also known as VR Teams during recon missions. *See also* **Skunk Hunt, Chumming, Aero Rifle Platoon, Heavy Hunter-Killer Team, Parakeet Missions.**

Hunter-Killer Teams, Navy A-6s *see* **Hunter-Killer Teams, Wild Weasels**

Hunter-Killer Teams, Wild Weasels Air Force Hunter-Killer teams composed of two Wild Weasel aircraft and two–four strike aircraft (usually F-105 or F-4). The Wild Weasels would seek out SAM sites and make the initial attack; the strike aircraft, representing the "killer" part of the team, followed up the attack on the SAM target. The Navy also operated SAM suppression Hunter-Killer teams. The Navy version usually consisted of three A-6 Intruders, one equipped for ECM (SAM acquisition) and two A-6s as the "killer" force. *See also* **Wild Weasel.**

HUS *see* **CH-34**

Hush Money *see* **Grievance Payment**

Hush Puppy (Smith & Wesson Mark 22, S & W 9mm) Smith & Wesson Mark 22, Model 0, 9mm pistol. The pistol was nicknamed the "Hush Puppy" and was fitted with a silencer. It was widely used by U.S. Navy Seals in Vietnam. The weapon was also popular with MACV-SOG teams that operated deep in enemy territory.

Huskie *see* **HH-43**

Husky *see* **HH-43**

Huyuh Phu So *see* **Hoa Hao**

HVY (Heavy, HH) Abbreviation for "heavy." Heavy Helicopters (HH) were designated by the lift capacity of the helicopter; the CH-53 and CH-54 were considered heavy lift helicopters with capacities in excess of 25,000 and 20,000 pounds, respectively. HH was also used as the letter designations for some Air Force helicopters, HH-3, HH-43, HH-53, etc.

I

I & I (R & R) (Intercourse and Intoxication) A variant of the GI's definition of R & R. *See also* **R & R.**

I & I Fires *see* **H and I**

I & R Platoon *see* **Intelligence and Reconnaissance Platoon**

I and I *see* **H and I**

I and I Fires *see* **H and I**

I Corps (I CTZ, I Corps Tactical Zone, Eye Corps) Northernmost tactical zone of the four Corps Tactical Zones in SVN. The Corps Tactical Zones were later renamed Military Regions. The headquarters for I Corps was located at Da Nang, Quang Nam Province. I Corps included the provinces of Quang Tri, Thua Thien, Quang Nam, Quang Tin and Quang Ngai. During the early phase of the war I Corps was primarily the responsibility of the U.S. Marines, later Army units of the 1st Cavalry, 82d Airborne,

101st Airborne, 5th Infantry and 23d Infantry divisions under the XXIV Corps Headquarters, also operated in I Corps. The primary ARVN units to operate in I Corps were 1st, 2d, 3d Infantry divisions, 20th Tank Regiment, the 1st Airborne Division and several Marine and Ranger groups. I Corps was also nicknamed "Marineland."

I Corps Tactical Zone *see* **I Corps**

I CTZ *see* **I Corps**

I Do Not Understand *see* **Toi Com (Khong) Biet**

I Don't Give a Damn... "I don't give a damn for Uncle Sam, I'm not going to Viet-Nam," one of many antidraft slogans chanted by antiwar protestors during the Vietnam War.

I-Feel-Like-I'm-Fixin'-to-Die Rag (Country Joe and the Fish) Popular song of the late sixties by Joe McDonald of the singing group Country Joe and the Fish. The song was about going to Vietnam, and the certainty of death.

I FFV *see* **I Field Force**

I Field Force (I FFV, First Field Force Vietnam) U.S. Army Corps level headquarters established at Nha Trang, II Corps. The headquarters was responsible for the coordination of the U.S. war effort in conjunction with Allied troops in II Corps, with special emphasis on the Central Highlands. The headquarters was originally deployed as Task Force Alpha in '65, but was renamed to I Field Force in March '66. The headquarters remained active until it was withdrawn from Vietnam in April '71, with functions of the I FFV transferred to the 2d Regional Assistance Command at that time. *See also* **TF Alpha.**

I Know I'm Going to Heaven... "I know I'm going to Heaven, cause I spent my time in hell." This phrase was often seen embroidered on the backs of souvenir jackets, brought home by GIs returning from Vietnam. The jackets varied in color, with black and gold being very popular. Along with the phrase was "Vietnam," an outline of the country and the date embroidered on the back. A variation of the phrase was, "When I die I'm going to Heaven, because I've already spent my time in hell."

I Love This Fuckin' Army... "I love this fuckin' Army and the Army loves to FUCK me." GI graffiti. A variant of the phrase featured the "Marine Corps" substituted for "Army."

I-Shit-You-Not A strong declaration that you are telling the truth, used in an effort to convince others that you are speaking with sincerity and truth. An attempt to convince them that you are not kidding, and know what you are talking about.

I'd Rather Be Dead... "I'd rather be dead than red, like the head on the dick of a dog." One of the charming Vietnam era DI phrases used to harass redhead recruits during basic training.

I'd Rather Throw Up... *see* **Reenlistment**

I'm Dreaming of a White Christmas *see* **American Service Radio**

I.V. *see* **Cut-Down**

Ia Drang *see* **Battle of Ia Drang**

Ia Drang Valley Valley located 25kms southwest of Pleiku, below the Chu Pong Massif along the Cambodian border in the Central Highlands of II Corps. Heavily jungled mountain area where the 1st Air Cavalry Division fought its first major battle, October '65. Elements of the Cavalry met three NVA regiments, and stopped their drive to cut SVN in half. The resulting communist defeat caused the NVA/VC to go on the defensive until Tet '68. In the Eastertide Offensive of '75, the NVA again launched their attack from the Ia Drang and successfully cut the country in two, speeding the collapse of SVN. *See also* **Battle of Ia Drang, Chu Pong Massif.**

IBS *see* **Inflatable Boat, Small**

ICAPS *see* **Intelligence Civic Actions Program**

ICC *see* **International Control Commission**

ICCS (International Commission of Control and Supervision) International Commission of Control and Supervision established to monitor the terms of the '73 Paris Peace Accords between the U.S., NVN, SVN, and the PRG. The ICCS was specifically sent to Vietnam to monitor the withdrawal of U.S. and NVA troops from SVN. The commission had no enforcement powers, and was ignored by the NVN and the VC. The members of the commission were Indonesia, Canada, Poland and Hungary. Canada withdrew from the commission in August '73 because NVN continued its aggression in the South and gave no indication of abiding by the terms of the Paris Peace Accords. Canada was replaced by Iran. *See also* **Im Cho Coi Sao.**

Ice Covered Volcano *see* **Nguyen Vo Giap**

Ice Cream Soldiers (U.S. Army Soldiers) One of the Marine nicknames for Army soldiers. The name was awarded to Army troops because of the luxuries they experienced at their base camps in Vietnam. Luxuries such as waitress service in the mess hall, hootch maids, civilian shit-burners and KPs, etc. *See also* **Infantry Soldier, The; Golden Ghettos.**

ICEX *see* **Intelligence Coordination and Exploitation Team**

ICM Round (Improved Conventional Munitions) Cluster bomb unit delivered by a 155mm shell. Sixty small antipersonnel grenades were carried to the target area via the 155mm ICM round. Over the target the shell casing ruptured dispersing the small grenades. The grenades were equipped with small fins to ensure that the detonating striker was correctly positioned on impact. The ICM grenades had an effect similar to regular grenades, throwing deadly fragments over a wide area. The rounds first saw service in '68 and were initially used, like the beehive round, for fire base defense. *See also* **Cluster Bomb Units, Firecracker.**

ICP *see* **Lao Dong**

ICSC *see* **International Control Commission**

ICU *see* **Intensive Care Unit**

ICU Patients *see* **Gorks**

ID Cards *see* **Good Guy Card**

IDAD *see* **Pacification**

Identification Panels *see* **Air Panels**

If It's Dead and Vietnamese... *see* **Body Count**

"If you are recovering my body..." *see* **Healy, General Mike**

If You Can See It, You Can Hit It *see* **Precision-Guided Munitions**

If You Kill for Money... *see* **Those Who Kill for Pleasure...**

IFS *see* **Landing Ship Medium Rocket**

IFS Ship *see* **Inshore Fire Support Ship**

IG *see* **Inspector General**

Igloo White Code name for a system used to detect and pinpoint enemy movement along the Ho Chi Minh Trail and SVN's border. Data from electronic sensors and aerial reconnaissance were fed into Air Force computers located at the Infiltration Surveillance Center at Nakhon Royal Thai Air Base which generated targets for Air Force strikes. The system was designed by the DCPG and employed a wide variety of electronic sensing devices. The system included both aircraft mounted sensors and detection devices, and remotely deployed ground sensors. *See also* **Electronic Sensors, Infiltration Surveillance Center, DCPG, INFANT.**

II Corps (II CTZ, II Corps Tactical Zone, 2 Corps) Tactical zone covering the 12 most central provinces of SVN, Headquartered at Pleiku, Pleiku Province. In November '65 NVA/VC units launched an attack from the Ia Drang Valley, attempting to drive across the II Corps Zone and cut SVN in half. The attack was stopped by U.S. units of the 1st Cav. Again in March '72 the NVA/VC attacked Dak To as part of their Eastertide Offensive; their drive was stopped by the ARVN 23d Inf Div backed by U.S. air support. Finally in March '75 the NVA/VC attacked at Ban Me Thuot and were successful in their drive to split SVN in half. The provinces of II Corps were Kontum, An Khe, Pleiku, Phu Bon, Phu Yen, Darlac Khanh Hoa, Ninh Thuan, Binh Thuan, Lam Dong, Tuyen Duc and Quang Duc. *See also* **Military Regions.**

II Corps Tactical Zone *see* **II Corps**

II CTZ *see* **II Corps**

II FFV *see* **II Field Force**

II Field Force (II FFV, Second Field Force Vietnam, The Plantation) U.S. Corps level headquarters, located at Long Binh, III Corps. II FFV first deployed to Vietnam in '66 to coordinate U.S. units operating in III and IV Corps and to provide support for ARVN units in the same area. Of the three U.S. Corps level headquarters in Vietnam, the II FF was the largest. Major U.S. units under the command of II FFV were elements of the 1st, 4th, 9th and 25th Infantry divisions; 82d and 101st Airborne divisions; 1st Cavalry Division; 173d, 196th, 199th Infantry brigades; 11th Armored Cavalry Regiment, 12th Combat Aviation Group and associated artillery groups. II FFV headquarters was nicknamed "the Plantation."

III Corps (III Corps Tactical Zone, III CTZ, 3 Corps) The 11 province area located around South Vietnam's capital. The CTZ was located between the Central Highlands and the IV Corps Delta. III Corps headquarters was located at Bien Hoa, Bien Hoa Province. The III Corps provinces were Phuoc Long, Binh Tuy, Long Khanh, Binh Long, Tay Ninh, Binh Duong, Hau Nghia, Long

An, Bien Hoa, Phuoc Tuy and Gia Dinh. *See also* **Military Regions.**

III Corps Tactical Zone *see* **III Corps**

III CTZ *see* **III Corps**

III MAF *see* **III Marine Amphibious Force**

III MAF Headquarters *see* **Camp Horn**

III Marine Amphibious Force (III MAF, Third Marine Amphibious Force, 3d Marine Amphibious Force) The III MAF was organized at Da Nang, I Corps, May '65 and provided support to SVN forces and control of U.S. Marine forces in the I Corps area. The III MAF was the controlling headquarters in I Corps until March '70 when control was turned over to the Army's XXIV Corps. The III MAF departed SVN April '71; Marine forces remaining in Vietnam after the departure of III MAF were placed under control of the 3d Marine Amphibious Brigade (3d MAB). The III MAF controlled two U.S. Marine divisions, two Regimental Landing Teams, and the 1st Marine Air Wing.

III Marine Expeditionary Brigade *see* **III Marine Expeditionary Force**

III Marine Expeditionary Force (III MEF, III Marine Expeditionary Brigade, III MEB) The 9th Marine Expeditionary Brigade controlled all Marine units in Vietnam until May '65. The III MEF was established to control the Marine forces, and within several days the III MEF was renamed the III Marine Amphibious Force (III MAF). The name change was an effort to keep the Marine presence from appearing to be colonial in nature as previous French Expeditionary Forces had been. *See also* **9th Marine Amphibious Brigade, III MAF.**

III MEB *see* **III Marine Expeditionary Force**

III MEF *see* **III Marine Expeditionary Force**

IL-28 (Beagle, Ilyushin-28) Small, Soviet made twin engine jet bomber. The North Vietnamese had several of the bombers in their inventory. The IL-28 was nicknamed the "Beagle" by American airmen, and was armed with four 23mm cannons, a maximum speed of 559mph, a range of 1,130kms and a bomb load of 6,600 pounds. The aircraft was not used offensively by the North Vietnamese during the war in Vietnam.

Illegal Drugs *see* **Illicit Drugs**

Illicit Drugs (Illegal Drugs, Drugs, Dope) Illicit drugs were readily available to U.S. troops in Vietnam. Drugs were available at many of the bars and massage parlors throughout Saigon and the cities of South Vietnam. In the shanty towns that sprung up outside of U.S. bases a wide variety of drugs could be purchased. Marijuana was by far the most available, but hashish, opium, heroin and an assortment of pills (uppers/downers) could be obtained. Drugs could also be obtained by military medical personnel through various channels, and resold. Drugs such as heroin and hashish distributed in Vietnam were much more potent than that which was available on the streets of America. Such drugs were available almost direct from their source and not "cut" or diluted to increase the seller's profit margin. In Vietnam, even small quantities of heroin were extremely addicting. Drug trafficking was highly profitable, and much money could be made by soldiers who shipped drugs and marijuana home for resale. Drug use by U.S. troops steadily increased after '67 reaching epidemic proportions by '72. *See also* **Marijuana, Hashish, Heroin, Dexamphetamines, Drug List, Mainliner, Quaaludes, STP, Speed, BTs, LSD, Morphine.**

Illumes *see* **Illumination Rounds**

Illumination Rounds (Illumes) Artillery fired flares which were fitted with parachutes, allowing the ignited flare to drift to the ground. The prime weapons used to fire "illumes" were the 105mm, 155mm howitzer and 4.2-inch mortar. Illumination rounds were also available for the M-79 Grenade Launcher. *See also* **Flares.**

Illuminator Name for the aircraft in a formation, carrying the laser gun that was used to mark a target. The laser was aimed at the target; when triggered it illuminated the target with its laser beam. The light reflected from the illuminated target was used by laser homing smart bombs (LGBs). The bomb locked on to the laser light guiding itself to the target. To increase LGB bombing accuracy the illuminating aircraft was required to keep the laser light focused on the target until the bomb was practically on top of it. One aircraft could serve as the illuminator for several LGBs or LGB bomb strikes. *See also* **Laser Guided Bomb.**

Ilyushin-28 *see* **IL-28**

Im Cho Coi Sao The South Vietnamese translation of the ICCS (International Commission of Control and Supervision), it meant "wait quietly and see how things turn out." The SVN were very skeptical of North Vietnam and the Viet Cong, and didn't believe the enemy would adhere to the terms of the '73 Paris Peace Accords. . . . They were correct. *See also* **ICCS.**

Image Intensifier *see* **Starlight Scope**

Immediates *see* **Triage**

Immersion Foot (Trench Foot, Tropical Impetico) Known as trench foot in WWI, a painful, and if untreated, incapacitating foot disorder caused by exposure to damp or wet conditions for extended periods of time. If the feet weren't kept dry the skin began to shrivel, crease, and peel into layers, leaving infected open sores. The raw, open sores were further irritated by the wet, rubbing of the boots, causing bleeding and resulting in repeated cycles of irritation, re-infection and temporary incapacity. In Vietnam the condition was called immersion foot and "tropical impetico." *See also* **Jungle Rot.**

Immigration and Naturalization Service (INS) At the direction of President Ford new guidelines were established at the INS that allowed thousands of Vietnamese refugees to enter the U.S. under special dispensation. Under the new parole, Asian refugees could be admitted to the U.S. as long as they could prove some type of "family tie" with an American, either in Vietnam or the United States.

Imperial City *see* **Citadel**

Improved Conventional Munitions *see* **ICM Round**

In Times of War . . . the First Casualty Is Truth From remarks made on February 24, 1965, by Secretary-General of the United Nations U Thant, eluding to the possibility that the American government was not being completely truthful in its explanations for the escalation of the war in Vietnam in '65. An escalation that entailed the bombing of targets in NVN by American and Vietnamese aircraft. *See also* **Tonkin Gulf Incident.**

In Vietnam, the Wind Doesn't . . . "In Vietnam, the wind doesn't blow, it sucks." . . . GI philosophy on Vietnam's seasonal winds. *See also* **Monsoons.**

In-Country Reference to "in South Vietnam," and the war fought on the ground, in and around South Vietnam.

In-Country R & R U.S. troops in Vietnam were eligible for one out of country R & R per one year tour of duty in Vietnam. Some in-country R & Rs were also made available to the troops. In-country R & R centers were established at Vung Tau (on the coast east of Saigon) and China Beach (on the coast near Da Nang). In-country R & Rs were generally three days long and awarded at the discretion of command. In some units in-country R & Rs were granted on a rotation basis (turns), or as reward for high enemy body count or for outstanding individual achievement. Many U.S. troops who served in Vietnam never experienced an in-country R & R at either of the two centers. *See also* **R & R, Meyercourt Hotel.**

In-Line *see* **On-Line**

In-Processing Reference to the procedures used to process troops returning to the U.S. at the end of their tour of duty in Vietnam. The process usually included medical and dental checks, hearing evaluations, records and payroll updating, equipment return, uniform issue and transportation arrangements. For the Vietnam returnee the process could take 2–3 days, if all the necessary records were available. Those troops being discharged on return from Vietnam usually encountered long delays before their release.

Incendiaries (Thermite Grenade) Fire bombs or grenades which burned with an intense heat or flame such as Molotov cocktails and thermite grenades. *See also* **Grenades, Thermite.**

Incendiary CBU *see* **M-35 CBU**

Incendijel *see* **Naphthenic-Palmitic Acid**

Incoming (Mail-Call) GI slang for enemy fire being received, usually in reference to enemy mortars, rockets or artillery. Some WWII veterans in Vietnam referred to "incoming" as "mail-call."

Incontinent Ordnance Delivery *see* **Friendly Fires**

Incursion A raid or attack into hostile or neutral territory. In April '70 US/ARVN ground units attacked into Cambodia in an effort to clear NVA/VC sanctuaries along the border. In June the US/ARVN forces began to withdraw back into SVN. In February '71 ARVN ground forces, with U.S. air support, attacked into Laos in an attempt to cut the Ho Chi Minh Trail at Tchepone, Laos. The force met with heavy enemy resistance and retreated from Laos back into SVN in March '71. The incursion into Laos resulted in heavy ARVN casualties, and their failure to cut the Ho Chi Minh Trail at Tchepone. *See also* **Cambodian Incursion, Lam Son 719.**

Independence *see* **USS Independence**

Independence Palace *see* **Gia Long Palace**

Independent Units (Separate Units) Units not directly assigned to a parent division or regiment. During Vietnam several U.S. units operated independently of the infantry divisions stationed in Vietnam. Several U.S. brigades operated throughout Vietnam controlled by MACV headquarters. Some examples of separate U.S. brigades or combat groups: 173d ABN Bde, 1st Aviation Bde, 18th Engineer Bde, 17th Aviation Group, 199th LIB, 20th Engineer Bde, 11th ACR, 3d Bde/82d ABN, and 3d Bde/101st ABN. The ARVNs and the NVA/VC also utilized independent regiments and battalions. Independent units were also referred to as "separate" units. *See also* **Organic.**

India *see* **ICC**

Indian Country (Bad Country, Contested Area) Grunt terms for extremely hostile enemy territory in Vietnam. A "Contested Area" was military jargon for any hostile area or place where Americans were fired on. Indian or Bad Country was exceptionally dangerous because it usually referred to an NVA base area, where the enemy operated in force and the area was

laced with defensive bunkers and or mines and booby traps. In such areas the civilian population was very hostile to American forces and actively supported the NVA/VC. *See also* **Boonies.**

Indiana *see* **Operation Indiana**

Indiana National Guard *see* **Hoosier LRRPs**

Indigenous Rations *see* **ARVN Long Rats**

Indigenous Rucksack *see* **ARVN Rucksack**

Indigenous Troops *see* **Civilian Irregular Defense Group**

Indirect Fire Weapons Weapons such as mortars and artillery pieces that fired at targets without having a direct line of sight to those targets. The targets' coordinates were determined by a friendly unit that could see the target, or the coordinates were plotted blind, from a map. Long-range rockets such as those used by the NVA were also indirect fire weapons. The mortar and rocket were strictly indirect fire weapons, whereas, the other weapons mentioned could be used in the direct fire role. *See also* **Flechette, Mortar, Howitzer, Cannon.**

Individual Fighting Position *see* **Foxhole**

Individual Load Carrying Equipment *see* **Web Gear**

Indochina (French Indochina [F.I.C.], Associated States of Indochina) French Indochina, at the start of the twentieth century, represented the French colonial empire in Southeast Asia; it included the following territories: Cochin China, Annam, Tonkin, and the Kingdoms of Laos and Cambodia. Modern references to Indochina refer to the southeastern part of Asia consisting of North and South Vietnam. Shortly after WWII the French established the Associated States. They installed Bao Dai as the figurehead ruler of Vietnam, in an attempt to stifle the independence movement throughout the former French colony. The members of the Associated States were Annam, Cochin China, Tonkin, Laos and Cambodia. *See also* **Cochin China, Annam, Tonkin.**

Indochina War (First Indochina

War, The Dirty War, La Sale Guerre) References to the war of independence waged by the Vietnamese forces of the Viet Minh against their colonial rulers, the French. Open warfare between the French and the Viet Minh broke out in '46 and ended in '54 with the defeat of the French Army. The French called their eight year war against the Viet Minh "La Sale Guerre," The Dirty War. French Union Forces suffered more than 74,000 dead and 65,000 wounded. The war between the NVA/VC and the Americans is referred to as the Second Indochina War. *See also* **Vietnam War.**

Indo-Chinese Communist Party *see* **Lao Dong**

Indo-Chinese Tiger *see* **Tiger**

Indoctrination Sessions *see* **Chinh Huan**

Indy *see* **USS Independence**

INFANT (Iroquois Night Fighter and Night Tracker) One of the DCPG systems developed under the Igloo White program. In '69 some U.S. Huey gunships were fitted with starlight and infrared scopes, enabling them to accurately engage the enemy at night and plot enemy movement. In addition to the scopes the choppers were fitted with special low light level TV (LLTV), Xenon searchlights and a Forward Looking Infrared (FLIR) imaging system that displayed images on a cockpit mounted CRT based on the thermal qualities of the target. The information was used with other intelligence gathered to generate targets for air strikes and ground assaults. *See also* **DCPG.**

Infantry Officer Advanced Course (IOAC) Follow-up Army officer course conducted at Fort Benning, Georgia. Officers who took the course during the Vietnam War era generally had some previous combat leadership experience. When the IOAC graduate returned to Vietnam for his second or third tour he was generally assigned to a staff position at the battalion or brigade level.

Infantry Search Patterns In Vietnam, Army patrols used several different types of search patterns, the most common were zigzag, starburst, checkerboard, and cloverleaf. In the starburst pattern, small patrol teams fanned out from the patrol base. After

traveling a prearranged distance, the patrol would swing around, form an oval pattern and return to the base. When all the patrol elements returned the base would be relocated. In the zigzag pattern the patrols weaved a zigzag search course to the patrol's final destination. The patrol would then turn about and begin a zigzag pattern covering different terrain on its way back to the patrol base. *See also* **Cloverleaf, Checkerboard.**

Infantry Soldier, The In Vietnam less than 15 percent of the U.S. forces were actual field combat troops. At the peak of U.S. troops in-country, 55,000 combat troops operated in the field, supported by over 450,000 troops at base camps and in rear areas. The combat infantryman was known by many names such as bluelegs, snuffies, grunt, boonie rat, ground pounder, crunchies, legs, beetle stompers, bush beetles, line doggies and doggies. The combat infantryman got the nickname of "grunt" because, as legend goes, it was an indication of his IQ. *See also* **Digger, The Shit.**

Infantry Training Company *see* **Infantry Training Regiment**

Infantry Training Regiment (ITR, ITC, Infantry Training Company) Army troops in basic training were officially assigned to established training units. The units were formed the same as regular Army units. An individual belonged to a squad, part of a platoon, part of a company, part of a battalion, all part of the training regiment. *See also* **Basic Combat Training.**

Infiltration Surveillance Center (ISC, Nakhon Phanom Royal Thai Air Base; 56th Special Operations Wing, NKP) Air Force intelligence and computer center located at Nakhom Phanom RTAFB (NKP), Thailand, code-named "Dutch Mill." Task Force Alpha of the 56th Special Operations Wing received and analyzed intelligence data on enemy activities along the Ho Chi Minh Trail and its surrounding area. The data was collected through ground observations by recon units, aerial overflights and electronic sensing/monitoring equipment. The analyzed information was forwarded to MACV headquarters and to other appropriate commands for action and targeting. NKP was located 400kms northwest of Da

Nang and 405kms southwest of Hanoi along the Thailand/Laos border. *See also* **Igloo White, Electronic Sensors, EC-121, OP-2E, F-4, U-8, Naked Fanny.**

Infinity Sight   Gun sight used by a helicopter gunship pilot to aim his forward facing weapons systems.

Inflatable Boat, Small (IBS, Rubber Raft)   Inflatable rubber rafts used in riverine operations in the Delta. The IBS were also carried aboard U.S. submarines for use in covert beach landings by recon or special mission forces. *See also* **TF 117.**

Information   *see*   **Skinny**

Infrared (IR, Pink Light, 2KW Searchlight)   Light not visible to the naked eye, but detectable through a special viewer or goggles. In Vietnam infrared viewers were available on a limited basis and were used for night aerial reconnaissance and as part of some base camp defenses. The American M-48 tank had infrared searchlights that allowed them to scan through the darkness. Infrared xenon searchlights were mounted on boats and vehicles and used for night surveillance duties. Infrared light was sometimes called "pink light" because of the way it looked when seen through a starlight scope. The 2KW was a hand operated infrared searchlight used by the Air Force. Aircraft mounted systems were called FLIR. *See also* **Xenon Light, LCPL, Nighthawks, FLIR.**

Infrared Binoculars   *see*   **SU-50 Electronic Binocular**

Infrared Scope   *see*   **IR Scopes**

Infusion   *see*   **Rotational Hump**

Ingress (Egress)   Terminology used by the military to describe an aircraft's inbound approach to a target (ingress), and the aircraft's departure from the target area (egress).

Initial Point (IP)   An imaginary reference point used by attacking aircraft to mark the starting point of the final attack run on a target. From the IP aircraft pressed the attack on the target without further course deviation.

Initiative   The combat force which had the initiative invariably was the force that determined when a battle would take place. Most of the initiative was with the NVA/VC in Vietnam. They chose when to attack,

attacking when they believed they had superiority in numbers or the element of surprise. U.S. forces were seldom able to use their initiative to engage large numbers of the enemy because the enemy chose not to fight on American terms. On those occasions when the enemy did stand and fight, superior American firepower inflicted heavy casualties on enemy units. For much of the war U.S. units were forced to "react" to the enemy, in the hope of containing him so he could be destroyed.

Ink Blot Policy   *see*   **Enclave Policy**

INS   *see*   **Immigration and Naturalization Service**

Insect Bar (Mosquito Netting)   Nylon netting used as protection against mosquitos. The netting fit over the bed or could be used over a suspended hammock and was supported on both ends by short bars. Mosquito bars were found at base camps and larger permanent facilities that actually had beds for their troops to sleep in. The grunts in the field lacked the requisite beds on which to hang the netting and bars. Mosquito protection in the field consisted of insect repellent. *See also* **Insect Repellent.**

Insect Repellent (Bug Juice)   Military insect repellent, more commonly known as "bug juice." It had marginal insect repellent qualities, but when mixed with C-Ration peanut butter made an excellent fuel for heating C-Rations. Bug juice, when applied directly on leeches, was very effective at causing the leeches to release their bite, allowing them to be removed without leaving their head under the victim's skin. *See also* **Peanut Butter.**

Insert(ion) (Extraction)   With reference to troops, insertion was the deployment of troops into an area. For airmobile forces the method of insertion was by helicopter. For riverine operations boats and or helicopters were used. Extraction was the military opposite of insertion. *See also* **Hot LZ.**

Insertions of Opportunity   "Minieagle flights" conducted by elements of Company E/75th Rangers operating in the Delta of IV Corps. If air reconnaissance detected a small enemy unit, the rangers would be inserted into the area in an attempt to make contact. If the "insertion of opportunity" resulted in contact with a larger enemy group than the rangers could handle, a larger assault force would immediately be inserted into the area. The mini-eagle flights consisted of a six man ranger team, with several teams available. *See also* **Eagle Flight.**

Inshore Fire Support Ship (IFS Ship, Task Force 70.8.9)   A naval ship assigned to give fire support to ground units. Targets of the IFS were located along the coast or anywhere inland within range of the ship's guns. During the Vietnam War the Navy kept several ships on station to provide fire support for Army and Marine units operating along the coast. The ships were designated Task Force 70.8.9, and operated along the coast of I Corps and the southern coast of North Vietnam. For several months in '68 the *Battleship New Jersey* was part of the shore bombardment group. *See also* **USS New Jersey, Operation Sea Dragon, TF 70.8.9, Landing Ship Medium Rocket.**

Inshore Undersea War Group   *see* **SEASHARP**

Inspector General (IG)   Watchdog department of the Army. The IG Department was responsible for monitoring the administrative operations of the Army. The IG used frequent, random, and (theoretically) unannounced inspections to check the Army's readiness and ability to perform its mission. The IG was outside the normal Army chain of command, so it was not controlled by lower level Army corps or division headquarters. Word that an IG Inspection was to take place sent a chill through the command that was targeted for the inspection. The IG also received, and acted on complaints from soldiers who believed some wrong had been done. The IG's office provided a soldier a chance to be heard if his complaint was squashed by the Army's normal bureaucratic chain of command.

Instant NCOs   *see*   **Shake 'n' Bake Sergeants**

Insurgency   *see*   **Guerrilla War**

Integrated Observation System   *see* **AN/GUQ-10**

Intel Unit   *see*   **S-2**

Intel-Reps   *see*   **Intelligence Reports**

Intelligence and Interdiction   *see*   **H and I**

Intelligence and Operations Coordination Center   *see*   **DIOCC**

Intelligence and Reconnaissance Platoon (I & R Platoon)   The I & R platoon was a standard unit of the SF/CIDG companies operating in Vietnam. Their mission was the gathering of intelligence on enemy activities in their area. The information gathered was relayed to Special Forces headquarters and later routed to MACV in Saigon for analysis and action. Most of the CIDG companies were composed of Montagnard tribesmen, who were excellent trackers and scouts. They were loyal to their American USSF leadership, even though they fought for pay. They had no loyalties to the South Vietnamese. *See also* **Montagnards.**

Intelligence Civic Actions Program (ICAPS)   A program similar to MEDCAP, but the emphasis was on intelligence gathering as Army units performed civic projects in a village. *See also* **Medical Civilian Aid Patrols.**

Intelligence Coordination and Exploitation Team (ICEX)   ICEX was a '67 CIA program to collect intelligence data on the National Liberation Front, the political arm of the Viet Cong. The program operated as part of CORDS, and was later renamed the Phoenix Program. Under the Phoenix Program not only was intelligence information gathered but the VCI were actively hunted down and arrested or eliminated. *See also* **Phoenix Program.**

Intelligence Reports (Intel-Reps)   Reports generated by the intelligence section of a unit. The reports were used for operations planning and defensive strategies.

Intensive Care Unit (ICU)   Intensive care unit of a medical facility, providing constant medical care for critically injured patients who required continuous monitoring and treatment.

Inter-Departmental Speaking Team   *see*   **Truth Team**

Intercourse and Intoxication   *see*   **I & I (R & R)**

Interior Lines   Military concept of lines of communication that allowed elements of a force to quickly move about a zone. In Vietnam NVN used interior lines of communication. The Ho Chi Minh Trail fed SVN between Laos/Cambodia and South Vietnam. From a centralized point near the middle of SVN, on the border with Cambodia, NVA forces could easily deploy to (and be supported from) almost any region of South Vietnam. South Vietnam forces did not control the interior of their country and thus had to move their units around its periphery. Such movements used critical amounts of time and resources, a disadvantage NVN did not have to contend with.

Interlocking Fire (Mutual Supporting Fire) Technique of establishing defensive weapons positions so that no one position alone had to cover a given area of the perimeter. The positions were set up so they were mutually supporting. This interlocking of fire reduced the weak link aspect of defensive positions. Ground units in combat also operated so that other nearby units could provide support when needed. Mutual support meant the units operated in such a way that they could provide support to each other if necessary. For companies this was usually accomplished by limiting the operational distance between companies to distances that could be covered, on the ground, in 2–4 hours. The helicopter greatly extended the mutual supporting range of infantry units in Vietnam. *See also* **DePuy Foxhole.**

Internal Defense and Development *see* **Pacification**

Internal Defense Operations *see* **Pacification**

Internal Net Company level radio net in which all the platoons and attached units of the company were on the same radio frequency for communication. There were usually several radios at the company CP, at least one set to the internal net linking the CP to the platoons, and at least one radio on the command net linking the company CP to the battalion headquarters. *See also* **Bullshit Net.**

Internal Security *see* **Pacification**

International Commission for Supervision *see* **International Control Commission**

International Commission of Control *see* **ICCS**

International Control Commission (ICC, ICSC, International Commission for Supervision and Control) International commission consisting of delegates from Canada, India and Poland, established by the 1954 Geneva Accords on Indo-China to monitor the armistice established between the French and the Viet Minh at the end of the First Indo-China War. The commission was officially known as the International Commission for Supervision and Control in Vietnam and had no real authority or power to make the involved parties comply with the terms of the Accords. *See also* **ICCS.**

International Red Cross *see* **Geneva Convention**

International Voluntary Services (IVS) International organization of volunteers that helped the peoples of Third World countries with agricultural training, teachers and other community services designed to "help the people help themselves." The IVS was similar in scope to the American Peace Corps. IVS groups worked throughout Asia, including South Vietnam.

Interrogation of Prisoner of War Team (IPW) Teams consisting of U.S. Military Intelligence, SVN Military Intelligence and the National Police. Their sole purpose was the interrogation of VC and VCS personnel captured in the field. *See also* **Interrogation-by-Altitude.**

Interrogation Room *see* **Quiz Room**

Interrogation-by-Altitude Rumored interrogation method used by some U.S. intelligence officers. Several VC or VCS were taken up in a helicopter; at two or three thousand feet the questioning began. If the first subject questioned refused to respond, he was thrown out of the chopper; the next subject was then asked the same questions. After the first or second man was thrown out of the helicopter, the remainder of the prisoners tended to be very cooperative, even to the point of inventing information they believed their interrogators wanted to hear. *See also* **Torture.**

Interrogator Translator Team (ITT) Marine intelligence teams that, through their ARVN interpreters, interrogated captured NVA/VC suspects or anyone else they believed could be a source of information on enemy movements or activities.

Intestinal Worms *see* Trichinosis

Intrenching Tool *see* Entrenching Tool

Intrepid *see* USS Intrepid

Intromycin *see* Polymagna

Intruder *see* A-6A

Invader *see* B-26

Invert *see* Naked Fanny

IOAC *see* Infantry Officer Advanced Course

Iodine Tablets *see* Water Purification Tablets

IOS Binoculars *see* AN/GUQ-10

IP *see* Initial Point

IPW *see* Interrogation of Prisoner of War Team

IQ Test   Part of the induction process in the military involved a battery of tests that gauged an individual's intelligence quotient. Based on test results the military decided the soldier's vocation, or Military Occupation Specialty (MOS). Based on the individual's test scores, and the particular needs of the service at the time, the Army and Marines awarded the soldier an MOS. Draftees were assigned an MOS based on the needs of the service. Those men who enlisted in the Army were sometimes allowed a choice in their MOS, but that choice was also tempered by the needs of the service. During the Vietnam War the needs of the service leaned heavily toward the combat MOS, and 40 percent of America's Vietnam era soldiers found themselves in Vietnam. *See also* Moron Corps, MOS.

IR *see* Infrared

IR Scopes (Infrared Scope, P-155 Scope)   The P-155 was an experimental infrared weapon's sight, tested in Vietnam in '65. The IR scope was designed to provide night vision by means of an "active" infrared system. The system was tested by the ARVNs under the guidance of the DOD Joint Research and Test Activity Agency (JRATA) and the ACTIV. The mounted scope weighed over thirty pounds and could operate for several hours on rechargeable ni-cad batteries. The P-155 scope proved impractical for combat use because of its limited effective range (100 meters), its excessive weight and the inaccessibility of a continuously reliable power source to recharge the batteries. *See also* Starlight Scope, Infrared.

IR8 Rice (Miracle Rice)   Strain of high yield rice developed in the States and used in Vietnam to increase their rice harvest. The Vietnamese did not like the flavor of the rice and avoided it as much as they could. Surplus amounts of the rice were usually forced on the occupants of the government refugee camps.

Iran *see* ICCS

IRB *see* SU-50 Electronic Binocular

IRC *see* Geneva Convention

Iron Bombs (Conventional Bombs)   Air Force slang for conventional bombs (nonnuclear bombs) carried by B-52s. The B-52 was originally designed as a heavy bomber for the delivery of nuclear bombs. B-52s were first used to bomb targets in Vietnam with conventional bombs in '65. The typical "iron bombs" carried by B-52s were 500- and 750-pounders. *See also* B-52.

Iron Bridge Ridge   Long ridge 16kms northwest of Da Nang which overlooked the Song Cu De River. The ridge was the southern extension of the Hai Van Mountain range which separated the Da Nang coastal basin from the coastal lowlands around Hue and Phu Bai. The Song Cu De River flowed along the southern edge of the ridge, and emptied into the Da Nang Harbor. *See also* Hai Van Pass.

Iron Brigade *see* 3d Brigade/1st Infantry Division

Iron Hand *see* Operation Iron Hand

Iron Idiot *see* Donkey Sight

Iron Land *see* Cu Chi

Iron Mike (O'Daniel, General John; American Friends of Vietnam, AFV Lobby)   Iron Mike O'Daniel served as U.S. Army MAAG Indo-China chief from '54 to '55 and worked closely with the newly formed Diem government. After Iron Mike's retirement from the Army in '55 he helped to found the American Friends of Vietnam lobby in the States. The AFV lobbied Congress for aid and support for the Diem regime.

Iron Triangle   Name given to a VC base area located in the roughly triangular area between the villages of Ben Suc (W), Ben Cat (N) and Phu Cuong (S), III Corps. The heavily forested Ho Bo Woods and plantation area was less than 25kms from Saigon and was laced with enemy tunnels. Several major U.S. operations were conducted in the area, but none of them ever permanently kept the VC out of the area. Most of the area was eventually classified a free-fire-zone. Among the operations conducted in the area were Atlas Wedge, Toan Thang, Uniontown. See also Ben Suc, Cedar Falls, Operation Uniontown, Ho Bo Woods.

Iron Triangle, I Corps Marine nickname for an extremely dangerous and hostile area located west of the Marine position on Hill 55, and southwest of Da Nang. The triangle was a longtime VC stronghold, with most of the hamlets in the heavily populated area supporting the Viet Cong. Marine patrols through the area were constantly the victims of enemy mines, booby traps, and snipers.

Iron Triangle, NVN Nickname for the triangle area formed by Hanoi–Haiphong–Thanh Hoa. The triangle area was saturated with North Vietnamese construction and repair facilities, airfields, power plants, storage depots, factories, radar installations and bridges. The area was named by American aircrews that attacked targets in the area during the air war against North Vietnam. The triangle was heavily fortified with AA/AAA gun positions and SAM missile sites. Much of the area was off limits to heavy bomb strikes during Rolling Thunder operations.

Ironing see **Restructuring**

Iroquois see **UH-1**

Iroquois Night Fighter and Night Tracker see **INFANT**

Irregulars see **Civilian Irregular Defense Group**

Irving see **Operation Irving**

ISC see **Infiltration Surveillance Center**

It's a Small War God, But... "It's a small war God, but it's the only war we've got..." Comment credited to anonymous career military officers on the positive aspects of a small "hot" war after years of "cold" war. Many factions within the military bureaucracy initially viewed Vietnam as a place for

combat officers to gain experience for the "real" war with the Russians, which they believed was inevitable. Shortly after U.S. combat forces were committed to Vietnam it became evident that American forces were not prepared for the necessities of the "hot" war in Southeast Asia. A variant sometimes heard was, "This is the only war we've got, don't knock it."

It's Not the Round with Your Name... It's not the round with your name on it you hav'ta watch out for, it's the one that's addressed "To Whom It May Concern." Concern shared by many grunts regarding the probability of being shot in Vietnam.

ITC see **Infantry Training Regiment**

Itchy Crotch see **Trichomoniasis, Jungle Rot**

Ithaca Model 37 see **Shotgun**

ITR see **Infantry Training Regiment**

ITT see **Interrogator/Translator Team**

IUWG see **SEASHARP**

IV Corps (IV CTZ, IV Corps Tactical Zone, 4 Corps) Corps Tactical Zone encompassing the 16 southernmost provinces of RVN, headquarters at Can Tho, Phong Dinh Province. The provinces in the IV Corps zone were Bac Lieu, An Xuyen, Chuong Thien, Kien Giang, Sa Dec, Phong Dinh, Vinh Binh, Kien Hoa, Kien Tuong, Dinh Tuong, Kien Phong, Chau Doc, Go Cong, Ba Xuyen, Vinh Long and An Giang. The U.S. 9th Infantry Division, in conjunction with the Navy's Mobile Riverine Force, worked the IV Corps Delta. The ARVN 7th, 9th and 21st Infantry divisions were also stationed throughout the Delta. See also Mekong Delta; Military Region, SVN.

IV Corps Tactical Zone see **IV Corps**

IV CTZ see **IV Corps**

Ivory Coast see **Son Tay Raid**

IVS see **International Voluntary Services**

Ivy Division see **4th Infantry Division**

Ivy Division Patch The unit patch of the 4th Infantry Division earned it the nickname of the "Ivy Division." During the Vietnam War the nickname was expanded to the "Poison Ivy Division." The patch was a white square standing on its pointed end. In each corner of the patch was a five-pointed ivy leaf. The brown stem of each leaf joined a brown ring in the center of the patch. *See also* 4th Infantry Division.

Iwo Jima   *see*   USS Iwo Jima

J

Js   *see*   Marijuana

J-1   *see*   G-1

J-2   *see*   G-2

J-3   *see*   G-5

J-4   *see*   G-4

J-5   *see*   G-5

JAs   *see*   Judge Advocate

Jack   *see*   LZ Jack

Jack Daniel's Whiskey (Jack-in-the-Black)   One of the more popular whiskeys available to Americans in Vietnam. Black labeled Jack Daniel's, like other hard liquor, could be purchased by the bottle from military stores. Officers and NCOs were allowed to purchase package liquor products. Enlisted men could legally only purchase hard liquor at the EM club, and only by the glass. But as with most everything else in Vietnam, it was available for a price. *See also* Juicers, Class Six Store.

Jack-in-the-Black   *see*   Jack Daniel's Whiskey

Jack-Off   *see*   Masturbate

Jackfruit (Cay Mit, Cay Champedak)   Commonly cultivated fruit in Vietnam, called "mit" in Vietnamese. The greenish-yellow fruit grew on 30–60-foot trees, and was 10–30 inches long, and up to 12 inches in diameter. The ripe jackfruit had a strong, foul smelling odor when first cut open; inside the fruit were bulbs of pulp that smelled of pineapple/banana. The sweet smelling pulp could be eaten raw or cooked. Seeds inside the fruit were boiled or roasted. The Vietnamese also ate the young leaves and flowers as vegetables. The Cay Champedak was a tree similar to the mit. The fruits of the trees were very much alike, but the mit had smooth, shiny leaves and the champedak had hairy leaves.

Jackson State   *see*   Kent State

Jackstay   *see*   Operation Jackstay

Jacob's Ladder   A long, flexible ladder, lowered and suspended from the rear cargo ramp of a CH-46 or CH-47 helicopter. The reinforced steel ladder was about 48 inches wide and up to 100 feet long, and was used to insert or extract troops through holes in jungle canopy when the helicopter was unable to land. The ladder could also be attached to the floor hatch of the CH-47; this offered troops two exits from the helicopter, facilitating loading and unloading of troops. The Jacob's ladder was a small version of the "Jungle Ladder" used in inaccessible areas. *See also* Jungle Ladder.

JAG   *see*   Judge Advocate

Jane   *see*   LZ Jane

Japanese Machine Guns (Type 92/96/99, Woodpecker)   WWII vintage Japanese machine guns were used by the Viet Minh and later by NVA/VC troops. The machine guns were taken by Chinese Nationalist troops from Japanese occupation forces on mainland China. The Japanese weapons fell into the hands of the Communist Chinese when they ran the Nationalist Chinese off the mainland. Large quantities of the weapons were given to the Viet Minh in their war against the French. Weapons used by the Viet Minh were later used by the Viet Cong and the NVA. The three main Japanese made machine guns used in Indo-China were the types 92, 96 and 99. The Type 92 was a 7.7mm heavy machine gun that was tripod mounted and was side fed by a 30-round strip of ammunition. The gun with its tripod weighed 122 pounds and because of a slight "stutter" when the weapon fired it was nicknamed the "woodpecker." The Type 96 and 99 were light machine guns. Both were magazine fed from a 30-round banana clip (that was mounted on the top of the weapon) and featured a carrying handle and bipod for support. The Type 96 was a 6.5mm machine gun that weighed 20 pounds unloaded. The Type 99 was a 7.7mm weapon weighing 23 pounds. The Japanese machine guns only fired automatic; no single or semiautomatic fire. *See also* **Machine Guns.**

Jarai *see* **Montagnards**

Jarhead *see* **U.S. Marines**

Jari *see* **Montagnards**

Jason Group *see* **Defense Communications Planning Group**

Jason Study Institute of Defense Analysis study ('66) on the effectiveness of U.S. military actions in the war in Vietnam. The study concluded that because North Vietnam's economy was agricultural based and primitive the massive U.S. bombings were having little negative effect on their economy, but were stiffening enemy resolve. The bombings failed to stop the infiltration of men and materiel from NVN into SVN and the continued resupply of NVN by the USSR, China and North Korea. NVN was willing to accept high casualties to accomplish its goals. Using the results of the study, Secretary of Defense McNamara began to change his opinion on America's ability to win the war in Asia. The study also suggested the construction of an electronic barrier across the DMZ to slow NVN infiltration activities into SVN. *See also* **McNamara's Wall.**

JATO Bottles (Jet Assisted Takeoff) Small jet engines that could be attached to the sides or wing pylons of an aircraft. The JATO bottles provided extra thrust, assisting heavily loaded aircraft on takeoff from short airstrips. The bottles had a burn time of several seconds and were used on both transport and tactical Air Force aircraft.

Jaunissement (Yellowing) During the First Indo-China War, the French made an effort to have South Vietnamese troops assume more of the burden of fighting the Viet Minh in South Vietnam. The French program was called Jaunissement; literally translated as "yellowing" (yellow and red

were the colors of the South Vietnamese flag). The French yellowing program was repeated by the Americans in Vietnam but under the name of "Vietnamization." The American program, when tested in '75, failed as miserably as the French program that preceded it. *See also* **Vietnamization.**

Jaws-Tight *see* **Pissed**

Jay *see* **Operation Jay**

JCRS *see* **Joint Casualty Resolution Center**

JCS *see* **Joint Chiefs of Staff**

JCS Conference Room *see* **Gold Room**

JCTG *see* **Son Tay Raid**

Jeep *see* **Gun Jeep**

Jeep Wash *see* **Water-Point**

Jefferson Glenn *see* **Operation Jefferson Glenn**

Jeh *see* **Montagnards**

Jehovah's Witness *see* **Conscientious Objector**

Jellied-Gasoline *see* **Fou Gas**

Jelly *see* **B-2 Unit**

Jenny *see* **LZ Jenny**

Jerry Can (Jerrican) Standard U.S. military, five-gallon liquid storage container. The rugged metal can had a built-in handle and a large gasket-sealed, angled opening. In Vietnam the container was used to store and transport a wide variety of liquids, especially water and fuels. A flexible spout, nicknamed a "donkey-dick," could be attached to the can to facilitate the refueling of vehicles. The can was an adaptation of a storage can originally designed for the German Army in WWII. *See also* **Donkey-Dick.**

Jesus Nut Master nut assembly that secured a helicopter's rotor blades to the vertical rotor drive shaft. The nut assembly was located on the top of the rotor mast and was absolutely critical to operation of the helicopter. Loss or loosening of the "Jesus Nut" in flight could convert the airworthiness of an 11,000-pound Huey to the aeronautical prowess of a rock. No nut, no blades, no lift, no helicopter.

Jet Aircraft see Flyboys

Jet Assisted Takeoff see JATO Bottles

Jet Fuel (JP-4, JP-5, Avgas, Mogas) JP-4 and JP-5 were high performance, kerosene based aviation fuels, nicknamed "Avgas." JP-4 was used for jets and older turbine equipped aircraft. JP-5 was a jet fuel that was used by the newer turbine equipped helicopters. "Mogas" was the abbreviation for motor fuel (gasoline) used by some vehicles and river craft. See also KC-135, High Drink.

Jet Jockeys see Flyboys

Jet Pilots see Zoomies

Jetstar see C-140

JGS see Joint General Staff

Jink see SAM Break

Jirene see U.S. Marines

Jitterbug Technique used by elements of the 9th Infantry Division operating in the Delta. Based on intelligence information and reconnaissance a list of enemy targets would be selected. A rifle platoon would be inserted into the target area seeking to make contact with the enemy. If no contact was made the platoon would be extracted and inserted into the next target site on the list. This would continue until contact was made, or the end of the day. If contact was made more troops would be inserted into blocking positions, the platoon reinforced, and massive air and artillery strikes brought to bear. This tactic allowed a maximum number of enemy sites to be investigated with maximum protection and flexibility.

JMC see Four Party Joint Military Commission

Job Codes see Military Occupation Specialty

JOC see Joint General Staff

Jock Itch see Jungle Rot

Jodie see Jody Calls

Jody see Jody Calls

Jody Calls (Jody, Jodie) Jody Calls were cadence calls sung by marching troops during drills and training, expounding the sexual escapades of "Jody." Jody was the generic name for a civilian back home who

had taken a GI's woman, or was "entertaining" her while the GI was away from home. Jody managed to worm his way out of military service and attempted to extend his phallic services to the wives, lovers, sisters and mothers of America's fighting men. The calls not only spoke of Jody's achievements, but also expanded upon the repercussions in store for Jody when the GI returned home. Many GIs spoke of becoming "Jody" when they returned to civilian life. The most memorable of the Jody Calls began: "Ain't no use in goin' home... Jody's got your girl an gone..." See also Dear John Letter.

John see Latrine

John F. Kennedy Center for Special Warfare see Army Special Warfare Center

John Wayne Cookies Marine nickname for C-Ration cookies. The hard dough, chocolate covered cookies came with one of three fillings: coconut, maple or vanilla. See also C-Rations.

John Wayne Crackers (Biscuits, C-Biscuits, C-Ration Crackers) Marine's nickname for the large round crackers found in the B-1 Unit of C-Rations, or the vacuum packed, rectangular crackers in LRRP Rations. The perfect field complement to C-Ration cheese, jelly or peanut butter. The crackers were sometimes simply referred to as "biscuits" or "C-Biscuits." See also C-Rations.

John-Wayne see P-38

Johnson, General Harold see Chief of Staff

Johnson, President Lyndon Baines (LBJ) America's president, '63–'69. As vice-president, Johnson assumed the presidency after the assassination of John Kennedy in November '63. As a politician Johnson served in both houses of Congress. During his administration he pushed for social reforms in the guise of his Great Society programs. In reaction to NVN aggression in SEA and the rapid decline in the military/political situation in SVN Johnson began a policy of military escalation that injected American combat troops into Vietnam in '65. Johnson attempted to move NVN to the peace table by a series of bombing escalations and halts. He refused to use the full air power of the U.S. against NVN;

instead he slowly increased the bombing of NVN and increased American troop strength to over 500,000 men. Reports from some of his advisors led him to believe that America was winning the war against the communists in '67. But the general communist offensive during Tet '68, though a military defeat for communist forces, was a political setback for the administration which had declared that the end of the war in Vietnam was near. NVN's refusal to negotiate, and continued U.S. domestic pressure against the war, led Johnson not to seek the presidency in '69. On advice from his advisors Johnson halted the bombing of NVN. War expenses and priorities caused his Great Society programs to suffer on the domestic front. But during his administration he was able to get the '64 Civil Rights Act passed and established Medicare for America's senior citizens. *See also* **Butcher of Vinh, Guns and Butter Financing, War on Poverty, The Great Society.**

Johnson City *see* **Logistic Support Area**

Johnson Island *see* **Detox, Rumors**

Johnson's War *see* **Army's War**

Johnsonvilles Nickname given by some Johnson administration opponents to the shantytowns and refugee camps that began to spring up across South Vietnam in late '65 as a result of U.S. combat operations and GVN forced relocation practices. *See also* **Restructuring.**

Joint *see* **Marijuana**

Joint Casualty Resolution Center (JCRS) Military center established at Nakhon Phanom, Thailand, in '73 to coordinate U.S. military activities regarding American MIA/POWs in SEA. The center collected data regarding POW sightings, aircraft wreckage locations, and possible unmarked American gravesites in the war zone.

Joint Chiefs of Staff (JCS, Chairman Joint Chiefs of Staff, CJCS) U.S. military advisory committee to the president, consisting of a Chairman (CJCS) and senior officers representing the Army, Navy, Marines and Air Force. The JCS operated under the Secretary of Defense. During the Vietnam War one of the duties of the JCS was to supply the White House with listings

of appropriate military targets in North Vietnam from which the Johnson and Nixon administrations made the final target selections. The JCS was created shortly after WWII to unify the different military services under one cabinet level office. *See also* **Gold Room, Joint General Staff.**

Joint Contingency Task Group Ivory Coast *see* **Son Tay Raid**

Joint General Staff (JGS, Joint Operations Center, JOC) South Vietnamese military equivalent to the U.S. Joint Chiefs of Staff. The JGS was located in Saigon and was responsible for overall command of all military functions in South Vietnam. The operational arm of the JGS was the Joint Operations Center (JOC) which extended control through Corps (CTZ) level command centers located in each of the four corps. *See also* **Joint Chiefs of Staff.**

Joint Grave (Mass Graves) Gravesite that was occupied by more than one body. There are several joint graves in Arlington National Cemetery occupied by the bodies of soldiers who had died together under circumstances that did not allow for their individual identity to be determined. Samples of such circumstances were the cremation of the bodies in the gun turret of a ship or within an armored vehicle, or the total pulverizing of several bodies by an extremely large mine or bomb. In Vietnam the enemy also made use of joint graves to bury their dead after an engagement. It was of utmost importance to the NVN/VC to recover their wounded and dead to prevent FWFs from knowing the exact casualties that had been inflicted upon them. For American troops it was a matter of honor to retrieve their dead. *See also* **Mass Graves.**

Joint Military Commission *see* **Four Party Joint Military Commission**

Joint Operations Center *see* **Joint General Staff**

Joint Research and Test Activity, Vietnam (JRATA) Department of Defense agency in Vietnam that worked with the ACTIV to test and evaluate new weapons systems for possible use in Vietnam. *See also* **Army Concept Team in Vietnam, IR Scopes.**

Joint U.S. Public Affairs Office (JUSPAO, PAO, PIO, U.S. Public Affairs Office) U.S. Public Affairs Office (Public

Information Office) located in downtown
Saigon that was the site for the daily MACV
press briefing. The office was located at
Nguyen Hue and Le Loi streets. Information
for the briefings was gathered from all over
Vietnam and condensed into a presentable
format at MACV's Office of Information
(MACOI), located at MACV Headquarters.
JUSPAO functioned as an official press center for MACV and the U.S. Embassy. *See
also* Five O'Clock Follies, MACOI, U.S. Information Agency.

Jolly Green Giant *see* CH-3

Jolly Green Giant, Super *see* CH-53

Jones, General David *see* Chief of
Staff

Jones Hat *see* Jungle Hat

JP *see* Penetrator

JP-4 *see* Jet Fuel

JP-5 *see* Jet Fuel

JRATA *see* Joint Research and Test
Activity, Vietnam

Ju-Ju (Mau Mau) Black racist groups
founded in the U.S. during the sixties. Factions of both the Ju-Ju and Mau-Mau sprang
up at several Marine and Army bases in Vietnam. The group's total membership was
small; for self-preservation they advocated
armed violence against whites. In their own
way the groups were as dangerous and unpredictable as the Ku Klux Klan. *See also* Klan.

Judge, Corporal Darwin *see* Last
American to Die...

**Judge Advocate (JAs, Judge Advocate
General [JAG])** Military attorney. Military officers who were members of the Judge
Advocate General's Corps (JAGC), and conducted the administration of the military
justice system. The JAG commanded the
corps and was its highest ranking officer. The
JAGC provided attorneys to process legal
cases within the military.

Judge Advocate General *see* Judge
Advocate

Juice Freaks *see* Juicers

**Juicers (Boozers, Juice Freaks, Alcohol-
ics, Alkies)** Soldiers who got "high" in the
field or at base camps were classified by their
peers as either Heads or Juicers (Boozers).
Heads got high on drugs (dope); primarily
marijuana, opium or hash. Juicers got high
on alcohol and as a group tended to be more
military oriented and hawkish in their view
of the VNW. The Heads tended to be more
philosophical and much more peace movement oriented. The two groups generally
didn't mix socially, but put their differences
behind them as they fought side by side during combat. Chronic alcoholism was more
prevalent among the higher ranking and
senior NCOs than it was in the lower enlisted ranks. *See also* Heads, Jack Daniel's
Whiskey.

Jump Pay Extra monthly pay received
by paratroopers on jump status; $55 for en-
listed men and $110 for officers. Jump status
and assignments were made by the Department of Defense which determined if it was
necessary for the paratroop unit to be
available for possible jumping missions. On
initial deployment to Vietnam several
paratroop units maintained their jump
status while functioning as ground or airmobile infantry. Most of the Army airborne
units in Vietnam were reclassified as airmobile, losing their jump pay. Normally, to
be eligible for jump pay paratroopers had to
make at least one jump within a three
month period. This requirement was waived
in Vietnam. The only major combat jump
on Vietnam by U.S. airborne units was conducted in February '67.

Jump School *see* Airborne Training

Jump Week *see* Airborne Training

Jump Wings (Blood Wings) Army
Airborne Jump Wings were awarded to
those who successfully completed the three
week jump training course at Ft. Benning,
Georgia. Paratroopers in training ran everywhere they went for the three weeks they attended the school. The physical training was
continuous. Soldiers graduated from the
school after completing five successful
jumps; they were awarded their Jump
Wings and joined an elite group, the Army
Airborne. Airborne soldiers called their
Jump Wings "Blood Wings" because of
what they went through to get them.

Jumping Junkies *see* Paratrooper

Jumping-Off-Point *see* Line of Departure

Jumpmaster NCO in charge of a group
of paratroopers making a jump. On the

ground the jumpmaster verified that parachute troops assigned to his aircraft were properly equipped and were ready to board. Once airborne and over the jump zone the jumpmaster verified the jumpers were hooked to the jump line for a static jump. When he got the green light, the signal for the jump to begin, he stood in the open door of the aircraft and verified that all of the troops exited.

Junction City *see* **Operation Junction City**

Junction City Alternate *see* **Operation Junction City Alternate**

Junction City FSBs *see* **1st Infantry Division Fire Bases**

Jungle Boots (Tropical Boots, DMS Boot) The U.S. Jungle Boot was specially designed for use in the jungle, constructed of leather and quick drying cotton or nylon. The outer soles were of synthetic Vibram DMS (direct molded-sole), which was falsely rumored to give the wearer extra protection against bamboo spikes (punji stakes). The cross hatch design of the sole allowed mud to collect, causing the GI to carry around extra weight in the form of mud clogged boots. The boots had side vents which allowed water collected in the boot to drain out, but these vents quickly clogged with mud. The Jungle Boot was standard Army/ Marine issue to all U.S. troops headed to Vietnam. *See also* **Brogans.**

Jungle Busting Technique using tanks to cut trails in heavy undergrowth and jungle, giving accompanying infantry units access to otherwise inaccessible terrain. The cutting of new trails made it almost impossible for the NVA/VC to booby-trap and mine the infantry's route, but eliminated the element of surprise for U.S. troops. *See also* **Dozer-Infantry.**

Jungle Camouflage Uniform (Cammies, Leaf Pattern Camouflage, ERDL Pattern) Various types of camouflaged uniforms were used by soldiers during the Vietnam War. Most U.S. and ARVN troops that wore cammies wore the Leaf Pattern or Tiger Stripe uniform. The Tiger Stripe was worn mostly by ARVN, CIDG and USSF/ LRRP units and consisted of a mix of dark blue/black, brown and green stripes on a light green background. The Leaf Pattern

(ERDL) was U.S. issue, mostly worn by FWF recon units and some aircrews. The pattern consisted of irregular shapes and swirls in black, brown, green, and yellow/green. The Leaf Pattern became standard issue to Army troops who required a cammo uniform. *See also* **Tiger Fatigues.**

Jungle Cover *see* **Cover**

Jungle Fatigues *see* **Jungle Utilities**

Jungle Hat (Boonie Hat, Bush Hat, Flop Hat, Jones Hat, Cowboy Hat, Tropical Hat) Officially known as "Hat, Jungle," the U.S. jungle hat was made of ripstop cotton fabric, had a wide, full brim and was fast drying when wet. It afforded more protection from the sun and rain than the standard issue baseball cap, and was initially made available to troops in the field. Most rear echelon troops wore the baseball cap. Even the ARVNs eventually had jungle hats available to them. Various copies of the bush hat appeared in Vietnam, many of them locally made by the Vietnamese. Other versions were made in Japan and Taiwan and sold in Vietnam. Marines called their jungle hats "bush covers." *See also* **NVA Jungle Hat, Baseball Cap.**

Jungle Jim Squadron *see* **4400th Combat Crew Training Squadron**

Jungle Ladders (Ladders) Flexible metal ladders used to insert or extract troops from areas where the terrain or vegetation made it impossible for helicopters to land. The ladders were six feet wide and 120 feet long and were attached to the rear ramp of a CH-47 or CH-46 helicopter. The ladder was lowered through a hole in the jungle canopy allowing troops ready access to areas that might otherwise take hours or days to get to on foot. A smaller version of the jungle ladder was called the "Jacob's Ladder." *See also* **Jacob's Ladder.**

Jungle Landing Nets Experimental Army landing net that was designed to create a stable surface for landing troops on dense canopied jungle. The system had nine steel nets, each 12 feet square, interconnected by steel rods. The nets were lifted into position and spread out over the jungle canopy. Troops could be off loaded from helicopters onto the nets. The net system was only effective if the canopy was less than

60 feet above the ground. The system proved ineffective for getting troops into the jungle because most of the deep jungle canopy was 100–150 feet above the ground, beyond the reach of the nets. *See also* **Jungle Ladders.**

Jungle Penetrator *see* **Penetrator**

Jungle Rot (Crotch Rot, Jock Itch, Pruritis Ani) GI name for a painful condition characterized by raw, open sores in the crotch and inner thighs. An extremely severe form of jock itch, or pruritis ani. Fungus infections were prevalent in Vietnam and were aggravated by the heat and constant damp and wetness. Troops in the field, unable to bathe or regularly change their clothes, were especially susceptible. The constant scraping action of their clothes caused chafing, itching and further infection. The rot was not limited to the crotch and the feet, but outbreaks in these areas were most severe. Treatment consisted of drying the affected area and application of antifungal medications. Many GIs in the field did not wear underwear because of the chafing. *See also* **Immersion Foot, Skivvies, Gook Sores.**

Jungle Rucksack (Tropical Rucksack) A modified version of the ARVN "X" frame rucksack. The U.S. version had three outside pockets and was made of water-resistant nylon. Waterproof liners were available for the outside pockets as well as additional straps and hangers for other equipment. The tropical ruck was more compact than the Army's lightweight rucksack and was more in demand by troops in the field. *See also* **ALICE, NVA Rucksack, ARVN Rucksack.**

Jungle Shoes *see* **NVA Boots**

Jungle Sweater (Heat Retentive and Moisture Resistant Sleeping Shirt) Army issued, OD Green, wool-polyester blend sweater. The sweater was typically used by reconnaissance troops that operated in the Central Highlands and in the mountains of I Corps. The long sleeved sweater offered some protection from the cooler mountain temperatures experienced during the early morning hours. The sweater provided warmth without the bulk and weight of the Army field jacket. The sweater was replaced in '66 by a lighter weight nylon/acetate shirt. The shirt had better insulating properties and was fast drying when wet. It was officially known within the Army Quartermaster Corps as the "Heat Retentive and Moisture Resistant Sleeping Shirt." After the Vietnam War the wool sweater became standard issue throughout the Army.

Jungle Tennis Shoes *see* **Bata Boots**

Jungle Utilities (Tropical Uniform, Tropical Utilities, Jungle Fatigues) Standard uniform issued to U.S. military personnel in Vietnam. The OD green uniform had four large bellow pockets on the shirt. The pants featured four regular pockets as well as one large bellow pocket located on the side of each thigh. The uniforms, commonly referred to as "Jungle Fatigues," were made of ripstop cotton poplin and were fast drying when wet. The jungle camouflage uniform was of similar design and fabric, and colored in the ERDL leaf pattern format. *See also* **Jungle Camouflage Uniform.**

Junk Force (Coastal Force, Junkies) Vietnamese Navy force used to patrol the coastal waters of South Vietnam. The force was formally created in '59 and was paramilitary by nature using motorized and sail junks, operated by the militia to patrol the coast. The Junk Force operated in conjunction with the South Vietnamese Navy Sea Force, the junks providing the patrol element, and the Navy ships the fire power and intercept element. In '65 the Junk Force was absorbed into the SVN Navy as part of the Coastal Force. The Junk Force was advised by U.S. Navy advisors, who often referred to the Vietnamese Junk Force crewmen as "Junkies." *See also* **South Vietnamese Sea Force, Junks, Junk Marines, Sat Cong, Gun Decking.**

Junk Marines (Viet Hy) Combat troops that operated with the South Vietnamese Coastal Junk Force. The Viet Hy functioned in a manner similar to the role U.S. Marines played aboard Navy ships at sea. The Junk Marines operated in small groups aboard coastal surveillance craft, boarding and searching suspected enemy junks and sampans. The small force also operated as an amphibious force conducting limited search operations along the coast. *See also* **Junk Force.**

Junkies *see* **Junk Force, Dopers**

Junks (Motor Junks) Junk ships were

used by the Vietnamese for coastal fishing and transport. The SVN Navy Junk Force made wide use of junks for coastal surveillance and patrol. Junks were 32–55 feet long, and were either motorized and or sail equipped. Most of the junks of the Force were only armed with individual crew weapons. The motorized command junks and the Yabuta class junks were armed with .30 and .50cal machine guns and a 60mm mortar. The junks patrolled the coastal waters of South Vietnam, and received fire support from larger naval ships when necessary. *See also* **Yabuta, Sail Junk, Command Junks.**

JUSPAO *see* **Joint U.S. Public Affairs Office**

Just and Lasting Peace *see* **Silent Majority**

Just Doin' My Time *see* **Don't Mean Nothin'**

K

K-20 *see* **UH-2**

K-44 Rifle *see* **Mosin-Nagant Rifle**

K-50M SMG *see* **Type 50 SMG**

K-Bar U.S. Marine combat knife.

K-Fifty *see* **Type 50 SMG**

KA-3, -3B *see* **B-66**

KA-6 Tanker *see* **A-6A**

KA-60 Gun Camera (Gun Camera, Strike Camera, KA-71 Gun Camera) Air Force gun camera that was activated when the fighter's guns were fired. The camera took "still" pictures from beneath the nose of the aircraft on a parallel line of sight with the guns, filming the effects of the fire. The KA-71 was a combat motion picture camera that was similarly mounted and activated. Combat pictures were used to evaluate the effectiveness of attack procedures and target verification.

KA-71 Gun Camera *see* **KA-60 Gun Camera**

Kadena Air Force Base Located on the Japanese island of Okinawa. From Kadena, U.S. B-52s of the 452d Strategic Wing flew routine bombing missions against targets in Southeast Asia from '65 to '70. *See also* **B-52.**

KAF *see* **Project Flycatcher**

Kalamazoo *see* **Operation Kalamazoo**

Kalashnikov 47 *see* **AK47**

Kam Nhe The Vietnamese hamlet of Kam Nhe, in I Corps, was destroyed by U.S. Marines in '65. The story was filmed and broadcast nationwide to American audiences showing the Marines burning the hamlet to the ground. The story was one-sided because it failed to show the enemy weapons captured or the casualties the Marines took in moving through the enemy ville. The American public was left with an impression of U.S. troops savagely burning a "helpless" village. *See also* **Boys-in-Saigon.**

Kampuchea *see* **Cambodia**

Kampuchean Front for National Salvation (Second Vietnamese Invasion of Cambodia) Vietnamese-backed front established in Vietnam for the purpose of overthrowing Pol Pot, the radical communist president of Kampuchea. In '79 the Vietnamese communists invaded Kampuchea, captured Phnom Penh, installed a puppet government, and occupied the country. Since the Vietnamese invasion, the Khmer Rouge and nationalistic Cambodians have been waging guerrilla war against the Vietnamese communists occupying their country.

Katha Montagnard talisman worn by the mountain tribesmen. The Katha was a small sack or pouch which was made of leather or animal skins, and contained magic that was believed to protect the wearer from evil spirits. The Katha was worn around the neck or carried in a pocket. *See also* **Montagnard Shaman.**

Kattenburg, Paul   U.S. State Department analyst who is recognized as the first American government official to recommend that the U.S. begin withdrawal of its advisory personnel and support from South Vietnam. Kattenburg made the recommendation at a National Security Council meeting in August '63 based on research and field trip information he had compiled about the Diem regime. His recommendations were dismissed by the Secretaries of State and Defense and he was excluded from any further such meetings on Vietnam.

Katu   *see*   **Montagnards**

Katushas   *see*   **DKZ-B**

KB-50   U.S. Air Force aerial tanker that saw limited use during the early stages of the U.S. airwar over Vietnam. The KB-50 was a modified B-50 Superfortress bomber that had a maximum speed of 380mph, a range of 7,800kms and a payload of 20,000 pounds. The Boeing four engine propeller driven aircraft was initially used to refuel attack aircraft for bomb runs against NVN. The KB-50 proved inadequate for the mission because bomb laden jet aircraft had a difficult time slowing down to meet the refueler's top speed in order to make the fuel transfer. The KB-50 was replaced by the jet driven KC-135 air tanker in '65. *See also* **Aerial Tankers.**

KBA (Killed by Air, Killed by Artillery, Killed by Action)   General abbreviation used by the military to identify the method used to kill an enemy; used primarily for reports and statistics. Such information was collected and analyzed as part of the overall system of body counts. Killed by Air — enemy killed by air strikes or gunships. Killed by Artillery — enemy killed by artillery. Killed by Action — enemy killed by nonspecific method, used when a body was found and the exact cause of death was unknown. *See also* **Body Count.**

KBH (Killed by Helicopter)   Abbreviation used for reports and communications to indicate that an enemy was killed as the result of helicopter gunships or door gunners, as opposed to being killed by any other method. The body count and cause of death information were used as statistical data. *See also* **Body Count.**

KC   *see*   **Khmer Rouge**

KC-130   Hercules C-130 transport aircraft refitted as airborne refueling stations, primarily used by the Marine Corps. The KC-130 was capable of refueling specially modified HH-53 helicopters that were used for SAR missions into North Vietnam. Beside the refueling mission the KC-130 saw extensive use as a transport with the Marines. *See also* **C-130, Aerial Tankers.**

KC-135 (Strato-Tanker, Young Tiger)   Military version of the commercial Boeing 707 aircraft, refitted for inflight refueling of jet aircraft. "Young Tiger" was one of the call signs used by tanker missions over SVN to refuel TAC Aircraft and Recon flights. The KC-135 had a refueling capacity of 26,000–30,000 imperial gallons and a max speed of 600mph and a range of 6,437kms. The KC-135 normally operated with a crew of ten. Tankers functioned as airborne refueling stations for fighter-bombers operating against targets in SEA. The ability to refuel while airborne allowed the planes to operate with larger bomb loads and for longer periods over hostile territory. *See also* **Boomers, C-135, Aerial Tankers.**

Kearsage   *see*   **USS Kearsage**

Keep Book   Slang, meaning to keep a record (written or mentally). To "keep book" on an AO meant to have knowledge regarding the AO, such info as possible enemy units active in the area, likely ambush sites, previous contacts, enemy methodology, terrain peculiarities, etc.

Keep on Steppin'   *see*   **Don't Mean Nothin'**

KEKN Crews (Korean Express Stevedoring Company)   Korean company under contract to the Navy to provide stevedore crews to unload U.S. cargo ships at American port facilities in Da Nang. The KEKN began operations in August '66 and continued at Da Nang until the U.S. Navy began its turnover of facilities to the Vietnamese as part of the ACTOV program in '70.

Kelly   *see*   **LZ Kelly**

Kennan, George   *see*   **Wise Old Men**

Kennedy, Edward M.   Born in 1932 and elected to the U.S. Senate in '62. After the death of his brother, Robert, Edward

Kennedy began to speak out against America's foreign policy in Vietnam, and was especially critical of U.S. military strategy and its ineffectiveness, and the ineptness and corruption of South Vietnam's government and military. He continued to blast the Nixon administration's war policies and called for the withdrawal of U.S. troops from Vietnam. Kennedy's hopes for future presidential bids were shadowed by the events at Chappaquiddick Island in '69, but he has successfully been reelected to the Senate since '68.

Kennedy, President John F. Born in 1917, served as a PT boat commander in WWII, and was elected to the U.S. Congress in '46 and to the Senate in '52. In '60 Kennedy defeated Richard Nixon to become the 35th president of the U.S. Kennedy opposed communist world domination attempts, and took special interest in stopping the spread of communism in Indo-China. Kennedy actively supported the creation of counterinsurgency forces (especially the U.S. Army Special Forces) and appointed retired General Maxwell Taylor as his special military advisor on the counterinsurgency program. As the communist position in Vietnam strengthened, Kennedy increased economic aid to Vietnam and increased U.S. advisors from several hundred to over 16,000 by the end of '63. Kennedy believed in supporting SVN in its struggle against communism by supplying SVN with military hardware and American training personnel, yet he opposed sending U.S. combat troops to take up the fight for the Vietnamese. Because of widespread corruption and mismanagement in the Diem regime, the political and military situation within SVN deteriorated rapidly. Kennedy, realizing the need for change in SVN, began to withhold support from the Diem regime. In early November '63 SVN's President Diem was assassinated during a coup, and three weeks later President Kennedy was assassinated in Dallas, Texas.

Kennedy, Robert Born in 1925, Robert Kennedy served as attorney general during his brother's administration ('60–'64). He was elected to the U.S. Senate in '64. He was assassinated in June '68 by Sirhan Sirhan in Los Angeles while campaigning for the Democratic presidential nomination. Kennedy originally backed administration

policy (Kennedy's and Johnson's) over Vietnam, but in early '68 after announcing his intention to seek the Democratic nomination for the presidency he began to oppose continued escalation of the war in Vietnam. Kennedy proposed an end to the bombing of North Vietnam and withdrawal of U.S. combat troops from South Vietnam. He was killed before the Democratic nominee for president was selected.

Kennedy Special Warfare Center *see* **Army Special Warfare Center**

Kennedy's War *see* **Army's War**

Kent State (Jackson State) During student protest against the use of American ground troops in Cambodia in April '70 four Kent State University of Ohio students were shot and killed by National Guardsmen attempting to maintain order on the campus. The Guard had been called out to protect the campus against rioting students who had burned the ROTC building in protest. On May 4, 1970, rioting student protestors refused to disperse, and attacked the Guardsmen. The Guardsmen opened fire, killing four and wounding fourteen. The Guardsmen involved were tried and acquitted. During similar protests at Jackson State University in May '70 police attempting to maintain order killed two black student demonstrators on campus; no charges were filed. *See also* **Cambodian Incursion.**

Kep *see* **MiG Airfields**

Key Radio *see* **AN/PRC-64**

Keys (Kilo, Lid) "Keys" and "kilo" were slang words representing kilograms, a metric unit of weight. One kilo equaled 2.2 pounds. In Vietnam large quantities of marijuana were bought and sold by the kilo. The "kilo" became the universal measure when referring to the weight of illicit drugs. Smaller amounts of "weed" were sold by the ounce and referred to as a "lid." A one-ounce lid contained enough dried marijuana leaves and stems (hopefully very few stems) to fill up a standard sized plastic sandwich bag. *See also* **Marijuana.**

Keystone Bluejay *see* **Keystone Increments**

Keystone Cardinal *see* **Keystone Increments**

Keystone Eagle *see* **Keystone Increments**

Keystone Increments (Operation Keystone: Robin, Bluejay, Cardinal, Eagle) Code name for the '69–'72 phases of withdrawal for U.S. combat troops from Vietnam. This phased withdrawal also included the transfer of some U.S. equipment and assets to the ARVN forces. Keystone: Eagle (June '69, 25,000 troops); Cardinal (September '69, 40,500 troops); Bluejay (December '69, 50,000 troops); Robin (April '70, 150,000 troops). Subsequent Keystone operations were also named after birds: Oriole, Mallard, Owl.

Keystone Mallard *see* **Keystone Increments**

Keystone Oriole *see* **Keystone Increments**

Keystone Owl *see* **Keystone Increments**

Keystone Robin *see* **Keystone Increments**

KHA *see* **Killed in Hostile Action, KIA**

Kha Tribes One of the indigenous mountain tribes of Laos that fought with the communist Pathet Lao and NVA against the forces of the Royal Lao government, and the Meo tribes supporting them. The Kha acted as guides and scouts for the Pathet Lao/NVA forces operating in the mountains of Laos. Not all of the Kha tribes fought for the NVA. Some of the southern tribes were trained by USSF teams and operated against the Pathet Lao/NVA in Southern Laos. *See also* **Meo**.

Khakis (Tans) Standard summer service uniform of the U.S. Army. The short sleeved khaki uniform, nicknamed "tans," was mostly worn for travel and at duty stations outside of Vietnam. During the Vietnam War, between '67 and '72, most enlisted troops traveling between the U.S. and Vietnam wore jungle fatigues, and officers wore their tans. Before '67 troops wore regular utility fatigues or their khaki uniforms enroute to RVN. From '72 on, troops returning from RVN usually wore khaki uniforms. The Navy and Marines also had a version of the khaki uniform.

Kham Duc Village which was the site of the isolated Kham Duc Special Forces Camp, located 80kms southwest of Da Nang in Quang Tin Province, just 20kms from the border with Laos. In May '68, when the camp was under siege by NVA troops, a reinforced U.S. infantry battalion and its artillery were moved to Kham Duc. NVA/VC forces pressed the attack. The camp was ordered evacuated before it could be overrun. All military and civilian personnel were evacuated from the area by helicopter and Air Force C-123 and C-130 aircraft. The camp was under constant attack resulting in the loss of two C-130s, but over 1,500 of the camp's survivors were airlifted out before Kham Duc was overrun by the NVA.

Khanh Hung Provincial capital of Ba Xuyen Province located along the coast of the South China Sea in IV Corps. Khanh Hung was located 145kms southwest and 50kms southeast of Can Tho. The U.S. helicopter base at Soc Trang was located on the outskirts of the capital.

Khau Hien Vietnamese phrase for "simple, easy to remember slogans." The Viet Cong and the GVN used many slogans as part of their propaganda and terror campaigns against the Vietnamese people.

Khe Sanh (Khe Sanh Combat Base, KSCB, Coney Island) Marine outpost near the DMZ and SVN/Laotian border. The outpost was surrounded and shelled by two NVA divisions for 77 days. American strategist believed the NVA were trying to create a defeat similar to the one the French suffered at Dien Bien Phu, believing such a defeat would weaken American resolve and crush morale. Six thousand U.S. Marines and ARVN Rangers withstood the siege. Supplied by air, and later relieved by a combined Marine, Army, and ARVN force under Operation Pegasus. The siege was officially lifted April 7, 1968. The enemy made several small attacks on KSCB and its outpost, but never tried to overrun the main base. During the siege the Marines were sometimes bombarded by the enemy with as many as a thousand rounds a day. *See also* **Niagara, Operation Pegasus, Siege of Khe Sanh, Coney Island.**

Khe Sanh Combat Base *see* **Khe Sanh**

Khe Sanh Quick Step During the NVA siege of the Marine combat base at

Khe Sanh, NVA shelling was accurate and frequent, severely limiting movement on the base. In order for the Marines to move about the base it became necessary to make quick dashes from bunker to bunker and shell hole to shell hole, dodging the enemy's incoming artillery and rockets. The Marines called those frantic dashes the "Khe Sanh quick step."

Khiem Cuong (Bao Tri) Provincial capital of Hau Nghia Province, III Corps. The town was located 30kms northwest of Saigon and less than 23kms east of the Parrot's Beak on the Cambodian border. In January '67 the NVA/VC attacked and overran the town's ARVN defenders, holding Khiem Cuong for a brief time until driven out by a combined ARVN and U.S. relief force. Khiem Cuong was also known as Bao Tri.

Khmer Air Force *see* Project Flycatcher

Khmer Communist *see* Khmer Rouge

Khmer Insurgents *see* Khmer Rouge

Khmer Issarak (Free Khmer) The Khmer Issarak (Free Khmer) were anti–French, noncommunist, Cambodian guerrillas fighting for independence from the French during the late forties and early fifties. The Issarak received limited support from Thailand and were a small, ineffective group. With the fall of the French in Vietnam in '54 came the independence of Cambodia, and the Khmer Issarak faded from the political scene. *See also* **Khmer Serei.**

Khmer Kampuchea Kron (KKK, Khmers) Kampuchea Kron was the name used to describe the northwestern provinces of South Vietnam's Delta, near the SVN/Cambodian border, in IV Corps. The area was inhabited by many ethnic Cambodians (Khmers). The Khmer Kampuchea Kron were an armed group of Cambodians from the area that advocated the return of the area to the control of the Cambodian government. The KKK fought against the Diem forces until the early sixties when they were convinced by the USSF to fight against the VC; at that time members of the KKK joined Delta based CIDGs. The ethnic Vietnamese considered the Khmers to be an inferior

and primitive people, on the same level as the Montagnards. *See also* **Khmer Serei, Vietnam's Niggers.**

Khmer Liberation Army *see* **Khmer Rouge**

Khmer People's National Liberation Front (KPNLF) Group of noncommunist Cambodian nationalists currently fighting Vietnamese occupation troops in Kampuchea. The KPNLF operated from bases along the Cambodia/Thailand border, conducting limited guerrilla warfare against the Vietnamese. The Front consisted of several different Cambodian groups seeking to remove the Vietnamese occupation force, and the puppet government it had established. Khmer Rouge factions were part of the Front, but supposedly Pol Pot and his radical communist element have been excluded from the KPNLF. *See also* **Vietnamese Invasion of Cambodia, Khmer Rouge.**

Khmer Republic *see* **Cambodia**

Khmer Rouge (Khmer Insurgents, KI, FUNK, National United Front of Kampuchea, Red Khmers) Cambodian Communist Party, led by Pol Pot. Originally the guerrillas of the Khmer Rouge were called the Khmer Insurgents (KI) or the Khmer Communists (KC). Officially, the communist forces called themselves the National United Front of Kampuchea (FUNK); the military arm of the party was the Khmer Liberation Army (Cambodian Liberation Army), more commonly known as the Khmer Rouge. The NVA began widespread support of the Khmer Rouge after '69 when the Cambodian government allowed U.S. planes to openly bomb NVA supply lines in Cambodia. Communist China also provided large quantities of materiel and weapons support to the Khmer Rouge. With NVA support, the Khmer Rouge defeated the anticommunist Cambodian Army (FANK) in '75, and seized control of the country, renaming it Kampuchea. After the communist takeover it was estimated that more than two million Cambodians were executed by Pol Pot's forces in his effort to create the perfect communist state. *See also* **Pol Pot, Vietnamese Invasion of Cambodia, Political Purification, Forces Armees Nationale Khmer, General Lon Nol.**

Khmer Serei The Khmer Serei (Free Khmer) were anticommunist, ethnic

Cambodians who lived in South Vietnam along the Cambodian border. Some Serei were recruited by the U.S. Special Forces to serve in the local CIDGs in defense of their homes against the NVA/VC in the III and IV Corps Delta region. Small bands of the Serei were active within Cambodia, branded as outlaws by the Sihanouk government. After Prince Sihanouk was ousted from Cambodia the new anticommunist government of Lon Nol encouraged the Serei to attack NVA/VC sanctuaries along the SVN/Cambodian border. Many of the Serei were CIA trained and supplied and fought the NVA/VC to the near extinction of the Serei. *See also* **Khmer Kampuchea Kron, Khmer Issarak.**

Khmers *see* **Khmer Kampuchea Kron**

Khoi Nghia Vietnamese phrase for "general uprising" [coy knee-ah]. One of the propaganda slogans of the Viet Cong. The VC had hoped that the general populace would support them in their all-out offensive, rising up to give them support and join them in overthrowing the Saigon government. During Viet Cong offensives in '64, and most notably '68, the popular support and general uprising they sought never materialized. *See also* **Tet Offensive.**

Khong Biet *see* **Toi Com (Khong) Biet**

Khong Quan *see* **Republic of Vietnam Air Force**

Khrushchev, Premier Nikita (Wars of National Liberation) USSR Premier ('58–'64) and First Secretary of the Soviet Communist Party ('53–'64). Khrushchev believed in world domination by the communists and in providing support to other nations attempting to follow the communist path by means of "Wars of National Liberation." Khrushchev supported Castro's Cuba, but backed down in a showdown with President Kennedy during the '62 Cuban Missile Crisis. In '64 Khrushchev approved major increases in military support provided to the NVA, provided North Vietnam would consider seeking a negotiated settlement with the U.S. over SVN. Khrushchev was ousted to internal exile by Kosygin and Brezhnev in '64, before he could bring pressure on NVN to seek a negotiated settlement with the U.S.

Khuong Biet *see* **Toi Com Biet**

KI *see* **Khmer Rouge**

KIA (Killed in Action, Kilo India Alpha) U.S. soldiers who died as a result of hostile fire were classified by the DOD as "Killed in Hostile Action," but were more commonly known as Killed in Action (KIA). Over 47,000 Americans died as a direct result of combat. In addition, another 11,000 died as a result of noncombat related circumstance. Noncombat related deaths included illness, traffic or aircraft accidents, homicides and suicides. Also included as a noncombat death were those soldiers killed by "friendly fire." Most of America's dead in Vietnam were men, but several women were also killed. A small number of the U.S. war dead were non–American citizens who joined the U.S. military as a means of obtaining their U.S. citizenship. *See also* **Friendly Fires; Vietnam War Casualties, U.S.; KHA; KIA/WIA Code Names; DOW; Killed in Hostile Action.**

KIA/WIA Code Names (Casualty Code Names) Slang and code names for KIAs and WIAs were often used over radio nets to disguise the exact extent of American casualties from the prying ears of the NVA/VC. Some nicknames were Kool-Aid, Cadillac, Kilos, Routines (KIA); Peanut, Ford, Whiskeys, Criticals (WIA).

Kickers Nickname for civilian aircrews that delivered supplies to remote areas of Southeast Asia. The crews delivered supplies in areas where U.S. military aircraft were not allowed to operate. The deliveries were made throughout Laos and Cambodia to government troops and militia fighting the communists in those countries. The aircrews got the name "kickers" because the majority of the supplies they delivered were air-dropped by parachute, the crates literally kicked out of the door of the aircraft.

Kidnapping Missions *see* **Snatch Missions**

Kien An *see* **MiG Airfields**

Kill (Coc Dau) There were many words and phrases used to express the act of "killing" in Vietnam; some of them were waste, off, dust, blow away, ding, DX, zap, grease, nail, hose, pop, do (did) someone, scatter their shit to the wind... Some of the phrases used to express to be killed or die:

caught-his-lunch, bought-the-farm, bring-the-max-on-you, deep-sixed. Some of the same words used for kill or killing also applied to wounding and being wounded. *See also* **Sanitize Operations, Terminate with Extreme Prejudice, Coc Dau, Neutralize.**

Kill Ratio   The ratio or proportion of enemy dead to friendly dead. After '65, U.S. and Allied progress in the Vietnam War was often measured by statistics. Kill ratios were very important for military briefings, and used as indicators of success. The American military put great emphasis on high kill ratios for their field units. Some units offered extra privileges for high enemy kill counts, and harassment for those units that were not killing enough enemy troops. Average kill ratios for American troops were 3–7:1, while some ROK and special American recon units managed kill ratios greater than 10:1. On some operations, U.S. kill ratios did climb well beyond 10:1, with artillery and air strikes contributing to the count. *See also* **Body Count.**

Kill the Viet Cong/Communists   *see* **Sat Cong**

Kill Them All...   *see* **Ultimate Weapon...**

Kill Zone (Artillery Kill Zone)   The deadliest part of an ambush, the area where all who entered were likely to be killed or wounded when the ambush was sprung. The greatest concentration of fire by the ambushers was focused on the kill zone. The term "Kill Zone" also applied to the range around the impact of an artillery shell that was considered to be lethal to anyone in the zone. The artillery kill zone was based on point detonation in open terrain. The kill zone diameters for a 105mm and 8-inch shell were 30 meters and 75 meters, respectively. These ranges were adjusted according to the terrain at the impact site.

Killed by Action   *see*   **KBA**

Killed by Air   *see*   **KBA**

Killed by Artillery   *see*   **KBA**

Killed by Helicopter   *see*   **KBH**

Killed in Action   *see*   **KIA, Killed in Hostile Action**

Killed in Hostile Action (KHA, WHA, Wounded by Hostile Action)   Because the war in Vietnam was not a "declared war," American soldiers killed as a result of enemy action in Vietnam were officially classified as "Killed in Hostile Fire." According to the U.S. Defense Department the term "Killed in Action" (KIA) was not authorized for use to describe American soldiers killed in battle with the enemy. A distinction that was lost on the dead and their survivors. Although unauthorized, the term "KIA" was universally used to describe both enemy and Americans killed as a result of combat. The term "Wounded by Hostile Action" was similarly used to classify Americans wounded in combat. *See also* **KIA, DOW, WIA.**

Killer Dolphins (Dolphins)   The U.S. Navy reportedly deployed dolphins to Vietnam to patrol beneath Navy ships anchored in coastal and bay areas subject to attack by Viet Cong frogmen. The dolphins were trained to attack any underwater swimmers they encountered in the immediate vicinity of their patrol areas. Confirmation of the existence of the "watch-dolphins" in Vietnam, and information regarding their enemy body count, are not available at this time.

Killer Junior (Killer Senior)   Tactic used by some U.S. artillery bases for defense against NVA/VC ground assaults. Artillery units used beehive rounds which were fired point-blank into attacking enemy formations, but the beehive darts could be avoided if the enemy low crawled along the ground. To counter this the "Killer Junior" tactic evolved. It consisted of 105mm and 155mm howitzers firing shells fused to explode 30 meters above the ground at ranges of 200–1,000 meters. The technique proved effective because the air bursts were difficult to avoid. Killer Senior was the same technique employing the 8-inch self-propelled howitzer. The technique was named by the 1st Battalion/8th Artillery/25th Infantry Division at Cu Chi. *See also* **Beehive Round.**

Killer Kiwis   *see*   **New Zealand**

Killer Patrol (Killer Teams)   A specially formed six-man ambush patrol from the 3rd/39th Infantry/9th Infantry Division, operating in the Rach Kien area of Long An Province, III Corps, August '67. The patrol's objective was to neutralize the VC that traveled by night through the area. The patrol was effective at reducing the VC's freedom to travel at will, and other units employed the same type of special patrols. The Marines also operated "killer patrols," which they called "killer teams," consisting of 5–6 man ambush teams which specialized in mobile ambush tactics, operating in Viet Cong or Viet Cong sympathetic areas at night.

Killer Senior *see* **Killer Junior**

Killer Teams *see* **Killer Patrol**

Killer-Weed Nickname for some of the more potent batches of marijuana that were available in Vietnam. Various regions throughout Southeast Asia cultivated marijuana, and GI connoisseurs prided themselves on their ability to identify the region based on the taste of the "smoke." *See also* **Marijuana**.

Kilo *see* **Keys**

Kilo India Alpha *see* **KIA**

Kilograms *see* **Keys**

Kilometers (Klics, Klicks, Ks, Click, km, Meter) Kilometer = 1km = 1000 meters, 6/10 mile, 3280 feet, 1090 yards. Meter = 1.09 yards, 3.28 feet, 39.36 inches. In Vietnam most military ballistic measurements of distance were in meters, as were references to map distances, contours and elevations.

Kim Son Valley Centered 20kms southwest of Bong Son, and 40kms northeast of An Khe. A rugged ridge separated the southern end of the valley from the Vinh Thanh Valley. The mouth of the Kim Son Valley opened onto the Bong Son Plain. The northern edge of the valley bordered on a ridge called the "Crow's Foot." The Kim Son Valley and the surrounding hills were a stronghold, and the site of several U.S. operations. *See also* **Bong Son Plain, Crow's Foot**.

Kimchi Tremendously odoriferous Korean vegetable dish, similar in content to German sauerkraut. Kimchi consisted of a mixture of cabbage, garlic, peppers, and seasonings, allowed to ferment. Aromatically similar to Vietnamese nuoc mam sauce. Many American GIs in Vietnam were introduced to it by ROK soldiers serving in-country. *See also* **Nuoc Mam**.

KIN (MAT, TOI MAT) Military document classification used on Vietnamese documents. "KIN," CONFIDENTIAL; "MAT," SECRET; "TOI MAT," TOP SECRET.

King, Reverend Dr. Martin Luther (Martin Lucifer Coon, Southern Christian Leadership Conference [SCLC]) Moderate leader of the Southern Christian Leadership Conference. King believed the way to bring change to American society, and its treatment of minorities, was through nonviolent protest and peaceful civil disobedience. King organized and participated in many demonstrations and marches against racial inequality and was awarded the Nobel Peace Prize in '64 in recognition of his work. He also believed the focus of the American government should have been on domestic reform within America. The biggest obstacle to that reform was the ever growing involvement of America in Vietnam. He helped bring attention to the inequities in the Selective Service draft system and its application to minorities. Dr. King argued that the draft was having an inordinate impact on the black and poor communities of America and that black casualties in Vietnam prior to '67 were much higher than blacks' proportional representation of the general American population. King was called many names, by friend and foe alike; in some Southern circles he was known as "Martin Lucifer Coon." King was assassinated in Memphis, Tennessee, by James Earl Ray on April 4, 1968.

Kingfisher *see* **Pacifier, Operation Kingfisher**

Kings *see* **Operation Kings**

Kingsmen *see* **Those Who Kill for Pleasure...**

Kinh Doi Canal *see* **Cholon**

Kiowa *see* **OH-58**

Kissinger, Henry (Shuttle Diplomacy) Diplomat and political scientist who became President Nixon's special assistant for security affairs. Kissinger served as the U.S.'s chief negotiator, opposite North Vietnam's Le Duc Tho, during the '69–'73 portion of the Paris Peace Talks. Kissinger and Tho were awarded the '73 Nobel Peace Prize for their efforts in finalizing the '73 Paris Peace Accords that resulted in the virtual abandonment of South Vietnam by the U.S. Kissinger was appointed Secretary of State in September '73 and remained at that post during the Ford administration where he orchestrated the U.S. attack on Cambodia in an effort to free the SS *Mayaguez* and her crew. Kissinger became known for his "shuttle diplomacy" during truce negotiations between Syria and Israel.

Kit Carson Scout (Loc Luong 66, Tiger Scout) Ex–NVA/VC working as scouts for U.S. combat units. NVA/VC who had rallied to the GVN under the Chieu Hoi program were encouraged to become scouts. The scouts were usually assigned to U.S. units operating in the same area that the rallier had operated in when he was part of the enemy force. He was aware of the locations of caches, bunkers, booby traps and assembly areas and specific enemy techniques. The scouts were paid for their services, and known officially as part of the Loc Luong 66 program. Some of the Kit Carson scouts worked as double agents for the VC, but most were considered reliable and became an integral part of the U.S. unit with which they worked. *See also* **Chieu Hoi Program.**

Kitchen Police *see* **Dining Room Orderly**

Kite-Tails (Staff Officers, Go-fers) Nickname for officers of a general's staff. Several such officers accompanied command generals wherever they went. The officers represented his staff advisors. The junior officers of the staff group usually amounted to "errand boys" and "go-fers."

Kitty Hawk *see* **USS Kitty Hawk**

Kiwis *see* **New Zealand**

KKK *see* **Khmer Kampuchea Kron, Klan**

Klacker *see* **Clacker**

Klan (KKK, Stars and Bars, Cross Burning) Evidence of racism in Vietnam surfaced shortly after the deployment of American combat troops to Vietnam. Stars and Bars flags of the Confederacy could be found waving from makeshift flagpoles at some small U.S. base camps, and the same type of flag could be found painted on the sides of some Army vehicles. Small groups of the Ku Klux Klan reportedly sprang up at several bases to counter some of the Black Power groups that had formed. During the war there were several "cross burning" incidents in Vietnam. Blacks and whites tended to naturally segregate themselves at the major base camps; while in the field, where soldiers depended on each other, there was little racial strife. Violent racial clashes in U.S. units occurred across Vietnam in '68, touched off by blacks' anger at the assassination of Dr. Martin Luther King and years of unofficial military policies that worked against black soldiers, fueling the fires of discrimination. *See also* **Human Relations Committee; Afro; Dap; Clenched Fist; Same Mud, Same Blood; Ju-Ju.**

Klaw II *see* **FSB Klaw II**

Klicks *see* **Kilometers**

Klics *see* **Kilometers**

KMAGV *see* **Korean Military Assistance Group, Vietnam**

Kms *see* **Kilometers**

KMU-351 *see* **Laser Guided Bomb**

Knife Grass *see* **Elephant Grass**

Koh Tang Island *see* **SS Mayaguez**

Koho *see* **Montagnards**

Kole Kole *see* **Operation Kole Kole**

Komer, Robert (DCC, Deputy Civilian Commander of MACV, Blowtorch) Former CIA agent who became a special assistant to President Johnson in '66, nicknamed the "Blowtorch." In '67 Komer was appointed deputy civilian commander of MACV and established CORDS. Komer believed that the best way to win the struggle against communism in Vietnam was with the support of the people through the efforts of the GVN to provide the people with social and economic development. Komer also established the Phoenix Program in '68, which was designed to eliminate the VCI and their supporters by means of assassination and imprisonment. Komer was replaced by William Colby in late '68. *See also* **Civil Operations and Revolutionary Development, Phoenix Program.**

Kompong Som *see* **Sihanouk Trail**

Kontum Capital of Kontum Province in II Corps, site of a major battle between NVA forces and ARVN units during the Eastertide Offensive of '72. The ARVNs held and eventually forced the two attacking NVA divisions to retreat back into Laos. Kontum was located deep in the Central Highlands 39kms north of Pleiku.

Kool-Aid   *see*   Water Purification Tablets

Kool-Aids   *see*   KIA/WIA   Code Names

Kools   *see*   Party-Pack

Korat Royal Thai Air Base (388th Tactical Fighter Wing, 553d Tactical Reconnaissance Wing)   Thailand air base leased by the U.S. Air Force to conduct missions throughout Southeast Asia. Korat was the home of the 388th Tactical Fighter and 553d Tactical Reconnaissance Wings. *See also* Thai Air Bases.

Korea, South   *see*   Republic of Korea

Korean Express Stevedoring Company *see*   KEKN Crews

Korean Military Assistance Group, Vietnam (KMAGV, Dove Unit)   KMACV was the Republic of Korea's military assistance program to the Vietnamese. The group provided medical and engineering assistance to the various branches of the South Vietnamese military. KMAGV started in '64. In '65 Korean combat troops began arriving in Vietnam and primarily operated along the coast of I and II Corps. *See also* Republic of Korea.

Korean Stevedores   *see*   KEKN Crews

Koster, Brigadier General Samuel W. Commanding general of the Americal Division at the time of the My Lai incident. Koster was accused of covering up the My Lai incident, and failure to report the incident to higher headquarters. For his part in the cover-up he received a letter of censure, medals and awards issued to him for the operation were revoked, and the general lost a grade, from major general to brigadier general. *See also* My Lai, Calley.

Kosygin, Aleksei   Became Soviet Union's prime minister, after the ouster of Nikita Khrushchev in '64. Kosygin continued to approve the supply of Soviet weapons to the North Vietnamese, and in '65 the first shipments of sophisticated radar controlled surface-to-air SAM missiles began arriving at Haiphong.

KP   *see*   Dining Room Orderly

KPNLF   *see*   Khmer People's National Liberation Front

KPV HMG (Krupnokalibernyi Pulemyoy Vladimirova, ZPU1, ZPU2, ZPU4, 14.5mm HMG)   Soviet-made 14.5mm heavy machine gun (HMG) used extensively by the NVA for air defense. The 14.5mm gun was gas operated, belt fed and weighed over 110 pounds when loaded, and had an effective AA range of 5,000 feet. The KPV was carriage mounted in either single barrel, dual, or quad barrel versions (ZPU1, ZPU2, ZPU4). The ZPU1 and ZPU2 were used throughout Vietnam by the NVA/VC, and the ZPU4 was used for antiaircraft defenses in NVN. The 14.5mm was similar to the U.S. 20mm cannon. *See also* AA, Machine Gun.

Krupnokalibernyi Pulemyoy Vladimirova   *see*   KPV HMG

Krypto   *see*   AN/PRC-77

Ks   *see*   Kilometers

KSCB   *see*   Khe Sanh

Kula Gulf   *see*   MSTS Card

Kunming   The city of Kunming was located in the People's Republic of China. Kunming, 930kms northwest of Hanoi, was a major railhead used by the Chinese to transport arms and supplies overland into North Vietnam. *See also* Nanning.

Ky Ha (Marine Air Group-36, MAG-36)   Village located along Highway 1, 10kms southeast of Hue, in Thua Thien Province, I Corps. The village was located just outside of Phu Bai and became the helicopter base for Marine Air Group-36 in September '65. *See also* Marine Air Group-36.

KY-38 Krypto Set   *see*   AN/PRC-77

L

L & M (Legal and Magnanimous Side) Tongue-in-cheek reference to the government of Vietnam and its allies. It was no small coincidence that the Viet Cong and the North Vietnamese also believed that their struggle against FWFs was just and proper. *See also* **GVN**.

L Zed *see* **Landing Zone**

L-19 (OE, Cessna 170, O-1E, Bird Dog, O-1) Light observation airplane used extensively by the U.S. military for reconnaissance and surveillance missions. The L-19 Bird Dog, designated the O-1, was the military version of the Cessna 170. First used by the Air Force in '50, over 3,100 of the planes eventually saw service with the Air Force, Army and Marines. The single engine prop had a max speed of 150mph and a range of 850kms. In Vietnam O-1s operated as observation and artillery/air strike spotter planes and were only armed with phosphorus rockets; used for marking targets. As a Forward Air Controller or "FAC" the O-1 was manned by a pilot and sometimes an observer. The L-19 was more popularly known as the "Bird Dog" or simply as a FAC. The Navy/Marines referred to their L-19s as "OEs" while the Army and Air Force referred to the aircraft as the O-1. There were several versions of the L-19 which ranged from the O-1A to the O-1E. The little planes were only 25 feet long with a wing span of 36 feet and typically operated at speeds less than 100mph. *See also* **73d Aviation Company, Forward Air Controller**.

L-20 *see* **U-6**

L-28 *see* **U-10**

L-Ambush *see* **L-Shaped Ambush**

L-Bush *see* **L-Shaped Ambush**

L-Shaped Ambush (L-bush, L-Ambush) An ambush set up in an L formation, usually in the following manner: The short leg of the L blocking the trail; claymore mines, aimed into the kill zone, were set up along the long leg of the L, and the machine guns and remaining troops lined both legs of the L. When the ambush was tripped, the claymores blew first, then grenades were thrown into the kill zone, and the whole area was raked with AW fire. The ambush lasted a few minutes at the most. The L-ambush was very effective and could be adjusted easily to accommodate the size of the unit conducting the ambush. In the NVA/VC L-ambush, the long leg of the L was often lined with punji stakes. *See also* **A-Shaped Ambush, Ambush**.

L.T. *see* **First Lieutenant, Second Lieutenant**

L/Cpl *see* **Lance Corporal**

L1A1 SLR (FN FAL) Standard infantry rifle of the Australian Army during the Vietnam War. The 7.62mm rifle was gas operated and fed by a 20-round magazine. The weapon weighed a little over 10 pounds when loaded and had a maximum effective range of 300 meters. The rifle fired semi-automatic, but could be modified for full automatic fire and was patterned after the Belgian FN FAL rifle.

L9A1 Pistol (FN GP35) Browning 9mm pistol, similar in appearance to the M-1911A1, .45cal pistol. The pistol had a maximum effective range of 50 meters and was fed from a 13-round clip. The pistol was the standard side arm used by the Australian military. The weapon was originally manufactured in Belgium as the FN GP35. *See also* **Pistols**.

L14 RCL (Carl Gustav) Swedish made medium antitank weapon, used in Vietnam by the Australians. The 31 pound, rear venturi loaded, single shot, spin stabilized rocket was very accurate with effective ranges of 450 meters with HEAT, 1,000 meters with HE, 1,300 meters with smoke, and 2,300 meters for illumination rounds. HEAT round weight was less than six pounds, allowing the weapon to be man carried in the field and used against NVA/VC bunkers and fortifications with great accuracy. *See also* **Recoilless Rifle**.

La Porte, Roger *see* **Burn Yourselves, Not Your Draft Cards**

La Rue Sans Joie *see* **Street Without Joy**

La Sale Guerre *see* Indochina War

Laager A defensive circle formed by elements of a unit, especially armored vehicles, to reduce the unit's susceptibility to attack while camped or resting. Helicopters were "laagered" by basing them, in twos and threes, at secure forward bases, or entire helicopter companies would laager near an assault area for quick response. From the forward bases, they could more quickly be used to support friendly troops in the more remote and forward areas.

LAAM *see* Hawk Missile

LAAW *see* M-72 LAW

Lace-In Zippers *see* Boot Zippers

Ladders *see* Jungle Ladders, Jacob's Ladder

Lagging *see* Goldbricking

Lai Day (Lai Mau) Vietnamese for "come here" [lie day]. "Lai Mau" [lie maow], meaning "come quickly." Two of the basic phrases learned by GIs for dealing with the Vietnamese civilians in the field.

Lai Khe Vietnamese town located on Highway 13 in Binh Duong Province, III Corps. Lai Khe was located 42kms north of Saigon and served as one of the base camps for units of the 1st Infantry Division. Nicknamed "Rocket City" because of frequent NVA, 122mm rocket attacks. *See also* Rocket City.

Lai Mau *see* Lai Day

Laird, Melvin Former congressman who served as Secretary of Defense during the first Nixon administration, '68–'72. Laird was a strong advocate of U.S. troop reductions in Vietnam and the speedy progress of the Vietnamization policy. Laird advised against any actions the administration might take to further escalate the war in Vietnam, stretching U.S. resources and increasing domestic opposition to the war.

Laissez-Passer (Exit Visa) Special document issued by South Vietnam's Ministry of the Interior to Vietnamese citizens allowing them to emigrate to the U.S. The document replaced the standard exit visa or passport normally issued by the Ministry. The laissez-passer was issued, during the last couple of weeks before Saigon fell in April '75, to Vietnamese who could prove they were an American dependent. The new laissez-passer policy was an attempt by the GVN to simplify and speed up the evacuation process of Vietnamese nationals who were dependents of Americans returning to the U.S. Instead of speeding up the process the laissez-passer clogged the system with thousands of Viets trying to leave the country. After the laissez-passer was obtained the Vietnamese with their American sponsors registered with the U.S. Embassy for evacuation. Marriage to a U.S. citizen and any children relating to the marriage (including children from previous marriages or out-of-wedlock) qualified as legitimate dependents and were eligible for evacuation.

Lam On *see* Cam On

Lam Son (Le Loi) Village in Thanh Hoa Province, North Vietnam, that was the birthplace of Vietnam's nationalist hero, Le Loi. Le Loi defeated and drove out of Vietnam an invading Chinese force in 1428. The ARVNs used "Lam Son" as a code name for many of their military operations during the Vietnam War. *See also* Black Market, Lam Son 719.

Lam Son 207 *see* Operation Pegasus

Lam Son 216 *see* Operation Delaware

Lam Son 719 (Laos-Lam Son 719, Laos Incursion) ARVN code name for their '71 incursion into Laos to disrupt NVN activities on the Ho Chi Minh Trail. The objective of the all–ARVN ground force was Tchepone, Laos, a major logistics center along the trail. The ARVNs met stiff enemy resistance, and suffered heavy losses before their hasty withdrawal back into SVN. Air support and air transport were provided by American aircraft and crews. U.S. ground units remained at the border and did not cross into Laos. The ARVNs destroyed large quantities of NVA supplies, but were unable to open Highway 9 to Tchepone for their ground forces, close Tchepone, or remain in Laos for extended operations. *See also* Conceived in Doubt..., Tchepone, Chup Rubber Plantation, Cooper-Church Amendment.

Lambretta Small three-wheel motorcycle used for taxi transportation and cargo. The vehicle consisted of a three-wheel motorcycle with a boxlike van mounted on the rear; the driver sat in the front. The little cabs could haul several Vietnamese and their loads, or four GIs. The small gas powered cabs were everywhere on the streets of Saigon and the larger towns of Vietnam. *See also* **Pedicab.**

Lame Duck   *see*   **Medic**

Lame Duck Ambush   Tactic of using decoys to draw an enemy into a prepared ambush. The decoy was one or two soldiers, perhaps appearing wounded, lost or otherwise an easy target; the enemy, believing the decoys to be easy targets, pursued and were trapped in an ambush. The NVA/VC were very good at the lame duck ambush. Year after year American units fell into the trap. Experience was the key to determining if the lame ducks were actually what they appeared to be or simply traps. *See also* **Baited Ambush.**

Lance Corporal (L/Cpl)   Marine Corps enlisted rank, grade E-3; equivalent to the Army's private first class, Air Force's airman second class or the Navy's seaman. In the Marines a lance corporal typically commanded a fire team. In Vietnam, due to shortages of qualified NCOs, L/Cpls were sometimes charged with the responsibility for an entire squad or the remnants of a platoon. *See also* **Private First Class.**

Land, Captain Jim   As a lieutenant in the 4th Marine Regiment, in '60, Land organized a scout/sniper school. At the time the Marine Corps had no dedicated scout/sniper units. October '66 saw the creation of a scout/sniper platoon as part of the 3d Marine Div., operating in SVN. Capt. Land commanded, and shot with the unit, operating from Hill 55, west of Duc Pho, I Corps. His shooting and organizational skills combined to form a unit that was a continual thorn in the side of the NVA/VC operating in the area. The NVA/VC eventually put a bounty on his head in an attempt to reduce his effectiveness. *See also* **Hathcock, Gunnery Sergeant Carlos.**

Land Clearing Operations   *see*   **Tree Crusher, Rome Plow**

Land Lines   *see*   **EE-8 Field Telephone**

Land Mine Detonator   *see*   **Ensure 202**

Land Mines   Various types of land mines were employed by the FWFs and the NVA/VC. Most of the land mines used by U.S. forces were either deployed by air or artillery. Viet Cong mines were initially homemade devices that were typically command detonated. Soviet and PRC–made land mines were used by the NVA/VC very effectively against U.S. vehicles. Over the course of the war, enemy land mines accounted for over 75 percent of all U.S. vehicles lost. *See also* **CBU Mines, Booby Traps, AN/PRS-3.**

Land of the Big PX   *see*   **U.S.A.**

Land Reform   *see*   **Collectivization**

Land-Tail   Those elements of airmobile units that deployed using ground vehicles. This included the support elements (logistics, maintenance, ordnance, fuels, medical, etc.) and heavy artillery.

Landgrab Campaign (Musical Villages)   The March '73 cease-fire (Paris Accords) between the U.S., RVN, PRG and NVN called for the freezing of all military units in their current location when the cease-fire took effect, and prohibited the seizing of new territory by either the PRG or GVN (the US/NVA were supposed to withdraw from SVN). All areas under PRG/GVN control at the time of the cease-fire were to remain unchanged. Shortly before the cease-fire took place, and thereafter, there were many pushes made by the PRG (VC), NVA and GVN to put more villages and areas of SVN under their control. These Landgrabs or "musical villages" continued until Saigon's fall in '75. The JMC was responsible for deciding control disputes, but it was ineffective in its cease-fire and control functions. *See also* **Four Part Joint Military Commission.**

Landing Craft Repair Ship   *see*   **ARL**

Landing Craft, Armored   *see*   **LCA**

Landing Craft, Mechanized   *see*   **LCM-6**

Landing Craft, Medium   *see*   **LCM-6**

Landing Craft, Personnel, Large   *see*   **LCPL**

Landing Craft, Tank   *see*   **LCT**

Landing Craft, Utility   *see*   **LCU**

Landing Craft, Vehicle/Personnel   *see*   **LCVP**

Landing Ship Dock (LSD)   Large landing ship used to transport smaller landing craft. The LSD was pressed into service in Vietnam and temporarily used as floating bases by river patrol craft of TF 116. The LSDs were equipped with helo landing decks which allowed Navy light fire teams to operate throughout the Delta, without the need of a fixed ground base. Because of their size and vulnerability the LSD operated along the coast, in the mouths of the Delta, and did not deploy further up the rivers. The LSDs were later replaced by specially equipped LSTs that could operate on the rivers. As a landing ship the LSD operated with a 300-man crew and had facilities for 3–8 helos, and up to 21 LCM-6s. *See also* **TF 116, LST, PBR.**

Landing Ship Medium Rocket (LSMR, Inshore Fire Support Ship [IFS]) U.S. naval ships used to provide rocket fire in support of on-shore friendly forces. The IFS and LSMR were similar ships, each equipped with eight 5-inch rocket launchers. Each launcher could fire 30 spin-stabilized rockets per minute. The ships operated with a 140-man crew, were capable of 15 knots, and were also armed with one 5-inch gun and several 40mm antiaircraft and machine guns. The LSMR and IFS ships operated along the coast of South Vietnam throughout the war. *See also* **TF 70.8.9, Operation Sea Dragon.**

Landing Ship, Infantry *see* **LSI**

Landing Ship, Infantry, Large *see* **LSIL**

Landing Ship, Medium *see* **LSM**

Landing Ship, Support, Large *see* **LSSL**

Landing Ship, Tank *see* **LST**

Landing Signal Officer *see* **LSO**

Landing Vehicle Tracked Engineer *see* **LVTE**

Landing Vehicle Tracked Howitzer *see* **LVTH-6**

Landing Vehicle Tracked Personnel *see* **LVT**

Landing Vehicle Tracked Retriever *see* **LVTR**

Landing Zone (LZ, L Zed, Lima Zulu, Helicopter Landing Zone [HLZ]) Aircraft landing zone. Most often used in reference to a helicopter landing zone (HLZ).

The LZs were used to insert or extract troops or supplies. The LZs were sometimes cut by hand in thick jungle to allow one helicopter to get into the LZ for resupply or to extract the wounded. If larger LZs were needed in jungle areas large bombs, called Daisy Cutters, were dropped to clear the LZ. Because there were so few natural LZs in the rugged mountains of the Central Highlands, the few that were available were often booby-trapped or ambushed by the NVA/VC. The Australians referred to LZs as L Zeds. LZs were sometimes enlarged and operated as fire bases to support troop operations for long periods of time. The name LZ was used interchangeably with fire base. *See also* **Daisy Cutter, Hot LZ, Fire Support Base.**

Lane Grader (Army Instructor, Course Instructor, LGs) Slang for an Army military instructor who taught or supervised military classes for troops in training. Lane graders taught specific classes and controlled the trainees during the class. When the class was over the trainees were returned to the control of the DI. The LGs simply instructed, while the DIs "mothered" the trainee through Basic Training. *See also* **Drill Instructor.**

Lang Bian Vietnamese mountain resort dedicated to the "art of lovemaking," located in the Central Highlands in the city of Da Lat. Lang Bian served as an exclusive resort retreat for high ranking GVN officials and was supposedly "off-limits" to the normal U.S. and ARVN military. Prior to the '68 Tet Offensive the Viet Cong also respected Lang Bian's special place in society and steered clear of the resort. *See also* **Da Lat, Lang Bian Relay Station.**

Lang Bian Relay Station Army operated radio relay station which was perched atop the mountains just north of the Vietnamese resort city of Da Lat, Tuyen Duc Province, II Corps. The Army station relayed VHF and microwave signals pulled from the southern section of the Central Highlands to I FFV and II FFV Headquarters. *See also* **Lang Bian, I FFV, II FFV.**

Lang Chi Power Plant The Lang Chi hydroelectric power plant was located less than 105kms northwest of Hanoi on the Red River. The Soviet built power plant was Hanoi's main source of electric power. The plant had been off limits to U.S. air strikes since '64, but in June '72 as part of Operation Linebacker I, the plant was struck by Air Force LGBs. The plant was destroyed without damaging the dam located behind it. Destruction of the dam would have flooded the densely populated valley below it, resulting in a significant reduction in the North Vietnamese population in the Red River Valley. *See also* **Linebacker I, Laser Guided Bomb, Surgical Bombing.**

Lang Vei (Lang Vei Special Forces Camp) The site of a Special Forces CIDG camp near the SVN/Laotian border, southwest of Khe Sanh. In February '68 the camp was overrun by the NVA using heavy artillery and Soviet made PT-76 light tanks. The surviving members of the camp withdrew. With the fall of Lang Vei the NVA siege of Khe Sanh had begun. The use of tanks by the NVA at Lang Vei marked the first use of communist armor in SVN. The tanks withdrew after taking Lang Vei, and NVA armor was not seen again in SVN until the NVA Eastertide Offensive of '72. *See also* **Khe Sanh.**

Language *see* **Military Paraphraseology**

Lansdale, Edward (Colonel/General Edward Lansdale, Saigon Military Mission [SMM]) Established the Saigon Military Mission in '54 after the defeat of the French. The SMM operated as a front for the CIA mission in Vietnam. Between '54–'56, CIA operatives in North Vietnam conducted covert operations to disrupt and destabilize Ho Chi Minh's new communist government. By keeping Ho busy in the North the CIA hoped to limit Ho's influence on the political scene in SVN. Lansdale's tactics included sabotage and rumor generation, some of which caused thousands of North Vietnamese Catholics to flee from North to South Vietnam. Lansdale worked behind the scenes of Diem's government attempting to strengthen the Diem regime and bring stability to the RVN. From '65–'68 he served as a Special Assistant at the U.S. Embassy in Saigon. *See also* **Black Psyche, Saigon Military Mission.**

Lao The majority ethnic population of Laos. The other major portion of the Laotian population consisted of the Meo mountain tribes. *See also* **Laos, Ta'i, Meo.**

Lao Dong (Communist Party, Workers Party, Indo-Chinese Communist Party [ICP], PRP) Vietnamese Communist Party or the Workers' Party (People's Revolutionary Party—PRP). The Indo-Chinese Communist Party was founded in '29 by Ho Chi Minh, Vo Nguyen Giap, Le Duc Tho, Le Duan and Pham Van Dong. Ho managed to consolidate Vietnamese nationalists and communists into the Viet Minh to operate against the French in the First Indochina War. The name of the party was changed in '52 to the Lao Dong. After the defeat of the French in '54, the Lao Dong was led by Truong Chinh and later Le Duan, under the direction of Ho Chi Minh (self-appointed leader of the new country of North Vietnam; the Democratic Republic of Vietnam). In SVN the PRP became the dominant communist party, at the core of the NLF. *See also* **Viet Minh, VCI, NLF.**

Lao Grass *see* **Marijuana**

Lao Liberation Front (LLF, Pathet Lao, Neo Lao Hak Sat) The Laos Communist Party was officially known as the "Neo Lao Hak Sat" (the Lao Liberation Front). The military arm of the LLF, which fought the anticommunist forces of the Royal Lao Government (RLG), were known as the Pathet Lao. The Pathet Lao were originally nationalists led by Prince Souphanouvong, who fought for Laotian independence from the French. After the French defeat in Indochina the Laotian monarchy retained control of the government. Laotian communists began to agitate for socialist reforms and took control of the Pathet Lao. In '59, NVN began furnishing supplies and weapons to the Pathet Lao. Eventually NVA troops were used to help the Pathet Lao defeat the troops of the RLG. From '64 to '73 the U.S. provided air support to the Royal Lao Government and waged a secret war against the Pathet Lao, attempting to destroy the communists. In August '75 the communists rolled back RLG forces and took control of Laos, renaming it the People's Democracy of Laos. *See also* **Laos, People's Democracy of Laos, Prince Souvanna Phouma.**

Laos (Royal Laotian Government [RLG]) Landlocked country located on the western border of North Vietnam, sharing part of its eastern border with SVN. The Royal Lao Government (RLG) was officially neutral in the VNW, but the NVA used the

NVN/Laotian border to funnel men and equipment in to SVN via the Ho Chi Minh Trail. The NVA backed the Laotian Communist Party (Pathet Lao) which overthrew the Royal Lao Government in August '75. There was no U.S. incursion into Laos to interdict the Trail, but the U.S. did support an ARVN incursion in '71. From '60–'62 USSF training teams organized Meo tribes to resist the NVA and Pathet Lao forces. In '62 a coalition government was formed in Laos and the country was declared independent and neutral. U.S. advisors were withdrawn at that time, but NVA troops remained with the Pathet Lao. After '62 the Lao communists, with NVN support, continued their efforts to subvert the Royal Lao Coalition government. In an effort to counter the communist buildup in Laos the U.S. began to secretly arm and train Meo tribesmen to fight the Pathet Lao/NVA. From '65–'73 the U.S. provided limited air and covert support to the RLG. With the withdrawal of U.S. forces from SVN, support for the RLG quickly dried up. In August '75 the communist NVA/Pathet Lao forces took control of Laos, renaming it the People's Democracy of Laos. During the early sixties the population of Laos was 2–3 million people. *See also* **Lao Liberation Front, Meo, People's Democracy of Laos, White Star Mobile Training Team.**

Laos Incursion *see* **Lam Son 719**

Laos-Lam Son 719 *see* **Lam Son 719**

Laotian Accords *see* **Geneva Agreement, '62**

Laotian Gold *see* **Marijuana**

Laotian Highlands *see* **Plaines Des Jarres**

LAPES *see* **Low Altitude Parachute Extraction System**

LARC (BARC [Barge, Amphibious Resupply Craft]; Lighter, Amphibious Resupply Craft) Army owned and operated craft used to transfer cargo from ship to shore. The Army used the WWII vintage vehicle in Vietnam to support supply operations for some units operating in I Corps. The LARC was available in 5-ton (LARC), 15-ton (BARC), and 60-ton (LARC-LX) cargo versions. The vehicle had large wheels and a boat-hull shape. After the LARC was loaded offshore it would drive onto the beach to be unloaded. LARCs and BARCs functioned as "lighters" moving cargo from ships to receiving facilities where no port or offloading piers were available. LARCs were also used by the Navy to move cargo from ships in Da Nang harbor to port facilities in the area. *See also* **LOB Base, LCU.**

LARC-LX *see* **LARC**

Larceny *see* **Midnight Requisition**

Large-Scale Operation *see* **Campaign**

LAS-4 *see* **Light Attack Squadron 4**

Laser Guided Bomb (LGB, KMU-351) A self-guiding, extremely accurate bomb that used a low level laser light as its aiming point. The target was marked by a laser light aimed by the attacking aircraft or a second "illuminator" aircraft. The LGB guidance system locked onto the light and homed onto the target. The LGB required the target to be continuously illuminated with the laser light while the bomb was inflight to the target. The KMU-351 was a guidance device that could be fitted onto the nose of a bomb allowing it to be laser guided. Laser guided bombs were typically 2,000 or 3,000 pounders. *See also* **Illuminator, Pave Fire, Lang Chi Power Plant.**

Last American to Die... (Cpl McMahon Jr., Cpl Judge, Capt Nystul, Lt Shea) The last American serviceman to die "on the ground" in SVN were U.S. Marine Corps corporals Charles McMahon Jr. and Darwin Judge. Both were killed in an early morning NVA rocket attack on Tan Son Nhut Air Base on April 29, 1975. The Marines were providing security for U.S. evacuation aircraft and their crews. Marine helicopter pilots Captain William Nystul and Lieutenant Michael Shea were the last American servicemen to die "in SVN" before the country collapsed to the communists. They were killed when their CH-53 crashed on its return to the USS *Hancock* during the final evacuation of the Marine security force from the Embassy, April 30, 1975. *See also* **Van de Geer, 2Lt. Richard; Vietnam War.**

Last Confucian *see* **Ngo Dinh Diem**

Last of the Mandarins *see* **Ngo Dinh Diem**

Last-Light Recon *see* **First-Light Recon**

Late Revolutionaries *see* April 30 Revolutionary

Laterite *see* Overbirth

Latrine (Privy, John, Shitter, Three-Holer) Military toilet. In Vietnam most U.S. bases used the bottom portion of a 55-gallon drum for fecal waste. Urine was deposited in a piss-tube near the latrine. Latrine size was referred to by the number of toilet seats, or "holes" available, i.e., three-holer, four-holer, etc. The waste was burned daily with kerosene. The shit burning detail was one of the worst of the base camp details, and was frequently used as a disciplinary action. The drum bottoms had to be collected and moved to the burn area. As they were moved they tended to slosh and slop the waste about. On some of the larger bases, Vietnamese civilians were employed to take care of the waste duties. *See also* Shit Burner, Cat Hole, Piss-Tube.

Latrine Detail *see* Latrine Duty

Latrine Duty (Latrine Detail, Latrine Police) Detail assignment requiring the participants to clean and maintain the latrine area. This could include digging new slit trenches, erecting new piss-tubes and enclosures, cleaning and general maintenance. In Vietnam latrine duty usually included the shit burning detail, for the disposal of human waste. Unless Vietnamese civilians were employed to burn the waste, GIs were detailed to take care of it. Latrine duty was one of the least popular assignments, and was often used by command as a punishment. *See also* Shit Burner, Latrine.

Latrine Police *see* Latrine Duty

LAU-3 Rocket Pod Rocket pod system used aboard American attack aircraft. Each pod was loaded with twenty-four 2.5-inch HEAT or HEAP rockets. The pods were usually mounted in pairs on the aircraft's wing pylons, two or four pods per plane. *See also* Aircraft Rockets.

LAU-59/A Rockets *see* XM-158 Rocket

LAU-74A Flare Launcher Air Force flare launcher used by some of its "AC" gunships in Vietnam. The LAU-74A allowed the flares to be fired automatically instead of the old method which required a crewman to "pull and drop" the flares manually. The old system was used on the older AC-47 gunship and flare ships. *See also* Flares.

LAU-77/78/80 (Pylons, Hard Points) Special vertical supports (pylons) used to carry ordnance and weapons on aircraft. The LAU-77/78/80 series wing mounted pylons were used to carry the AGM-78A ARM missile. The LAU-77 was used on the Navy's A-6 Intruder and the LAU-78/80 were used on Air Force F-105. Aircraft hard points on fixed-wing and helicopter aircraft were used to mount a wide array of weapons systems. The points were designed into the aircraft's structure, allowing equipment to be externally bolted onto the aircraft. Pylons not designed into the structure of the aircraft were attached to the hard points.

Launch and Move SAM (Relocatable SAM) Tactic used by the North Vietnamese to relocate their SAM missile launchers after firing at American aircraft. During attacks American pilots noted when SAMs were launched, and the coordinates of the launch site. The coordinates were then used for future SAM suppression missions. The North Vietnamese believed they could increase the survivability of their launch sites if they could keep them hidden until the missiles were fired. After the North Vietnamese fired their SAMs from a site, they would pack up the launcher and its guidance radar system and relocate to a new site. The launch and move system was only partially effective because U.S. SAM suppression missions primarily relied on enemy radar emissions for targeting. *See also* Wild Weasel.

Laundry Bag (Barracks Bag) Cloth bag with a string pull top used by troops to carry "odds and ends." In the training barracks environment the bag was used to hold dirty laundry until the weekly ritual of washing clothes took place. In Vietnam the bags were found as low as the base camp level, but it was rare to see one in the field. The bags were either white or OD green in color.

Lavelle, General John D. General Lavelle commanded the U.S. 7th Air Force in Vietnam during the opening days of the NVA's Eastertide Offensive in April '72. Lavelle was relieved of command on April 11 and accused of violating the rules of engagement as issued by Washington. Under those rules U.S. aircraft could not strike enemy

SAM or AA/AAA sites unless the sites showed "hostile intent." Supposedly several SAM sites north of the DMZ had been attacked as part of protective reaction air strikes before they had fired on U.S. aircraft. According to Lavelle the strikes were valid because some of the same sites had fired on U.S. aircraft in the days preceding the protective attack. *See also* **Rules of Engagement, Protective Reaction Strikes.**

Laverack   *see*   **Operation Laverack**

LAW   *see*   **Light Antitank Weapon, M-72 LAW**

Lay Down the Line   *see*   **Skinny**

LBE   *see*   **Web Gear**

LBJ   *see*   **Long Binh Jail; Web Gear; Johnson, President Lyndon Baines**

LBJ Ranch   *see*   **Long Binh Jail**

LCA (Landing Craft, Armored)   Armored landing craft used by the French to transport their engineer units in Vietnam. The LCAs carried the engineer troops and supplies to repair bridges and construct fortifications. The Vietnamese later used these craft to fill out their naval river forces. *See also* **RAG, LCT.**

LCM   *see*   **LCM-6, LCM-8**

LCM-6 (Landing Craft Medium [Mechanized])   Standard armored landing craft used by American, French and South Vietnamese riverine forces in Vietnam. The LCM-6 was used to transport and land assaulting troops during riverine operations. The LCM-6 was 65 feet long, powered by two diesel engines and could make 9 knots. It was usually armed with 20mm cannons and .50cal machine guns, could transport 120 troops or 32 tons of cargo and was operated by a crew of seven. The LCM had a front mounted ramp that was lowered to disembark troops. Modified versions of the LCM were used as command and fire support boats and were called Commandements or Monitors. *See also* **Commandement, Monitor, ATC, LCM-8, Lighter.**

LCM-8 (Mike Boat)   Standard landing craft used in Vietnam. The LCM-8 "Mike Boat" was 73 feet long, 21 feet wide, and was powered by three engines to a max speed of 9 knots. The craft was used for troop and supply transport by river units. It was also used at coastal ports as a "lighter" for cargo

transfers between ships and port facilities. The LCM was operated by the Navy, but the Army did operate several of its own as part of the MRF in the Delta. The LCM-8 had a large front-drop ramp and could transport up to 300 troops, tanks and vehicles. Several LCM-8s were modified to function as mobile riverine command post and fire direction centers. LCMs of the MRF were transferred to the ARVN and VNN as part of the Vietnamization program in the early seventies. *See also* **Artillery Barge, Lighter, LCM-6.**

LCPL (Landing Craft, Personnel Large)   Small Navy boats used for harbor patrol duties. The steel hulled LCPLs were 36 feet long, had a max speed of 13 knots and were armed with two .50cal machine guns and usually a crew of three. Some LCPLs were outfitted with large xenon gas searchlights and used to patrol the waterways at night to discourage VC mining activities. The LCPLs that were fitted with searchlights carried extra M-60 or .30cal machine guns to increase their firepower. TF 116 LCPLs were used for river patrols in the Delta until '66 when they were replaced by the faster PBRs. LCPL craft were extensively used by TF Clearwater for river patrols in I Corps. *See also* **TF 116, TF Clearwater.**

LCT (Landing Craft, Tank)   Armored landing craft originally used during WWII to land tanks during amphibious operations. In Indochina the French used LCTs to transport their engineering elements and their heavy equipment. Some of the LCTs were transferred to the South Vietnamese for use by their River Assault Group. *See also* **LCA.**

LCU (Landing Craft, Utility; U's, U-Boats, YFU, Harbor Utility Craft)   American built utility landing craft used by the U.S., French, and SVN in Vietnam. Seven LCUs were available to the Vietnamese Navy and were part of the River Transport Group. The 180-ton LCU could make 10 knots, was powered by three diesel engines and armed with two 20mm cannons. The LCU, 105 feet long, was larger than the LCM and could transport up to 180 tons of cargo and was fitted with a front drop ramp for access to the storage bay. The YFU was an old version of the LCU used in harbors for cargo transfers. Navy LCU and YFUs were used extensively to move cargo from Da Nang to other supply points in I Corps. The

LCUs and YFUs were nicknamed the "U-Boats" or "U's." *See also* LARC, Skilak, Lighter.

LCVP (Landing Craft, Vehicle/Personnel) Small American made landing craft used by the French and South Vietnamese navies in riverine operations. The LCVP could transport and land 36 troops or one small vehicle. In Indochina the boat was armored, armed with a 20mm cannon, three machine guns and used as a combined troop assault and fire support boat. The 35-foot-long boat was made of wood and fiberglass and could make 9 knots. *See also* Lighter, LCM-6/8.

LCW *see* Limited Conventional War

LD *see* Line of Departure

LDNN *see* South Vietnamese SEAL Force

Le Cercle Sportif *see* Cercle Sportif

Le Col des Nuages *see* Hai Van Pass

Le Duan One of the original founders of the Vietnamese Communist Party. In '60 he became the First Secretary General of the Lao Dong, Vietnam's Communist Party. During the First Indochina War Le Duan directed Viet Minh military activities against the French in SVN. In the Second Indochina War Le Duan was instrumental in supporting the guerrilla war of the Viet Cong against the U.S. and the GVN. He succeeded Ho Chi Minh at the top of North Vietnam's power structure after Ho's death. *See also* Lao Dong.

Le Duc Tho (Ducky) Primary negotiator representing North Vietnam during the Paris peace negotiations with the U.S. The Paris Accords resulted in the signing of peace agreements between the U.S., North Vietnam, the PRG (Viet Cong) and the South Vietnamese government. Tho, along with Henry Kissinger, the U.S. principal negotiator, was awarded the '73 Nobel peace prize for their efforts. Tho refused to accept the prize because there was no real peace in Vietnam in '73, only an agreement that the U.S. would pull out of the war. Tho was also one of the founders of the Vietnamese Communist Party. Behind closed doors, the American negotiating team reportedly nicknamed Le Duc Tho "Ducky." *See also* Lao Dong, Paris Accords.

Le Loi *see* Accelerated Pacification Program, Black Market, Lam Son

Le Mal Jaune (Yellow Fever) French for "yellow fever," but not the yellow fever associated with the killer viral infections prevalent in tropical rain forest. Yellow fever was the French description of the Western world's intoxicating attraction to Indochina. To the French in Indochina, and later, to the Americans, the lure of the women, drugs and the lifestyle made Indochina, and later Vietnam, a very special place to be. The women of Euro-Asian background were beautiful and available; the cost of living was so low that a man could live very well, indeed, on even the lowly wages of a government (U.S.) employee.

Le Van Vien *see* Hall of Mirrors

Lead Sled *see* F-105, F-100

Leadership Bankruptcy A reference to the state of U.S. military leadership and ability during the last five years ('69–'73) of U.S. involvement in Vietnam, particularly the Army. These references were made by post–Vietnam critics and scholars. Cited as major contributing factors to the leadership decline were the draft, the lowering of service entrance requirements (intelligence), careerism in the Officer Corps, shortages of experienced low and mid level leaders, and the restrictions of using conventional tactics to fight an unconventional war. *See also* Frag(ging), Calley, Project 100,000.

Leaf Pattern Camouflage *see* Jungle Camouflage Uniform

Leaflet Missions *see* Controlled Littering

League for Vietnamese Independence *see* Viet Minh

Leaning-Rest Position most Army and Marine Corps Basic Trainees frequently assumed on command from their DI. The position consisted of placing the body horizontal to the ground, supported by the extended arms and balls of the feet; the "up" part of the push-up. Many DIs believed the troops "listened" better when in this position. While in training the usual rule was that after completing push-ups troops remained in the leaning rest until commanded to get to their feet. The leaning-rest was not only used during "PT," but was often used for punishment when troops were in full field gear. For most troops, once they got out of Basic and AIT, their leaning-rest days were over. *See also* **PT, Push-Ups.**

Leaping Lena *see* **Project Delta, Operation Leaping Lena**

Leary, Timothy (Turn-On, Tune-In, and Drop-Out) One of the leaders of the illicit LSD drug movement in the mid-sixties. Leary stressed the spiritual possibilities of LSD, believing that many of the world's problems could be solved through its use. Leary believed in the mystical power of the drug, and was a strong advocate of its widespread public use. LSD quickly became one of the major drugs of the new hippie generation. Timothy Leary's message to the world was "tune in, turn on and drop out." He advocated the use of LSD to free the mind and spirit. *Turn-on:* use of LSD or any other drugs to open the mind and get into the scene. *Tune-in* to what was happening, the spiritual awakening. *Drop-out:* give up the old ways of life (school, work, commitments) and follow Leary. *See also* **Ginsberg, Allen; Hippie; Illicit Drugs; Lysergic Acid.**

Leather Gloves *see* **Recon Gloves**

Leatherneck Square (Gio Linh, Cam Lo, Dong Ha, Con Thien) Nickname for the 3d Marine Division AO located in the northeastern corner of I Corps. The "square" consisted of the area encompassed by the Marine bases at Con Thien and Gio Linh along the DMZ, to Cam Lo and Dong Ha along the Cam Lo River.

Leathernecks *see* **U.S. Marines**

Leavenworth Plan *see* **Hammer-and-Anvil**

LEC Compound *see* **TIARA Project**

Leeches (Brown, Green, White, Black Leech) Vietnam was home for several varieties of blood sucking leeches. Black land leeches, less than two inches long, hung in the trees and crawled along the ground under the dense jungle canopies. White ground leeches clung to the low bushes. Brown and green water leeches, 6–10 inches long, occupied many of the streams, canals, rice paddies and stagnant pools. Leeches clung to the body, embedding their head in the skin, feeding off the blood of their

"host." Leeches were a constant problem for troops operating in the field. The leech was found in the dank undergrowth of the jungle and in slow flowing streams and canals. Removal was best accomplished with a burning cigarette or a squirt of Army issue insect repellent. Either method would cause the leech to loosen its bite and drop off. Leeches could sometimes be repelled by soap, salt, or tobacco. If the body of the leech was grabbed and pulled loose, the leech's head remained embedded in the skin and caused infection. The Army suggested "a slight knife cut" be made just back of the leech's head. Most GIs had neither the time or the patience for an anatomy lesson on the leech. When there were many leeches attached to the body, it was sometimes easier to let them suck their fill, after which they would drop off. This "wart" method wasn't used if the leech tried to make his way up the urethra or rectum.

Leg Armor Leg armor was used on a limited basis in Vietnam. Leg armor was available in steel, weighing 38 pounds, and a 10-pound version that used ceramic plates. The armor was used by some helicopter door gunners, but was not widely utilized because of its weight and uncomfortable fit. It was also very awkward to work in and only provided protection to the front of the lower legs. *See also* **Body Armor.**

Leg Unit *see* **Legs**

Legal and Magnanimous Side *see* **L & M**

Legislative Liaison Office of the Congress *see* **Congressionals**

Legs (Leg Unit, Straight-Legged Division) Airborne trooper slang for a nonairborne infantryman. Any nonmechanized, regular infantry unit. Straight-legged divisions were regular Army infantry. Air cavalry or air mobile units did not consider themselves "leg" units, but "cav." *See also* **Infantry Soldier, The.**

Lejeune *see* **Operation Lejeune, Camp Lejeune**

LeMay, General Curtis (Bomb Vietnam Back into the Stone Age) Famous WWII bomber commander who served as Air Force chief of staff from June '61 to February '65. The general once commented that the U.S. could "bomb Vietnam back into the stone age" and that the U.S. should use whatever means was available to bring a quick end to the war in Vietnam. During the '68 presidential elections Le May ran as George Wallace's vice-presidential candidate. *See also* **We Ought to Nuke the Chinks.**

Lemnitzer, General Lyman *see* **Chief of Staff**

Let's Bring the Troops Home Now Sixties antiwar protest slogan often heard at demonstrations and rallies.

LeTournear Tree Crusher *see* **Tree Crusher**

Levies (Levy List) Mass troop call-ups within the Army for the purpose of meeting an external threat. During the VNW levy lists were generated containing the names of the troops that were to be sent to Vietnam as replacements. Levy lists were forwarded to the various Army bases throughout the U.S. where troops eligible for Vietnam service were staged until needed.

Levy List *see* **Levies**

Lexington *see* **Operation Lexington**

LFT *see* **Light Helicopter Section**

LGs *see* **Lane Grader**

LGB *see* **Laser Guided Bomb**

LHC (LLC, Light Salvage Ship, Heavy Salvage Ship) Heavy landing craft used for salvage work by the Navy. LHCs were normally assigned to an amphibious force: In Vietnam they were assigned to the river patrol and riverine forces of TF 116 and TF 117. The LLC was a small salvage boat used for light duty and was part of the river task force support group. *See also* **LCM-6, -8.**

LHFT *see* **Light Helicopter Section**

Liaison Section (Go-Fors, Gophers) Supply acquisition team. By '67 the large buildup of U.S. troops in Vietnam was creating huge logistic supply problems. Units operating in the field were running short of a variety of supply items and the normal supply channels were unable to move the items to the field fast enough. In order to expedite resupply, Army divisions sent special teams to rear area supply depots to seek out the items the division needed. These "liaison sections" or "go-fors" would locate supplies and arrange for the material to be transported by assets (vehicles/aircraft) from

their division. By '70 changes made to the resupply system, and the overall reduction of troops in-country increased the efficiency of the logistics system.

Liberated Zones Viet Cong terminology for hamlets and villages under their control. The VC considered such locations to be under their control as long as the location provided material, psychological or intelligence support to the NLF, even if enemy troops (US/ARVN) were active in the area. Such "liberated villages" were required to provide the VC with manpower and intelligence information on the enemy, and to pay taxes in the form of food or other needed items. Villages that did not actively cooperate with the VC were coerced into submission. American troops provided some protection for rural villages during the day, but most were open to the VC at night.

Liberation Radio (PRG Radio) Low power clandestined radio station used by the PRG for propaganda broadcast in South Vietnam. The portable station moved frequently to avoid capture or identification of its location. After the '73 Paris Peace Accords the PRG established a permanent station to continue its attacks on the Saigon regime. *See also* **Radio Hanoi.**

Liberty *see* **Operation Georgia**

Liberty Bridge Marine name for the bridge just north of An Hoa that crossed at the junction of the Vu Gia and Thu Bon rivers about 22kms southwest of Da Nang. The bridge, which was on the main road link between An Hoa and Da Nang, was located at the mouth of the "Arizona Valley," an area of intense enemy activity throughout the war. The French had originally constructed a bridge in the same general area, but the VC destroyed it in the early sixties. The Marines provided support while the Navy SEABEES worked on constructing a new bridge. *See also* **Arizona Territory.**

Liberty Call (Cinderella Liberty) U.S. Navy and Marine name for authorized absence or break from duty, and permission to leave the base for a period of less than 48 hours. All troops on "cinderella liberty" were required to be back on base by midnight.

Liberty Canyon *see* **Operation Liberty Canyon**

Liberty Street *see* **Tu Do Street**

Lice Head lice were a part of everyday life for many Vietnamese. Searching for lice was a minor social event. Several of the older women in a group would sit on a stool or a box, each with a young girl or woman sitting at their feet. The old ladies would carefully search the younger women's heads looking for the elusive head lice. As they searched the old ladies would chew their betel nut and jabber socially to each other. The young ones being preened would sit quietly and listen. When lice were found the old women would pinch them with their fingernails or crush them with their teeth. *See also* **People Detector.**

Lichee *see* **Dragon Fruit**

Lid *see* **Keys, Marijuana**

Lidocaine *see* **Drug List**

Lien Ket 18 *see* **Operation Harvest Moon/Lien Ket 18**

Lien Ket 52 *see* **Operation Colorado**

Lien Tinh Lo *see* **Highways**

Lieutenant *see* **First Lieutenant, Second Lieutenant**

Lieutenant Colonel (Light Colonel, Lt Col, Trung-Ta) Officer above the grade of major and below the officer grade of colonel. Insignia; silver oak leaves. Trung-Ta was the equivalent Vietnamese rank.

Lieutenant General (LtG) A three-star general officer in the U.S. Army, Marines and Air Force. The equivalent rank in the Navy was vice admiral. *See also* **General Officers.**

Lifer's Dream (SKS Rifle) Some weapons captured by U.S. soldiers were allowed to be brought home as war trophies. The most sought after weapon was the SKS semiautomatic rifle. The Marines called the SKS a "lifer's dream" because they all wanted to capture one and take it home. The AK47 was an automatic rifle and not eligible to be classified as a war trophy for return to the U.S. Normal procedure was to tag the captured rifle and store it at the man's headquarters; when he departed RVN he would take the rifle with him. Because the SKS was so popular they were often stolen by rear echelon troops and never

made it back to the States with their rightful owners. *See also* **SKS Carbine, Rifle.**

Lifers (Hard-Case Lifers) Derogatory term used to refer to soldiers who made a career out of the military, most notably senior NCOs. The name was most often used by draftees who had to function under NCOs who didn't have a very high regard for those who didn't voluntarily enlist in the Army or plan to make it their home. "Hard-case" lifers were the worst of the lot. They harassed troops unnecessarily and were usually at the top of the list of candidates for "fragging." *See also* **Frag(ging).**

Lifers Are the Same as Flies . . . "Lifers are the same as flies, they eat shit and won't leave you alone." GI graffiti.

Lift *see* **Sortie**

Liftmaster *see* **C-118**

Light Antiaircraft Missile *see* **Hawk Missile**

Light Antitank Weapon (LAW) Man-carried light antitank weapons, shoulder fired, single shot and short ranged. The primary U.S. antitank weapon in Vietnam was the M-20 Rocket Launcher and the M-72 LAW. The NVA/VC forces used the Rocket Propelled Grenade as their primary antitank weapon. The antitank weapons found widespread usage against enemy troop concentrations, fortifications and installations. In the direct fire support role the recoilless rifle was widely used as an antitank/antibunker and antipersonnel weapon. *See also* **M-72, Rocket Propelled Grenade, Recoilless Rifle.**

Light Artillery *see* **M-101A1 Howitzer**

Light Arty *see* **M-101A1 Howitzer**

Light at the End of the Tunnel Reference by Gen. William Westmoreland (via the French) to his view of the war in Vietnam just prior to the '68 Tet Offensive; the view that the U.S. effort in Vietnam was successful and that the U.S. was winning the war against the NVA/VC, a war that would soon be over. The NVA/VC Tet '68 Offensive blew out the "light at the end of the tunnel." After Tet the phrase was used sarcastically to reference the ineffectiveness of the military and political leadership regarding their claims of control and imminent victory in

Vietnam. Although the offensive was a military defeat for the NVA/VC, the psychological and political implications of their attacks began to turn the tide of American public opinion against the war.

Light at the Top... "Light at the Top, Heavy at the Bottom," President Thieu's name for his defensive strategy employed against the NVA/VC in early '75. The tactic involved concentrating ARVN forces around the main population centers such as Saigon and the coastal enclaves, instead of trying to defend the entire country. By giving up remote and strategically unimportant areas Thieu hoped his military units would be able to hold out against a full scale NVA offensive. It was Thieu's order to abandon ARVN outposts in the Central Highlands that precipitated the ARVN rout that eventually led to the total collapse of SVN. *See also* **Final Offensive.**

Light Attack Helicopter Squadron 3 *see* **Seawolves**

Light Attack Squadron 4 (Black Ponies, LAS-4, VAL-4, Ponies) U.S. Navy fixed-wing aircraft that provided close air support for friendly units operating in the Delta. The Black Ponies, flying the OV-10A Bronco, operated in support of TF 116. The twin engine, propeller driven Bronco could be armed with a combination of weapons including rockets, machine and miniguns, bombs, and 20mm cannon pods. The maneuverability, navigational aids and armament made VAL-4 a valuable asset in the skies over the Delta. Aircraft of VAL-4 began operations in March '69 from airfields at Vung Tau and Binh Tuy. VAL-4 operated over the Delta until April '72 when the unit was deactivated. During the war VAL-4 represented the Navy's only land based, fixed-wing squadron in-country. *See also* **Seawolves, Navy's Delta Air Force, VARS, OV-10.**

Light Colonel *see* **Lieutenant Colonel**

Light Fire Team *see* **Light Helicopter Section**

Light Helicopter Section (Light Fire Team [LFT], Light Helo Fire Team [LHFT]) Army term for two helicopter gunships operating together. The Navy called their two helicopter gunship fire teams "Light Helo Fire Teams." Navy LHFTs

operated in support of riverine operations in the Delta. Light Helicopter Sections were also referred to as "Red Teams," "Light Fire Teams," and "Helo Fire Teams." *See also* **Heavy Helicopter Section, Seawolves.**

Light Helicopter Squadron *see* **HML**

Light Helo Fire Team *see* **Light Helicopter Section**

Light Infantry (Mechanized Infantry, Regular Infantry) "Light" infantry operated primarily with the equipment they carried into combat: small mortars, rockets, recoilless rifles, machine guns, and rifles. Modern light infantry tended to be airborne or helimobile, deployed for combat with enough supplies and munitions to only last a few days before resupply was necessary. "Regular" infantry deployed by truck or on foot with its organic heavy artillery support. Mechanized infantry deployed by means of armored personnel carriers and tanks. The NVA was acknowledged by many U.S. military leaders as some of the best light infantry of the twentieth century.

Light Machine Gun (LMG) Several different types of light machine guns saw service in Vietnam. *See also* **M-60, M-1919A6, RPD, Japanese Machine Guns, M-63A1 Stoner, Mle 24/29, RPK.**

Light Salvage Ship *see* **LHC**

Light SEAL Support Boat (LSSB, Light SEAL Support Craft [LSSC]) Small aluminum boats used by Navy SEAL teams for mission insertion and extraction. The boats were operated by crews permanently assigned to support SEAL units. The 24-foot-long boats were driven by gasoline powered water jets and were capable of 30 knots. The boats were armed with machine guns and grenade launchers and typically operated with a three man crew. The terms craft and boat were used interchangeably in reference to the craft. *See also* **SEAL Team Assault Boat.**

Light SEAL Support Craft *see* **Light SEAL Support Boat**

Light Section Term used to describe two tanks or two helicopters operating together under the same command. A light helicopter section was usually composed of two gunships, but could be an LOH and a gunship. *See also* **Hunter Killer Team.**

Light(s) Term for moving or maneuvering in the field with weapon and ammo, and without full field gear or rucksack. Temporarily removing the field gear to improve performance in a firefight. *See also* **Field Load.**

Light-Emitting Chemical Compound *see* **TIARA Project**

Lighten-Up (Cut...Some Slack, Cut ...a Hus) Not to take a situation seriously. To ease off, reduce the pressure, not be so intense. To take it easy on someone, help them out or do them a favor. If you asked someone to "cut you some slack," you were asking them to take it easy on you; give you a break.

Lighter Small ships and boats used to transfer cargo from larger ships to shore facilities when dock facilities capable of supporting large ships were lacking or nonexistent. Cargo from the larger ship would be offloaded onto the smaller ships for transfer to port or beach receiving facilities. Several different types of craft were used as lighters by the Navy in Vietnam. Because of limited dock facilities at Da Nang and Vung Tau lighters were used to unload ships in the harbor. At sites where no harbor existed, such as Tuy Hoa, Chu Lai and Cua Viet, lighters moved the cargo. Some craft used as lighters were LCU, LCM, AKL, YFR, YFU. *See also* **NSAD, NSAS, LCU, LCM, AKL, YFR, YFU, LARC.**

Lighter, Amphibious Resupply Craft/ Cargo *see* **LARC**

Lightning Bug *see* **Firefly**

Lightning Joe *see* **Collins, General Joseph L.**

Lightship *see* **Firefly, C-123 Lightship**

Lightweight Entrenching Tool *see* **Entrenching Tool**

Lightweight Rucksack *see* **ALICE**

Lima *see* **LZ Lima**

Lima Charlie (Loud and Clear, Five-by-Five, Five-Square) Response given during a communications check of radio equipment testing the voice transmission quality between two sets. If the quality at the receiving set was good, the receiver announced "Lima Charlie" or "Loud and Clear" or "five-

by-five." The response number decreased according to the quality of reception; four-by-four, three-by-three...etc.

Lima Zulu *see* **Landing Zone, LZ Lima Zulu**

Limited Conventional War (LCW) Description of the Vietnam War after September '65. According to conflict classification by the U.S. Department of Defense, U.S. combat units in Vietnam were involved in a "Guerrilla War," but when the size of a single U.S. unit exceeded 4,000 men, the conflict was reclassified a "Limited Conventional War." In September '65 the 1st Cavalry Division deployed to Vietnam followed by the entire 1st Infantry Division in October; each division totaled nearly 20,000 men. Prior to the arrival of the divisions the largest Army combat unit in Vietnam was the 173d Airborne Brigade. *See also* **Guerrilla War.**

Limited War Laboratory (LWL) One of the technical branches of the Army Concept Team in Vietnam that developed new weapons for use in counterinsurgency warfare. The laboratory was established in '62 in Maryland and over the years of the Vietnam War developed several interesting projects such as an effective leech repellent, a 1,100 calorie meal in a 10-ounce package, and a radar set able to penetrate foliage. Some of the LWL's more noteworthy failures were tunnel weapons and exploration kits, the PDM, and a seismic tunnel detector. *See also* **ACTIV, Tunnel Exploration Kit, TELACS, Tunnel Weapon, Seismic Tunnel Detector, Tunnel Exploration Kit, PDM.**

Limpet Mine (Moored Mines, Floating Mines) An explosive charge attached to a ship's hull. The mine was placed by a swimmer, under the waterline of the ship. The Viet Cong made use of limpet mines in their effort to disrupt Allied shipping on the rivers and harbors of South Vietnam. The VC also made use of floating mines, but because floating mines were indiscriminate in their attack, the VC favored the command detonated mine. Command detonated mines were usually moored just below the surface and electrically detonated from an observation point along the river. Such mines allowed the VC to be very selective in the types of ships they attacked. *See also* **Killer Dolphins.**

Lin Dei Nugel Nghai (LLDN, Vietnamese SEALs [VNS], ARVN SEALs) South Vietnamese naval units that trained under the guidance of U.S. Navy SEALs and special naval warfare advisors. Most SEAL field duties were transferred to the LLDN by '72. The LLDN were sometimes referred to as "ARVN SEALs," by GIs who referred to all South Vietnamese forces as "ARVNs." *See also* **SEAL.**

Line, The *see* **Shit, The**

Line Backer I Code name for U.S. air strikes which began in May '72 against supply routes feeding the North Vietnamese invasion of SVN. During the NVA Eastertide Offensive, April '72, several NVA divisions with heavy artillery and armor support launched massive attacks from Laos and across the DMZ. President Nixon authorized the renewed bombing of North Vietnam to cut the NVA lines of communication, choking off the invasion. Line Backer II was initiated in December '72 as an extension of Linebacker I. *See also* **Eastertide Offensive, Christmas Bombing.**

Line Doggies *see* **Infantry Soldier, The**

Line Numbers Field identification system used by the 2d Brigade/9th Infantry Division to track troops during operations. The troops were part of the Mobile Riverine Force that operated in the swamps and mangroves of the Delta. In such terrain it was easy for a man to get lost during night operations, falling into a stream or canal, drowning, or becoming pinned in quicksand. Each man on an operation was given a line number as an identifier. The troops were landed ashore by boat or helicopter to conduct operations. When the operation was over a head count would be taken, by line number, as the returning troops filed onto the extraction boats. A missing number would generate a search to find the missing man. The system was crude but effective.

Line of Departure (Jumping-Off Point, LD) Imaginary line from which an exercise or field operation began. The units that would participate in the operation remained on one side of the line, holding, until the operation commenced. Once the units crossed the line they were committed to the action.

Line Units *see* **Shit, The**

Line-Abreast *see* **On-Line**

Line-Ahead *see* **On-Line**

Linear Ambush Typical ambush in which most of the ambush force was deployed to one side of a trail or kill zone. Such ambushes were most effective when security elements were placed up and down the trail from the ambush site. The security element could signal the main ambush when the enemy approached and was also in position to kill any enemy troops that attempted to escape along the trail when the ambush was sprung. With the ambush force positioned along one side of the trail they could easily withdraw together if the enemy charged the ambush site. *See also* **Ambush.**

Linebacker I *see* **Operation Linebacker I**

Linebacker II *see* **Christmas Bombing**

Lines *see* **Bunkerline**

Lines of Communication (LOC) Any general reference to the lines or methods used by military units to communicate with each other and higher headquarters and logistics centers. The LOC more specifically referred to the supply lines and methods used to connect combat units with their logistic support. Such lines/methods included air, land, and water routes.

Lions of Contigny *see* **28th Infantry Regiment**

Liquor Store *see* **Class Six Store**

Listening Post *see* **Observation Post**

Lister Bag (Water Bag) Large canvas water bag used by troops in the field. Lister bags were usually found at the smaller base camps where water trailers were not available or practical. *See also* **Fat Rats.**

Lit-Up/Lite-Up *see* **Fire (Shoot)**

Litchi Fruit *see* **Dragon Fruit**

Litter *see* **Bamboo Litter**

Little Appalachia *see* **Four Corners**

Little Bulldog Tank *see* **M-41 Light Tank**

Little Detroit *see* **Van Dien**

Little Guys *see* **Enemy, The**

Little IRT   see   Tunnels of Cu Chi

Little People   see   Enemy, The

Little Vegas   see   Hanoi Hilton

Live and Let Live (Accommodations)
A view of the ARVN/VC relationship in many of the rural areas of Vietnam. In some places the ARVNs and the Viet Cong had reached an accommodation. The ARVNs wouldn't go looking for the VC, and in turn the VC would leave the ARVNs alone. GVN tax collectors roamed the countryside by day, and Viet Cong tax collectors roamed by night. The peasants were caught in the middle. The ARVNs could no more protect the peasants from the Viet Cong than the VC could totally eliminate the ARVNs. The accommodation worked well until North Vietnam decided it was time for reunification of North and South, and the U.S. decided it was not going to allow North Vietnamese expansion to continue unchecked. *See also* **Search and Avoid.**

Living Allowance   see   Allotment

Liz   see   LZ Liz

LKA   see   Attack Cargo Ship

LLC   see   LHC

LLDB   see   Luc Luong Dac Biet

LLDN   see   Lin Dei Nugel Nghai

LLF   see   Lao Liberation Front

LLTV   see   Low Light TV

LMG   see   Light Machine Gun

Loach   see   OH-6

Loach Alley   Nickname for the area along the Song Sai Gon River approximately 30kms northwest of Saigon, between Cu Chi in the west and Lai Khe in the east. The area along the river between Dau Tieng and Phu Cuong was a major NVA/VC base area. The area was nicknamed by Army helicopter pilots who worked the area. A high number of "Loaches" who had been shot down during reconnaissance and surveillance missions along that particular stretch of the river in '68–'69.

Load Bearing Equipment   see   **Web Gear**

Load Bearing Junk   see   **Web Gear**

Loadmaster   Air Force transport crewman responsible for the loading operations of the aircraft. The loadmaster maintained the flight manifest of passengers and cargo, and verified the proper loading and securing of those loads. On transport helicopters this was normally done by the crew chief. *See also* **Shoe Tags.**

Loan, General Nguyen Ngoc   see   Nguyen Ngoc Loan

Loan-Shark   see   Shylocker

LOB Base (Logistics-over-the-Beach Base, Wunder Beach, LOTS)   Logistical supply base established on a coastal beach. The base was supplied from ships moored offshore, using small amphibious craft that transferred the supplies between ship and shore. "Wunder Beach" was the LOB base located 14kms east of Quang Tri, originally established by the Marine Corps and later taken over by the Army. Army LARC and BARC vehicles transported the cargo to the beach. The large, wheeled amphibious vehicles made their way to the supply ships offshore; on their return they would drive onto the beach to be unloaded. Several LARCs also operated at Da Nang, off-loading cargo from ships anchored in the harbor. Army LOB operations were referred to by the Navy as "LOTS," Logistics Over the Shore. *See also* **LARC.**

Lob-Bombs   Name for one of the methods used by the NVA/VC to get satchel charges inside the perimeter of an enemy combat base. A small explosive charge was placed under a shielded satchel charge, the fuse was ignited on the satchel charge, and as it burned the small charge under it was detonated. The small charge blew the satchel over the US/ARVN defensive wire, where it exploded within the perimeter of the base. This lobbing of the satchel charge reduced NVA/VC sapper losses, and was very hard for the Americans to defend against. The range of the lob-bomb was very short. *See also* **Satchel Charge, Sapper.**

LOC   see   Lines of Communication

Loc Luong 66   see   Kit Carson Scout

Loc Ninh   Village located 120kms north of Saigon in III Corps, near the SVN/Cambodian border. The ville was declared the capital of the Provisional Revolutionary Government of South Vietnam by the Viet Cong (NLF). Loc Ninh was captured by the NVA/VC during the '72 Eastertide Offensive and remained in their control until the fall of SVN in '75. After the fall of SVN the VC/PRG disappeared from the political landscape of Vietnam. During U.S. involvement in Vietnam, Loc Ninh had been a Special Forces Camp, and was the scene of heavy fighting and attempts by two NVA/VC regiments to take the camp in '67. *See also* **Battle of Loc Ninh.**

Local Force Viet Cong   *see*   **Local VC**

Local Military Confinement Facility *see*   **Long Binh Jail**

Local VC (Local Force Viet Cong, Vung VC)   Viet Cong who operated primarily in the areas in which they lived. Local VC ("Vung VC" in Vietnamese) operated in small groups, usually platoon size or smaller and were usually poorly equipped. A large percentage of their weapons and supplies were captured from American and South Vietnamese forces, the remainder filtering down through the Ho Chi Minh Trail or fabricated in secret VC workshops. The local VC tended to have legitimate jobs by day, and engaged in attacks and ambushes by night. Those VC who were not gainfully employed during the day hid out to avoid capture or detection. The primary uniform of the VC was the "black pajama." *See also* **Viet Cong, Main Force VC.**

Lock 'n' Load   Ready a weapon for firing by cocking and chambering a round. When field troops were inside the perimeter of a patrol or fire base, or boarding a helicopter, they were required to keep the chamber of their weapon empty. This was done to avoid an accidental discharge of the weapon. On the way out of the base the call would go up and down the line to lock 'n' load in preparation for action. During basic training on the weapons range, a familiar call was "lock 'n' load one live round." *See also* **Clear a Weapon.**

Lockjaw   *see*   **Marine Medium Helicopter Squadron 362**

Lodge, Ambassador Henry Cabot, Jr. Served as the Massachusetts state representative to the U.S. Senate from '36–'52, when he was replaced by John F. Kennedy. From '53–'60 he served as the U.S. representative to the United Nations. In '63 he was appointed the U.S. ambassador to South Vietnam and held the post until '64. He was appointed to the same position from '65–'67, and ambassador-at-large from '67–'69. He headed the U.S. delegation to the Paris peace talks with NVN from '69–'70. Lodge believed in a negotiated settlement in Vietnam, but was unable to convince NVN and the VC to cooperate.

Log Bird (Log Ship, Logged, Log Day, Log Run)   GI name for resupply helicopters. The resupply operations were referred to as "log runs" (logistical resupply). To be logged or waiting for the log ship meant being resupplied or waiting for the resupply helicopter to come in. While operating in the field grunts looked forward to "Log Day" because it usually signaled a limited or no "hump" day. Besides food, water and ammunition the log ships would bring in fatigues, mail and replacement troops to units that spent long successive periods of time in the field. Log Runs for helicopter crews were generally routine assignments. *See also* **Back Bird.**

Log Day   *see*   **Log Bird**

Log Run   *see*   **Log Bird**

Log Ship   *see*   **Log Bird**

Logged   *see*   **Log Bird**

Logistic Support Area (LSA, Johnson City)   Small Marine logistic and support bases that provided fuel, ammunition, supplies and medical treatment for operating Marine forces in the field. The LSAs were strategically placed throughout the Marines' area of operation in I Corps, providing quick access to support and greatly increasing the mobility of Marine ground operations against the NVA/VC. The LSAs received their support directly from Da Nang and Chu Lai. One particular LSA used by Marine Task Force Delta, in January '66, also had limited helicopter maintenance support; this LSA was called "Johnson City."

Logistics Over the Shore   *see*   **LOB Base**

Logistics-Over-the-Beach Base   *see* **LOB Base**

LOH, LOH-6   *see*   **OH-6, OH-13, OH-23, OH-58**

Loincloth   *see*   **Breechcloth**

Loiter Time (Hang Time)   The amount

of time an aircraft can remain over an area and still have sufficient fuel remaining to return to base. Long loiter times allowed attack and surveillance aircraft more time over enemy target areas. Jet aircraft and helicopters had some of the shortest loiter times, while the AC-47 and light observation aircraft had longer loiter times. Sometimes referred to as "hang time." Helicopters that were able to rearm and refuel at FREARF points were able to increase their loiter time on station.

LOLEX *see* **Low Level Extraction System**

Lolo *see* **LZ Lolo**

Lomotil Antidiarrhea drug widely used by American forces in Vietnam to combat the frequent cases of dysentery and unspecific cases of diarrhea. Lomotil was the trade name for "diphenoxylate hydrochloride." When taken regularly Lomotil did reduce attacks of diarrhea, but it could also produce side effects such as cramps, drowsiness, fatigue, and a general skin rash. Continued use could also lead to drug dependency. *See also* **Drug List.**

Lon Nol *see* **Nol, General Lon**

Long Binh (Camp Long Binh, Long Binh Junction) Major city 24kms northeast of Saigon, in Bien Hoa Province, III Corps. Long Binh became the largest U.S. logistics center in Vietnam and was USARV (U.S. Army Vietnam) Headquarters, site of the U.S. military stockade and the home of the 90th Replacement Center. The 90th Replacement Center was one of two replacement centers where most Army troops, arriving from the U.S. (assigned to III or IV Corps), started their tour of duty in SVN. The big U.S. military complex at Long Binh was called "Long Binh Junction" and "Camp Long Binh," but to everyone in-country it was simply "Long Binh." *See also* **Long Binh Jail, 90th Replacement Battalion, 22d Replacement Battalion, Cu Chi Express.**

Long Binh Heliport *see* **Castle**

Long Binh Jail (LBJ, Long Binh Stockade, Local Military Confinement Facility, Stockade) U.S. multiservice jail located at Long Binh, Bien Hoa Province, III Corps. Hard-core disciplinary cases served time at LBJ. The military referred officially to the maximum security stockade as a "Local Military Confinement Facility." The 284th MP Company operated the stockade with support from the 720th MP Battalion. A second American stockade in Vietnam was located at Da Nang. The Long Binh Stockade was also nicknamed the "LBJ Ranch," or just "LBJ" for short. Many accusations about prisoner abuses and mistreatment surfaced during the stockade's operation. *See also* **Good Time.**

Long Binh Junction *see* **Long Binh**

Long Binh Stockade *see* **Long Binh Jail**

Long Green Line "Poetic" reference to troops advancing through the jungle as seen from above in an aircraft.

Long Hai *see* **Project Rapid Fire**

Long Hai Hills Small stretch of hills located 15kms northeast of Vung Tau in Phuoc Tuy Province, III Corps. The hills were one of several Viet Cong strongholds in the area.

Long John Antenna (Whip Antenna, RC-292) GI slang for long, RC-292 antenna used on field radios to increase the radios' range. The long John antennas were not normally used in dense jungle because of their tendency to snag in the brush. The long antenna also acted as a signpost to the enemy; the long jointed antenna could be seen from a considerable distance. The short "whip" antenna was typically used in the jungle; it was flexible and less than six feet long, but it did reduce the radio's range. *See also* **U.S. Radios.**

Long Lance *see* **Operation Long Lance**

Long Nguyen Secret Zone Viet Cong name for a major base area centered about 56kms northwest of Saigon, just east of the Michelin Rubber Plantation in Binh Duong Province, III Corps. *See also* **Michelin Rubber Plantation, Iron Triangle.**

Long-Range Patrol *see* **Long-Range Reconnaissance Patrol**

Long-Range Patrol Rations *see* **LRRP Rations**

Long-Range Planning Task Group (LORAPL) Group formed by MACV commander, General Abrams, in July '68 consisting of his staff and advisors. Their task was to review U.S. military strategy in Vietnam from '64–'68 and make recommendations for a change in strategy.

Long-Range Reconnaissance Patrol (LRRP, Lurps, LRP, Long-Range Patrol, Animals of the Army) Special "long-range patrols" designed, outfitted and operated for the purpose of gathering intelligence data on the enemy; his movements and bases. The LRRPs (Lurps) operated deep in enemy territory seeking out the enemy and performing special tasks such as raids, POW rescues, sabotage and ambushes. In Vietnam LRRP duties were performed by units of the U.S. Special Forces and by LRRP companies organized from regular Army units and trained by the USSF. In February '69 Army LRRP companies were converted to Ranger Companies of the 75th Infantry Regiment. Australia's SAS units performed as LRRPs while in Vietnam. LRRPs were nicknamed the "Animals of the Army" because of their aggressiveness. *See also* **SAS, MACV-SOG, USSF LRRPs, 75th Infantry, SEAL, Force Recon, MACV Recondo School.**

Long Rats *see* **LRRP Rations**

Long Son Island Small island located 8kms north of Vung Tau in the Ganh Rai Bay. The bay was situated between Vung Tau and the Rung Sat Special Zone (in the Mouth of the Mekong). The island served as a base of operations for Viet Cong units operating out of the RSSZ and in Phuoc Tuy Province. *See also* **Rung Sat Special Zone.**

Long Tan (Battle of Long Tan) Village located 4kms east of the Australian base camp at Nui Dat in Phuoc Tuy Province, III Corps. In August '66 an ATF company was on patrol in a rubber plantation near Long Tan and became heavily engaged with an estimated 5 battalions of main force VC and NVA. The company was eventually reinforced by an armored cavalry troop and two infantry companies. Supported by artillery and the reinforcements, the battle of Long Tan resulted in 245 confirmed enemy KIA (and much higher estimates of probable enemy KIA/WIA) and the capture of several enemy prisoners. The Australian force suffered 18 KIAs and 21 WIAs.

Long Tau River *see* **Song Long Tau River**

Long Thanh *see* **Bear Cat**

Long Tra'ng du K'ich *see* **Hathcock, Gunnery Sergeant Carlos**

Long Xuyen Provincial capital of An Giang Province located in the northwest portion of the Delta in IV Corps. The town was located 135kms southwest of Saigon and 50kms northwest of Can Tho on the southern bank of the Song Hau Giang River.

Long-Controls Experimental controls used on the M-113 APC. Long rods were attached to the controls, extending through the driver's hatch, allowing the driver to operate the APC while sitting on top of the vehicle. This reduced his vulnerability to road mines, but exposed him to enemy weapons fire. The extended controls made the steering overly sensitive; unexpected bumps and drop-offs in terrain could throw the driver from the vehicle. *See also* **M-113.**

Longhairs *see* **Hippie**

Longhouse Montagnard communal house. The longhouse was 40–100 meters long, made of bamboo, had a heavy thatched roof, and housed several families. Usually the families that resided in the longhouse were related either by blood or marriage. The house was built on stilts, raising it several feet in the air. The raised house was drier during the rainy season and the area beneath the house was used for storage (animal pens, wood, etc.). The raised house also had the advantage of protecting the residence from snakes and small animals which were abundant in the jungles where the Montagnards lived. *See also* **Montagnards, Happy House.**

Look Long, Duck Back *see* **Luc Luong Dac Biet**

Looking for Golf Balls... "Looking for golf balls in the field" was a euphemism used by American women in the field (Red Cross or Special Services) meaning having to go to the bathroom. ARC or Special Services workers in the field were not always privy to latrine facilities, and had to do as the troops did; wherever and whenever possible, bush or no bush. *See also* **Special Services, Donut Dollies.**

Loose Threads *see* **Cables**

LORAN *see* **Pave Nail**

LORAPL *see* **Long-Range Planning Task Group**

Lost Unit Triangulation *see* Marking Mission

Lost-in-the-Woods   Army nickname for Fort Leonardwood, Missouri.

LOTS *see* LOB Base

Loud and Clear *see* Lima Charlie

Louies (Spit)   GI slang for "spit," or saliva, especially that less than clear variety, complete with green, embedded iridescent modules.

Louisville Slugger *see* Operation Louisville Slugger

Love by Nature, Live by...   *see* Death on Call

Lovett, Robert *see* Wise Old Men

Low Altitude Parachute Extraction System (LAPES)   Air Force system used to deliver supplies to combat bases in the field without the aircraft having to land. The supplies were loaded onto pallets. The supply plane flew five feet above the landing strip at 130 knots. A parachute attached to the pallet was deployed at the rear cargo door of the plane pulling the pallet out, and slowing its fall and slide. This system allowed bases under fire, or without adequate runways, to receive larger resupply shipments than would normally be possible by helicopter or smaller aircraft. The system was used for a time to resupply Khe Sanh, but was not as productive as direct parachute drops. The system was an adaptation of the Army's Low Level Extraction System used by the C-2. *See also* LOLEX, GPES, CDS.

Low Level Extraction System (LOLEX) Cargo delivery system developed by the Army for use with their C-2 Caribou transports. The system was designed to provide cargo resupply in the field when a cargo plane was unable to land due to hostile fire or inadequacies of the landing strip. The cargo was loaded on a large pallet with a drag chute attached. The pilot would approach the landing strip at an altitude of 3–5 feet at slow speed; the chute would be deployed behind the aircraft. Once the chute filled with air it snatched the pallet off the cargo ramp of the aircraft where it would slide to a halt. The LOLEX system was adapted by the Air Force for their C-130s and was called "LAPES." *See also* LAPES, GPES.

Low Light TV (LLTV)   Night observa-

tion device used by Air Force and Navy surveillance and reconnaissance aircraft during the Vietnam War. The LLTV system magnified and intensified the existing light conditions to create a real time picture that was displayed on a small monitor carried in the aircraft. The enhanced night picture was used for targeting and surveillance. Several different aircraft carried versions of the Low Light TV system. LLTV was used in conjunction with detection systems such as SLAR, FLIR, ignition detectors, other NOD devices and sensors to monitor and select enemy targets along the Ho Chi Minh Trail. *See also* Black Spot, VAH-21, Electronic Sensors, Commando Hunt, SLAR, FLIR.

Low Quarters   Standard military shoes. The black, lace tie shoes were standard issue in all branches of the service.

Lowboy Trailer *see* M-123 Tractor

LP *see* Observation Post

LP Bladder *see* Collapsible Canteen

LPA *see* Attack Transport Ship

LPD *see* Amphibious Transport Dock

LPD-9 *see* USS Denver

LPH (Assault Hospital Ship)   Navy ship that provided medical services to the units of an amphibious assault group. Initial treatment took place on board the ship with the more serious cases being transported to other hospital facilities, either land based hospitals or hospital ships such as the USS *Repose* or *Sanctuary*.

LPH-4 *see* USS Boxer

LPH-5 *see* USS Princeton

LPH-8 *see* USS Valley Forge

LPH-10 *see* USS Tripoli

LRP *see* Long-Range Reconnaissance Patrol

LRP Rations *see* LRRP Rations

LRRP *see* Long-Range Reconnaissance Patrol

LRRP Rations (LRP Rations, Long-Range Patrol Rations, Long Rats, Lurp Rations)   Special freeze-dried and dehydrated rations issued to Long-Range Reconnaissance Patrol units. The rations were lighter and easier to carry than standard C-rations and left no waste that the enemy could use to make booby traps. The meals could be consumed dry, but water greatly improved the taste of the dehydrated food, and hot water was most effective for softening the food. A full LRRP meal included extra items similar to C-rations and weighed less than 12 ounces. LRRP rations or "long rats" were also used by other units that operated on long extended patrol where resupply would be difficult or would affect the success of the mission. By '71 Lurp rations were generally available to most units in the Army. Lurp rations were tastier than their C-ration counterparts and were of much more recent vintage. They included such meals as chicken stew, spaghetti with meat sauce, chicken with rice, beef stew, and chili with beans. The meals came packaged in a watertight, OD green plastic bag and included a candy wafer bar of chocolate, coconut or vanilla. The candy bars were nicknamed "John Wayne Bars" by the GIs. Some Lurp meals also included an orange flavored, high energy "cornflake" bar, similar to a modern-day granola bar. The cornflake bar had such "appeal" that it was seldom eaten. Long rats were packaged with the same accessory packet as the boxed C-rations. *See also* C-Rations, ARVN Long Rats.

LSA *see* **Lubricant, Small Arms or Logistic Support Area**

LSD *see* **Lysergic Acid, Hallucinogens, Landing Ship Dock**

LSI (Landing Ship, Infantry) Armored ships used to land infantry during amphibious operations. The French and Vietnamese navies made use of LSIs for command and support duties during river and coastal operations in Vietnam. The large landing ships were armed with 3-inch and 40mm cannons and machine guns, and were usually used as the command center during operations. The LSI came in two variations: LSSL (Landing Ship, Support, Large) and the LSIL (Landing Ship, Infantry, Large). *See also* **LSIL, LSSL.**

LSIL (Landing Ship, Infantry, Large) American made troop landing ship used by the French and Vietnamese navies as a command and fire support ship for riverine operations. The 393-ton LSIL could make 12 knots and was armed with 3-inch, 40mm and 20mm cannons. Although the ship was designed to land up to 76 troops, it was primarily used as a command and fire vessel.

LSM (Landing Ship, Medium) American made landing ship used for the transport and landing of troops during amphibious operations. The French and Vietnamese used the LSM primarily as a cargo vessel operating along the coast of Vietnam. The 1,905-ton LSM was 206 feet long, could make 12 knots and was armed with two 40mm and four 20mm cannons. The LSM could transport 400 troops or 250 tons of cargo and was equipped with two large bow doors that opened on beaching to allow access to the ship's storage bay.

LSMR *see* **Landing Ship, Medium Rocket**

LSO (Landing Signal Officer) Officer who stood on the deck of an aircraft carrier and guided landing aircraft during their final approach to the carrier deck. His job has been mostly replaced by automatic mirrors and electronic landing sights.

LSSB *see* **Light SEAL Support Boat**

LSSL (Landing Ship Support, Large) American made landing ships used by the French and Vietnamese navies in Vietnam. The LSSL was used as a command and fire support ship during riverine operations. The 385-ton LSSL was 137 feet long, could make 15 knots, and was armed with a 3-inch forward gun, three 40mm and four 20mm cannons and could transport sixty combat troops.

LST (Landing Ship, Tank; Ts) Navy landing ships originally designed to transport and land armored vehicles during amphibious operations. Several LSTs were refitted for riverine operations and included extra boat cranes, a helo landing deck, and updated communications and navigational equipment. The 4,080-ton LST, nicknamed "Ts," was capable of 11 knots and was armed with eight 40mm cannons. The ship served as a mobile base for PBRs operating as part of Operation Game Warden, each ship supporting up to 30 patrol boats. Other converted LSTs served as motorized barracks and river craft repair ships. American riverine forces made extensive use of the LST as did the Navy's logistics support operations in I Corps. *See also* **TF 115, Market Time, Game Warden, ARL, APB.**

Lt Col *see* **Lieutenant Colonel**

LtG *see* **Lieutenant General**

LTH *see* **Bad Paper**

LTL *see* **Highways**

Lubricant, Small Arms (LSA) Lubricant extensively used in the M-16 rifle to keep the bolt from jamming. *See also* **M-16 Rifle.**

Luc Luong Dac Biet (LLDB, Tony-the-Tiger Patch, VNSF, SVNSF, ARVNSF, ARVN Special Forces) Vietnamese name for the South Vietnamese Special Forces. The unit patch for the LLDB featured a picture of "Tony the Tiger," of cereal box fame, with a red polka dot scarf around his neck and an opened parachute behind him. The LLDB were trained by the CIA and USSFs. The LLDB worked extensively with the Phoenix Program to identify and eliminate the VCI. Some GIs claimed that LLDB stood for "Look Long, Duck Back." Some GIs perceived the ARVN attitude towards combat with the enemy as being "very cautious" about engaging into combat. *See also* **Biet-Dong-Quan, ARVN.**

Luc Luong Dai Doan Ket (Greater Unity Force) Catholic organization founded in SVN in '54 by Father Hoang Quynh, whose members primarily consisted of refugees and transplanted Catholics from North Vietnam. Thousands of Catholics fled to South Vietnam after the defeat of the French in Indochina in '54. The Luc Luong Dai Doan Ket was extremely anticommunist and anti–Buddhist and strongly supported the Diem regime. Under Diem most of the upper civil service and military positions were filled by Catholics. This created resentment among the Buddhists who lacked representation in the Diem government. The relocated northern Catholics, as a group, tended to be less educated and more agrarian oriented, settling away from the large cities. *See also* **Southern Catholic Laity.**

Luc Quan *see* **ARVN**

Lucifer Match (Friction Detonator) A wooden stemmed friction match. Often used by the Viet Cong to make small, homemade antipersonnel mines. The match was positioned in such a way that a friction plate of metal or bamboo scraped against the head of the match ignited it, causing the explosive charge in the mine to detonate. A very simple detonating device and very effective if the match could be kept dry. *See also* **Booby Trap.**

Lucky Stars of the 61st Aviation Company *see* **61st Aviation Company**

Lucky Towel (GI Towel; Towel, OD; Go-to-Hell Rag, Sweat Towel) Standard issue to all American troops in Vietnam was the "Towel, OD." The OD green (22 × 44 inches before shrinkage) terry cloth towel was used at base camps and REMF facilities for the purpose for which it was designed. But for the field grunt the towels fell into other uses. Grunts wore the towels around their necks to wipe the sweat away as they humped the boonies and ease the bite of rucksack straps. Towels shaded the back of the neck in 103-degree heat and at night provided a small screen from mosquitos and other pests. Many GIs were superstitious about their "lucky towel" and felt naked and vulnerable without it.

Lucrative Targets *see* **Luctars**

Luctars (Lucrative Targets) Navy pilot slang for "lucrative targets." A lucrative target was loosely defined as enemy targets of opportunity that were readily accessible to U.S. aircrews. Targets such as truck convoys out in the open or traveling the roads by day, uncamouflaged truck parks or railroad cars and other relatively "easy" targets.

Lug-a-Lug *see* **Blivet**

Luke the Gook *see* **Enemy, The**

Luke's Castle *see* **1st Infantry Division Fire Bases**

Lunar New Year *see* **Tet**

Lunch, BA 609 *see* **Operation Menu Targets**

Lurp Rations *see* **LRRP Rations**

Lurps *see* **Long-Range Reconnaissance Patrol**

LVT (Landing Vehicle Tracked, Amtrac) Marine amphibious cargo tractors used to transport personnel and or equipment. The vehicles were originally designed to move troops and equipment between landing ships and beach landing zones, but were employed offensively by the Marines for river and coastal operations, and base security sweeps. Four variants of the LVTP-5 were used by the Marines in Vietnam. The

LVTP served as a personnel/cargo transport, and as a command vehicle. The LVTE was an engineering vehicle fitted with a plow/dozer blade. The LVTR was used as a maintenance and Amtrac retriever, and the LVTH was equipped with a turret mounted 105mm howitzer. The bottom of the LVTP was lightly armored and susceptible to mine damage, and the vehicle's fuel tanks were located in the floor. Because of the fire danger combat troops normally rode on the outside of the vehicle. The LVTs were usually armed with a combination of .30cal, .50cal, and M-60 machine guns. *See also* **LVTP-5, LVTH-6, LVTR, LVTE, LVT-4.**

LVT-4 (LVTA-4) American-made armored amphibious landing vehicle used for riverine operations by the French in Indochina. Two versions of the LVT were used by the French. The 16-ton LVT-4 was the standard transport and could carry thirty troops; it was armed with .30cal and .50cal machine guns and was equipped with a rear ramp for access to its interior. The 18-ton LVTA-4 had an open turret mounting a 75mm howitzer and one .50cal machine gun, and was used for fire support. *See also* **LVT.**

LVTA-4 *see* **LVT-4**

LVTE (E-1, Potato Digger, Landing Vehicle Tracked Engineer) Marine amphibious tractor used as an engineering vehicle. The LVTE was an LVTP-5 fitted with a moveable, pointed plow/dozer blade, and was used for clearing mines. LVTEs were used by the Marines in Vietnam. The blade of the plow had a row of tines that looked like huge teeth. With a pair of eyes painted on the plow blade, the tracked carriers looked like huge monsters with eyes and teeth. The painted face gave the LVTE a unique and memorable personality. The amtrac was nicknamed the "E-1" and the "Potato Digger." *See also* **LVT.**

LVTE Engineering Track *see* **LVTP-5**

LVTH Howitzer Track *see* **LVTP-6**

LVTH-6 (How-Six, Landing Vehicle Tracked Howitzer, H-6) Marine version of the LVT-5 with a turret mounted 105mm howitzer. The LVTH-6, nicknamed the "H-6," or "How-Six," provided the Marine Amphibious Tractor Battalion with organic direct/indirect fire support. *See also* **LVT.**

LVTP-5 (LVT, Amtrac[k], Amphibious Landing Vehicle, P-5s, LVTP-CMD) U.S. Marine, amphibious tracked personnel carrier, used to transport and land supplies and personnel. Officially known as a "Landing Vehicle, Tracked Personnel." The LVTP was lightly armored, fully tracked, and armed with a machine gun. The track could carry 6–9 tons of cargo or 25–34 combat troops. Access to the cargo/passenger compartment was through a large hatch at the front of the vehicle covered by a drop down ramp. The LVTP could be outfitted as an ambulance/aid station. Equipped with medical equipment and medics, it had a 12-litter capacity. The LVTP-CMDs were equipped with additional radio equipment and used as mobile command posts. The LVTs carried nicknames such as the P-5s, Hogs, Amtracs, and Gators. *See also* **AMCRASH, LVT.**

LVTP-CMD *see* **LVTP-5**

LVTR (R-1 Amtrac, Landing Vehicle Tracked Retriever) Marine amphibious tractor used for maintenance and retrieval of the LVTPs. The LTVR was a modified LVTP-5 fitted with booms, towing, and repair equipment, and used to support LTVs in the field. The LVTR was nicknamed the "R-1," and operated in the field with a large spare parts inventory. *See also* **LVT.**

LWL *see* **Limited War Laboratory**

LWR *see* **WR-300**

Lychee *see* **Dragon Fruit**

Lynx II Armored Car *see* **Armored Cars**

Lysergic Acid (LSD, Acid, Lysergic Acid Diethylamide 25) Psychedelic drug of the '60s hippie generation. Caused strange and bizarre hallucinations with gradually increasing episodes of schizophrenia. In the mid-60s Timothy Leary was one of the main advocates for using LSD to create a spiritual revolution within the user. LSD was originally used in clinical research. The drug was relatively easy to produce and it soon found its way to that segment of society that was looking for a better life and enlightenment through drugs. LSD was outlawed in California in October '66. The drug continued to be illegally manufactured and distributed, some finding its way to U.S. troops in Vietnam. *See also* **Leary, Timothy.**

Lysergic Acid Diethylamide 25 *see* Lysergic Acid

LZ *see* **Landing Zone, Fire Base**

LZ Aloui   LZ used by the ARVN Task Force during Operation Lam Son 719, the '71 Laos Incursion. Aloui was located about 35kms from the old Marine combat base at Khe Sanh, and just north of Highway 9. *See also* **Operation Lam Son 719.**

LZ Baldy   Large U.S. fire support base located 33kms south of Da Nang and 28kms east of An Hoa along Highway 1.

LZ Barboa   Temporary LZ used by elements of the 1st Cavalry Division during their '67 campaign in the Ia Drang Valley. A battery of 105mm howitzers was inserted into the LZ to support the Cav's operations. *See also* **Ia Drang.**

LZ Bird   Located 45kms northeast of An Khe in the Kim Son Valley, just west of the Crow's Foot in Binh Dinh Province, II Corps. The LZ was located on the valley floor near the village of Phu Xuan along the Song Lon River. Elements of the 1st Air Cav assaulted into the area to establish the LZ for operations against a large NVA/VC force in the valley.

LZ Blackbird   One of several LZs used during Operation Jackstay during March '66 by elements of the Marine Special Landing Force. The LZ was located 8kms northwest of Can Gio in the center of the Long Thanh Peninsula, in the Rung Sat Special Zone, III Corps. *See also* **Operation Jackstay.**

LZ Bluejay   *see*   **Operation Tailwind**

LZ Cates   LZ used during Operation Pegasus in '68, the relief of the Khe Sanh. Cates was located east of Khe Sanh Combat Base and north of Highway 9. The LZ was used by elements of the 5th Battalion/7th Cavalry/1st Cavalry Division.

LZ Cobra   LZ Cobra was used as a fire support base by batteries of the 2d/17th Arty and 2d/19th Arty during operations conducted by elements of the 1st Cavalry Division. The LZ was located in the Vinh Thanh Valley, 20kms northeast of An Khe and 32kms northwest of Phu Cat.

LZ Crow   One of several LZs used by the Marine SLF during Operation Jackstay in March '66 during operations in the RSSZ. LZ Crow was located on the eastern shore of the Song Soi Rap River, 12kms south-southeast of Nha Be. *See also* **Operation Jackstay.**

LZ Delta   LZ used by the ARVN Task Force during Operation Lam Son 719, the incursion into Laos. LZ Delta was located in Laos about 20 kms southwest of Khe Sanh, and south of Highway 9. *See also* **Lam Son 719.**

LZ Dog   Temporary LZ used by elements of the 1st Cavalry Division during operations in the Bong Son Valley in early '66.

LZ Eagle   LZ established during Operation Nathan Hale, near the village of Trung Luong, northwest of Tuy Hoa, II Corps.

LZ English (LZ English North)   Base camp for the 503d Infantry/173d Airborne Brigade, '69–'71. The camp was located about 10kms west of the coast near the village of Hoai Nhon (Bong Son), 77kms north of Qui Nhon. LZ English North was located 4kms farther north of LZ English and was the base camp for the 4th Battalion/503d Infantry.

LZ English North   *see*   **LZ English**

LZ Hope   LZ used by the ARVN Task Force during Operation Lam Son 719 in '71. The LZ was located 50kms west of KSCB, and 3kms northeast of Tchepone, Laos. The LZ was used to land ARVN troops attacking Tchepone, an NVA logistics center and feed point for the Ho Chi Minh Trail. *See also* **Operation Lam Son 719.**

LZ Hotel   LZ used by the ARVN Task Force during Operation Lam Son 719, the '71 incursion into Laos. LZ Hotel was located in Laos about 12kms southwest of Khe Sanh, south of Highway 9. *See also* **Lam Son 719.**

LZ Jack   LZ established in the Ho Bo Woods by elements of the 1st Infantry Division during Operation Crimp, in January '66. *See also* **Operation Crimp.**

LZ Jane   Temporary fire base established by elements of the 501st Infantry on a small hill outside of Hue, near the village of Hai Lang.

LZ Jenny   LZ used by elements of the 327th Infantry during Operation Hawthorne. The LZ was located north of

Tuomorong, at the base of the mountain. *See also* **Operation Hawthorne.**

LZ Kelly (FSB Kelly) LZ Kelly functioned as a fire support base for elements of the 2d Battalion/12th Cavalry. LZ Kelly was located at Loc Ninh, 110kms north of Saigon in Binh Long Province, III Corps.

LZ Lima LZ used by the 1st Air Cav, located 16kms east of An Khe at the junction of Highway 19 and the northern road to Vinh Thanh in Happy Valley (Vinh Thanh Valley).

LZ Lima Zulu Hastily established LZ, about 35kms north of Kontum, used as a fire base by elements of the 2d Battalion/30th Artillery. The battalion was part of the 52d Artillery Group, during Operation Hawthorne One in June '66. *See also* **Operation Hawthorne.**

LZ Liz LZ used by the ARVN Task Force during their '71 Laos Incursion, Operation Lam Son 719. LZ Liz was located in Laos about 44kms west of Khe Sanh and south of Highway 9.

LZ Lolo LZ used by the ARVN Task Force during their '71 Laos Incursion, Operation Lam Son 719. LZ Lolo was about 38kms west of Khe Sanh. *See also* **Lam Son 719.**

LZ Mary LZ used by elements of the 1st Squadron/9th Cavalry Regiment/1st Cavalry Division, during the Battle of the Ia Drang, October '65. The LZ was located 55kms southwest of Pleiku, II Corps, and 5kms from the Cambodian border. The 1st/9th was lifted in at night, set up and sprung a night ambush on NVA units attempting to retreat back into sanctuaries in Cambodia. The night lift and subsequent reinforcement of the 1st/9th Cavalry represented the first such night helimobile activity for the 1st Cav in their early history in Vietnam. *See also* **Battle of Ia Drang.**

LZ Mike Temporary LZ used by the 1st Battalion/7th Cavalry during Operation Pegasus in '68. The LZ was located south of Highway 9. *See also* **Operation Pegasus.**

LZ Montezuma Originally the base camp for 3d Bn/7th U.S. Marines located at Duc Pho, in Quang Ngai Province, I Corps. The Marines later moved further north into I Corps and the base was later occupied by

2d Brigade/1st Cavalry Division in February '67. Later the base was taken over by the 3d Brigade/4th Infantry Division. *See also* **Operation Lejeune, Duc Pho.**

LZ Phillips Temporary fire base which was located in Cambodia, established by elements of the 4th Infantry Division in '70 during the Cambodian Incursion.

LZ Red Devil Fire base used by elements of the 1st Brigade/5th Infantry Division (Mechanized), established in their AO near Quang Tri, I Corps.

LZ Robin Marine LZ used during Operation Pegasus, the relief of Khe Sanh. LZ Robin was located east of Khe Sanh, and northwest of Highway 9. LZ Robin was also the name of an LZ used by the Marine SLF during Operation Jackstay in March '66 conducted in the Rung Sat Special Zone, southeast of Saigon. During Jackstay, LZ Robin was located about 5kms west of Can Gio and 1km north of the beach. *See also* **Operation Pegasus, Operation Jackstay.**

LZ Savoy LZ located next to the U.S. Special Forces CIDG camp located at Vinh Thanh, II Corps.

LZ Snapper LZ located south of Khe Sanh and used by elements of the 1st Cavalry Division during Operation Pegasus. The 1st/8th and the 1st/12th Cavalry established Snapper as the last LZ in a string of LZs used to support the relief of Khe Sanh. *See also* **Operation Pegasus.**

LZ Sparrow One of the LZs established as part of Operation Jackstay in March '66 by elements of the Marine SLF on Long Thanh Peninsula in the Rung Sat Special Zone, southeast of Saigon. The LZ was located 1km north of the beach and 2kms west of Can Gio. *See also* **Operation Jackstay.**

LZ Stud (Ca Lu) LZ established in March '68, near the village of Ca Lu, east of Highway 9, east of Khe Sanh in I Corps. LZ Stud became the jump-off point for elements of the 1st Cav during Operation Pegasus.

LZ Ten Alpha Small abandoned U.S. airstrip which in May '66, during Operation Paul Revere, became the site of a major victory for elements of the U.S. 35th Infantry against the NVA. Five entrenched, and working, 12.7mm heavy machine guns were captured by American troops that CA'ed into the area. The NVA attempted to recapture the guns using an infantry battalion, and failed. The 35th suffered heavy casualties, but did not give up the captured guns.

LZ Thor   LZ used during Operation Pegasus, the relief of Khe Sanh. The LZ was used by elements of the 2d Battalion/7th Cavalry/1st Infantry Division. LZ Thor was located just south of Highway 9.

LZ Tom   LZ used during the relief of Khe Sanh, Operation Pegasus. The LZ was located southeast of Khe Sanh, and used by elements of the 2d Battalion/5th Cavalry/1st Cavalry Division.

LZ Vicki   Established in the A Shau Val-ley to support ground operations during Operation Delaware, April '68.

LZ Wharton   LZ used during the relief of Khe Sanh, Operation Pegasus. The LZ was used by the 2d Battalion/5th Cavalry/1st Cavalry Division, and was located southeast of Khe Sanh.

LZ Xray   LZ used by elements of the 1st Cavalry Division during the battle of the Ia Drang Valley in October '65. LZ Xray was located 57kms southwest of Pleiku, 10kms from the Cambodian border in the foothills of the Chu Pong Massif. Elements of the U.S. 5th and 7th Cavalry engaged NVA units attempting to retreat back across the border into sanctuaries in Cambodia. *See also* **Battle of Ia Drang.**

M

M & Ms (tm)   *see*   **SP Pack**

M Force   *see*   **Mobile Strike Force**

M-1 81mm Mortar   *see*   **M-29 81mm Mortar**

M-1 Carbine (M-2 Carbine, M-1A1 Carbine)   American made, .30cal, vintage WWII light rifle (carbine). The M-1 was developed as a carbine to be used by paratroops and other troops who did not require a full size rifle. The carbine weighed 5.5 pounds. The M-1 rifle, which was standard Army issue during WWII, weighed nearly twice as much. The M-1 Carbine had a max effective range of 250 meters, was gas operated, and was fed by a 15 or 30-round magazine. The M-1 fired only semiautomatic; the M-2 Carbine had a selector switch that enabled it to fire semi- or full automatic. Large numbers of the carbine were given to the French and ARVNs, and initially issued to the CIDGs. The M-1A1 Carbine had a folding metal stock. The carbine was popular with U.S. air and armor crews that initially did not have access to the M-16 rifle.

M-1 Helmet   *see*   **GI Helmet**

M-1 Mortar   Old version of the Ameri-can 81mm mortar, replaced by the M-29 mortar. The NVA/VC used captured M-1s as well as PRC and Soviet made 82mm mortars. *See also* **M-29.**

M-1 Rifle (Garand Rifle)   WWII standard U.S. infantry rifle that was distributed worldwide. The Garand .30cal (7.62mm) rifle was gas operated, fired semiautomatic, weighed over 10 pounds when loaded, had a maximum effective range of 460 meters, and was fed by an 8-round clip that automatically ejected out of the weapon after the last round was fired. Large quantities of the rifle were given to the French in Indochina, and later the M-1 was used to equip ARVN units. ARVN soldiers did not do well with the rifle; it was heavy and over 43 inches long, compared to the ARVN soldier who averaged only 64 inches tall. ARVN M-1 rifles and carbines were eventually replaced with the M-16 rifle. The M-1 was the standard training rifle for U.S. troops until replaced by the M-14 rifle in the early sixties.

M-1A1 Carbine   *see*   **M-1 Carbine**

M-1A1 SMG (Thompson Submachine Gun)   U.S. made .45cal submachine gun. The gun was first manufactured in 1928, with the military version, the M-1A1 entering service during WWII. The weapon could fire from a 100-round drum or a 20- or 30-round magazine, to an effective range of 50 meters. Most "Thompsons" used in Vietnam were fed by the 20- or 30-round magazine. The gun weighed 11.8 pounds when loaded (20-round magazine). The Thompson used the same ammunition as the M-3 Grease Gun and the .45cal Colt pistol. The gun was used by some rural South Vietnamese defense forces and captured weapons were used by the VC. *See also* **M-3A1 SMG.**

M-2 Bounding Mine *see* **Bouncing Betty**

M-2 Carbine *see* **M-1 Carbine**

M-2 HMG (.50, Fifty-Cal, Browning Heavy Machine Gun, 50 Cal) U.S. heavy machine gun, air cooled and belt fed from a metallic link belt. The gun weighed about 83 pounds (without tripod), with a maximum effective range of 1,800 meters at a sustained rate of fire of 50–400 rounds per minute. The gun was used tripod-mounted (14-pound tripod) or pedestal- or ring-mounted on APCs, jeeps, trucks, tanks and helicopters. Normally every fifth round of the machine gun's ammo belt was a tracer round; tracer rounds helped the gunner more accurately place his fire. The .50cal required two hands to aim the gun. The "butterfly" shaped trigger was located between the two hand grips at the rear of the weapon. The butterfly was depressed once for single shots, or held down for automatic fire.

M-2 Mortar *see* **M-19 60mm Mortar**

M-2A17 Flamethrower (Zippo) U.S. portable flamethrower. The man-packed "zippo" weighed about 43 pounds, and was filled with a napalm mixture. The flame range was from 20–45 meters depending on the thickness of the napalm mixture. *See also* **M-67A2 Flame Tank.**

M2M *see* **May Second Movement**

M-3 Airborne Personnel Detector *see* **XM-3**

M-3 APD *see* **XM-3**

M-3 SMG *see* **M-3A1 SMG**

M-3 TAP Suit The M-3 Toxicological Agents Protective suit was used by some Army EOD teams. The suit provided protection from chemical agents in hazardous

areas. The suits were awkward to use and very hot, requiring help to get into and out of. Outer coveralls were used to provide some cooling for the suit. The suit saw limited service in Vietnam.

M-3A1 SMG (Grease Gun, Burp Gun, M-3) U.S. made, .45cal submachine gun. The gun, which used a 30-round magazine, was first produced in '42 for use in WWII, and later was dispersed worldwide. The M-3 was a favorite of armor crews because they yielded fair firepower in a small package. The weapon was good at close range but lacked accuracy and stopping power beyond 100 meters. The gun acquired its nickname, the "grease gun," because it resembled a tool used for injecting grease into vehicle axles. Also called a "burp gun" because of its distinctive sound. *See also* **Submachine Gun.**

M-4 Tank (Sherman) American made, WWII vintage medium tank used by the French during the First Indochina War. The 30-ton Sherman had a maximum speed of 24mph which reduced its usefulness in the swift flowing guerrilla war in Indochina. The Sherman was armed with a 75mm gun and three .30cal machine guns, and operated with a five-man crew. The ARVNs only had a few of the Shermans in their inventory after the French departed Vietnam, and those few Shermans were quickly replaced by the new and faster M-24 light tank. *See also* **M-24.**

M-5 Grenade Launcher (XM-5, Thumper, Chunker) The M-5 was a turreted, single barrel, link belt fed, 40mm grenade launcher. The turret was fitted under the nose of the helicopter gunship and was aimed and fired by the pilot. The round turret allowed the launcher tube to be swiveled and pivoted up and down allowing the pilot to fire on targets his ship was not facing directly. The M-5 was fitted on some Cobra and Huey gunships. The XM-5 was the experimental version. The launcher had a maximum range of 1,500 meters and was fed by a 150-round box and chute system, or a 305-round rotary drum. Max rate of fire was 220 rounds per minute. *See also* **M-75 Grenade Launcher Turret.**

M-5 Medical Kit *see* **Unit One**

M-5 Triggers (Antimotion Triggers) Antimotion switches used in U.S. booby traps. The switch, which was wired to a detonator, was attached to the item to be booby-trapped. When the item was moved the switch activated the detonator, exploding the charge/booby trap. *See also* **Booby Trap.**

M-6 Blasting Caps *see* **Blasting Caps**

M-6 Quad MG *see* **XM-6 Machine Gun**

M-7 CS Hand Grenade *see* **Grenades, Gas**

M-7A1 Flame Gun *see* **M-67A2**

M08 MMG *see* **Type 24 MMG**

M-8 Armored Car (Greyhound) U.S. WWII vintage, six wheel, light armored car. First produced in '42 it came in turret and nonturret versions, armed with one or more of the following: 37mm gun, .30cal or .50cal machine gun. The M-8 was used in Vietnam by the French and early in the war by the South Vietnamese military. The M-8 "Greyhound" had a maximum speed of 55mph, and a range of 550kms. *See also* **Armored Cars.**

M-8 Smoke Grenade *see* **Grenades, Smoke**

M-8A1 Dozer Blade *see* **Dozer Tank**

M-14 Antipersonnel Mine *see* **M-16 Antipersonnel Mine, Toe-Poppers**

M-14 Rifle Standard U.S. infantry rifle from 1959 to 1966, when it began to be replaced by the M-16. The M-14 fired 7.62mm ammunition, was gas operated, magazine fed, with an effective range of 460 meters. It weighed 12 pounds when loaded with a 20-round magazine. The rifle was used at U.S. training centers during the VNW, and found some use with the Army in Vietnam as a sniper weapon. U.S. Marines used the M-14 early in the Vietnam War when the M-16s they were issued repeatedly jammed and proved hazardous to use in the field. The problem with the M-16 was subsequently corrected, but many Marines still favored the M-14, even after the M-16 became the standard rifle of the Army and the Marine Corps. *See also* **M-16.**

M-14 Sniper Rifle (XM-21, M-21, ART Scope) The Army began using dedicated sniper teams in '69. The Army snipers were equipped with the M-14 semiautomatic rifle and an adjustable ranging telescope (ART). The M-16 and other scope combinations were tried but the M-14/ART, designated the XM-21, proved the best combination for the Army. The ART scope was adjustable from 3–9 power and provided accuracy out to 900 meters. After field trials the XM-21 was designated the M-21. Army night sniper teams consisted of four men: a shooter, spotter and two soldiers for security. Army snipers trained at Ft Benning, Georgia, and in SVN at the 9th Infantry Division sniper school, the "Reliable Academy." *See also* **Sniper; Waldron, Sergeant A.F., III.**

M-15 Land Mine U.S. land mine used as part of perimeter defenses at some American bases.

M-15A1 Semitrailer Lowboy *see* **M-123 Tractor**

M-16 Antipersonnel Mine (M-14 Antipersonnel Mine) A bounding mine (Bouncing Betty) used by U.S. forces in Vietnam. The 8.25-pound mine was cylinder shaped, 4 inches in diameter, and almost 8 inches high. Three short prongs extending from the top of the mine served as the triggering mechanism. Once tripped a small charge launched the mine into the air; at a height of 3–4 feet the main charge of the mine exploded, spraying deadly fragments for several meters. The M-14 was a much smaller version of the M-16 mine and weighed a little over 3 ounces. *See also* **Bouncing Betty.**

M-16 Rifle (Mattel Toy Rifle, AR-15, Black Magic, Widow Maker, M-16A2, Black Rifle) Replaced the M-14 as the standard U.S. infantry rifle in '67. The black plastic and steel M-16A1 was a 5.56mm assault rifle, automatic, 7.6 pounds in weight with a 20–30 round magazine, and an effective range of 460 meters. The 3,250fps muzzle velocity caused the bullet to spin, greatly increasing the tissue damage done to impacted body areas. Early versions (M-16) used in Vietnam were prone to jamming and were eventually recalled and reworked using a chrome chamber and buffer system; the powder used in the 5.56mm cartridges was also changed and bottles of LSA were liberally issued with each weapon. Reworking and frequent cleaning improved the weapon's effectiveness and serviceability. Developed as the CAR-15, the rifle was first tested in '62. Production deliveries to the field began in '64 under the new designation of M-16. The reworked M-16A1 became the standard rifle of the U.S. military. The Air Force versions of the M-16A1 were designated as the AR-15. The M-16A2 was an improved version of the original M-16A1 and entered service in the early '80s. The CAR-16 was a slightly shortened version of the M-16. The rifle was nicknamed the Widow Maker, Mattel Toy Rifle, Black Rifle and Black Magic. *See also* **CAR-15, Armalite.**

M-16A2 *see* **Armalite**

M-17 Protective Mask (Gas Mask, XM-28 Protective Mask) Standard U.S. Army gas mask. The mask was widely used in Vietnam as protection against CS gas used by the Army in flushing the enemy from bunkers and tunnel systems. On occasion the enemy would use CS gas against U.S. units. If the mask filter element was wet no air could filter through, causing the outside air to be leaked into the mask. Starting in '68, the Army began replacing the mask with the XM-28, a more compact and effective mask that was less susceptible to damage by moisture. The M-17 mask carrier was worn strapped around the waist, secured by a leg strap; the XM-28 carrier fit into the large pocket of the jungle fatigues. *See also* **CS Gas.**

M-18 Claymore Mine (Claymore Mine) The American M-18A1 Claymore was a directional, 3.5-pound antipersonnel mine, approx. $8.5 \times 3.5 \times 1.3$ inches thick and slightly curved, containing 600–700 metal balls in a plastic box and 1.5 pounds of C-4 explosive. The kill range of the blast was about 50 meters, within a 60-degree arc. The M-18 was usually electrically detonated; multiple claymores could be detonated with det cord. U.S. troops used the claymores around defensive positions and in ambush sites. The M-18 kit included an M-7 bandolier containing the claymore, an M-57 pulse firing device (clacker), M-6 electric blasting cap, tape, 100 feet of wire and a small bag to carry it all in. *See also* **VC Claymore, Claymore Bag, Gravel Mine, Clacker, Snatch Mission, Mouse Trap Detonator.**

M-18 Smoke Grenade *see* **Grenades, Smoke**

M-18A1 Antipersonnel Mine Carrier *see* **Claymore Bag**

M-18A1 RCL (57mm RCL) U.S. made 57mm recoilless rifle primarily used by the ARVNs. The 57mm RCL weighed almost 45 pounds and was usually found mounted on an APC or tripod mounted for base defense. *See also* **Recoilless Rifle.**

M-19 Mortar (60mm Mortar, M-2 Mortar, 60mm Tubes, Free-Tubing) U.S. light mortar, smooth bore, drop fired and muzzle loaded. Range: 1,800 meters; weight: about 45 pounds. Prior to the Vietnam War the M-19 was the standard company support mortar, but was phased out because of its limited range. It was replaced by the M-29, 81mm mortar. The M-29 was uncomfortably heavy for humping in the field, and some units operating in the hills and jungles of Vietnam retained the M-19 for direct support at the company level. The M-19 fired HE, smoke, and illumination rounds. The M-2 was a slightly improved version. Mortars were more commonly referred to as "tubes" in the field. The tube was normally bipod and base mounted, but could be supported on the ground and hand fired in an emergency; this was known as "free-tubing."

M-20 Rocket Launcher (Super Bazooka, Type 51, 3.5-Inch Rocket Launcher) The U.S. M-20 antitank rocket launcher was an upgraded version of the WWII bazooka. The weapon fired a 3.5-inch HEAT rocket, fin stabilized, with a maximum effective range of 110 meters against armor (800 meters against soft targets). In Vietnam it was used against NVA/VC bunkers and fortifications. The firing tube broke into two pieces and weighed 12 pounds. Each rocket weighed 9 pounds. It saw limited use by FWFs and was primarily used by the Marines. The M-20 was not popular with troops in the field because of its short range, low powered warhead and overall heavy weight. The M-20 was nicknamed the "Super Bazooka." The Type 51, the PRC copy of the M-20, was used by the NVA/VC. *See also* **Light Antitank Weapon.**

M-21 *see* **M-14 Sniper Rifle**

M-22 AGM *see* **SS-11 AGM or XM-22 AGM System**

M-24 20mm Cannon *see* **XM-31 20mm Cannon Pod**

M-24 Light Tank (Chaffee) American light tank used by the French in Indochina, and later transferred to ARVN armor forces. The M-24 was developed at the end of WWII; it was armed with a 75mm gun and two .30cal machine guns. The tank normally operated with a crew of five, had a max road speed of 30mph, and a range of 160kms. The "Chaffee" was later replaced by the M-41 ("Walker Bulldog" tank) in ARVN armor units. Prior to '65 ARVN armor units carried out their operations within easy commuting range of the larger cities. *See also* **Coup Troops.**

M-24A1 Cannon *see* **SX-35 Cannon**

M26 Frag *see* **M26A1/M57**

M-26 Hand Grenade U.S. fragmentation hand grenade, weighed 1 pound, had a 40-meter burst range and a lethal radius of about 10 meters. The grenade could be thrown out to 45 meters, or with the addition of a special attachment, it could be rifle fired (rifle grenade) out to 160 meters. The M-26 was oval, or egg shaped and had a 5–7 second fuse. The acid fuse was activated by removing the safety pin and releasing the handle (spoon). The steel grenade casing covered a coil of pressed steel that broke into several hundred sharp fragments when the grenade exploded. *See also* **Hand Grenades.**

M-26 NVA Armor Group Was based along the Cambodian border in the III Corps area after '72. The group consisted of three armor battalions and a light armored reconnaissance battalion. The M-26 overran Song Be in January '75, prior to the NVA's Final Offensive in April of that year. *See also* **Final Offensive.**

M26A1/M57 Hand Grenade (M26 Frag, M57 Frag) U.S. fragmentation grenades that were widely used during the Vietnam War. The M26 was about 4 inches long and 2.25 inches in diameter, weighed nearly one pound and was egg shaped. The outer shell of the grenade was smooth. Under the shell was a spring coil that broke into many small and deadly fragments when the grenade detonated. The M26 had a delayed fuse that detonated the grenade 5–7 seconds after the handle was released. The M57 grenade was identical to the M26 except it detonated on impact. The casualty blast radius of the M26 was about 15 meters. *See also* **Hand Grenades.**

M-28 Rifle Grenade U.S. antitank, rifle grenade. The grenade was attached to the end of a rifle (M-14) and fired. The 1.5-pound grenade could be lobbed out to a distance of 90 meters. *See also* **Hand Grenades.**

M-29 81mm Mortar (81mm Mortar, 81 Mike-Mike, 81mm Tubes, M-29A1) The American standard medium mortar was the M-29. It replaced the M-1 81mm mortar. The M-29 weighed 106 pounds, with a maximum range of 4,500 meters, depending on the charge. This mortar could fire HE, WP, illumination and CS gas. Because of its weight the mortar was seldom packed into the field, and was primarily used as fire support from base camps. A self-propelled version with the mortar tube mounted inside on an APC was designated the M-125. The M-29A1 was an improved version of the M-29. HE rounds weighed 6.5 pounds. *See also* **M-125 81mm Mortar, Mortar.**

M-29C (Weasels, Crabs) American made amphibious cargo carrier which first saw service with U.S. forces during WWII and was called a "weasel." The French later acquired the cargo carriers and called them "crabs," using them for riverine operations in Indochina. The fully tracked, lightly armored crabs weighed two tons, and could transport about 1,100 pounds of cargo or personnel. The crabs worked well in the swampy areas of the Delta, but their vulnerability to enemy fire, slow speed and low cargo capacity reduced their effectiveness in the riverine war.

M-30 4.2-Inch Mortar (4.2-Inch Mortar, Four-Deuce, Four Point Twos) The U.S. M-30 was a 4.2-inch (107mm), drop fired, muzzle loaded, rifled barrel, spin stabilized, heavy mortar. The mortar round was comparable in size to the rounds fired by the 105mm howitzer. At 670 pounds the heavy mortar was used at base camps for fire support, and was assigned to the battalion level. The M-106 was a self-propelled version of the 4.2-inch mortar, which was mounted in the troop section of an M-113 APC. The Four-Deuce fired smoke, chemical, illumination and HE rounds out to a range of 6,800 meters. The typical HE round used, the M-329A2, had an 18-pound warhead. *See also* **M-106 Four Deuce.**

M33 Frag *see* **M33/M59 Fragmentation Grenade**

M33/M59 Fragmentation Grenade (M59 Frag, Baseball Grenade) U.S. fragmentation grenade used in Vietnam. The baseball shaped grenade weighed 14 ounces and was 2.5 inches in diameter and about 3.5 inches long. The outer shell of the grenade was smooth. The effective kill radius of the grenade in the open was 17 meters. The M33 used a 5–7 second delayed fuse for detonation and the M59 detonated on impact.

M-34 *see* **Grenades, White Phosphorus**

M-35 Cannon *see* **SX-35 Cannon**

M-35 CBU (Incendiary CBU) The M-35 was an Air Force cluster bomb packed with small, incendiary bomblets. When released over the target, the bomblets were dispersed over a wide area, detonating on impact, generating a small fire storm. *See also* **Fuel-Air CBU, Cluster Bomb Units.**

M-35 Truck (Deuce-and-a-Half, 2½-Ton Truck, 6 × 6, Six-By) Standard U.S. military 2½-ton cargo truck. The deuce-and-a-half had a maximum speed of 55mph, and a cargo capacity of 2.5 tons. Some were fitted with mounts for the M-60 and .50cal machine guns. Still other trucks were fitted with armor plate and used as gun trucks for base defense and convoy work. The trucks performed a multitude of functions, ferrying supplies and troops between bases and facilities. The M-35 chassis was also used for several other variants of the truck; for example, the M-49A was a 1,200-gallon tanker, the M-109A2 had a van mounted on the chassis, and the M-292A1 also was van mounted, but the sides of the van extended, increasing its size to 12 × 12 feet. *See also* **Hardened Convoy.**

M-35 Vulcan Gun Pod *see* **SUU-23**

M37 Mortar *see* **Type 53 Mortar**

M-37B1 (Three-Quarter Ton Truck, ¾-Ton Truck) U.S. ¾-ton utility truck used throughout the military. This truck, made by Dodge, had four-wheel drive and was used for a wide variety of duties.

M38 Mortar (120mm Mortar, M43 120mm Mortar, Type 55) The NVA made use of three different versions of 120mm mortar: the M38 and M43 Soviet and the PRC Type 55. The mortars had a maximum range of 5,700 meters and were fitted with a two wheel carriage which allowed the tube to be moved without disassembly. The tubes could further be broken down and man or animal packed into position. *See also* **Mortar.**

M-40 Rifle (Remington 700, Varmint) One of the high powered rifles used by American Marine sniper teams in Vietnam. The military designated M-40, was a .308cal, 7.62mm, bolt action rifle, usually fitted with a Redfield 3–9 power or a Unertl 8-power scope. Effective range was over 1,300 meters. The rifle was manufactured by the Remington Arms Company and known commercially as the Varmint. *See also* **Sniper.**

M-40A1 RCL (106mm Recoilless Rifle, 106mm RR, Big Shotgun) U.S. 106mm recoilless rifle, breech loaded, single shot gun with a maximum effective HEAT range of 1,100 meters. The gun used a 105mm round, but was more commonly referred to as the 106mm Recoilless. The gun could fire the APERS-T antipersonnel round with a maximum effective range of 3,300 meters. The 17-pound HE round had a range of nearly 7,700 meters. The 462-pound gun was usually jeep or APC mounted; it had a maximum range of 8kms, and was used as a lightweight artillery piece for direct fire against enemy positions and bunkers. The 106mm RR was nicknamed the "Big Shotgun" when it was used to fire antipersonnel canister (beehive) rounds, each round containing 10,000 steel darts. *See also* **Recoilless Rifle.**

M-41 Light Tank (Walker Bulldog, Little Bulldog) Post-WWII American light tank which saw extensive service during the Korean War. The M-41 was armed with a 76mm gun, and .30cal and .50cal machine guns. The tank operated with a four man crew, had a maximum road speed of 45mph, and a range of 160kms. The M-41 was used in Vietnam to replace the M-24 light tanks in the ARVN inventory. The M-41 was originally named the "Little Bulldog," but the tank was renamed the "Walker Bulldog," in honor of General Walton W. Walker, who was killed in the Korean War.

In '72 ARVN armor units began operating with the M-48 tank. The M-41s were organized into tank squadrons as part of an armored cavalry regiment. The M-48s were organized into tank battalions.

M41 Mortar (50mm Mortar) Soviet made 50mm light mortar used by the VC. *See also* **Mortar.**

M-42 Duster (Bofors Guns, Pom-Pom Guns) Self-propelled antiaircraft tank armed with twin Bofors 40mm, AA guns. Since the NVA/VC had no aircraft operating in SVN, the Duster was used against enemy personnel and fortifications. Dusters were used for convoy duty and defensively at base camps and other security locations. The Duster turret was open topped, with low armored sides, which left the crew partially exposed to enemy fire. The turret was mounted on a modified M-41 tank chassis. Against ground targets the twin 40mm Bofors guns had a maximum effective range of 5,000 meters at 240 rounds per minute, and it was very effective in the fire suppression role. Three battalions (64 vehicles) of M-42 (Automatic Weapon, Self-Propelled) guns deployed to Vietnam. *See also* **M-55 Quad.**

M43 120mm Mortar *see* **M38 Mortar**

M43 160mm Mortar (160mm Mortar) The Soviet made 160mm mortar had a maximum range of 5,100 meters and was mounted on a two wheel carriage that allowed the tube to be moved without first disassembling it. The short range of the tube meant it had to be located fairly close to the target, but with the wheels for mobility it could be moved after several rounds were fired, and set up in a new location. The 160mm mortar was not drop fired like most mortars; instead it was breech loaded and fired like a cannon or howitzer. *See also* **Mortar.**

M-48A2 AVLB *see* **M-60 AVLB**

M-48A3 Tank (Patton Tank) Main Battle Tank used by U.S. armor forces during the VNW. The tank was officially named after General George Patton and featured a 90mm cannon, and two .50cal machine guns. The 50-ton diesel powered tank had a maximum speed of 30mph, a road range of 460kms, and operated with a four-man crew. The M-48 deployed to Vietnam organized in tank battalions and as tank companies of the armored cavalry. The M-48 was used by the Army and Marines, and in '72 two ARVN M-48 tank battalions were created from American tank assets left in Vietnam as U.S. forces were withdrawn. The tanks proved effective in Vietnam, but were limited by the terrain. The enemy was able to damage the M-48, but it was difficult to destroy with the weapons available to the NVA/VC prior to '72. *See also* **M-67A3.**

M-49 Scope (Spotting Scope) Standard spotting telescope used by Marine sniper teams in Vietnam. The scope had a power of twenty and was tripod mounted. *See also* **Sniper.**

M-49A2 Tanker Truck *see* **M-35 Truck**

M-50A1 Ontos (The Thing, Self-Propelled Multiple Rifle) The Ontos was armed with six, 106mm recoilless rifles; two of the rifles could be removed and tripod mounted for ground use. The 10-ton air transportable antitank "tank" had a crew of three, and was fully tracked. The Ontos was used by the Marines for convoy security and base defense. The "Thing" was especially effective against enemy bunkers and entrenchments, but its light armor made it vulnerable to enemy fire and mines. During the reloading of the tubes the loader was fully exposed, and vulnerable to enemy fire. The Ontos' RCL tubes could elevate and depress, and had a limited traverse. Four tube-mounted .50cal spotting rifles were used for aiming the Ontos. The M-50A1 had a max speed of 30mph, and was officially designated the "M-50A1 Self-Propelled Multiple Rifle."

M-51 HRV (Heavy Recovery Vehicle) Heavy Recovery Vehicle (HRV) used by the Marines in Vietnam to support their armor operations. The M-51 was assigned to the company level and was fitted with a large towbar and a low profile crane. The M-51 was nicknamed the "Ox." The Marines scheduled the M-51 for replacement by the M-88 VTR, but the replacement process did not begin until the Marines had departed Vietnam. *See also* **M-88 VTR.**

M-52 Tractor *see* **M-123 Tractor**

M-53 155mm SPA Marine 155mm Self-Propelled Howitzer. The Korean War vintage SPA was phased out of service with the Marines in '69. Marine M-53 units in Vietnam were replaced with the M-107, 175mm SPA. Marine units in Vietnam also operated M-109 SPAs as division artillery. *See also* **M-109.**

M-54 Truck (5-Ton Truck) Standard Army 5-ton, 6 × 6 truck. Like the M-35, 2½-ton truck, the M-54 was available in several variations. The M-54 chassis was used for tankers, wreckers, vans, etc. Versions of the 5-ton capacity truck were armor-plated and sandbagged and used as convoy escorts. The engine of the M-54 was designed to operate on several different fuels (gasoline, diesel, methanol, etc.), at a max speed of about 55mph. *See also* **M-35 Truck.**

M-55 8-inch SPA Korean War vintage 8-inch Self-Propelled Howitzer used by the Marines in Vietnam. The M-55 was replaced in '67 by the M-110 8-inch Self-Propelled Howitzer. The 8-inch guns were assigned as division artillery. *See also* **M-110 8-inch SPA.**

M-55 Quad (Quad 50s) Motorized gunmount fitted with simultaneously fired, and parallel aimed .50cal machine guns. In Vietnam the Quad 50 was mounted on an M-35 truck bed, or boat deck, and was used for base camp defenses and convoy duty. The Quad 50 was sometimes permanently mounted on a ground pedestal and used for perimeter defense. The M-55s were deployed to Vietnam in four separate companies, approximately 32 Quads per company. The gun sections were divided and parceled out to provide support to various headquarters throughout Vietnam. The typical gun fired 1,800 rounds per minute to a range of 1,800 meters. M-55s were sometimes paired with M-42 Dusters to form composite batteries. *See also* **M-42 Duster.**

M-56 Harness *see* **Butt Pack**

M-56 SPAT (Scorpion SPAT, 90mm SPAT) Army 90mm self-propelled anti-tank gun, SPAT. At 6 tons, the small fully tracked gun was air transportable, but in Vietnam it was not deployed by air. The gun crew was vulnerable to enemy small arms and mortar fire. A very small shield was attached to the front of the gun, but it was totally ineffective at protecting the crew.

The M-56 had a max speed of 25mph, and operated with a four-man crew. The Scorpion was later replaced in Army units by the M-551 Sheridan tank. *See also* **M-551 ARV.**

M57 Frag *see* **M26A1/M57 Hand Grenade**

M-57 Hand Detonator *see* **Clacker**

M59 Frag *see* **M33/M59 Fragmentation Grenade**

M-60 AVLB (Armored Vehicle Launched Bridge, Scissors Bridge, M-48A2 AVLB, M-113 AVLB) Portable bridge deployed for use by armored forces. In Vietnam two versions of AVLBs were used. Both the M-60 AVLB and the M-48A2 AVLB deployed a folded 60-foot bridge. The folded bridge was carried on top of modified M-48 and M-60 tanks. The turret was replaced with a hydraulic assembly that automatically unfolded the bridge as it was deployed. The bridge could span 30 feet, and had a 60-ton capacity which could support the largest armored vehicles operating in Vietnam. The bridge was lifted back onto the tank by the same mechanism. The M-48 AVLBs were gasoline powered and were eventually phased out in favor of the diesel M-60 AVLB. An experimental version of the AVLB called the "Marginal Terrain Assault Bridge" (MTAB) was used by armored cavalry units. The experimental bridge was a smaller version of the 60-foot AVLB. The MTAB, when extended, was about 38 feet long, and it was carried and deployed by the M-113 APC. The M-113 AVLB (MTAB) deployed the bridge in a manner similar to the M-60 AVLB and could span a maximum of 30 feet. The AVLBs were sometimes referred to as "scissors bridges" or "porta-bridges." *See also* **Bailey Bridge, Balf Bridge.**

M-60 LMG (The Gun, The Pig, General Purpose Machine Gun [GPMG]) Standard U.S. general purpose light machine gun, 7.62mm, belt fed, 1,100-meter effective range, 3,700-meter max range, 23 pounds without ammo or tripod. The M-60 used disintegrating link belts and fired standard ball, tracer, armor piercing and AP incendiary cartridges, with a muzzle velocity of 2,800fps. Carried at the squad level by infantry in Vietnam, the M-60 was also mounted on vehicles and helicopters. Called "The Pig" or "The Gun" by GIs in the field because of its weight and firepower. M-60 gunners were prime targets during enemy attack because of the amount of firepower the gun could bring to bear. ARVN units began receiving the M-60 as replacements for their .30cals in '69. *See also* **M-1919A6 MMG, XM-6 Machine Gun.**

M-60 Main Battle Tank (M-60A1, M-60A2, M-60A3) U.S. main battle tank used during the '60s and early '70s, currently being replaced in front line armor units by the M-1 MBT. The M-60 MBT was not used by U.S. forces in Vietnam, but armored vehicles based on the M-60's chassis did see service in-country. The M-728 CEV and the M-60 AVLB were both used extensively by Army armor units. The M-728 was a combat engineering vehicle, and the M-60 AVLB carried and deployed a 60-foot scissors bridge. *See also* **M-728 CEV, M-60 AVLB.**

M-61 Vulcan (XM-12 Gun Pod) Version of the 20mm Vulcan cannon used on the AC-130 gunship. The M-61 was also used in the XM-12 aircraft gun pod. *See also* **SX-35, AC-130.**

M-63A1 Stoner LMG (Stoner) Light machine gun used by the U.S. Navy SEALs. The Stoner LMG used 5.56mm ammunition and was fed from a 150-round box magazine. The Stoner weighed 7.75 pounds.

M-67 RCL (90mm RCL, 90mm Recoilless Rifle) U.S. 90mm recoilless rifle, man portable, shoulder fired, breech loaded, firing a single shot HEAT round. The 35-pound gun had an effective range of 400 meters and a maximum range of 2,000 meters. The M-67 was lighter than the older 57mm RCL, and more effective against enemy targets. The M-67 was sometimes packed into the field, but it was usually brought to the field by helicopter for use by ground troops or it was mounted on a mule, jeep or APC. The gun was served by a crew of two and it was primarily used against NVA/VC bunkers and fortifications. *See also* **Recoilless Rifle.**

M-67A2 Flame Tank (Zippo Tank, Zippos, Rod, M-67A1) Modified M-48 Patton tank fitted with an M-7A1 flame gun instead of the 90mm cannon. The range on the flamethrower was 100–250 meters. A burst of napalm fired by the M-67 was nick-

named a "rod" by the Marines. The M-67 was deployed to Vietnam with the U.S. Marine Corps, and was assigned as part of H & S Company of a tank battalion. The M-67A1 was the Army version of the flamethrower tank. *See also* **M-132 Flamethrower APC.**

M-72 LAW (LAAW) U.S. light antitank weapon, 66mm HEAT rocket, shoulder fired, one shot disposable launcher, 250-meter effective range and a 1,000-meter maximum range. The M-72 weighed 4.8 pounds and several were normally carried in each infantry platoon; used in SVN exclusively against enemy bunkers and crew served weapons until '72. In '72 the NVA started using armor in combat and the M-72 was used effectively, at close range, by the ARVNs against NVA armor. When used against personnel the M-72 had a kill range equivalent to that of a hand thrown grenade. *See also* **Light Antitank Weapons, M-20.**

M-73 Machine Gun Dual 7.62mm machine gun. The dual version of the M-60 machine gun was sometimes mounted in place of the single machine gun used by helicopter door gunners, or on gun jeeps and armored vehicles.

M-75 Grenade Launcher Turret (Hognose) Nicknamed for the "hognose" turret used to house the automatic, belt fed 40mm grenade launcher attached beneath the nose of the AH-1 Cobra and Huey Hog gunships. The helicopter grenade launcher came in two flavors; the XM-28 was a double tube system that featured a minigun along with the grenade launcher; and the M-5 (XM-5) single barrel turreted grenade launcher. The grenade launcher had a range of 2,000 meters, and a rate of fire of 220rpm. *See also* **XM-28 Turret; M-5 Grenade Launcher; Grenade Launchers, 40mm.**

M-76 Cargo Carrier (Amphibious Cargo Carrier, Otter) U.S. Marine Corps, tracked cargo carrier, nicknamed the "Otter." The lightly armored 5-ton tractor could transport 1.5 tons of cargo or ten men and was armed with one .50cal machine gun. *See also* **LVT.**

M-79 Buckshot Round *see* **M-576 Canister Round**

M-79 Flare *see* **Grenades, Illumination**

M-79 Flechette Round *see* **M-576 Canister Round**

M-79 Grenade Launcher (Thumper, Blooper Gun, Thump Gun, M-79 Pig, Bloop Tube) U.S. single shot, single barrel, 40mm grenade launcher. The weapon weighed 6.5 pounds, loaded, and had an effective range of 340 meters. The M-79 could fire several different types of rounds: WP, smoke, HE/fragmentation, CS gas, flares, and a canister round containing buckshot or flechettes. The 6-ounce HE rounds were spin-armed requiring the grenade to travel several meters before it could detonate. At very close range enemy soldiers were often hit by unexploded rounds. The M-79 was nicknamed the "blooper" because of the way it lobbed rounds out to 300 meters, and nicknamed "Thumper" because of the distinct sound it made when it fired. Sometimes called the M-79 "Pig" or "Blooker." *See also* **Grenadier; M-75 Grenade Launcher Turret; Grenade Launchers, 40mm; M-406; M-576.**

M-79 Pig *see* **M-79 Grenade Launcher**

M-88 VTR (Vehicle Tracked Retriever) Army medium armored recovery vehicle. The VTR weighed over 55 tons, was fitted with an A-frame boom and was armed with two .50cal machine guns. The M-88 was built on the M-48 tank chassis, was fitted with a front mounted dozer blade, normally operated with a four-man crew, and was assigned to the company/troop level. *See also* **M-578.**

M-101A1 Howitzer (M-102, 105mm Howitzer, Dime-Nickel, 105 Howie, 105s, Light Arty) The standard American light field artillery piece was the 105mm towed howitzer. There were two versions used in Vietnam, the M-101A1 and the M-102. The M-101 had a range of 11,000 meters, and weighed 2.5 tons. The M-102 was an improved 105mm howitzer with a range of 11,500 meters and a weight of 1.5 tons. The "Dime-Nickel" fired a wide variety of rounds including HE, WP, CS, antipersonnel, antitank, beehive, illumination, and propaganda leaflets. The 105-Howie was easily transported by CH-46 or CH-47 helos. The 105mm HE warhead weighed 33 pounds, and the overall weight of the shell was 55 pounds. The M-108 was a self-propelled version of the 105mm Howitzer. *See also* **M-108 105mm SPA, Howitzer, RAS Shell.**

M-102 *see* **M-101A1 Howitzer**

M-106 Four-Deuce (4.2-Inch Mortar Carrier) An M-113 with a 4.2-inch mortar mounted in the troop compartment, at the rear of the APC. In Vietnam the M-106 provided armored cavalry units with organic heavy mortar support. The M-106 was operated by a six-man crew. The mortar tube was attached to the floor of the APC and could be fired through the overhead hatch on the rear deck of the APC. The mortar could also be removed from the APC and fired normally. In American armored cavalry units the M-106 was assigned to the armored cavalry platoon. In tank battalions they were assigned as the battalion support battery. ARVN armored cavalry units also used the M-106. In ARVN units it was assigned to the regimental headquarters. *See also* **M-125.**

M107 *see* **M107/M38 Mortar**

M-107 175mm SPA (175mm Gun, 175s, 175mm Self-Propelled Gun) U.S. 175mm self-propelled gun. The M-107 provided long-range artillery support. The long barreled 175mm gun could fire a 174-pound HE warhead 32,000 meters. The gun was mounted, open-topped on a fully tracked chassis. During operation of the gun the 8–10 man crew was exposed. The 175mm gun had the longest range of any American field artillery piece in Vietnam, but it was also the least accurate. Due to the high powder charges the barrel life of the gun was about 400–500 rounds, after which the barrel was replaced. The 175mm barrel was interchangeable with the 8-inch barrel of the M-110. Both guns were sometimes assigned as a composite battery at the Field Force or Division Artillery level. The gun was used by the Marines and Army artillery. *See also* **M-110 8-inch SPA.**

M107/M38 Mortar (M107, 107mm Mortar) The 107mm mortar used by the NVA was of Soviet manufacture and used as a heavy mortar by the NVA infantry. The mortar was drop fired and had a five or six man crew. The tube was mounted on a two wheel carriage giving the weapon mobility along with effective firepower. The maximum effective range of the mortar was 6,300 meters. *See also* **Mortar.**

M-108 105mm SPA (105mm SPA)
Fully tracked, 105mm self-propelled howitzer. The 105mm howitzer tube was completely enclosed in an armored turret. The turret protected the gun's crew from enemy fire during operation of the howitzer. The M-108 had specifications similar to the 105mm towed howitzer. The M-108 was only operated in Vietnam by U.S. Army artillery units. *See also* **M-101A1 Howitzer.**

M-109 155mm SPA (155s, 155mm Self-Propelled Howitzer, 155mm SPA, Penny Nickle-Nickle) Fully tracked, self-propelled 155mm howitzer. The 155mm howitzer tube was enclosed in an armored turret that protected the gun and gun crew from enemy fire. The M-109 could fire a 95-pound HE warhead to a range of 14,600 meters. The M-109 was also armed with a roof mounted .50cal machine gun. Marine and Army 155mm SPA (Self-Propelled Artillery) battalions deployed to Vietnam to provide artillery support. The M-109 weighed over 23 tons and had a maximum road speed of about 35mph. The M-114A1 was the towed version of the 155mm howitzer, and the M-53 was an older version of the 155mm SPA. *See also* **M-53 155mm SPA, M-114A1 155mm Howitzer.**

M-109A2 Truck *see* **M-35 Truck**

M-110 8-Inch SPA (Eight-Inchers, 8-Inch Howitzer, 8-Inch SPA, 8-Inch Howie) U.S. self-propelled, 8-inch howitzer. The M-110 was mounted on a fully tracked chassis. Weighing 29 tons, it could fire a 104-pound warhead to a range of 16.8kms. The full weight of the shell (warhead, charge, fuse, and brass) weighed 200 pounds. The howitzer barrel was mounted open-top on the chassis leaving the five-man crew exposed during the weapon's operation. The 8-inch howitzer was mounted on the same chassis as the M-107, 175mm gun, and the barrels of the two weapons were interchangeable. Both Army and Marine artillery battalions operated in Vietnam. Marine 8-inch SPA batteries operated the M-55 until '67 when they were replaced by the M-110s. *See also* **M-107 175mm Howitzer, M-55 8-Inch SPA, Howitzer.**

M-113 APC (M-113A1, APC, Green Dragon, Armored Personnel Carrier, Track, PCs) Primary armored tracked personnel carrier used by Allied forces in Vietnam. Nicknamed the "Green Dragon" by the Vietnamese because of its green color and the fire it spit from its top mounted .50cal machine gun. ACAV was a modified version used as a Cavalry Assault Vehicle featuring gunshields for the main .50cal and the two side mounted M-60 machine guns. The M-113 was gasoline powered, while the M-113A1 was the diesel version; both had a max road speed of 40mph, and were able to "swim" 4mph in water. Some versions of the ACAV featured turret mounted guns. Other variants based on the M-113 included the M-163, M-132, M-106, M-125, M-548, and M-577. The M-113 had a crew of two (driver, vehicle commander/gunner). The APC could transport ten fully equipped troops, who dismounted from the interior troop compartment through a fold down ramp at the rear of the APC. Due to the M-113's light armor and susceptibility to mine damage, troops usually rode on top of the vehicle. A portable, vehicle launched bridge was also available as an M-113 variant. *See also* **Armored Cavalry Assault Vehicle, M-60 AVLB.**

M-113 AVLB *see* **M-60 AVLB**

M-113 MTAB *see* **M-60 AVLB**

M-114 CRV U.S. lightly armored amphibious tracked carrier. The M-114 was a smaller version of the M-113 APC, and was designed to be used as an armored command and reconnaissance vehicle (CRV). The M-114 was armed with a .50cal machine gun. Several M-114s were sent to ARVN armor units for field testing and evaluation in Vietnam. The M-114 was used as a command vehicle and for reconnaissance and deployed with the M-113 APC. During tests of the vehicle in Vietnam it broke down frequently, and had trouble negotiating the same terrain as the M-113. The M-114s were judged to be inadequate for use in Vietnam and were eventually withdrawn from service. *See also* **M-113.**

M-114A1 155mm Howitzer (155s, Heavy Artillery, Penny-Nickle-Nickle) U.S. 155mm towed howitzer. During the Vietnam War the 155mm howitzer was the standard infantry heavy artillery weapon. The 6-ton howitzer could be moved by helicopter (CH-53/CH-54) or conventionally towed by truck. The M-114s were typically assigned as division artillery or as batteries of a separate artillery group. In Vietnam some composite 155mm and 8-inch howitzer batteries were created. The M-114A1 could fire a 95-pound warhead (104 pounds total shell weight) to a range of 14.6kms. The 155s fired a variety of shells including HE, smoke, illumes, antitank, beehive, gas and leaflet. The M-109 was the self-propelled version of the howitzer. A typical crew consisted of 9–11 men. *See also* COFRAM Round, M-109 155mm SPA, Howitzer.

M-116 Cargo Carrier   Fully tracked, amphibious cargo carrier used by the Marine Corps. The M-116 was similar to the M-548 used by the Army, but had a slightly larger cargo capacity. The M-116 saw very limited service with the Marines in Vietnam. *See also* M-548 Cargo Carrier, Tracked Cargo Carriers.

M-123 Tractor (Tank Transporter, Tractor Trailers)   The M-123 was the standard U.S. military 10-ton, 6 × 6 tractor. The tractor towed a variety of trailers which were used to move supplies and equipment. The M-52 was the 5-ton version of the tractor. Both tractors looked similar, but the M-123 had a slightly higher profile. Examples of semitrailers towed by the tractors were the M-127 flatbed (12-ton), M-15A1 lowboy flat (45-ton), M-131 tanker (5,000-gallon), M-129 van (12-ton), and various sized vans and refrigerated trailers. The M-15A1 was sometimes called a "tank transporter."

M-125 81mm Mortar (81mm Mortar Carrier)   M-113 modified as a fire support vehicle, equipped with an 81mm mortar, floor mounted in the rear of the APC. The mortar could be fired from inside the "track," through the overhead hatch, or the mortar could be removed and fired normally. The M-125 operated with a 5–6 man crew. M-125s were assigned to the mortar troop in ARVN Armored Cavalry Assault Squadrons. The troop consisted of three M-125s and an M-113 as the troop headquarters track. U.S. armored cavalry units field modified M-113s to function as mortar carriers to provide fire support at the platoon level. M-125s were not widely used by U.S. cavalry units in Vietnam. *See also* M-106 Four-Deuce.

M-127   *see*   **Hand Flare**

M-127 Semitrailer, Flatbed   *see*   **M-123 Tractor**

M-129 Grenade Launcher   Helicopter mounted, 40mm, automatic grenade launcher. *See also* **M-75 Grenade Launcher, Grenade Launcher.**

M-129 Semitrailer Van   *see*   **M-123 Tractor**

M-131 (Fuel Trailer, Fuel Tanker)   Standard Army fuel semitrailer. The tanker trailer had a capacity of 5,000 gallons.

M-131 Tanker   *see*   **M-123 Tractor**

M-132 Flamethrower APC (Zippo Track)   An M-113 APC with a flamethrower mounted as its main weapon. A machine gun was also fitted in the turret, coaxially mounted with the flamethrower cannon. Napalm fuel used by the flamethrower was stored in a large tank in the rear troop compartment. The flamethrower had a range of 100–200 meters. During the early formation days of the Mobile Riverine Force, M-132s were loaded onto ATC river transports and used against NVA/VC positions along the river. The technique was so successful that modifications were eventually made to several river Monitors equipping them with organic flamethrowers. *See also* M-67A3.

M-134 Minigun   *see*   **XM-134 Minigun**

M-151 Jeep   *see*   **Gun Jeep**

M-151 TOW (M-151E2, TOW, BGM-71, XM-26)   The Hughes Co. M-151 TOW, tube launched, optically tracked, wire guided, antitank missile first saw service with U.S. units during the NVA Eastertide Offensive. The TOW was considered a HAW (Heavy Antitank Weapon). The 54-pound HEAT missile was fin stabilized, with a range of 3,000 meters, and excellent kill ability. The missile was guided to the target by the gunner. In Vietnam the system was usually jeep or APC mounted. The XM-26 was a three TOW pod that was mounted, in pairs, on selected Cobra and Huey Gunships. *See also* **Antitank Guided Missiles.**

M-151E2   *see*   **M-151 TOW**

M-163 Vulcan (Vulcan APC)   M-113 APC fitted with a turret mounted Vulcan 20mm Gatling gun. The M-163 was used in the ground support role and was attached to the armored cavalry platoon as a fire support weapon. *See also* SUU-23, SX-35, M-113.

M-203 Rifle (XM-203, Over-and-Under Gun, XM16E1/XM-148)   M-16 rifle with a 40mm grenade launcher tube mounted under the rifle barrel. The single shot grenade launcher was fired independently of the rifle, and required the man carrying the weapon to pack both grenades and rifle magazines. The XM16E1/XM-148 was the experimental version of the combined rifle/grenade launcher; it was tested in Vietnam in '67 and proved unsatisfactory. In '69 an improved version of the combination M-16/grenade launcher, the XM-203, was successfully tested in Vietnam. The weapon went into mass production in '71 and was designated the M-203. Due to a reduction in the U.S. war effort in Vietnam the number of M-203s that saw combat with U.S. troops were limited, but many of the M-203s were issued to the ARVNs. It eventually became standard issue in the U.S. Army. *See also* **M-79 Grenade Launcher, M-16 Rifle.**

M-274 Mule (Mechanical Mule)   Small field utility vehicle used by the Marines and the Army. The ½-ton capacity "mechanical mule" consisted of a low flatbed platform with four-wheel drive. The steering wheel swung out of the way to allow full access to the flatbed. The mule weighed 1,000 pounds and could be easily air-dropped or moved by helicopter. Mules were used to move supplies and equipment around the battlefield, and they were sometimes equipped with 90mm recoilless rifles and used to support troops. A portion of the mule's flatbed was designed to uncomfortably accommodate a seated driver.

M-292A1 Truck   *see*   **M-35 Truck**

M-329A2 Mortar Round   *see*   **M-30 4.2-Inch Mortar**

M-383 Grenade   *see*   **M-406 Grenade**

M-406 Grenade (M-383 Grenade)   Standard high explosive (HE) fragmentation round used by the 40mm, M-79 grenade launcher. The M-406 round weighed 9 ounces; the HE/fragmentation grenade weighed 6 ounces and had a maximum range of 400 meters. The steel casing that encased the grenade became the fragmentation projectiles when the HE detonated. The round had a kill zone of 5 meters and a casualty zone of 10 meters in diameter. The M-383 was a 40mm grenade round used by

aircraft grenade launchers and featured a heavier warhead and longer cartridge casing, and it had a higher velocity when fired. Both rounds detonated on impact and were spin-armed, requiring the round to travel 5–10 meters before it was armed for detonation. *See also* **M-79 Grenade Launcher, M-576 Canister Round.**

M-520 Cargo Carrier   *see*   **M-553 Cargo Carrier**

M-546 Beehive Round (Canister Round, XM-546)   U.S. 105mm artillery shell that contained 8,000 steel darts used as an antipersonnel weapon against attacking enemy formations. Each of the two-inch-long, finned darts weighed about eight grams. When fired, the spinning shell casing broke apart and the explosive charge, located behind the darts, detonated blasting the darts forward in a 30-degree arc. The beehive round was extremely effective at stopping enemy charges. The Australian version of the beehive round was called a "Splintex Round." Beehive rounds were also available for the 2.75-inch rocket and the 106mm recoilless rifle. *See also* **Flechette.**

M-548 Cargo Carrier (XM-45E1 Armored Cargo Carrier)   Tracked vehicle cargo carrier which was based on the M-113 APC chassis. In Vietnam the M-548 was found in Army mechanized/armored units. The M-548 operated as an ammunitions carrier for self-propelled artillery batteries. The M-548 functioned as a standard cargo vehicle (5-ton capacity) and was also deployed with Army land clearing engineer teams, transporting parts and fuel. The track was armed with a ring mounted .50cal machine gun. The XM45E1 was an armored version of the M-548 that was used to transport the liquid napalm used by the M-132 Flamethrower APC. *See also* **M-113, Tracked Cargo Carriers.**

M-551 ARV (Sheridan Tank)   Army turreted armored reconnaissance vehicle (ARV). The lightly armored M-551 deployed to Vietnam in '69 to replace some of the M-113 used in armored cavalry units. Troops in the field referred to the M-551 as a "tank," but it was designed as an assault vehicle. The M-551 was armed with a 152mm gun capable of firing combustible case HEAT rounds or antitank guided missiles, but vehicles which deployed to SVN were armed only with HEAT rounds. The M-551 was also armed with 1–2, .50cal machine guns. The M-551 was not very popular with the crews that operated them. The aluminum hull of the Sheridan was vulnerable to mines and enemy RPG rounds. The interior of the ARV was subject to flash fires caused by leakage of the propellant powder used to fire the HEAT round. Gases from the fired rounds sometimes collected in the turret. The 152mm XM409 HEAT round was very effective against enemy bunkers. The M-551 also fired the XM625 canister round which contained over 9,000 flechettes. The Sheridan was equipped with night imaging sites that allowed it to engage enemy targets at night and the 17-ton "tank" was so light that when it fired, the front end lifted several inches off the ground. The M-551 had a max speed of 45mph, a 500km range, and in Vietnam it operated with a three man crew. The field addition of titanium belly plates lessened the effects of mines on the M-551, but RPGs easily penetrated the tank's armor, igniting the ARV's combustible case ammunition, destroying the vehicle.

M-553 Cargo Carrier (M-520 Cargo Carrier, GOER) Four wheel, 4 × 4 rough terrain vehicle used by the Army. The "GOER" was manufactured by the Caterpillar Corp. and had a max road speed of about 30mph. The vehicle was mounted on four large wheels and was available in ten-ton (M-553) and eight-ton (M-250) versions.

M-561 Cargo Carrier (Gamma Goat) Small utility cargo truck used by the Army. The 6 × 6 articulated truck had a 1.25-ton cargo capacity, and a maximum road speed of 55mph. The body of the truck pivoted at the center of the vehicle allowing it to traverse rough terrain that a normal truck would have had difficulty crossing.

M-576 Canister Round (M-79 Buckshot Round, M-79 Flechette Round) On an experimental basis a flechette round was developed for the M-79 Grenade Launcher. The round featured 45 steel finned darts that were used by the grenadier for close range combat. Later the M-576 canister round was developed. It contained 27 lead, 00-buckshot pellets. The flechette and buckshot rounds gave the grenadier the ability to provide close range support when

the enemy was too close for the effective use of the standard M-79 HE round. *See also* **Flechette, M-79 Grenade Launcher, M-406 Grenade.**

M-577 ACC (Commo Track, Hightop, Armored Command Carrier [ACC]) A modified M-113 used for a mobile command post or as an artillery fire direction center. The M-577 was filled with extra radio and communication equipment, and carried an externally mounted auxiliary power generator. The normal top of the M-113 was extended upward to accommodate the extra gear. Because of the added head room some M-577s were used as mobile aid stations in armored cavalry units. *See also* **M-113.**

M-578 VTR (Vehicle Tracked Retriever, Cherrypicker) Tracked vehicle retriever designed to support the M-113 APC. The VTR was based on the same tracked chassis used by the M107/110 SPA guns. The M-578 had a box-like turret located on the rear deck of the chassis which mounted the crane used for repairs of the M-113s. Additional repair equipment and parts were stored in the M-578. The VTR was nicknamed the "Cherrypicker" because of the crane's repair boom. The M-578 was lightly armored, and armed with a roof mounted .50cal machine gun, had a max speed of 35mph, and operated with a three-man crew. The M-578 supported the M-113 and other light armor vehicles. Heavier armored vehicles were serviced by the M-88 VTR. *See also* **M-88 VTR.**

M-706 Armored Car *see* **V-100**

M-728 CEV Army Combat Engineering Vehicle (CEV) used in Vietnam to support armor operations. The CEV was a modified M-60 Main Battle Tank, equipped with a front mounted dozer blade, a 165mm demolition gun, and a turret mounted A-frame boom with an 8.75-ton capacity. The tank weighed over 57 tons and provided support to the armored units to which it was assigned. The short range (4,800 meters) 165mm gun was designed for demolitions use, and it was often used against enemy bunkers. The CEV was armed with two machine guns, and operated with a four-man crew. Max speed of the heavy tank was 30mph.

M-733 APC Fully tracked carrier used experimentally by the Marine Corps in Vietnam. The M-733 was armed with machine guns and a grenade launcher. The carrier was evaluated, but never deployed tactically by the Marines in Vietnam. *See also* **Tracked Cargo Carriers.**

M1891/30 Rifle   *see*   **Mosin-Nagant**

M-1905 Bayonet   Army bayonet with a 12-inch blade.

M1911 ACP   *see*   **M-1911A1**

M-1911A1 Pistol (45 Pistol, .45 Pistol, M-1911 ACP)   Standard U.S. military issue, Colt, .45cal, automatic pistol. The ".45," as it was more commonly known, was magazine loaded (7 rounds), recoil operated, weighing a little over two pounds with an effective range of 50 meters and a muzzle velocity of 860 feet per second. The .45 has seen service worldwide and fires M-1911 ACP (Automatic Cartridge, Pistol) ammunition, the same ammunition fired by the Thompson M-1A1 and the M-3A1 .45 submachine guns. *See also* **Pistols.**

M-1918A2   *see*   **Browning Automatic Rifle**

M-1919A4   *see*   **M-1919A6**

M-1919A6 MMG (Browning Medium Machine Gun, .30cal MG, Thirty-Cal, M-1919A4)   M-1919A4 .30cal medium machine gun used throughout Vietnam. The 32-pound, belt fed, air cooled weapon was normally tripod or bipod mounted in the field. Some versions were used on vehicles and boats for fire support. This machine gun had a maximum effective range of 1,000 meters, and could only fire automatic and was fitted with a pistol type grip and a large trigger lever. The A6 version was equipped with a shoulder stock, lighter barrel and a carrying handle. The heavy weight of the weapon restricted its use in the field by the Vietnamese. For field use the ARVNs were eventually supplied with the M-60 machine gun. *See also* **Machine Gun.**

M1937 Mortar   *see*   **Type 53 Mortar**

M-1944 AA Gun   *see*   **8mm AA**

M-1951 Field Cap   Cotton field cap similar to the baseball cap. The soft cap was blocked with plastic or metal inserts. It was primarily worn by high ranking officers with access to air conditioning. The cap was replaced with the standard utility cap in '64. *See also* **Baseball Cap.**

M-1951 Field Coat (Field Jacket, M-1965 Field Jacket)   Standard issue Army cold weather field jacket. The wind-resistant, OD Green coat had four pockets, a drawstring around the waist, and button sleeves. A later model, the M-1965, featured a built-in rain hood, zipped into the collar, and velcro tape at the sleeves. Units that operated in the Central Highlands and the mountains of Vietnam frequently used the cold weather field jackets. *See also* **Jungle Sweater.**

M-1952 Body Armor   *see*   **Flak Jacket**

M-1955 Flak Jacket (Armor-Plated Shorts, Armored Girdle, Porcelain Plates)   The Marine's flak jacket was a wraparound vest similar to the Army flak jacket, but six pounds heavier and able to significantly slow down small caliber rounds. The zipper front nylon vest was made of 22 overlapping fiberglass or ceramic (porcelain) plates. In comparison to Army field troops, a greater number of Marines wore their vest in the field. In addition to the vest, the Marines had access to an 8½-pound armored girdle that could be worn in the field. The Marines called the armored girdles "armor-plated shorts" or "armored pants." These were seldom worn by field Marines. *See also* **Body Armor, Flak Jacket.**

M-1956/1961 Combat Field Pack   *see*   **Butt Pack**

M-1956/1967 Individual Load Carrying Equipment   *see*   **Web Gear**

M-1965 Field Jacket   *see*   **M-1951 Field Coat**

M-Day   *see*   **Moratorium Day**

M-SID   *see*   **MAGNA-SID**

M.J.   *see*   **Marijuana**

MA   *see*   **Mechanical Ambush, Montagnards**

Ma Ruoc Hon (Ancestral Ghost)   Vietnamese ancestral ghost which guided the spirit of the dead into the "next world."

MAAG   *see*   **Military Assistance Advisory Group, Vietnam**

MAAGI   *see*   **Military Assistance Advisory Group, Vietnam**

MAAGV   *see*   **Military Assistance Advisory Group, Vietnam**

MAAGV, Navy Section   *see*   **Naval Advisory Group**

MAB   *see*   **III Marine Amphibious Force**

MAC *see* Military Airlift Command

Macaque *see* Rock Apes

MacArthur *see* Operation MacArthur

Machete (Mak, Rice Hook, Bush Knife)
Long blade knife used by U.S. forces to cut
a path through dense jungle brush and
vines. The Army issue machete had a steel
blade 18 inches long, about 3 inches wide, a
6-inch wood/plastic handle, and was issued
in a canvas sheath. The point man cut
through the brush, and the rest of the unit
followed. In particularly dense jungle the
point was rotated often. Cutting a new trail
was the best way to avoid enemy mines,
booby traps, and prepared ambush sites
while moving through the jungle. The
NVA/VC used a "rice hook" as a machete.
The tool was used in the harvesting of rice
and had a 10–12 inch curved blade with a
hook on the end, attached to a 12–14 inch
bamboo handle. *See also* **Cut(ting) Trail.**

Machine Gun (MG) Various types of
machine guns, and submachine guns were
used in Vietnam. A new type of machine
gun was also introduced in Vietnam, the
minigun. Machine guns were generally classified as light, medium, and heavy. Machine
guns featured a high rate of fire and were
usually a crew served weapon. *See also* **Light
Machine Gun: M-60, RPD, Japanese
Machine Guns, M-63A1 Stoner. Medium
Machine Gun: SG43, Type 24 MMG, M-
1919A6. Heavy Machine Gun: M-2, Type 54
HMG, KPV, Japanese Machine Guns. Minigun, Submachine Gun.**

MACOI *see* **MACV Office of Information**

Macon *see* **Operation Macon**

MACT *see* **Military Assistance
Command, Thailand**

MACV *see* **Military Assistance
Command, Vietnam**

MACV Compound *see* **Military Assistance Command, Vietnam**

MACV Daily Press Briefings *see*
Five O'Clock Follies

**MACV Forward (Provisional Corps
Vietnam)** An MACV Command Center
established near Phu Bai in I Corps in February '68 and commanded by Gen. C.W.

Abrams. The temporary center was placed to
control and coordinate the efforts of Army
and Marine units in I and II Corps. Since
'65, the Marines had controlled U.S. I Corps
operations and some Marine commanders
were reluctant to share their assets with other
non–Marine units in the area. This reluctance, coupled with an increase in enemy activity, and reduced Marine effectiveness,
caused MACV to put an Army HQ in command of I Corps. In March '68 MACV Forward was redesignated Provisional Corps
Vietnam, and remained in place until the
XXIV Corps Headquarters was established
to oversee all American operations in I
Corps. *See also* **XXIV Corps.**

MACV Headquarters *see* **Pentagon
East**

MACV Office of Information (MACOI)
MACV office responsible for the collection
and dissemination of information to the
public and the media. MACVOI gathered
the information that was used for the Five
O'Clock (Follies) briefings that took place
daily at the JUSPAO. *See also* **Five O'Clock
Follies, Joint U.S. Public Affairs Office.**

**MACV Recondo School (Recondo
School)** U.S. Special Forces training facility located at Nha Trang on Hon Tre
Island in II Corps, established in September
'66 under the command of Detachment
B-52. The USSF conducted three week training courses on reconnaissance techniques,
tracking, infiltration, signaling, map and
compass reading, air and artillery strike
direction, and other skills required to enable
the students to successfully operate behind
enemy lines. The course was taught to CIDG
recon elements, American LRRP units, and
others required to work undetected in
enemy territory. *See also* **Project Delta.**

MACV Tigers Small defense force organized to augment the Military Police force
that guarded the MACV complex near Tan
Son Nhut in Saigon. The force was formed
after Tet '68. The MACV Tigers consisted of
personnel that worked (RATS) at the headquarters. In the event of an enemy attack
they would assemble to defend the complex.
See also **REMF.**

**MACV-SOG (MACV–Studies and Ob-
servations Group)** U.S. Military Assistance Command Vietnam–Studies and Observations Group: A highly classified unit

composed of members of the Army Special Forces, Air Force Commandos, Navy SEALs, and Marine Recon. This special unit carried out various secret missions both in and out of SVN: missions of intelligence gathering, raiding and other unconventional wartime activities against the enemy. MACV-SOG units were perhaps the most independently operated U.S. units in all of SVN. MACV-SOG's operations were carried out by various U.S. specialized forces and CIDGs, under the SOG's direction. SOG operations were conducted by one of four SOG study groups. *See also* **Projects Omega and Sigma; SES; STD; TDAT; SOG Groups.**

MACV-SOG Command and Control (CCN, CCC, CCS)   MACV-SOG operations, Project Sigma and Omega, were carried out from one of three Forward Operating Bases designated CCN (north), CCS (south) and CCC (central). The southern FOB was located at Ban Me Thuot in Darlac Province, II Corps. The central FOB was located at Kontum in Pleiku Province, II Corps. And the northern FOB was located at Da Nang, I Corps. USSF and CIDG troops which operated from these FOBs were organized into special groups in order to carry out their missions. The groups were called Spike Recon Teams, Hatchet Forces, SLAM Companies, and the Hoc Bao. *See also* **MACV-SOG, Project Omega and Sigma, Forward Operating Base.**

MACVNAG   *see*   **Naval Advisory Group**

Mad Minute   *see*   **Area Recon by Fire**

MAD System   *see*   **Mortar Air Delivery System**

Madame Ngo Dinh Nhu   *see*   **Madame Nhu**

Madame Nhu (Madame Ngo Dinh Nhu, Tran Le Xuan, Vietnam's Marie Antoinette, Dragon Lady)   Tran Le Xuan (in Vietnamese; Beautiful Spring) was the flamboyant and outspoken wife of Ngo Dinh Nhu, brother of South Vietnam's President Diem. Madame Nhu acted as South Vietnam's official hostess—Diem was a bachelor. When Buddhist monks began burning themselves alive in protest against government oppression, Madame Nhu and her husband referred to these sacrifices as "barbecues" and offered to provide gasoline

to any other monks who desired to commit suicide. Such callous remarks and anti–American sentiment turned U.S. public opinion against Diem's Regime. Traveling in the U.S. when the '63 coup took place, she never returned to Vietnam; she now lives in Italy. *See also* **Thich Quang Duc, Dance Ban.**

Maddox   *see*   **Tonkin Gulf Incident**

Maeng Ho II   *see*   **Operation Fierce Tiger II**

MAF   *see*   **III Marine Amphibious Force**

MAG-11   *see*   **Marine Air Group-11**

MAG-12   *see*   **Marine Air Group-12**

MAG-13   *see*   **Marine Air Group-13**

MAG-16   *see*   **Marine Unit Vietnam, Marine Air Group-16**

MAG-16   *see*   **Marine Air Group-16, Marine Unit Vietnam**

MAG-36   *see*   **Marine Air Group-36**

MAG-39   *see*   **Marine Air Group-39**

Maggie's Drawers   On military firing ranges a "miss" was registered by a pair of bright red silk (cotton or polyester) panties waved in front of the missed target. On several occasions during the NVA siege of Khe Sanh, Marines waved a pair of Maggie's Drawers at the NVA gunners. *See also* **Khe Sanh.**

MAGNA-SID (M-SID, Magnetic Sensing Intrusion Device)   Unattended ground sensor used by the U.S. The Magnetic Sensing Intrusion Device, MAGNA-SID, was a metal sensitive remote sensing device used in conjunction with other ground sensors. The device, also called an M-SID, consisted of a 12-inch square waterproof box with an 18-inch antenna and a thick magnetic coil located on top. The box was buried near a trail with only a short length of the antenna exposed. Any metal objects such as ammunition, weapons or the large iron ring in the nose of a water buffalo would activate the sensor causing it to transmit a coded signal to a receiver. The sensing radius of the M-SID was about 10 feet. The device was fitted with a self-destruct mechanism like that of the G-SID. *See also* **G-SID, Electronic Sensors.**

Magnesium Flares Aerial flares dropped from aircraft in support of ground units. The flare, when released, floated to the earth attached beneath a small parachute. The output of the flare was in excess of one million candlepower. *See also* **Flares.**

Magnetic Sensing Intrusion Device *see* **MAGNA-SID**

Magnificent Bastards (2d Battalion/4th Marine Regiment) Nickname for the 2d Battalion/4th Marine Regiment. Most of the regiment deployed to Vietnam in May '65, and operated along the DMZ until the unit's departure from Vietnam in November '69. The regiment operated as part of the 3d Marine Division.

Magpie (No. 2 Squadron Royal Australian Air Force) Call sign of the No. 2 Squadron, RAAF, which operated Canberra bombers out of the Air Force base at Phan Rang, Ninh Thuan Province, II Corps. The squadron first deployed to Vietnam in April '67. The Canberra bombers used by the RAAF were the English Electric Version, built in Australia. The performance of the RAAF Canberra was similar to that of the American made B-57 Canberra except the RAAF models had a range of 6,000kms. The U.S. B-57 had a range of 3,600kms. *See also* **Royal Australian Air Force, B-57 Bomber.**

Mahone *see* **1st Infantry Division Fire Bases**

Mail-Call *see* **Incoming**

Main Chute *see* **T-10 Parachute**

Main Force VC (Chu Loc) Full-time VC soldiers. The Viet Cong operated with two types of combat forces, part-time VC and main force VC. Part-time VC were farmers, shopkeepers or various other workers by day, and VC by night. The part-time VC was usually part of a local squad, platoon or company. Main Force VC or "Chu Loc" fought in company- to division-size units, and operated out of areas they controlled, or moved constantly from area to area, frequently crossing into Cambodia or Laos to train, or to evade American units. Main force VC were armed and equipped with some of the same equipment issued to NVA soldiers. The VC wore the black pajama or khaki NVA style uniform. *See also* **Viet Cong.**

Main Line of Resistance (MLR, Defensive Line) Imaginary line marking a unit's defensive boundary; the defensive line between a unit and the enemy.

Main Man Nickname for a close friend, buddy, or someone you trust. Sometimes used as a general greeting, especially among urban blacks. *See also* **Soul Brother.**

Mainliner (Shooter, Speedball) Nickname for a heroin or morphine addict who injected the drug directly into the vein, usually in the arm. Mainlining put the drug directly into the bloodstream speeding the effects of the drug. Morphine could be administered into the muscles of the body; i.e., the thigh, buttocks, arm, which resulted in a slower body response to the effects of the drug. Besides the hard drugs, methedrine could also be injected for an instant rush; the nickname for injected meth was a "speedball." *See also* **Illicit Drugs, Morphine, Speed.**

Maj. *see* **Major**

Maj Gen *see* **Major General**

Major (Maj, Thieu-Ta) Field grade officer in the U.S. Army, Marines and Air Force. The equivalent rank in the Navy was a lieutenant commander. In Army field units a major normally functioned as an executive officer, second in command to the battalion commander, a lieutenant colonel. Majors not at the battalion level usually worked as division or brigade staff officers. The insignia of rank for a major was a gold oak leaf. Thieu-Ta was the Vietnamese equivalent rank. *See also* **Field Grade Officers.**

Major General (Maj Gen, Trung-Tuong) A two-star general officer in the U.S. Army, Marines and Air Force. The equivalent rank in the Navy was rear admiral (upper). In the Vietnamese Army the equivalent rank was "trung-tuong." *See also* **General Officers.**

Mak *see* **Machete**

Makarov Pistol *see* **Type 59 Pistol**

Make Love Not War One of the most widely voiced slogans of the 60s hippie movement.

Make-a-Hat *see* **Book**

Malaria (Falciparum, Volvax, Blackwater Fever) Falciparum and Volvax (vivax) were two of the most common forms of malaria found in Vietnam. U.S. soldiers were issued two different preventative medicines to reduce their chances of contracting malaria. Dapsone was taken daily and Chloroquine Primaquine was taken weekly. Later in the war some GIs avoided taking the malaria preventative medicine hoping they would contract malaria and be pulled out of the field. The malaria mosquito stands on its head when it bites; the normal mosquito lies down to suck the blood. Parasites transmitted by the female mosquito invaded the red blood cells causing them to burst leading to fever and various degrees of diarrhea, jaundice, fits, and shock. Without timely treatment the parasites spread to the liver and spleen, causing their enlargement and malfunction. Malaria, insufficiently treated, can lead to repeated attacks of fever and fits. One severe complication of malaria, Blackwater Fever, resulted in heavy destruction of red blood cells, causing them to be excreted in the urine, giving the urine a brownish-red color. Accompanying the cell destruction was unusually high fever and jaundice, sometimes requiring blood transfusions to stabilize the patient. *See also* **Dapsone, Chloroquine, Primaquine.**

Malaria Pills *see* **Dapsone, Chloroquine, Primaquine, Malaria**

Malay Log *see* **Malayan Gates**

Malay Whip Log *see* **Malayan Gates**

Malaya *see* **Malaysia**

Malayan Gates (Malay Log, Malay Whip Log, Malaysian Whip) One type of booby trap used by the VC in Vietnam. One end of a long bamboo pole was tied to a tree; attached to the free end of the pole were several pointed stakes. The pole was bent back, away from the trail, and secured with a quick release mechanism. A trip wire was stretched across the trail and attached to the release. When the wire was tripped, the bent pole was released, arching across the trail, impaling those in the pole's path. A variant of the whip was the "Malay Log," which featured a spike-embedded log suspended above a trail; when tripped, the log would swing down into the enemy force moving on the trail. *See also* **Booby Trap.**

Malayan Krait Extremely toxic snake. The snake was 3–4 feet long, brownish in color with ring bands starting several inches behind the head, going all the way down its body. The snake could be found near cultivated fields and hiding near hootches or other structures. The snake was not overly aggressive, but the venom dose from one bite could kill five men. *See also* **Snakes.**

Malayan Pit Viper Poisonous snake found in the lowlands and near the coastal plains. The snake was 3–5 feet long and was a slow mover. The pit viper attacked without provocation inflicting a painful bite, injecting a blood-poison venom that could result in death in several days. The snake had a small hollow between its nose and eyes that was able to sense temperature. It used this sensor to target its strikes. *See also* **Snakes.**

Malaysia (Malaya) In '49 communist Chinese insurgents attempted to take control of Malaya using guerrilla warfare. The British fought the guerrillas in a ten year battle that resulted in the communists being driven out of Malaya. One of the more successful British programs was the relocation of the people out of communist rebel areas to safe, protected zones. Without the people the rebels lost their base of support. SVN attempted a similar relocation plan, the Strategic Hamlet Program, which failed completely. The British Malaysia campaign was the only successful counterinsurgency program waged against communist forces by a Western power. *See also* **Thompson, Sir Robert Thompson; Strategic Hamlet Program.**

Malaysian Whip *see* **Malayan Gates**

Malheur *see* **Operation Malheur**

Malingering A GI who continually went on sick call or feigned injury to avoid work details or combat. There was no physical basis for the sick call, only a fear or an unwillingness to perform, cooperate or obey. *See also* **Goldbricking, REMF, Sick Call.**

Mama-San GI name for an aged or mature Vietnamese woman, or the mother in charge of a family or woman in charge of a whorehouse. Used by GIs to refer to any Vietnamese woman of undetermined age. *See also* **Papa-San.**

Mameluke Thrust *see* **Operation Mameluke Thrust**

Man, The Black American reference to the white power structure, courts, authority, and especially the police. Also applied to the power and upper command structure within the military. *See also* **Caucasian.**

Man Who Never Was *see* **Unit That Never Was**

Maneuver Aggressively Military jargon calling for a unit to move forward with speed, and little regard for safety; advance and attack.

Mang Yang Pass Strategic pass, on Route 19, located 37kms west of An Khe, II Corps. Route 19 was the main access road from Kontum, through An Khe, to the coast. It was at this pass that French Mobile Group 100 was destroyed by Viet Minh forces in June '54. *See also* **Groupement Mobile 100.**

Manhattan *see* **Operation Manhattan**

Manilla Treaty Treaty that established Southeast Asia Treaty Organization in '54. *See also* **Southeast Asia Treaty Organization.**

Manpack Personnel Detector–Chemical *see* **XM-2 People Sniffer**

Mao Tse-Tung (One Slow-Four Quick) Considered to be the father of modern communist guerrilla warfare in Asia. His doctrine was used by the NVA/VC as the basis for their combat tactics. The NVA/VC version: When the enemy advances, withdraw; when he defends, harass; when he tires, attack; when he withdraws, pursue. They also had the "one slow—four quick" rule: Slowly prepare each operation . . . advance quick . . . quickly exploit success and pursue the enemy . . . quickly clear the battlefield of weapons, ammo, the dead and wounded . . . quickly withdraw.

MAP *see* **Military Assistance Program**

Marauder *see* **Operation Marauder**

Marble Mountain (Marble Mountain Marine Air Facility) Marine air facility located on the Tien Sha Peninsula, 4kms southeast of Da Nang. Marble Mountain served as the Marines' main helicopter base.

The base shared the peninsula with several other facilities, and Monkey Mountain. *See also* **Tien Sha Peninsula.**

Marble Mountain Marine Air Facility *see* **Marble Mountain**

Marching *see* **Close-Order Drill**

Marching Fire Troops marching, sweeping forward, firing and throwing hand grenades ahead of them as they move. It was effective if the enemy was not well dug in. The troops marching forward, on-line, were exposed and vulnerable if the enemy was bunkered with machine gun support.

Marching Fires (Walking Rounds, Walking Fires) Artillery fires walked along a travel route (road or trail), ahead of an advancing column. The fires were designed to break up any enemy ambushes that might be set up along the route to be traveled by the advancing column. Also referred to as "walking rounds," where the impact of the artillery rounds is slowly adjusted in a specific direction. Walking fire was used to sweep an area with artillery. Assaulting infantry often approached an objective from behind the walking fires; this kept the enemy under cover until the assaulting troops were almost on top of them. The effectiveness of the assault was dependent on how closely the troops followed the sweeping artillery. *See also* **Recon by Fire.**

Marching-Fire *see* **On-Line**

Marginal Terrain Assault Bridge *see* **M-60 AVLB**

Marginals *see* **Recycle**

Margret, Ann *see* **Hope, Bob**

Marigold *see* **Operation Marigold**

Marijuana (Dew, Pot, Grass, Weed, Stash, Joints, Mary Jane, Js, OJs, Smoke, Doobie) Marijuana (cannabis) was one of many illicit drugs available in Vietnam: Known by many names, marijuana was most frequently smoked either in a pipe or rolled into a cigarette (roach). Marijuana cigarettes were referred to as joints, Js or OJs. In the U.S., pot was used illegally on a widespread basis, and there were several failed attempts by activists to legalize its use. The Vietnamese word for opium was "thuoc phien," which GIs mistakenly called marijuana ("phien" or "thuoc phien") when buying it from the Viets. There were many varieties of pot available such as Cambodian Red or Black, Laotian Gold, Lao Grass, Buddha Grass. Marijuana was also called M.J. (Mike-Juliet), Dinky-Dau Smoke, Happy Smoke. *See also* **Illicit Drugs, OJs, Opium, Hashish, Dexamphetamines, Bowls, Shot-Gun, Heroin, Lid.**

Marijuana Cigarettes *see* **Party-Pack**

Marine Air Group-11 (MAG-11) Deployed to Da Nang in July '65 as part of the 1st Marine Air Wing. Mag-11 operated F-4 and A-6 aircraft. *See also* **1st Marine Air Wing.**

Marine Air Group-12 (MAG-12) Initially stationed at Chu Lai under the control of the 1st Marine Air Wing.

Marine Air Group-13 (MAG-13) MAG-13 operated out of Chu Lai as part of the 1st Marine Air Wing. The group operated A-4s in support of Marine ground operations in the I Corps area. *See also* **1st Marine Air Wing.**

Marine Air Group-16 (MAG-16) Marine helicopters of MAG-16 operated as part of the 1st Marine Air Wing. The group operated from Da Nang in support of Marine operations in the I Corps area. *See also* **1st Marine Air Wing.**

Marine Air Group-36 (MAG-36) Deployed to Vietnam in September '66 under control of the 1st Marine Air Wing. MAG-36 was based at Chu Lai and consisted of helicopters to support Marine ground units. The group was later moved to the helicopter base at Ky Ha near Phu Bai. *See also* **Ky Ha.**

Marine Air Group-39 (MAG-39) Provided Marine helicopter support to elements of the 3d Marine Division from a base constructed at Quang Tri in April '68.

Marine Air Squadron Designations (VMA, VMFA, VMCJ, VMGR, VMO, HML, HMM, HMH) Several Marine air squadrons operated in Vietnam; their designations roughly identified their mission. HMH—Heavy lift helicopters, originally CH-37, replaced by CH-53. HMM—Medium lift helicopters, originally CH-34, replaced by CH-46. HML—High lift helicopters; the UH-1E. VMO—O-1 and OV-10 observation aircraft and AH-1 Cobra gunships. VMGR—KC-130 transport and re-

fueling aircraft. VMCJ—Recon photo and electronic warfare aircraft; RF-8, RF-4, EA-6A. VMFA—Attack aircraft; F-4s. VMA—Attack aircraft; A-4s and the all weather (AW) A-6s.

Marine Air Station, Chu Lai *see* **Chu Lai**

Marine Air Wing (MAW) The Vietnam era Marine Air Wing consisted of approximately 500 fixed and rotary wing aircraft. The "wing" was further subdivided into Air Groups of 75 aircraft. One Marine Air Wing was active in Vietnam. *See also* **1st Marine Air Wing.**

Marine Aircraft Group-16 *see* **Marine Unit Vietnam, Marine Air Group-16**

Marine Code *see* **Semper Fidelis**

The Marine Corps Builds Men One of the U.S. Marine Corps recruiting slogans.

The Marine Corps Is a... "The Marine Corps is a communist plot to take over the world"; Vietnam era GI graffiti.

Marine Corps Recruit Depot (MCRD, Hollywood Marines, Parris Island, San Diego) U.S. Marine Corps training centers, located at Parris Island, South Carolina, and San Diego, California. Initial "boot" camp training took place at one of the two training centers. Parris Island MCRD was established in 1919 and San Diego MCRD became operational in 1923. Marines who took their basic training at the San Diego MCRD were known as "Hollywood Marines." *See also* **Basic Training Camps, U.S. Marines.**

Marine Expeditionary Force (MEF) U.S. Marine Corps force which initially deployed to Vietnam consisted of a Marine Infantry Division and a Marine Air Wing. MEFs were used for temporary deployment under combat conditions. Later the MEF was replaced by the Marine Amphibious Force (MAF). The 9th Marine Expeditionary Brigade was used as the expeditionary force originally sent to South Vietnam in March '65. *See also* **9th Marine Amphibious Brigade, III Marine Amphibious Force.**

Marine Field Equipment/Gear *see* **782 Gear**

Marine Fishing (Stun-Fishing) Technique using hand grenades or explosive charges to catch fish. Explosives or a grenade was thrown over the side of the boat or from a riverbank, exploding underwater; fish in the area of the blast were stunned and floated to the surface. Marine CAP teams in I Corps sometimes used the technique to help the local fishermen.

Marine Force Recon *see* **Force Recon**

Marine Logistical Command (MAR-LOG) U.S. Marine logistics group that handled Marine resupply efforts in Vietnam. MARLOG delivered supplies and equipment to Marine units throughout I Corps. The command was also responsible for U.S. mail distribution to the Marines.

Marine LOH *see* **Sperm**

Marine Medical Battalion *see* **C & C Company**

Marine Medium Helicopter Squadron 163 *see* **Marine Medium Helicopter Squadron 362**

Marine Medium Helicopter Squadron 362 (HMM-362, Shufly, HMM-163, Operation Lockjaw) First U.S. Marine helicopter unit assigned duty in South Vietnam. HMM-362, known as "Shufly," arrived in Vietnam April '62 at Soc Trang, Ba Xuyen Province, IV Corps. The H-34 squadron, based at Soc Trang, transported ARVN units into combat around the Delta. The unit remained at Soc Trang until replaced by HMM-163 in August '62. The following month HMM-163 deployed to Da Nang. The first Marine air assault mission was conducted in April '62 when Marine CH-34 helicopters ferried an ARVN infantry battalion into combat; the operation was code-named "Lockjaw." *See also* **Marine Unit Vietnam, USS Princeton.**

Marine Nicknames *see* **U.S. Marines**

Marine Recon *see* **Force Recon**

Marine Stove *see* **C-Rat Stove**

Marine Unit Vietnam (MUV, Marine Aircraft Group-16) The first Marine air units in Vietnam were H-34 helicopter squadrons, code-named "Shufly," used to transport ARVN forces on strike missions. In '64 the Marine helicopter units in Vietnam were designated MUV (Marine Unit Vietnam). With the addition of Marine attack aircraft and additional helicopters MUV was redesignated Marine Aircraft Group-16

(MAG-16), and placed under control of the 9th Marine Expeditionary Brigade. In August '65 MAG-16 moved from facilities at Da Nang to a new airstrip located at Marble Mountain, just southeast of Da Nang. *See also* **Marine Medium Helicopter Squadron 362.**

Marineland GI reference to U.S. Marine Area of Operations, covering most of I Corps.

Marines *see* **U.S. Marines**

Marines' My Lai *see* **Son Thang**

Maritime Studies Group *see* **SOG Groups**

Mark 5 *see* **Centurion**

Marker Round *see* **Marking Round**

Market Place *see* **TF 71**

Market Time (Operation Market Time) In March '65 U.S. Navy ships were authorized and directed to assist the South Vietnamese Navy in its coastal surveillance and anti-infiltration patrol efforts. This was in response to NVN's infiltration of weapons and supplies along the coast. Operation Market Time was under control of the newly formed Coastal Surveillance Force, TF 115, responsible to MACV. The ships patrolled the entire coast of SVN which had been divided into four naval zones. The patrols were carried out by ships and aircraft of the U.S. 7th Fleet and Coast Guard Squadron One. *See also* **TF 115.**

Marketplace *see* **Cho**

Marking Mission (Lost Unit Triangulation) Triangulation technique that used artillery fire to help a unit lost in the jungle find its bearings. An artillery battery would fire a WP (smoke) shell at a given grid coordinate or an easily recognizable terrain feature. The lost unit would attempt to spot the smoke, using a compass to plot an azimuth (on the map) to the smoke round. A second round would be fired at another coordinate; the azimuth plotting procedure would be repeated. Where the extended lines of the two azimuths intersected on the map was the location of the lost unit. The technique only worked when the lost unit could identify the direction of the marking rounds, a difficult task in triple canopy where the trees were up to 200 feet tall.

Marking Round (Spotting Round, Marker Round, Spotter Round, Put Smoke) Single round fired by artillery, mortars, or spotter aircraft used to mark a target. From its impact other rounds were adjusted to hit the desired target location. HE or WP rounds were used by artillery and FACs used WP rockets to mark their targets. The FACs would "put smoke" on the target and fighter-bombers would strike as directed by the FAC.

Marlin *see* **P-5**

MARLOG *see* **Marine Logistical Command**

Marmalade *see* **B-2 Unit**

Marmite Cans *see* **Mermite Cans**

MARS *see* **Military Affiliated Radio Stations**

Mars Air Generator Commercial air blower that saw limited use with the Army in Vietnam. The Mars unit weighed 175 pounds and required 12 gallons of fuel per hour for operation. The unit was usually air transported to the field and positioned near an enemy tunnel entrance where it forced smoke or gases through the tunnel complex. The Mars could run continuously, and be refueled while operating. Tunnel Rats did not usually operate in the tunnel when the blower was operating because the 1,000-degree heat exhaust from the Mars unit was also blown through the tunnel. *See also* **Tunnel Warfare, Air Blowers.**

Martin, Graham Career diplomat who was America's last ambassador to South Vietnam. Martin replaced Ellsworth Bunker in '73. Martin was a strong supporter of U.S. actions in Vietnam and had a misguided belief that the ARVN forces could hold out against the sweeping NVA offensive of '75. There is some question as to whether Martin's embassy kept administration officials in Washington apprised of the critical and fast deteriorating status of the Saigon government, and the military, in '74, months prior to Saigon's final collapse. Martin and his wife were two of the very last Americans to leave South Vietnam during the embassy evacuation on April 30, 1975. *See also* **Operation Frequent Wind.**

Martin Lucifer Coon *see* **King, Reverend Dr. Martin Luther**

Marvelous Speed, Boldness, Surprise ... *see* **Final Offensive**

Marvin-the-Arvin *see* **ARVN**

Mary *see* **LZ Mary**

Mary Jane *see* **Marijuana**

MAS36 (MAS36/51, MAS36/CR39, MAS36/LG48) French made, 7.5mm rifle. Captured MAS36s were used by the NVA/VC. The MAS36 was a bolt action rifle with a five round integral magazine. The NVA/VC used captured French weapons against the FUF in the First Indochina War, and later some of the same weapons against the Americans. The MAS36/51 and /LG48 were capable of firing rifle grenades and the /CR39 had a folding aluminum stock and was originally used by French paratroopers.

MAS36/51 *see* **MAS36**

MAS36/CR39 *see* **MAS36**

MAS36/LG48 *see* **MAS36**

MASH *see* **Mobile Army Surgical Hospital**

Masher *see* **Operation Masher-White Wing**

Mass Graves *see* **Joint Grave, Hue Massacre**

Mass-Focus Weapon *see* **Carolina Moon**

Massachusetts Striker *see* **Operation Massachusetts Striker**

Massacre, Hue *see* **Hue Massacre**

Massacre, My Lai *see* **My Lai**

Massage Parlor *see* **Whorehouse**

MASSCAL Hospital *see* **12th Evacuation Hospital (Semimobile)**

MASSTER (Mobile Army Sensor Systems Test and Evaluation Resources) A DOD group which designed and tested devices to be used for detecting enemy personnel in the field. The most remembered of their personnel detectors was the XM-3 People Sniffer. *See also* **XM-3 People Sniffer.**

Master Chief Petty Officer *see* **E-9**

Master Gunnery Sergeant *see* **E-9**

Master Sergeant *see* **E-8, E-7**

Masturbate GI translations for masturbation: jack-off, pull-your-pud, strokin'-

your-tube, beat-off, shavin'-your-palms, whack-off and get-your-rocks-off.

MAT *see* **Mobile Advisor Team, KIN**

Mat Tran *see* **National Liberation Front**

MAT49 SMG (Pistolet Mitrailleur 1949) French made 9mm submachine gun. The MAT49 had a 32-round magazine and was used by the French in Indochina. The VC modified captured MAT49s for their own use. The guns were modified to use 7.62mm ammunition, a 35-round magazine and had their cyclic rate of fire increased from 600 to 900 rounds per minute. *See also* **Submachine Gun.**

Matador *see* **Operation Matador**

MATSB *see* **Mobile Advance Tactical Support Base**

Mattel Toy Rifle *see* **M-16 Rifle**

Mau Mau *see* **Ju-Ju**

Maureen *see* **FSB Maureen**

Maverick (Stolen Military Vehicles) GI slang for a stolen military jeep or truck. It was not unusual in Vietnam for military vehicles to be "reappropriated" by other units or individuals. If the stolen vehicle was to remain within or near the unit it was originally stolen from for any length of time, the painted serial numbers were usually changed. Sometimes the stolen vehicles would be used for temporary one-way transportation and left abandoned at the thief's final destination. *See also* **Midnight Requisition.**

MAW *see* **Medium Antitank Weapon, Marine Air Wing**

Maxi-Ward (Maxillofacial Unit) Hospital ward that primarily handled facial wounds.

Maxillofacial Unit *see* **Maxi-Ward**

Maxim MMG *see* **Type 24 MMG**

May Second Movement (M2M) 1960s Yale University antiwar movement protesting America's involvement in Vietnam, claiming that the "war is for the suppression of the Vietnamese struggle for national independence." The M2M was principally led by members of the Progressive Labor Party (former members of the Communist Party), and had a very small following.

May Tao Mountains (May Tao Zone) Southernmost extension of the mountains of the Central Highlands. May Tao was 2,867 feet high and at its eastern base was 10kms from the coast. May Tao was located several kms northwest of Ham Tan in Binh Tuy Province, III Corps. The mountain area was called the "May Tao Zone," and served as a major base for elements of the 5th Viet Cong Division. *See also* **FSB Castle.**

May Tao Zone *see* **May Tao Mountains**

May Tree *see* **Palm Trees**

Mayaguez *see* **SS Mayaguez**

Mayflower *see* **Operation Mayflower**

MB I/II *see* **River Division 55**

MC-1 Hourglass Spray System *see* **Operation Ranch Hand**

MCC *see* **Code of Conduct**

McCain, Admiral John *see* **Commander-in-Chief, Pacific Command**

McCloy, John *see* **Wise Old Men**

McCone, John Director of the CIA under Presidents Kennedy and Johnson. In '65 McCone voiced the opinion that President Johnson's gradual escalation of force in SVN would lead the U.S. into a war it couldn't win or easily extricate itself from once engaged. McCone advocated the use of massive air strikes against NVN if American ground forces were to be effective and he further predicted a serious erosion of popular support in the U.S. for the war effort as time went on.

McConnell, General John *see* **Chief of Staff**

McDonald, Admiral David *see* **Chief of Naval Operations**

McElroy, Neil *see* **Secretary of Defense**

McGovern, Senator George U.S. Senator from South Dakota, elected in '63. McGovern opposed the war in Vietnam, advocating the withdrawal of all U.S. troops. Running on a peace platform he lost the '68 Democratic nomination for president to Hubert Humphrey. He won the nomination in '72 and was buried by the Nixon presidential win in the same year.

McGuire Rig Harness assembly used to

extract troops by helicopter. The rig was used by USSF troops from '64 to '68 to extract troops from locations in which the helicopter could not land. The rig featured three web slings the troops sat in, holding on to the straps as they were raised out of the PZ. The troops were vulnerable to enemy fire and returning fire had to be done with one hand, the other being required to hold on to the rig for balance. The McGuire Rig was replaced by the Stabo Rig. *See also* **Stabo Rig, Swiss Seat.**

McMahon, Corporal Charles, Jr. *see* **Last American to Die...**

McNamara, Robert Strange Former president of Ford Motor Company who became the U.S. Secretary of Defense from '61–'68. McNamara believed strongly in the U.S. mission in Vietnam and the military's ability to win the war if sufficiently backed with modern technology. In '67 reports indicated that McNamara's technological advances used were not deterring the NVA/VC. In fact the enemy's tenacity, increasing U.S. casualties, faltering ARVN performance, and GVN corruption brought McNamara to the conclusion that the war in Vietnam would be lost. He began advising President Johnson in '67 to end the bombing of NVN, seek a negotiated settlement, and turn the war over to the ARVN. In November '67 Johnson asked for McNamara's resignation, and got it. *See also* **McNamara's Wall.**

McNamara's Line *see* **McNamara's Wall**

McNamara's Wall (Operation Dye Marker, McNamara's Line, Project Practice Nine, Electric Fence) Operation started in April '67 to build a solid barrier across the DMZ between NVN/SVN to eliminate or slow NVA infiltration into the south. The barrier was to consist of a network of mines, wire, and electronic sensing equipment. The project was never completed because other defense needs in the area took priority. The project was one of Secretary of Defense Robert McNamara's pet projects, and was so labeled in the field. The project was originally named Practice Nine, and renamed Illinois City in '67. It was again renamed Dye Marker before it was suspended and eventually abandoned. *See also* **Operations: Kingfisher, Beau Charger, Hickory,**

Jason Study.

MCRD *see* **Marine Corps Recruit Depot**

MDH-7 Antipersonnel Mine NVA directional antipersonnel mine. The pan shaped mine was 8 inches in diameter, 2 inches high and weighed 8.4 pounds. *See also* **Booby Traps.**

MDMAF *see* **TF 117**

Me Wal Plantation One of many plantations located around Ban Me Thuot. The Me Wal plantation was located near the town of Quang Nhieu. Quang Nhieu was located 14kms north of Ban Me Thuot in Darlac Province, II Corps. The area around Ban Me Thuot was part of the 4th Infantry Division's area of operations. *See also* **4th Infantry Division.**

Measured Response *see* **Operation Rolling Thunder, Escalation**

Meat Factories *see* **Evacuation Hospital (Semimobile)**

MEB *see* **III Marine Expeditionary Force**

Mech *see* **Mechanized**

Mechanical Ambush (MA, Widow Maker) U.S. Army terminology for an ambush setup using claymore mines or other types of mines or booby traps. In Vietnam after '69 Army policy dictated that more mechanical ambushes were to be employed in an effort to reduce the number of U.S. casualties. The typical ambush consisted of a string of several claymores aimed along the kill zone. The claymores would be command detonated, and the small ambush force would fire into the zone and conduct a quick sweep after the ambush. *See also* **Booby Trap, Ambush.**

Mechanical Mule *see* **M-274 Mule**

Mechanized (Mech) Reference to mechanized infantry; mounted infantry using armored personnel carriers and armor. Mechanized units in Vietnam used the M-113 as their APC as well as the M-48 tank and M-551 ARV for support. *See also* **M-113, M-48A3 Tank, M-551 ARV, 5th Infantry Division (Mechanized), Light Infantry, 11th Armored Cavalry.**

Mechanized and Armor Combat Operations, Vietnam *see* **Go/No Go**

Mechanized Infantry see Light Infantry

Med-Techs see Medical Technicians

Medal of Honor see Congressional Medal of Honor

MEDCAP see Medical Civilian Aid Patrols

Medevac (Dustoff, 57th Medical Detachment) Medical evacuation (medevac) helicopter flights. Early in the war any available helicopter was used for medical evacuation of the wounded, but in '62 the first UH-1 Hueys were deployed to Vietnam for medevac duties. The Hueys proved to be ideally suited for the role. The large open doors on the side allowed for easy loading and unloading of litters and the aircraft was maneuverable and relatively agile. Dustoff pilots and their crews experienced a much higher casualty rate than other helicopter crews. Because of the medevacs, wounded troops were usually only minutes from hospital facilities. The term "Dustoff" was the call sign of the first medevacs deployed to Vietnam, the 57th Medical Detachment. According to the terms of the Geneva Convention, ambulance vehicles were not to be fired on by hostile forces. The vehicle had to clearly display the red cross symbol (red cross on a background square or circle of white) and could only be used as an ambulance. Neither the NVA nor the Viet Cong signed the Geneva Convention; they ignored the articles of the Convention and went to great lengths to attack American medevacs and hospital facilities. The UH-1 was the standard medevac helicopter while the larger CH-46, CH-47, and CH-53 were used for larger casualty loads. On occasion the little OH-6 was fitted with two skid mounted litters and used for medevacs. "Casevac" was the Australian term for medical evacuations.

Medevac Priorities In Vietnam medevacs for field casualties were primarily transported by helicopter. Request for medical evacuation was based on a priority system. Marine and Army designations for the priorities differed mainly in name. "Emergency Evac" meant the casualty needed to be evacuated immediately; his wounds were life threatening. Helicopters attempted to pick up emergency casualties even if the unit was under fire. "Priority" or

"Urgent Evac" meant serious wounds, but not life threatening; evacuation could wait until the helicopters could come in without being fired on. "Routine Evac" casualties were lightly wounded and evacuated per convenience of helicopter availability. See also Casualty Classifications.

Medic American combat medics were one of the prime targets for the NVA/VC. One of the enemy tactics was to purposely wound a U.S. soldier so they could kill the medic that came to treat his wounds. Medics attempted to disguise themselves by carrying rifles or toting their medical bags inside their rucksacks. Medics were sometimes given code names allowing them to be called for aid without revealing their identity to the enemy. Some of the code names used were Bravo, and Lame Duck, or whatever the members of the unit agreed on. There were also code names for the type of casualties; "Cadillac" was a KIA, "Ford" was a WIA, again dependent on what the unit agreed upon. See also Combat Medic, Corpsmen, KIA/WIAs, Zulu.

Medical Civic Action Program see Medical Civilian Aid Patrols

Medical Civilian Aid Patrols (MEDCAP, Medical Civilian [Civic/Civil] Assistance [Aid/Action] Program) U.S. Army program similar to the Marines' CAP patrols. An armed patrol with a medic and sometimes a doctor would enter a village or hamlet in the unit's current AO, and provide first aid and hygiene assistance to the people of the village. MEDCAP patrols were sometimes referred to as "Medical Civic Action Patrols" or programs. The Navy also conducted MEDCAP programs as part of their riverine mission. See also Intelligence Civic Action Programs, Combined Action Platoon, TF 116, TF 117.

Medical Civilian Assistance Program see Medical Civilian Aid Patrols

Medical Clearing Station see C & C Company

Medical Corpsmen see Corpsmen

Medical Holds Personnel scheduled to be released from the military, but held due to wounds suffered or illness. Wounds or illnesses had to be sufficiently corrected to allow the individual to be released from the military and returned to civilian life. Medical hold patients were usually undergoing repeated orthopedic or reconstructive surgery or were suffering severe mental problems.

Medical Kit *see* **Unit One**

Medical Profile (Profile, Permanent Profile, Temporary Profile) The "profile" was a record of a soldier's medical problems, maintained in his medical record. There were two types of profiles, the permanent and the temporary. Temporary and permanent conditions that would impact a person's performance of his duties were listed, and restrictions to duty were noted. Illness, injury, or disability allowed the soldier with such a profile to be excluded from certain military duties. In Vietnam a profile could keep a GI out of the field, or get him sent home. Temporary profiles could be granted for anything (medical or psychological) that affected the GI's performance. Permanent profiles were more difficult to obtain.

Medical Tags Heavy stock paper tags carried by medics in the field. The 4 × 7-inch tag was attached by a string to a wounded man's uniform. On the tag was recorded any drug that had been administered to the man before he was evacuated from the field. The tag also included other pertinent information such as the man's name, rough description of the wounds, and treatment provided. A similar tag was used for identification of bodies held in the morgue, the tag unceremoniously attached to the dead man's toe or body bag. *See also* **Unit One.**

Medical Technicians (Med-Techs) Army medical technician that performed nonphysician and nonnursing duties with a medical unit. The med-techs performed the blood testing, x-rays, chemical analysis, etc.

Medical Unit, Self-Contained, Transportable (MUST) U.S. Army field hospital that contained all the facilities necessary to support its surgical and personnel needs, helipads, and a 30- to 90-bed hospital, all transportable by truck. MUST units provided life-saving surgery to the wounded. After surgery the patient was held in the hospital until his condition stabilized, and he could be transferred to larger evacuation and field hospitals for more extensive care. MUST units were a more portable version of the Army's MASH units. In Vietnam the 22d and 45th Surgical Hospitals deployed as MUST units. The 3d and 18th MASH units were MUST equipped in '67. *See also* **3d Field Hospital; 18th, 22d, 45th Surgical Hospitals; Mobile Army Surgical Hospital.**

Medicare *see* **Johnson, President Lyndon Baines**

Medina, Capt. Ernest L. Commander of Charlie Company/1st Bn/20th Inf/11th Inf Bde/Americal Division, Medina was Lt. Calley's company commander during the My Lai incident in March '68. Medina was reportedly aware of the war crimes that had transpired in the hamlet but he made no attempt to stop them or report them afterwards. Medina was later tried for war crimes in '70 along with several other officers and NCOs of the unit, and found not guilty. *See also* **Lt. William Calley, My Lai.**

Medium Antitank Weapon (MAW) During most of the Vietnam War the U.S. and NVA/VC used recoilless rifles to fill the medium antitank weapon's role. U.S. units used the MAWs against fortified enemy positions. The NVA/VC used the MAWs against U.S. vehicles, river craft, and fortifications. *See also* **Recoilless Rifle, Light Antitank Weapon.**

Medium Helicopter Company (MHC) The Army medium helicopter company consisted of CH-47 Chinooks which provided transport for troops and equipment. The Chinook could move the 105mm artillery pieces into places that would normally be considered inaccessible. In Vietnam the CH-47 replaced the CH-37 as the Army's main medium lift helicopter. *See also* **Avn, CH-37, CH-47.**

Medium Helicopter Squadron *see* **HMM**

Medium Machine Gun Several different medium machine guns were used in Vietnam. *See also* **M-1919A6, SG43 MMG, Type 24 MMG.**

MEDMAF *see* **TF 117**

MEDTC *see* **Military Equipment Delivery Team Cambodia**

MEF *see* **Marine Expeditionary Force**

Mekong Delta (The Delta, Rice Bowl) Mekong River delta area in southernmost provinces of SVN, in IV Corps. A vast area of swamps, and mud flats, covering over 5,600-kms of rivers, streams and canals. Longtime

VC stronghold, breadbasket of the RVN, richest, most fertile rice growing region in all of SVN; called South Vietnam's "rice bowl." The Delta represented the agriculturally richest and most populated area in South Vietnam. Prior to '65, over 80 percent of all rice grown in SVN was grown in the Delta of IV Corps. GIs typically referred to the Mekong Delta area as "the Delta" or "the Mekong." *See also* **IV Corps.**

Mekong Delta Mobile Afloat Force (MEDMAF) *see* **TF 117**

Mekong Delta Mobile Riverine Force *see* **TF 117**

Mekong River (Song Mekong, Song Tien Giang River) Over 4,000km-long river with its headwaters in Tibet and its mouth in South Vietnam, emptying into the South China Sea. The Mekong provided a major inland waterway for commerce and transport; the delta area was rich in fertile silt deposits, providing abundant rice growing areas. In an effort to increase the use of the delta lands a system of interconnecting canals and channels was constructed over the years by the Cambodians, Vietnamese and the French. Once inside the borders of Vietnam the Song Mekong, called the Song Tien Giang, split into four branches: the Bassac at Cho Moi, and at Vinh Long the river split into the Song My Tho, Ham Luong and Co Chien. *See also* **Mekong Delta; Fence, The; Upper Mekong River.**

Men with Painted Faces Nickname given to American LRRPs by the NVA/VC. U.S. LRRP and recon troops usually wore camouflage face paint when conducting operations. *See also* **LRRP.**

Mennonites *see* **Conscientious Objector**

Menu *see* **Operation Menu**

Meo (General Vang Pao, Hmong, Miao) Mountain tribes that inhabited the Laotian Highlands of the Plaine des Jarres; also known as the Hmong or Miao. The CIA/USSF-trained Meo troops, led by General Vang Pao, fought the communist Pathet Lao and harassed the NVA along the Laotian segment of the Ho Chi Minh Trail. The Pathet Lao, with NVA support and troops, eventually took control of Laos. Meo troops were effective jungle fighters, but they suffered heavy casualties when NVA

regulars began operating with the Pathet Lao. Meo troops and soldiers of the Royal Laotian Army, with the support of U.S. air power, fought the Pathet Lao and NVA, but Laos fell to the communists in August '75 and was renamed the People's Democracy of Laos. *See also* **Plaines des Jarres, Laotian Accords.**

Meprobate Depressive drug administered as a tranquilizer and muscle relaxer to combat high anxiety reactions. The drug was available in pill form and could cause severe adverse reactions. Meprobate was one of several drugs that were abused in Vietnam. *See also* **Drug List.**

MER *see* **Triple Ejector Rack**

Mercenaries *see* **Nungs**

Mere-Gook-Rule An attitude by some U.S. personnel in SVN that the Vietnamese, as a people, were an inferior race. This belief allowed the mistreatment and abuse of the Vietnamese to seem less of a crime, tolerable or even justified. The moral standard applied to the Vietnamese was not the same as would have been applied to the average American back in the U.S. This led to a widespread tolerance of injustices, and verbal and physical abuses against the Vietnamese. Many GIs considered the enemy (NVA/VC) to be subhuman "gooks," eventually classifying all Vietnamese as "gooks." *See also* **Gook Syndrome.**

Meritorious Unit Citation (MUC) Awarded to an entire U.S. unit for exceptional combat service under hostile conditions for a period of at least six months.

Mermite Cans (Vac Cans, Marmites) Large, vacuum sealed, insulated food containers used for transporting hot food to the field, sometimes called "vac cans." Using Mermite containers and helicopters, field troops could have lukewarm meals delivered to base camps on special occasions such as Thanksgiving and Christmas. When weather and combat conditions were favorable some field units were able to get one warm meal a day. This not only applied to units on garrison duty or at small outposts, but also applied to battalion and some company size units operating in the boonies. *See also* **Hots.**

Mescaline *see* **Hallucinogens**

Mess Hall Food *see* **Hots**

Mess-Up see Fuck-Up

Metal Detector see AN/PRS-3

Meter see Kilometers

Meterological Unit (Metro Unit)
Army Metro units were assigned to artillery
units and collected data on air temperatures
and density, wind speed and direction, and
humidity. This data was submitted to the
Fire Direction Center and entered into the
gun computers which calculated fire mission
gun settings. Metro units also provided
general weather information for aircraft
units.

Meth see Speed

Meth Heads see Speed

Methamphetamine Hydrochloride see
Speed

Methaqualone see Quaaludes

Methedrine see Speed

Methodology of War see Principles
of War

Metrecal Division see Americal Division

Metro Unit see Meterological Unit

METTW Mission, Enemy, Terrain,
Tactics, Weather—Critical factors used to
evaluate a given situation. Army officers
were taught to use these factors to formulate
commands to accomplish their mission.

Meyercourt Hotel One of the hotels
used by U.S. troops on "in-country" R & Rs
in Saigon. See also In-Country R & R.

MFL see Multiple Fragment Lacerations

MFW see Multiple Fragment
Wounds

MG see Machine Gun

MGC see Blackjack Operations

MGF see Blackjack Operations

MH see Congressional Medal of
Honor

MHC see Medium Helicopter
Company, Avn

MIA see Missing in Action

Miao see Meo

Michelin Rubber Plantation Large
French rubber plantation located about
50kms northwest of Saigon, near Dau Tieng
(Tri Tram), in Binh Duong Province, III
Corps. The Binh Duong Province area was
part of the NVA/VC infiltration route into
Saigon and central III Corps. Part of the
plantation was used as an enemy base camp.
During operations by elements of the 1st Infantry Division and the 11th ACR much of
the plantation was destroyed. The 10–15
foot spacing of the rubber trees was con-
ducive to armor operations, and several were
carried out in the plantation. During the
war Dau Tieng served as one of the base
camps of the 1st Infantry Division which
made routine sweeps through the plantation. See also Dau Tieng.

Michigan State University Advisory
Group (MSUAG, MSU Advisory Group)
MSUAG was headed in '54 by Wesley Fishel
and was under contract with the GVN to
provide training for government employees
in the fields of civil service, guards and police. The MSUAG was also responsible for
the reorganization of SVN's National Administration Institute and the reorganization of Diem's administration. The contract
was dissolved by Michigan State University
in '61 when the U.S. government attempted
to keep some returning members of the
MSUAG from publicly speaking out about
the abuses and excesses of the Diem regime.

Mickey Mouse Bullshit see Stateside Bullshit

Mickey Mouse Mission see Milk
Run

MicroGravel Mines see Gravel
Mine, U.S.

Midnight Requisition (Larceny, Reappropriation, Out of Channel Procurement) Nickname for acquiring equipment through nonofficial channels, during
nonofficial hours, with no official approval;
taking what was needed from a supply
depot, another unit without official consent,
knowledge or approval. Your basic military
field reappropriation. See also Maverick,
Strategic Reappropriation.

Midway see USS Midway, TG 76.8

Mien see Montagnards

MiG (MiG-15, MiG-17, MiG-21, Fagot,
Fresco, Fishbed) Soviet made jet fighter

aircraft, piloted by the North Vietnamese. The NVN used the MiG-15 (Fagot), MiG-17 (Fresco) and the MiG-21 (Fishbed) for air defense over NVN. The NVN did not use their Air Force in support of military actions by their ground forces in SVN, but MiGs were used in the air defense role. Due to political restrictions enemy MiGs on the ground were initially safe from attack by U.S. aircraft. U.S. fighters were allowed to engage enemy MiGs if airborne, but pre-emptive ground strikes were not allowed until very late in the war. One of the first MiGs downed in the air war was by a Navy propeller-driven A-1 in June '65. *See also* **Shenyang J-6 (MiG-19), Tail-Gunner, USS Chicago.**

MiG Airfields (Phuc Yen, Kep, Gia Lam, Hoa Loc, Kien An) The North Vietnamese Air Force operated its MiG aircraft from five bases in North Vietnam. Gia Lam was in Hanoi; Phuc Yen and Hoa Lac were within 30kms of Hanoi; Kep was 55kms northeast of Hanoi and Kien An was located just outside of Hai Phong. In April '67 U.S. Air Force and Navy aircraft bombed all NVAF, MiG fields except Gia Lam. Several MiGs were destroyed on the ground and escaping MiGs flew to Communist Chinese bases at Ning Ming, Wuyu and Tianyang for sanctuary. Gia Lam was restricted from attack by the White House because it was NVN's only international airport facility.

MiG CAP *see* **MiG Combat Air Patrol**

MiG Combat Air Patrol (MiG CAP) U.S. aircraft assigned to MiG CAP; were responsible for protecting U.S. strike aircraft from attack by North Vietnamese MiG fighters. F-4 aircraft were assigned the bulk of MiG CAP patrols. *See also* **EC-121, Operation Bolo.**

Mig Watch *see* **EC-121**

MiG-15 (Fagot, Fantail) Soviet built, single seat jet fighter that initially made up part of North Vietnam's Air Force. The "Fantail" or "Fagot" as it was called by Western observers, had a maximum speed of 664mph and a range of 1,960kms. The fighter was armed with one 37mm and two 23mm cannons and could carry up to 1,100 pounds of ordnance. The MiG-15 was initially used against U.S. aircraft, but was not as manueverable or as survivable as the

MiG-17s and 21s that later entered service with the North Vietnamese. *See also* **MiG.**

MiG-17 (Fresco) Soviet made, single seat jet fighter. The MiG-17 was called the "Fresco" by NATO countries and had a maximum speed of 711mph, a range of 2,250kms and was armed with three 23mm cannons. The MiG-17 could also carry 1,100 pounds of bombs or rockets, but its primary mission was that of an interceptor. The North Vietnamese had a number of MiG-17s in their inventory. *See also* **MiG.**

MiG-19 *see* **Shenyang J-6**

MiG-21 (Fishbed) Soviet built, single seat jet fighter, designated the "Fishbed" by NATO observers. The Fishbed had a maximum speed of 1,230mph, a range of 560kms and was armed with one 30mm cannon and two air-to-air missiles. The MiG-21 was an interceptor with sophisticated electronic navigational systems allowing it to operate at night and in all types of weather. The North Vietnamese had several such MiG-21s in their inventory, all supplied by the Soviet Union. *See also* **MiG, Atoll Missile.**

Mighty Mouse Rockets *see* **XM-159C Rocket**

Mighty-Mite (Mity-Mite) Small, gas operated, portable blower used to force smoke and CS gas through enemy tunnel systems. The blowers were not carried by U.S. troops in the field, but were delivered by helicopter if a large enemy tunnel complex was discovered. Smoke was forced through the tunnels in an attempt to locate other tunnel exits, and gas was used to force the NVA/VC out of the tunnels. *See also* **Tunnel Warfare, Air Blowers.**

Mike *see* **LZ Mike**

Mike Boat *see* **LCM-8**

Mike Force *see* **Mobile Strike Force**

Mike-Juliet *see* **Marijuana**

Mike-Mike (Millimeter) Slang for millimeter. *See also* **Area Recon by Fire.**

Mil *see* **Mil Setting**

Mil Setting (Mil) A unit of angular measurement equal to 1/6,400 of a circle. Mil settings were used on aircraft bomb sites, mortars, and artillery pieces to make aiming adjustments to the weapon or bombs. Field artillery pieces were aimed according to the mil setting calculated by the FDC.

Military Affiliated Radio Stations (MARS, Military Amateur Radio Service) Network of ham radio stations and equipment that allowed free phone calls to be made from Vietnam to the U.S., by radio, via the U.S. Signal Corps. GIs with access to a military telephone could place calls to the States, weather and traffic permitting. The military station would make a connection with a ham operator, and the ham would patch the call into the local telephone network. The linkup was made over a two-way radio using standard radio procedures, i.e., callers could not talk at the same time; instead they would take turns, saying "over" when it was the other person's turn to speak. MARS was also known as the Military Amateur Radio Service.

Military Airlift Command (MAC) U.S. Air Force Command responsible for the strategic air movement of U.S. forces worldwide. MAC moved soldiers, their equipment, and supplies, and also functioned in the aeromedical evacuation role. MAC also provided transportation for soldiers bound for R & R destinations outside of Vietnam. In '65 MAC started the "Red Ball Express" program that expedited the processing and delivery of critical cargos to Vietnam. When U.S. troops began to withdraw from Vietnam, MAC played a major role in their redeployment. MAC support continued to Vietnam until April '75 when Saigon fell to the communists. *See also* **Priority 999.**

Military Alphabet *see* **Alphabet**

Military Amateur Radio Service *see* **Military Affiliated Radio Stations**

Military Assistance Advisory Group, Indochina *see* **Military Assistance Advisory Group, Vietnam**

Military Assistance Advisory Group, Vietnam (MAAGV, MAAG, MAAGI) Prior to the establishment of MACV in '62, U.S. military assistance to the RVN was carried out by the members of MAAGV. They coordinated and monitored U.S. aid to the French from '50–'54 and trained and advised the South Vietnamese Armed Forces from '54 to '64. MACV took over responsibility for advising the South Vietnamese in '65

and MAAG was disbanded. MAAG was originally designated MAAG Indochina, which was changed to MAAGV in '55. The original purpose of the group was to provide instructional assistance to French forces acquiring American equipment, but after the French defeat in Indochina, the advisory group focused its efforts on the Vietnamese. *See also* **MACV.**

Military Assistance Command, Thailand (MACT) U.S. command that coordinated military aid and assistance to the Royal Government of Thailand. MACT was established in '62 and was under the command of General Paul Harkins, who was also the first commander of the Military Assistance Command in Vietnam.

Military Assistance Command, Vietnam (MACV) Created in '62 as an advisory command to the South Vietnamese Armed Forces. Later as the war escalated MACV had overall command of all U.S. combat operations in the RVN as well as the training of the South Vietnamese Armed Forces. MACV Headquarters were located in Saigon at the MACV complex at Tan Son Nhut. The MACV commander had operational control of USARV, III MAF, 7th Air Force, Naval Forces Vietnam, 5th SFG, XXIV Corps, I & II Field Force and various pacification programs, and reported directly to the CINCPAC Commander. MACV commanders were Generals Paul Harkins, William Westmoreland, Creighton Abrams and Frederick Weyland. *See also* **Military Assistance Advisory Group, Vietnam; Combat Assistance Teams.**

Military Assistance Program (MAP) Generic name for the many U.S. programs that provided military aid to foreign countries around the world. Under such programs arms, equipment, and advisory personnel could be provided to countries seeking U.S. military aid.

Military Bullshit *see* **Stateside Bullshit**

Military Bus *see* **Chicken Bus**

Military Code of Conduct *see* **Code of Conduct**

Military Crest The military's version of the crest of a hill, the highest defendable point on a hill, providing maximum cover for friendly forces with maximum visibility for sighting and direct fire. The military crest was not always the same as the topographical crest, or physically the highest point on the hill. *See also* **Hill.**

Military Equipment Delivery Team, Cambodia (MEDTC) Team of U.S. personnel stationed in Cambodia which coordinated the delivery of supplies and equipment to the Cambodian Army for use in their struggle against the communist Khmer Rouge. The team was operational from October '71 until April '75. The team was headquartered at Phnom Penh.

Military Hill *see* **Hill**

Military Lawyer *see* **Judge Advocate**

Military Occupation Specialty (MOS, Primary MOS) Number designation used by the military to identify a job skill. The numbers supposedly correlated with equivalent jobs and professions in the civilian work force. The initial classification a soldier received was based on his training and skills. A soldier's job assignments were usually based on his "MOS." In the Army soldiers were initially trained in basic combat and military skills. After basic they were trained in a specific field. After training the soldier was assigned a Primary MOS which was his basic job function in the Army. Cooks, clerks, medics, artillerymen, etc., all had a different MOS. Some soldiers had multiple MOSs depending on their training and time in service. Army MOS codes consisted of two digits and a letter designation for the basic job category; 11B for infantry, 91B medic, 71H for admin clerk, 32E microwave communications. Two additional digits indicated the specialty within the general job code; 71H20 personnel records specialist, 71H30 clerk typist, etc. Additional MOSs were obtained by training or on the approval of the commanding officer. The Marines used a similar system of MOS codes; their codes consisted of four digits. All Marines carried a Primary MOS of infantryman, and their Secondary MOS was their actual job classification. A Marine armor MOS was "1802," and an amphibious tractor operator was a "1806." "0311" was an infantryman, "0369" was a platoon sergeant, "0842" was an artillery RTO, "0321" was a Recon Marine, and "0801" was a field artillery officer. *See also* **11 Bravo, IQ Test.**

Military Paraphraseology Some examples of military paraphraseology: In military terminology you do not "shoot" at someone, you "take the enemy under fire"; you do not "drop bombs" on the enemy; you "expend ordnance" on the target. You do not get "shot" at, you "take hostile fire"; you do not "retreat when you are outnumbered"; you "break contact and make a retrograde movement from a numerically superior enemy force." Civilian property was not "bombed by mistake"; it "suffered collateral damage due to its proximity to the target." You didn't say "assassinations of enemy spies was approved by higher headquarters"; you said "terminations of indigenous personnel were sanctioned by the appropriate control authority." An NCO was not "busted to private," but was "reduced in grade." A soldier didn't have a "job to do"; a soldier "fulfilled his Primary MOS." Enemy food supplies were not destroyed or poisoned; they were "subjected to military resource control." "Enemy troops in the village" were not "napalmed," but "multiple dispersed soft targets, in the vicinity of the specified coordinates, were engaged with soft ordnance." Troops weren't "jailed at LBJ," but "offenders were incarcerated at the Local Military Confinement Center located at Long Binh." FWF troops weren't mistakenly attacked by friendly aircraft; they were "engaged by incontinent ordnance." Troops weren't told to "leave the whores alone"; they were told "not to fraternize with the local indigenous population." A village was not "bulldozed flat," and its occupants "forcibly relocated to a refugee camp"; instead it was "restructured," and the villagers were "resettled to government hamlets."

Military Payment Certificates (Funny Money, Scrip, Play Money, Military Scrip, MPC, Monopoly Money) Military scrip used in place of U.S. currency. Scrip was issued in place of greenback dollars in Vietnam. Regulations ordered that all U.S. currency be exchanged for scrip when troops processed into Vietnam. Scrip could be exchanged for Vietnamese piasters, but scrip brought a higher exchange rate on the black market, and greenbacks brought an even higher return. Scrip was multicolored paper money, 2.5 × 4.5 inches and covered all the usual denominations of U.S. currency and coins. Nicknamed play money, monopoly money, and funny money. *See also* **MPC Changeover.**

Military Peace Corps *see* **SEABEE Technical Assistance Teams**

Military Police (MP) The military maintained its own police force for troop discipline, traffic control, convoy escort, and installation guards. The Army police were called MPs, the Air Force police were called APs, and the Navy and Marines used Shore Patrols (SPs). The criminal division of the military police was called the Criminal Investigations Division. In Vietnam a military "SWAT" team was maintained to handle violent or hostage incidents involving American soldiers at the major U.S. base camps or in the cities. *See also* **Air Police, Shore Patrol, 18th MPs, Criminal Investigations Division, Composite Military Police Strike Force.**

Military Region 4 *see* **Military Regions SVN or NVA/VC**

Military Region 5 *see* **Military Regions, NVA/VC**

Military Region B-3 *see* **Military Regions, NVA/VC**

Military Region Tri-Thien-Hue *see* **Military Regions, NVA/VC**

Military Regions, NVA/VC The NVA/VC subdivided South Vietnam into Military Regions (MR) for control purposes. There were five regions. MR Tri-Thien-Hue consisted of the provinces of Quang Tri and Thua Thien. MR B-3 consisted of the western Central Highlands provinces of Kontum, Pleiku, Darlac and parts of Quang Tin, Binh Dinh, Phu Bon, Phu Yen and Khanh Hoa. MR 5 consisted of the coastal areas of Khanh Hoa, Phu Yen, Binh Dinh, Quang Nam, Quang Tin and Quang Ngai. The rest of SVN fell under COSVN which controlled the provinces of III/IV Corps and Quang Duc, Tuyen Duc, Ninh Thuan, Binh Thuan and Lam Dong provinces. Within the COSVN area was MR 4, which included Saigon and the provinces surrounding it.

Military Regions, SVN (MR 1, MR 2, MR 3, MR 4) In July '70 the name used to describe the four Military Corps Zones in SVN was changed to Military Regions I–IV (1–4) instead of Corps Tactical Zones I–IV. *See also* **Corps Tactical Zones.**

Military Reporting *see* **Friendly Initiated Incident**

Military Scrip *see* **Military Payment Certificates**

Military Scrip Changeover *see* **MPC Changeover**

Military Sealift Command (MSC, MSTS, Military Sealift Transport Service [System]) U.S. naval command responsible for worldwide sea transport of military personnel and supplies. During the VNW most supplies for the war were transported by ship, and very early deployments of entire U.S. units were by ship. Later in the war replacement personnel arrived in RVN by aircraft, but most supplies and munitions were transported by the MSC. Critically short, or emergency supply or equipment items were transported by air. Military Sea Transport Service was the original name of the current MSC. During the fall of South Vietnam in April '75 thousands of Vietnamese refugees were evacuated from Vietnam by MSC. *See also* **Military Airlift Command, Pioneer Commander, Sealift.**

Military Sealift Transport Service (System) *see* **Military Sealift Command**

Military Security Service (MSS) Counterespionage service of the South Vietnamese Army. The CIA speculated that the Chief of the MSS might be an NVA spy passing secret, high level decisions made by the Thieu government directly to North Vietnam. The CIA station in SVN never pursued the issue because the CIA had been instrumental in the MSS Chief's acquisition of his position within the Thieu regime.

Military Solution An attempt to destroy an armed force, using an opposing military force. The attempt only had value if the enemy's will to resist and his aggression could be broken through the use of military power. Ultimately military power could gain physical objectives and apply pressure, but could not in itself end the conflict. A modified "military solution" was attempted in Vietnam by America. It included an escalation which gradually increased U.S. manpower in Vietnam, and increased air attacks against NVN in a series of phased steps. The early American air campaign against NVN did not weaken their resolve of significantly decreasing NVN's support for the war in SVN.

Military Store *see* **Post Exchange**

Military SWAT Team *see* Composite Military Police Strike Force

Militia *see* People's Self-Defense Force

Milk *see* Real Whole Milk

Milk Run (Walk in the Sun, Mickey Mouse Mission) An easy or nonhazardous mission or task. Some GIs in the field referred to such movements or operations as a "Walk in the Sun" or "Mickey Mouse" mission.

Miller, David *see* Catholic Worker Movement

Millimeter *see* Mike-Mike

Million Dollar Wound A wound received in combat that by its nature was not life threatening or crippling, but was serious or incapacitating enough to get the wounded soldier sent home. Some examples of "million dollar wounds" were loss of toes, fingers, hearing, and some stomach wounds. Million dollar wounds were an "automatic ticket back to The World." *See also* Wounded.

Mimot Rubber Plantation *see* Central Office South Vietnam

Min Mine NVA/VC antipersonnel mine made with a cast iron body and a wooden cap. The mine was detonated when the friction fuse in the cap was pulled away from the main body of the mine. A variant of the mine featured a triggering device that was activated when a nail was driven into the detonator charge. *See also* Booby Trap.

Min Xe Dap *see* Bicycle Bomb

Mine Detector *see* AN/PRS-3

Mine Division 112/113 (Detachment Alpha [Alfa]) Special minesweeping forces used to clear the shipping lanes connecting the port of Saigon with the South China Sea. The first minesweep units were deployed to SVN in '67 and were designated Detachment Alfa and operated 57-foot, wooden hulled MSBs. The size of the detachment was increased and renamed Mine Division 112 in early '68. Mine Division 113 was formed in '68 from assets operating in the Rung Sat Special Zone. Both Mine Divisions operated along the Song Nha Be and Song Long Tau attempting to keep the shipping lanes open. *See also* Minesweeper, River.

Minesweeper, Coastal *see* MSC

Minesweeper, Oceangoing *see* MSO

Minesweeper, River (MSB, MSM, MSR, MLMS) Four types of minesweepers were used by the U.S. Navy riverine force in Vietnam. The MSB was a 30-ton, 57-foot, wooden hulled boat. The nonmagnetic boats were armed with two .30cal or M-60 machine guns in the bow and a .50cal machine gun position located at the stern. The minesweepers were very active along Nha Be and Long Tau rivers, which provided access to port facilities located in Saigon. A detachment of minesweepers was also deployed to I Corps to keep the river links to Dong Ha and Hue open. Converted LCM-6s (MSM) were also used as river minesweeps. The MSR was a modified ASPB which was used extensively for minesweep duties. The MLMS was a 50-foot Navy launch modified for the river minesweeping task. *See also* Mine Division 112/113, TF Clearwater, River Division 55.

Minh *see* Duong Van Minh

Minh Thanh Village located 75kms north/northwest of Saigon and 35kms northeast of Tay Ninh, in Binh Duong Province, III Corps. The village was located just north of the Michelin Rubber Plantation and was a Viet Cong base area.

Mini-Arc Light Strikes (Area Fire) Artillery barrage technique developed to enhance normal area fire by ground based artillery. The procedure involved a large number of artillery pieces firing individually at interlocking target zones. The target area covered by the interlocking fires was 500 x 800 meters, with all guns firing simultaneously and continuously for 10–15 minutes. The resulting airbursts saturated the target area with deadly shell fragments. These mini-strikes were compared to the massive Arc Light strikes by B-52 bombers. Targeting and coordination time required for the artillery guns was about an hour. *See also* Arc Light.

Mini-Eagle Flights *see* Insertions of Opportunity

Mini-Pacification Operations *see* County-Fair Operations

Mini-SID *see* Ground Seismic Intrusion Device

Mini-Tet In May '68 shortly after the NVA/VC Tet Offensive the NVA launched a second series of attacks in the Saigon area in an effort to sway public opinion in SVN. The minioffensive was met with stiff and heavy resistance and was quickly put down. *See also* Tet.

Mini-Tet Offensive *see* **Operation Toan Thang**

Minigun Extremely high speed machine gun capable of firing up to 6,000 rounds per minute. The minigun featured an electrically rotated barrel similar to the Gatling gun. In Vietnam the miniguns were 7.62mm and could be found mounted on a variety of vehicles, boats, and aircraft. SUU-11 and GAU-2/A—Air Force minigun pods used on AC gunships. XM-27E1—GP minigun. XM-134/M/134—minigun used in various gun systems (XM-18, -21, -28, -50). XM-93—swivel mounted/pedestal for use on a Huey. XM-18—minigun encased in a pod-helicopter mount.

Minimums "Minimums" referred to the minimum visibility and weather conditions at which an aircraft was allowed to operate. Minimums were established by the major command HQ. In some units subordinate commands were allowed to waive the "below minimum" flying restrictions if the unit's pilots were willing to fly. Army helicopter pilots frequently disregarded the minimums if friendly units were in desperate need of support. Army medevacs were typically flown in extremely bad weather, including fog and rain. Some Marine helicopter pilots tended to avoid flying below the minimums, even though in many instances they operated more powerful or instrument equipped helicopters such as the CH-46 and CH-53.

Mink, Patsy *see* **Abzug, Bella**

Miracle *see* **Operation Miracle**

Miracle Rice *see* **IR8 Rice**

Misfire *see* **Hang Fire**

Missing in Action (MIA) Currently over 2,300 Americans from the Vietnam War are unaccounted for, and are listed as Missing in Action. According to U.S. policy an MIA is carried as missing until his remains are recovered, or there is irrefutable evidence of his death. Many Americans believe that some of our servicemen are still alive in SEA, and are being held by the communists. Since '73, Asian refugees have reported seeing "Americans" being held captive in Southeast Asia. The U.S. has sought to place GR teams in Vietnam to search for all the bodies of American servicemen killed in Vietnam, but the communist government of Vietnam has been reluctant to cooperate. Over the years since the war ended the SRV has allowed several U.S. teams to visit specific aircraft crash sites to recover bodies, but no widespread search activities. SRV has returned the remains of several bodies to the U.S., some of which were American MIAs. SRV denies that there are any Americans held in Vietnam, but communist countries have a history of not releasing all the POWs they have held. Some POWs held by Russia after WWII, and North Korea and China after the Korean War, were held for several years before being released. Some POWs held by NVN after the defeat of the French in '54 were not released by the communists until '79. Based on the communists' past record there is a possibility that some Americans are still being held prisoner in SEA. SRV refuses to cooperate fully in the search for American MIAs as long as the U.S. refuses to accept the SRV communist government as the true, chosen representative of the Vietnamese people. *See also* **Discrepancy Case.**

Mission Council Weekly meeting by various U.S. agencies operating in Vietnam. The meeting covered the previous week's events and the coordination of upcoming agency activities. The meetings were first organized and chaired by U.S. Ambassador Maxwell Taylor in '64, and eventually became the responsibility of CORDS. *See also* **Civil Operations and Revolutionary Development.**

Mission Ready (Not Operationally Ready, NORS, NORS-G) Military status indicating that the labeled item was ready to perform its assigned mission. This status applied to equipment, vehicles, aircraft and units. The opposite of the ready status was NORS (Not Operationally Ready for Service). For aircraft it was specified as NORS-G (Not Operationally Ready for Service—Grounded). *See also* **Down.**

Mission, Enemy, Terrain, Tactics, Weather *see* **METTW**

Mister *see* Warrant Officer

Mister Charlie *see* Caucasian

Misty FACs *see* Commando Sabre Missions

Mit *see* Jackfruit

Mites *see* Annamese, Vets

Mitterand, François *see* We Have Granted Vietnam "Full Independence"...

Mity-Mite *see* Mighty-Mite

MIUWG *see* Mobile Inshore Undersea War Group

Mixed Artillery *see* Composite Battery

Mixmaster *see* Operation Mixmaster

Mk-2 Hand Grenade (Pineapple Frag) U.S. fragmentation grenade, 4.5 inches long and 2.25 inches in diameter, elongated (egg) in shape and weighing about 22 ounces, commonly called a "pineapple frag." The grenade's outer shell was made of serrated cast iron, and it was filled with TNT. The Mk-2 was fitted with a safety pin; when the pin was pulled and the grenade's handle released, detonation took place in 7–10 seconds. The effective blast radius of the Mk-2 was about ten meters. *See also* **Hand Grenade.**

Mk-3A2 Offensive Hand Grenade (Concussion Grenade) U.S. antipersonnel hand grenade used against enemy bunkers, tunnels and enclosures. When the grenade detonated it released a shock wave that could kill or render unconscious the occupants of a closed vehicle or bunker. The cylinder shaped grenade was 5.3 inches in diameter and weighed one pound. When used in the open the blast range was about 35 meters, and would only cause serious injury if the grenade exploded within 10 meters of the target. The grenade was extremely effective, and lethal, if detonated in a confined space. *See also* **Hand Grenades.**

Mk 5 *see* **Centurion**

Mk-10/18/19/20 Grenade Launchers *see* **Grenade Launchers, Navy**

Mk-20 CBU (Antitank CBU) Antitank cluster bomb unit. The Mk-20 was designed to be used against armored vehicles but it proved to be very effective as an antipersonnel weapon. The CBU featured 9-inch finned, armor piercing darts that were dispersed as the CBU broke up over the target. *See also* **Cluster Bomb Unit.**

Mk 30 AAM *see* **Sidewinder Missile**

Mk-81/82 Retarded Bombs *see* **Retarded Bombs**

Mk-81/82/83/84 GP Bombs *see* **GP Bombs**

Mle 24/29 (Fusil Mitrailleur Modeles 1924/29, Modele 24/29) French light machine gun. The 7.5mm, gas operated gun could use a 150-round drum, but in Indochina it used a 25-round magazine. The gun was used by French forces and captured weapons were later used by the NVA/VC. The weapon weighed over 22 pounds when loaded and had a cyclic rate of fire of 500 rounds per minute. *See also* **Light Machine Gun.**

MLMS *see* **River Minesweepers**

MLR *see* **Main Line of Resistance**

MN-19 Runway Panels Interlocking steel panels that were used in Vietnam to create all-weather runway and taxi surfaces. The ground surface for the panels was graded and leveled before the four-foot-square steel panels were installed. *See also* **Perforated Steel Plate.**

Mnong *see* **Montagnards**

Mnong Plateau (Plateau Du Mnong) Plateau located at the southwestern edge of the Central Highlands near the border of II and III Corps. The City of Song Be was perched on the edge of the plateau overlooking the flat jungles of northern III Corps.

Mo-Fo *see* **Do Ma**

Mobile Advance Tactical Support Base (MATSB) A mobile base used by the Navy to support its river and coastal activities in the Delta of IV Corps. An MATSB consisted of several "Ammi barges" strung together and anchored near the center of a major waterway. The base consisted of sandbagged shelters, defensive positions and berthing facilities for the Navy patrol craft. The base also had a helipad that could support several helicopters. The base was towed into place and could be easily shifted to new locations within the AO to provide mobility and support to riverine operations. *See also* Operation Sea Float.

Mobile Advisor Team (MAT) Vietnamese advisory teams that trained RF/PF forces throughout SVN. The MAT teams were trained by U.S. Army advisors, who also accompanied some of the MAT teams in the field. The U.S. Advisory MAT team consisted of two officers, three enlisted men and an interpreter. The MAT training center was located at Di An, northeast of Saigon, and began operation in February '68. The center closed down in September '71.

Mobile Army Sensor Systems Test and Evaluation *see* **MASSTER**

Mobile Army Surgical Hospital (MASH) Small, mobile Army hospital units that provided emergency, life-saving surgery to wounded soldiers. The MASH 30–120 bed units typically treated field casualties suffering from immediate life-threatening wounds. After the MASH unit stabilized the patient he was transferred to the larger evacuation or field hospitals. A patient's stay at a MASH unit was not usually longer than three days. Some MASH units were MUST equipped in '67. The MUSTs were more portable than the MASHs, allowing the entire hospital facility to be disassembled, moved by truck, and reassembled in a matter of hours. *See also* **Medical Unit, Self-Contained, Transportable.**

Mobile Camp Operations Operations conducted in the IV Corps area by Mobile Strike Force units. A patrol base would be established in a known enemy area with one or two MSF companies. The companies would operate against the NVA/VC for a period of thirty days, conducting ambushes, searches, and harassment of the enemy base area. After thirty days one of the MSF companies was replaced with a new company. The rotation continued until enemy activity in the area shifted to another location. The patrol base or "mobile camp" would be extracted and moved to a new location and the process began again. The mobile camps were completely self-supporting and resupplied by air. *See also* **Mobile Strike Force.**

Mobile Crotch Rot *see* **Venereal Diseases**

Mobile Defense *see* **Dynamic Defense**

Mobile Fire Support Base *see* **Artillery Barge**

Mobile Guerrilla Company *see* **Blackjack Operations**

Mobile Guerrilla Force *see* **Blackjack Operations**

Mobile Inshore Undersea War Group (MIUWG) U.S. Navy group that provided temporary harbor and port security for Navy vessels in RVN, from '65 to '67. The MIUWG was used in Vietnam until a permanent harbor security force, the IUWG, could be deployed and sufficiently trained. The IUWG took over harbor security duties in SVN's harbors in '67 and operated as part of TF 115. *See also* **TF 115, SEASHARP.**

Mobile River Base *see* **Mobile Riverine Base**

Mobile River Group (MRG) As the assets of the Mobile Riverine Force increased in '68, two mobile river groups within TF 117 were formed. Mobile River Group Alpha was based in Kien Hoa Province and operated five RADs while Mobile River Group Bravo was based in the central Delta around Can Tho with three RADs. The groups continued operations until their assets were transferred to the Vietnamese in '69. The five RADs of Group Alpha were 91, 92, 111, 112 and 151. Group Bravo consisted of RAD 121, 132 and 152. *See also* **TF 117, RAD, RAS.**

Mobile Riverine Base (MRB, Mobile River Base, Afloat Base) Mobile base used by U.S. riverine forces in support of operations conducted throughout the Delta of IV Corps. The MRB provided billets for combat troops, repair facilities for the boats of the MRF, hospital facilities, and limited direct fire support. Navy LSTs and APBs were used to house troops and support personnel. Deck mounted helo pads were attached to some of the MRBs, allowing the helicopters to be remotely supported from the base. The MRB was motorized and could operate on the larger rivers of the Delta. *See also* **LST, APB, ASpB, TF 116, TF 117.**

Mobile Riverine Force *see* **TF 117**

Mobile Strike Force (Mike Force, M Force, MSF) In '64 company sized CIDG Mobile Strike Forces were enlarged from 150 men to 500-men battalion Mobile Strike Forces or Mike Forces, divided into companies. The Mike Forces were trained and led by USSF A-Teams and provided a heavily armed reaction and recon force to aid CIDG camps in their area. Assigned to each Mike Force was a special recon platoon or company that conducted intelligence gathering, ambushes and raids behind enemy lines, and also a Nung platoon or company used to provide security. Until the Mike Forces were transferred to Vietnamese control they were under command control of Detachment B-55, U.S. Special Forces. *See also* Strike Force, Detachment B-55, Mobile Strike Force Command, Black Hawk.

Mobile Strike Force Command (MSF Command, MSFC) Command established to control the operations of Mobile Strike Force battalions. An MSF Command was established in each of the four Corps Tactical Zones in '65. The command typically controlled several Mobile Strike Forces, each consisting of several CIDG battalions, a recon company, a Nung security company and a controlling USSF A-Team. The command dissolved with the withdrawal of the USSFs in '71. *See also* Mobile Strike Force.

Mobile Support Base *see* River Division 55

Moc Hoa Provincial capital of Kien Tuong Province located in the northern Delta of IV Corps, 75kms west of Saigon and 7kms south of the Cambodian border. Moc Hoa also served as an ARVN outpost and a U.S. Special Forces Camp. Moc Hoa was strategically situated near the center of the Plain of Reeds, a longtime Viet Cong base and training area.

Model 70 Winchester (Winchester) 30-06 sniper rifle used by the Marines in Vietnam. *See also* Sniper.

Modele 24/29 *see* Mle 24/29

Modified Table of Equipment (MTOE, Modified Table of Organization and Equipment) An Army unit was assigned certain equipment and personnel as outlined in the unit's Table of Organization and Equipment. Because of combat conditions and field expedience in Vietnam, the table was found to be inappropriate or lacking for the current situation. The MTOE al-

lowed temporary changes to a unit's TOE requirements allowing the unit to fulfill its required mission. An example of such a change was the 81mm mortar. Normally an infantry company had 2–3 mortars assigned, but infantry companies of the 9th Infantry Division operated in the field without their mortars. The mortars were kept at the base camp and not usually humped to the field. *See also* Table of Organization and Equipment; Organic.

Mogas *see* Jet Fuel

Mohawk *see* OV-1

Moi *see* Montagnards, Nguoi Thuong

Mojave *see* CH-37

MON *see* Monitor

Mon Ky *see* Monkey Mountain

Monday Pill *see* Chloroquine

Money Order *see* Finance

Mongoose *see* Eight-Klick Ville

Monitor (River Battleship, Heavies, MON) Modified LCMs used as command and fire support boats for riverine operations in Vietnam; designated MON. Armored LCMs were modified by having their bow ramps replaced with a rounded bow, and a gun turret mounted in the front of the boat. The turret weapon was usually a 40mm cannon, 105mm howitzer or flamethrower. In addition, the boat had an assortment of 20mm cannons, .30 and .50cal machine guns, grenade launchers and an 81mm mortar. The American version was sometimes fitted with miniguns and grenade launchers, as well as special protective RPG screens. The 60-foot boats, nicknamed "heavies," could do 8 knots and had a crew of eleven. *See also* CCB, Standoff Armor, Water Cannons.

Monkey Mountain (Mui Da Nang, Mon Ky) 2,228-foot mountain located on the northern end of the Tien Sha Peninsula northeast of Da Nang. The peninsula comprised the southern arm of Da Nang Bay and was called "Mui Da Nang" or "Mon Ky" mountain by the Vietnamese. During the war the Air Force established a radar station on the mountain (Panama Station) and the Marines deployed Hawk missiles to protect the air base at Da Nang from air attack. *See also* 1st LAAM, Da Nang.

Monkey Strap *see* **Bunji Strap**

Monkeys *see* **Rock Apes**

Mono Buoy *see* **Swivel-Top Buoy**

Monom *see* **Montagnards**

Monopoly Money *see* **Military Payment Certificates**

Mons Six *see* **1st Infantry Division Fire Bases**

Monsoons (Rainy Season, Southeast Monsoons, Northeast Monsoons) Seasonal wind-blown rains that were prevalent in Asia and India. In Vietnam the summer (southeast) monsoon season extended from June–September and mostly affected III and IV Corps; the winter (northeast) monsoons hit I and II Corps October–March. The monsoons played a large part in the war. During the wet seasons, ground, especially armor movement, was greatly reduced, and air cover was dependent on favorable skies. Successful large-scale operations had to be planned to coincide with the dry periods. The southeast monsoons were characterized by daily, sudden, drenching downpours. The northeast monsoons covered the area with low clouds and drizzle, restricting air operations. *See also* **Dry Monsoons, Crachin.**

Monster *see* **AN/PRC-77, PACV**

Monster Net *see* **Secure Net**

Montagnard Rice Wine *see* **Numpai**

Montagnard Shaman (Yard Witch Doctor) Tribal medicine man and spiritual priest of the Montagnard tribes. Montagnard shamans worked for the good of the tribe, healing the sick, fighting evil spirits and prophesying. The yard shaman also acted as the tribal teacher in the ways of the Montagnards, passing on the verbal history of his people. *See also* **Katha.**

Montagnard Witch Doctor *see* **Montagnard Shaman**

Montagnards (Yards, Tribes: Rhade, Jarai, Bahnar, Sedang, Bru, Moi, Katu, Koho, Chru, Hre, Ma, Chil, Drung, Nongao, Halang, Ragulai [Roglai], Rongao, Bong, Tuong, Mien, Mnong, Stieng, Cau [Ca], Chrau, Pacoh, Jeh, Hroy, Duan, Takua, Tem, Monom, Strieng)** Aboriginal tribes of the Central Highlands mountain range in South Vietnam and Laos. In '61 the U.S. Special Forces began organizing the various tribes into armed village defense forces, called CIDGs, capable of defending themselves against the NVA/VC. The "Yards" were discriminated against by the Vietnamese people, but fought the NVA/VC under USSF's direction. There were many different tribes scattered throughout the Annamitique mountain range running north-south through North Vietnam, South Vietnam and Laos. During the course of the Vietnam War the U.S., South Vietnam and North Vietnam tried to control and win the support of the mountain tribes. The U.S. originally hired Yards as a defensive force to protect the mountain villages, paying them as mercenary soldiers. The USSF respected the Yards and the Yards, in turn, trusted and were loyal to their American advisors. The GVN relocated many Yard villages, placing the inhabitants in camps and making them conform to Vietnamese society. The Vietnamese generally looked down upon the Yards, treating them as inferiors and called them "Moi," which meant "savage." The conflict between the two peoples continued throughout the war. The Yards would fight for the Americans but wanted nothing to do with the Vietnamese. The North Vietnamese also tried to win the support of the Yards who lived in the mountain regions of North Vietnam. Under Ho Chi Minh's direction in '54 many Yards were trained as teachers, medics, soldiers and government spokesmen and relocated throughout the various tribal zones. Some of the zones were allowed to govern themselves on a limited basis and were even granted recognition in NVN's National Assembly. Some members of the Katu tribe operated with NVA/VC as guides; members of other Yard tribes were often "drafted" into the service of the NVA as guides and bearers, operating in the jungle areas near the Ho Chi Minh Trail. The majority of the mountain tribes wanted little to do with the war, the Americans or the Vietnamese. Both sides, north and south, had their "friendly Yards." It is estimated that less than 600,000 Montagnards survived the war and more than 90 percent of the survivors have been displaced from their ancestral lands. The name Montagnards was the French name for the mountain aboriginal tribes. The lowland Vietnamese were small and light skinned with slanted eyes, some resembling the Chinese. By comparison the "Yards" had dark brown skin, large eyes and tended to be larger in stature than the Vietnamese, and were of Malayo-Polynesian heritage. *See also* FULRO, Chams, Longhouse, Happy House, Nguoi Thuong, Vietnam's Niggers.

Montezuma *see* **LZ Montezuma**

Monument to the Countries Aiding South Vietnam *see* **Turtle Monument**

Moonbeam Call sign for one of the Air Force's night duty airborne battlefield command and control centers that coordinated night bombing missions. *See also* Airborne Battlefield Command and Control Center.

Moonshine *see* **Flares**

Moore, Mary Tyler *see* **Hope, Bob**

Moore *see* **FSB Moore**

Moored Mines *see* **Limpet Mine**

Moorer, Thomas *see* **Chief of Naval Operations**

MOOSE *see* **Project MOOSE**

Mopping Up Actions *see* **Clear and Hold**

Morality Law *see* **Dance Ban**

Moratorium Day (M-Day, Vietnam Moratorium Committee) A nationwide, one-day demonstration in October '69 designed to show the Nixon administration and the Congress the depths of the antiwar movement and the sentiment of the American people. Millions participated in the demonstration in a variety of ways. At college campuses across the country moderate and radical antiwar speakers spoke to crowds of students and faculty. Some supporters of the moratorium handed out leaflets on street corners and door-to-door; others rode with their car headlights on. Mayor Lindsay of New York City declared a day of mourning, and ordered the city's flags flown at half mast. Several large labor unions supported the demonstration and more than 250,000 people marched in Washington, D.C., on M-day.

Morgue Facilities *see* **Zipper Room**

Morning Report (DA Form 1, Morning Reports Clerk) Army report that tracked the wounded, missing, killed, AWOLs, sick calls, and leave and on-duty status of every man assigned to the unit. From the Morning Report Form (DA Form 1), in theory, the status of every American soldier in the Army could be monitored. Information for the report was collected each morning by an assigned clerk who passed the information on to higher headquarters. At the higher levels there were clerks whose primary duty was the Morning Report (Morning Reports Clerk). Platoon leaders passed personnel information to the Company Clerk, who relayed the numbers to higher headquarters. Troop status was more difficult to track in Vietnam because of R & Rs, extended patrols, DEROS, replacement troops, and the vagaries of combat.

Morning Reports Clerk *see* **Morning Report**

Moron Corps (Armed Forces Qualification Test [AFQT]) Nickname given to men who were inducted into the military as part of Project 100,000. The project inducted over 350,000 men into the military during the Vietnam War. The normal passing score on the Armed Forces Qualification Test (AFQT) was 31 percent. The minimum for Project 100,000 applicants was only 10 percent. The normal minimum score had been waived by the Johnson administration to fill out the ranks of the military, and get some of America's "disadvantaged youth" off the streets. The vast majority of men caught in the Project 100,000 sweeps were poor blacks from the South and urban ghettos, poor Southern whites, and Mexican-Americans. With the lowering of entrance requirements some men who had flunked out of college, or barely finished high school were able to enlist in the Army to become officers. The needs of the service for low level leaders caused the Army to lower its OCS requirements, which resulted in the graduation of some "marginal" officers. *See also* **Project One-Hundred Thousand, Black American Soldier.**

Morphine (Morphine Syrettes) Medics carried a supply of syrettes and some recon and Special Forces troops carried individual syrettes for self-injection if wounded. Syrettes were typically ¼–¾ grams of morphine. Standing orders in the field were no morphine for those with stomach, head or chest wounds. The morphine caused swelling in the head; it also caused the body functions to slow down, starting from the area of injection first and working its way into the rest of the body. In the field, once a syrette of morphine was administered, the empty vial was pinned to the wounded man's collar; this allowed anyone treating him later to know how much morphine had been administered. *See also* **Morphine Restrictions.**

Morphine Restrictions   During the early days of the war many U.S. troops, operating in the field, carried individual syrettes of morphine for self-injection when wounded. After '67 restrictions were placed on the individual soldier carrying morphine syrettes due to an increase in drug abuse and the relative speed with which a wounded soldier could be pulled out of the field for hospitalization. Combat medics still carried a supply of syrettes, but the individual field soldier was no longer issued the morphine for self-injection. Troops in high risk operations such as long-range reconnaissance, USSF and SOG teams still carried their individual syrettes.

Morphine Syrettes *see* **Morphine**

Morrison, Norman *see* **Burn Yourselves, Not Your Draft Cards**

Morse, Senator Wayne (Senator Ernest Gruening)   Wayne Morse and Ernest Gruening were the only two members of the U.S. Senate to vote against the Southeast Asia Resolution (Gulf of Tonkin Resolution); the vote was 88–2, in favor of the resolution. Morse challenged the Johnson administration's version of the incidents in the Gulf of Tonkin. Other senators were critical of the resolution, fearing it would give the President the power to make war, a congressional power established by the Constitution. Critical or not, the Senate passed the resolution. The House of Representatives unanimously endorsed the resolution with all "yes" votes except for Adam Clayton Powell's vote of "present," which was recorded as a "yes" vote. *See also* **Powell, Representative Adam Clayton.**

Mort *see* **Mortar**

Mortar (Tubes, Mort, Piss-Tube)   Small artillery pieces, man portable or vehicle mounted, carried by infantry and providing them with organic fire support. Rounds were dropped down the mortar tube and lobbed towards the target. Nicknamed tubes, piss-tubes. In Vietnam the US/ARVNs used 60mm, 81mm and 4.2-inch mortars (Tubes). The NVA/VC used 50mm, 60mm, 81/82mm, 120mm and any captured weapons available. Enemy 82mm mortar tubes were capable of firing both U.S. 81mm mortar rounds and their own 82mm rounds, whereas U.S. 81mm mortars could not use the enemy 82mm rounds. *See also* **M-30 4.2-Inch Mortar, Type 31 Mortar, Type 53 Mortar, M-1 Mortar, M-19, M-29 81mm Mortar, M43 160mm Mortar, M41 Mortar, M38 Mortar.**

Mortar Air Delivery System (MAD System)   Field expedient system devised by helicopter crews of the 173d Airborne Brigade. The system consisted of a box attached to the side door area of a UH-1D/H helicopter. Attached to the box was a slide chute. The box was filled with stacked and armed 81mm mortar rounds. The helicopter would hover over a target and the crew chief would release the mortar rounds. The MAD System gave the "Herd" a limited bomber capability.

Mortar Fire *see* **High Angle Hell**

Mortar Increment (Powder Charge)   Premeasured charges used to propel mortar rounds. U.S. mortars used small bags containing the explosive propellant; NVA mortars used small paperlike disks. The charges were placed around the fins, and the combination of charge and the elevation of the mortar tube determined the range of the round. Some artillery guns also used individual bags of propellant called "powder charges" to launch their projectiles.

Mortar Magnets   Marine nickname for the C-130 aircraft that kept Khe Sanh Combat Base supplied during the NVA siege in early '68. Whenever one of the C-130s (Hercs) made an approach or landed on the airstrip at Khe Sanh, enemy mortars and rockets bombarding the base would greatly increase in an attempt to hit the aircraft. *See also* **C-130, Khe Sanh, LAPES.**

MOS *see* **Military Occupation Specialty**

Mosby *see* 1st Infantry Division Fire Bases

Mosin-Nagant Rifle (M1891/30, Type 53 Carbine, K-44, Red Stock Rifle, Red Butt Rifle) The standard sniping and infantry rifle used by the NVA/VC. The Russian made Mosin-Nagant Model 44 (K-44), bolt action rifle fired .30cal (7.62mm) cartridges, with a maximum effective range of 900 meters. The rifle used a 5-round, integral magazine and was normally fitted with a 3.5-power PU or the 4-power PE telescopic sight. American scopes used cross hairs in their reticle; the NVA/VC scopes used a pointed aiming post instead. The PRC version of the weapon was called the Type 53 Carbine and both versions were used by the NVA/VC. The K-44 was nicknamed the "Red Butt" because of its red, wooden stock. *See also* **Sniper, SVD Rifle.**

Mosquito Netting *see* Insect Bar

Most Ricky-Tick[y] *see* Book

Mothball Fleet *see* National Defense Reserve Fleet

Mother Green *see* Crotch, The

Mother Vietnam *see* House 7 Radio Group

Mother-Fucker *see* Do Ma

Motor Junks *see* Junks

Motorcycles (Honda, Suzuki) One of the main forms of motor transportation available to the individual Vietnamese was the motorcycle. Thousands of motorcycles and motorscooters were used in the towns and cities across South Vietnam. Many of these found their way to the VC and were used for transport along sections of the Ho Chi Minh Trail. Most of the cycles and scooters used very small engines, usually less than 60cc. Harley Davidson didn't have any impact on the Vietnamese cycle market, but Honda, Suzuki and Lambretta were much in evidence on the streets of Saigon. *See also* **Lambretta.**

Mountain Aborigines The mountain aborigines of Vietnam's Central Highlands were called the "Montagnards" by the French. The name applied to all the mountain tribes that inhabited the I and II Corps areas. *See also* **Montagnard.**

Mountain Commandos (Mountain Scouts) USSF's trained, CIDG units who conducted offensive patrols in their area. The CIDGs were originally established to provide defensive support for their mountain villages, but in the mid-sixties the focus of the CIDG program changed from a strictly defensive nature to a program of defense combined with active offensive patrols and surveillance of the NVA/VC.

Mountain Men *see* Montagnards

Mountain Scouts *see* Mountain Commandos

Mourning Clothes *see* Tang Phuc

Mouse Trap Detonator Nickname for the trip wire release mechanism that was used to detonate the M-18A1 Claymore mine. The claymore was normally electrically detonated. The cylinder shaped "mouse trap" detonator screwed into the top of the claymore and when tripped, detonated the blasting cap, firing the claymore. *See also* **M-18 Claymore Mine.**

MP *see* Military Police

MP SWAT Team *see* Composite Military Police Strike Force

MPC *see* Military Payment Certificates

MPC Changeover (Military Scrip Changeover, Changeover Day) Changeover consisted of American soldiers turning in their MPC to their finance unit. Several days later new MPC was issued to the soldiers. The new issue MPC was a different series and became the current legal tender used by the U.S. military in Vietnam. Only Americans were to possess and use MPC, but it invariably found its way to the black market. Since only Americans were to have MPC and be involved in the exchange, others holding MPC would be excluded from the exchange and left holding worthless MPC. The changeover was an unsuccessful attempt by MACV to discourage the use and exchange of MPC in the black market. *See also* **Military Payment Certificates.**

MPD-C *see* XM-2 People Sniffer

MPQ-4 Radar *see* AN/MPQ-4 Radar

MR 1 *see* Military Regions, SVN

MR 2 *see* Military Regions, SVN

MR 3 *see* Military Regions, SVN

MR 4   see   Military Regions, SVN

MR 4 (NVA/VC)   see   Military Regions, NVA/VC

MR 5 (NVA/VC)   see   Military Regions, NVA/VC

MR B-3   see   Military Regions, NVA/VC

MR I   see   Military Regions, SVN

MR II   see   Military Regions, SVN

MR III   see   Military Regions, SVN

MR IV   see   Military Regions, SVN

MR Tri-Thien-Hue   see   Military Regions, NVA/VC

MRB   see   Mobile Riverine Base

MRF   see   TF 117

MRG   see   Mobile River Group

MSB   see   Minesweeper, River

MSC (Minesweeper, Coastal)   American made minesweeper used by the French and Vietnamese for coastal mine clearing patrols. The 270-ton MSC was capable of making 13 knots, was metal hulled and armed with two 20mm cannons. *See also* TF 115.

MSC   see   Military Sealift Command

MSF   see   Mobile Strike Force

MSF Command   see   Mobile Strike Force Command

MSFC   see   Mobile Strike Force Command

MSG   see   SOG Groups

MSM   see   River Minesweepers

MSO (Minesweeper, Oceangoing)   U.S. Navy oceangoing minesweeper used for coastal surveillance and interdiction along the coast of South Vietnam. The minesweepers were part of TF 115, Operation Market Time. MSOs began operations off the coast of SVN in '61 using their radar to detect targets and vector South Vietnamese Navy forces to intercept those targets. The MSOs began their own intercepts in '65 as part of TF 115. *See also* TF 115, Market Time.

MSQ-77   see   Combat Skyspot

MSR   see   River Minesweepers

MSS   see   Military Security Service

MSTS   see   Military Sealift Command

MSTS Card (MSTS Kula Gulf)   Military sea transports that moved the 1st Cavalry Division to Vietnam in '65. During WWII the ships had been "Jeep Carriers" or escort carriers, and the small "flat tops" made an excellent helicopter transport. In December '61 the first load of CH-21 "Flying Bananas" arrived on board the Card and were unloaded at Saigon. The choppers were manned and maintained by U.S. Army helicopter crews of the 8th and 57th Transportation Company. The Card made several trips delivering helicopters and their crews. In May '64 Viet Cong frogmen placed underwater charges on the Card and sank her while she was off-loading helicopters in Saigon. The Card was later raised and returned to the U.S.

MSTS Kula Gulf   see   MSTS Card

MSU Advisory Group   see   Michigan State University Advisory Group

MSUAG   see   Michigan State University Advisory Group

MTAB   see   M-60 AVLB

MTOE   see   Modified Table of Equipment

Mu Gia Pass   Strategic mountain pass located in Quang Binh Province, NVN. The pass through the Truong Son Mountains was used by NVN to move war materiels to South Vietnam. The pass was a frequent target of U.S. strike aircraft. Mu Gia Pass was located on the border between North Vietnam and Laos, 110kms south of Vinh and 78kms west of Quang Khe (on the coast of NVN). Early in the war there was talk of a U.S. invasion into the southern panhandle of NVN to seize the pass, but no invasion of NVN was ever seriously considered by the U.S. administration. U.S. military experts believed it was essential to cut the flow of supplies from NVN to SVN if the American effort in Vietnam was to succeed.

Muang Xepon   see   Tchepone

MUC   see   Meritorious Unit Citation

Mud Ball   Viet Cong booby trap that consisted of a large, weighted mud ball bristling with sharpened bamboo spikes.

The ball was hung on a vine and suspended out of sight; when tripped, the ball was released to swing into the path of approaching troops. *See also* Booby Trap.

Mud River *see* Igloo White

Muhammad Ali *see* Ali, Muhammad

Mui Da Nang *see* Monkey Mountain

Mule GI nickname for a Viet civilian who transported arms, ammunition and supplies for the NVA/VC. These mules made their way down the Ho Chi Minh Trail, or along the numerous resupply routes within South Vietnam transporting their goods on their backs or by bicycle. The mules were generally in their early teens, male or female. *See also* M-274 Mule.

Mule Train (Operation Mule Train) Code name for a squadron of Air Force C-123 transports deployed to SVN in November '61. The transports provided lift support to the South Vietnamese Armed Forces. The squadron, the 346th Tactical Control Squadron, was under the command of the 2d ADVON located at Tan Son Nhut. *See also* Operation Saw Buck II, 2d Air Division, Project Mule Train.

Multiple Ejector Rack *see* Triple Ejector Rack

Multiple Fragment Lacerations *see* Multiple Fragment Wounds

Multiple Fragment Wounds (MFW, Multiple Fragment Lacerations, MFL) Military terminology for fragmentation or shrapnel wounds.

Multiple Rocket Launcher (MRL) Artillery rocket launcher system employing multiple tubes. In Vietnam MRLs were found on U.S. Navy LSMR ships. The NVA/VC used MRLs sparingly, but widely used the single tube versions of the MLRs. *See also* LSMR, BM14/21, Type 63, DKZ-B.

Multiple Unit Training Assembly (MUTA) Multiple National Guard or Army Reserve units assembled for a combined training exercise.

Multiple-Shot Grenade Launchers *see* Grenade Launchers

Muscle Shoals *see* Igloo White

Musical Villages *see* Landgrab Campaign

MUST *see* Medical Unit, Self-Contained, Transportable

Mustang (Field Commission) An officer who started his career in the military as an enlisted man and worked his way up through the ranks and was offered, and accepted, a commission based on his leadership abilities and performance. Such field commissions were usually only awarded during wartime conditions.

MUTA *see* Multiple Unit Training Assembly

Mutilations (Ears, Noses) The VC often tortured and mutilated captured GIs, leaving them in a place their unit would surely find them. The most common VC technique was to cut the man's ears and nose off, or to cut off his penis and testicles, stuffing them in his mouth. GIs speculated that the soldiers were not always dead when the mutilations took place. Some U.S. soldiers also mutilated dead enemy bodies by cutting off the ears. The severed ears were kept as war trophies and were worn on a string around the soldier's neck or carried in a sack in his ruck. Many U.S. units outlawed such practices while others ignored them. A string of dried ears looked a lot like shriveled apricots. *See also* Calling Cards.

Mutiny *see* Combat Refusal

Mutter's Ridge (Nui Cay Tre) During Operation Prairie in September '66 U.S. Marines engaged a large NVA force just south of the DMZ. The resulting battle ended with the Marines taking the hill from the entrenched NVA, causing them to retreat back across the DMZ into NVN. The battle resulted in heavy casualties on both sides and marked one of the first occasions of U.S. ground forces making contact with a large Regular NVA force in SVN. The Marines remember the battle and the hill at Nui Cay Tre as "Mutter's Ridge."

Mutual Supporting Fire *see* Interlocking Fire

MUV *see* Marine Unit Vietnam

Muzzle Velocity A measure of the speed of a traveling bullet after being fired from a weapon, usually measured in feet per second (fps). Some examples of muzzle velocities of weapons used in the Vietnam War: M-14 Rifle, 2,800fps; M-16 Rifle, 3,250fps; M-79 Grenade Launcher, 250fps; M-60 Machine Gun, 2,800fps; .45cal Pistol, 830fps; AK47 Rifle, 2,350fps, and the SKS Rifle, 2,410fps. The high muzzle velocity of weapons like the AK47 and the M-16 caused the bullets to inflict excessive damage to the tissue and bones of the human body.

MXD *see* **Composite Battery**

My (American, Diem My, Ong My, My Kim) Vietnamese for American or America [me]. Viet Cong propaganda often referred to South Vietnam's President Diem as "Diem My"; American Diem, or America's puppet. Americans were usually referred to as "Ong My." "My Kim" was the American dollar, and "My Quoc" was the United States.

My Chanh During the communist Eastertide Offensive of '72, their push south was stopped by the ARVNs at My Chanh, 30kms northwest of Hue, on Highway 1, I Corps. The ARVNs halted the NVA's armored push south, and rolled them back north to the DMZ and near the Laotian border. *See also* **Eastertide Offensive.**

My God!!! *see* **Choi Oi**

My Kim *see* **My**

My Lai (My Lai Massacre, Pink Ville, Son My, My Lai 4) In March '68 elements of the U.S. Americal Division were operating around Son My Village, Quang Ngai Province, I Corps. A platoon under command of Lt. W.L. Calley entered the hamlet of My Lai and killed the civilian population (200+) men, women and children. Ronald Ridenhour, formerly a member of Calley's platoon (after the fact), wrote to President Nixon and to several congressmen about the incident, prompting an investigation, and

later charges. Of the 14 men and officers charged with war crimes only Calley was convicted and sentenced to life imprisonment in '71. He was later paroled March '74. In '68 the 11th Brigade/Americal Division received a special Army commendation for its body count during the operation, before the facts of My Lai were known. *See also* **Son Thang, Calley, Koster, Peers Inquiry.**

My Lai Incident *see* **My Lai**

My Lai Massacre *see* **My Lai**

My Quoc *see* **U.S.A.**

My Shit Don't Stink (Hot Shit, Hot Shot) Phrase used to imply confidence, high self-esteem; prideful, invulnerable, invincible belief in one's self, verging on the point of arrogance and vanity—really "hot shit." A belief that you were so good at what you did that you stand out from the rest; are different, special. Others' "shit may stink," but you're above all that; no way your "shit stinks." *See also* **Hot Shit.**

My Thi POW Camp ARVN maximum security prison located near China Beach, in a suburb of Da Nang, I Corps. The prison was used to hold captured Viet Cong and interrogate suspects VC or VC sympathizers. The prison was known for its torture and harsh treatment of prisoners.

My Tho One of South Vietnam's autonomous cities, and provincial capital of Dinh Tuong Province, IV Corps, located on the Mekong River 50kms southwest of Saigon. During Tet '68 Viet Cong forces occupied part of the city. It required the use of air strikes, artillery and house-to-house fighting to drive them out of the city.

My Tho RPG *see* **Game Warden River Groups**

Myron *see* **FSB Myron**

N

N-1   *see*   S-1

N-2   *see*   S-2

N-3   *see*   S-3

N-4   *see*   S-4

N-5   *see*   S-5

NAG   *see*   Naval Advisory Group

Nail   *see*   Kill

Nails   *see*   2.75-Inch Flechette Rocket

Naked Fanny (Invert)   Air Force pilot's nickname for the Air Force control center at Nakhon Phanom RTAFB. "Naked Fanny" was the site of the Air Force computer center that collected and digested information gathered on the Ho Chi Minh Trail. A special computer center was also established to monitor air traffic over Laos and North Vietnam. The computer, labeled "Invert," was used to identify enemy air traffic and was instrumental in supporting U.S. fighters engaging NVNAF MiGs. *See also* Infiltration Surveillance Center, NKP, RTAB.

Nakhon Phanom Royal Thai Air Base *see* Infiltration Surveillance Center, NKP RTAB

Nam, The *see* Republic of Vietnam, Vietnam (GI Names)

Nam *see* Republic of Vietnam, Vietnam (GI Names)

Nam Bo *see* Republic of Vietnam

Nam Can (Old Nam Can, New Nam Can) Capital of Nam Can district on the Cau Mau Peninsula, located on the Song Cua Lon River in An Xuyen Province, IV Corps. During the enemy Tet Offensive of '68, Nam Can was overrun by the VC and abandoned by the GVN. The VC operated throughout the Cau Mau Peninsula, infiltrating supplies and distributing them throughout the Southern Delta. The abandoned Nam Can was called "Old Nam Can" and a new settlement for Nam Can's refugees was established near the village of Xom Cai Keo, 15kms north of Old Nam Can. The new settlement was called "New Nam Can." In August '69 as part of Operation Sea Float

a successful effort was made to reestablish GVN control in the area. *See also* Operation Sea Float, Solid Anchor.

Nam O Bridge Bridge 10kms northwest of Da Nang over which Highway 1 crossed the Song Ca De River. The bridge was destroyed by the Viet Cong in April '67. The bridge also carried the tracks for Vietnam's sole railroad, the Trans-Vietnam. Due to enemy activity much of the railroad was unusable. *See also* Railway Security Agency.

Nam Phong Royal Thai Air Base *see* Thai Air Bases

Nam-Bo *see* Cochin China

Nam-Viet *see* Republic of Vietnam

Nan Trach *see* Nhon Trach

Nancy *see* FSB Nancy

Nanh Dan (Communist Daily Newspaper) North Vietnam's "Communist Daily Newspaper" that spewed the Communist Party line.

Nanning The city of Nanning was located in the People's Republic of China. Nanning, 300kms northeast of Hanoi, was a major rail head used by the Chinese to transport arms and supplies overland into North Vietnam. *See also* Kunming.

Nap-of-the-Earth (NOE, Going-Low-Level, Contour Flying) Technique of flying an aircraft as close to the terrain (the ground) as possible (3–5 feet), making it harder for the enemy to detect and fire on the aircraft. Helicopters employing this skimming technique followed along roads and riverbeds at high rates of speed, avoiding enemy radar and AA fire. During contour flying (low level flying) the aircraft followed the contours of the terrain, maintaining a low fixed altitude above the contour/terrain and obstacles. Contour flying was used by helicopters and fixed wing aircraft. Helicopters flying NOE flew between obstacles, along the same paths a vehicle would take. Aircraft flying contour flew slightly above the terrain and any obstacles encountered. *See also* Air Strike Technique.

Napalm *see* **Naphthenic-Palmitic Acid**

Napalm Canisters Empty napalm canisters were sometimes used for resupply efforts to SF or reconnaissance units operating in enemy areas. The empty canisters were filled with supplies such as ammunition, rations, medical supplies or food. The canisters could then be dropped by regular attack aircraft such as A1s or A-37s. Attached to the canister was a small parachute that was deployed to slow the fall of the canister. To the enemy, the aircraft would appear to be making another attack. Canister resupply missions were used when ground elements did not want to give their position away to the enemy by receiving a regular resupply drop.

Napalm Victims *see* **Crispy-Critters**

Napalm, Homemade *see* **Fou Gas**

Nape *see* **Naphthenic-Palmitic Acid**

Naphthagel *see* **Naphthenic-Palmitic Acid**

Naphthenic-Palmitic Acid (Napalm, Hot-Stuff, Nape, Naphthagel, Incendijel, Selective Ordnance) Jellied gasoline mixture used in flame-throwing weapons and bombs. When air dropped the napalm container ruptured on impact and ignited; the sticky, jellied, burning contents spread and clung to anything or anybody in its path. Napalm burned with an intense radiating heat, which rapidly consumed oxygen, suffocating those caught in the center of the strike. Napalm was effectively used against bunkers and troop concentrations. Most of the U.S. napalm used in Vietnam was manufactured by Dow Chemical Company. Antiwar protestors in the U.S. used several slogans to condemn the use of napalm in Vietnam: "Dow shalt not Kill," and "Napalm Is Johnson's Baby Powder." Also known as naphthagel, incendijel, and as "selective ordnance." *See also* **Crispy-Critters, Napalm Canisters, Ord.**

NAS *see* **Navy Advisory Group**

Nathan Hale *see* **Operation Nathan Hale**

Nation Building *see* **Pacification**

National Assembly South Vietnam's legislative body.

National Conference for New Politics (NCNP) A group organized in early '66 to provide political and moral support for peace candidates running in the '66 elections. The group consisted of nationwide antiwar and civil rights groups with the same general political slant as the candidate. The NCNP pushed several candidates, but was unable to sustain the drive.

National Coordinating Committee to End the War (NCC) Organization formed in '65 to demonstrate nationwide against the war in Vietnam. The committee consisted of a coalition of more than 30 antiwar and peace groups. The NCC sponsored a nationwide protest in October '66 which attracted over 100,000 participants. The NCC also organized teach-ins, marches, draft card burnings, and rallies across the U.S.

National Council of Reconciliation and Concord The '72 Paris Peace Accords included a provision that established a special council to provide the Viet Cong a vehicle to participate in the political climate of South Vietnam. The council was to consist of representatives from the GVN, Viet Cong (PRG), DRV and the U.S. North Vietnam accepted this provision in lieu of a coalition government. It was through this council that the political conflict in South Vietnam was to have been resolved by establishing democratic processes and the organization of elections. President Thieu opposed such a council and any coalition government with the communists. Reconciliation or formation of the coalition government never took place.

National Defense Reserve Fleet (Mothball Fleet) Several hundred U.S. cargo ships of various sizes and usages were stored at facilities on the East and West Coast. Also stored were many out-of-commission Navy ships. Some of the vessels dated back to WWII and the Korean War. The ships were kept in storage by the government in the event a national emergency should arise and a fleet of cargo and support ships be required. The fleet of storage ships was known as the "Mothball Fleet." During the Vietnam War several hundred ships were taken out of mothballs and reconditioned for use as transports to move supplies and equipment to Vietnam. The cargo ships were manned by the Merchant Marines.

National Defense Ribbon *see* **National Defense Service Medal**

National Defense Service Medal (National Defense Ribbon, Republic of Vietnam Campaign Medal) Was awarded to all U.S. military personnel that served in the armed forces in recognition of their national service to America. The Republic of Vietnam government authorized the issuance of the Vietnam Campaign Medal, to be worn by all U.S. military personnel that served in Vietnam during the war.

National Guard *see* **Reserves**

National Intelligence Estimates (NIEs) Official intelligence reports issued by the U.S. Central Intelligence Agency. The reports projected political and military trends worldwide. The reports were often used by Congress and the Administration to make foreign policy decisions or to substantiate claims or requests for funding. The reports were based on information gathered by the CIA and subjected to the agency's analysis.

National Interrogation Center (NIC) GVN interrogation center located in Saigon. The center housed the more important political prisoners of the Thieu regime and served as the primary collection and holding point for high ranking NVA/VC prisoners. The center was directly controlled by the South Vietnamese who were advised by U.S. military intelligence and the CIA.

National Leadership Council (NLC, Nguyen Brothers, Three Stooges) An interim council established to govern South Vietnam until nationwide elections could take place to select a president. The council was established by three of SVN's strongest generals after the coup that ended the Diem regime. In the period between Diem's overthrow and the establishment of the council a succession of military leaders attempted to consolidate enough power to lead the country. The generals originally on the '65 council were: Nguyen Van Thieu, Nguyen Huu Co and Nguyen Cao Ky. Unconfirmed sources in some diplomatic circles referred to the members of the new council as the "Nguyen Brothers" or the "Three Stooges." The three men were not related, but did share the same last name. *See also* **Nguyen.**

National Liberation Front (NLF, Mat Tran) The political arm of the communist party in SVN, the Mat Tran. The NLF was formed in '59 when it was billed as a nationalist group, but most of the organization consisted of South Vietnamese communists, fully backed by the communist government in NVN. The primary aims of the NLF were reunification of North and South Vietnam, the overthrow of the Diem regime, the withdrawal of all American advisors (forces), establishment of a representative system of government, education, and land reform. In '69 the NLF merged into the PRG. *See also* **Provisional Revolutionary Government of SVN.**

National Police Field Force *see* **National Police Force**

National Police Force (Canh-Sat Quoc-Gia, White Mice, NPF, QC, NPFF, Quoc Canh) The South Vietnamese National Police Force (SVNNP) consisted of two branches; the Special Branch, or QC, dealt primarily with police and intelligence matters in Saigon and the larger cities; the Field Force operated with regular army units in rural hamlets and villages. The NPF was notorious for its corruption and the tortures they applied to political prisoners. The NPF was responsible for enforcing SVN's criminal justice system, but their primary goal was the elimination of the VC and VCI. U.S. military intelligence units worked closely with the National Police. The National Police Field Force (NPFF) operated in the rural areas and accompanied ARVN units during their sweeps of villages, checking the villagers' identity cards and searching for the VC and VCI. The NPF kept detailed records on the VC and VCS they arrested, and worked closely with the Phoenix Program in its attempt to exterminate the Viet Cong. The National Police in the cities wore white or dark blue helmets (helmet liners) with "QC" painted on the sides, white gloves and shirt, and gray pants. GIs nicknamed them the "White Mice" because of their small stature and bright outfits. The NPFF in the rural areas usually wore military uniforms, and dark "QC" helmets. QC was the abbreviation for "quoc canh" [k-woc can], or National Police.

National Priority Areas A '66 US/GVN plan to designate four areas of SVN to be the initial start areas for pacification. Under the plan U.S. units would defend American installations and the ARVN would defend the government centers in those areas. The plan called for limited offensive operations in an effort to build up the ARVN forces. When the ARVN were strong enough, they would strike outside the four areas to eliminate the VC and restore government control throughout SVN. The four areas were around Saigon, Qui Nhon, Da Nang and Can Tho.

National Revolutionary Movement *see* **Can Lao Nhan Vi Cach Mang Dang**

National Salvation *see* **Cuu Nuoc and Thong Nhat**

National Security Adviser *see* **National Security Council**

National Security Agency (NSA, Signal Intelligence Agency [SIGINT]) The NSA operated the code breaking operations of the U.S. The agency intercepted and analyzed signals and communications of all types attempting to break foreign codes and correspondence in the name of National Security. The NSA functioned as part of the Executive Branch, under the President. "SIGINT" was short for "Signal Intelligence." The NSA worked directly with the Army's ASA in Vietnam in the intercept and analysis of NVA/VC radio transmissions. *See also* **Army Security Agency.**

National Security Council (NSC, National Security Adviser) Council established in '47 to advise the President on matters of U.S. national security, including affairs related to domestic, foreign and military issues. The council was composed of the president, vice-president, secretaries of state and defense, and during the VNW, directors of the Office of Emergency Planning, the Central Intelligence Agency and the Joint Chiefs of Staff. The NSC was headed by the National Security Adviser. During the Vietnam War the NSC was headed by Gordon Gray, McGeorge Bundy, Walt Rostow and Henry Kissinger.

National Servicemen (Conscripts) Australian military conscripts (draftees) were known as "National Servicemen," and first started serving in Vietnam with the 1st Australian Task Force in mid '66. *See also* **Draftee.**

National United Front of Kampuchea *see* **Khmer Rouge**

National Vet Center Program *see* **Psychological Readjustment Act**

National War College (NWC) Located at Fort McNair, Washington, D.C. The NWC represented the military's highest academic institution, and conducted studies in national and international policy development, the use of military and political power, the use of American and world resources to form political policy. Students at the college consisted of high level civilians within the government and military personnel at, or above the equivalent rank of lieutenant colonel.

Nationalist China (Taiwan, Republic of China, Ching Chuan Kang [CCK]) Provided a small group of military assistants to SVN (less than 50 advisors). The ROC offered to send combat troops, but the U.S. declined their offer in fear that the use of Nationalist Chinese troops in Vietnam would give the Red Chinese an excuse to send in massive numbers of "volunteers" to assist the North Vietnamese, greatly expanding the war in Asia. The U.S. did make use of the ROC air base at Ching Chuan Kang (CCK). The base was used to support Air Force elements of the 314th and 317th Tactical Airlift Wings (C-130), which flew support missions in Vietnam. The U.S. "borrowed" several F-5 fighter aircraft from Roc which were then "loaned" to VNAF in '73, to augment their jet fighter squadrons. *See also* **Free World Military Forces.**

Nationalist Party of Vietnam *see* **Dai Viet**

Native Sport GI slang phrase for "hunting" the Viet Cong.

Naval Academy *see* **U.S. Naval Academy**

Naval Advisory Group (Navy Advisory Section [NAS], NAG, MACVNAG, CNAG, NAVFORV/NAG) Prior to '65, the American naval advisory function to the South Vietnamese Navy was carried out by MAAGV, Navy Section. In '64 MACV took over advisory duties from MAAG, and the Navy Section of MAAG was reorganized under Naval Force Vietnam (NAVFORV) as the Naval Advisory Group (NAG), and was called MACVNAG or more formally,

NAVFORV/NAG. The commander of the advisory group was known as "CNAG." *See also* Naval Forces, Vietnam; MAAGV.

Naval Assault Division, French *see* **Dinassauts**

Naval Construction Action Teams (NAVCATS) Construction teams that operated under the guidance of the SEABEES. NAVCATS constructed housing and facilities at U.S. Navy bases in Vietnam that were transferred to the Vietnamese Navy as part of the Vietnamization process. The bases originally did not have adequate housing to support the families of the VNN sailors who took over the U.S. bases. Without such shelter the VNN would not have been able to maintain its force and fulfill its naval mission in SVN. Other Navy programs were also initiated to help the VNN dependents with housing and support during the Vietnamization process. *See also* **Operation Helping Hand, Project Buddy Base.**

Naval Forces Vietnam (NFV, NAVFORV) U.S. Navy forces that operated in and off the coast of Vietnam; TF 115, 116 and 117. The Navy forces of the task forces were under the command of the MACV Commander. The NFV did not include the naval forces of the 7th Fleet that operated off Vietnam's coast. The NFV was formally known as NAVFORV, Naval Forces Vietnam. *See also* **TF: 115, 116, 117; Commander U.S. Naval Forces, Vietnam.**

Naval Mobile Construction Battalions *see* **SEABEES**

Naval Operations Center *see* **Combat Information Center**

Naval Support Activity, Da Nang (NSA, Da Nang; NavSuppAct, Da Nang; They Shall Not Want, NSAD) The NSA, headquartered at Da Nang, had overall responsibility for all Navy logistics activities throughout I Corps. NSA's responsibilities included operation and transfer of ship cargos and munitions, U.S. POL requirements in I Corps, hospital facilities, harbor defense and security, and improvements to the port facility. NSA was established at Da Nang in July '65 and took over the duties formerly covered by TG 76.4. By September '70 most of the Navy logistics support had been reduced as part of the American reduction of forces in Vietnam.

The remaining Navy forces were reorganized into the NSF, Da Nang. The motto of the NSA was "They Shall Not Want." *See also* **SEASHARP, TG 76.4; Navy Support Facility, Da Nang; Southern Shipping Company, Camp Tien Sha.**

Naval Support Activity, Saigon (NSA, Saigon; NSAS) Navy logistical support command that coordinated naval activities in the II, III and IV Corps of South Vietnam. Navy support operations for the three Corps Tactical Zones were headquartered in Saigon. NSA, Da Nang had responsibility for Navy logistics and support in I Corps. *See also* **Southern Shipping Company.**

Naval Support Activity Resupply Mission *see* **Southern Shipping Company**

Naval War College (NWC) The Navy's highest academic institution, located at Newport, Rhode Island.

Navarre, General Henri Commanding general of French forces in Vietnam during the final months of the First Indochina War. It was the Navarre Plan in '54 that eventually led to the defeat of the French at Dien Bien Phu. *See also* **Dien Bien Phu.**

Navarre Plan *see* **Dien Bien Phu**

NAVCATS *see* **Naval Construction Action Teams**

NAVFORV *see* **Commander U.S. Naval Forces, Vietnam**

NAVFORV/NAG *see* **Naval Advisory Group**

Navigator/Weapon Systems Officer *see* **Weapons Systems Operator**

NavSuppAct, Da Nang *see* **Naval Support Activity, Da Nang**

Navy Advisory Section *see* **Naval Advisory Group**

Navy Aircrews *see* **Brown Shoes**

Navy Amphibious Training Center *see* **Coronado Island**

Navy Cook *see* **Stew Burner**

Navy Cross United States' second highest award for valor, awarded to Navy personnel on behalf of the President. Comparable to the Air Force Cross and the Army's Distinguished Service Cross.

Navy Hat *see* **Dixie Cup**

Navy Helicopter Gunships *see* Rowell's Rats, HAL-3

Navy Hospital Corpsmen *see* Corpsmen

Navy Medical Battalion *see* C & C Company

Navy Sailors (Squids, Swabbies, Bluejackets, Admiral) Nicknames for U.S. Navy sailors: squids, swabbies, bluejackets. Non-Navy personnel sometimes facetiously referred to any sailor as an "admiral."

Navy SOG *see* Navy Special Operations Group

Navy Special Operations Group (NSOG, Navy SOG) Navy SEAL elements that operated as part of the MACV-SOG in Vietnam. The SEALs operated as part of the Maritime Studies Group conducting missions in the Delta and against enemy installations in North Vietnam. *See also* SEAL, MACV-SOG, SOG Groups.

Navy Special Warfare Operations Training Center *see* Coronado Island

Navy Support Facility, Da Nang (NSF, Da Nang) The NSF was formed in September '70 to carry out the Navy's plan of Vietnamization, the ACTOV. The NSF took responsibility for supplying the remaining Navy units operating in I Corps. Responsibility for such support had been the duty of NSA, Da Nang. The NSF trained the Vietnamese Navy on the care and use of Navy craft that had been transferred to the Vietnamese as part of the ACTOV program. NSF also instructed and assisted the Vietnamese in assuming the logistics effort at Da Nang. Logistic support to ARVN units in the I Corps area was the responsibility of the VNN. *See also* Naval Support Activities, Da Nang.

Navy's Delta Air Force (Delta Air Force) In support of U.S. Navy riverine operations in the Delta of IV Corps, the Navy formed three specialized air units. The units operated as part of TF 116 and were stationed at various bases throughout the IV Corps area. Helicopter gunship and lift capacity were provided by HAL-3; close air support was provided by the OV-10 Broncos of VAL-4 and fixed-wing gunships were provided by the Neptunes of VAH-21. *See also* Light Attack Squadron 4, Seawolves, VAH-21.

NBC *see* Non-Battle Casualty

NC-123K *see* Black Spot

NCC *see* National Coordinating Committee to End the War

NCNP *see* National Conference for New Politics

NCO *see* Noncommissioned Officer

NCO Course *see* Shake 'n' Bake Sergeants

NCOC *see* Shake 'n' Bake Sergeants

NCOIC *see* Noncommissioned Officer

NCR 500 *see* Cu Chi Computer Center

NDB *see* Radio Beacon

NDP *see* Night Defensive Position

Nem (Vietnamese Sausage) Ground pork mixed with powdered rice and seasonings and packed into rolled banana leaves and cooked.

Nematodes *see* Trichinosis

Neo Lao Hak Sat *see* Lao Liberation Front

Neptune *see* P-2

Neptune Gunships *see* VAH-21

Nervous *see* Tight

Net *see* Radio Net

NETT *see* New Equipment Training Teams

Neutralize Military/CIA verbiage meaning to kill, eliminate or otherwise render ineffective. Rather than make statements point-blank, the military tended to shroud much of what it said. Example: "Neutralize suspected VC sympathizer, with extreme prejudice," meant to kill a suspected VC sympathizer, as quickly and directly as possible, regardless of any possible consequences. Neutralize could pertain to an individual, a group, a weapons site or anything that was a threat or could be perceived as a threat. *See also* Kill, Operation Neutralize.

Nevada Eagle *see* Operation Nevada Eagle

Nevah Happen (Never Happen) GI

phrase used to express an opinion that an event was an impossibility, or near impossibility. Was also used to express the hope that a possible situation or circumstance wouldn't happen. An emphatic form of "no." The Vietnamese were quick to pick up on the phrase, and their rendition sounded more like "neb-bah hop-pen."

Never Happen *see* **Nevah Happen**

New City Part of Hue City, south of the Perfume River, the more modern part of the city. Hue was located in Thua Thien Province, I Corps. *See also* **Hue.**

New Economic Zones (Forced Rural Resettlement, Resettlement Camps) Forced rural resettlement carried out by the communists in Vietnam after their victory in '75. From '75 to '80 over 5 million Vietnamese city dwellers and refugees were forcibly moved to resettlement camps located in rural areas of South Vietnam. The communists moved people out of the cities to reduce congestion and the constant drain on the cities' limited resources. Those sent to the "new economic zones" lived a spartan lifestyle and were forced into working the land and surviving on its yield. *See also* **Restructuring.**

New Equipment Training Teams (NETT) DOD teams assigned to Vietnam to introduce new and complex equipment or technology to the military. Units assigned the new equipment were initially trained by the NETT teams.

New Guy Village *see* **Hanoi Hilton**

New Jersey *see* **USS New Jersey**

New Life *see* **Operation New Life**

New Life Hamlet (Relocation Camps) GVN controlled and defended hamlets and villes. The occupants of these New Life Hamlets were relocated villagers from VC controlled or VC sympathetic villes in other areas. These relocation camps were similar to a concentration camp; more effort was often spent on keeping the occupants inside, and away from joining the VC, than efforts made by the government to keep the VC outside. The objective of the program was to win the trust and support of the people, but the program was honeycombed with corruption, graft, and many of the relocated people

resented the GVN for displacing them from their ancestral lands. *See also* **Strategic Hamlet Program, Forced Urbanization, Fishes-and-the-Sea, Really New Life Hamlets, Gom Dan, Restructuring, New Economic Zones.**

New Meat *see* **New Troop**

New Mobe *see* **New Mobilization Committee to End the War**

New Mobilization Committee to End the War (New Mobe) Antiwar group that sponsored a protest march against the Pentagon in October '67. The demonstration drew an estimated crowd of 150,000 people. The New Mobe also helped to organize the nationwide Moratorium Day demonstration in October '69. The group changed its name in '71 to the People's Coalition for Peace and Justice, and continued to organize protest against the war in Vietnam. *See also* **Moratorium Day.**

New Nam Can *see* **Nam Can**

New Pleiku Name given to the section of Pleiku that housed II Corps headquarters and the U.S. Air Force base. New Pleiku was located just northeast of Pleiku City beyond the junction of Highway 19 and Highway 14. *See also* **Pleiku, Turkey Farm.**

New Troop (Fuckin' New Guy [FNG], Boot, Cherry, Newfer, Newby, Brown Bar, Green Troop) Any soldier new to the field lacking combat experience, regardless of whether he was straight from the States or from a base in the rear. Brown Bar was exclusively used to refer to new 2nd lieutenants. "Cruit" was another name for "new meat" in the field. Anyone new to Vietnam was considered a "virgin" by those who were already there. "Cherry" was probably the most widely used term for a new, inexperienced and untested soldier. "Baby-san" was used to denote the sexual virgin soldier, and a Cherry Baby-san was not an oddity in Vietnam. Troop replacements were also called "Turtles" because it seemed to take forever until they arrived. "Fenuge" was a variant of "fuckin' new guy" (FNG). *See also* **Baby-San, Cash Sales, Twinks.**

New York *see* **Operation New York**

New Zealand (Kiwis, Killer Kiwis, NZSAS, NZ) New Zealand SAS, infantry, engineers, artillery and medical units deployed in support of SVN from '64 to '71. The NZ forces combined with some Australian units to form ANZAC (RAR/NZ). The Kiwis, as they were nicknamed, operated in Phuoc Tuy Province. The New Zealand SAS (NZSAS), along with the ASAS, trained and operated with CIDG forces in the area. New Zealand troops also participated in pacification and civic action projects around Nui Dat. The New Zealand force peaked in '69 at 550 troops, and by '72 all the combat Kiwis (Killer Kiwis) had returned home. *See also* **Australian–New Zealand Army Corps, Royal New Zealand Army.**

New-Man-on-the-Block Rule *see* **New-Man-Rule**

New-Man-Rule (New-Man-on-the-Block Rule) Long-standing tradition among some field GIs in Vietnam that new men (replacements) to the unit walk point soon after joining the unit. Walking point was one of the most hazardous infantry assignments; ambush, snipers, and booby traps were a constant threat. Many veteran grunts were of the opinion that if a new man could survive walking point for a few days his chances of making it in Vietnam were better than 50–50. But one of the most important aspects of making new men walk point was to give the veteran grunts a chance to get off point, and out of the "bull's-eye" for a while, greatly increasing their own chances of survival.

Newbee *see* **New Troop**

Newby *see* **Second Lieutenant**

Newfer *see* **New Troop**

Newport *see* **Newport Terminal Facility**

Newport Terminal Facility U.S. Army port facility built to increase Saigon's port handling capacity to accommodate the increase in supplies and equipment arriving in-country. The Newport facility was managed by the Army Transportation Corps and construction was completed in '67. The only other deep water ports available to Allied shipping in SVN were Da Nang, Qui Nhon and Cam Ranh Bay. *See also* **Army Transport Corps.**

Newsmen in Vietnam *see* **Boys-in-Saigon**

Newton, Huey P. *see* **Black Panthers**

Newy Bac Viet *see* **Noi Bac-Viet?**

Newyoricans (Puerto Ricans) Street slang for New York born or raised Puerto Ricans, a general nickname for Puerto Ricans who were relatively fluent in English. During the Vietnam War Puerto Ricans that joined the Army and were not fluent in English most often found their way into the infantry.

Next *see* **Short-Timer**

Next of Kin (NOK) Those persons to be notified when a member of the military service was missing in action, wounded or died while on active duty. NOK usually received notification of wounds by telegram. Notification of a serviceman's death or MIA was usually personally delivered by an officer from the man's branch of service.

NFG *see* **Number Ten**

NFV *see* **Naval Forces Vietnam**

NG *see* **Reserves**

Ngo Dinh Can *see* **Ngo Dinh Family**

Ngo Dinh Diem (Last Confucian, Last of the Mandarins, America's Puppet, Churchill of Asia) Dictator-President of South Vietnam ('55 –'63) originally backed by the U.S. government. The U.S. later allowed his overthrow in a coup by ARVN officers in '63. Diem and his brother were assassinated during the coup. A Mandarin and Catholic by birth, Diem was fiercely anticommunist and anti–French. In '54 he was appointed premier under Emperor Bao Dai. In '55 Diem led the drive to dethrone Bao Dai and establish Vietnam as a Republic. One-sided elections were held October '55 that resulted in Diem becoming the President of the Republic of Vietnam. He was accused by the Viet Cong and the North Vietnamese of being "America's Puppet" (Diem My), but many of his actions were contrary to American wishes. Diem kept tight control over the country, and ignored internal and international requests for political and social reforms. In '61, then VP Johnson referred to Diem as "the Churchill of Asia." Under Diem South Vietnam did begin to stabilize, but his excesses in dealing with Buddhist dissidents eventually led to a coup against him by his own army officers, resulting in his assassination. Because of his excesses and methods Diem was referred to as a fascist dictator. *See also* **Ngo Dinh Family, Night of the Pagodas.**

Ngo Dinh Family (Ngo Dinh Kha, Khoi, Thuc, Diem, Can, Nhu, Luyen) Ngo Dinh Kha had six sons; the most well known was Ngo Dinh Diem who established himself as President of the Republic of Vietnam in '55. The father of the family, Ngo Dinh Kha, was a counselor to Vietnam's Emperor Thanh Thai. The sons of Kha were born in the following order: Khoi, Thuc, Diem, Can, Nhu and Luyen. Luyen served as SVN's ambassador to Great Britain until '63 when his brother was deposed in a coup. Nhu served as SVN's chief of the Secret Police and the head of the Vietnamese Special Forces. He was killed with his brother Diem during the '63 coup. Can lived in, and unofficially administered the area around Hue. He was arrested, tried and executed by the military junta that deposed his brother Diem in '63. Diem established himself as RVN's president in '55 and was executed during the '63 coup to overthrow his regime. Thuc became a Catholic priest and attained the position of Archbishop of Hue; during the coup against his brother he was recalled to Rome and eventually excommunicated from the Church for his "religious extremism." Khoi was killed by the Viet Minh in '45.

Ngo Dinh Kha *see* **Ngo Dinh Family**

Ngo Dinh Khoi *see* **Ngo Dinh Family**

Ngo Dinh Luyen *see* **Ngo Dinh Family**

Ngo Dinh Nhu Brother of President Ngo Dinh Diem. Nhu was the head of the Vietnamese Secret Police and used them to control those around him and his brother, and especially the enemies of the Ngo Dinh family. Nhu used terror and extortion to manage the affairs of state within Vietnam. Nhu also commanded the Vietnamese Special Forces, which he kept armed with the latest weapons; their primary role was to act as the personal bodyguard for Nhu and his brother Diem. Nhu used extreme force to put down antigovernment riots and demonstrations by Buddhists in '63. Nhu was executed in November '63, with his brother, during a coup by disgruntled ARVN officers. *See also* **Ngo Dinh Family, Madame Nhu.**

Ngo Dinh Thuc *see* **Ngo Dinh Family**

Ngu Hanh Son Program (Five Mountain Program, Nine Village Program) Pacification effort carried out by the GVN and supported by the Marines in I Corps. The program took place around a cluster of villages located south of Hoi An. After Marine units cleared the area of the VC, RF/PF forces were to provide security for the GVN Cadre and their pacification programs. The program faltered because the GVN was unable to support the program and the efforts of the poorly trained and equipped RF/PF forces were unable to keep the VC out of the area. *See also* **Pacification.**

Nguoi Thuong (Montagnard, Moi, Savage) Derogatory name for Vietnam's ethnic aboriginal people that lived in the mountains of the Central Highlands. "Nguoi Thuong" [new-e tongue] meant "highlands citizen." The South Vietnamese, who were of Chinese descent, looked upon the Montagnards as inferiors, and called them the "Moi" or savages. The French called the mountain people the "Montagnards," which meant "mountaineers." The "Yards," as they were called by the Americans, were Austro-Asiatic/Malayo-Polynesian in ethnic heritage. The Yards were a dark-complexioned people. The Vietnamese considered all dark skinned people "inferior," and treated the Yards accordingly. *See also* **Montagnards, Vietnam's Niggers, Chams.**

Nguy (Puppets) NVA/VC nickname for the ARVN and GVN troops. It meant "puppet" in Vietnamese. South Vietnam's government and armed forces were always perceived as puppets, first under control of the French and later controlled by the Americans.

Nguyen (Vietnamese Name) One of the most common Vietnamese names. The equivalent of Jones or Smith in the States. To the GI it seemed as though half of the Vietnamese were named Nguyen. Formal Vietnamese names begin with the last name, middle name and then the first name. To the GI who was unenlightened on the order of Vietnamese names, it appeared the many Vietnamese had the same first name. Many Vietnamese took the name of

Nguyen from the dynasty that ruled and culturally advanced Vietnam in the 1600s and 1700s. *See also* **Gia Long; Enemy, The.**

Nguyen Ai Quoc *see* **Ho Chi Minh**

Nguyen Brothers *see* **National Leadership Council**

Nguyen Cao Ky (The Cowboy) Flamboyant South Vietnamese Air Force officer who was part of a military coup in '65 that consolidated power under the National Leadership Council in an effort to stabilize the political scene in SVN. Ky served as prime minister from '65 to '67, when he became SVN's vice-president under President Thieu. In '71 Thieu stopped Ky from challenging him in the presidential elections, appointing Ky South Vietnam's air marshal. In April '75 he left SVN as part of the U.S. evacuation of Saigon, prior to his country's collapse to Communist forces. Ky was nicknamed "the Cowboy" because of his flashy style. *See also* **National Leadership Council.**

Nguyen Charlie *see* **Enemy, The**

Nguyen Chi Thanh North Vietnamese commander of NVA/VC forces in South Vietnam. Nguyen Chi Thanh infiltrated into South Vietnam in '65 to head COSVN. He died in Hanoi in '67.

Nguyen Dan *see* **Tet**

Nguyen Dynasty *see* **Gia Long**

Nguyen Hue Offensive *see* **Eastertide Offensive**

Nguyen Ngoc Loan (General Nguyen Ngoc Loan) Head of South Vietnam's National Police, he became known worldwide when he executed a Viet Cong prisoner, with a single shot to the head, on a Saigon street in front of news cameras during the '68 Tet offensive. Just before his capture, the VC had butchered the family of one of General Loan's officers. As director of the NPF, Loan ruled with an iron fist, and had little sympathy for the communists. The NPF was notoriously brutal and corrupt. Loan was later crippled and lost a leg to a VC mine, but continued to operate in the GVN as a special assistant to General Cao Van Vien, chairman of SVN's Joint General Staff.

Nguyen O Phap *see* **Ho Chi Minh**

Nguyen Phuc Anh *see* **Gia Long**

Nguyen Sinh Cung *see* **Ho Chi Minh**

Nguyen Tat Thanh *see* **Ho Chi Minh**

Nguyen Thi Binh Traveling spokesman for the National Liberation Front (Viet Cong). She traveled around the world attempting to generate support for the NLF. In '68 she became the principal negotiator and public spokesman for the NLF at the Paris peace talks. She was named minister of education of the newly united Vietnam in '75.

Nguyen Van Thieu A military coup in '65 established Thieu as SVN's chairman and chief of state. In '67, in a national election, Thieu was elected president of SVN, with Nguyen Cao Ky as his vice-president. Thieu resigned as president April 21, 1975, just 9 days prior to the collapse of SVN to Communist forces. Thieu claimed South Vietnam had been abandoned by America after its promise to come to his country's aid in the event of a major violation by the NVA/VC of the '73 Paris Peace Accords. Thieu did not like the condition of the Accords, but was threatened with abandonment by the U.S. if he did not sign the Accords. He reluctantly signed the Accords in '73. When the North Vietnamese began their Final Offensive in March '75, Thieu repeatedly requested American support to blunt the Communist drive. He also pleaded with America's President Ford to honor the promises made by the previous administration to come to SVN's aid if the NVA/VC violated the Paris Peace Accords. Congress and the administration turned a deaf ear to South Vietnam's pleas. No U.S. combat air support was provided to the Vietnamese, and the ARVNs were unable to stand alone against the twenty NVA/VC divisions that made the final push against Vietnam. *See also* **Operation Frequent Wind, You Have My Absolute Assurance....**

Nguyen Vo Giap (Nui Lua, Ice Covered Volcano, General Nguyen Vo Giap) Under Ho Chi Minh, he directed the NVA war effort until the end of '72. Giap was Ho's military strategist in the early '40s and advised and directed the Viet Minh efforts against the French and later the NVA/VC against the Americans. Giap was an expert at guerrilla warfare and was willing for his forces to accept mass casualties in order to accomplish his goals. His friends called him Nui Lua, the "Ice Covered Volcano." Giap was replaced by Van Tien Dung in '74 after suffering over 100,000 casualties as a result of his '72 Eastertide Offensive and his deteriorating health. *See also* Every Day in the World..., You Can Kill Ten of My Men....

Nha Be River *see* Song Nha Be

Nha Dac Biet (Special House) Vietnamese for an intelligence "safe house" or house used for intelligence gathering activities. Nha [naa] meaning "house," and Dac Biet [doc b-ett] meaning "special."

Nha Trang Provincial capital and port city of SVN's Khanh Hoa Province, II Corps, also home of the U.S. 5th Special Forces in Vietnam, I Field Force Vietnam and a major logistics and Air Force base. Nha Trang was centrally located on South Vietnam's eastern coast and fell to the communists in early April '75.

Nhaques (Peasants) French nickname for the Vietnamese peasants.

Nhon Trach (Nan Trach) Southern district of Bien Hoa Province which formed the northern boundary of the RSSZ. From base areas in the Nhon Trach the VC operated in the RSSZ, attacking allied shipping and operating without restraint in the heavy mangrove and swamp that made up the RSSZ. The Rung Sat Special Zone was assigned to the VNN, but they were unable to stop VC attacks in the zone. In '69 several large scale operations combining U.S., Australian, Thai and Vietnamese forces were launched in the RSSZ and against the Nhon Trach to reduce enemy influence in the area. *See also* Rung Sat, Song Long Tau, Doan-10, Operations: Platypus, Wolf Pack.

Niagara *see* Operation Niagara

NIC *see* National Interrogation Center

NIEs *see* National Intelligence Estimates

Night Angel Code name for night flare dropping missions conducted by U.S. Air Force and VNAF SC-47 aircraft. Night Angel missions were used to provide support

to remote ARVN outposts early in the war. Flare missions were gradually taken over by artillery and armed flare ships that could provide fire support as well as illumination. *See also* Gunship, Flares.

Night Defensive Position (NDP, Remain Overnight Position [RON], Night Location [NL]) A temporary defensive perimeter set up at night by U.S. troops operating in the field. Company sized and larger NDPs usually had LPs set out from the camp to give early warning of enemy activity that might be directed towards the camped troops. The NDP was also referred to as a unit's RON (Remain Overnight Position) or the Night Location (NL, November Lima). The Australian infantry referred to their NDPs as "harbour sites." *See also* Harbour Site, Wagon Train Defense, Wagon Wheel Defense.

Night Fire One of the live-fire courses in Army basic training. Troops negotiated a series of night fire exercises during which they were taught the techniques of target selection, firing with flares and familiarization with the starlight scope.

Night Government of Vietnam *see* Enemy, The

Night Hawk *see* Night Hunter Operations

Night Hunter Operations (Night Hawk) Night operations conducted by helicopters of the 1st Cavalry. The ops were conducted around the 1st Cavalry base camp at Duc Pho and involved four helicopters: a flare ship and three gunships. The flare ship flew around the perimeter of the base dropping flares; following the flare ship were two gunships, the door gunners using starlight scopes to select targets. The selected targets were marked with tracer rounds fired by the gunners. The third gunship would then attack the area marked by the tracers. The technique was effective at keeping the NVA/VC in the area off guard. The 25th Infantry conducted similar night missions which they called "Night Hawks." *See also* Firefly, Nighthawks.

Night Location *see* Night Defensive Position

Night Observation Devices (AN/TVS-4 NOD, AN/TVS-2 NOD) A passive night observation scope (starlight scope) used by U.S. troops in Vietnam. The TVS-4 was hand-held, cylindrical, and about 12 inches long. It intensified existing light to allow objects to be viewed at night. The TVS-4 was also used to view objects illuminated by infrared light sources from U.S. IR searchlights. Other NODs used by the military for night observation were IR scopes, antipersonnel radar, and electronic sensors. *See also* **Starlight Scope, Nighthawks.**

Night of the Pagodas (Xa Loi Temple) Incident in August '62 when South Vietnamese police and soldiers attacked Buddhist temples in most of Vietnam's major cities, including the most sacred of the Buddhist pagodas, Xa Loi in Saigon. The police and troops looted and burned the temples. The Diem government later stated that the ARVN had instigated the attack, but it was more widely believed that the attacks had been ordered by the Diem regime, most likely Diem's brother Ngo Dinh Nhu. The attacks further incited the non–Catholic Vietnamese against Diem, and all but eliminated American support for Diem. *See also* **Ngo Dinh Diem.**

Night Owls Code name for U.S. night air operations to interdict NVA activity along the Ho Chi Minh Trail. The Night Owl missions used flare and gunships for aerial reconnaissance missions along the trail. The AC gunships were able to directly engage targets they encountered and call in additional support from fighter-bomber aircraft in the area. The Night Owl missions were part of the Operation Steel Tiger. *See also* **Operation Steel Tiger.**

Night Patrol (Suicide Patrols) U.S. patrols that maneuvered out from a base or NDP at night, seeking to make contact with the NVA/VC, disrupting a possible attack on the NDP. At a company size NDP perhaps one or two squads would go out, in different directions. The squad out on night patrol actually functioned as bait, attempting to draw enemy fire. Once the enemy opened up on the patrol the NDP or base could call in artillery on the patrol's position, and hopefully get a good enemy body count. Night patrols weren't popular among the troops that had to pull them. The GIs didn't like being used as bait and labeled the patrols as suicidal. Sometimes, in the interest

of self-preservation, a squad would "sandbag" the patrol. *See also* **Sandbagging a Patrol.**

Night Phantom *see* **OV-1**

Night Sun Searchlight A 20,000-watt xenon searchlight used by the Army for its Night Hawk operations. From an altitude of 2,000 feet (above small arms range) the Night Sun Searchlight could light up an area 200 meters in diameter. *See also* **Xenon Searchlight, Night Hawk, Night Hunter Operations.**

Night Vision Goggles *see* **SU-50 Electronic Binocular**

Nighthawks Nighthawk missions were similar to the three ship "firefly" missions used for night surveillance and interdiction of in-country, enemy infiltration routes. Nighthawk missions also consisted of three aircraft, the lightship and two gunships. The Nighthawk lightship was equipped with a Xenon searchlight, night vision scope and armed with miniguns. The Xenon searchlight was capable of producing white or infrared light. The lightship would troll slowly attempting to draw enemy fire, using its spotlight and night scope to identify targets. Once a target was identified the minigun could be used to mark the target for the gunships. *See also* **Firefly, C-123 Lightship, Starlight Scope, Xenon Light, Night Hunter Operations.**

Nights Belong to Charlie Phrase used to describe the amount of control the NVA/VC had in Vietnam, as perceived by many of the Vietnam War's observers and combatants. FWF and ARVN forces tended to conduct most of their combat operations during the daylight hours when air superiority and mobility could best be used. At night the same forces tended to set up in NDPs, only venturing into the night when absolutely necessary. U.S. units sent out small night patrols and ambushes, but rarely conducted any large unit operations or movements after dark. The NVA/VC, on the other hand, hid during the day, usually avoiding contact and moved at night.

Nine Village Program *see* **Ngu Hanh Son Program**

Nine-Rule Card Early in the war U.S. military personnel arriving in SVN were issued a small card of important rules regarding how to interact with the Vietnamese. The rules were 1) We are guests, make no demands, seek no special treatment; 2) Join with the people, understand their life, use phrases from their language, honor their customs and laws; 3) Treat women with politeness and respect; 4) Make friends among the soldiers and common people; 5) Always give the Vietnamese the right of way; 6) Be alert to security and to react militarily; 7) Do not attract attention by loud, rude or unusual behavior; 8) Avoid separating ourselves from the people by a display of wealth and privilege; 9) Above all else as members of a U.S. military force on a difficult mission, be responsible for all personal and official actions. Reflect honor upon ourselves and the United States of America.

Nine-to-Five War   An expression used to describe how America fought the war in Vietnam. Major U.S. combat units typically started operations early in the morning, moving during the day then stopping just before dark to camp for the night, perhaps setting out a small defensive ambush or two. Major offensive operations were usually limited to the daylight hours; this was in part due to the rules and restrictions placed on combat operations, and no clear-cut objectives other than killing as many enemy soldiers as possible. There was no systematic recapture of enemy held territories and holding of those territories to keep them out of the hands of the enemy. U.S. operations frequently cleared the same piece of real estate several times.

Nineteen   *see*   **19**

Ninety-Day Loss   Term that referred to rear area and base camp GIs with less than 90 days to go in Vietnam before their DEROS. Such troops were expected to continue their normal duties, but being "short-timers" were not expected to be very enthusiastic about their military obligations. Troops in the field were often rotated into base camp duties, but some units kept their people in the field up to the last week of their tour. *See also* **Short-Timer.**

Nipa Palms (Dua Nuoc, Dua La, Nipple Palm)   Feathery leafed palm tree commonly found along the coastal swamps and river mouths in South Vietnam. The Nipa Palm was also planted by farmers because of its food value. The buds could be eaten raw

or cooked and the tree sap could be converted to syrup or sugar. The sugar could also be fermented, converting to vinegar. The seeds of the kernel were sweet and edible if boiled for a short time. The ashes of burned palm leaves could also be used as salt. The Vietnamese called the Nipa Palm "Dua Nuoc" or "Dua La." The leaves of the Nipa Palm were used to make thatched roofs and hootches. GIs nicknamed the palm "nipple palm." *See also* **Palm Trees.**

Nipple Palm   *see*   **Nipa Palms**

Nitze, Paul   *see*   **Ad Hoc Task Force on Vietnam**

Nixon, President Richard M. (Tricky Dick)   Served as vice-president in the Eisenhower administration and was defeated by John F. Kennedy in the '60 presidential election, but narrowly defeated Hubert Humphrey in the '68 presidential election. The main plank in the Nixon platform was achieving an "honorable peace" in Vietnam. Nixon began the withdrawal of U.S. troops from Vietnam in '69 while his NSC advisor, Henry Kissinger, talked peace with the North Vietnamese in Paris. A major part of the Nixon peace plan called for ARVN troops to take up the defense of their country; the program of gradually shifting the burden of fighting to the ARVN was called Vietnamization. As Vietnamization continued and U.S. troops withdrew NVN continued to infiltrate troops south. In an effort to slow NVA troop movement on the Ho Chi Minh Trail Nixon authorized the secret bombing of infiltration routes in Cambodia and in '70 the US/ARVN incursion into Cambodia to cut the NVA supply lines. Negotiations remained stalemated. A U.S. backed ARVN incursion into Laos to cut the NVA supply lines ended in disaster for the ARVNs. Three of their elite divisions assaulted into Laos and suffered 50 percent casualties as they retreated from heavy NVA resistance. NVN continued to be uncooperative at the peace table and in March '72 launched another all-out offensive to seize SVN. U.S. air power was brought in to help the ARVN and the NVA offensive was turned back. In an effort to get NVN talking in Paris Nixon ordered intensified bombings of NVN. The bombings encouraged NVN to talk peace terms and the Paris Peace Accords were signed in January '73. The Accords were not well accepted by SVN's

Thieu, but he was threatened with a cut in U.S. aid if he did not sign. Nixon had achieved his honorable peace on paper. The Accords did not force the NVA to withdraw from SVN. The Accords simply allowed the U.S. the return of its POWs and to fully withdraw from SVN. SVN was left on its own with the promise that the United States would come to their aid if NVN broke the Accords. Due to the events of Watergate and the spectre of impeachment, Nixon resigned the Presidency in August '74. Nixon's promises of help were not fulfilled when the NVA made their final push against SVN.

Nixon Doctrine   President Nixon's public doctrine on the U.S. presence in Asia. Under the Nixon doctrine, Asian allies of the U.S. would, in the future, be required to fight their own ground wars without U.S. ground troops. The U.S. would provide air support and a nuclear deterrent, but no longer would U.S. ground troops be committed to internal Asian wars. The Nixon plan for Asia was scheduled to take effect as soon as the Vietnam War was settled. An important aspect of the doctrine was Nixon's belief that his Vietnamization program would allow U.S. ground troops to disengage from Vietnam and the GVN would be able to hold out against the NVA/VC with only U.S. equipment support and possibly U.S. air support.

Nixon's War   see   **Army's War**

NKP RTAB (Nakhon Phanom, 56th SOW, 633d SOW)   One of the Thai air bases leased by the U.S. Air Force to conduct air operations in SEA. From NKP (Nakhon Phanom Royal Thai Air Base) the Air Force operated the 56th and 633d Special Operations Wings. The base also served as the control center for computers of the Infiltration Surveillance Center which monitored NVA/VC traffic along the Ho Chi Minh Trail. NKP was located 600kms northeast of Bangkok along the Laotian border, and was nicknamed "Naked Fanny." The special operations wings operated gunships (AC-119) on interdiction missions along the enemy infiltration routes along South Vietnam's border. See also **Thai Air Bases, Infiltration Surveillance Center, Naked Fanny.**

NL   see   **Night Defensive Position**

NLC   see   **National Leadership Council**

NLF   see   **National Liberation Front**

NLF Guerrillas   see   **Bung**

NMCB   see   **SEABEES**

No Bic   see   **Toi Com (Khong) Biet**

No Biet   see   **Toi Com (Khong) Biet**

No Bit   see   **Toi Com (Khong) Biet**

No Fire/No Fly   Designation for an area in which air and artillery missions were temporarily restricted. Such "recon zones" were declared when ground reconnaissance units were operating in the area. LRRP and USSF recon units sometimes dressed in captured enemy clothing when conducting long-range reconnaissance. From the air it was difficult to identify disguised recon units. The areas were declared off limits to fly-overs by aircraft that might jeopardize the ground recon. Air and arty strikes into the area were restricted unless requested by the recon unit. There were several instances of recon units suffering friendly fire because of a breakdown in communication or coordination with other friendly units in the area. See also **Recon Box.**

No Lie GI   Phrase commonly used by a Vietnamese to try to convince GIs that they were telling the truth.

No Mission Too Difficult, No Sacrifice...   see   **1st Infantry Division**

No Problem   see   **No Sweat**

No Sweat (No Problem)   Slang for "no problem" or requiring little effort, risk or trouble; everything is okay or all right, an affirmative response to a task request or question.

No Viet Cong Ever Called...   see   **Ali, Muhammad**

No Wider War   During Lyndon Johnson's campaign for president in '64, he repeatedly promised the American public that there would be "no wider war" in Vietnam involving American forces, and that American troops would not be sent to Southeast Asia to fight South Vietnam's war. Although "no wider war" was the Johnson administration's public stance, his military advisors urged him to take swift action against NVN. For a short period after the Gulf of Tonkin Incident NVN antiaircraft defenses were minimal. At this time NVN lacked sophisticated radar or SAMs and had less than three dozen combat MiGs in their inventory. During the Vietnam War, Johnson's slow escalation of the war allowed NVN time to build its air defenses to become the most successful in the world.

No-Doze Mission   U.S. airborne PSYOPS missions that continually broadcasted propaganda and music during the hours of darkness, aimed at convincing the Vietnamese of the worthiness of their government and ruining their sleep. *See also* **Psychological Operations.**

No-Fire-Zone   *see*   **Free-Fire-Zone**

No-Fuckin'-Good   *see*   **Number Ten**

No-Go Pills   *see*   **Polymagna**

No-No War in Never-Never Land   *see* **Secret War, Laos**

No. 2 Squadron Royal Australian Air Force   *see*   **Magpie, Royal Australian Air Force**

No. 9 Squadron   *see*   **Royal Australian Air Force**

NOC   *see*   **Combat Information Center**

NOD   *see*   **Starlight Scope**

NOE   *see*   **Nap-of-the-Earth**

Noel, Cris   American Armed Forces Radio Network personality. Cris' hour-long shows, "A Date with Cris," were produced in the States and rebroadcasted throughout the Armed Forces Network worldwide. She produced shows from '66–'70, and toured Vietnam several times, visiting the troops.

NOFORN   "NO FOREIGN EYES," document classification used by Americans in Vietnam meaning the document was not to be seen by foreign eyes, including and especially the South Vietnamese.

Noggies   Australian slang for NVA/VC troops. *See also* **Enemy, The.**

Noi Bac-Viet? (Newy Bac Viet)   "Noi Bac-Viet?" [newy bac Viet], Vietnamese phrase approximately translated as "Are you North Vietnamese?". One of the questions GIs in I and II Corps quickly learned.

Noise Discipline   Military reference to the amount of noise a man or unit made while moving or in position. Poor noise discipline indicated the unit made a lot of

noise as it moved, or while it was set up in an ambush, etc. Poor noise discipline aided the enemy, allowing him to determine the unit's location, disposition and strength. Good noise discipline meant the unit was moving quietly, greatly increasing its survivability. U.S. LRRP and USSF units had excellent noise discipline. Regular line units had good to poor noise discipline, and had to constantly work at improving their techniques. Most ARVN units had generally poor noise discipline, announcing their location to the Viet Cong well in advance of their approach. *See also* **Breaking Tape.**

NOK   *see*   **Next of Kin**

Nol, General Lon (Lon Nol)   General Lon Nol, Cambodia's premier, seized power of the government of Cambodia in '70 from Prince Norodom Sihanouk. Prior policies of the Sihanouk government had allowed the NVA/VC to use eastern Cambodia as a sanctuary for attacks on South Vietnam and the Cambodian port of Sihanoukville became a major supply entry point for the NVA/VC. Lon Nol was extremely anticommunist and encouraged U.S. attacks on communist bases in Cambodia. Lon Nol ineffectively guided the Khmer Republic against the communists until April 17, 1975, when the communist Khmer Rouge defeated Cambodia's FANK Army with the fall of Phnom Penh.

NOMEX Flight Suit (NOMEX Gloves) Two-piece (and single-piece) flight suit worn by helicopter crewmen and some aircraft pilots. The nylon suit was OD green, flame resistant and became generally available to aircraft crews after '69. The two-piece flight suits were primarily worn by Army helicopter crews. A long-sleeved NOMEX glove was also available. It featured thin, sheepskin palms which improved the wearer's ability to manipulate objects with his gloved hands. The gloves were also worn by some Special Forces and Recon troops.

NOMEX Gloves   *see*   **NOMEX Flight Suit**

Non (Conical Hat, Vietnamese Hat) The ever-present cone shaped hat worn by the Vietnamese. The hat was worn by men and women alike, and was made of latania leaves or woven reeds. Used to shade the face from the sun, and functioned as a rain hat and a hand fan.

Non Gratum Anus Rodentum *see* **Diehard Tunnel Rats**

Nonbattle Casualty (NBC) Military casualty classification for a soldier who was wounded or died away from the battlefield, under noncombat related circumstances. This would normally apply to casualties caused by illness, accidents, suicides, etc. Some commands in Vietnam reported combat WIAs who died en route to or in hospital as nonbattle casualties. This erroneous practice allowed the ratio of enemy dead to friendly dead appear much more favorable to the reporting unit.

Noncom *see* **Noncommissioned Officer**

Noncommissioned Officer (NCO, Noncom, Noncommissioned Officer in Charge [NCOIC]) Ranks sergeant E-5 to E-9, led and directed troops. Sergeants took orders issued by officers and filtered those orders down to the troops in the unit, and insured they were carried out. The enlisted man made up the bulk of the manpower in the military, but it was the NCO that translated orders from the officer corps into something meaningful, reasonable and hopefully obtainable. In Vietnam the NCO ranks accounted for a significant number of casualties; where officers typically spent six months leading in combat, combat NCOs usually spent their full 12-month tour on the line. Leaders and RTOs were a special target of the enemy. An NCOIC was an NCO placed in charge of a unit or group. *See also* **Shake 'n' Bake Sergeants.**

Noncommissioned Officer in Charge *see* **Noncommissioned Officer**

Nondirectional Beacon *see* **Radio Beacon**

Nondivisional Aviation Assets *see* **Nonorganic Aviation Unit**

Nonevac *see* **Casualty Classifications**

Nongao *see* **Montagnards**

Nonorganic *see* **Organic**

Nonorganic Aviation Unit (Nondivisional Aviation Assets, Separate Helicopter Companies) Helicopter units which were not assigned to any specific division, and were under the control of MACV.

MACV assigned these separate helicopter companies to assist field units as necessary. The infantry divisions and brigades which the helicopter companies were assigned to had temporary operational control of the helicopter units. In some instances one or several helo companies repeatedly worked with the same units, and came to be identified with those units. The separate helicopter companies were organized as separate battalions and parceled out as necessary. *See also* **Organic Avaiation Unit.**

Nonpersistent CS Gas *see* **CS Gas**

Nonspecific Urethritis (Clap) One of the many "rank has its privileges" jokes that circulated through the Army was that when it came to venereal diseases "officers contracted nonspecific urethritis, while enlisted men caught the clap." *See also* **Venereal Diseases.**

Nooky *see* **Boom-Boom**

Norodom Complex Complex of Quonset huts located on the grounds of the U.S. Embassy in Saigon. Most of the complex housed CIA offices.

NORS *see* **Mission Ready**

NORS-G *see* **Mission Ready**

North Vietnam *see* **Democratic Republic of Vietnam**

North Vietnamese *see* **Tonkinese, Democratic Republic of Vietnam**

North Vietnamese Air Force (NVAF, Vietnamese People's Army Air Force [VPAAF]) The North Vietnamese Air Force consisted mostly of Soviet made Il-28 bombers and MiG 15, 17 and 21 aircraft, and several light helicopters. The air force was officially known as the "Vietnamese People's Army Air Force"; VPAAF.

North Vietnamese Army *see* **People's Army of North Vietnam**

North Vietnamese Flag *see* **Flags...**

North Vietnamese Newspaper *see* **Quan Doi Nhan Dan**

North Vietnamese Regulars *see* **Enemy, The**

North Vietnamization Prior to the '68 Tet Offensive the primary task of the Viet Cong was aimed at the villages and hamlets located near urban centers and in rural areas.

The VC staged small attacks on US/ARVN outposts and made extensive use of ambushes and booby traps. The NVA primarily operated from sanctuaries across the border in the dense jungle areas of I and II Corps. Because of heavy casualties suffered by the VC during Tet, the NVA took on a greater share of the fighting in SVN, and virtually took complete control of the NVA/VC war. The NVA outfitted the remaining VC with newer, more powerful weapons and slowly absorbed them into their ranks. The NVA's Vietnamization efforts were directly opposite those of the U.S. in '69.

Northeast Monsoons *see* **Monsoons**

Nose Mutilations *see* **Mutilations**

Not Operationally Ready for Service-Grounded *see* **Mission Ready**

Not Operationally Ready *see* **Mission Ready**

Not Worth a Rat's Ass *see* **Diehard Tunnel Rats**

Nothing Is More Precious... "Nothing is more precious than independence and liberty." Quote from Ho Chi Minh that was constantly used by him and later as a propaganda centerpiece by NVA/VC cadre.

November Lima *see* **Night Defensive Position**

November Victor Alpha *see* **Enemy**

NPF *see* **National Police Force**

NPFF *see* **National Police Force**

NSA *see* **National Security Agency; Naval Support Activity, Saigon or Da Nang**

NSA Courier Service *see* **Air Cofat**

NSA, Da Nang *see* **Naval Support Activity, Da Nang**

NSA, Saigon *see* **Naval Support Activity, Saigon**

NSAD *see* **Naval Support Activity, Da Nang**

NSAS *see* **Naval Support Activity, Saigon**

NSC *see* **National Security Council**

NSF, Da Nang *see* **Navy Support Facility, Da Nang**

NSOG *see* **Navy Special Operations Group**

Nuc-Bom Vietnamese soup made from vegetables, rice and fish. After preparation the soup was sealed in a jar, buried, and allowed to ferment. The Viet Cong buried nuc-bom throughout the remote areas they operated, allowing them to move about without having to carry food. The buried jars were readily available, and the VC enjoyed the rotting contents. Although high in protein and carbohydrates, most GIs were repulsed by the soup's horrible odor, unable to get by the smell in order to taste it.

Nuclear Reactor *see* **Atoms for Peace**

Nuclear Threat Shortly after the Korean War ended in July '53, the Communist Chinese increased their military aid to the Viet Minh. President Dwight Eisenhower warned China that if they sent troops into Indochina to aid the Viet Minh, as they had done in Korea, the U.S. would use all available force, including nuclear weapons if necessary, to dissuade Chinese intervention. *See also* **Nuclear Weapons.**

Nuclear Weapons (Tactical Nuclear Weapons) During the NVA siege of Khe Sanh Combat Base, General William Westmoreland considered the tactical strengths and weaknesses of using low yield, tactical nuclear weapons. Westmoreland felt that if enough enemy forces could be massed around a remote base, it would provide an excellent opportunity to annihilate a large number of enemy troops and "demonstrate American resolve in Vietnam." The nuclear possibilities and contingency plans were discussed at secret meetings, but no formal plan for the use of tactical nuclear weapons in the Vietnam War was ever approved by President Johnson. *See also* **Nuclear Threat.**

Nui Ba Dinh (Black Virgin Mountain) 3,225-foot mountain located just north of Tay Ninh City, Tay Ninh Province, III Corps. The mountain was located about 83kms northwest of Saigon, near the SVN/Cambodian border, part of the U.S. 25th Inf. Div.'s area of operations. Tay Ninh was a major NVA/VC base area. Nui Ba Dinh translated to "Black Virgin Mountain."

Nui Cam Highest peak (2,325 feet) of the Seven Mountains area of the Delta, located along the Cambodian border in

Chau Doc Province. The mountain area was heavily infested with Viet Cong throughout the war.

Nui Cay Tre *see* **Mutter's Ridge**

Nui Coto (The Rockpile) Southernmost mountain of the Seven Mountains located in Chau Doc Province, IV Corps. The mountain was honeycombed with tunnels and served as a Viet Cong base camp. Nui Coto was located 182kms west of Saigon and 95kms northwest of Can Tho. Repeated assaults by Mobile Strike Force companies in '69 temporarily cleared most of the VC off the mountain. Nui Coto was nicknamed "the Rockpile" by the MSF survivors. Eventually three NVA regiments were brought into the Seven Mountains area to support VC operations and the entire area fell to the NVA/VC.

Nui Dat *see* **Australian Task Force**

Nui Lua *see* **Nguyen Vo Giap**

Nui Thi Mountain (Dinh Hills) Small mountain located just northwest of Phuoc Le (Baria). The 1,654-foot hill was a base area for elements of the 5th Viet Cong Division that operated in the area. The hill was located 18kms northeast of Vung Tau, and 50kms southeast of Saigon. *See also* **Phuoc Le.**

Numba One *see* **Number One**

Numba Ten *see* **Number Ten**

Number One (#1, Numba One) Top of the line, the very best, cream of the crop, excellent. Referred to a person, place or thing. In Vietnam the Vietnamese and GIs used it to describe many conditions, moods and preferences, "numba one" being the best; "numba ten" was the very worst. The terms were brought to Vietnam by American advisors and support troops in the early days of the war, terms adopted from the Japanese scale of values. *See also* **Number Ten.**

Number Ten (#10, Numba Ten, Number Ten-Thousand, NFG [No-Fuckin'-Good]) The very worst, no good, rotten, unacceptable, unworthy, bottom of the barrel or without value. Used by the Vietnamese and GIs to communicate value. Could refer to a person, place or thing. To be #10 was bad news, compared to being #1, which was the greatest. In Vietnam there was no rating in between. The situation or the person or the thing was either rated as #1 or #10. The very worst of the worst was "Number Ten-Thousand." The terms #1 and #10 were brought to Vietnam by American advisors and support troops in the early days of the war, terms adopted from the Japanese scale of values. "NFG" (no-fuckin'-good), was an abbreviated form of a #10 condition. *See also* **Number One.**

Number Ten-Thousand *see* **Number Ten**

Number-10s (Dimes) GI name for an especially potent mixture of barbiturates used to get high (Quaaludes and speed); also nicknamed "dimes." *See also* **Speed, Quaaludes, Illicit Drugs, Drug List.**

Numpai (Montagnard Rice Wine) [Num pie.] Extremely sweet Montagnard rice wine. *See also* **45 Whiskey.**

Nungs (Mercenaries) Nungs were an ancestral mix of Chinese-Thai-Muong-Tibetan, simply referred to as being of Chinese ancestry. The Nungs were tribal with the largest population located in NVN. Nungs fought as mercenaries during the VNW; they were recruited and paid by the U.S. Special Forces. They were ruthlessly effective fighters. Most of the Nungs fought for the USSF against the NVA/VC, but there were some instances of Nungs fighting for the NVA/VC for pay. The Nungs were considered excellent fighters and were the highest paid of the American mercenaries and, in general, despised all Vietnamese except other Nungs. Nung platoons and companies were often used to provide security for American A-Teams at USSFs camps. *See also* **Montagnard.**

Nuoc Mam (Fish Sauce) Concentrated Vietnamese fish sauce/paste used to flavor food. The sauce was made from rotten fish and had a long-range odor factor. The fish was ground up and allowed to ferment (spoil). The very best quality nuoc mam was allowed to ferment for about a year; the lesser (cheaper) grades generally were fermented for at least a month. The sauce was used to flavor rice and vegetables and was a Vietnamese staple, more common than "ketchup" in the U.S. The area around the Vietnamese village of An Thoi on the island of Phu Quoc, in the Gulf of Thailand, supposedly produced the best nuoc mam [new-ook mom] in all Vietnam. GIs had a wide variety of unflattering names for the foul smelling sauce such as Rotten Fish Head Sauce, Armpit Sauce, Viet Kimchi, Shit Sauce. *See also* **An Thoi, Nuc-Bom, Kimchi.**

Nurse Corps *see* **U.S. Army Nurse Corps**

Nurse Hat *see* **Dixie Cup**

Nurses Do It for Free, but... "Nurses do it for free, but the Red Cross girls charge." A well-worn phrase based on the belief by some antiwar activists and GIs that the Red Cross women and nurses went to Vietnam to service the troops sexually. The rumor was also spread by REMFs whose advances had been turned down by nurses and Red Cross workers. ARC workers had the highest regard for the grunts in the field. The grunts in the field respected and protected the Delta-Deltas when the women made their field visits. The women would catch a ride on a mail ship or log run and spend a few hours with the grunts, returning home before dark. *See also* **Donut Dollies.**

Nuts *see* **FSB Nuts**

NVA *see* **People's Army of North Vietnam; Enemy, The**

NVA Army *see* **People's Army of North Vietnam**

NVA B-52 *see* **Dac Cong**

NVA Boots (Pataugas, Tropical Boots, Jungle Shoes) NVA troops headed south were issued jungle boots very similar to American high top tennis shoes. The NVA jungle shoes were manufactured in North Vietnam and the PRC. The design of the shoe was fashioned after the "pataugas," the tropical boots worn by the French in Indochina. *See also* **Binh-Tri-Thien, Bata Boots.**

NVA Combat Engineers *see* **Dac Cong**

NVA Flag *see* **Flags...**

NVA Haircut *see* **White-Sidewalls**

NVA Hammock *see* **Hammock**

NVA Helmet (Sun Helmet, Reed [Sun] Helmet, Pith Helmet, Palm Hat) Sun helmet frequently worn by NVA soldiers. The true "pith helmet" was made of cork; the helmets most frequently worn by the

NVA were made of cardboard or plastic. The cardboard version was covered with cloth and issued to troops. The plastic version was made in the PRC and was primarily issued to civilian workers and the militia. Another version of the sun helmet made of woven, split bamboo shoots was called the Reed Sun Helmet. These helmets served as rain and sun hats, having no protective value against bullets or shrapnel. A U.S. version was available, but was rarely issued to U.S. troops. *See also* **NVA Jungle Hat.**

NVA I Corps (1st NVA Corps) Corps level headquarters formed in '73. The Corps consisted of the 308th, 312th, and 320th NVA divisions, which operated in the northern I Corps area of South Vietnam.

NVA II Corps (2d NVA Corps) NVA corps level headquarters formed in '74. The corps consisted of the 304th, 324th and 325th NVA divisions, which operated in the Central Highlands of South Vietnam.

NVA III Corps (3d NVA Corps) NVA corps level headquarters formed in '74. The corps consisted of the 2d and 711th NVA divisions, which operated in the central I Corps area of South Vietnam.

NVA IV Corps (4th NVA Corps, 301st NVA Corps) The 4th NVA Corps was formed in '74 from the 7th and 9th NVA divisions, and the 3d Phuoc Long Division. The divisions operated in the northern provinces of South Vietnam's III Corps. The corps was also known as the 301st NVA Corps.

NVA Jungle Hat The most common form of headgear worn by the NVA/VC was a jungle hat, similar to the U.S. jungle hat. The NVA version was made of cotton, fashioned after the jungle hat worn by French forces in Indochina. *See also* **Jungle Hat.**

NVA Prison Camps *see* **Hanoi Hilton**

NVA Rucksack The rucksack used by NVA troops was similar in overall design to that of the American rucksack, with one large main compartment, and three smaller outer pockets. The NVA ruck was made of heavy khaki cotton material and rode lower on the wearer's back, making it more comfortable to carry. Versions of the rucksack were manufactured in the PRC and NVN. American Special Forces and Lurps used captured NVA rucksacks, when they were available, because they were more comfortable to wear when humping in the boonies. *See also* ALICE.

NVA Trucks *see* Zils

NVA/VC Base Camps Those base camps located in areas controlled by the NVA/VC were well hidden and heavily fortified with interconnecting bunkers and fighting positions. Base camps hidden along the border areas and the mountains of the Central Highlands were extremely difficult to locate from the air, and featured more permanent facilities. In contested areas near villages the NVA/VC base camps were highly mobile, and moved between a number of fortified locations. During the war U.S. intelligence identified several enemy base areas, but knew the exact location of relatively few base camps. For example, the enemy's COSVN headquarters in III Corps was the subject of several U.S. search operations, but it was never captured. *See also* **Central Office South Vietnam.**

NVA/VC Frags The NVA/VC used Soviet, PRC and North Korean manufactured fragmentation grenades. The frags came in various shapes, but they all weighed about one pound and most were slightly smaller in size than their American counterpart. The Viet Cong also manufactured some of their own grenades which they used for booby traps. *See also* **F1 Frag, RG-42 Frag, RGD-5 Frag, F1 Frag NK, Type 59 Grenade; Grenades, Fragmentation.**

NVA/VC Radios (Captured Radios, R-105M, R-104M, R-108M, R-126) The NVA/VC made use of radios down to the battalion level, and in some special instances lower echelons had radios, temporarily. The NVA/VC primarily used Soviet radio equipment, but also utilized captured American/ARVN AN/PRC-25s. The captured radios were used for normal command communications and were also used to monitor American and ARVN transmissions. On some occasions captured radios were used to give false information regarding air strikes and artillery adjustments. The primary Soviet radios used were the R-104M, R-105M, R-108M and the R-126. *See also* **Radios.**

NVAF *see* **North Vietnamese Air Force**

NVN *see* **Democratic Republic of Vietnam**

NVR *see* **Enemy, The**

NWC *see* **National War College, Naval War College**

Nystul, Captain William *see* **Last American to Die...**

NZ *see* **New Zealand**

NZSAS *see* **New Zealand**

O

O-1 *see* **L-19**

O-2 (Cessna O-2, Pusher-Puller, Super Skymaster) Light observation aircraft used by the Air Force as a forward air controller (FAC). The O-2 featured twin in-line engines, one facing front pulling the aircraft; the other engine faced to the rear, pushing the plane. The aircraft was manufactured by Cessna, and along with the OV-10 replaced the much older O-1 Bird Dogs the Air Force had previously used. *See also* **Forward Air Controller.**

O Club *see* **Officer's Club**

OAB *see* **Oakland Army Base**

Oak Leaf Cluster (Rat-Turds) A decoration added to a previously awarded decoration or citation to indicate the bearer had received the award or decoration more than once, as in multiple Purple Hearts or Bronze Stars. Nicknamed Rat-Turds by field grunts in Vietnam.

Oakland Army Base (OAB) Main point of debarkation for replacement troops going to Vietnam, '66 to '73. Replacement troops en route to RVN were staged at OAB and then bused to Travis Air Force Base for air transport to SVN. OAB was also the main West Coast receiving station for troops returning from Vietnam at the end of their tour. OAB, California, was the site of the U.S. Army Mortuary, point of entry for all remains returning from Southeast Asia.

Oasis *see* **FSB Oasis**

OBC *see* **Officer Basic Course**

Observation Post (OP, Listening Post [LP]) In Vietnam "observation post" and "listening post" were used interchangeably. The OP/LP was a station or position set up forward of the main body of the unit. The OP/LP acted as early warning to the rest of the unit for enemy advance or attack. One or more LPs acting as early warning were put out from an NDP in the path of the most likely avenues of enemy approach. The most important aspect of an LP was that it must not be detected by the enemy. If the enemy could slip by the LP, the main body and the LP were in big trouble. At night LPs were placed 100–300 meters beyond the perimeter depending on the terrain, and pulled in at first light. OPs were deployed further out during the day and withdrawn at dark.

OCO *see* **Office of Civil Operations**

OCS *see* **Officer Candidate School**

OD *see* **Olive Drab, Officer of the Day**

OD Towel *see* **Lucky Towel**

O'Daniel, General John *see* **Iron Mike**

OE *see* **L-19**

OER *see* **Officer Efficiency Report**

Of Their Own Accord *see* **75th Infantry (Rangers)**

Ofay *see* **Caucasian**

Off *see* **Kill**

Off Duty Hours *see* **Ghost Time**

Offensive Sweeps *see* **Search and Destroy**

Office of Civil Operations (OCO) Embassy staffed group that coordinated all U.S. civilian pacification efforts in SVN prior to the establishment of CORDS. OCO was established in '66 by Ambassador Henry Cabot Lodge, Jr. In '67 all pacification efforts were placed under the control of CORDS and became directly subordinate to MACV. CORDS was originally directed by Robert Komer. Neither the OCO or CORDS was very successful in its mission to separate the people from the VC and win the people's trust and support. *See also* **CORDS.**

Office of Secretary of Defense *see* **Secretary of Defense**

Office of Special Investigations (OSI) Branch of the Air Force military police that conducted criminal investigations. *See also* **CID.**

Office of Strategic Services (OSS) Established in '42, during WWII, the OSS (American Office of Strategic Services) conducted special and clandestine operations for the United States. The OSS operated outside of the States and was the forerunner of today's Central Intelligence Agency. OSS officers made the initial contacts with Ho Chi Minh in the mid-forties, seeking Ho's help in America's efforts against the Japanese in WWII. *See also* **Deer Team; Patti, Archimedes L.A.**

Office of the Special Assistant *see* **OSAFO**

Office of U.S. Air Attaché *see* **OUSAIRA**

Officer *see* **Tuong- Si**

Officer Basic Course (OBC) Name of the officer training course for prospective candidates at OCS. *See also* **Officer Candidate School.**

Officer Candidate School (90 Day Wonders, OCS) Army officer training school. During the Vietnam War the educational requirements for entry into OCS were gradually lowered in an effort to fill the Army's depleted company grade ranks. The term of training and preparation for command was very short compared to the time and education required to graduate from the Army's West Point Military Academy. The OCS course was 90 days in length, and field troops referred to OCS graduates as "90 day wonders."

Officer Efficiency Report (OER) Annual (supposedly objective) evaluation of an officer by his superiors, used in determining career progress, duty assignments and promotions. During the Vietnam era and, somewhat, today, so much emphasis was placed on OERs that many officers neglected their duty to their men in their efforts to secure a good OER. A bad OER could ruin an officer's career. For many, Vietnam was a place where they could enhance their careers, and their actions were focused on improving their image, rather than working for the good of the country. *See also* **Ticket Punchers, Frag, The Best Go West.**

Officer of the Day (OD)   Officer of a unit charged with responsibility for overseeing the security of a post or facility during the 24 hours of his duty watch. ODs were usually rotated through a list of junior officers who worked with the CQ during his watch. ODs were most noticeable during the unit's off duty hours and in the absence of the unit commander. In Vietnam the OD's primary concern was base security, and verification that the guard was adequately maintained around the base's perimeter. *See also* **CQ.**

Officer's Award   *see*   **Bronze Star, Gongs**

Officer's Club (O Club)   Service club for officers only, no enlisted men allowed, except to work in the club.

Officers   U.S. Army officers fell into four major classes based on their training and experience: West Pointers, Mustangs, ROTC, and OCS. West Point officers attended the Army academy and studied war for four years. The Mustang officer was promoted in the field based on his leadership qualities and experience (plus the needs of the service). The ROTC officer attended a regular college and studied war on a part-time basis. The OCS officer attended the Army's 90 day officer training course. Officers within the Army fell into three grades: general (all generals), field (major, lieutenant colonel, colonel), and company (lieutenant, captain) grade.

Offshore Fuel Station   *see*   **Swivel-Top Buoy**

OH-6 (Cayuse, LOH-6, Loach, White Bird, Flying Egg)   Small, light observation helicopter (LOH) designed by Hughes Aircraft, designated the Model 369. The LOH, or "Loach" entered service with the

U.S. Army in '67 as the OH-6A "Cayuse" and proved to be a highly maneuverable and dependable aircraft. The egg-shaped fuselage helicopter had a max speed of 152mph, a range of 600kms. The small cabin allowed for the transport of four passengers or limited cargo. In Vietnam the OH-6 was primarily used for observation, scouting and surveillance duties, sometimes working with teams of one or two Cobra gunships. Some Loaches were armed with a fixed, skid mounted minigun, or a door mounted M-60 LMG. Later versions were sometimes armed with TOW antitank missiles. *See also* **Helicopter Scouts, Doghouse, Loach Alley.**

OH-13 (Sioux, H-13, Flying Bubble, Bubble, Goldfish Bowl, Sperm)   Primary Army light observation helicopter (LOH) in the late '50s and early '60s. The H-13 was developed by Bell Helicopter Company and several hundred were in the Army's inventory. The H-13 was initially nicknamed the "goldfish bowl." The Army Sioux, OH-13, had a range of 507kms and a max speed of 105mph, weighed 1,795 pounds and could seat three men or carry two skid mounted litters. In Vietnam the OH-13 was used for short-range scouting and many were distributed throughout South Vietnam at various Army bases. Several H-13s were used by the Navy for antisubmarine warfare and liaison duties in the early fifties. The Marines nicknamed their OH-13s "Sperm," and used it for air recon and spotting. *See also* **Helicopter Scouts, Sperm.**

OH-23 (Raven, H-23)   Unarmed, three seat, light observation helicopter used by the Army for reconnaissance and observation in Vietnam. The 1,700-pound helicopter developed by Hiller Aircraft had a max speed of 96mph, a range of 360kms and a large plexiglass cockpit canopy similar to the OH-13. The Raven was used throughout the war, but it was gradually replaced by the OH-6 and OH-58 helicopters which provided greater speed, range and maneuverability. *See also* **OH-6, OH-13, OH-58, Helicopter Scouts.**

OH-43   *see*   **HH-43**

OH-58 (Kiowa, Bell Jet Ranger, Sea Ranger)   Light observation helicopter manufactured by Bell Helicopters as the Jet Ranger. The OH-58 entered service with the Army in late '67 and began deployment to

Vietnam in '69. The single engine, twin blade helo had a max speed of 135mph and a range of 480kms, and was the planned replacement for the old Army OH-13 and OH-23 helicopters. The OH-58 was called the "Kiowa" and operated with a two man crew, with room for three passengers or cargo. The Navy also used the Jet Ranger designated TH-57, "Sea Ranger," as a liaison aircraft.

Oil Spot Technique Nickname for some of the early French attempts at pacification in Vietnam. A base of operations was established in a town or village under GVN control, operating from the base into the surrounding area, gradually increasing the area of control and popular support. Early American pacification efforts used the "oil spot technique," but they eventually failed due to the ARVN's inability to provide security and corruption by the GVN that limited the effectiveness of such programs in the field. *See also* **Pacification.**

OJs (Marijuana Cigarettes) (100s, Big O's) Marijuana cigarettes that had been soaked in or "painted" with an opium solution, multiplying the effects of the opium and marijuana. The opium laced joints were somewhat larger than regular cigarettes and were sometimes called "100s" or "Big O's." *See also* **Marijuana.**

OJT *see* **On the Job Training**

Okinawa (The Rock) Largest of the Japanese Ryukyu Islands, current home of a large U.S. base supporting both Army, Navy, Marine and Air Force units. Prior to '64 the U.S. 1st Special Forces HQs was located at Okinawa, operating SF teams in SVN. In '64 the 5th Special Forces was organized and deployed to SVN, taking over many of the in-country duties of the 1st Special Forces group. Several Marine units were based on Okinawa during and preceding the VNW and the Marines nicknamed it "the Rock." *See also* **USS Okinawa.**

Old Breed, The *see* **1st Marine Division**

Old City *see* **Citadel, Hue**

Old Man, The *see* **Commanding Officer**

Old Nam Can *see* **Nam Can**

Old Reliables *see* **9th Infantry Division**

Old-Salt *see* **Salty-Dog**

Olfractronic Personnel Detector *see* **XM-2 People Sniffer**

Olive Drab (OD) Standard Army green color, olive in color — drab in luster, found on everything from underwear to helicopters.

Omega *see* **Project Omega**

On the Job Training (OJT) Training one received while actually doing the job; nonformal training or education. OJT was the primary method used by U.S. units to train Vietnamese forces during Vietnamization. Because of a lack of language skills on the part of the Vietnamese and the Americans in each other's language, OJT was the only satisfactory method available to quickly orient the Vietnamese to the operation and maintenance of U.S. equipment. *See also* **Vietnamization, ACTOV.**

On-Call Targets Prearranged artillery targets; the target information was on record with an artillery battery. When it became necessary to fire on the target, a call was made and the stored gun data was used. This method resulted in reduced fire reaction time to request for artillery support. On-call targets were usually plotted against likely avenues of enemy approach to a unit's position. For field units the FO or unit commander designated the targets and registered the guns on each target.

On-Line (In-Line, Line-Ahead, Line-Abreast, Marching-Fire, Trail Formation) Military maneuver or formation. Units "on-line" were side by side, facing the same direction. For troops, this would be shoulder to shoulder; line-abreast. The distance between the elements in the line determine the frontal area covered by the line. This differed from the "in-line" or "line-ahead" formation which placed the elements of the unit in "trail formation" (single file line) with the front of one element facing the back of the element to its front. Units marching on-line, firing their weapons ahead of them, were using "marching-fire," which was not terribly effective against dug-in NVA troops.

On-Station Aircraft in a holding

pattern above a particular area, available and waiting, to be used in that area. The term also applied to naval ships in a holding pattern at sea.

On-the-Block   Black slang for the inner city streets of urban America, and particular reference to a black GI's "home" street and neighborhood. *See also* **U.S.A.**

On-the-Rag   *see*   **Pissed**

One Buck Deployment   *see*   **Strike Force One Buck**

One Country, One Flag; Love It or Leave It (America, Love It or Leave It) Sentiments expressed on signs during a Veterans of Foreign Wars sponsored "Loyalty Day Parade" in New York. The April '67 parade was organized to show support for the soldiers in Vietnam and President Johnson. Nearly 10,000 people showed up for the parade.

One Shot, One Kill   U.S. Marine sniper's motto. *See also* **Hathcock, Gunnery Sergeant Carlos.**

One Slow — Four Quick   *see*   **Mao Tse-Tung**

One, Two, Three, Four, the NLF... "One, two, three, four, the NLF will win the war. Five, six, seven, eight, the U.S. will capitulate." One of the chants used by Australian antiwar protestors during the late 60s.

One War Plan   In February '69 the U.S. outlined a new plan of operation and strategy for South Vietnam. The plan stressed the need for accelerated pacification and territorial security; it also stressed the development of the SVN military as an independent fighting force. The plan gave the highest priority to Vietnamization of the war and limited U.S. forces to defensive operations and support of the Vietnamese military. In the following months and years the same plan changed names several times. *See also* **Dynamic Defense.**

One Year Tour   The tour of duty for the American serviceman in Vietnam was one year (13 months for the Marines, 8 months for SEABEES). The year tour was established to quickly bring America's youth home. The Johnson administration believed the public would not support a long war in far off Asia if America's youth were tied up there for several years. Support for the war had to come from middle America, and Johnson believed he could hold that support if he could honestly tell America that he only needed their sons for a year in Vietnam. For the military establishment the one year tour did not bode well. The Viet Cong, by way of the NVA and the Viet Minh, had been fighting a guerrilla war in Vietnam for over ten years. Some of the same men that fought the French were fighting the Americans. American combat troops typically trained 4–6 months before they arrived in Vietnam. It took several months of survival in the war zone to understand the enemy. By the time the average U.S. field soldier was proficient in fighting the enemy his tour was nearly complete and he was due to return home. The constant turnover of troops put immense pressures on soldiers who were struggling to survive and learn the enemy's ways, and at the same time keep the new, green troops being fed into the line alive long enough to learn the tricks of survival. The one year tour was a good gimmick in the States, but it proved disastrous for America's military in Vietnam. *See also* **We Weren't in Vietnam for Ten Years....**

One-Buck (Vietnam Ready Reserve) Code name for an Army reserve force held on 48-hour standby in the States for immediate deployment to Vietnam. During Tet '68 the 3d Brigade/82d Airborne Division made a rapid deployment to Vietnam to counter the NVA/VC offensive. The brigade was attached to the 101st Airborne Division, and operated in I Corps until the end of '69 when it returned to the States.

One-Oh-Worst   *see*   **101st Airborne Division (Airmobile)**

Ong Dong Jungle   Heavy jungle area located 27kms north of Saigon along the Song Dong Nai River. The area served as a major VC base and was the site of numerous U.S. jungle clearing operations.

Ong My   *see*   **My**

Onion Heads (Skin Jobs)   Nickname for the close-cut, shaved haircuts of the U.S. Marines. During Vietnam lifers in the Corps and some officers tended to keep their heads shaved. And shaved heads were the order of the day for Marine recruits. Once in the field the haircut rules were a little more relaxed. The Army haircut rules were not as strict as the Marines'. In basic training the hair was initially shaved off and afterwards kept short; except for some Special Forces and Rangers, the shaved head was not typical among combat troops. *See also* **White-Sidewalls.**

The Only Good Gook Is a Dead Gook *see* **Gook Syndrome**

Only You Can Prevent Forest *see* **Operation Ranch Hand**

Ontos *see* **M-50A1 Ontos**

OP *see* **Observation Post**

OP-2E   The twin engine, propeller driven "Neptune" was originally used by the Navy for antisubmarine surveillance. Navy P-2 Neptune aircraft were modified in '67 to be used for implant operations of electronic sensors along the Ho Chi Minh Trail. The Neptune seeded the trail with hundreds of sensors before being withdrawn from implant duty when they were replaced by the less vulnerable F-4 Phantoms of the Air Force. The sensors used in the implant operations were the ADSID and ACOUSID. The OP-2E was used in conjunction with the AP-2H gunship as part of TRIM operations against the Ho Chi Minh Trail. *See also* **Electronic Sensors, ADSID, ACOUSID, F-4, VAH-21, P-2.**

Op-Orders   Abbreviated term for Operational Orders used by a unit, containing the objective, route of attack, radio frequencies, support and other pertinent information relevant to an operation or mission.

OPCON *see* **Operation Control**

Open Arms Program *see* **Chieu Hoi Program**

Open City   Opposing enemy forces occupying the same city, each aware of the presence of the other, but neither taking any action against the other; an unspoken, informal truce between opposing forces. Prior to Tet '68, Hue was an open city. The Viet Cong were known to be in the city, but neither the ARVN nor the Police pressed the matter. In turn, the ARVN 1st Div HQ and their U.S. advisors located in Hue, where mostly unmolested by terrorist acts from the Viet Cong. The NVA/VC attacks during Tet

'68 ended Hue's "open city" status. After the communists were cleared out of Hue the GVN made routine sweeps of the city in an attempt to keep the Viet Cong from reestablishing a foothold.

Open Sheaf *see* **Sheafs of Fire**

Operating Room *see* **ER/OR**

Operation Abel Mabel (TF Abel Mabel)   Operation conducted by Air Force reconnaissance aircraft of the 45th Tactical Reconnaissance Squadron in late '61 from air facilities located at Don Muang air base in Thailand. The Air Force group flew recon missions over Laos and the Ho Chi Minh Trail. *See also* **Operation Pipe Stem.**

Operation Abilene   Operation conducted in April '66 by elements of the 1st Infantry Division in Phuoc Tuy Province, III Corps.

Operation Ala Moana   Conducted by elements of the 25th Infantry Division in the rice growing areas of Saigon, and the Ho Bo Woods. The Ho Bo Woods were located just north of Cu Chi, and served as a major NVA/VC base area. The operation was conducted in December '66 and ended in January '67, just prior to the start of Operation Cedar Falls.

Operation Apache Snow (Hamburger Hill)   Operation Apache Snow was conducted by elements of the 3d Bde, 101st ABN, the 9th Marines and the ARVN 3d Regiment, 1st ARVN Inf Div., in May '69. The objective of the operation was to disrupt enemy activity building up in the A Shau Valley in Thau Thien Province. Units of the 101st ABN made contact with two NVA battalions on Hill 937, Ap Bia Mountain. Ten days, and 70 American KIAs later, the hill was taken from the NVA. The Americans abandoned the hill shortly thereafter. Within days the NVA had returned to the hill. Public controversy exploded over the military's leadership of the operation and its objectives. *See also* **Hamburger Hill, Operation Massachusetts Striker.**

Operation Arc Light *see* **Arc Light**

Operation Atlanta   Operation conducted by elements of the 25th Infantry Division in early '68 in their AO northwest of Saigon.

Operation Atlas *see* **Iron Triangle**

Operation Atlas Wedge   Operation conducted by elements of the 11th Armored Cavalry in the old Michelin Rubber plantation in March '69. The 11th ACR engaged units of the 7th Viet Cong Division.

Operation Attleboro   September '66 operation by elements of the U.S. 1st, 4th and 25th Infantry divisions in the area of Soui Da Special Forces Camp in War Zone C, Tay Ninh Province. The units engaged the 9th VC Division and the 101st NVA Regiment. The operation resulted in heavy enemy casualties and the withdrawal of the NVA/VC force into sanctuaries in Cambodia. *See also* **Soui Da Special Forces Camp.**

Operation Austin II   Conducted by elements of the 101st Airborne Division in the vicinity of Phan Thiet, along the coast of SVN, in April '66.

Operation Babylift   USAID operation executed by the U.S. Air Force in early April '75 to evacuate Vietnamese orphans from Saigon before its collapse to the communists. Most of the 2,000+ orphans that were evacuated were Amer-Asians, the children of Vietnamese mothers and American GI fathers. Such Amer-Asian children were outcasts in Vietnamese society and it was feared they would suffer even more under communist rule. During one of the lifts a C-5A transport lost cabin pressure shortly after takeoff and crash landed near Saigon; over 200 children and 43 crew and escorts aboard the plane were killed. The babylift ended May 9, 1975, after evacuating over 2,600 orphans. *See also* **Healy, Kenneth; Amer-Asian.**

Operation Baker   Conducted in Binh Dinh Province, II Corps, in April '67 by elements of the 4th Infantry Division.

Operation Barn Door *see* **Tactical Air Control System**

Operation Barrel Roll   Code name for a U.S. Air Force and Navy operation that provided air support to the Royal Lao government in its fight against the communist forces of the Pathet Lao. The operation started in December '64 providing air support throughout the southern Laos area. Operation Steel Tiger was initiated in the northern Laos area to interdict the flow of supplies through Laos for North Vietnam to South Vietnam. *See also* **Operation Steel Tiger.**

Operation Barrier Reef   January '69 operations carried out by elements of TF 194 in Kien Tuong and Kien Phong provinces, IV Corps. The operations were designed to interdict NVA/VC supply activities across the Plain of Reeds area. Barrier Reef, in conjunction with other operations across the northwestern provinces of the Delta, temporarily slowed the infiltration of men and supplies from Cambodia into SVN. *See also* **TF 194.**

Operation Bastogne   Army operation by elements of the 3d Squadron/5th Cavalry, which operated as the reconnaissance element for the 9th Infantry Division. The operation was conducted in the division's AO just south and west of Saigon.

Operation Beau Charger   May '67 operation by elements of the 1st Battalion/3d Marine Division conducted in the DMZ. The search and destroy operations were designed to clear the NVA from the DMZ, enabling the construction of the Project Practice Nine (McNamara's Wall) antiinfiltration and detection barrier. The Marines encountered stiff enemy resistance from several NVA regiments. The operation was in conjunction with other Marine and ARVN operations throughout the DMZ. Part of the operation involved the forced relocation of the village of Trung Loung. *See also* **McNamara's Wall, Operation Hickory, Trung Loung.**

Operation Big Patch (Operation Hot Spot, 315th ARVN Troop Carrier Group)   Crop denial operations carried out by Detachment 1, 315th Troop Carrier Group in October/November '64. The group consisted of C-123 defoliation aircraft operating under the control of the ARVN, and advised by U.S. Air Force members of Operation Ranch Hand. Big Patch took place in War Zone D and Hot Spot took place in a fertile VC crop area located along the Cambodian border in Phuoc Long Province, III Corps. The ARVN pilots refused to fly the missions alone, even though fighter escort was provided. American pilots eventually flew the spray missions with ARVN pilots accompanying the flights as "aircraft commanders." *See also* **Crop Denial, Operation Ranch Hand.**

Operation Billings   Operations conducted by elements of the 1st Infantry Division in Phuoc Long Province, III Corps, in June '67.

Operation Binh Tay Part of the '70 invasion of Cambodia by elements of the U.S. 4th Infantry Division and the 49th ARVN Regiment. *See also* **Cambodian Incursion.**

Operation Blackjack *see* **Blackjack Operations**

Operation Blastout Combined U.S. Marine and ARVN operation in August '65 around Da Nang. The operation was designed to increase the area of control of the Marine enclave at Da Nang.

Operation Blastout I *see* **Cam Ne**

Operation Blue Light '65 Combined Army and Air Force operations to deploy the 3d Brigade 25th Infantry Division, from its base in Hawaii to Pleiku, II Corps. The 3d Brigade was deployed to counter an enemy offensive designed to overrun the Central Highlands and cut South Vietnam in half.

Operation Blue Marlin Combined U.S. and South Vietnamese Marine amphibious operation near Tam Ky in November '65. This operation represented the first combined amphibious operation by U.S. and Vietnamese Marines in South Vietnam.

Operation Bold Dragon I The initial part of Bold Dragon was conducted in March '68 by elements of TF 116 against enemy bases on the Delta island of Tanh Dinh. Subsequent parts of the operation followed in the area of Chau Doc, in northern IV Corps. The operation was designed to interdict the flow of enemy men and supplies from Cambodia into Viet Cong bases along the border.

Operation Bolling September '67 Army operation conducted near Tuy Yoa in Phu Yen Province, II Corps, by elements of the 173d Airborne Brigade and the 1st Cavalry Division.

Operation Bolo Code name for January '67 Air Force operation to engage and destroy NVN Air Force MiGs. Attached to a normal American air strike force were several flights of F-4 fighters whose primary mission was to attack enemy MiGs. When a group of MiGs approached the strike group, the F-4s jumped in: The result was seven MiGs

downed in less than 15 minutes with no loss of American aircraft. *See also* **MiG CAP.**

Operation Bravo A plan devised by SVN's President Diem and his brother Nhu in October '63, which called for the staging of a fake revolt, by the military, against the Diem regime. Diem planned to escape from the capital and hide outside Saigon. There would be rioting and some assassinations of Diem's enemies and general upheaval throughout Saigon. The plan called for Diem and his supporters to return to Saigon and put down the revolt and restore order. Diem believed the plan would show the people of SVN that he alone could guide the country and fight off the communists. Some of the military that were supposed to participate in the plan were actually planning the coup that did overthrow Diem in late October '63.

Operation Breakfast *see* **Operation Menu Targets**

Operation Buckskin Operation conducted in the Ho Bo Woods by elements of the 1st Infantry Division, 173d Airborne Brigade and the Royal Australian Regiment in January '66. The operation was an extension of Operation Crimp which attempted to clear the VC from the Ho Bo Woods area north of Cu Chi. During the operation a massive tunnel complex was discovered, initiating the U.S. and Australian forces to tunnel warfare. *See also* **Operation Crimp.**

Operation Buffalo July '67 operation conducted by elements of the 3d Marine Division near the DMZ in I Corps.

Operation Burlington Trail Operation by elements of the Americal Division in the area west of Tam Ky, in Quang Tin Province, I Corps. The operation was conducted along the road between Tam Ky and the rich rice growing area located around Tien Phuoc. The operation started in April '68, as elements of the Americal made continuous sweeps along the road attempting to keep it open for civilian traffic moving the harvested rice to markets along the coast. The Americans were opposed by the 2d NVA Division. Large numbers of U.S. troops were required to make the continual sweeps to keep the road open, and the operation ended in September '68.

Operation Byrd   Operation conducted by a battalion task force centered around the 2d Battalion/7th Cavalry/1st Cavalry Division, over a 17-month period in '66 and '67. The force operated around Phan Thiet in Binh Thuan Province, II Corps, clearing the Viet Cong from the area and allowing the GVN and ARVN troops to establish control over the area. The battalion task force was self-supporting; it had its own artillery, aeroweapons support, signal, intelligence and civil support groups.

Operation Carolina Moon   *see* **Carolina Moon**

Operation Cedar Falls   First U.S. multidivisional operation in III CTZ. Elements of the Army's 1st and 25th divisions conducted search and destroy operations in the VC base area known as the Iron Triangle in January '67. The area was honeycombed with a mass of tunnels and bunkers. As part of the operation the VC village of Ben Suc was evacuated (5,000+ people), the village leveled and some of the tunnel system beneath it destroyed. The villagers were relocated to government controlled villages outside of the area. Following this operation the units moved on to War Zone C, in Operation Junction City. Within weeks the VC were back in the Iron Triangle rebuilding their tunnel system. *See also* **Junction City.**

Operation Certain Victory   *see* **Operation Quyet Thang**

Operation Chaos   Code name for secret surveillance operations conducted by elements of the CIA against selected antiwar activists and groups in the States. The operations were at the request of President Nixon, who wanted more information on those who were against his administration. The use of the CIA for any operations within the U.S. was strictly forbidden by the CIA's charter. Because of this abuse of CIA authority Congress established a number of "oversight" committees to continually monitor the CIA.

Operation Chopper   Operation conducted in February '62 by ARVN infantry units and their U.S. advisors into a Viet Cong area located 16kms west of Saigon. The operation represented the first time helicopters had been used in a major assault. The helicopters were U.S. CH-21s operated by American Army crews which had recently arrived in SVN in December '61. The choppers and crews were from the 8th and 57th Transportation companies.

Operation Chuong Duong   *see* **Operation Platypus**

Operation Circle Pines   Successful U.S. operation conducted by elements of the 25th Infantry Division, 20kms north of Saigon against a Viet Cong base camp area. This May '66 operation represented the first multibattalion armor operation to take place in SVN by U.S. units. *See also* **25th Infantry Division.**

Operation Cochise Green   Operation conducted by elements of the 173d Airborne Brigade in Binh Dinh Province, II Corps. The operation began in March '68 and continued until January '69.

Operation Colorado (Lien Ket 52)   Combined operation conducted by U.S. Marines and ARVN infantry near the Que Son Valley, in the area west of Chu Lai. The operation took place in August '66 and involved sweeps by the Marines toward ARVN blocking positions. The ARVNs named the operation Lien Ket 52.

Operation Commando Hunt (Operation Tiger Hound)   U.S. air operations against the Ho Chi Minh Trail in Laos from '68–'73. Operations focused on trail activities along the Laos/SVN border with the Air Force, Navy and Marines providing the strike support. Operational control was under MACV, with targeting information provided by air and ground recon missions into Laos, and responses from electric sensors. From '65–'68 operations against the trail were code named Tiger Hound and Steel Tiger. The operations were designed to stop NVA infiltration of supplies and troops down the trail. Because there were so many branches and side routes to the trail system the bombings were never able to completely shut down the trail. *See also* **Electronic Sensors, DART, C-123K.**

Operation Concordia   Operation in June '67 by elements of the Mobile Riverine Force conducted in Long An Province, III Corps. During a second phase of the operation (Concordia II), elements of TF 116, the River Patrol Force, operated with elements of the MRF in a combined operation in the same area. Concordia operations were a series of suboperations conducted under Operation Coronado, TF 117's name for operations in the Delta.

Operation Coronado   Series of Mobile Riverine Force operations started in the Kien Hoa and Dinh Tuong provinces area of the Delta in June '67 by elements of the 60th Infantry/9th Infantry Division. Operation Coronado was carried out in several parts which were designated I–X and lasted into '68. Suboperations were also carried out under the operation name of Concordia.

Operation County Fair   Code name for major Marine cordon and search operation in I Corps shortly after their original deployment to SVN in '65.

Operation Crazy Horse (Battle of Vinh Thanh)   Concluded in the hills above Vinh Thanh, in Binh Dinh Province, II Corps. Elements of the 1st Cavalry Division engaged units of the 2d NVA Regiment in May '66. Some of the first tactical air strikes by B-52s were used against entrenched NVA/VC positions during the battle.

Operation Cricket   Air Force operations which provided FACs for use in Steel Tiger and Barrel Roll operations. The FACs used O-1s and A-1s to spot and fly surveillance for fighter and bomber aircraft. The Cricket FACs were based in Thailand. *See also* **FAC, Operation Barrel Roll and Steel Tiger.**

Operation Crimp   Conducted by elements of the 1st Infantry Division, 173d Airborne, during January '66 in the Ho Bo Woods north of Saigon. The densely forested area had been a longtime VC base area. Elements of the 1st Royal Australian Regiment which were attached to the 173d ABN also participated in the operation. The operation was conducted in preparation for the deployment of the U.S. 25th Infantry Division, which established its divisional base camp at Cu Chi, south of the Ho Bo Woods. *See also* **Operation Buckskin.**

Operation Crimson Tide   September '67 operation by elements of the U.S. Riverine Force on the Bassac River in the Delta.

Operation Daniel Boone (Operation Thot Not, Operation Salem House)   Code name for secret ground operations into Cambodia in '67. The operations included recon and raids carried out by small mixed forces of ARVN LRRPs, CIDGs and U.S. Special Forces. The operation was renamed Salem House until '71, when it was renamed Thot Not. Daniel Boone operations gathered intelligence on enemy infiltration routes and sanctuaries, information that was used to plan air strikes and the '70 Cambodian Incursion.

Operation Deckhouse IV   Marine combat assault by helicopter into the coastal area northeast of Dong Ha in September '66. The assault was conducted by elements of the 26th Marine Regiment. Deckhouse IV was one of a series of Marine operations conducted in the area.

Operation Defiant Stand   September '69 combined amphibious assault by elements of the U.S. Marines, ROK Marines and ARVN troops against Barrier Island, located south of Da Nang.

Operation Delaware–Lam Son 216   April '68 operations in the NVA/VC controlled A Shau Valley. The operation was conducted by elements of the 1st Cavalry, 101st Airborne, 196th LIB, 1st ARVN Division and the 3d ARVN Airborne Task Force. During the operation over 20 helicopters were shot down in the valley that was heavily defended by 23mm and 37mm antiaircraft guns. The ARVN part of the operation was code-named Lam Son 216. *See also* **A Shau Valley.**

Operation Dessert   *see*   **Operation Menu Targets**

Operation Dewey Canyon (Dewey Canyon I and II)   Marine operation conducted in the upper A Shau Valley in January '69 and later in January '71. Elements of the 9th Marines and the 1st ARVN Division conducted search and destroy operations from FSB Vandergrift, south to the Laotian border and Highway 9. During the three-month operation, six small fire bases were established to support Dewey Canyon. The operation resulted in the capture of large numbers of enemy crew-served weapons and supplies, and over 1,600 enemy killed. At the end of the operation the fire bases were closed down and the Marines and ARVNs withdrawn. *See also* **Dewey Canyon Fire Bases.**

Operation Dinner *see* **Operation Menu Targets**

Operation Double Eagle *see* **Task Force Delta**

Operation Dye Marker *see* **McNamara's Wall**

Operation Eagle Pull (TG 76.8, Refugee Assistance Group [RAG 76.8], Fall of Cambodia) Code name for the evacuation of U.S. personnel from Phnom Penh, Cambodia, prior to its collapse to the Khmer Rouge, April 16, 1975. The group assigned the task were elements of the U.S. Navy's 7th Fleet, TF 76, designated Task Group 76.8, the Refugee Assistance Group. TG 76.8 evacuated 276 American, third country nationals and Cambodia embassy personnel and their families before the operation was halted. The task group also evacuated American personnel from Saigon before its fall to the communists in April '75. High ranking Cambodian government officials refused U.S. offers to be evacuated from their country. Less than 1,200 Cambodians left their country in the three weeks prior to its collapse in April. *See also* **Operation Frequent Wind, TG 76.8.**

Operation El Paso I & II Operations in Binh Long Province, III Corps, by elements of the 1st Infantry Division and the 5th ARVN Division in June '66. The first part of the operation involved search and destroy operations in the area of Loc Ninh. The second part of the operation shifted west from Loc Ninh into War Zone C. El Paso ended in July '66.

Operation Embankment *see* **Dewey, Major Peter**

Operation Endsweep U.S. Navy operations conducted in '73 to clear the U.S. implanted mines from the harbors of North Vietnam. The mines were placed in '72 as part of Operation Linebacker II, and under the terms of the '73 Paris Peace Accords the U.S. was responsible for clearing the mines. Elements of the Navy's Task Force 78 cleaned the mines.

Operation Enhance Plus (Project Enhance) Code name for the accelerated buildup of U.S. military equipment to the Thieu government of South Vietnam in October '72, just prior to the formal signing of the Paris Peace Accords. The operation also involved the transfer of U.S. military equipment and bases to the South Vietnamese. Over $2 billion in equipment was poured into SVN before the Accords were signed in January '73. The Nixon administration used the equipment as an incentive to force the Thieu regime to compromise at the Paris Peace Accords. Thieu had taken a hard-line against a coalition government with the NLF and refused to cooperate in the peace talks. Enhance Plus was an extension of Project Enhance which had started in '71 to expedite the transfer of U.S. equipment and facilities to the Vietnamese. *See also* **Four No's.**

Operation Enterprise Combined operations conducted by elements of the 3d Brigade/9th Infantry Division, ARVN and RP/PF units in Long An Province, III Corps. The search and destroy operations started in February '67 and were intended to clear the province of the Viet Cong. The operation continued until March '68. The province was never cleared, and in fact, the Viet Cong were able to substantially participate in the Tet '68 Offensive.

Operation Fairfax Operations conducted in the II Corps area designed to protect the tactical approaches to Saigon. The operations were conducted by the 199th Light Infantry Brigade in conjunction with USSFs and the 5th ARVN Rangers. Fairfax, which lasted most of '67, was designed to protect Saigon and work ARVN units into the defense of the city. By the end of the operation in '67 the ARVN units were responsible for most of the patrolling and screening, with the American units providing backup and reaction support. The results of the Tet '68 Offensive proved the ARVNs were unable to protect their objective from enemy attack.

Operation Farmgate Code name for U.S. Air Force advisory operations to the VNAF started in '61, based at Bien Hoa Air Base. Farm Gate operations were later expanded to allow its aircraft to provide combat support (attack enemy positions) to ARVN ground forces if a Vietnamese pilot accompanied the American pilot in VNAF aircraft. The Farm Gate force primarily consisted of T-28 fighters and B-26 bombers. In mid-'63 the Air Force replaced the Farmgate team with the 1st Air Commando Squadron. The new squadron continued to provide combat support to ARVN forces. *See also* **1st Air Commando Squadron, Jungle Jim Squadron, Dirty Thirty.**

Operation Field Goal Operation conducted by U.S. Air Force pilots, flying reconnaissance aircraft borrowed from the Philippine Air Force, painted with the markings of the Royal Laotian Air Force. The operations were conducted in April '61 out of the Royal Thai air base located at U Dorn. The flights were conducted to provide reconnaissance support to the Royal Laotian Government in its fight against the communist Pathet Lao. The operation continued until the '62 Geneva Agreement formally established Laotian neutrality. Direct support of Royal Lao forces by the U.S. was ended, but covert support by the CIA continued. *See also* **Geneva Agreement, '62.**

Operation Fierce Tiger II (Maeng Ho II) ROK operation along the rivers of Qui Nhon, II Corps, in conjunction with a detachment of U.S. Navy PBRs from TF 116. *See also* **TF 116.**

Operation Flaming Dart I and II Code name for U.S. retaliatory air strikes against North Vietnamese installations at Dong Hoi, Chanh Hoa and Vit Thu Lu in February '65. The raid was in response to attacks by NVA/VC units on U.S. installations in Pleiku, Tuy Hoa, Soc Trang and Qui Nhon in December '64 and February '65. The strikes were in two parts: Flaming Dart I hit the NVN military installation at Dong Hoi, and Flaming Dart II strikes hit installations at Chanh Hoa and Vit Thu Lu.

Operation Foul Deck (Operation Tran Hung Dao) November '68 operations conducted in the northwestern corner of Kien Giang Province, near the Cambodian border. The operations were conducted by elements of TF 194 and involved patrolling and interdiction of enemy supply routes in the area. As the operation continued into '69 it was renamed Tran Hung Dao as more of the responsibility for the operation was assumed by the South Vietnamese Navy. *See also* **Operation Tran Hung Dao.**

Operation Fractured Cross Alpha Joint Air Force and Navy air operations conducted in March '71 against North Vietnamese SAM sites north of the DMZ.

Operation Francis Marion April '67 operation involving units of the 4th Infantry Division. Two brigades of the division worked the area along the Cambodian border, north and south of the Special Forces camp at Duc Co on Highway 19. The operation lasted into October with the 4th Infantry engaging in heavy fighting with enemy elements of the 32d, 66th and 95B NVA regiments. The operation was merged with Operation Greeley in western Kontum Province in October '67; the merged operations were renamed MacArthur. *See also* **Operation Greeley, Operation MacArthur.**

Operation Freedom Deal *see* **Operation Menu**

Operation Freedom Porch Bravo *see* **Bullet Shot I–V Deployments**

Operation Freedom Train (Operation Pocket Money) Sustained air strikes conducted by Air Force and Navy/Marine air units against North Vietnamese targets south of the 19th Parallel. The operation started in early April '72 in response to the NVA invasion of SVN, their '72 Eastertide Offensive. In May '72 the air campaign was renamed Linebacker I and a series of suboperations commenced attacking targets throughout North Vietnam. One of the first operations of Linebacker, Operation Pocket Money, was the mining of Haiphong Harbor by aircraft of TF 77, delivering water mines. *See also* **Haiphong, Operation Linebacker, Operation Prime Choke.**

Operation Freeze In response to increasing "fragging" of Marine officers and NCOs, the Marine Corps in Vietnam instituted Operation Freeze. Fraggings were usually directed at platoon or company level leaders. When a fragging attack took place the platoon/company involved was isolated from the other units and all members of the unit interrogated. A roll call was taken to determine if anyone was missing. All members of the unit were completely restricted and could not take leave, rotate out of the country or transfer to another unit until suspects were identified. Members of the unit were promised reassignments and protection if they provided investigators with information. Such instant response to fraggings greatly reduced the number of incidents incurred by the Marines. *See also* **Frag(ging).**

Operation Frequent Wind (Refugee Assistance Group [RAG 76.8], Task Group 76.8 [TG 76.8], Talon Vise) Operation code name for the evacuation of U.S. personnel from Saigon in April '75, just prior to the fall of SVN to the communists; originally coded "Talon Vise." Elements of the U.S. Navy's Task Force 76 were organized into Task Group 76.8, the Refugee Assistance Group, expressly for the evacuation of Phnom Penh, Cambodia and South Vietnam. The operation terminated in the early hours of April 30, 1975, after evacuating 978 U.S. personnel and 1,120 Vietnamese military and civilians from the U.S. Embassy. The operation also covered the evacuation of Vietnamese military and civilians that made it by boat or helicopter out to the ships of the task group waiting just offshore. *See also* **Eagle Pull, Option IV, TG 76.8, Black Flights.**

Operation Friendship *see* **Operation Platypus**

Operation Game Warden *see* **TF 116**

Operation Garfield Conducted in the Central Highlands by elements of the 3d Brigade/25th Infantry Division in '66.

Operation Georgia (Operation Liberty) Operation conducted in early '66 by elements of the 9th Marine Regiment. The operation represented the initial movement in force by the Marines into the An Hoa Valley. This operation was followed by Operation Liberty which brought elements of the 1st Marine Regiment into the area. *See also* **Arizona Territory.**

Operation Giant Slingshot Late '68 operation conducted by elements of TF 194, in an NVA/VC base area in the vicinity of the Parrots Beak, bordered by the Song Vam Co Dong and Song Vam Co Tay rivers. The area, just 50kms west of Saigon, had long been an NVA/VC base and training area. During the operation, U.S. and ARVN units met stiff enemy resistance that resulted in over 2,500 dead or captured enemy soldiers.

Operation Gibraltar Operation conducted by elements of the 173d Airborne Brigade around An Khe in '65. The operation was designed to provide protection for the newly arrived 1st Cavalry Division while

they established their base camp at An Khe.

Operation Golden Fleece U.S. Marine operation in '65–'66 designed to protect rice farmers and their crops from confiscation by the VC operating in the I Corps area. Subsequent rice protection operations were mounted yearly by the Marines at harvest and market time.

Operation Greeley June '67 operation around Dak To in Kontum Province. Elements of the 173d Airborne Brigade, 1st Cavalry and ARVN Paratroopers engaged units of the 24th NVA Regiment. During the initial fighting Company A/503d Infantry was nearly destroyed. In October the operation was merged and renamed Operation MacArthur. *See also* **Operation MacArthur, Battle of Dak To.**

Operation Green Wave September '67 operation in I Corps conducted by a small group of Navy PBRs to field test the boats for patrol duties along the coastal river mouths of I Corps. The boats proved to be too small to operate effectively in the heavy seas off the coast and were restricted for use on the rivers and canals. Responsibility for patrolling the mouths of the rivers was given to the larger craft of TF 115.

Operation Hades *see* **Operation Ranch Hand**

Operation Hammersley Conducted by elements of the 8th Royal Australian Regiment in February '70 in the vicinity of the Long Hai Hills, which were located 20kms northeast of Vung Tau, III Corps.

Operation Harvest Moon/Lien Ket 18 Combined operation by U.S. 7th Marines and ARVN forces in Phuoc Ha Valley, north of Chu Lai in December '65. The ARVN code name for the operation was Lien Ket 18. The operation was conducted along the road linking Highway 1 with the village of Hiep Duc, deep in the valley. Elements of the 5th ARVN Division were hard hit by the NVA/VC in the valley; eventually three U.S. Marine battalions were brought in to cordon off the enemy, and B-52 strikes and artillery were used to pound the area.

Operation Hastings Joint operations by elements of the 1st, 4th and 5th Marines and ARVN forces in the Song Ngan Valley in July '66. The Marines and ARVNs were locked in heavy fighting with elements of the 324B NVA Division. The Marines nicknamed the Song Ngan Valley "Helicopter Valley" because several Marine helicopters were shot down or crashed during CAs into the valley. *See also* Helicopter Valley, Operation Prairie.

Operation Hawthorne I and II Joint American and ARVN operation conducted June '66, in the mountains of the Central Highlands, 60kms northeast of Kontum. The objective of the operation was to engage enemy units of the 24th and 88th VC regiments believed to be based in the area, and to evacuate a Montagnard militia outpost located at Toumorong. Units originally involved were elements of the 1st Bde/101st Infantry Division, 42d ARVN Infantry Regiment, 21st ARVN Rangers, 43d ARVN Infantry and attached CIDG companies. Following the successful evacuation of the Montagnards Hawthorne II commenced when elements of the 101st Airborne Division continued sweeps in the area.

Operation Helping Hand Foundation (Project Pay Dirt) One of several programs sponsored by the Navy and U.S. businessmen to help improve the living conditions of VNN dependents. The Helping Hand Foundation was founded in '70 and collected contributions and materials to help raise the standard of living for VNN personnel that were to occupy U.S. Navy bases in SVN as part of the ACTOV program. Other programs such as "Project Pay Dirt" raised money to enhance and expand animal husbandry programs that provided livestock to VNN families. It was hoped that improving conditions for VNN dependents would improve the performance of the VNN and increase enlistments. *See also* NAVCATS, Project Buddy Base.

Operation Hickory (Army) Army operation conducted by elements of the 11th ACR in October '66 in their AO, east of Bien Hoa.

Operation Hickory (Marine) Marine operation conducted in the DMZ in May '67 by elements of the 3d, 4th and 9th Marine regiments. The operation was designed to clear the DMZ of enemy units prior to construction of an electronic infiltration barrier. The Marines encountered stiff resistance from several NVA regiments operating south of the DMZ. *See also* McNamara's Wall, Operation Beau Charger.

Operation Highland Clear and hold operation in August '65 conducted in the An Khe area by 1st Brigade/101st Airborne Division. An Khe later became the base camp of the 1st Cavalry Division, which deployed to the area in October '65.

Operation Hollyhock Code name for Bob Hope's '70 troop show in South Vietnam.

Operation Homecoming Operation that processed the return of American POWs from Vietnam. As part of the '73 Paris Peace Accords there was an exchange of prisoners of war held by all participants in the war. Operation Homecoming was responsible for the return of 591 American POWs to the States. American prisoners were released at three locations. POWs held by the Viet Cong were released at Saigon, POWs held by NVN were released in Hanoi and three POWs held by the PRC were released in Hong Kong. The American POWs were transported to Clark AFB in the Philippines for medical exams and debriefing and then returned to U.S. military hospitals near their homes for recovery and further medical attention as required. *See also* American POWs.

Operation Homecoming '79 *see* Orderly Departure Program

Operation Homestead Operation carried out by elements of the Mobile Riverine Force in Kien Hoa Province in the fall of '68.

Operation Hot Spot *see* Operation Big Patch

Operation Hump Operation conducted by elements of the 173d Airborne Brigade and the 1st Australian Regiment near the Iron Triangle in late '65. During the operation the 1st Battalion/503d Infantry engaged an estimated Viet Cong regiment. The battalion suffered nearly 20 percent casualties before the enemy regiment was beaten back and the battalion extracted.

Operation Indiana Operation conducted by elements of the 7th Marine Regiment northwest of Quang Ngai in March '66.

Operation Iron Hand Code name for Air Force and Navy missions flown by "Wild Weasel" aircraft designed to destroy SAM missile sites around NVN targets. The primary aircraft used in the Weasel flights were initially twin seat F-100s and the F-105. Later the F-100 was replaced by the F-4C. *See also* **Wild Weasel.**

Operation Irving Operation conducted by elements of the 1st Cavalry Division and ROK troops in Binh Dinh Province, II Corps, in October '66. The search and destroy operation was centered around the Phu Cat Mountain area.

Operation Ivory Coast *see* **Son Tay Raid**

Operation Jackstay (LZ Robin, LZ Sparrow, Red Beach) Amphibious operation conducted by the Navy and Marine Special Landing Force in March '66. The SLF made amphibious assaults into the Rung Sat Special Zone at Red Beach, on the southwest tip of the Long Thanh Peninsula, and by helicopter at LZ Sparrow and LZ Robin on the peninsula. *See also* **Operation Tailwind.**

Operation Jay Conducted by elements of the Marines' 1st and 4th regiments operating 20kms northwest of Hue in July '66.

Operation Jefferson Glenn (OPORD 13-70) Joint US/ARVN operation conducted in I Corps by elements of the U.S. 101st Airborne during September '70–October '71. The operation represented the last major offensive operation conducted by U.S. combat units in the Vietnam War. During the operation US/ARVN units established a ring of fire bases in the foothills surrounding the coastal lowlands of Thua Thien province. The units continued to actively patrol and search out the enemy within the enclave. 101st Airborne participation dropped off until most of the patrolling was being done by ARVN units, with the 101st providing support and a reserve force. The operation was renamed OPORD 13-70, in July '71.

Operation Junction City February '67, a massive operation against NVA/VC base areas north of Tay Ninh, near the Cambodian border, War Zone C. Elements of the 1st, 4th, 9th and 25th Infantry divisions, 11th ACR and the 196th LIB as well as units

from the 503d/173d Airborne Brigade captured large quantities of food and supplies and inflicted heavy casualties on enemy units based in the area. During the operation the 2d Bn/503d Infantry conducted the only major American parachute jump into Vietnam during the war. *See also* **Operation Junction City Alternate.**

Operation Junction City Alternate Army operation conducted in February '67 in War Zone C, 85kms northwest of Saigon, in Tay Ninh Province, III Corps. War Zone C was a longtime enemy base area, and believed to be the location of COSVN. The operation involved infantry, armored cavalry and an 800-man parachute jump by the 2d Battalion/503d Infantry/173d Airborne Brigade. Numerous enemy structures, tunnel systems and facilities were uncovered and destroyed. The operation followed the successful Cedar Falls campaign in the nearby Iron Triangle. Both operations accounted for tons of enemy war materiel destroyed and over 3,700 enemy KIAs. *See also* **Cedar Falls, Operation Junction City, Drop Zone.**

Operation Kalamazoo Army operation in April '66 involving armor units from the 5th Infantry Regiment (Mechanized) near Cu Chi. The 5th Mech was operating as part of the 25th Infantry Division.

Operation Keystone... *see* **Keystone Increments**

Operation Kingfisher Operations conducted by elements of the 3d Marine Division along the DMZ in July '67. The operation was used to provide security and screening for military efforts to establish an electronic barrier along the DMZ to monitor NVA movement into Quang Tri Province from North Vietnam. *See also* **McNamara's Wall.**

Operation Kings Marine operation conducted by elements of the 3d Marine Division south of Da Nang near Highway 14 and the An Hoa Valley. The operation was conducted in March '66.

Operation Kole Kole Operation by elements of the 25th Infantry Division conducted around Cu Chi in the last half of '67.

Operation Laverack Australian operation conducted by elements of the 6th Battalion RAR/NZ Task Force. The operation was conducted in the northern area of Phuoc Tuy Province, II Corps. Phuoc Tuy Province was the RAR's primary AO.

Operation Leaping Lena Early (February '64) CIA sponsored operations involving Vietnamese reconnaissance teams parachuted into areas along the Laos/NVN border. The teams were to survey the Ho Chi Minh Trail and report back to USSF/CIDG outposts located along the Laos/SVN border. Most of the Vietnamese reconnaissance teams were never heard from again. Official speculation is that the teams were captured or "Chieu Hoi'ed" to the other side. Eventually the program was transferred to the USSF which conducted their own Leaping Lena long-range reconnaissance patrols along the border. The operation was later expanded and renamed Project Delta. *See also* **Project Delta, MACV-SOG.**

Operation Lejeune April '67 operation by 3d Battalion, 7th Marines and the 2d Brigade, 1st Cavalry, to clear the Duc Pho area of VC control. The operation was based out of the Marine base at LZ Montezuma, located at Duc Pho in Quang Nhai Province, I Corps. After the operation the Marines deployed further north into I Corps and the 1st Cav took over responsibility for the area.

Operation Lexington Series of operations in the Rung Sat Special Zone during '66 conducted by elements of the 1st Battalion/18th Infantry Regiment. The operations were designed to interdict Viet Cong supply activities in the swamp zone east of Saigon.

Operation Liberty *see* **Operation Georgia**

Operation Liberty Canyon Code name for the '68 shift of the entire 1st Cavalry Division from its operational area in I Corps to the III Corps area.

Operation Lincoln Army operation by elements of the 25th Infantry Division conducted south of Pleiku.

Operation Linebacker I In May '72, after the NVA Eastertide offensive, President Nixon authorized renewed air operations against North Vietnam. Operation Linebacker I covered all of North Vietnam including areas in and around Hanoi and Haiphong that had previously been restricted. As part of the effort to reduce the import of weapons and supplies to NVN, the port of Haiphong and three other major North Vietnamese ports were mined and patrolled by the U.S. Navy. The renewed bombings and the mining of NVN's harbors induced NVN to return to the Paris Peace Talks and seek a resolution of the war. Linebacker I ended in October '72, but was followed up by Linebacker II in December. *See also* **Christmas Bombing, Haiphong, Freedom Train.**

Operation Linebacker II *see* **Christmas Bombing**

Operation Lockjaw *see* **Marine Medium Helicopter Squadron 362**

Operation Long Lance Marine operation conducted in the Vu Gia Valley area, 32kms southwest of Da Nang in early '66.

Operation Louisville Slugger February '71 Air Force air operation against North Vietnamese SAM sites. The strike was part of the "protective reaction" response authorized by the Nixon White House in retaliation for NVN attacks against U.S. aircraft flying reconnaissance missions over North Vietnam.

Operation Lunch *see* **Operation Menu Targets**

Operation MacArthur October '67 operation involving elements of the 4th Infantry Division and the 173d Airborne Brigade, plus units of the 42d ARVN Infantry Regiment and the ARVN Airborne. The operation was centered around Dak To in the Central Highlands of Kontum Province. During heavy fighting in the area the 174th NVA Regiment was engaged. Elements of the enemy regiment were dug in on Hill 875, 20kms west of Dak To. After several costly assaults the hill was taken by the remnants of the U.S. 2d/503d, 4th/503d, and 1st/12th Infantry in November '67. American casualties had been high, but the 32d, 66th and 174th NVA regiments had been temporarily pushed back into Cambodia. *See also* **Battle of Dak To, Hill 875, Operation Greeley.**

Operation Macon Operation conducted from July–September '66 in the An Hoa Valley by elements of the 9th Marine Regiment. There were numerous bloody clashes with hard-core Viet Cong units in the area and the Marines suffered many casualties from mines and booby traps. The An Hoa Valley came to be known as "Arizona Territory" because of the hostility of the area. The Vietnamese who lived in the area were either VC or direct supporters of the Viet Cong. *See also* **Arizona Territory.**

Operation Maeng Ho II *see* **Operation Fierce Tiger II**

Operation Malheur Two-part operation conducted from May–August '67 by elements of Task Force Oregon, conducted in the Duc Pho area of Quang Ngai Province, I Corps. The operations (Malheur I and II) operated along the coast sweeping the southern I Corps area for the NVA/VC and providing security for traffic along Highway 1. Later some elements of Task Force Oregon were used to form the 23d Infantry Division; Americal Division.

Operation Mameluke Thrust Marine operation carried out in central Quang Nam Province by elements of the 7th and 27th Regiment/1st Marine Division in May '67.

Operation Manhattan U.S. operation conducted in early March '67 in the Michelin rubber plantation, west of Lai Khe and south of Dau Tieng, in III Corps. Elements of the 1st and 25th Infantry divisions participated in the operation.

Operation Marauder January '66 operation by elements of the 173d Airborne Brigade and the 1st Royal Australian Regiment in the VC base area known as the Plain of Reeds. The operation represented the first time American combat units had operated in IV Corps. Marauder lasted eight days and inflicted heavy casualties on the 506th Viet Cong Battalion Headquarters and the 267th Viet Cong Battalion.

Operation Marigold Code name for secret peace overtures made by the U.S. government to Hanoi in June '66. The exchange was carried out through the Polish representative of the ICC and the Italian Ambassador to SVN. NVN publicly rejected the proposal because the U.S. was still bombing NVN.

Operation Market Place *see* **TF 71**

Operation Market Time *see* **Market Time**

Operation Masher-White Wing (Bong Son Campaign) January '66 operation by elements of the 1st Cav Div., the 22d ARVN Division and the Korean Capital Division on the Bong Son Plain in Binh Dinh Province, II Corps. The operation engaged units of the 2d Viet Cong, 18th and 22d NVA regiments. At the same time the Marines (Operation Dougle Eagle) swept south of Bong Son trapping the enemy forces between the forces of Masher and Double Eagle. Masher received a name change to White Wing in an effort to downplay the destructive tone of "Masher." The operation caused the temporary withdrawal of enemy forces from the area. *See also* **Double Eagle.**

Operation Massachusetts Striker Conducted by elements of the 101st Airborne Division in the A Shau Valley of Thau Thien Province, I Corps, in March '69. During the two-month-long search and destroy operation, a large enemy base camp was discovered. In an effort to locate more enemy bases Operation Apache Snow was launched in the same area in May. *See also* **Operation Apache Snow, Hamburger Hill.**

Operation Matador January '66 operation by elements of the 1st Cavalry Division in the Central Highland provinces of Pleiku and Kontum, II Corps.

Operation Mayflower Code name for the two-day bombing halt of NVN called by President Johnson as an incentive to the North Vietnamese to engage in peace negotiations. But North Vietnam refused any type of negotiations, direct or indirect, with the U.S. Operation Mayflower was terminated on May 15, 1966, and bombing of NVN resumed.

Operation Menu (Operation Freedom Deal) Code name for the secret bombing of NVA sanctuaries inside Cambodia. The operation was active from March '69 to August '73. U.S. bombing missions in Cambodia were aimed at NVA/VC sanctuaries along Cambodia's eastern border. In May '70 the operation was renamed Freedom Deal and expanded to include Khmer Rouge positions. The Khmer Rouge were included as targets by the U.S. in an effort to help the Lon Nol government fight the Cambodian communists. Before bombing operations were expanded to include other areas of Cambodia and Laos the selected sanctuary targets were located in the Fish Hook area and were code-named Breakfast,

Lunch, Dinner, Supper, Dessert and Snack. *See also* **Operation Menu Targets, Secret Bombing of Cambodia, Skyspot.**

Operation Menu Targets (Operation: Breakfast, Lunch, Dinner, Supper, Snack, Dessert) During Operation Menu secret U.S. Air Force strikes were made against NVA/VC sanctuaries in the Fish Hook along the Cambodian border. For targeting purposes the base areas (BA) were designated 353, 609, 352, 740, 351, and 350; these were further code-named Operation Breakfast, Lunch, Dinner, Supper, Snack, and Dessert, respectively. According to MACV the target areas were not inhabited by Cambodian civilians, but independent military reports indicated that civilian villages were located in or near the target zones and would suffer from the effects of the operations. *See also* **Operation Menu, Secret Bombing of Cambodia, Base Area.**

Operation Miracle Operation by elements of the Americal Division, February '68, south of Da Nang.

Operation Mixmaster Marine operation to stagger the rotational replacement of its personnel in Vietnam during '65–'66. The Marine tour of duty in Vietnam was 13 months. Some units that originally deployed to Vietnam in early '65 were scheduled to rotate out of Vietnam in '66; this would require the Marines to replace entire units. By staggering the rotation of individuals and units the Marines were able to replace personnel over a longer period of time as opposed to all the personnel from a given unit departing Vietnam at the same time. This increased unit efficiency, and eased the transition of command, services, and combat support.

Operation Monster *see* **Operation Quai Vat**

Operation Mule Train *see* **Mule Train**

Operation Nathan Hale June '66 operation in Phu Yen Province, II Corps, in the area northwest of Tuy Hoa, near Dong Tre. Elements of the U.S. 327th Infantry and the 7th and 8th Cavalry engaged units of the 18B NVA Regiment.

Operation Neutralize Concentrated air effort to silence NVA long-range gun positions just north of the DMZ which were hampering American efforts to construct new fire bases along the DMZ. Especially hard-pressed by the guns were the Marines at Con Thien. The operation started in September '67, ran for 49 days and involved air strikes and B-52 raids on the suspected enemy gun positions. Special ground reconnaissance teams infiltrated into North Vietnam to assess bomb damage and select new targets for the operation. The successful operation resulted in the destruction or damaging of over 200 enemy guns and allowed American efforts to fortify the area to continue. *See also* **Con Thien, SLAM.**

Operation Nevada Eagle May '68 operation by elements of the 101st Airborne in the rich rice growing region south of Hue in Thua Thien Province, I Corps. The NVA/VC routinely confiscated much of the rice crop grown in the region. The rice denial program was an effort by American forces to deny the NVA/VC the rice crop and ensure that the rice was harvested and delivered to the South Vietnamese marketplace. The operation lasted nine months.

Operation New Life November '65 operation by Army elements of the 173d Airborne Brigade and the 1st Royal Australian Regiment. The operation provided security for rice harvesting and marketing activities for the farmers around Vo Dat, in the flat rice region located 65kms northwest of Phan Thiet, in Binh Tuy Province, III Corps.

Operation New York Operation conducted by elements of the 1st Marine Regiment northeast of Phu Bai, Thau Thien Province, I Corps. The Marines made a night helicopter assault into the area to relieve an ARVN battalion hard hit by the Viet Cong; February '66.

Operation Niagara Joint U.S. Air Force, Navy and Marine air campaign focused on the destruction of NVA units built up around the Marine combat base at Khe Sanh. The operation ran continuously from January 14 to March 31, 1968, dropping over 100,000 pounds of ordnance on suspected NVA positions. The name "Niagara" was personally selected by General Westmoreland, MACV Commander. By April surviving elements of the NVA divisions surrounding Khe Sanh withdrew to sanctuaries in Laos. *See also* **Khe Sanh.**

Operation Passage to Freedom   Operation conducted by ships of the Navy's Western Pacific Amphibious Group in August '54. The 9-month operation evacuated refugees from North Vietnam, primarily Haiphong, to ports in South Vietnam. The evacuation was part of the nearly one million Vietnamese that fled North Vietnam after the defeat of the French in the First Indochina War. During the operation an estimated 300,000 refugees were moved to SVN. During the same period less than 100,000 South Vietnamese opted to move to North Vietnam. *See also* **Voting with Their Feet.**

Operation Patio   Air Force operations conducted in support of the pro–Western Cambodian Army fighting NVA/Khmer Rouge forces in various locations across Cambodia. The support strikes began in April '70 shortly after the pro–West government of Lon Nol was established in Cambodia. The Lon Nol government unsuccessfully ordered an end to North Vietnamese usage of the port of Sihanoukville and the supply and infiltration trail that led across Cambodia to South Vietnam. Lon Nol requested U.S. assistance in his fight against the communist forces. *See also* **Secret Bombing of Cambodia.**

Operation Paul Revere (I–IV)   Army operation involving the units of TF Walker, conducted during May '66, in the Pleiku area of the Central Highlands, II Corps. Units of the 4th and 25th Infantry divisions, and 1st Cavalry Division operated out of Fire Base Oasis, located 25kms southwest of Pleiku until December '66. Operation Paul Revere was divided into four parts (I–IV) which eventually drove the 1st NVA Division back into the safety of their sanctuaries across the Cambodian border. *See also* **TF Walker, LZ Ten Alpha, FSB Oasis.**

Operation Pave Eagle   Aerial relay operations conducted by the Air Force over the Ho Chi Minh Trail. The Air Force used unmanned, remotely controlled aircraft to monitor electronic sensors placed along the Trail. The aircraft used was a civilian version of the single engine Beechcraft "Debonair." "Pave Eagle" aircraft flew along the trail system radio-relaying information gathered from sensors to the ISC at NPK for evaluation and targeting. The unmanned flights

were more cost effective in terms of manpower and equipment than the manned EC-121 aircraft that were also used in similar data collection operations. *See also* **Electronic Sensors, Commando Hunt, EC-121.**

Operation Pegasus–Lam Son 207A   Combined operation to lift the siege of the 26th Marines at Khe Sanh. The Marine base at Khe Sanh was completely surrounded by elements of three NVA divisions. Pegasus involved elements of the 1st Cavalry Division, 1st and 3d Marine regiments, Navy SEABEES and Army 11th Engineers, and the 3d ARVN Airborne which attacked overland opening the route along Highway 9, from the American fire base at Ca Lu to Khe Sanh Combat Base. The Marines and ARVN Airborne moved along Highway 9 while the 1st Cavalry established a series of LZs and fire bases on either side of the road to protect the flanks of the advancing Marines. The operation started April 1, 1968, with the siege declared over on April 11. *See also* **Khe Sanh.**

Operation Pennsylvania   Code name for a U.S. State Department approved peace feeler mission to Hanoi by Herbert Marcovich and Raymond Aubrac in '67. Marcovich was a French biologist and Aubrac a worker from the Food and Agriculture Organization; both knew Ho Chi Minh personally and were willing to sound him out on the possibility of a negotiated settlement to the war in Vietnam. The men met with Ho and his prime minister, Pham Van Dong. Ho's prime condition for any possible settlement at the time was the removal of the Thieu government in Saigon and reunification of North and South Vietnam. Operation Pennsylvania made no progress towards settlement talks because the U.S. was not willing to remove the Thieu regime at that time.

Operation Pershing   Year-long operation started in February '67 by elements of the 1st Cavalry Division in the An Lao Valley area of Binh Dinh Province. The focus of the operation was the elimination of Viet Cong control of the population within the province. The 1st Cavalry conducted several other operations aimed at eliminating the VC infrastructure and the NVA units in the area. One of the larger battles took place at Tam Quan where over 600 NVA/VC were killed. 1st Cavalry operations within the province were so successful that when the Tet '68 Offensive broke out across SVN,

Binh Dinh Province was one of the least active areas in terms of NVA/VC attacks. *See also* **Battle of Tam Quan.**

Operation Phu Dung *see* **Operation Shining Brass**

Operation Pierce Arrow Navy code name for the initial retaliatory strikes against North Vietnam in August '64 for NVN torpedo boat attacks against the USS *Maddox* and *Turner Joy* in the Gulf of Tonkin earlier in the month. Strike aircraft from the aircraft carriers *Ticonderoga* and *Constellation* attacked North Vietnamese PT boat bases along the coast and also struck the oil refinery and storage facility located at Vinh. *See also* **Tonkin Gulf Incident.**

Operation Pink Rose Experimental jungle defoliation program tested by the Air Force in Vietnam. The method of defoliation involved a small target area being sprayed with a chemical herbicide. A subsequent spraying took place with a chemical drying agent. B-52s then dropped cluster incendiary bombs on the target. The result was an intense and destructive fire reportedly capable of destroying all vegetation in the target zone as well as enemy fortifications and personnel. *See also* **Defoliation.**

Operation Pipe Stem (TF Pipe Stem) Conducted by elements of the Air Force's 15th Tactical Reconnaissance Squadron in October '61. The group operated four RC-101 reconnaissance aircraft, designated TF Pipe Stem, over Laos and the Ho Chi Minh Trail. They were temporarily based at Tan Son Nhut Air Base near Saigon. The flights were stopped in November when the North Vietnamese complained that the U.S. was in violation of the '62 Geneva Agreement on Laos and the '54 Geneva Accords on Vietnam. The recon aircraft of Pipe Stem were withdrawn. *See also* **Operation Abel Mabel.**

Operation Piranha September '65 operation conducted on the Batangan Peninsula in Quang Tin Province, I Corps. The operation involved an amphibious landing by the 3d Battalion/7th Marines against a base area used by the 1st Viet Cong Regiment. The operation was further supported by ARVN troops airlifted into the area by helicopter. *See also* **Batangan Peninsula.**

Operation Platypus (Operation Friendship, Operation Chuong Duong) Series of operations started in August '69 conducted by elements of the 1st Australian Task Force, Royal Thai Army Volunteers, Vietnamese Navy, ARVN, and U.S. Navy, against enemy bases located in the Nhon Trach district of southern Bien Hoa Province, III Corps. The Nhon Trach district was located along the northern edge of the Rung Sat Special Zone, and was used by the Viet Cong to launch attacks against Allied shipping traveling between Saigon and the South China Sea. Operations against the enemy bases were code-named Platypus, Friendship and Chuong Duong. *See also* **Rung Sat, Nhon Trach, Operation Wolf Pack.**

Operation Pocket Money *see* **Operation Freedom Train**

Operation Prairie Series of Marine operations conducted around Con Thien by elements of the 3d Marine Division in August '66 and March '67. The Marines engaged elements of the 324B NVA Division that were infiltrating across the DMZ and massing for an attack on Quang Tri Province. The Marines succeeded in breaking up the NVA division, causing them to withdraw across the DMZ. *See also* **Operation Hastings.**

Operation Prairie Fire *see* **Operation Shining Brass**

Operation Prime Choke Operation by U.S. aircraft to strike at rail communication lines in the previously off limits buffer zone along the Chinese/NVN border. Initially Washington declared a 48km-wide zone along the border off limits to all U.S. air attacks. In September '72 the bombing restriction on the zone was removed and railheads and bridges in the area were struck. The strikes were code-named Prime Choke and were part of the overall Linebacker I campaign against NVN. In April '72 NVN launched an all-out offensive against the South and refused to pull back. U.S. air power was used against NVN positions and installations throughout NVN in an effort to cut military supplies that were fueling the invasion. *See also* **Operation Linebacker I, Eastertide Offensive.**

Operation Proud Deep   Air Force operations against North Vietnamese installations below the 20th Parallel conducted in December '71. The strikes were in retaliation for the North Vietnamese downing of several U.S. reconnaissance aircraft over NVN. The strikes were the first major air strikes against NVN since the '68 bombing halt, and lasted for five days. Several other retaliatory strikes against NVN were initiated with individual SAM or AA sites targeted, but no large scale sustained strikes took place until the December '72 Linebacker bombings. *See also* **Bombing Pause, Operation Linebacker I, Christmas Bombing.**

Operation Quai Vat (Operation Monster)   Combined operation by USSFs and Navy PACVs to test the machine's combat abilities in the Plain of Reeds. The '66 operation was conducted out of Muc Hoa which was located 75kms west of Saigon and less than 8kms south of the Cambodian border. The operation proved the PACV was effective in combat but the high fuel consumption, limited payloads, and noise made the PACV no more effective than heliborne operations. "Quai Vat" was Vietnamese for "monster," the adopted call sign for the PACVs of Navy Division 107. *See also* **PACV.**

Operation Quyet Chien (Cai Be, Sung Hieu)   Combined ARVN and U.S. operation in the Delta in November '68 along the Mekong River west of My Tho and north of Cai Be (Sung Hieu). The town of Cai Be, also called Sung Hieu, was located on the northern bank of the Mekong River, 36kms west of My Tho, Dinh Tuong Province, IV Corps.

Operation Quyet Thang (Operation Certain Victory)   Conducted by elements of the U.S. 1st Infantry Division in March '68 in the Phu Loi-Phu Cuong area north of Saigon. The operation was designed to search out and destroy surviving enemy units that had participated in the '68 Tet Offensive. "Quyet Thang" in Vietnamese meant "certain victory."

Operation Ranch Hand (Hades, Only You Can Prevent Forest, We Prevent Forest Fires, MC-1 Sprayer)   Code name for U.S. Air Force defoliation operations conducted from '62 to '71 over parts of SVN and Laos. The defoliants were sprayed by U.S. aircraft of the 12th Air Commando Squadron in an effort to deny the enemy cover by destroying dense growth along roads and rivers that could be used for ambush and attacks. Operation Hades was the original name of the operation, but it was later changed to Ranch Hand. The herbicides used were code-named Agents Blue, White, Pink, Purple and Orange. Ranch Hand's mottos: "Only you can prevent forest" and "We prevent forest fires." Ranch Hand flights were typically carried out at an altitude of 100 feet with a flight of three to five C-123s. Each plane could carry 950 gallons of defoliant, dispensed by the MC-1 Hourglass spray system at the rate 3 gallons per acre, in a path 80 meters wide and 16kms long. The spraying missions required the planes to fly at slow speed (140 knots or less) and low altitude which made them vulnerable to enemy fire and left them no room to maneuver in the event of mechanical problems. The planes were fitted with light armor plate under the cockpit area, but on several occasions planes were downed by enemy ground fire. An estimated 19 million gallons of herbicide were dispersed over SVN before the program ended. *See also* **Defoliation; Resource Management; Crop Denial; Agent: Orange, White, Blue, Pink, Purple; C-123; Operation Big Patch.**

Operation Red Beach II   Code name for the Marine amphibious landing operation and the landing beach area used by the U.S. 9th Marine Expeditionary Brigade. Red Beach was located just west of Da Nang, inside Da Nang Harbor. As the Marines waded ashore in March '65 they were greeted by local Vietnamese government officials and school girls welcoming them to Vietnam. This landing plus the airlift of elements of the 3rd Marine Div. to Da Nang marked the start of U.S. ground combat forces in support of South Vietnam. The Marines were deployed by Task Group 76.7. *See also* **9th Marine Expeditionary Brigade, TG 76.7.**

Operation River Raider   Riverine operation conducted by U.S. forces of the MRF in February '67 in the Rung Sat Special Zone of Gia Dinh Province, III Corps.

Operation Rock Crusher   Code name

for elements of the American forces involved in the Cambodian Incursion in '70. *See also* **Cambodian Incursion.**

Operation Rolling Stone Conducted by elements of the 1st Infantry Division and the 1st Royal Australian Regiment in the Ben Cat area of Binh Duong Province. The units conducted security operations for road construction performed by U.S. Army Engineers.

Operation Rolling Thunder Code name for U.S. February '65–November '68 bombing campaign against NVN. The bombing objectives of the initial campaign were transportation routes, but this was soon expanded to include POL centers, power stations, war essential factories and NVN airfields. The campaign was a "measured" response to NVN aggression against the U.S. and SVN. A list of targets was created by the JCS from which the White House made target selections. The White House believed the campaign would discourage NVN from continuing their support of the VC in SVN. Over 300,000 sorties were directed against North Vietnam, delivering 643,000 tons of bombs during Operation Rolling Thunder. *See also* **Rolling Thunder Coordinating Committee.**

Operation Russell Beach Joint Army/ARVN operation on the Batangan Peninsula in '69.

Operation Safeside *see* **Combat Security Police**

Operation Salem House *see* **Operation Daniel Boone**

Operation Sam Houston January '67 operation by elements of the 4th Infantry Division in the Central Highlands along the Cambodian border. The extremely heavily forested mountain area along the border was believed to be the home of the 1st and 10th NVA divisions. Contact with the enemy was sharp and sporadic. Troops of the 4th Infantry Division were often ambushed by NVA troops at such close ranges that it was difficult to bring artillery fire and air strikes to bear without hitting friendly troops. The operation was terminated in early April. The 4th Infantry Division suffered moderate casualties throughout the operation, many of them from heat fatigue.

Operation Saw Buck II (777th Tactical Control Squadron [TCS]) Air Force deployment of the 777th Tactical Control Squadron to Da Nang in June '62 to support South Vietnamese military operations. The 777th TCS consisted of 16 C-123 transports, maintained and operated by U.S. Air Force personnel. *See also* **Mule Train.**

Operation SCOOT (Support Cambodia Out of Thailand) Air Force operations started in April '73 to provide Cambodian forces with air support in their war against the communist Pathet Lao and NVA troops in Cambodia. U.S. combat aircraft had ceased operations out of SVN per the Paris Peace Accords, but Lon Nol's forces in Cambodia were still at war. The SCOOT operation provided combat support as well as the airlift of supplies and ammunition to Phnom Penh. *See also* **Project Flycatcher.**

Operation Scotland Two part Marine operation conducted in the area of Khe Sanh Combat Base by elements of the 3d Marine Division. The first part of the operation started in November '67 and ended with the start of the siege of Khe Sanh in January '68. Part two of the operation began at the end of the seige in April '68. *See also* **Khe Sanh.**

Operation Sea Dragon U.S. naval offshore bombardment operation designed to interdict and harass NVN supply and military facilities along the coast of North Vietnam, from the 20th Parallel near Thanh Hoa, south to Cat Son Phuong. U.S. and Australian ships attacked NVN coastal shipping, radar and gun batteries from October '66 to October '68. As part of the '68 bombing halt, Sea Dragon was terminated. *See also* **USS New Jersey, TF 70.8.9.**

Operation Sea Float (Operation Tran Hung Dao III, Sea Float Annex) Operation by elements of the Navy's TF 115 and the VNN in the Nam Can area of the Ca Mau Peninsula in IV Corps. A mobile float base (MATSB) was placed on the Song Cua Lon river near the old village of Nam Can, 135kms southwest of Soc Trang, in June '69. The area around Nam Can was heavily infested with VC. U.S. Navy and VVN units patrolled from the Sea Float base, and supporting the sparse rural population, gradually reduced the VC's effect in the area. Sea Float established an "Annex" several kilometers east of the base which provided the local population with medical treatment and protection from the VC. Because of the effectiveness of the base a permanent base was later established at Old Nam Can. *See also* **Solid Anchor.**

Operation Search Turn   November '68 operation conducted by elements of TF 194 along the Rach Gia-Long Xuyen canal in Kien Giang and An Giang provinces, IV Corps. The operation was designed to interdict enemy infiltration routes that honeycombed the Western Delta and was one of several operations to establish barrier patrols in the Delta. *See also* **Delta Barrier Operations.**

Operation Shenandoah II   September '67 operation conducted by elements of the 1st Cavalry and 1st Infantry divisions, and the 173d Airborne Brigade in the area around Loc Ninh, Binh Long Province, III Corps.

Operation Shining Brass (Prairie Fire, Phu Dung)   Shining Brass was the operational code name for the first MACV-SOG recon missions into Laos, started in '65. The objectives of the missions were to pinpoint the route of the Ho Chi Minh Trail, gather intelligence on its management and conduct BDAs of U.S. air strikes on the trail. In '68 the name of the operation was changed to Prairie Fire, and again changed in '71 to Phu Dung.

Operation Silver Bayonet   Conducted by elements of the 1st Cavalry Division in October '65, shortly after their initial deployment to South Vietnam. The 1st Cavalry Division operated in the Central Highlands near the Plei Me Special Forces Camp, south of Pleiku in II Corps. The Cavalry engaged NVA units which were attempting to overrun Plei Me. The Cav drove the enemy back into sanctuaries across the Cambodian border. *See also* **Battle of Ia Drang, Task Force Ingram.**

Operation Silver Mace   December '68 operations by elements of TF 115 on coastal inlets around the southern tip of South Vietnam, in the vicinity of the village of Old Nam Can, on the Cau Mau Peninsula. Silver Mace II commenced in January '69 against the same area by a combined force of U.S. Navy ships and Air Force air support, and a small task force from the Vietnamese Army, Navy and Marines.

Operation Silver Spring   Army operation conducted by elements of the 3d Brigade/1st Infantry Division in the area of Phuoc Vinh, Binh Duong Province, III Corps.

Operation Slingshot   May '69 Navy riverine operation conducted by TF 116 in the area of Tan An, Long An Province, IV Corps. The area was located along the eastern edge of the Plain of Reeds, 35kms southwest of Saigon.

Operation Snack   *see*   **Operation Menu Targets**

Operation Somerset Plain   Combined operation by elements of the 101st Airborne Division, 1st Cavalry Division and the 1st ARVN Infantry Division, conducted in August '68 in the A Shau Valley of I Corps. During the operation several small fire bases were established in the area to support the operation. *See also* **FSB: Birmingham, Eagle's Nest, Son, Georgia, Berchtesgaden.**

Operation Speedy Express   Extensive operation by elements of the 9th Infantry Division's 2d Brigade conducted in the Northern Delta area of IV Corps, December '68 to May '69.

Operation Stable Door   Code name for operations of TF 115 to provide harbor security for facilities at Cam Ranh Bay. *See also* **TF 115.**

Operation Starlite (Van Tuong)   August '65 operation by elements of the 3d and 4th Marine regiments which engaged the 1st VC Regiment at Van Tuong, 18kms southeast of Chu Lai in Quang Ngai Province, I Corps. The 3/3 Marines landed during the first enemy opposed amphibious Marine assault in Vietnam. The 2/4 Marines air assaulted into blocking positions, trapping the Viet Cong regiment along the coast where it was destroyed by the combined efforts of offshore Navy shelling, air strikes, Marine armor and infantry. The operation represented the first major U.S. operation in SVN using armor.

Operation Steel Tiger   U.S. air operation started April '65 designed to interdict the Ho Chi Minh Trail in the eastern portion of the southern Laotian Panhandle. Aircraft from the Air Force, Marines and the Navy struck at enemy supply lines in the Laos corridor located along the Laos/NVN border from the DMZ, north about 300kms. In '68 the operation was expanded to cover the entire southern Panhandle of Laos and the Ho Chi Minh Trail. In conjunction with the Steel Tiger missions, Barrel Roll operations were expanded to provide the Royal Laotian Government air support in its fight against communist Pathet Lao and NVA troops in Laos. The Panhandle area south of the DMZ was under control of Operation Tiger Hound. *See also* **Operation Barrel Roll, Operation Tiger Hound, Night Owls.**

Operation Sunrise   Code name for one of the earliest attempts at pacification in South Vietnam by its leader, Ngo Dinh Diem in '62. The pacification plan called for the relocation of several rural villages to government controlled camps. Many of the people were eventually forced by the military to relocate when they were reluctant to relocate voluntarily. Like many other pacification plans that followed, the Sunrise plan failed, due in part to the GVN's insensitivity to the ancestral attachments of its people to their land, GVN corruption, and the placement of the camps in areas distant from market and agricultural areas. The operation encountered stiff VC resistance. *See also* **Pacification, New Life Hamlet, Restructuring.**

Operation Supper   *see*   **Operation Menu Targets**

Operation Swift   Marine operations conducted in Quang Nam and Quang Tin provinces, I Corps, September '67. The operation was conducted by elements of the 5th Marine Regiment/1st Marine Division.

Operation Switchback   MACV operation for the takeover of the responsibility from MAAG to MACV. Switchback put many of the CIA sponsored programs in SEA under direct and indirect control of MACV. Programs such as the CIDG, fortified hamlets, crossborder reconnaissance, and intelligence nets were originally established and controlled by the CIA and executed in large part by the U.S. Special Forces.

Operation Tailwind (LZ Bluejay, Blue Beach)   Conducted as part of Operation Jackstay in March '66. Elements of the Marine SLF made an amphibious landing at Blue Beach to follow up on a B-52 strike that had been conducted in the area between the Song Vam Sat and Song Soi Rap rivers, 28kms south of Saigon, on the western edge of the RSSZ. LZ Bluejay was established at the same time, and artillery brought into the LZ to provide fire support to the troops at Blue Beach. Blue Beach was located on the east shore of the Song Soi Rap River about 27kms south of Saigon; LZ Bluejay was located about 5kms south of Blue Beach and a kilometer east of the river. *See also* **Operation Jackstay.**

Operation Tally Ho   Combined Air Force and Marine air effort in July '66 to strike at NVA supply points and infiltration routes just north of the DMZ.

Operation Talon Vise   *see*   **Operation Frequent Wind**

Operation Texas   March '66 operation conducted by elements of the 3d Battalion/7th Marines, 2d Battalion/4th Marines, and the 5th ARVN Airborne at An Hoa in Quang Nam Province, I Corps. The 1st Viet Cong Regiment had attacked the RF outpost at An Hoa, and was surrounded and trapped by the Marines and ARVN Airborne. The Viet Cong suffered heavy casualties, leaving more than 400 dead in four days of fighting.

Operation Texas Star   Pacification operations conducted by elements of the 101st Airborne Division in conjunction with the 1st ARVN Division from April–September '70 in Thua Thien and Quang Tri provinces, I Corps.

Operation Thayer I & II   September '66 operation by elements of the 1st Cavalry Division which engaged elements of the 18th NVA Regiment. The operation was conducted in the 506 Valley area, which was located along the coast in Binh Dinh Province, II Corps. A second part of the operation, Thayer II, resumed in October '66.

Operation Thot Not   *see*   **Operation Daniel Boone**

Operation Tiger Hound   Air operations by Air Force and Navy aircraft to interdict the Ho Chi Minh Trail in the southern Laotian Panhandle along the Laos/SVN border in the corridor south of the DMZ. Operation Steel Tiger targeted trail activity in the northern Laotian Panhandle, while

Tiger Hound focused on the southern Panhandle area. Tiger Hound truck-busting operations began in December '65 and were later expanded to cover the entire Ho Chi Minh Trail. This expansion was merged with the Steel Tiger missions and renamed Commando Hunt in '68. See also Operation Steel Tiger, Operation Commando Hunt, Project Big Eagle.

Operation Tiger Hunt see Operation Commando Hunt

Operation Toan Thang   In Vietnamese Toan Thang meant "total victory." The ARVN named a series of operations Toan Thang with a series number appended to the name. In May '68 the NVA/VC launched a Mini–Tet Offensive aimed at Saigon. Over 75 U.S. and ARVN battalions responded, encircling Saigon and engaging any enemy units they were able to find. The first phase of Toan Thang officially ended May 31, 1968, with an MACV body count of over 7,000 NVA/VC KIA. Because of Operation Toan Thang the enemy's mini–Tet Offensive was unable to do any major damage in the city. Subsequent phases of the operation continued to the end of '69. See also Iron Triangle.

Operation Total Victory see Cambodian Incursion

Operation Tran Hung Dao   Conducted by elements of ARVN (Rangers, Marines and Airborne) in February '68. The operations were in response to enemy activity during the '68 Tet Offensive and involved the ARVN units dislodging the NVA/VC from their positions in Cholon, the Chinese section of Saigon. It took the ARVN forces a month to clear Cholon of the Viet Cong and restore order. Operation Tran Hung Dao was also the name for SVNN operations conducted against enemy infiltration routes in the northwestern Delta of IV Corps. Tran Hung Dao was a rename of Operation Foul Deck. See also Operation Foul Deck.

Operation Tran Hung Dao III see Operation Sea Float

Operation Tran Hung Dao XI   Code name for the Navy operations conducted as part of the U.S. incursion into Cambodia in May '70. Navy riverine and air support units of HAL-3 operated along the Mekong River

near the Cambodian border. See also Cambodian Incursion, HAL-3, TF 116.

Operation Truong Cong Dinh   March '68 operation conducted by elements of the U.S. 9th Infantry Division in Dinh Tuong and Kien Tuong provinces in IV Corps.

Operation Union I & II   Operations conducted by elements of the 1st Marines in Quang Nam and Quang Tin provinces in April '67. The Marines engaged elements of the 2d NVA Division in the Phuoc Ha Valley area, with the operations continuing into June '67.

Operation Uniontown   Conducted in December '67 by elements of the 199th Light Infantry Brigade in the Iron Triangle area near Bien Hoa in III Corps. The operations continued into March when the 199th LIB engaged Viet Cong forces during the '68 Tet Offensive. See also Iron Triangle.

Operation Utah   Operation in March '66 conducted by elements of the 1st, 4th and 7th Marine regiments which engaged troops of the 36th NVA Regiment just south of Chu Lai in I Corps. The Marines remained in contact with the NVA for several days before the enemy retreated from the area.

Operation Utah Mesa   Conducted by elements of the 5th Infantry Division (Mechanized) in the A Shau Valley in July '69.

Operation Utah/Lien Ket 26   Combined U.S. 1st Marine Division and SVN Marine operation conducted northwest of Quang Tri in March '66. The ARVN part of the operation was code-named Lien Ket 26.

Operation Vulture   Plan devised by the Eisenhower administration in '54 to provide direct American military aid to the French in Indochina, at their request. The plan called for American air strikes against Viet Minh positions around Dien Bien Phu by U.S. Air Force planes from Philippine air bases, supported by U.S. Navy carrier aircraft stationed off the coast of Vietnam. The plan also considered the use of U.S. ground troops to help relieve the French at Dien Bien Phu. The plan was dropped due to a lack of support from the French and the British (both countries with colonial interest in Asia), and a reluctance by Congress to get militarily involved in Vietnam. *See also* **Dien Bien Phu, B-29 Bomber.**

Operation Wallowa *see* **Operation Wheeler/Wallowa**

Operation Washington Green April '69 operation conducted by elements of the 173d Airborne Brigade in the area of Phu My, 24kms north of Phu Cat, Binh Dinh Province, II Corps. The primary purpose of the operation was to secure the area around Phu My allowing for the continuation of pacification efforts. In addition to the pacification mission the operation focused on training the local RF/PF units in the area and conducting combined security operations with them.

Operation Water Glass Air Force protective security operations conducted in March '62. The operations involved the deployment of several F-102s to Tan Son Nhut AB as interceptors in the event the air base was attacked by enemy aircraft. The Air Force rotated detachments of aircraft, on temporary duty from Clark Air Force Base in the Philippines, into Tan Son Nhut air base until May '63 when the practice was ended, primarily due to a lack of participation by enemy aircraft (North Vietnamese).

Operation Wedge *see* **Iron Triangle**

Operation Wheeler/Wallowa Operations by elements of the Americal Division in Quang Nam and Quang Tin provinces of I Corps. The operations started in November '67 and lasted until November '68 yielding large enemy body counts. *See also* **My Lai.**

Operation White Star *see* **White Star Mobile Training Team**

Operation Wolf Pack Series of operations first conducted in October '69 by the combined forces of the Australian Task Force, Royal Thai Army, Vietnamese and U.S. units against the Viet Cong's Doan-10 Battalion which was primarily responsible for attacks against Allied shipping on the Song Long Tau River in the Rung Sat Special Zone. *See also* **Rung Sat, Song Long Tau River, Operation Platypus.**

Operation Yankee Team Code name for the resumption of U.S. reconnaissance missions over Laos in May '64. Aerial reconnaissance by U.S. aircraft over Laos had been terminated by the '62 Geneva Agreement on Laos. The U.S. resumed the flights in March when fighting broke out between the three political factions in Laos. Some of the recon flights operated with armed aircraft which were authorized to attack enemy targets of opportunity deep in Laos. The flights confirmed the buildup of NVA anti-aircraft gun sites on the Plain of Jars, a direct violation of the Geneva Agreement (as were the armed recon flights). During the course of the reconnaissance flights several U.S. aircraft were fired on and downed.

Operation Yellowstone Operations conducted by elements of the 25th Infantry Division in War Zone C during January and February '68. During the operations the 271st and 272d Viet Cong regiments attempted to overrun FSB Burt, but were thrown back with heavy losses sustained on both sides. *See also* **FSB Burt.**

Operational Bases Unsuccessful GVN plan established after the '72 Eastertide Offensive. The plan called for the establishment of fixed bases to be manned by RFs and PFs in an effort to deprive the enemy of the ability to move freely.

Operational Command (Operational Control) A commander who had "operation command" of a unit had the authority to assign missions and direct the unit. A commander with "operation control" of a unit had overall responsibility for the unit (logistics, administration, personnel) and had the authority to place the unit under the operation command of another force. MACV had command control of naval units in Vietnam and could assign them missions and duties, yet CINCPAC had overall control of all Navy units in the Pacific, including those in Vietnam, and was responsible for logistics support, staffing, rotations and administrative operations of those units. In rough terms MACV defined the mission, and CINCPAC decided how it was to be executed.

Operational Control (OPCON, Temporary Assigned Duty [TAD]) Referred to the headquarters that had operational control of a unit. If a unit was temporarily put under the command control of a headquarters other than its own, the unit was said to be OPCON'ed to the new command headquarters. OPCON was generally temporary, for the duration of a given operation or mission. Temporary assignments for men or units for specific assignments were also called "Temporary Assigned Duty," TAD. *See also* **Operational Command.**

Operational Exhaustion *see* **Combat Fatigue**

Operational Order *see* **Op-Orders**

Operations Plan-34A *see* **OPLAN-34A**

Operations Report/Lessons Learned (ORLL) Quarterly report prepared by a unit's headquarters detailing the combat actions of the unit, its response and the results. The report was required by the Army from units of battalion size or larger. Through the reports the Army hoped to learn from its combat experiences and adjust its techniques and tactics to better adapt to the fluid combat situation in Vietnam. The ORLL was one of many reports the Army required of its commanders in the field.

Opium (Phien, Thuoc Phien, Yen) One of several illicit drugs available to U.S. troops in Vietnam. Opium was also one of the many illegal drugs and substances in use within the U.S. In Vietnam opium was called "thuoc phien." "Yen" was opium used for smoking. The hippie movement made extensive use of the drug throughout the sixties and seventies. In Vietnam opium was usually smoked in a pipe or in opium laced cigarettes. The NVA also made use of opium, sometimes using it before an attack to fortify the spirits of their soldiers, making them feel invulnerable to enemy fire. *See also* **OJs, Ta'i, Drug List.**

OPLAN-34A (Operations Plan-34A) A '64 secret program of CIA planned and MACV-SOG directed raids using South Vietnamese forces, landed by U.S. PT boats, on the coast of NVN. The object of the raid was to destroy NVN coastal facilities and otherwise harass NVN in an effort to demonstrate to them that they were not immune to attack on their home ground. The raids were ineffective, and the damage created was minor. *See also* **Tonkin Gulf Incident.**

OPORD 13-70 *see* **Operation Jefferson Glenn**

Opposition, The *see* **Enemy, The**

Ops Abbreviated form of "operations." Also referred to the G-3, S-3, or N-3 command sections of a unit which were responsible for operations of the unit. *See also* **S-3, G-3.**

Optical Rectosis Slang for having a "shitty" outlook on life: a very negative attitude.

Option IV Code name for the planned evacuation of American personnel from Saigon by helicopter. The plan called for Americans and "high risk Vietnamese" to be evacuated from the U.S. Embassy compound by helicopter. Option IV was activated when the airfield at Tan Son Nhut could no longer be used for evacuation. Tan Son Nhut was closed by enemy fire and runway damage on April 29, 1975. The closure triggered the helicopter deployment of a Marine ground force to provide security for the Embassy compound during the evacuation. Air America helicopters assisted in the final lift by collecting Americans and Vietnamese from various locations around Saigon and transferring them to the Embassy for evacuation. Americans and several thousand Vietnamese were eventually extracted from the Embassy grounds and rooftops across Saigon in the early hours of April 30 when the evacuation ended. Option IV was part of Operation Frequent Wind. The evacuation resulted in the helicopter airlift of over 7,050 Americans, Vietnamese and third country nationals. *See also* **Operation Frequent Wind.**

OR *see* **ER/OR**

Ord (Ordnance, Soft Ordnance) Military abbreviation for "ordnance." Ordnance referred to any type of bombs, rockets, napalm, cannon fire, etc., delivered against a target. Ordnance was most often used in reference to air delivered weaponry. "Soft ordnance" was used in reference to napalm, CS gas and FAE-type weapons.

Order of Battle Detailed record of a unit's size, disposition, composition, deployment (current and future), equipment, and identification. An order of battle was kept on all friendly units. Orders of battle were also kept on all known enemy units. One of the primary functions of the intelligence section of a military headquarters was to constantly update and seek out new information to maintain an accurate order of battle on enemy units.

Orderly Departure Program (Operation Homecoming '79)   As a part of Operation Homecoming '79 the U.S. Congress appropriated funds to assist the emigration of Amer-Asian children from South Vietnam (SRV) to the United States. An estimated 7,000–12,000 Amer-Asian children were believed to have survived the communist takeover in South Vietnam and continued to live in the country. Under the Orderly Departure Program the Vietnamese authorities were to screen applicants for the program, issuing the exit visas. The U.S. would then provide transport out of the country and resettlement in the U.S. The program was scheduled to expire in '90 and the Vietnamese authorities have intermittently cooperated with the program. *See also* **Amer-Asian.**

Orderly Room   Administrative office of a unit (company, battery, troop). The unit's company clerk and records were housed in the orderly room. The orderly room also had offices for the company first sergeant and the company commander. In Vietnam company orderly rooms for line units were usually located at the battalion, brigade, or division base camp. The orderly room also handled the unit's mail, military and personal, and was located near the company's supply room.

Ordnance *see* **Ord**

Oreo (Uncle Tom, Uniform Tango)   As in Oreo Cookie, black on the outside, white on the inside. Black reference to another black who catered to whites in order to gain their favor, especially at the cost of other blacks. A black trying to act white in order to be accepted by whites and ignoring, or working against other blacks to achieve that end. Blacks saw Oreos as untrustworthy, dangerous, spineless and useless. Phonetically known as "Uniform Tangos." *See also* **Token Nigger.**

Organic (Nonorganic)   Referred to a unit, section, or weapons system that was a permanent part of a larger unit. Organic weapons were those that were normally required for the unit to carry out its mission. Organic weapons and equipment were listed in a unit's Table of Organization and Equipment (TO&E). Equipment, or another unit, attached to a unit was said to be "nonorganic." Example: a 155mm howitzer battery consisted of six guns; if two 105mm guns were assigned to the battery they were considered nonorganic to the 155mm battery, yet they were still under command of the battery headquarters. *See also* **Table of Organization and Equipment, Independent Units, Composite Battery.**

Organic Aviation Unit (Division Aviation Assets)   A helicopter unit attached to a regular infantry unit. The infantry unit provided the troops to be lifted, while the separate helicopter unit provided the aircraft. In Vietnam a helicopter battalion was assigned to an infantry division on a permanent basis. The battalion consisted of two lift companies and an air cavalry troop. The organic aviation unit was also referred to as a Divisional Aviation Asset. *See also* **Nonorganic Aviation Unit.**

Orion *see* **P-3**

Oriskany *see* **USS Oriskany**

ORLL *see* **Operations Report/Lessons Learned**

OSAFO (Office of the Special Assistant for Field Operations)   Following the '73 Paris Peace Accords and the withdrawal of U.S. combat forces, the U.S. CORDS agency was reorganized and renamed the "Office of the Special Assistant for Field Operations." The OSAFO had many of the same functions as those of CORDS, but there was more emphasis placed on helping the GVN with its pacification efforts. *See also* **Civil Operations and Revolutionary Development.**

OSD *see* **Secretary of Defense**

OSI *see* **Office of Special Investigations**

OSS *see* **Office of Strategic Services**

Other War, The (Real War, Hot War, Political War, Shooting War)   U.S. military perception that there were two wars going on in SVN. The "real war," by military standards, was the actual combat and the elimination of the NVA/VC—the "shooting war." The "other war" was the pacification and security effort, winning the people over to the side of the GVN. The military dealt with the real war (the hot war) and less effectively with the other war (the political war): One could not be fought effectively without including the other. Much of the time the "other war" received low priority which resulted in the Americans being isolated from the very people they were trying to help. The Marines realized the importance of the "other war" and focused more attention on WHAM than did the Army. *See also* **MEDCAP, Combined Action Platoon, WHAM.**

Otter *see* **U-1A or M-76 Cargo Carrier**

Our Goal Is Peace in Vietnam Slogan often used by President Johnson to describe America's goal in Vietnam, while he escalated U.S. involvement to the tune of billions of dollars and hundreds of thousands of combat troops.

Our Vietnamese *see* **ARVN**

OUSAIRA (Office of U.S. Air Attaché) Embassy level office responsible for the coordination of U.S. air assets within a foreign country.

Out of Channel Procurement *see* **Midnight Requisition**

Out-Country Popular Air Force and Navy term for the air war conducted outside of South Vietnam, particularly against North Vietnam.

Out-of-Country Patrols *see* **Cross Border Patrols**

Outguard Referred to the security duties provided by a separate unit assigned to guard a base. In Vietnam infantry units provided the guard for fire support bases. The assigned infantry unit manned the bunker line around the perimeter of the base and provided the initial reaction to an enemy attack. At forward battalion FSBs the outguard was usually rotated among the companies of the battalion. Two to three of the battalion's companies would be out on operations, while the remaining company provided security for the battalion headquarters and attached artillery battery. Units on outguard were considered "standing-down," and normally did not conduct offensive operations around the base, but rested, refitted, and guarded the base.

OV-1 (Mohawk, Night Phantom) Grumman manufactured, twin engine, light observation aircraft. The Army Mohawk was very maneuverable with a high payload capacity, allowing it to be armed to support ground troops. The Mohawk carried various types of radar and was originally designed for reconnaissance and surveillance. Later in the war the aircraft was sometimes armed and used to support ground troops, although the Air Force contested such practices. The Mohawk was officially the Army's only armed, fixed-wing aircraft. The OV-1 contained sophisticated navigational and targeting equipment that allowed it to conduct night missions against enemy positions, carried out under the code name of Night Phantom. The OV-1 started combat trials in South Vietnam in '62 and was used throughout the war. The aircraft had a maximum speed of 317mph, a range of 2,700-kms, and a crew of two. Various versions of the OV-1 were fitted with side-looking radar (SLAR) and infrared surveillance systems. OV-1s were armed with a variety of weapons that included bombs, rockets, napalm and gun pods. *See also* **23d Special Warfare Aviation Detachment.**

OV-10A (Bronco) The twin propeller Bronco was manufactured by North American Rockwell and operated as an armed reconnaissance and observation aircraft with the Marine Corps and the Air Force. The Bronco gradually replaced the older O-1 Bird Dog as FACs. The Navy version of the OV-10A was more heavily armed and was used for air strikes in support of riverine operations in the Delta of Vietnam. The OV-10 had a max speed of 281mph, range of 960kms, a payload of 3,600 pounds and was armed with four belly mounted machine guns. The aircraft could carry a combination of rockets, bombs and cannon pods. *See also* **Light Attack Squadron 4.**

Over-and-Under Gun *see* **M-203 Rifle**

Overbirth (Laterite) U.S. Army engineering term used to describe the tunnel structures at Cu Chi. The tunnels were primarily dug in laterite clay and were woven around and between tree root systems. The tree roots served to strengthen the tunnels making overhead bracing and side wall support rarely necessary. *See also* **Tunnels of Cu Chi.**

Overrun   When an enemy force entered and overwhelmed a defensive position, taking control of the position, inflicting sufficient casualties on the defensive force, and rendering it unable to repel the attack or hold the position. The NVA/VC frequently overran the smaller RF/PF and ARVN outposts, usually holding on to the outpost only long enough to remove captured weapons and ammunition, and remove their wounded. USSF camps in remote areas were a favorite target of the NVA/VC, but the liberal use of U.S. air support often kept the camps from being completely overrun. On several occasions the NVA/VC launched major ground assaults against USSF camps resulting in high U.S. and CIDG casualties and the abandonment of the targeted camps. *See also* **Kham Duc, A Shau, Lang Vei.**

Ovnand, Master Sergeant Chester   *see* **First American to Die...**

Ox   *see*   **M-51 HRV**

OZM-3 Antipersonnel Mine   *see* **Bouncing Betty**

P

P   *see*   **Piasters**

P-2 (Neptune, P2V, SP-2H)   Twin engine, propeller aircraft manufactured by Lockheed and used in the late fifties by the U.S. Navy for surveillance and antisubmarine duties. During the Vietnam War the P-2 "Neptune" was used off the coast of South Vietnam for surveillance and interdiction of NVA/VC waterborne infiltration routes. The planes were ground based, operating out of Cam Ranh Bay and Tan Son Nhut as part of TF 115, Operation Market Time. The P-2 had a max speed of 345mph, a range of 3,540kms and operated with a 10-man crew. Several of the P-2s were armed and used as gunships to engage enemy boat traffic along the coast. *See also* **VAH-21, OP-2E.**

P2N/V   *see*   **P-2**

P-3 (Orion, P3A, EP-3C)   All-weather, four engine turboprop aircraft manufactured by Lockheed Aircraft. The P-3 was the military version of the Lockheed Electra used by commercial aviation. The P-3 was equipped with sophisticated radar and navigational equipment, and used for surveillance and antisubmarine patrol. During the Vietnam War the P-3 operated as part of the Navy's Operation Market Time, TF 115, from bases at Vung Tau and the Philippines. The P-3 had a max speed of 473mph, range of 3,385kms and operated with a 10-man crew. The EP-3C was used as an airborne radar center; it was also used

to monitor NVN radar emissions. *See also* **TF 115, Market Time, SAM Suppression.**

P-4 Torpedo Boat (Torpedo Boat, PT Boat, Swatow)   Soviet built torpedo patrol boats used by the North Vietnamese Navy. The P-4 Swatow PT boat had a max speed of 40 knots and carried torpedoes and 12.7mm machine guns. On August 2, 1964, three NVN PT boats attacked the U.S. Navy destroyer *Maddox* in international waters, over 40kms from the North Vietnamese coast. The Maddox returned fire and was assisted by aircraft from the aircraft carrier *Ticonderoga*. *See also* **Tonkin Gulf Incident.**

P-5 (Marlin, Flying Boat, SP-5)   U.S. Navy seaplane used for surveillance duty off the coast of South Vietnam during Operation Market Time, TF 115. The Martin Marlins operated until '67 when they were phased out of service and replaced by the P-2 Neptune. The P-5, twin engine, propeller driven seaplane had a max speed of 251mph, a range of 3,300kms and operated with a crew of 11. Marlins operated from bases at Cam Ranh Bay and the island of Con Son. *See also* **TF 115, Market Time.**

P-5 Amtrac   *see*   **LVTP**

P5 Marlin   *see*   **P-5**

P-38 (Can Opener, John-Wayne)   Small, collapsible GI field can opener. Several were found in the bottom of each case of C-Rations. The Marines called their P-38s

John-Waynes. The P-38 was used for a variety of functions other than opening C-Ration cans. In an emergency the P-38 could slit open a windpipe for a tracheotomy; as a screw driver to remove the locking pins on an M-16 rifle; bottle opener; fingernail cleaner. Many grunts wore their P-38 around their neck on the same chain as their dog-tags.

P-155 Scope *see* **IR Scopes**

P-SID *see* **Portable Seismic Intrusion Device**

PACAF *see* **Pacific Air Force**

Pacific Air Force (PACAF) Designation for U.S. Air Force units assigned to the Pacific area.

Pacific Command (PACOM) A unified command center responsible for all U.S. military units operating in the Pacific. PACOM reported directly to the Joint Chiefs of Staff.

Pacific Stars and Stripes Newspaper available to U.S. servicemen in the Pacific. The paper claimed to be an "Authorized Publication of the Armed Forces Far East," and later an "Authorized Unofficial Publication of the Pacific Command." The daily paper was published in Tokyo and distributed to U.S. bases throughout the Pacific area at a cost of 10 cents per copy. The paper consisted of several pages of world and national news, with a "slight" optimistic slant that tended to "favor" the American position around the world.

Pacification (COIN Operations) In Vietnam, pacification theory entailed a government program whose objective was to end the war, restore the peace, develop democracy and reform the society. Under the plan the army was to provide protection to a village, allowing the internal security force of the village to weed out the VC. The government would institute civil improvements, provide schools, agricultural enhancements, and medical services and help the people. Because of this government effort, the people would be free of the VC influence, putting a distance between the war and the people. The people in turn would recognize the efforts of the government, throwing their support to the GVN and making it even more difficult for the VC to gain ground. The theory was sound but

the execution was poor. Corruption in the military and the government greatly reduced the effectiveness of the plan, and the entrenchment of the VC in the rural society was too much to overcome. Many of the methods used by the GVN to accomplish their goal only alienated the people they were seeking to help. The GVN forced the relocation of whole villages, moving the people away from their ancestral lands and their normal social and economical environments, only increasing the hostilities of the people. Programs administered by the GVN were full of corruption resulting in the needs of the people falling behind those of the administrators. The Viet Cong capitalized on the distrust of the people against the GVN. GVN cadres sent into villages to do pacification and development work were understaffed and undertrained. GVN troops assigned to provide security during pacification efforts were rarely able to keep the VC from adversely impacting the GVN efforts. ARVN troops further complicated the efforts by conscripting villagers to build defensive works or facilities for the enhancement of the troops. The attempt to combine civil improvements with military operations in an effort to win over the allegiance of the people and make the central government more responsive and equitable to the people's needs had worked on an extremely limited basis. One of the most important components lacking was a desire by the people to participate in the pacification program. The military aspect of the program focused on killing the local VC, but the local VC were the sons, daughters, fathers and husbands of the same villagers who were the targets of the program. It was difficult for them to accept the GVN's killing of their family members in order to free them of the influences of the VC. As each new version of the pacification program took effect, it compounded the mistakes of the previous program, repeating and enlarging them. Pacification programs attempted to separate the people from the VC, but the VC were not outsiders or foreigners; the VC were the people. The GVN could neither overcome nor understand that they were one and the same. Pacification was known by many names over the years: Nation Building, Revolutionary Development, Internal Security, Counterinsurgency (COIN Operations), Rural Construction, Rural Reconstruction, Internal

Defense Operations, Stability Operations, Internal Defense and Development, and Civil Support for Revolutionary Development. *See also* **Revolutionary Development Peoples Group; Operation Sunrise; Strategic Hamlet Program; Thompson, Sir Robert; Oil Spot Technique.**

Pacification by Assassination A reference to the means and methods of the Phoenix Program which sought to pacify rural areas of Vietnam by elimination of the Viet Cong, its political infrastructure, and local Vietnamese supporters. *See also* **Phoenix Program, Provisional Reconnaissance Unit.**

Pacifier (Kingfisher, Sparrow Hawk) Names for a Marine technique similar to the Army's Eagle Flight. Marine helicopters would provide transport for an infantry rifle platoon acting as a quick reaction/reserve force or as a follow-up force if the enemy was found. Observation aircraft would scout out an area; when the enemy was detected the rifle platoon would be inserted. CH-46s provided the troop lift while a UH-1 Huey provided command and control, and several gunships were available for fire support. Should the platoon discover a larger force than it could handle, more infantry could be lifted into the area. *See also* **Eagle Flight, Parakeet Missions.**

Pack Bicycle *see* **Xe Tho**

Package A/B Awards (General's Awards, Award Packet) Most generals who spent any command time in Vietnam received a number of awards and decorations. GIs labeled these "General Awards, Package A and B." Packages usually included the following: Silver Stars, Distinguished Flying Cross, Bronze Stars, Distinguished Service Medals, and others. GIs believed generals received the awards simply because of their rank, since few generals spent any time in the field, ever came under fire, or ever flew into a hot LZ. Award packets were also available for battalion and brigade commanders as they departed the unit. The A Package was reserved for staff and division generals, and the B Package went to the other "deserving" generals and colonels at the brigade and battalion level. *See also* **Gongs.**

Packboard Plywood board frame used by U.S. infantry troops to transport heavy or irregular shaped loads. The packboard was worn on the back using shoulder straps. The load was tied or lashed to the packboard for transport.

Packs (NVN Target Areas) *see* **Route Packages**

Pacoh *see* **Montagnards**

PACOM *see* **Pacific Command**

PACV (Patrol Air Cushioned Vehicle, SRN-5, SK-5, Hovercraft, ACV, Monster) Air cushioned vehicles that were a cross between a helicopter and a boat. The ACV skimmed across the land or water on a cushion of air. Three ACVs were used for evaluation by the Navy in SVN. The ACV was 40 feet long, weighed 5 tons, max speed of 55 knots (75mph), payload capacity of 2 tons/17 troops, a crew of three and was armed with .50cal machine guns and grenade launchers. The ACV was tested in the Delta and in I Corps but proved to be inadequate for large scale operations. The ACVs were expensive, noisy, had limited transport capacity, consumed excessive quantities of fuel and were prone to numerous mechanical breakdowns, and deemed no more effective than helicopters. The PACVs operated with the call sign "Monster." *See also* **TF 116, Airboat, Operation Monster, Army ACV.**

PACV Division 107 *see* **PACV**

Paddy Dikes *see* **Berm or Red River Delta**

Paddy Strength (Combat Strength, Foxhole Strength) GI slang for "combat strength" of a unit. For field infantry units "paddy strength" was the actual number of troops in the field on combat operations. In Vietnam the actual number of troops in the field was usually much less than the "authorized strength" of the unit. A typical Army infantry company had an authorized strength of about 140–180 men, yet in the field the paddy strength of the company was usually closer to 90–120 troops. The only time full strength units (fat units) were fielded in Vietnam was during their initial deployment, when whole units arrived in SVN and went into the field. Casualties, R&Rs and rotations quickly reduced the combat strengths of all U.S. units in Vietnam. *See also* **Fat Unit.**

PAEs (Parachutist Adjustable Equipment Bag) Equipment bag sometimes carried by Army parachutist. The bags were carried below the reserve chute during the jump. Shortly before the jumper made his landing the PAE was released and lowered below, to dangle at the end of a 20-foot-long strap. The PAE would hit the ground before the jumper, reducing his total impact weight. The PAE bag had a capacity of nearly 100 pounds. *See also* **T-10 Parachute.**

Pair Off Program In an effort to speed up Vietnamization some U.S. combat units were divided and assigned to work directly with larger ARVN units in an attempt to increase their training and improve their confidence.

Palace Air Strike In February '62 two VNAF AD-6 Skyraiders attacked the presidential palace in Saigon. The AD-6s were piloted by two disgruntled VNAF pilots who bombed and strafed Diem's residence. None of Diem's staff was killed, but three of the "civil population," including Madame Nhu's maid, died as a result of the bombing expertise of the VNAF pilots. Diem's sister-in-law, Madame Nhu, broke her arm while running for the bomb shelter located in the basement of the palace. During the course of the attack one of the AD-6s was shot down and the other flew west across the Cambodian border. *See also* **Tactical Air Control System.**

Palm Hat *see* **NVA Helmet**

Palm Trees (Cay Dua Nuoc, Cay May, Cay Dua) There were several varieties of palm trees in Vietnam that were used for food. The Cay Dua was a large palm tree that produced edible coconuts. The trees grew to heights of over 100 feet and were found in coast areas or cultivated by farmers. Cay Dua coconuts were also boiled to extract the oil. The Cay May rattan palm grew in dense clumps 20–250 feet high. It was usually found in dense canopy areas of the highland forest. The buds could be boiled or roasted for eating, and the hollow stems collected potable drinking water. The Cay Dua Nuoc nipa palm provided the most in edible food. The leaves of the nipa and coconut palm trees were used to make roofs and thatched huts (hooches). *See also* **Nipa Palms, Cay Thien Tue.**

Palmer, General Bruce, Jr. *see* **Bien Hoa Commute**

Pan American Airlines *see* **Commercial Carriers**

Pan-SEA Pike (SEA Freeway, Pan-Southeast Asia Pike) U.S. Army plan formulated in the early sixties that proposed to open a single secure route across South Vietnam, Laos and Thailand. The plan would utilize Highway 9 that began at Dong Ha on South Vietnam's eastern coast, heading west across northern SVN, crossing the Laotian border near Khe Sanh, west to Savannakhet on the Thai border. From there the highway would proceed west to Khon Kaen and then southwest to Bangkok. The plan called for several countries to participate in the engineering work with joint U.S. and Allied combat units providing security along the highway. The plan was one of many military ideas that never came to pass or saw the light of serious consideration.

Pan-Southeast Asia Pike *see* **Pan-SEA Pike**

Panama Station *see* **Monkey Mountain**

Panji Pit *see* **Punji Pit**

Panther *see* **F-9**

Pao, General Vang *see* **Meo**

PAO *see* **Joint U.S. Public Affairs Office**

Papa Delta Round *see* **VT Round**

Papa Zulu *see* **Pickup Zone**

Papa-San GI slang for an old Vietnamese man, or the head of a family, or an older male in charge. For GIs any older Vietnamese male was called a papa-san. *See also* **Mama-San.**

Paper Pushers *see* **Rear Echelon Personnel**

Paper Soldiers *see* **Rear Echelon Personnel**

Parachute Flare Aerial flares used to illuminate an area at night. The flares were of various sizes and burning duration and could be hand launched, pistol fired, M-79 fired, artillery fired or air dropped. The flare was fired and rose to its peak altitude; it then opened, and the burning flare drifted back to earth suspended under a small parachute. *See also* **Flares.**

Parachutist Adjustable Equipment Bag *see* PAEs

Parade Ground *see* **Grinder**

Parakeet Missions Modified Hunter Killer missions employed by the 9th Infantry Division. A Hunter Killer helicopter team (Loach and Cobra) was accompanied by a slick which carried a Ranger team. The Loach would locate the enemy followed by an attack by the Cobra. The Ranger team would be immediately inserted into the area to assess the damage and retrieve any enemy weapons and documents. If the enemy was encountered in larger numbers than the LRRPs could handle, additional troop support would be flown in. Typically a platoon of regular troops was on alert for such missions. *See also* **Hunter Killer Team, ARP, Pacifier.**

Parallel Sheaf *see* **Sheafs of Fire**

Parapets (Gun Pets) Fortified position used to protect artillery pieces. Gun parapets in Vietnam used for the 105mm and 155mm howitzers were constructed to provide the most protection from enemy direct fire and bombardment and yet leave the gun with a 360-degree field of fire. The "gun pets" were circular and large enough to allow the gun and its trails to be rotated full circle. Sandbags were stacked around the position and dirt piled up to provide cover. Around the inside of the gun pet were bunkered storage for artillery shells, fuses, powder, and a bunker for the gun crew.

Pararescuemen *see* **Aerospace Rescue and Recovery Service**

Paras *see* **Paratrooper**

Paratrooper (Paras, Jumping Junkies) Nicknames for paratroopers: Sky Soldiers, Jumping Junkies, Paras.

Parcel Bomb An experimental bomb used by the U.S. Army in Vietnam. The 1,000 pound bomb was dropped from a helicopter, and the casing ruptured over the target, dispersing small antipersonnel bomblets across a wide area. *See also* **Cluster Bomb Unit.**

Pardon, Draft Dodgers *see* **Carter, President Jimmy**

Paris Call sign for the Saigon-Tan Son Nhut Air Control Center. The center coordinated all air traffic in the Saigon area.

Paris Accords (Paris Peace Accords, Peace Talks, Cease Fire) On January 27, 1973, the U.S., RVN, PRG, and NVN signed the Paris Peace Accords to end the fighting and restore peace in SVN. The agreement called for the withdrawal of NVN and U.S. troops from SVN, a cease-fire would be in effect between the ARVN and the NVA/VC, and POWs would be repatriated. The Accords also established a commission to monitor and supervise the terms of the agreement. SVN's President Thieu did not want to sign the Accords, but was threatened with the total cutoff of U.S. aid if he did not. U.S. promises of support for SVN by President Nixon were not honored by the Ford administration and SVN was overrun by North Vietnam in April '75. The Paris peace talks between the U.S. and North Vietnam began in May '68 and continued "off and on" until the signing of the final agreement in January '73. Le Duc Tho was NVN's chief negotiator with Averell Harriman and Henry Kissinger negotiating for the U.S. The talks were mostly a public affair until '71 when the Nixon administration, through Kissinger, decided to use secret negotiations. Secret negotiations allowed concessions to be explored and manipulated without immediate reaction from the public or the lesser participants (South Vietnam and the National Liberation Front). *See also* **Four Party Joint Military Commission, Four No's, Operation Enhance Plus.**

Paris of the Orient *see* **Saigon**

Paris Peace Accords *see* **Paris Accords**

Parker-51 Booby Trap A Viet Cong booby trap made from either a "Parker-51" or "Parker-75" pen. The hollow body of the pen was packed with explosives and a small friction detonator attached in the cap. When the cap was removed the explosives were detonated. The small booby trap could blow off several fingers. The pen was used by the VC for terrorist attacks at GVN offices. The pen was also left behind at VC command centers and bases that were overrun by FWF troops. FWF troops often confiscated enemy equipment as souvenirs when they happened upon them. *See also* **Booby Trap.**

Parker-75 Booby Trap *see* **Parker-51 Booby Trap**

Parris Island *see* **Marine Corps Recruit Depot**

Parrot's Beak An area in Cambodia, along the SVN/Cambodian border used by the NVA/VC as a base for operations into SVN. On a topographical map the boundary between SVN and Cambodia in this area roughly resembles a parrot's beak. The beak pointed southwest and was located 50kms west of Saigon at the junction of III and IV Corps, and the Cambodian border.

Part of the Way with LBJ Slogan printed on a Students for a Democratic Society (SDS) button circulated during '64 election activities. The slogan "Part of the way with LBJ," was in support of Lyndon Johnson's pledge of not widening the war in Vietnam. The SDS was in agreement with that part of Johnson's platform, but was not very happy with the other parts of his platform dealing with civil rights and poverty. They believed the platform stand on those issues was too weak to accomplish any meaningful progress.

Partial Body Count A method used by American commanders in calculating total body count. Normally a whole body was used in totaling the count of enemy soldiers killed in a battle. In Vietnam the "partial body count" came into being. This method counted partial body remains as a whole body. For instance if two arms and a leg were found after an attack, the parts could indicate they were from three separate individuals or perhaps just one. In an effort to increase the body counts, some officers would claim three KIAs instead of one; statistically, it was more impressive. *See also* **Body Count, Confirms.**

Party-Pack (Kools, Marijuana Cigarettes, Decks) A pack of ten prerolled marijuana cigarettes, wrapped in plastic and sold by local Vietnamese vendors in some of the more industrious villes and shantytowns that sprang up outside the gates of U.S. bases. A variant of the party-pack was "Kools." Kools were regular cigarettes stuffed with a mixture of regular tobacco and marijuana. Some GIs rolled their own, but many of the village sources around U.S. bases also offered the Kools or "decks" for sale. *See also* **Marijuana, OJs.**

Passage to Freedom *see* **Operation Passage to Freedom**

Passage to Freedom Program (Catholic Refugee Program) U.S. sponsored program in '54 that provided refugees from North Vietnam food, clothing, medical aid and relocation assistance. Nearly one million North Vietnamese fled the North after the fall of the French and the temporary partitioning of North and South Vietnam. The U.S. also provided funding to assist the Ngo Dinh Diem government with its efforts to settle the refugees. Most of the refugees were Catholics, many fearful of the repression or reprisals that might be directed against them by the Ho Chi Minh government. Many of the rumors spread about the Ho government were generated by CIA agents in the north. *See also* **Black Psyche, Operation Passage to Freedom.**

Passive Light System *see* **Starlight Scope**

Pataugas *see* **NVA Boots**

Pate, General Rudolph *see* **Commandant**

Pathet Lao *see* **Lao Liberation Front**

Pathfinders *see* **Black Hats**

Patio *see* **Operation Patio**

Patricia Lynn *see* **Project Patricia Lynn**

Patrol Air Cushioned Vehicle *see* **PACV**

Patrol Base (PB, Platoon Patrol Base [PPB]) Small, temporary combat base established in enemy territory from which patrols and ambushes could be launched. U.S. patrol bases were generally company size and supplied by air. The bases were large enough to be defensible and small enough to be mobile. Platoons generally operated out of patrol bases during the day and returned before dark to pass the night. An LP, or two, and at least one squad size ambush from each platoon operated out of the PB during the night. Sometimes the company was split up and the platoons established small patrol bases (PPBs) one to three kilometers out from the company CP. *See also* **Harbour Site, Fire Base, Fire Support Base.**

Patrol Boat, River *see* **PBR Mark I/ II**

Patrol Craft *see* **PC**

Patrol Craft Fast *see* **PCF**

Patrol Gunboat, Motorized *see* **PG**

Patrol Motor Gunboat *see* **PG**

Patrol Patterns *see* **Cloverleaf, Checkerboard**

Patrol Seismic Intrusion Device *see* **Portable Seismic Intrusion Device**

Pattern Activity Analysis Jargon for the lengthy reports compiled by military computers regarding enemy activity and predictions of future activity. Various types of information were included in the reports analysis; such information included river traffic, identification check results, number of enemy contacts in an area, number of draft age males in a district or village, disposition of wood supplies (used for coffin making), sniper incidents, prisoner interrogations, ARVN defections, border sanctuary activity, etc. *See also* **Cu Chi Computer Center.**

Patti, Archimedes L.A. OSS Officer, became the first American to make official contact with Ho Chi Minh, April '45. Ho was leading a group of Vietnamese rebel communists against Japanese occupation forces in Indochina when Patti, on behalf of the U.S. government, recruited Ho to harass the Japanese and help rescue downed U.S. aircrews in the area. *See also* **Deer Teams, OSS.**

Patton Tank *see* **M-48A3 Tank**

Paul Doumer Bridge Strategic bridge crossing the Red River in NVN, less than 16kms from Hanoi; heart of NVN transportation system. Four of NVN's five major railroad lines crossed the mile-long, 19-span bridge. In March '65 the JCS urged President Johnson to strike at NVN's major rail lines and in particular at the Paul Doumer Bridge. The administration rejected the plan to bomb rail lines around Hanoi. The bridge was not attacked and brought down until August '67. The bridge was repaired, but follow-up air attacks brought the bridge down again. NVN opted not to repair it again until after the '68 bombing halt. In May '72 several spans of the bridge were destroyed during Operation Linebacker I. *See also* **Linebacker.**

Paul Revere (I–IV) *see* **Operation**

Paul Revere (I–IV)

Pave Eagle *see* **Operation Pave Eagle**

Pave Fire Code name for one of the laser bomb systems used by the Air Force in Vietnam. Pave Fire consisted of an aircraft mounted laser designator which "lit up" the target with a laser beam. Other aircraft in the attack group dropped "smart bombs" on the laser illuminated target. The smart bomb used the laser illuminated target for guidance. Laser guided bombs were extremely accurate and could be dropped at greater distances from the target, reducing the aircraft's vulnerability to enemy AA fires. *See also* **Smart Bombs, Laser Guided Bomb.**

Pave Nail (LORAN, Towel-Rack) Code name for the LORAN navigation equipment used on the OV-10 Bronco. The OV-10 operated with a crew of two. The aircraft featured long-range navigational equipment, a light intensified viewer, laser designator and an onboard navigation/targeting computer. LORAN equipment was used on various U.S. aircraft. The distinctive LORAN antennas used on the F-4 were nicknamed "towel-racks" by aircrews.

PAVN *see* **People's Army of North Vietnam**

Pay Advance (Advance, Temporary Advance) A monetary payment made to a soldier charged against his next regular pay period. Soldiers could request advances if they were taking leave in conjunction with their moving to a new duty assignment. Temporary advances against the soldier's pay were also granted if pay records were lost and he could prove he had not been paid for several months. Such proof was hard to come by if the pay records were lost or misplaced. When a soldier changed duty stations his finance and personnel records were usually sent ahead of him, and lost records were a constant problem. On some occasions the soldiers were allowed to hand-carry their records. During the Vietnam War Army pay records were not completely computerized and the only record of a soldier's last pay was in his finance record. Many a pay voucher disappeared from hand-carried finance records, between a soldier's last duty station and Vietnam, allowing the soldier to sometimes receive double pay for a month or two. *See also* **Finance, Advance Leave.**

Pay Voucher *see* **Finance**

Payback Slang for "revenge." *See also* **Get Some...**

PB *see* **Patrol Base**

PBDB *see* **Provisional Base Defense Battalion**

PBR Mark I/II (Patrol Boat, River [PBR]) The PBR Mark I was a 31-foot-long, fiberglass hulled, twin waterjet propelled patrol boat capable of 25 knots and armed with one twin .50cal machine gun in the bow and a single .50cal aft, an M-60 located amidship and one 40mm grenade launcher. The PBR Mark II was similar to the Mark I, with a slightly longer hull and the twin machine gun located closer to the bow of the boat. Both versions of the boat were radio and radar equipped. Some of the boats were eventually armed with such weapons as miniguns, flamethrowers, mortars and 20mm cannons. Although both versions had lightly armored hulls, they were still susceptible to damage by heavy automatic weapons and RPG fire. The PRB was the Navy's primary river patrol craft. *See also* **TF 116, Guntub.**

PBR Mini-Dock LCM-8 used as a mini-drydock to perform maintenance and repairs on Navy PBRs. The PBR was floated into the well of the LCM-8; when the water was pumped out the PBR was supported on skids in the well. The PBR mini-dock was used to support the PBRs of TF Clearwater that patrolled the Song Perfume and Song Cua Vet rivers in I Corps. The mini-dock was able to move between Tan My and Cua Vet, repairing the PBRs as it moved. *See also* **TF Clearwater.**

PC (Patrol Craft) Seagoing patrol ships used by the French and South Vietnamese navies in Vietnam. The 450-ton PC was armed with a 3-inch gun forward, one 40mm and four 20mm cannons. The PCs were used by the Vietnamese for coastal patrols.

PCs *see* **M-113**

PC-6 (Pilatus Porter) Swiss-made, single engine, prop-driven STOL utility transport. The PC-6 could take off and land on a rough strip less than 205 meters long, trans-

porting up to ten passengers or small cargo. The small craft was manufactured in America by Hiller Aircraft under the name Pilatus Porter, and had a maximum speed of 174mph and a range of 1,090kms. The PC-6 could be lightly armed and used in COIN operations. The CIA had several PC-6s in the inventory of its SEA airline, Air America. *See also* **Air America.**

PCF (Swift Boat, Patrol Craft Fast, Swifties) A patrol boat used by the Navy to patrol the inshore coastal waters and rivers of South Vietnam. The aluminum hulled Swift boat was 50 feet long, had a crew of 6, was capable of 25 knots and was armed with twin .50cal machine guns forward and a combination .50cal machine gun and 81mm mortar mounted aft. Individual crew weapons included the M-60 machine gun and M-79 grenade launcher. Swift crews were sometimes referred to as "Swifties." Swift boats carried HF and VHF-FM radios. *See also* **TF 115, Market Time, Game Warden.**

PCOD (Pussy Cutoff Date) Last day a GI could indulge in boom-boom with the Vietnamese women, and still have enough time to detect and treat any lingering cases of VD. The normal cutoff date was 6–8 weeks prior to the soldier's DEROS. U.S. military personnel rotating home were required to pass a VD test before they could leave Vietnam. If the test returned positive (VD found), their tour in-country was extended until the VD was treated and cleared up. *See also* **Rumors, Venereal Disease.**

PDF *see* **Principal Direction of Fire**

PDJ *see* **Plaines des Jarres**

PDL *see* **People's Democracy of Laos**

PDM *see* **Portable Differential Magnetometer**

PE Scope *see* **Mosin-Nagant Rifle**

Peace Corps — Not Marine Corps One of many antiwar movement slogans aimed at American servicemen en route to Vietnam.

Peace Freak *see* **Peacenik**

Peace Movement (Antiwar Movement) Organized antiwar movements started about '64, aimed at ending American involvement in Vietnam and bringing U.S.

troops home, leaving Vietnam to resolve its own issues. The movement was borne out of small groups, many of them students active in other areas of social reform, moving towards civil rights and liberties and a more democratic society. As the war went on the size of the movement grew, fueled in part by the actions of the American government and its use of secrecy, misrepresentation and manipulation. In the beginning support for the antiwar groups came mostly from college campuses. As the war continued and the American people became more disillusioned with the war and its effects, the antiwar movement secured a larger base of support: government employees, scholars, economists, blue collar workers and the media. Some factions of the movement supported North Vietnam; others wanted an end to the war; still others just wanted our troops to come home and the killing to stop. For the most part the movement was peaceful, although there were increasing instances of violence. The government attempted to explain its position in Vietnam, but it was unable to maintain the popular support of its people. In the mid-sixties the peace movement and antiwar movement were blending together. As this blending was taking place, the hippie movement was growing. Eventually the peace movement and the hippie movement tended to blend together with the general public viewing the peaceniks and the hippies as one and the same. *See also* **Hippie Movement.**

Peace Offensive   Reference to the Johnson administration's attempts during the end of '65, and the beginning of '66 to induce Hanoi to begin conditional peace negotiations.

Peace Sign   *see*   **Fuck-Peace Sign**

Peace Talks   *see*   **Paris Accords**

Peace Through Fire Superiority   GI helmet graffitti seen around many fire support bases.

Peace with Honor   The aim of U.S. peace negotiations with North Vietnam, as coined by President Lyndon Johnson. After Richard Nixon became president in '68 his policy toward Vietnam was an "honorable peace." *See also* **Honorable Peace.**

Peacemakers of the 334th Avn   *see*

334th Aviation Company, Camp Woodson

Peaceniks (Peace Freak)   Nickname for members of the peace movement. The name generally applied to anyone who opposed the Vietnam War, who was under the age of thirty. *See also* **Peace Movement.**

Peanut   *see*   **KIA/WIA Code Names**

Peanut Butter   Came to Vietnam in the form of a 2 ½-inch diameter × ½-inch high, 1 ½-ounce tin found inside selected boxes of C-rations; it was one of three spreads packed in every box of Cs. High in protein and an excellent lightweight energy food, peanut butter did have its down side: eating it made you very thirsty. In the field, good drinking water was scarce, so wiser GIs avoided peanut butter when water supplies were a problem. Peanut butter did have other uses. When mixed with military issued insect repellent and ignited, it would burn for several minutes and could be used to heat rations or water. Peanut butter also served as a field expedient, temporarily causing constipation and marginal relief from diarrhea. *See also* **B-2 Unit.**

Pearl Beer   *see*   **Vietnamese Beer**

Pearl of the East   *see*   **Saigon**

Peasants   *see*   **Nhaques**

Peckerwood   *see*   **Caucasian**

Pedicab (Rickshaw, Cyclo)   Vietnamese taxicab, also known as a "cyclo." The pedicab was a three-wheeled bicycle with two wheels in front on either side of the basket chair used for passengers, and one wheel in back, also loosely known as a "rickshaw." The operator sat over the third wheel at the rear and provided the locomotion. Steering was accomplished by turning the front of the cab. Some of the cabs were fitted with an accordion-like top that could be swung into position to provide the passengers with partial protection from the rain. The pedicab was a common sight in the cities and larger towns of Vietnam. The true rickshaw was a two-wheeled carriage powered by the operator running along the street pulling the cab behind. *See also* **Lambretta.**

Pedro   Nickname for the survival winch mounted on some Air Force rescue helicopters operated in Vietnam. "Pedro" could be used to extract downed flyers, or a wire-basket stretcher could be attached to remove casualties when the helicopter was unable to land. Most Army helicopters, including "Dustoffs," were not equipped with a winching device. In situations where a winch extraction was necessary Air Force "Pedro" equipped choppers were requested. Air Force SAR helicopters were based at the larger airfields such as Tan Son Nhut, Phang Rang, Tuy Hoa, Phu Cat and Da Nang. *See also* **Dustoff.**

Peers Inquiry   May '70 report on the investigation of the '68 My Lai Incident conducted under the direction of Lt. Gen. W.R. Peers. The report resulted in the filing of criminal charges against several officers of the 11th Light Infantry Brigade and members of the platoon that murdered Vietnamese civilians at My Lai. *See also* **My Lai, Calley.**

Pegasus   *see*   **Operation Pegasus–Lam Son 207A**

Pegged Fatigues (Designer Fatigues) Tailored fatigues. Most ARVN soldiers wore pegged fatigues. The fatigues were tailored so they fit very close to the body unlike the baggy, loose fitting fatigues worn by Americans in the field. Some U.S. soldiers in the larger base areas and cities also had their fatigues altered to make them form-fitting. Tight fitting pants tended to be uncomfortable for prolonged field operations, and were avoided by U.S. grunts.

Pelican   *see*   **CH-3**

Pencil Pushers   *see*   **Rear Echelon Personnel**

Penerine   *see*   **Peta-Prime**

Penetrator (Forest Penetrator, Jungle Penetrator, JP)   Rescue device attached by cable to a helicopter and dropped through dense jungle canopy, allowing a soldier to be lifted from areas too dense for the helicopter to land. The penetrator was about three feet long and constructed of heavy metal. The blunt pointed nose of the device allowed it to break through jungle canopy when it was dropped from the helicopter. A fold-down metal seat was attached to the sides of the penetrator to accommodate a single soldier. The soldier, or a body, could be strapped in place and lifted out of the jungle. *See also* **Horse Collar.**

Penicillin   *see*   **Tetracycline**

Penis (Tool, Dong, Tube Steak, Dick, Cock, Prick, Bird, Dork, Hon Dai) Some of the more colorful names for the "male member." The Vietnamese euphemistically referred to the penis as a "bird," and "hon dai" [hon die] was Vietnamese for testicles. Vietnamese whores often complained that American penises were too large; they used that argument as leverage to negotiate higher prices to be paid by the GI. The same argument was used to avoid a GI's advances. *See also* **Shrinking Bird Disease, Mutilations.**

Pennsylvania   *see*   **Operation Pennsylvania**

Penny-Nickle-Nickle   *see*   **M-114A1 or M-109 155mm SPA**

Pentagon   *see*   **Puzzle Palace**

Pentagon East (MACV Headquarters) Nickname for the U.S. MACV Headquarters complex located near Tan Son Nhut Air Base, in Saigon. After the withdrawal of U.S. combat troops in '73, the complex became headquarters center for the DAO. The complex was destroyed by U.S. Marine demolitions April 29, 1975, as Saigon fell to the NVA.

Pentagon Papers (The History of U.S. Decision Making Process on Vietnam) Top secret history of the U.S. government's decision making regarding SVN from '54 to '68, commissioned by Secretary of Defense, Robert McNamara in '67. The report, entitled "The History of U.S. Decision Making Process on Vietnam," was completed in '68 and remained secret until it was leaked to the press in '71 by Daniel Ellsberg, one of the coauthors of the report. The report, nicknamed the "Pentagon Papers," detailed the government's political and military decision making policies on Vietnam and listed, in detail, classified sources and methods of intelligence gathering used to make those decisions and create the report. The report indicated the government's acknowledgment of opinions by its experts voicing doubts about the U.S.'s ability to win militarily in SVN. The report indicated that the government had misled the public on the extent of U.S. involvement in Vietnam prior to '64. Copies of the secret documents were given to the *New York Times* which began publication of the report. The Nixon administration tried unsuccessfully to stop the publications. Ellsberg and Anthony Russo were tried in '72 for conspiracy, espionage and the theft of government documents. The case was dismissed in '73 because of misconduct by the government in processing the case; White House staff members, with the help of the CIA, had burglarized Ellsberg's psychiatrist's office in '71 searching for evidence. Some evidence in the hands of the administration (FBI wiretap transcripts) mysteriously disappeared before it could be entered into the trial proceedings. Another reason for the dismissal of the case was misconduct on the part of the Nixon White House which offered the trial judge the directorship of the FBI in return for a favorable ruling. *See also* Jason.

Pentagon Papers Trial *see* **Pentagon Papers**

Pentomic Division A '50s plan drawn up by General Maxwell Taylor to reorganize U.S. Army units to meet battlefield conditions in the atomic age. Each division would contain five battle groups; each group consisted of five companies; a company would consist of five platoons. This dispersal of troops and leadership was to insure survival of the combat force. The plan never went into effect because of various command problems.

PEO *see* **Program Evaluations Office**

People Detector (Bedbug People Detector) U.S. DOD researchers attempted to develop a device that could be used to detect the presence of the Viet Cong. A device that literally consisted of a microphone and headset attached to a jar of bedbugs. In theory when the bedbugs got near the Viet Cong they would get excited and make audible clicking noises. The noises would be picked up by the microphone, amplified and heard through the headset. Troops moving through the jungle could use the device to locate the enemy. The project failed when researchers realized the bedbugs could not distinguish between friendly and enemy Vietnamese. The bugs also had a short life span and their excitability could not be guaranteed. *See also* XM-2, Lice.

People Sniffer *see* **XM-2, XM-3**

People's Army of North Vietnam (PAVN, NVA Army) Official name of the North Vietnamese Army. The NVA soldier was generally well trained and well equipped (compared to the ARVN); he was organized and disciplined, a regular, full-time soldier. In the early days of the war the infiltration trip to SVN took several months, a trip made on bicycle and on foot, and eventually by truck. During the Final Offensive in '75, there were more than half a million NVA troops in SVN. By '75 the NVA consisted of 4 armored, 20 infantry, 15 SAM, 10 artillery and 24 AA regiments.

People's Democracy of Laos (PDL) When the communists seized power in Laos in August '75, they renamed the country the People's Democracy of Laos. *See also* Lao Liberation Front, Laos, Meo.

People's Liberation Armed Forces (PLAF, People's Liberation Army [PLA]) The official name of the military army of the National Liberation Front (NLF). The Viet Cong were the actual combat element of the NLF, fighting in the role of the insurgent guerrilla until the NLF Army could take over the war effort. The PLA existed in the form of main force Viet Cong divisions and regiments that operated from strongholds in remote areas of South Vietnam or from sanctuaries located along the Cambodian border. *See also* Viet Cong.

People's Liberation Army *see* **People's Liberation Armed Forces**

People's Party *see* **Spock, Dr. Benjamin**

People's Republic of China (PRC, Red China, China, Trung Cong) The largest supplier of military equipment to the North Vietnamese. Communist Chinese weapons and equipment were commonly referred to as Chi-Com. The Soviet Union and other Warsaw Pact countries also supplied large quantities of weapons and materials to the North Vietnamese. One of the fears of the U.S. government during the early years of the war was the possibility of the PRC sending in troops to aid NVN, as had been the case in North Korea. China and the Vietnamese had long been enemies even though they shared similar communist ideology. NVN neither sought nor would have willingly accepted any large scale troop intervention by the PRC, had the Chinese been inclined or capable of such intervention. Trung Cong, Vietnamese for "Communist China."

People's Republic of Kampuchea *see* **Vietnamese Invasion of Cambodia**

People's Revolutionary Party *see* **Lao Dong, Viet Cong Infrastructure**

People's Self-Defense Force (PSDF, Militia, Hamlet Militia) SVN militia force (Dan Quan) that consisted of men outside of draft age (16–17 and 39–50) to provide defense at the hamlet level. Unpaid, poorly equipped and virtually untrained, the PSDF leaders tended to be corrupt and interested in their own comforts, using their position to increase their own power. All SVN males under the age of 50 and not eligible for the draft were required to participate in the PSDF. The PSDF was designed to fill the gap left by RF/PF forces which were not stationed in every village. The PSDF was totally ineffective as a defensive force and was further weakened by the large numbers of VC that were secretly part of the force.

Pepper Frags *see* **U.S. Frags**

Peppering the LZ *see* **Prep**

Peregrine Group (Asian-American Special Forces) U.S. Special Forces program that created an all Asian-American force to be used for covert operations in Vietnam. USSF troopers deployed to SVN in late '67 and operated along the Cambodian border of III and IV Corps. Because of their Asian appearance it was hoped the USSF troops could get closer to the VC. The force usually dressed in black pajamas, was heavily armed and sought out the VC and their supporters. The group also worked with the PRU of the Phoenix Program.

Perfect Bush *see* **Ambush**

Perforated Steel Plate (PSP) U.S. manufactured reinforced steel plate used to make hard stands and helipads. The plates were 3 × 5 feet and weighed 100 pounds. The plates were also used for bunker construction and bolt on armor for trucks and jeeps. Another version of the PSP was reinforced steel planking. The 2 × 12-foot planks were reinforced with steel bars along the plank's width. Like the steel plate the PSP planks were used in bunker construc-

tion, and cut and mounted on armored vehicles and river craft for additional protection.

Perfume River (Hue River, Song Ta Trach) Flowed through the heart of Hue City in I Corps and opened on the South China Sea 8kms east of Hue. The Perfume was the main shipping channel used to move supplies to the city. Because of increased enemy attempts to close the river, a U.S. riverine patrol and task force was formed to keep the river open. *See also* **TF Clearwater, River Division 55.**

Perimeter (Perim) Military abbreviation for the outer edge or outer line of defense around a base or area.

Perishable Food *see* **Class I Provisions**

Permanent Party Term used to distinguish between troops assigned duty (permanent) at a base, and troops that were in transit through, or only temporarily assigned to the base. Permanent party generally referred to soldiers assigned to a specific base, as opposed to troops who rotated through the base on a temporary basis. On Army training bases the term distinguished between the training cadre and the trainees who were processed through the facility. *See also* **Holding Barracks.**

Permanent Profile *see* **Medical Profile**

Pershing *see* **Operation Pershing**

Persistent CS (CS-1) Crystal form of CS irritant used to make CS gas. The crystals could be sprinkled on the ground causing excessive irritation upon contact with the skin. The CS-1 crystals were used in Vietnam to contaminate enemy bunkers and abandoned fire bases. Enemy tunnels were sometimes contaminated with the crystals. A length of det cord would be laid along the floor of the tunnel and covered with the crystals; when the cord was detonated the crystals would be imbedded in the tunnel walls, rendering the tunnel temporarily hostile to the enemy (effective underground for about a week). The crystals were sometimes used around the defensive perimeter of a fire base to make the job of enemy infiltrators more difficult. *See also* **CS Gas.**

Personal Engineering Implement *see* **Entrenching Tool**

Peta-Prime (Penerine) Oil based coating spread on helipads and open areas in base camps to reduce the dust blown about by helicopters. The black sealant tended to get very sticky and messy in the heat, and stuck to clothing and equipment. The sealant was also known as "penerine" and was applied in the dry season when dust was at its corrosive best.

Petroleum, Oil, Lubricants *see* **POL**

Petty Officer First Class *see* **Staff Sergeant**

Petty Officer Second Class *see* **Buck Sergeant**

Petty Officer Third Class *see* **E-4**

PF *see* **Popular Forces**

PFC *see* **Private First Class**

PG (Patrol Motor Gunboat [PGM]; Patrol Gunboat, Motorized) American made motorized patrol boat used by the South Vietnamese Navy for coastal and inlet patrol duties. The 95-ton, twin diesel patrol ship was armed with one 40mm cannon, two 20mm cannons and two .50cal machine guns.

PGM *see* **PG, Precision-Guided Munitions**

Pham Van Dong One of the founders of the Lao Dong, the Vietnamese Communist Party. Dong served under Ho Chi Minh as North Vietnam's prime minister from '54 to '86. Early in the war with America, Dong said "Americans do not like long, inconclusive wars—and this [the war in Vietnam] is going to be a long, inconclusive war. Thus we are sure to win in the end." Put another way, all the communists had to do to win in Vietnam was simply survive the American occupation. *See also* **War of Attrition.**

Phan Rang Port city and provincial capital of Ninh Thuan Province. Phan Rang was located 55kms south of the U.S. base at Cam Ranh Bay, II Corps. Phan Rang served as a major Air Force base from '66 to '72, and as Vietnam Headquarters for the USAF 14th Commandos, 35th Tactical Fighter Wing and 315th Tactical Airlift Wing.

Phan Thiet Provincial capital of Binh Thuan Province, located on the coast,

145kms east of Saigon, II Corps. Phan Thiet served as a base of operations for several U.S. units and was the Vietnamese's main shipyard for the construction of junk ships used by the coastal Junk Force.

Phantom *see* **F-4**

Phien *see* **Opium, Marijuana**

PHILCAG *see* **1st Philippine Civic Action Group**

Philippine Civic Action Group *see* **1st Philippine Civic Action Group**

Philippines (Subic Bay Naval Base, Clark Air Force Base) U.S. military facilities, located in the Philippines, which provided logistic and combat support to U.S. forces operating in Vietnam. The Philippines, located less than 1,300kms from Vietnam, served as a major staging base for U.S. air and naval forces en route to Vietnam, as well as ship repair facilities for the 7th Fleet. The Philippine government of Ferdinand Marcos also provided a small complement of combat, engineering and medical troops to South Vietnam as part of the 1st Philippine Civic Action Group. After the fall of SVN in '75, Soviet air and naval forces were awarded the use of Cam Ranh Bay and Da Nang as bases of operation, making U.S. bases in the Philippines even more critical to U.S. security. *See also* **1st Philippine Civic Action Group.**

Phillips *see* **LZ Phillips**

Phnom Penh *see* **Cambodia, Operation Eagle Pull**

Phoenix Program (Phuong Hoang, Pacification by Assassination, Assassination Bureau) Phoenix (Phuong Hoang), part of the '68 US/GVN Accelerated Pacification program, was designed to identify members of the VC and VCI, and capture or eliminate them, thus allowing the GVN pacification program a chance to succeed. The CIA sponsored program ended in '72 and was accused of being an assassination bureau, used for reprisals against the VC, GVN critics and personal enemies. Torture was common, and "elimination" was the preferred method of dealing with Phoenix's suspects. A quota system relating to the number of VC and VCS turned up by Phoenix teams resulted in further program abuses. Sometimes referred to as Pacification by Assassination. *See also* **CORDS, Do Unto the VC. . . , Colby, ICEX, PRU.**

Phonetic Alphabet *see* **Alphabet**

Phou Pha The   U.S. radio navigational outpost in the mountains of Laos. The station provided navigation aid to U.S. aircraft attacking NVN targets in Hanoi's Red River Valley area. The NVA made several attempts to push the station off the mountain. In February '68 the NVA successfully attacked, and overran the outpost, with three battalions of the 766th NVA Regiment. The outpost was defended by a small force of Meo tribesmen and the U.S. Air Force technicians who operated the equipment.

Phougas   *see*   **Fou Gas**

Phrases   *see*   **Military Paraphraseology**

Phu Bai   *see*   **Camp Eagle**

Phu Cat   Town located 29kms northwest of Qui Nhon in Binh Dinh Province, II Corps. Located at Phu Cat was a U.S. Air Force base that provided Tac Air support to friendly units in the area.

Phu Cuong   Capital of Binh Duong Province, III Corps. Phu Cuong was located 13kms north of Saigon.

Phu Dung   *see*   **Operation Shining Brass**

Phu Loi   Town located 15kms north of Saigon in Binh Duong Province, III Corps. Phu Loi served as one of the major base camps of the 1st Infantry Division, home of the division's 1st Aviation Battalion, division artillery, and the 1st Squadron/4th Cavalry. The squadron provided the division with ground and air reconnaissance. *See also* **Viet Cong Phu Loi Battalion.**

Phu Loi Battalion   *see*   **Viet Cong Phu Loi Battalion**

Phu My   *see*   **Crescent, The**

Phu My Hung   *see*   **Ho Bo Woods**

Phu Nu Can Bo (Viet Cong Cadre Girl) Vietnamese phrase meaning "Viet Cong cadre girl."

Phu Quoc Island (Dao Phu Quoc, To Chau Training Center)   Large island used by USSF to conduct a limited basic training program for CIDG troops, located in the Gulf of Thailand, 37kms west of SVN's mainland, less than 14kms from the Cambo-

dian mainland. The 8-week CIDG course ended with the trainees participating in actual operations against the enemy along the Cambodian border in IV Corps. A small training center was also opened at To Chau in Kien Giang Province, IV Corps. Phu Quoc's proximity to enemy forces along the border in Cambodia and the lack of U.S. support units in the southwestern IV Corps area made it difficult, and at times impossible, for Army medevacs to remove combat casualties from the island. During the collapse of SVN in '75 several thousand refugees were relocated to the island until they could be evacuated.

Phu Tai   Rear support base for the 173d Airborne Brigade, located north of Qui Nhon, Binh Dinh Province, II Corps.

Phu Vinh   Provincial capital of Vinh Binh Province, IV Corps, wedged between two of the main branches of the Mekong River. Phu Vinh was located 47kms south of My Tho.

Phuc Yen   *see*   **MiG Airfields**

Phung Hoang   *see*   **Phoenix Program**

Phuoc Binh (Rocket Alley, Song Be) Provincial capital of Phuoc Long Province, III Corps. Phuoc Binh was located 120kms north of Saigon and 25kms from the Cambodian border in the foothills of the Central Highlands. The border area and the mountains of Phuoc Long were a longtime stronghold of NVA/VC forces operating in the II/III Corps area. Phuoc Binh was repeatedly attacked by enemy forces and was rocketed so often it was nicknamed "Rocket Alley." During the NVA's Final Offensive in '75, Phuoc Binh was the first provincial capital to fall. Corruption was reportedly so bad among the ARVN at Phuoc Binh that ARVN infantry units had to pay ARVN artillery units in order to receive fire support. Phuoc Binh was also referred to as Song Be. *See also* **Corruption.**

Phuoc Le (Baria)   Provincial capital of Phuoc Tuy in III Corps. Phuoc Le was located 62kms southeast of Saigon and 17kms northeast of Vung Tau. Phuoc Le was also known as Baria.

Phuoc Long Province   In January '74 Phuoc Long Province, III Corps, became the first of South Vietnam's provinces to fall under complete military and political control of the NVA/VC. The province was taken by elements of the 3d, 7th and 9th Viet Cong Infantry divisions. The capital of Phuoc Long Province was Phuoc Binh.

Phuoc Thanh Province   Former South Vietnamese province located in III Corps. The province was centered about 75kms northeast of Saigon. In '66 its territorial and administrative boundaries were dissolved and it ceased to exist as a province. The provincial boundaries of Phuoc Long, Long Khanh, Binh Duong and Bien Hoa were expanded to include the former territory of Phuoc Thanh. *See also* **Province.**

Phuoc Thuan Peninsula   Peninsula centered 12kms southeast of Chu Lai, extending northward. The northern tip of the peninsula was due east of the U.S. air base at Chu Lai. The entire peninsula was a VC base area until Marines began operations in '65. The first major operation on the peninsula was a combined air and amphibious assault code-named Operation Starlite. *See also* **Operation Starlite.**

Phuoc Vinh   Town located 38kms north of Bien Hoa, Binh Duong Province, III Corps. Phuoc Vinh was located along Highway 14 and served as the base camp for the 1st Brigade/1st Infantry Division. *See also* **War Zone D.**

Phuong Ho   *see*   **Horseshoe, The**

Phuong Hoang   *see*   **Phoenix Program**

Phy Loi   Resettlement (refugee) camp established to house the previous residents of Ben Suc after they were relocated by elements of the U.S. 1st Infantry Division and ARVN troops. Phy Loi was located near Phu Cuong, west of Bien Hoa in III Corps. *See also* **Ben Suc, Operation Cedar Falls.**

Physical Training (PT)   Military version of calisthenics or exercise.

Piasters (P, Dong, Vietnamese Money)   Vietnamese money came in paper denominations (piasters) and coins (dong). Compared to American money, a piaster was worth less than one cent; one dong was about one-twentieth of a cent, depending on the rate of exchange. In '69, 120 piasters were worth one U.S. dollar. Military scrip could be converted to piasters, and vice versa. The black market exchange rate was much higher than the official rate, and the black

market exchange rate on U.S. greenbacks was even higher. Under military order, all U.S. personnel were required to exchange their greenback currency for military scrip on entry into Vietnam. *See also* **Military Payment Certificates.**

Picardy   *see*   **FSB Picardy**

Pickle Switch   *see*   **Pickling**

Pickling (Bomb Release Switch, Pickle Switch)   Slang reference by pilots to the release of ordnance (bombs and canisters) over a target, one at a time in close sequence, on one pass. Such a release allowed the ordnance to cover a larger linear area. Pickling of bombs was used against tree lines, enemy bunker lines, or as a blocking screen when a wide area needed to be attacked. A "pickle switch" was the nickname for the bomb-release switch located on the control stick of a fighter-bomber aircraft.

Pickup Zone (PZ, Papa Zulu)   Designated area used to pick up troops by helicopter, generally in preparation for a heli-mobile operation. The PZ was usually a secured area near the perimeter of a base camp, large enough to accommodate several helicopters at one time, and secure enough to allow troops to relax before they would be picked up.

Picolonic Acid   *see*   **Agent White**

A-Piece-of-Tail   *see*   **Boom-Boom**

Pierce Arrow   *see*   **Operation Pierce Arrow**

Pig, The   *see*   **M-60, M-79**

Pig Shit Run   Part of the duties performed by the first American helicopter units assigned to Vietnam in '62 included the transport of supplies to remote government outposts. The helicopters transported ammunition and the typical foodstuffs (packaged goods, rice, etc.) as well as live animals such as chickens, ducks and pigs. The Marine helicopter crews nicknamed such supply runs "Pig Shit Runs" because of the lasting aroma the pigs left on the floor of the helicopter. The animals were loaded aboard in bamboo cages with less than watertight bottoms, and the dripping pig waste tended to filter into the floor crevices of the Marines' H-34s.

Pigasus   *see*   **Yippie**

Piggyback 60s *see* **XM-23 Machine Gun**

Pilatus Porter *see* **PC-6**

Pile-On Nickname for a tactic employed by American units in Vietnam. When a friendly unit made contact with the enemy, heavy firepower was called in to pin the enemy in position. Reinforcements were quickly deployed in an effort to completely overwhelm the enemy and keep him from breaking contact and slipping away. Air and armored cavalry were most effective at "piling on," because of the speed with which they could be deployed.

Pilot Systems Operator *see* **Weapons Systems Operator**

Pineapple Frag *see* **MK-2 Hand Grenade**

Pineapple Stick Grenade *see* **Type 59 Grenade**

Pinhead Caps *see* **Baseball Cap**

Pink Light *see* **Infrared**

Pink Rose *see* **Operation Pink Rose**

Pink Sheet Nickname for secret documents or communications. Such documents and communications were usually covered by a "pink" cover sheet with the security clearance "SECRET" or "TOP SECRET" stamped on them.

Pink Team *see* **Hunter Killer Team**

Pink Ville (My Lai) Nickname for the My Lai area, called Pink Ville because it happened to be colored pink on the military maps used by the Americal Division units operating in the area. *See also* **My Lai.**

PIO *see* **Joint U.S. Public Affairs Office**

PIOCC *see* **DIOCC**

Pioneer Commander (Pioneer Contender, USS Miller, Transcolorado) The *Pioneer Commander, Pioneer, Transcolorado* and the USS *Miller* were four of the merchant vessels that participated in the evacuation of refugees from Da Nang in March '75 as the city was near capture by the North Vietnamese during their Final Offensive. The *Pioneer Commander* was the last ship to leave Da Nang before the city fell to the communists. The ships were under contract to the Military Sealift Command, spe-

cifically assigned for evacuation duties. Refugees evacuated from Da Nang were taken to Cam Ranh Bay. *See also* **Military Sealift Command.**

Pioneer Contender *see* **Pioneer Commander**

Pipe (Smoking) (Bong) A "bong" was a native Vietnamese pipe used for smoking opium and marijuana. Constructed of a long bamboo tube, sealed at one end with a small hole in the top of the tube near the sealed end. The burning opium or marijuana smoke was sucked through the small hole by the smoker at the open end of the bong. U.S. soldiers used various types of bongs while in Vietnam. A variant of the bong was the barrel of a shotgun, called "shot-gunning." *See also* **Shot-Gun.**

Pipe Cleaning *see* **Prostitute**

Pipe Stem *see* **Operation Pipe Stem**

Pipes *see* **Bowls**

Pipesmoke *see* **CH-47**

Pipper (Target Indicator) Nickname for the visual gunsight target indicator seen on the pilot's targeting screen in fighter/bomber aircraft. When the "pipper" dot was superimposed on the target the aircraft's guns or rockets were aimed for the kill.

Piranha *see* **Operation Piranha**

Piss-Cutter *see* **Cunt Cap**

Piss-Pot *see* **GI Helmet**

Piss-Tube (Pisser, Urinal) Vertical tube, partially buried, used for a urinal in the field at small base camps. Fecal waste was kept separate from urine waste to prevent the cutoff 55-gallon drums (honey pots) used for the latrine from filling up too quickly. The honey pots were removed daily and their contents of waste burned with diesel fuel. The burning process was greatly hampered if the honey pots also contained large amounts of urine. A "piss-tube" was also slang for a mortar tube. *See also* **Mortar.**

Pissed (Case-of-the-Ass, Jaws-Tight, Tight-Jawed, Got-the-Ass, On-the-Rag) Slang for being upset, angry, or not too pleased with a situation. A situation or individual that makes you angry "gives-you-the-ass." This could range from mild displeasure to almost psychotic hostility. Someone being "on-the-rag" signified the individual was irritable, upset, or just basically in a bad mood.

Pisser *see* **Bummer, Piss-Tube**

Pistolet Makarova *see* **Type 59 Pistol**

Pistolet Mitrailleur 1949 *see* **MAT49 SMG**

Pistolet-Pulemyot Shpagina 1941 SMG *see* **Type 50 SMG**

Pistols Various types of pistols were used by combat and police forces in Vietnam. The most widely distributed American pistol was the .45cal and the most widely used NVA/VC pistol was the Chinese Type 51. *See also* **M-1911A1, Type 51 Pistol, Type 59 Pistol, L9A1 Pistol.**

Pith Helmet *see* **NVA Helmet**

PJs *see* **Aerospace Rescue and Recovery Service**

PLA/PLAF *see* **People's Liberation Armed Forces**

Plain of Reeds (Plaine des Joncs) A large grassy plain located along the SVN/Cambodian border, west of Saigon, in the northern part of the Mekong Delta. The plain covered over 6,400 square kilometers in the provinces of Kien Phong and Kien Tuong, IV Corps, also extending into parts of Long An and Hau Nghia provinces. The plain served as a major VC base and was one of the southern termini of the Ho Chi Minh Trail. The eastern edge of the Plain was marked by the Song Vam Co Dong River and the Mekong marked the western edge. The French called it the Plaine des Joncs.

Plaine des Joncs *see* **Plain of Reeds**

Plaines des Jarres (Laotian Highlands, PDJ) Remote area of Laos mostly inhabited by the Meo mountain tribes. Many of the Meo tribes in the area were organized to fight the communist Pathet Lao, who were supported by the NVA. The Pathet Lao pressed to take control of Laos from the Royal Lao Government. The Meos were trained by the CIA/USSF in a program similar to the Montagnard CIDG program in South Vietnam. After years of fighting the Pathet Lao/NVA were able to overcome the Meos, led by Gen. Vang Pao, and the Royal

Laotian Army, putting Laos under total communist rule in '75. *See also* **Meo, Laos.**

Plains, The *see* **Bong Son**

Plantation, The *see* **Hanoi Hilton, II Field Force**

Plateau du Darlac *see* **Central Highlands**

Plateau Du Mnong *see* **Mnong Plateau**

Platoon (Plt) A basic infantry unit consisting of 22–40 men, usually commanded by a lieutenant, with a sergeant as second in command. A U.S. gunship platoon in Vietnam consisted of 6 helicopter gunships. A tank platoon consisted of 3–5 tanks. An infantry company consisted of 2–4 platoons usually configured as 3 rifle or maneuver platoons and a weapons or support platoon. In Vietnam, line platoons rarely operated at full strength, their actual strength being closer to 20–35 men.

Platoon Leader (Plt Ldr) Leader of a platoon size unit. In Vietnam, U.S. platoons were commanded by 1st and 2nd lieutenants. On occasions when there was a shortage of officers, sergeants were placed in command of line platoons. Authorized infantry platoon strength was 43–45 men, but in line units the actual strength was between 20–35 men.

Platoon Patrol Base *see* **Patrol Base**

Platoon Sergeant *see* **E-7**

Platypus *see* **Operation Platypus**

Play Money *see* **Military Payment Certificates**

Playboy of Paris *see* **Bao Dai**

Please *see* **Cam On**

Plebiscite, 1956 According to the terms of the '54 Geneva Accords, a nationwide election was to take place in '56 for the Vietnamese people to determine which political power would govern Vietnam. Vietnam was temporarily partitioned at the 17th Parallel, with Ho Chi Minh's communist party in control of the north and the anticommunist government of Bao Dai/Diem in the south. SVN and the U.S. did not sign the '54 Geneva Accords and claimed the provisions of the Accords were not binding upon them. The '56 national vote never took place and the NVA/VC stepped up their efforts to take control of SVN.

Plei Do Lim   *see*   **Plei Lim**

Plei Lim (Plei Do Lim)   One of the 4th Infantry Division's base camps, located 20kms southeast of Pleiku, II Corps.

Plei Me Special Forces Camp   U.S. Special Forces Camp located near Plei Me, 50kms southwest of Pleiku, in the Central Highlands of II Corps. The camp was attacked by units of the 32d, 33d and 66th NVA regiments in the first large scale offensive in South Vietnam by NVA troops. To counter the NVA attack on Plei Me the newly arrived U.S. 1st Cavalry Division engaged the NVA. *See also* **Battle of Ia Drang, Ia Drang Valley.**

Pleiku (Rocket City)   Provincial capital of Pleiku Province in the Central Highlands, II Corps. The February '65 attack by the VC on the U.S. compound at Camp Holloway served as partial justification for expanded air strikes against NVN in '65. Pleiku served as ARVN II Corps HQs, as a major U.S. air base, and as a major HQ for US/ARVN units in the area. During the NVA Final Offensive in '75, the ARVNs abandoned Pleiku and the Central Highlands on orders from President Thieu. Because of its proximity to the border (60kms) and the Ho Chi Minh Trail, Pleiku was often rocketed by the NVA/VC, and came to be nicknamed "Rocket City." Pleiku was also noted for the fine red dust that filtered into everything: animate and inanimate. *See also* **Camp Holloway, New Pleiku.**

Plt Ldr   *see*   **Platoon Leader**

Plt   *see*   **Platoon**

PMD-6/7 Antipersonnel Mine   Soviet made antipersonnel mines used by the NVA/VC. The mine consisted of explosives in a small wooden box, detonated by a fuse mechanism. The PMD-7 was $6 \times 2 \times 2$ inches and weighed one pound. The PMD-6 was slightly larger and used a seven pound explosive charge. *See also* **Booby Trap.**

PMN Antipersonnel Mine   Soviet nonmetallic antipersonnel mine. The plastic mine was cylinder shaped, 4.5 inches in diameter, 2.2 inches high and weighed 1.8

pounds. Detonation was by means of a pressure plate located at the top of the mine. Since the mine was not made of metal it could not be detected by the metal detectors used by U.S. Engineer troops during mine clearing operations. *See also* **Booby Trap.**

Pneumatic Mattress   *see*   **Rubber Bitch**

Poags   *see*   **Rear-Echelon-Mother-Fuckers**

Pocket Belt   *see*   **Belts, Machine Gun**

Pocket Money   *see*   **Operation Freedom Train**

Pod   *see*   **Blivet**

Pogey Bait   Marine term for any foodstuffs, candy, drinks or goodies offered to clerks or other rear echelon personnel, in trade for a favor or administrative help with a task. *See also* **Rear-Echelon-Mother-Fuckers.**

Pogues   *see*   **Rear-Echelon-Mother-Fuckers**

Point, The   *see*   **West Point Military Academy**

Point Detonation Fuse   *see*   **VT Round**

Point Welcome, U.S. Coast Guard Cutter   *see*   **CGC Point Welcome**

Pointman   *see*   **Walking Point**

Poison   *see*   **Resource Management, Defoliation**

Poison Ivy Division   *see*   **4th Infantry Division**

Pok (Siesta)   "Pok" Montagnard word for their 2–3 hour afternoon nap or "siesta."

POL   Military abbreviation of "Petroleum, Oil, Lubricants."

POL Depot   *see*   **Tank Farm**

Pol Pot (Saloth Sar)   Leader of the Khmer Rouge, the Cambodian Communist Party. Pol Pot led his troops to victory over the anticommunist Army of Cambodia in '75. He was educated in Paris, and between '70 and '75 received support from NVN in his attempt to take over Cambodia. In his effort to achieve the "Perfect State," more than 2 million Cambodians were exterminated and millions more sent to reeducation camps. In '78 the Vietnamese Army invaded

Cambodia, drove out Pol Pot and established a puppet government under the name of the People's Republic of Kampuchea. The Vietnamese army remained in Cambodia to support the new government and fight a guerrilla war against Pol Pot. *See also* **Year Zero, Vietnamese Invasion of Cambodia, Khmer Rouge, Political Purification.**

Poland *see* **ICC, ICCS**

Polar Bears *see* **31st Infantry Regiment (Light)**

Polei Kleng Site of a U.S. Special Forces camp, located about 25kms west of Kontum, Kontum Province, II Corps.

Polgar, Thomas *see* **Polgarize**

Polgarize (Thomas Polgar) Reference by Saigon CIA personnel to the reported manipulation of agent reports by the station chief, Thomas Polgar in '72–'73. Agent reports related to the exposure of corruption in the Saigon government and military deficiencies were amended to glowing, upbeat reports of the stability and strengths of the Saigon government and the military. *See also* **The Elephants Have Moved Out in Front...**

Police Call (Burn Call) Military term for trash collection and general cleanup. At major U.S. installations police call generally entailed a unit, walking online, across an area, picking up trash and cigarette butts. Basic Training platoons spent a considerable part of their time doing police calls. A burn call was a police call in which the collected trash was deposited in a central location and burned. Units operating in the field in Vietnam often conducted a burn call after an all night attack by the enemy. If the unit was to remain in the location, trash from C-Ration boxes, ammo boxes, pieces of clothing, used battle dressings, and other trash would be collected and burned.

Political Officer, Viet Cong *see* **Cadre**

Political Purification (Blood Bath) Communist phrase used to describe the mass deaths and massacres inflicted on the South Vietnamese population as the NVA/VC seized control of towns and villages. Political purifications resulted in the deaths of several thousand Vietnamese at the hands

of the communists in '68 after they took over the city of Hue during the Tet Offensive. Those "purified" were GVN officials, their families, teachers, military and paramilitary personnel and anyone else on the Viet Cong's "black list." The U.S. and GVN believed there would be widespread massacres if the communists ever gained control of South Vietnam. *See also* **Hue Massacre, Khmer Rouge.**

Political Struggle (Vietnamese) *see* **Dau Tranh**

Political War *see* **Other War, The**

Politically Sensitive Vietnamese *see* **Black Flights**

Polluted *see* **Drunk**

Pollution System *see* **XM-52 Smoker**

Polymagna (Intromycin, No-Go Pills) Antidiarrhea drug widely used by U.S. troops in Vietnam, nicknamed "no-go pills." Polymagna offered temporary relief from the stomach cramps that frequently accompanied diarrhea. Some USSF/LRRPs took the polymagna before going out on a mission to create a temporary state of constipation. This allowed them to accomplish their long-range patrol missions with less interference from "nature's call." *See also* **Ho Chi Minh's Revenge.**

Pom-Pom *see* **Boom-Boom**

Pom-Pom Guns *see* **M-42 Duster**

Poncho Rip-stop nylon, waterproof, field rain gear worn over the body and field equipment as a rain shelter. The 92 × 60-inch poncho was worn folded over the shoulders with a hooded hole in the center. The poncho weighed 1.5 pounds had a row of snap fasteners along two sides and was stored rolled. Two ponchos attached together could be pitched like a tent. The poncho was available in OD Green and camouflage pattern. USSF and LRRP units did not usually use the poncho in the field because when it was wet, the slick surface of the poncho easily reflected light, which could give away their position. *See also* **Poncho Liner.**

Poncho Liner Nylon insert, camouflage pattern, used under a standard military rain poncho. The 1.7-pound liner was designed to be used as a lightweight blanket by troops in the field. It had the equivalent insulating rating of a four-pound wool blanket. *See also* **Poncho.**

Poncho Litter *see* **Bamboo Litter**

Pongi Stakes *see* **Punji Pit**

Ponies *see* **Light Attack Squadron 4**

Pontoon Barges *see* **Ammi Barge**

Pony Express (Errand Boy) Daily courier flights conducted by Army aircraft between command locations, sometimes called "errand boy" flights. The "Pony Express" was also the nickname given to one of the forms of intracamp communication practiced by some U.S. POWs in Hanoi. The method involved writing notes on scraps of paper and attaching them to the bottoms of their toilet bowls, which were placed outside of their cells and emptied daily. The Pony Express Rider was one of the POWs who was assigned to collect the "honey pots" and empty them. As he emptied the bowls he collected the notes, redistributing them at a later time.

Pony Soldiers Nickname for soldiers of the 1st Cavalry Division. The name also applied to members of some LRRP units.

Pool Hall, The American POW nickname for one of the prison buildings located at the "Zoo" on the outskirts of Hanoi. *See also* **Zoo, The.**

Poontang *see* **Vagina**

Poop Meeting Informal meeting by the leaders of a unit. At the company level this would be the platoon leaders (sergeants and/or lieutenants). At the platoon level the meeting would be between the squad and fire team leaders. The meetings usually dealt with the unit's movement orders, objectives, resupply, etc.

Poor Man's War After '73 the U.S. Congress made drastic cuts in U.S. funding for the war in Vietnam. The cuts affected economic and military aid to the Thieu regime. During the '72 communist offensive ARVN forces used large quantities of munitions and supplies to halt the NVA thrust to overrun South Vietnam. After the signing of the '73 Paris Peace Accords, and the final withdrawal of U.S. combat forces, Congress was reluctant to continue funding the war at the previously established levels. ARVN combat units no longer had an endless supply of ammunition and were required to use their remaining reserves cautiously.

Pop *see* **Kill**

Pop Bleeders Slang term for a previously operated-on wound that would erupt and begin heavy bleeding.

Pop Smoke Military jargon for igniting a smoke grenade. Smoke grenades had a pin and handle similar to that of a fragmentation grenade. The smoke was most commonly used as a signal to aircraft, or as an obstruction to the enemy's line of sight (smoke screen).

Pop-Up *see* **Star Cluster, Air Strike Technique**

Poppers (Amyl Nitrate) Slang for the drug amyl nitrate, normally prescribed for the relief of angina attacks, but taken by some GIs as an upper. The drugs were usually acquired through medics who had the ability to order drugs. *See also* **Drug List.**

Popular Forces (Ruff-Puffs, PF, Home-guard, [Village] Self-Defense Force or Corps [SDC/SDF]) SVN local defense force used to protect their villages from the VC. Originally known as the Village Self-Defense Force (Corps), these local defense forces were renamed Popular Forces in '64. The forces received GVN backing, but were generally poorly trained and armed. PFs were platoon size village defense forces, controlled by the district chief. A larger, company size force, called Regional Forces, performed a similar task for a group of villages in a region. Prior to '64 the PFs were called the Self-Defense Corps (SDC) and were controlled by the Province Chief. In '64 the PFs became part of the ARVN forces. GIs nicknamed the PFs and RFs Ruff-Puffs. *See also* **Regional Forces, Dan Ve.**

Population and Resource Control Military term used to describe one of the missions of the Navy patrol boats that operated in the Delta. The PBRs operated on the rivers and channels, stopping Vietnamese sampans and junks. The PBR crews checked ID cards, verified cargo manifest and generally inspected river traffic in search of the VC and their supplies. The 12–14 hour "population and resource control" patrols were slow and boring duty. *See also* **TF 116.**

POR Training *see* Processing Overseas Replacement Training

Porcelain Plates *see* M-1955 Flak Jacket

Porcupine Fence (Abatis) Defensive works used to slow enemy ground assaults. The abatis design was usually used around ARVN outposts, hamlet defenses, and Special Forces camps. The abatis employed in Vietnam consisted of rows of bamboo stakes driven into the ground at various angles of slant (30–90 degrees). The ends were sharpened and, when practical, hardened by burning. The slanted stakes pointed out from the defense position, forming a row around the perimeter similar to the quills on the back of a porcupine.

Porta-Bridge *see* M-60 AVLB

Portable Differential Magnetometer (PDM, Tunnel Cache Detector) One of the DOD's Limited War Laboratories projects experimentally tested in Vietnam. The PDM was designed to analyze soil and was supposedly able to detect freshly dug earth, as would be found near a fresh tunnel site. The unit weighed over 100 pounds and proved totally ineffective during field trials and was dropped by the Army. *See also* Limited War Laboratory.

Portable Seismic Intrusion Device (P-SID, Patrol Seismic Intrusion Device, Beep Codes) Small portable seismic sensors used to monitor enemy traffic in conjunction with ambushes and intelligence gathering. The sensors were short-range devices most effective as an early warning signal of approaching enemy traffic along a trail. The sensors could be planted and operational in a matter of seconds, and easily retrieved and reused. The P-SID kit consisted of four transmitters and one receiver, each about twice the size of a pack of cigarettes. When activated each transmitter radioed a series of beep tones which could be heard through an earphone attached to the receiver. The beep tone for transmitter one was a single beep; for transmitter two it was two quick beeps, etc. A small, spike shaped geophone was attached to each transmitter by a 6-foot wire cord. The geophone would be shoved into the ground along a trail and the transmitter placed out of sight. The receiver could monitor all the transmitters simultaneously, and was activated by ground vibrations. An ambush setup along a trail used the P-SID to monitor the approaches warning the ambush of the approximate number and speed of the approaching enemy. After use the P-SID was simply turned off and picked up for use elsewhere. The effective range of the P-SID was about 100 meters with a battery life of 40–60 days. P-SIDs entered service with U.S. troops on a limited basis in '68. *See also* Electronic Sensors.

Portable Truth Detector *see* Ultimate Weapon…

Possession *see* Holdin'

Post Exchange (PX, BX, Base Exchange, Military Store, AAFES, Quan Kho) On-post store, used exclusively by military personnel and their dependents. Items in the PX were generally less expensive than the same item in a civilian store but the availability and range of items were usually not as extensive. Called a Base Exchange on Air Force bases. The Army and Air Force base/post exchanges were operated by the AAFES (Army and Air Force Exchange System). "Quan Kho" [k-wan co] in Vietnamese. *See also* Cash Sales.

Post-Traumatic Stress Disorder (Delayed Stress Syndrome [DSS], PTSD, PTS) A psychological disorder characterized by an individual's inability to come to terms with the violence and destruction he experienced during combat or other traumatic experiences. As related to the war, the violent and destructive experiences haunted the veteran after his war was over. Some of the symptoms were nightmares, flashbacks, emotional numbness, insomnia, survivor guilt, depression, anxiety, and difficulties with interpersonal relationships. PTSD is still a legal and psychological problem, but work continues on identifying its exact causes and ramifications. Post-Traumatic Stress (PTS) had also been experienced by veterans of other wars. In WWI it was called shell shock; in WWII, battle fatigue or battle neurosis; in Korea, operational exhaustion; in Vietnam it was called combat fatigue. Delayed Stress Syndrome was an early name sometimes used to describe PTSD and its effects. *See also* Combat Fatigue, Combat Veteranitis, Survivor Guilt.

Pot *see* Marijuana

Pot, Pol *see* Pol Pot

Potassium Nitrate *see* **Saltpeter**

Potato Digger *see* **LVTE**

Potato Masher *see* **Type 59 Grenade**

Pothead *see* **Doper, Heads**

Poulo Condore (Prison Island, Con Son Island, Con Son Correctional Center) The Island of Con Son, located 220kms south of Saigon, 117kms southeast of Soc Trang, IV Corps. The island was used as a political prison by the French and called Poulo Condore. After the French, the South Vietnamese used the prison on Con Son as a major holding facility for the Viet Cong, NVA POWs, and other South Vietnamese political prisoners such as Buddhist dissidents. After the takeover of Southern Vietnam by the communists, Con Son was used to hold former GVN and military officials. Many of the 5 × 9-foot cells, called "tiger cages," were underground. The cells were poorly ventilated, bug and parasite infested, and prisoners were usually chained to the walls, denied exercise and generally abused. *See also* **Tiger Cage.**

Poulo Wai Island *see* **SS Mayaguez**

POW *see* **Prisoner of War**

POW Cigarettes *see* **Vinh Binh Cigarettes**

POW Handling Practices (SSSSS, Five S's) Army units in Vietnam were given specific instructions as to the handling of captured enemy soldiers. The procedure was condensed into the "Five-S's." POWs were to be S-earched, S-ilenced, S-afeguarded, S-egregated and S-ped out of the area of capture. Most U.S. units adhered to the policy, but some abuse of prisoners did take place. Enemy soldiers, captured in the field, were usually turned over to the ARVNs who frequently proceeded to interrogate the prisoners on the spot, often resorting to beating and torture to extract information. U.S. troops were ordered not to interfere in the Vietnamese interrogation process, but ARVN excesses sometimes caused U.S. commanders to intervene.

Powder Charge *see* **Mortar Increment**

Powell, Representative Adam Clayton Member of the House of Representatives. During the August '64 House vote on the Southeast Asia Resolution, Powell, like all the other representatives, was asked for a yea or nay note on the resolution. Powell responded with a vote of "present." This was his attempt to register a protest to what the resolution might mean to Americans in the future. The House vote was 416–0, in favor of the resolution. *See also* **Morse, Senator Wayne.**

Power Sign Common hand greeting between blacks to demonstrate their solidarity. In Vietnam, a form of racial identification primarily used between black enlisted men. The Power Sign was banned by higher officers in some units; their reasoning was that it was adding to the racial strife experienced by some commands in SVN.

Powerplant, The *see* **Hanoi Hilton**

PPB *see* **Patrol Base**

PPS-4/5 Radar *see* **Ground Radar**

PPS43 SMG Russian-made submachine gun used by the NVA/VC. The gun was firing blowback operated, full automatic with a maximum effective range of 200 meters. The submachine gun used a 35-round magazine and was equipped with a folding, metal stock. *See also* **Submachine Gun.**

PPSh41 SMG *see* **Type 50 SMG**

Prairie *see* **Operation Prairie**

Prairie Fire *see* **Operation Shining Brass**

Pranging *see* **Skids**

Pray for War Marine slogan used during peace time and by troops seeking action in an active combat zone.

Prayer Meeting (Propaganda Session) GI slang for the mandatory propaganda sessions held by the Viet Cong. In rural hamlets the VC would round up all the occupants and give them a propaganda lecture on the virtues of the communist cause and the decadence of the GVN and its primary supporter, the U.S. These sessions tended to be more instructional than violent and sometimes included skits or plays and communal sing-alongs; however, executions and torture were used at the sessions if a communist "point" was to be made, or an example set.

PRC *see* People's Republic of China

PRC-4 Mine PRC–manufactured mine used by the NVA/VC. The mine could be used against vehicles or personnel. The PRC-4 was round with a flat top and bottom, 3.9 inches high, and 8.9 inches in diameter, and weighed 11.4 pounds. The mine was buried below ground and detonated by means of a pin release. The mine could be trip wired or command detonated. *See also* **Booby Trap.**

PRC-10 *see* **AN/PRC-10**

PRC-25 *see* **AN/PRC-25**

PRC-41 *see* **AN/PRC-41**

PRC-74 *see* **AN/PRC-74**

PRC-77 *see* **AN/PRC-77**

PRC-90 *see* **Survival Radios**

PRC RCL (Type 36, Type 52, Type 56) The PRC recoilless rifles (Type 36, 52, 56) were copies of Soviet and U.S. made RCLs. The Type 52, 75mm RCL was capable of using both PRC and U.S. ammunition, weighed only 115 pounds and could fire HEAT rounds out to 800 meters and HE out to 6,000 meters. The Type 56 was a variant of the Type 52, but it could only fire PRC ammunition. The Type 36, 57mm recoilless gun, weighed 44 pounds and fired a 3-pound shaped charge to a range of 450 meters. The Type 36 could be shoulder fired; the Type 52 and 56 were mounted and fired from a two-wheel gun cart. All the PRC RCLs could defeat the armor on the U.S. M-113. The RCLs were effectively used against enemy armored targets and base fortifications. The PRC Type 65 weighed more than 125 pounds and fired an 8-pound shaped charge to a maximum effective range of 900 meters. The B-11 was a Soviet made 107mm RCL that weighed over 650 pounds and could fire a 30-pound round over 6,500 meters. The 57mm and 75mm RCLs were used by main force VC and NVA units as direct support weapons. *See also* **Recoilless Rifle.**

Precision-Guided Munitions (PGM; If You Can See It, You Can Hit It) During the Vietnam War the U.S. developed many different types of advanced weapons systems. Precision-Guided Munitions were one part of this technological advance. The PGM weapons increased payloads and bombing accuracy. Laser and TV guided bombs were part of the development, as was the TOW antitank missile. The Soviet Union was also developing their own line of PGMs such as the AT-3 and Strela missiles. One of the advertising slogans used by American PGM developers was, "if you can see it (the target), you can hit it." *See also* **Laser Guided Bombs, SAM, EOGB.**

Predictability Perhaps one of the greatest allies of the NVA/VC was American predictability. American units that followed predictable routines, based on previous patterns, were prime targets for the enemy. Units that repeatedly followed the same patrol route at the same times, moved in the same pattern or formation day after day or reacted in the same way to small arms or sniper fire, gave the enemy a decided advantage. The enemy could plan an attack knowing the way the American unit would react. American units that varied their patterns and kept the enemy guessing were much less likely to be ambushed or surprised by the enemy and were much more successful against the enemy.

Prep (Peppering the LZ) Target areas of assault or landing were attacked by artillery or aircraft prior to the assault in an effort to reduce enemy resistance for the units making the assault. Prepping was not always used in helimobile assaults because it revealed the exact location of the attack; this advanced knowledge would often work against the landing troops. Helicopter gunships, artillery and fighter-bombers were used to prep LZs. Sometimes referred to as "peppering the LZ." *See also* **Soften the LZ.**

Prepared Ambush Ambush site that was prepared in advance. The ambush force moved into the site and waited for the enemy to enter. The site had previously been selected based on enemy movement or the likelihood of enemy movement in the selected area. The prepared ambush was planned, unlike the hasty ambush which was quickly set up by a moving unit that encountered a moving enemy force. The NVA/VC were experts at ambush techniques and often hit U.S. units as they patrolled. USSF/LRRP and recon units were extremely effective at ambushing the enemy, using many of the NVA/VC's own tactics of camouflage and stealth against them. *See also* **Ambush, Hasty Ambush.**

Preserve the Fighting Strength Motto of the U.S. Army medical corps.

Presidential Body Guard *see* **Diem's Angels**

Presidential Palace *see* **Gia Long Palace**

Press Camp Group of media reporters sharing temporary living space at a military location or other accommodations shared by correspondents.

Pretty *see* **Dep**

Pretty Kittens All-woman American band that toured South Vietnam entertaining American troops. The band consisted of four women dressed in miniskirts and white go-go boots. The group toured from May–September '67.

PRG *see* **Provisional Revolutionary Government**

PRG Radio *see* **Liberation Radio**

PRGVN *see* **Provisional Revolutionary Government of SVN**

Prick *see* **Penis**

Prick-25 *see* **AN/PRC-25**

Prima Cord *see* **Detonator Cord**

Primaquine Primaquine phosphate was used for the treatment of recurring vivax malaria. In Vietnam primaquine was mixed with chloroquine and taken in tablet form by U.S. troops as an antimalarial agent. *See also* **Dapsone, Chloroquine.**

Primary MOS *see* **Military Occupation Specialty**

Prime Choke *see* **Operation Prime Choke**

Prince *see* **Vinh**

Prince Souphanouvong *see* **Souvanna Phouma, Prince**

Prince Souvanna Phouma *see* **Souvanna Phouma, Prince**

Princeton *see* **USS Princeton**

Principal Direction of Fire (PDF) Marine term for the direction in which an infantryman fired when under attack. In theory, each man around a defensive perimeter had a PDF which overlapped the PDFs of the men on either side of him. *See also* **Field of Fire.**

Principles of War (Methodology of War) There were nine basic principles of war that U.S. military forces ascribed to. The principles roughly determined how the military would function in time of war or conflict. 1) Objective—Identify the overall and specific objectives of the mission. 2) Offensive—Assume an offensive posture, control the situation. 3) Unity of Command—Responsibility and authority of the force are to be under one commander as are all subordinate commands, not command by committee. 4) Surprise—The element of surprise is most difficult to defend against; use it against the enemy whenever possible. 5) Concentration of Force—Mass forces against the enemy. 6) Economy of Force—Do not attempt to fortify every position; mass force for specific use. 7) Security—Secure lines of communication and concealment of command decisions from the enemy. 8) Maneuver—Keep the force mobile; such forces are harder to find and fix. 9) Simplicity—Keep the plans simple and straightforward; complex plans greatly increase the chance of error or omission. During the Vietnam War most of the principles were ignored or negated by political considerations and restraints. The NVA/VC effectively employed the nine principles and were able to stalemate a superior enemy force.

Priority 999 (999, Red Ball Express) Special priority code used by the U.S. Air Force's Military Airlift Command during the Vietnam War. The "999" was the highest priority classification a cargo item could receive; such items were immediately expedited for delivery to Vietnam, and the classification was reserved for critically needed items such as spare parts or medical supplies. In '65 MAC instituted a special cargo service for Vietnam-bound cargo that provided for shipment of cargo within 24 hours of receipt at the MAC transport terminal. The Air Force called the service the "Red Ball Express." *See also* **Military Airlift Command.**

Priority Evac *see* **Medevac Priorities, Casualty Classifications**

Priority Vietnamese *see* **Black Flights**

Prison Grapevine *see* **Tap Codes**

Prison Island *see* **Poulo Condore**

Prison Morse Code *see* **Tap Codes**

Prisoner of War (POW, PW)   Military personnel or nationals of a country held as prisoners by the enemy. During the Vietnam War NVA personnel held as prisoners were under the direct control of the GVN. Most Americans held prisoner by NVN were kept in prison camps in NVN and Laos. Americans held by NVN were subject to torture, physical and psychological abuse and murder, totally ignoring the terms of the Geneva Convention of '49 on the treatment of prisoners of which NVN was a signing party. NVA/VC troops under the control of the GVN were also tortured and mistreated on a regular basis. In early '73, 591 Americans, 5,000 South Vietnamese and 26,500 NVA/VC were repatriated. *See also* American POWs, 4th POW Wing, Operation Homecoming, Yankee Air Pirates, Fink Release Program, MIA, Commander Jeremiah Denton, Repatriate.

Private   *see*   E-2

Private First Class (PFC, Private-Fucking-Civilian, Ha-Si)   U.S. Army enlisted grade E-3. Equivalent in the Air Force to airman second class; Marines, lance corporal; Navy, seaman. It was also translated as "private-fucking-civilian" by many GIs on the verge of their ETS, in response to the question of what they would be when they got out of the Army. Ha-Si was the Vietnamese equivalent meaning corporal. *See also* Lance Corporal.

Private First Class, ARVN   *see*   E-2

Private-Fucking-Civilian   *see*   Private First Class

Privy   *see*   Latrine

Probe   Small attacks made against a position to gain knowledge about the position's defenses. Probes would be made of the defenses of a base camp to determine where the automatic weapons were placed and the exact positions of the bunkers. Probes were also used to test for weak points in a defensive line or perimeter. The NVA/VC made extensive use of probes around U.S. bases. To counter probes, U.S. troops tossed out hand grenades and avoided firing their weapons or machine guns so as not to give away their exact position. *See also* Standoff Attack, Recon by Fire.

Processing Overseas Replacement Training (POR Training)   Stateside troops going to Vietnam as replacements were sometimes given a short familiarization course on Vietnam prior to their departure. The course briefly covered tactics, conditions and some expectations of the difficulties the new replacements would encounter in RVN. In the sixties most BCT troops trained with the M-14 rifle. POR training was used to quickly train RVN bound replacements on the M-16, the primary U.S. Infantry combat weapon in Vietnam.

Processing Stations   *see*   Stations of the Cross

Professionals, The   *see*   46th Infantry Regiment (Light)

Profile   *see*   Medical Profile

Profile Suits   *see*   Club Cammies

Program Evaluation Office (PEO)   Office established as part of the U.S. Embassy in Laos as a front for CIA activities in Laos in '58. The PEO was similar to the Combined Studies Group set up in SVN. Due to the terms of the '54 Geneva agreements, the U.S. was unable to establish an official military presence in Laos to help the Royal Lao forces combat the North Vietnamese backed communist Pathet Lao. The PEO operated covertly against the Pathet Lao and organized the Meo Tribesmen in the Laotian Central Highlands into an anticommunist force. Under CIA direction, Special Forces White Star teams trained the forces of the Royal Lao Army and helped with the organization of the Meo force. *See also* White Star MIT.

Programming   *see*   American Red Cross

Prohibition Against Dancing   *see*   Dance Ban

Project 100,000   *see*   Project One-Hundred Thousand

Project Agile   *see*   Advanced Research Project Agency

Project Banner Sun (Banner Sun)   Code name for the October '70 redeployment and deactivation of several Air Force squadrons based in Thailand and South Vietnam. Many of the redeployed units returned to Southeast Asia in early '72 when the NVA invasion of South Vietnam took place. *See also* Eastertide Offensive.

Project Big Eagle (Big Eagle, Truck-Busting)   Air Force operation conducted by specially equipped B-26 bombers that flew "truck-busting" missions against the Ho Chi Minh Trail. The project started in June '66 and was operated from Nakhon Phanom AB in Thailand. The B-26s were armed with fourteen .50cal machine guns and 5,000 pounds of bombs as well as an increased fuel capacity. Project Big Eagle aircraft were part of the 1st Air Commando Wing and were used to replace the slower AC-47s that had been attacking enemy trucking along the trail. *See also* **B-26, AC-47, Steel Tiger, Tiger Hound.**

Project Buddy Base   U.S. program established in '70 that encouraged the U.S. Navy to provide help to dependents of Vietnamese Navy personnel in Vietnam. Some surplus Navy equipment at U.S. bases was sent to Vietnam to help the Vietnamese with housing and other facilities that would be needed by the families of Vietnamese sailors taking over U.S. naval bases in Vietnam. *See also* **NAVCATS, Operation Helping Hand Foundation.**

Project Carolina Moon   *see* **Carolina Moon**

Project Delta (Leaping Lena, Detachment B-52)   Code name for Detachment B-52 of the U.S. Special Forces Group operating in SVN. The Nha Trang based group trained CIDG and LLDB units, and later U.S. Army LRRP units, to perform long-range recon, raids, bomb damage assessments, air strike direction and other missions as required against the NVA/VC in their base and infiltration areas. The project originally conducted long-range recon under the code name Leaping Lena in May '64 and was redesignated Project Delta in '65 under the control of the USSF. The final organization consisted of 12 Roadrunner Teams, 12 Recon Teams, one company of Nungs for camp security and one battalion of ARVN Rangers as a reaction force. *See also* **Roadrunner Teams, Operation Leaping Lena.**

Project Enhance Plus   *see* **Operation Enhance Plus**

Project Flycatcher (Fly Catcher, KAF, Khmer Air Force)   Code name for the Air Force program established to upgrade the Cambodian (Khmer) Air Force. The program involved Air Force personnel training Khmer aircrews in the use, tactics and support maintenance of the U.S. supplied T-28, C-47 and O-1 aircraft. The O-1s were used by the Khmers for reconnaissance and air/artillery spotting. The T-28 was used in support of ground troops and the C-47 was used for transport and flare dropping missions. The project was terminated in June '73 with the withdrawal of most U.S. Air Force units from SEA. *See also* **Operation SCOOT.**

Project Gamma (Detachment B-57)   A special long-range reconnaissance group organized and directed by the U.S. Special Forces that conducted intelligence gathering activities deep into Cambodia. Many of the missions performed by the group were originated by the CIA. Project Gamma was the code name given to Detachment B-57, the control element of the USSF that operated the LRRP patrols. *See also* **LRRP, Greek Operations, Rheault Affair.**

Project Illinois City   *see*   **McNamara's Wall**

Project Leaping Lena   *see*   **Project Delta**

Project MOOSE (MOOSE)   Project "Move Out of Saigon Earliest" (MOOSE) was the Navy plan to relocate the Naval Support Activity headquarters in Saigon to another location outside of the city. The Navy chose the town of Nha Be to become the new headquarters. Nha Be was located on the west bank of the Song Nha Be River, south of Saigon. The move was scheduled for summer '68, but due to events of the war the move was postponed, and never really took place because of the drawdown of U.S. combat forces in Vietnam. *See also* **Naval Support Activity.**

Project Mule Train (Mule Train, 315th Air Commando Wing)   U.S. project conducted by elements of the Air Force's 315th Air Commando Wing. The 315th deployed to SVN in '61 with C-123 aircraft to provide South Vietnamese troops with air transport capacity. The C-123 had good short landing strip capabilities and could move cargo or up to 70 Vietnamese troops. The 315th operated from Tan Son Nhut and later from Phan Rang. *See also* **C-123.**

Project Omega (Detachment B-50)

MACV-SOG reconnaissance operation started in '66. Detachment B-50 operated out of Ban Me Thuot in II Corps, gathering intelligence from deep in enemy territory. The Omega force consisted of CIDG and USSF troops conducting roadrunner and reconnaissance ops in enemy controlled areas. Information gathered was fed to I and II Field Force for use in designing battle plans to counter NVA/VC activity. Omega operations were carried out from one of three Forward Operating Bases, designated MACV-SOG CCC, CCN, CCS. Omega operations were expanded in '67 and redesignated the Mobile Guerrilla Force. *See also* **MACV-SOG, MACV-SOG Command and Control, Greek Operations, Blackjack Operations.**

Project One-Hundred Thousand (Project 100,000, Subterranean Poor) U.S. government program to fill the ranks of the military during the early years of the Vietnam War. The '66 project was a Great Society program designed to reduce poverty nationwide by providing military training to a large portion of America's disadvantaged youths, teaching them new skills that could be utilized beyond the military. Those who enlisted in the program were also eligible for Veteran's benefits which could lead to higher education, and a notable improvement in their lifestyles. The program waived the military's normal IQ level and physical requirements, and accepted people with IQ scores as low as 62. Most of the lower intelligence individuals found their way to Vietnam as riflemen, and some even qualified as officers. Men who had previously been denied military enlistment or induction because they did not meet the military's minimum mental and physical requirements were allowed to enlist under Project 100,000. The majority of those who enlisted under the program were the impoverished: urban and Southern minorities, and poor whites. The goal of the project was the recruitment of one-hundred thousand new soldiers per year, and the program greatly exceeded its goal, sweeping over 350,000 men into the military, with most of those entering the Army. Over 40 percent of the Project 100,000 men were black, and more than 140,000 men were combat trained only: not a skill typically in demand beyond the military. Secretary of Defense McNamara nicknamed the Project 100,000 soldiers the "subterranean poor." *See also* **Moron Corps, Black American Soldier.**

Project Patricia Lynn (Patricia Lynn) Code name for the deployment of Air Force RB-57 bombers to South Vietnam. The RB-57 Canberra was the reconnaissance version of the twin engine jet bomber. The Canberras were equipped with photographic and infrared cameras and operated from Tan Son Nhut. *See also* **B-57 Bomber.**

Project Pay Dirt *see* **Operation Helping Hand Foundation**

Project Practice Nine *see* **McNamara's Wall**

Project Rapid Fire (Long Hai, Detachment B-36) Code name for a U.S. Special Forces Reconnaissance project conducted by Detachment B-36. B-36 was raised as a provisional element and operated from Long Hai, which was located on the coast, 16kms northeast of Vung Tau in III Corps.

Project Sigma (Detachment B-56) MACV-SOG organized and directed long-range reconnaissance force that operated from Ho Ngoc Nau, near Saigon, and fed its intelligence information to II Field Force Headquarters, III Corps. Detachment B-56 consisted of USSF and CIDG troops operating in enemy controlled areas gathering information, directing air strikes, raiding, harassing enemy base areas and conducting special ambushes. The operation started in '66 and continued until '71. In '67 the operations were expanded and redesignated part of the Mobile Guerrilla Force. *See also* **MACV-SOG, MACV-SOG Command and Control, Greek Operations, Mobile Guerrilla Force.**

Promotion from Within *see* **Grow-Your-Own**

Propaganda Session *see* **Prayer Meeting**

Prostitute (Saigon Ho, Short-Time Girl) Prostitution was widespread in the cities and larger villages of Vietnam. The GIs had many names for the prostitutes they encountered. The NVA/VC also made use of prostitutes to service their troops. Sometimes the same women servicing Americans during the day, found themselves servicing the NVA/VC that same night. Prostitution was a way of life for many of Vietnam's young women, especially those in the urban areas where the glut of the refugee populations made well-paying jobs scarce. For many the rule-of-thumb was, if you couldn't work for the Americans, then sell yourself to them; brothers traded on their sisters, fathers on their daughters and sons. *See also* **Cowboys.**

Protective Reaction Strikes (Reinforced Protective Reaction Strikes)   As a concession to peace talks, air and naval bombardment of North Vietnam was halted in '68. The U.S. continued to fly reconnaissance flights over NVN to monitor enemy supply and infiltration efforts. When these recon flights began taking fire from North Vietnamese gunners and missiles, President Nixon authorized "protective reaction" air strikes against NVN, AAA and SAM sites. When NVN continued to fire on recon aircraft "reinforced protective reaction" strikes were initiated. These strikes involved large groups of American strike planes hitting offending AA, AAA, SAM sites and MiG airfields in North Vietnam. *See also* **Lavelle, U.S. Air Rules of Engagement.**

Protest Busters   *see*   **Hell's Angels**

Proud Deep   *see*   **Operation Proud Deep**

Provider   *see*   **C-123**

Province (Province Chief, District, District Chief, Village Chief, Hamlet Chief) South Vietnam, as a country, was divided into 44 provinces, a province being equivalent to a state in the United States. The provinces were further subdivided into districts, a total of 240. A district consisted of a number of villages, and a village was a cluster of hamlets. The province was under the control of the province chief who was usually a ranking officer in the ARVN. At each level below the province (district, village and hamlet) a chief was appointed who was responsible for the GVN administrative task and the associated military mission. In some VC controlled areas, a GVN village or hamlet chief might be nonexistent and the district chief afraid to sleep at night in his own district capital. Prior to '67 SVN consisted of 45 provinces. In '67 the island province of Con Son was converted to a district administered from Saigon and the province

of Phuoc Thanh was eliminated, its territory split between the provinces of Phuoc Long, Long Khanh, Bien Hoa and Binh Duong. Also, the southern delta portion of Bien Hoa was added to the extended province of Gia Dinh, at which point Gia Dinh included Saigon and the immediate area around it and a narrow corridor and the river delta area that opened on the South China Sea. The Province of Sa Dec was created from the western tip of Vinh Long Province in IV Corps. *See also* **I, II, III, IV Corps; Provincial Capitals.**

Province Chief   *see*   **Province**

Province Intelligence and Operations Center   *see*   **DIOCC**

Province Senior Advisor (PSA)   A U.S. Army officer, under command of MACV, assigned to aid and advise the GVN's individual province chief. The rank of the PSA was usually a colonel. The PSA advised the province chief regarding matters of security, police and medical operations and economic improvement programs. The provinces were further divided into districts, with advisory functions carried out by U.S. District Advisory Teams. *See also* **District Advisory Team.**

Provincial Capitals   Each of SVN's provinces had a provincial capital that administered the province. The province chief was an appointed position and was usually occupied by an ARVN officer. The provincial capitals (prov/cap): An Giang/Long Xuyen, An Xuyen/Ca Mau, Ba Xuyen/Khanh Hung, Bac Lieu/Vinh Loi, Bien Hoa/Bien Hoa, Binh Dinh/Qui Nhon, Binh Duong/Phu Cuong, Binh Long/An Loc, Binh Thuan/Phan Thiet, Binh Tuy/Ham Tan, Chau Doc/Chau Phu, Chuong Thien/Duc Long, Darlac/Ban Me Thuot, Dinh Tuong/My Tho, Gia Dinh/Gia Dinh, Go Cong/Go Cong, Hau Nghia/Khiem Cuong, Khanh Hoa/Nha Trang, Kien Giang/Rach Gia, Hien Hoa/Truc Giang, Kien Phong/Cao Lanh, Kien Tuong/Moc Hoa, Kontum/Kontum, Lam Dong/Bao Loc, Long An/Tan An, Long Khanh/Xuan Loc, Ninh Thuan/Phan Rang, Phong Dinh/Can Tho, Phu Bon/Cheo Reo, Phu Yen/Tuy Hoa, Phuoc Long/Phuoc Bing, Phuoc Tuy/Phuoc Le, Pleiku/Pleiku, Quang Duc/Gia Nghia, Quang Nam/Hoi An, Quang Ngai/Quang Ngai, Quang Tin/Tam Ky,

Quang Tri/Quang Tri, Sa Dec/Sa Dec, Tay Ninh/Tay Ninh, Thua Thien/Hue, Tuyen Duc/Da Lat, Vinh Binh/Phu Vinh and Vinh Long/Vinh Long.

Provincial Reconnaissance Unit *see* **Provisional Reconnaissance Unit**

Provisional (Wartime-Expediency Unit) A unit composed of smaller unassigned or uncommitted units formed to fill a specific need or task. The newly formed unit was usually raised within the war zone. Some provisional units raised in Vietnam operated for years in-country, being dissolved when American troops were withdrawn. Provisional forces also applied to small groups of troops assembled into a named, temporary unit, sometimes called "wartime-expediency units."

Provisional Base Defense Battalion (PBDB) A Marine defense force organized from support and service personnel stationed at the air base at Da Nang. The PBDB was hastily assembled after a Viet Cong ground attack on the base in July '65 destroyed and damaged several parked aircraft. The PBDB was organized to augment the Marine combat force assigned to protect the base. Prior to the enemy attack, elements of the 9th Marine Regiment were responsible for the northern and western perimeter of the base; the ARVNs had been assigned the southern and eastern perimeter. It was through the eastern side of the air base that the Viet Cong made their attack. The PBDB was dissolved in August '65 when the 3d Battalion/9th Marines took responsibility for air base defense.

Provisional Corps Vietnam *see* **MACV Forward**

Provisional Reconnaissance Unit (PRU, Hit Teams, Provincial Reconnaissance Unit) Under the '68 Phoenix Program a special SVN police force was created to identify and eliminate the VC and VCI. Working within the framework of the program, special teams worked to assassinate the VC and VCI. These teams were called Provisional (or Provincial) Reconnaissance Units. The U.S. Special Forces nicknamed the teams Hit Teams. The teams were composed mostly of mercenary soldiers and other shady types who received a bounty for each elimination they carried out. USSF and SEAL teams also participated in the Phoenix

Program. *See also* **Pacification by Assassination, Phoenix Program.**

Provisional Revolutionary Government of SVN (PRG, PRGSVN, PRGVN) In June '69 the National Liberation Front changed the name of their organization to the Provisional Revolutionary Government of South Vietnam. This new name for the political arm of the Viet Cong was recognized as the legal government of SVN by North Vietnam. This new government requested formal help from NVN to free SVN of the oppression placed upon it by the government in Saigon and the United States. The PRG/NLF was a communist group displaying a nationalist front, supported by NVN. Shortly after the fall of Saigon in '75 the PRG/NLF were stripped of their power; military and political control of South Vietnam was directed from Hanoi. *See also* **National Liberation Front.**

Provost Marshal Military command position overseeing the operations of the Military Police on a base or in an area.

Prowler *see* **EA-6A**

PRP *see* **Viet Cong Infrastructure, Lao Dong**

PRS-3 Mine Detector *see* **AN/PRS-3**

PRU *see* **Provisional Reconnaissance Unit**

Pruritis Ani *see* **Jungle Rot**

PSA *see* **Province Senior Advisor**

PSDF *see* **People's Self-Defense Force**

Pseudomonas One of several severe infections that plagued the recovering wounded in military hospitals in Vietnam. Pseudomonas were especially virulent in the burn wards, where moist, burned tissue was susceptible to infection. The infection was treated with penicillin, and debridement of the infected tissue, and draining of abscesses. Pseudomona infections were even worse in the Vietnamese hospitals which lacked the manpower and equipment to properly care for the military and civilian population.

PSG *see* **SOG Groups**

Psilocybin *see* **Hallucinogens**

PSO *see* **Weapons Systems Operator**

PSO-1 Scope *see* **SVD Rifle**

PSP *see* **Perforated Steel Plate**

Psychedelic Cookie *see* **9th Infantry Division**

Psychiatric Discharge *see* **Section 212**

Psychological Operations (PSYOPS, PSYWAR, Psychological Warfare) The practice of influencing enemy morale in an effort to reduce his battlefield effectiveness and his will to continue to fight. In Vietnam the U.S. used propaganda in the form of leaflets, radio, and loudspeaker broadcasts aimed at the NVA/VC. The U.S. Army had a Psychological Warfare battalion in each of the CTZs dispersing millions of leaflets, posters and banners. The USIA broadcasted anticommunist programs on Vietnamese radio. NVN used radio broadcasts in Vietnam and made extensive use of the news media to spread its propaganda. In hindsight, it seems the NVN PSYOPS were more successful against the American people back in the States than they were on U.S. troops in the field. *See also* **No-Doze Missions, Bullshit Bombers, Controlled Littering.**

Psychological Readjustment Act (National Vet Center Program) '79 congressional act that established a series of counseling centers to help Vietnam veterans and their families cope with their Vietnam War experience. As part of the act the National Vet Center Program was established to house the counseling centers in local, storefront operations to provide the greatest access to the veterans. Over the years the program experienced increasing funding cuts under the Reagan administration.

Psychological Studies Group *see* **SOG Groups**

Psychological Warfare *see* **Psychological Operations**

Psychological Warfare Expert *see* **Psywarrior**

PSYOPS *see* **Psychological Operations**

PSYWAR *see* **Psychological Operations**

Psywar Officers *see* **Psywarrior**

Psywarrior (Psychological Warfare Expert) Nicknames for psychological warfare officers: Psywar Officer, Psychological Warfare Expert, and Psywarriors.

PT *see* **Physical Training**

PT Boat *see* **P-4 Torpedo Boat**

PT-76 Tank (Type 62 Light Tank) Soviet-made light amphibious tank used by the NVA. PT-76s made their first appearance in the VNW when they were used to overrun the Special Forces camp at Lang Vei in January '68. North Vietnamese tanks were not used again in South Vietnam until the NVA Eastertide Offensive of '72. The PT-76 was armed with a 76mm turret mounted gun, and a 7.62mm coax machine gun. The tank was also armed with a 12.7mm heavy machine gun for air defense, and was manned by a three man crew. The PT-76 weighed 14 tons, had a max road speed of 30mph, and a max armor thickness of 15mm. The Chinese Type 62 weighed 18 tons, and was armed with an 85mm gun. The NVA had a mix of both types of light tanks in their armor units.

PTD *see* **Ultimate Weapon...**

PTS *see* **Post-Traumatic Stress Disorder**

PTSD *see* **Post-Traumatic Stress Disorder**

PTT Exchange *see* **Tiger Phone Exchange**

PU Scope *see* **Mosin-Nagant Rifle**

Public Affairs Office *see* **Joint U.S. Public Affairs Office**

Public Information Office *see* **Joint U.S. Public Affairs Office**

Public Works, Da Nang SEABEE group assigned to conduct public works projects in I Corps. The group functioned under NSA, Da Nang and contracted with civilian firms (U.S., Vietnamese, Korean, Filipinos and Nationalist Chinese) to provide a work force to carry the projects out. Under Public Works, support was given to Vietnamese towns in the form of road and bridge improvements, irrigation, wells, housing and other civic improvements. The group also provided military facilities with a force that could maintain runways, rebuild structures and provide maintenance and construction needs to large, secure bases. For bases in more hostile environments the CBMU was usually used. *See also* **SEABEES**.

Pucker Factor   A field measurement of the amount of fear, anxiety, nervousness or stress associated with a given situation or mission. The scarier the circumstances, the "tighter your asshole puckered, as it tried to withdraw into the safety of your body."

Pueblo   *see*   **USS Pueblo**

Puerto Ricans   *see*   **Newyoricans**

Puff-the-Magic-Dragon   *see*   **AC-47**

Pugil Stick   Six foot long stick with heavy padding on each end used during basic recruit training. The stick was used to simulate combat with a rifle with fixed bayonet. Troops in training were required to combat each other, practicing the techniques of bayonet combat. The troops wore padded gloves, a football helmet and a padded groin cup for protection during the exercises. A DI conducted the exercises and usually made an example out of one of the padded recruits by "beating the hell out of him" with the pugil stick, by way of demonstration.

Pukin' Buzzards   *see*   **101st Airborne Division (Airmobile)**

Pull Pitch   Warning sometimes announced by a helicopter pilot to the crew indicating the aircraft was preparing to take off. Pitch controlled the angle of the rotating rotor blades. Increasing the pitch of the blades caused the helicopter to rise; decreasing the pitch caused the aircraft to descend.

Pull-Your-Pud   *see*   **Masturbate**

Punch-Out (Bail Out, Eject)   Aircraft slang for bailing out or ejecting from a damaged aircraft.

Pungi Stakes   *see*   **Punji Pit**

Punji Pit (Spike Trap Pit, Pungi Pit, Ham Chong, Tiger Pit, Punji Trap)   VC booby trap, various sized pits, the bottoms lined with punji stakes or barbed spikes. When an enemy soldier fell through the camouflaged covering over the pit he was impaled on the stakes in the bottom. The ends of the stakes or spikes were often covered with feces or a poison the Vietnamese called "Elephants Trunk"; both

caused infection should the victim survive the impaling. The pits varied in size from just large enough to accommodate a foot, to large pits several feet deep and 3–5 feet square. The larger pits were called "tiger pits." Stakes were also concealed in the grass along the sides of trails or in clearings. They were also used to booby-trap helicopter LZs with the stakes hidden in tall grass. "Cay Chuong" was Vietnamese for "punji stake," and "Ham Chong" was Vietnamese for "punji pit." *See also* **Tiger Trap, Booby Traps**.

Punji Trap   *see*   **Punji Pit**

Puppets   *see*   **Nguy**

Purple Heart (Three Hearts and You're Out, 3 Heart Ticket, Cheap Heart, Heart, Third-Heart)   U.S. medal awarded for wounds received in combat or as a result of hostile action. On the receipt of a third Purple Heart in Vietnam the recipient's tour of duty was considered complete and he was eligible for return home to the States. A "cheap heart" was a very minor wound not requiring medical evacuation, hospitalization or any major treatment; any combat wound was grounds for a Purple Heart.

Purple Heart Trail   Nickname for RVN Highway 1 leading along the coast of SVN into Saigon. Shortly after the start of the NVA Final Offensive in '75, the highway was clogged with refugees and routed ARVN soldiers fleeing to Saigon. The road was under constant artillery attack from advancing NVA units, and was littered with the bodies of ARVN and civilians alike, from Hue to Saigon. "Purple Heart Trail" was also a nickname given to various local paths, trails and roads where GIs frequently died or were wounded. The thing most of the Purple Heart Trails had in common was they were usually heavily mined or booby-trapped. *See also* **Highway 1**.

Purple-Out-Zone (Emergency Evacuation LZ)   Coded field reference to an LZ set up as an emergency evacuation point used for the extraction of casualties and troops.

Push   *see*   **Radio Frequency, Pushes**

Push Package   Special air deliveries of needed field equipment. Freight processing using the normal overseas shipping channels was not fast enough to keep up with the

Army's demand for field equipment in Vietnam. To reduce the time it took for equipment to get from the manufacturer to the field, special deliveries, via air cargo, were employed. These "push package" deliveries, as they were called, continued until '67 when sufficient supplies of equipment were available in-country.

Push-Ups (Leaning Rest Position, Chinese Push-Ups)   Push-ups were probably the most prevalent exercise during basic (boot) training. Push-ups were used during training to discipline soldiers for infractions, screwups, bad judgment or at the whim of the DI. The usual response by a DI to recruit screwups was "drop and give me 20" or perhaps 30, push-ups. Entire platoons or the company would find itself in the "leaning-rest position," pumping out push-ups. Push-ups were as much a part of basic training as were the rifle range, saluting and KP. The Marines had a special variant called the "Chinese Push-Up" in which only the head and toes supported the body and the push-up was completed with the hands behind the back. See also **Leaning-Rest.**

Pusher-Puller Plane   see   **O-2**

Pushes (Casualties)   Medical personnel's slang for a large group of casualties received at one time.

Pussy   see   **Candy-Ass, Vagina**

Pussy Cut-Off Date   see   **PCOD**

Put Smoke   see   **Marking Round**

Putnam Tiger   see   **Operation Putnam Tiger**

Puzzle Palace   Nickname for the Pentagon in Washington, and MACV headquarters (Pentagon East) in Saigon. Viewed by GIs in Vietnam as an accurate nickname in view of the fact that neither location appeared to have any real concept of what was going on in-country.

PVS-2 Starlight Scope   see   **Starlight Scope**

PW   see   **Prisoner of War**

PX   see   **Post Exchange**

PX Cowboys   see   **Rear-Echelon-Mother-Fuckers**

Pylon Turn   Flying technique used by AC-47, AC-119 and AC-130 gunships to direct their fire at ground targets. The technique involved the banked aircraft flying in a tight circle at a fixed altitude. Miniguns firing from inside the aircraft were able to impact their gun runs on a target area that was about 100 meters in diameter. By allowing the aircraft to slip wider in the turn the area of minigun coverage could be expanded. See also **AC-47, AC-119G, AC-119K, AC-130.**

Pylons   see   **LAU-77/78/80**

PZ   see   **Pickup Zone**

Q

QC   see   **National Police Force**

QL   see   **Highways**

QM   see   **Quan Nhu**

QNH   see   **Qui Nhon**

QU-22 Bonanzas   see   **U-8**

Qua Chuoi   see   **Souvenir Me**

Quaaludes (Methaqualone)   Oral medication prescribed as a sedative. The drug was a derivative of methaqualone and had hypnotic and depressive side effects.

Quaaludes were one of many drugs abused during the sixties and seventies. See also **Illicit Drugs.**

Quack   see   **Corpsmen**

Quad 50s   see   **M-55 Quad**

Quad 60s   see   **XM-6 Machine Gun**

Quadrillage   see   **Hop Tac Plan**

Quadriplegic   see   **Blinker**

Quads   see   **M-55 Quad, Blinker**

Quai Vat   see   **Operation Quai Vat**

Quaker Prosthetics Center (Quang Ngai Prosthetics Center, AFSC, Xa Hoi Quaker, Quang Ngai Rehab Center) A prosthetics center located at Quang Ngai, I Corps, sponsored by the American Friends Service Committee (AFSC). The center, established in '66, provided artificial limbs, rehabilitation and physical therapy to any Vietnamese civilian who sought their services. Many of their patients were children who had lost limbs due to the war. "Xa Hoi Quaker" was Vietnamese for "Quaker Services." The AFSC was also known as the Quang Ngai Rehabilitation Center. They left VN in '75. *See also* VISA.

Quan Doi Nhan Dan (North Vietnamese Newspaper) North Vietnamese newspaper that carried the North Vietnamese Communist Party line.

Quan Kho *see* Post Exchange

Quan Loi (Terre Rouge Rubber Plantation) Town located 48kms north of Phuoc Vinh, and 8kms east of Highway 13, in Binh Long Province, III Corps. Quan Loi was located just east of An Loc, and served as one of the base camps of the 1st Infantry Division. The Terre Rouge Rubber Plantation was located near Quan Loi.

Quan Long *see* Ca Mau Peninsula

Quan Nhu (Quartermaster, QM) Vietnamese for "Quartermaster" Corps. The Quan Nhu was responsible for providing the uniforms used by the SVN Armed Forces. Many of the ARVN uniforms were made in SVN, but some uniforms and materials were imported from Japan, Korea and Taiwan.

Quan Su Vietnamese for "military advisor." *See also* MACV.

Quan-Y-Si *see* Bac-Si

Quang Duc *see* Thich Quang Duc

Quang Khe *see* Blockade

Quang Nam *see* Operation Quang Nam

Quang Ngai Capital of Quang Ngai Province, I Corps, located 32kms southeast of Chu Lai along the Song Tra Khuc River.

Quang Ngai Prosthetics Center *see* Quaker Prosthetics Center

Quang Ngai Rehabilitation Center *see* Quaker Prosthetics Center

Quang Tri Capital of Quang Tri Province, I Corps, near the DMZ, and the largest, northernmost city in South Vietnam. Quang Tri was located 28kms northwest of Hue on Highway 1. During the '72 Eastertide Offensive the 304th NVA Division, supported by armor, put Quang Tri City under siege in March, capturing the city in May when ARVN soldiers surrendered the garrison. Quang Tri was later retaken by members of the ARVN 1st Inf Div and SVN Marines, with U.S. fire support. Quang Tri became the prisoner of war exchange point between SVN and NVN in '73. Quang Tri Province was the northernmost province in South Vietnam.

Quarter Cav *see* 1st Squadron/4th Cavalry (Division Recon)

Quartermaster *see* Quan Nhu

Que Son Hills *see* Que Son Valley

Que Son Valley (Que Son Hills) Valley located along the border of Quang Nam and Quang Tin provinces in I Corps. The Que Son Hills consisted of a 3,000-foot high ridge separating the Que Son Valley (to the south) from the An Hoa Valley (to the north). The hills started 30kms south of Da Nang and ran southwest for about 23kms. The Que Son Valley, located south of the ridge, continued southwest where it narrowed, ending just east of Kham Duc. The NVA/VC were active throughout the area. The area was patrolled by the Marines and later by elements of the Americal Division. *See also* Arizona Territory, An Hoa.

Queen of the Battles (Army Infantry) Self-description of the U.S. Army infantry.

Queen's Cobras (Royal Thai Army Volunteer Regiment, Queen's Cobras Regimental Combat Team) Unit name for the Royal Thai Army Infantry Regiment (Queen's Cobras Regimental Combat Team) deployed to Vietnam in '67 in support of the GVN. The regiment operated in III Corps until '68 when it was replaced by the Royal Thai Expeditionary Division. Before their deployment to Vietnam the Thai units serving in SVN were trained by members of the U.S. 1st SFG in Thailand. *See also* Black Panther Division.

Queen's Cobras Regimental Combat Team *see* Queen's Cobras

Queers *see* ARVN Queers

Qui Nhon (QNH)   Port city and capital of Binh Dinh Province, II Corps, site of a major U.S. logistics center. At the start of the war the port was enlarged and the harbor deepened by U.S. forces making Qui Nhon (QNH) a major base for support of units along the coast and in the Central Highlands. Ground security for the port area was provided by the Korean Capital Division. Qui Nhon was located on the eastern coast of SVN, 168kms north of Nha Trang, and was South Vietnam's third largest city.

Qui Vat   see   **PACV**

Quick Fuse   see   **VT Round**

Quick-Wash   see   **Water-Point**

Quickies   see   **Boom-Boom**

Quiz Room (Interrogation Room, Chicken Coop)   American POW slang for a North Vietnamese interrogation room. Some interrogation rooms were given specific names by the POWs such as "Chicken Coop," the interrogation room at the "Zoo." During the interrogations the North Vietnamese subjected American POWs to various forms of torture in attempts to get them to divulge military information about flight procedures and targeting, personal information or confessions to war crimes credited to their aircraft bombing raids. See also **Zoo, The; Torture, NVA Methods.**

Quoc Canh   see   **National Police Force**

Quoc Lo   see   **Highways**

Quonset Hut   A metal building, originally designed for the U.S. military. The building looked like a section of corrugated pipe, cut in half and laid on its side. The ends were capped with walls in which doors and windows were placed. The huts found widespread use during WWII and continued to be used and built through the Vietnam War. The building could be erected quickly, providing shelter for personnel, vehicles and supplies.

Quy Chanh   see   **Hoi Chanh**

Quyet Chien   see   **Operation Quyet Chien**

Quyet Thang   see   **Operation Quyet Thang**

R

R & R (Rest and Relaxation, Rape and Ruin, Rest and Recreation, Four Fs)   Official break for rest and recreation away from the combat zone; a GI's vacation from the war. U.S. soldiers in Vietnam were eligible for one 7-day R & R. Transport to one of ten R & R locations was provided by the government. The sites were Manila, Penang, Tai Pei, Kuala Lumpur, Tokyo, Singapore, Hong Kong, Bangkok, Australia and Hawaii. Only married men were eligible for Hawaii, and black soldiers were discouraged from applying for Australia. GIs referred to R & R as "rape and ruin" and the cardinal rule for dealing with women on R & R was the "Four Fs": "Find 'em, finger 'em, fuck 'em and forget 'em." See also **In-Country R & R, I & I.**

R & R Quotas   Under most major commands in Vietnam a quota system was established to handle troop R & Rs. The system was designed to enable a steady flow of men to take their R & Rs and still maintain adequate troop levels in the field. The result was inadequate troop levels on the line.

R and R   see   **R & R**

R-1 Amtrac   see   **LVTR**

R4D   The Navy/Marine version of the C-47 transport aircraft used by the Army Air Force and later the Air Force. The R4D featured a slightly longer fuselage and more powerful engines allowing it to haul more cargo or passengers. The R4D was used early in Vietnam by Marine advisory elements of MAAGV. See also **C-47.**

R-104M/105M/108M   Radio   see   **NVA/VC Radios**

R-126 Radio   *see*   NVA/VC Radios

RA   *see*   US (Serial Number)

RA-3   *see*   B-66

RA-5   *see*   A-5

RAAF   *see*   Royal Australian Air Force

Rabbit   *see*   Dog Collar

Rabbits   *see*   Caucasian

RABFAC (Radar Beacons, Beacon Drops)   Small, portable ground radar beacons used by ground bound FACs. Marine ground FACs made use of navigational radar beacons to direct air strikes. The A-6 aircraft used by the Marines and Navy featured advanced avionics systems that allowed the aircraft to use the beacon to pinpoint targets called by the FACs. The FAC identified the target's distance and bearing from the beacon for the aircraft, which made the necessary adjustments to attack the target. The radar beacon reduced the effectiveness of cloud cover and darkness to conceal targets. Air strikes controlled by the radar beacons were called "beacon drops." *See also* Radio Beacon.

RAC   *see*   Reconnaissance Airplane Company, Avn

Race Relations Board   *see*   Human Relations Committee

Rach Gia (Rock Jaw)   Provincial capital of Kien Giang, located on the western coast of SVN on the Gulf of Thailand. The "Rock Jaw" as it was nicknamed, was 75kms west of Can Tho and 113kms northwest of Soc Trang.

Rach Kien   Village located 15kms south of Saigon and 18kms east of Tan An in Long An Province, III Corps. U.S. and ARVN units stationed at bases around Rach Kien were part of the ring of strategic bases providing security for Saigon.

Racism in Vietnam   For American–American racism *see:* **Black American Soldier, Project 100,000, Klan, Ju-Ju, Clenched Fist, Soul Handshake, Black Power, Undesirable Discharges.** For American–Vietnamese racism *see:* **Mere-Gook-Rule, Gook Syndrome.** For Vietnamese–Montagnard racism *see:* **Vietnam's Niggers, Nguoi Thuong, Montagnards.**

RAD   *see*   River Assault Division

Radar Beacons   *see*   RABFAC

Radar Burnthrough   The ability of radar to operate through enemy countermeasures designed to inhibit or otherwise render the radar ineffective. U.S. aircraft on strike missions into NVN used electronic countermeasures to reduce the enemy's ability to radar track and target the aircraft. The enemy used radar controlled AAA guns and surface to air missiles. ECM screens were effective at long range, but a close range enemy radar could sometimes penetrate (burnthrough) the ECM defenses of the attacking formation. *See also* ECM.

Radar Controlled Bombing   *see*   TPQ Missions, RABFAC.

Radar, Ground   *see*   Ground Radar

Radar Homing and Warning Equipment   *see*   Wild Weasel, RHAW System

Radar Image   *see*   Radar Paint

Radar Intercept Officer (RIO)   Navy air officer whose duties were similar to those of a Weapons Systems Operator with the Air Force. The RIOs rode in the backseat of F-4 fighters, operating radar, ECM equipment and weapons systems. *See also* Weapons Systems Operator.

Radar Paint (Radar Image)   Pilot's slang for the image that was displayed on a radar scope.

Radar Picket   *see*   DER

Radio   Radios were used extensively in Vietnam by Free World Forces. For American forces radios were sometimes found as low as the squad level and some aircraft crewmen carried their own portable survival radios. The NVA/VC also made use of radios, but not as extensively as the U.S., and their lowest level of radio support was usually the company. Soviet radios were the NVA/VC's main source of equipment, although they did make use of captured ARVN/American equipment for communications, and for monitoring and jamming American nets. *See also* NVA/VC Radios, U.S. Radios, AM/FM Radio.

Radio Amplifier   *see*   Bitch Box

Radio Beacon (Nondirectional Beacon [NDB]) Small navigational beacons that were used by aircraft for target acquisition. The NDB broadcasted a radio signal which was used by attacking aircraft for direction to the target. The location of the beacon was known to the aircraft, and they delivered their ordnance based on the relative location of the target to the beacon. The small radio beacons were usually deployed by USSF/MACV-SOG teams. The use of radio beacons for targeting was similar to the use of radar beacons. *See also* **RABFAC.**

Radio Call Signs *see* **Call Signs**

Radio Check *see* **Commo Check**

Radio Code Book *see* **Signal Operating Instructions**

Radio Code Sheets *see* **Shackle Cards**

Radio Frequency (Freq, Push, Freak, Uniform, Surgical Push) Field terms for a radio frequency. The word "uniform" was used to refer to a UHF radio frequency; i.e., battalion uniform, the battalion's UHF radio frequency. A "Surgical Push" was the radio frequency of a specific U.S. field hospital. Medevac aircraft en route could notify the receiving hospital of the type of casualties being brought in, allowing the hospital extra minutes to prepare.

Radio Hanoi (VNA) NVN radio programs that targeted U.S. troops in SVN. The English speaking broadcasts were made over VNA, Radio Hanoi. The principal broadcaster was an NVN woman called "Hanoi Hanna." Her program consisted of music, communist slanted news stories, and propaganda messages. She sometimes mentioned U.S. units by name and even told stories about individual U.S. soldiers. The source of information for many of the stories was from bits and pieces of information collected from recent combat areas (personal effects, letters, etc.), or salvaged from U.S. trash sites. The broadcast was an attempt to weaken U.S. troop morale in Vietnam. Hanoi Hanna was the equivalent of Japan's Tokyo Rose of WWII. *See also* **Hanoi Hanna, Liberation Radio.**

Radio Liberation Clandestine communist radio station controlled by the NLF/PRG that broadcasted news and propaganda into South Vietnam.

Radio Net (Net) Radios that were on the same frequency made up a net. The radios within a command used the same frequency. The platoons within a company were on the same net, and the companies within a battalion would be on a different net, etc. This reduced the confusion of radio traffic. There were usually at least three radios at a company CP, each on a separate frequency: one net with the companies' platoons, a net to the battalion headquarters, and one radio that could be used to switch to other nets such as aircraft, artillery, medevac, etc.

Radio Operators *see* **Radio Telephone Operator**

Radio Relay (RR) Technique used to extend communications for units in the field beyond the range of their radio equipment. Messages, coordinates, requests, etc., were passed to a friendly unit within range; the friendly unit would in turn pass the information on. This relay continued until the message reached its final destination. Ground units and airborne units were used to relay messages. Such messages were kept short to reduce the error rate. *See also* **Airborne Radio Relay.**

Radio Research Unit (Group) *see* **Army Security Agency**

Radio Saigon SVN government radio station that broadcasted from Saigon. The station's format included music, news and progovernment propaganda. *See also* **House 7 Radio Group.**

Radio Spooks *see* **Army Security Agency, Spook**

Radio Telephone *see* **Field Radio**

Radio Telephone Operator (RTO, Radio Operators [RO]) Soldier in the field who carried and or manned radio equipment. Field RTOs or radio operators usually carried either a PRC-25 or PRC-77, along with their normal combat gear. Extra radio batteries were dispersed throughout the platoon or unit to insure their supply while operating in the field. In most cases the radio served as the only link to support from the rear: support in the form of artillery, air cover, medical evacuation, supply, reinforcements or extraction. RTOs were one of the prime targets of enemy snipers and gunners. *See also* **U.S. Radios, Army Security Agency.**

Radio Vietnam *see* **American Forces Vietnam Network**

Radios *see* **Field Radio**

RAF *see* **TF 117**

RAF One *see* **River Assault Flotilla One**

RAG (River Assault Group) Elements of the South Vietnamese Navy's River Force. RAGs transported troops during river assaults and provided them with fire support, performed minesweeping, logistics transport and patrol escorts. The typical RAG consisted of a command boat, monitor, five LCMs, six armored LCVPs and six STCAN/FOM patrol boats. The River Force continued operations in conjunction with American forces that entered the war in '65. The RAGs had no organic infantry and had to rely on ARVN and RF/PF infantry units for their riverine operations. *See also* **South Vietnamese Navy.**

RAG 76.8 *see* **Operation Frequent Wind, Eagle Pull**

Ragulai *see* **Montagnards**

RAID *see* **River Assault, Interdiction Division**

Railroad Tracks *see* **Captain**

Railway Security Agency (RSA) South Vietnamese government agency responsible for railroad security on the South's limited rail system, the Trans-Vietnam. The agency used ground patrols and specially armored rail cars in attempts to secure the rail lines. Rail traffic across Vietnam was virtually shut down by the Viet Cong, except in the large cities where the GVN presence was highest. *See also* **Wickums, Nam O Bridge.**

Rain Making Operations *see* **Cloud Seeding Operations**

Rainy Season *see* **Monsoons**

Rakassans *see* **187th Infantry Regiment**

Raking/Raking Over *see* **H and I**

Rallier *see* **Hoi Chanh**

Ramp Alert (Strip Alert) Readied strike aircraft, fully armed and fueled, that could be airborne in less than 15 minutes. Such aircraft remained on standby at air bases across Vietnam and Thailand to provide support to ground units. The number of ramp alert aircraft was at its peak during the hours of darkness, when enemy units were most active. Ramp alert aircraft included a variety of fixed and rotary wing craft. *See also* **Whiplash, Razor Back Fire Team, Hot Pad Alert.**

RAN *see* **Australia, HMAS Hobart**

Ranch Hand *see* **Operation Ranch Hand**

Rand Corporation U.S. operational research corporation, headquartered in Santa Monica, California. Rand was a nonprofit corporation providing a "think tank" environment for various research projects, most of which were government funded. Rand performed systems analysis for various branches of the government and was used to analyze intelligence information gathered from the field in RVN, making recommendations to the government and the military on how best to deal with, and disrupt VC and VCI operations in Vietnam. Many of the Rand recommendations surfaced in the operations of the Phoenix Program and throughout the military.

Randall Knife Randall Model 14 attack knife was one of the knives carried by USSF troops in Vietnam. The knife featured a 7.5-inch, single edged blade, carried in a leather sheath which included a sharpening stone.

Randy Australian slang for "horny."

Range Card A card containing the designated target area of responsibility for a gun position on the perimeter of a base. The base TOC maintained a copy of the gun position's areas of responsibility, which allowed more control of the perimeter defenses. Gun positions were deployed with interlocking fields of fire, allowing them to protect each other and bring extra fire to bear as required. Range cards were only maintained at the larger American base camps.

Range-Gunnery Computer (Armor) *see* **Donkey Sight**

Ranger *see* **USS Ranger**

Ranger Handbook *see* **Ranger's Bible**

Ranger Hat *see* **Campaign Hat**

Ranger Pack *see* **ARVN Rucksack**

Ranger's Bible (Ranger Handbook, TC 21-76, FM 31-18 LRRP Manual) Nickname for the "Ranger Handbook," originally published by the Army Infantry School at Fort Benning, Georgia, as a reference guide for the school's ranger course. The small handbook was used as a training guide by LRRP schools in the U.S. and Vietnam. The book detailed patrolling techniques, first aid, communications, aerial resupply, field survival, fire and maneuver, demolitions, and various other subjects critical to the LRRP mission. The Ranger Handbook was not an "official" Army manual but was issued as a supplemental training document (TC 21-76). The handbook proved to be much more valuable and practical than the official Army Ranger Field Manual (FM 31-18), Long-Range Reconnaissance Patrol Company.

Rangers (Sneaky Petes) U.S. Army LRRP units operating in Vietnam were re-designated as the 75th Infantry, Rangers, in '69. There had been no active Ranger companies in the U.S. Army since the end of the Korean War. The Rangers continued their LRRP functions as well as the training and advising of ARVN Ranger units. In Vietnam the LRRP units were renamed Ranger companies C thru I, and K thru P. The Rangers were also nicknamed the "Sneaky Petes." *See also* **75th Infantry (Rangers)**.

Rangers Lead the Way *see* **75th Infantry (Rangers)**

Rap Slang for talk, converse, discuss.

Rape and Ruin *see* **R & R**

Rapid Engineer Deployment Heavy Operation Squadron *see* **RED HORSE Engineers**

Rapid Fire *see* **Project Rapid Fire**

Rapist-Killer *see* **Double Veteran**

Rappelling Descending rapidly down a rope. In Vietnam most rappelling done by FWF troops was from a helicopter. In areas where the vegetation was too dense for helicopters to land, troops were inserted by rope or rope ladder.

RAR *see* **Royal Australian Regiment**

RAR/NZ *see* **New Zealand or Royal Australian Regiments**

RAS *see* **River Assault Squadron**

RAS Shells (Rocket Shells, Rocket-Assisted Artillery Shells) Rocket-assisted artillery shells that extended the range of a 105mm howitzer shell as much as 3,200 meters. The normal range of a 105mm shell was 11,000 meters. *See also* **M-101A1 Howitzer**.

Rat Patrols Nickname given to night ambush patrols conducted by elements of the 6th Infantry/198th Light Infantry Brigade operating in the Que Son Valley. The ambushes were conducted along Highway 535, the road link between LZ Ross and LZ Baldy. Before the "Rat Patrols" started in late '67 the road was mined daily and road convoys were ambushed on a regular basis by local VC. The Rat Patrols consisted of an infantry company deployed in squads which conducted stationary ambushes and roving patrols after dark. The patrols successfully eliminated much of the VC activity against Highway 535 and in the Que Son Valley. "Rat Patrol" was also the nickname for armed gun jeeps that conducted mine clearing operations along the roads traveled by supply convoys.

Rat Trap Marine nickname for a two- or three-man spider hole used by the Viet Cong. In areas patrolled by U.S. troops the VC would hole up in the spider hole during the day and come out at night to visit the nearby villages for their food, supplies and operations, and other needs. The VC would regroup for night operations and disperse again before daybreak, returning to their rat traps. *See also* **Spider Hole**.

Rat-6 *see* **Diehard Tunnel Rats**

Rat-Turds *see* **Oak Leaf Cluster**

Ratcheting Secretary of Defense Robert McNamara's term for the gradual incrementation of American troop strength in Vietnam. *See also* **Escalation, Gradualism**.

Ratfuck Operation *see* **Cluster Fuck**

Ration-of-Shit GI slang, meaning to give (or receive) a hard time, to complain, to cause trouble, to make life miserable.

Rations *see* **C-Rations, LRRP Rations**

A Rat's Ass   see   Give-a-Fuck

RATS   see   Rear-Echelon-Mother-Fuckers

Rattlesnakes (ARVN Deserters)   Nickname for armed ARVN deserters who roamed the streets during the final days of South Vietnam in April '75. The rattlesnakes used their weapons to rob and loot as they made their way down the coast of Vietnam and into the streets of Saigon.

Raven   see   OH-23

Raye, Martha (Margie Yvonne Read)   Martha Raye, singer and comedienne, toured Vietnam entertaining and visiting U.S. troops. She started her troop visits in '65, and they continued yearly until the end of U.S. involvement in Vietnam. Martha Raye was wounded twice in Vietnam while visiting with U.S. troops, and was awarded two Purple Hearts. Martha Raye's private name is Margie Yvonne Read. See also Hope, Bob.

Raymond-Morrison-Knudsen Construction   see   RMK-BRJ

Razor   see   Dewey Canyon Fire Bases

Razor Back Beach   Code name for a beachhead established near Duc Pho to provide added logistics support for 1st Cavalry Division operations out of LZ Montezuma. The beachhead was fed by LSTs and LCMs.

Razor Back Fire Team   Team of two helicopter gunships used as a quick reaction force that remained on standby alert until needed. When called, the team could be airborne in three minutes. See also Ramp Alert.

Razor Grass   see   Elephant Grass

Razor Wire   see   German Wire

Razorbacks   see   120th Aviation Company

RB-26   see   B-26

RB-57   see   B-57

RBF   see   Recon by Fire

RC-47   see   C-47

RC-130   see   C-130

RC-135   see   EC-135, C-135

RC-292   see   Long John Antenna

RCL   see   Recoilless Rifle

RD Cadre   see   Rural Development Cadre

RD-55   see   River Division 55

RDC   see   Rural Development Cadre

RDPG   see   Revolutionary Development Peoples Group

Re-Up   see   Reenlistment

Reaction Force (Reaction Team)   Force designed and organized to move to the aid of friendly forces under attack. During Vietnam, the size of such reaction forces varied from company to battalion size units, and were deployed as armor, infantry and airmobile forces. In the early days of the war, the NVA/VC would attack a small ARVN outpost causing the post to request assistance. An ARVN reaction force would start out to relieve the post, and then be ambushed by a large enemy force waiting in ambush for them. Such Viet Cong ambushes against American units became less popular with the VC due to the Americans' mobility and readily available firepower. See also Sparrow Hawk.

Reaction Team   see   Reaction Force

Read, Margie Yvonne   see   Raye, Martha

Ready Rifles   see   52d Infantry Regiment (Light)

Ready to Strike, Anywhere, Anytime   see   25th Infantry Division

Real War   see   Other War, The

Real Whole Milk (Reconstituted Milk, Whole Milk)   Because of a lack of local dairy facilities most Americans in Vietnam did not have access to "real whole milk." Instead, when available, they were given a reconstituted oily version of milk. Many troops returning home from Vietnam on commercially chartered aircraft were amazed at the taste of the "real whole milk" served on board, a taste that the troops had not experienced for at least a year.

Really New Life Hamlets (Ap Doi Moi)   Name for the CORDS pacification program that followed the New Life Hamlet program. The program "really" wasn't any more effective than the program that preceded it. See also Fishes-in-the-Sea, Strategic Hamlets, New Life Hamlets.

Reappropriation   see   Midnight Requisition

Rear, The *see* **Sitdown**

Rear Admiral *see* **Admiral**

Rear Area Types (RATS) *see* **Rear-Echelon-Mother-Fuckers**

Rear Echelon Personnel (Paper Pushers, Pencil Pushers, Paper Soldiers) The number of administrative and support personnel required to keep combat units operational in the field was very high. On an average, the military required 5–8 rear area troops to support each combat troop operating in the field. These rear area troops consisted of clerks, cooks, medical staff, transportation, maintenance, logistics personnel, etc. Rear echelon troops were resented by many grunts in the field, while other grunts envied them their relatively secure positions at base camps, away from the daily humps and firefights of the boonies. *See also* **Rear-Echelon-Mother-Fuckers.**

Rear Guard *see* **Closing the Back Door**

Rear Security *see* **Tail-End Charlie**

Rear-Echelon-Mother-Fuckers (Headquarters Specialist, Remington Warriors, REMF, Pogues, Spoons) General class of troops, EM, NCOs, and officers looked upon with distaste by field soldiers. Such rear support troops, known as "pogues" to the Marine grunt, spent most of their tour in rear area base camps and rarely saw the war, let alone combat. Yet some of the REMFs (clerks, cooks, drivers, etc.) were quick to boast of their war tales and imagined actions. A special place of disgust was kept in the grunt's heart for the officers who directed combat operations from rear area CPs or high above in C & C helicopters. The staff and support personnel and Remington Typewriter Commandos will long be unflatteringly remembered. Also known as Remington Raiders, Desk Jockeys, Rearies, Combat Clerks, Base-Camp-Desk-Jockey, Clerks and Jerks, Rear Area Types (RATS), PX Cowboys, Spoons (cooks). *See also* **Saigon Warriors.**

REARF *see* **Forward Rearm and Refuel Point**

Rearies *see* **Rear-Echelon-Mother-Fuckers**

Reburial *see* **Cai Tang**

Recce *see* **Reconnaissance**

Receiving *see* **Triage**

Recoilless Rifle (RCL, Backblaster, RR) Designed primarily for use against armored targets, recoilless rifles (RCLs) were used extensively by both NVA/VC and FWFs throughout the war. The NVA/VC used Soviet, Czech and PRC made weapons, most of which fired a fin stabilized HEAT rocket. FWF recoilless weapons were the U.S. 57mm, 90mm, and 106mm, and a Swedish made 84mm gun. Recoilless rifles typically discharged their exhaust gases and vapors through a vent system located at the rear of the rifle tube, greatly reducing the weapon's recoil when fired, but emitting an easily enemy observable, and dangerous backblast. *See also* **M-67 RCL, M-40A1, L14 RCL, B10/11 RCL, T21 RCL, PRC RCL, M-18A1 RCL.**

Recon *see* **Reconnaissance**

Recon Box (Recon Zone) Army term for the typical recon area patrolled by an LRRP team. The box covered a 2 × 2kms square area and was sometimes referred to as a "recon zone." An LRRP team would be inserted into the area to conduct reconnaissance for 5–7 days. Some of the recon missions involved ambushes set up by the recon team. If the team discovered a large enemy force, additional friendly units would be moved into the area to engage the enemy. If the recon force was detected it was usually extracted. *See also* **No Fire/No Fly, LRRP.**

Recon by Fire (RBF) Technique of firing into an area in an attempt to force concealed enemy units to return fire, thus revealing their position or intentions. RBF was effectively used by U.S. units along suspected ambush routes, sometimes causing the enemy to spring the ambush prematurely before the entire unit entered the kill zone. *See also* **Area Recon by Fire, Marching Fires, Probe, Mad Minute.**

Recon Gloves (Leather Gloves) Field name for the standard Army issue, black leather glove shells. The glove shells were designed to be worn with wool glove liners. In Vietnam the fingers and thumb of the leather glove shells were cut off to allow unobstructed use of weapons. The cutoff gloves were worn by recon and some heavy weapons troops.

Recon Zone *see* **Recon Box**

Recondo School *see* **MACV Recondo School**

Recondos Name for small units of platoon size or smaller, that conducted search operations seeking to make contact with NVA/VC forces. The Recondos were specialized, operating as independent recon units, forwarding their recon results to higher headquarters. The Recondos used a checkerboard search pattern that allowed them to cover more ground. *See also* **Checkerboard.**

Reconnaissance (Recon, Recce, Reconnoiter) Operation with the specific purpose of gathering information (intelligence) about the enemy, his defenses, disposition and any other pertinent information. Such operations could also include gathering information on terrain, resources, weather conditions or other information that could affect future operations in an area. Various types of recon missions were used in Vietnam, but they were all based on gathering information about the enemy and pinpointing his haunts and habits. *See also* **Reconnaissance in Force, Recon by Fire, Recondos, Marine Force Recons, Reconnaissance Airplane Company, Spike Recon Teams.**

Reconnaissance Airplane Company (RAC) Army reconnaissance airplane company which primarily consisted of the OV-1 Mohawk. The Mohawk was configured as a recon and surveillance aircraft, with the extra capability of operating armed. In Vietnam the OV-1 was armed with a variety of weapons including machine guns, bombs, napalm and rockets. *See also* **Avn, OV-1.**

Reconnaissance in Force (RIF) A recon mission combining intelligence gathering with combat. Normally a recon mission involved the covert gathering of information, hopefully, without enemy contact. In a RIF the recon force purposely made contact with the enemy in order to determine his strength, disposition, location and any other information that could be gathered from the contact. Similar to a small scale probe, or large scale search and destroy. *See also* **Search and Destroy, Battalion RIF.**

Reconnaissance Teams (MACV-SOG) *see* **Spike Recon Teams**

Reconnoiter *see* **Reconnaissance**

Recons *see* **Marine Force Recons**

Reconstituted Milk *see* **Real Whole Milk**

Reconstruction Aid A provision of the '73 Paris Peace Accords called for the U.S. to provide North Vietnam with economic aid to assist in their reconstruction. According to the Nixon administration, $4.25 billion in economic aid was to be given to NVN, pending U.S. congressional approval. The aid package was not approved because Congress did not believe NVN was cooperating fully regarding the U.S. MIA issue. Following the Nixon resignation the Ford administration did not actively pursue the aid issue. Two years after the signing of the peace accords NVN was flagrantly violating the accords with their all-out offensive to take over SVN. A full accounting of U.S. MIAs, by NVN, has continued to stand in the way of economic aid to NVN.

Recycle (Cuts, Unsats, Marginals) To be put back to a lower level in the training cycle. DIs used the threat of recycling to encourage troops to improve, to avoid forced repetition of some phases of basic training. Those recruits that had difficulties completing the training were sometimes called "cuts" or "unsats" and were repeatedly recycled until they were able to complete the training cycle, were released from the military as "unfit," went AWOL or committed suicide. Marine DIs labeled recruits on the verge of recycling as "marginals" and stayed "on their case" in an effort to make them break or succeed.

Red Alert *see* **Alerts**

Red Ball Express Nickname for special convoys of the 1st Brigade/5th Infantry Division (Mechanized), which made depot runs to get spare parts needed by their armored vehicles in the field. *See also* **Priority 999.**

Red Beach *see* **Operation Jackstay, Operation Red Beach II**

Red Beach II *see* **Operation Red Beach II**

Red Bird *see* **AH-1G**

Red Bombs Air Force slang for their high-powered sleeping pills used by airmen after they returned from a combat mission so "keyed up" that they were unable to sleep.

Red Butt Rifle   *see*   **Mosin-Nagant Rifle**

Red China   *see*   **People's Republic of China**

Red Cross   *see*   **Donut Dollies**

Red Cross Package   Small packages of utility items furnished to troops in the field by the American Red Cross. The packages usually found their way to troops around holidays and contained such items as playing cards, soap, toothpaste, washcloths, toothbrushes, chewing gum, paperback books, writing paper, shaving kit, etc. A similar Red Cross Package was provided for U.S. POWs held in North Vietnam, but the packages were usually held up by the North Vietnamese and not allowed to be distributed to the POWs.

Red Crown   Code name for a U.S. Navy ship operating in the Gulf of Tonkin, off the coast of NVN, as an air controller for U.S. aircraft operating in the area and over NVN.

Red Devil   *see*   **LZ Red Devil**

Red Devil Road (FSB Elliot)   Road cut by U.S. Army Engineers from FSB Elliot to just east of Khe Sanh, I Corps. The road was cut through dense jungle and enemy territory, and was used by the ARVNs during their incursion into Laos in February '71. FSB Elliot was established at the junction of Highway 9 and Red Devil Road.

Red Devils   *see*   **1st Brigade/5th Infantry Division (Mechanized)**

Red Golf Balls   *see*   **Cotton Balls**

Red Haze (Cooking-Fire Recon)   Aerial recon photos taken by Air Force RF-4C Phantom jets. The red haze photos were specialized pictures that revealed the locations of cooking fires spotted during the aircraft's flight. Such locations, if determined to be in hostile territory, were usually targeted for air or artillery strikes at a later time.

RED HORSE Engineers (Rapid Engineer Deployment Heavy Operation Squadron)   Air Force combat engineer squadrons that operated in Vietnam. The engineer squadrons consisted of a small force that deployed on a temporary basis making improvement to airfield facilities and fortifications. RED HORSE engineers

normally did emergency field repairs, built revetments and perimeter defenses. During the initial buildup of U.S. air power in SVN, RED HORSE engineers participated in the construction of several air base facilities. "RED HORSE": Rapid Engineer Deployment Heavy Operation Repair Squadron, Engineering. *See also* **Engineers.**

Red Khmers   *see*   **Khmer Rouge**

Red LZ   *see*   **Hot LZ**

Red Menace   *see*   **Domino Theory**

Red Platoon   *see*   **Aero Weapons Platoon**

Red River Delta (Red River Valley, Dikes, Bombing the Dikes)   Rich delta region around Hanoi in North Vietnam, part of the Red River Valley. The area around Hanoi, east and southeast, was a major part of the Delta. April '72 marked the first time B-52 bombers had been used against targets near Hanoi, or anywhere in the Red River Delta area. The area was NVN's major industrial area and site of a major harbor. Because of seasonal monsoon flooding a series of dikes was constructed throughout the valley to control the river's flood waters. Numerous "hawks" suggested bombing the ancient systems of dikes in order to flood Hanoi. The proposal was never adopted by Presidents Johnson or Nixon.

Red River Valley   *see*   **Red River Delta**

Red Smoke   *see*   **Hot LZ**

Red Stock Rifle   *see*   **Mosin-Nagant Rifle**

Red Team   Nickname for helicopter team composed of two or three gunships. The teams provided support to ground units and escort for airmobile operations. *See also* **Light Helicopter Section, Heavy Helicopter Section.**

Red Tracers   *see*   **Tracer Round**

Red-Baiting   Practice used by conservative politicians and groups to discredit another group, movement, or position by claiming that the communists were somehow connected to the group. Antiwar groups were frequently accused of being communist-backed, supported or influenced. In some cases antiwar groups were communist-backed or oriented. Such groups as W.E.B. DuBois Clubs, M2M, and the Progressive Labor Party were believed to be communist involved.

Redball In military terms a redball was a high speed transportation route. During WWII, redballs were the high speed road routes used to transport supplies and equipment to the front. In Vietnam a redball was a high speed enemy trail or road. The trails were usually concealed beneath jungle and canopy, and well maintained, and allowed the enemy to move large quantities of material swiftly, and undetected.

Redcatchers *see* **199th Light Infantry Brigade**

Redlegs (Artillerymen, Cannon Cockers) GI nickname for artillery troops, or "Cannon Cockers."

Redneck *see* **Caucasian**

Reds *see* **Aero Weapons Platoon**

Reduction in Force (RIF) When the military became overstaffed, they used a reduction in force to bring their numbers down. One method used was the mandatory retirement of career military personnel who had at least 20 years of active duty service. *See also* **Reconnaissance in Force.**

Reduction in Grade *see* **Busted**

Reed (Sun) Helmet *see* **NVA Helmet**

Reeducation Camps (Concentration Camps) Name used by NVN and the Khmer Rouge to describe political prisons and labor camps set up by the NVA in SVN after the fall of Saigon in April '75, and in Cambodia. Much of the population, especially those in the cities, GVN workers and the ex-military, were interred in the camps until they were reeducated in the communist way. The camps were located in various locations throughout North and South Vietnam. It is estimated that over 500,000 South Vietnamese were arrested; many have never returned home and to this day are still in reeducation prisons or are dead. *See also* **Reeducation Program, Camouflaged Concentration Camps.**

Reeducation Program After the fall of Saigon in '75 the communists established a program of reeducation to be applied to former teachers, GVN personnel, politi-

cians, the military, and in general, anyone who was associated with the U.S. or the GVN and its suborganizations. The program called for three levels of reeducation. Level one applied to minor GVN employees and soldiers and was to last three days. Level two applied to junior officers and middle GVN staff, and was to last one week. Level three was to consist of the higher level GVN leaders, senior military officers and members of the National and Secret Police; their stay was to last one month. According to NVN the purpose of the program was to reeducate the South Vietnamese in the ways of the new communist government and the history of the Vietnamese struggle for independence. NVN was still working behind the front of the PRG and NLF, which was encouraging the South Vietnamese to voluntarily enter the reeducation program. Over 500,000 South Vietnamese were sent to reeducation camps—some voluntarily, others by arrest; many never returned to Vietnamese society. The status of these people is not completely known, but many are known to have been executed for their participation in the GVN and the military. *See also* **Reeducation Camps.**

Reefer Trucks *see* **Reefers**

Reefers (Refrigerated Conex, Temporary Morgue, Reefer Trucks) Conex containers with self-contained refrigeration units attached. On some of the larger bases the reefer units were used to store perishable goods such as meats and medicines. The reefer units were also used as temporary morgues, holding the dead until they could be transported to the larger morgue facilities for processing back to the States. "Reefer trucks" in Vietnam were refrigerated trailers in the 7.5 to 10-ton range, used to transport perishable foodstuffs and medical supplies. *See also* **Body Cooler, Zipper Room.**

Reenlistment (Re-Up, Reopt, I'd Rather Throw Up...) The act of extending one's military career by agreeing to further enlistment in the service. During the Vietnam War, draftees were the least likely to reenlist when their current active duty enlistment was up. It was often necessary for a man to reenlist if he wanted to attend a particular service school or get an assignment to a particular area of the world. A three-year enlistment was standard, but as the VNW dragged on the term was lowered to two years. Many draftees summed up their view of reenlistment as, "I'd rather throw up than re-up!" *See also* **Hash Marks.**

Refrigerated Conex *see* **Reefers**

Refrigerated Food *see* **Class I Provisions**

Refugee (Displaced Person, DP) The war in Vietnam created tens of thousands of refugees. Prior to the introduction of U.S. ground combat troops, the refugee situation in Vietnam was relatively stable. The NVA/VC were not making widespread attacks across the country. Most refugees generated at that time were a result of government programs to move villagers from enemy controlled areas to fortified government hamlets. Much of the relocation work of the GVN was forced upon the people. The war, at that time, was primarily a rural war. Vietnamese civilians who chose to avoid the war or communist influence moved to the cities. After '65 there was an explosion of refugees which continued to increase throughout the war. As U.S. combat operations expanded large segments of the population were displaced. The refugees continued to flock to the cities. Vietnam's economy was based on the American presence. Thousands of homes and hamlets were destroyed over the course of the war. When the U.S. departed Vietnam, the refugee problem remained, and gradually grew worse as fighting between the NVA/VC and the GVN continued. Tens of thousands lived in the squalor of cardboard and tin camps along the streets of the city. The NVA's Final Offensive in '75 caused a mass exodus from SVN's rural areas as the population tried to outrun the communist forces. During the final collapse of Saigon in April '75 several thousand Vietnamese managed to get to American ships waiting offshore. After the fall of SVN refugees continued to escape the country by boat. *See also* **Forced Relocation, Johnsonvilles.**

Refugee Assistance Group *see* **Operation Frequent Wind, Eagle Pull**

Regiment, Army (Regt) A basic unit of organization traditionally used within the Army. The U.S. Army regiment of the Vietnam era only existed officially in the Armored Cavalry. Regiment size infantry and artillery units were organized into, and

designated as brigades; 3–4 battalions per brigade. Unofficially the Army continued to recognize the traditional regimental names of units, i.e., 2d Infantry Regiment, but officially the unit name excluded "regiment," i.e., 2d Infantry (Infantry). This only applied to infantry, artillery units and nonarmored cavalry. The 11th Armored Cavalry was the only official Army "regiment" to serve in Vietnam. *See also* **Brigade, Reorganization Objective Army Divisions.**

Regiment, Marine (Regt) The regiment formed one of the basic elements of the U.S. Marine divisional organization. The Marine regiment consisted of three combat battalions and its associated artillery support. The Marines deployed eight infantry (1st, 3d, 4th, 5th, 7th, 9th, 26th, 27th) and two artillery (11th, 12th) regiments to Vietnam. For identification purposes the term "Marines" in the unit name referred to the regiment, i.e., 2/4 Marines; 2d Battalion/4th Marine Regiment.

Regiment, NVA/VC The NVA/VC deployed large numbers of regiments to support the communist struggle in Vietnam. Regiments were assigned to individual divisions such as the 2d, 7th, 10th, 316th, 320th, etc. In addition there were several independent regiments that operated in each of the communist military regions of South Vietnam. The NVA fielded infantry, artillery, and later in the war armored regiments. The size of NVA/VC infantry regiments varied greatly and consisted of from 1,200 to 2,100 men, including support and artillery units. Enemy regiments and battalions that suffered heavy losses were usually pulled into Laos or Cambodia to regroup and refit. The rebuilt units would return to SVN under the same regimental name, or under a different name to confuse U.S. intelligence efforts.

Regimental Aid Station *see* **Battalion Aid Station**

Regimental Landing Team (RLT, Battalion Landing Team [BLT]) U.S. Marine amphibious regiment. In Vietnam the 5th Marines had three RLTs: the 26th, 27th, and the 28th. Sometimes disparagingly called "Reluctant Landing Teams." An RLT consisted of a regimental size infantry force reinforced by armor, artillery, engineers and associated units capable of making amphibious assaults. The regiment, likewise, consisted of infantry battalions organized into Battalion Landing Teams (BLTs). *See also* **Battalion Landing Team, 5th Marine Division.**

Regional Communications Group *see* **Strategic Communications Command**

Regional Forces (RFs, RF/PF, Ruffs, Civil Guard) South Vietnamese territorial forces organized as company size militia units deployed to guard strategic points and act as a reaction force to aid Popular Force units within their province. The Regional Forces were officially renamed the Civil Guard, but throughout the war were referred to as RFs. The units were defensive in nature, generally lacking military training and poorly equipped. The RF/PF's defensive skills against VC units were marginal at best, and ineffective at stopping NVA units unless the RF/PFs were heavily supported by air and artillery. They were under the control of the province chief until '64 when control was transferred to the ARVN. GIs called them Ruffs or Ruff-Puffs. *See also* **Popular Forces, Dan Ve.**

Regional Officer in Charge (ROIC) CIA chief of a regional area in Vietnam.

Registration Fire *see* **Battery Registration**

Regt *see* **Regiment**

Regular Army *see* **US (Serial Number)**

Regular Infantry *see* **Light Infantry**

Regulars *see* **6th Infantry Regiment (Light); Enemy, The**

Reinforced Protective Reaction Strikes *see* **Protective Reaction Strikes**

Reliable Academy *see* **M-14 Sniper Rifle**

Relocatable SAM *see* **Launch and Move SAM**

Relocation Camps *see* **New Life Hamlet**

Remain Overnight Position *see* **Night Defensive Position**

REMAINS NONVIEWABLE This note was stenciled on the outside of some caskets containing the bodies of American service personnel returning home from Vietnam. The note indicated the body was disfigured, mutilated or incomplete and not, in the opinion of the Department of Defense, in a condition appropriate for viewing in an open casket.

REMF *see* **Rear-Echelon-Mother-Fuckers**

Remington 700 *see* **M-40 Rifle**

Remington 870 One of the shotguns used by U.S. troops in Vietnam. The shotgun was an effective close range weapon and was used on combat patrols and by base security forces. The Remington 870 was a pump action shotgun with an 8-shot internal magazine. The standard shotgun shell in Vietnam was packed with nine 00-Buck lead pellets which gave the shotgun a kill range of about 20 meters in clear terrain and a wounding range out to 40 meters. At ranges of less than 10 meters it was hard to miss a target in the open. Due to projectile deflection by the foliage, jungle targets were more difficult to hit, but enemy ranges in dense jungle were typically less than 25 meters. *See also* **Shotgun.**

Remington Raiders *see* **Rear-Echelon-Mother-Fuckers**

Remington Typewriter Commandos *see* **Rear-Echelon-Mother-Fuckers**

Remington Warriors *see* **Rear-Echelon-Mother-Fuckers**

Remote Image Intensifier System *see* **Batship**

Rendezvous *see* **FSB Rendezvous**

Reopt *see* **Reenlistment**

Reorganization Objective Army Divisions (ROAD, Reorganization of Army Divisions) A U.S. Army plan to restructure the traditional makeup of a division. ROAD started in '61, before U.S. combat troops were involved in Vietnam. The reorganization called for the composition of a division to be based on the needs of the situation, with brigades assigned accordingly. This system allowed for the mixing of armor and infantry into a combined unit, under one command. Previously, the regiment/battalion was the main divisional unit component, but after ROAD the division components were brigade/battalion. Traditional Army regiments retained their names but were incorporated into brigades, several regiments per brigade.

Reorganization of Army Divisions *see* **Reorganization Objective Army Divisions**

Reparations *see* **Grievance Payment**

Repatriate The return of a captured soldier to his native country. According to the terms of the '73 Paris Peace Accords between the U.S. and North Vietnam, all POWs were to be returned to their country of origin. When it came time for repatriation, some NVA POWs held by the South Vietnamese refused to return to North Vietnamese control. Of the American POWs held by North Vietnam, PFC Robert Garwood willingly did not return to the States with the initial exchange of American prisoners in March '73. *See also* **Prisoner of War.**

Replacement Center (Repo Depo, Repple Depple, 90th Repo, 90th Replacement Center) Facility where new troops were processed prior to their permanent duty assignments. In Vietnam, the 90th Replacement Center was located at Long Binh, III Corps, and handled all III and IV Corps Army replacements. New troops were flown into Tan Son Nhut, then bused to Long Binh and held at the 90th Repo until assigned to a regular unit in-country. The stay at the Repo center was usually short as most assignments were arranged before the new troops arrived. Repple Depple was WWII slang for such a facility. Replacements were nicknamed "Turtles," because it took so long for them to arrive. *See also* **90th Replacement Battalion, 22d Replacement Battalion.**

Repo Depo *see* **Replacement Center**

Repose (USS Repose, AH-16) U.S. Navy hospital ship initially stationed off the coast of SVN at Chu Lai, I Corps, February '66. The *Repose* had a capacity of 800–920 hospital beds. It primarily operated along SVN's I Corps coastal zone in order to be near the areas of heaviest action. The *Repose* operated with a 370+ man crew, and a medical staff of over 500 people. *See also* **Sanctuary.**

Repple Depple *see* **Replacement Center**

Republic of China *see* **Nationalist China**

Republic of Korea (ROK, Korea) South Korean troops in Vietnam were known as ROKs (rocks) by GIs. Korea provided a significant combat force to operate in Vietnam: two infantry divisions, a brigade of Marines, and the accompanying artillery and support personnel operated in RVN from September '65 to March '73. ROK units in Vietnam were Capital Div, 9th Infantry Div and the 2nd Marine Corps Bde. The ROK's primary area of responsibility was the central coast area of II Corps from Qui Nhon to Phan Rang. During the war the ROKs suffered over 4,400 KIAs. In '68, over 50,000 ROK troops were in-country. The Korean Military Assistance program to the South Vietnamese was called the KMAGV or the "Dove Unit." *See also* **Korean Military Assistance Group, Vietnam; Tae Kwon Do.**

Republic of Korea Marine Corps (ROK Marines, Blue Dragons, Dragon Eye Regiment, 2d ROK Marines) In October '65 the Republic of Korea deployed the 2d Marine Brigade to South Vietnam. The ROK Marines initially deployed in defense of Cam Ranh Bay, but later moved north to operate from their base at Hoi An, just south of Da Nang, I Corps. The Dragon Eye Regiment (Blue Dragon Brigade) continued to operate along the I and II Corps coast until their withdrawal in '73. *See also* **Republic of Korea.**

Republic of Vietnam (Vietnam, South Vietnam, SVN, 'Nam, RVN, Nam Bo, Nam-Viet) South Vietnam was referred to by several names, including SVN, Republic of Vietnam, RVN, Vietnam and 'Nam. The Vietnamese called South Vietnam "Nam Bo" or "Nam-Viet." After the '54 Geneva Accords, the partitioned country of Vietnam was divided into North Vietnam (Democratic Republic of Vietnam) and South Vietnam. In '60 over 12 million people lived in South Vietnam. In October '55 Diem proclaimed himself president of the new Republic of Vietnam. Throughout the course of the war the Republic of Vietnam was alternately referred to as SVN, RVN, Vietnam, The Nam, and South Vietnam. *See also* **Vietnam (GI Names), Government of Vietnam.**

Republic of Vietnam Air Force (RVNAF, VNAF, South Vietnamese Air Force [SVNAF], VeeNAF, Khong Quan) The South Vietnamese Air Force (VNAF) consisted almost entirely of aircraft supplied by the United States, beginning in '55.

VNAF personnel were trained in Vietnam, and some flight officers were trained in the United States. The U.S. Air Force advisory program for the South Vietnamese was code-named Farm Gate and started in '61. At its peak VNAF numbered 2,000 aircraft. Most of the aircraft used by VNAF were propeller driven although there were several squadrons of F-5A/E and A-37 jet fighters. "Air Force" in Vietnamese was "Khong Quan."

Republic of Vietnam Army *see* **Army, Republic of Vietnam**

Republic of Vietnam Campaign Medal *see* **National Defense Service Medal**

Republic of Vietnam Marine Corps (VNMC, Thuy-Quan Luc-Chien, ARVN Marines, South Vietnamese Marines [SVNMC]) VNMC (Thuy-Quan Luc-Chien) was one of the best units available in the South Vietnamese armed forces. Formed in '65, the VNMC were trained by U.S. Marine Corps advisors and were well armed and disciplined combat troops. The VNMC as well as the ARVN Rangers and Airborne troops were often used as a "fire brigade" to be sent to trouble spots to fill the gaps in South Vietnam's line of defense. Although they were some of the best in the SVN military, they were plagued by low morale, high casualties and corrupt leadership. The ARVN Marines participated in the Laos Incursion, Lam Son 719, and suffered heavy casualties during their withdrawal from Laos. The Marines operated throughout SVN, but primarily operated in I Corps. *See also* **Special Landing Force, SVN.**

Republic of Vietnam Navy (RVNN, Vietnamese Navy [VNN], South Vietnamese Navy [SVNN], Hai Quan) Naval forces of the Republic of South Vietnam. The first ships available to the VNN were French craft used for riverine operations. This small fleet was later expanded by the Americans. VNN personnel were trained by American naval advisors and participated in coastal surveillance operations. When the U.S. Navy departed Vietnam in '72 they turned over their riverine fleet to the Vietnamese, bringing the VNN fleet to over 1,600 ships which included a large assortment of river craft and coastal patrol ships. As with most of the military, morale was extremely low in the VNN after the departure

of U.S. troops and the Navy's efficiency suffered. "Hai Quan" meant Navy in Vietnamese. *See also* **South Vietnamese Armed Forces, Sea Force.**

Republican Troops *see* **ARVN**

Republican Youth South Vietnamese youth group founded by President Diem. The progovernment group was a "flag-waving" organization whose main purpose was to participate in parades and demonstrations in support of Diem.

Request Mast *see* **Captain's Mast**

RESCAP *see* **Rescue Combat Air Patrol**

Rescue Combat Air Patrol (RESCAP) U.S. fighter and fighter-bomber aircraft that provided air cover for rescue operations during the retrieval of downed aircrews, especially in NVN. In June '65, propeller driven Navy A-1 fighters on RESCAP were attacked by NVAF jet MiG-17s. The A-1 Sandys were providing air cover for rescue operations. One of the A-1s outmaneuvered the jets and using his 20mm cannon, shot down one of the attacking MiGs.

Rescuemaster *see* **C-54**

Reserve Chute *see* **T-10 Reserve Parachute**

Reserve Officer Training Corps (ROTC) College students participating in on-campus programs which involved the study of military courses in addition to regular academic courses. The military courses prepared the students for military leadership and the Officer Corps. Graduates of the course were required to serve active duty in the military and entered the service as second lieutenants. As the VNW became increasingly unpopular on campus, enrollment in the ROTC declined. The ROTC was one of the four major sources of officer material for the Army. *See also* **Officers.**

Reserve Troops *see* **Weekend Warriors**

Reserves (Citizen Soldiers, National Guard [NG], the Guard) One of the recommendations made by the U.S. Joint Chiefs of Staff in '65 for conducting the war in SVN was to call up the American Reserves. It was argued that calling up the reserves would increase the military manpower base and at the same time provide a large, trained and experienced source of troops. The reserves could be deployed in a support role in Vietnam or used to maintain U.S. military commitments worldwide, allowing regular combat units to be used in Vietnam. The Johnson administration did not mobilize the reserves on a nationwide scale for fear of the growing antiwar sentiment that had begun to grow within the nation. Several reserve units were activated, but not the wholesale mobilization the JCS sought. Over one-million men served in the Reserves and National Guard during the Vietnam War. Of the total manpower available to the regular military, only 15,000 Reserves and National Guardsmen served in Vietnam. *See also* **USS Pueblo, Hoosier LRRPs, FSB Anzio, Weekend Warriors.**

Resettlement *see* **Restructuring**

Resettlement Camps *see* **New Economic Zones**

Resistance, The Nationwide antiwar group organized in San Francisco to resist the draft. The group organized protest demonstrations and encouraged men to return their draft cards to the Selective Service. In October '66 a rally was held at the U.S. Department of Justice and over 1,000 draft cards were collected and turned in to the attorney general's office. The AG returned the cards to the Selective Service for redistribution. Those individuals who refused the card were immediately inducted into the military; if they refused induction, under the law, they were subject to prosecution.

Resojet Air Generator Air blower used experimentally for tunnel warfare by the Army in Vietnam. The air generator was used to force smoke or gases through enemy tunnel complexes. The Resojet weighed over 100 pounds and required 10 gallons of gasoline an hour for operation. The Army rejected the Resojet for field use because of its high fuel consumption and poor mechanical performance under combat conditions. The Resojet operated with a 2.5-gallon fuel tank that did not allow for continuous operation of the unit while refueling. *See also* **Tunnel Warfare, Air Blowers.**

Resolution 9 One of the few official communist documents captured in Vietnam that indicated in '68 that the NVA/VC war against the US/GVN was not going well.

Because of the continued bombing of the North, large scale American ground operations and the NVA/VC losses suffered during Tet '68, Hanoi began to privately rethink its policy and goals.

Resolution 1975 Overall plan for NVN's conduct of the war in South Vietnam approved by North Vietnam's Politburo in '75. The Resolution outlined, in general terms, North Vietnam's continued commitment to maintain military pressure on South Vietnam and gradually bring more territory under their control. Political negotiations were to continue between NVN, SVN and the PRG, but the military was to continue a slow advance.

Resource Control *see* **Resource Management**

Resource Management (Resource Control, Thuoc Dao) Military phrase for the poisoning and destruction of crops or livestock which was used by, or was of potential use by the enemy. The spraying of defoliants was the method used when the military determined that crops in a specific area were destined for the VC or were being cultivated by the VC or its sympathizers. This was not a widespread policy because it was difficult to determine if the poisoned crops would find their way into the friendly food supply. The Vietnamese called chemical defoliants "Thuoc Dao"; poison. *See also* **Defoliation, Ranch Hand, Crop Denial.**

Respect 1954 Geneva Accords Sixties antiwar protest slogan which encouraged the Johnson administration to adhere to the '54 Geneva Accords which specifically called for a vote by the Vietnamese people on the reunification of North and South Vietnam, establishment of a central government representing all Vietnam. *See also* **Geneva Accords.**

Rest and Recreation *see* **R & R**

Rest and Relaxation *see* **R & R**

Restructuring (Forced Relocation, Resettlement, Ironing) The military term for the forced relocation of Vietnamese civilians from their hamlets. When the civilians were removed, the hamlet was destroyed (either by fire, explosives or bulldozer) and the area was declared a free-fire-zone. Relocations most frequently occurred in VC controlled areas where the population supported the VC. The term "relocation" for the displacement of the civilian population was later changed by the military to "resettlement" in an effort to give the impression that the people being relocated were doing it completely voluntarily. The Vietnamese nicknamed the restructuring "ironing a village." *See also* **Strategic Hamlet, Operation Sunrise, Johnsonvilles, Forced Urbanization, Scorched Earth Policy.**

Retarded Bombs (Snakeye Bombs, Mk-81, Mi-82, Drag Bombs, High Drag Bombs) High explosive aircraft bombs used for low level ground attacks. The "Snakeye" bombs were fitted with air brakes (drag fins) that deployed when the bomb was released, slowing its descent. This slowed descent was required to allow the aircraft to release the bomb from a much lower altitude and still have time to clear the bomb blast. Low level deliveries (500–700 feet) greatly increased the accuracy of the air strike allowing the ordnance to be dropped on enemy positions in closer proximity to friendly forces. Two of the most commonly used retarded bombs were the Mk-81 (250-pound) and the Mk-82 (500-pound). Without the retard fins the Mk-81 and the Mk-82 were also used as conventional GP bombs. *See also* **GP Bombs.**

Retire (Retirement) The movement of a force away from an opposing enemy force. This movement was made before contact was made with the enemy force in an attempt to avoid engaging the enemy. *See also* **Retreat, Retrograde Movement.**

Retirement *see* **Retire**

Retreat (Tactical Redeployment) The hasty movement to the rear, away from an enemy force, with all speed by the units involved. The retreating force was usually intact, but overwhelmed after contact with the enemy force. The unit attempted to fall back with its equipment; excess equipment was destroyed. Sometimes referred to as a "tactical redeployment." *See also* **Retrograde, Retire, Rout.**

Retrograde Cargo (Returning Cargo) Military terminology for cargo returning from the battlefield or combat zone. Such cargo could include empty brass from artillery shells, empty cargo containers, surplus equipment or any other items being shipped out of the area.

Retrograde Movement (Withdrawal) Considered, by the military, to be a controlled movement away from the enemy (voluntary or involuntary). This movement could be for the purpose of regrouping or to seek another route to advance, and was usually associated with a unit that was in contact with the enemy. Such movements were not considered retreats, merely the "repositioning" of combat forces. Contact with the enemy was broken and the engaged force attempted to withdraw from the enemy. Sometimes referred to by the military as "Tactical Redeployment." *See also* **Retreat, Retire, Delaying Action.**

Returnee *see* **Hoi Chanh**

Returning Cargo *see* **Retrograde Cargo**

Rev-Dev Nickname for Revolutionary Development programs. *See also* **Pacification.**

Revenge *see* **Payback**

Revetment A protective area, with reinforced sides (walls). The reinforcement could be made of wood, steel, earth or stacked sandbags. Large revetments were used on airfields in Vietnam to protect aircraft from enemy bombardment. In the field smaller structures were used for ammo dumps, gun pits, etc. The enemy, likewise, made use of revetments on a regular basis. Concrete revetments with overhead cover were used to protect American aircraft at many of South Vietnam's air bases.

Revolutionary Development *see* **Pacification**

Revolutionary Development Cadre *see* **Rural Development Cadre**

Revolutionary Development Peoples Group (RDPG) Part of the US/GVN '67 plan for Revolutionary Development called for the people of the RD hamlets and villages to defend themselves. Local villagers would be trained and armed, and their village fortified. The villagers were very reluctant to take up arms against the VC, leaving the RDPG plan on shaky ground. *See also* **Pacification.**

Revolutionary Guerrilla Warfare (Wars of Liberation) The use of guerrilla warfare to subvert and overthrow the standing government of a nation. Many of the revolutionary guerrilla wars in recent history have involved small groups of communist led or inspired insurgents seeking to overthrow the target government. Many of these "wars of liberation" have been supported, and in some instances instigated, by countries outside the target country. Wars of liberation were fought by antigovernment elements seeking to forcibly remove the existing government from power, a government usually accused of ineffectiveness, oppressiveness and a lack of regard for the general population.

Revolutionary Personalist Labor Party see **Can Lao Nhan Vi Cach Mang Dang**

Revolutionary Youth League see **Thanh Nien Cach Menh Dong Chi Hoi**

Revolving Door Command Nickname for Army policy in Vietnam. A line officer spent only six months in the field in command of a combat unit. This six month limit allowed more officers the opportunity to serve as combat unit commanders, a vital necessity for career advancement. This was a detriment to the Army as field commanders had less experience than the troops they were attempting to lead. Officers were not encouraged to specialize in any one field because the Army's overall goal was to have officers that were proficient in many areas. Time was not allowed for specialization if an officer expected to advance in the new military of the sixties and seventies. See also **Ticket-Punching, OER.**

RFs see **Regional Forces**

RF-4 Photo reconnaissance version of the F-4 Phantom II fighter which provided day and night reconnaissance. The RF-4 used infrared sensors and other sensors and film for intelligence gathering. See also **F-4.**

RF-8 see **F-8**

RF-100 see **F-100**

RF-101 (Voodoo, F-101) Photo reconnaissance version of the F-101 "Voodoo," manufactured by McDonnell Aircraft. The twin engine jet was built in a single and two seat version, operated at a max speed of 1,220mph and had a range of 2,400kms. The Voodoo was designed as an interceptor and bomber escort fighter armed with air-to-air missiles. The unarmed RF-101 was a late fifties vintage aircraft that was used by the Air Force for photo reconnaissance missions

over Vietnam early in the war.

RF/PF see **Regional Forces**

RG-42 Frag Soviet made fragmentation grenade used by the NVA/VC. The grenade was cylinder shaped with a flat bottom, 2.5 inches in diameter and 3.5 inches long, weighing about one pound. The grenade had a blast radius of 22 meters. See also **Hand Grenade.**

RGD-5 Frag Soviet made fragmentation grenade used by the NVA/VC. The elongated grenade was 2.5 inches in diameter and 3.75 inches long and weighed just over a pound, with a blast radius of 22 meters. The smooth shell of the grenade fragmented when detonated. See also **Hand Grenade.**

Rhade see **Montagnards**

RHAW see **Wild Weasel**

RHAW System (Radar Homing and Warning System) ECM equipment manufactured by the Bendix Corporation. The RHAW system was initially used by U.S. Wild Weasel aircraft for suppression missions against North Vietnamese SAM sites. The system tracked enemy radar emissions and sounded a warning to the pilot when enemy search radar was detected. See also **Wild Weasel.**

Rheault Affair (Thai Khac Chuyen) Colonel Robert Rheault, Commander of the U.S. 5th Special Forces Group, Vietnam, and six fellow officers were charged with the murder of a Vietnamese national, Thai Khac Chuyen. Chuyen was executed, under the responsibility of USSF, when it was discovered he was a double agent feeding the NVA information on Top Secret Project Gamma. The case was dismissed when the CIA (Project Gamma sponsor) refused to release information on the project because of national security, September '69. See also **Project Gamma.**

Rice Belts see **Elephant Intestines**

Rice Bowl see **Mekong Delta**

Rice Cakes see **Banh Giay**

Rice Cookies see **Banh Da**

Rice Hook see **Machete**

Rice Paddy see **Berm**

Rice Rolls *see* Elephant Intestines

Rice Tubes *see* Elephant Intestines

Rice Whiskey *see* 45 Whiskey

Rice Wine *see* Numpai

Rice-Denial Program US/GVN program to deny the availability of rice to the NVA/VC. Methods of rice denial included destruction of crops in remote areas and the guarding of a rice harvest and its transport to market. After the harvest, the GVN took control of the rice and issued small quantities to the villagers involved. The quantities given out were just enough to sustain a family, with no extra rice that could be passed on to or taken by the VC. American units participated in the program, conducting operations to screen the NVA/VC from the crop. *See also* **Crop Denial.**

Richardson, Elliot *see* **Secretary of Defense**

Rickshaw *see* **Pedicab**

Ride Bareback (Bareback) GI slang for having sexual intercourse without using a condom. *See also* **Boom-Boom.**

Ride Shotgun Troop(s) that watched for enemy ambush and whose job it was to return fire from the vehicle or aircraft in which they were riding; a mounted guard. Helicopter door gunners "rode shotgun" for their choppers, manning door mounted machine guns. *See also* **Door Gunner.**

Ridenhour, Ronald *see* **My Lai**

RIF *see* **Reconnaissance in Force, Reduction in Force**

Rifle Grenade Hand grenade fired from the end of a rifle instead of thrown by hand. Some rifle grenades were specifically designed to be attached to the muzzle of a rifle, and some regular hand grenades could be rifle-fired by means of a special adapter. The rifle grenade allowed the infantryman to lob the grenades at ranges well beyond the reach of the hand-thrown grenade (50–100 meters). Versions of the rifle grenade saw limited service with ARVN and NVA/VC forces. American and ARVN units used the M-79 Grenade Launcher to replace the rifle-fired grenade. *See also* **Grenade Launcher.**

Rifle Range, The Nickname for a large open area near Phu Cat that was used as a temporary laager by helicopters of the 1st Cavalry Division. The area had previously been used as a rifle range by the ARVNs and was located just east of Highway 1 in Binh Dinh Province, about 18kms north of Qui Nhon, II Corps.

RIIS *see* **Batship**

Riley *see* **Dewey Canyon Fire Bases**

Ring Knocker Society *see* **West Point Protective Association**

Ringing-the-Perimeter *see* **Defensive Contact Artillery Fire**

Ringworm *see* **Gook Sores**

RIO *see* **Radar Intercept Officer**

Riot Guns *see* **Shotgun**

Ripcord *see* **FSB Ripcord**

Ripped *see* **Drunk, Get High**

RITA *see* **Deserters**

River *see* **Song**

River Assault and Interdiction Division (RAID) South Vietnamese Navy riverine force that operated similarly to the U.S. River Assault Division. The RAIDs were formed from the assets of U.S. riverine units transferred to the Vietnamese as part of the Vietnamization program in '69. *See also* **River Assault Division.**

River Assault Division (RAD) Navy element that provided boat support for the Army infantry units of the Mobile Riverine Force, TF 117. Two RADs, along with their assigned infantry or artillery battalion, composed one River Assault Squadron. The RADs originally numbered four when the MRF began operations in '67; by the time U.S. units were withdrawn from the MRF there were eight RADs. As more vessels became available, the unit size an individual RAD could support increased. *See also* **TF 117, River Assault Squadron.**

River Assault Flotilla One (RAF One) In June '67 the U.S. Navy River Assault Flotilla One, consisting of the first of two River Assault Squadrons (RAS) and one River Support Squadron (RSS), was operational. Each RAS was further divided into River Assault Divisions (RAD). The Flotilla operated throughout IV Corps using riverine warfare, mobile artillery, gunships, air assault and units of the Army's 2d Brigade/ 9th Infantry Division to strike at NVA/VC base areas. In early '69 the Navy began to transfer its assets to the Vietnamese; by June '69 the U.S. Flotilla was history. *See also* **TF 117, RAS, RSS, RAD, ACTOV.**

River Assault Force   *see*   **TF 117**

River Assault Group   *see*   **RAG**

River Assault Squadron (RAS) Combined Army/Navy river assault force. The initial Mobile Riverine Force, TF 117, was composed of two infantry battalions of the 2d Bde/9th Inf and river craft from the Navy's River Assault Flotilla One. Navy craft were split into two River Assault divisions to support each battalion of infantry (River Assault squadrons 9 and 11). RAD 91/92 supported RAS 9, and RAD 111/112 supported RAS 11. The assault squadrons were used for amphibious operations along the riverbanks and swamps of the Delta. The MRF eventually expanded to four RASs before its assets were transferred to the Vietnamese Navy. *See also* **River Support Squadron, TF 117.**

River Battleship   *see*   **Monitor**

River Division In March '68 the five Navy river divisions that patrolled the Delta were redesignated River Patrol Flotilla 5. The river divisions were designated River Squadrons. The squadrons, designated RIVRON 51, 53, 55, 57 and 59, each operated 4–5 river divisions. Each division consisted of PBRs and helicopter gunships. Most of the divisions included SEAL units and LSTs. Because of heavy enemy mine activity in the RSSZ, RIVRON 59 operated several minesweepers in place of the LSTs. Prior to the designation of the Flotilla, the RIVRONs were called River Patrol Groups. Two separate river divisions (521/453) operated in I Corps as TF Clearwater. *See also* **Game Warden River Groups, TF 116, TF Clearwater, River Division 55.**

River Division 55 (RD-55, MB I/II, Mobile Support Base, Division 55) Navy riverine force established in late '67 to provide security and surveillance duties on the rivers that linked Dong Ha and Hue with the South China Sea. Two PBR Mobile Support Bases (MB) were established on the Cua Vet River (Dong Ha) and the Perfume River (Hue). The PBR bases were designated MB

I and MB II. The two rivers, patrolled by the units of RD-55, were the primary supply routes used for shipment of heavy equipment and munitions destined for the Marine support base at Dong Ha and military units operating out of Hue. During the Tet '68 Offensive, RD-55 was reorganized into Task Force Clearwater in an effort to keep the river LOC open. *See also* **TF Clearwater.**

River Force   *see*   **South Vietnamese River Force**

River Mines In February and March '67 the first mining of rivers in North Vietnam occurred. Navy A-6 aircraft dropped floating naval mines in the mouths of the Cua Sot, Song Ma, Kien Giang, Song Ca and South Giang rivers. The mines proved effective at limiting NVN river traffic in the area. The major NVN deep water ports of Cam Pha, Hon Gai and Haiphong were not mined until '72.

River Minesweepers   *see*   **Minesweeper, River**

River Patrol Boat, French   *see*   **STCAN/FOM**

River Patrol Craft   *see*   **RPC**

River Patrol Flotilla 5   *see*   **Game Warden River Groups**

River Patrol Force   *see*   **TF 116**

River Patrol Groups   *see*   **Game Warden River Groups**

River Raider   *see*   **Operation River Raider**

River Rats   *see*   **TF 116**

River Support Squadron (River Support Squadron 7, RSS) Part of River Assault Flotilla One of TF 117 (MRF). The RSS handled the support functions of TF 117. Boat repair facilities and logistics support were provided through the RSS. The ships of the RSS were the troop barracks ships (APB, APL); the repair ship (ARL); and the logistic supply ship (LST). In addition, there were barges used as artillery firing platforms, and the tugs (YTB) necessary to position them. Some of the RSS vessels had deck mounted helicopter landing pads. Additional support facilities were located at TF 117's land base at Dong Tam. *See also* **RAF One, River Assault Squadron.**

River Support Squadron 7   *see*   **River Support Squadron**

River Transport Escort Group   see
RTEG

River Transport Group   see   RTG

River Warfare (Riverine Warfare)
"River warfare," as described by the Navy in
Vietnam, consisted of the naval effort to engage the enemy on the rivers and canals of
the Delta of IV Corps. Navy river craft attacked enemy shore positions and inter-
dicted supply and infiltration activity.
"Riverine warfare" involved the use of a
ground force combined with naval elements
to operate against the enemy. In Vietnam,
the ground forces used were elements of the
9th Infantry Division which operated as part
of TF 117 with Navy river units. The river
and ground force combined amphibious
and air assaults to engage enemy units in the
Delta. See also TF 116, TF 117, Riverine
Operations.

Riverine Assault Force   see   TF 116

Riverine Blocking Group   see   TF 194
Groups

Riverine Operations   Military operations conducted against enemy units and activities on rivers and canals. In Vietnam prolonged riverine operations were conducted
by specialized and combined forces of the
Navy and Army, with air support provided
by the Army, Navy and the Air Force. On
several occasions Marine SLFs conducted
riverine operations on a limited basis. Navy
TF 116 patrolled the waterways of the Delta.
TF 117 was a combined Army/Navy force
that conducted riverine operations in the
Delta. See also TF 116, TF 117, River Warfare.

Riverine Patrol Force   see   TF 116

Riverine Raiding Group   see   TF 194
Groups

Riverine Strike Group   see   TF 194
Groups

Riverine Warfare   see   River Warfare

Rivet Top   see   EC-121

RIVPATFLOT 5   see   Game Warden
River Groups

RIVRON 51–59   see   Game Warden
River Groups

RL   see   Rocket Launchers

RLA   see   Royal Laotian Army

RLAF   see   Royal Laotian Air Force

RLG   see   Laos

RLT   see   Regimental Landing
Team, 5th Marine Division

RLT 26   see   5th Marine Division

RLT 27   see   5th Marine Division

RLT 28   see   5th Marine Division

RMK-BRJ (Raymond-Morrison-Knudsen Construction, Brown-Root-Jones
Construction)   U.S. based construction
companies that combined operations in
Vietnam to undertake widespread military
construction projects for the U.S. government. RMK-BRJ employed thousands of
Vietnamese, Koreans and Filipino construction workers on hundreds of major projects
such as bases, roads, bridges, airstrips, harbor facilities and civic projects. During the
peak years of RMK-BRJ construction, '65–
'69, less than 10 percent of the construction
staff were Americans. See also Engineers,
Tiger Ladies.

RNZA   see   Royal New Zealand
Army

RNZIR   see   Royal New Zealand
Army

RO   see   Radio Telephone Operator

Ro-Ro Containers (Roll-On, Roll-Off
Containers; Containerized Cargo)   After
'66 some U.S. military cargos began arriving
in Vietnam loaded in 35-foot containers.
The new containerized delivery system
greatly decreased the time it took for a ship
to off load its cargo. The containers were
lifted off the ship by crane and loaded onto
the backs of trailers. A more expedient
method of handling the containers was
called "Ro-Ro"; roll-on, roll-off. Loaded
containers were left mounted on their
trailers and driven onto specially designed
ships. When the ship reached its destination, the trailers were simply driven off the
ship. Ro-Ro container method further increased the Navy's logistical support capabilities. See also Conex.

Roach   see   Cockroach Races, Marijuana

ROAD   see   Reorganization Objective Army Divisions

Road Recce   Aerial reconnaissance

mission flown by armed aircraft looking for enemy road traffic. If the aircraft spotted enemy vehicles they immediately took them under fire, expending their ordnance, then returning to base. Road Recce missions were standard in both the Navy and Air Force and were typically flown against NVA infiltration routes in NVN, Laos and Cambodia.

Road Repair Crews   *see*   **Binh Tram**

Road Runners   A U.S. armor technique used to provide security for convoys and roads similar to Thunder Runs, except larger units were used and the runs were made mainly during daylight hours. Road runners attempted to trigger enemy ambushes before they could attack supply convoys, reducing the enemy's ability to tie up the LOCs. Units that performed these runs called themselves Road Runners. Road Runner units sought contact with the enemy, making sweeps along roads used by friendly convoys. *See also* **Thunder Runs.**

Roadrunner Teams   Special Forces recon teams from Detachment B-52, assigned to perform surveillance and harassment of the NVA/VC along the Ho Chi Minh Trail network in and outside of SVN. The teams, 4–10 men dressed in NVA/VC uniforms, roamed the enemy trails performing surveillance and ambushing enemy units. The teams also directed air and artillery strikes, and organized attacks on the enemy by larger friendly forces. *See also* **Project Delta, Operation Leaping Lena.**

Robbins, Barbara   *see*   **First American Woman to Die. . .**

Robin   *see*   **LZ Robin**

Robin Hood   *see*   **173d Aviation Company**

ROC   *see*   **Nationalist China**

Rock, The   *see*   **Okinawa, Guam**

Rock Apes (Monkeys, Gibbon, Donc, Macaque)   Nickname for large gibbons, doncs, and macaques that inhabited the mountains of Northern I Corps. Several monkey species were spread throughout Southeast Asia. The "Rock Apes" of Vietnam were in the 12–40 pound range, and on occasion, reportedly pelted remotely located Marine LPs and NDPs with rocks.

Rock Crusher   *see*   **Operation Rock Crusher**

Rock Island East   *see*   **City, The**

Rock Jaw   *see*   **Rach Gia**

Rock 'n' Roll   GI slang for firing a weapon on full automatic, instead of single shot or short burst. Mostly applied to the M-16 rifle which had a selector switch that allowed single shot (semiautomatic), or full automatic fire.

Rock Pile   *see*   **Chu Pao Pass**

Rock Pile, The (Thon Son Lam, FSB Sheraton Rock Pile)   U.S. Marine fire support base located along the DMZ near Dong Ha. The base was also known as Fire Support Base Sheraton Rock Pile. Along with the Marine artillery, the Army's 8th Battalion/4th Artillery provided heavy fire support to Marine, and later Army units operating in northern I Corps. The 8th/4th Arty was a composite 175mm gun and 8-inch Self-Propelled Howitzer unit. *See also* **Dong Ha.**

Rock Quarry (Hill 64)   Rock Quarry located on a small hill (Hill 64), 1,600 meters west of Khe Sanh Combat Base (KSCB) in I Corps. During the siege of Khe Sanh the 1st Battalion/9th Marines and A Company/3d Battalion/26th Marines occupied the hill protecting the western approach to KSCB. *See also* **Khe Sanh.**

Rock Regiment   *see*   **503d Infantry Regiment (Airborne)**

Rocket Alley   *see*   **Phuoc Binh**

Rocket Artillery   Unguided rockets used for long-range bombardment. In Vietnam the NVA used various sized rockets for attacking fixed targets. The U.S. use of artillery rockets was primarily provided by Navy LSMR rocket ships which provided U.S. units with fire support. The NVA used 107mm, 122mm, and 140mm rockets, with ranges of 6–20kms. The launchers came in single tube and 12–40 tube versions, called Multiple Rocket Launchers. The MLRs required a vehicle or trailer for transport. *See also* **BM14/21, DKZ-B, Type 63 Rocket, LSMR.**

Rocket Belt   A defined zone around a city or installation from which enemy artillery rockets could be launched against the location. In Vietnam the NVA/VC used the PRC Type 63, and DKZ-B single tube artillery rockets, with ranges of 11–17kms.

The rockets could be broken down and man-packed to firing locations around cities and military installations. A large part of the U.S. ground effort after '70 was in patrolling these rocket belts to keep the NVA launchers out of range. *See also* **Rocket Artillery.**

Rocket City   A common local nickname for a base that was frequently attacked by NVA rockets. Bases such as Pleiku, Phu Loi and Lai Khe were continually harassed by NVA 122mm rockets. *See also* **Pleiku, Phu Loi, Lai Khe.**

Rocket Launchers   Small man-carried devices used to fire a rocket, usually an anti-tank weapon. In Vietnam rocket firing weapons were used against armored targets and fortifications. On occasion the NVA/VC used small rocket weapons against helicopters. The rocket was typically fin stabilized, as opposed to a finless shell which was spin stabilized. *See also* **M-20, M-72, RPG2, RPG7, Type 51.**

Rocket Shells   *see*   **RAS Shells**

Rocket-Assisted Artillery Shell   *see* **RAS Shells**

Rocket-Propelled Grenade (RPG, B40, RPG7, RPG2, Type 69, Type 56, B41, B50)   Soviet made antitank weapons that fired a shaped charge. The RPG was shoulder fired, single shot, and reloadable, and was widely used by the NVA/VC. The range of the RPG2 was 180 meters. The range of the RPG7 was 350–500 meters and it featured a more effective warhead and target sight. The B40 was the NVA version of the RPG2 and the B41/B50 their version of the RPG7. The RPG2 used a 4-pound, 82mm rocket and the RPG7 used a 5-pound, 85mm rocket. The RPG was used against vehicles, fortifications and helicopters. The Chinese versions of the Soviet RPG2 and RPG7 were the Type 56 and Type 69. The RPG2 and RPG7 could penetrate up to 210mm and 330mm of armor, respectively. The rockets detonated on impact or after traveling to their max range of 900 meters. *See also* **M-72.**

Rocketeers   *see*   **Aerial Rocket Artillery**

Rockets   Various types of rockets were used during the Vietnam War. Rockets were an aim-and-shoot weapon, unguided once fired. Rockets in use in Vietnam varied from man portable RPGs and RCLs, ground launched artillery rockets, aircraft fired rockets, to U.S. Navy ships firing rockets for onshore support. *See also* **RCL, RL, RPG, LSMR, ARA, Aircraft Rockets, Rocket Artillery.**

Rockpile, The   U.S. Marine observation post located atop a small mountain peak in northern I Corps. The post, perched on top of a 700-foot cliff, gave a commanding view of the central and western area of Quang Tri Province. The Rockpile was located halfway between Quang Tri City in the east and the Laotian border in the west, just off Route 9 (connecting Khe Sanh and Dong Ha), overlooking a fork in the Cam Lo River. The outpost was less than 20kms from the DMZ and 9kms north of Ca Lu (LZ Stud). The strategically located OP was resupplied and supported by air.

Rockpile, The (IV Corps)   *see*   **Nui Coto**

Rod   *see*   **M-67A2 Flame Tank**

ROE   *see*   **Rules of Engagement**

Rogers, William P.   *see*   **Secretary of State**

Roglai   *see*   **Montagnards**

ROIC   *see*   **Regional Officer in Charge**

ROK   *see*   **Republic of Korea**

ROK, Capital Division   *see*   **Capital Republic of Korea Infantry Division**

ROK Marines   *see*   **Republic of Korea Marine Corps**

Roll-On, Roll-Off Containers   *see* **Ro-Ro Containers**

Roll-Up Force   Small security force detached from the main body of a unit, assigned to cover and protect the withdrawal of the main force. The roll-up force distanced itself from the main force, and continued to slowly withdraw from the area, maintaining contact with the enemy in an effort to keep the enemy from overtaking the main force. The tactic was similar to a delaying force, except the delaying force tended to hold its ground, while the roll-up force slowly withdrew. The NVA/VC made widespread use of both tactics and was very effective in the execution of the maneuvers. *See also* **Delaying Action.**

Rolling Hot *see* **Gun Run**

Rolling Stone *see* **Operation Rolling Stone**

Rolling Thunder *see* **Operation Rolling Thunder**

Rolling Thunder Coordinating Committee (RTCC, Tuesday Lunch) Joint U.S. Navy and Air Force group responsible for coordinating air strikes between the two services against targets in NVN. The list of Rolling Thunder targets was presented to the White House, which made the final selection as to which targets would be hit. President Johnson took an active part in the selection process. During the Johnson administration target selection was done at weekly meetings, referred to as the "Tuesday Lunch." *See also* **Joint Chiefs of Staff, Operation Rolling Thunder.**

Roman Collar *see* **Dog Collar**

Rome Plow (Hogjaws) A special blade and protective cab fitted to the D7E bulldozer and used in land clearing operations by the U.S. Army Engineers in Vietnam. The plow blade was manufactured by the Rome Company of Georgia and nicknamed "Hogjaws." The 4,600-pound blade was capable of slicing through a tree trunk up to three feet in diameter, and was used for jungle clearing along roads and around bases. The protective cab shielded the driver from falling branches, but was not bulletproof. *See also* **Caterpillar D7E Tractor, Dozer-Infantry, Tree Crusher, Headache Bar.**

RON Position *see* **Night Defensive Position**

Rongao *see* **Montagnards**

RONONE *see* **WPB**

RONTHREE *see* **WPB**

Ross *see* **LZ Ross**

Rostow, Walt Served as a special assistant to both Presidents Kennedy and Johnson, and later was appointed Special Assistant to the President for National Security Affairs. Rostow was instrumental in supporting U.S. military and political aid for fighting the communists in Southeast Asia. Rostow actively supported wide scale bombing of North Vietnamese supply and POL facilities. He was awarded the Medal of Freedom by President Johnson in recognition of his services to the nation. *See also* **Ad Hoc Task Force on Vietnam, Sonic Boom Raids.**

Rostow's Plan 6 *see* **Sonic Boom Raids**

Rotate (Rotation, Unit Rotation) For the U.S. military in Vietnam, rotation was directly related to a soldier's tour of duty in Vietnam. The rotation period for the average Army soldier was 12 months in SVN; at the end of that time he would leave Vietnam (rotate out), and a replacement would rotate in to take his place. The Marines rotated their soldiers at 13 months. The Australians rotated entire units, for infantry and artillery battalions, and SAS, cavalry, and armor squadrons. Navy SEABEE ACBs rotated after an 8-month tour, returning for another tour in 6 months. Other SEABEE units followed the individual, one year rotation schedule. Navy SEALs operated on a 6-month tour, spending several tours in Vietnam. *See also* **Tour of Duty.**

Rotation *see* **Rotate**

Rotational Hump (Infusion) The rotation of more than 25 percent of a unit within a thirty-day period. This occurred in Vietnam when combat troops first deployed to Vietnam as whole units which resulted in large numbers of troops from the same unit being due for rotation at the same time. To counter this, a program of "infusion" was instituted. The program transferred troops between other units and commands to reduce the impact of rotation. The transferred troops had varying lengths of time remaining before their rotation. This produced a staggered rotation that allowed the units to maintain efficiency.

ROTC *see* **Reserve Officer Training Corps**

Rotor Bumpers *see* **Helicopter Ambush**

Rotor Wash (Flaring) Air turbulence created on the ground by the rotor blades of a helicopter. The rotor wash was most severe when the helicopter was descending and just a few feet above the ground. The severity of the wash could be intensified by making a fast approach to the ground, then suddenly pulling up the nose of the ship, or "flaring." The result was a severe rotor wash generating air turbulence in excess of 60mph. The turbulent air kicked up dust, dirt and small rocks that were as deadly as the winds of a small tornado. Some helicopter pilots in Vietnam used the rotor wash as a form of harassment against the civilian population. *See also* **Autorotation.**

Rotten Fish Head Sauce *see* **Nuoc Mam**

Round Eyes (American Women) GI slang for an American woman in Vietnam, or more generally, any non–Asian or non-slant-eyed woman encountered in Vietnam. GIs in the field saw few women other than the Vietnamese unless they were in a field hospital or in one of the major cities or base camps. The closest a grunt would come to a "round eye" would be pictures in magazines, books or in letters from home, or nurses in an evacuation hospital. Approximately 15,000 American women served in Vietnam, half of them with the military (primarily in nursing), and the remainder as civilian workers (contractors, Embassy employees, relief workers, Red Cross, etc.). *See also* **Army Nurse Corps, Donut Dollies.**

Rout The hasty and uncontrolled movement of a defeated force away from the attacking enemy. The routed force moved as quickly as possible, without regard for unit safety or form; it was an "every man for himself mentality." Routed units frequently abandoned their weapons, ammunitions, supplies, and sometimes their wounded. Their consuming desire was escape and survival; their will to fight had been broken, and they ceased to be a fighting force. The ARVNs were routed during several major engagements with the NVA/VC, and their rout in March '75 led to the eventual collapse of the South Vietnamese military, and the fall of the country to the communists in April '75. *See also* **Retreat, Retire, Retrograde Movement, Final Offensive.**

Rout of the Central Highlands *see* **Abandonment of the Central Highlands**

Route Packages (RP I–VI) For U.S. bombing purposes, NVN was divided into six attack areas, known as Route Packages I–VI. The Navy and Air Force coordinated their attacks based on these attack areas. Route Package VI (Pack 6) was the Hanoi-Haiphong area in the Red River Delta and Pack 1 was the southernmost area of North Vietnam. RP I was primarily an Air Force AO, with targets selected by MACV. RP II, III, and IV were Navy/Marine AOs. RP V was controlled by the Air Force and RP VI was a joint Air Force and Navy/Marine AO.

Route-Step A military marching formation used by troops over rough or uneven terrain. The members of the formation moved in loose order and did not march in step or to a cadence.

Routine Evac *see* **Casualty Classifications, Medevac Priorities**

Routine Missions *see* **Ass-and-Trash Runs**

Rowell's Rats (Helicopter Detachment 1, HC-1) Nickname for one of the four Navy helicopter gunship detachments that began operating in Vietnam in August '66. Each detachment consisted of two UH-1B gunships on loan from the Army. The Navy operated in support of the riverine operations conducted by TF 116, the Navy's Delta river patrol units. HC-1, Rowell's Rats, operated out of Vung Tau, while the other detachments operated out of Nha Be, Vinh Long and from the USS *Comstock,* an LSD stationed off the coast. In April '67 the detachment's assets were increased and the unit was designated Helicopter Squadron HAL-3. HAL-3 continued operations until '72. *See also* **Seawolves.**

Royal Australian Air Force (RAAF, Wallaby Airlines, No. 2 Squadron, No. 9 Squadron) The RAAF deployed several air units to Vietnam between '64 and '73. No. 2 Squadron consisted of Canberra jet bombers used for close air support. No. 9 Squadron was an Australian assault helicopter group which consisted of slicks, UH-1D gunships and Chinook transports. RAAF Transport Flight Vietnam, better known as "Wallaby Airlines," consisted of seven C-2 Caribou transports. Other RAAF crews operated U.S. aircraft performing a variety of missions in support of Australian troops of the 1st ATF. *See also* **B-57, Magpie.**

Royal Australian Engineers *see* **Sapper, Australian**

Royal Australian Navy *see* **HMAS Hobart**

Royal Australian Regiments (RAR)
Australian ground combat troops from the 1st Battalion, Royal Australian Regiment, deployed to SVN in '65 and were initially attached to the U.S. 173d Airborne. As more Australian troops arrived in-country a separate Australian Task Force was established and assigned the Province of Phuoc Tuy as their area of operations. The Australians rotated whole units in and out of Vietnam, unlike the Americans who rotated individual soldiers, with several battalions of the RAR usually in RVN at any one time. The last of the RAR departed Vietnam in early '72. *See also* **Australia.**

Royal Laotian Air Force (RLAF)   Consisted primarily of American supplied T-28 fighters. The Royal Laotian Air Force pilots were trained and advised by U.S. Air Force personnel.

Royal Laotian Army (RLA, FAL-FAR)
Prior to '59 the Royal Lao Army was very small and its primary duty was to provide security at the Royal Palace in Vientiane. Under the leadership and training of the USSFs the quality of the RLA improved, yet they were still hard-pressed to hold back the communist Pathet Lao, backed by NVA troops. To assist the RLA, USSF troops trained and helped equip Meo tribesmen in Southern and Central Laos to fight the communists. The operation to equip and train Laotians to fight the Pathet Lao were part of CIA operations in Southeast Asia. *See also* **White Star Mobile Training Teams.**

Royal Laotian Government   *see*
RLG

Royal New Zealand Army (RNZA, RNZIR)   New Zealand deployed several units to Vietnam in support of the South Vietnamese. In addition to medical and civic action units the New Zealanders deployed two companies of infantry from the RNZIR (Royal New Zealand Infantry Regiment), a battery of 105mm howitzers from the RNZA (Royal New Zealand Artillery) and Number 4 Troop of the NZSAS (New Zealand Special Air Services). The units operated in Phuoc Tuy Province, III Corps, departing Vietnam between '70–'71. *See also* **New Zealand.**

Royal New Zealand Artillery   *see*
Royal New Zealand Army

Royal New Zealand Infantry Regiment
see **Royal New Zealand Army**

Royal Thai Air Force Base   *see* **Thai Air Bases**

Royal Thai Army Force   *see* **Black Panther Division**

Royal Thai Army Volunteer Force   *see* **Black Panther Division**

Royal Thai Army Volunteer Regiment
see **Queen's Cobras**

Royal Thai Expeditionary Division
see **Black Panther Division**

RP I–VI   *see*   **Route Packages**

RP46 LMG   *see*   **RPD LMG**

RPC (River Patrol Craft)   River patrol boat used by the SVN River Force. The RPC was 36 feet long, had a max speed of 15 knots, operated with a three or four man crew, was armed with a twin .50cal machine gun in the front and two .30cal machine guns mounted aft, and could transport up to 14 troops for combat assault. The RPC was also used for harbor patrol duties.

RPD LMG (Type 58, Type 53, RP46, RPDM, Ruchnoy Pulemyot Degtyaryov)
General name for Soviet and PRC–made light machine guns used by the NVA/VC during the VNW. The PRC–made versions were Type 56 (53–58); the Soviet versions were the RP46, RPD, and RPDM. All versions were gas operated, 7.62mm, automatic fire only and most could be drum or belt fed; effective range was 800 meters. Of the group, the most commonly used by the NVA/VC was ᵗhe RPD which was belt fed from a 100-round drum and weighed about 20 pounds (loaded). The RPD series was the forerunner of the AK47. *See also* **RPK LMG, AK47, Light Machine Gun.**

RPDM LMG   *see*   **RPD LMG**

RPG   *see*   **River Patrol Group, Rocket-Propelled Grenade**

RPG Screen (Venetian Blind Armor)
The NVA/VC made widespread use of rocket propelled grenade launchers, particularly the RPG2 and the RPG7. RPG rounds detonated on contact, the explosion of the shaped charge penetrating the target. By shielding a possible RPG target with wire, cyclone fencing, PSP or sandbags the round would explode prematurely, greatly reducing

the shaped charges' effect. APCs, tanks and boats used the screening to increase vehicle survivability. Many bunker locations also used RPG screens. The slat armor (RPG screens) on river boats made them appear as if they were surrounded by venetian blinds. *See also* **Standoff Armor.**

RPG2 *see* **Rocket-Propelled Grenade**

RPG7 *see* **Rocket-Propelled Grenade**

RPK LMG (TUL1) The RPK was a Soviet made light machine gun based on the design of the RPD. The NVN produced a version of the RPK called the TUL1. The 7.62mm LMG had a range of 800 meters, was gas operated and could be drum/box fed from 30, 40, or 75-round magazines. The gun had an attached carrying handle and a built-in bipod. The RPK/TUL1 functioned as the main LMG used by the NVA/VC during the VNW. *See also* **Light Machine Gun.**

RR *see* **Recoilless Rifle, Radio Relay**

RRB *see* **Human Relations Committee**

RRU *see* **Army Security Agency**

RSA *see* **Railway Security Agency**

RSS *see* **River Support Squadron**

RSSZ *see* **Rung Sat**

RT *see* **Field Radio**

RTs *see* **Spike Recon Team**

RT-10 *see* **Survival Radios**

RT-28 *see* **T-28**

RT-33 *see* **T-33**

RTAB *see* **Thai Air Bases**

RTAFB *see* **Thai Air Bases**

RTAVF *see* **Black Panther Division**

RTCC *see* **Rolling Thunder Coordinating Committee**

RTEG (River Transport Escort Group) South Vietnamese Navy River Force element responsible for providing river security for transport boats of the RTG. The RTEG was based out of Saigon and consisted of four monitors, six STCAN/FOM patrol boats, and twenty armored LCVPs. *See also* **South Vietnamese Navy.**

RTG (River Transport Group) South Vietnamese Navy River Force element responsible for river transport. The force was equipped with seven LCUs, and the RTEG provided convoy security for the transports. *See also* **South Vietnamese Navy.**

RTO *see* **Radio Telephone Operator**

Rubber Bag *see* **Body Bag**

Rubber Bitch (Air Mattress, Pneumatic Mattresses) Marine slang for the 4-pound, standard issue, rubber air mattresses slept on in the field. The air mattresses (pneumatic mattresses) had a history of leakage problems due to extremes in the combat zone. Grunts rarely carried the "rubber bitch" to the field because of its excess weight and the lack of opportunity to use it.

Rubber Go-Aheads *see* **Rubber Thongs**

Rubber Raft *see* **Inflatable Boat, Small**

Rubber Thongs (Shower Shoes, Flip Flops, Shower Clogs, Rubber Go-Aheads, Zorries) Foam rubber sandals with a split thong strap. The cheap sandals were imported from Japan and widely worn by the Vietnamese as well as the Americans. GIs used their thongs for base camp trips to the showers while the Vietnamese wore them as shoes. Many an ARVN or RF/PF soldier patrolled in a pair of the colorful foam sandals. The thongs were known by a variety of names.

Rubberneck Flight Nickname for an administrative flight in which correspondents were ferried about the battlefield. The flight usually consisted of one or two planned stops at various bases. The aircraft was only committed to those initial stops and any other stops or fly-overs the correspondent onboard might request. Flights were authorized subject to the availability of the aircraft. Such flights were difficult to obtain after '65 when U.S. aircraft were committed to support the operations of American combat forces.

Rubin, Jerry *see* **Chicago 8, Vietnam Day Committee**

Ruchnoy Pulemyot Degtyaryov *see* **RPD LMG**

Ruck(sack) *see* **ALICE**

Ruck-Up *see* **Saddle-Up**

Rue Catinat *see* **Tu Do Street**

Ruff-Puffs *see* **Popular Forces**

Ruffs *see* **Regional Forces**

Rules of Engagement (ROE)   U.S. Department of Defense directives and guidelines that defined when U.S. forces could actively engage in combat. In Vietnam the ROE changed frequently. U.S. troops could not always return fire when fired on by the enemy. A Free-Fire-Zone was the only area where enemy fire could be returned or any target engaged without permission from a higher headquarters. In most cases, fire into a populated area had to be cleared with the Vietnamese province chief and the unit's headquarters; automatic return of fire was not allowed in populated areas. ROE also varied, and were often ambiguous, for aircraft crews attacking NVN. *See also* **U.S. Army Rules of Engagement, U.S. Air Rules of Engagement, Lavell.**

Rumor Control (Scuttlebutt)   The control point or most accurate source of information about a pending event or action before the event took place. Information (rumors) on an event was much more credible if the source of the information was verifiable or from a responsible source. *See also* **Bullshit Net.**

Rumors   There were more rumors circulating in SVN than there were GIs; a few of them were: If you contracted the incurable strain of syphilis called the "Black Syph" you would be either sent to Johnson Island, in the Pacific, and listed as an MIA, or sent to Camp-Crotchrot on Okinawa and listed as a KIA so your next-of-kin could collect your GI insurance. You were never to fall asleep after sex in a whorehouse because the VC might sneak in and cut your balls off. It was said that the bottled coke sold by some Vietnamese children and roadside vendors was filled with ground glass or poison. Two basic training rumors were: there was saltpeter added to the food to kill sexual desire, and that the trainee's first series of inoculations were administered to the left testicle. ROK soldiers were rumored to be paid a bounty for each pair of enemy ears they brought into their headquarters; the bounty was paid by the ROK government as an incentive to the ROKs to kill more VC.

Some VC whores that offered to service U.S. troops were said to have razor blades or glass shards in their vaginas. If you wanted to find an alcoholic in the Army, you were told to find an "Army Cook." Most of the stateside medics who didn't go to Vietnam were queers. A GI's field test for VD was conducted by the GI putting earwax on his finger and inserting the waxed finger into the woman's vagina; if it burned her he could take the indication as "gospel" that she had the "clap."

Run *see* **Gun Run**

Rung Sat (Rung Sat Special Zone, RSSZ, Forest of Assassins)   Large, dense mangrove swamp area of the Delta where the Saigon and Dong Nai rivers meet, known as the Rung Sat Special Zone. The zone was located between Saigon and the South China Sea, southeast of Saigon. The zone was a VC base area for the 9th VC Division, from which they attacked river traffic moving to and from Saigon. The VC also operated from bases in Southern Bien Hoa Province (Nhon Trach) striking into the RSSZ. In '64 the RSSZ was primarily policed by forces of the SVN Navy. Rung Sat in Vietnamese meant "dense jungle," and was nicknamed the "Forest of Assassins." *See also* **Nhon Trach, Doan-10, Song Long Tau, Long Son Island.**

Rung Sat RPG *see* **Game Warden River Groups**

Rung Sat Special Zone *see* **Rung Sat**

Running Takeoff   Helicopter technique used to get an overloaded ship airborne. Normal helicopter takeoffs began from a hover, but an overloaded ship was usually unable to maintain a hover. In order to get the ship airborne the aircraft rose to the hover position, the nose was tipped down and the ship skimmed along the ground, gradually gaining speed and altitude. Such running takeoffs required plenty of open space for the helicopter to make the run.

Runs *see* **Ho Chi Minh's Revenge**

Runway Panels *see* **MN-19 Runway Panels, PSP**

Runways (East-West / North-South) *see* **Vagina**

Rural Construction *see* **Pacification**

Rural Development *see* **Pacification**

Rural Development Cadre (RD Cadre, Revolutionary Development Cadre [RDC])   GVN personnel assigned to assist the people as part of the Rural Development Program. The RD Cadre represented the GVN and lived with the people, aiding them in such projects as self-defense, sanitation, roads, schools, agricultural assistance, etc. The RD cadre used some of the same techniques and tactics as those used by the VC cadre. It was hoped that the people being helped would be able to identify the cadre with the GVN, thus supporting the government and turning away from the VC. GVN troops were assigned to provide security for the RDC, but they were seldom effective. Like the many names for "pacification" programs, the cadre were known as a "rural" or "revolutionary" cadre under the GVN.

Rural Reconstruction   see   Pacification

Rusk, David Dean (The Buddha) Served as secretary of state in the Kennedy and Johnson administrations. Rusk was strongly anticommunist and believed in the U.S. war effort in Vietnam and a military solution. Rusk was nicknamed "the Buddha" because of his quiet dedication to his superiors.

Russel's Viper   Common lowland poisonous snake. The viper grew to 4–5 feet in length and was similar in appearance to a small python. The snake's venom was twice the lethal dose required to kill a man, and the fangs and jaws of the snake would sometimes remain clamped onto the victim after biting. The snake was usually dormant during the day and quite active at night, considered one of the most deadly of the Southeast Asian snakes. See also **Snakes.**

Russell Beach   see   **Operation Russell Beach**

Russia   see   **Union of Soviet Socialist Republics**

Russians   see   **Americans Without Dollars, USSR**

Russo, Anthony   see   **Pentagon Papers**

Rusty Calley   see   **Calley, Lt. William, Jr.**

RVN   see   **Republic of Vietnam**

RVN Flag   see   **Flags**...

RVNAF   see   **Republic of Vietnam Air Force**

RVNMC   see   **Republic of Vietnam Marine Corps**

RVNN   see   **Republic of Vietnam Navy**

Ryan, General John   see   **Chief of Staff**

Ryan 147D   see   **147D Drone**

S

S & C Files (Secret and Confidential Files)   Military files containing sensitive information that was not to fall into enemy hands. The files included unit radio frequencies, shackle codes, secret messages, emergency procedures, etc. At major U.S. commands where the files were kept, clerical soldiers under command of an officer were assigned to guard the files and destroy them if there was a reasonable possibility that an enemy attack might capture the files. See also **Shackle Cards.**

S & D   see   **Search and Destroy**

S & W 9mm   see   **Hush Puppy**

S and D   see   **Search and Destroy**

S and S   see   **Supply and Service**

S-1 (Adjutant's Office, N-1)   Battalion or brigade level staff officer responsible for personnel administration: a position usually filled by a captain or a major. The adjutant's officer was responsible for such things as replacements, decoration processing, mail,

PX facilities, service clubs, casualty reports and processing, and a series of odds-and-ends. At the low end the adjutant interfaced with the company and battalion headquarters, and interfaced with the division G-1 at the high end. The N-1 was the Navy's equivalent. *See also* **G-1.**

S-2 (N-2, Intel Unit)   Battalion or brigade level staff officer responsible for intelligence functions related to the unit, including the direction of gathering, analysis, and presentation of intelligence information to the unit commander. The N-2 was the Navy's equivalent. *See also* **G-2.**

S-3 (N-3, Ops)   Battalion or brigade level staff officer charged with the operations (Ops) and training of the unit. The S-3 advised the unit commander on matters relating to operation and training, and carried out the directions of the commander. The S-3 took command of the unit during the commander's absence. The N-3 was the Navy's equivalent. *See also* **G-3, Ops.**

S-4 (N-4)   Brigade or battalion level staff officer responsible for supply and logistics support of the unit. In the Navy the N-4 filled the logistics position. *See also* **G-4.**

S-5 (N-5)   Brigade or battalion level staff officer responsible for civil affairs between the unit and the local civilian populace. This position was not always filled in all units. The Navy's counterpart was called N-5. *See also* **G-5.**

S-55   *see*   **H-19**

S-56   *see*   **CH-37**

S-58   *see*   **CH-34**

S-60 Antiaircraft Gun   *see*   **57mm AA**

S-61 Sikorsky   *see*   **SH-3**

S-65A   *see*   **CH-53**

SA   *see*   **Small Arms Fire**

SA-2 (Guideline)   Soviet made surface-to-air (SAM) antiaircraft missile. The SAM was a 35-foot long, radar guided, two stage rocket with a maximum altitude of 85,000 feet and speeds in excess of 1,800mph. SAMs were guided to their target by the Fan Song radar of "intercept control." A typical SAM site featured six SAM launchers around a central Fan Song radar unit. The 349-pound HE warhead on the SAM could be set to detonate at a specific altitude, or using a proximity fuse, detonated within a certain range of the target aircraft. The SAM's biggest asset was its speed, but because the missile was not very maneuverable, an alert pilot who saw one coming could usually evade the missile. *See also* **Fan Song, Surface-to-Air Missile, Ballistic Firing.**

SA-7   *see*   **Surface-to-Air Missile**

SA-16   *see*   **HU-16**

Sabotage   *see*   **Foreign Object Damage**

Sabreliner   *see*   **T-39**

SAC   *see*   **Strategic Air Command, Surveillance Airplane Company, Avn**

SACB   *see*   **Subversive Activities Control Board**

Sack-Out   *see*   **Zs**

SAD   *see*   **Search and Destroy**

Saddle-Up (Ruck-Up)   Lingering cavalry term meaning to make your equipment ready and prepare to move out. For the infantryman in Vietnam rucking-up was the equivalent, and both were used interchangeably.

Sadec   Large river village in Sadec Province, IV Corps, that was suspected of being a Viet Cong R & R center. After '67 the territory around Sadec was formed into Sadec Province, and the village was designated the provincial capital. Sadec was located 18kms west of Vinh Long, on the south bank of the Song Tien Giang River.

Sadler, Sergeant Barry   Former Special Forces Green Beret sergeant who wrote several songs about the Vietnam War and the Special Forces, the most famous of which was "THE BALLAD OF THE GREEN BERETS." *See also* **Ballad of the Yellow Beret.**

SAF   *see*   **Small Arms Fire**

Safe Conduct Passes   *see*   **Controlled Littering**

Safe House   *see*   **Nha Dac Biet**

Safety Pin   *see*   **Spoon**

Safety Strap   *see*   **Bunji Strap**

SAG   *see*   **Senior Advisory Group**

Sagami Mount   Special tubular weapons support used to mount machine guns and miniguns in the doorways of the UH-1 helicopter. The sagami mounted weapons were operated by helicopter door gunners.

Sagger *see* **ATGM-3**

Saigon (Paris of the Orient, Pearl of the East, The Ville, Gia Dinh) The capital, largest city, and the largest sea port in South Vietnam. The city and the area immediately surrounding it made up the Capital Military Region. Saigon was located in Gia Dinh Province, III Corps, and served as Government Headquarters, location of the U.S. Embassy, MACV Headquarters and the Headquarters Command for various other units. Saigon was also the location for SVN's international airport and major air base, Tan Son Nhut. Saigon and the RVN fell to the communists during the Final Offensive, April 30, 1975. Saigon was originally named Gia Dinh and in ancient times served as the capital of Cochin China. It was renamed Ho Chi Minh City after the NVA victory in April '75. *See also* **Ben Nghe River, Capital Military District, Gia Dinh.**

Saigon Commandos *see* **Saigon Warriors**

Saigon Ho *see* **Prostitute**

Saigon Military Mission (U.S. Saigon Military Mission, SMM) U.S. mission established in Saigon in '54 to provide military assistance to Vietnamese forces in the Saigon region who were fighting the Viet Minh. The CIA sponsored mission worked independently of the French and much of their work was covert in nature, until the French defeat in Indochina. The mission was initially headed by Colonel Edward Lansdale, USAF. The mission also carried out psychological warfare against the new communist government of North Vietnam and conducted numerous other CIA-type covert activities in South Vietnam. *See also* **Black Psyche, Edward Lansdale.**

Saigon Police Boy Scouts Association (SPBSA) Saigon area Boy Scouts Association, sponsored in part by the U.S. 716th Military Police Battalion. The 716th MP's duty area was Saigon, and their prime duties were VIP escorts, traffic control, guardpost and roving patrols. During the MP's off-duty time they worked with South Vietnamese youngsters in the Boy Scouts in a program similar to Police Athletic Leagues of today.

Saigon Post Saigon's only English-language newspaper. News reported in the daily paper had a decidedly pro–GVN and pro–American slant since the paper was almost entirely controlled by the CIA.

Saigon River *see* **Ben Nghe River**

Saigon Syndrome Unofficial reference by some Americans in Vietnam to the high rate of ARVN troops who deserted their units and escaped to Saigon to hide out. ARVN military performance was very low over the period of '64 to '68. After Tet '68 more U.S. military emphasis was placed on upgrading and strengthening South Vietnam's Armed Forces. The ARVN's yearly desertion rate outpaced the rate of volunteer enlistments. The ARVNs depended heavily on their mandatory draft to maintain troop levels.

Saigon Tea Colored, scented water, or diluted tea which sold for $1–$5 a glass in Saigon bars. The drink was bought by a GI for one of the bar girls (prostitutes) whom he selected (or a girl who selected him) to keep him company while he was in the bar. The GI drank beer or booze, while the bar girl drank the Saigon tea. The usual routine upon entering the bar was for the bar girl to swish up to the GI and tell him how handsome he was and then lay a "You buy me Saigon tea?" on him. The prices of the tea were inflated to whatever the market would bear. If the GI refused he was usually rebuffed and declared a "cheap charlie," and the girl would "hit" on another bar patron. While the GI was in the bar he could talk to the bar girl, but the Mama-San that operated the bar usually didn't allow the GIs to touch or fondle the girls. Arrangements could be made between the bar girl and the GI for a later meeting. In some bars a whorehouse was attached, and after Mama-San was paid the bar girl and her "new love" would maneuver to a cot in the back of the bar for a "short-time." *See also* **Boom-Boom.**

Saigon Warriors (Saigon Commandos) Rear echelon military personnel working at the various facilities in and around Saigon. They had (more or less) regular jobs (noncombat) with regular hours (8–12 hour days), and their assigned weapons were usually stored under lock and key in one of the base armories. Grunts who operated in the boonies had various derogatory names for these REMFs. *See also* **Rear-Echelon-Mother-Fuckers.**

Saigon-Cowboy Suits *see* **Jungle Camouflage Uniform**

Saigon-TSN Air Control Center *see* **Paris**

Sail Junks Used by the South Vietnamese Navy as part of their Junk Force which patrolled the coastal waters of South Vietnam. The sail junks were 32 feet long and fitted with two sails. The junks were unarmed except for the weapons carried by the crew. *See also* **Junk Force, Junks.**

Saint Paul *see* **USS Saint Paul**

Salem House *see* **Operation Daniel Boone**

Salisbury, Harrison E. Salisbury was an American journalist and one-time Pulitzer prize winner who visited North Vietnam in December '66. Like others before him, and others who followed, he was given a guided tour of several bomb damaged areas around Hanoi. North Vietnamese officials lectured Salisbury about how American planes had deliberately bombed schools and churches or attacked villages where there were no military targets. Salisbury relayed the tour, via the American press, to the world. Many of his "facts" on the bombings were disputed by the U.S. government and later disproved. It was a regular practice of the NVN to locate AA sites, military storage and factories near villages because of American reluctance to bomb near civilian population centers.

Saliva *see* **Louies**

Saloth Sar *see* **Pol Pot**

Saltpeter (Potassium Nitrate) One of the more prevalent rumors that surfaced during Army basic training was that the Army put "saltpeter" (potassium nitrate) into the trainee's food. The potassium nitrate supposedly killed any sexual desires that might arise during the eight weeks of basic when the trainees were separated from women. *See also* **Rumors.**

Salty Marine slang for an individual who was conceited, stuck-up, pushy, or arrogant. It also applied to combat troops that had spent a lot of time in the field and tended to be unimpressed by REMFs.

Salty-Dog (Old-Salt) Marine slang for a piece of equipment lost (or abandoned) as a result of enemy action. Not to be confused with an "old salt," which was a nickname for a veteran sailor.

SALUTE (Size-Activity-Location-Unit-Time-Equipment) Acronym used to describe the customary reporting procedure used by Army reconnaissance units who encountered the enemy in the field. SALUTE stood for S-ize of enemy force, A-ctivity of the enemy, L-ocation of the sighting, U-nit or uniforms of the sighted enemy, T-ime of sighting and E-quipment carried by the enemy. *See also* **Situation Report.**

SAM *see* **Surface-to-Air Missile**

SAM, U.S. *see* **Hawk Missile**

SAM Break (Jink) Evasive maneuver used by U.S. pilots to avoid NVA SAM missiles. The maneuver involved the aircraft making a hard-breaking dive as the missile approached. The break (dive) and subsequent zig zag moves would confuse the missile tracking system causing it to detonate prematurely. Sudden evasive maneuvers to avoid SAMs or any enemy fire were also called "Jinking" (jinked, jink).

Sam Houston *see* **Operation Sam Houston, Fort Sam Houston**

SAM Launch Detector *see* **WR-300**

SAM Site *see* **Star-of-David**

SAM Suppression During the air war against North Vietnam, enemy surface-to-air missiles were a constant threat to U.S. attack aircraft. The threat was serious enough that the Air Force formed special units to attack and suppress enemy SAM activity. The Wild Weasels were formed to function in the SAM suppression role. The Weasels attacked detected SAM sites with homing rockets, and bombed sites with conventional bombs. The Navy also conducted SAM suppression operations in conjunction with its normal strikes against NVN targets. Both the Air Force and the Navy used ECMs to jam and disrupt enemy radar that was used to guide the SAMs. *See also* **Wild Weasel, Iron Hand, SA-2, P-3, A-4, A-6A, F-105F/G, F-100, F-4.**

Same Mud, Same Blood View of the war shared by most black and white grunts.

There were few racial incidents in the field between blacks and whites, where they depended on each other for their survival. Racial flare-ups and confrontations occurred among rear area troops at the larger base camps, and increased in number and intensity in '68, after the assassination of Dr. Martin Luther King. *See also* **Klan, Clenched Fist, Dap, Afro.**

Same Old Shit *see* **SOS**

Same-Same GI-Vietnamese slang for "same" or nearly identical.

Samozaryadnyi Karabin Simonova Rifle *see* **Type 56 SKS**

Sampan (Vietnamese Boats) Small Vietnamese boats used for fishing and river commerce. The boats were generally flat bottomed, powered by a combination of sail, poles or small outboard motors. The Viet Cong used the sampan to smuggle supplies from border sanctuaries into the interior of SVN. *See also* **Bassac River.**

Sampan Alley *see* **Bassac River**

Sampan Road *see* **Bassac River**

Sampan Valley *see* **Bassac River**

San Antonio Formula Name for a secret plan offered to the NVN in August '67. The U.S. offered to stop the bombing of NVN if Hanoi would agree to begin peace talks and not use the bombing halt to send more NVA troops and equipment into SVN. President Johnson, in a speech in San Antonio in September '67, publicly revealed the proposal to the NVN and repeated it again in March '68. NVN rejected the offer in October '67 in the belief that they could win militarily against the U.S. and did not want to make possible concessions during cease-fire negotiations.

San Diego *see* **Marine Corps Recruit Depot**

Sanctuaries Safe areas from which enemy troops could launch attacks; areas free from retaliation by the opposition. During the VNW Laos and Cambodia claimed neutrality. NVN used the border areas of both countries to build the Ho Chi Minh Trail and send supplies and men south to fight in SVN. NVA/VC units operated from sanctuaries along the border. Although the U.S. launched air strikes on the sanctuaries and the trail, it wasn't until April '70 that a large U.S. ground force attacked NVA bases in Cambodia. *See also* **Hanoi-Haiphong Sanctuaries, Cambodian Incursion, Lam Son 719.**

Sanctuary (USS Sanctuary, AH-17) U.S. Navy hospital ship that operated off the coast of SVN, near Da Nang from April '67 until the end of U.S. involvement in the war. The USS *Sanctuary* was a 750-bed floating hospital similar to the USS *Repose*. The *Sanctuary* normally operated with a ship's crew of about 375 men. The medical staff aboard the ship numbered 24 doctors, 3 dentists, 29 nurses, and 258 enlisted men and NCOs. *See also* **Repose.**

Sand Table Scale model of a target used for training and preparation for an attack or operation. Available intelligence on the target area was translated into a scale model constructed to show the overall terrain and fortifications of the target. The model was used to plan the assault and instruct the various commanders on the operation. The NVA/VC made use of sand tables in many of their larger assaults on GVN and U.S. base camps. U.S. sand tables in Vietnam were primarily models of areas since there were practically no large scale NVA/VC fortifications in South Vietnam.

Sandbagging *see* **Goldbricking**

Sandbagging a Patrol/Ambush Technique used to avoid a patrol. One of the SOPs of Army units in the field during Vietnam was to send out night patrols or ambushes from a unit's NDP. The roaming patrol was sent out to locate enemy units that might be massing to attack the NDP. In reality the night patrols were bait, attempting to lure the enemy into revealing his position. Once the enemy opened fire on the patrol, artillery would be called onto the patrol's position. The patrols were not popular with most GIs. To avoid getting caught in an enemy ambush some of the patrols would sandbag. The patrol would move out beyond the perimeter of the NDP and lay low for the night, periodically calling in radio reports to the NDP as though the patrol was moving. In the morning the patrol would reenter the perimeter. Sometimes the technique backfired with the sandbagged patrol being mistaken for the enemy. A similar technique was sometimes used when a squad was sent to a night ambush site one or two kms from the NDP into exceptionally hostile territory. The ambush patrol would leave the perimeter and set up a short distance away. Through the night the squad would call in reports as if it were in the assigned ambush site. This tactic could also backfire if the NDP was actually attacked by the enemy. The NDP commander would assume the ambush squad was well out of the area and call in artillery on the attacking enemy force. The fires sometimes were directed at the same area where the ambush squad was sandbagging. *See also* Gundecking.

Sandbags   Two types of sandbags were used by U.S. forces in Vietnam. The older burlap bags were available, as well as the newer reinforced nylon bags. Some U.S. units carried the bags as they patrolled, each man carrying several empty bags. When the unit stopped for the night they would dig in, filling the sandbags, using them around their foxholes. The dirt from the bags was used to refill the holes when the troops left the NDP. When patrol bases were established for an extended period helicopters flew in the sandbags, and later removed them when the base was dismantled. The bags were used for defensive fortifications or stacked on top of, and inside armored vehicles. To protect a truck's cargo/ driver, sandbags were used to line the truck's bed and cab floor. A full bag weighed 50–80 pounds.

Sandy   *see*   A-1

Sanitized (Sterilized)   Many operations of the Special Forces required them to cross the border into Laos, Cambodia or North Vietnam. The teams operating on these missions were sanitized before crossing the border. This meant the Americans wore no insignia, name tags, or unit patches. They carried no other form of identification or personal items and they used foreign weapons and equipment. In the event a team member's body was recovered by the enemy, there would be no conclusive proof that the body was American or officially linked to U.S. military operations. LRRP and Ranger units also sterilized their equipment before conducting cross-border operations. *See also* Unit That Never Was.

Sanitizing Operations   Assassination operations of the Phoenix Program, designed to seek out, identify and eliminate the Viet Cong and its support structure (personnel). Sanitizing of suspected VC or their supporters was routinely carried out by special assassination squads employed by the program. Assassination was the preferred method of dealing with the VC/VCI/VCS. An estimated 20,000 South Vietnamese are believed to have been killed under the program. Because of corruption within the system the program was sometimes used to settle personal grudges. When an individual was "fingered" as a VC/VCS/VCI by an informant, a check into the accuracy of the informant's information might not be done, and the fingered VC "sanitized." *See also* Phoenix Program, Provisional Reconnaissance Unit.

Santa Fe   *see*   Operation Santa Fe

SAO   *see*   Survival Assistance Officer

SAPs   *see*   Watch List

Sapper (Suicide Squads)   Specially trained NVA/VC commandos. Their prime function was the destruction of enemy equipment and fortifications; the satchel charge was their primary weapon. They were experts in infiltration techniques, booby traps and mines. The sappers cleared paths through minefields for their attacking friendly troops and entered military installations to destroy aircraft or fortifications. Many sapper missions were suicidal, but very effective. The NVA sappers were special members of the NVA combat engineers, the Dac Cong. The sapper's training lasted 6–18 months and encompassed the various FWF defensive techniques, mines and anti-intrusion devices. *See also* Dac Cong, Tourniquet, F-100 Battalion, Anti-Intrusion Devices.

Sapper, Australian (Royal Australian Engineers)   Combat engineers of the Australian Army who were demolition and fortification specialists. While in Vietnam the Australian sappers usually performed the job of searching and destroying enemy tunnels. *See also* Royal Australian Regiment, Tunnel Rats.

Sapphire   *see*   Sister

SAR   *see*   Search and Rescue, AIM-7

Saratoga   *see*   USS Saratoga

SARTAF   *see*   Search and Rescue Task Force

SAS   *see*   Australian Special Air Services

Sat Cong (Kill the Communists, Kill the Viet Cong, Diet Cong, Exterminate Communists) Vietnamese phrase that meant "kill the communists" or "kill the Viet Cong." In the early days of the South Vietnamese Junk Force it was required of the force personnel to have "Sat Cong" tattooed on their chest. With such a tattoo, members of the force were totally committed to the effort against the Viet Cong. The Viet Cong showed no mercy to the Junkies they captured, thanks to the tattoo. "Diet Cong" meant to "exterminate communists." *See also* **Junk Force, Ban.**

Satchel Charge An explosive device containing several blocks of explosives tied or taped together and designed to detonate simultaneously. The explosives were carried in a pack and detonated by a time or burning fuse. The pack had a handle to allow for easy carrying and throwing. In U.S. units, engineers used satchel charges for demolishing enemy fortifications. In Vietnam enemy sappers used the charges to destroy aircraft, vehicles and bunkers. The charge was placed by hand or thrown at the target. *See also* **Lob-Bombs, Sapper.**

SATS *see* **Short Airfield for Tactical Support**

Saturation Bombing *see* **Carpet Bombing**

Saturation Patrolling Military term for platoon size patrols used to draw out the enemy. A patrolling technique used by some U.S. units in Vietnam. Units employing the technique flooded an area with small patrols in hopes that one of them would make contact with the enemy. If contact took place, other patrolling units were vectored into the contact to surround and destroy the enemy. Patrolling GIs saw themselves as bait to entice enemy units to attack; this revealed the enemies' position, but didn't do much for the bait that was chewed up during the initial contact with the enemy.

Sauced *see* **Drunk**

Saucer Cap Army service cap, usually worn with the Class A, dress green uniform. The official name for the hat was "Cap, Service, Wool Serge, AG-44." The cap had a round flat top and a short front brim, similar in design to the hats worn by civilian police officers and hotel doormen. A similar type of hat was worn by Air Force, Marine and Navy personnel.

Savage Shotgun *see* **Shotgun**

Savages *see* **Nguoi Thuong, Montagnards**

Save-a-Plane Number In Vietnam when an artillery battery was preparing to fire, clearance procedures required friendly aircraft traveling through the area of fire to be warned of the impending artillery fire mission. This clearance was generally handled by an air liaison officer who was responsible for the notification and verification of friendly aircraft in the area. He would then issue a number that was recorded as part of the official firing record. This safety procedure was designed to eliminate accidentally hitting friendly aircraft, along the gun line, between the target and firing battery. This added clearance step increased the battery's response time, delaying the fire support.

Savoy *see* **LZ Savoy**

SAW *see* **Small Arms Fire**

Saw Buck II *see* **Operation Saw Buck II**

SAWTOC (Special Asian Warfare Training and Orientation Center) Special Asian Warfare Training and Orientation Center located on the Hawaiian island of Oahu. The SAWTOC center was established in '56 to train U.S. troops in counterinsurgency operations. The center consisted of several mock Asian villages. Troops of the 25th Infantry Division trained at SAWTOC until the center was closed in '63. *See also* **Camp Cobra.**

SC-47 *see* **C-47**

SC-54 *see* **C-54**

Scag *see* **Heroin**

Scared Horse Regiment *see* **11th Armored Cavalry Regiment**

Schlesinger, James *see* **Secretary of Defense**

Science Fiction *see* **Special Forces**

Scientific-Wild-Assed-Guess *see* **WAG Principle**

Scissors Bridge *see* **M-60 AVLB**

SCLC *see* **King, Reverend Dr. Martin Luther**

SCOOT *see* **Operation SCOOT**

Scooter *see* **A-4**

Scorched Earth Policy Military policy of total annihilation of the enemy and his support structures and systems. In Vietnam an unofficial "scorched earth policy" included the burning and leveling of enemy villages (and suspected enemy sympathetic villages), the destruction of agricultural crops and feed animals that could support the enemy; and the relocation and confinement of enemy family members and sympathizers. Such a policy meant virtual war against some of the very people that America was attempting to protect and save from the communists. As author Robert Taber put it, "There is only one way of defeating an insurgent people who will not surrender, and that is extermination.... There is only one way to control a territory that harbors resistance, and that is to turn it into a desert. Where these means cannot, for whatever reason, be used, the war is lost," from *The War of the Flea*. The French also utilized a "scorched-earth policy" during the First Indochina War: Any town in or near enemy territory they could not hold they destroyed as they left. *See also* **Operation Ranch Hand, Crop Denial, Restructuring.**

Score Slang word meaning to obtain illicit drugs or contraband. Also used to indicate a sexual conquest. *See also* **Gettin' Over.**

Scorpion SPAT *see* **M-56 SPAT**

Scorpion Trap Method used by the Viet Cong to booby trap their tunnels. A box of 15–20 scorpions was concealed in the wall or roof of a tunnel. A GI searching the tunnel would trigger the release of the angry scorpions. A box full of angry scorpions posed a sizable barrier to an unsuspecting GI exploring the tunnel. *See also* **Booby Trap.**

Scotland *see* **Operation Scotland**

Scoutships *see* **Helicopter Scouts**

Screamers (Whistlers) Small pieces of metal (usually razor blades) inserted between an artillery shell and the screwed-on fuse. The metal made the shell scream as it cut through the air en route to the target. The added pieces of metal voided the aerodynamic efficiency of the shell's design,

reducing its target accuracy. Screamers were most often applied during H & I fires when the accuracy of the shells was not critical. GIs thought the "screaming" shells added terror to the lives of the NVA/VC who were the nightly targets of H & I fires. Screamers were also called "whistlers."

Screaming Chicken Patch During the Vietnam War the 101st Airborne Division acquired several nicknames. Two of them were based on the division's screaming eagle patch. The names were the "pukin' buzzard" and the "screaming chicken." The shield shaped patch was flat on top and flared at the upper corners. The bottom of the patch was rounded into a scrolled point. The border and background of the patch were black. In the center was the profile of an eagle head with its beak open. The eagle was white with a gold beak, black eye and a red tongue. Worn above the patch was a black crescent shaped tab with "Airborne" embroidered in gold. *See also* **101st Airborne Division.**

Screaming Chickens *see* **101st Airborne Division (Airmobile)**

Screaming Eagle Replacement Training School (SERTS) An indoctrination, acclimatization and training course for new replacements assigned to the 101st Airborne Division in Vietnam. The 7–10 day course was conducted at Division Headquarters in Phu Bai, I Corps. Topics included dealing with the Vietnamese, health, hygiene, strategy and tactics. Division Headquarters believed preparation was one of the best ways to insure a soldier survived the tour in Vietnam. *See also* **Camp Eagle.**

Screaming Eagles *see* **101st Airborne Division (Airmobile)**

Screen(ing) Using a force to protect or shield friendly forces from enemy attack, harassment or discovery. Screening forces acted as an early warning to the main body if enemy units were encountered. In Vietnam, various sized units performed screening duties. USSF units sometimes screened for larger regular infantry operations. During a company movement, four squads were deployed as a screening force, one ahead of the company, one on each flank, and one at the rear. Screening forces were generally small units, operating at a distance from the main body. Both aircraft and naval vessels performed screening missions. On occasion the NVA/VC forced civilians and livestock to act as a screen to protect them from enemy fire.

Screw *see* **Boom-Boom**

Screw-Up *see* **Fucked-Up**

Scrip *see* **Military Payment Certificates**

Scunnions *see* **Fire (shoot)**

Scut Duty (Scut Work, Chickenshit Details, Shitty Details) Slang for the routine daily duties performed at military, medical, and field facilities, such as bandage and tissue disposal, supplies inventory, floor/wall cleaning, instrument sterilization, latrine duty, bunker repair, burning shitters, filling sandbags for the general's bunker, raking the general's sand, and a host of other menial tasks. Scut jobs were the dirty, sometimes degrading, jobs that no one wanted to do, so they fell to the low men on the "totem pole" or were used as disciplinary assignments. In Vietnam, as elsewhere, they were referred to as "chickenshit" or "shitty" details. *See also* **Shit Burner, Holding Company.**

Scut Work *see* **Scut Duty**

Scuttlebutt *see* **Rumor Control**

SDC/SDF *see* **Popular Forces**

SDS *see* **Students for a Democratic Society**

SEA *see* **Southeast Asia**

Sea Cobra *see* **AH-1J**

Sea Dragon *see* **Operation Sea Dragon**

Sea Float *see* **Operation Sea Float**

Sea Float Annex *see* **Operation Sea Float**

Sea Force *see* **South Vietnamese Sea Force**

SEA Freeway *see* **Pan-SEA Pike**

Sea King *see* **SH-3**

Sea Knight *see* **CH-46**

Sea Load Lines *see* **Swivel-Top Buoy**

Sea Ranger *see* **OH-58**

Sea Snakes *see* **Hook-Nosed Sea Snake**

Sea Stallion *see* **CH-53**

Sea Tiger A locally produced information newspaper printed and distributed to members of the III Marine Amphibious Force, Vietnam. The Information Services Office of the III MAF had overall responsibility for the *Sea Tiger*'s publication and distribution.

Sea-Air-Land *see* **SEAL**

Sea-Tac *see* **Commercial Carriers**

SEAAS *see* **Southeast Asia Airlift System**

Seabag *see* **Dufflebag**

Seabat *see* **CH-34**

SEABEE Teams *see* **SEABEE Technical Assistance Teams**

SEABEE Technical Assistance Teams (SEABEE Teams, STATS, Military Peace Corps) Navy SEABEE teams initially deployed to Vietnam in '63 to assist in the construction of USSF camps and support facilities throughout SVN. The teams worked in the remote areas where the Special Forces camps were located, improving the fortifications and constructing small airstrips used to resupply some of the camps. After the camps were established teams spent much of their time on local civic projects in the area making improvements to wells, roads, bridges and communal buildings. Each team consisted of a hospital corpsman and 12–14 men skilled in various fields of construction. Because of the SEABEES' civic action efforts in Vietnam, they came to be nicknamed the "Military Peace Corps." *See also* **SEABEES, Amphibious Construction Battalions, CAP.**

SEABEES (Naval Mobile Construction Battalions, NMCB) U.S. Navy SEABEES began deploying to SVN in '63. They directed the construction of schools, roads, dams, housing, airstrips and USSF fortifications. In '65 the 30th Naval Construction Regiment was activated at Da Nang, I Corps, and began large scale construction on military facilities throughout the I Corps area. The 32d Naval Construction Regiment deployed to RVN in August '67. As the SEABEE Force grew, they spread over SVN constructing facilities as required. The first Navy Medal of Honor awarded during the Vietnam War went to SEABEE CMA3

Marvin G. Shields, June '65, Dong Xoai, III Corps. *See also* **Dong Xoai, STATS, ACB, Rotate, TSFC, CBMU.**

Seahorse *see* **CH-34**

SEAIR *see* **Southeast Asia Airlift System**

SEAL (Sea-Air-Land, Black Berets) Elite U.S. Navy commando force which specialized in covert intelligence gathering, sabotage, long-range patrolling and raiding. SEALs could deploy by sea, air or land and in RVN operated as part of the River Patrol Force (TF 116) and MACV-SOG operations. They were especially adept at small ambush and raiding techniques. The SEALs wore black berets as their distinctive headgear. SEAL teams usually contained 3–4 men and operated out of bases at My Tho, Binh Tuy and Nha Be. The SEALs conducted covert missions into NVN and trained the LLDN, the Vietnamese version of the SEALs. SEAL teams first deployed to SVN in '66 and operated with one of the highest kill ratios of any U.S. force in Vietnam. *See also* **LLDN, Coronado Island.**

Seal and Search *see* **Search and Destroy, Clear and Hold**

Seal Bin *see* **Blivet**

SEAL Team Assault Boat (Strike Assault Boat, STAB, BSU, Boat Support Unit) Specially outfitted Boston Whaler boats used by SEAL teams in the Delta for mission insertion and extraction. The fast boats were armed with a variety of armaments and were the boat of choice by SEAL teams because of its speed and maneuverability. SEAL teams eventually switched from the propeller driven STAB boats to the faster LSSC (Light SEAL Support Boat) boats. In Vietnam SEAL teams were supported by their own boat support units (BSU) which were familiar with SEAL tactics and modified boats. *See also* **Boston Whaler, Light SEAL Support Boat.**

SEAL Training Center *see* **Coronado Island**

Seale, Bobby *see* **Chicago 7, Chicago 8, Black Panthers**

Sealift The movement of cargo or personnel by means of ships and boats across the world's oceans and seas. Sealift was the primary method of cargo delivery for equipment and supplies used by U.S. forces in Vietnam. The Military Sea Transportation Service and the Merchant Marine provided for the movement of bulk cargo to Vietnam. MSTS was later reorganized into the Military Sealift Command. *See also* **Military Sealift Command.**

SEALORDS *see* **TF 194, Air Cofat-Sealords**

Seaman *see* **Private First Class**

Seaman Apprentice *see* **E-2**

Search and Avoid Phrase used by some GIs to describe ARVN field operations against the NVA/VC. For a variety of reasons, many ARVN combat units avoided contact with the NVA/VC. The ARVN operations often resulted in no contact, despite ops being in known NVA/VC areas. This unwillingness or inability to confront the enemy haunted the ARVNs until they collapsed as a fighting force during the NVA Final Offensive of '75. There were some ARVN units that gave a good accounting of themselves such as the 1st ARVN Division and the ARVN Marine and Airborne units, but they were the exception to the rule. *See also* **25th ARVN Division.**

Search and Clear *see* **Search and Destroy**

Search and Destroy (S & D, SAD, Sweep and Clear, Search and Clear, Snoop 'n' Poop, Seal and Search) U.S. operations in Vietnam designed to utilize technology and superior firepower to locate and destroy the enemy, his bases and supply caches. Units constantly moved; searching, instead of taking and holding territory or terrain, eliminating the enemy through combat attrition. As the war dragged on, "Search and Destroy" made a less than favorable impression in the news media, and SAD missions were given less sinister names such as "Reconnaissance in Force," "Offensive Sweeps," "Sweep and Clear," "Seal and Search," or "Search and Clear" operations. The Marines nicknamed their SAD missions "Snoop 'n' Poop." *See also* **Reconnaissance in Force, Battalion RIF, War of Attrition, Zippo Raid, Aggressive Defense.**

Search and Rescue (SAR) Specially designed techniques for the search and rescue of downed aircrews. In Vietnam, U.S. Air Force and Navy SAR operations involved air, sea and land components in their rescue operations. On some occasions, MACV-SOG teams would be used to aid in ground search and recovery. Various helicopters and aircraft were involved in rescue operations. Rescue squadrons and helos which composed the Southeast Asia SAR were based at Da Nang, Udorn, Saigon, Tuy Hoa, Takhli, Korat and Nakhon Phanom. *See also* **Aerospace Rescue and Recovery Service, Search and Rescue Task Force.**

Search and Rescue Task Force (SAR-TAF)   Force organized for search and rescue work. In Vietnam, the force usually included several A-1 Sandys for search and aircover, and two or three helicopters from the ARRS for pickup. The ARRS used the HH-3 and HH-53 Jolly Green Giant helos for rescue work. Some of the HH-53 Super Jolly Green Giants were specially equipped allowing them to be refueled inflight, and enabling them them greater penetration into enemy territory and increased loiter on station waiting to pick up downed crewmen. The SAR-TAF operated from bases in SVN and Thailand. *See also* **Aerospace Rescue and Recovery Service.**

Search Turn   *see*   **Operation Search Turn**

Search-Locate-Annihilate-Mission *see*   **SLAM Company**

Searchlight Boats   *see*   **LCPL**

SEASHARP (Southeast Asia Semi-permanent Harbor Protection, HOMS, HECP, HPE, HEOD, IUWG)   U.S. Navy security unit organized and deployed to SVN in '64 to provide protection for ships in SVN's harbors. SEASHARP consisted of four specialized units: Harbor Operations and Maintenance Support (HOMS), Harbor Entrance Central Post (HECP), Harbor Patrol Element (HPE), and Harbor Explosive Ordnance Disposal Teams (HEOD). The HOMS provided land based support for the SEASHARP elements. HECP was the command center for all SEASHARP operations. HPF was the patrol force that checked civilian vessels using the harbor. HEOD teams inspected ship hulls and anchorage sites for enemy placed explosives and mines. SEASHARP was later designated the Inshore Undersea War Group (IUWG) and placed under command of TF 115 in '67. *See also* **MIUWG.**

Seasprite   *see*   **UH-2**

SEATO   *see*   **Southeast Asia Treaty Organization**

Seawolves (Light Attack Helicopter Squadron 3, HAL-3, Blue Hueys)   Navy helicopter gunship squadron which operated in the Delta in support of riverine operations of TF 194. The "Blue Huey" was the nickname for Navy helicopter gunships that were painted blue-green instead of the olive drab color used by the Army. Both colors were found on the choppers of HAL-3. The squadron was commissioned in April '67 from a Navy helicopter detachment that previously had supported Navy riverine operations since August '66. HAL-3 operated with UH-1B/C aircraft and later the upgraded -1L/M. HAL-3 also provided AIR COFAT with logistic and lift capacity. *See also* **Light Attack Squadron 4, TF 194, Rowell's Rats, Air Cofat.**

SecDef   *see*   **Secretary of Defense**

Second Advon   *see*   **2d Air Force**

Second Air Force   *see*   **2d Air Force**

Second Field Force Vietnam   *see*   **II Field Force**

Second Indochina War   *see*   **Vietnam War**

Second Lieutenant (Second Louie, Boot Brown Bar, Butter Bar, Newby, 2d Lt, Gold-Bar, 2Lt)   Lowest ranking officer in the Army, Air Force and Marines, excluding warrant officers. The 2d Lieutenant insignia of rank was a single gold bar. GIs in Vietnam were sometimes heard to say that "a 2d lieutenant with a map and a .45 was almost as dangerous as facing the enemy." A variant of the phrase was "the most dangerous thing in the world was a 2d lieutenant armed with a compass and a map." Promotion from 2Lt was to 1st lieutenant. In the field, "L.T." was a commonly used nickname for lieutenants who were liked by the enlisted men. Army and Marine 2d Lts generally commanded a platoon. Thieu-Uy was the equivalent Vietnamese rank. *See also* **Company Grade Officers.**

Second Louie   *see*   **Second Lieutenant**

Second Regional Assistance Command

(SRAC) U.S. advisory command for II Corps, responsible for all American advisory functions and CORDS operations in the II Corps zone. *See also* Vann, John Paul.

Second Vietnamese Invasion of Cambodia *see* **Kampuchean Front for National Salvation**

Second-Eight *see* **Advanced Infantry Training**

Secondaries *see* **Secondary Explosions**

Secondary Explosions (Secondaries) Explosions resulting from a previous explosion or fire. Fire attacks by bombs, artillery or weapons fire sometimes caused hidden ammunition, fuels or other explosives to detonate creating a "secondary explosion." *See also* Sympathetic Detonations.

Secondary MOS *see* **Military Occupation Specialty**

Secret and Confidential Files *see* **S & C Files**

Secret Bombing of Cambodia (Bombing of Cambodia) In March '69 President Nixon authorized the U.S. Air Force to begin secret bombings of NVA/VC base areas inside the Cambodian border. The bombings were made in "neutral" territory, supposedly with the secret approval of Cambodia's leader, Prince Sihanouk. Since Cambodia was officially neutral, by international law the bombings were illegal. At the insistence of Nixon, no public releases were allowed concerning the targeting, damage assessments or aircraft losses associated with the bombing of the NVA/VC sanctuaries. Air Force records were falsified in order to maintain the secrecy of the bombing missions. The missions remained secret until '70. *See also* Operation Menu & Patio, Operation Menu Targets, Kent State.

Secret Evacuations *see* **Black Flights**

Secret Police *see* **Can Lao**

Secret War, Laos (No-No War in Never-Never Land) "No-No War in Never-Never Land," description of the secret war the CIA waged against the communists in Laos. In '62 a Geneva agreement declared Laos neutral and called for the withdrawal of U.S. troops supporting the Royal Lao forces, and the withdrawal of NVN troops support-

ing the communist Pathet Lao. North Vietnam covertly continued to support the Laotian communists. In response to the NVN support the U.S. CIA began its own secret support activities of the Royal Lao anticommunist forces. In addition, the CIA raised and equipped the mountain Meo tribesmen to fight the Pathet Lao/NVA in the Central Highlands of Laos. *See also* Secret Wars.

Secret Wars Reference to the covert war waged in Laos and Cambodia by U.S. military forces and the CIA. Open warfare against Cambodia did not begin until '70. Prior to '70, operations against the Ho Chi Minh Trail and NVA/VC base camps were very limited, strictly secret, and were primarily raids by small groups of USSF units. Operations in Laos were conducted by the CIA to counter the communist Pathet Lao who were supported by the NVA. In '70 the secret bombings of the Ho Chi Minh Trail were made public and US/ARVN forces launched ground attacks against NVA/VC sanctuaries in Cambodia. In '71, ARVN ground forces met disaster when they attempted to cut the NVA supply lines at Tchepone in Laos. *See also* Secret Bombing of Cambodia; Secret War, Laos; Operation Lam Son 719.

Secret Zones Navy nickname for Viet Cong base areas that lined the rivers of the Delta. The VC controlled much of the Delta until the efforts of Task Force 115, 116, and 117 began operations in '65. VC Secret Zones referred to enemy areas where little, if any, hard intelligence information about the area was available to the U.S. military.

Secretary of Defense (SOD, Department of Defense [DOD], SecDef, OSD) As a member of the U.S. presidential cabinet, the secretary of defense controlled the Department of Defense, which controlled all aspects of the U.S. military establishment. During American involvement in Vietnam, from '59 to '73 the SODs were: Thomas Gates, Jr., Neil McElroy, Robert McNamara, Clark Gifford, Melvin Laird, Elliot Richardson and James Schlesinger. Officially the SOD was referred to as the "Office of Secretary of Defense" (OSD).

Secretary of State (SOS, State, Department of State, State Department) The U.S. secretary of state advised the president in matters concerning foreign affairs, and headed the U.S. Department of State. During U.S. involvement in the Vietnam War there were five different SOSs: John Foster Dulles, Christian Herter, Dean Rusk, William Rogers and Henry Kissinger. The State Department was generally referred to simply as "State."

Section 8 *see* **Section 212**

Section 212 (Two-Twelve, 212, Psychiatric Discharge, Section 8) Army Regulations section detailing the grounds for a discharge from military service for psychiatric reasons. Comparable to the "Section 8" of WWII fame. *See also* **Discharges.**

Secure Net (Monster Net) Radio net connecting PRC-77 radios. The PRC-77 scrambled and descrambled radio transmission, allowing units in the field and higher headquarters to communicate with each other without the enemy intercepting the traffic. All radios in the net had to be on the same settings in order to transmit and receive valid recognizable information. *See also* **AN/PRC-77.**

Security Holdover Army term for personnel held in confinement, pending assignment, because they were considered security risks. During Vietnam this applied to returned AWOLs and deserters. The Army held these individuals on the base until it could be established that they could be trusted to perform their assignment. The holdovers were confined to base and in some instances placed under arrest and held in the stockade.

Security Police *see* **Air Police**

Sedang *see* **Montagnards**

Seek-Locate-Annihilate-and-Monitor *see* **SLAM**

Seger, Bob *see* **Ballad of the Yellow Beret**

Segmented Round *see* **Tunnel Weapon**

Seismic Intrusion Devices (SID) Ground sensors used to detect enemy movement. In Vietnam the sensor was planted in the ground; when activated, it transmitted a number code to a receiver, representing the sensor number. By planting the sensors in line an estimate of the number of enemy, speed and direction of travel could be determined. This information was most often used to determine firing coordinates for artillery and for future ambushes or operations. Impacting artillery, passing civilians or even water buffalo could activate the sensors. *See also* **Electronic Sensors, Unattended Ground Sensors.**

Seismic Tunnel Detector (STD, ACG-35/68M) One of the DODs, Limited War Laboratory projects evaluated in Vietnam. The device was designed to detect enemy tunnels by means of seismic signals. In theory, enemy movement underground could be detected by the device. The STD required two men to operate and transport the device. The device proved so sensitive and inaccurate that it picked up erroneous signals generated by friendly troops and artillery strikes in the area. The STD project was cancelled by the Army and the devices returned to the States. *See also* **Limited War Laboratory.**

Selected Reserve Force (SRF) U.S. military program designed to update and train selected Army-Reserve and National Guard units with the latest available military equipment. This training and equipping of AR and NG units with frontline Army equipment provided the Army with a pool of manpower that could quickly be absorbed into the system in time of need, with a minimum of disruption. Normally AR and NG units trained with older, outdated equipment that had previously been frontline hardware used by regular Army troops.

Selective Ordnance *see* **Naphthenic-Palmitic Acid**

Selective Service (SSS) The Selective Service System (SSS) was the responsible government agency that administered the nation's draft requirements. The DOD projected its manpower needs and the SSS used the projections to determine draft quotas. The draft calls were made through local Selective Service Boards. Because of the system of deferments and inequities in the selection process, an inordinate proportion of the draftees, prior to '69, were from those segments of American society not likely or able to avoid the draft; the poorly educated, poor whites, blacks and Hispanics. *See also* **Draft Lottery; Draft, U.S.**

Selective Service Youth Advisory Committee *see* **Draft Lottery**

Self-Defense Corps *see* **Popular Forces**

Self-Determination in Mississippi and Vietnam (Self-Determination—Vietnam for the Vietnamese) 1960s antiwar protest slogans that reflected the liberal view that the repression suffered by blacks in America's Southern states was comparable to the repression suffered by the South Vietnamese at the hands of their own government—a government backed by the same American political leaders who were ignoring the injustices of blacks in the deep South. Slogan also heard as "Self-Determination—Vietnam for the Vietnamese."

Self-Immolation *see* **Thich Quang Duc; Burn Yourselves, Not Your Draft Cards**

Self-Propelled Antitank Gun *see* **M-56 SPAT**

Self-Propelled Multiple Rifle *see* **M-50A1 Ontos**

Semiactive Radar Guidance *see* **AIM-7**

Semi-inverted Chute *see* **T-10 Chute Malfunctions**

Semimobile Evacuation Hospital *see* **Evacuation Hospital (Semimobile)**

Seminole *see* **U-8**

Semitruck *see* **M-123 Tractor**

Semper Fidelis (Always Faithful, Esprit de Corps, Marine Code) U.S. Marine Corps motto: "Always Faithful," to the Corps; the individual's spirit and devotion to the Marine Corps, "Esprit de Corps." Variants: "Semper Fi," "Semper Fi, Do or Die." The Marine code: Never retreat, never surrender as long as you have the means to resist (translated: "as long as you're alive") and never leave your casualties on the battlefield.

Senior Advisory Group (SAG) A group of senior policymakers who advised President Johnson on a wide variety of policy matters, foremost of which was the Vietnam War. The group recommended that the U.S. should "disengage itself" from the war; they were concerned that by the time SVN was able to bear the war effort on its own, U.S. public support for the war would have deteriorated to unacceptable levels. In March '68, on advice of the SAG, Johnson

announced the bombing halt of North Vietnam and asked the North Vietnamese to seek peace in the region. Johnson also announced he would not run for another term as president. *See also* **Wise Old Men.**

Senior Grade Officers *see* **General Officers**

Sensitive Vietnamese *see* **Black Flights**

Sensor Receiver *see* **Sensor String**

Sensor String (Sensor Receiver) Group of several sensors placed together allowing an area to be remotely monitored using electronic devices. A typical string consisted of 5–7 sensors implanted along an enemy trail. Each ground sensor's exact location was known because the sensors were implanted by hand. The string was monitored from a remote station, and based on the frequency, duration, and sequence of the activations of the individual sensors in the string, the size, speed and direction of an enemy force moving near the sensors could be determined. From such information artillery strikes could be called in or ambush missions planned. Activations from the sensors were monitored by a special "sensor receiver" which received coded activation signals on one of four different channels; each channel could monitor up to 99 sensors. Each sensor device transmitted a unique two-digit number code (01–99) that was displayed on the receiver. The receivers were a high priority security item and special efforts were made to insure they were not captured by the enemy. A captured receiver could be used by the enemy to discover the radio frequencies used by the sensors; once the frequencies were known the enemy could jam the air and render hundreds of sensors useless. *See also* **Electronic Sensors, Unattended Ground Sensors.**

Separate Helicopter Companies *see* **Nonorganic Aviation Unit**

Separate Units *see* **Independent Units**

Separation Program Numbers *see* **SPN Number**

Sequential Turnover Plan *see* **Accelerated Turnover to Vietnam**

SERE Course *see* **Survival Evasion Resistance and Escape Course**

Serenity, Tranquility, Peace *see* STP

Sergeant E-5 *see* **Buck Sergeant**

Sergeant Major *see* **E-9**

Sergeant Rock *see* **Gungi Marine**

Sergeants' Scandal Late in the VNW a scandal surfaced regarding "irregularities" that had taken place within the NCO Club system. Sgt Maj William O. Wooldridge and four other managing sergeants in the club system were indicted, accused of bribery, extortion, kickbacks, misuse of equipment and negligence of duty.

Serial Nickname for a flight of "slicks." Seven slicks were usually sufficient to transport a platoon of American infantry, and twenty-two slicks were capable of transporting an entire infantry company.

Serial Number *see* **US (Serial Number)**

SERTS *see* **Screaming Eagle Replacement Training School**

Serum Albumin (Blood Expander, Albumin, Dextran) A protein based blood expander that was carried in the field by medics and was administered to the severely wounded as a temporary blood filler. The albumin was available bottled in glass or in a sealed plastic bag and was administered through an IV. On long-range patrols some USSF and LRRP troops carried albumin, to be self-administered, packaged in protective metal cans. Dextran was also available as a blood expander. The interaction of the expander with the body caused absorption of fluids from the area surrounding the blood vessels, increasing blood volume.

Services Techniques des Construction et Armes *see* **STCAN/FOM**

SES *see* **Special Exploitation Service**

Set Slang for a drug related party, in Vietnam, held in a private, secure area of the base camp.

Set-In (Deploy) Take up a position, offensive or defensive.

Set-Piece Battle (Conventional Warfare) A battle between two opposing military forces, using conventional weapons and warfare tactics. Both forces used detailed plans and had foreknowledge of the impending battle. The war in Vietnam saw very few set-piece battles between U.S. and NVA/VC forces. The U.S. initially used conventional warfare methods in Vietnam to fight the NVA/VC guerrilla warfare. The NVA/VC seldom stood their ground to fight if they were outnumbered or outgunned, choosing instead to fight on their terms. On those few occasions that NVA/VC did stand their ground to fight, they suffered heavy casualties from superior U.S. firepower. *See also* **Guerrilla War, Expend Shells Not Men.**

Seven Mountains (Superstition Mountain, Nui Coto) Rough mountainous area along the SVN/Cambodian border in Chau Doc Province, IV Corps. NVA/VC units operating out of mountain caves and tunnels used the area as a base. The principal peak of the mountain group, Nui Coto, was called Superstition Mountain by the locals because for years the VC had operated untouched from the mountain. In March '69 a combined CIDG and LLDB force led by USSF Mobile Strike Forces attacked and eventually (but temporarily) cleared the mountain of the VC base camps. *See also* **Nui Coto.**

Seventeenth Parallel *see* **Geneva Accords**

Sex *see* **Boom-Boom**

SF Team A-222 *see* **Dong Tre Special Forces Camp**

SFAS *see* **Special Forces Association of Saigon**

SFC *see* **E-7**

SFG *see* **Special Forces**

SG43 MMG (Stankovyi Goryunova 1943, Type 53 HMG, SG43M, SGM, Type 57 HMG) Soviet made medium machine gun. The 7.62mm gun was used for infantry support and antiaircraft fire. The gun weighed over 31 pounds and was usually mounted on a two wheel carriage, was pocket belt fed (250 rounds) and had a maximum effective range of 1,000 meters. The SG43M or SGM was a modified version of the SG43. Some of the modifications included a relocated operating handle, dust cover for feed and ejection ports and an improved barrel. The PRC copy of the SG43 was called the Type 53 Heavy Machine Gun.

The PRC version of the SGM was called the Type 57 HMG. *See also* **Medium Machine Gun, Heavy Machine Gun.**

SGF-2 Fog Oil *see* **XM-52 Smoker**

SGM MMG *see* **SG43 MMG**

SH-3 (Sea King, Big-Mothers, Fetch, S-61 Sikorsky, H-3)   Navy helicopter used for SAR. In Vietnam, the helicopter was armored and armed with M-60 machine guns. The Sea Kings were affectionately known as "Big-Mothers" to those who flew and depended on them for rescue. They operated under the call sign "Fetch." The SH-3 (S-61) was manufactured by Sikorsky. The 5-blade rotor was powered by two turbine engines with a max speed of 166mph and a range of 1,000kms. A modified version of the SH-3, the CH-3/HH-3, was used by the Air Force and Coast Guard. *See also* **CH-3.**

SH-34 *see* **CH-34**

Shackle Cards (Radio Code Sheets, Compromised Codes, Shackle Codes) Series of codes used by the Marines for radio transmission. The preprinted codes were carried by the RTO. If any of the code cards fell into enemy hands, then all the codes on those cards were considered "compromised," and no longer secure. A new set of codes would have to be issued to all Marine units who were using the compromised code set. *See also* **S & C Files.**

Shackle Codes *see* **Shackle Cards**

Shackup   Slang for GIs who lived off base with one of the locals. In Vietnam military personnel were supposed to be barracked on base, but in places like Saigon and Da Nang it was not unusual for a GI to live in the city, off the military base. Many NCOs rented apartments and houses in the city and had Vietnamese "girlfriends" who lived with them. The girlfriend functioned as a surrogate "wife," doing the cooking, cleaning and providing nocturnal companionship. The off post "shackups" were against military policy, but the policy was usually not enforced. Enlisted men also had their shackups, but there were periodic crackdowns on the EM; even so, the practice continued throughout the war. *See also* **Bedcheck.**

Shadow *see* **AC-119G**

Shadow Government of Vietnam *see* **Enemy, The**

Shake 'n' Bake Sergeants (Instant NCOs, NCO Course, NCOC)   Field reference to hastily trained NCOs; recent graduates of NCO courses in the States. Army requirements for experienced low level NCOs (Sgt/SSG) greatly increased as the war in Vietnam expanded. In order to fill the need, new NCOs were pushed through a 21-week leadership and advanced infantry course at Fort Benning. After '68 there was a severe shortage of platoon and company level leaders often forcing new NCOs, lacking experience in combat and leadership, to be assigned to lead squads and platoons. The result was poor troop performance and a general decline in morale and discipline. The newly hatched NCOs were called "Shake 'n' Bake" sergeants or "Instant NCOs."

Shakedown (Amnesty Box)   The military's search of its troops for contraband and or illicit drugs. American troops departing Vietnam at the end of their tour of duty were subject to search for items such as drugs, weapons, explosives, and any other military hardware. "Amnesty Boxes" were provided at the DEROS Centers where troops could deposit such contraband, prior to their departure from Vietnam, with no questions asked. After '70 American troops leaving Vietnam were thoroughly searched for drugs before being allowed to leave the country.

Shaman *see* **Montagnard Shaman**

Shamin' *see* **Goldbricking**

Shamnesty Board *see* **Ford Clemency Review Board**

Shangri-La *see* **USS Shangri-La**

Shantytowns *see* **Dogpatch, Johnsonvilles**

Sharp, Admiral U.S. Grant *see* **Commander-in-Chief, Pacific Command**

Sharper-Than-the-Average-Gook *see* **STAG**

Shavin'-Your-Palms *see* **Masturbate**

Shawnee *see* **CH-21**

Shea, Lt. Michael *see* **Last American to Die...**

Sheafs of Fire (Open Sheaf, Converged Sheaf, Parallel Sheaf)   Artillery term used to describe burst patterns against a target area. An "open sheaf" covered a wide area with the batteries' fire spread along an axis allowing the individual burst ranges of the impacting rounds to slightly overlap. In the "parallel sheaf," the rounds of the battery impacted in parallel burst as they were adjusted or walked over the target. In the "converged sheaf," the batteries' fires were plotted to converge on one point.

Shell Fragments When a high explosive shell exploded it ripped its metal casing into thousands of sharp pieces, capable of destroying the human body in a multitude of ways. A fragmentation grenade was designed to perform in the same manner. These jagged fragments of metal were sometimes incorrectly referred to as "shrapnel." *See also* **Shrapnel, Grenade Fragmentation.**

Shell Oil Company (Esso, Caltex) The three major oil companies that operated in South Vietnam were Shell, Esso, and Caltex. The companies provided commercial fuels for civilian needs as well as selling fuel supplies, on occasion, to various U.S. and GVN military organizations in-country.

Shell Shock *see* **Combat Fatigue**

Shelter Half (GI Tent) Cotton or canvas tent-half used in the field. Two shelter halves snapped together could accommodate two soldiers. Each soldier would normally carry several tent pegs and a three piece tent pole. Because of the shelter half's weight (several pounds), grunts usually did not take them to the field, but used their rain ponchos for shelter. *See also* **Poncho.**

Shenandoah *see* **Operation Shenandoah II**

Shenyang J-6 (MiG-19, Farmer, Chinese MiGs) Chinese manufactured version of the Soviet MiG-19. The twin engine, single seat jet fighter had a max speed of 900mph, a range of 2,100kms and was armed with a combination of three 20mm and 30mm cannons and AAM missiles. The US/NATO name for the MiG-19 was the "Farmer." During the course of the Vietnam War, Chinese Shenyangs shot down two U.S. fighter planes that had strayed into Chinese airspace. *See also* **MiG.**

Sheridan Tank *see* **M-551 ARV**

Sherman Tank *see* **M-4 Tank**

Shields, CMA3 Marvin G. *see* **SEABEES, Dong Xoai**

Shines Derogatory name for black GIs. *See also* **Soul Brother.**

Shining Brass *see* **Operation Shining Brass**

Ships *see* **Birds**

Shit, The (The Line, Line Units) The day-to-day combat operations endured by GIs in the field. The humping up and down numbered hills, the trudging through rice paddies and the trail-breaking through dense jungle in search of an elusive and deadly enemy. The Vietnam that only some 10–15 percent of the U.S. ground force in-country saw and survived. These units were referred to as "line units," and their time spent in the field was referred to as being "on the line." *See also* **Boonies, Lines, Infantry Soldier, Bush Time.**

Shit Burner (Willie the Shit Burner, Burning Shit) An individual assigned to dispose of the waste collected in the latrine. The duty consisted of removing the buckets (sections of 55 gal. drums) used as toilets and burning the contents with kerosene, gasoline, or a combination of both. The resulting fire had an unbelievable stench, a plume of thick black smoke, and could have a burn time of several hours. The buckets had to be stirred as they burned to insure complete consumption of the contents by the fire; sloshing and splattering of the contents were unavoidable at some bases, the buckets were emptied into a trench for burning. On larger U.S. bases, Vietnamese were paid to do the task, and the shit burner was universally named "Willie" by the GIs. On smaller U.S. bases, the duty was rotated among the enlisted men, and it was often used as a highly negative disciplinary action. *See also* **Honey Bucket, Scut Duty.**

Shit Burning Detail *see* **Shit Burner, Latrine**

Shit Details *see* **Shit Burner, Scut Duty**

Shit Paper (Toilet Paper) The source of toilet paper for grunts in the field was the pack of tissue paper that was enclosed in the C-Ration accessory packet. Each packet contained twenty 4.5-inch square pieces of thin, scratchy tissue paper. The squares were folded in half and then rolled together. Rolls of toilet paper were reserved for the base camps where formal latrines and "pissers" could be found. Grunts in the field often carried their "shit paper" under the elastic band that secured the helmet cover or inside the helmet to provide "dry" insurance against sweat and rain. *See also* **Accessory Packet.**

Shit Pots *see* **Honey Buckets**

Shit Sauce *see* **Nuoc Man**

Shit, Shine, Shower & Shave *see* **Four Ss**

Shit-Bird Marine slang for a GI who was continually screwing up or getting into trouble. *See also* **Goldbricking.**

Shit-Eatin'-Grin (Vietnamese Smile, Frozen Smile) The Vietnamese perpetual grin in response to Americans' questions they didn't understand, had no adequate English response for, or just didn't care to answer. The GI consensus was, if you asked a Vietnamese a question, especially rural and farm types, you'd get a grin in response (regardless of the question) and the typical "toi com biet" (I don't understand). The perpetual "Vietnamese smile" or "frozen smile" was more likely related to fear or confusion than some inside joke shared universally by the Vietnamese. For the GI in the field the Vietnamese "perpetual grin," to all manner of questions, was maddening. The Vietnamese peasant would grin when asked questions about VC in the area or the location of booby traps. After a GI tripped a booby trap in a village or was killed by a sniper, the villagers would respond with the same grin when asked why they did not warn the Americans of the booby trap or the presence of the enemy. For the GI in the field, the Vietnamese's inscrutable "grin of innocence" was not an endearing trait. *See also* **Toi Com (Khong) Biet.**

Shit-Faced *see* **Drunk**

Shit-Hook *see* **CH-47**

Shit-Kicker Nickname for a cowboy, farmer or hillbilly.

Shit-on-a-Shingle (Creamed Beef on Toast, Chipped Beef on Toast, SOS) GI slang for one of the Army's longest surviving mess hall items, creamed beef or chipped beef on toast. Even with all the hardships of Vietnam, the Army managed to keep up the tradition, and "SOS" found its way to Vietnam. In Vietnam "SOS" was usually cold, lumpy chipped beef, on soggy toasted bread.

Shitbirds *see* **Goldbricking**

Shits, The *see* **Ho Chi Minh's Revenge, Fucked-Up**

Shitter *see* **Latrine, Honey Buckets**

Shitty Details *see* **Scut Duty**

Shock Deadliest enemy of the wounded soldier in the field. After stopping the bleeding of a seriously wounded soldier a prime concern was to keep him from going into shock. Shock was typically caused by a loss of, or severe restriction of, blood circulation. Soldiers suffering from shock had a weak, fast pulse, low blood pressure, shallow breathing, skin pale and sweaty to the touch, and, if untreated, slipped into unconsciousness. The reduced blood flow could result in death in a matter of minutes due to kidney or liver failure. It was essential to keep such a wounded man awake; if allowed to sleep, shock would easily set in. Treatment included immediate use of blood expanders and drugs to stabilize the patient's deteriorating condition.

Shock Brigades (Youth Shock Brigade) North Vietnamese volunteer laborers who repaired and maintained the Ho Chi Minh Trail. The workers were civilian youths that were officially known along the trail as the "Youth Shock Brigade Against the Americans for National Salvation."

Shoe Mine *see* **Toe-Poppers**

Shoe Tags Method used by the 2d Battalion/503d Infantry to keep track of its troops during the unit's parachute assault into War Zone C in February '67. The normal procedure involved a manifest of the soldiers that boarded and jumped from the transport aircraft. The "shoe tag" method was derived to simplify the record keeping. The tag was divided into four parts, each containing the soldier's name, rank, serial and chalk numbers. The soldier kept one part for identification; battalion operations, the jumpmaster and the loadmaster also received a part of the tag. Using this method troops could be easily moved between jump aircraft, and their status and location more easily tracked. *See also* **Operation Junction City.**

Shoebox Mine   During the early stages of the Vietnam War terrorist attacks against U.S. servicemen in the larger cities of Vietnam were frequent. The attacks took several forms, one of which involved the VC planting a bomb in a shoeshine boy's shoebox, sending him into the streets in search of American servicemen. Sometimes the shoeshine boy had no idea that explosives were packed in the bottom of the box. On other occasions the VC would casually put the box down near a restaurant or location frequented by GIs; later a time fuse would detonate the bomb. *See also* **Bicycle Bomb, Booby Trap.**

Shoot   *see*   **Ban, Kill**

Shoot an Azimuth   *see*   **Azimuth**

Shoot Down   *see*   **Down**

Shooter   *see*   **Mainliner**

Shooting Star   *see*   **T-33**

Shooting the Donut   The "donut hole" was represented by U.S. troops set up in their NDP; the area around the hole was where defensive artillery fire was called, in the event of attack. Supporting artillery fire had to be very accurate because of the enemy's tactic of "hugging," which required artillery fires to be brought in very close to friendly troops. Rounds that landed short would fall into the friendly position, and long rounds would be ineffective against the enemy. In Vietnam, the greatest number of friendly fire casualties were caused by artillery fires. "Shooting the donut" also worked in reverse with U.S. troops encircling an enemy position and calling artillery into the "hole." *See also* **Friendly Fires, Short Round, Defensive Contact Artillery Fire.**

Shooting War   *see*   **Other War, The**

Shore Patrol (SP)   U.S. Navy military police.

Short   *see*   **Short-Timer**

Short Airfield for Tactical Support (SATS, Tinfoil Strip)   Airfield concept used by U.S. Marine aircraft to provide tactical support to their ground forces. The concept centered around the ability of Marine aircraft to operate from short airstrips in a fashion similar to air operations

from the deck of a carrier. The airstrip used was 2,000 feet long and made of AM-2 aluminum matting. The "tin foil strip" could accommodate the Marines' jet aircraft and heavier C-130 transports. A ground arresting hook system was devised to "catch" landing aircraft. To launch heavy aircraft from the short strip JATO bottles were employed and a catapult system was developed. The SATS strip was tried at Chu Lai, but the strip was lengthened to 4,000 feet to increase aircraft performance.

Short Round   Artillery round or aircraft ordnance that fell short of the target area by such a great distance that it didn't even qualify as a miss. If the artillery was being fired over friendly troops there was always a chance that a round falling short would fall among the friendlies. Short rounds were usually the result of a failure of the explosive launching the shell to detonate properly or completely, but short rounds could also be attributed to errors in the coordinates requested for the strike, or gun laying errors. In Vietnam the term "short round" eventually came to mean any firing or bombing errors that put ordnance on friendly troops or civilians. *See also* **Friendly Fires, Shooting the Donut, Gun-Target-Line.**

Short Term Recon and Target Acquisition Team   *see*   **STRATA Team**

Short-Time   *see*   **Boom-Boom**

Short-Time Fever   *see*   **Short-Timer Syndrome**

Short-Time Girl   *see*   **Prostitute**

Short-Timer (Short, Two-Digit Midget, Single-Digit Midget, Next)   Slang for a soldier nearing the end of a tour of duty, assignment or an enlistment. For soldiers in Vietnam "short" referred to being close to their DEROS date, the end of their tour in Vietnam. Troops kept track of the date on special calendars, and some "short" troops carried a short carved stick (similar to a swagger stick) on which they notched each passing day as they neared their DEROS. Two-digit midgets had less than 100 days to DEROS and those under 10 days were called "single-digit midgets" or simply "Next." Some short-timers displayed a phobia for field operations as they became short. *See also* **Short-Timer's Stick, Short-Timer Calendar, Short-Timer Jokes.**

Short-Timer Calendar GI calendar used to track the number of days a man had remaining on his tour in Vietnam. There were almost as many different calendars as there were short-timers in Vietnam. One of the more popular types was a picture of a nude woman, her body divided into tiny sections representing the remaining number of days; each day a section was marked off or colored in; usually the pubic area was reserved for the last few remaining days. Most GIs didn't start their calendars until they had 60–90 days left in their tour.

Short-Timer Jokes *He's so short:* . . . he sleeps in his helmet; . . . his legs don't reach the ground; . . . he can't even see his shadow; . . . he's not short any more, he's "next"; . . . he can walk under the white stripes in the middle of the road; . . . he has to look up to look down; . . . he better not take a long piss or he'll miss his plane home. *See also* **Short-Timer.**

Short-Timer Syndrome (Short-Time Fever) For some combat GIs as their total days remaining in-country shrank, their fears and anxieties about making it out of the field, and getting home, greatly increased. Their anxiety level increased as their remaining tour time decreased. Some GIs talked continuously of home and what they would do when they got back to "the World." The short-timer became reluctant to take chances, became overcautious and, in some cases, acted extremely paranoid. Some units tried to get their short-timers out of the field and into base camp assignments, while other units required them to hump in the boonies until their DEROS. For some grunts, REMF jobs were very appetizing when they reached the "sixty-and-a-wake-up" point of their tour.

Short-Timer's Stick A short stick carried by some short-timers in Vietnam as their tour of duty neared its end. The sticks often had ornate designs, and some GIs carved notches in the stick as they counted down the days to DEROS. Some GIs cut the stick down a little with each passing day; when his tour was up he was left with a short stub. The stick was mostly found with individuals at the larger base camps and cities, and was carried as a sign to all that the carrier was "short," and would be going home soon. An enlisted man's swagger stick.

Shortie *see* **CAR-15**

Shorts *see* **Skivvies**

Shot Card Military regulations specified that all personnel maintained an up-to-date record of their inoculations. The records of those inoculations and shots were maintained on the "shot card." Troops en route to Vietnam were required to have several additional inoculations; for typhoid, yellow fever, plague and tetanus. For Army troops, a copy of the shot card was usually kept in the individual's 201 File, but some officers kept the card with them. If the shot card was lost or could not be produced the individual had to retake the series of shots. Without an up-to-date shot card troops could not go to Vietnam, or return home via the normal DEROS procedures. *See also* **Bubonic Plague.**

Shot-Gun Name for a technique used to smoke marijuana in Vietnam, involving the use of a long tube (bong) to intensify the effect of the drug. At one end of the tube marijuana smoke was blown into a small opening in the tube, and the recipient, at the opposite end, drew the smoke down the tube and into his lungs. A variety of tubes were used including stacked beer cans, bamboo, metal rods and shotgun barrels. *See also* **Pipe.**

Shotgun (Ithaca Model 37, Remington 870, Savage, Winchester, Stevens, Riot Guns) Shotguns (Riot Guns) were used in Vietnam by MPs, recon, and various other units in the field. They were a favorite weapon of point men because of their wide angle of fire at close range. The shotguns used were 12 gauge, single barrel pumps; the most popular models were the Ithaca and the Remington, with a limited number of Winchester, Stevens, and Savage models also used. LRRP and USSF troops used shotguns with sawed-off barrels when operating in the field. The standard shotgun shell used 00 lead buckshot, but flechette rounds containing finned darts were used on a limited basis. *See also* **Remington 870, Shotgun Flechette, Riding Shotgun.**

Shotgun Alley Nickname for the patrol area around the U.S. Special Forces camp located in the A Shau Valley. *See also* **A Shau Valley.**

Shotgun Beehive Round *see* **Shotgun Flechette**

Shotgun Flechette (XM-258) Shotgun flechette or beehive rounds were used experimentally in Vietnam. Several manufacturers developed flechette rounds for the Army and Marine 12-gauge shotguns used in Vietnam. Each shell carried 20–26 steel or cadmium, finned darts, each about 25mm long and weighing .49–8.0 grams each. The maximum effective range of the flechettes was 300 meters, with an optimum range of 30–35 meters. The darts traveled at 500–700 meters per second when fired and did considerable damage to the human body when they made contact. Jungle foliage reduced the effectiveness of the darts, but the shotgun flechette added an additional weapon to the U.S. infantryman's firepower. The XM-258 was Winchester's flechette shell. *See also* **Shotgun.**

Shotgunner *see* **Door Gunner**

Shoulder Patches Army personnel wore the unit patch of their current parent unit on their left shoulder, and on their right shoulder the patch of the unit to which they were previously assigned.

Shoulder Tabs (Tabs) Descriptive ornamental cloth shoulder tabs worn on the military uniform. For Army personnel, the embroidered crescent shaped tabs were worn on the shoulder sleeve above the unit patch. The tabs indicated special skill, training or unit affiliation. The most frequently worn tabs during the Vietnam War were "Ranger" and "Airborne." In Vietnam many other specialized units, such as LRRPs, snipers, EOD teams, etc., created their own tabs which were embroidered by local Vietnamese tailors. These special unit tabs were not officially authorized by the Army, but generally tolerated in Vietnam in the name of "esprit de corps." The specialized tabs (excluding Ranger and Airborne) were not authorized to be worn outside of the war zone.

Shoup, General David *see* **Commandant**

Shower Clogs *see* **Rubber Thongs**

Shower Shoes *see* **Rubber Thongs**

Shrapnel The contents of an exploding shell that scattered its contents over a wide area. The shrapnel charge was used against enemy personnel. The words "shrapnel" and "shell fragments" were sometimes used interchangeably, although technically they were not equivalent. *See also* **Shell Fragments.**

Shrike ARM *see* **AGM-45**

Shrinking Bird Disease Vietnamese men worried that their Vietnamese women would be less interested in them sexually once they had discovered the discrepancy in size between the American "birds" (penis) and the Vietnamese "birds." To save face, a rumor was started by the Vietnamese men claiming that they had caught the "Shrinking Bird Disease" from the Americans, who had been immunized against the disease and were not affected by the shrinking effects.

Shrinks *see* **Combat Psychiatrist**

Shudder-and-Shitboxes *see* **CH-34**

Shufly *see* **Marine Medium Helicopter Squadron 362**

Shuttle Diplomacy *see* **Kissinger, Henry**

Shylocker (Financier, Loan-Shark) Slang for a moneylender or loan shark. Most U.S. military units had at least one man who would make high interest money loans to other soldiers. For most grunts out in the field, money held little significance; there was usually nowhere to spend it and paydays were once a month. For troops in the rear with access to local massage parlors, whorehouses, shops, PXs and booze, money had a much greater significance.

Sick Call Open period in the morning and afternoon when soldiers with injuries or illnesses reported to the unit's medical center for treatment. Most units had a sick call twice a day, each session lasting from 1–2 hours. A pilot could put himself on sick call, relieving himself from flight duty. Those who placed themselves on sick call were not usually subjected to disciplinary action unless it could be proved that they were malingering. During Army basic training soldiers were not encouraged to visit sick call and were often harassed by their DIs for the training they missed (or attempted to avoid). *See also* **Malingering, Recycle.**

SID *see* **Seismic Intrusion Devices**

Side Cap *see* **Cunt Cap**

Side Kicks of the 92d Avn *see* **92d Aviation Company**

Side Looking Airborne Radar *see* **SLAR**

Sidewinder Missile (AIM-9, Mk 30 AAM) Heat-seeking air-to-air missile used by the Air Force, Navy, and Marines for aerial combat with enemy jets. The 165-pound missile was solid fuel powered with a 22-pound warhead, a max speed of about 1,500mph, and a range of nearly 3.2kms. The Sidewinder homed in on its target using infrared and semiactive radar (SAR) tracking.

Sidge *see* **Civilian Irregular Defense Group**

Siege of Khe Sanh (Battle of Khe Sanh) For 77 days North Vietnamese units surrounded the isolated Marine base at Khe Sanh, near the Laotian border in Quang Tri Province, I Corps. From February to April '68 the NVA bombarded the base with long-range artillery and rocket fire. The siege was officially lifted April 5, 1968, when a combined Marine, Army, and ARVN force under Operation Pegasus cleared Highway 9, which was the overland link between Khe Sanh and the Marine bases east of Khe Sanh. Over 200 Marines died at Khe Sanh, and another 1,600 were wounded. The NVA launched one major ground probe against the base, which was repelled by the Marines. An estimated 3,000 NVA soldiers died in the area of the base, during the siege. The base was destroyed and abandoned by the Marines on June 17, 1968. *See also* **Khe Sanh, Operation Niagara or Pegasus.**

Siege of the Pentagon Massive antiwar demonstrations staged outside of the Pentagon in Washington, D.C., in October '67. The aim of the demonstration was an attempt to shut down operations at the military center and voice antiwar sentiment on a large scale. The Pentagon continued to function and the demonstration fizzled after two days.

Siesta *see* **Pok**

Siff *see* **Syphilis**

SIGINT *see* **National Security Agency**

Sigma *see* **Project Sigma**

Sigma I/II *see* **Sigma War Games**

Sigma War Games (Sigma I/II) Code name for war games conducted by the U.S. military in '63 and '64. The '63 Sigma I war game was an evaluation of what would be required of the U.S. military to defeat the Viet Cong in Vietnam. Analysis of the game's results indicated that more than 500,000 U.S. troops would be required to accomplish a military victory over the VC. The Sigma II games of '64 were used to evaluate the effectiveness of a U.S. air war against NVN. The results of Sigma II indicated that such a war against NVN would not eliminate their support for the VC. Based on Sigma I/II the JCS concluded that military victory in Vietnam using conventional weapons and tactics was highly improbable.

Signal Flare *see* **Star Cluster**

Signal Intelligence Agency *see* **National Security Agency**

Signal Operating Instructions (SOI, Radio Code Book) Specific radio codes, frequencies and instructions used by a unit. Such information was usually kept in a small book which also detailed special codes for data encryption and communication. In larger units the SOI was the responsibility of the RTO. In smaller units or patrols, such as recon and LRRPs, the SOI was maintained by the RTO, but all team members were familiar with it and were capable of assuming the RTO's duties if he was killed or wounded.

Signature (Backblast) When certain weapons were fired the weapon released a large blast of smoke and/or flame from the rear of the weapon. This rearward blast was called the weapon's "signature." Weapons such as recoilless rifles, rocket launchers, and LAWs left a visible signature after the weapon was fired. The signature could be used by the enemy to pinpoint the weapon's firing location. The term signature also applied to the exhaust pattern displayed by some aircraft. From the aircraft's signature antiaircraft missiles could home in for the kill. Heat seeking missiles locked on to the exhaust emitted by aircraft and tracked it to the target.

Sihanouk, Prince Norodom Royal Cambodian head of state from '47 to '70. Sihanouk claimed Cambodia to be neutral in the Vietnam War, but allowed NVN to move supplies into the IV Corps area of SVN through the Cambodian port of Sihanoukville. In '70 Cambodian army general Lon Nol seized power in Cambodia, exiling Sihanouk. Lon Nol ordered NVN out of Cambodia. NVN retaliated by backing the Cambodian communists: Cambodia fell to the Khmer Rouge in April '75. *See also* Cambodia.

Sihanouk Trail (Sihanoukville Trail, Kompong Som)   Series of trails and roads that originated at the Cambodian port of Sihanoukville (Kompong Som) on the Gulf of Thailand and extending northeast, terminating along the Cambodian border in III and IV Corps. The trail was used as the main supply and infiltration route by the NVA/VC through Southern Cambodia. Until mid-'70 it was thought that the Ho Chi Minh Trail was the main supply line to the NVA/VC in the south, but enemy documents captured during the '70 Cambodian incursion indicate that as much as 80 percent of the NVA/VC supplies infiltrated into SVN came across the Sihanouk Trail. *See also* Ho Chi Minh Trail, the Tram.

Sihanoukville Trail   *see*   Sihanouk Trail

Silent Majority (Vocal Minority, Just and Lasting Peace)   In October '69 the Moratorium Day demonstration was staged against the war in Vietnam. The nationwide antiwar protest was supported by Americans from all walks of life. To counter the massive antiwar sentiment generated, President Nixon gave a televised speech to the nation in which he attacked the antiwar movement and labeled its participants the "vocal minority." He then announced his plans to withdraw U.S. troops from SVN and "Vietnamize" the war. He called on the American public, the "great silent majority" who were not speaking out, to patriotically support him in his efforts to achieve a "just and lasting peace" in Vietnam. *See also* Moratorium Day, Vietnamization.

Silicone Injections   *see*   Falsies

Silver Bayonet   *see*   Operation Silver Bayonet

Silver Iodide Crystals   *see*   Cloud Seeding Operations

Silver Mace   *see*   Operation Silver Mace

Silver Spring   *see*   Operation Silver Spring

Silver Spurs   *see*   17th Aviation Company

Silver Star (SS)   United States' third highest award for valor, awarded by the president for bravery in combat; all branches of the service were eligible.

Simons, Colonel Arthur "Bull"   Led the original White Star Training Teams in Laos and also commanded the commando force that raided Son Tay, the North Vietnamese prison camp that held American POWs. *See also* Son Tay.

Sin City   Name of a small, alleged U.S. Army sponsored brothel for the use of U.S. troops located in Pleiku. The whorehouse was reputedly supervised by the military and the women inspected and treated by Army medics in an attempt to reduce the spread of various venereal diseases rampant in Southeast Asia. Sin City was established for the use of the enlisted men, but officers were known to seek service in the house. The name also applied to a similar arrangement of bars and whorehouses, allegedly Army monitored, located outside of the 1st Cavalry Division base camp at An Khe, Binh Dinh Province, II Corps. *See also* Whorehouse.

Sin Loi   *see*   Sorry 'bout That

Sin-Loi-Motherfucker   *see*   Sorry 'bout That

Sinatra, Nancy   *see*   Hope, Bob

Sine Qua Non   Latin phrase meaning essential or absolutely necessary. The phrase was used in reference to the importance of the helicopter to the Army's doctrine of air mobility.

Single File Formation   *see*   On-Line

Single-Digit Midget   *see*   Short-Timer

Single-Shot Pistol   *see*   Deer Gun

Sinh-Vien Sy-Qu   *see*   Aspirant

Sioux   *see*   OH-13

Sister (Black Woman, Ho[e], Sapphire, Hamma)   Slang nicknames referring to black women. "Sapphire" was more WWII vintage, but it remained active in the black vernacular. "Sister" was most commonly used by black men in reference to black women during the sixties and seventies. "Ho," as in whore or hole, was one of the more derogatory black nicknames for any woman. "Hamma," as in hammer, was heard on the streets of America's big cities, and was used to describe a good-looking woman; i.e., a "fine hamma." *See also* Soul Brother.

Sister Elizabeth McAlister *see* Father Philip Berrigan

Sit Map *see* Situation Map

Sit Rep *see* Situation Report

Sitdown (The Rear, The Front) Marine slang for the "rear" area. Rear areas in Vietnam were primarily the larger base camps and towns, locations that were infrequently mortared or rocketed, and seldom hit with a ground attack (a notable exception was Tet '68 when "rear" areas across South Vietnam were attacked by the NVA/VC in a massive offensive). In Vietnam the main difference between the "front" and the "rear" was the attitude of the command elements and the creature comforts available to the troops. *See also* Boonies, FEBA.

Sitmap *see* Situation Map

Situation Map (Sitmap) Large scale map kept at the command level showing the location of all friendly units and known enemy units in the area of operation. The map was used for reference by the command staff to determine unit deployment and possible enemy intentions. The map was updated from field reports and intelligence gathered on the enemy.

Situation Normal, All... *see* SNAFU

Situation Report (Sit Rep, Spot Report, SpotRep) Part of U.S. Army policy to keep higher headquarters informed of activities in the field. Field units maintained contact with their headquarters who monitored the unit's progress. SitReps were called in on a periodic basis to notify headquarters of the unit's position, proposed course and enemy situation. During enemy contacts or sightings, "spot reports" were passed on to headquarters and updated as the combat situation changed. Spot reports were referred to as "SpotReps." The Navy and Marines maintained strict policies on situation reporting and updating of higher headquarters. *See also* Alpha-Sierra-Sierra-Romeo-Sierra, SALUTE.

Situational Trauma *see* Combat Fatigue

Six-By *see* M-35 Truck

Size-Activity-Location-Unit-Time-Equipment *see* SALUTE

SK-5 PACV *see* PACV

Skag *see* Heroin

Skate Duty *see* Skatin'

Skatin' (Skate Duty, Fat Rat Jobs) GI slang for taking it easy, no hassles, having it made, getting by smoothly or getting away with something. "Skate Duty" or "Fat Rat Jobs" were easy, or choice assignments, off the front line, of the boonies and the terror filled humps characterized by field operations. Some examples of "fat rat jobs" were mail clerk, cook's assistant, courier, clerks, bugler, DRO, etc. *See also* Milk Run, Goldbricking.

SKE *see* Station Keeping Equipment

Skids (Pranging) Helicopter landing gear. The Hueys, Cobras, LOHs and the Kiowa helicopter used landing skids instead of wheels to support the chopper when it was on the ground. The skids were designed to absorb the shock of landings. During combat assaults, GIs would sit in the open door of the slicks with their legs dangling out over the side; just before the slick landed, the GIs would stand on the skids so they could make a quick exit from the helicopter. "Pranging" was slang for a helicopter making a hard landing on its skids (literally a crash or bounce). The skids banging against the ground made a distinctive "prang" when they hit and the chopper bounced.

Skilak (Eskimo Boats) Commercially designed cargo vessel used by the Navy in Vietnam to transfer cargo from ships off the coast of Vietnam to receiving facilities on shore. The boat was originally designed to operate in Alaskan waters and carried the name "Skilak," which was Eskimo for "strange craft." The Skilak could carry up to 360 tons of cargo and could operate in SVN's coastal waters or on the rivers. It featured better navigational equipment than was available on WWII vintage craft used by the Navy for the same purpose. The Skilak first arrived in Vietnam in late '67. *See also* LCU.

Skimmer *see* **Boston Whaler**

Skin 1... Fuzz 1... *see* **American GI Film Ratings**

Skin Jobs *see* **Onion Heads**

Skinny (Information, The Word, Lay Down the Line) As in "what's the skinny?" Slang for information or enlightenment on a subject or situation. The "word" referred to the official version of the information. To "lay down the line" was to tell the facts, as they were known or perceived.

Skip Shot *see* **Bank Shot**

Skivvies (Shorts, Briefs, Underwear) Slang reference to underwear, especially men's shorts and T-shirts. Field troops rarely wore skivvies (shorts) because the extra layer of clothing irritated the chafed skin, causing rashes and crotch rot. During the wet season in Vietnam, Army issued boxer shorts worn beneath the baggy tropical fatigue pants were continually wet and clung to the skin increasing the irritation and chafing caused by the constant wetness. *See also* **Jungle Rot.**

Skoshi Tiger *see* **F-5 Tiger**

SKS Carbine or Rifle *see* **Type 56 SKS**

SKS Rifle/Carbine *see* **Type 56 SKS**

Skulled-Out *see* **Get High**

Skunk Hunt Name for joint missions involving U.S. Army gunships and Air Force fighters. Gunships would fly low and slow in an attempt to draw enemy fire; the gunships would then attack the area and pull out of the way. Air Force fighters, on station above and out of sight, would then dive and unload their ordnance on the enemy position. *See also* **Hunter Killer Team.**

Sky (Exfiltrate, Beat-Feet) GI slang for leaving, escaping or departing an area quickly. Also related to "beat feet" and "book"; militarily known as "exfiltrate." *See also* **Book, Di Di.**

Sky Cav *see* **1st Cavalry Division (Airmobile)**

Sky Crane *see* **CH-54**

Sky Honcho *see* **God**

Sky Pilot *see* **God Squad**

Sky Soldiers Nickname for the troopers of the 173d Airborne Brigade, also sometimes used to refer to the airmobile troopers of the 1st Cavalry Division. *See also* **173d Airborne Brigade.**

Sky Spot Code name for the U.S. Air Force computer controller that circled Khe Sanh during the siege in early '68. Air Force technicians manned the airborne control center coordinating air traffic over the Marine base. *See also* **Airborne Battlefield Command and Control Center.**

Skycrane *see* **CH-54**

Skyhawk *see* **A-4**

Skyknight *see* **F3D-2**

Skymaster *see* **C-54**

Skyraider *see* **A-1**

Skyservant *see* **Do-28**

Skyspot *see* **Combat Skyspot**

Skytrain *see* **C-47**

Skywagon *see* **U-17**

Skywarrior *see* **B-66**

Slack Time *see* **Ghost Time**

Slacking *see* **Goldbricking**

Slackman Slang for the man following the point man in a formation.

SLAM (Seek-Locate-Annihilate-and-Monitor) Tactic of concentrating massive firepower to attack a given target. The tactic was formalized by Air Force General William Momyer and used for the defense of Con Thien during Operation Neutralize in '67. B-52, fighter-bomber, naval bombardment, and artillery fires were massed against NVA targets around the base. After Con Thien, SLAM attacks became SOP whenever assets were available. SLAM fires were also a method by which some U.S. artillery batteries could expend large amounts of artillery rounds, thus reducing the buildup of excess rounds in storage at the FSB. "SLAM fires" better guarded the true nature of the fires from the media as opposed to the phrase "seek-locate-annihilate-monitor" fires. *See also* **Fireballing, Time on Target.**

SLAM Company Specially organized company of USSF and CIDG troops that conducted raids and ambushes deep in enemy controlled territory. The SLAM (Search-Locate-Annihilate-Mission) companies operated as part of the MACV-SOG Projects Omega and Sigma missions which were designed to harass and hurt the NVA/VC in their base areas. The companies struck from bases located in I and II Corps conducting operations in Laos, Cambodia and North Vietnam. The companies also provided backup for Spike Recon Teams and Hatchet Force operations. *See also* **MACV-SOG Command and Control; Projects Omega, Sigma; Hatchet Force; Spike Recon Team.**

Slanteyes *see* **Vietnamese, The**

Slap Flare *see* **Hand Flare**

SLAR (Side Looking Airborne Radar, Forward Looking Airborne Radar [FLAR]) Aircraft mounted radar system used for ground surveillance. The radar scanned the ground to the sides of the aircraft. The SLAR system was used specifically for the detection of enemy movement at night. Several different Air Force and Navy surveillance/reconnaissance aircraft used the SLAR system. The system featured a large, long boom fitted to the fuselage of the aircraft which was connected to instrumentation mounted inside the aircraft. A Forward Looking Airborne Radar system (FLAR) was developed and used for ground target acquisition. *See also* **OV-1, VAH-21.**

Sleep *see* **Zs**

Sleep Shirt *see* **Jungle Sweater**

SLF *see* **Special Landing Force, U.S.**

Slick *see* **UH-1D**

Sling-Load *see* **Slung-Load**

Slingshot *see* **Operation Slingshot**

Slopes *see* **Enemy, The**

Slumpflation *see* **Stagflation**

Slung-Load (Sling-Load) Loading of cargo or an item to be moved, slung beneath a helicopter. In Vietnam, loads of supplies were either loaded in nets or on large wooden pallets for transport by helicopter. This method allowed quick movement of materials without the need for loading and unloading the aircraft. Artillery pieces,

ammunition, damaged aircraft and many other items too large or awkward to fit inside the helicopter could still be transported with a minimum of handling and delay.

Slushies (Vietnamese Workers) Australian slang for the Vietnamese civilians that worked on U.S. bases performing a wide variety of tasks such as KPs, cleaning, laundry, shit-burners, bilingual clerks, latrine duty, etc. *See also* **Tiger Ladies, Willie the Shit Burner.**

Smack *see* **Heroin**

SMaj *see* **E-9**

Small Arms Fire (SAF, SA, SAW) Military shorthand used for reports and briefings, indicating the use of small arms, generally in reference to friendly units receiving small arms fire, or friendlies returning enemy fire with small arms fire. Small arms included rifles, submachine gun, light machine gun, and automatic weapons fire. Sierra Alpha Foxtrot. "SA" or "SAW" was the abbreviation for small arms weapons.

Small Arms Range *see* **Standoff Range**

Small Gravel Mines *see* **Gravel Mine, U.S.**

Small Starlight Scope (SSS) *see* **Starlight Scope**

Smart Bombs (Glide Bombs) Sophisticated U.S. ordnance used to increase bombing accuracy. The two main types of smart bombs used in Vietnam were laser-guided and electro-optically guided bombs. The bombs featured extremely high accuracy and allowed the bombs to be released at greater distances from the target, thus reducing the aircraft's vulnerability to enemy fire. The bombs were fitted with steerable fins and were also referred to as "glide bombs." *See also* **Electro-Optical Guided Bomb, Laser Guided Bomb, AGM-12.**

SMG *see* **Submachine Gun**

Smith & Wesson *see* **38 Smith & Wesson, Hush Puppy, Tunnel Weapon**

Smith & Wesson Mark 22 *see* **Hush Puppy**

SMM *see* **Saigon Military Mission**

Smoke *see* **Toke, Marijuana**

Smoke Canister Grenade *see* Grenades, Smoke

Smoke Grenade *see* Grenades, Smoke

Smoke Pots *see* Smudge Pots

Smokeless Kitchen *see* Dien Bien Phu Kitchen

Smoker System *see* XM-52 Smoker

Smokers *see* XM-23 Machine Gun, Heads

Smokey Bear (Smokey) Nickname for early C-47s used to drop aerial flares. The name was also used to refer to a helicopter with a mounted smoke generator, used to make smoke screens. *See also* Flares.

Smokey-Bear Hat *see* Campaign Hat

Smudge Pots (Smoke Pots) Portable smoke pots used by the Army to generate dense clouds of smoke. The smoke was used to flood enemy tunnels in an attempt to force the enemy to the surface and reveal tunnel openings and air holes. The smoke pots came in 10- and 30-pound dispensers.

Snack *see* Operation Menu Targets

Snack, BA 351 *see* Operation Menu Targets

SNAFU "Situation normal, all fouled up" ("situation normal, all fucked up"). A military expression of the normal state of confusion regarding a situation or happening, or when something unexpectedly went wrong. *See also* Cluster Fuck.

Snaggletooth Island Marine nickname for a small Viet Cong controlled island located in the bay just northwest of Chu Lai.

Snake *see* AH-1G

Snakes There were several varieties of highly poisonous snakes in Vietnam. The Viet Cong sometimes used the snakes in conjunction with booby traps or as an obstacle in their tunnel complexes. When used in tunnels, the snakes were usually wired or tied down allowing them to move and strike but not leave the area of the tunnel where they were placed. The primary poisonous snakes encountered in Vietnam were the Asiatic cobra, Malayan krait, Russell's viper, Malayan pit viper, hook-nosed sea snake,

Hardwick's sea snake, brown krait, banded krait, paradise flying snake and the bamboo viper. The python and Wagler's pit viper and Asiatic file were common nonpoisonous snakes in Vietnam.

Snakeye Bombs *see* Retarded Bombs

Snapper *see* LZ Snapper

Snatch *see* Vagina

Snatch Missions (Kidnapping Missions) Nickname for USSF and MACV-SOG kidnap missions aimed at capturing a specific VC/VCI target individual. USSF/LRRP teams also sought to capture VC/NVA soldiers to enhance intelligence information on a given area. Concussion grenades were frequently used in ambush to subdue a potential prisoner. Sometimes claymore mines were employed for a similar effect. Several claymores would be placed so their back blast covered a trail. When the enemy entered the kill zone, the back blast from the detonated claymores would knock the enemy unconscious. The claymores allowed for a larger coverage area and reduced the chance of serious injury to the captive and captor.

SNCC *see* Student Nonviolent Coordinating Committee

Sneaky Petes (Army Peace Corps) One of the nicknames for the U.S. Special Forces and the Army Rangers. The Special Forces also nicknamed themselves the "Army Peace Corps." *See also* Special Forces, Rangers.

Snick *see* Student Nonviolent Coordinating Committee

Sniper During the Vietnam War the NVA/VC made extensive use of snipers. The enemy snipers harassed base camps, picked at convoys and were used to pin and slow down FWF units during all levels of their operations. The U.S. Marines had a dedicated sniper unit of their own and organized a scout/sniper school in Vietnam that operated throughout I Corps. The Army did not have dedicated sniper units, but did have some specialized teams that operated with LRRP and recon forces. *See also* Hathcock, Mosin-Nagant, Model 70 Winchester, M-40 Rifle, M-14 Sniper Rifle, SVD, Waldron.

Sniper Hide A concealed position,

used by a sniper, to fire on a target. The sniper frequently used the same hide over and over, unless it became known to the enemy.

Snoop 'n' Poop *see* **Search and Destroy**

Snoopys *see* **120th Aviation Company**

Snuffies *see* **Infantry Soldier, The**

Snuffy *see* **Infantry Soldier, The**

Soc Trang (Bugville) Located in Ba Xuyen Province, IV Corps. Soc Trang served as a major helicopter base providing combat transport to the South Vietnamese Army in '62. Marine helicopters operated out of the base until they redeployed to Da Nang. They were replaced by Army helicopter units of the 93d Transport Company. Soc Trang was nicknamed "Bugville" and was located 148kms southwest of Saigon, and 27kms west of Vietnam's eastern coast.

Socialist Republic of Vietnam (SRV) Official name for Vietnam adopted in '75 after the reunification of what was North and South Vietnam. The capital of the "new" Vietnam is "old" Hanoi. *See also* **Democratic Republic of Vietnam.**

SOD *see* **Secretary of Defense**

Soda Ration *see* **Beer and Soda Ration**

Soft Cap *see* **Cunt Cap**

Soft Cover *see* **Baseball Cap**

Soft Ordnance *see* **Ord**

Soft Targets *see* **Hard Targets**

Soften the LZ Technique of using air strikes, artillery or gunships to strike an LZ before the troops were inserted. In theory, softening up, or "prep-ing" the LZ reduced the chances that the enemy would be able to shoot up the assault troops as they jumped from the helicopters. If the first troops on the ground started taking enemy fire, they called for additional gunship or artillery support and would "pop red smoke" to indicate to all other assaulting aircraft that the LZ was hot—under enemy fire. *See also* **Prep.**

Softliners *see* **Hardliners**

SOG *see* **MACV-SOG**

SOG Groups (PSG, ASG, MSG, GSG, SOG Study Groups: Psychological, Ground, Air, Maritime) Operations conducted by MACV-SOG units during the VNW were operated by one of four subgroups within the organization. The Air Studies Group (ASG) operated its own small air force which was used in operations throughout NVN, Laos and Cambodia. The Psychological Studies Group (PSG) conducted psyops and bandit radio broadcasts aimed at the NVA/VC. The Ground Studies Group (GSG) was the largest subgroup and conducted ground operations against the enemy in SVN, NVN, Laos and Cambodia. The Maritime Studies Group (MSG) conducted missions against NVN coastal areas and in SVN's Delta. *See also* **MACV-SOG, Unit That Never Was.**

SOI *see* **Signal Operating Instructions**

Soi Rap River *see* **Song Soi Rap**

Solatium *see* **Grievance Payment**

Soldier *see* **Bo Doi, GI**

Sole Survivor Rule Dictated that the sole surviving son of a family could not be ordered by the military to serve in a combat zone where there was a chance of hostile fire. A sole surviving son could volunteer for service in Vietnam, but the military could not legally order such service. If two brothers of one family were serving in Vietnam, and one of them was killed, the remaining son could request to be assigned out of the combat zone. *See also* **Compassionate Loan.**

Solid Anchor Name for the combined U.S. Navy and VN Navy base located at Old Nam Can on the Song Cua Lon River in the extreme southern portion of the Delta. The base was established at the site of the old village of Nam Can which the VC had forced the GVN to abandon during the '68 Tet Offensive. An MATSB was established on the river in August '69 as part of Operation Sea Float which eventually reestablished GVN control in the area. The success of Sea Float led to the creation of a permanent base at Old Nam Can in October '69. From the base, coastal and river patrols were conducted in the Cau Mau Peninsula, and civic improvements were made in support of the area's residents. *See also* **Operation Sea Float, Nam Can.**

Solitary Confinement Cell *see* **Calcutta**

Somerset Plain *see* **Operation Somerset Plain**

Son *see* **FSB Son**

Son My *see* **My Lai**

Son Tay Raid (Bull Simons, Ivory Coast, Joint Contingency Task Group [JCTG], Camp Hope) November '70 combined U.S. Army, Air Force and Navy (Joint Contingency Task Force Ivory) raid on the North Vietnamese Son Tay prison camp, 32kms northwest of Hanoi, near the Red River. The raid, code-named "Ivory Coast," was designed to rescue U.S. POWs held at the compound. Three helicopters (code-named Redwine, Greenleaf and Blue Boy) carried a 56-man ground rescue force which attacked the compound. No POWs were in the camp; they had been moved 3–4 months before because of seasonal river flooding in the area. Most of the NVA defenders at the camp were killed before the rescue force withdrew. The rescue force suffered no serious casualties but one damaged helicopter was destroyed by the force as it was extracted. Even though the raid did not rescue any American POWs it did cause North Vietnam to institute some changes in its POW program. POWs in the remote camps around Hanoi were consolidated into camps in the immediate Hanoi area. This redistribution of POWs caused some of them to share cells where they had been in solitary confinement before. The raid also boosted the spirits of the POWs; the North Vietnamese had continually told them that America had forgotten them. The raid, led by Col. Arthur "Bull" Simons, showed the POWs they had not been forgotten. Son Tay prison camp was nicknamed "Camp Hope" by U.S. POWs. *See also* **Cloud Seeding Operations.**

Son Thang (Marines' My Lai) One of several hamlets located in the Que Son Valley south of Da Nang. In February '70 a Marine ambush team entered the hamlet at night and tried to round the people up; when some of them started to run, the Marines opened fire killing eleven women and five children. A low level attempt was made to cover up the incident, but eventually four of the five members of the "Killer Patrol" ambush team were brought to trial; the fifth member became a prosecution witness and was not charged. The leader of the patrol and one member of the patrol were acquitted while the other two members were convicted and served a year in the stockade. *See also* **My Lai.**

Song (River) Vietnamese word for river; i.e., Song Hau Giang, Song Sai Gon, Song Tien Giang, etc.

Song Be *see* **Phuoc Binh**

Song Ben Hai (River) *see* **Ben Hai River, Demilitarized Zone**

Song Ca (River) *see* **River Mines, NVN**

Song Cam Lo (River) *see* **Song Cua Viet River**

Song Cau Lon (River) *see* **Nam Can, Operation Sea Float**

Song Cau Viet (River) (Cau Viet River, Song Hieu Giang, Song Cam Lo) The mouth of the Cau Viet River opened onto the South China Sea about 15kms north of Quang Tri in I Corps. The river served as a major supply route used by U.S. Marines and Army troops operating along the DMZ. Supplies were off-loaded from ships anchored just off the coast and transferred by small craft up the river to the logistics centers located at Dong Ha (on the Song Cam Lo) and Quang Tri. The entire area was in range of long-range NVA guns located just north of the DMZ, and was a frequent target of NVA/VC attack. The river was essential to units operating along the DMZ because it provided them an all-weather supply route into the area. The river was also known as the Song Hieu Giang. *See also* **TF Clearwater, Cua Viet.**

Song Co Chien (River) *see* **Mekong River**

Song Cu De (River) (Cade River) South Vietnam river that emptied into the South China Sea at Da Nang, I Corps. The mouth of the river was located about 10kms northwest of Da Nang, within the harbor. Americans called the Song Cu De the Cade River.

Song Cua Sot (River) *see* **River Mines, NVN**

Song Dong Nai (River) Merged with the Song Sai Gon just east of Saigon becoming the Song Nha Be. The Dong Nai had its origins in the mountains of the Central

Highlands 140kms northeast of Saigon. The river flowed through the outskirts of Bien Hoa before it merged with the Song Sai Gon.

Song Giang (River) *see* **River Mines, NVN**

Song Ham Luong (River) *see* **Mekong River**

Song Hau Giang (River) *see* **Bassac River**

Song Hien Giang (River) *see* **Song Cua Viet River**

Song Kien Giang (River) *see* **River Mines, NVN**

Song Long Tau (River) (Long Tau River) Main shipping channel that roughly paralleled the Song Nha Be and Song Soi Rap. The Song Long Tau forked from the Nha Be about 12kms southeast of Saigon and continued south through the Rung Sat Special Zone to its mouth, near the mouth of the Song Nha Be, just west of Vung Tau and north of Can Gio. The Song Long Tau connected Saigon with the sea, and was continuously patrolled by U.S. Navy riverine minesweeps until such duties were transferred to the RVN Navy. The areas along the river were frequently defoliated in an attempt to prevent VC ambush of river traffic. *See also* **Mine Division 112/113, Song Nha Be, Doan-10, Rung Sat.**

Song Ma (River) *see* **River Mines, NVN**

Song Mekong (River) *see* **Mekong River**

Song My Tho (River) *see* **Mekong River**

Song Ngan Valley *see* **Helicopter Valley**

Song Nha Be (River) Main waterway connecting Saigon with the South China Sea by way of the Song Soi Rap. The Song Nha Be wound south from Bien Hoa to Nha Be; from Nha Be south the river was known as the Song Soi Rap. The Saigon River opened onto the Song Nha Be about 4kms east of Saigon. Because of repeated enemy attempts to close the river, Song Nha Be was continuously patrolled by U.S. and RVN Navy minesweeps. *See also* **Song Long Tau, Mine Division 112/113, Song Soi Rap.**

Song Sai Gon (River) *see* **Ben Nghe River**

Song Soi Rap (River) (Soi Rap River) Large river that flowed south from Nha Be. From Nha Be north, the river was called the Song Nha Be. The Soi Rap was very wide, but not very deep. Because of its shallows and underwater obstacles the river was not used by the larger oceangoing ships to move cargo from the South China Sea to the port at Saigon. The Song Long Tau River was the main shipping channel for access to Saigon. Small, shallow draft boats made extensive use of the Soi Rap. *See also* **Song Long Tau (River).**

Song Ta Trach (River) *see* **Perfume River**

Song Tien Giang (River) *see* **Mekong River**

Song Tra (Batangan Peninsula) More than 5,000 villagers were relocated from the peninsula coastal area by American units of Task Force Oregon in September '67. The villagers were relocated to a New Life Hamlet called Song Tra, along the Song Tra Khuc River, east of Quang Ngai. The hamlets left behind on the peninsula were systematically destroyed by the American units and the remaining area declared a free-fire-zone. The Batangan Peninsula had long been an area of VC support, and was located southeast of Chu Lai. The people were relocated along the coast, southeast of Chu Lai. *See also* **Batangan Peninsula, TF Oregon.**

Song Tra Khuc (River) *see* **Quang Ngai**

Song Trach Han (River) *see* **Song Cua Viet (River)**

Song Vam Co Dong (River) With its headwaters in southeastern Cambodia, the Song Vam Co Dong crossed into Vietnam west of Tay Ninh, and wound its way south through Hau Nghia Province into Long An Province, terminating at the mouth of the Mekong, 30kms south of Saigon. The river flowed through the heart of Long An Province and served as the eastern edge of the Plain of Reeds. The rich, fertile agricultural area around the river was heavily populated and a prime rice growing region.

Sonic Boom Raids (Rostow's Plan 6) One of the tactics to be used in a plan to escalate the war against North Vietnam. The plan, originally drafted in '61 by Walt Rostow, detailed possible tactics and procedures that could be used to increase the war effort against NVN. Sonic booms would be created over Hanoi in an effort to show the NVN government that the U.S. was serious about its support role in SVN. The plan also called for the eventual bombing of targets in Hanoi and NVN. The plan was never completely accepted, but was occasionally discussed, and in '65 various parts of it were implemented.

SOP *see* **Standard Operating Procedure**

Sophia *see* **FSB Sophia**

Sorry 'bout That (Xin Loi, Sin Loi, Sin-Loi-Motherfucker) "Xin Loi" [sin loy] was a Vietnamese phrase loosely translated as "sorry about that" or "too bad." Sing Loi or Sin Loi, as the Americans said it, was widely used by GIs, as was their literal translation, "sorry 'bout that," the standard answer to a mistake or screwup. It was usually applied sarcastically, but on occasion was used sincerely by GI and Vietnamese alike.

Sorry 'bout That Trap Nickname for one of the Viet Cong's traps used in their tunnel systems in the Cu Chi area. The trap consisted of a man-sized pit in the floor of a tunnel. When a GI Tunnel Rat fell into the pit a VC positioned in an adjacent pit would kill the GI with repeated stabs from a bamboo spear. *See also* **Booby Trap.**

Sorry-Assed-Pussies *see* **War Zone VIPs**

Sortie (Lift) One round-trip flight by a military aircraft, to include supply missions, air strikes, medevacs, gunship runs and observation flights. The term "lift" applied specifically to a helicopter making a single cargo or troop transport run from the PZ, where the cargo/troops were loaded, to the LZ, where the troops/cargo were unloaded.

SOS (Same Old Shit) Slang description for the status of a situation or condition. *See also* **Special Operations Squadron, Secretary of State, Shit-on-a-Shingle, Strongpoint Obstacle System.**

SOTAS (Stand Off Target Acquisition System, AN/APS-94) Experimental target acquisition system tested aboard the UH-1 Huey helicopter in '74. The system featured the AN/APS-94 rotating radar boom mounted below the fuselage of a UH-1H helicopter. The system was used for targeting "moving targets" on the ground. The system was later replaced by more efficient systems aboard the new EH-60 Blackhawk helicopter.

Soui Da Special Forces Camp In October '66 elements of the 9th VC Division and the 101st NVA Regiment attempted to overrun the Soui Da USSF Camp located near the heart of War Zone C. The defenders were reinforced by units of the U.S. 173d Airborne, 1st, 4th, and 25th divisions. Operations in the area by the American units killed more than a thousand enemy troops and captured large quantities of weapons and supplies. *See also* **War Zone C, Operation Attleboro.**

Soul Alley *see* **Soul Kitchen**

Soul Brother (Bro, Brother, Brother Black, Home Boy, Home, Blood[s], Spade, Spook, Splib) Particular reference to a black GI. Used as a general and familiar greeting. "Bro," "Home," "Home Boy" could also apply to a person of any color who was a close friend or close member of the same unit. Generally not used by officers or stuffier NCOs. Bro, Home or Home Boy usually referred to a close friend. Blood(s) exclusively referred to black GIs. Splibs was a Marine Corps nickname for blacks, supposedly first originated by black Marines. *See also* **Black American Soldier, Black Woman, Shines, Main Man.**

Soul City Sections of Saigon and Da Nang that catered to blacks. Most of the bars, massage parlors, and Americanized restaurants in the area were frequented by blacks who brought a little of their culture to the city's streets. As on the base camps, blacks and whites tended to segregate themselves. The Vietnamese, as a whole, did not approve of the black GIs, but they did approve of the GIs' money, and swallowed their prejudices in pursuit of the American dollar. The soul city sections were small, encompassing several blocks. The areas were unofficially off limits to whites, as some white areas of the city were restricted for blacks. In some instances, white MPs refused to patrol the soul cities. *See also* **Vietnam's Niggers.**

Soul Handshake (Dap)   Handshake greeting primarily used between black soldiers as a form of race identification, and also used by grunts from the same unit as a greeting. Not your typical handshake, varied hand and arm moves involved could last for many seconds. At one time the dap was outlawed by the Army in an attempt to reduce racial tensions. Some white officers objected to what they perceived to be a lack of military courtesy and a bonding of black soldiers in a nonmilitary manner. The Army later rescinded the ban. *See also* **Clenched Fist, Black Power, Afro, The Klan, Ju-Ju.**

Soul Kitchen (Soul Alley)   Name of a Vietnamese bar in Saigon whose clientele were mostly black GIs. After '69 the Army desertion rate in Vietnam climbed, and the Soul Kitchen was one of many bars in Saigon that became hangouts for AWOL soldiers. Soul Kitchen was located on what was known as "Soul Alley," a street of bars, shops and restaurants that catered to black GIs. Soul Alley was located just outside the main gate of Tan Son Nhut Air Base. *See also* **Soul City.**

Souphanouvong, Prince *see* **Souvanna Phouma, Prince; Lao Liberation Front**

South Korea *see* **Republic of Korea**

South Vietnam *see* **Republic of Vietnam**

South Vietnamese Air Force *see* **Republic of Vietnam Air Force**

South Vietnamese Armed Forces (SVAF)   Like the U.S. military, South Vietnam's armed forces consisted of four branches of service (Republic of Vietnam: Air Force, Army, Navy and Marine Corps). Within the individual branches some specialized units existed such as the ARVN Airborne, Rangers and Special Forces, and the Navy SEALs. The term ARVN was used in general terms to apply to South Vietnamese military personnel from any branch of service unless specific reference to a branch or organization was necessary. *See also* **Republic of Vietnam: Air Force, Army, Navy, Marine Corps; ARVN: Airborne, Rangers, SEALs, Special Forces.**

South Vietnamese Army *see* **Army, Republic of Vietnam**

South Vietnamese Identification Card *see* **Good Guy Card**

South Vietnamese Liberation Army *see* **SVNLA**

South Vietnamese Marines *see* **Republic of Vietnam Marine Corps**

South Vietnamese Navy *see* **Republic of Vietnam Navy**

South Vietnamese Rangers *see* **Biet-Dong-Quan**

South Vietnamese River Force (River Force)   Was organized in '53 with the responsibility for river operations within South Vietnam. Most of the craft at their disposal was WWII vintage, well adapted for river operations. The force was divided into three main groups: River Assault, River Transport Escort, and River Transport Groups. The forces contained a mixture of patrol boats and modified landing craft. The U.S. Navy began riverine operations in '65 under the code name "Game Warden." When U.S. forces withdrew from Vietnam they left behind over 700 river craft to be added to the Vietnamese River Force. *See also* **RAG, RTEG, RTG.**

South Vietnamese Sea Force (Sea Force) The South Vietnamese Navy became an independent organization in '55 and was divided into two forces, a sea and a river force. The Sea Force was designed to patrol the coastal waters of South Vietnam and support the River Force in its riverine operations. By '65 the Sea Force consisted of 45 ships: PGMs, MSCs, LSSLs, LSILs, LSMs and LSTs. The SVNN also organized a paramilitary force of motor and sail junks, manned by civilian militia, trained and commanded by the Navy. This Junk Force was absorbed into the regular Navy in '65 as part of the Coastal Force. *See also* **Junk Force, Republic of Vietnam Navy.**

South Vietnamese SEAL Force (LDNN) The LDNN was the South Vietnamese Navy commando force designed to operate in a similar fashion to the U.S. Navy SEALs. The Vietnamese were trained and advised by the American SEALs.

South Vietnamese Special Forces *see* **Luc Luong Dac Biet**

Southeast Asia (SEA)   Referred to the Southeast Asian countries of Thailand,

Laos, Cambodia, North Vietnam and South Vietnam. For most U.S. Army and Marine troops SEA meant South Vietnam. For Air Force and Navy pilots SEA meant North and South Vietnam.

Southeast Asia Airlift System (SEAAS, SEAIR) Air Force transportation system established in Vietnam to insure timely delivery of Air Force munitions and supplies throughout SEA. The system also provided transport assets in support of MACV from '62 to the end of the war. *See also* **Air Force Logistics Command.**

Southeast Asia Lake, Ocean, River, Delta Strategy *see* **TF 194**

Southeast Asia Resolution (Gulf of Tonkin Resolution, Tonkin Gulf Resolution) A resolution requested by the president and passed by both U.S. houses of Congress, August 7, 1964, gave the president the power to "take all necessary measures to repel an armed attack against the forces of the United States and prevent further aggression." This was in response to North Vietnamese torpedo boat attacks against two U.S. Navy destroyers operating in the Gulf of Tonkin, off the coast of NVN, August 2, 1964. The resolution unanimously passed the House of Representatives and was passed in the Senate with Senators Morse and Grueing casting the only "no" votes. The resolution was repealed in '70. *See also* **Tonkin Gulf Incident; Morse, Senator Wayne.**

Southeast Asia Semipermanent Harbor Protection *see* **SEASHARP**

Southeast Asia Treaty Organization (SEATO) U.S. conceived organization formed in '54 to fight the spread of communism among its member nations. The members of SEATO were Australia, Britain, France, New Zealand, Pakistan, Philippines, Thailand and the U.S. South Vietnam, Laos and Cambodia were nonmember nations that received protection and aid under a separate SEATO agreement. France and Britain, though members of SEATO, gave it little support believing the U.S. was trying to take control of SEA. Britain, France and Pakistan sent no combat forces to aid SVN. SEATO was based on the NATO alliance in Europe, but did not include provisions for a joint military force of its member nations. Ineffective at its primary goal,

SEATO was dissolved in '77.

Southeast Monsoons *see* **Monsoons**

Southern Catholic Laity Loose organization of native South Vietnamese Catholics. There were two main groups of Catholics in SVN after '54: those who were born in the south and followed Archbishop Paul Nguyen Van Binh and those who fled from NVN after the fall of the French in '54. Many of the relocated northern Catholics were part of the Luc Luong Dai Doan Ket under the organization of Father Hoang Quynh. Southern Catholics, while being anti–Buddhist and anticommunist, were less extreme in their opposition and less supportive of the Diem regime and its excesses against the Buddhists. The southern Catholics tended to be more middle class, better educated and more urbanized than their northern counterparts. *See also* **Luc Luong Dai Doan Ket.**

Southern Christian Leadership Council *see* **King, Reverend Dr. Martin Luther**

Southern Cracker *see* **Caucasian**

Southern Shipping Company (Naval Support Activity Resupply Mission) Nickname for resupply operations conducted by the Naval Support Activity. The NSA was responsible for the resupply and logistics support of TF 115, 116 and 117 base facilities. Resupply was accomplished by several Navy AKL and YFR craft making supply runs along the coast to Cat Lo, An Thoi, Qui Nhon and Da Nang, and river runs up the Mekong as far as Tan Chau. Resupply items included food, ammunition, and equipment. Emergency needs were usually handled by air supply or a special boat run. *See also* **NSAD, NSAS, AKL, YFR.**

Southern Vietnam *see* **Cochin China**

Souvanna Phouma, Prince (Prince Souvanna Phouma) Led the neutral coalition government of Laos from '62 to '75 when the communist Pathet Lao took complete control of Laos. The Pathet Lao was organized in the early fifties by Souvanna Phouma's half brother, Prince Souphanouvong, to fight the French for an independent Laos. After the defeat of the French in '54, the nationalists in the Pathet Lao were replaced by communists. *See also* **Laos, Lao Liberation Front.**

Souvenir Me (You Souvenir Me, Qua Chuoi, Banana) American-Vietnamese slang meaning "you give to me...." Used to request or trade items. Vietnamese children would say to a GI, "You souvenir me cigarette," meaning they wanted the GI to give them a cigarette. Or a GI might tell a mama-san in a village, "Mama-san you souvenir me qua chuoi," etc. "Qua Chuoi" [kwa choy], banana in Vietnamese.

Soviet Union *see* **Union of Soviet Socialist Republics**

SOW *see* **Air Commando Wing**

SP *see* **Shore Patrol, Air Police**

SP Pack (Sundries Pack, Supplemental Pack) Cellophane packet containing toiletries and cigarettes, issued to troops in the field. The packet contained candy, razor blades, shave cream, toothpaste, toothbrushes, pencils, writing paper, playing cards, chewing tobacco, pipe cleaners and various other small items. In Vietnam, the packets were usually issued during resupply along with C-Rations and fresh water. *See also* **C-Rations, Accessory Packet, Tropical Chocolate Bars.**

SP-2H *see* **P-2**

SP/4 *see* **Specialist 4th Class**

SP-5 *see* **P-5, Specialist 5th Class**

SP/5 *see* **Specialist 5th Class**

SP/6 *see* **Specialist 6th Class**

SP/7 *see* **E-7**

SP/8 *see* **E-8**

SP/9 *see* **E-9**

Spad *see* **A-1**

Spade *see* **Soul Brother**

Sparrow *see* **AIM-7, LZ Sparrow**

Sparrow Hawk *see* **Pacifier**

Spartan Call sign for the Army heliport located at Bien Hoa.

SPAT *see* **M-56 SPAT**

SPBSA *see* **Saigon Police Boy Scouts Association**

Spec 4 *see* **Specialist 4th Class**

Spec 5 *see* **Specialist 5th Class**

Spec 6 *see* **Specialist 6th Class**

Spec 7 *see* **E-7**

Spec-8 *see* **E-8**

Spec-9 *see* **E-9**

Special Asian Warfare Training Center *see* **SAWTOC**

Special Attention Personnel *see* **Watch List**

Special Boots (Footprintless Boots, Barefoot Boots) Two experimental boot designs that were tried in Vietnam were the footprintless boot and the barefoot boot. The barefoot boot had a sole designed to leave a ground imprint like that of a barefoot Vietnamese. The footprintless boot had a sole design that imprinted leaf and branch designs on the ground instead of a discernible boot print. As a result of experimental tests by USSF troops in the field, the boot designs were not permanently incorporated into the Army's footwear program. The barefoot print left by the boot was about a "size 12," which was about five sizes larger than the average Vietnamese.

Special Exploitation Service (SES, Strategic Technical Directorate [STD]) The Special Exploitation Service, later renamed the Strategic Technical Directorate, was the South Vietnamese counterpart of the U.S. MACV-SOG (Studies and Observations Group). The SES/STD performed highly classified intelligence gathering missions, psychological and terror missions and other special duties against the enemy, as required. The SES/STD functioned as a Vietnamese extension of the MACV-SOG. *See also* **MACV-SOG.**

Special Flak Suit (Fragmentation Suit) Protective armor suit created by the 199th Light Infantry Brigade in '68. The suit was used by some of the 199th's infantry pointmen as they tried to explode and trip enemy booby traps. The suit consisted of armored pants or a long skirt made from armor fragmentation vests. A flak jacket was worn along with a protective head wrap and helmet. The suit was extremely heavy and hot for field operations, but it was effective in reducing casualties from booby trap blasts on those limited occasions when it was worn. *See also* **Body Armor.**

Special Forces (U.S. Special Forces [USSF], Green Berets, SFG, Greenie Beanies, USASF) U.S. Army Special

Forces (USASF) organized in '52 to conduct unconventional warfare and counterinsurgency operations. The Special Forces performed a much broader function in Indochina. The USSF trained regular army and special warfare units in Thailand, Cambodia, RVN, South Korea, Taiwan, and the Philippines. The Green Berets of the USSFs trained and directed CIDGs across Vietnam, advised the Vietnamese and operated special intelligence gathering missions. Officially each SF camp was under the command of an ARVN Special Forces officer and was "advised" by an American Special Forces officer. In some cases this was the case; in other cases the USSF team controlled the camp's operation. CIDG camps were constructed from materials provided through the USSF and the troops were armed and paid by the USSF. The Montagnard tribes of the Central Highlands constituted the bulk of the CIDG. The USSFs directed the CIDGs until the Special Forces departed Vietnam. Control of the CIDG was turned over to the ARVN who quickly opened old ethnic wounds between the Vietnamese and the "Yards." Due to the ARVN's leadership the CIDG quickly ceased to be a fighting force with which the NVA/VC had to reckon. The motto of the U.S. Special Forces: "De Oppresso Liber," To Liberate from Oppression. Nicknames for the USSF were "Greenie Beanies," "Sneaky Petes," "Army Peace Corps," and "Science Fiction." See also MACV-SOG; 1st, 5th, 7th Special Forces Groups.

Special Forces Association of Saigon (SFAS) Small group of American "civilians" that lived in Saigon in '74–'75. The members were former U.S. Special Forces soldiers who returned to Saigon after their discharge from the military. The association's purpose in life was fraternal and if the U.S. ever decided to return to Vietnam the SFAS would already be there and ready to carry on the work that had been abandoned in '73. Members of the SFAS, as well as other American civilians, were evacuated from Saigon before the city fell to the NVA in April '75.

Special Forces Company   see   C-Team

Special Forces Popcorn   see   Dexamphetamines

Special Forces School, CIDG   see   Phu Quoc Island

Special Forces School, In-Country   see   Hon Tre

Special House   see   Nha Dac Biet

Special Landing Force, SVN   South Vietnamese Marine units that operated as an amphibious landing force. The South Vietnamese SLF was equivalent in function to the U.S. Marines, and was one of South Vietnam's best units. See also **Republic of Vietnam Marine Corps.**

Special Landing Force, U.S. (SLF) Special U.S. Marine landing force, composed of units from a Marine Amphibious Ready Group. The SLF was a combined group of Marine infantry, armor, artillery and helicopters used for small scale landing operations. The SLF made several amphibious assaults during the Vietnam War. SLF units rotated within the Marine Corps units that operated in Vietnam. The Marine SLF was typically a battalion size force with several different naval ships which provided support (landing craft, gunfire support, hospital, etc.).

Special Mobile Corps   see   Biet-Dong-Quan

Special Operations Squadron (SOS) U.S. Air Force squadrons that operated special COIN (counterinsurgency) mission aircraft in Vietnam and SEA. SOS squadrons operated the Air Force's A-37s, A-26 bombers, gunships, and psychological warfare operations. SOS squadrons also operated special missions such as COIN training for the Vietnamese and MACV-SOG operations. The focus of the SOS was utilization of the Air Force for counterinsurgency, as opposed to tactical and strategic missions of the Air Force. See also **AC-47, -119G, -119K, -130, Waterpump, Air Commando Wing, 1st Air Commando Squadron.**

Special Operations Wing   see   **Air Commando Wing**

Special Services Army Special Services was a club program supported by the military, employing civilian workers to provide off-duty troops with recreational facilities. Special Services operated cookouts, libraries, lounges, games and other forms of diversion at secured major base camps and the larger South Vietnamese cities.

Specialing (Specials)   Army nurses' term used to describe extended care given to especially critically wounded patients (Specials). Some patients suffered from so many wounds, and the complications of these wounds, that they required extra nursing care, on a 24-hour basis. Typically the nursing staff was extremely busy and often shorthanded. After a normal 12–14 hour shift some of the nurses would volunteer to spend some of their off-duty time with those patients requiring extra care. When there were sufficient nurses on staff a "Special" would be assigned one nurse whose primary job was to care for him while he was at the Evac Hospital.

Specialist 4th Class (Spec 4, SP/4) U.S. Army enlisted grade E-4. Highest ranking non–NCO enlisted rank. The E-4 rank was equivalent to a specialist 4 or a corporal. Corporals were usually only found in Army artillery and infantry units, and Spec 4s were found throughout the Army. During the Vietnam War there was a shortage of low level sergeants to lead squads and platoons, and some squads were led by Spec 4s. Other Spec 4s were temporarily assigned the rank of sergeant E-5 and led under-strength platoons. See also Specialist Class, E-4.

Specialist 5th Class (Spec 5, SP/5) Army grade of E-5. Equivalent in grade to a sergeant E-5, but more technically oriented. An SP/5 would lead a specialty section or platoon such as communications, administration, etc., but would not normally be placed in a field command position such as an infantry platoon sergeant.

Specialist 6th Class (Spec 6, SP/6) Army grade E-6. Equivalent to a staff sergeant, but not a combat field command position. See also Specialist Class, Staff Sergeant.

Specialist 7th Class   see   E-7

Specialist 8th Class   see   E-8

Specialist 9th Class   see   E-9

Specialist Class (Hard Stripes)   Classification within the Army for the ranks E-4 to E-9. The specialist class, E-4 to E-9, primarily dealt with operations, while the other enlisted ranks, corporal to sergeant E-9 (hard stripes), dealt with leadership. Corporals and sergeants led combat units in the field while the specialists operated equipment and performed most of the other tasks of the Army. Specialists were not normally placed in command of a unit although they might command a section. Though the ranks might be equivalent (Sgt.—SP/5), "hard stripe" sergeants had the command authority. This relationship was similar to the relationship between warrant and commissioned officers.

Specials   see   Specialing

Spectre   see   AC-130

Speed (Methamphetamine Hydrochloride, Amphetamines, Methedrine, Speed Freaks, Meth)   One of the more widely used drugs during the hippie movement. Speed was originally taken orally, and medically prescribed for diet control. In '67 the practice of shooting up, or injecting the speed directly into the bloodstream became popular throughout the world. The injected dose of amphetamines caused an immediate and intensified feeling of euphoria and hyperactivity for the user. Addiction to the drug was swift, and prolonged use could result in severe depression and paranoia. Addicts were called speed freaks and meth heads. In Vietnam "Number 10s" were the street equivalent to the speed type drugs. Amphetamines were also used by some USSF and LRRP troops to improve their endurance. See also Dexamphetamines, Mainliner.

Speed Freaks   see   Speed

Speed Shift   Technique used to allow quick repositioning of 105mm and 155mm howitzers in a full 360-degree circle. The technique was first used in Vietnam and involved the placement of a metal or concrete pedestal under the gun carriage. When the gun needed to be positioned to a new direction it was lowered onto the pedestal; the gun trails could then be lifted and the gun pivoted into position. Using this method reduced gun crew fatigue and allowed the howitzers to have a 360-degree field of fire.

Speedball   see   Mainliner

Speedy Express   see   Operation Speedy Express

SPH-3 Helmet (Flying Helmet)   Standard flying helmet used by Marine and Navy helicopter crews. The SPH-3B was an Army version of the Navy's SPH-3. The Army adopted the new SPH-3B as its standard flight helmet in '69 and redesignated it the SPH-4 Flight Helmet. The SPH-4 used an improved microphone and could be fitted with either a clear or sunshading visor. The SPH-3/4 provided improved acoustic and crash protection for the wearer. The Army SPH-4 replaced the APH-5 and AFH-1 Flying helmets. *See also* **APH-5 Helmet.**

Spider Hole   Single man foxhole with a hinged roof for concealment used by the NVA/VC. The NVA/VC used such positions for sniping and observation. The holes were usually linked to a more extensive tunnel complex that afforded the VC a means to escape after sniping attacks against U.S. troops. The holes were excellently camouflaged and resistive to air and artillery strikes. *See also* **Rat Trap.**

Spike Recon Team (RTs)   Special recon teams (RTs) operating as part of MACV-SOG Projects Omega and Sigma. The 12-man recon team consisted of three USSF and nine CIDG troops operating from bases in I and II Corps. Their missions carried them into enemy controlled areas of Laos, Cambodia, North Vietnam and enemy base areas along South Vietnam's border. The RTs were backed up by platoon sized Hatchet Forces and SLAM Companies. Some of the names of the Spike Recon Teams were FORK, ADDER, LIGHTNING, HOT-CAKES, ANACONDA, ASP, BUSH-MASTER, PLANE, CRUSADER, SPIKE, HUNTER, TROWEL, WEATHER, WASP, VIPER, INTRUDER, KRAIT, MAMBA, SIDEWINDER, MOCCASIN, RATTLER, MIKE FACS. Teams also frequently used the names of U.S. states for team names. *See also* **MACV-SOG Command and Control; Project Omega, Sigma; Hatchet Force; SLAM Company.**

Spike Trap Pit   *see*   **Punji Pit**

Spiked Guns   The act of destroying one's own artillery pieces to keep them from falling into the hands of the enemy. In the ARVN's haste to abandon their base or outpost (under imminent threat of being overrun), they often neglected to "spike" their artillery pieces before they "beat-feet" out of the area. The NVA/VC captured the abandoned weapons but seldom took the large artillery pieces with them. At weights of 2 and 6 tons the towed 105mm and 155mm howitzers could not be easily transported by the NVA/VC troops who did not have the luxury of vehicles in the contested zones of SVN. The NVA/VC typically destroyed the ARVN artillery pieces before they withdrew from the ARVN camp.

Spiked Rounds   *see*   **AK Booby Trap**

SPINS   *see*   **SPN Number**

Spit   *see*   **Louies**

Spit Shine   *see*   **Brasso**

Splash   Artillery radio slang used to indicate to the party requesting artillery fire that the requested shells were on the way and would detonate in 5 seconds. *See also* **Down (Shoot Down).**

Splib   *see*   **Soul Brother**

Splintex Round   *see*   **M-546 Beehive Round**

Split   *see*   **Vagina**

Split Battery   Firing technique used by the larger calibre artillery guns in Vietnam. Normally all the guns of a given artillery battery fired at the same target, but the 175mm and 8-inch guns fired such large shells that their battery targets were often split. Two or three guns of the battery would fire at one target, while the remaining guns fired elsewhere. When necessary the battery guns would be combined, but splitting the battery fire allowed a wider dispersal of the big guns' fire support. *See also* **Composite Battery.**

SPN Number (Separation Program Numbers [SPNS or SPINS])   Three-digit number stamped on a soldier's military discharge certificate. The "Spin" number corresponded to one of 446 codes, many of which indicated a negative reason for discharge associated with Honorable and General Discharges from '52 to '74, when Spins were discontinued by the DOD. Negative Spins could be used by businesses to deny employment, and the VA or other government agencies could use the numbers to restrict or deny the veteran services. Spin numbers were associated with such activities as homosexuality, bed wetting, behavioral deficiencies, social inadequacies, and a host of other personal traits that the DOD deemed unacceptable. *See also* **Discharges.**

SPNS   *see*   **SPN Number**

Spock, Dr. Benjamin (The Baby Doctor, The People's Party) Noted American baby doctor who became an avid antiwar activist in the late sixties. Spock was best known for his bestseller, "The Common Sense Book of Baby and Child Care," which later became a bible on child care for many of America's fifties and sixties "baby-boom" generation. Spock was arrested in '68 for violations against the Selective Service System, but his conviction was later overturned. Spock participated in several major antiwar demonstrations and was arrested in '71 during anti–Vietnam War protests in Washington, D.C. In '72 the People's Party nominated him as their presidential candidate. The People's Party was one of several left-wing antiwar and antiestablishment groups that sponsored candidates to oppose Richard Nixon for President in '72.

Spoiling Attacks *see* **Spoiling Operations**

Spoiling Operations (Spoiling Attacks) Attacks on enemy bases and troop concentrations in an effort to keep the enemy off-balance, reducing his ability to mass troops and equipment for an attack or planned offensive. American forces made wide use of ground operations to break up enemy concentrations, and American air power was very effective in hitting enemy bases and staging areas. Some of the most successful spoiling attacks were those aimed at enemy base areas. Such attacks and the eventual discovery of large amounts of supplies, weapons, and ammunition set enemy efforts back several months at a time. But because the flow of supplies down the Ho Chi Minh and Sihanouk Trail continued, enemy losses could be rebuilt relatively quickly.

Sponson Box A storage or tool box located on the side or fender of an armored vehicle.

Spook (Case Officer, Foreign Service Reserve Officer, Radio Spooks) Nickname for a CIA agent. CIA agents that handled or operated local spy networks using indigenous personnel were also known as "case officers." CIA employees at the embassy in Saigon were officially classified as employees of the embassy in the capacity of a "Foreign Service Reserve Officer." Radio technicians of the Army Security Agency were referred to as "Radio Spooks" because of their NVA radio monitoring activities. Also a reference by some older blacks to another black. *See also* **CIA, Tech Rep, Soul Brother.**

Spook Plane Aircraft operated by the CIA. In Vietnam the planes were unmarked, not part of any formal military organization, and not subject to the usual military regulations and procedures relating to flight plans, minimum altitudes, scheduling or load limits. Special Forces troops made widespread use of the "Spook Planes" during the early days of the war (pre-'65) when air support was limited. *See also* **Air America.**

Spooky *see* **AC-47**

Spoon (Hand Grenade Handle, Cotter Pin, Safety Pin) Field term for the spoon shaped, curved handle of a hand grenade. The handle was spring loaded, and when released popped off, igniting the fuse. The handle was secured in place by a safety pin (a bent cotter pin) with an attached ring for pulling out the safety pin. Because of the possibility of the safety pin being accidentally pulled out of the grenade while moving through dense jungle, grenade handles were often secured with tape to avoid accidental detonation. *See also* **Hand Grenade.**

Spoons *see* **Rear-Echelon-Mother-Fuckers**

Spot Report *see* **Situation Report**

SpotRep *see* **Situation Report**

Spotter Second member of a U.S. Army or Marine sniper team. The spotter helped the sniper in the selection of targets, advising him as necessary. Marine spotters in Vietnam used the M-49, 20-power, spotting scope.

Spotter Round *see* **Marking Round**

Spotting Scope *see* **M-49 Scope**

Spring Offensive *see* **Eastertide Offensive**

Spy Plane *see* **SR-71**

Sq *see* **Squadron**

Sqd *see* **Squad**

Sqdn *see* **Squadron**

Squad (Sqd) Basic fighting unit in the U.S. Army and Marines. Army infantry squads were normally commanded by a sergeant and consisted of 8–11 men, divided into two fire teams. An armor squad consisted of a tank and its crew. In the artillery a squad consisted of one artillery piece and its crew. An infantry platoon usually consisted of three rifle squads and sometimes a fourth squad designated as a weapons squad. *See also* **Platoon.**

Squad-Leaders in the Sky *see* **Flying-Squad-Leader**

Squadron (Sq, Sqdn)   An organization of units within the military. A Navy squadron usually consisted of two or more divisions of ships/flights under one command. U.S. Air Force, Marines, and Navy air squadrons consisted of several flights of aircraft under the same command. In the U.S. Army an air or armored cavalry squadron was equivalent in size to an infantry battalion; the squadron consisted of two or more cavalry troops. A troop was equivalent in size to an infantry platoon. *See also* **Cavalry Troop, Tactical Fighter Squadron, Wing, Flight.**

Squared Away *see* **Get-Your-Shit-Together**

Squash Bomber *see* **F-105**

Squat-Thrust Exercises *see* **Bends-and-Motherfuckers**

Squids *see* **Navy Sailors, Corpsmen**

Squirts, The *see* **Ho Chi Minh's Revenge**

SR-71 (Black Bird)   Air Force, high altitude reconnaissance aircraft which conducted aerial reconnaissance missions over Vietnam. The Lockheed-manufactured "spy plane" had a maximum speed of over Mach 3 and an altitude of over 80,000 feet. The twin engine jet operated with a crew of two.

SRAC *see* **Second Regional Assistance Command**

SRAO *see* **Supplemental Recreational Activities Overseas**

SRF *see* **Selected Reserve Force**

SRN-5 PACV *see* **PACV**

SRU-21/P *see* **Survival Vest**

SRU-21/P Survival Vest *see* **Survival Vest**

SRV *see* **Socialist Republic of Vietnam**

SS *see* **Silver Star**

SS Card *see* **MSTS Card**

SS Mayaguez (USS Holt, USS Wilson, Poulo Wai Island, Koh Tang Island)   In May '75 a communist Cambodian gunboat captured the SS *Mayaguez* in the Gulf of Thailand and charged the crew with spying. President Gerald Ford denounced the seizure and demanded the release of the U.S. ship and crew. When the crew was not released Ford ordered Navy and 3d Marine Div. units to rescue the crew and retrieve the ship. A Marine force CA'ed onto Koh Tang Island, 55kms from the Cambodian mainland, and were pinned by enemy fire on the beach. The crew was actually held on the mainland and not at Koh Tang. The USS *Holt* seized the ship at Poulo Wai. During the assault the crew was released by the Cambodians and transferred by a Thai fishing boat to the USS *Wilson*. With the crew's return the rescue attempt was called off, but a naval bombardment was required against Khmer positions on Koh Tang to allow the pinned Marines to be extracted. Estimated casualties: 5–15 KIA, 50–80 WIA and 16 MIA. It became known later that Secretary of State Henry Kissinger did not make the National Security Council aware that the Chinese were using their influence to gain the release of the American crew and that their efforts were close to succeeding when the attack was launched. The U.S. response was viewed by critics as excessive, but the Ford administration wanted to demonstrate it was prepared to protect U.S. interests in the region (just two weeks before the U.S. had been forced to evacuate SVN and Cambodia).

SS Vulcanus   The SS *Vulcanus* was equipped with a special furnace which was used to incinerate U.S. stockpiles of the chemical herbicide Agent Orange. An estimated 1.2 million gallons of the defoliant were burned at sea, in a remote area of the North Pacific Ocean. The last stockpiles of Vietnam era Agent Orange were destroyed in '77. *See also* **Agent Orange, Defoliation, Operation Ranch Hand.**

SS-11 AGM (M-22 AGM)   First generation air-to-ground missile used by the U.S. Army in Vietnam. The SS-11 was a French designed, short-range, wire guided missile which was carried by some U.S., ARA helicopters early in the war. The SS-11 was originally designed as an antitank missile, but it was used in Vietnam as a bunker-buster. It had a minimum range of 500 meters and a maximum range of 3,000 meters, but its effective range against bunkers was less than 2,000 meters. The 4-foot-long missile had a speed of 335mph, a launch weight of 66 pounds, and was available with either an antitank or antipersonnel warhead. The U.S. designation for the missile was the "M-22," but it was usually referred to as the SS-11. *See also* **XM-22 AGM System.**

SSG *see* **Staff Sergeant**

SSM *see* **Lansdale, Edward**

SSS *see* **Selective Service, Starlight Scope**

SSSSS *see* **POW Handling Practices**

SSYAC *see* **Draft Lottery**

ST-Special Text Manual *see* **Field Manual**

St. John, Jill *see* **Hope, Bob**

STAB *see* **SEAL Team Assault Boat**

Stability Operations *see* **Pacification**

Stable Door *see* **Operation Stable Door**

Stabo Extraction Harness *see* **Stabo Rig**

Stabo Rig (Stabo-Ring, D-Ring, Stabo Extraction Harness) Equipment harness worn by USSFs and some LRRP troops. The rig was made of nylon, passed over the shoulders and under the legs, similar to the paratrooper harness. Attached at the top of each shoulder was a Stabo-Ring or D-Ring, which allowed the wearer to be lifted out by rope or cable from a helicopter, leaving his hands free to use his weapon; it also allowed for the quick retrieval of the dead and wounded. The Stabo extraction harness replaced the McGuire Rig. Stabo was named after its USSF inventors: Maj. Stevens, Cpt. Knabb, Sfc. Roberts in '68 (STevens knABb rOberts). *See also* **Swiss Seat, McGuire Rig.**

Stabo-Ring *see* **Stabo Rig**

Staff Officers *see* **Kite-Tails**

Staff Sergeant (SSG, Petty Officer First Class, Technical Sergeant) U.S. Army sergeant, grade E-6. Normally an SSG led a platoon, or platoon size unit. During the Vietnam War there were shortages in the low level NCO positions (Sgt/SSG), and sometimes a buck sergeant would lead a platoon, while a staff sergeant would end up at the company level, in a position normally held by an E-7, SFC. The E-6 grade in the Marines was also called a staff sergeant. The grade in the Air Force was equal to a technical sergeant. For the Navy an E-6 was a petty officer first class. There was no direct ARVN equivalent rank to the American staff sergeant's rank. *See also* **E-6, Buck Sergeant.**

STAG (Sharper-Than-the-Average-Gook) American POW slang for a few North Vietnamese prison camp officials who seemed to be a little more intelligent or better educated than the rest.

Stagflation (Slumpflation) Sixties buzzword for a condition typified by price inflation in the midst of economic stagnation; price inflation within a nation while the nation's growth indicators stood still or slipped backwards.

Stallions of the 92d Avn *see* **92d Aviation Company**

Stand Lines *see* **Bunkerline**

Stand Off Target Acquisition System *see* **SOTAS**

Stand-Down Military term for relieving troops from combat operations to allow them to prepare for redeployment or to perform maintenance duties on their equipment; a general rest from combat ops. For infantry troops stand-down meant returning to base camp for the repair and refit of their equipment; relatively easy duty compared to the daily humps in the boonies. Units on stand-down usually provided security and perimeter guard at their stand-down base. For armor units, repairs and maintenance of their vehicles were performed during stand-downs. Stand-downs allowed time for troops to take care of personnel and payroll problems and drink up their beer ration. *See also* **Ghost Time, Holiday Inns.**

Stand-To (First-Light-Readiness [FLR], Wildcat) Name for an operational technique that put all troops on a base on full alert and readiness in preparation for a possible enemy attack. Troops at patrol bases and small base camps in enemy territory frequently were attacked by the NVA/VC at or near dawn. In an effort not to be caught by surprise, troops within the base were put on full alert and standing-to (literally next to their guns), and ready for any possible attack. Stand-tos were referred to as "FLR" (First Light Readiness) by REMF, TOC officers. In the field a stand-to was also called a "wildcat."

Standard ARM *see* **AGM-78**

Standard Operating Procedure (SOP) Detailed operating procedures. In the military there was an SOP for most contingencies.

Standoff Armor (Bar Armor) Defensive armor used to reduce the effectiveness of NVA/VC, RPGs and recoilless rifle rounds. The standoff armor consisted of a series of bars or rods placed out from the hull and superstructure of armored vehicles and riverine craft. Enemy fired RPGs would detonate on the standoff armor before they could penetrate the vehicle or boat, greatly reducing the RPG's effectiveness. The bar armor on riverine craft was sometimes called "venetian blind" armor. Sandbags and cyclone fencing were also used to provide similar standoff protection to vehicles and defensive positions. *See also* **RPG Screen.**

Standoff Attack, NVA/VC Attack in which the attacking force fires on a target from a distance but does not follow up the attack by closing on the target, similar to a probe. The NVA/VC frequently used standoff attacks to test an enemy unit's response to attack. The NVA/VC would later use information gathered from the probes to launch a full scale ground attack on the enemy position. The standoff attack could be used for harassment or as a means to keep the enemy from mounting an attack of their own. Standoff attacks were most successful against fixed installations where the attacking force had the advantage of moving around the perimeter of the camp, controlling the duration of the attack and its initialization. *See also* **Probe.**

Standoff Attack, U.S. U.S. units used a variant of the standoff attack technique. Helicopter gunships armed with .50cal machine guns and/or 20mm cannons would attack entrenched NVA/VC positions. The increased range of the larger caliber weapons allowed the gunships to attack enemy targets, yet the gunships were beyond the range of enemy small arms fire. The typical enemy light machine gun had a range of 900–1,100 meters, while the .50cal machine gun had a range of over 1,400 meters. Standoff attacks were effective until the enemy started using larger caliber automatic weapons such as the 12.7mm and 14.5mm heavy machine guns.

Standoff Jammers Nickname for aircraft that operated beyond the range of AA fire and SAM missiles jamming enemy radar with aircraft-mounted ECM equipment.

Standoff Range (Small Arms Range) Range at which aircraft could operate without threat from enemy small arms fire. Most enemy small arms fire consisted of rifles (AKs) and carbines (SKS) with effective ranges of less than 500 meters (1,600 feet); thus helicopters making routine runs and approaches over hostile areas generally flew at 1,500–2,000 feet. In areas where known enemy machine gun activity was prevalent helicopters had to fly at 3,500–4,000 feet to avoid the enemy fire. Helicopters fitted with the heavier .30 and .50cal machine guns could standoff beyond small arms range and continue to fire on their targets due to the 1,400-meter (4,400-foot) effective ranges of the heavier machine guns. *See also* **Standoff Attack, U.S.**

Stankovyi Goryunova 1943 MMG *see* **SG43 MMG**

STANO (Surveillance, Target Acquisition and Night Observation) U.S. Army acronym for fundamental operating procedures employed during combat, the overall responsibility of the unit commander. The importance of these fundamentals was underscored by combat experiences in Vietnam against an enemy who was an expert at STANO techniques.

Star Cluster (Signal Flare, Pop-Up) Signal flare, available in various colors, hand-held, about one foot long and launched to a height of 30 meters. To use the flare the top was removed and reseated on the base of the flare; the base would then be struck with the hand or against another surface causing the flare to be fired. The flare shot up to explode at the top of its flight, bursting into four or five balls of fire, similar to skyrockets used in fireworks displays. The flare was used for signaling or identification. In the field a green star cluster indicated a "friendly position"; red indicated enemy troops in the area. *See also* **Flares.**

Star-of-David (SAM Site)   Air Force nickname for SA-2 SAM sites concentrated around Hanoi and Haiphong. A SAM battery consisted of 4–6 missile launchers that were located, equally spaced, in a pattern similar to the six-pointed Star of David, with a SAM on each point. Located in the center of the star was the Fan Song radar van used to track and target enemy aircraft. Single and double launcher sites were widely used throughout the southern portion of North Vietnam, with the sites often located in the center of villages. The NVN located the sites in or near villages because of American pilots' hesitancy to bomb civilian villages or populated areas. *See also* **SA-2, Surface-to-Air Missiles, Fan Song.**

StarCom   U.S. military phone system installed in South Vietnam linking the various major American installations and facilities. The system was notorious for its disconnections and line static qualities. *See also* **Tiger Phone Exchange.**

Starfighter   *see*   **F-104**

Starlifter   *see*   **C-141**

Starlight   *see*   **Operation Starlite, Starlight Scope**

Starlight Operations   U.S. night reconnaissance operations conducted by various units using night vision devices to gather information on the enemy. The operations sometimes included the setting of ambushes, using night scopes to identify the targets. *See also* **Starlight Scope.**

Starlight Scope (AN/PVS-2, Night Observation Device [NOD], Image Intensifier, CSWS, SSS)   Night sighting device that magnified the light from the moon or the stars by a magnitude of 50–60,000 times at ranges out to 1,200 meters. The magnified starlight seen through a special scope illuminated the view allowing the user to easily detect enemy movement. Such image intensifiers used existing light in a "passive" system, unlike the "active" IR systems that broadcasted infrared light that was detected by an infrared viewer. In '66 ACTIV began testing the passive image itensifiers under combat conditions. There were three classifications of night viewing devices: SSS, Small Starlight Scope; CSWS, Crew Served Weapons Scope; NOD, Night Observation Device. The 6-pound, 18-inch-long SSS was hand-held or could be rifle/machine gun mounted and had a maximum range of 300 meters. The CSWS was about 4 times the size and 6 times the weight of the SSS and had a range of 1,200–1,800 meters. The NOD was a much larger device and was pedestal mounted. After successful field testing the SSS was adopted and designated the AN/PVS-2 and was slowly introduced into the Army. Starlight scope operations were sometimes enhanced by the use of infrared searchlights. The starlight scopes picked up the IR light, which appeared pink through the scope. *See also* **Starlight Operations, IR Scopes, SU-50 Electronic Binocular, Twinkles, Infrared, Night Observation Devices.**

Starlight Scope Operator   *see*   **Twinkles**

Starlite   *see*   **Operation Starlite**

Stars and Bars   *see*   **Klan**

Starshell   Aerial flares fired from large caliber guns, especially naval guns. *See also* **Flares.**

Start-Reactions   Clinical name for extreme sensitivity to sudden moves or loud noises, experienced by some Vietnam veterans who were exposed to heavy combat. Such individuals were easily startled by loud noises that reminded them of their combat experiences. *See also* **Post-Traumatic Stress.**

Stash   *see*   **Marijuana**

State   *see*   **Secretary of State**

State Department   *see*   **Secretary of State**

State of Vietnam   This was the official name of South Vietnam during the '54 Geneva Convention on Indochina. The conference was convened to arrange for the cessation of hostilities between France, its allies and the Viet Minh; the Democratic Republic of Vietnam (North Vietnam). The State of Vietnam encompassed the area of Vietnam below the 17th Parallel, and was more often referred to as South Vietnam. At the time of the truce the area south of the 17th Parallel was occupied by the French and a large number of anticommunist South Vietnamese. *See also* **Republic of Vietnam.**

Stateside Bullshit (Mickey Mouse Bullshit, Military Bullshit)   Terms used by some GIs to refer to the type of duty experienced at U.S. Army bases. The duty was characterized by strict adherence to military protocol, dress codes and conduct, repetitious, trivial tasks, and busy work. This included such things as clean-shaved faces, short hair, spit-shined boots, cleaned and pressed fatigues, saluting, grounds cleaning details and a host of other menial military tasks. To many soldiers returning from Vietnam, the stateside military life was much too constraining and regimented. For field troops in Vietnam clean uniforms and saluting were only found at the largest base camps; boots were scuffed white, dirt and filth were the norm, survival was paramount, there was no time for the "Mickey Mouse Bullshit" that plagued the stateside duty stations. Many troops returning home from combat assignments in Vietnam, with time remaining to serve in the Army were warehoused at various military posts across America. Many of those troops became so fed up with the hassles and harassment that they volunteered for another tour in Vietnam. *See also* **Mickey Mouse.**

Stateside Fatigues   *see*   **Fatigues**

Static Defense   *see*   **Aggressive Defense**

Static Defensive Position   *see*   **Base Camp**

Station Keeping Equipment (SKE) Electronic equipment on board cargo aircraft used to keep precise spacing between aircraft to insure accurate supply drops while using the AWADS delivery system. The SKE equipment established the timing used by the aircraft making the drop. *See also* **Combat Skyspot.**

Stations of the Cross (Processing Stations)   Marine slang for the various processing points a soldier was required to clear before he could be reassigned to another unit, depart for R & R or rotate out of Vietnam. The processing points included, but were not limited to, the medical aid station, operations, quartermaster supply, armory and the unit's Orderly Room.

Statistical Indicators of Military Success *see*   **Body Count**

STATS   *see*   **SEABEE Technical Assistance Teams**

Stay-Behind Ambush Team (Tail Gun-

ner Team)   An ambush team left behind as the main force moved through the area. An enemy unit following behind the main body would run into this concealed ambush. The main body remained close enough to support the ambush if needed, but far enough away for the enemy to think the area was safe. This tactic was often employed by U.S. units patrolling in heavy jungle areas. Usually a company size patrol, deploying a squad, was the smallest unit to use the stay-behind ambush. Stay-behind ambush teams were nicknamed "tail gunner teams." *See also* **Button Hook Bush.**

STCAN/FOM (River Patrol Boat, French)   French built and operated patrol boat used in riverine operations during the Indochina War. After the French left Vietnam the boats were used by the South Vietnamese Navy in their riverine operations. The boat was 36 feet long, with a V-shaped metal hull, 13 tons in weight, a maximum speed of 10 knots and a crew of eight. The boat was usually armed with three .30cal and one .50cal machine gun. Because of its hull shape and armor it was often used for minesweeping operations. In a pinch the boat could transport about ten troops. STCAN/FOM was an acronym for "Services Techniques des Construction et Armes Navales/France Outre Mer."

STD   *see*   **Special Exploitation Service, Seismic Tunnel Detector**

Steel Arrow Trap   *see*   **Bay Ten Sat**

Steel Cows   *see*   **B-52**

Steel Pot   *see*   **GI Helmet**

Steel Tiger   *see*   **Operation Steel Tiger**

Step-and-a-Half Snake   *see*   **Bamboo Viper**

Sterilized   *see*   **Sanitized**

Stevens, Connie   *see*   **Hope, Bob**

Stevens Shotgun   *see*   **Shotgun**

Stew Burner (Navy Cook)   Nickname for Navy cooks in particular, and military cooks in general. *See also* **REMF.**

Stick Grenade   *see*   **Type 59 Grenade**

Sticks, The   *see*   **Boonies**

Stieng   *see*   **Montagnards**

Stinger   *see*   **AC-119K**

Stingers of the 116th Avn *see* 116th Aviation Company

Stingray Missions U.S. Marine Force Recon missions conducted in enemy base areas in I Corps, North Vietnam and Laos. The Force Recon elements directed air and artillery strikes against targets they selected during their recon operations. *See also* **Force Recon.**

Stitch Slang for bullets piercing the skin of an aircraft resulting in a series of equally spaced holes that look like sewing stitchwork.

Stockade *see* **Long Binh Jail**

Stolen Military Vehicles *see* **Maverick**

Stoned *see* **Get High**

Stoner LMG *see* **M-63A1 Stoner LMG**

Stop *see* **Dung Lai**

Stop the Bombing . . . Now! One of the most frequently heard American antiwar protest slogans of the sixties and seventies.

Stopper GI slang for artillery or air strikes available to seal off an enemy escape route. During sweep and clear operations, an attempt was made to drive the enemy into a blocking, friendly force, or down a prearranged route that could be attacked by air or artillery. Air and/or artillery fire could provide the necessary blocking fire if the enemy could be driven into the target area. *See also* **Hammer-and-Anvil.**

Stove *see* **C-Rat Stove**

STP (Dom; Serenity, Tranquility, Peace) Highly potent, experimental hallucinogen developed by DOW Chemical Company for treating mental illness. "Dom," as it was called, somehow made its way into the hippie drug scene in the mid-sixties. On the street it was simply called STP (Serenity, Tranquility and Peace). *See also* **Illicit Drugs.**

Strac (Strak, Strack) Military slang for a neat, clean, professional appearance or one who strictly adheres to military rules, regulations and formalities. The stack trooper had spit shined shoes, sharp creases, a spotless uniform and every item in place. Sometimes referred to as "being squared away" or "having your shit together."

Strack *see* **Strac**

Straddle The firing of artillery or naval guns so that the rounds fell on either side of the target; the target's left and right sides. *See also* **Bracket.**

Straight Arrows *see* **42d Artillery Regiment**

Straight-Legged Division *see* **Legs**

Strak *see* **Strac**

Straphanger Nickname for an individual who accompanied a unit to the field, but was not an official part of, or assigned to, the unit, i.e. correspondents and military observers from other branches, units or nations. Such individuals usually performed no useful purpose for the unit and were "along for the ride." Officers who took helicopter rides in order to log in "flight time" towards air medals and awards were sometimes called straphangers by the troops.

STRATA Team (Short-Term Reconnaissance and Target Acquisition Team) U.S. Special Forces teams which performed short recon missions to select targets, directed air strikes (especially B-52 strikes), and conducted after strike bomb damage assessment. The teams functioned throughout the Vietnam War but took on special significance from '72 on as U.S. combat troops withdrew from SVN and intelligence on enemy positions gathered by the ARVN became much less timely and accurate. It was through the efforts of the STRATA teams that some large enemy concentrations were dispersed by U.S. air strikes during the NVA invasion of SVN in '72. *See also* **Eastertide Offensive.**

STRATCOM *see* **Strategic Communications Command**

Strategic Air Command (SAC) The bomber command provided B-52s for Arc Light strikes in Southeast Asia from June '65 to January '73. SAC directed and had responsibility for all B-52 missions conducted during the Vietnam War. Most other Air Force activities related to Vietnam were under the command of the 7th Air Force, headquartered at Ton Son Nhut Air Base in Saigon. SAC B-52s operated from bases in Thailand, Guam and Okinawa. *See also* **B-52.**

Strategic Communications Command (STRATCOM, Regional Communications

Group, Defense Communications System [DCS]) U.S. Army command that operated the Army's portion of the worldwide Defense Communications System (DCS). The system was designed to maintain strategic communications nets between U.S. military facilities and stations throughout the world. In Vietnam STRATCOM was maintained by USASTRATCOM, Vietnam, until the deployment of the 1st Signal Brigade in July '66. Prior to that time STRATCOM also coordinated local combat communications traffic in Vietnam. In July '66 the 1st Bde. took over support of combat traffic and STRATCOM was redesignated the Regional Communications Group assuming sole responsibility for the DCS. *See also* **1st Signal Brigade.**

Strategic Defense *see* **Economy of Force**

Strategic Hamlet Program The Strategic Hamlet Program was an extension of the Diem Agroville Program of '59. The '61 program was designed to turn agroville hamlets into fortified defense strongholds or camps that could protect their inhabitants from VC attack and harassment. It was hoped that by protecting the people, the GVN would win their support. Model villages of the program were established, fortified and surrounded by barbed wire. The object was to keep the VC out of the ville and away from the people. The villages were located near existing ARVN military facilities. Protection for the ville was provided by a locally organized militia force, which usually lacked adequate training, was sparsely equipped and poorly led. The GVN villes were far from the relocated farmer's fields and the markets where he sold his goods. And the long hours of curfew made it difficult for the farmer to put a full day's work into his farming. Many of the GVN camps were filled with villagers, forcibly relocated from VC controlled areas, unable to return to their ancestral homes and traditional way of life. The program was unpopular with rural Vietnamese and was discontinued in '64. *See also* **Agroville Program, Restructuring, Buon Enao, Fishes-and-the-Sea, New Life Hamlets, Forced Urbanization, Operation Sunrise, Pacification, Malaya, Camouflaged Concentration Camps.**

Strategic Offensive Military theory, opposite of Strategic Defense, calling for the military to take the offensive against the enemy, attack, and occupy his territory and eliminate his will and ability to fight, denying him safe bases from which to operate. In Vietnam this would have meant U.S. ground forces attacking and occupying most of NVN. The NVA employed Strategic Offense; the U.S. struggled with Strategic Defense. *See also* **Economy of Force.**

Strategic Reappropriation (Cannibalization, Controlled Cannibalization) Taking parts from one vehicle or device to get another up and running. Usually the donor device was inoperable, disabled, wrecked or left unattended for too long. In controlled cannibalization the removed parts were not used immediately, but stored for future use. *See also* **Midnight Requisition.**

Strategic Technical Directorate *see* **Special Exploitation Service**

Strato-Tanker *see* **KC-135**

Stratofortress *see* **B-52**

Stratolifter *see* **C-135**

Strawberry Patch Nickname for the site of numerous executions and burials committed by the communists during the Hue massacres. The site was located outside of Gia Hoi, a residential area in the northwestern part of Hue City. *See also* **Hue Massacre.**

Street Without Joy (La Rue Sans Joie) Name given to that section of Vietnamese road located between Highway 1 and the coast. The road ran between Quang Tri and Tan My. Many small fortified villages lined the road and French troops operating in the area were constantly ambushed and booby-trapped by the Viet Minh. Highway 1 was of strategic importance to the French and U.S. logistics effort, and the enemy launched repeated attacks against the highway. The French, and later the U.S., went to great lengths to keep the road open. The French called it "la rue sans joie"; the street without joy. *See also* **Highway 1.**

Strela *see* **Surface-to-Air Missile**

Strela Suppressor Retrofit exhaust funnel used on the UH-1 and AH-1 helicopters. During the enemy Eastertide Offensive in '72 the NVA began using the SA-7 Strela SAM. The SA-7 was a heat seeking, shoulder fired missile capable of bringing down aircraft. A special adapter was mounted on U.S. Huey and Cobra helicopters consisting of an inverted funnel that directed the chopper's exhaust into the downward flow of air from the rotors, defusing the hot exhaust. The Strela was designed to home in on the heat generated by the aircraft's engine exhaust. Installation of the kits began shortly after the NVA's use of the SA-7 was verified. *See also* **Surface-to-Air Missile.**

Stretch Huey *see* **UH-1D**

Strieng *see* **Montagnards**

Strike (Air Strike)   Military terminology for an attack or assault made by aircraft against ground or water based targets.

Strike Assault Boat *see* **SEAL Team Assault Boat**

Strike Camera *see* **KA-60 Gun Camera**

Strike Damage *see* **Hit Parade**

Strike Force   Company size CIDG units led by USSF deployed as a reaction force to help smaller, remote CIDGs protect their villages. One Strike Force was originally assigned to provide support to several CIDG hamlets in its area. In '64 the company level Strike Force was enlarged to battalion and brigade strength and renamed Mobile Strike Forces, or Mike Forces. The increased size and effectiveness of these larger CIDG Mike Forces (under USSF leadership) allowed them to be more effective in battle against NVA Regulars. *See also* **Mobile Strike Force.**

Strike Force One Buck (One Buck Deployment)   Initial Air Force deployment of combat aircraft to Southeast Asia beginning in August '64 following the Tonkin Gulf Incident. The deployment involved the aircraft from several fighter squadrons deploying to bases in Thailand, Clark in the Philippines, Tan Son Nhut and Da Nang in SVN. *See also* **Tonkin Gulf Incident.**

Striking Ninth *see* **9th Marine Amphibious Brigade**

Strip Alert *see* **Ramp Alert, Whiplash**

Strobe Lights   Battery powered, high intensity strobe lights were used by FWF to mark night LZs and PZs in the field. Gener-

ally only used in secure areas or for emergencies, i.e., medevacs, resupply or reinforcements. In the field the strobe lights acted as "bullet magnets," drawing enemy fire to the area where the strobe was deployed.

Strokin'-Your-Tube *see* **Masturbate**

Strong Point   Military term for a defensive position established to protect and defend a specific area or feature. In Vietnam strong points were set up to protect road junctions, bridges, depots, etc. In base camps a strong point would be one of the many heavy gun positions located around the perimeter of the base.

Strongpoint Obstacle System (SOS)   U.S. plan developed in '66 to strategically place a string of fire bases along the coast of SVN from the DMZ to Nha Trang. The bases were to be manned by U.S. Marines and Korean units, patrolling out from the bases, forming a shield to act as an obstacle to NVA/VC movement into the populated coastal areas. The plan was a modified enclave plan that would have concentrated the bulk of U.S. forces as a screening force to keep the NVA/VC from the population and rich rice growing areas along the coast. The plan was not fully activated by U.S. and Korean troops in Vietnam.

Stud *see* **LZ Stud**

Student Nonviolent Coordinating Committee (SNCC, Snick)   Founded in '60 by Stokely Carmichael and organized by black civil rights leaders intent on establishing the rights of black Americans as first class citizens of the United States. The group was active in nonviolent demonstrations, and civil disobedience, and pushed for more black voter registration throughout the South. The SNCC included many white supporters and participants from across the country. As the Vietnam War began to escalate, so did opposition to the war by the SNCC and other civil rights groups. These groups argued that the government should have been focusing on America's civil rights issues, not issues of politics in South Vietnam. In '66 Carmichael turned against the white members of the SNCC. He argued that if SNCC was to be successful it had to truly represent blacks in America, and it had to be staffed, controlled, and financed by blacks. Carmichael pushed for the exclusion of whites from SNCC. In '67 H. Rap Brown became the leader of the SNCC and changed the name to the Student National Coordinating Committee, and actively supported the use of armed revolt to accomplish social change in America. Brown's militant views and support of the black power movement turned many of SNCC's ("Snicks") white supporters away, further distancing the group from the mainstream of the civil rights movement. *See also* **Brown, H. Rap; Black Power; Black Panthers.**

Student Officer *see* **Aspirant**

Students for a Democratic Society (SDS, Weathermen) 1960s antiwar and civil rights protest group that urged U.S. withdrawal from SVN. The Michigan based group became increasingly violent in its protest, and radical in its views, and later spawned a subgroup called the Weathermen. The Weathermen advocated violence as a means to bring about change within the U.S. The SDS originally started out as a student group on the University of Michigan campus. The members, mostly white, focused on a democratic system that would work equally at all levels of society. The SDS expanded its protest to the draft, military research, and the use of napalm as a weapon.

Studies and Observations Group *see* **MACV-SOG**

Stun-Fishing *see* **Marine Fishing**

SU-50 Electronic Binocular (Night Vision Goggles, AN/PAS-8, AN/PVS-5, Infrared Binoculars [IRB]) Night vision binoculars that saw limited service in Vietnam. The battery powered goggles were head/helmet mounted leaving the wearer's hands free. The SU-50 was used in conjunction with the AN/PAS-8 Night Aiming Light. The light was attached to a weapon and was used to illuminate the target. Both the SU-50 and the AN/PAS were infrared devices. The special illumination could be picked up by the SU-50. Because of the limited production of the SU-50 they were only found in some special air and ground recon units. An improved version of the night vision goggles, the AN/PVS-5, was under development when the Vietnam War ended. *See also* **IR Scopes, Starlight Scope.**

Sua Sponte *see* **75th Infantry (Rangers)**

Subic Bay Naval Base *see* **Philip-**pines

Submachine Gun (SMG) Individual automatic or semiautomatic small arms weapon with a short range but capable of a high volume fire. The submachine gun was lighter and smaller than a machine gun, and allowed the individual soldier increased firepower at the cost of range and accuracy. *See also* **MAT49, Type 50, M-3, M-1A1, PPS43.**

Submunitions Military term for multiple bombs or explosives contained inside of other munitions. Bomblets inside of a bomb, or explosive gases or fuels dispersed from a single bomb or projectile. *See also* **Cluster Bomb Units, COFRAM Round.**

Subterranean Poor *see* **Project One-Hundred Thousand**

Subversive Activities Control Board (SACB) Department of the U.S. attorney general's office that monitored the activities of political action groups within the country to determine if the group was subversive in nature.

Suckie-Suckie *see* **Fellatio**

Sucking Chest Wound Major chest wound typically caused by a bullet or shell fragments entering the chest and piercing the lung. As the victim breathed, frothy pink bubbles could be seen collecting at the wound indicating the lung had been pierced. The first procedure in dressing the wound was to seal off the air loss through the wound, preventing collapse of the lung. In the field, a piece of plastic or cellophane was used to seal the hole making it as airtight as possible, before the dressing was applied. Multiple punctures of the lung required that all such holes be sealed to keep the lung from collapsing and suffocating the victim. In Vietnam C-Ration plastic or the cellophane from a cigarette package was often used to seal wounds in the field.

Sucks *see* **Bummer**

Sugar Reports *see* **FREE**

Suicidal Burnings *see* **Burn Yourselves, Not Your Draft Cards**

Suicide Patrols *see* **Night Patrol**

Suicide Squads *see* **Sapper**

Summer Institute of Linguistics Religious missionary organization that translated the Bible into local languages. The institute operated a mission in the Central Highlands translating the Bible into the Montagnard language. During the '68 Tet Offensive one of the American members of the mission was taken prisoner by the VC near Ban Me Thuot and later died after several months of captivity in the jungle.

Sun Helmet *see* **NVA Helmet**

Sundries Pack *see* **SP Pack**

Sung Hieu *see* **Operation Quyet Chien**

Sunrise *see* **Operation Sunrise**

Super Bazooka *see* **M-20 Rocket Launcher**

Super Connies *see* **EC-121**

Super Constellation *see* **EC-121**

Super Jolly Green Giant (HH-53B/C) Air Force heavy lift helicopter used in Vietnam for Search and Rescue missions. The first Air Force HH-53s arrived in Vietnam in September '67. In '69 the HH-53C, an upgraded version of the HH-53, arrived for SAR duties. The helicopter, nicknamed the "Super Jolly Green Giant," featured inflight refueling capabilities, extra fuel tanks, armor protection for the crew and were armed with three miniguns. While in Vietnam the primary mission of SAR aircraft was the recovery of downed airmen, most of their work being done in hostile areas of Laos and North Vietnam. *See also* **CH-53.**

Super Sea Stallion *see* **CH-53E**

Super Skymaster *see* **O-2**

Super Stallion *see* **CH-53**

Super-Gaggle Nickname for the combined efforts of Marine helicopters and fighter-bombers to deliver cargo and extract the wounded from the hill outposts around Khe Sanh during the NVA siege of the base in early '68. Several flights of fighter-bombers would hit NVA positions around one of the hill outposts with a combination of bombs, napalm, and CS gas. 10–12 Marine helicopters would quickly maneuver into the outpost's LZ, offload their cargo and take on a load of wounded. The fighter-bombers, along with helicopter gunships, would continue to pound the area until all the choppers got out. Within a matter of minutes the choppers had off-loaded their cargo, loaded the wounded, and were departing the LZ.

Supersabre *see* **F-100**

Superstition Mountain *see* **Seven Mountains**

Supper, BA 704 *see* **Operation Menu Targets**

Supplemental Pack *see* **SP Pack**

Supplemental Recreational Activities Overseas (SRAO) Official title of the Red Cross workers who served in Vietnam, working with the troops in the field, hospitals and at Red Cross centers across Vietnam. The women of the Red Cross were known to the troops as Donut Dollies. *See also* **Donut Dollies.**

Supply and Service (S and S) U.S. Army command supplying logistics and services to combat units.

Supply Boats and Ships *see* **Waterborne Logistical Craft**

Support Cambodia Out of Thailand *see* **Operation SCOOT**

Support Our Men in Vietnam... "Support our men in Vietnam—Don't stab them in the back." Slogan sometimes used by pro–Vietnam groups holding counter-demonstrations at antiwar rallies and marches.

Supreme-6 *see* **God**

Surface-to-Air Missile (SAM, SA-2, SA-7, Strela, Grail, Guideline, Flying Telephone Pole) Antiaircraft missiles, surface launched, used to shoot down enemy aircraft. The Soviet made SA-2 (Guideline) was NVN's prime defensive SAM. U.S. pilots called the SA-2 the "flying telephone pole." SA-2s first deployed in NVN in '65 and had a range of 85,000 feet. The SA-7 (Strela or Grail) was a 4-foot-long, shoulder fired, infrared homing SAM that entered service with the NVA during the '72 Eastertide Offensive; it had a range of 10kms, a maximum altitude of 5,000 feet, and a speed of 1,100mph. *See also* **Fan Song; SA-2; Star-of-David; SAM, U.S.; Dr. Pepper; Ballistic Firing; Strela Suppressor.**

Surgical Bombing U.S. coined phrase for high accuracy bombing of a target, using a very narrow bombing pattern to insure that only the desired target was damaged or destroyed, thus eliminating or reducing collateral damage. Surgical bombing also described the U.S. bombing plan employed in '64 against NVN in an effort to force them to seek peace in Southeast Asia. The plan entailed bombing a series of targets one at a time, escalating the bombing until the NVN agreed to peace talks. The Johnson policy of three years of escalated bombing did little to encourage the North Vietnamese to consider negotiations. But in the course of 11 days of intensified strikes, the Nixon '72 Christmas bombing campaign managed to get North Vietnam's attention. *See also* **Collateral Damage, Lang Chi Power Plant, Christmas Bombing.**

Surgical Push *see* **Radio Frequency**

SURV *see* **Surveillance Aircraft Company, Avn**

Surveillance Airplane Company (SAC, SURV) Fixed-wing aircraft, flown by Army pilots, used for spotting and reconnaissance, part of an Aviation Brigade. The primary aircraft of the surveillance company was the O-1 Bird Dog and the OV-1 Mohawk. *See also* **Avn, O-1, OV-1.**

Surveillance, Target Acquisition and Night Observation *see* **STANO**

Survivability Chance of an individual, unit, facility, vehicle or craft surviving an enemy attack. The chance was usually expressed as a percentage, odds, or as a ratio.

Survival Assistance Officer (SAO) An active duty man detailed by the military to accompany the body of a soldier on its return home for burial. The SAO was to be of the same rank as, or greater than that of the deceased. The SAO's duties included offering assistance to the next of kin with the burial arrangements, and he represented the U.S. government during the burial ceremony. The SAO generally had served with, or knew the deceased, or lived near the home of the deceased's next of kin. *See also* **Casualty Assistance Call Officer.**

Survival Evasion Resistance and Escape Course (SERE Course) Survival and evasion course taught during the Vietnam War to Navy personnel who would be operating in Vietnam as part of the River Patrol or Mobile Riverine Forces, or to Navy personnel who might be operating behind enemy lines, such as SEALs or selected pilots.

Survival Radios (AN/PRC-90, ARC/ RT-10, AN/URC-10, Emergency Radio) Small emergency survival radios carried by U.S. airmen while on missions in SEA. Air Force, Navy, and Marine crews usually carried the radio in their SRU-21/P survival vest, while a small number of Army pilots carried the radio in the cockpit. Several versions of the FM band radios were available; they were battery powered and had a limited range. The URC-10 allowed two-way communication while the RT-10 was limited to transmission only. The radio allowed communications between downed crews and rescue aircraft. Some LRRP teams carried survival radios to insure communications with aircraft in their recon area. *See also* **Survival Vest, U.S. Radios, Beeper.**

Survival Sling *see* **Horse Collar**

Survival Vest (SRU-21/P) A sleeveless vest worn by Air Force combat aircrews over their flying suit. The zippered vest featured many pockets for storage of survival items in the event the crewman was shot down. The vest included such items as survival radio and batteries, signal flares, first aid kit, tourniquet, folded plastic water bag, survival knife, .38cal revolver and 20 rounds of ammo, insect repellent, compass, 2 × 2-foot rubber map of Vietnam, signal strobe light, signal mirror, gill net and mosquito netting. Some Army pilots also wore the survival vest when operating over remote enemy areas. *See also* **Survival Radios.**

Survivor Guilt (Why Me Syndrome) Also known as the "why me syndrome." A condition suffered by some of America's Vietnam veterans. The veteran suffered varying degrees of guilt for having survived combat in Vietnam while many of his friends and those around him died or were maimed. The guilt manifested itself in a number of ways from insomnia to acute cases of social withdrawal. Most Vietnam combat veterans have overcome any guilt they may have had for surviving the war but some continue to wrestle with thoughts of why they survived a firefight or an ambush while a buddy next to them died. *See also* **Post-Traumatic Stress Disorder.**

SUU-11 and GAU-2/A Minigun Pods Air Force 7.62mm minigun pods used on AC gunship aircraft. The SUU-11 pod was used on Air Force gunships, notably the

AC-119G which was armed with four pods, along with the aircraft's other weapons. The GAU-2/A pod was used primarily on the older AC-47 gunships. The pod could fire 6,000 rounds per minute and was fed from huge boxes of ammunition on the floor of the ship. *See also* **Minigun, AC-119G, AC-47.**

SUU-23 (Vulcan Gun Pod, M-35 Vulcan Gun Pod) 20mm gun pod used on the F-4 fighter. The Phantom did not have an internal machine gun or cannon, so the SUU-23 was mounted on the aircraft to give it the ability to dogfight with NVAF MiGs and provide strafing support to ground units. The M-35 Vulcan gun pod was an adaptation of the SUU-23 which was used on some AH-1 Cobra gunships. The pod was mounted on one of the Cobra's wing pylons. *See also* **SX-35 Cannon.**

SUU-42 Pod *see* **F-4**

Suzuki *see* **Motorcycles**

SVA *see* **Army, Republic of Vietnam**

SVAF *see* **South Vietnamese Armed Forces**

SVD Rifle (Dragunov, PSO-1 Scope) The Dragunov SVD was a Soviet made sniping rifle used by the NVA. The SVD was a 7.62mm semiautomatic rifle with a 10-round magazine. The SVD was specifically designed as a sniper rifle and incorporated the PSO-1 sniping scope. The scope featured ranging and an infrared detector. *See also* **Sniper, Mosin-Nagant Rifle.**

SVN *see* **Republic of Vietnam**

SVN Flag *see* **Flags...**

SVNAF *see* **Republic of Vietnam Air Force**

SVNLA (South Vietnamese Liberation Army) Shortly after the establishment of the communist Provisional Revolutionary Government in '69, the combat forces of the NLF began referring to themselves as "liberation forces." To the rest of the world, the South Vietnamese Liberation Army was still the Viet Cong. *See also* **NLF, PRG.**

SVNMC *see* **Republic of Vietnam Marine Corps**

SVNN *see* **Republic of Vietnam Navy**

SVNNP *see* **National Police Force**

SVNSF *see* **Luc Luong Dac Biet**

Swabbie *see* **Navy Sailors**

SWAG *see* **WAG Principle**

Swat Team *see* **Composite Military Police Strike Force**

Swatow *see* **P-4 Torpedo Boat**

Sweat Towel *see* **Lucky Towel**

Swedish K Swedish made submachine gun used by U.S. Special Forces and Navy SEALs in Vietnam. The weapon featured a built-in sound suppressor and was automatic fire only. The Swedish K was a 9mm automatic that weighed 7.5 pounds unloaded and could use a 36- or 50-round magazine. The submachine gun featured a folding stock and looked much like the U.S. M-3 Grease Gun. *See also* **M-3A1 SMG.**

Sweep (Village Sweep) Movement of a combat force through an area for the purpose of providing security or seeking out the enemy. A village sweep involved a unit search through a ville, checking for weapons, food caches or signs of the enemy. The sweep was the most common maneuver experienced by grunts in the field. *See also* **Search and Destroy, Clear and Hold.**

Sweep and Clear *see* **Search and Destroy**

Swift *see* **PCF, Operation Swift**

Swift, Deadly, Silent *see* **3d Marine Division Reconnaissance Company**

Swift, Silent and Deadly (Celer, Silens et Mortalis; 3/3 Marines) "Celer, Silens et Mortalis"; motto of the 3d Reconnaissance Battalion/3d Marine Regiment/9th Marine Amphibious Brigade.

Swifties *see* **PCF**

Swimming-Pool-Maker (1,000-Pounders) Nickname for 1,000-pound bombs that created large craters on detonation. During the monsoons the craters filled up with water and from the air looked like swimming pools dotting the landscape.

Swiss Seat A strap harness used as a seat. The harness was attached to a rope and used to lower or raise a single man. The Swiss seat was used by Army tunnel rats, allowing them to be lowered into some of the deeper tunnel shafts. One arm was required to hold onto the rope, leaving the other hand free to operate a weapon. *See also* Stabo Rig, McGuire Rig.

Switchback *see* **Operation Switchback**

Swivel-Top Buoy (Mono Buoy, Offshore Fuel Station, Sea Load Lines) Special buoy used to support Navy refueling operations at Phu Bai. Tankers connected fuel lines to swivel fittings on the buoy and pumped the fuel ashore. The buoy was fixed in position by sea anchors and connected to the fuel storage area by two 8-inch hoses. Fuels pumped ashore were used to support Marine air and ground operations in the Phu Bai-Hue area.

SX-35 Cannon (20mm Cannon, M-24A1, XM-31, 20 mike-mike, M-35 Cannon, 20mm Vulcan) The SX-35 Vulcan (M-35) was the standard 20mm cannon used by the AH-1 Cobra gunship and was not enclosed in a pod shell. The M-24A1 was the standard aircraft cannon and was found in several configurations. The XM-31 was an experimental weapons pod that used the M-24A1 cannon. The XM-31 was mounted on Huey gunships allowing them to fire at targets from a greater distance while they stayed out of enemy machine gun range. Maximum sustained rate of fire was 2,000 rounds per minute which sounded like an aerial buzzsaw when the cannon fired. The 20mm was similar to the Russian/NVA 14.5mm HMG. *See also* M-61 Vulcan, SUU-23.

Sydney Opera House Nickname for the 1st Australian Armoured Regiment's tank workshop located at Nui Dat. *See also* Australian Task Force.

Syme's Amputation Amputation of the foot, just below the ankle. A common amputation among soldiers and civilians who survived explosive encounters with the smaller land mines and booby traps. *See also* Booby Traps; Gravel Mine, U.S.

Sympathetic Detonations Detonation of explosives caused as a result of the close proximity detonation of another explosive device. A mine or mortar round exploding near a man could sometimes cause the hand grenades he carried to suddenly detonate. The military phrase for such accidental detonations was called "sympathetic detonations" or "secondary explosions." *See also* Secondary Explosions, Blasting Caps.

Syph *see* **Syphilis**

Syphilis (Syph, Siff, Black Syph, Tim-La) Black syphilis was the nickname for an extremely virulent strain of syphilis, difficult to treat and highly resistant to penicillin. "Tim-La" [tim laa] was Vietnamese for syphilis. One of the rumors regarding the Black Syph was that if you caught it you were sent to a small island in the Pacific, and remained there until a cure could be found or you died; you were carried as MIA. A variant of this was that you were carried as a KIA so your next-of-kin could collect your GI insurance. *See also* Venereal Diseases, Rumors.

Syrette *see* **Morphine**

T

T and E Tripod (Traversing and Elevating Tripod, T-and-E) Large tripod used for mounting the .50cal machine gun. The tripod held the gun firmly in place and used geared controls to position the gun. The tripod allowed for precision adjustments of the machine gun enabling its use as a long-range sniper weapon. *See also* M-2 HMG.

T M & B School (Tunnels, Mines and Booby Trap School) Special school of the 25th Infantry Division located at the unit's headquarters at Cu Chi, Hau Nghia Province, III Corps. The school was conducted to orient new troops to the dangers of mines and booby traps and what to look for with regard to the enemy's tunnel system.

Captured enemy tunnels beneath the base camp were used to train prospective tunnel rats under controlled conditions. *See also* **Tunnel Rats.**

Ts *see* **LST**

T6 Bulldozer *see* **Caterpillar D7E Tractor**

T-10 Chute Malfunctions (Cigarette Roll, Bra Chute, Semi-inverted Chute) Two of the more common chute malfunctions were the cigarette roll and the bra chute. The cigarette roll was a rigging error which caused the parachute to unfold, but not fill with air, not opening to full deployment. The bra chute or semi-inverted chute resulted when the rigging lines were routed incorrectly causing the lines to split the chute canopy into two sections. Both conditions were fatal if the reserve chute was not deployed.

T-10 Maneuverable Parachute *see* **T-10 Parachute**

T-10 Parachute (T-10 Maneuverable Parachute, Main Chute) The T-10 was the Army's standard parachute which used the MC-1 nylon canopy. The chute was available in two varieties; the standard chute deployed a 35-foot diameter, full canopy. The T-10 maneuverable chute deployed a 35-foot canopy with a small oval hole (39 square feet) in the top of the canopy. In February '67, the 2d Battalion/503d Infantry/173d Airborne Brigade made the only parachute assault by a U.S. airborne battalion in Vietnam, the only such jump of the war. *See also* **T-10 Reserve Parachute, T-10 Chute Malfunctions, PAEs.**

T-10 Reserve Parachute (Reserve Chute) The T-10 Reserve Parachute was the standard Army reserve chute. The chute was worn on the chest, about stomach level and was released for deployment by pulling the manual release ring (ripcord). The reserve chute was smaller than the main chute, deploying to about 24 feet in diameter. If the main chute failed to deploy correctly, it had to be released completely from the harness before attempting to use the reserve chute. If the main chute was not released from the harness there was a chance the reserve chute would twist and tangle with the main chute. *See also* **T-10 Parachute.**

T21 RCL Czech made recoilless rifle, single shot, breech loaded with a maximum effective HEAT range of 450 meters. The 44-pound gun was man portable, shoulder fired and used by the NVA/VC against both armored and fortification targets. *See also* **Recoilless Rifle.**

T-28 (RT-28, Trojan) Single engine American propeller aircraft used for training by the Air Force and Navy. In Vietnam the T-28 Trojan was armed and used as a fighter by South Vietnam's Air Force (VNAF). The RT-28 was equipped with cameras and used for aerial photo reconnaissance by the VNAF. The T-28 Trojan was manufactured by North American Aviation, had a maximum speed of 280mph, a range of 1,600kms, was armed with two .50cal machine guns, and could carry 200 pounds of bombs or rockets. The T-28 proved to be a good trainer, but was inadequate for close support because of its limited bomb load.

T-33 (RT-33, Shooting Star, F-80) Lockheed single engine jet fighter, designated the F-80 by the Air Force, and the T-33 by the Navy. The aircraft first entered service in '48. Later as more advanced aircraft became available the F-80 was used as a jet trainer. The RT-33 was the reconnaissance version and it saw limited service with the Navy early in the war in Southeast Asia. The Shooting Star had a max speed of 600mph, a range of 2,100kms and was armed with six .50cal machine guns and 2,000 pounds of bombs or rockets.

T-34/85 WWII vintage Soviet tank used by NVA armor units. The T-34 was armed with an 85mm cannon, and two machine guns. The 32-ton tank operated with a five-man crew, and had a maximum road speed of 34mph. NVA T-34s first appeared in combat in '72 during the NVA Eastertide Offensive. *See also* **Armor.**

T-37 *see* **A-37**

T-39 (Sabreliner, Teeny Weeny Weasel, Willie Weasel College) U.S. Air Force/Navy twin engine jet transport manufactured by North American Rockwell. The T-39, Sabreliner, could transport 4–8 passengers or nearly two tons of cargo. Several T-39Fs were used by the Air Force as trainers for Wild Weasel crews starting in '68. The Wild Weasel T-39F trainer was nicknamed the "Teeny Weeny Weasel." The Wild Weasel school was located at Nellis AFB, Nevada, and was nicknamed the "Willie Weasel College." The T-39 had a cruising speed of 502mph and a range of 3,100kms. The Navy used their T-39s for radar and weather training. *See also* **Wild Weasel.**

T-54 Tank (T-59) Soviet made medium tank used by NVA armor units. The T-54 medium tank weighed over 35 tons and was armed with a 100mm cannon and two machine guns. The tank had a maximum road speed of 30mph and was operated by a four-man crew. The T-54's first major actions in South Vietnam were in early '72 during the NVA invasion of SVN. The T-59 was the PRC version of the Soviet T-54. *See also* **Armor.**

T-56 *see* **AK47**

T-59 Tank *see* **T-54 Tank**

TA-4F Twin seat version of the Douglas Aircraft Co. A-4 Skyhawk fighter, used by the Marine Corps for reconnaissance and in the high speed tactical air coordinator mode. *See also* **Tactical Air Coordinator, A-4.**

TAADS *see* **Army Authorization Document System**

Table of Equipment *see* **Table of Organization and Equipment**

Table of Organization and Equipment (TOE, Table of Equipment) An Army organizational outline of the number of personnel, their specialties (jobs) and equipment authorized for a given unit in order for the unit to perform its mission. Such equipment was said to be "organic" to the unit. In order to accomplish their mission in Vietnam TOEs had to be modified to allow the unit to adjust for the terrain, climate, personnel shortages and new equipment being brought into service. These authorized changes to the TOE were considered temporary and were allowed as part of a Modified Table of Organization (MTOE). TOE was sometimes referred to as "Table of Equipment." *See also* **Modified Table of Equipment, Organic.**

Tabs *see* **Shoulder Tabs**

TAC *see* **Tactical Air Command, Tactical Air Coordinators**

Tac Air *see* **Tactical Air Support**

TAC-E *see* **Tactical Emergency**

TACA *see* **Tactical Air Controllers Airborne**

TACAN (Tactical Air Navigation System, VHF Omnidirectional Range Navigation System) U.S. military navigational system which provided aircraft with a bearing (azimuth) and distance to a ground reference station. A pilot could determine where he was in reference to a known ground station. The TACAN system had a line-of-sight range of over 600kms. The VOR (VHF Omnidirectional Range) system provided aircraft with precise directional information in reference to a ground station. Pilots flew from one reference station to the next until they reached the area near the target. Deviations between stations were displayed by the VOR system. The VORTAC was a combination of the TACAN system and the VOR system. The VORTAC system significantly reduced navigational errors in SEA.

TACC *see* **Tactical Air Control Center**

Tacos *see* **EKA-3**

TACS *see* **Tactical Air Control System**

Tactical Air Command (TAC) Air Command managing the use of fighter and fighter-bomber aircraft in support of ground combat units. TAC provided air support for combat and personnel transport within the conflict area of responsibility. *See also* **Tactical Air Support.**

Tactical Air Control Center (TACC) Control center that managed and directed TAC assets. In Vietnam, the 7th Air Force operated a TACC out of Tan Son Nhut AB, controlling Vietnamese and American Air Force operations, countrywide. Prior to the creation of the TACC, U.S. and Vietnamese military traffic was controlled by the Air Force's Tactical Air Control System (TACS) which was located at Tan Son Nhut. Under the old system traffic monitoring and direction were carried out under command of Air Operations Center. As U.S. involvement in Vietnam increased more air control was required and AOC operations were expanded into the TACC. *See also* **Tactical Air Control System.**

Tactical Air Control System (TACS, Operation Barn Door) Air Force radar system used to control and monitor aircraft. A TACS deployed to SVN in December '61 (Operation Barn Door) to coordinate both Air Force and South Vietnamese Air Force aircraft operating in Vietnam. The TACS controlled air strike, transport and recon aircraft, with radar installations located at Da Nang, Pleiku and Tan Son Nhut. The radar centers were called Control and Reporting Post (CRP) and directed their information to the Control and Reporting Center (CRC) at the Air Operations Center at TSN. As the system was expanded it came under command control of the Tactical Air Control Center, based at TSN under overall command of the 7th Air Force. *See also* **Tactical Air Control Center, Control and Reporting Post.**

Tactical Air Controllers Airborne (TACA) Military air controllers who directed air traffic from the air. Airborne controllers were used for special operations when numerous aircraft were active in a particular area, and tactical considerations, or time, did not allow for a ground-bound air traffic controller to be inserted into the area.

Tactical Air Coordinators (TAC[A]) Marine Forward Air Controllers who did their spotting and strike coordination from jet aircraft. The Marine TACs used the two-seat F-9, later replaced by the TA-4F. The TACs primarily dealt with the coordination of air strikes, but on occasion were able to adjust supporting artillery fire. FAC aircraft flew the slower propeller driven aircraft low and slow over friendly forces, while TACs flew the high performance aircraft high over enemy controlled areas. *See also* **Forward Air Controller, TA-4F.**

Tactical Air Navigation System *see* **TACAN**

Tactical Air Support (Tac Air) Aircraft attacks against enemy ground targets in support of friendly ground operations. The tactical air strike was carried out by fixed-wing aircraft.

Tactical Air Support Squadron (TASS) Official parent unit of U.S. Air Force Forward Air Controllers (FACs). *See also* **Forward Air Controller.**

Tactical Air Warfare Center (TAWC) Department of Defense center established to design and develop weapons and techniques for use in tactical air warfare. One of their "achievements" was large pancake shaped bombs, floated down the Song Ma River, unsuccessfully used in an attempt to destroy the Thanh Hoa Bridge in North Vietnam. *See also* **Thanh Hoa Bridge, Operation Carolina Moon.**

Tactical Airlift Military term for the transport of military supplies and personnel by fixed-wing aircraft. Primarily a function of the Air Force. *See also* **Military Airlift Command.**

Tactical Area of Responsibility (TAOR) Military designation for a specific area under command and control of one headquarters. All friendly units operating in the TAOR were responsible to, and under the control of, the headquarters command assigned to the TAOR. ARVN and U.S. TAORs often overlapped, but the forces did not operate under one unified command. The TAOR was similar to the AO (Area of Operations), but the TAOR generally covered a wider area. *See also* **AO.**

Tactical Areas of Interest American name for the areas where the remaining U.S. troops in Vietnam focused their attention after '71. American units pursued a defensive strategy concentrating their limited offensive efforts on trouble spots in-country. In theory this "focusing" allowed the ARVNs to take on the responsibility for wide area patrolling and security around South Vietnam's key areas.

Tactical Armament Turret 101 *see* **TAT 101 Turret**

Tactical Bomb Squadron (TBS, 8th TBS, 13th TBS) U.S. Air Force squadron consisting of aircraft whose prime function was that of a bomber. The 8th and 13th TBSs operated B-57 bombers in Vietnam until their return to the States in October '69 and January '68, respectively. The squadrons operated from air bases at Bien Hoa and Phan Rang. *See also* **B-57.**

Tactical Crusher *see* **Tree Crusher**

Tactical Emergency (TAC-E) Military code used in Vietnam by U.S. units to define a tactically critical condition in which U.S. forces were under heavy attack and in danger of being wiped out and/or overrun. Only a general was authorized to declare a Tactical Emergency. When a TAC-E was declared any available units could be moved in to support the unit in trouble. The reinforcement units were moved in by whatever means were available. Such reinforcements could be pulled from units that were already committed to other operations.

Tactical Fighter Squadron (TFS, Tactical Fighter Wing [TFW]) Air Force squadron composed of tactical fighter and fighter-bomber aircraft. TFSs operated such aircraft as F-4, F-104, F-101, F-100, F-105, F-111, etc. Squadrons were organized into Tactical Fighter Wings, two or more squadrons per wing. *See also* **TFW.**

Tactical Fighter Wing *see* **Tactical Fighter Squadron**

Tactical Nuclear Weapons *see* **Nuclear Weapons**

Tactical Operations Center (TOC, Combat Operations Center [COC]) U.S. command center responsible for the coordination and operation of combat units assigned to it. Individual base camps had a TOC to direct and coordinate the camp's defenses; a division had a TOC (DTOC) to manage all of its combat elements in the field. The TOC was found at many command levels (battalion, task force, brigade, etc.) and represented the command center for the unit's tactical operations. The Marine equivalent was called the Combat Operations Center. *See also* **Combat Information Center, Command of Camp.**

Tactical Reconnaissance Squadron (TRS, TRW, Tactical Reconnaissance Wing) U.S. Air Force squadron composed of reconnaissance and surveillance aircraft such as the RB-57, RB-66, RF-101, RF-4, etc. Two or more squadrons under one command were called a wing.

Tactical Reconnaissance Wing *see* **Tactical Reconnaissance Squadron**

Tactical Redeployment *see* **Retreat**

Tactical Support Functional Components (TSFC) SEABEE construction kits held in reserve for use by Marine and Navy units in Vietnam. The kits included bridge assemblies, airstrip matting, bunker components, defensive perimeter materials (stakes, concertina wire, etc.), water distribution kits, combat support hospitals, POL storage,

revetments and many other kits. The kits could be quickly deployed to meet the tactical situation and needs of the unit. The kits were managed by, and ultimately erected by, the SEABEES.

TAD *see* **Operation Control**

Tae Kwon Do Martial arts practiced by the Koreans. During the Vietnam War some South Korean troops were used as instructors offering Tae Kwon Do training to the ARVNs and U.S. troops. *See also* **Republic of Korea.**

Ta'i One of the mountain tribes living in the area along the eastern border of Laos, near Dien Bien Phu. The Ta'i were known for their opium crop which they traded with other mountain tribes such as the Hmong. A limited number of Ta'i were recruited by USSF teams as mercenaries and scouts and used in operations against the NVA/VC in Laos.

Tai Kwon Do *see* **Tae Kwon Do**

Tail Gunner Team *see* **Stay-Behind Ambush Team**

Tail-End Charlie (Drag, Rear Security) Last element or man in a formation. The drag usually provided rear security and watched for stragglers. *See also* **Closing the Back Door, Dust Eater.**

Tail-Gunner B-52 bombers used during the Vietnam War were fitted with a remote controlled 20mm gun turret positioned at the tail of the aircraft. During the intensified B-52 raids on Hanoi in Dec '72, two NVAF MiGs were shot down by separate B-52 tail-gunners. *See also* **B-52, MiG, Christmas Bombing.**

Tailwind *see* **Operation Tailwind**

Taipans *see* **135th Aviation Company**

Taiwan *see* **Nationalist China**

Takeoff Instructions Takeoff instructions scribbled on the wall inside the latrine located along the landing strip at Pleiku: "C-130 Takeoff Instructions for Passengers: In the event of a power failure on takeoff, bend over at the waist, grasp your ankles firmly with your hands, tuck your head between your knees and kiss your ass goodbye."

Takhli Royal Thai Air Base (355th

Tactical Fighter Wing, Buick Flight)
Thai air base leased by the U.S. Air Force to
launch missions throughout Southeast Asia.
Takhli served as home for the U.S. 355th
TFW, 49th TFW, and 366th Tactical Fighter
Wings. "Buick Flight" was one of the regular
F-105 flights that operated out of the base.
Takhli was located about 160kms north of
Bangkok. See also Thai Air Bases.

Takua   see   Montagnards

Talk-Quick Radio   see   AN/PRC-77

Tally Ho   see   Operation Tally Ho

Talon Vise   see   Operation Frequent
Wind

Tam Ky   Provincial capital of Quang
Tin Province, I Corps. Tam Ky was located
along Highway 1, 27kms northwest of Chu
Lai and 60kms southeast of Da Nang.

Tam Quan   see   Battle of Tam Quan

Tan An   Provincial capital of Long An
Province, III Corps. Long An was the most
populated province in South Vietnam during the war and was one of Vietnam's main
rice growing regions. Tan An was located
32kms southwest of Saigon on Highway 4.
Tan An served as the headquarters for the 3d
Brigade/9th Infantry Division until the brigade departed Vietnam in October '70.

Tan Chau   Remote Navy outpost located on the Upper Mekong River, 14kms
northeast of Chau Duc and 10kms south of
the Cambodian border. Elements of TF 116
intermittently operated from the base conducting interdiction operations against
NVA/VC infiltration routes in the area. See
also TF 116.

Tan Hiep (Battle of Tan Hiep)   Village
located 7kms west of Bien Hoa, III Corps,
site of heavy fighting between elements of
the U.S. 18th Infantry/1st Infantry Division
and NVA/VC units trying to infiltrate into
Bien Hoa for a renewed offensive in May '68.
See also Mini-Tet.

Tan My (Vinh Loc Peninsula)   Large
village located on the tip of the Vinh Loc
Peninsula. The peninsula paralleled the
South Vietnamese coast, northwest from
Tan My. Tan My was about 8kms north of
Hue. The coastal area northwest of Tan My
had a long history of Viet Minh and Viet
Cong activity. Tan My also served as a small
naval base used to support the PBRs of TF

Clearwater that operated on the Perfume
River. See also Street Without Joy, TF Clearwater.

Tan Son Nhut (Ton Son Nhut, TSN
Air Base)   South Vietnam's International
Airport and a major air base located near
Saigon. It also functioned as the head-
quarters for the VNAF and the U.S. 7th Air
Force. Also located on the air base was the
MACV headquarters complex. The complex
was nicknamed "Pentagon East" and be-
came the home of the DAO, ICCS, and the
FPJMT after U.S. troops withdrew from
SVN in '73. The MACV Complex was de-
stroyed by the U.S. Marines April 29, 1975,
before the fall of Saigon to the communists.
See also Pentagon East.

Tan Son Nhut Air Base   see   Tan Son
Nhut

Tan Trao   Village in the hills, 120kms
northwest of Hanoi, where Ho Chi Minh, in
August '45, established the Democratic Republic of Vietnam. Ho proclaimed himself
president of the new republic, which was to
be an independent country operating as part
of the French Union.

Tang Phuc (Mourning Clothes)   Traditional white mourning clothes worn by the
Vietnamese.

Tanglefoot (Barbed Wire, Day Thep
Gai)   Barbed wire used as a defensive barrier around the perimeter of an installation
or base camp. The wire was staked to the
ground in a criss-cross pattern, designed to
entangle the feet of enemy troops attempting to cross the perimeter. "Day Thep Gai"
was Vietnamese for "barbed wire." See also
German Wire, Concertina Wire.

Tango Boat   see   ATC, Armored
Troop Carrier

Tango India Charlie   see   Troops in
Contact, Adrenaline Junkie

Tango November   see   Token Nigger

Tank, The   see   Gold Room

Tank Commander (TC, Track Commander)   Commander of an individual
tank or "track" (APC).

Tank Crewman   see   Tread-Head

Tank Farm (Fuel Depot, POL Depot)
General term for a large fuel storage facility.

The fuels were usually stored in several large fuel tanks, ranging from 25 to 60 feet high. Tank farms in Vietnam were located near the major coastal and river logistics centers where fuels off-loaded from seagoing tankers were stored for distribution to military units across the country. Some of the first targets struck in North Vietnam by U.S. warplanes were North Vietnam's coastal POL facilities. The U.S. raids were in retaliation for NVA/VC attacks against U.S. installations and ships in Southeast Asia.

Tank Loader   *see*   **Bullet Stabber**

Tank Transporter   *see*   **M-123 Tractor**

Tank Treads   *see*   **Blocs**

Tanked   *see*   **Drunk**

Tanker   *see*   **Tread-Head**

Tanker Boots (Wrap Boots)   Combat boot that featured double-wrap leather straps over the regular bootlaces. This style boot had been a favorite of U.S. tank crews during the Korean War, but enjoyed only limited popularity among Vietnam era tankers.

Tanker's Grenade   Two pounds of TNT or C-4 explosive wrapped with barbed wire, and used as a grenade by some tank crews. The grenade was thrown from the tank, aimed at enemy troops too near the tank to be fired on by the tank's guns. *See also* **Daisy Cutter (Homemade)**.

Tans   *see*   **Khakis**

Taon Thang #40–#43   *see*   **Toan Thang**

TAOR   *see*   **Tactical Area of Responsibility**

Tap Codes (Prison Morse Code, Prison Grapevine)   American POWs held in NVA prison camps were usually kept apart from each other and isolated as much as possible. In order for the POWs to maintain contact with each other they developed a communications network that could be used without arousing the guard's suspicion. They used a simplified series of taps similar to Morse code to spell out words using 25 letters of the alphabet, with the letter "C" used for the letter "K." The letters were arranged in five rows of five characters each—a 5 × 5 matrix. Many methods of transmitting the taps were used, from whistles, to scratching,

to coughing: whatever would work.

TAP Suit   *see*   **M-3 TAP Suit**

Taping Up   *see*   **Breaking Tape**

Tapioca Mill   *see*   **Whorehouse**

Target Indicator   *see*   **Pipper**

Targets of Intelligence   *see*   **H and I**

Targets of Opportunity   Targets that could be fired on by a unit, as the targets appeared, without the firing unit seeking approval or clearance from a higher headquarters. Such orders were generally issued to units operating in known enemy areas. *See also* **Rules of Engagement**.

Tarhe   *see*   **CH-54**

Task Force (TF, Task Group [TG], Task Unit [TU])   Special military force assembled for a predefined objective or task. Within a task force a separate group of units could be assigned a specific task or mission; this group was referred to as a "task group" (TG). The individual units of a task force or group were also referred to as "task units" (TU).

Task Force 70.8.9   *see*   **TF 70.8.9**

Task Force 71   *see*   **TF 71**

Task Force 73   *see*   **TF 73**

Task Force 76   *see*   **TF 76**

Task Force 77   *see*   **TF 77**

Task Force 115   *see*   **TF 115**

Task Force 116   *see*   **TF 116**

Task Force 117   *see*   **TF 117**

Task Force 194   *see*   **TF 194**

Task Force Alpha   *see*   **TF Alpha**

Task Force Alpha, 56th Special Operations Wing   *see*   **Infiltration Surveillance Center**

Task Force Clearwater   *see*   **TF Clearwater**

Task Force Delta (Operation Double Eagle)   Double Eagle was a two-month operation by a combined force of the 2d and 22d ARVN Infantry divisions, 1st Cavalry Division (Op Masher) and the Marines of Task Force Delta. The task force consisted of elements of the 4th and 7th Marine regiments. The operation involved the ARVN and 1st Cavalry blocking the area south of

Quang Ngai while the Marines made an amphibious assault at Thach Tru and swept south towards Minh Long in the hills west of the beachhead. The units were in search of the elusive 325th NVA Division. There were no significant enemy contacts during the sweep. Thach Tru was located on the coast, 28kms south of Quang Ngai, I Corps.

Task Force Garry Owen *see* **TF Garry Owen**

Task Force Ingram (TF Ingram) 1st Cavalry Division task force which deployed to Pleiku in October '65 to provide support to the U.S. Special Forces camp at nearby Plei Me in the Ia Drang Valley. TF Ingram consisted of a brigade of infantry and its artillery. The task force was later enlarged with additional units from the 1st Cavalry Division, opening the Battle of the Ia Drang. *See also* **Battle of Ia Drang, Operation Silver Bayonet.**

Task Force Ivory *see* **Son Tay Raid**

Task Force Oregon *see* **TF Oregon**

Task Force South *see* **TF South**

Task Force Walker *see* **TF Walker**

Task Group *see* **Task Force**

Task Group 76.4 *see* **TG 76.4**

Task Group 76.7 *see* **TG 76.7**

Task Group 76.8 *see* **TG 76.8**

Task Unit *see* **Task Force**

Task Unit 70.8.9 *see* **Inshore Fire Support Ship**

TASS *see* **Tactical Air Support Squadron**

TAT 101 Turret (Tactical Armament Turret 101, TAT 102 Turret) Experimental machine gun turret used by the Marine Corps on their UH-1E helicopter gunships. Two M-60 machine guns were positioned in the turret that was mounted to the chin of the chopper and operated by the pilot. The guns each had a 1,000-round supply of ammunition and the turret, operated by the pilot, could be pivoted and the guns raised and depressed. The TAT 102 turret was originally used on the AH-1 Cobra helicopter and featured a single minigun. The TAT 102 was later replaced by the XM-28 which combined a minigun and gre-

nade launcher in one turret. The experimental TAT 101 continued to be used by the Marines until '72. *See also* **XM-28 Turret.**

TAT 102 Turret *see* **TAT 101 Turret**

TAWC *see* **Tactical Air Warfare Center**

Tax Collection The Viet Cong collected taxes from the farmers in the rural areas of Vietnam primarily in the form of food. In areas where GVN or FWF troops were active the VC entered the hamlets at night to collect their "taxes." In areas of low GVN presence the VC tax collectors would circulate through the villages and hamlets during daylight collecting rice and other foodstuffs that were used to supply NVA/VC forces. Taxes were also collected by the VC on small roads and trails used by the farmers to move their crops to market. It was one of the responsibilities of U.S. units in Vietnam to eliminate these VC pressures. Rice was the number one tax commodity. Many rural farmers faced a double plague because they were forced not only to pay the Viet Cong, but were also obligated to pay similar taxes to the government of South Vietnam. The farmers found themselves trapped between the night government of the Viet Cong and the day government of South Vietnam. The farmer's grudging allegiance usually went to the force that provided him the most security or offered the largest threat to his survival. In the long run it was the NVA/VC who posed the largest threat with the GVN unable to provide the rural farmers the security they needed.

Taxi Dancer Vietnamese bar girls who danced with the bar's customers for a fee. The girls would dance and carry on conversation but were not allowed to leave with the customers or drink alcoholic beverages. Taxi dancers were outlawed by Madame Nhu's "Dance Ban" which forbade all forms of public dancing. After the fall of Diem dancing was again allowed but the influx of U.S. troops changed the world of the taxi dancer from hand holding, conversation and after-hours rendezvous to quick sex for pay in back rooms while the bar was open. *See also* **Dance Ban.**

Tay Ninh City Provincial capital of Tay Ninh Province, located in the northwestern corner of III Corps along the Cambodian border. The capital was located 75kms northwest of Saigon and was the second largest city in SVN.

Taylor, Maxwell (General Maxwell Taylor) Appointed as America's ambassador to South Vietnam, July '64, replacing Henry Cabot Lodge. Taylor served as the chairman of the joint chiefs of staff from '62 until his appointment to SVN. He repeatedly called for the build-up of American troops in SVN, an increase in aid, and recommended President Diem institute political and social reforms throughout the country. By the beginning of '65 Taylor's outlook on how successful America could be in Vietnam took a pessimistic turn. In June '65 Taylor left Vietnam as ambassador, returning the position to Henry Cabot Lodge. *See also* **Ad Hoc Task Force on Vietnam.**

Taylor Common *see* **Operation Taylor Common**

TBS *see* **Tactical Bomb Squadron**

TC *see* **Tank Commander**

TC 21-76, Ranger Handbook *see* **Ranger's Bible**

TCBs *see* **Tropical Chocolate Bars**

Tchepone (Base Area 604, Muang Xepon) Village in Laos, about 30kms from the border of SVN where the NVA had stockpiled large quantities of war supplies for use in SVN. Tchepone was one of the main objectives of the ARVN incursion into Laos in February '71. MACV designated the area around Tchepone as Base Area 604, following its scheme of numbering enemy base areas along the border. The small town served as a major hub for NVA supply activities down the Ho Chi Minh Trail. *See also* **Lam Son 719.**

TCS *see* **Operation Saw Buck II**

TDAT *see* **Technical Directorate Assistance Team**

TDY *see* **Temporary Duty**

Tea Plantation, The Nickname for an infantry base camp established south of Pleiku, adjacent to an old French tea plantation. The camp was used by several different U.S. units that conducted operations in the Ia Drang Valley.

Teach-In Loosely formatted gathering of college students, faculty members and others who opposed the war in Vietnam. The practice started in the early '60s and saw hundreds and sometimes thousands of people gathered together to discuss the war and its effects. The teach-ins lasted from hours to several days, and were usually held on the college campus in the dorms, gym or auditorium. In addition to discussions among the teach-in's groups, there were usually formal speakers, berating the war or administration policies. *See also* **Fuck-the-Army.**

Team, The *see* **Australian Army Training Team, Vietnam**

Team A-222 *see* **Dong Tre Special Forces Camp**

Teamhouse Combination dayroom, kitchen, off duty and storage area found at U.S. Special Forces camps in Vietnam. The teamhouse served as a gathering place for off duty team members and was generally off-limits to non–Special Forces personnel, except by personal invitation.

Teamwork, Enthusiasm, Stamina... *see* **TESTICLES**

Tear Gas *see* **CS Gas**

Tear Gas Grenades *see* **Grenades, Gas**

Tech Rep The CIA was constantly seeking new devices and techniques in the counterinsurgency war in Vietnam. One method of testing new devices was to give them to USSF/LRRP units that conducted COIN missions on a regular basis. CIA agents, claiming to be "Tech Reps" from the company that manufactured the device, would take the device to the field unit, explain its use and turn it over to USSF/LRRPs. The success or failure of the device or technique would quietly be passed back to the CIA for evaluation. On occasion, legitimate company reps would introduce the device. *See also* **DCPG, ARPA, Spook.**

Technical Directorate Assistance Team (TDAT) When MACV-SOG was deactivated in April '72, as part of the U.S. withdrawal from Vietnam, SOG duties were taken over by the South Vietnamese Technical Directorate Assistance Team. Some USSF troops continued to operate with the TDAT until March '73. *See also* **MACV-SOG.**

Technical Sergeant *see* **Staff Sergeant**

Tee-Tee *see* Ti Ti

Teeny Weeny Weasel *see* T-39

TEK *see* Tunnel Exploration Kit

TELACS *see* Tunnel Explorer, Locator & Communications System

Tem *see* Montagnard

Tempest *see* FSB Tempest

Temporary Assigned Duty *see* Operation Control, TDY

Temporary Duty (TDY) Military terminology for a temporary assignment. In the early stages of the Vietnam War, before U.S. combat troops were deployed, U.S. military personnel served in Vietnam on TDY performing aircraft maintenance, communications and liaison duties.

Temporary Equipment Recovery Mission (TERM) U.S. mission established in Vietnam in '56 to coordinate the recovery of military equipment that had been given to the French to assist them in their war against the Viet Minh. The recovered equipment was turned over to the armed forces of South Vietnam. TERM was under control of MAAG, Vietnam.

Temporary Morgue *see* Body Cooler

Temporary Profile *see* Medical Profile

Temporary Sergeant *see* Acting Jack

Ten Alpha *see* LZ Ten Alpha

TER *see* Triple Ejector Rack

TERM *see* Temporary Equipment Recovery Mission

Terminate with Extreme Prejudice One of the colorful phrases used by the CIA to refer to killing, assassination or elimination of a target individual. The CIA and the U.S. military command used a host of words and phrases to cloak their actual meanings or intentions. *See also* Kill, Sanitizing Operations.

Terpin Hydrate *see* GI Gin

Terre Rouge Plantation French operated rubber plantation located near the village of Quan Loi, about 100kms north of Saigon in Binh Long Province, III Corps. The entire area was used by the NVA/VC as a base and infiltration route. The plantation

was operated on a marginal basis and was not subjected to NVA/VC attacks or harassment because of an accommodation which had been reached between the French owners and the NVA/VC. The French made payments to the VC and allowed them the use of areas of the plantation; in return the NVA/VC avoided damaging the remaining rubber trees. *See also* Accommodation, Quan Loi.

Terri Lynn *see* FSB Terri Lynn

Territorial Forces Local South Vietnamese defense forces organized to protect their home hamlets and villages. The forces were later renamed the Popular and Regional Forces. The defensive forces were poorly trained, disciplined, armed and led, and did poorly when pitted against regular NVA troops. Early in the war, RF and PF outposts were a regular source of arms and ammunition for raiding VC forces. When attacked by the VC, surviving occupants of the outposts would often flee, leaving their weapons behind. *See also* Regional Forces.

TESTICLES Acronym for the qualities that LRRP team members should possess in the opinion of the 2d Ranger Battalion. The qualities were Teamwork, Enthusiasm, Stamina, Tenacity, Initiative, Courage, Loyalty, Excellence, and a Sense of humor. *See also* LRRP.

Tet (Chinese New Year, Lunar New Year, Nguyen Dan, Tet Mau Than) Annual celebration of Buddha's birthday, occurring at the end of January, coinciding with the start of the lunar new year. This period in Vietnam parallels the Western world's celebration of the Christmas and New Year holidays. The Vietnamese followed the Buddhist tradition of naming each new year with one of the twelve animals of the 12-year cycle. For Americans the year of the monkey is most remembered for the communist offensive launched during the '68 Tet celebrations. *See also* Tet Offensive, Year of the...

Tet '68 *see* Tet Offensive '68

Tet '69 *see* Tet Offensive '69

Tet Mau Than *see* Tet

Tet Offensive '68 (Tet '68, Year of the Monkey, Great General Offensive and People's Uprising) During the '68 Tet celebrations communist forces launched a country-wide offensive against US/ARVN military installations and major population centers. Their aim was to seize power in the South, causing mass SVN Army defections and the population to rise up against the GVN and join forces with the communists. These objectives were not realized; the NVA/VC suffered a tactical defeat, over 32,000 NVA/VC KIA compared to less than 2,100 US/ARVN KIAs. But the NVA/VCs' ability to launch such an attack created doubt in the U.S. as to the "winnability" of the war against the communists. Because of the offensive and the Hue massacre more support among the general population was temporarily generated for the GVN.

Tet Offensive '69 (Tet '69)   During the later months of '68 and early '69, NVA/VC units operating from bases along the Cambodian border of III Corps were quietly attempting to move closer to Saigon. The NVA/VC objective was to stage another large scale offensive around Saigon. In the fall of '68 the 1st Air Cavalry Division was moved from I Corps to operate in the III Corps area. Airmobile tactics by the 1st Cav and other American units in the III Corps area kept the NVA/VC off balance, eliminating the threat of another NVA/VC offensive similar to Tet '68.

Tetracycline (Penicillin)   One of several antibiotics used to treat venereal diseases. The old standby was penicillin, but several strains of VD in Vietnam were extremely resistant to antibiotics normally used to treat venereal disease. *See also* **Venereal Diseases.**

Texas   *see*   **Operation Texas**

Texas Star   *see*   **Operation Texas Star**

TF   *see*   **Task Force**

TF 70.8.9 (Task Force 70.8.9)   Provided offshore fire support to ground units along the I Corps coast of South Vietnam. The task force consisted of a cruiser/destroyer group, and for six months in '68, the battleship USS *New Jersey*. Coastal bombardment support started in '65 and ended in late '72. *See also* **USS New Jersey, Inshore Fire Support Ship.**

TF 71 (Task Force 71, Operation Market Place)   Operation Market Place was the early U.S. Navy program of coastal surveillance and patrolling started in March '65.

Coast Guard cutters, destroyers and aircraft were used and designated Task Force 71. TF 71 later became TF 115 and was redesignated Operation Market Time. *See also* **TF 115.**

TF 73 (Task Force 73)   U.S. Seventh Fleet elements responsible for logistics support of the fleet.

TF 76 (Task Force 76)   Task force of the U.S. Navy's 7th Fleet that conducted amphibious operations in conjunction with Marine units in Vietnam. The task force provided the equipment and support used for amphibious operations. The task force also participated in the evacuation operations conducted during the collapse of South Vietnam in '75. *See also* **Operation Frequent Wind.**

TF 77 (Task Force 77, CTF-77)   U.S. Navy Carrier Task Force (CTF) operating in the Western Pacific, part of the U.S. 7th Fleet. The force consisted of several aircraft carriers, destroyers, cruisers and support vessels, conducting Rolling Thunder raids against NVN. TF 77's operational area was the Gulf of Tonkin and South China Sea, with carrier stations located just off the coast of NVN and SVN. The carrier station, located off NVN, was code-named "Yankee Station" and the southern station was called "Dixie Station." *See also* **7th Fleet, Yankee Station, Dixie Station.**

TF 115 (Task Force 115, Coastal Surveillance Force, CSF, Coast Guard Squadron 1 & 3)   The U.S. Navy created the Coastal Surveillance Force (Task Force 115) in July '65 to aid the South Vietnamese Navy in its patrol and surveillance of SVN's coastal waters. The patrol zone ran from the 17th Parallel in the North to the Cambodian border at Ha Tien. Under Operation Market Time, U.S. Navy ships and aircraft of the 7th Fleet, and patrol boats of Coast Guard Squadron One and Three were used as barrier patrols to reduce the infiltration of arms and supplies into SVN by NVN. The CSF was directly assigned to MACV Hqs. By '71 most of TF 115's smaller vessels had been transferred to the VNN. *See also* **Market Time, TF 115 Assets, WPB, TF 71.**

TF 115 Assets   The major ships and aircraft used during Operation Market Time for coastal and sea patrols were WPM coast guard cutters, DER destroyer escorts, MSO minesweepers, LST fitted with radar, PCF patrol boats, P-3A radar aircraft, P2V radar aircraft, P-5 seaplanes.

TF 116 (Game Warden, Task Force 116, Riverine Patrol Force, Brown Water Navy) Code name for U.S. Navy operation started in December '65, aimed at disrupting the transport and distribution of enemy supplies to NVA/VC units by means of the inland waterways of SVN. The operation was performed by units of TF 116, the Riverine Patrol Force (Riverine Assault Force), supported by U.S. Army helicopters, Navy Attack Helicopter Squadron 3, Neptune gunships of VAH-21, and Navy Light Attack Squadron 4. The latter manned armed OV-10 Bronco aircraft. The force was nicknamed the Brown Water Navy after the dirty brown waters of the Delta which they patrolled. The Navy boat crews called themselves "River Rats." The primary patrol craft of TF 116 were the Mark I and II, PBR. The task force consisted of 200 PBRs deployed in 10-boat sections. The boat sections were members of five different PBR divisions that patrolled the inland waterways of the Delta. The boat crews were supported by shore based facilities and from mobile bases established on converted Navy LSTs. The mobile LST bases were located in the mouths of IV Corps major river outlets. *See also* **PBR Mark I/II, TF 117, Game Warden River Groups, Navy's Delta Air Force, River Division.**

TF 117 (MRF, Task Force 117, River Assault Force, Mobile Riverine Force, MEDMAF) Combined U.S. Army-Navy task force conducting riverine operations in the Delta of IV Corps, officially designated the Mekong Delta Mobile Afloat Force (MEDMAF), but more commonly known as the Mobile Riverine Force. Army troops operated from Navy craft as a self-contained strike force based at Dong Tam; operations began June '67. The MRF consisted of four River Assault Squadrons, and operated until June '69. At that time, the ARVNs began to assume full responsibility for riverine operations in the Delta. MRF assets eventually became part of SEALORDS Operations before being permanently transferred to the Vietnamese. *See also* **River Assault Flotilla One, ACTOV, Mobile River Group.**

TF 194 (Task Force 194; SEALORDS; Southeast Asia Lake, Ocean, River, Delta Strategy) A combined task force consisting of US/RVN units operating in the IV Corps Delta area. The objective of the force was to eliminate enemy supply routes from Cambodia into SVN, and attack enemy base areas in the Delta. Operations later expanded to include I & II Corps waterways. The operation started in '68 and U.S. participation ended in April '71, when RVN units took over full responsibility for the operations. The operations were referred to as SEALORDS (Southeast Asia Lake, Ocean, River, Delta Strategy). The initial focus was interdiction of enemy supply lines along the Cambodian border between the Gulf of Thailand and the Parrot's Beak area. TF 194 was divided into five operational groups. *See also* **TF 194 Groups.**

TF 194 Groups (Coastal Raiding, Blocking, Riverine Strike, Riverine Raiding, Riverine Block) TF 194, SEALORDS operations, were conducted by U.S. Navy units and elements of the Army's 9th Infantry Division. In addition, ARVN forces were involved and gradually took on more of the responsibility for SEALORDS operations. The task force was divided into five operational groups. The coastal raiding and blocking groups operated along the coastal inlets of SVN. The riverine strike, blocking and raiding groups operated inland on the rivers. *See also* **TF 194.**

TF Abel Mabel   *see*   **Operation Abel Mabel**

TF Alpha (Task Force Alpha) A headquarters task force deployed to SVN in August '65 to control U.S. troops in SVN and provide support to SVN armed forces in the area. TF Alpha deployed to Nha Trang in II Corps, and was upgraded to the I Field Force, Vietnam, in March '66. *See also* **I Field Force.**

TF Clearwater (Task Force Clearwater, Hue River Security Group, Dong Ha River Security Group) Special riverine task force formed in February '68 to operate in I Corps. The task force's primary assignment was to keep the Cua Viet and Perfume rivers open between the sea, Hue and Dong Ha. The task force was divided into two groups: the Hue, and the Dong Ha River security groups. Both groups operated in conjunction with the existing forces of River Division 55 and consisted of PBR, ATC, Monitors, CCB, and minesweeper LCM craft. The Cua Viet was the most difficult of the two rivers to keep open because it was so close to the DMZ where the NVA could easily cross over to ambush and attack river traffic. *See also* **River Division 55.**

TF Garry Owen (Task Force Garry Owen) Task force composed of the 1st Battalion/7th Cavalry Regiment which operated July '72 until the battalion's departure in August of the same year. The task force operated around Saigon and Bien Hoa as a "fire brigade" or reaction force for the area. The regiment's name was "Garry Owen."

TF Ingram *see* **Task Force Ingram**

TF Ivory *see* **Son Tay Raid**

TF Oregon (Task Force Oregon) U.S. Army task force consisting of elements of the 3d Brigade/25th Infantry Division, 196 Light Infantry Brigade and 1st Brigade/101st Airborne Division under command of the III MAF. The force operated in southern I Corps eventually allowing U.S. Marine units in the area to be moved north, concentrating along the DMZ and the border with Laos. Some units of TF Oregon were later used to form the 23d Infantry Division, the Americal. *See also* **Americal Division.**

TF Pipe Stem *see* **Operation Pipe Stem**

TF South (Task Force South) Combined force consisting of units from 1st Battalion/173rd Airborne Brigade, and various other units that temporarily operated in the boundary area between II and III Corps.

TF Walker (Task Force Walker) Army task force assembled in May '66 to conduct Operation Paul Revere. The force consisted of elements of the 4th and 25th Infantry divisions and the 1st Cavalry, and was named after its leader Gen. Glenn Walker. TF Walker operated in the Central Highlands, from the Cambodian border east to the Pleiku area. The force consisted of three infantry battalions, an armored and air cavalry troop, one armor company and four artillery batteries. The task force base camp was located at Oasis, 25kms southwest of Pleiku. *See also* **Operation Paul Revere (I–IV), FSB Oasis.**

TFS *see* **Tactical Fighter Squadron**

TFW *see* **Tactical Fighter Squadron**

TG *see* **Task Force**

TG 76.4 (Task Group 76.4, White Elephant, Amphibious Logistics Support Group [ALSG]) Temporary task group of the U.S. 7th Fleet organized as the Amphibious Logistics Support Group in June '65. The group coordinated the delivery of military cargo to port facilities in I Corps. The ALSG was headquartered at Da Nang and consisted of several elements that managed such tasks as harbor security and defense at Da Nang, UDT and EOD services, cargo transfer and other freight related services. The shore based office of TG 76.4 was located in an old French office/warehouse called the "White Elephant," which was situated on the Da Nang River near the port facilities. As U.S. operations expanded in I Corps the Naval Support Activity was created to control the functions of TG 76.4. *See also* **NSA, Da Nang.**

TG 76.7 (Task Group 76.7, USS Vancouver, USS Henrico, USS Union) Navy TG 76.7 that deployed the first American ground combat forces to South Vietnam. The task group deployed elements of the 9th Marine Expeditionary Brigade at Red Beach II on the shore of Da Nang Harbor on March 8, 1965. The ships of the task group were the USS *Union,* USS *Vancouver* and the USS *Henrico. See also* **9th Marine Amphibious Brigade.**

TG 76.8 (Task Group 76.8) Special Navy task group created from elements of TF 76 assigned to conduct the evacuations of Phnom Penh and Saigon in April '75. Some of the ships of the evacuation fleet were the USS: *Okinawa, Denver, Blueridge, Durham, Dubuque, Midway. See also* **Operations Frequent Wind, Eagle Pull.**

TH-55A Helicopter Light helicopter manufactured by Hughes and used by the Army as a helicopter trainer. The TH-55 (Model 269) was less than 23 feet long and could seat 2–3 people on the bench seat in the small plexiglass cockpit. The chopper had a maximum speed of 86mph and a range of 320kms. The TH-55 served as the Army's initial training helicopter in '65. *See also* **Fort Rucker.**

TH-57 Sea Ranger *see* **OH-58**

Thach Tru Village located along

Highway 1, 28kms south of Quang Ngai, Quang Ngai Province, I Corps. In November '65 enemy forces attacked the government outpost at Thach Tru which was defended by ARVN Rangers. The Rangers, assisted by U.S. naval gunfire support, held the outpost. A follow-up sweep by elements of the U.S. 7th Marines discovered that the attack had been carried out by elements of the 95th NVA Regiment, representing the first confirmed instance of North Vietnamese troops taking part in battles in South Vietnam's I Corps.

Thai Air Bases (Royal Thai Air Force Base, RTAFB, RTAB) The U.S. Air Force operated several bases in Thailand from facilities leased to the U.S. by the Thai government. The bases were officially designated as "Royal Thai Air Bases" (RTAB). Those bases leased from the Thais were Nam Phong, Korat, Takhli, Nakhon Phanom, U Tapao, U Dorn and U Bon. From these bases American aircraft carried out raids and surveillance throughout Southeast Asia. *See also* Individual Bases.

Thai Guerrillas *see* **U Dorn Royal Thai Air Base**

Thai Khac Chuyen *see* **Rheault Affair**

Thailand Began providing troops (pilots and aircraft mechanics) to aid South Vietnam in mid-'64. In '67 the first Thai combat troops, the Queen's Cobras Regimental Combat Team, deployed to Bien Hoa Province. In '68 the Cobras returned home and were replaced by a division of Royal Thai combat troops, the Black Panther Division. In addition to the combat troops, Thailand provided Air Force and Navy advisors to the Vietnamese. Thai troops began returning to Thailand in August '71. Over 350 Thai soldiers died in Vietnam. *See also* Queen's Cobras, Black Panther Division, Thai Air Bases.

Thanh Dien Forest *see* **Trapezoid, The**

Thanh Hoa (Port) *see* **Blockade**

Thanh Hoa Bridge (Ham Rung Bridge, Dragon's Jaw) Strategic road/rail bridge spanning the Song Ma River, 130kms south of Hanoi in NVN. The bridge, an important supply and communications line to the NVN war effort against SVN, was one of the more difficult NVN targets for U.S. air strikes. The bridge was 164 meters long, 17 meters wide, and 15 meters above the Song Ma River. The heavily reinforced bridge was damaged several times, but not completely downed until May '72, when smart bombs succeeded in bringing the bridge down. The original bridge was destroyed by the Viet Minh during the First Indochina War by crashing two locomotives loaded with dynamite, started from opposite ends, in the center of the bridge. *See also* **Carolina Moon, Smart Bombs.**

Thanh Long *see* **Hanoi**

Thanh Nien Cach Menh Dong Chi Hoi (Revolutionary Youth League) Independence movement organized by Ho Chi Minh in '24. The small group was founded during Ho's stay in China and, through papers and speeches, advocated Vietnamese independence from the French. French agents shadowed Ho for his anti–French subversive activities and in '27 he escaped to Russia to avoid arrest. When Ho left China his Revolutionary Youth League collapsed. *See also* **Ho Chi Minh.**

Thank You *see* **Cam On**

That Others May Live *see* **Aerospace Rescue and Recovery Service**

Thayer I & II *see* **Operation Thayer I & II**

There It Fuckin' Is *see* **There It Is**

There It Is (There It Fuckin' Is) GI phrase used to emphasize an obvious truth or situation, sometimes used in an "I told you so..." context.

Thermite Grenade *see* **Grenades, Thermite**

They Shall Not Want *see* **Naval Support Activity, Da Nang**

Thich Nu Thanh Quang *see* **Thich Quang Duc**

Thich Quang Duc (Bonze, Ho Thi Thien, Thich Nu Thanh Quang) The 73-year-old Bonze (Buddhist monk) was the first to burn himself alive in protest of discrimination and oppression against the Buddhists by the Catholic government of Ngo Dinh Diem, June '63. Later, six more Buddhist priests and two nuns (Ho Thi Thien and Thich Nu Thanh Quang) burned themselves to protest Buddhist oppression by the government. Government troops used massive force to stop the demonstrations. This strong response by the government turned world opinion against Diem, and eventually led to the collapse of his government, and his assassination. Madame Nhu, Diem's sister-in-law, called the self-immolations "Buddhist barbecues." *See also* Madame Nhu.

Thien Tue *see* **Cay Thien Tue**

Thieu, Nguyen Van *see* **Nguyen Van Thieu**

Thieu-Ta *see* **Major**

Thieu-Tuong *see* **General Officers**

Thieu-Uy *see* **Second Lieutenant**

Thing, The *see* **M-50A1 Ontos**

Third Marine Amphibious Force *see* **III Marine Amphibious Force**

Third Marine Division *see* **3d Marine Division**

Third Vietnam, The During the NVA Eastertide Offensive in '72 they captured and held South Vietnamese territory along the Cambodian and Laotian border. From the captured territory they began to expand their presence in SVN until they controlled most of SVN's western border from the DMZ to the Gulf of Thailand. Their area of control was sometimes referred to as the "Third Vietnam." North Vietnamese troops and civilian workers occupied the area creating fortifications, roads and fuel pipelines. From the "Third Vietnam" the NVA massed their forces, undisturbed by the ARVN, and prepared for the final assault on SVN which followed in early '75.

Third-Heart *see* **Purple Heart**

Thirty-Cal MG *see* **M-1919A6 MMG**

This Is the Only War We've Got... *see* **It's a Small War God, But...**

Tho, Le Duc *see* **Le Duc Tho**

Thompson, Sir Robert British guerrilla warfare specialist and expert on the insurgency in Malaysia and the application of counterinsurgency techniques. Sir Thompson's efforts and tactics were instrumental in defeating the communist insurgents in Malaysia during the fifties. Thompson helped develop the Strategic Hamlet Program which was adopted by the Diem regime in Vietnam as a method to counter the Viet Cong offensive in rural areas. The program called for the relocation of rural villagers to fortified hamlets where the government could protect them from the VC and at the same time improve the villagers' living conditions. The program was successful in Malaysia but failed in SVN. *See also* Pacification, Malaysia.

Thompson SMG *see* **M-1A1 SMG**

Thompson Submachine Gun *see* **M-1A1 SMG**

Thon Son Lam *see* **Rock Pile**

Thong Nhat *see* **Cuu Nuoc & Thong Nhat**

Thong-Thong *see* **General Officers**

Thongs *see* **Rubber Thongs**

Thor *see* **LZ Thor**

Those Who Kill for Pleasure... (Gunslingers, Kingsmen) Motto of the Gunslingers: "Those who kill for pleasure are sadists; those who kill for money are professionals; those who kill for both are GUNSLINGERS." The motto of the Kingsmen of the Company B/101st Aviation Battalion was similar: "If you kill for fun you're a sadist; if you kill for money you're a mercenary; if you kill for both you're a KINGSMAN." *See also* Calling Cards.

Thot Not *see* **Operation Daniel Boone**

Thousand Yard Stare The distant look in the eyes of a soldier who has seen and been involved in a great deal of combat. A soldier with the "stare" was withdrawn, quiet, sullen, glassy-eyed and generally only concerned with his immediate survival in the combat zone.

Three Heart Ticket *see* **Purple Heart**

Three Hearts and You're Out *see* **Purple Heart**

Three Stooges *see* **National Leadership Council**

Three-Holer *see* **Latrine**

Three-Quarter Cav *see* **3d Squadron/4th Cavalry (Division Recon)**

Three-Quarter Ton Truck *see* **M-37B1 Truck**

Three-Sevens *see* **37mm AA**

Throwin' Hands (Fist Fight, Fight, Buckle) Slang for a fistfight. In Marine slang "buckle" was to fight, as in "buckle for your dust"; to fight violently.

THUD *see* **F-105**

Thud Ridge A small rugged mountain range running northwest from Hanoi, often used for cover by U.S. aircraft in their attacks on targets in the Hanoi area. The ridge provided attacking planes some cover from NVA antiaircraft fire from the ground. The ridge also provided a visual landmark for aircraft attacking the Red River area.

Thump Gun *see* **M-79 Grenade Launcher**

Thump Gunner *see* **Grenadier**

Thumper *see* **M-79 or M-5 Grenade Launcher**

Thumperman *see* **Grenadier**

Thunder I–III *see* **Fire Base Thunder**

Thunder Mountain Nickname for a small, 980-foot mountain located about 3kms south of Duc Pho along Highway 1 in I Corps. The mountain was nicknamed by elements of the 14th Infantry/4th Infantry Division in '67.

Thunder One *see* **FSB Thunder One**

Thunder Road (Highway 13) Nickname for Vietnamese National Highway 13, between Loc Ninh in Binh Long Province, and Phu Cuong, just north of Saigon. The road provided the main overland link between Saigon and the northern border areas of III Corps. The road wound through heavy areas of enemy activity and was nicknamed by U.S. armor units conducting thunder runs in support of convoy traffic on the highway. *See also* **Thunder Run**.

Thunder Run In Vietnam, a small armor force would speed down the road at night firing into the roadsides as they drove, attempting to keep the VC off guard and limit the enemy's ability to set up ambushes and mine the roads. The start times of the runs were randomly selected to reduce the chances of the Viet Cong setting up ambushes against the runs. *See also* **Road Runners**.

Thunderbirds of the 118th Avn *see* **118th Aviation Company**

Thunderchief *see* **F-105**

Thuoc Dao *see* **Resource Management**

Thuoc Phien *see* **Opium, Marijuana**

Thuong-Si-Nhat *see* **E-9**

Thuy-Quan Luc-Chien *see* **Republic of Vietnam Marine Corps**

Ti Ti (Tee-Tee) [tee tee] Vietnamese meaning very little or small, so simple to say it was not even phonetically bastardized by the American GI.

TIA Airlines *see* **Commercial Carriers**

TIARA Project (LEC Compound, Light-Emitting Chemical Compound, the Funky-Light Project) ARPA project that experimented with a luminous chemical compound code-named "TIARA." When exposed to air the compound emitted low-level light similar to the luminous paint on a clock dial. Used in large quantities the TIARA could be seen from greater distances than luminous paint and it did not have to be exposed to light before it became operational. TIARA was tested in Vietnam as a marking agent for equipment used in night operations, but the hot and humid conditions of Vietnam reduced its luminous qualities and it proved totally unusable. Its biggest drawback, however, was that when applied to clothing or equipment the LEC compound gave off a clinging and lingering putrid odor that was resistant to soap and normal washing. Testing was discontinued. *See also* **ARPA**.

TIC *see* **Troops in Contact, Adrenaline Junkie**

Ticket Home *see* **Million Dollar Wound**

Ticket-Punching An unofficial policy that emerged within the Army Officer Corps after the Korean War. In order for a career soldier to advance in rank there were certain unofficial requirements or "punches" that had to be achieved, such as airborne training, college degrees, SF or Ranger training, combat command time, highest possible OERs, and a host of others. This policy stressed careerism instead of professionalism and weakened the Army's command structure during the VNW. The policy of careerism was in part imposed by civilian authorities who sought to have military leaders proficient in a wide range of fields. This led to a marked reduction in officers who were willing to specialize in any field. *See also* **Revolving Door Command, The Best Go West, OER.**

Tico *see* **USS Ticonderoga**

Ticonderoga *see* **USS Ticonderoga**

Tiec Lon *see* **Bua Chen**

Tien Sha Peninsula Peninsula that formed part of Da Nang Harbor in I Corps. The prominent feature of the peninsula was the 2,200-foot Mui Da Nang, more popularly known as Monkey Mountain. The peninsula was the site of many logistical and command facilities for the I Corps area including Camp Horn, III MAF Headquarters until March '70, and later, XXIV Corps Headquarters.

Tiger (Indo-Chinese Tiger) Several incidents of tiger encounters were reported by U.S. troops operating in deep jungle areas of Vietnam. Some of the reports indicated sightings of tigers, while others reported attacks by a tiger on troops in NDPs or night ambush positions. In '68, naturalist V. Mazak identified a subspecies of tiger living in Southeast Asia. The subspecies, a descendant of the Indian and Chinese tiger, was sometimes referred to as the Indo-Chinese Tiger and was generally about the size of a leopard, or 6–8 feet long, compared to the 13-foot size of the Indian or Siberian Tiger.

Tiger Balm (Vietnamese VAPORUB) A Vietnamese medicinal ointment used for a wide variety of nonspecific afflictions; a Vietnamese version of America's "Vicks VAPORUB" ™.

Tiger Beer *see* **Vietnamese Beer**

Tiger Cage Small bamboo boxes used to confine and punish prisoners. The boxes were too small for the prisoner to stand erect or move around freely. Prisoners were kept in the boxes for weeks at a time. Prolonged confinement in the boxes eventually led to crippling and disfigurement of the prisoner. The tiger cages and their variants were used by both the VC and some intelligence gathering groups within the South Vietnamese military. The tiny cells on the prison island at Con Son were also referred to as "tiger cages." The 5 × 9-foot underground concrete cells "featured" poor ventilation and a host of parasites and bugs. A variant of the tiger cage was used by the ARVNs to temporarily hold their interrogation subjects. The modified tiger cage consisted of a small area enclosed with barbed wire. The top of the enclosure was 10–12 inches above the ground and made of closely spaced, strung barbed wire. Interrogation subjects were made to lie in the enclosure, stripped nude or seminude. The enclosures were placed so that most of the day they were under direct sunlight. Victims in the low cage were unable to turn over without being cut by the wire and there was no relief from the hot sun. Victims in the cage were usually denied water as long as they refused to cooperate with their interrogators. To increase the prisoners' discomfort, the ARVNs would dowse them with salt water, which irritated the multitude of nicks the prisoners' bodies suffered from the barbed wire. *See also* **Poulo Condore.**

Tiger Country Australian infantry slang for enemy territory, especially those areas where the enemy was active or the infantry was operating in a known enemy base area. The same sort of areas referred to by American GIs as the "Bad Bush," "Arizona Territory," "Indian Country," "The Shit," etc. *See also* **Boonies.**

Tiger Division *see* **Capital Republic of Korea Infantry Division**

Tiger Fatigues (Tiger Suit, Tiger Stripes) Tight fitting camouflage fatigues worn by ARVN soldiers. The fatigues' pattern (irregular black and green stripes on a green background) blended well with the jungles of Vietnam. American recon and Special Forces also wore the tiger stripe uniform, although such uniforms were not officially authorized or available through normal logistical supply. The Americans purchased their fatigues locally and had them altered to accommodate their larger physical size. Eventually the Army began to issue the ERDL pattern camouflage uniform which had a four color woodland pattern. *See also* **Jungle Camouflage Uniform, Club Cammies.**

Tiger Force (Tiger Team) An all-volunteer recon force from 1st Battalion/327th Infantry/101st Airborne Division, also known as "Tiger Teams." It was also the name for a late '62 reinforced platoon of RF/PF troops which was kept as a reserve/reaction force in the I Corps area. The force was lifted into action by elements of the Marine helicopter force that provided support to the Vietnamese military in I and II Corps. *See also* **Tigers.**

Tiger Force Recon *see* **Tigers**

Tiger Hound *see* **Operation Tiger Hound**

Tiger Island *see* **Ho Co Island**

Tiger Ladies (Civilian Construction Workers) Nickname for Vietnamese women who worked as civilian laborers for military engineers and U.S. engineering contractors. The Tiger Ladies were hard, able workers in the construction of U.S. air bases, roads and port facilities throughout South Vietnam. *See also* **Engineers, Slushies.**

Tiger Mountains Nickname for the small mountain range running west from the coast, approximately 85kms north of Qui Nhon, Binh Dinh Province, II Corps. The mountains were nicknamed by elements of the 503d Infantry/173d Airborne Brigade operating in the area.

Tiger Phone Exchange (PTT Exchange, Arvin Telephone Exchange) One of three semi-public telephone systems that were available in South Vietnam. Telephoning by means of the quasi-military/commercial exchanges in Vietnam was a nightmare because there was no one system installed countrywide; instead calls had to be routed through three different, and mutually antagonistic systems. The three phone systems involved were the Arvin, PTT and Tiger exchanges. *See also* **StarCom.**

Tiger Pit *see* **Punji Pit**

Tiger Scout *see* **Kit Carson Scout**

Tiger Stripes *see* **Tiger Fatigues**

Tiger Suit *see* **Tiger Fatigues**

Tiger Team *see* **Tiger Force**

Tiger Trap A large hole used to trap APCs. Early in the war, after the U.S. introduction of the APC to SVN, the Viet Cong used such traps in an attempt to reduce the effectiveness of the APC. The practice gradually disappeared as more effective antitank weapons became widely available to the Viet Cong. *See also* **Punji Pit.**

Tigerpiss (Gook Booze, Gook Beer) Generic GI nickname for Vietnamese beer and alcohol, more frequently referred to as "gook booze" and "gook beer." *See also* **Vietnamese Beer.**

Tigers (Tiger Force Recon) Long-range reconnaissance teams for the 1st Brigade/101st Airborne Division. The teams were organized in '65 after the division's arrival in Vietnam. The Tiger recon teams consisted of volunteers from the 1st Battalion/327th Infantry (Airborne). The teams conducted reconnaissance and special ambushes for the battalion. The Tiger teams were later classified as LRRP teams as part of Company F/58th Infantry (LRP). The LRRPs were redesignated Company L/75th Infantry (Rangers) in February '69. *See also* **Hawk Team, Tiger Force.**

Tiger's Lair Nickname for the four fire bases of the 3d Battalion/47th Infantry/2d Brigade/9th Infantry Division established in Kien Hoa Province, IV Corps in September '68. Operations continued in the area until the division's departure in mid-'69. The four fire bases and an artillery fire support base were located along Highway 26 southeast of Ben Tre near the center of Kien Hoa Province. *See also* **47th Infantry Regiment.**

Tight (Nervous) To be very good friends with or very close to someone. Also meant anxious, edgy or nervous. To be "wrapped-too-tight" was to be a little crazy. *See also* **Crazy.**

Tight-Jawed *see* **Pissed**

Tim-La *see* **Syphilis**

Time Fuse *see* **VT Round, Time Pencil**

Time on Target (TOT) Designated time for attacking aircraft to be over an assigned target. Also referred to the scheduled impact time of artillery rounds fired from different batteries, massed against one target, allowing for the simultaneous arrival of the rounds on the target. Coordination of fuse time was such that air burst rounds would all detonate over the target area at the same time. Such TOT artillery strikes required extensive coordination by the batteries involved, but the massed TOT greatly improved the effects of the artillery fires. *See also* SLAM.

Time Pencil Time delayed detonator about the size of a fat wooden pencil. The timers, which were available in fixed time intervals, detonated when the time elapsed. The pencils could be attached to hand grenades, claymores or explosives, and used as delayed booby traps. *See also* Booby Trap.

Tin City *see* Guam

Tin Foil *see* Chaff

Tinfoil Airstrip Early reference to the U.S. Marines' airstrip located at Chu Lai. The strip was constructed out of aluminum matting, and from the air looked like tinfoil spread out on the sand. *See also* Chu Lai, Short Airfield for Tactical Support

Tinh Bien Large village located at the northeast entrance to the Seven Mountains area of the Delta, along the Cambodian border.

Tinh Lo *see* Highways

Tinh Nguyen (Volunteer Worker) Vietnamese for "volunteer worker." The NVA made heavy use of "volunteer" laborers to maintain the Ho Chi Minh Trail. Many members of the work force were rural mountain tribespeople forced by the NVA to work on the trail system along the border areas of Laos and Cambodia. *See also* Dan Cong.

Tissue Paper *see* Shit Paper

Titty Hill Nickname for the 4th Infantry Division headquarters located at Pleiku. The division base camp was located on a low rounded hill that from a distance was reminiscent of a woman's breast. *See also* 4th Infantry Division.

Titty-Deep *see* Foxhole

TK-2 GFS Kit (TK-2 Ground Fire Armament Suppression Kit) Weapons system kit mounted on Marine Corps UH-1E gunships. The kit consisted of a mount on each side of the chopper that supported an electrically fired M-60 machine gun and a pair of 2.75-inch FFAR rocket pods. The UH-1Es became available to the Marines in

Vietnam in May '65. *See also* UH-1E.

TK-2 Ground Fire Armament Suppression Kit *see* TK-2 GFS Kit

TL *see* Highways

TM-41 Antitank Mine Soviet antitank mine used by the NVA/VC. The metallic mine was cylinder shaped, 5.7 inches high, 9.9 inches in diameter and weighed 12 pounds. The mine was detonated by a pressure cap that extended slightly above the top of the mine. The mine was designed for anti-vehicle use. *See also* Booby Trap.

TM-Technical Manual *see* Field Manual

TNT (Trinitrotoluene) High explosive used worldwide. The enemy in Vietnam made wide use of TNT for booby traps and demolitions. The U.S. military used TNT primarily for construction purposes. Early in the war TNT was used in the field for demolitions, but the damp climate reduced the explosive's shelf life and greatly affected its stability in the field. TNT used by U.S. military units in the field was usually packaged in tin-covered 4oz blocks, and was detonated by blasting caps. TNT was eventually replaced by the more stable and reliable C-4 explosive. *See also* C-4, C-3 Explosive; Amatol.

To Chau Training Center *see* Phu Quoc Island

To Cong Campaign (Denounce the Communist Campaign) Campaign by South Vietnam's President Ngo Dinh Diem to round up and jail or eliminate former members of the Viet Minh who were believed to be communist or procommunist.

Toan Thang *see* Cambodian Incursion, Operation Toan Thang

Toan Thang 40–45 (Cambodian Invasion) Code name for the combined US/ARVN incursion into Cambodia to attack and destroy NVA/VC sanctuaries along the Cambodian/South Vietnam border in April '70. In addition to the incursion, part of the Toan Thang operation was conducted to secure the area around Saigon, reducing a possible recurrence of the NVA/VC attacks of Tet '68. U.S. and Australian forces operated around Saigon, while ARVN forces operated in the Saigon Military District. Toan Thang [tone th-ang] meant "complete" or "total victory" in Vietnamese. *See also* Cambodian Incursion; City, The.

Tobasco Sauce™   A staple of field grunts. Hot sauce was used extensively to add some flavor to the boringly bland C-Rations grunts were required to eat. The hot sauce also had a secondary benefit in that it seemed to make the high heat of the day a little more tolerable. After a meal of "Cs" liberally laced with Tobasco sauce, the heat of the day didn't seem nearly as uncomfortable as the overall burning sensation caused by the sauce. *See also* C-Rations.

TOC   *see*   Tactical Operations Center

TOE   *see*   Table of Organization and Equipment

Toe-Poppers (M-14 Antipersonnel Mine, Shoe Mine)   Small pressure detonated mines with the power to blow off a hand or part of a foot, used for booby traps. The Viet Cong used crude, but effective, homemade devices to booby-trap a wide variety of articles that might be handled or inspected by GIs. The use of such booby traps against the Viet Cong by Americans was not widespread. In areas that were not inhabited or frequently traveled by civilians, the M-14 Antipersonnel Mine was used by some USSF/LRRP troops. The pressure sensitive plastic mine was about 3 inches in diameter and 1 inch thick. Military gear that the enemy might attempt to recover was sometimes booby-trapped: items such as used radio batteries, C-Ration cans, packing material, empty ammo cans, etc. *See also* Booby Trap, M-16 Antipersonnel Mine.

Toi Com (Khong) Biet (No Biet, No Bit, No Bic, I Don't Understand)   Vietnamese for "I don't know." During the questioning of the Vietnamese "toi com (khong) biet" [toy kong b-et] was often heard in answer to the questions, "Are you VC?" "Where is the VC?" "How many VC?" or "You help VC?" It came to be that any American question the Vietnamese didn't want to answer they pretended they didn't understand: "no bic" as the GIs would say. This held true for friend and foe, laborer and hooker, officer or magistrate. "Khong biet" [kong b-et]: "I don't know," "Toi khong hieu" [toy kong hue]: "I do not understand." The Vietnamese's inscrutable

"grin" usually accompanied their response. *See also* Shit-Eatin'-Grin.

Toi Khong Hieu   *see*   Toi Com (Khong) Biet

TOI MAT   *see*   KIN

Toilet Paper   *see*   Shit Paper

Tokarev   *see*   Type 51 Pistol

Toke (Smoke)   Drag or inhale from a pipe or cigarette, particularly relating to the smoking of marijuana or opium.

Token Nigger (Tango November)   Slang for a sole black soldier in a previously all white group or organization, particularly the officer corps. In Vietnam, some field commands used "tokens" to avoid accusations of segregation by the media or higher command. Tokenism was not endemic to the military in Vietnam, but was seen across corporate America in the sixties as issues of racial equality surfaced, and the public image of many of America's private companies was dodging the "spotlight" of accusations of segregation and inequality. In some instances the "Tango November" used his position to further his own goals. In the eyes of those blacks not so fortunate the "token" was perceived as being an "Uncle Tom," or an "Oreo." *See also* Oreo.

Tom   *see*   LZ Tom, Oreo

Tomcat   *see*   F-14

Ton Son Nhut   *see*   Tan Son Nhut

Tong Le Chan   *see*   Tonle Chan

Tonkin (Bac-Ky, Bac-Bo)   Northernmost of the three subdivided regions of ancient Vietnam. It included the area north of the 20th Parallel to the Chinese border. To the Southern and Central districts, the inhabitants of the Tonkin area were known as Tonkinese. Hanoi was the major city and capital of Tonkin. Tonkin was known as "Bac-Ky" (Tonkin) and "Bac-Bo" (Northern Vietnam) by the Vietnamese. *See also* Cochin China, Annam.

Tonkin Gulf Incident (USS C. Turner Joy DD-951, USS Maddox DD-731)   Incident that took place August 2, 1964, in the Gulf of Tonkin, off the east coast of North Vietnam. The U.S. destroyer *Maddox* (DD-731) was on an intelligence gathering patrol in international waters in the Gulf of Tonkin when it was attacked by NVN torpedo boats. In the same general area on August 4, the U.S. destroyer *C. Turner Joy* (DD-951) reported being attacked by NVN torpedo boats, but there is some question as to whether the second attack actually took place. These two attacks were used by President Lyndon Johnson to request of Congress a resolution giving him the power to deal with NVN and any further attacks. *See also* **Southeast Asia Resolution, Ferret Operations, Operation Pierce Arrow.**

Tonkin Gulf Resolution *see* **Southeast Asia Resolution**

Tonkinese (North Vietnamese) The South Vietnamese name commonly used to refer to anyone from North Vietnam (Tonkin and its inhabitants). *See also* **Tonkin, Democratic Republic of Vietnam.**

Tonle Cham (Tong Le Chan) Small South Vietnamese outpost located 85kms north of Saigon and 47kms northeast of Tay Ninh City. The outpost was one of the very few areas along the border still controlled by South Vietnamese forces after '72. The outpost was completely surrounded by the NVA. In April '74 President Thieu secretly ordered the ARVN troops at the post to withdraw; he then publicly claimed that the NVA had flagrantly violated the terms of the '73 Paris Peace Accords. Thieu used the fall of Tonle Cham (Tong Le Chan) as a pretext to end bilateral talks between the GVN and the PRG regarding a coalition government. He also appealed to the U.S. Congress for their further support in the face of "continued communist aggression."

Tony-the-Tiger Patch *see* **Luc Luong Dac Biet**

Tool *see* **Penis**

Tooth-to-Tail Ratio Army reference to the number of near echelon troops required to support one combat soldier in the field. The tooth was the combat soldier, and the tail, the troops required to support him. In Vietnam the ratio varied from 1:5 to 1:8. At the end of WWII the Army's ratio was about 1:4. During '68 over 500,000 American military personnel were in Vietnam, and of that total, only 50–55,000 of those Americans were actual combat troops (grunts) operating in the field. *See also* **Ass-in-the-Grass-Test.**

Top *see* **Gunnery Sergeant**

Topographical Maps (Comics, Funny Papers) Multicolored American military maps of Vietnam which showed the terrain elevations, population centers, lines of transportation and other pertinent military data dealing with the terrain. GIs in the field referred to these maps as the "comics" or the "funny papers."

Topper, The *see* **Gunnery Sergeant**

Torching Pilot slang for an external fire fed by fuel sprayed from a ruptured fuel tank, usually the result of AA fire damage. The AA fire pierced the fuel tanks allowing the fuel to blow out, which was ignited by the AA tracer rounds. The jet was moving so fast that a trail of fire "torched" behind it. External fires allowed the pilot time to maneuver the aircraft into position for bailout, and the aircraft was flown until the fuel ran out. Fires which occurred within the engine compartment were considered internal fires and were much more critical, allowing only a matter of seconds before the aircraft exploded.

Torpedo Boat *see* **P-4 Torpedo Boat**

Torture, ARVN Methods Various methods of torture were used by the ARVNs to obtain information from captured NVA/ VC, VCI, and VCs. Torture was not limited to the ARVN; the ROKs were very effective at obtaining information, and on occasion U.S. interrogators tortured prisoners to obtain information. American methods typically involved physical beatings or the classic "interrogation-by-altitude." Most of the hard-core torture techniques were inflicted on the Vietnamese by their fellow Viets. Some of the methods used included stuffing a rag down the victim's throat and continuously soaking it with water (slow drowning); electrocution by cattle prod or hand cranked radio generator; dunking underwater until nearly drowned; skinning; beating the soles of the feet with split bamboo; staking to a post and putting a coating of honey on the body or the feet, causing black ants to swarm and bite; placing a nonpoisonous (yet very hostile) water snake in the victim's blouse or shirt; beatings and prolific verbal abuse; and the "Arabic method" of questioning. *See also* **Tiger Cage, Arabic Method.**

Torture, NVA Methods During captivity American POWs were repeatedly subjected to various types of torture. Some of the North Vietnamese techniques included sleep deprivation; solitary confinement (lasting years); being placed in blood circulation restrictive irons for long periods of time (weeks); starvation and thirst; beatings with rubber hoses, belts and bamboo; tying the body into various positions to cut off the circulation and nerves; breaking bones; opening lacerations to cause infection; withholding medical treatment for wounds and disease; electric shock treatments. *See also* **Torture, ARVN.**

TOT *see* **Time on Target**

Total Victory *see* **Cambodian Incursion, Operation Toan Thang**

Toumorong *see* **Operation Hawthorne I & II**

Tour of Duty *see* **Date Eligible to Return from Overseas Service**

Tour of Duty Phases The U.S. combat soldier typically went through three phases during his tour of duty in Vietnam, providing he survived the tour. Phase one: new troop in-country, basically afraid of everything: the unknown, the enemy's capabilities, his own limitations. Phase two: the troop has been in-country for a while; he has learned some of the tricks of survival; he has become confident, callous, perhaps even a little crazy in his personal disregard for the dangers of war. Phase three: the ultimate paranoia; he is "short"; he knows the enemy's capabilities, and the random factors controlling his life; he does all he can to insure he survives his tour, knowing full well his limitations and vulnerability.

Tourane *see* **Da Nang**

Tourniquet Besides the traditional medical usage of a tourniquet to reduce the blood flow to a bleeding wound, it was sometimes used by NVA/VC sappers to aid them during assaults. The sapper would tourniquet his arms and legs just prior to an attack on an enemy position. The tourniquet would allow the sapper to take several limb wounds and still continue to his target. The tourniquet limited some of the immediate blood loss caused by wounds; this combined with use of opium before the attack could give the sapper an extra edge in fulfilling his suicide mission. *See also* **Sapper.**

TOW *see* **M-151 TOW**

Towel, OD *see* **Lucky Towel**

Towel-Rack *see* **Pave Nail**

Tower Week *see* **Airborne Training**

TPQ Missions (Radar Controlled Bombing) Radar controlled bombing missions performed by Marine fighter-bombers. The aircraft flew to a predesignated point where they would be picked up by a groundbound guidance system. The system automatically directed the aircraft to the target and released the ordnance; the pilot would resume control of the craft after the bombs were released and return to base. If there was a malfunction the attack planes could be guided by voice from the ground, with the pilot taking manual control of the attack and releasing his ordnance on command from the ground station. *See also* **Combat Skyspot.**

TPQ-10 Portable radar system used by the Marines to direct and monitor aircraft. The system could be used to direct bombing runs or resupply deliveries under poor weather or low light conditions. Marine TPQs were operated by Air Support Radar Teams (ASRT). Maximum range of the TPQ-10 was 80kms, but typically the maximum effective range of the unit was closer to 30kms. The TPQ could be linked to equipment on board the aircraft; signals from the TPQ initiated the drop of the ordnance or supplies. *See also* **Combat Skyspot.**

TPS-25 *see* **Ground Radar**

TPS-33 *see* **Ground Radar**

TR-5 *see* **TR-20**

TR-20 (TR-5) Two-way AM voice radio that was widely distributed to GVN villages in South Vietnam. The radio had a 20-watt power output and was used to provide a communications link between the larger villages, district offices and the provincial capitals. The TR-5 was distributed at the hamlet level, under the responsibility of the hamlet chief. *See also* **U.S. Radios.**

Tra Khuc River *see* **Song Tra**

Tracer Round (Red Tracers, Green Tracers) A phosphorus tipped round that ignited when fired. The glowing trail left by machine gun tracer rounds indicated the direction and impact area of the fire. Many weapons had tracer rounds available to them, but they were primarily used by machine guns, with every fifth round on the belt a tracer round. While increasing accuracy against a target, they also indicated to the enemy the firing position of the gun. In Vietnam, U.S. tracer rounds were tipped with red, while NVA rounds were tipped with green phosphorus.

Trach Tube *see* **Tracheotomy**

Tracheotomy (Trach Tube, Endotracheal Tube) When the trachea, or windpipe, collapsed or was obstructed, death occurred due to suffocation. In basic training American soldiers were taught to perform emergency tracheotomies in the field. When a wounded solder experienced breathing difficulties the procedure was to cut a small slit in the throat (using a knife or the P-38 can opener), above the breast bone, piercing the trachea. A tube was then inserted (intubation) into the trachea to facilitate breathing. Any small hollow tubular device could be used: a ballpoint pen case, rolled plastic, anything that could keep the slit in the trachea open and allow air to enter the lungs. "Endotracheal tubes" were used at the hospitals and aid stations to accomplish intubation.

Track *see* **M-113**

Track Commander *see* **Tank Commander**

Tracked Cargo Carriers *see* **M-116, M-76, M-548, M-733**

Tractor Trailers *see* **M-123 Tractor**

Trader *see* **C-1 Trader**

Trail, The *see* **Ho Chi Minh Trail**

Trail Blazing *see* **Cut(ting) Trail**

Trail Formation *see* **On-Line**

Trail Marker *see* **Cairn**

Trail Watcher The NVA/VC had a system of trail watchers to monitor the areas they controlled and or operated in. The trail watchers were usually extremely well hidden and sat for hours watching various jungle trails that led to hidden NVA/VC base camps. Sometimes the watchers sniped at U.S. units as they moved through the area.

The sniping tended to slow the advance of the unit and the sniper fire alerted other watchers and NVA/VC units in the area. The VC also used farmers, children and peasants as watchers, tracking U.S. units as they operated; signaling the VC of the unit's approach or change in direction.

Trail Watcher Program *see* **Border Surveillance Program**

Trails and Road Interdiction, Multisensor Program *see* **TRIM Program**

Train Wrecks Slang used by some medical personnel in Vietnam to describe the severely wounded. Train wrecks were cases suffering from multiple injuries, requiring immediate surgery: head, chest, eye, face, stomach wounds and broken bones.

Trained Bears *see* **Weapons Systems Operator**

Training, Relations and Instruction Mission *see* **Advisory, Training and Operations Mission**

Tram, The Flat marsh and rice paddy area covering much of the IV Corps provinces of Kien Giang, An Giang and Chau Doc. The "Tram," as the Vietnamese called it, was part of a heavily used Viet Cong infiltration route. Supplies used to support the VC were moved by boat through the numerous canals and channels that crisscrossed the area. Enemy supplies originated from shipments received at the port of Sihanoukville, Cambodia, on the Gulf of Thailand. *See also* **Sihanoukville Trail.**

Tran Do Deputy commander of North Vietnamese Army and Viet Cong forces in South Vietnam. Tran Do planned and executed the communist Tet '68 Offensive. The offensive resulted in high casualties among the NVA/VC, especially the VC, and was considered a military defeat. But the offensive was seen as a political victory for the NVA/VC as it proved to be the turning point in U.S. public opinion against the war. *See also* **Tet Offensive.**

Tran Hung Dao *see* **Operation Tran Hung Dao**

Tran Hung Dao III *see* **Operation Sea Float**

Tran Hung Dao XI *see* Operation Tran Hung Dao XI

Tran Le Xuan *see* Madame Nhu

Tranh Grass *see* Elephant Grass

Transcolorado *see* Pioneer Commander

Transit Barracks Most large military bases had a separate barracks that provided temporary sleeping quarters for troops moving through their command. The barracks featured beds and bedding, and usually a wall or foot locker for personal storage. *See also* **Permanent Party, Holding Barracks.**

Trapezoid, The (Thanh Dien Forest) 1st Infantry Division nickname for the Thanh Dien Forest located about 50kms northwest of Saigon in Binh Duong Province, III Corps. The southern border of the forest was located along the Iron Triangle area and was a major NVA/VC base and infiltration route. The heavily forested area was situated south of Minh Thanh and the Michelin Plantation, between Dau Tieng and Lai Khe.

Trash (Fruit-Salad) GI slang for the assorted ribbons, badges, decorations, awards and patches worn on the military uniform. Fruit-salad usually applied to generals and senior NCOs who wore an abundance of decorations on their breasts.

Trash (Garbage) *see* **Burn-Bash-Bury (Garbage)**

Traumatic Amputation (Dismemberment) Term for bodily dismemberment; limbs blown or shot off.

Traversing and Elevating Tripod *see* **T and E Tripod**

TRC-90 *see* **AN/TRC-90**

Tread-Head (Tanker, Tank Crewman) GI nickname for the crewman of an armored vehicle.

Tree Crusher (LeTournear Tree Crusher, Triphibian Tree Crusher, Tactical Crusher) Three-wheeled tree demolition machine used by Army engineers in land clearing operations. The operations were designed to deny the enemy access and cover near U.S. base camps and along main roads and highways. Each of the three wheels was diesel powered and fitted with huge knife edges that cut the trees in the machine's path.

The cut trees were then crushed under the machine's 60-ton weight. A larger 100-ton version, called a "Tactical Crusher," was also used and was capable of operating in swamps and marshes. The machines were effective at land clearing but they broke down frequently, and their large size made them difficult to protect from the enemy when they were being repaired. The Rome Plow was more cost effective at stripping the jungle. *See also* **Rome Plow.**

Tree Line *see* **Wood Line**

Trench Foot *see* **Immersion Foot**

Tri Tam *see* **Dau Tieng**

Tri Ton Village in the center of the Seven Mountains area of the Delta. Tri Ton was located 47kms north of Rach Gia near the Cambodian border in western South Vietnam.

Tri-Thien Front North Vietnamese military zone. The zone consisted of the two northernmost provinces of South Vietnam, Quang Tri and Thua Thien. NVA/VC military units in the zone were under the direct control of North Vietnamese military officers. VC units in the other provinces of SVN were controlled by COSVN, while NVA units in the same provinces were indirectly controlled through COSVN. The NVA/VC '68 Tet Offensive greatly reduced the number of Viet Cong soldiers. After '68 NVA troops were used to fill the ranks of many VC units, which resulted in more direct control of the VC forces by the NVA military. *See also* COSVN.

Tri-Thien-Hue *see* **Military Regions, NVA/VC**

Triage (Receiving, Triaged-Out) Medical screening and prioritizing of incoming casualties. In Vietnam, triage was done by doctors and nurses in the "Receiving" area. Casualties were divided into one of three types: walking wounded, immediates, and expectants. Expectants were casualties so severely wounded that they weren't expected to survive, even with medical care; they were "triaged-out" to an area a discreet distance from the operating room to die. Immediates required immediate surgery or medical care, and time was critical to their survival. Walking wounded suffered non-life-threatening casualties and had to wait for medical attention. *See also* **Casualty Priorities.**

Triaged-Out *see* Triage

Triangulation *see* Marking Mission

TRICAP Division (Triple Capacity Division) After departing South Vietnam the 1st Cavalry Division was converted to a three element division consisting of infantry, helicopters, and armor. In Vietnam the division did not have organic armor units, but on occasion armored and mechanized units were temporarily attached to the division.

Trichinosis (Worms) Parasitic disease caused by the ingestion of nematode (round) worms. The worms lodged in the intestines or muscles and caused infection, diarrhea, nausea, fever, pain, stiffness, swelling and insomnia. The typical source of the worms was from infected, improperly cooked pork. Sometimes acoustically confused with trichomoniasis.

Trichomoniasis Parasitic infection affecting the reproductive and intestinal tract. The parasite caused troublesome symptoms such as itchy crotch, tiny bumps and blistering of the penis and general discomfort while urinating. The parasite could also lodge in the intestinal tract causing cramps and diarrhea. The parasite was transmitted through sexual intercourse or ingested in contaminated drinking water (drinking water improperly collected and treated in the field).

Tricky Dick *see* Nixon, President Richard M.

Trigger Time *see* Bush Time

TRIM *see* Advisory, Training and Operations Mission

TRIM Program (Trails and Road Interdiction, Multisensor Program) Late '67 through '68 program that incorporated various types of Air Force and Navy aircraft in road interdiction along the Ho Chi Minh Trail. Under the program electronic sensors were seeded along the trail and monitored. From information gathered, air strikes were called in. There were also flights by specially armed and equipped planes that flew the trail, day and night, seeking targets of opportunity, based on observation and information from the sensors. *See also* **F-4, VAH-21, OP-2E, Igloo White, Electronic Sensors, Black Crow.**

Trinitrotoluene *see* TNT

Trioxane *see* Fuel, Compressed, Trioxane

Trip Flare Small ground mounted flare. The flare was placed into the ground and a trip wire stretched from the safety pin on the flare across an area of approach. When the trip wire was pulled the flare ignited, giving off a bright shower of light that lasted for several minutes. Trip flares were used at night in ambushes and around the perimeter of a position as an early warning device. Trip flares were SOP for American infantry units operating in the field. *See also* **Flares.**

Trip Wire Wire or nylon string used to trip (activate or detonate) booby traps or mines. The Viet Cong used wire or nylon trip wires when available, or cloth string or vines.

Triphibian Division Name for a division that was to be formed in Vietnam consisting of one brigade of riverine infantry (three battalions), one brigade of mechanized infantry (two battalions) and one brigade of airmobile infantry (four battalions). The idea for this division came from U.S. Defense Secretary McNamara who was seeking the creation of a second airmobile division in Vietnam. The division never materialized. The 2d Brigade/9th Infantry Division did operate as riverine infantry in the Delta until July '70. *See also* **2d Brigade/9th Infantry Division, TF 117.**

Triphibian Tree Crusher *see* Tree Crusher

Triple Canopy *see* Canopy

Triple Capacity Division *see* TRICAP Division

Triple Ejector Rack (TER, Multiple Ejector Rack [MER]) Bomb ejector racks mounted on the pylons of attack aircraft. The TER rack supported three bombs and the MER (Multiple Ejector Rack) could support up to six 500-pound bombs.

Triple-A's *see* **Antiaircraft Artillery**

Tripoli *see* **USS Tripoli**

Tripping *see* **Get High**

Trippy Slang for someone who was functioning under the influence of drugs or experiencing hallucinations or an LSD induced "trip."

Trojan *see* T-28

Troop *see* Trooper, Cavalry Troop

Troop H/16th Cavalry *see* 1st Squadron/9th Cavalry (Aerial Recon)

Trooper Traditionally a cavalryman. In Vietnam, "trooper" was used in reference to any soldier in a cavalry unit, especially the 1st Cavalry. In general, throughout the Army, "troop" referred to a soldier. A "Cavalry Troop" was a maneuver element of a cavalry squadron. *See also* Cavalry Troop.

Troops in Contact (TIC, Engaged) Military designation for friendly "troops in contact" with enemy troops. Tango-India-Charlie, used in radio communications to notify headquarters of troops engaged with the enemy. *See also* Contact.

Tropic Lightning *see* 25th Infantry Division, Electric Strawberry

Tropic Moon III *see* B-57G

Tropical Boots *see* NVA Boots, Jungle Boots

Tropical Chocolate Bars (TCBs) Chocolate bars that came in the C-Ration Sundry Pack. The bars were made of light colored chocolate and had the taste and texture of chalk. The bars were designed for use in tropical climates and did not melt easily. To most GIs the chocolate bars tasted bad. Sometimes when the GIs threw the TCBs to the Vietnamese children whom they passed, the Viets threw the bars back at the GIs. *See also* SP Pack.

Tropical Hat *see* Jungle Hat

Tropical Impetico *see* Immersion Foot

Tropical Rucksack *see* Jungle Rucksack

Tropical Tree *see* Air Delivered Seismic Intrusion Device

Tropical Uniform *see* Jungle Utilities

Tropical Utilities *see* Jungle Utilities

Tropical Worsted Uniform *see* Army Tan Uniform

TROPO Radio *see* AN/TRC-90

Tropospheric Radio *see* AN/TRC-90

Trp *see* Cavalry Troop

TRS *see* Tactical Reconnaissance Squadron

Truc Giang *see* Ben Tre

Truce *see* Christmas Truce, Paris Accords

Truck Drivers *see* Wheel Jockeys

Truck Wash *see* Water-Point

Truck-Busting *see* Big Eagle, Steel Tiger, Tiger Hound

Trung Cong *see* People's Republic of China

Trung Lap One of South Vietnam's strategic hamlets located near Cu Chi in Hau Nghia Province, northwest of Saigon in III Corps.

Trung Luong Large village located just south of the DMZ near Highway 1. During Operation Beau Charger in May '67, U.S. Marine and ARVN units provided security for a GVN police force that evacuated the village of its 13,000 inhabitants, relocating them to a refugee camp near Cam Lo. *See also* Operation Beau Charger, Restructuring.

Trung-Bo *see* Annam

Trung-Si *see* Buck Sergeant

Trung-Si-Nhat *see* E-7

Trung-Ta *see* Lieutenant Colonel

Trung-Tuong *see* General Officers, Major General

Trung-Uy *see* First Lieutenant

Truong Cong Dinh *see* Operation Truong Cong Dinh

Truong Son Corridor Supply and infiltration route in South Vietnam that ran parallel to the north-south sections of the Ho Chi Minh Trail. *See also* Ho Chi Minh Trail.

Truth Team (Interdepartmental Speaking Team on Vietnam Policy) The "truth team," as labeled by *TIME* magazine, was a four-man team of government experts organized by the Johnson administration in '65. The goal of the team was to spread the "truth" about U.S. involvement in Vietnam by means of speaking engagements at various colleges, and teach-ins. The team represented an effort by the Johnson administration to attempt to overcome the objections to the Vietnam War held by the academic community. The team consisted of two members of the USAID and two Army officers familiar with the war.

TRW *see* **Tactical Reconnaissance Squadron**

TSFC *see* **Tactical Support Functional Components**

TSN *see* **Tan Son Nhut**

TSN Air Base *see* **Tan Son Nhut**

TT 33 Pistol *see* **Type 51 Pistol**

TU *see* **Task Force**

Tu Do Dan Chu (Freedom and Democracy) Vietnamese slogan meaning "Freedom and Democracy."

Tu Do Street (Duong Tu Do, Rue Catinat) One of Saigon's most colorful and animated streets during the height of the U.S. troop buildup in Vietnam. The street was located in the heart of downtown Saigon in the eastern section of the city near the river. On its northwestern end were the large Catholic cathedral and the hotels such as the Caravelle and the Continental Palace. At the southeastern end of the street, near the river, were a host of bars, whorehouses and opium dens. The street was called the Rue Catinat under the French, and renamed to Duong Tu Do (Liberty Street) after they left.

Tu Ve Viet Minh security forces in Hanoi after the close of WWII. The force was controlled by Nguyen Vo Giap, Ho Chi Minh's chief military tactician.

Tube Artillery (Field Artillery) "Tube artillery" was slang for mortars and artillery field guns; howitzers and cannons. "Tubes" generally referred to mortars but was often used in reference to artillery pieces. With the advent of helicopters "Aerial Rocket Artillery (ARA) was born. *See also* **Artillery, ARA.**

Tube Socks *see* **Elephant Intestines**

Tube Steak *see* **Penis**

Tubes *see* **Mortar, Howitzer, Tube Artillery**

Tuesday Lunch *see* **Rolling Thunder Coordinating Committee**

TUL1 LMG *see* **RPK LMG**

Tunnel Cache Detector *see* **Portable Differential Magnetometer**

Tunnel Exploration Kit (TEK) Experimental tunnel exploration kit developed by one of the Army's research facilities. The kit included a hat-mounted light which could be turned on by a switch the tunnel rat held in his mouth, a throat mike and earphone communications set, a .38cal revolver with silencer and attached aiming light. The kit proved to be inadequate for tunnel work. The revolver was too heavy and awkward with the light and silencer attached. The head light switch didn't work correctly and the earpiece of the communications set wouldn't stay in place. The kit was tested in Vietnam in August '66, and withdrawn shortly thereafter. *See also* **Limited War Laboratory.**

Tunnel Exploration Personnel *see* **Tunnel Rats**

Tunnel Explorer, Locator & Communications System (TELACS) Experimental communications system for use by tunnel rats during exploration of enemy tunnel systems in Vietnam. The system consisted of an earphone and throat mike for communications with the surface; there was also a tracking monitor that allowed the progress of the tunnel rats to be tracked from above ground. The communications system proved inadequate because of voice distortion and the large amount of wire that had to be dragged behind the explorer. The tracking system proved to be too slow and not always accurate. The system was tested in '69, and shortly withdrawn. *See also* **Limited War Laboratory.**

Tunnel Ferrets *see* **Tunnel Rats**

Tunnel Flusher *see* **Air Blowers**

Tunnel Rats (Tunnel Ferrets, Tunnel Runners, Tunnel Exploration Personnel) Nickname for U.S. and Allied soldiers who sought and fought the NVA/VC in underground tunnel systems. Tunnel rats were initially called "tunnel runners." Australian tunnel specialists were called "tunnel ferrets." In '65 the 1st and 25th Infantry divisions organized specialized teams to search and explore enemy tunnels encountered in the III Corps area. Tunnel rats were all volunteers and were usually armed only with a pistol or shotgun, knife and flashlight. The name "tunnel rat" came to apply to anyone who ventured into NVA/VC tunnels in search of the enemy; they were officially known as "Tunnel Exploration Personnel." *See also* **Tunnels of Cu Chi, Diehard Tunnel Rats, Tunnel Warfare.**

Tunnel Runners *see* **Tunnel Rats**

Tunnel School *see* **T M & B School**

Tunnel Warfare   The VC made extensive use of tunnels in SVN. The tunnels were used to house troops, for storage, hospitals, repair shops and headquarters. 200kms of tunnel systems were discovered in the Iron Triangle, north of Saigon. As the tunnels were discovered the job of searching them fell to a group of U.S. Army volunteers who called themselves Tunnel Rats; they became experts in the deadly art of searching and flushing the VC from tunnels. Many tunnels were damaged by demolitions and bombings, but the systems were never fully destroyed or uncovered. *See also* **Tunnel Rats, Air Blowers, Diehard Tunnel Rats, Carpet Bombing, Booby Traps.**

Tunnel Weapon (.44 Magnum, Segmented Round)   Experimental revolver used by U.S. troops exploring Viet Cong tunnel systems in '69. The 6-shot Smith & Wesson snubnosed .44 magnum handgun fired a special pellet round. Each round contained 15 small pellets. When fired the revolver was almost noiseless with very little smoke or muzzle flash. The pellets proved to lack stopping power and the weapon was seldom used by tunnel teams. A special "segmented" bullet was developed for the weapon, but after six months of service the weapon and the new round were withdrawn. The segmented round split into four pieces when fired and was especially lethal. The weapon was withdrawn because of possible violations of the Geneva Convention on allowable war weapons. *See also* **Limited War Laboratory.**

Tunnels, Mines and Booby Trap School *see* **T M & B School**

Tunnels of Cu Chi (Little IRT)   Interconnecting tunnel system located in the northern section of Hau Nghia Province and the southwestern section of Binh Duong Province in III Corps. The tunnels interconnected hamlets, villages and provinces in the area and were originally dug to support the Viet Minh guerrilla war against the French. There were over 200kms of underground tunnels in the area, reaching to less than 30kms from the outskirts of Saigon. Some GIs nicknamed the tunnels the "Little IRT" after the New York City Subway. The tunnel system was up to four levels deep in some locations, interconnected by a series of trap doors, channels, shafts, wells and communication tunnels. The tunnels were connected to nearly bombproof bunkers and ground level bunkers. The system featured various sized chambers that served as rest areas, hospitals, weapons and ammunition storage, kitchens, workshops, barracks rooms, communications equipment rooms and storage rooms of all types. Enemy dead were often buried in the system to keep U.S. forces from knowing the exact extent of VC casualties. Due to tactical conditions the dead sometimes didn't get buried before U.S. tunnel rats discovered them. Sometimes the VC would even hide GI bodies in the tunnels in an attempt to unnerve and demoralize U.S. troops. *See also* **Cu Chi, Tunnel Rats, Ho Bo Woods, Overbirth, Communication Tunnel, Dien Bien Phu Kitchen, Vets.**

Tuong *see* **Montagnards**

Tuong-Si (Officer, Tuong-Soai)   Tuong-Si was Vietnamese for "officer." "Tuong-Soai" meant general. *See also* **General Officers.**

Tuong-Soai *see* **Officer, General Officers**

Tuongs *see* **General Officers**

TurdSID   A small seismic intrusion device constructed in the shape of dog droppings. The TurdSID was one of the creations of the DCPG, and was designed to be dropped along the Ho Chi Minh Trail and used to monitor enemy movements along the trail. *See also* **Ground Seismic Intrusion Device.**

Turkestan (Cam Pha)   The *Turkestan* was a Soviet merchant ship unloading coal and supplies at the North Vietnamese port of Cam Pha about 60kms northeast of Haiphong. During June '67, American aircraft flying over the port were fired on by NVN AAA guns around the port. The aircraft returned fire, strafing NVN AAA gun positions around the port. The Soviet ship was hit by several rounds of 20mm cannon fire from the U.S. aircraft. The Soviets verbally complained, and U.S. aircrews were reminded that Cam Pha was off-limits, even if fire was received from the port. At that time, the port of Cam Pha was not on the "authorized" target list for American aircraft. It was not until much later in the war that Cam Pha became an "authorized" target. *See also* Haiphong.

Turkey Farm Nickname for a large LZ just east of Pleiku used by the 1st Cavalry Division during its '65 operations in the Ia Drang. The temporary pad was located between New Pleiku in the north and Camp Holloway in the south, and just east of Pleiku City. *See also* **New Pleiku, Pleiku, Camp Holloway, Ia Drang.**

Turn-On, Tune-In, and Drop-Out *see* **Leary, Timothy**

Turnage *see* **Dewey Canyon Fire Bases**

Turner Joy *see* **Tonkin Gulf Incident**

Turning back the tide... "Turning back the tide of communist aggression." Slogan which echoed the anticommunist sentiment of the Johnson administration.

Turtle Monument (Countries Aiding South Vietnam, Monument to the Countries Aiding SVN) Official list of nations providing aid to South Vietnam was inscribed on a monument, riding on the back of a large marble turtle in the square in Saigon. The list: Argentina, Australia, Austria, Belgium, Brazil, Canada, Republic of China, Costa Rica, Denmark, Ecuador, France, Federal Republic of Germany, Greece, Guatemala, Honduras, India, Iran, Ireland, Israel, Italy, Japan, Republic of Korea, Laos, Liberia, Luxembourg, Malaysia, Morocco, Netherlands, New Zealand, Norway, Pakistan, Philippines, Singapore, South Africa, Spain, Sweden, Thailand, Tunisia, Turkey, United Kingdom, Uruguay, Venezuela and the U.S.A. *See also* **Free World Military Forces.**

Turtles *see* **New Troop, Replacement Center**

Tuy Hoa Provincial capital of Phu Yen Province, II Corps. Tuy Hoa served as a major U.S. military base and was located on the coast, 120kms north of Cam Ranh Bay. It was headquarters for the USAF 31st Tactical Fighter Wing. Security for the installation was provided by the 28th Regiment/9th Infantry Division, ROK.

TVS-2 NOD *see* **Night Observation Devices, Starlight Scope**

TVS-4 NOD *see* **Night Observation Devices**

TW Uniform *see* **Army Tan Uniform**

Twat *see* **Vagina**

Twelve-Seven *see* **Type 54 HMG**

Twenty-Third Psalm *see* **23d Psalm**

Twinkles (Starlight Scope Operator) GI nickname for a starlight scope operator. *See also* **Starlight Scope.**

Twinks (Army Recruit) Slang for a new Army recruit, also called "boots" and "cruits." *See also* **New Troop.**

Two Shades of Soul *see* **173d Airborne Brigade**

Two-Digit Midget *see* **Short-Timer**

Two-Shop *see* **G-2**

Two-Twelve *see* **Section 212**

Type 24 MMG (M08, Maxim) WWI vintage Soviet made Maxim medium machine gun which was a modified version of the Germany-08 machine gun. The 7.62mm Maxim had an effective range of 1,100 meters, was belt fed, water cooled, could only fire on automatic and weighed over 54 pounds when loaded. It could be tripod mounted, but was usually mounted on a two wheel carriage. The PRC version of the gun was called the Type 24. The Type 24/Maxim was used by the NVA/VC against the French, and later against the Americans for ground support and as an antiaircraft weapon. *See also* **Medium Machine Gun.**

Type 31 Mortar (61s, 61mm Mortar, 61mm Tubes) Light mortar used by the NVA/VC. The Type 31 was a PRC copy of the American 60mm mortar, the M-19 (M-2). The Type 31 had a range of 1,500 meters and fired 61mm mortar rounds. The PRC mortar could fire American 60mm ammo and PRC 61mm ammunition. The Chinese 61mm mortar rounds were not interchangeable with the American 60mm tubes, and could not be fired in the American mortar. The Type 63 was an improved version of the 61mm mortar. It had an increased range and weighed only 27 pounds. *See also* **Type 63 Mortar.**

Type 36 RCL *see* **PRC RCL**

Type 50 SMG (PPSh41, Pistolet-Pulemyot Shpagina 1941, K-50M) 7.62mm blowback operated submachine gun used by the NVA/VC. The weapon had an effective range of 150 meters and used either a 71-round drum or 35-round box magazine. The Soviet version was called the PPSh41 (Pistolet-Pulemyot Shpagina 1941) and the PRC version was the Type 50. The NVA version, K-50M, modified the design, shortening the barrel and changing the stock. It weighed 7.5 pounds (unloaded), 1.1 pounds lighter than either the Soviet or PRC versions, and only used the 35-round magazine (banana clip). The Soviet and PRC versions featured a wooden stock while the NVA version had a collapsible wire butt. The K-50 was widely distributed to NVA/VC troops. *See also* **Submachine Gun.**

Type 51 Pistol (TT 33, Tokarev, Type 54) Soviet made TT 33 Tokarev, 7.62mm pistol used by the NVA. The PRC version of the pistol was called the Type 51. A second version of the Type 51 was produced, designated the Type 54. All three versions used an 8-round clip and featured a safety lever similar to the type used on the U.S. .45cal M-1911A1 pistol. *See also* **Type 59 Pistol, M-1911A1.**

Type 51 Rocket Launcher *see* **M-20 Rocket Launcher**

Type 52 RCL *see* **PRC RCL**

Type 53 Carbine *see* **Mosin-Nagant Rifle**

Type 53 HMG *see* **SG43 MMG**

Type 53 LMG *see* **RPD LMG**

Type 53 Mortar (82mm Mortar, 82 Mike Mike, 82s, M1937, M37) The M1937 or M37 was the standard Soviet medium, 82mm mortar. The mortar could fire its standard 82mm round or it could use American/NATO 81mm mortar rounds (81mm mortar tubes were not able to use the 82mm mortar round). The minimum range of the M37 was 100 meters; the maximum range was 3,000 meters. The mortar tube,

legs and base weighed about 115 pounds, each round weighing 6.5 pounds. The M37 was used by the Viet Minh and later the NVA/VC. A popular Viet Cong tactic was to quickly fire 3 to 5 rounds and then move the tube to a new position for firing, making it difficult to pinpoint the mortar's exact location. After dropping 15–30 rounds on a U.S. position the tube and crew would fade back into the jungle before American artillery could effectively be brought to bear. *See also* **M1 Mortar, M-29, Mortar.**

Type 54 HMG (DShK, Degtyaryov Shpagin 38, DShK38/46, .51cal, 12.7mm Machine Gun) The DShk, Soviet made, 12.7mm (.51cal) heavy machine gun. The gun weighed over 80 pounds when loaded and was usually mounted on a two-wheel carriage when used against ground targets. The antiaircraft version was mounted on a tall, three-legged stand. The weapon was belt fed and had a maximum effective range of 2,000 meters. The PRC version of the gun was called the Type 54. The NVA/VC used the gun in the ground support and AA roles, and it was very effective against helicopters. Also known to GIs as a "twelve-seven." *See also* **Heavy Machine Gun.**

Type 54 Pistol *see* **Type 51 Pistol**

Type 55 Mortar *see* **M38 Mortar**

Type 56 *see* **AK47**

Type 56 RCL *see* **PRC RCL**

Type 56 RPG *see* **Rocket-Propelled Grenade**

Type 56 SKS (SKS Carbine, Samozaryadnyi Karabin Simonova [SKS]) The Simonov SKS was a Soviet made 7.62mm semiautomatic rifle similar to the U.S. M-14 rifle. The Chinese copy of the SKS was the Type 56 SKS, which they called a carbine. The rifle weighed almost 9 pounds, was over 3 feet long, with a range of 450 meters and a 10-round, integral box magazine. Because of its size and weight the Type 56, or SKS as it was more commonly known, was not popular with NVA/VC troops although it was widely used. The SKS had a permanently attached bayonet which pivoted into position. *See also* **Lifer's Dream.**

Type 56-1 *see* **AK47**

Type 57 HMG *see* **SG43 MMG**

Type 58 LMG *see* **RPD LMG**

Type 59 Grenade (Stick Grenade, Pineapple Stick Grenade, Potato Masher, Chicom Hand Grenade)   PRC-made fragmentation grenade used by the NVA/VC. The Type 59 (Chicom hand grenade) was 8–16 inches long and 2–3 inches in diameter and weighed .5–1.5 pounds. The head of the grenade was either elongated like the U.S. MK2 grenade or cylindrical like the Soviet RG-42 grenade. The head was attached to a wooden handle 4–12 inches long. The stick grenade with the cylinder head was sometimes called a "potato masher," similar to the WWII German stick grenades. The serrated stick grenade was referred to as a "pineapple." The Chicom was known for its high dud rate. Along with the manufactured Chicom, the VC made their own potato masher grenades similar in design and operation to that of the Type 59. *See also* **Grenade.**

Type 59 Pistol (Makarov, 9mm Pistol, Pistolet Makarova)   The Soviet made Makarov 9mm pistol was used by NVA forces. The pistol featured an 8-shot magazine and was similar in appearance to the U.S. .45cal pistol. The PRC version of the pistol was called the Type 59. Pistols were generally only carried by NVA/VC officers or troops on special assignment. *See also* **Type 51 Pistol, M-1911A1, Browning 9mm.**

Type 62 Light Tank *see* **PT-76 Tank**

Type 63 Mortar   PRC 60mm mortar used by the NVA/VC. The mortar was an upgraded version of the PRC Type 31 Light Mortar. The Type 63 weighed 27 pounds, had a range of 1,800 meters, and was drop fired. The 60mm mortar was widely used by the Viet Cong. *See also* **Type 31 Mortar.**

Type 63 Rocket (107mm Rocket)   PRC made 107mm Multiple Rocket Launcher used by the NVA during the VNW. The Type 63 was a 12 tube system, spin stabilized, mounted on a two-wheel cart. A man portable version was used to allow the system to be packed to the field. A single round launcher version was also widely used by the NVA/VC.

Type 65 RCL *see* **B10/11 RCL, PRC RCL**

Type 69 RPG *see* **Rocket-Propelled Grenade**

Type 92/96/99 MG *see* **Japanese Machine Guns**

U

U Bon Royal Thai Air Base (8th Tactical Fighter Wing)   Thai air base used by the U.S. Air Force to launch missions throughout Southeast Asia. U Bon served as the home of the U.S. 8th Tactical Fighter Wing, nicknamed the "Wolfpack." In January '70 a small group of communist Thai guerrillas attacked the base with satchel charges. The attackers were killed or captured before they could damage any aircraft. U Bon was located 500kms east of Bangkok and less than 40kms west of the Laotian border. *See also* **Thai Air Bases.**

U Bon RTAB *see* **U Bon Royal Thai Air Base**

U Dorn Royal Thai Air Base (7/13th Air Force Headquarters, 432d Tactical Reconnaissance Wing)   Thailand air base used by U.S. Air Force to launch missions throughout Southeast Asia. Home of the 4th TFW and the 432d Tactical Reconnaissance Wing. U Dorn was one of several military bases leased to the U.S. by the Thai government. In July '68 communist sappers attacked the base with satchel charges, damaging several planes and killing two Americans. After the attack security at all Air Force installations in Thailand was tightened. The attack was supposedly carried out by a small group of Thai communist guerrillas. U Dorn was located 480kms northeast of Bangkok and less than 40kms south of the Laotian border. *See also* **Thai Air Bases.**

U Dorn RTAB *see* **U Dorn Royal Thai Air Base, Thai Air Bases**

U Minh Forest (Forest of Darkness)
VC base area located in a dense mangrove
swamp area, along the western coast of SVN
in An Xuyen and Kien Giang provinces, IV
Corps. Site of major American riverine operations in August '68 and most of '71. The
forest was nicknamed the "Forest of Darkness" by the Vietnamese.

**U Tapao Royal Thai Air Base (635th
Combat Support Group, 307th Strategic
Wing)**   Thailand Air Base leased by the
U.S. Air Force to conduct missions through-
out Southeast Asia. In April '67, B-52s de-
ployed to U Tapao and began conducting air
strikes against targets in Southeast Asia. U
Tapao served as home for the 635th Combat
Group and B-52s of the 307th Strategic
Wing. *See also* **Thai Air Bases.**

U's *see* LCU

**U-1A (Otter, 18th Transportation
Company)**   Canadian   made   utility
transport used by the Army in Vietnam. The
Otter, designated the U-1 by the Army, had
a max speed of 160mph and a range of
1,500kms. The U-1 had a large single engine
prop and could transport cargo or up to 11
passengers. The Otter was used for resupply
and liaison missions by the Army. The 18th
Aviation Company of U-1A Otters deployed
to SVN in February '62 and operated until
their withdrawal in April '71. *See also* **45th
Transportation Battalion.**

U-2   Air Force high altitude reconnaissance and surveillance aircraft manufactured
by Lockheed Aircraft. The U-2 entered service in '55. The single engine jet operated at
a max speed of 520mph and at an altitude
of 36,000 feet. During the Vietnam War
U-2s were used for weather recon, targeting,
and bomb damage assessments. Flights over
North Vietnam started as early as April '65.

U-6 (Beaver, L-20)   Canadian made,
single engine, prop aircraft used by the U.S.
Air Force and Army as a utility transport.
The small plane had a max speed of 140mph
and a range of 1,220kms. The U.S. designation for the plane was the U-6. The "Beaver"
saw service with the Army in Vietnam as a
small strip supply and liaison plane, capable
of transporting small loads of cargo or 5–7
passengers.

U-8 (Seminole, QU-22 Bonanzas)

Small twin engine utility transport used by
the Army and Air Force. The U-8 was manufactured by Beech Aircraft and could transport four passengers or light cargo, had a
max speed of 239mph and a range of
1,900kms. The Army U-8 Seminole was
used in Vietnam as a STOL courier aircraft.
The Air Force version was designated the
QU-22 Bonanza, and several were equipped
with special sensor monitoring and radio
relay equipment, and used to gather and
transmit surveillance/sensor information to
the Air Force intelligence center at Nakhon
Phanom RTAFB. *See also* **Infiltration
Surveillance Center, Igloo White.**

U-10 (Helio Courier, L-28)   Single engine, STOL prop aircraft used by the Army
and Air Force in Vietnam. The U-10 had excellent STOL qualities allowing it to land on
rough airstrips less than 65 meters long, and
take off in less than 110 meters. The U-10
could fly as slow as 30mph (necessary for
short landings), with a max speed of
167mph and a range of 984kms. The U-10
could transport small cargo loads or up to
four passengers. Prior to the widespread use
of helicopters in Vietnam, the U-10 was used
to resupply small remote Special Forces outposts and camps. Several of the U-10s were
in the Air American inventory, used to support COIN operations. *See also* **Air
America.**

U-17 (Skywagon)   Utility transport aircraft used by the Vietnamese Air Force. The
U-17 was manufactured by Cessna Aircraft
and was powered by a single prop engine.
The U-17 was called the Skywagon and had
a max speed of 178mph and could carry light
cargo or up to three passengers. U-17s were
used by VNAF mostly for liaison duties. The
Skywagon looked similar to the 0-1 Bird Dog
but had a slightly longer cockpit/passenger
compartment.

U-21 (Ute)   Light utility transport aircraft used by the Army in Vietnam. The
twin engine turbo-prop was manufactured
by Beech Aircraft, could carry up to 10 passengers or cargo and was fully instrument
equipped. Several of the U-21 Utes were
used by the Air Force as VIP transports.

U-Boats *see* LCU

U-Shaped Ambush   *see*   **A-Shaped
Ambush**

U.S. Agency for International Development (USAID, AID) Program established by executive presidential order in '61 to provide economic aid to developing Third World countries. The agency provided funding to developing countries to assist them with education, public health and agricultural expansion. AID also sent teams of workers to Third World countries to channel funding and help local populations with developmental problems. AID programs were designed to be nonpolitical, but in Vietnam they tended to support the U.S. and GVN anticommunist policy. In '73 before the fall of Saigon, AID organized Operation Babylift, the air evacuation of Amer-Asian orphans from SVN. *See also* **Operation Babylift, USOM, CORDS.**

U.S. Air Force Academy (Air Force Academy) Established in 1958, the Air Force Academy was located at Colorado Springs, Colorado. Graduates of the academy received a Bachelor of Science degree, a commission in the U.S. Air Force (2d lieutenant) and a four-year commitment to serve in the Air Force. The academy represented a prime source of career Air Force officers. *See also* **West Point, Annapolis.**

U.S. Air Rules of Engagement (Hostile Intent) During initial use of U.S. air power in Vietnam strict rules of engagement were defined. U.S. aircraft attacking targets in NVN were not allowed to hit population centers; only "military" trucks on roads could be fired on; unused bomb ordnance had to be dumped at sea or over uninhabited terrain and not on secondary enemy targets; prestrike air reconnaissance was not allowed and bomb damage assessment had to be carried out immediately after the attack by aircraft that accompanied the strike group. Aircraft were restricted to certain air corridors for attacks over Vietnam and once the enemy identified the corridors he moved large numbers of antiaircraft weapons to line the corridors. U.S. aircraft were not allowed to attack a 48km buffer strip located along the Chinese/NVN border. It was several years into the war before air attacks were allowed on NVN MiG airfields. During the period following the '68 bombing halt, U.S. aircraft were not allowed to fire on NVN AA positions unless the position had "hostile intent," which meant it had to fire first, before

it could be engaged by American planes. The NVN port of Cam Pha could only be attacked if no foreign ships were in port. These and many other restrictions placed on aircraft crews by politicians in Washington made conduct of the air war over Vietnam very difficult and much of the time wholly ineffective. *See also* **Rules of Engagement, Lavelle, Protective Reaction Strikes.**

U.S. Aircraft Losses An estimated 8,700 U.S. aircraft were lost in Southeast Asia between 1961 and 1975. Aircraft losses were sustained by all branches of the service and included in the total were aircraft lost by the CIA. The losses include both combat and noncombat aircraft. Army helicopters accounted for over 89 percent of the 4,900 choppers lost. Total fixed-wing losses were approximately 3,800 aircraft of which 58 percent, 22 percent, 11 percent and 7 percent belonged to the Air Force, Navy, Army, Marines, respectively.

U.S. Army Health Services Group, Vietnam *see* **44th Medical Brigade**

U.S. Army Hospital, Saigon *see* **3d Field Hospital**

U.S. Army Medical Command, Vietnam *see* **44th Medical Brigade**

U.S. Army Medical Motto *see* **Preserve the Fighting Strength**

U.S. Army Mortuary, Oakland *see* **Army Mortuary**

U.S. Army Nurse Corps (ANC, Nurse Corps, Army Nurse Corps, Combat Nurses) U.S. Army Nurse Corps provided nurses to all elements of the Medical Corps. Combat nurses served in field, surgical, and evacuation hospitals, in locations that sometimes came under enemy fire and ground attack. The Army estimates that 60 percent of its nurses who served in Vietnam had been in the Army less than a year. Second lieutenant was the starting rank for a nurse and nursing duty in Vietnam was a volunteer assignment. Estimates of the number of American women nurses who served in Vietnam range from 7,000 to 50,000. *See also* **Round Eyes.**

U.S. Army Pacific (USARPAC) Army command headquarters for units operating in the Pacific region. *See also* **CINCPAC.**

U.S. Army Rules of Engagement   The Army established a series of rules of engagement for their troops to follow in Vietnam. If hostile fire was taken from a village containing civilians, the unit taking the fire could not fire on the village, unless it was granted special permission by the province chief and the unit's higher headquarters. If the village was in a Free Fire Zone, hostile fire could be returned without special permission. Random artillery fires could only be directed into FFZs. Indigenous personnel encountered in an FFZ were considered to be enemy and could be freely fired upon. *See also* Rules of Engagement.

U.S. Army Security Agency Group, Vietnam   *see*   Army Security Agency

U.S. Army Soldiers   *see*   Ice Cream Soldiers

U.S. Army Special Forces (USASF)   *see*   Special Forces

U.S. Army Support Command Vietnam   *see*   U.S. Army Vietnam

U.S. Army Vietnam (USARV, USARV/MACV Support Command, U.S. Army Support Command Vietnam)   Army headquarters organized at Long Binh, III Corps, July '65, to control logistics support of U.S. units in SVN. U.S. Army troops were previously under the command of U.S. Army Support Command Vietnam. In '72 the headquarters was renamed USARV/MACV Support Command. This command was deactivated March '73 with the departure of the last U.S. combat troops from South Vietnam.

U.S. Defectors to the Viet Cong   *see*   Garwood, PFC Robert (Bobby)

U.S. Disciplinary Barracks   *see*   Fort Leavenworth

U.S. Draft   *see*   Draft, U.S.

U.S. Economic Mission   *see*   USECOM

U.S. Embassy, Saigon Bombing   *see*   First American Woman to Die...

U.S. Embassy, Tet '68   During the NVA/VC Tet '68 Offensive on January 31, elements of the C-10 Viet Cong Sapper Battalion attacked the U.S. Embassy compound in Saigon. The sappers broke into the compound killing several of the embassy security force, but they never were able to blast into the embassy building itself. Eight hours after the enemy assault had begun the compound was cleared. *See also* Tet Offensive '68.

U.S. Foreign Aid to North Vietnam   *see*   Reconstruction Aid

U.S. Fragmentation Grenades   *see*   U.S. Frags

U.S. Frags (Frags, Pepper Frags)   The U.S. and FWFs used a variety of fragmentation hand grenades during the Vietnam War. The two main types were the small, round grenades referred to as baseball grenades and the elongated or egg shaped pineapple grenades. The grenades were fitted with either delayed, instantaneous, or impact detonation fuses. The fragmentation grenade was nicknamed a "pepper frag" because of the manner in which the grenade "peppered" the target with deadly fragments. *See also* MK-2, M26A1/M57 Hand Grenade, M33/M59 Frag, MK3A2 Offensive Grenade.

U.S. Information Agency (USIA, U.S. Information Service [USIS])   U.S. government agency that disseminated official news, books, and information overseas about the U.S.A. The USIA had offices worldwide. During the Vietnam War the USIA directed anticommunist radio broadcasts to the Vietnamese and established pro–American libraries in several of Vietnam's larger cities. *See also* Joint U.S. Public Affairs Office.

U.S. Information Service   *see*   U.S. Information Agency

U.S. Marine Corps   *see*   Crotch, The

U.S. Marines (Marine Nicknames)   Nicknames for the Marines: Jarheads, Leathernecks, GI-rines, Gyrenes. *See also* U.S.M.C.

U.S. Military Academy   *see*   West Point Military Academy

U.S. Naval Academy (Naval Academy, Annapolis)   U.S. naval academy, located at Annapolis, Maryland, established in 1845. The academy awarded its graduates a Bachelor of Science degree, a commission in the U.S. Navy or Marine Corps (2d lieutenant) and a four-year commitment to continued military service. Annapolis was the prime source for career Navy and Marine officers. *See also* West Point, U.S. Air Force Academy.

U.S. Operations Mission (USOM) The USOM originally conducted the U.S. AID program in South Vietnam. Under the program South Vietnam was given technical help and economic support to make improvements within the country. *See also* U.S. Agency for International Development, CORDS.

U.S. Public Affairs Office *see* Joint U.S. Public Affairs Office

U.S. Radios The U.S. and its allies made wide use of radio equipment throughout the Vietnam War. Some of the radio sets used were TR-20, TR-5, AN/PRC-77, AN/PRC-64, AN/PRC-25, AN/PRC 524, AN/PRR-9, AN/PRT-4, AN/PRC-10, 32S-3, AN/PRC-41, AN/PRC-90, ARC/ RT-10, AN/URC-68, AN/TRC-90, AN/ ASC, AN/PRC-74, HT-1, Collins 32S-3. *See also* Bitch Box, Radios.

U.S. Saigon Military Mission *see* Saigon Military Mission

U.S. Special Forces *see* Special Forces

U.S. Support Activities Group (USSAG) U.S. headquarters established in January '73 at Nakhon Phanom, Thailand, to take control of U.S. air and naval forces still present in Southeast Asia. The group was colocated with 7th Air Force Headquarters that had been relocated from South Vietnam to Thailand.

U.S. Support Activities Group/7th Air Force *see* 7th Air Force

U.S. Troops in Vietnam An estimated 2.7 to 3.8 million American forces served in Vietnam between 1954 and 1975. Nearly 10 million personnel served in the military, worldwide, during the same period of time.

U.S.A. (The Big PX, The World, Zone of the Interior [ZI], Land of the Big PX, CONUS) References to home, the U.S.A. Generally any place except Vietnam. The Zone of the Interior, ZI, was the military designation for the Continental United States (CONUS). The Vietnamese called the U.S.A. "My Quoc." *See also* On-the-Block.

U.S.M.C. *see* United States Marine Corps

UAC *see* Fixed-Wing Utility Company

UCMJ *see* Uniform Code of Military Justice

UD *see* Undesirable Discharge

UDTs *see* Underwater Demolition Teams

UF-1 *see* HU-16

UH-1 (Iroquois, Huey, Choppers, HU-1A) Workhorse helicopter of the VNW. First deployed to Vietnam in '62, functioned as transport, gunship, weapons platform, assault ship and a full spectrum of other uses. Army helicopters were named after Indian tribes; the UH-1 was officially called the Iroquois, but most GIs referred to it as a chopper or "Huey" after the UH-1's original designation of HU-1A. The two most frequently encountered models were the UH-1C gunship (Huey Hog) and the UH-1D transport (Slick). Marine, Air Force and Navy versions of the helicopter used different designator numbers: -1E, -1F, -1H, etc. *See also* UH-1A, -1B, -1C, -1D, -1F, -1N, -1H, HH-1K.

UH-1A First in a series of Bell utility helicopters. The UH-1A Huey Iroquois became the first operational U.S. armed helicopter, deploying to Vietnam in '62. The chopper was originally designed as a utility transport that could accommodate 6 passengers or 2 litters. Some Hueys were used for medical evacuation of wounded; others were armed with .30cal machine guns and rockets and used as gunships. Due to the six-man troop limit, the -1A was limited in its effectiveness as a combat assault transport. The ship had a 44-foot rotor and a maximum speed of 120 knots (138mph). *See also* UH-1.

UH-1B (Huey Gunship, Huey Hog) An upgraded version of the Huey-1A. It had a greater range and more powerful engine and could accommodate 3 litters or 8 combat troops. Some ships were outfitted with rockets and machine guns allowing them to function as gunships. Because of the cabin size, gunship versions were unable to function as troop transports. Maximum speed on a fully armed gunship was about 80 knots

(92mph); an empty -1B transport had a maximum speed of 120 knots (138mph). The -1B gunship was originally nicknamed the "Cobra," but the name was later transferred to the AH-1 Cobra helicopter and the -1B was referred to as the "Huey Gunship" or "Huey Hog."

UH-1C (Hog, Huey Hog, Huey Gunship, Huey Cobra Gunship, Hog Flight) The -1C was an upgraded version of the -1B, with improved handling and increased payload. The -1C was used almost exclusively as a gunship and mounted a variety of weapons systems including 2.75-inch rockets, grenade launcher, miniguns, machine guns, guided missiles, 20mm/30mm/40mm cannons and TOW missiles. The -1C was the Army version; the Marines, Air Force and Navy versions were designated -1E, -1F, -1L. The -1B and -1C were sometimes called Huey Cobra Gunships. Flights of the Huey gunship were called Hog Flights and consisted of 2–3 Hogs. The -1C had a maximum speed of 140 knots and increased range over the -1B. *See also* **Heavy Hog.**

UH-1D (Slick, Stretch Huey) The -1D was a stretched version of the -1B, featuring an enlarged cargo area, larger engine and fuel capacity, and a 48-foot rotor. The -1D could carry 14 combat troops or 6 litters, although in Vietnam the normal load was much less (6–7 combat troops or 3–4 litters). It was armed with only door mounted machine guns. The -1D acquired the nickname "Slick" because it was not equipped with externally mounted weapons systems as were the gunships. The Slick was the prime assault helicopter of the Army, and the cavalry "horse" of the Air Cav. Heavily armed gunship versions of the -1D were used by the RAAF and VNAF. *See also* **UH-1H.**

UH-1E Marine Corps version of the UH-1B, featuring an aluminum airframe (-1B used magnesium) which was more resistive to the deterioration caused by salt air. The -1Es served as troop transports and gunships entering limited Marine service in Vietnam in May '65. The original -1Es were upgraded to the specifications of the -1C which included a more powerful engine and a larger fuel tank. The -1E as a gunship was armed with a variety of armament including chin mounted gun turrets, rocket pods, machine guns and grenade launchers. *See*

also **Gunship, HH-1N, TAT 101 Turret.**

UH-1F (H-48, UH-1P, Green Hornets) Air Force version of the UH-1B helicopter, designated the H-48. The -1F featured a more powerful engine, larger fuel tank and larger rotor than the -1B. The helicopter was primarily used as a personnel transport. Several of the -1Fs were assigned to the 606th Air Commando Squadron, operating from Thailand during the Vietnam War. Other -1Fs were assigned to the 20th Special Operations Squadron which operated with MACV-SOG units throughout Southeast Asia. The 20th SOS were known as the "Green Hornets" and also operated the -1P which was a gunship version of the -1F.

UH-1H The -1H Huey helicopter was a slightly modified version of the UH-1D featuring a later model engine (T-53-L-13) and a more crash resistant fuel tank. The -1H arrived in Vietnam for use by the Army in '67, with the -1D and -1H used extensively for transport. The HH-1H was the Air Force version of the UH-1H. *See also* **UH-1D.**

UH-1L (UH-1M) Navy version of the Marine Corps' UH-1B. Navy -1Ls in Vietnam were assigned to HAL-3 Seawolves operating with riverine forces in the Delta of IV Corps. The Seawolves had previously operated with borrowed Army UH-1B/C helicopters; some of these were eventually replaced with the -1L model. The -1M was the Navy's version of the UH-1C. *See also* **Seawolves.**

UH-1M *see* **UH-1L**

UH-1N (HH-1N, VH-1N) The -1N Huey was a twin engine version of the UH-1D/H helicopter. The most notable difference between the -1N and the -1D/H series helicopters was the -1N had a pointed nose while earlier UH-1s had a blunt, rounded nose. The twin engine Huey had more power, but the same cargo space limitations as the -1D/H models. The -1N entered service with the Air Force in '70 (as the HH-1N), and the Navy and Marine Corps a year later. Air Force -1Ns were used in SAR and transport duties, while the Marine -1Ns (VH-1N) were used for transport and VIP services. *See also* **UH-1E.**

UH-1P *see* **UH-1F**

UH-2 (Seasprite, K-20) The Seasprite, developed by Kaman Aerospace, was used by the Navy for search and rescue duties and antisubmarine warfare. During the Vietnam War the Seasprite, UH-2, was used on carriers and larger destroyers for SAR work. The UH-2 had a max speed of 165mph with a range of 680kms.

UH-19   *see*   **H-19**

UH-34   *see*   **CH-34**

UH-46   *see*   **CH-46**

Ultimate Weapon... (Portable Truth Detector [PTD])   In the fantasy world of the combat soldier many "ultimate weapons" to fight the war in Vietnam were conceived. Perhaps one of the most universally accepted weapons was the "PTD," the Portable Truth Detector. The PTD could be attached to the end of a rifle or machine gun or be mounted in the cockpit of a fighter-bomber or a helicopter; when aimed at the Vietnamese the PTD could instantly identify them as either "friend or foe." The DOD never solved the dilemma and for many GIs the problem of determining friend or foe was reduced to a simple axiom: "Kill them all, let God sort them out!"

Ultra Hog   *see*   **F-105**

UMP   *see*   **Universal Military Pod**

Un-Ass   Slang for disembark or unload, get off or out of, get away from or otherwise evacuate in a hasty manner. *See also* **Book.**

Unaccompanied Tour   *see*   **Accompanied Tour**

Unattended Ground Sensors (Sensor String)   Electronic Sensing equipment used by the U.S. in Vietnam. There were three main types of sensors: seismic, magnetic and audio. The sensors were implanted along trails and areas of suspected enemy activity in groups called "strings," and monitored remotely. Monitoring was done locally by units in the area while more remote sensor locations were monitored from the air. Seismic sensors responded to ground vibrations; the magnetic sensor could detect a mass of metal and the audio sensor was triggered by noise, enemy voices, etc. From information gathered from the sensors air or artillery strikes could be called in or ambush missions arranged. *See also* **P-SID, G-SID, MAGNA-SID, ACOU-SID, Electronic Sensors, Sensor String, Seismic Intrusion Devices.**

Unblouse   *see*   **Blouse**

Uncle Ho   *see*   **Ho Chi Minh**

Uncle Tom   *see*   **Oreo**

Unconventional Warfare   *see*   **Guerrilla War**

Underwater Demolition Teams (UDTs)   Special Navy underwater teams that performed a variety of services, including placement and disarming of underwater explosives, underwater ship patrolling, underwater beach reconnaissance (prior to Marine amphibious landings), and landing beach obstacle removal.

Underwear   *see*   **Skivvies**

Undesirable Discharge (UD)   A soldier charged with a court-martial offense could sometimes plea-bargain, taking an administratively issued Undesirable Discharge, and leaving military service. In Vietnam many UDs were issued to troops held for drug related crimes, disobedience, insubordination, disrespect, and a host of other minor offenses. Those with a UD were ineligible for VA benefits, and employers were very hesitant to hire anyone with "bad paper." Blacks made up nearly 60 percent of the stockade population in Vietnam and received a very large number of the 657,000 Less-Than-Honorable discharges issued to Vietnam era veterans. *See also* **Discharges, SPN Number, Bad Paper.**

Unification   *see*   **Cuu Nuoc & Thong Nhat**

Unified Command   The overall command of U.S. forces in Vietnam was under CINCPAC. Within the command was MACV, the responsible command for U.S. ground forces in Vietnam. Air Force and Naval operations in South Vietnam and against North Vietnam were under separate commanders who reported directly to CINCPAC; thus there was no one unified commander who was actually "in" Vietnam directing the war. Direction of the war was more by "committee" and required agreement to get anything accomplished. Command of South Vietnamese forces was also separate and not unified under the U.S. command, further creating difficulties in planning, coordination, and execution of a common goal. *See also* **Unity of Command.**

Uniform (Radio Frequency)   *see* **Radio Frequency**

Uniform Code of Military Justice (UCMJ)   Justice and legal system used in the U.S. Army.

Uniform Tango   *see*   **Oreo**

Uniforms   *see*   **Fatigues**

Union I & II   *see*   **Operation Union I & II**

Union of Soviet Socialist Republics (USSR, Soviet Union, Russia)   The USSR diplomatically recognized the rebel communist government of the SRV several days after the announcement of its formation by Ho Chi Minh in January '50, but did not provide any military or economic support to the Viet Minh. The USSR participated in the '54 Geneva Accords which resulted in the partitioning of NVN and SVN. As U.S. aid and support to South Vietnam began to increase in the late fifties, so began Soviet military and economic aid to North Vietnam. During the course of the war, NVN received military support from both Red China and the USSR, with the bulk of the aid coming from the USSR. Aid to NVN included weapons, supplies, and a small contingent of advisor/trainers for the more sophisticated equipment. In '65 the first SAM missiles from Russia were deployed to NVN. The U.S. perception of the Soviet-NVN relationship was that the USSR had control of, or was somehow behind, NVN's aggression in SVN. And through this relationship, the Johnson and Nixon administrations tried to get the USSR to put pressure on NVN to negotiate for peace. But NVN was fiercely independent, accepting aid from both the USSR and China, but controlled by neither. After the collapse of SVN in '75 the DRV granted the USSR use of Cam Ranh Bay for a naval base and the airfield at Da Nang for a Soviet air base. *See also* **Americans Without Dollars.**

Uniontown   *see*   **Operation Uniontown**

Unit One (Medical Kit, Aid Bag, First Aid Kit, B-1 Kit, M-5 Medical Kit)   Unit One (B-1) was the field medical kit carried by Navy corpsmen attached to Marine units. The Army version was called an Aid Bag (M-5 Kit). The contents of both kits were similar and included battle dressings, tourniquet, plastic trach-tube, surgical tub-

ing and tape, gauze, wire splints, compresses, needle and sutures, hemostats, scalpel, forceps, probes, tweezers, Band-Aids™, scissors, isopropyl alcohol, penicillin, Mercurochrome™, morphine syrettes, phosphorous burn powder, bug repellent, foot powder, blood-volume expander, heat-salt-malaria tablets, benzoin, cotton applicators, antiseptic soap, antibacterial ointment, Darvon and aspirin, peroxide, casualty tags, instruction booklet, and miscellaneous other items as needed by the medics.

Unit Rotation   *see*   **Rotate**

Unit That Never Was   Nickname for MACV-SOG units that conducted top-secret, cross-border operations. Because the SOG units were entering neutral or hostile territory outside of Vietnam the U.S. government would disavow any knowledge of such operations or the personnel that conducted them, should members of the SOG unit be captured or their bodies recovered by the enemy. The members of such operations were referred to as the "men who never were, members of the unit that never was." *See also* **Sanitized.**

Unit Training Assembly   *see*   **Annual Active Duty for Training**

United Hearts and Minds   *see*   **Dong Tam**

United Services Organization (USO, United States Overseas)   A private, nonprofit organization formed to support the members of the U.S. Armed Forces and their families. The USO assisted with the social welfare of military families and provided social clubs and facilities for American military personnel. The USO operated clubs and facilities worldwide, wherever U.S. servicemen were stationed. During the war in Vietnam there were more than twenty USO clubs which provided soldiers with such facilities as overseas phones, gift shops, recreational activities, hamburger and soda stands, and libraries. Volunteer personnel operated the USO, visited the wounded in hospitals, and made visits to base camps. The USO's motto was, "Your home away from home." USO was sometimes defined as the "U.S. Overseas."

United States Marine Corps (U.S.M.C.)   The first major Marine unit to arrive in

Vietnam was MMH Squadron 362 in April '62. The first ground combat Marines arrived in Vietnam in March '65. The last combat Marines pulled out of Vietnam in June '71. An estimated 14,700 Marines died in Vietnam, and over 51,000 Marines were wounded.

United States Overseas *see* **United Services Organization**

Unity of Command (Unified Command) One of the nine modern principles of war observed by the U.S. military. "Unity of command" stated that the authority and responsibility for the command of military forces must be under one unified commander with subordinate commands likewise under the command of a single individual, all the way down the chain of command. There was no FWF unity of command during the Vietnam War. ARVN forces were not under the direct control of the U.S. military commander in Vietnam. The war against NVA/VC was fought by separate factions that were not united in their purpose nor unified in their goals. *See also* **Principles of War, Unified Command.**

UNIVAC 1005 *see* **Cu Chi Computer Center**

Universal Military Pod (UMP, Cargo Pod, Detachable Cargo Pod) A cargo pod developed by Sikorsky Helicopter for the CH-54 Flying Crane. The pod measured 27 × 9 × 8 feet high, and could be outfitted with seats for troops, carry cargo or equipped for communications, command, or field surgical hospitals. The CH-54 came in two versions with a maximum lift capacity of 47,000 pounds. Both versions saw duty in the Vietnam War and moved a variety of cargo pods and retrieved damaged aircraft. *See also* **CH-54.**

Unload *see* **Un-Ass**

Unsats *see* **Recycle**

Unwilling, Led by the Unqualified... *see* **UUUU**

Up-Country *see* **Boonies**

Upper Delta *see* **Upper Mekong River**

Upper Delta RPG *see* **Game Warden River Groups**

Upper Mekong River (Song Tien Giang, Upper Delta River) The stretch of the Mekong River between the Cambodian border and Cho Moi was called the Song Tien Giang and was sometimes referred to as the "Upper Mekong" or "Upper Delta." *See also* **Mekong River, Game Warden River Groups.**

Uppers *see* **Dexamphetamines**

URC-10 *see* **Survival Radios**

URC-68 *see* **AN/URC-68**

URC-68 Radio Military radio carried by some USSF SOG team members.

Urgent Evac *see* **Medevac Priorities**

Urinal *see* **Piss-Tube**

US (Serial Number) (Regular Army [RA], Enlisted Reserve [ER]) On induction into the Army, new recruits were issued a serial number. For draftees, the number was preceded by "US." For those who enlisted in the Army, the serial number was preceded by "RA" for Regular Army. Those who enlisted in the Reserves had the prefix "ER." Army officer serial numbers were preceded by "O." Some field soldiers referred to this as their officer's IQ.

USAID *see* **U.S. Agency for International Development**

USARPAC *see* **U.S. Army Pacific**

USARV *see* **U.S. Army Vietnam**

USARV Cobra Transition School (Cobra Training School) The Cobra Training School was located at Vung Tau, 65kms southeast of Saigon. The school was operated to train Huey helicopter pilots to make the transition from flying the UH-1s to piloting the new AH-1 Cobra gunship.

USARV/MACV Support Command *see* **U.S. Army Vietnam**

USASA *see* **Army Security Agency**

USASAGV *see* **Army Security Agency**

USASF *see* **Special Forces**

USECOM (U.S. Economic Mission) Circa 1950s U.S. missions established in various foreign countries to administer and coordinate U.S. economic aid. The first U.S.

mission was established in South Vietnam in '50.

USIA *see* **U.S. Information Agency**

USIS *see* **U.S. Information Agency**

USNS Barrett Navy ship that transported the U.S. 9th Infantry Division support group to Vietnam in December '66.

USNS Corpus Christi Bay (USS Albemarle, Army Aircraft Carrier) Shortly after the 1st Cavalry Division deployed to Vietnam the Navy provided the Army with a ship that could be used as an offshore helicopter repair facility while the Cavalry was organizing at An Khe. The USS *Albemarle,* which had previously been used as a seaplane tender, was stationed in the bay at Qui Nhon ('66), 70kms from An Khe. The converted tender was used to provide repair facilities and support for Army choppers. It was nicknamed the "Army's Aircraft Carrier," but was officially renamed the USNS *Corpus Christi Bay.* She had a max speed of 19 knots, and operated with a 150-man Navy crew. A 300-man Army support crew operated aboard the ship.

USNS Darby (USNS Patch) Two Navy ships used to transport the 196 Light Infantry Brigade to Vietnam in July '66. The voyage took 30 days to complete.

USNS Greenville Victory U.S. Navy ship positioned off the coast of South Vietnam at Vung Tau at the end of April '75. The ship was part of the task force used for the evacuation of South Vietnam. *See also* **Operation Frequent Wind.**

USNS Patch *see* **USNS Darby**

USO *see* **United Services Organization**

USO, Viet Cong Version *see* **Cu Chi Music Ensemble**

USOM *see* **U.S. Operations Mission**

USS Albemarle *see* **USNS Corpus Christi Bay**

USS America (CVA-66) U.S. Navy aircraft carrier that operated off the coast of Vietnam, part of TF 77. The USS *America* was a Kitty Hawk class carrier. *See also* **USS Kitty Hawk, TF 77.**

USS Benewah *see* **APB**

USS Blueridge *see* **TF 76.8**

USS Bon Homme Richard (Bonnie Dick, CVA-31) U.S. attack aircraft carrier that operated off the coast of Vietnam. Nicknamed the "Bonnie Dick," CVA-31 operated as part of TF 77, conducting air operations against enemy targets in Vietnam. She was an Essex class attack carrier. *See also* **TF 77, USS Yorktown.**

USS Boxer (LPH-4) Navy escort carrier that deployed the helicopters and heavy vehicles of the 1st Cavalry Division to South Vietnam in October '65. The *Boxer* was part of a small group of ships that transported the Cav's equipment and the bulk of its troops. The division unloaded at Qui Nhon and moved west to its base camp located in the Central Highlands at An Khe. The *Boxer* was armed with several 5-inch guns and was capable of 33 knots. The normal ship's crew was 1,000 men, and she could transport 30 helicopters and 1,500 combat troops and their equipment. The *Boxer* was converted from an attack carrier (Essex class) to the LPH class in the early sixties. *See also* **1st Cavalry Division (Airmobile).**

USS Card *see* **MSTS Card**

USS Chicago (CG-11) In May '72 in response to the NVA invasion of South Vietnam, the U.S. Navy was allowed to attack NVN targets along North Vietnam's coast from the DMZ to Xuan Bo, 40kms up the coast. During operations in the area the USS *Chicago,* guided missile cruiser, was approached by an unidentified aircraft; when the aircraft continued to press towards the *Chicago* it was shot down by a Talos surface-to-air missile. The *Chicago* kill was the only SAM missile kill by U.S. forces in the entire Vietnam War. The *Chicago* was converted from a heavy cruiser to a guided missile cruiser in '64. She had a max speed of 33 knots and operated with a 1,000-man crew. *See also* **MiG.**

USS Colleton *see* **APB**

USS Constellation (Connie, CVA-64) U.S. aircraft carrier which operated off the coast of Vietnam, part of TF 77. The USS *Constellation* was a Kitty Hawk class carrier. *See also* **USS Kitty Hawk, TF 77.**

USS Coral Sea (CVA-43) Operated off the coast of Vietnam, part of TF 77 and also as part of Task Group 76.8, the evacuation of Saigon in April '75. The *Coral Sea* was a Midway class aircraft carrier. *See also* **USS Midway, TF 77.**

USS Denver (LPD-9)   U.S. Navy LPD assault ship used during the evacuation of Saigon in April '75. The LPD-9 was normally used for amphibious assaults, and carried helicopters and landing craft capable of supporting a 900-man Marine landing force. *See also* **Operation Frequent Wind, TG 76.8, Amphibious Transport Dock.**

USS Dubuque   *see*   **TF 76.8**

USS Durham   *see*   **TF 76.8**

USS Enterprise (Big E, CVAN-65) U.S. Navy aircraft carrier that conducted air operations off the coast of Vietnam, part of TF 77. The carrier also participated in Operation Frequent Wind as part of TF 76, the evacuation of Saigon in April '75. The *Enterprise* was a 4-shaft nuclear powered carrier with a speed of 30 knots, a typical aircraft load of 80 aircraft and 6 helicopters. In January '69 during maneuvers off the coast of Hawaii, an aircraft rocket accidentally discharged on the flight deck. The ensuing fire destroyed several aircraft and killed 28 crewmen. After eight months of repair the "Big E" deployed to the waters off Vietnam in October for air operations.

USS Forrestal (CVA-59)   U.S. aircraft carrier that operated off the coast of Vietnam, part of TF 77. The Forrestal class carrier was driven by a 4-shaft steam turbine with a speed of 33 knots and a typical load of 80 aircraft and 6 helicopters. In July '67, while preparing for flight operations, a Zuni rocket was accidentally fired from a parked aircraft causing fire and explosion of ordnance-loaded aircraft on the carrier's deck. 134 crewmen lost their lives and the carrier was out of action for seven months while repairs were made. *See also* **TF 77.**

USS Franklin D. Roosevelt (CVA-42) U.S. Navy aircraft carrier that operated off the coast of Vietnam, part of TF 77. The *Roosevelt* was a Midway class carrier. *See also* **USS Midway, TF 77.**

USS Hancock (CVA-19)   U.S. Navy aircraft carrier that operated off the coast of Vietnam as part of TF 77, conducting air operations against enemy targets in Vietnam. The *Hancock* was an Essex class attack carrier. *See also* **TF 77, USS Yorktown.**

USS Henrico   *see*   **TG 76.7**

USS Holt   *see*   **SS Mayaguez**

USS Hornet (CVS-12)   U.S. Navy aircraft carrier that conducted air operations off the coast of Vietnam, part of TF 77. The *Hornet* was an Essex class carrier normally fitted for antisubmarine warfare. During the Vietnam War her complement of attack aircraft was increased to allow her to support air operations against North Vietnam. *See also* **TF 77, USS Yorktown.**

USS Independence (CVA-62, Indy) U.S. aircraft carrier that conducted air operations against North Vietnam, part of TF 77. The "Indy" was a Forrestal class aircraft carrier. *See also* **USS Forrestal, TF 77.**

USS Intrepid (CVS-11, Fighting I) U.S. aircraft carrier which operated off the coast of Vietnam, part of TF 77. The *Intrepid* was nicknamed the "Fighting I," and was an Essex class antisubmarine warfare aircraft carrier. Her attack aircraft were used in support of air operations against North Vietnam. *See also* **TF 77, USS Yorktown.**

USS Iwo Jima   Helicopter aircraft carrier (amphibious assault ship) used by the Navy in support of Marine helicopter operations off the coast of South Vietnam. The Iwo Jima class assault ship usually carried 28 helicopters and was driven by a single shaft steam turbine, with a speed of 20 knots.

USS Kearsage (CVS-33)   U.S. Navy aircraft carrier that operated off the coast of Vietnam as part of TF 77. The *Kearsage* was an Essex class aircraft carrier normally fitted for antisubmarine warfare. During the Vietnam War her normal complement of attack aircraft was increased, allowing her to better support air operations against North Vietnam. *See also* **TF 77, USS Yorktown.**

USS Kitty Hawk (CVA-63)   U.S. aircraft carrier which operated off the coast of Vietnam, part of TF 77. The Kitty Hawk class carrier was powered by a 4-shaft steam turbine with a speed of 30 knots and an aircraft complement of 80 aircraft and 6 helicopters. *See also* **TF 77.**

USS Krishna   *see*   **An Thoi**

USS Maddox (DD-731)   On August 2, 1964, the U.S. Navy destroyer USS *Maddox* was attacked by NVN gunboats in the Gulf of Tonkin off the coast of NVN. The *Maddox* was in international waters on routine intelligence patrol. Two days later the *Maddox* and the USS *Turner Joy* were reportedly attacked again by NVN gunboats. The U.S. retaliated with air strikes against the NVN port city of Vinh, the first bombing of NVN by the U.S. *See also* **Tonkin Gulf Incident, Southeast Asia Resolution.**

USS Mercer *see* **APB**

USS Midway (CVA-41) U.S. aircraft carrier operated off the coast of Vietnam, part of TF 77. The Midway class carrier was steam turbine driven with 4 geared shafts and a speed of 32 knots. This class of carrier usually carried 65–70 aircraft. The *Midway* also participated in the evacuation of Phnom Penh and Saigon in '75 as part of TG 76.8. *See also* **TF 77, TG 76.8.**

USS Miller *see* **Pioneer Commander**

USS New Jersey (BB-62) U.S. battleship *New Jersey* arrived off the coast of Vietnam September '68. Under control of TF 70.8.9 she provided fire support to ground units operating along the coast for six months. The *New Jersey*'s 16-inch guns had a range of 38kms when firing a 1,900-pound shell. The *New Jersey* was an Iowa class battleship with nine 16-inch and twenty 5-inch guns, and a variety of antiaircraft guns. She could accommodate three observation helicopters, and her four engines could turn 33 knots. *See also* **TF 70.8.9, Operation Sea Dragon.**

USS Nueces (Nieces) *see* **APB**

USS Okinawa The helicopter carrier USS *Okinawa* operated as part of TF 76 in the South China Sea off the northern coast of South Vietnam. In early '75 it participated in the evacuation of Phnom Penh and Saigon as part of TF 76.8. *See also* **TF 76.8.**

USS Oriskany (CVA-34) 7th Fleet attack aircraft carrier. One of the Navy's carriers that operated off the coast of Vietnam during the war, part of Task Force 77. During the *Oriskany*'s tour on Yankee Station in October '66 a fire broke out in the ordnance storage area which resulted in the deaths of 44 Navy crewmen. The *Oriskany* was an Essex class carrier. *See also* **TF 77, USS Yorktown.**

USS Princeton (LPH-5) U.S. Navy amphibious assault carrier which deployed the first Marine aviation units to South Vietnam. The *Princeton* arrived off the coast of SVN near Soc Trang in April '62 and deposited Marine helicopter squadron HMM-362 which assisted the ARVN with combat transport and support. In March '65 the *Princeton* deployed Marine helicopters (HMM-162) to Da Nang in support of the 9th MEB, the first American ground combat troops to operate in Vietnam. The *Princeton*, LPH-5, was an amphibious assault ship, which was formerly an Essex class aircraft carrier, capable of 33 knots, with a ship's complement of 1,000 men. She supported a Marine Battalion Landing Team and their 25–28 helicopters. *See also* **Marine Medium Helicopter Squadron 362.**

USS Pueblo (Air National Guard [ANG]) U.S. Navy intelligence gathering ship captured by the North Koreans, off their coast, in the Sea of Japan in January '68. Because of the North Korean actions and the possibility of an increased conflict President Johnson mobilized a limited number of Air National Guard (ANG) squadrons. Four of the squadrons were deployed to Vietnam and two were deployed to South Korea. The four squadrons deployed to Vietnam in May '68 and were deactivated in '69; the ANG squadrons were 120th TFS from Colorado, 136th TFS from New York, 174th TFS from Iowa and the 188th TFS from New Mexico. During their tour in Vietnam the ANG squadrons participated in normal combat missions. *See also* **Reserves.**

USS Ranger (CVA-61) Operated off the coast of Vietnam, part of TF 77. The *Ranger* was a Forrestal class aircraft carrier. *See also* **USS Forrestal, TF 77.**

USS Repose *see* **Repose**

USS Saint Paul (CA-73) U.S. Navy heavy cruiser that provided long-range gun support to friendly ground units in South Vietnam. The *Saint Paul* operated with a 1,700-man crew, and was armed with nine 8-inch, ten 5-inch, and twelve 3-inch guns. She was not armed with antiaircraft missiles, but she was armed with several antiaircraft guns.

USS Sanctuary *see* **Sanctuary**

USS Saratoga (CVA-60) U.S. Navy aircraft carrier that conducted air operations off the coast of Vietnam, part of TF 77 in mid-'72. The USS *Saratoga* was a Forrestal class carrier and the Navy's only Atlantic Fleet aircraft carrier to see duty off the coast of Vietnam. *See also* **USS Forrestal, TF 77.**

USS Shangri-La (CVS-38) U.S. Navy attack aircraft carrier that operated off the coast of Vietnam as part of TF 77. The Shangri-La was an Essex class carrier. *See also* **TF 77, USS Yorktown.**

USS Ticonderoga (CVA-14, Tico) U.S. Navy aircraft carrier that conducted air operations off the coast of Vietnam, part of TF 77. Nicknamed the "Tico." The *Ticonderoga* provided air support to the destroyers *Maddox* and *Turner Joy* during the '64 Gulf of Tonkin incident. The *Tico* operated with TF 77 from '65 to '69 and in '73 was decommissioned and sold to brokers for scrap metal. *Tico* was an Essex class attack carrier. *See also* **TF 77.**

USS Tripoli (LPH-10) Navy amphibious assault carrier, used by the Marines, off the I Corps coast of South Vietnam. The Iwo Jima class helicopter carrier was operated by a crew of 528 men, and could transport and deploy a Marine Battalion Landing Team of over 2,000 men and their equipment. The *Tripoli* carried a squadron of 22–25 helicopters to accomplish her assault support mission. Maximum speed of the LPH-10 was about 20 knots.

USS Turner Joy *see* **Tonkin Gulf Incident**

USS Union *see* **TG 76.7**

USS Valley Forge (LPH-8) Navy amphibious assault ship. The LPH class ship transported Marines and their assault helicopters. The *Valley Forge* could transport up to 28 helicopters and nearly 2,100 combat troops at a max speed of 33 knots. The 600-foot-long helicopter carrier was armed with defensive SAMs and had the appearance of a small aircraft carrier. The LPH-8 was actually a converted Essex class aircraft carrier, and operated with a 1,000-man crew.

USS Vancouver *see* **TG 76.7**

USS Wilson *see* **SS Mayaguez**

USS Yorktown (CVS-10) U.S. Navy aircraft carrier that conducted limited air operations off the coast of Vietnam. The *Yorktown* was primarily an antisubmarine warfare ship, but her aircraft did participate

in the air operations of TF 77. The *Yorktown* was an Essex class (CVS) aircraft carrier capable of 33 knots, and operated by a 2,000-man crew. The Essex class carriers were primarily used for fleet antisubmarine support duties, and usually deployed squadrons and detachments of antisubmarine helicopters, surveillance and tracking aircraft, and a small detachment of attack planes (several A-4s). CVS class carriers used in Vietnam operated in the attack mode and deployed several squadrons of A-4s and F-8s in place of the surveillance squadrons. *See also* **TF 77.**

USSAG *see* **U.S. Support Activities Group**

USSAG/7AF *see* **7th Air Force**

USSF *see* **Special Forces**

USSF LRRPs *see* **Greek Operations, Detachments B-50, 52, 56, 57**

USSR *see* **Union of Soviet Socialist Republics**

UTA *see* **Annual Active Duty for Training**

Utah *see* **Operation Utah**

Utah Mesa *see* **Operation Utah Mesa**

Utah/Lien Ket 26 *see* **Operation Utah/Lien Ket 26**

Ute *see* **U-21**

Utilities *see* **Fatigues**

Utility Airplane Company *see* **Fixed-Wing Utility Company**

Utility Cap *see* **Baseball Cap**

Utility Fatigues *see* **Fatigues**

Utility Tactical Transport Company (UTTCO, Utility Transport Helicopter Company [UTTHCO], UTT Avn) In July '62, UH-1A helicopters of the U.S. Army's 53d Aviation Detachment deployed to Vietnam as UTTHCO (UTT Avn) to test armed helicopters in support of ARVN airmobile operations. UH-1As were field fitted with 2.75-inch rockets and .30cal machine guns. The armed helicopter proved suitable for combat and the Army ordered more choppers to support ARVN ground operations. UTTCO was later equipped with UH-1Bs which had more powerful engines and were armed with rockets, XM-6 Flex guns, and M-60 door mounted machine guns. UTTCO was also known as UTTHCO before the company started operating the gunships. In August '64 UTTCO became the 68th Aviation Company. *See also* **Gunship, UH-1, XM-6 Machine Gun.**

Utility Transport Helicopter Company *see* **Utility Tactical Transport Company**

UTT Avn *see* **Utility Tactical Transport Company**

UTTCO *see* **Utility Tactical Transport Company**

UTTHCO *see* **Utility Tactical**

Transport Company

UUUU (Unwilling, Led by the Unqualified, Doing the Unnecessary. . .) Abbreviation for a well circulated slogan among U.S. troops in SVN, "The Unwilling, led by the Unqualified, doing the Unnecessary, for the Ungrateful." The word order was sometimes switched around, but the meaning was the same: troops not overly enthusiastic to be in Vietnam believed they were being led by hastily trained, inexperienced officers and NCOs performing ineffective and unnecessary tasks for the South Vietnamese people who didn't support the war or want the Americans in their country.

V

V, The *see* **V-100**

V-100 Armored Car (Commando, XM-706, The Duck, The V) Armored car manufactured by Cadillac-Gage as the V-100, and introduced into Vietnam as the XM-706 Commando. The Army version of the four-wheel drive armored car was later designated the M-706. The V-100 was used for convoy duty and base defense by Army MP units and Air Force base security units. Over 100 of the cars were part of the ARVN inventory and were used for security. The M-706 had a road speed of over 60mph, and was available in turret and opened top models. The car was nicknamed the "Duck" or the "V," and was usually armed with two or three machine guns. In '67 the V-100 replaced the M-8 Armored Car in ARVN units. *See also* **Armored Cars.**

V.D. *see* **Venereal Diseases**

V/STOL *see* **Vertical Takeoff and Landing Aircraft**

VA *see* **Green Machine**

VAC *see* **Vietnam Action Committee**

Vac Cans *see* **Mermite Cans**

Vagina (Pussy, Box, Runways, Snatch, Twat, Poontang, Split) GI slang references to the female pubic area were many, some of which included snatch, box, runways, twat, poontang and pussy. A popular pilots' joke referred to women by the direction of the slit in the pubic area, their "runways." If the runway ran north-south, she was non–Asian, for Asian runways reportedly ran east-west; this was associated with the slope of their eyes.

VAH-21 (AP-2H, Neptune Gunships, AN/APQ-92) In '67 the U.S. Navy equipped four P-2 Neptunes as gunships and designated them the AP-2H. The gunships were fitted with 20mm cannons, miniguns and a grenade launcher. The aircraft was also equipped with various types of NOD systems, navigational and detection radar (AN/APQ-92). The squadron was redesignated VAH-21 in '68 and operated until mid-'69. VAH-21 primarily operated at night seeking out enemy river traffic in support of TF 116 operations. The gunships were also fitted with general purpose and incendiary bombs. Part of the aircraft's detection equipment included night sniper scopes and the Black Crow Detector. The squadron was disbanded in mid-'69. *See also* **P-2, OP-2E, TRIM Program, Black Crow.**

VAL-4 *see* **Light Attack Squadron 4**

Valorous Unit Award A U.S. Army award, bestowed upon an entire unit for extraordinary heroism in action against the enemy. The unit award was equivalent to the Silver Star, awarded for individual acts of valor.

Valpak *see* **B-4 Bag**

Vam Co Dong River *see* **Song Vam Co Dong**

Van de Geer, 2 Lt. Richard (Last American to Die in the Vietnam War...) Second Lt. Richard Van de Geer is officially listed by the DOD as the last American to die "in the Vietnam War," killed May 15, 1975. He was a helicopter pilot of the Air Force's 21st Special Operations Squadron, Nahom Phnom, Thailand. His helicopter was destroyed by enemy fire as he was approaching Kaoh Tang Island, Cambodia, as part of the U.S. force attempting to rescue the crew of the S.S. *Mayaguez,* which was seized by the Khmer Rouge off the coast of Cambodia in '75. Officially, the last Americans to die in Vietnam were two Marine guards at Tan Son Nhut during the evacuation of Saigon, and two Marine helicopter pilots killed at the end of the evacuation operation. *See also* **Operation Frequent Wind, Last American to Die....**

Van Dien (Little Detroit) Village located south of Hanoi, NVN, that was nicknamed "Little Detroit" by U.S. pilots because it served as a major enemy truck repair and staging area. Van Dien was often targeted for U.S. air strikes during the air war. Van Dien also had a large cemetery where some U.S. POWs who had died in captivity were buried.

Van Tien Dung, General Assumed the planning and direction of the NVA from General Giap at the end of '72. General Dung planned the Final Offensive of '75 and commanded the NVA to its victory which resulted in the collapse of South Vietnam to the communists, April 30, 1975.

Van Tuong *see* **Operation Starlite**

Vanderdrift *see* **FSB Vanderdrift**

Vang Pao *see* **Meo**

Vann, John Paul Served in the Army as an advisor to the Vietnamese in '61–'62. Vann was an ardent anticommunist and had strong views on how the war should have been waged in Vietnam. Vann repeatedly raised questions of the ARVN's combat deficiencies, and the seeming ignorance of the U.S. government about the political situation in Vietnam. Vann accused the U.S. government of covering up the ARVN's dismal combat record, and tried to enlighten Washington of the Diem regime's false statistics on the pacification programs and Saigon's exaggerated claims of the territories it controlled. Vann repeatedly tried to make his voice heard through the Army chain of command and protocol channels, but he was largely ignored, even though he had an excellent record reflecting his duty in Vietnam. Vann resigned from the Army in '63, and returned to Vietnam as a civilian working for the USAID mission. Vann attempted to make the pacification program work in Vietnam, believing that the key to defeating the communists was with the Vietnamese people. Under CORDS, Vann became the director of the Second Regional Assistance Command (SRAC), in '71, with responsibility for all CORDS operations in II Corps. John Paul Vann was killed in June '72 during a low level night flight between Pleiku and Kontum. Vann's helicopter plowed into a clump of trees along Highway 14 when the pilot became disoriented during bad weather. Vann's methods of dealing with the communists were largely effective, and communist radio hailed his death as a major setback for U.S. efforts in Vietnam.

Variable Time Fuse *see* **VT Round**

Varmint Rifle *see* **M-40 Rifle**

VARS *see* **Visual Aerial Reconnaissance and Surveillance**

VATS *see* **Civic Action Teams**

VC *see* **Enemy, The**

VC Cell *see* **Viet Cong Cell**

VC Claymore (C-40 Claymore, DH-5/ DH-10 Claymores) Locally fabricated VC claymore mines made from captured American military equipment. These homemade mines usually had a much greater kill range than their American equivalents. The VC, DH-5 and DH-10 directional claymores were dish shaped and weighed 5 kilos (11 pounds) and 10 kilos (22 pounds) each, and contained several hundred steel pellets and rocks that were blasted forward by several pounds of TNT. The VC claymores were pressure or command detonated and were bipod mounted or sometimes buried. The VC also used a PRC copy of the U.S. M-18 Claymore, designated the C-40. It functioned the same as the M-18, but contained more explosive and pellets. *See also* **M-18 Claymore; Booby Trap; Gravel Mine, U.S.; Gravel Mine, Viet Cong.**

VC Draft   As the war continued it became difficult for the VCI to interest the populace into volunteering support for the communist war effort. To compensate for this, the VC began drafting villagers into service. Services included ammo bearing, fortification construction, food collection and the use of villagers for the sexual releases of NVA/VC troops. A combination of fear and violence was used to keep control. Village males were often drafted into combat forces, threats on their families used to insure their cooperation. VC draft age was 12 years and up.

VC Hand Grenade   *see*   **C-Rat Grenade**

VC Song and Dance Teams   *see* **Cadre**

VCC   *see*   **Viet Cong Suspect**

VCI   *see*   **Viet Cong Infrastructure**

VCS   *see*   **Viet Cong Suspect**

VD   *see*   **Venereal Diseases**

VDC   *see*   **Vietnam Day Committee**

VDGI   *see*   **Department of Information**

Veenaf   *see*   **Republic of Vietnam Air Force**

Veghel   *see*   **FSB Veghel**

Vehicle, Tracked Retriever (VTR)   *see* **M-88, M-578**

Venereal Diseases (V.D., Clap, Gonorrhea, Syphilis, Chancroid)   Group of sexually transmitted diseases, referred to as the "syph" and "clap." In Vietnam a number of factors contributed to high rates of V.D. throughout the Vietnamese civilian population and the U.S. military. Hygiene habits, lack of adequate medical care and screening, nontreatment and a lack of responsiveness by the military to the problem of V.D. contributed to the wide spread of the disease.

Some military units unofficially established and monitored their own whorehouses for use by their troops in an effort to reduce the spread of the disease. The women in the houses were checked by military doctors on a regular basis and not allowed to work if they were sick. This worked on a small scale but the problem was much too large for such measures. There were various strains of venereal diseases in-country, some of which were highly resistant to normal penicillin treatments, and nicknamed the "Black Syph." In an effort to keep the Asian strains of V.D. from returning to the U.S. with infected soldiers, all soldiers scheduled to rotate out of SVN were required to pass a V.D. test before they would be allowed to leave Vietnam. If they did not pass they received treatment and stayed in Vietnam until they could pass the test. In addition to the threat of V.D., whoring in Vietnam could also lead to tuberculosis and "crabs," a form of mobile (animated) crotch rot. *See also* Syphilis, Trichomoniasis, Tetracycline, Cock-Rot, PCOD.

Venetian Blind Armor   *see*   **RPG Screen**

Venice of the East   *see*   **Bangkok**

Vertical Assault   *see*   **Combat Assault**

Vertical Butt Stroke (Butt Stroke) One of the classic rifle/bayonet moves taught to Army and Marine recruits in basic training. The move involved holding the rifle at a modified "port arms," with the bayonet end of the rifle pointed skyward; the butt end of the rifle was quickly swung upward, pivoting in the left hand, the butt end of the rifle guided by the right hand. The object of the move was to strike the enemy soldier under the chin with an upward motion of the rifle butt. Or as the DIs said, "To knock Charlie's fuckin' head off."

Vertical Envelopment (Encircle)   Military terminology for "surrounding the enemy," using troops parachuted or helicoptered into position, to completely encircle the enemy. *See also* **Combat Assault.**

Vertical Takeoff and Landing Aircraft (VTOL, V/STOL)   Fixed-wing aircraft capable of lifting straight up, off the ground, without the necessity of the traditional rolling takeoff. The aircraft was viewed as a cross between a helicopter and a fixed-wing aircraft. The Marine Corps saw the need for such an aircraft and ordered several from the British, who were successfully operating the Hawker Harrier VTOL. The Harrier VTOLs were delivered to the Marines and designated the AV-8A but they did not see combat duty in Vietnam. The carrier-based AV-8A had a max speed of 700mph, a range of 3,700kms, was armed with two 30mm cannons and could deliver up to 5,000 pounds of ordnance. VTOL aircraft were sometimes referred to as V/STOL (Vertical/Short Takeoff and Landing) aircraft.

Very Small *see* **Ti Ti**

Veterans Administration *see* **Green Machine**

Vets (Chiggers, Mites) One of many parasites that infected the inhabitants and visitors to Southeast Asia. The tiny parasitic larvae lodged beneath the skin, feeding on the flesh, causing intense itching and inflammation. Typical treatment was to remove the chiggers ("vets," to the Vietnamese) by pulling them out from under the skin with tweezers or a needle. The mites thrived in dark, damp places and were rampant in the Viet Cong's tunnel and bunker systems. *See also* **Tunnels of Cu Chi, Gook Sores.**

VH-1N *see* **UH-1N**

VHF Omnidirectional Range Navigation System *see* **TACAN**

Vi Thanh *see* **Duc Long, Chuong Thien**

Vice Admiral *see* **Admiral**

Vicki *see* **LZ Vicki**

Victor Charlie *see* **Enemy, The**

Victor Tango Round *see* **VT Round**

Victory Medals, Viet Cong Victory medals were awarded by the NLF to Viet Cong who performed heroic actions under fire. There were three classes of the award: Class I, II and III. The Victory medal was also awarded to a VC soldier on the basis of the number of Americans killed. For three "confirmed" enemy kills a Class I Victory medal was awarded; six enemy killed rated a Class II and nine Americans killed by one soldier rated a Class III award. *See also* **Body Count.**

Victory/Victory 12 *see* **FSB Victory**

Viet Cong (Viet Nam Cong San) A derogatory name (contraction) for the Vietnamese Communists in SVN (Viet Nam Cong San), a name supposedly originated by President Diem in '58. The Viet Cong, who called themselves the "Bung," became the combat arm of the NLF (National Liberation Front). The NLF was organized in SVN to oppose the GVN and "free the oppressed peoples" of the South and reunify North and South Vietnam. In '59 the VC began guerrilla war against the GVN, and in '64 NVN began sending "volunteers" to SVN to aid the VC in their struggle. As the war expanded NVN increased its support to the VC in the form of materiel and combat soldiers. After '68, vacant troop positions in VC units were filled by NVA soldiers as VC casualties increased, and popular support for the VC among the South Vietnamese decreased. Initially the VC consisted of volunteers, fighting the GVN part-time: farmer or a laborer by day, guerrilla fighter by night. The VC were organized into local cells, main force units, and the VCI. Local cells were the part-timers operating locally and at the province level. Main force VC were full-time guerrillas operating out of fixed mountain or jungle bases. The VCI was the infrastructure responsible for recruitment, tax collecting, propaganda, etc. The VC waged guerrilla war against the GVN; the NVA war effort was more conventional. The VC operated independently of the NVA, but provided the NVA with local scouts and information. During the all-out Communist offensive of Tet '68, the VC were destroyed as an independent, viable force. In '69 the NLF became the PRG. With the fall of Saigon in '75, the PRG was stripped of its power by NVN, and rule of all Vietnam came directly from Hanoi. *See also* **National Liberation Front; Viet Cong Infrastructure; South Vietnamese Liberation Army; Enemy, The.**

Viet Cong Cadre Girl *see* **Phu Nu Can Bo**

Viet Cong Cell (VC Cell) The basic unit of organization of the Viet Cong was the "cell." Each cell consisted of three members. Each member kept an eye on his other cell members to insure they followed the straight and narrow path set by the Viet

Cong cadre. The individual cells operated in their local villages, joining to form squads and platoons for offensive operations.

Viet Cong Coffins *see* **Coffins, Viet Cong**

Viet Cong Flag *see* **Flags...**

Viet Cong Infrastructure (VCI, People's Revolutionary Party [PRP]) The VCI was the political arm of the South Vietnamese Communist Party (PRP) and was responsible for such activities as tax collecting, recruitment, propaganda, indoctrination, social programs and, in general, the noncombative functions of the war against the GVN; sometimes called the Viet Cong Cadre. The upper levels of the VCI were referred to as the "People's Revolutionary Party" (PRP), which was established in '62 as the southern arm of the Lao Dong. The VC as a combat force were severely weakened in the '68 Tet Offensive. The vacuum created by this loss was filled by NVN which assumed direct control of the surviving VC/VCI elements. *See also* **Cadre.**

Viet Cong Phu Loi Battalion VC battalion formed near Phu Loi, north of Saigon in '59. The battalion consisted of main force VC which were based in the area. The battalion was named after a reported massacre of communist and political prisoners being held at the government prison in Phu Loi. Several hundred prisoners were reportedly poisoned to death by prison authorities on command from Saigon. *See also* **Phu Loi.**

Viet Cong Special Forces *see* **Dac Cong**

Viet Cong Suspect (VCS, VCC [Confirmed VC]) Vietnamese in the South were routinely questioned and detained by the National Police and the military. The physical features of a VC were no different from those who were pro–GVN. It became automatic to assume that any Vietnamese who ran from the authorities or was reluctant to cooperate was a suspected VC, and if he was carrying a weapon, he was, without doubt, a VC. Among the more cynical GIs a VCS was defined as an "unarmed Vietnamese stranger; if he was armed he was a confirmed VC." A confirmed Viet Cong was referred to as "VCC." *See also* **Doubtfuls.**

Viet Cong Tax Collectors *see* **Tax Collection**

Viet Cong USO *see* **Cu Chi Music Ensemble**

Viet Hy *see* **Junk Marines**

Viet Kimchi *see* **Nuoc Mam**

Viet Minh (Vietnam Doc Lap Minh Hoi, Vietnamese Independence League, VN-Communist) Vietnam Doc Lap Don Minh Hoi (Viet Minh), the official name for a coalition of Vietnamese groups fighting for independence from the French in the First Indochina War, '46–'54. The name meant the "League for Vietnamese Independence," and was generally referred to as the Viet Minh. The league was formed by the Vietnamese Communist Party in '41 and was led by Ho Chi Minh in a war of independence against the French. During WWII the U.S. used the Viet Minh to aid in the recovery of downed airmen and the gathering of intelligence on the Japanese forces occupying Indochina. American OSS agents provided training and weapons to members of the Viet Minh. The Viet Minh were very successful at spreading anti–Japanese sentiment and propaganda among the peasants of Vietnam. After Japan's surrender the French returned to Indochina to reclaim their former colony, but met resistance from the Vietnamese who demanded and fought for their independence. The First Indochina War began in '46 and ended with the defeat of the French in '54. The Communist Viet Minh was the forerunner of the Viet Cong who began conducting open guerrilla warfare against the GVN in '59.

Viet Nam Cong San *see* **Viet Cong**

Viet Nam Quoc Dan Dang (Vietnamese Nationalist Party [VNP], VNQDD) Vietnamese Nationalist party first organized in '25 in China. The party was pro–Chinese and advocated the independence of Vietnam from the French but also was anticommunist and opposed Ho Chi Minh's Communist Party of Independence. The VNP managed to survive in South Vietnam and in '64 began to increase its membership. The VNP called for democratic socialism and an end to government sponsored repression of the Buddhists: over 60 percent of the party members were Buddhist.

Viet Tri Power Plant Major North Vietnamese thermal power plant located

48kms northwest of Hanoi at the junction of the Red River and the Song Lo. The plant was destroyed during the U.S. bombing of North Vietnam.

Vietcong Security Service (VSS) Terrorist arm of the Viet Cong. The VSS routinely performed assassinations, kidnappings and mutilations of GVN officials and workers, religious leaders, and anyone in a position to support or benefit from the GVN. The VSS also was effectively used to intimidate the rural peasants into not cooperating with the GVN and FWFs.

Vietminh *see* **Viet Minh**

Vietnam *see* **Republic of Vietnam**

Vietnam (GI Names) GIs had many names for Vietnam; some of them were Across the Pond, Disneyland East, Armpit of the World, Asshole of the World, The Country, 'Nam, The Nam.

Vietnam Action Committee (VAC, Communist Party of Australia [CPA]) An early anti–Vietnam protest group organized in Australia. The group was believed to have ties with the Australian Communist Party (CPA). The group held protest strikes and demonstrations in opposition to Australian involvement in the Vietnam War. The group was primarily made up of students.

Vietnam Conflict *see* **Vietnam War**

Vietnam Day Committee (VDC) One of the many antiwar groups that sprang up during the sixties. The VDC tended to focus on the moral issues of the war in Vietnam and U.S. intervention. The VDC was also militant in its demonstrations, sometimes attempting to physically block the movement of troops and inductees within the States. One of the VDC's well known founders was Jerry Rubin, who also co-founded the Yippies in '68. *See also* **Chicago 8, Yippie.**

Vietnam "Dead" Memorial *see* **Vietnam War Memorial**

Vietnam Doc Lap Don Minh *see* **Viet Minh**

Vietnam Era Veterans Members of the military who served in the U.S. Army, Air Force, Marines, Navy, and Coast Guard during the period '62 to '75. This period covered the first large influx of American military

personnel, which consisted of several helicopter units, their ground support, and over 3,200 military personnel. The period ended one week after the evacuation of Americans from Saigon and the collapse of SVN, April 30, 1975. Another period sometimes referenced as the Vietnam Era is '64 to '73. This period covers the first overt attacks by the NVA/VC against U.S. installations in SVN, and U.S. Navy ships at sea off the coast of NVN. The period ended in '73 with the withdrawal from SVN of the last U.S. combat troops.

Vietnam Individual Training Group *see* **Forces Armees Nationale Khmer**

Vietnam Moratorium Committee *see* **Moratorium Day**

Vietnam Ready Reserve *see* **One-Buck**

Vietnam Reds (Vietnamese Communist) Late 1950s American political slang for the Vietnamese communists. *See also* **Viet Cong, Viet Minh.**

Vietnam Service Medal (VSM) U.S. medal, authorized to be worn by all personnel who served in Vietnam between July '65 and May '73.

Vietnam Solution, The "Assemble all the 'good' Vietnamese at coastal enclaves, load them onto ships and move the ships out into the South China Sea, 'nuke' all of South Vietnam then cover the whole country with blacktop, and then sink the ships." One of many cynical GI solutions to the Vietnam War and the difficulties in stopping the flow of men and materiel from North Vietnam, identifying the Viet Cong among the people, the overall corruption rampant in the South Vietnamese Government and the ineptness of its military forces. *See also* **Any One Who Runs Is. . . .**

Vietnam Syndrome The tendency to compare all post–Vietnam War communist led "wars of liberation" in which the U.S. is involved, to Vietnam (especially if the U.S. strongly backs the anticommunist forces). Such wars and conflicts invariably are compared to Vietnam if there is any indication of U.S. military aid, or the possibility of American military advisors or troops becoming involved in the conflict. The Vietnam Syndrome has been used by military critics to denounce the U.S. efforts to supply Central and South American countries with military aid in combating the illicit drug trade in those countries.

Vietnam Veterans Against the War (VVAW, Winter Soldier Investigation) Antiwar organization formed by Vietnam veterans in '67. The group actively participated in demonstrations against the war and in '71 held an open investigation and hearings in Detroit, into U.S. war crimes in Vietnam. The "Winter Soldier Investigation" was primarily funded by Jane Fonda and featured testimonies by several Vietnam War veterans on war crimes they either participated in or witnessed in Vietnam. Testimony was also included on weapons, tactics, POW (NVA/VC) care and abuse, and defoliation and its relationship to negligence on the part of the U.S. government. Selected testimonies were published in '72 but the effects on the public were countered by government moves to discredit the hearings. *See also* **Fonda, Jane.**

Vietnam Veterans Leadership Program (VVLP) Government program established in '81 that attempted to mobilize successful white-collar Vietnam veterans into an organization that could provide support to other less organized or successful veterans. The government provided funding to help the members of the VVLP with the task. Membership in the VVLP was on a voluntary basis. The program lasted until '84 when Reagan administration funding for the program began to dry up.

Vietnam Veterans Memorial   *see* **Vietnam War Memorial**

Vietnam War (Second Indochina War, Vietnam Conflict) War between forces of the Republic of Vietnam, its allies and communist insurgents backed by the forces of North Vietnam. Open hostilities between South Vietnamese forces and communist insurgents began in '56. In '60, American military support to the South Vietnamese increased. In '65, American combat forces began deploying to South Vietnam and the war between North and South quickly escalated. Some U.S. officials referred to the war as the "Vietnam Conflict" since no official "state of war" existed between the U.S. and the North Vietnamese. American and allied combat forces withdrew from SVN in '73

and the country collapsed to the North Vietnamese in '75. For Americans the war ended in Vietnam after the return of the crew of the SS *Mayaguez* in May '75. *See also* **Indochina War.**

Vietnam War Casualties, NVN Exact figures are extremely difficult to obtain relating to North Vietnam and Viet Cong casualties during the Second Indochina War. In '69 General Nguyen Vo Giap, North Vietnam's military commander, estimated NVA losses to be in excess of 500,000 KIA. American estimates for the war range between 600,000 and 1,000,000 NVA KIAs, and an additional 250,000–350,000 Viet Cong KIAs. North Vietnamese civilians killed by U.S. attacks are estimated to be 65,000–100,000 people.

Vietnam War Casualties, SVN Exact casualty figures are not available for South Vietnamese forces but an estimated 243,000 soldiers died and more than 570,000 suffered serious wounds. South Vietnamese civilian casualties were estimated to be between 250,000 and 1,100,000 people.

Vietnam War Casualties, U.S. An estimated 2.7 million Americans served in Vietnam ('61–'75). Estimates of casualties (killed/wounded) are as follows: Army, 38,000/208,000; Marines, 15,000/89,000; Navy, 2,400/4,100; Air Force, 2,300/3,500; Coast Guard, 7/100. As of January 1990, more than 2,300 Americans were still listed as Missing in Action.

Vietnam War Memorial (VWM, The Wall, Black Gash of Shame, Vietnam Veterans Memorial [VVM]) Black granite memorial to the more than 58,000 dead and missing Americans of the Vietnam War. The memorial was dedicated in November '82 and lists the names of the dead and missing on black granite panels, chronologically, by date of death (date declared missing). The memorial was designed by Maya Lin; both she and her design were the subject of heated controversy. Many veterans resented the fact that an Asian-American's design was chosen and others resented the design itself which featured a large black sublevel V-shaped monument, gouged out of the earth near the Lincoln Memorial. Also referred to as the "black gash of shame," the "black ditch for the dead," and the "Vietnam 'Dead' Memorial." President Reagan is remembered by his absence from the dedication ceremonies; he did not visit the memorial until six months after its dedication.

Vietnam's Marie Antoinette *see* **Madame Nhu**

Vietnam's Niggers The Vietnamese were of mostly Chinese ancestry, and they had a loathing for the aboriginal mountain people of Vietnam, called the Montagnards. The relationship between the Montagnards and the Vietnamese was sometimes compared to that of early black Americans and white America. Before the Montagnards were recruited as mercenary soldiers by the U.S. Special Forces (CIDG), they were discriminated against, harassed, persecuted, and killed by the Vietnamese. Under the USSFs the Montagnards fought the NVA/VC, and were tolerated by the South Vietnamese. When the Americans left Vietnam the ARVN took control of the CIDG forces. In a short time the old prejudices resurfaced and the Yards fought for survival against the NVA/VC and the South Vietnamese. *See also* **Montagnards, Nguoi Thuong, Khmers, Chams.**

Vietnamese, The (Yoane, Yellow Annamese) GIs had many different names for the people of Vietnam. Sometimes the same names used to refer to NVA/VC were used for the South Vietnamese people in general. Some of those names were Dinks, Garbage-Pickers, Gooks, Dicks, Little People, Slopes, Zips, Zipperheads, Viets, Slant-eyes, Yellow People. The Montagnard word for the Vietnamese was "Yoane," literally meaning "Yellow Annamese from the coastal plains." *See also* **Enemy, The.**

Vietnamese Astrological Signs *see* **Year of the...**

Vietnamese Beer (Pearl Beer, Tiger Beer, 33 Beer, Ba-Mi-Ba) There were several brands of Vietnamese beer popular with Americans in Vietnam. The one thing the beers had in common was their high concentration of formaldehyde. Some of the most popular brands were Pearl Beer, Tiger Beer, 33 Beer, and Ba-Mi-Ba. *See also* **33 Beer, Rice Whiskey, Tigerpiss.**

Vietnamese Boats *see* **Sampan**

Vietnamese Car Wash *see* **Water-Point**

Vietnamese Civil War (Civil War) Some critics of American policy on Vietnam argued that the war in Vietnam was a civil war and that the U.S. government was confusing communism with nationalism. The critics argued that the struggle between North and South Vietnam was over the unification of the nation, and not the outside intervention of a communist power as claimed by successive U.S. administrations. The argument continued that the fight was between the Vietnamese and the war was not instigated by either of the major communist powers. They compared the intervention of the U.S. in Vietnam to a foreign power arming the KKK in America and sending in troops to assist them.

Vietnamese Civilian *see* **VNC**

Vietnamese Communist *see* **Viet Minh, Viet Cong, Vietnamese Reds**

Vietnamese Dress *see* **Ao Dais**

Vietnamese General Officers *see* **General Officers**

Vietnamese Hat *see* **Non**

Vietnamese Independence League *see* **Viet Minh**

Vietnamese Information Service (VIS) One of several South Vietnamese intelligence gathering organizations.

Vietnamese Interpreters *see* **Cowboy Scouts**

Vietnamese Invasion of Cambodia In December '78 Vietnamese Army forces invaded Cambodia, supposedly in response to excesses by the communist Cambodian government of Pol Pot. The Vietnamese drove out Pol Pot and established a new puppet government and renamed the country the People's Republic of Kampuchea. The Vietnamese army remained in Kampuchea to support the new government and insure that guerrilla warfare, waged by Pol Pot against the new regime, did not succeed. *See also* **Pol Pot, Khmer People's National Liberation Front.**

Vietnamese Money *see* **Piasters**

Vietnamese Names *see* **Nguyen**

Vietnamese National Army *see* **Army, Republic of Vietnam**

Vietnamese Nationalist Party *see*

Viet Nam Quoc Dan Dang

Vietnamese Navy *see* **Republic of Vietnam Navy**

Vietnamese Nuclear Reactor *see* **Atoms for Peace**

Vietnamese Officer Corps Perhaps the weakest link in the South Vietnamese military. Most ARVN officers for higher ranking positions were chosen according to their social station and promotions were awarded based on their loyalty to higher ranking officials. Those officers aligned with the current leadership in Saigon received the promotions, the support and the better positions within the regime. Officer capability was of limited importance in choosing who commanded ARVN forces. The American advisory effort attempted to make changes in the system, but they were unable to flush out deep-seated Vietnamese traditions. Although there were several outstanding Vietnamese officers, the majority were ineffective at their command.

Vietnamese People's Army Air Force *see* **North Vietnamese Air Force**

Vietnamese Rangers *see* **Biet-Dong-Quan**

Vietnamese Sausage *see* **Nem**

Vietnamese SEALs *see* **Lin Dei Nugel Nghai**

Vietnamese Smile *see* **Shit-Eatin'-Grin**

Vietnamese Telephone System *see* **Tiger Phone Exchange**

Vietnamese VAPORUB *see* **Tiger Balm**

Vietnamese Workers *see* **Slushies**

Vietnamization An American term for the program initiated in June '69 that was to gradually shift more of the combat responsibility for the war from the U.S. and FWFs to the South Vietnamese military. It was hoped that the Vietnamese would be able to stand on their own in the fight against the communists succeeding, as the South Koreans had done in Korea. The U.S. would continue to supply and support the Vietnamese and at the same time eliminate the presence of U.S. combat forces in Vietnam. Some ARVNs called the program "America's program of fighting communism, to the last ARVN." *See also* Jaunissement, Double Force, Buddy System, ACTOV, Dong Tien.

Viets *see* **Vietnamese, The**

Viggie *see* **A-5**

Vigilante *see* **A-5**

Village (Ville) Several hamlets grouped together. A ville was larger than a hamlet and smaller than a town. The ville was generally the lowest level of government organization with a government appointed village chief installed at those villages protected by RF/PF or ARVN troops. Progovernment village chiefs had a very high mortality rate in areas not directly controlled by GVN or FWF forces. Some village chiefs worked in their home village by day, and spent their nights in the relative safety of a government outpost or district headquarters. *See also* Hamlet.

Village Action Teams *see* **Civic Action Teams**

Village Chief *see* **Province**

Village Deer (Dog) Vietnamese nickname for the mixed strain of dogs that inhabited many of Vietnam's rural villages. Like many Asian societies, the Vietnamese ate dog meat. Because of their penchant for dog meat, the Vietnamese never really had a problem with canine overpopulation.

Village Ironing *see* **Restructuring**

Village Militia *see* **Dan Ve**

Village Self-Defense Force (Corps) *see* **Popular Forces**

Village Self-Development Program South Vietnamese government program designed to encourage rural villages to control their own priorities regarding civic projects and economic development. The early seventies program was ultimately used as a political tool by the Saigon regime to improve its rural support base. Money was given to the village chief for civic projects, giving him the authority over how the money was spent. In order for the villagers to get any of the money for projects they had to "dance" to the village chief's tune. In turn the village chief had to dance to Saigon's tune if he expected to be allowed to control the funds. The corruption of the system doomed the program to failure.

Village Sweep *see* **Sweep**

Ville *see* Village

Ville, The *see* Saigon

Vinh (Prince) Vietnamese word meaning "Prince," or a reference to royalty. Vinh was also a North Vietnamese port city located on the Song Ca, 243kms south of Hanoi, and about 11kms from the South China Sea. Vinh was one of the initial targets of U.S. retaliation for the Gulf of Tonkin incident in '64. Vinh served as a POL depot, and at the time contained an estimated 10 percent of North Vietnam's storage fuels. The river port was mined in May '72 by the U.S. Navy as part of Operation Linebacker, closing Vinh to foreign shipping and war materiel supply. *See also* **Blockade, Butcher of Vinh.**

Vinh Binh Cigarettes (Done-Beens) Vietnamese cigarettes sometimes given to American POWs being held in NVN. The POWs nicknamed them "done-beens." POWs were sometimes given 1–3 cigarettes a day, depending on the attitude of the prison camp commander and guards.

Vinh Linh North Vietnamese city located just north of the DMZ. The population of 70,000 moved underground, into a series of interconnected villages, as a result of heavy bombardment by American aircraft against NVA staging and supply areas near the city. The primary task of the city's inhabitants was the maintenance of nearby NVA supply routes across the DMZ into SVN.

Vinh Loc Island (Colco Island, Cocoa Beach) Long (32kms) skinny island located east of Hue. The U.S. Navy had a fuel depot located at the northern tip of the island. At the southern end of the island was the village of Vinh Loc. The island was as wide as 4kms and as narrow as several hundred meters. Security for the base was provided by Marine, and later Army, units that took turns rotating into the base. The Navy called the base Coloc Island but the grunts called it "Cocoa Beach." Providing security at the base was considered good duty. The southern portion of the island was sympathetic to the VC and several operations were run in the area to clear out enemy bases. *See also* **Acey-Deucy Club.**

Vinh Loc Peninsula *see* **Tan My**

Vinh Loi Provincial capital of Bac Lieu Province located along the eastern coast of IV Corps. Vinh Loi was located 40kms southwest of Soc Trang, 63kms east of Ca Mau (Quan Long), and less than 15kms from the coast.

Vinh Long Provincial capital of Vinh Long Province located in the heart of the Delta of IV Corps, along the Mekong River, 90kms southwest of Saigon. Vinh Long was temporarily overrun by the Viet Cong during the '68 Tet Offensive.

Vinh Thanh Valley (Happy Valley) Valley located in Binh Dinh Province, II Corps. The southern mouth of the valley was located just off of Highway 19, 17kms east of the 1st Cavalry Division base at An Khe in the Central Highlands. The village of Vinh Thanh was located at the northern end of the valley about 11kms from Highway 19. A U.S. Special Forces camp was also located in the valley. The valley was nicknamed "Happy Valley" by units of the 1st Cavalry that began operations in the area after their arrival in Vietnam in '65. *See also* **Operation Crazy Horse.**

VIP *see* **Volunteer Informant Program**

VIPs *see* **Watch List**

Virgin Soldier *see* **Baby-San, New Troop**

VIS *see* **Vietnamese Information Service**

VISA A program sponsored by the Quaker's American Friends Service Committee. The VISA program sponsored American civilian volunteers to work with the Vietnamese population in the area of Saigon, providing aid, assistance and social services to the Vietnamese through the Buddhist School for Social Services. The program started in '66 and ended in '68. *See also* **Quaker Prosthetics Center.**

Visits to Hanoi Starting in '65, groups of American antiwar activists and pacifists made trips to NVN at Hanoi's invitation. Hanoi used their visits for propaganda purposes, highlighting the destruction caused by U.S. bombers. On occasion Hanoi even released some American POWs to the visiting party. The visitors returned to the U.S. with new fuel for the antiwar fires. Visitors to Hanoi were seen by some Americans as unpatriotic, even traitorous, and were accused of "giving aid and comfort" to the enemy. Movie star Jane Fonda is most identified with the antiwar activists who visited Hanoi. During her highly publicized visit she posed for pictures atop an NVN AA gun, a gesture which did not endear her to GIs who survived Vietnam. Since there were no diplomatic ties with NVN, all such visits were unauthorized by the U.S. government. Some of the visits were '65—Tom Hayden, Herbert Aptheker, Staughton Lynd; '66—Harrison E. Salisbury; '67—Carol Brightman (Bertrand Russell Tribunal); '72—Jane Fonda, Ramsey Clark; '73—Joan Baez, Mike Allen, Barry Romo, Telford Taylor.

Visual Aerial Reconnaissance and Surveillance (VARS)   Aerial reconnaissance and surveillance conducted by aircraft of the Navy's Light Attack Squadron 4, VAL-4. VAL-4 began VARS missions in late '71 when their primary responsibility of supporting TF 116 operations was reduced by the withdrawal of Navy surface forces. The VAL-4 Black Ponies continued VARS and interdiction missions until the unit was deactivated in April '72. *See also* **Light Attack Squadron 4.**

Visual Reconnaissance Team   *see* **Hunter Killer Team**

Vitamin B *see* **B-12**

VITG *see* **Forces Armees Nationale Khmer**

Vivax *see* **Malaria**

VMA *see* **Marine Air Squadron Designations**

VMCJ *see* **Marine Air Squadron Designations**

VMFA *see* **Marine Air Squadron Designations**

VMGR *see* **Marine Air Squadron Designations**

VMO *see* **Marine Air Squadron Designations**

VN-Communist *see* **Viet Minh, Viet Cong**

VNA *see* **Radio Hanoi; Army, Republic of Vietnam**

VNAF *see* **Republic of Vietnam Air Force**

VNC   American military abbreviation for "Vietnamese Civilian."

VNMC *see* **Republic of Vietnam Marine Corps**

VNN *see* **Republic of Vietnam Navy**

VNP *see* **Viet Nam Quoc Dan Dang**

VNQDD *see* **Viet Nam Quoc Dan Dang**

VNS *see* **Lin Dei Nugel Nghai**

VNSF *see* **Luc Luong Dac Biet**

Vo Dat   Small Vietnamese town located near the base of the southern foothills of the Central Highlands. The town was located 92kms northeast of Saigon and 68kms northwest of Phan Thiet, in Binh Tuy Province, III Corps. Between Vo Dat and the foothills was a flat, fertile, rice growing area. This made Vo Dat and several other farming villages around the area frequent targets of Viet Cong tax collection attempts. *See also* **Operation New Life.**

Vocal Minority *see* **Silent Majority**

Voice of Southern Nam Bo   *see* **House 7 Radio Group**

Voice of the Sacred Sword   *see* **House 7 Radio Group**

Voice of Vietnam (VOV)   A propaganda broadcast by North Vietnam Radio aimed at breaking the spirit of U.S. POWs held at various prison camps across NVN, Laos, and Cambodia. *See also* **Hanoi Hanna.**

Volpar   Small twin engine utility transport used by Air America for missions throughout Southeast Asia. The Volpar was a modified Beach Craft Model 18, light transport. The Model 18 was normally equipped with landing gear under the wings, and a tail wheel. The Volpar modified the Model 18 to tricycle landing gear, adding a retractable nose wheel. The Volpar could transport 7–9 passengers, had a max speed of about 230mph, and a range of 300kms.

Volunteer Informant Program (VIP)   Program initiated by some U.S. units that operated in heavily populated rural areas. The program paid Vietnamese civilians who offered U.S. units help or information regarding the NVA/VC. The informants were usually paid in piasters, but sometimes other forms of payment were used such as food, building materials, cigarettes, etc. The information received and its accuracy varied. Because of retaliation by the VC against informants the program was only successful after U.S. units controlled an area or established a base camp and demonstrated that they could protect the people from the VC.

Volunteer Worker *see* **Tinh Nguyen, Dan Cong**

Volvax *see* **Malaria**

Voodoo *see* **RF-101**

VOR System *see* **TACAN**

VORTAC Navigational System *see* **TACAN**

Voting Machines *see* **Coup Troops**

Voting with Their Feet   Reference to the '54 Geneva Accords that partitioned Indochina at the 17th Parallel into North and South Vietnam, allowing the civilians to freely relocate to either of the two zones created by the partition. Nearly one million Vietnamese moved from the North to the South. A nationwide vote was to be taken on whether the two Vietnams were to be united, and under which government. The actual vote never took place. But to the embarrassment of the communists, less than 100,000 people opted to move from the South to the North; this was often referred to as the Vietnamese "voting with their feet." The term also applied to Vietnamese civilians who moved out of VC controlled areas. *See also* **Operation Passage to Freedom.**

VOV *see* **Voice of Vietnam**

VPAAF *see* **North Vietnamese Air Force**

VR Team *see* **Hunter Killer Team**

VS17 *see* **Air Panels**

VSM *see* **Vietnam Service Medal**

VSS *see* **Viet Cong Security Service**

VSS-3 Searchlight *see* **Xenon Light**

VT Round (Variable Time Fuse, Time Fuse, Point Detonation Fuse, Quick Fuse)   Artillery rounds that contained a variable time fuse to trigger detonation of the round. The fuse timing was set so the rounds exploded over the target causing an airburst. Airbursts covered a wider area than ground impacted rounds, showering the area with fragments. The mechanically timed fuse could be set to detonate at various heights above the target. The quick (point detonation — Papa Delta) fuse detonated on impact with the ground or dense vegetation. The VT (variable time — Victor Tango) fuse used radar to sense when the shell was 20 meters above the ground, detonating above the target. VT fuses were less reliable in the rain because of false radar readings.

VTOL *see* **Vertical Takeoff and Landing Aircraft**

VTR *see* **M-88 VTR, M-578 VTR, M-51 HRV**

Vulcan APC *see* **M-163 Vulcan**

Vulcan Gun Pod *see* **SUU-23, SX-35 Cannon**

Vulcanus *see* **SS Vulcanus**

Vulture *see* **Operation Vulture**

Vultures *see* **162 Aviation Company**

Vung Ro Bay *see* **Vung Ro Incident**

Vung Ro Incident (Vung Ro Bay)   In February '65 a 130-foot NVN trawler was spotted in Vung Ro Bay, 75kms north of Nha Trang, II Corps. The ship was bombed and ARVN forces directed to search the bay. Three days later the ARVNs reluctantly agreed to go into the area and conduct a search (this area was a suspected VC base area). Large quantities of weapons, ammunition and medical supplies were found. After much foot-dragging by the Vietnamese military, some of the ammunition was destroyed. Based on this information the U.S. joint chiefs of staff decided to commit U.S. naval forces in the area to aid the South Vietnamese in their coastal patrol efforts under Operation Market Time. *See also* **TF 115, Market Time, Battle of Ap Bac.**

Vung Tau (Cap St. Jacques)   SVN port city in Phuoc Tuy Province, III Corps. Vung Tau served as a major FWF base and the operational support base for the Mobile Riverine Force. The city also served as an in-country R & R center, used by U.S. troops. It was rumored that the VD rate in Vung Tau was 133 percent, meaning all the women had VD, and one-third of them harbored more than one kind of venereal disease. During French occupation of Vietnam Vung Tau was known as Cap St. Jacques.

Vung VC *see* **Local VC**

Vuon Chuoi *see* **Chuoi**

VVA *see* **Vietnam Veterans of America**

VVAW *see* **Vietnam Veterans Against the War**

VVLP *see* **Vietnam Veterans Leadership Program**

VVM *see* **Vietnam War Memorial**

VWM *see* **Vietnam War Memorial**

W

WAAPM-CBU (Wide Area Antipersonnel Munition CBU) Air Force cluster bomb unit that dispersed hundreds of small antipersonnel mines. After impact, triggering wires were opened around the small mines; contact with the wires caused the mines to detonate. The WAAPMs were used to "seed" areas of suspected NVA/VC activity and were very effective because they could not easily be reused by the enemy. *See also* **Cluster Bomb Unit.**

WAC Detachment *see* **Women's Army Corps**

WAC Uniform *see* **Green Cord Uniform**

WACs *see* **Women's Army Corps**

WAG Principle (Wild-Assed-Guess Principle, Scientific-Wild-Assed-Guess [SWAG]) When there was insufficient data or the parameters had not been sufficiently specified to make a decision, the WAG Principle was employed: you simply made a wild-assed-guess and hoped for the best. WAGs that were partially based on valid information or pertinent data were referred to as SWAGs (scientific-wild-assed-guesses). When questioned about how a decision was made, "SWAG" or "WAG" had a more official ring to it than admitting the decision was based on a wild guess.

Wagler's Pit Viper A common snake found in Vietnam. The snake's bite was not normally fatal to man, but could kill small animals. Some Vietnamese farmers kept several of the snakes around their hootches and food storage areas to keep the rats and other varmints away. The snake had a hollow point

between its nose and eyes that was temperature sensitive. It used the sensor to detect warm-blooded animals. The pit viper was light green in color and could climb trees. *See also* **Snakes.**

Wagon Train Defense GI nickname for the defensive perimeter used by units operating in the field when they planned to stop for a long period of time, or as an overnight defense. Elements of the unit positioned themselves in a circle (circling the wagons), around the headquarters element; this applied to both infantry and armor units. Keeping the circle large reduced the effects of enemy mortar or RPG attack on the perimeter. The unit commander, from the center of the circle, had better command control of his units, but was also the focal point of enemy attacks, since the NVA/VC knew where the American Command Post would be located. *See also* **Night Defensive Position.**

Wagon Wheel Defense Defensive position used by LRRPs and small reconnaissance teams in which the team members lay in a circle with their feet pointed to the center and their bodies pointed outward. The "wagon wheel" was used for static positions and NDPs. *See also* **Night Defensive Position.**

Waikiki East *see* **Holiday Inns**

Wait-a-Minute Vines (Getcha Vines) Heavy, thorn covered vine growth encountered by troops moving through dense jungle. The vines slowed troop movement by snagging on equipment or tangling the feet. The sharp thorns easily ripped through fatigues and skin. In high, moist jungle heat such wounds quickly became infected. Though moving through such thick brush was slow and painful, it reduced the risk of being ambushed. Travel along trails was easier but the probability of running into an ambush or booby traps was extremely high. (As troops moved through the jungle quiet cries of "wait-a-minute" could be heard as a GI would get snagged in the vines, and did not want to be left behind.) Also called "Getcha Vines."

Wake Island Small coral atoll located 6,100kms east of Vietnam in the Pacific Ocean. The U.S. maintained a small base on the island. In '75 the island was used as a resettlement point by Vietnamese refugees evacuated from South Vietnam. *See also* **Guam.**

Waldron, Sergeant Adelbert F., III Sergeant Waldron was the U.S. Army's top sniper during the Vietnam War. In two months of sniping in '69, Sergeant Waldron accumulated 109 confirmed enemy kills, one of which was a VC target at 900 meters, shot while the sergeant was in a moving patrol boat. Sergeant Waldron was part of the 9th Infantry Division operating in the Delta of IV Corps. *See also* **Sniper; Hathcock, Gunnery Sergeant Carlos.**

Walk in the Sun *see* **Milk Run**

Walker Bulldog Tank *see* **M-41 Light Tank**

Walking Fires *see* **Marching Fires**

Walking Point (Point, Pointman) First man in a patrol or formation. Walking point in Vietnam was one of the most hazardous positions in a moving patrol. The pointman generally walked out beyond the main body and was the forward eyes and ears of the patrol or column, often drawing the initial enemy fire in an attack. The point also attempted to detect booby traps and possible enemy ambush sites. Some units had men who specialized in walking point; in other units point duties rotated through the unit. Some units placed FNGs on point in an effort to break them in sooner and perhaps limit the veterans' time on point. A squad or fire team could also be called the point element because of their advanced position in the formation. *See also* **Double Point, Slackman.**

Walking Rounds *see* **Marching Fires**

Walking Tracers Slang reference to a machine gunner using the tracers from his gun to more accurately aim his fire. The tracers indicated the vicinity the rounds were impacting. The gunner made adjustments to his fire by moving his weapon, bringing the tracers onto the target.

Walking Wounded Ambulatory, wounded soldiers able to walk under their own power. The wounds suffered by the "walking wounded" were usually not severe; no serious leg or spinal wounds. The "Walking Wounded" also referred to a class of Vietnam veterans who suffered psychological and or emotional wounds because of their war experience. The impact of those "wounds" was not immediately apparent by simply looking at the veteran. *See also* **Triage.**

Wall, The *see* **Vietnam War Memorial**

Wallaby Airlines *see* **Royal Australian Air Force**

Walled City *see* **Citadel**

Walleye *see* **Electro-Optical Guided Bomb**

Wallowa *see* **Operation Wheeler/Wallowa**

Wandering Soul Operations Nickname for U.S. psychological warfare operations aimed at the NVA/VC. Funeral music and eerie sounds were broadcast over helicopter-borne loudspeaker systems in an attempt to unnerve, agitate and terrorize the enemy. The Vietnamese were very superstitious about death. One of the basic Vietnamese fears was to be buried in an unmarked grave; such improper burial would not allow him to link up with his ancestors or enable his family to honor his grave. *See also* **Psychological Operations, Coffins.**

War Crimes Tribunal *see* **Bertrand Russell War Crimes Tribunal**

War Erodes the Great Society Antiwar slogan highlighting the drain of funds from President Johnson's Great Society programs in order to finance the war in Vietnam. *See also* **Guns and Butter Financing.**

War of Attrition War conducted with the object of inflicting as many casualties as possible on the enemy. At some point the casualties inflicted would outweigh the purpose or intent of the war and the side suffering the most casualties would concede. The U.S. waged war in Vietnam based on this policy. The military and the administration believed American technology and firepower would overwhelm the NVA/VC, creating casualties at such levels that they would be unable to sustain the war effort. NVN's policy was much the same, inflicting unacceptable casualty levels on U.S. troops making the American public grow weary of the war, and demanding an end to further U.S. involvement. NVN achieved its goal. *See also* **Search and Destroy, Pham Van Dong.**

War of the Flags   Reference to the tug of war between the PRG and the GVN after the '73 cease-fire. According to the Paris Accords, areas held when the cease-fire took effect were to remain in the control of the party that held the area (PRG or GVN). Areas in dispute were to be settled by the members of the Four Party Joint Military Commission. One of the guidelines used by the JMC was the number of "flags" visible when the JMC made an inspection tour of the disputed area, thus the "war of the flags." Both the GVN and the PRG attempted to sway the decision of the JMC by saturating a disputed hamlet with flags.

War on Poverty Programs   President Johnson's first real initiative, and his favorite domestic program was his war on poverty. The effort against poverty in America was part of Johnson's Great Society program, and involved stimulating the labor market and preparing the labor force to meet the needs of industry. Under the Office of Economic Opportunity (OEO) programs were funded which supported VISTA, Job Corps, Migrant Workers, Work Experience, Project Head Start, Legal Services, Neighborhood Services, Neighborhood Health Centers, and a host of other programs aimed at increasing employment and supporting the work force. Part of the program to train low income youths was Project 100,000, which lowered entrance requirements for joining the military. *See also* **Great Society, The; Project One-Hundred Thousand.**

War Powers Act (War Powers Resolution, Declaration of War)   A congressional resolution passed by Congress November '73 which, by law, required the president of the United States to consult with Congress before committing military units to combat. If Congress agreed with the use of combat forces, those forces could be deployed at the president's discretion for a period not to exceed 90 days. A formal "Declaration of War" was required if the troops were to be activated for a period in excess of 90 days. U.S. combat forces fought in Vietnam for over 8 years without a Declaration of War. The law was intended to stop another "Vietnam" type action from recurring. The original resolution was vetoed by President Nixon, but Congress passed the resolution over his veto. *See also* **Cooper-Church Amendment, Hatfield-McGovern Amendment.**

War Powers Resolution   *see*   **War Powers Act**

War Resisters League (WRL)   Antiwar group that called for the immediate withdrawal of all U.S. military forces from Vietnam and an end to all military aid to South Vietnam. The group described itself as "a secular organization that advocates Gandhian nonviolence to create a democratic society without war, racism, sexism and exploitation."

War to the End   *see*   **Guerre a Outrance**

War Zone C (C Zone)   Major VC base area north of Saigon, centered around Tay Ninh City in Tay Ninh Province, III Corps. The area bordered on Cambodia and covered most of Tay Ninh Province and large parts of Binh Long and Binh Duong provinces. War Zone C was adjacent to War Zone D, separated by Highway 13. The zones were originally named by the French during the First Indochina War, and the U.S. military referred to them by those names throughout U.S. involvement in the war.

War Zone D (Phuoc Vinh, D Zone) Major VC base area north of Saigon, east of War Zone C. The location of the area covered portions of four provinces of Phuoc Long, Long Khanh, Bien Hoa and Binh Duong. The city of Phuoc Vinh was located roughly near the center of the zone and was used by U.S. units as a base of operations against VC. The western boundary of the zone was Highway 13 and the Song Dong Nai served as the eastern boundary.

War Zone VIPs   *see*   **Watch List**

War Zones   *see*   **Free-Fire-Zone**

Warning Order   Preparatory order issued to troops which briefly detailed an upcoming mission or operation. Based on the order, the troops prepared themselves and their equipment for the mission.

Warnke, Paul   *see*   **Ad Hoc Task Force on Vietnam**

Warrant Officer (WO, Warrant Officer Candidate [WOC], Chief Warrant Officer [CWO], Mister)   Military officers who obtain their rank by appointment or warrant. Such officers were not commissioned but were specialists in various skills such as piloting, electronics, etc. Warrant officers enjoy the same privileges as commissioned officers and similar command responsibilities within their specialty. Warrant officer ranks were WO-1, CW-2 (chief warrant), CW-3 and CW-4, and were equivalent to the commissioned officer ranks of 2d lieutenant, 1st lieutenant, captain and major. In the Army the relationship between the warrant and commissioned officer was similar to the relationship between NCO sergeants and specialists. Warrant officers were usually referred to as "Mister." For some GIs the difference between a warrant officer and a commissioned officer was defined as, "a warrant officer 'earned' his rank, and a commissioned officer 'acquired' his rank through an act of Congress." *See also* **Boatswain Mate.**

Warrant Officer Candidate   *see*   **Warrant Officer**

Wars of Liberation   *see*   **Revolutionary Guerrilla Warfare**

Wars of National Liberation   *see*   **Khrushchev, Premier Nikita**

Wartime-Expediency Unit   *see*   **Provisional**

Washington Green   *see*   **Operation Washington Green**

Waste   *see*   **Kill**

Watch List (Special Attention Personnel [SAPs], War Zone VIPs)   Unofficial Army list containing the names of troops serving in Vietnam who required "special attention" (SAPs—field translation was "sorry-assed-pussies"). VIP troops were the sons of high ranking government officials, politicians, generals and stateside celebrities. Normally such individuals arrived in Vietnam with special orders assigning them duties in the least hostile areas. The "watch list" tracked them through their tour of duty in Vietnam; determined efforts were made to keep them out of harm's way. Not all those on the list allowed themselves to be special handled. Of several hundred military aged sons of U.S. legislators, very few saw military service, and even fewer saw service in Vietnam; only one congressman's son was wounded, and one, killed in action.

Water Bag   *see*   **Lister Bag**

Water Biscuits   *see*   **B-2 Unit**

Water Bladder   *see*   **Fat Rats**

Water Bottle Break   Pilot slang for taking a break during a flight to drink water. Pilots would freeze water-filled plastic bottles (usually baby bottles) prior to a mission. They would then take the bottles with them on their mission. One bottle was usually consumed just prior to takeoff; the other bottle was usually consumed sometime during the flight. The bottles were usually tucked into a pilot's flight bag or his survival vest. In the Southeast Asian heat the ice melted very quickly. The combination of combat stress and Asian heat resulted in weight losses of 2–3 pounds (water and bodily fluids) per mission for some combat aircrewmen. The water bottles were necessary to help prevent dehydration.

Water Buffalo (Water-Bo, Buffs, Buffalo Boy)   Vietnam's beast of burden, with an unexplained dislike for American GIs. The Vietnamese used the buffs for pulling plows and carts. A "Buffalo Boy" was a Vietnamese or Montagnard child who tended the water buffalo.

Water Cannons   Some riverine Monitors were fitted with high pressure water cannons. The cannons were used to spray enemy fortifications along the river causing the normally dry fortifications to erode and crumble. The cannons used water pumped directly from the river. The cannons performed double duty, sometimes being used to hose down the unit's dirty river craft during the dry season. *See also* **Monitor.**

Water Glass   *see*   **Operation Water Glass**

Water Leech   *see*   **Leeches**

Water Purification Tablets (Kool-Aid, Iodine Tablets) Iodine tablets were used to purify the water supplies collected by GIs operating in the field. The tablets made the water from the streams, swamps and wells potable. Although the treated water was drinkable, it tasted of chemicals and had a gritty texture. When available, troops mixed unsweetened Kool-Aid with their treated water to slightly improve the taste. One or two iodine tablets were used per quart of water and at least half a package of Kool-Aid. The Vietnamese used human feces to fertilize most of their crops. The runoff from those crops entered the water system. It was also common practice for the Vietnamese to use their rivers and streams as open "latrines," further polluting the available water resources.

Water-Bo *see* **Water Buffalo**

Water-Point (Quick-Wash, Jeep/Truck Wash, Vietnamese Car Wash) A location near a U.S. base with a source of water, usually a well, small river or stream. GIs would stop and Vietnamese children would throw some water on the truck to give the appearance that it was being washed. While the "truck washing" was going on the GI would wander inside a strategically placed shack near the water-point for a little sexual release with the wash's resident whore. *See also* **Whorehouse.**

Waterborne Logistical Craft (Supply Boats and Ships) Military terminology for supply craft, boats, and ships.

Waterpump *see* **1st Air Commando Squadron**

Wave *see* **Bomber Cell**

WC-135 *see* **C-135**

WCT *see* **Bertrand Russell War Crimes Tribunal**

WD-1 Communication Wire *see* **Commo Wire**

We Gotta Get Out of This Place Song by the British group "Eric Burdon and the Animals," one of the most popular songs of American troops in Vietnam during the late sixties and early seventies.

We Had to Destroy the Town... *see* **Ben Tre**

We Have Granted Vietnam "Full Independence"... (Francois Mitterrand) "We have granted Vietnam 'full independence' eighteen times since 1949. Isn't it about time we did it just once, but for good?" A 1954 comment by Francois Mitterrand on France's historical, and unfulfilled, grants of freedom to the Vietnamese people. The French government granted Vietnam independence in various forms on several occasions, but each time they blocked true independence from French rule and interference. Mitterrand held ministerial posts with the French government and was a dedicated member of the French Socialist Party. After two unsuccessful attempts at the French presidency he was elected president in '81. *See also* **Elysee Agreement.**

We Ought to Nuke the Chinks Comment attributed to General Curtis LeMay, the Air Force's chief of staff during the mid '60s. The general was a firm believer in air power and had every confidence that the way to end the war in South Vietnam was through massive force. He was of the opinion that the Viet Cong in South Vietnam were being supported by the regime in Hanoi, and Hanoi was in turn supported by the Chinese government in Peking. His solution was simply stated: "We are swatting flies when we should be going after the manure pile." *See also* **General Curtis LeMay.**

We Prevent Forest Fires *see* **Operation Ranch Hand**

We Weren't in Vietnam for Ten Years... "We weren't in Vietnam for ten years ... we were in Vietnam one year, ten times," or as John Paul Vann put it in '72, "We don't have twelve years' experience in this country (Vietnam). We have one year's experience twelve times." This remark is frequently used to refer to the U.S. military's role in SVN. It is based on the fact that troops were rotated into Vietnam on a one-year basis; the result was experience learned by a troop in the field was not easily passed to a replacement; this required replacements to relearn the lessons of the war over and over again. *See also* **One Year Tour, Tour of Duty.**

We-Eat-This-Shit-Up *see* **WETSU**

Weapon Systems Officer *see* **Weapons Systems Operator**

Weapons Platoon   Under the U.S. Army T O & E, the Vietnam era infantry company consisted of three maneuver platoons and a weapons platoon. The weapons platoon consisted of the company's crew served weapons: machine guns, antitank, and mortar sections. Some weapons platoons also had a Redeye SAM missile section for air defense. In Vietnam the extra machine guns of the weapons platoon and the troops of the antitank section were usually parceled out to the company's maneuver platoons, and the mortar section operated as a reduced platoon or as part of the company headquarters. The weapons platoon of an armored unit consisted of self-propelled mortars (M-106 and M-125), and antitank sections (recoilless rifles and M-150 TOW equipped APCs).

Weapons Systems Operator (WSO, Wizzo, Backseater, Trained Bears, Guy in Backseat [Gibs], PSO)   The backseater in an Air Force F-4, F-100 or F-105, his primary mission was the operation of the electronic weapons, detection, ECMs and targeting systems onboard the aircraft. The Air Force backseaters were initially referred to as "Pilot Systems Operator" (PSO), but locally known as "Gibs" (Guy in Backseat) or "Trained Bears." Later in the war the backseater was officially designated a Navigator/Weapon Systems Officer (WSO). The Navy equivalent of an RIO. *See also* **Radar Intercept Officer.**

Weasels   *see*   **M-29C, Wild Weasel**

Weather   *see*   **WX**

Weather Micro-Modification Projects *see*   **Cloud Seeding Operations**

Weathermen   *see*   **Students for a Democratic Society**

Web Gear (M-1956/1967 Individual Load Carrying Equipment, LBE, LBJ) Cotton or nylon belt and suspender straps worn by a soldier, used to carry equipment and ammunitions in the field. Cotton web gear, also known as load bearing equipment (LBE), was worn by U.S. soldiers in Vietnam. But the cotton gear was very heavy when wet and was very slow drying; it was replaced with lighter weight nylon. The web gear was officially known as either M-1956 or M-1967 Individual Load Carrying Equipment. Some GIs nicknamed the web gear

"LBJ" "load bearing junk." *See also* **Stabo Rig, 782 Gear.**

Web Seats   Temporary seats used aboard military cargo aircraft. The seats were easily stored aboard the aircraft when not in use and consisted of webbing hung from the ceiling of the aircraft. They were far from comfortable, especially on long-distance flights.

Wedge   *see*   **Iron Triangle**

Weed   *see*   **Marijuana**

Weekend Warriors (Reserve Troops) GI nickname for military reservists who assembled for training one weekend a month and were activated for two weeks during the year. Reserve units represented America's second line of defense, behind the regular, full-time military. Many critics believed that many of the Army's troubles in Vietnam could have been lessened if the reserves had been called for active duty during the Vietnam War. Several units were activated, but there was no general mobilization. Many logistical and administrative support positions during the war were filled by regular troops. Those positions could have been filled by reserve units, freeing more troops for combat operations. *See also* **Reserves.**

Weiner, Lee   *see*   **Chicago 8**

Welch, Raquel   *see*   **Hope, Bob**

Well Connected   *see*   **Drag**

West Point Military Academy (The Point, U.S. Military Academy)   U.S. Army military academy located at West Point, New York, established in 1802. Graduates from West Point were awarded a Bachelor of Science degree, a commission in the U.S. Army (second lieutenant), and a commitment of four years' military service in the regular Army. *See also* **U.S. Naval Academy, U.S. Air Force Academy, Beast Barracks.**

West Point Protective Association (WPPA)   Imaginary association which consisted of the graduates of the Army's West Point Military Academy. Supposedly all graduates of the Point were members of the WPPA, and looked out for one another whenever possible. No actual organization existed, but the camaraderie among West Point graduates was a fact, and the imaginary WPPA no doubt played a more important part in some of the Army's decisions over the years than the Pentagon would care to admit. The WPPA was also loosely known as the "Ring Knocker Society," based on the large class ring worn by West Point graduates.

Westmoreland, General William C. (Westy, General Waste-More-Land) Commander of MACV June '64 to July '68. Westmoreland commanded U.S. Army ground combat and advisory forces in South Vietnam until his appointment as the Army's Chief of Staff. MACV command was passed to General Creighton W. Abrams on Westmoreland's return to Washington. Westmoreland was accused in a CBS documentary in '82 of having under-reported enemy strength in Vietnam in an effort to conceal increasing enemy troop levels and U.S. forces' inability to contain them. "Westy" sued CBS for slander and the suit was settled out of court. Some antiwar groups referred to Westmoreland as "General Waste-More-Land." *See also* **GROWN; Adams, Sam.**

Westy *see* **Westmoreland, General William C.**

Wet Thrust *see* **Afterburner**

WETSU   (We-Eat-This-Shit-Up) "WETSU" was used as a coded password by some Mobile Guerrilla Force units that operated in Vietnam. Also used as a "catch" phrase by a variety of post–Vietnam "macho" forces. *See also* **Mobile Guerrilla Force.**

Weyand, General Fred *see* **Chief of Staff**

WHA *see* **Wounded**

Whack-Off *see* **Masturbate**

Whale, The *see* **B-66**

WHAM (Winning the Hearts and Minds, Developing Community Spirit) The object of the U.S. counterinsurgency program in Vietnam was to win the trust and loyalty of the people. By providing the people with security from VC harassment and increasing their well-being through civic improvements, it was believed that the people would come to trust, support and strengthen the GVN in its fight against communism. Winning the hearts and minds was

essential, but never really happened on a wide scale. Some cynical GIs were heard to say of the Vietnamese and WHAM, "Grab 'em by the balls, and their hearts will follow." The Army later changed the WHAM phrase to "Developing Community Spirit."

Wharton *see* **LZ Wharton**

What Are They Going to Do... "What are they going to do, send me to Vietnam?" Typical attitude of the American grunt in Vietnam regarding any disciplinary action the military might threaten him with: From the grunt's perspective, what more could the military do; he was already pounding the ground in Vietnam.

WHEC (High Endurance Cutters) Large Coast Guard cutter that was used to augment the WPB force in Vietnam. The WHEC was 311 feet long and provided additional firepower and speed to Market Time operations. Five WHECs were eventually deployed for use in SVN. *See also* **WPB.**

Wheel Blocks *see* **Chocks**

Wheel Jockeys (Truck Drivers) Slang for Army truck drivers of the Transportation Command.

Wheeler, General Earle Served as Army Chief of Staff from '62 to '64, and also advised President Johnson on the Vietnam War. *See also* **Ad Hoc Task Force on Vietnam.**

Wheeler *see* **Operation Wheeler**

Wheels *see* **Command**

When I Die I'm Going to Heaven... *see* **I Know I'm Going to Heaven...**

When They're Not Red... "When they're not red, they're yellow." A phrase used by some GIs to describe their attitude towards the Vietnamese. It was also used to describe the colors of the South Vietnamese flag: three "red" stripes on a bright "yellow" background. *See also* **Flags..., Gook Syndrome.**

Whip Antenna *see* **Long John Antenna**

Whiplash Code name for U.S. Air Force F-105s on strip alert at Thailand air bases. The fighters flew in support of Operation Steel Tiger, the interdiction of NVA traffic on the Ho Chi Minh Trail. When USSFs conducting reconnaissance missions along the Ho Chi Minh Trail found a viable target, they requested an Air Force strike. In an effort to decrease aircraft response time, several F-105s were kept on "strip alert," fueled and armed, with aircrews standing by. *See also* Ramp Alert, Hot Pad Alert.

Whiskey-Papa *see* **White Phosphorus**

Whistlers *see* **Screamers**

White, General Thomas *see* **Chief of Staff**

White Alert *see* **Alerts**

White Bird *see* **OH-6**

White Christmas *see* **American Service Radio**

White Elephant *see* **TG 76.4**

White Envelope Missions *see* **Controlled Littering**

White Feather, The *see* **Hathcock, Gunnery Sergeant Carlos**

White Horse Division *see* **9th Infantry Division, ROK**

White Knights of the 114th Avn *see* **114th Aviation Company**

White Leech *see* **Leeches**

White Light *see* **Xenon Light**

White Man's War Many blacks, both in and out of the military, viewed the war in Vietnam as a "White Man's War." Blacks were fighting and dying in Vietnam for Vietnamese freedom while in America blacks were fighting for dignity and basic civil rights denied them by the white power structure. Because of inequities in the draft system higher percentages of blacks and Hispanics were drafted into the military in comparison to the percentage of the American population they represented. Initially black and Hispanic soldiers in Vietnam saw more combat and suffered higher casualty percentages. Militant blacks preached war against the white man and argued that blacks in the military should be home fighting for "their own" freedom and recognition, and not fighting to keep the Vietnamese free from communism. As the Johnson administration became sensitive to the plight of blacks in America, changes were instituted to make the draft more equitable. The "White Man's

War" argument found its way into the Army via militant blacks drafted into the service, but their argument did not sway large numbers of black soldiers from performing admirably under combat conditions. *See also* Project 100,000.

White Mice *see* **National Police Force**

White Paper: Aggression from the North 1965 White Paper published by the U.S. State Department explaining how America became involved in Vietnam. The paper cited facts and statistics regarding U.S. involvement and the aggression of North Vietnam against the South. The paper, aimed at the academic community, was fact filled, but it ignored some aspects of the involvement and misled the reader on others. The paper was extremely proadministration in its slant. Of the critiques written about the White Paper, "A Reply to the White Paper" by I.F. Stone was one of the most critical, and in effect shot gaping holes in the State Department's White Paper.

White Phosphorus (Willie Peter, WP, Willy-Pete, Whiskey-Papa, Wilson-Pickett) Long-burning, incendiary material. Used in bombs, rockets, artillery shells and hand grenades. It burned with an intense flame when exposed to the air and was used for generating a concealing smoke screen, target marking, and as an antipersonnel weapon. When the device exploded, small WP fragments ignited when exposed to the air, and continued to burn until the air supply was removed or the fragment was completely consumed. WP had several nicknames; among them were Willie Peter, Whiskey-Papa and Wilson Pickett (nickname used by predominantly black units after soul singer Wilson Pickett). *See also* Grenades, White Phosphorus.

White Phosphorus Grenade *see* **Grenades, White Phosphorus**

White Pill *see* **Dapsone**

White Platoon *see* **Aero Scout Platoon**

White Power As a backlash to the rise of Black Power among militant black groups, small groups of whites began to protest against blacks who were seeking equality within American society. Groups such as the

KKK and the American Nazi Party frequently showed up at black rallies to heckle, and on occasion, attack civil rights demonstrators. These antiblack groups began appealing for White Power, to counter the black civil rights movement. *See also* **Klan, The.**

White Psyche   CIA term for favorable propaganda aimed at strengthening the position of a regime, heads of state or other factions supported by the CIA or their interest. The opposite of favorable propaganda was called Black Psyche. *See also* **Black Psyche.**

White Star Flare   *see*   **Hand Flare**

White Star Mobile Training Team (White Star MTT, Operation White Star)   U.S. Special Forces mobile training teams, activated in '59 to train Royal Laotian Army units in counterguerrilla operations in an effort to counter the buildup of the NVN backed communist Pathet Lao. The White Star teams also organized and trained Laotian Meo, Kha, and Montagnards of the Hmoung tribe to harass and monitor NVA traffic along the Ho Chi Minh Trail. The White Star mission was originally led by Col. Bull Simons. Training teams continued to work with the Hmoung tribes throughout the sixties, while the Laotian Army troop training ended in '62. *See also* **Meo.**

White Star MTT   *see*   **White Star Mobile Training Team**

White Team   Helicopter team composed of two observation ships. The choppers were used for reconnaissance and observation and worked in pairs. Normally one ship worked at low altitude while the other observed from a higher altitude. The higher ship could provide support should the lower ship come under fire or go down. *See also* **Pink Team, Aero Scout Platoon**

White Wing   *see*   **Operation Masher–White Wing**

White-Beast   *see*   **Caucasian**

White-Sidewalls (NVA Haircut, Whitewalls)   Field reference to the NVA/VC haircut. The finished haircut looked as if a rice bowl had been placed on the head and all the hair not under the bowl, cut and shaved off, leaving a white shaved area around the ears and back of the head. U.S. Army and Marine lifers wore a similar cut

they called "Whitewalls" or "White-Sidewalls." *See also* **Onion Heads.**

Whites   *see*   **Aero Scout Platoon**

Whitewalls   *see*   **White-Sidewalls**

Whitey   *see*   **Caucasian**

Whole Milk   *see*   **Real Whole Milk**

Whom the Gods Would Destroy...   "Whom the gods would destroy, they first make Marines." More American graffiti.

Whorehouse (Tapioca Mill, Brothel, Barbershop)   Brothels in Vietnam had many different names and appearances. Outside of most major U.S. bases and in the larger cities "truck washes" were established on the main road near the base. Here a GI could stop to get his vehicle washed, and himself, a "short-time." Many bars, massage parlors, and barbershops were equipped with a backroom containing a bed and a prostitute for servicing the troops. Some of the whorehouses were backed by the U.S. military which provided the girls with medical checks and treatment in order to reduce the exposure of American troops to venereal diseases. The GI's need for sexual release was recognized by enterprising Vietnamese, who hastened to provide those needs in return for the economic independence of the American dollar. *See also* **Water-Point, Sin City, Prostitute.**

Whup-Whup-Whup   Unmistakable sound made by the UH-1 helicopter as its blades slapped the air....

Why Me Syndrome   *see*   **Survivor Guilt**

WIA   *see*   **Wounded**

Wickums (Armored Rail Cars)   Self-propelled armored railroad cars, nicknamed "Wickums," used by the Vietnamese Railway Security Agency (RSA). The slow moving rail cars were armed with a variety of machine guns and charged with the task of keeping South Vietnam's limited rail lines open. The railroad was an easy target for the VC, and the RSA was only able to effectively provide security on the portion of the track the armored car rested on. *See also* **Railway Security Agency.**

Wide Area Antipersonnel Munition CBU   *see*   **WAAPM-CBU**

Widow Maker *see* **Mechanical Ambush, M-16 Rifle, Booby Trap**

Wild Goose Chase *see* **Dry Hole**

Wild Weasel (First in and Last Out, RHAW, Radar Homing and Warning Equipment)   Code name for U.S. flights against NVN designed to detect, suppress and destroy enemy SAM and AAA sites interfering with U.S. air strikes against targets in NVN. The primary aircraft of the Wild Weasels were the F-100 and F-105 armed with AGM-45 Shrike missiles, which homed on the radar emissions of enemy tracking radar. Wild Weasel strikes first began in '65 after NVN began using SA-2 missiles against U.S. strike aircraft. Wild Weasels, along with other strike aircraft jamming tactics, reduced SAM effectiveness to the point that the NVN kill ratio of SAMs fired, to U.S. aircraft destroyed, was about 150:1. F-100 Weasels began operations in December '65 and F-105s began Wild Weasel operations in June '66, slowly replacing the F-100s. Weasel aircraft were also equipped with RHAW (Radar Homing and Warning) equipment which allowed them to detect enemy radar signals. When the signal was detected, the Weasel would visually locate the radar site and either launch his Shrike missile or mark the target for other aircraft in the flight to attack. The unofficial Weasel motto was "First in and Last Out." Wild Weasel Squadron (WWS). *See also* **Iron Hand, 6234th TFW, T-39.**

Wild Weasel Squadron *see* **Wild Weasel**

Wild-Assed-Guess Principle *see* **WAG Principle**

Wildcat *see* **Stand-To**

Willie Peter *see* **White Phosphorus**

Willie Peter Grenade *see* **Grenades, White Phosphorus**

Willie the Shit Burner *see* **Shit Burner**

Willie Weasel College *see* **T-39**

Willy-Pete *see* **White Phosphorus**

Wilson Pickett *see* **White Phosphorus**

Wimp *see* **Candy-Ass**

WIN *see* **Workshop in Nonviolence**

Winchester *see* **Model 70 Winchester, Shotgun**

Wing (Air Wing)   Major organizational element of U.S. Air Force, Marine and Navy aviation units. An Air Force wing generally consisted of three fighter squadrons of 25–50 aircraft each. A Marine Corps Wing (MAW) consisted of about 500 aircraft. A Navy carrier base wing consisted of about 75 aircraft, which included attack and special purpose aircraft (recon, helicopters, surveillance, etc.). *See also* **Tactical Fighter Squadron.**

Wing Helo (Wingman)   Reference to the second helicopter in a light fire team; the first helicopter in the pair was called the "lead helo." The second ship was also referred to as the "wingman," which was the same terminology used by Air Force and Navy fixed-wing pilots.

Wing Wipes *see* **Flyboys**

Winged Warrior *see* **Chickenman**

Wingman *see* **Wing Helo**

Wink and Gin *see* **Gwink**

Winning the Hearts and Minds *see* **WHAM**

Winter Soldier Investigation *see* **Vietnam Veterans Against the War**

Wise Old Men (WOMs)   Unofficial group that advised President Johnson on national policy matters. The group advised Johnson in '68 that they believed the war in Vietnam was lost and U.S. troops should be withdrawn. The Wise Old Men consisted of Dean Acheson, McGeorge Bundy, Joseph Goldberg, Averell Harriman, Paul Nitze, George Kennan, John McCoy, Robert Lovett and Charles Bohlen. Some antiwar protesters called Johnson's advisory group "WOMs" and accused them of having started the war in Vietnam.

Witch Doctor *see* **Montagnard Shaman**

Withdrawal *see* **Retrograde Movement**

Wizzo *see* **Weapons Systems Operator**

WMs *see* Women Marines

WO *see* Warrant Officer

WOC *see* Warrant Officer

Wolf Pack *see* Operation Wolf Pack

Wolfhounds *see* 27th Infantry Regiment

Wolfpack *see* Ubon Royal Thai Air Base

WOMs *see* Wise Old Men

Woman *see* Ba

Women *see* Round Eyes

Women Marines (WMs)   Several women Marines served in Vietnam between '67 and '73. They were primarily assigned to staff liaison duties with MACV and worked at MACV headquarters in Saigon and the Marine base at Da Nang.

Women's Army Corps (WACs, WAC Detachment)   Until the late '70s women in the U.S. Army were either part of the Medical or Nursing Corps, or were part of the regular army in the Women's Army Corps. During Vietnam women were not assigned to combat units operating in the field. They were assigned to rear and base camp areas. Over 7,000 military women served in Vietnam. The USARV, WAC Detachment was stationed at Long Binh, III Corps.

Wonderful White Winged Weekend Warrior *see* Chickenman

Wood Line (Tree Line)   Line of trees at the edge of a field, clearing or a rice paddy. The tree line was often used as an ambush site by the NVA/VC who frequently had bunkers and firing positions located at the base of the trees.

Woodpecker Machine Gun *see* Japanese Machine Guns

Woodson *see* Camp Woodson

Wooldridge, Sergeant Major William O. *see* Sergeants' Scandal

Word, The *see* Skinny

Workers Party *see* Lao Dong

Workshop in Nonviolence (WIN) 1960s antiwar group located in New York City. In July '65 during an antidraft demonstration outside New York's Whitehall Army Induction Center, members of the group participated in a draft card burning; a picture of the event eventually appeared in *Life* magazine. This and other card burnings helped spur Congress into passing tough anti-draft-card-burning legislation. *See also* Bill 392.

World, The *see* U.S.A.

World Airways   One of several commercial airlines that were chartered by the U.S. military to ferry troops between the United States and South Vietnam. During the final collapse of South Vietnam in March '75 World Airways crews operated continuously to evacuate refugees from major cities such as Da Nang, Hue, Qui Nhon and eventually Saigon. World Airways was based in Oakland, California. *See also* Commercial Carriers.

World News *see* FREE

World of Hurt (Deep Shit)   GI phrase generally applied to a multitude of situations: if the situation was bad; the outlook was bleak; if there was little or no hope; if there was pain; if the news was bad or things looked very dark; a "world of hurt" applied. These three words covered not only the physical problems that could occur, but also the emotional and intellectual pit in which any one or any group could find themselves. Also called being in "deep shit."

World's Biggest Sand Trap *see* Cam Ranh Bay

Worms *see* Trichinosis

Wounded (Wounded in Action [WIA], Wounded by Hostile Action [WHA])   In Vietnam, in order for a wounded soldier to be classified as a WIA, his wounds had to be the result of hostile action. This WIA classification entitled him to be eligible to receive a Purple Heart. On the battlefield the wounded were often removed by means of medical helicopter flights called "Dustoffs." In order to better control the transport of casualties, the extraction of the wounded was prioritized by the severity of the wounds and the availability of Dustoff aircraft. Over 248,000 Americans were Wounded in Action as a result of hostilities in Vietnam. The DOD officially declared Americans wounded in Vietnam to be "Wounded by Hostile Action (WHA)" since no state of war existed for U.S. troops in

Vietnam. The priority codes were Priority—Urgent—Tactical Urgent—Routine. *See also* KIA/WIA Code Names, Million Dollar Wound, DOW.

Wounded by Hostile Action *see* **Wounded**

Wounded in Action *see* **Wounded**

WP *see* **White Phosphorus**

WP Grenade *see* **Grenades, White Phosphorus**

WPB (Coast Guard Cutter, Coast Guard Squadrons One and Three, RONONE, RONTHREE) U.S. Coast Guard cutters used in Operation Market Time (TF 115) to patrol the coastal waters of South Vietnam. The 64-ton WPB was 82 feet long, had a crew of 11, was capable of 20 knots and armed with a combined .50cal machine gun and 81mm mortar on the bow, 2 × 20mm guns or 4 × .50cal machine guns mounted aft, and carried HF, VHF-FM and UHF communications equipment. The first of the 26 boats and their American crews arrived in Vietnam in July '65 and operated until the boats were turned over to the South Vietnamese Navy in '70. Between '65 and '70 Coast Guard Squadrons One (RONONE) and Three (RONTHREE) operated the Coast Guard cutters of TF 115. *See*

also TF 115, Market Time, An Thoi, YR-71.

WPPA *see* **West Point Protective Association**

WR-300 (SAM Launch Detector, LWR, APR-26 Launch Warning Receiver) ECM device mounted on Wild Weasel aircraft. The WR-300 monitored Fan Song radar guidance signals for the SA-2 SAM missile and was capable of detecting the missile's launch and displaying a visual and audio warning to the pilot. The WR-300 was the test version of the device and after acceptance, the Air Force redesignated the device the "APR-26 Launch Warning Receiver (LWR)." *See also* **Wild Weasel.**

Wrap Boots *see* **Tanker Boots**

Wrapped-Too-Tight *see* **Crazy**

WRL *see* **War Resisters League**

WSO *see* **Weapons Systems Operator**

Wunder Beach *see* **LOB Base**

WV-1 *see* **EC-121**

WWS *see* **Wild Weasel**

WX Abbreviation for "weather" commonly used by aircrews for communications, reports, briefings, etc.

X

Xa Hoi Quaker *see* **Quaker Prosthetics Center**

Xa Loi Temple *see* **Night of the Pagodas**

Xe Tho (Pack Bicycle) Vietnamese bicycles, fitted with packs, used to transport supplies. The NVA made use of pack bicycles to transport troops and supplies down the Ho Chi Minh Trail during infiltration into SVN. The xe tho [z tho] frame was reinforced, which allowed it to carry up to 400 pounds in equipment, supplies or rice. The heavily loaded bike could be ridden when the terrain permitted, but initially, much of the Ho Chi Minh Trail was so rough that many of the NVA soldiers pushed their

bikes from North Vietnam to South Vietnam. *See also* **Bicycle.**

Xenon Light (White Light, AN/VSS-3 Searchlight) High intensity searchlight with an output of 75 million candlepower. The light could be found mounted on U.S. M-48 tanks and was capable of either white light or infrared emissions. Larger, 24-inch xenon infrared searchlights were also fitted on LCPL riverine boats used to patrol the waterways at night. Nighthawk helicopter missions used the searchlight for targeting and surveillance. *See also* **LCPL, Nighthawks, Night Sun Searchlight.**

Xin Loi *see* **Sorry 'bout That**

XM (Experimental Model) Department of Defense designation for experimental equipment. During the VNW the U.S. often experimented with new weapons, equipment, and techniques. Some of the experimental models, such as the XM-148, XM-21, and XM-706, were later accepted for regular Army use. When accepted by the Army the production model of the experimental equipment retained the name, less the "X" (M-21, M-706, etc.). Many other experimental devices such as the XM-2 and the XM-52 never progressed beyond the experimental stage.

XM-2 People Sniffer (Manpack Personnel Detector-Chemical [MPD-C], Olfractronic Personnel Detector) Officially the "Olfractronic Personnel Detector," an experimental, man-portable people sniffer developed under the DCPG for use by the Army in Vietnam. The XM-2 was a portable version of the XM-3 People Sniffer used experimentally on Army helicopters. The XM-2 sensing probe attached to the end of a rifle, where it sampled the air for ammonia content. Body sweat and waste were high in ammonia which the device was designed to detect. The XM-2 was first field tested in Vietnam in '68. The "People Sniffer" proved to be too sensitive for use in the field because it could not distinguish between friend or foe and was so sensitive that it reacted to water buffalo urine as easily as it did human waste. *See also* **XM-3 People Sniffer, People Detector.**

XM-3 People Sniffer (People Sniffer, M-3 APD, M-3 Airborne Personnel Detector) Experimental personnel detector, attached to a helicopter, and used to collect and test air samples over the jungle. The device tested for high ammonia content which was an indication that there was a buildup of excrement or sweat in the area where the sample was taken. This was used as an indicator of a possible hidden enemy base camp. The accuracy of the detector was questioned because water buffalo urine was sufficiently high in ammonia to register on the device. A man-portable version was used experimentally, and was called the "XM-2 Manpack Personnel Detector-Chemical." *See also* **People Detector, XM-2.**

XM-3 Rocket Launcher The XM-3 system was a helicopter (UH-1B/C) mounted 2.75-inch folding fin rocket launcher. The system consisted of 48 rockets in two 24-tube

launching pods. The launchers were fixed in position on the sides of the aircraft and aimed by the pilot maneuvering the aircraft into position for firing. The rockets were fired in pairs or bursts of several pairs. *See also* **XM-158 Rocket, XM-159C Rocket.**

XM-5 Grenade Launcher   *see*   **M-5 Grenade Launcher**

XM-6 Machine Gun (Quad 60s, XM-153, Flex Guns, XM-16, M-6 Quad MG) Machine gun mount that featured four fixed M-60 machine guns synchrofired. The XM-6 was experimentally mounted on some of the early Huey gunships. The machine guns were mounted in pairs, one over the other, on each side of the helicopter and fed by flexible metal ammunition feed chutes that were attached to large ammo trays on the floor of the ship. Each machine gun could fire at a rate of over 500rpm out to a range of 1,000 meters and had limited vertical movement, allowing aiming by the pilot. The system was nicknamed the "Quad 60s" or "Flex Guns," and later designated the M-6 Quad MG. The XM-153 was the original designation of the system using the M-73 machine gun. The XM-16 was the same system with the addition of a mount for attaching rocket pods. *See also* **M-60 MG.**

XM-8   Experimental mount used to arm the OH-6 Loach with the M-75 Grenade Launcher. *See also* **M-75 Grenade Launcher.**

XM-12 Gun Pod   *see*   **M-61 Vulcan**

XM-13 Gun Pod Experimental gun pod that was equipped with a 40mm grenade launcher. *See also* **Grenade Launchers.**

XM-14 Gun Pod Experimental gun pod used on some U.S. attack aircraft. The pod enclosed a .50cal machine gun.

XM-16 Machine Gun   *see*   **XM-6 Machine Gun**

XM16E1/XM-148   *see*   **M-203 Rifle**

XM-18 Minigun (7.62mm Minigun Pod) 7.62mm minigun pod used by helicopter gunships. The pods were mounted in pairs, one on each side of the gunship. The minigun was completely enclosed by the pod and had a maximum rate of fire of 4,400 rounds per minute. The XM-18 was primarily used on the AH-1G Cobra gunship. *See also* **Minigun.**

XM-21   *see*   **Minigun, M-14 Sniper Rifle**

XM-21 Minigun   Twin minigun system used on Huey helicopter gunships. The system featured two belt fed rotary barrel M-134 miniguns, one on each side of the aircraft. The guns were usually fixed in position and aimed by the pilot's positioning of the aircraft. The minigun mount could also accommodate at least one rocket pod (XM-158). The guns were fed by flex chutes which were attached to large boxes of ammo on the floor of the chopper. The guns could fire out to 1,500 meters at a max rate of 4,000rpm. *See also* **Minigun.**

XM-22 AGM System   Experimental air-to-ground missile system used by the Army in Vietnam. The system used the SS-11 AGM missile. There were six missiles in the helicopter mounted system, each attached to a bar mount attached to the helo's rear hard point, three missiles per side. The missiles had a range of 3,000 meters and were wire guided by the pilot. The XM-22 was designed as an antitank system but saw limited use in Vietnam against enemy bunkers. When the system was operationally deployed it was designated the M-22 AGM. *See also* **AGM, SS-11 AGM.**

XM-23 MG (Smokers, Piggyback 60s)   Dual M-60 machine gun mount used on some helicopters. The dual machine guns were attached to the mount in one of two configurations: an over and under mount (Piggyback 60s), or mounted side by side (Smokers). The guns were fixed together on the mount allowing them to swivel, elevate and fire together. The XM-23 was most often mounted on "slicks" providing them extra firepower during CA missions. *See also* **M-60 MG, XM-59.**

XM-24 MG   Experimental gun mount system used on the CH-47 helicopter. The system used a 7.62mm M-60 light machine gun mounted in the forward crew window of the helicopter, in the cargo bay.

XM-25 20mm Gun Pod   Aircraft gun pod that housed a 20mm high speed cannon. The pod could be mounted on fixed-wing or rotary-winged aircraft. *See also* **XM-12.**

XM-26 TOW   *see*   **M-151 TOW**

XM-27 Mine   *see*   **Gravel Mine, U.S.**

XM-27E1 Minigun   Belt fed minigun with a selectable rate of fire, either 2,000 or 4,000 rounds per minute. Some OH-6 Loach helicopters carried the minigun mounted on the side of the chopper. The system used the M-134 minigun, with a typical ammo load of 2,000 rounds. *See also* **Minigun.**

XM-28 Protective Mask   *see*   **M-17 Protective Mask**

XM-28 Turret (Chin Turret, M-28 Turret)   One of the variations of chin turrets used on the AH-1G Cobra helicopter. The XM-28 featured a minigun and grenade launcher. The turret could be pivoted from left to right and the minigun/grenade launcher could be elevated and depressed. The moveable chin turret allowed the gunner in the Cobra to fire on targets the ship was not directly pointed towards. The M-28 was the production model of the turret. The Cobra carried 4,000 rounds of 7.62mm ammunition for the M-134 minigun and 300 40mm rounds for the grenade launcher. *See also* **Chin Turret.**

XM-30 Cannon   *see*   **XM-140**

XM-31 20mm Cannon Pod (M-24 20mm Cannon)   20mm cannon pod that was mounted to some Huey gunships. The pod featured a single barrel M-24 20mm cannon mounted in pairs, on the rear hard points of the UH-1B/C. The M-24 could fire 700rpm at ranges out to 3,000 meters. The pods were belt fed from ammunition boxes located on the floor of the helicopter. *See also* **SX-35 Cannon.**

XM-31 Cannon   *see*   **SX-35 Cannon**

XM-32 MG   Experimental gun system used on the CH-47 helicopter. The system used .50cal or M-60 machine guns mounted in pairs on the sides of the ship. *See also* **Go-Go Bird.**

XM-33 MG   Experimental weapons system used on the CH-47 Go-Go bird. Forward facing .50cal or M-60 machine guns were mounted on each side of the ship. The guns gave the big helicopter plenty of firepower, but the helicopter was slow and a very large target, and use of the CH-47 as a gunship never got beyond the experimental stage. The armed Go-Go Bird was used in combat, but the system was not approved for addition to the Army's T O & E. *See also* **Go-Go Bird.**

XM-35 20mm Cannon   *see*   **SX-35 Cannon**

XM-45E1 Armored Cargo Carrier   *see*   **M-548 Cargo Carrier**

XM-52 Smoker (Smoker System, Pollution System)   Experimental system developed to allow the Huey helicopter to lay down a smoke screen. SGF-2 fog oil was injected in the helicopter's engine exhaust, creating a dense cloud of black smoke. The smoke was used to cover hot LZs to assist troop landings. The helicopter was able to produce a great deal of smoke but in order to do so it was required to fly at a slow speed which made it highly vulnerable to enemy fire.

XM-59 HMG   M-2 .50cal machine gun mount used on some Huey helicopters. The .50cal machine gun was mounted on one side of the helicopter while a dual M-60 machine gun was mounted on the other. The machine guns were operated by the crew chief and the door gunner. *See also* **XM-23 Machine Gun.**

XM-93 Minigun   Helicopter door mounted 7.62mm minigun system. The system could be operated manually by the gunner/crew chief, or the guns could be locked into position and fired by the pilot. The M-134 miniguns could fire at a rate of 2,000 or 4,000rpm to a range of 1,500 meters. The guns were fed by flex chutes from large ammo boxes stored on the floor of the chopper. Typical ammo loads ranged from 8,000–12,000 rounds per gun. The guns were mounted in pairs, on each side of the aircraft, in the doorway. *See also* **XM-134 Minigun.**

XM-94 Grenade Launcher (XM-129 Grenade Launcher)   Door mounted 40mm grenade launching system. Two automatic grenade launchers were mounted in the doorways of Huey gunships used by the Air Force. The launchers could be fired by the crew or fixed in position and fired by the pilot. The design saw limited service with the Air Force. *See also* **UH-1F.**

XM-129 Grenade Launcher   *see*   **XM-94 Grenade Launcher**

XM-134 Minigun (M-134 Minigun)   Six-barrel minigun, the barrels electrically rotated; an electric Gatling gun. The minigun fired 7.62mm ammunition, with a maximum fire rate of 6,000 rounds a minute to a range of 1,500 meters. The minigun was used in various weapons systems and in numerous configurations. The XM-134 was the experimental version and the M-134 was the final production model. The M-134 was used in several different minigun weapons systems which were developed for aircraft and vehicle mounting. *See also* **Minigun, XM-21 Minigun, XM-93 Minigun, XM-28 Turret.**

XM-140 (30mm Cannon, 30 Mike-Mike, XM-30)   Experimental version of a helicopter mounted 30mm cannon. The cannon provided the helicopter with good standoff range, but required an inordinate amount of ammunition to be practical for widespread tactical deployment. The automatic cannon was used mounted on the AH-1G Cobra.

XM-148   *see*   **M-203 Rifle**

XM-153 Machine Gun   *see*   **XM-6 Machine Gun**

XM-157 Rocket   *see*   **XM-158 Rocket**

XM-158 Rocket (LAU-59/A XM-157)   2.75-inch folding fin aerial rocket pod. The pod contained seven replaceable tubes that were loaded with the FFAR rockets. The pod was used on Huey and Cobra gunships. The XM-157 was an early version of the pod, but the tubes that carried the rockets were not readily accessible. The XM-157 was eventually replaced with the XM-158. The rockets were fired by the pilot and aimed by positioning the ship. LAU-59/A was the Air Force designation for the rocket pod. Rockets were available with a 10- or 17-pound warhead in HE or WP. Later in the war a flechette rocket was available. *See also* **XM-3 Rocket Launcher, XM-159C Rocket.**

XM-159C Rocket (2.75-Inch Rocket, Mighty Mouse Rockets, Folding Fin Aerial Rockets [FFAR])   The XM-159/SM-200 was the standard rocket pod carried by ARA helicopter gunships. Each pod contained 19 2.75-inch folding fin aerial rockets (FFAR). Pods were mounted in pairs, two or four pods per helicopter. The 2.75-inch rocket was the standard unguided rocket used by most American aircraft. The fins that stabilized the rocket inflight were folded while the rocket was in the tube launcher; when launched, the tail of the rocket cleared the tube, and spring loaded fins extended, guiding the rocket's flight to the target. The

XM-159 could fire the rockets at the rate of six per second. *See also* **2.75-Inch Flechette Round, XM-158 Rocket, XM-3 Rocket Launcher, ARA.**

XM-174 Grenade Launcher An experimental, multiple-shot, automatic grenade launcher. The XM-174 weighed 27 pounds, was pedestal mounted and fed by a 12-round magazine. The weapon fired the standard M-406 HE round at a maximum rate of 300 rounds per minute. Maximum range of the XM-174 was 400 meters and was used by the Army. The grenade launcher was sometimes jeep or APC mounted, or tripod mounted and used for base defense. *See also* **Grenade Launchers.**

XM-177E2 *see* **CAR-15**

XM-200 *see* **XM-159C**

XM-203 *see* **M-203 Rifle**

XM-258 Flechette Round *see* **Shotgun Flechette**

XM409 HEAT Round *see* **Combustible Case Ammunition, M-551 ARV**

XM-546 *see* **M-546 Beehive Round**

XM625 Canister Round *see* **M-551 ARV, Flechette**

XM-706 *see* **V-100**

XO *see* **Executive Officer**

Xoi Dao (GVN by Day, NLF by Night) Vietnamese phrase used to refer to some rural hamlets of South Vietnam, government controlled by day, Viet Cong controlled by night. Xoi Dao [zoi dow] figuratively translated, "black and white together." *See also* **Enemy, The.**

Xray Commonly used radio call sign for a reconnaissance patrol operating from a company NDP. *See also* **NDP, FSB Xray, LZ Xray.**

Xuan Loc (Blackhorse Base Camp, Camp Blackhorse) Provincial capital of Long Khanh, in III Corps, 64kms northeast of Saigon. During the NVA's Eastertide offensive in April '75, Xuan Loc was defended by the ARVN 18th Inf Div. Four NVA divisions attacked the ARVNs at Xuan Loc; three of the enemy divisions were destroyed before heavy casualties to the ARVN 18th caused the ARVN survivors to retreat to Saigon. Camp Blackhorse was located 13kms south of Xuan Loc, which served as the regimental base camp for the U.S. 11th Armored Cavalry Regiment.

Xuan Thuy North Vietnam's chief negotiator at the Paris peace talks from the start of the talks in '68 to '70 when Le Duc Tho became the chief negotiator. *See also* **Le Duc Tho.**

Xuyen Oc (House Fighting, VC Style) Method of house-to-house city fighting used by the VC. Many of the houses on a block in the more populated areas were built sharing a common wall. The VC would enter a house on the end of the block and open up holes in the common walls of several of the connected houses; they would then begin sniper fire. The Americans' response to the sniper fire was to call in an air strike or artillery on the house; the VC would move to the next house and fire again. By the time the VC were killed or escaped much of the block had been destroyed and the people who owned the homes came to hate the Americans whose planes and artillery brought the destruction. "Xuyen" [swen] meant to perforate or go through, and "Oc" [ock] meant house.

XXIV Corps (24th Corps) A corps level headquarters dating back to WWII. It was reactivated in August '68 to control Army and Marine units operating in I Corps. XXIV Corps Headquarters was located at Phu Bai until March '70, when it relocated to Da Nang (Camp Horn) after the departure of the Marines. The remaining Army units assigned to the Corps Hq. were the Americal, 1st Cavalry and 101st Airborne Division and the 1st Brigade/5th Infantry Division. *See also* **Camp Horn, MACV Forward.**

Y

Yabuta   Main motorized junk used by the South Vietnamese Junk Force. The Yabuta was a Japanese designed, wooden hulled junk, 55 feet long and armed with .30cal and .50cal machine guns, and a 60mm mortar. *See also* **Junks, Junk Force.**

Yankee Air Pirates (American Pilots, Air Pirates)   Ho Chi Minh labeled American aircraft pilots "Yankee air pirates" and criminals. The North Vietnamese claimed American bombing of NVN was a criminal and "genocidal bombing campaign" and therefore the aircrews that conducted the bombing were war criminals and were not considered prisoners of war and subject to the protections of the 1949 Geneva Convention on the treatment of prisoners. NVN also stated that since no formal declaration of war had been announced by America there was no war, and therefore no POWs.

Yankee Go Home   Familiar chant heard around the world by those in opposition to a U.S. policy and presence in their country (U.S. bases, installations, embassies, etc.). Opposition groups shouted the chant at American dignitaries visiting their country, or when media news crews were in the area.

Yankee Station   Code name for the U.S. Navy's 7th Fleet, Attack Carrier Strike Force (TF-77), operational area in the Gulf of Tonkin, off the coast of NVN at 17 degrees, 30 minutes north and 108 degrees, 30 minutes south. Navy strikes against NVN and against the northern provinces of South Vietnam were launched from Yankee Station. *See also* **Dixie Station.**

Yankee Team *see* **Operation Yankee Team**

Yard Witch Doctor *see* **Montagnard Shaman**

Yards *see* **Montagnards**

YAWF *see* **Youth Against War and Fascism**

Yea, Though I Walk Through the Valley Of... *see* **23d Psalm**

Year of the... (Vietnamese Astrological Signs)   The Chinese Buddhists (and Vietnamese) celebrate the years on a 12-year astrological cycle, each of the 12 years having the name of a different animal, each with different traits. The cycle of names repeated every 12 years. '61/73 — ox; '62/74 — tiger; '63/75 — rabbit (hare); '64 — dragon; '65 — snake (serpent); '66 — horse; '67 — goat (ram); '68 — monkey; '69 — rooster; '70 — dog; '71 — pig (boar); '72 — rat.

Year of the Monkey *see* **Tet '68**

Year Zero   When the communist Khmer Rouge, led by Pol Pot, captured Phnom Penh in April '75, "Year Zero" was pronounced. Year Zero was to be the start of the new rural socialism in Cambodia. The name of the country was changed to Kampuchea and the residents of Phnom Penh driven out of the city. Millions of Cambodians were interned in "reeducation camps" where they died of starvation or were executed. *See also* **Khmer Rouge, Pol Pot.**

Yellow Alert *see* **Alerts**

Yellow Annamese *see* **Vietnamese, The**

Yellow Fever *see* **Le mal Jaune**

Yellow People *see* **Enemy, The**

Yellow Star Division *see* **1st NVA Division**

Yellowing *see* **Jaunissement**

Yellowstone *see* **Operation Yellowstone**

Yen *see* **Opium**

YFND   Non–self-propelled Navy barge. The barge had a covered well and was used for storage of various Navy stores. *See also* **Ammi Barge.**

YFR   Small Navy ship used as a lighter and resupply vessel during the Vietnam War. The YFR had refrigerated storage, allowing it to move perishable goods. As a lighter, the YFR was used to transfer cargo from larger ships to shore facilities. YFRs operated under the Naval Security Activity and were also used for resupply missions of

TF 116 and TF 117 outposts in the Delta. The YFR had a shallow draft and a max speed of 10 knots. *See also* **Southern Shipping Company, AKL, Lighter.**

YFU *see* **LCU**

Yippie (Youth International Party, Pigasus)   Quasi-political party founded by Ed Sanders, Paul Krassner, Jerry Rubin and Abbie Hoffman in '68. The party was an attempt to combine the hippie and antiwar movements into one faction. The Yippies, as they were known, held their own presidential nominating convention in Chicago in '68, nominating a pig named Pigasus as their candidate. The main planks of their platform were based on a society of free love, free drugs, no war and no commitments.

YMS (Auxiliary Minesweeper)   Minesweepers used by the French and Vietnamese navies during the Indochina War.

YO3A   Army light observation aircraft, used experimentally in Vietnam. The single engine, two-seater plane was used for reconnaissance and observation. Its quiet running engine allowed the plane to get closer to enemy units before detection.

Yoane *see* **Vietnamese, The**

Yorktown *see* **USS Yorktown**

You Can Kill Ten of My Men. . .   "You can kill ten of my men for every one I kill of yours, but even at those odds, you will lose and I will win." This quote was attributed to Ho Chi Minh during his fight against the French in the First Indochina War. Ho Chi Minh did not hold the lives of his troops sacred and he and his military commanders were willing to suffer extensive casualties in their quest to unite Vietnam under Ho's communist domination. *See also* **Nguyen Vo Giap; Every Day in the World. . . .**

You Have My Absolute Assurance. . .   "You have my absolute assurance that if Hanoi fails to abide by the terms of this agreement it is my intention to take swift and severe retaliatory action." This statement by President Richard Nixon in November '72 was part of a letter hand-carried by General Alexander Haig to South Vietnam's President Thieu. The letter and Haig's visit to SVN were designed to encourage Thieu to accept the terms of the peace agreement hammered out in Paris between Kissinger and Le Duc Tho (NVN). Nixon's promise of support was short-lived when he resigned from the Presidency in August '74 and his replacement, Gerald Ford, and the U.S. Congress chose not to honor his pledge. *See also* **Nguyen Van Thieu.**

You Souvenir Me *see* **Souvenir Me**

Young Socialist Alliance (YSA)   Sixties antiwar group, Trotskyist in their orientation, which attempted to take control of the National Coordinating Committee in '65.

Young Tiger *see* **KC-135**

Your Home Away from Home *see* **United Services Organization**

Youth Against War and Fascism (YAWF)   American antiwar group of the sixties believed to have ties with the Communist Party.

Youth International Party *see* **Yippie**

Youth Shock Brigade *see* **Shock Brigades**

YR-71   Repair barge located in Da Nang Harbor and used to support the operations of Coast Guard Squadron Three. The squadron operated from the DMZ south to Cam Ranh Bay as part of the coastal surveillance force of TF 115. *See also* **WPB.**

YRBM Barge   Navy barge used as a floating river patrol base by elements of TF 116. The barge provided housing and mess facilities for boat and support crews. The barge had a repair shop that was used for PBR boat maintenance. The YRBM was not self-propelled and had to be towed for deployment. Several of the barges were used on the rivers of the Delta in conjunction with LSD and LSTs. *See also* **TF 116, LST, Landing Ship Dock.**

YSA *see* **Young Socialist Alliance**

YTB Tug (Harbor Tug, Large)   Large tug boat used by the MRF to position barges and non–self-propelled barracks ships of the Mobile Riverine Base. *See also* **TF 116, TF 117.**

YTL Tug (Auxiliary Tug, Small)   Small tug boats used by the Mobile Riverine Force to position boats of the Mobile Riverine Base. *See also* **TF 117.**

Z

Z, The *see* **Demilitarized Zone**

Zs (Sleep, Sack-Out, Crash, Catch Some Zs) Slang for sleep.

Z-15 NVA Regiment (Z-18 NVA Regiment, 24th NVA Regiment, 8th NVA Division) The Z-15 was a composite NVA regiment that appeared in the central Delta area in '72. Sometime later the Z-18 was also formed. The regiments were formed from several independent battalions operating in the IV Corps area. Both regiments were independent, and did not become part of a regular division until '74, when, along with the 24th NVA Regiment, they formed the 8th NVA Division.

Z-18 NVA Regiment *see* **Z-15 NVA Regiment**

Zais, General Melvin Commanded the 101st Airborne Division from July '68 to May '69 and ordered the assault and capture of Hamburger Hill, Hill 937, in May '69. Critics of the war claimed the hill had no strategic importance and the hill was abandoned shortly after having been taken by the 187th Infantry. General Zais stated that the enemy was on the hill and that alone was reason enough for the costly assault. Later in the month command duties of the 101st Division were assumed by General John Wright. *See also* **Hamburger Hill.**

Zap *see* **Kill**

Zero (Zero a Weapon) The sighting adjustments required to hit a selected target, at a specific range. On most rifles there were two adjustments, windage and elevation. These two adjustments had to be made on all new weapons, and for each individual who used the weapon. Zeroing a weapon involved adjusting the windage and elevation scales in order that a target, at a specific range, would be hit on a consistent basis.

Zero a Weapon *see* **Zero**

Zero Population Growth (ZPG) A seventies movement started in the U.S. that preached the possibility that the world might be destroyed by overpopulation. ZPG called for a reduction in the birth rate by such means as abortion, contraception, birth limits and whatever other means were available to keep the world population from exceeding the world's ability to support its growth. The ZPG movement gained visibility as a result of the new social and environmental awareness that surfaced in the world in the late sixties.

Zero-Delay The amount of delay between the time a pilot ejected from a disabled aircraft, separating from the seat, until his parachute was automatically deployed. Zero-delay indicated the parachute deployed immediately.

ZI *see* **U.S.A.**

Zils (NVA Trucks) Soviet-made trucks used by the NVA. The Model 130 was a four-ton payload, two-wheel-drive truck. The Model 157 was a six-ton payload, six-wheel-drive truck. The tire pressure on the Model 157 could be adjusted from inside the truck to accommodate the terrain.

Zipper Room (Morgue Facilities) Nickname for morgue rooms where bodies received from the field were stored until processed for return to the States. Bodies that arrived at medical facilities unbagged, and soldiers who died at the facility, were stored in the "zipper room" until they could be placed in a zippered body bag. At some smaller field medical units the morgue consisted of a tent or shaded area. At larger bases the holding room might be a refrigerated van, conex container, or a dedicated refrigerated storage room. *See also* **Reefers, Body Coolers.**

Zipperheads *see* **Enemy, The**

Zippo *see* **Zippo Lighter, M-2A17 Flamethrower**

Zippo Lighter (Zippo) The most common cigarette lighter found in Vietnam. The flip top lighter was wind resistant and very popular with U.S. troops. The lighter was made by the Zippo Lighter Company. The name "Zippo" also applied to U.S. flamethrower tanks and APCs, and was also used in reference to the portable flamethrower sometimes used by U.S. troops; M-2A17. *See also* **M-132 Flamethrower APC, M-67A2, M-2A17 Flamethrower.**

Zippo Missions *see* **Zippo Raid**

Zippo Raid (Zippo Missions) Field name for operations that resulted in the burning of hootches and villages by ground troops. Zippo missions were often part of search and destroy operations that sought to kill as many of the enemy as possible and destroy anything of which he might make use. The homes and crops of suspected enemy supporters were put to the torch in an effort to eliminate the VC's sources of survival and rural support. The Zippo lighter was the most popular lighter available to GIs at the time, and was the usual source of the flame used to burn the hootches. *See also* **Restructuring, Search and Destroy.**

Zippo Squad Some field units had soldiers who took special delight in the burning of hootches and villes, whether or not it was tactically required. These individuals were commonly called the "Zippo Squad," because the Zippo lighter was carried by so many field troops.

Zippo Tank *see* **M-67A2 Flame Tank**

Zippo Track *see* **M-132 Flamethrower APC**

Zippos Common nickname applied to any number of flamethrower type weapons. The name applied to the M-67 flamethrower tank, the M-132 flamethrower APC and riverine Monitors fitted with flamethrowers. *See also* **M-67A1, M-132.**

Zips *see* **Enemy, The**

Zone of the Interior *see* **U.S.A.**

Zoo, The (Cu Loc Prison, The Zoo Annex) American POW nickname for NVN Cu Loc Prison Camp. The prison camp was located in Hanoi and was part of the NVN prison camp system holding American POWs. The Zoo was used as a meeting place where POWs could be shown to visiting dignitaries and the news media. *See also* **Hanoi Hilton.**

Zoo Annex *see* **Zoo, The**

Zoomies *see* **Flyboys**

Zorries *see* **Rubber Thongs**

ZPG *see* **Zero Population Growth**

ZPU *see* **KPV HMG**

Zulu Marine field name for "casualty report" called in to higher headquarters. Casualty reports were often coded to keep the enemy from knowing the exact extent of casualties a unit had suffered, with coded names used to reference KIA and WIA status. *See also* **Medic.**

Zuma *see* **Camp Zuma, U.S. Army Evacuation Hospital**

Zumwalt, Vice Admiral Elmo Commander, U.S. Naval Forces, Vietnam (COMNAVFORV), September '68 to May '70. Admiral Zumwalt established the Navy's program of Vietnamization shortly after assuming his command duties in Vietnam. In '70 he became the chief of naval operations. *See also* **Accelerated Turnover to Vietnam.**

Zuni (5-Inch Rockets, 127mm Rocket) Five-inch (127mm) unguided rocket primarily used by Navy and Marine aircraft for air-to-ground combat. The high explosive rockets were packed four to a pod, with at least a pair of pods mounted on the aircraft. In some instances an aircraft might carry four pods. *See also* **AGM.**

Numerals

This listing is firstly in strict numerical order and secondly in alphabetical order.

.30cal MG   *see*   M-1919A6 MMG

.38 S & W   *see*   38 Smith & Wesson

.38 Smith & Wesson   *see*   38 Smith & Wesson

.38 Special   *see*   38 Smith & Wesson

.44-Magnum Pistol   *see*   Tunnel Weapon

.45 Pistol   *see*   M-1911A1 Pistol

.50cal HMG   *see*   M-2 HMG

.51cal HMG   *see*   Type 54 HMG

¾-Ton Truck   *see*   M-37B1 Truck

#1   *see*   Number One

1/4 Cav   *see*   1st Squadron/4th Cavalry (Division Recon)

1/9 Cav   *see*   1st Squadron/9th Cavalry

1-A   *see*   Draft Classification

1-AO   *see*   Draft Classification

1Lt.   *see*   First Lieutenant

1-O   *see*   Draft Classification

1st Air Cav   *see*   1st Cavalry Division (Airmobile)

1st Air Cavalry Division   *see*   1st Cavalry Division (Airmobile)

1st Air Commando Squadron (Waterpump)   In '63 the U.S. Air Force crews of Operation Farmgate were replaced by the 1st Air Commando Squadron. The squadron continued training programs initiated by the Farmgate teams. The squadron's role in combat support of the Vietnamese was also expanded. The 1st Air Commandos deployed a detachment to Thailand in March '64, where they trained aircrews of the Royal Lao and Cambodian air forces in the operation of the T-28. The detachment, nicknamed the "Waterpump," was located at U Dorn Royal Thai Air Base, 70kms south of Vientiane (capital of Laos). *See also* Operation Farmgate.

1st Army Inf Div   *see*   1st Infantry Division

1st ARVN Infantry Division (1st ARVN; 1st, 3d, 51st, 54th ARVN Regiments)   One of the best ARVN fighting units of the Vietnam War. The 1st ARVN shared such distinction with the ARVN Airborne and ARVN Marines. The 1st ARVN operated in I Corps throughout most of the war in Vietnam and suffered heavy casualties during the Laos Incursion, Lam Son 719. The division consisted of the 1st, 3d, 51st and 54th Infantry regiments and attached artillery. *See also* Operation Lam Son 719, Hac Bao.

1st ARVN Infantry Division Recon Company   *see*   Hac Bao

1st ARVN Regiment   *see*   1st ARVN Infantry Division

1st Australian Task Force   *see*   Australian Task Force

1st Aviation Brigade (First Aviation Brigade, 1st Avn Bde)   Aviation brigade organized at Tan Son Nhut, May '66, to provide fire support, transport, medevac and recon support to Army units throughout SVN. The brigade relocated to Long Binh in December '67, and was one of the last major units to depart Vietnam, March '73. The 1st Avn Bde controlled 20 aviation battalions and four air cavalry squadrons, accounting for more than 4,200 aircraft. The 1st Aviation controlled most of the nonorganic Army aviation units in Vietnam and also provided support to ARVN forces.

1st Aviation Company (1st Avn)   U.S. Army fixed-wing transportation company which deployed to Vietnam in July '62. The unit operated the twin engine, CV-2 Caribou. The 1st Avn was located at Vung Tau and provided support to ARVN troops throughout the region. *See also* CV-7.

1st Avn Bde   *see*   1st Aviation Brigade

1st Battalion/8th Artillery Regiment *see* **Killer Junior**

1st Bde/5th Mech *see* **1st Brigade/ 5th Infantry Division (Mechanized)**

1st Brigade/1st Infantry Division The 1st Brigade deployed to Vietnam in October '65 and operated primarily in the III Corps area until the unit departed in April '70. The brigade was headquartered at Quan Loi and consisted of the 1st/2d, 1st/26th, and 1st/28th Infantry battalions, as well as the 1st/5th Arty. *See also* **1st Infantry Division.**

1st Brigade/4th Infantry Division The brigade deployed to Vietnam in October '66 and operated in the upper II Corps area. Brigade headquarters was located at Dak To, Kontum Province. The brigade consisted of the 1st/8th, 3d/8th, and 3d/12th Infantry battalions. Artillery support was provided by the 6th/29th Arty Battalion. The brigade departed Vietnam in December '70. *See also* **4th Infantry Division.**

1st Brigade/5th Infantry Division (Mechanized) (1st Bde/5th Mech, Red Devils, 1st/5th Mech) The 1st Bde deployed to the Quang Tri area of I Corps in July '68, operating along the DMZ and along the SVN/Laos border. The 1st Bde participated in Operation Dewey Canyon II as part of the preliminaries to the ARVN incursion into Laos, Operation Lam Son 719, February '71. The brigade was withdrawn from SVN in August '71. The 1st/5th consisted of three maneuver battalions: armor, infantry and mechanized infantry. Also attached to the brigade was a 155mm SPA artillery battalion, an air cavalry troop and an engineer company which specialized in armored vehicle bridge support. *See also* **5th Infantry Division.**

1st Cavalry Division (Airmobile) (1st Cav, 1st Air Cav, First Cavalry Div., First Team, Blanket Division) The first U.S. division to deploy to SVN, September '65, was also the first U.S. Army division to be helicopter based, or airmobile, and was also the first major U.S. unit to engage NVA units in SVN (Ia Drang Valley). The "First Team" consisted of nine airmobile infantry battalions, five artillery batteries, one aerial rocket artillery battalion, air recon units and the 11th Aviation Group. Nicknamed the "Blanket Division" because of the unit's large shoulder patch. The "1st Cav" deployed to II Corps and eventually served in all four Corps Zones while in Vietnam. Troopers of the 1st Cav were sometimes called "Pony Soldiers." During the VNW the 1st Cav was the only division awarded a Presidential Citation (for its performance in the Battle of the Ia Drang Valley). The 1st Cavalry and its troopers received more awards than any other U.S. unit that fought in Vietnam. The Cav started redeployment to the States in '70; its last unit, the 3rd Brigade, returned June '72. After Vietnam the Division was redesignated as Mechanized and lost its airmobile status. *See also* **11th Air Assault Division, An Khe, Blanket Division.**

1st Infantry Division (1st Inf Div, Big Red One, 1st Army Inf Div, First Infantry Div., Bloody One) The U.S. Army's 1st Infantry Division arrived in Vietnam in October '65. The division consisted of seven light infantry and two mechanized infantry battalions as well as an armored recon squadron and five artillery battalions. The "Big Red One" deployed and operated in the III Corps area until its departure from Vietnam, April '70. The division worked extensively with the 5th ARVN Infantry Division during pacification efforts and combat operations throughout III Corps. The motto of the 1st Infantry Division was "No mission too difficult. No sacrifice too great. Duty first." Nicknamed the "Big Dead One" by some of its less inspired troopers. *See also* **Big Red One Patch.**

1st Infantry Division Fire Bases (Aachen II, Bandit Hill, Holiday Inn, Mons Six, Mosby, Mahone, Luke's Castle) Series of temporary fire bases established by elements of the 1st Infantry Division in the division's area of operation north of Saigon in '67–'69. The fire bases included Aachen II, Bandit Hill, Holiday Inn, Mons Six, Cantigny, Junction City, Julie, Mahone, Luke's Castle and Mosby.

1st Kien Hoa Battalion *see* **516th Viet Cong Battalion**

1st LAAM *see* **1st Light Antiaircraft Missile Battalion**

1st Lieut. *see* **First Lieutenant**

1st Light Antiaircraft Missile Battalion (1st LAAM) Marine surface-to-air missile battery deployed to Vietnam in February '65 to provide antiaircraft defense to the Marine air base at Da Nang, I Corps. Since NVN aircraft never attacked south of the 17th Parallel (South Vietnam) the Hawk missiles of the 1st LAAM were never fired in anger. The battalion deployed four batteries in defense of Da Nang. The Marines also deployed the 2d LAAM Battalion to Chu Lai. *See also* **Hawk Missile.**

1st Logistical Command (First Logistical Command, 1st Log)   Deployed to South Vietnam in March '65 and provided logistical support to U.S. and FWF forces. The 1st Log had responsibility for II, III and IV Corps logistics support until the end of '68 and was headquartered at Long Binh, III Corps. After '68, the 1st Log also assumed logistics support for I Corps, previously supported by the U.S. Navy. Functions of the 1st Log were consolidated under USARV in '70, with USARV assuming responsibility for logistics support throughout all Vietnam. After the consolidation, the 1st Log Command was withdrawn from Vietnam.

1st Lt.   *see*   **First Lieutenant**

1st Marine Air Wing (1st MAW, First Marine Air Wing)   The 1st MAW consisted of six Marine Air Groups. The groups consisted of fighter-bombers or helicopters. The first of these units deployed to Da Nang, May '65. The 1st MAW provided air support throughout the I Corps area, and specifically, supported U.S. Marine operations of the 1st and 3rd Marine divisions. Marine Air Groups 16, 36 and 39 provided helicopter support. Marine Air Groups 11, 12 and 13 provided fighter-bomber support. *See also* **MAG-11, -12, -13, -16, -36, -39; Marine Air Wing.**

1st Marine Division (First Marine Division, The Old Breed)   Was the second U.S. Marine division to deploy to SVN, February '66. The division was initially headquartered at Chu Lai in I Corps and later moved to Da Nang. The 1st Marines primarily operated in the three southern I Corps provinces of Quang Tin, Quang Ngai and Quang Nam. In Vietnam the division consisted of the 1st, 5th and 7th Marine regiments and the battalion recon. The 26th and 27th Marine regiments of the 5th Marine Division were also temporarily at-

tached to the 1st Marines. Division assets included tank, amphibious tractor, engineer, recon and 155mm howitzer battalions. The 1st Marine Division, nicknamed "the Old Breed," departed Vietnam April '71. *See also* **III MAF.**

1st Marine Regiment (1st Marines)   The 1st Marines were part of the 1st Marine Division and operated in the central I Corps area. The regiment consisted of three battalions of infantry (1/1, 2/1, 3/1) and artillery support from 1/11 Marines, a battalion of 105mm howitzers. *See also* **1st Marine Division.**

1st Marines   *see*   **1st Marine Regiment**

1st MAW   *see*   **1st Marine Air Wing**

1st NVA Corps   *see*   **NVA I Corps**

1st NVA Division (Yellow Star Division, 44th NVA Sapper Regiment; 52d, 101D NVA Regiments)   Crack NVA Infantry Division which operated in the Central Highlands of II Corps. The division frequently crossed back and forth across the Cambodian border to avoid major contact with U.S. units operating in the same area. The division consisted of the 52d and 101D Infantry regiments and the 44th NVA Sapper Regiment.

1st NVA Regiment   *see*   **2d NVA Division**

1st Philippine Civic Action Group (PHILCAG)   The Philippines deployed several units to assist the South Vietnamese. In '64 an advisory element arrived and focused on pacification efforts in Tay Ninh Province, III Corps. In '66, combat elements arrived to protect the members of the Philippine civic action group. The primary Philippine units in Vietnam included a battalion of infantry, a battery of artillery (105mm), medical/dental battalion, engineering battalion and several support companies. By January '70 all Philippine forces had been withdrawn from Vietnam.

1st Sergeant   *see*   **Gunnery Sergeant**

1st SFG   *see*   **1st Special Forces Group**

1st Signal Brigade (First Signal Brigade, 1st Signal)   The brigade consisted of four signal groups, subdivided into signal battalions and companies. These sub units were stationed across SVN and Thailand, providing the military communications network used by the U.S. and FWFs throughout the war. The brigade, headquartered in Saigon, arrived April '66 and departed SVN November '72. The 1st Signal assumed the responsibilities for combat communications traffic and support throughout Vietnam, which was previously handled by STRATCOM, Vietnam. *See also* **Strategic Communications Command.**

1st Special Forces Group (1st SFG, First Special Forces Group) U.S. Special Forces group based in Okinawa, Japan, began operations in SVN in '57. USSF teams organized and trained the CIDG and advised the LLDB; in addition to these tasks, the 1st SFG trained Thai units in unconventional warfare and conducted counterinsurgency operations in Thailand until '73. The 1st SFG also trained Laotian irregular army personnel and Cambodian Special Forces in counterguerrilla operations. Throughout the VNW the 1st SFG continued to operate teams in SVN as well as the rest of SEA. *See also* **Special Forces.**

1st Squadron/4th Cavalry (Division Recon) (1st/4th Cav, 1/4 Cav, Quarter Cav) The squadron deployed to Vietnam in October '65 and was assigned to the 1st Infantry Division operating north of Saigon. The squadron provided the 1st Infantry Division with ground and aerial reconnaissance. The aerial reconnaissance troop (Troop D) operated as part of the 1st Aviation Battalion based at Phu Loi. The squadron departed Vietnam in February '70, and was nicknamed the "Quarter Cav."

1st Squadron/9th Cavalry (Aerial Recon) (1st/9th Cav, Troop H/16th Cavalry, 1/9 Cav, Apaches) The 1st/9th Cav consisted of six cavalry troops that operated as the reconnaissance element of the 1st Cavalry Division. Troops A–F were Air Cav recon, except Troop D which was ground recon. Each air troop consisted of three platoons: scout, rifle, and weapons, called white, blue, and red teams. Scouts conducted recon, and were reinforced by the rifle platoon while the weapons platoon provided aerial fire support. Recon forces sought out the enemy, engaging him until larger Cav elements could be "piled-on." Troop F was also known as Troop H/16th Cavalry. These air recon units had their own air assets and functioned as the eyes, ears

and nose of the 1st Cav in Vietnam. The squadron's code name in Vietnam was "Apache," and they were nicknamed the "Cav of the Cav" because of their highly effective mobile aerial reconnaissance and follow-up contact methods. The 1st/9th was also referred to as the "Buffalo Soldiers," the original nickname of the elite, all black, 9th Cavalry, formed in the American West in the 1800s to fight the Plains Indians. *See also* **1st Cavalry Division.**

1st VC Regiment *see* **1st Viet Cong Regiment**

1st Viet Cong Regiment (1st VC Regiment, DT-1 VC Regiment, Dong Thap Regiment) Believed to have operated in Binh Dinh Province, along the coast of I Corps. Sometimes referred to as the DT-1 VC Regiment. The regiment was also called the Dong Thap Regiment and operated independent of other NVA/VC units in the area. In '74 the regiment was placed under the control of the 6th NVA Division. *See also* **6th Viet Cong Division.**

1st/4th Cav *see* **1st Squadron/4th Cavalry (Division Recon)**

1st/5th Cav *see* **5th Cavalry**

1st/5th Mech *see* **1st Brigade/5th Infantry Division (Mechanized)**

1st/5th Mech/25th Infantry *see* **5th Infantry Regiment (Mechanized)**

1st/6th Infantry *see* **6th Infantry Regiment (Light) or Gunfighters**

1st/8th Arty *see* **8th Artillery Regiment**

1st/8th Infantry *see* **1st Brigade/4th Infantry Division**

1st/9th Cav *see* **1st Squadron/9th Cavalry**

1st/11th Infantry *see* **5th Infantry Division (Mechanized)**

1st/12th Infantry *see* **2d Brigade/4th Infantry Division**

1st/14th Infantry *see* **14th Infantry Regiment**

1st/16th Infantry *see* **16th Infantry Regiment**

1st/22d Infantry *see* **2d Brigade/4th Infantry Division**

1st/35th Infantry *see* **3d Brigade/4th Infantry Division**

1st/39th Arty   see   39th Artillery Regiment

1st/46th Infantry   see   46th Infantry Regiment (Light)

1st/52d Infantry   see   52d Infantry Regiment (Light)

1st/61st Mech   see   5th Infantry Division (Mechanized)

1st/77th Armor   see   5th Infantry Division (Mechanized)

1st/501st Infantry   see   501st Infantry Regiment (Airborne)

1st/502d Infantry   see   502d Infantry Regiment (Airborne/Airmobile)

1st/503d Infantry   see   503d Infantry Regiment (Airborne)

1-Y   see   Draft Classification

2—Call Sign   see   Army Call Signs

2-4-5-D   see   Agent Orange

2-4-5-T   see   Agent Orange

2/12 Marines   see   9th Marine Regiment

2 × 2s   Surgical bandage carried in field medical kits, 2 by 2 inches square, requiring tape to hold it in place. *See also* **Unit One.**

2 Corps   see   II Corps

2-Quart Canteen   see   Collapsible Canteen

2d Advanced Echelon   see   2d Air Division

2d ADVON   see   2d Air Division

2d Air Division (2d ADVON, 2d Advanced Echelon, 2d Air Force)   Command group responsible for American aircraft operating in support of South Vietnam. The 2d ADVON was located at Tan Son Nhut, and began operations in late '61, commanded by General R.H. Anthis. The 2d ADVON operated as a detachment of the 13th Air Force and was sometimes referred to as the "2d Advanced Echelon" or the "2d Air Force." The 2d ADVON was reorganized into the 7th Air Force in April '66. *See also* **Operation Farmgate, 7th Air Force.**

2d Air Force   see   2d Air Division

2d Battalion/3d Marine Regiment (2d/3d Marines)   Deployed to Vietnam in April '65. The 2d/3d Marines performed the first U.S. night helicopter assault in the Vietnam War. Elements of the battalion were air assaulted into the Elephant Valley in August '65. The battalion departed Vietnam in November '69. *See also* **Elephant Valley.**

2d Battalion/4th Marine Regiment   *see* **Magnificent Bastards**

2d Battalion/138th Artillery Regiment (2d Bn/138th Arty)   The 2/138th Artillery was a National Guard self-propelled M-109, 155mm howitzer battalion. The unit, from Louisville, Kentucky, operated in the I Corps area for one year starting in October '68. It was one of the few National Guard or Reserve units to see action in Vietnam during the war. *See also* **Reserves.**

2d Battalion/503d Infantry Regiment (2d/503d, 2/503 Airborne, Camp Zinn)   The 2d Battalion/503d Infantry operated as part of the 173d Airborne Brigade first deployed to SVN in May '65. The battalion was the only major U.S. combat unit to perform a combat parachute jump during the Vietnam War. The jump took place in February '67 into DZ Charlie located near the Cambodian border in War Zone C. The entire battalion plus its artillery support of 105mm howitzers, 4.2-inch mortars and several small vehicles made the drop. The DZ was located in enemy territory and the paratroopers and their equipment made a successful and virtually unopposed drop. Camp Zinn was the battalion's base camp located at Bien Hoa. *See also* **Operation Junction City, Drop Zone, 503d Infantry Regiment.**

2d Brigade/1st Infantry Division   The brigade deployed to Vietnam in July '65 and operated throughout the III Corps Zone. Like most of the other elements of the 1st Division, the 2d Brigade departed in April '70. The brigade consisted of the 2d/16th, 1st/18th, and 2d/18th Infantry battalions, and was supported by the 1st/7th Artillery Battalion. *See also* **1st Infantry Division.**

2d Brigade/4th Infantry Division   The brigade deployed to Vietnam in August '66 in the Central Highlands around Ban Me Thout. The brigade consisted of the 1st/12th and 1st/22d Infantry battalions, the 2d/8th

Mechanized Infantry Battalion, and the 4th/42d Artillery Battalion. The bulk of the brigade departed Vietnam in December '70. *See also* 4th Infantry Division.

2d Brigade/9th Infantry Division The 2d Bde deployed to Vietnam, January '67, and operated on the rivers of the Delta. The brigade was organized into three riverine battalions and operated as a part of the Mobile Riverine Force, TF 117. The brigade was based at Dong Tam until its departure from RVN, July '69. *See also* 9th Infantry Division, TF 117.

2d Infantry Regiment (Black Scarves, 2d/2d Mech) Two battalions of the 2d Infantry Regiment served in Vietnam. The 1st and 2d battalions deployed to Vietnam as part of the 1st Infantry Division operating as part of the 1st and 3d brigades. The 1st Bn operated as regular infantry and the 2d Battalion converted to APCs, became mechanized in '67 and was known as the 2d/2d Mech. The regiment departed Vietnam in April '70 having operated throughout most of central and northern III Corps. The 1st Battalion was nicknamed the "Black Scarves." *See also* 3d Brigade/1st Infantry Division.

2d LAAM *see* Hawk Missile

2d Light Antiaircraft Missile Battalion *see* Hawk Missile

2d Lt. *see* Second Lieutenant

2d Marine Brigade, ROK *see* Republic of Korea Marine Corps

2d NVA Corps *see* NVA II Corps

2d NVA Division (1st, 141st, 31st, 38th NVA Regiments; 52d VC Regiment) Operated in the I Corps area of South Vietnam and consisted of the 1st and 141st NVA Infantry regiments. Later in the war the 52d VC Regiment was placed under the command of the 2d NVA Division. The division was reformed in '74 with the 31st and 38th NVA regiments. These two units had previously formed part of the 711th NVA Division, but the morale of the 711th Division was so low that it adversely affected the unit's combat effectiveness. NVA higher command had hoped a name change and a shift in division leadership would correct the morale problem. There are no indications that during the '75 NVA Final Offensive the reformed 2d NVA Division performed in a more inspired manner.

2d NVA Regiment *see* 2d Viet Cong Regiment

2d ROK Marines *see* Republic of Korea Marine Corps

2d VC Regiment *see* 2d Viet Cong Regiment

2d Viet Cong Regiment (2d NVA Regiment) Operated in the Central Highlands of II Corps in the Vinh Thanh Valley region and along the coast in Binh Dinh Province. After engaging American units in Binh Dinh Province in '66, the 2d VC withdrew to Quang Nhai Province to regroup and rebuild. The regiment was originally part of the 3d Viet Cong Division. After heavy losses the regiment was rebuilt with NVA troops and redesignated the 2d NVA Regiment. *See also* 3d NVA Division.

2d/2d Mech *see* 2d Infantry Regiment

2d/3d Marines *see* 2d Battalion/3d Marine Regiment

2d/5th Cav *see* 5th Cavalry

2d/8th Mech *see* 2d Brigade/4th Infantry Division

2d/9th Arty *see* 3d Brigade/4th Infantry Division

2d/14th Infantry *see* 14th Infantry Regiment

2d/16th Infantry *see* 16th Infantry Regiment

2d/35th Infantry *see* 3d Brigade/4th Infantry Division

2d/138th Arty *see* 2d Battalion/138th Artillery Regiment

2d/501st Infantry *see* 501st Infantry Regiment (Airborne)

2d/502d Infantry *see* 502d Infantry Regiment (Airborne/Airmobile)

2KW Searchlight *see* Infrared

2Lt. *see* Second Lieutenant

2-S *see* Draft Classification

2½-Ton Truck *see* M-35 Truck

2.75-Inch Flechette Rocket (Flechette Rocket, Nails) Helicopter gunship rocket that contained a flechette filled warhead. Each rocket contained several thousand steel finned darts that were very effective at close range and used exclusively against enemy personnel. Helicopter crews nicknamed the rockets "nails." *See also* **Flechette.**

2.75-Inch Rocket *see* **XM-159C Rocket**

3 – Call Sign *see* **Army Call Signs**

3/3 Marines *see* **Swift, Silent and Deadly**

3/4 Cav *see* **3d Squadron/4th Cavalry (Division Recon)**

3 Corps *see* **III Corps**

3 Heart Ticket *see* **Purple Heart**

3d ARVN Regiment *see* **1st ARVN Infantry Division**

3d Binh Dinh Division *see* **3d NVA Division**

3d Brigade Task Force *see* **3d Brigade/82d Airborne Division**

3d Brigade/1st Infantry Division (Iron Brigade) As part of the 1st Infantry Division, the 3d Brigade deployed to Vietnam in October '65, operating in the III Corps area. The brigade departed Vietnam April '70 and consisted of four battalions, the 2d/2d and 1st/16th Mechanized Infantry, the 2d/28th Infantry and the 2d/33d Arty. *See also* **1st Infantry Division.**

3d Brigade/4th Infantry Division The brigade deployed to Vietnam in October '66 for operations in the Pleiku area of the Central Highlands. The brigade consisted of the 1st/14th, 1st/35th, and 2d/35th Infantry battalions, and the 2d/9th Artillery Battalion. The brigade departed Vietnam in April '70. *See also* **4th Infantry Division.**

3d Brigade/82d Airborne Division (3d Brigade Task Force) The 3d Brigade/82d ABN, deployed to SVN for emergency service after the start of the communist Tet Offensive of '68. The brigade consisted of three airborne infantry battalions, an artillery battalion and support units. The 3d/82d deployed to SVN February '68, was attached to the 101st Airborne, and provided security for Hue City in I Corps. In Septem-

ber '68 the brigade relocated to the Saigon area, under the control of the Capital Military Command. The brigade departed RVN, December '69, and consisted of the 3d/187th, 1st/506th, and 2d/506th Airmobile Infantry battalions. Also assigned to the brigade was the 2d/319th Artillery Battalion.

3d Field Hospital (U.S. Army Saigon Hospital, 3d Field) Main U.S. Army field hospital, located at Tan Son Nhut in Saigon. 3d Field deployed to Vietnam in April '65 and was combined with the 51st Field Hospital to form the U.S. Army Saigon Hospital. The military components of the hospital departed Vietnam in May '72.

3d MAB *see* **III Marine Amphibious Force**

3d Marine Amphibious Brigade *see* **III Marine Amphibious Force**

3d Marine Amphibious Force *see* **III Marine Amphibious Force**

3d Marine Division (Third Marine Division) Elements of the U.S. Marines 3d Division deployed to SVN in March '65 at Da Nang, I Corps, and operated in the I Corps area until their departure, November '69. The division primarily consisted of the 3d, 4th, and 9th Marine Infantry regiments, 12th Marine Artillery Regiment, and the division's tank, antitank, engineer, 155mm howitzer, amphibious tractor, and recon battalions. The 3d Marine Division was primarily responsible for the northern part of Quang Tri Province and the line of defense along the DMZ. The 3d Marine Division also was the controlling headquarters for Khe Sanh in '68. *See also* **Leatherneck Square, SS Mayaguez.**

3d Marine Division Reconnaissance Company (Swift, Deadly, Silent; Eyes of the 26th Marines) Marine company, the "Eyes of the 26th Marines," provided ground reconnaissance for the 26th Marine Regiment. The motto of the company was "Swift, Deadly, Silent." Marine recon teams of 4–12 men normally operated far removed from the regiment. During the siege of Khe Sanh the recon company remained at KSCB as a reserve reaction force. *See also* **3d Marine Division.**

3d Marine Regiment (3d Marines) The 3d Marines were part of the 3d Marine

Division and saw extensive service along the DMZ in South Vietnam. The regiment consisted of three infantry battalions, designated 1/3, 2/3, and 3/3 Marines. Artillery support was provided by a 105mm howitzer battalion, the 1/12 Marines. *See also* 3d Marine Division.

3d NVA Corps *see* NVA III Corps

3d NVA Division (3d Viet Cong Division, 3d Binh Dinh Division; 2d, 12th, 21st NVA Regiments) The 3d NVA Division was previously known as the 3d Viet Cong Division. After heavy VC losses the VC division was reorganized and renamed as the 3d NVA Division. As a VC division the unit was composed of the 2d, 18th and 22d VC regiments. The 2d VC Regiment was replenished with NVA troops and designated the 2d NVA Regiment. The decimated 18th and 22d VC regiments were replaced by the 12th and 21st NVA regiments. During the war the division operated throughout Binh Dinh Province and was sometimes referred to as the 3d Binh Dinh Division. *See also* 2d Viet Cong Regiment.

3d Phuoc Long Division (274th VC, 33d, 201st NVA Regiments) NVA division formed in '74 from independent regiments that had operated in the Phuoc Long Province area during the war. The regiments that formed the division were the 274th VC, and the 33d and 201st NVA Infantry regiments.

3d Reconnaissance Battalion/3d Marines *see* Swift, Silent and Deadly

3d Squadron/4th Cavalry (Division Recon) (3d/4th Cav, Three-Quarter Cav, 3/4 Cav) Elements of the squadron deployed to Vietnam in March '66 and operated as the ground reconnaissance force for the 25th Infantry Division. The 3d Squadron consisted of APCs and Sheridan tanks for armored recon, and a separate air cav troop (Troop D) for aerial recon. Troop D was assigned to the 25th Aviation Battalion. The squadron operated in the II Corps area until its departure from Vietnam in December '70. After the squadron departed, the air recon troop remained in Vietnam and operated as part of II Field Force. The troop was reorganized into Troop F, 4th Cavalry in February '71 and operated as recon until its departure from Vietnam in February '73.

See also 25th Infantry Division.

3d Viet Cong Division *see* 3d NVA Division

3d/4th Cav *see* 3d Squadron/4th Cavalry (Division Recon)

3d/5th Cav *see* 5th Cavalry

3d/8th Infantry *see* 1st Brigade/4th Infantry Division

3d/12th Infantry *see* 1st Brigade/4th Infantry Division

3d/16th Arty *see* 16th Artillery Regiment

3d/39th Infantry *see* 39th Infantry Regiment (Infantry)

3d/187th Infantry *see* 187th Infantry Regiment

3d/503d Infantry *see* 503d Infantry Regiment (Airborne)

3.5-Inch Rocket Launcher *see* M-20 Rocket Launcher

4—Call Sign *see* Army Call Signs

4 Corps *see* IV Corps

4-F *see* Draft Classification

4th Battalion/42d Artillery Regiment *see* 42d Artillery Regiment

4th Inf Div *see* 4th Infantry Division

4th Infantry Division (4th Inf Div, Ivy Division, Poison Ivy Division, Famous Fourth, Funky Fourth) The 4th Inf Div deployed to SVN in September '66, and consisted of three infantry brigades. The 3d Bde operated in III Corps, and was eventually transferred to the control of the 25th Inf Div at Cu Chi. The other two brigades operated in the Pleiku and An Khe areas of II Corps. The division participated in the '70 Cambodian Incursion. The Funky Fourth, as it came to be known in the later days of the war, started its withdrawal from Vietnam in December '70. *See also* Titty Hill, Ivy Division Patch, Camp Enari.

4th Marine Regiment (China Marines, Fourth Marine Regiment, 4th Marines) The 4th Marines began deploying to I Corps, Vietnam in April '65. The "China Marines" operated extensively along the

DMZ until their departure from Vietnam the end of '70. The regiment consisted of three infantry battalions, designated the 1/4, 2/4, and 3/4 Marines. The 3/12 Marines provided the regiment with a battalion of 105mm howitzer support. The regiment was part of the 3d Marine Division.

4th Marines *see* **4th Marine Regiment**

4th NVA Corps *see* **NVA IV Corps**

4th NVA Regiment Participated in the attack on Hue during the '68 Tet Offensive. The 4th NVA operated as an independent regiment, reporting directly to the NVA's Tri-Thien Military Region Headquarters. *See also* **Tri-Thien Front.**

4th POW Wing Americans who were held prisoner by the North Vietnamese at the Hao Lo Prison called themselves the 4th POW Wing. The January '73 Peace Accords between the U.S. and North Vietnam required the release of all American POWs within 60 days of the signing of the accords. Five hundred ninety-one prisoners were eventually released. *See also* **American POWs, Prisoner of War.**

4th Tactical Fighter Wing *see* **Udorn Royal Thai Air Base**

4th/12th Cav *see* **5th Infantry Division (Mechanized)**

4th/39th Infantry *see* **Hardcore Battalion**

4th/42d Arty *see* **42d Artillery Regiment**

4th/503d Infantry *see* **503d Infantry Regiment (Airborne)**

4.2-Inch Mortar Carrier *see* **M-30 4.2-Inch Mortar**

5—Call Sign *see* **Army Call Signs**

5 × 5 *see* **Lima Charlie**

5-Inch Rockets *see* **Zuni**

5-Quart Bladder (Flotation Bladder Assembly) Five-quart capacity bladder first used by the U.S. military in '68. The vinyl bladder was used to carry water or could be inflated with air and used as a flotation device. The bladder was fitted with a nylon cover that featured eyelets and string ties for attaching the bladder to field equipment. *See also* **Collapsible Canteen.**

5-Ton Truck *see* **M-54 Truck**

5th ARVN Division (7th, 8th, 9th ARVN Regiments) Operated in the III Corps area. After the withdrawal of U.S. combat forces the 5th ARVN operated primarily in the area north of Saigon. The division consisted of four artillery battalions and the 7th, 8th, and 9th ARVN Infantry regiments. The 5th ARVN established its division headquarters at Lai Khe after the departure of the U.S. 1st Infantry Division in '70.

5th Battalion/42d Artillery Regiment *see* **42d Artillery Regiment**

5th Cav *see* **5th Cavalry**

5th Cavalry (Black Knights, 5th Cav, 1st/5th Cav, 2d/5th Cav, 3d/5th Cav) The 5th Cav deployed its 1st and 2d battalions to Vietnam September '65 under control of the 1st Cavalry Division. The two battalions operated in II and III Corps, as airmobile infantry, until their withdrawal in April '71. The 3d Squadron, which was the 5th Cav's recon squadron, arrived in Vietnam in February '70 and operated with the 9th Inf, 1st Cav and the 5th Mech divisions. The 3d Squadron departed Vietnam in November '71. *See also* **1st Cavalry Division.**

5th Inf Div *see* **5th Infantry Division (Mechanized)**

5th Infantry Division (Mechanized) (5th Mech, 5th Inf Div, 1st Bde/5th Inf Div, Diamond Division) The 5th Infantry Division was stationed at Fort Carson, Colorado. In July '68 the 1st Brigade of the division deployed to Vietnam, and operated in the Quang Tri area of I Corps. The brigade consisted of mechanized infantry (1st/61st) and cavalry (4th/12th), armor (1st/77th), engineers (Co A/7th) self-propelled artillery (5th/4th) and a battalion of airmobile infantry (1st/11th). After participating in Operation Lam Son 719, the brigade began its withdrawal from Vietnam in August '71. The division was nicknamed the "Diamond Division" because of the unit's small, bright red, diamond shaped unit patch. *See also* **1st Brigade, 5th Infantry Division (Mechanized).**

5th Infantry Regiment (Mechanized) (1st/5th Mech, Bobcats) The 1st Battalion/5th Infantry deployed to Vietnam in January '66 as part of the 25th Infantry

Division. The battalion was nicknamed the "Bobcats" and operated around the Saigon areas of Cu Chi and Xuan Loc until its departure in April '71. The unit was originally assigned to the 2d Brigade as regular infantry, but later operated from APCs as mechanized infantry. See also 25th Infantry Division.

5th Marine Division (5th Marines, 26th/27th/28th Regimental Landing Teams, RLT 26, 27, 28) The 5th Marine Division consisted of three Regimental Landing Teams: the 26th, 27th and 28th, and the 13th Regimental Artillery. The 26th and 27th RLTs deployed to Vietnam in September '66, under the control of the 1st and 3d Marine divisions and operated in I Corps. The 26th RLT was ultimately assigned the defense of the Khe Sanh Combat Base in '67/68. The regiments continued operations in I Corps until September '68 when the 27th RLT began redeployment to the U.S.; the 26th RLT remained in Vietnam until March '70. See also 1st and 3d Marine Divisions.

5th Marine Regiment (5th Marines) The regiment operated along the coast of I Corps between Chu Lai and Da Nang as part of the 1st Marine Division. The regiment consisted of three infantry battalions (1/5, 2/5, 3/5) and a battalion of 105mm artillery, the 2/11 Marines. See also 1st Marine Division.

5th Marines see **5th Marine Regiment**

5th Mech see **5th Infantry Division (Mechanized)**

5th NVA Regiment see **324B NVA Division**

5th SFG (Airborne) see **5th Special Forces Group**

5th Special Forces Group (5th SFG [Airborne]) The 5th SFG deployed to Vietnam in October '64 for the purpose of reconnaissance, organization and direction of CIDGs, and to provide training and support to the South Vietnamese Special Forces. The group consisted of four field companies (battalion sized) subdivided into detachments. C detachments controlled B detachments, with B detachments controlling the actual field units, or A-Teams. In addition to training the Vietnamese and directing Montagnard forces, the SFG operated special missions into North Vietnam, Laos, and Cambodia. The missions included recon, targeting and aircrew retrieval. As part of their anticommunist guerrilla efforts, the Special Forces also assisted in establishing schools, medical clinics and public works projects to help the civilian population of South Vietnam. Based in Nha Trang, II Corps, the 5th SFG was the largest Special Forces group operating in SEA. The group operated teams throughout Vietnam performing recon and raids, and organizing CIDGs and Strike Forces. As the war continued, the 5th SFG also trained and advised the SVN Special Forces and LRRP units of the U.S. Army. The 5th SFG group conducted special projects under the code names Delta, Sigma, Rapid Fire, Omega and MACV-SOG. SF teams operated not only in SVN, but also in Laos, Cambodia and North Vietnam. The SFG began withdrawing from Vietnam in March '71.

5th VC see **5th Viet Cong Division**

5th Viet Cong Division (5th VC; 6th, 174th, 275th NVA/VC Regiments) Operated primarily in the III and IV Corps areas of Vietnam. The division participated in the attacks on Saigon during the '68 Tet Offensive. Elements of the division operated throughout Phuoc Tuy and southern Gia Dinh provinces. Because of heavy casualty losses, the division consisted almost entirely of NVA replacements by '74. At that time the division consisted of the 6th, 174th, and 275th NVA/VC Infantry regiments. Also attached to the division were two Sapper regiments.

5th/4th Arty see **5th Infantry Division (Mechanized)**

5th/16th Arty see **16th Artillery Regiment**

5th/42d Arty see **42d Artillery Regiment**

5th/46th Infantry see **46th Infantry Regiment (Light)**

6 — Call Sign see **Army Call Signs**

6 × 6 Truck see **M-35 Truck**

6 — Actual see **Army Call Signs**

6th Infantry Regiment (Light) (Regulars, 1st/6th Infantry) The 1st Battalion of the 6th Infantry Regiment deployed to Vietnam in October '67 as part of the 198th Infantry Brigade. The regimental nickname of the 6th Infantry was the "Regulars." The battalion operated in the southern area of I Corps with the Americal Division. The battalion departed from Da Nang in November '71. *See also* **198th Light Infantry Brigade, Gunfighters.**

6th NVA Division   *see*   **6th Viet Cong Division**

6th NVA Regiment   Independent NVA infantry regiment that operated in Thua Thien Province, I Corps. The regiment captured the walled Citadel in Hue during the '68 Tet Offensive. *See also* **Hue, 324B NVA Regiment.**

6th NVA/VC Regiment   *see*   **5th Viet Cong Division**

6th VC Division   *see*   **6th Viet Cong Division**

6th Viet Cong Division (6th VC Division; 24th, 207th, 320th, 812th NVA Regiments)   The 6th VC Division primarily operated in the IV Corps area of South Vietnam and consisted of the 24th, 207th, and 320th NVA Infantry regiments. In '73 the division was disbanded, but reformed in '74 and consisted of the 207th and 812th NVA Infantry regiments, and the 1st VC Regiment. The reformed division was designated the 6th NVA Division.

6th/29th Arty   *see*   **1st Brigade/4th Infantry Division**

6th/56th Arty   *see*   **Air Defense Artillery**

6th/71st Arty   *see*   **Air Defense Artillery**

7/1 Cavalry   *see*   **7th Squadron, 1st Cavalry Regiment (Dragoons)**

7/13th Air Force Headquarters   *see*   **Udorn Royal Thai Air Base**

7th Air Force (USSAG/7AF, U.S. Support Activities Group/7th Air Force)   U.S. Air Force command responsible for conducting air operations in South Vietnam. The command group USSAG was organized in April '66 and was headquartered at Ton Son Nhut Air Base in Saigon. In addition to controlling Tactical Fighters and Fighter-Bombers, the command also coordinated military airlift duties throughout South Vietnam. In early '73 the USSAG command was relocated from Tan Son Nhut, SVN, to Nakhon Phanom Air Base, Thailand, to be later deactivated in June '75, after the fall of Saigon. All Air Force operations in Vietnam were under the command of the 7th Air Force, with the exception of the B-52 Bomber Command, which was controlled by Strategic Air Command. *See also* **2d Air Division.**

7th ARVN Division (10th, 11th, 12th ARVN Regiments)   Operated in the northern part of IV Corps during most of the Vietnam War. The division was headquartered at My Tho in Dinh Tuong Province. The 7th ARVN consisted of four 105mm artillery battalions and the 10th, 11th, and 12th Infantry regiments.

7th ARVN Regiment   *see*   **5th ARVN Division**

7th Fleet   The responsible command for U.S. Navy operations in the Western Pacific Ocean. Part of the command's duties were to provide naval support to American efforts in Vietnam. The 7th Fleet deployed five Task Forces for operations in Southeast Asia: Task Force 70.8, 73, 76, 77 and 117. These TFs provided offshore fire support for Free World Forces, supply and medical aid, naval air support, amphibious operations and riverine assault operations. In '75 elements of TF 76, Task Group 76.8, assisted in the evacuation of Phnom Penh and Saigon. *See also* **TF: 70.8, 73, 76, 77, 117; TG 76.8.**

7th Marine Regiment (7th Marines)   The 7th Marines operated in the central I Corps area as part of the 1st Marine Division. The regiment consisted of three infantry battalions (1/7, 2/7, 3/7) and artillery support from the 3/11 Marines, a battalion of 105mm howitzers. *See also* **1st Marine Division.**

7th Marines   *see*   **7th Marine Regiment**

7th NVA Division (141st, 165th, 209th NVA Regiments; 312th NVA Division)   Operated out of Cambodia and participated in the attacks to seize Saigon during the '68 Tet Offensive. The 7th primarily operated in the northern provinces of III Corps, but later in the war it moved into I Corps. The division consisted of the 141st, 165th and 209th Infantry regiments and also operated under the designation of the 312th NVA Division.

7th SFG *see* **7th Special Forces Group**

7th Special Forces Group (7th SFG) Based out of Fort Bragg, North Carolina, the 7th Special Forces Group operated advisory teams in SVN. The teams organized and directed CIDGs, and advised the South Vietnamese Special Forces stationed in defensive camps located along South Vietnam's western border. Teams of the 7th SFG conducted border surveillance, raids and ambushes against NVA/VC units operating in the area.

7th Squadron/1st Cavalry Regiment (Dragoons) (7/1 Cavalry, Dragoons) The 7th Squadron of the 1st Cavalry (First Regiment of Dragoons) deployed to SVN February '68. The 800-man squadron was a helicopter based search/attack cavalry force that operated as part of the 164th Aviation Group/1st Aviation Brigade. The 7/1 Cav operated out of Vinh Long in IV Corps. The original Dragoons were infantrymen who rode into battle mounted on horseback. As wars modernized the mounts became armored cars and halftracks. During Vietnam, the cavalrymen's mounts were the Armored Personnel Carrier and the helicopter.

7th/8th Arty *see* **8th Artillery Regiment**

7.62mm Minigun Pod *see* **Minigun, XM-18 Minigun**

8-Inch Howie *see* **M-110 8-Inch SPA, M-55 8-Inch SPA**

8-Inch Howitzer *see* **M-110 8-Inch SPA, M-55 8-Inch SPA**

8-Inch Self-Propelled Howitzer *see* **M-110 8-Inch SPA, M-55 8-Inch SPA**

8-Inch SPA *see* **M-110 8-Inch SPA, M-55 8-Inch SPA**

8-Inchers *see* **M-110 8-Inch SPA, M-55 8-Inch SPA**

8mm AA (M-1944 AA Gun) Soviet-made antiaircraft artillery used by the NVA for air defense. The 8mm AA fired 20-pound shells to an altitude of 30,000 feet at a rate of 20 rounds per minute. *See also* **Antiaircraft Guns.**

8th Artillery Regiment (Automatic 8th) The 8th Arty deployed two battalions to Vietnam. The 1st/8th Arty was a 105mm howitzer battalion which arrived in Vietnam in January '66 as part of the 2d Brigade/25th Infantry Division and operated from the division base camp at Cu Chi, III Corps. The 7th/8th Arty was a composite 8-inch howitzer and 175mm gun battalion. The 7th/8th arrived in June '67 and operated from Bear Cat and Bien Hoa under control of the II FFV Artillery. The two battalions departed Vietnam in mid-'71. The regiment was nicknamed the "Automatic Eight." The 1st/8th Arty had the distinction of naming a specialized artillery technique called "Killer Junior," which was used against massed enemy ground attacks at point-blank range. *See also* **Killer Junior.**

8th ARVN Regiment *see* **5th ARVN Division**

8th Cavalry *see* **8th Cavalry (Airborne/Airmobile Infantry)**

8th Cavalry (Airborne/Airmobile Infantry, 8th Cavalry) The 8th Cav deployed two battalions to Vietnam, September '65, as part of the 1st Cav Div. As originally deployed, the battalions were airborne infantry, but in November '66 the battalions lost their jump status and were redesignated as Airmobile Infantry.

8th Field Hospital Deployed to Vietnam, April '62, departed, August '71. The 8th was located on the coast at Nha Trang, Khanh Hoa Province, II Corps, until September '70 when it was relocated to An Khe, II Corps. In '71 the hospital was relocated to the coast at Tuy Hoa, II Corps. The 8th Field Hospital was the first U.S. Army field hospital to be deployed to SVN.

8th NVA Division *see* **Z-15 NVA Regiment**

8th Tactical Bomb Squadron *see* **Tactical Bomb Squadron**

8th Tactical Fighter Wing *see* **Ubon Royal Thai Air Base**

8th TBS *see* **Tactical Bomb Squadron**

8th TFW *see* **Ubon Royal Thai Air Base**

9-to-5 War *see* **Nine-to-Five War**

9mm Pistol *see* **Type 59 Pistol, Browning 9mm**

9th ARVN Division (14th, 15th, 16th ARVN Regiments) Initially operated in Binh Dinh and Phu Yen provinces of II Corps, but shortly after '63 the division was relocated to IV Corps with headquarters located at Sa Dec. The division consisted of the 14th, 15th, and 16th Infantry regiments as well as four artillery battalions.

9th ARVN Regiment *see* **5th ARVN Division**

9th Cavalry *see* **1st Squadron/9th Cavalry (Aerial Recon)**

9th Inf Div *see* **9th Infantry Division**

9th Infantry Division (Old Reliables, Flower Power, Psychedelic Cookie, Bloody-Assholes) The 9th deployed to Vietnam in December '66, the 1st and 3d brigades to III Corps; the 2d Brigade operated with the Mobile Riverine Force in IV Corps. By the beginning of '69, the primary operations area of the 9th Inf Div was IV Corps. Elements of the division departed July '69, the first U.S. combat units to leave Vietnam. The 3d Brigade remained in Vietnam until October '70. It was assigned to the 25th Infantry Division and operated from Tan An in III Corps. The 9th acquired several nicknames related to its colorful octofoil unit patch which looked like a scalloped edge cookie. *See also* **TF 117, Flower Power Patch, Delta Butcher, 2d Brigade/9th Infantry Division.**

9th Infantry Division Reliable Academy *see* **M-14 Sniper Rifle**

9th Infantry Division, ROK (White Horse Division) South Korea's 9th Infantry Division deployed to SVN in September '66, and was headquartered near Cam Ranh Bay, Khanh Hoa Province, II Corps. The division consisted of three infantry regiments, four artillery battalions, a recon and a tank company. The 9th remained in SVN until their withdrawal in '73. *See also* **Republic of Korea.**

9th MAB *see* **9th Marine Amphibious Brigade**

9th Marine Amphibious Brigade (Striking Ninth, 9th Marine Expeditionary Brigade, 9th MAB, 9th MEB) The U.S. Marine force originally deployed to Vietnam in March '65 was called the 9th Marine Expeditionary Brigade, but the name was later changed to the 9th Marine Amphibious Brigade to sound less "colonial." The brigade consisted of two battalions, the 1st Bn/3d Marines and the 3d Bn/9th Marines. The brigade was assigned to provide security for Da Nang Air Base. In May '65 the III MAF was formed to take control of all Marine units in I Corps and the 9th MAB battalions rejoined their parent units in Vietnam. At the end of the war the 9th MAB assisted with the evacuation of Saigon. In May '75 the 9th MAB attempted to rescue the crew of the SS *Mayaguez*. *See also* **III Marine Expeditionary Force, Operation Frequent Wind, SS Mayaguez.**

9th Marine Expeditionary Brigade *see* **9th Marine Amphibious Brigade**

9th Marine Expeditionary Force *see* **9th Marine Amphibious Brigade**

9th Marine Regiment (9th Marines) The 9th Marines deployed to Vietnam in March '65 as part of the first American ground combat forces to enter South Vietnam. The regiment consisted of three battalions of infantry designated 1/9, 2/9, and 3/9 Marines. Artillery support was provided by the 2/12 Marines, a 105mm howitzer battalion. The regiment was part of the 3d Marine Division and operated in the northern I Corps area. *See also* **3d Marine Division.**

9th Marines *see* **9th Marine Regiment**

9th MEB *see* **9th Marine Amphibious Brigade**

9th MEF *see* **9th Marine Amphibious Brigade**

9th NVA Regiment *see* **304th NVA Division, 320th NVA Division, 968th NVA Division**

9th VC Division *see* **9th Viet Cong Division**

9th Viet Cong Division (9th VC Division) Operated in the areas of Phuoc Tuy and Gia Dinh provinces in the early and mid-sixties. In '67, operating from sanctuaries along the Cambodian border, elements of the 9th VC attempted to overrun Loc Ninh. Loc Ninh was reinforced by ARVN and U.S. combat units, resulting in heavy VC casualties and the retreat of the VC units back into their sanctuaries in Cambodia. The 9th was organized by the NVA and consisted of the 95C NVA, 271st and 272d Viet Cong regiments. The division made its debut during an attack against Binh Gia in '64. By the time of the '72 Eastertide Offensive the two VC regiments were manned entirely by NVA troops. *See also* **Battle of Loc Ninh, Operation Attleboro.**

#10 *see* **Number Ten**

10th Aeromed *see* **Aeromedical Evacuation Units**

10th Aeromedical Evacuation Group *see* **Aeromedical Evacuation Units**

10th ARVN Regiment *see* **7th ARVN Division**

10th NVA Division (F-10 Division; 28th, 66th, 95B NVA Regiments) One of the NVA's divisions that operated in the Central Highlands northwest of Nha Trang in Khanh Hoa Province, II Corps. The 10th NVA was sometimes referred to as the F-10 Division. The division consisted of the 28th, 66th, and 95B NVA Infantry regiments and division artillery.

11 Bang-Bang *see* **11 Bravo**

11 Bravo (11B, 11 Bush, Eleven Bravo, 11 Bang-Bang, 0311) MOS for a U.S. Army infantryman, the "infantry light weapons specialist." In Vietnam infantrymen in the field referred to themselves as "11 Bush," the "grunt." For the Marines the MOS code for the infantryman was "0311." Some other Army combat MOSs were 11C (11 Charlie)—Infantry Mortars, 11D (11 Delta)—Reconnaissance Specialist/Cavalry Scout, 11E (11 Echo)—Armor, 12B (12 Bravo)—Combat Engineer, and 13B (13 Bravo)—Field Artillery. *See also* **Military Occupation Specialty, The Infantry Soldier.**

11 Bush *see* **11 Bravo**

11B, 11C, 11D, 11E *see* **11 Bravo**

11th AAD *see* **11th Air Assault Division (Test)**

11th ACR *see* **11th Armored Cavalry Regiment**

11th Air Assault Division (Test) (11th AAD) Army division raised in '62 to test a new concept in mobile warfare using the helicopter. The division was designated the 11th Air Assault Division (Test) and was formed at Fort Benning. It conducted various tests and trials at Fort Rucker and Fort Bragg. The division consisted of less than 15,000 men, fixed and rotary-wing aircraft, and less than 1,000 vehicles. The Air Force opposed the division having its own fixed-wing assets, but their complaints were overruled by Secretary of Defense Robert McNamara. The division was converted from "test" to full active combat status in July '65, and redesignated the 1st Cavalry Division (Airmobile). Shortly afterward America's first helicopter equipped combat division deployed to South Vietnam. *See also* **1st Cavalry Division.**

11th Armored Cavalry Regiment (11th ACR, Blackhorse Regiment, Scared Horse Regiment) The 11th ACR deployed to Vietnam in September '66 and operated in the III Corps area until its departure in '71. The Blackhorse Regiment's base camp was located at Xuan Loc, 60kms east of Saigon. The regiment consisted of three armored cavalry squadrons and an air cavalry troop, with associated artillery. The unit patch of the 11th ACR featured the black silhouette of a rearing horse. The unit was nicknamed the "Scared Horse Regiment." *See also* **Cambodian Incursion, Blackhorse Patch.**

11th ARVN Regiment *see* **7th ARVN Division**

11th Aviation Group Aviation assets assigned to the 1st Cav in Vietnam. The group consisted of several companies of assault, support, gunship aircraft and three separate Air Cav troops. The group first deployed to RVN August '65, and returned to the States in March '73.

11th Inf Bde *see* **11th Infantry Brigade (Light)**

11th Infantry Brigade (Light) (11th Inf Bde, Butcher Brigade) The 11th, as part of the U.S. Americal Division, conducted most of its operations in the southern portion of I Corps against NVA regulars. The 11th was nicknamed the Butcher Brigade after the My Lai Incident in '68 (Lt. William Calley's platoon was part of the brigade at the time). The brigade was poorly trained and poorly led, and was known for its inflated body counts.

−12 *see* Dash-Twelve

12 Bravo *see* 11 Bravo

−12 Logbook *see* Dash-Twelve

12.7mm Machine Gun *see* Type 54 HMG

12B−12 Bravo *see* 11 Bravo

12th Air Commando Squadron *see* Ranch Hand

12th ARVN Regiment *see* 7th ARVN Division

12th Evac *see* 12th Evacuation Hospital (Semimobile)

12th Evacuation Hospital (Semimobile) (12th Med, 12th Evac, MASSCAL Hospital) The 12th Evac deployed to Vietnam in September '66 with the hospital located at Cu Chi, base camp for the 25th Infantry Division. The 300-bed hospital primarily served the 25th Infantry and other units in the area, providing normal, emergency and intensive care medical treatment. The 12th Evac was also a designated "MASSCAL Hospital" with facilities to handle mass casualty situations. The hospital served as an evacuation hospital for preparing the seriously wounded for transport to larger field hospitals and also had a small ward available for civilian (Vietnamese) casualties. *See also* Bunker Bunnies.

12th Med *see* 12th Evacuation Hospital (Semimobile)

12th NVA Regiment *see* 3d NVA Division

13B−13 Bravo *see* 11 Bravo

13 Bravo *see* 11 Bravo

13th Air Force U.S. Air Force command group located at Clark Air Force Base in the Philippines which provided the tactical and materiel support for 7th Air Force operations in Southeast Asia.

13th Aviation Battalion (Combat) (13th Combat Aviation, Guardian) The 13th Aviation was initially formed from the 114th and 121st Aviation companies. The 13th eventually consisted of nineteen aviation companies which included four assault helicopter companies, a surveillance aircraft company and a fixed-wing transport company. The battalion operated in the IV Corps area providing support to riverine operations until its departure from Vietnam in April '72. The 13th was assigned to four higher headquarters during its tour in Vietnam: 12th Aviation Group, 164th Aviation Group, 1st Aviation Brigade and the Delta Provisional Aviation Group.

13th Aviation Group *see* 13th Aviation Battalion (Combat)

13th Combat Aviation *see* 13th Aviation Battalion (Combat)

13th Tactical Bomb Squadron *see* Tactical Bomb Squadron

13th TBS *see* Tactical Bomb Squadron

14.5mm HMG *see* KPV HMG

14th ARVN Regiment *see* 9th ARVN Division

14th Infantry Regiment (14th Infantry, Golden Dragons, 1st/14th, 2d/14th Infantry) The 14th Infantry deployed two battalions and a separate rifle company to SVN. The 1st and 2d battalions deployed to Vietnam in January and April '66 as part of the 25th Infantry Division. The 1st Battalion later was moved to Duc Pho, I Corps, and transferred to the 3d Brigade/4th Infantry Division. A separated rifle company (Company E) was deployed to III Corps in June '71 to provide security for the base at Long Binh. The 14th was nicknamed the "Golden Dragons." Both battalions departed Vietnam in December '70, and Company E (Rifle Security) departed November '72. The 2d Battalion operated in the III Corps area as part of the 1st and 3d brigades of the 25th Infantry Division. *See also* 3d Brigade/4th Infantry Division.

14th Special Operations Wing *see* Air Commando Wing

15th ARVN Regiment *see* 9th ARVN Division

16th Artillery Regiment (16th Arty, 5th/16th Arty, 3d/16th Arty) The 16th Arty Regiment deployed two battalions and one additional 155mm howitzer battery to Vietnam. 3d Battalion (155mm howitzers) deployed in June '67 and operated out of Chu Lai in support of the Americal Division in I/II Corps. The 5th Battalion (155mm howitzer/8-inch SPA) deployed in October '66 and supported the 4th Infantry Division in II Corps. The additional battery that deployed to Vietnam in June '66 operated in support of the 1st Cavalry Division in II Corps. After '68 the battery operated in I and III Corps until its withdrawal in April '70. The two battalions withdrew from Vietnam in '71. *See also* **Cherry Hill.**

16th Arty *see* **16th Artillery Regiment**

16th ARVN Regiment *see* **9th ARVN Division**

16th Cavalry *see* **1st Squadron, 9th Cavalry (Aerial Recon)**

16th Infantry Regiment (1st/16th, 2d/16th Infantry)   The 1st and 2d battalions of the 16th Infantry operated as part of the 1st Infantry Division in III Corps. The 1st Battalion deployed in October '65 and primarily operated with the 1st and 3d brigades of the division. The 2d Battalion deployed to Vietnam in July '65 and operated under the 2d Brigade. Both battalions departed Vietnam in April '70. In September '68 the 1st and the 9th Infantry divisions traded units; infantry troops from the 1st/16th transferred to the 5th/60th at Dong Tam, while the mechanized units of the 5th/60th transferred to the 1st/16th at Lai Khe; the 1st/16th became mechanized and the 5th/60th became ground (riverine) infantry.

17th Aviation Company (Silver Spurs, 17th Avn)   The 17th Aviation Company operated as part of the 214th Aviation Battalion under the call sign "Silver Spur." The 17th Avn was a lift company providing airmobile support to the 9th Infantry Division from '68 to '69. Later in '69 the Silver Spurs flew support for the 7th and 9th ARVN divisions operating in the Delta. Prior to '68, the company had operated as part of the 12th Aviation Group in support of U.S. operations in III Corps. *See also* **214th Aviation Battalion.**

17th Parallel *see* **Geneva Accords**

18th ARVN Infantry Division (43d, 48th, 52d ARVN Regiments)   One of South Vietnam's least effective combat infantry divisions for much of the war. The 18th ARVN did distinguish itself briefly during the NVA Final Offensive in April '75. The 18th ARVN, reinforced by armor and paratroop units, defended Xuan Loc, provincial capital of Long Khanh, III Corps.

The 18th ARVN managed to destroy three of the four attacking NVA divisions before casualties to the 18th caused the surviving ARVNs to retreat toward Saigon. The division consisted of the 43d, 48th, and 52d Infantry regiments, and attached artillery. *See also* **Xuan Loc.**

18th Engineer Brigade (18th Engr Bde)   U.S. Army engineers provided support in the I and II Corps area from '65 to '71, and consisted of the 35th, 45th and 937th Engineer groups. *See also* **Engineers.**

18th Engr Bde *see* **18th Engineer Brigade**

18th MASH *see* **18th Surgical Hospital (Mobile Army)**

18th Military Police Brigade (18th MPs)   U.S. Military Police Brigade, deployed RVN September '66. The brigade had overall responsibility for Army police units throughout South Vietnam and operated as part of USARV. Military police duties included security, convoy escort, traffic control, prisoner handling, and stockade management. The brigade was headquartered at Cam Ranh Bay.

18th MPs *see* **18th Military Police Brigade**

18th NVA Regiment   NVA infantry regiment operated in the Central Highlands of II Corps as early as '66. During heavy fighting around Khe Sanh in mid-'67, the 18th NVA Regiment suffered heavy casualties at the hands of U.S. Marines operating in the area. The survivors of the regiment retreated into Laos to rebuild. *See also* **325C NVA Division.**

18th Surg *see* **18th Surgical Hospital (Mobile Army)**

18th Surgical Hospital (Mobile Army) (18th MASH, 18th Surg)   The U.S. Army 18th MASH deployed to Vietnam in June '66 at Pleiku as part of the 55th Medical Group servicing the 4th Infantry Division. The 18th was MUST equipped in November '67 and subsequently relocated to Lai Khe, Quang Tri, Camp Evans, and finally back to Quang Tri before its departure from Vietnam in August '71. The hospital had 70 beds and provided emergency surgery for casualties too severely wounded for immediate evacuation to other hospital facilities.

18th Transportation Company *see* U-1A

18th VC Regiment *see* 3d NVA Division

19 Average age of the U.S. combat soldier in Vietnam, the children of the "Baby Boom," '45–'55. The average age of the U.S. soldier in WWII was 26. *See also* Baby Boomers.

19th NVA Regiment *see* 968th NVA Division

19th Tactical Air Support Squadron (19th TASS) Air Force squadron activated at Bien Hoa in '63. The squadron provided forward air controller support to American Army advisors operating with ARVN units in the field. The 19th's FACs primarily used the O-1A for support.

19th TASS *see* 19th Tactical Air Support Squadron

20 Mike-Mike *see* SX-35 Cannon

20mm Cannon *see* SX-35

20mm Vulcan *see* SX-35, SUU-23

20th ARA *see* 20th Artillery (Aerial Rocket)

20th Artillery (Aerial Rocket) (20th ARA, Bobcats, Blue Max, Armed Falcons) The 20th ARA consisted of a battalion of rocket armed helicopter gunships. The 20th ARA deployed to Vietnam in September '65 as part of the 1st Cavalry Division, providing them with aerial rocket artillery. The 20th deployed to An Khe and later moved to Phuoc Vinh in '68. Call signs used by the battalion were "Bobcats," "Blue Max" and "Armed Falcons." ARA helicopters were heavily armed UH-1Cs, equipped with rockets and machine guns.

20th Engineer Brigade (20th Engr Bde; 34th, 79th, 159th Engineer Groups) Deployed to SVN in August '67 at Bien Hoa, III Corps. The brigade was responsible for all II FFV engineering duties and was withdrawn from Vietnam in September '71. The brigade controlled the 34th, 79th and 159th Engineer groups. The individual groups were composed of combat and construction engineer battalions. Engineering duties of the brigade were carried out throughout the III and IV Corps Zones.

20th Engr Bde *see* 20th Engineer Brigade

20th Special Operations Squadron *see* UH-1F

21st ARVN Division (31st, 32d, 33d ARVN Regiments) Initially operated in the southern portion of I Corps, but later deployed to the IV Corps Delta region. The division consisted of a headquarters element, the 31st, 32d, and 33d Infantry regiments, and four artillery battalions.

21st Infantry Regiment (Light) (21st Infantry, 21st Light Infantry, Gimlet) The 21st Infantry consisted of the 3d and 4th battalions. Their regimental unit name was "Gimlet." The 3d Battalion arrived in SVN in August '66 as part of the U.S. 196th Light Infantry Brigade. The 4th Battalion arrived April '68 as part of the 11th Infantry Brigade. Both battalions later became part of the Americal Division in February '69. The 4th Battalion departed RVN June '71. The 3d Battalion, the last U.S. combat battalion in Vietnam, departed August '72. The units operated throughout the northern II Corps and southern I Corps area.

21st Light Infantry *see* 21st Infantry Regiment (Light)

21st NVA Regiment *see* 3d NVA Division

22d ARVN Division (40th, 41st, 42d, 47th ARVN Regiments) The 22d ARVN was headquartered in Binh Dinh Province. The division consisted of five artillery battalions and the 40th, 41st, 42d, and 47th Infantry regiments. The 41st ARVN Regiment was transferred to the division in '73. The division primarily operated throughout the II Corps provinces of Binh Dinh, Phu Bon and Phu Yen.

22d MUST *see* 22d Surgical Hospital

22d NVA Regiment Operated in the Central Highlands of II Corps, in the area of the Vinh Thanh Valley. After engaging American units during the '66 Operations, Thayer and Irving, the 22d NVA withdrew into Quang Nhai Province to rebuild and regroup.

22d Replacement Battalion (22d Replacement, 22d Replacement Center) The 22d Replacement deployed to SVN in August '66 and processed Army replacement personnel for units operating in I and II Corps. The center, located at Cam Ranh

Bay, II Corps, also processed troops returning to the U.S. at the end of their tours. The 22d departed Vietnam April '72. *See also* Replacement Center.

22d Replacement Center   *see*   **22d Replacement Battalion**

22d Surg   *see*   **22d Surgical Hospital**

22d Surgical Hospital (22d MUST, 22d Surgical, 22d Surg) Army surgical field hospital located at Phu Bai, Thua Thien Province, I Corps. The unit arrived in Vietnam December '67 and deployed to Phu Bai January '68 in support of units of the 101st Airborne Division. The hospital was self-contained and transportable. The 22d was part of the 43d Medical Group. *See also* Medical Unit, Self-Contained, Transportable.

22d VC Regiment   *see*   **3d NVA Division**

23d Infantry Division (Americal)   *see* **Americal Division**

23d Psalm (Twenty-Third Psalm) Vietnam grunts' versions of the 23d Psalm: "Yea, though I walk through the Valley of the Shadow of Death, I shall fear no evil, because I am the baddest mother-fucker in the Valley." Depending on the helmet cover this prayer was written on, "baddest" might be substituted with "meanest," and "mother-fucker," interchanged with "son-of-a-bitch."

23d SAD   *see*   **23d Special Warfare Aviation Detachment**

23d Special Warfare Aviation Detachment (23d SAD, 23d Special Aviation Detachment) One of the Army's fixed-wing support units. The 23d operated twin-engine OV-1 Mohawks providing recon and aerial photo support services to the ARVN command, deploying to Nha Trang, II Corps in September '62. Later in '62 the detachment's aircraft were armed with .50cal machine guns and allowed to return fire when fired upon. *See also* OV-1.

23mm AA Soviet made 23mm antiaircraft gun used by the North Vietnamese for air defense. *See also* Antiaircraft Guns, AA Gunsites.

24B NVA Regiment   *see*   **304th NVA Division**

24th Corps   *see*   **XXIV Corps**

24th Evacuation Hospital (Semi-mobile) (24th Evac) Deployed to Vietnam in July '66, and was located at Long Binh, III Corps, until it departed South Vietnam in November '72. The 320-bed hospital was part of the 68th Medical Group. *See also* Evacuation Hospital.

24th NVA Regiment Elements of the regiment operated in the Central Highlands, and in June '66 the 4th, 5th, and 6th battalions engaged units of the 101st ABN during Operation Hawthorne I and II. The regiment was part of the 6th Viet Cong Division until '74 when it was transferred to the 8th NVA Division. *See also* Z-15 NVA Regiment.

25th ARVN   *see*   **25th ARVN Infantry Division**

25th ARVN Division (25th ARVN; 46th, 49th, 50th ARVN Regiments) Consisted of four artillery battalions and the 46th, 49th, and 50th Infantry regiments. Based in Quang Ngai Province until '63, the division was transferred to III Corps. Division Hq. was located at Duc Hoa until late '70 when it was relocated to Cu Chi, former base camp for the U.S. 25th Infantry Division. The division had responsibility for the provinces of Hau Nghia, Long An, and Tay Ninh. The 25th was one of the ARVN's worst divisions, elevating search-and-avoid operations to an art form. The division had an excellent intelligence net which allowed them to avoid major contacts with the enemy until the '75 Final Offensive. In '74 the division commander was jailed for selling rice and other supplies to the Viet Cong.

25th Infantry Division (Tropic Lightning, 25th U.S., Cu Chi National Guard) Elements of the division deployed to SVN in January '66. The division was headquartered at Cu Chi in III Corps, northwest of Saigon. 2d Brigade operations covered the Tay Ninh and Hau Nghia Province areas. The 3d Brigade operated in the Central Highlands of II Corps, under control of the 4th Infantry Division. The division consisted of one aviation, twelve infantry, two armor and six artillery battalions as well as division recon. Among other ops, the division participated in the Cambodian Incursion of April '70. Nicknamed the "Cu Chi National Guard," the division was referred to as the 25th U.S. so as not to be confused with the 25th ARVN Infantry Division which was stationed in the same area. The division motto: "Ready to strike, anywhere, anytime." *See also* **Electric Strawberry.**

25th U.S. *see* **25th Infantry Division**

26th Infantry Regiment (Blue Spaders) The 1st Battalion of the 26th Infantry Regiment deployed to Vietnam in October '65 as part of the 1st Infantry Division. The 26th's regimental name was the "Blue Spaders." The unit operated throughout the central and western III Corps area with the 1st and 3d brigades. The battalion departed Vietnam in April '70.

26th Marine Regiment (26th Marines) The 26th Marines, Regimental Landing Team deployed to Vietnam in August '66. The regiment operated throughout I Corps, but primarily along the DMZ. The unit is best remembered for having garrisoned Khe Sanh Combat Base during the siege of the base by several NVA divisions during early '68. The 26th Marine Regiment remained in Vietnam until March '70. The regiment consisted of three infantry battalions (1/26, 2/26, 3/26) and a battalion of 105mm howitzers, the 1/13 Marines. When not functioning as an RLT the regiment was assigned to the 5th Marine Division. *See also* **5th Marine Division.**

26th/27th/28th Regimental Landing Teams *see* **5th Marine Division**

27th Infantry Regiment (Wolfhounds) The 27th consisted of two battalions of infantry, both arriving in South Vietnam in January '66 as part of the U.S. 2d Brigade/25th Infantry Division. Both battalions operated in the III Corps area until their withdrawal from Vietnam in April '71 and December '70, respectively.

27th Marine Regiment (27th Marines) The 27th Marines functioned as a Regimental Landing Team, conducting amphibious assaults during various Marine operations in I Corps. The regiment was controlled by the 1st Marine Division and was headquartered at Da Nang. The regiment consisted of three infantry battalions (1/27, 2/27, 3/27) and artillery support from the 2/13 Marines, a 105mm howitzer battalion. The 27th's

parent unit was the 5th Marine Division, prior to its assignment to the 1st Marine Division. *See also* **1st Marine Division.**

27th Marines *see* **27th Marine Regiment**

27th NVA Regiment (27th PAVN Regiment) Independent regiment sometimes referred to as the "27th PAVN Regiment." Elements of the regiment operated in the Vinh Thanh area of Binh Dinh Province, II Corps. After '73 it was redeployed to I Corps and continued to operate as an independent regiment.

27th PAVN Regiment *see* **27th NVA Regiment**

28th Infantry Regiment (28th Infantry, Lions of Contigny) The 28th Infantry consisted of two infantry battalions which arrived in SVN in October '65 as part of the U.S. 1st Infantry Division. The 1st Battalion operated with the 1st Brigade while the 2d Battalion operated with both the 1st and 3d brigades of the 1st Infantry Division. Both battalions departed Vietnam in April '70. The regiment was known as the "Lions of Contigny," but GIs in Vietnam simply called them the "Black Lions." The regiment operated throughout the central and northern areas of III Corps.

28th NVA Regiment *see* **10th NVA Division**

29th CA *see* **29th Civil Affairs Company**

29th Civil Affairs Company (29th CA) The 29th CA deployed to Vietnam in May '66 and operated around Da Nang, I Corps. Army members of the 29th worked with the Vietnamese civilian population on civic projects such as the construction of schools and medical clinics, agricultural improvements and providing medical services and other help to the population. The 29th departed Vietnam in December '71.

29th NVA Regiment *see* **324B NVA Division**

30 Mike-Mike *see* **XM-140**

30mm Cannon *see* **XM-140**

31st ARVN Regiment *see* **21st ARVN Division**

31st Infantry Regiment (Light) (31st Infantry, Polar Bears) Two battalions of the

31st Regiment, the 4th and 6th, arrived in Vietnam in August '66 and April '68 respectively. The 4th Battalion operated as part of the 196th LIB in I Corps until February '69 when it became part of the Americal Division. The 6th Battalion operated under the 9th Infantry Division in the Delta. The 6th departed Vietnam in October '70; the 4th departed a year later.

31st NVA Regiment *see* **2d NVA Division**

31st Security Police Squadron U.S. Air Force security police force assigned to provide on-base security for the airfield at Tuy Hoa, Phu Yen Province, II Corps.

32d ARVN Regiment *see* **21st ARVN Division**

32d Naval Construction Regiment *see* **Camp Haskins**

32d SEABEES *see* **Camp Haskins**

32S-3 Radio *see* **Collins 32S-3**

33 Beer Locally manufactured Vietnamese beer which contained a high quantity of formaldehyde, rendering the beer extremely potent. Since formaldehyde was typically used as an embalming fluid, GIs claimed you could go directly "from the bar to the grave, and bypass the undertaker." *See also* **Vietnamese Beer.**

33d ARVN Regiment *see* **21st ARVN Division**

33d NVA Regiment *see* **3d Phuoc Long Division**

34th Aeromed *see* **Aeromedical Evacuation Units**

34th Aviation *see* **34th General Support Group (Aviation Support)**

34th Engineer Group *see* **20th Engineer Brigade**

34th General Support Group (Aviation Support) (34th GSG, 34th Aviation) The 34th Aviation was formed at Tan Son Nhut air base January '66 to provide support and supply for Army aircraft. Full maintenance and repairs were provided for the Army's helicopters and fixed-wing aircraft. Many civilian mechanics, from the States, were contracted to provide the necessary services for the Army at Tan Son Nhut. The 34th departed SVN in November '72, leaving its duties to be performed by its ARVN counterpart.

34th GSG *see* **34th General Support Group (Aviation Support)**

35th Infantry Regiment (35th Infantry, Cacti) The 1st and 2d battalions of the 35th deployed to SVN in January '66 as part of the U.S. 25th Infantry Division. Both battalions operated primarily in the Central Highlands of II Corps. In August '67 the battalions were transferred to the 4th Infantry Division operating in II Corps. The 1st Battalion departed Vietnam in April '70, and the 2d Battalion followed in December. The unit name was the "Cacti" Regiment.

36th NVA Regiment *see* **308th NVA Division**

37mm AA (Three-Sevens) The North Vietnamese made extensive use of 37mm antiaircraft guns for air defense. The 37mm guns had a maximum rate of fire of 80 rounds per minute, each round weighing about 1.5 pounds with a maximum vertical range of 9,000 feet, and an effective range of about 4,500 feet. American pilots simply called the guns "Three-Sevens." *See also* **Antiaircraft Guns.**

38 Smith and Wesson (.38 S & W, Smith & Wesson, .38 Special) The Model 10, .38cal pistol had a two-inch or four-inch barrel. The .38 Special was carried by many American pilots in Vietnam, some aircrewmen, Army officers and by many Special Forces troops.

38th NVA Regiment *see* **2d NVA Division**

39th Artillery Regiment (1st/39th Arty) The 1st Battalion/39th Artillery arrived in Vietnam in October '66. The battalion was equipped with 155mm self-propelled howitzers (M-109). The battalion was later reequipped with the M-107 and M-110 self-propelled 175mm gun and 8-inch howitzer. Operating as part of the 108th Artillery Group the battalion provided support to the 101st Airborne operating in I Corps. The 1st/39th was based at FSB Nancy until their departure from Vietnam in December '71. *See also* **FSB Nancy.**

39th Infantry Regiment (Infantry) (AAA-0; Anything, Anywhere, Anytime, Bar Nothing; 3d and 4th/39th Infantry)

The 39th Infantry deployed three battalions to Vietnam in January '67: 2d, 3d, and 4th. The battalions were part of the 9th Infantry Division and operated throughout the IV Corps Delta until their departure in mid-'69. The regiment was known as the "AAA–0": "Anything, Anywhere, Anytime, Bar Nothing." The 4th Battalion operated as a counterguerrilla force in the Delta and was known as the "Hardcore Battalion." The battalions operated as part of the MRF using air assault and river boat tactics against the Viet Cong. *See also* **Hardcore Battalion.**

39th NVA Regiment *see* **968th NVA Division**

40mm Grenade Launcher *see* **Grenade Launchers, 40mm**

40th ARVN Regiment *see* **22d ARVN Division**

41st ARVN Regiment *see* **22d ARVN Division**

42d Artillery Regiment (4th & 5th/42d Arty, Straight Arrows, Highland Redlegs) Two battalions of the 42d Artillery Regiment saw service in Vietnam. The 4th Battalion deployed in August '66; the 5th deployed in April '68. The regimental name was the "Straight Arrows," but in Vietnam the 4th Battalion was known as the "Highlands Redlegs." Both battalions operated in the II Corps area; the 4th/42d fielded 105mm howitzers and the 5th/42d fielded 155mm howitzers. The 4th Battalion withdrew from Vietnam in December '70; the 5th Battalion followed in April '72.

42d ARVN Regiment *see* **22d ARVN Division**

43d ARVN Regiment *see* **18th ARVN Infantry Division**

44th Med *see* **44th Medical Brigade**

44th Medical Brigade (44th Med; U.S. Army Medical Command, Vietnam; U.S. Army Health Services Group) The 44th Med arrived in Vietnam in April '66. The brigade was headquartered in Saigon, and later moved to Long Binh. The brigade was responsible for all U.S. Army related medical duties in SVN, and consisted of four medical groups and one medical depot (43d, 55th, 67th, 68th Medical groups and the 32d Medical Depot). In December '70 the 44th Med combined with the Surgeon General's Office of USARV and became the U.S. Army Medical Command, Vietnam. In April '72 the command was reduced to the U.S. Army Health Services Group, Vietnam, which departed Vietnam in March '73.

44th NVA Sapper Regiment *see* **1st NVA Division**

45 Pistol *see* **M-1911A1 Pistol**

45 Whiskey (Rice Whiskey) One of the more potent Vietnamese rice-based whiskeys was called "45." The rice whiskey was locally brewed in the Phu Loi/Lai Khe area, just north of Saigon. *See also* **Vietnamese Beer, Numpai.**

45th MUST *see* **45th Surgical Hospital**

45th Surg *see* **45th Surgical Hospital**

45th Surgical Hospital (45th MUST, 45th Surgical, 45th Surg) The 45th deployed to Vietnam in October '66 and operated at Tay Ninh, III Corps, until its departure in October '70. The 45th was a MUST unit, the first to deploy to Vietnam, and operated as part of the 68th Medical Group. MUST units were self-contained surgical hospitals capable of rapid relocation by truck. *See also* **Medical Unit, Self-Contained, Transportable.**

45th Trans *see* **45th Transportation Battalion**

45th Transportation Battalion (45th Trans) The 45th Trans deployed to Vietnam in '62 and operated five transport helicopter companies (8th, 33d, 57th, 81st and 93d) and a company of fixed-wing, U-1 Otters (18th). The 45th Trans represented the U.S. Army's initial aircraft commitment in support of South Vietnamese forces.

46th ARVN Regiment *see* **25th ARVN Division**

46th Infantry Regiment (Light) (The Professionals, 46th Infantry; 1st/46th, 5th/46th Infantry) Two battalions of the 46th Infantry deployed to Vietnam in October '67 and March '68. Both battalions operated as part of the 198th LIB until August '71 when they became part of the Americal Division, conducting operations in the Chu Lai area of I Corps. The 5th Battalion departed Vietnam in May '71; the 1st Battalion departed in June '72.

46th SFC *see* 46th Special Forces Company

46th Special Forces Company (46th SFC) Elements of the U.S. Special Forces provided counterinsurgency training to the troops of Thailand from '66–'74. The 46th SFC consisted of Green Berets from the 1st Special Forces Group headquartered on Okinawa, Japan.

47th ARVN Regiment *see* 22d ARVN Division

47th Infantry Regiment The 47th Infantry deployed three battalions to Vietnam in January '67 which were assigned to the 9th Infantry Division. The 2d/47th was mechanized and primarily operated in the division's AO south and east of Saigon, and did participate in the '70 Cambodian Invasion. The 3d and 4th battalions operated with the division's 2d Brigade as part of TF 117, the Mobile Riverine Force. *See also* Tiger's Lair, TF 117.

48th ARVN Regiment *see* 18th ARVN Infantry Division

48th Aviation Company (48th Avn, Blue Stars) The 48th Avn deployed to Vietnam in November '65 and served with various aviation battalions. The call sign of the 48th Avn was the "Blue Stars"; they operated primarily in the I Corps area. During their time in Vietnam they served as part of the 11th Aviation Group and the 10th, 223d and 268th Aviation battalions.

48th NVA Regiment *see* 320th NVA Division

49th ARVN Regiment *see* 25th ARVN Division

49th Tactical Fighter Wing *see* Takhli Royal Thai Air Base

50mm Mortar *see* M41 Mortar

50th ARVN Regiment *see* 25th ARVN Division

51st ARVN Regiment *see* 1st ARVN Infantry Division

52d ARVN Regiment *see* 18th ARVN Infantry Division

52d Aviation Battalion (Flying Dragons) The 52d deployed to RVN in March '63, as part of the 17th Aviation Group/1st Aviation Brigade. The battalion operated in the II Corps area providing airlift, recon and combat support for the 4th Infantry Division located in the Central Highlands.

52d Infantry Regiment (Light) (52d Infantry, Ready Rifles, 1st/52d Infantry) The 52d Infantry provided a full battalion and four separate companies for service in SVN. The 1st Battalion deployed to Vietnam, February '68, as a part of the 198th LIB (the 1st later became part of the Americal Division when it was formed in February '69). Company C and D served as security with MP units and Company E and F served as Long-Range Recon with the 1st Cav and the 1st Inf. Div. *See also* Company C/D/E/F/52d Infantry.

52d NVA Regiment *see* 1st NVA Division

52d VC Regiment *see* 2d NVA Division, 320th NVA Regiment

52d Viet Cong Regiment *see* 2d NVA Division

53d Aviation Detachment *see* Utility Tactical Transport Company

53d USASA Special Operations Command *see* Army Security Agency

54th ARVN Regiment *see* 1st ARVN Infantry Division

55th Aeromed *see* Aeromedical Evacuation Units

56th Aeromed *see* Aeromedical Evacuation Units

56th Special Operations Wing, Task Force Alpha *see* Infiltration Surveillance Center, NPK

57mm AA (S-60 Antiaircraft Gun) Antiaircraft gun used by the NVA for air defense. The Soviet made gun could fire a six-pound shell to an altitude of 15,000 feet at a rate of 70 rounds per minute. *See also* Antiaircraft Guns.

57mm Recoilless *see* M-18A1 RCL, PRC RCL

57th Aeromed *see* Aeromedical Evacuation Units

57th Aviation Company (57th Avn, Cougars, Gladiators, Gray Tigers) The 57th Avn first deployed to Vietnam in '65 under the call sign "Gray Tigers" and operated fixed-wing CV-2 Caribou aircraft to provide Army units with transport and supply support. The 57th redeployed to SVN in October '67 as an assault and airmobile helicopter company under the call signs "Gladiators" and "Cougars." The 57th Avn primarily operated out of Kontum, II Corps, until they withdrew from Vietnam in March '73.

57th Medical Detachment   *see* **Medevac**

60mm Mortar   *see*   **M-19 60mm Mortar**

60mm Tubes   *see*   **M-19 60mm Mortar**

60th Infantry Regiment   Deployed three battalions to Vietnam in December '66, as part of the 9th Infantry Division. The 2d/60th operated with the division's 1st and 3d brigades in their AO south and east of Saigon. The 3d/60th operated with the 2d Brigade as part of the Mobile Riverine Force in the Delta. The 5th/60th was mechanized, and operated with the 3d Brigade until '68 when its mechanized equipment was transferred to the 16th Infantry/1st Infantry Division. The 5th/60th operated as regular infantry after '68. The 2d and 5th battalions departed Vietnam in '70, and the 3d Battalion departed in mid-'69. *See also* **16th Infantry Regiment.**

61mm Mortar   *see*   **Type 31 Mortar**

61s   *see*   **Type 31 Mortar**

61st Aviation Company (61st Avn, Lucky Stars)   U.S. Army fixed-wing transportation company. The unit deployed to Vietnam in July '63 operating the twin engine, CV-2 Caribou. The 61st Avn was located at Vung Tau and provided support to ARVN troops throughout the region. The 61st AVN operated under the call sign "Lucky Stars." *See also* **C-7A.**

64th NVA Regiment   *see*   **320th NVA Division**

66th NVA Regiment   Operated in the Dak To/Kontum region of II Corps as part of the 10th and 304th NVA divisions. The 66th participated in the '67 battles around Dak To. *See also* **10th NVA and 304th NVA Divisions.**

68th Aviation Company   *see* **Utility Tactical Transport Company**

68th NVA Artillery Regiment (164th NVA Artillery Regiment)   The 68th and the 164th NVA Artillery Regiment participated in the siege of the U.S. Marine combat base at Khe Sanh in early '68. The 68th was part of the 304th NVA Division; the 164th NVA Arty was an independent artillery regiment operating under the command of the NVA's B-5 Front. *See also* **304th NVA Division.**

73d Aviation Company (73d Avn)   U.S. Army observation airplane company that deployed to Vietnam in May '62. Elements of the company were dispersed across Vietnam and were used for aerial observation, artillery fire adjustments, radio relays, aerial command posts, targeting and emergency supply operations. The O-1 "Bird Dog" aircraft used by the Army had proved its usefulness in the skies over Korea several years before. *See also* **O-1.**

74th Infantry LRRP   *see*   **Delta Teams**

75mm Recoilless   *see*   **PRC RCL**

75th Infantry (Rangers) (Sua Sponte)   Elite Army force that conducted long-range reconnaissance patrols (LRRP), special ambush teams, and intelligence gathering. In Vietnam Ranger companies worked directly with division, brigade, and Field Force headquarters. The Rangers were originally designated LRP (Long-Range Patrol) companies and operated for their parent brigade/division. The LRP/LRRP companies were reclassified as Ranger companies of the 75th Infantry in February '69; their motto: "Sua Sponte" ("Of their own accord"). The all-volunteer force also carried the unofficial motto of "Rangers lead the way." Ranger companies were typically organized into 10–14 6-man recon teams. *See also* **Long-Range Reconnaissance Patrol.**

77th Artillery Regiment (77th Arty)   The 77th Arty deployed four battalions to Vietnam: the 1st, 2d, 4th, and 6th. The 1st/77th's 105mm howitzers were assigned to 2d Bde/1st Cavalry. The 2d/77th's 105mm howitzers were assigned to the 4th Infantry Division and later the 25th Infantry Division. The 4th/77th were ARA helicopters assigned to the 101st Airborne. The 6th/77th's 105mm howitzers were assigned to II FFV and attached to the 25th Infantry Division. In '71 the headquarters of the

6th/77th was reorganized into ARA and designated Battery F/77th Arty. *See also* **Death on Call.**

77th Arty *see* **77th Artillery Regiment**

79th Engineer Group *see* **20th Engineer Brigade**

81 Mike-Mike *see* **M-29 81mm Mortar**

81mm Mortar *see* **M-29 81mm Mortar**

81mm Mortar Carrier *see* **M-125 81mm Mortar**

81mm Tubes *see* **M-29 81mm Mortar**

82 Mike-Mike *see* **Type 53 Mortar**

82d ABN *see* **82d Airborne Division**

82d Airborne *see* **82d Airborne Division**

82d Airborne Division (82d ABN, 82d Airborne, Eighty-Deuce, Air Mattress, All-Afro) During the Vietnam War the 82d Airborne Division was a part of the United States strategic force, an emergency force held in reserve to be used worldwide. The self-contained division could be transported anywhere, and air-dropped if suitable landing facilities were not available. As a result of the widespread communist offensive of Tet '68, a task force was organized around the 3d Brigade of the 82d ABN, which deployed to SVN in February '68. The brigade returned to the U.S. in December '69. During its tour in Vietnam the 3d Bde/82d ABN was attached to the 101st Airborne Division, and was nicknamed the "Air Mattress" and the "All-Afro" Division. *See also* **3d Brigade, 82d Airborne Division, Almost Airborne.**

82d USASA Special Operations Unit *see* **Army Security Agency**

82mm Mortar *see* **Type 53 Mortar**

82s *see* **Type 53 Mortar**

85mm AAA Antiaircraft artillery used by the NVA for air defense. *See also* **Antiaircraft Guns.**

85th Evac *see* **85th Evacuation Hospital (Semimobile)**

85th Evacuation Hospital (Semimobile) (85th Evac) The 85th Evac deployed to Vietnam in August '66, departing December '71. The 130-bed hospital was originally located at Qui Nhon, II Corps, part of the 43d Medical Group. The 85th was later transferred to Phu Bai in I Corps under control of the 67th Medical Group.

88th NVA Regiment *see* **308th NVA Division**

89th Military Police Group (89th MPs) The 89th deployed to Vietnam in March '66 as the controlling command for four U.S. MP battalions operating in the II and III Corps areas. The four battalions were the 92d MPs at Tan Son Nhut, the 95th and 720th MPs at Long Binh and the 716th MPs in Saigon. The 89th Group headquarters departed Vietnam December '71, but its battalions stayed in Vietnam until '72 and '73. *See also* **716th Military Police Battalion, 720th Military Police Battalion.**

89th MPs *see* **89th Military Police Group**

90-Day Wonders *see* **Officer Candidate School**

90mm RCL *see* **M-67 RCL**

90mm Recoilless Rifle *see* **M-67 RCL**

90mm SPAT *see* **M-56 SPAT**

90th Replacement Battalion (90th Replacement) The 90th Replacement Battalion was located at Long Binh and was the processing center for U.S. replacements entering SVN who were assigned to the III or IV Corps area. The 90th deployed to Vietnam in August '65, under command of USARV, and was one of the last units to leave, departing March '73. New replacements arrived by plane at Tan Son Nhut airport, and were then bused to Long Binh for processing to their new units. The 90th also processed DEROS personnel returning to the States at the end of their tour of duty in South Vietnam. *See also* **Replacement Center.**

90th Replacement Center *see* **Replacement Center**

90th Repo *see* **Replacement Center**

91 Bravo *see* **Military Occupation Specialty**

91st Evac *see* 91st Evacuation Hospital (Semimobile)

91st Evacuation Hospital (Semimobile) (91st Evac) Deployed to Vietnam in December '66 at Tuy Hoa, Phu Yen Province, II Corps. The 320-bed hospital unit was relocated to Chu Lai, I Corps, in July '69. While stationed at Tuy Hoa, the 91st was part of the 43d Medical Group, and later became part of the 67th Medical Group after its relocation to Chu Lai.

92d Aviation Company (92d Avn, Stallions, Sidekicks) The 92d Avn first deployed to Vietnam in January '64 outfitted with the CV-2 Caribou Army transport. When the Army lost command of the Caribous, the unit departed Vietnam in January '67 and returned as an AHC in November '67. The unit provided lift and gunship support, used the call signs "Stallions" and "Sidekicks," and departed Vietnam in January '72. During both tours the 92d worked the II Corps area.

92d MPs *see* 89th Military Police Group

95B NVA Regiment *see* 10th NVA Division

95C NVA Regiment *see* 9th Viet Cong Division

95th Evac *see* 95th Evacuation Hospital (Semimobile)

95th Evacuation Hospital (Semimobile) (95th Evac) The 95th Evac deployed to Vietnam in March '68 at Da Nang as part of the 67th Medical Group. The 300-bed hospital serviced both Army and Marine personnel in the area.

95th MPs *see* 89th Military Police Group

95th NVA Regiment *see* 325th NVA Division

97th Artillery Group *see* Air Defense Artillery

98th NVA Regiment *see* 316th NVA Division

100 Missions (Hundred-Mission Crunch) The Air Force established a 100 Mission minimum for its fighter-bomber pilots in Vietnam before their combat tour was considered complete. When a pilot had completed the limit he was eligible for reassignment. The reassignment normally meant return to the U.S. or another Air Force installation outside of the SEA combat zone. Sometimes the reassignment took the form of a noncombat flying position within the squadron or wing. Pilots referred to the mission requirements and the difficulties in surviving such missions as the "hundred-mission crunch."

100mm AAA Antiaircraft artillery guns used by the NVA for air defense. The 100mm guns could fire a 35-pound shell to an altitude of 45,000 feet at a rate of 15 rounds per minute. The guns were towed into position and were initially located in North Vietnam but later protected the Ho Chi Minh Trail. *See also* **Antiaircraft Guns.**

100s (Marijuana Cigarettes) *see* OJs (Marijuana Cigarettes)

101D NVA Regiment *see* 1st NVA Division

101st ABN *see* 101st Airborne Division (Airmobile)

101st Air Cavalry Division (Airmobile) In July '68 the 101st Airborne Division was officially redesignated the 101st Air Cavalry Division (Airmobile). The division traded in its parachutes for helicopters, and though officially an air cavalry division, it was still referred to as the 101st Airborne. *See also* **101st Airborne Division.**

101st Airborne (Airmobile) *see* 101st Airborne Division (Airmobile)

101st Airborne Division (Airmobile) (101st ABN, Screaming Eagles, Pukin' Buzzards, 101st Airborne [Airmobile]) Units of the 101st ABN Div deployed to SVN July '65, and the division was redesignated Airmobile. The division, nicknamed the "Screaming Eagles," consisted of 10 airmobile infantry battalions, five battalions of ground artillery, an artillery battalion of ARA, a squadron of air recon and its own aviation group of assault and gunship helicopters. The division operated in the Central Highlands of II Corps, and is remembered for its operations in the A Shau Valley, especially at "Hamburger Hill," May '69. Unofficial division nicknames were "The Pukin' Buzzards," "One-Oh-Worst" and "Screaming Chickens." Field motto:

"Above the rest." *See also* **101st Air Cavalry Division, Screaming Chicken Patch.**

101st NVA Regiment   Operated in the Tay Ninh Province region. In late '66 the 101st NVA and the 9th VC Division attacked and overran the Special Forces Camp at Sui Da. *See also* **325C NVA Division.**

102d NVA Regiment   *see*   **308th NVA Division**

105-Howie   *see*   **M-101A1 Howitzer**

105mm Howitzer   *see*   **M-101A1 Howitzer, M-108 105mm SPA**

105mm Recoilless   *see*   **M-40A1 RCL**

105mm SPA   *see*   **M-108 105mm SPA**

105s   *see*   **M-101A1 Howitzer, M-108 SPA, F-105**

106mm RCL   *see*   **M-40A1 RCL**

106mm Recoilless Rifle   *see*   **M-40A1 RCL**

106mm RR   *see*   **M-40A1 RCL**

107mm Mortar   *see*   **M107/M38 Mortar**

107mm Recoilless   *see*   **PRC RCL**

107mm Rocket   *see*   **Type 63 Rocket**

114th Aviation Company (114th Avn, White Knights)   The 114th deployed to Vietnam in September '64 and provided airmobile support to ARVN and U.S. units as part of the 13th Aviation Battalion. The company operated in the IV Corps area throughout its stay in Vietnam. In October '69 the 114th Avn transferred to the 214th Aviation Battalion and departed Vietnam in February '72. The call sign of the 114th Avn was the "White Knights."

114th Avn   *see*   **114th Aviation Company**

116th Aviation Company (116th Avn, Hornets, Stingers)   The 116th Avn deployed to Vietnam in October '65 as an AHC providing lift and gunship support in the II and III Corps area. The call signs used by the unit were the "Hornets" and the "Stingers." The unit departed Vietnam in December '71.

118th Aviation Company (Thunderbirds, Bandits, Choppers; 118th Avn)   The company provided assault support to

Army and ARVN units for the eight years it operated in Vietnam. The 118th first arrived in Vietnam in June '63. Nickname and call signs used by the helicopters of the 118th Aviation Company were the "Thunderbirds," "Bandits" and "Choppers."

119th Aviation Company (119th Avn, Crocodiles, Gators)   Helicopters of the 119th Avn deployed to Vietnam in June '63 and operated primarily from Pleiku in II Corps. The company provided airmobile and assault helicopter support under the call signs "Gators" and "Crocodiles." The company withdrew from SVN in December '70.

120mm Mortar   *see*   **M38 Mortar**

120th AHC   *see*   **Razorbacks**

120th Assault Helicopter Company   *see*   **Razorbacks**

120th Aviation Company (120th Avn, Razorbacks, The Deans, Snoopies)   The 120th deployed to Vietnam in June '63, operated throughout the III Corps area from its base at Long Binh, and used the following call signs: the Deans, Snoopies and Razorbacks. The 120th Avn provided lift and gunship support and were based at Tan Son Nhut during Tet '68. The 120th departed Vietnam in October '72.

120th TFS–Colorado ANG   *see*   **USS Pueblo**

122mm Rocket   *see*   **DKZ-B**

127mm Rocket   *see*   **Zuni**

130mm AAA   Antiaircraft artillery gun used by the North Vietnamese for air defense. The 130mm gun could fire a 74-pound shell to an altitude of 45,000 feet at a rate of 12 rounds per minute. *See also* **Antiaircraft Guns.**

130mm Cannon (130s)   Soviet-made, long-range cannon used by the NVA. The 130mm cannon first saw widespread use during the NVA's '72 Eastertide Offensive. The cannon had a range of 27kms.

130s   *see*   **130mm Cannon**

135th Aviation Company (135th Avn, Emus, Taipans)   The 135th Avn was a combined company of U.S. Army and Australian Navy aircrews. During '65–'67 the company operated CV-2 Caribous out of Dong Ba Thin. In '67 the company was equipped with helicopters and was based at

Vung Tau. The 135th operated under the call signs "Emus" and "Taipans," supporting Australian operations in Phuoc Tuy Province, AO of the 1st ATF. The 135th was originally designated an EMU (Experimental Military Unit) to evaluate joint operations by U.S. and Australian crews. *See also* **Australia, Royal Australian Navy.**

136th TFS–New York ANG   *see* **USS Pueblo**

140mm Rocket   *see*   **BM14/21**

141st NVA Regiment   Operated along the Cambodian border on the plateau northeast of Song Be, where the II and III Corps boundaries met the Cambodian border. The regiment eventually worked its way south to bases in the central area of III Corps. During the course of the war the 141st Regiment suffered extremely heavy losses at the hands of American troops on several occasions. In each case the survivors of the regiment retreated to border sanctuaries in Cambodia where the unit was rebuilt, and reentered South Vietnam. During the war the regiment operated with the 2d, 3d, 7th, and 312th NVA divisions. *See also* **2d or 7th NVA Division.**

147D Drone (Ryan 147D)   Drone aircraft used by the Air Force to gather intelligence information. The drone saw service over the Hanoi and Haiphong areas of North Vietnam. The drone was transported by the DC-130, and dropped near its surveillance zone. The drone was later recovered by helicopter.

150-Day Early-Out   *see*   **Early-Out**

151st Infantry (LRP)   *see*   **Hoosier LRRPs**

155mm Howitzer   *see*   **M-114A1, M-109 155mm SPA, M-53 155mm SPA**

155mm Self-Propelled Howitzer   *see* **M-109 155mm SPA, M-53 155mm SPA**

155mm SPA   *see*   **M-109 155mm SPA, M-53 155mm SPA**

155s   *see*   **M-114A1, M-109 155mm SPA, M-53 155mm SPA**

159th Engineer Group   *see*   **20th Engineer Brigade**

160mm Mortar   *see*   **M43 160mm Mortar**

162d Aviation Company (162d Avn,

Vultures, Copperheads)   The 162d deployed to SVN in March '66 and consisted of assault helicopters operating under the call signs the "Vultures" and the "Copperheads." In '68 the 162d Av was assigned to support air operations of the 2d Brigade/9th Infantry Division that was operating in the Delta of IV Corps. The 162d Avn operated out of brigade headquarters at Dong Tam.

164th NVA Artillery Regiment   *see* **68th NVA Artillery Regiment**

165th NVA Regiment   Operated as part of the 7th NVA Division in the northwestern and central areas of III Corps, and participated in the overrun attempt against the Special Forces Camp at Loc Ninh in October '67. By '73 the regiment operated as part of the 312th NVA Division in I Corps. *See also* **7th NVA Division.**

173d ABN   *see*   **173d Airborne Brigade**

173d Airborne Brigade (173d ABN, The Herd, Flying Butterknife, Sky Soldiers, Two Shades of Soul)   The first major U.S. Army ground combat unit deployed to SVN, May '65. The unit, originally assigned TDY duty in Vietnam, remained in-country until August '71, and operated in both II and III Corps. The brigade consisted of the 503d Infantry (Airborne) Regiment. The brigade nicknames were "Sky Soldiers," "Two Shades of Soul," and "The Herd"; their shoulder patch was a winged bayonet (nicknamed the Flying Butterknife). Elements of the 173rd participated in the only major U.S. combat parachute jump of the VNW, February '67, during Operation Junction City. The brigade consisted of four infantry and one artillery battalion and several attached units. Motto: "All the way." *See also* **Hill 875, Dak To, 503d Infantry, Flying Butterknife.**

173d Aviation Company (173d Avn, Crossbows, Robin Hood)   The 173d Avn deployed to Vietnam in March '66 and primarily operated with the 1st Infantry Division providing them with lift and gunship support. The 173d operated with the call signs "Crossbow" and "Robin Hood" and departed Vietnam in March '72, having operated as part of the 1st, 11th, and 223d Aviation battalions performing airmobile and assault helicopter missions.

174th NVA Infantry Regiment   Operated in the Central Highlands, and was believed to be one of the units to have mutilated the bodies of dead GIs in an attempt to intimidate other American units operating in the area. Not to be outdone, some American units mutilated NVA/VC bodies, until higher command outlawed the practice. The 174th was originally a Viet Cong regiment of the 5th VC Division. Casualties in the regiment were replaced by NVA soldiers until the regiment consisted entirely of NVA troops. *See also* 316th NVA Division.

174th NVA/VC Regiment *see* 5th Viet Cong Division

174th TFS–Iowa ANG *see* USS Pueblo

175mm Gun *see* M-107 175mm SPA

175mm Self-Propelled Gun *see* M-107 175mm SPA

175mm SPA *see* M-107 175mm SPA

175s *see* M-107 175mm SPA

175th Medical Detachment (175th Vets) U.S. Army medical unit that provided veterinary services in Vietnam. The 175th Vets were attached to the 101st Airborne at Camp Sally and primarily provided veterinary services for American scout dog units operating in-country.

175th Vets *see* 175th Medical Detachment

176th NVA Regiments *see* 316th NVA Division

177mm SPA *see* M-107 175mm SPA

178th Aviation Company (178th Avn, Boxcars) The 178th was a medium helicopter company which deployed to Vietnam in March '66. The Chinook equipped unit operated in the I Corps area from its base at Chu Lai, providing medium lift support to units in the area. The 178th call sign was the "Boxcars." The unit departed Vietnam in March '72.

178th Avn *see* 178th Aviation Company

187th Infantry Regiment (Rakassans, 3d/187th Infantry) 3d Battalion/187th Infantry, part of the 101st ABN, operated in the A Shau Valley of I Corps. The regiment

was named the "Rakassans." Elements of the battalion, during Operation Apache Snow, made contact on Hill 937 with enemy units of the 7th and 8th battalions of the 29th NVA regiment. The 3d Battalion made repeated attacks up the hill to dislodge the enemy. After several days, the battalion was reinforced by two battalions from the 101st, and the hill, dubbed "Hamburger Hill," was taken on May 20, 1969. Two hundred and forty-one U.S. soldiers were killed in the battle for a hill that was ordered abandoned shortly after its capture. *See also* Hamburger Hill, Operation Apache Snow.

188th TFS–New Mexico ANG *see* USS Pueblo

196th Infantry Brigade (Light) *see* 196th Light Infantry Brigade

196th LIB *see* 196th Light Infantry Brigade

196th Light Infantry Brigade (196th LIB, 196th Infantry Brigade [Light]) The 196th deployed to Vietnam in August '66 and was headquartered at Tay Ninh, III Corps. The brigade operated throughout Tay Ninh Province until April '67, when it was redeployed to Chu Lai, I Corps, as part of Task Force Oregon. In September '67 the brigade became the backbone for the newly formed Americal Division (23d Infantry Division) operating from Tam Ky. The 196th Brigade continued to operate in the I Corps area until its withdrawal from Vietnam, June '72. *See also* Americal Division.

197th Infantry Brigade (Dollar Ninety-Worst) When it was decided that U.S. combat troops would be sent to SVN, a decision was made to use troops from other units to bring the 1st Cav up to strength for deployment to Vietnam. The 197th was a training unit at Fort Benning, Georgia, and all of its soldiers that could be deployed overseas were transferred into the 1st Cav. The 197th eventually became a holding brigade for those troops who could not be deployed to Vietnam because of physical limitations, discipline problems or insufficient time remaining in service. Because of the calibre of troops which filled the ranks of the unit it was nicknamed the "Dollar Ninety-Worst." The brigade never went to Vietnam.

198th Infantry Brigade (Light) (198th

Light Infantry Brigade, 198th LIB) The 198th deployed to SVN in October '67, and operated in the I Corps area as part of Task Force Oregon. The brigade consisted of four infantry and one artillery battalion. The 90th later became part of the Americal Division and continued to operate in I Corps until its departure from Vietnam in November '71. *See also* **Americal Division.**

198th LIB *see* **198th Infantry Brigade (Light)**

198th Light Infantry Brigade *see* **198th Infantry Brigade (Light)**

199th Infantry Brigade (Light) *see* **199th Light Infantry Brigade**

199th LIB *see* **199th Light Infantry Brigade**

199th Light Infantry Brigade (199th LIB, 199th Infantry Brigade [Light], Redcatchers) The 199th was organized in the U.S. and deployed to Vietnam in December '66. The brigade was headquartered out of Long Binh and operated around Saigon until its departure in October '70. The 199th Bde was one of the first units used to experiment with the combining of U.S. and ARVN combat units in the field. This combining was called "the double force," and was the forerunner of the U.S. plan of Vietnamization. The brigade operated under direct command of MACV during its training of the Vietnamese, and its protection duties around Saigon. The brigade consisted of four infantry battalions, one artillery battalion and a troop of air cavalry. *See also* **Double Force.**

201 File (Army Personnel File) U.S. Army personnel file containing a record of an individual's military service. While on active duty, the file was kept by the headquarters unit to which the individual was assigned. When the man was assigned to another unit his records were forwarded to his new headquarters. Normally, enlisted personnel were not allowed to view their records. If the records were to be hand carried to the new unit they were sealed; otherwise, the records were mailed or sent by courier. Officers were allowed to view their records and usually hand carried them between duty stations. The 201 File contained information on a soldier's training, education, IQ test, shot record, awards and decorations, duty stations, and any disciplinary actions.

201st NVA Regiment *see* **3d Phuoc Long Division**

207th NVA Regiment *see* **6th Viet Cong Division**

209th NVA Regiment *see* **7th NVA Division**

212 *see* **Section 212**

214th Aviation Battalion (Cougars, 214th Avn Bn) The battalion deployed to Vietnam in April '67 as part of the 12th Aviation Group providing helicopter support to U.S. units in the III Corps area. In '68 the battalion moved to Dong Tam to provide support to the 9th Infantry Division. In late '69 the battalion moved to Vinh Long in the Delta as part of the 164th Aviation Group to provide support to the 7th and 9th ARVN Infantry divisions working the Delta. The battalion consisted of surveillance, lift, and gunship helicopters, as well as two fixed-wing reconnaissance aircraft companies. The battalion's nickname was the "Cougars." *See also* **Delta Regional Aviation Command.**

267th VC *see* **Operation Marauder**

271st Viet Cong Regiment *see* **9th Viet Cong Division**

272d Viet Cong Regiment (272d VC Regiment) This VC regiment was believed to have operated in the northwestern portion of III Corps and participated in the October '67 attacks on the Special Forces Camp at Loc Ninh. The regiment was part of the 9th Viet Cong Division formed in '64. *See also* **9th Viet Cong Division.**

273d Viet Cong Regiment (273d VC) Believed to have been an independent VC unit that operated in the northwest areas of III Corps. Elements of the VC regiment were known to have participated in the October '67 attacks on the Special Forces Camp at Loc Ninh and later attacked the 1st Infantry Division base camp at Phu Loi during the '68 Tet Offensive. The regiment operated in conjunction with the 9th Viet Cong Division but was not part of it. *See also* **9th Viet Cong Division.**

274th Viet Cong Regiment (274th VC) The regiment was formed in late '64 near Song Be in Phuoc Long Province, III Corps.

The unit operated as an independent regiment until '74 when it became part of the 3d Phuoc Long Division. By this time most of the troops in the unit were NVA, the VC having been killed off in previous battles. *See also* 3d Phuoc Long Division.

275th NVA/VC Regiment *see* **5th Viet Cong Division**

282d Aviation Company (282d Avn, Black Cats)   The 282d AHC deployed to Vietnam in June '66 and operated throughout I Corps providing lift and gunship support to Army and Marine units in the area. The call sign of the 282d was the "Black Cats." The unit withdrew from Vietnam in January '72.

301st NVA Corps   *see*   **NVA IV Corps**

304th NVA Division (9th, 24B, 66th NVA Regiments)   Believed to have participated in the siege of the U.S. Marine combat base at Khe Sanh in early '68. The division consisted of the 9th, 24B and 66th NVA Infantry regiments. The 66th NVA operated with the 10th NVA Division when the regiment operated in the II Corps area. *See also* 10th NVA Division.

307th Strategic Wing   *see*   **U Tapao Royal Air Base**

308B NVA Division   *see*   **308th NVA Division**

308th NVA Division (308B NVA Division; 36th, 88th, 102d NVA Regiments)   Operated in the I Corps area, and was especially active during the '68 Tet Offensive. The sister division of the 308th was the 308B NVA Division, and was deployed in the Hanoi area. The 308th NVA consisted of the 36th, 88th, and 102d NVA Infantry regiments.

0311 Infantry   *see*   **11 Bravo**

312th NVA Division   *see*   **7th NVA Division**

314th Tactical Airlift Wing   *see*   **Nationalist China**

315th Air Commando Wing   *see*   **Project Mule Train**

315th ARVN Troop Carrier Group   *see*   **Operation Big Patch**

316th NVA Division (98th, 174th,

176th NVA Regiments)   Operated in northern Laos. After the cease-fire in '73 the division returned to NVN. The division consisted of the 98th, 174th, and 176th NVA Infantry regiments.

317th Tactical Airlift Wing   *see*   **Nationalist China**

320th NVA Division (9th, 48th, 64th NVA Regiments; 52d VC Regiment)   Believed to have operated primarily in the western region of I Corps and participated in the siege of Khe Sanh in early '68. After Khe Sanh the division withdrew into Laos to refit before moving into II Corps. The division consisted of the 48th and 64th NVA Infantry regiments, and the 52d VC Regiment. In '74 the 9th NVA Regiment replaced the 48th Regiment. The 52d VC Regiment also operated with the 2d NVA Division during the course of the war.

320th NVA Regiment   *see*   **6th Viet Cong Division**

324B NVA Division (5th, 6th, 29th, 803d, 812th NVA Regiments)   The NVA 324B Infantry Division infiltrated across the DMZ in June '66. Their target was the provincial capital Quang Tri City, Quang Tri Province, I Corps. In July '66 Operation Hastings began with U.S. and SVN Marines engaging the NVA 324B Division and inflicting heavy losses on the division. The 324B withdrew back across the DMZ to rebuild. The 324B returned during Tet '68 to participate in the attack on Hue. The 324B was the first major NVA unit to enter Saigon after its collapse on April 30, 1975. The division consisted of the 29th, 803d, and 812th Infantry regiments until '74 when the 812th transferred to another division and 324B Division was reinforced with the 5th and 6th NVA Infantry regiments.

325C NVA Division   *see*   **325th NVA Division**

325th NVA Division (18th, 95th, 101st NVA Regiments; 325C NVA Division)   Headed down the Ho Chi Minh Trail from NVN in September '64 to infiltrate into SVN, sometimes called the 325C NVA Division. The NVA division operated in the I Corps area and was involved in the Hill Fights with the U.S. Marines in April '67 and later participated in the siege of Khe Sanh. The division consisted of the 18th, 95th, and 101st

NVA Infantry regiments. *See also* **Hill Fights.**

327th ABN *see* **327th Infantry (Airborne) Regiment**

327th Infantry (Airborne) Regiment (327th ABN, Bastogne Bulldogs, 327th Infantry, 327th Infantry [Airmobile]) The 1st and 2d battalions of the 327th Inf deployed to SVN in July '65 as part of the 1st Brigade, 101st Airborne Div. By August '68 both battalions were redesignated as airmobile and operated in the III Corps area until November '69, when they were deployed to the Hue/Phu Bai area of I Corps. Both battalions departed RVN in early '72. *See also* **101st Airborne Division.**

327th Infantry (Airmobile) *see* **327th Infantry (Airborne) Regiment**

334th Aviation Company (334th Avn, Dragons, Peacemakers) The 334th Avn was an Army aerial weapons helicopter company (AWC) that provided gunship support in the III Corps area. The unit deployed to Vietnam in November '66 and was stationed at Bien Hoa. The call signs of the 334th Avn were the "Dragons" and the "Peacemakers." The unit was originally armed with Huey Hog gunships but quickly converted to the AH-1 Cobra in '67–'68. The company departed Vietnam in March '72. *See also* **Camp Woodson.**

335th Aviation Company (Cowboys, Falcons, 335th Avn) The 335th Avn deployed to Vietnam in November '66 and operated in the II and III Corps areas until its departure in November '71. The 335th used the call signs "Cowboys" and "Falcons," providing troop assault and gunship capabilities.

341st NVA Division Operated north of the DMZ throughout most of the war, occasionally sending regiments across the DMZ to attack US/ARVN positions. During the Final Offensive in '75, the 341st NVA operated in III Corps and was part of the final push against Saigon. Just prior to the NVA capture of Saigon, VNAF planes dropped several 15,000-pound Daisy Cutter bombs on NVA troop concentrations. One of the Daisy Cutters destroyed the 341st headquarters near Xuan Loc. *See also* **Daisy Cutter.**

346th Tactical Control Squadron *see* **Mule Train**

355th Tactical Fighter Wing *see* **Takhli Royal Thai Air Base**

366th Tactical Fighter Wing *see* **Gunfighters, Takhli Royal Thai Air Base**

388th Tactical Fighter Wing *see* **Korat Royal Thai Air Base**

400th USASA Operations Unit *see* **Army Security Agency**

432d Tactical Reconnaissance Wing *see* **Udorn Royal Thai Air Base**

501st Infantry Regiment (Airborne) (Geronimo Regiment, 1st/501st Infantry, 2d/501st Infantry) Two battalions of the 501st Infantry deployed to Vietnam in December '67 as a part of the 2d Brigade/101st Airborne. The 501st operated in the I and III Corps areas for five years before its return to the U.S. The battalions were later designated as Airmobile when the units were removed from jump status. *See also* **101st Airborne Division.**

502d Infantry Regiment (Airborne/Airmobile) (1st/502d Infantry, 2d/502d Infantry) Two battalions of the 502d deployed to Vietnam as part of the 101st Airborne. The 2d Battalion arrived in July '65 and operated throughout II and III Corps until December '69 when it relocated to I Corps. The 1st Battalion deployed to Vietnam in December '67 and operated under control of the 2d Bde/101st ABN. Both battalions departed Vietnam in early '72. *See also* **502d Light Infantry Brigade, 2d Battalion/503d Infantry Regiment.**

502d Light Infantry Brigade (Five-O-Deuce) At one time the 2d Battalion/502d Infantry operated a special force that consisted of the 2d Battalion, a platoon of the 326th Engineers, a unit of the Bu Prang RF Company, a squad of National Police, a company of the 4th Bn/9th ARVN Regiment, a Recondo platoon for scouting, a platoon of Montagnard trackers and a platoon of Montagnard porters. The force was nicknamed the "502d Light Infantry Brigade." The unit operated throughout the II and III Corps area. *See also* **502d Infantry Regiment.**

503d Infantry Regiment (Airborne) (503d Infantry, Rock Regiment) The 503d Infantry fielded four battalions in Vietnam. The 1st and 2d battalions deployed to South Vietnam in May '65. The 3d and 4th battalions deployed in October '67 and June '66, respectively. The regiment operated as part of the 173d Airborne Brigade in the II and III Corps area. The 2d/503d was the only U.S. battalion to make a combat jump in Vietnam during the war (February '67, War Zone C). The regiment departed Vietnam in April '71. The regiment was named the "Rock Regiment." *See also* **Operation Junction City, 2d Battalion/503d Infantry.**

506 Valley   North-south valley located north and west of Bong Son in Binh Dinh Province, II Corps. The valley extended from the village of My Duc in the south to Nuoc Dip Thuong in the north, 14kms south of Duc Pho. The NVA/VC used the valley as a base area and transport route. The western edge of the valley led into the Central Highlands. *See also* **FSB Floyd, Bong Son, The Crescent.**

506th VC Battalion   *see*   **Operation Marauder**

507th Tactical Control Group   *see* **Control and Reporting Post**

509th USASA Operations Group   *see* **Army Security Agency**

516th Viet Cong Battalion (1st Kien Hoa Battalion)   The 516th VC battalion was an independent main force VC unit based in Kien Hoa Province, IV Corps, and operated throughout the province and adjacent areas. Prior to '68 the VC "owned" Kien Hoa Province. During Tet '68 the 516th VC attacked the town of Ben Tre which was the headquarters of the 10th ARVN Regiment. The 516th VC held the headquarters and most of the town for several days before they were bombed out by U.S. aircraft. *See also* **Ben Tre.**

525th MI Group   *see*   **525th Military Intelligence Group**

525th Military Intelligence Group (525th MI Group)   Military intelligence group organized under the Defense Intelligence Agency. The 525th deployed to Vietnam in November '65 under control of MACV and coordinated U.S. Army intelligence activities throughout South Vietnam.

553d Tactical Reconnaissance Wing *see*   **Korat Royal Thai Air Base**

606th Air Commando Squadron   *see* **UH-1F**

631st Combat Support Group   *see* **Don Muang Royal Thai Air Base**

632d Security Police Section   *see* **Devil Flight**

633d Special Operations Wing   *see* **NPK**

635th Combat Support Group   *see* **U Tapao Royal Air Base**

711th NVA Division   *see*   **2d NVA Division**

716th Military Police Battalion (716th MPs)   The 716th deployed to SVN in August '65 and operated in the Saigon–Tan Son Nhut area until its departure in March '73. The MPs worked with the South Vietnamese police conducting traffic control and security, and maintaining military order among the troops. MP duties included the handling of enemy prisoners and the apprehension of U.S. AWOLs and deserters. The 716th was part of the 89th MP Group.

716th MPs   *see*   **89th Military Police Group**

720th Military Police Battalion (720th MPs)   The 720th MP Battalion deployed to RVN, October '66, to provide military police functions for the Long Binh area; they were temporarily relocated to Da Nang in August '70. In '71 the battalion returned to Long Binh and remained there until its return to the U.S. in August '72. In addition to its other duties, the 720th assisted in providing security for the military stockade at Long Binh Jail. Primary responsibility for the jail was handled by the 284th MP Company. The 720th MPs were part of the 89th Military Police Group. *See also* **89th Military Police Group, Long Binh Jail.**

720th MPs   *see*   **720th Military Police Battalion**

766th NVA Regiment   *see*   **Phou Pha The**

777th Tactical Control Squadron   *see* **Operation Saw Buck II**

782 Gear (Marine Field Equipment/ Gear, Field-Transport Pack)   "782 Gear" was the Marine term for the standard combat equipment fielded by a U.S. Marine, and included blanket, poncho, shelter half with accessories (tent pole, guy line, tent pegs), extra boots and socks, extra underwear, first aid kit, ammunition, K-Bar knife, E-Tool, shaving kit, two canteens, extra uniform, haversack, mess kit, pack and weapon. In Vietnam the typical grunt carried his ammo, E-Tool, poncho, knife, first aid kit, grenades, canteens, mess kit, pack and weapon (roughly 60–75 pounds of gear, depending on the amount of ammunition and Cs carried) plus extra gear such as LAWs, ropes, smoke grenades, claymores, etc. *See also* **Web Gear, Field Load.**

803d NVA Regiment *see* **324B NVA Division**

812th NVA Regiment *see* **6th Viet Cong Division, 324B NVA Division**

834th AD *see* **834th Air Division**

834th Air Division (834th AD) The U.S. Air Force 834th Air Division deployed to SVN in October '66 and was the responsible headquarters controlling the tactical airlift within South Vietnam. The 834th was part of the 7th Air Force based out of Tan Son Nhut and was dissolved in '70, with most of its aircraft being transferred to the Vietnamese Air Force.

968th NVA Division (9th, 19th, 39th NVA Regiments) Believed to have operated in Laos until '73 providing security for the Ho Chi Minh Trail. After the cease-fire it moved into the Central Highlands of SVN. The division consisted of the 9th, 19th and 39th NVA Infantry regiments.

999 *see* **Priority 999**

1,000-Pounders *see* **Swimming-Pool-Maker**

1041st Security Police Squadron *see* **Combat Security Police**

1802 Armor *see* **Military Occupation Specialty**

1806 Amtrac *see* **Military Occupation Specialty**

4400th CCTS *see* **4400th Combat Crew Training Squadron**

4400th Combat Crew Training Squadron (Jungle Jim Squadron, 4400th CCTS) Air Force squadron established at Elgin AFB, Florida, for the purpose of training and familiarization of Air Force crews in the role of aircraft in guerrilla warfare and counterinsurgency, and later to train the VNAF. The squadron was established in April '61, and in October '61 a detachment of the 4400th was deployed to SVN to begin advising and training VNAF. The initial advisory operation was code-named "Farmgate." In '63 the training squadron was redesignated the 1st Air Commando Squadron. *See also* **Operation Farmgate.**

6234th Tactical Fighter Wing (6234th TFW) The 6234th was the first Wild Weasel detachment to operate in Southeast Asia. The detachment was based at Korat AFB in Thailand and began operations in December '65 with newly equipped F-100F (twin seat) fighters. *See also* **Wild Weasel.**

6234th TFW *see* **6234th Tactical Fighter Wing**

#10,000 *see* **Number Ten**

$10,000 *see* **GI Insurance**